INTERNATIONAL FINANCE

TRANSACTIONS, POLICY, AND REGULATION

NINTH EDITION

By

HAL S. SCOTT
Nomura Professor of International Financial Systems
Harvard Law School

PHILIP A. WELLONS
Deputy Director
Program on International Financial Systems
Harvard Law School

NEW YORK, NEW YORK
FOUNDATION PRESS
2002

COPYRIGHT © 1995–2001 FOUNDATION PRESS
COPYRIGHT © 2002 By FOUNDATION PRESS
                395 Hudson Street
                New York, NY 10014
                Phone Toll Free 1–877–888–1330
                Fax (212) 367–6799
                fdpress.com

ISBN 1–58778–433–5

TEXT IS PRINTED ON 10% POST CONSUMER RECYCLED PAPER

PREFACE

This is the ninth edition of our textbook on international finance. Several major changes in the area occurred since the eighth edition was published a year ago. The consequences of Enron appear for U.S. securities markets in Chapter 2 and for swaps in Chapter 17. The Argentine crisis is covered in Chapter 6, on foreign exchange regimes, and Chapter 21, on emerging market debt. The new Lamfalussy reforms for European securities markets are discussed in Chapter 7. Chapter 17, on swaps, includes an expanded coverage of credit derivatives. Chapter 23 examines the IMF's new sovereign bankruptcy proposal.

The book is organized into four parts. Part One deals with the international aspects of major domestic markets, Part Two with instruments and offshore markets, Part Three with emerging markets, and Part Four with international financial architecture. There are also four infrastructure chapters woven throughout the book covering capital, foreign exchange, the payment system and clearance and settlement. We have updated information throughout the book wherever possible, and continue to reedit existing material to increase the book's readability.

While our approach is rooted in government policy and regulation, the book introduces the student to basic financial concepts and transactions. Exchange rate regimes, for example, are necessary background for an understanding of the European Monetary Union. And a student of futures, options and swaps must understand the basic characteristics and functions of these instruments. Only the most basic financial theory is presented. We believe our approach is original and complements existing texts written for finance or economics courses.

We gratefully acknowledge the dedicated assistance of our secretary Betsy Rempel.

Hal S. Scott
Philip A. Wellons

Cambridge, Massachusetts
June 2002

ACKNOWLEDGMENTS

We gratefully acknowledge permission to publish excerpts from the following material.

M. Carter, "The Impact of Pension Investments on the World's Financial Market Structure," a paper given at Harvard Law School, November 15, 1993

Reprinted with permission from M. Carter and Y. Zhou.

P. Cooke, excerpts from Bank Capital Adequacy, Price Waterhouse, London (July 1991)

Reprinted with kind permission from Price Waterhouse.

G. Dufey and T. Chung, "International Financial Markets: A Survey," in R. L. Kuhn, ed., *International Finance and Investing* (1990)

Reprinted with permission from G. Dufey and T. Chung; reprinted with permission of Richard D. Irwin, all rights reserved.

Euroclear, Cross-Border Clearance, Settlement and Custody: Beyond the G30 Recommendations (June 1996)

Reprinted with permission from Morgan Guaranty Trust Company of New York, as operator of the Euroclear System.

Goldman, Sachs & Co., Marketing Documents for Roadshow of Telmex ADS Offer (1991)

Copyright © 1991 by Goldman, Sachs & Co.

F. Graaf, *Euromarket Finance: Issues of Euromarket Securities and Syndicated Eurocurrency Loans* (1991)

Reprinted by permission of Kluwer Publishers.

S. Miller and L. Mullen, "Alternative Trading Systems," Traders Magazine, Vol. 17, No. 3 (March 1999)

Reprinted by permission of Securities Data Publishing.

E. Greene, A. Beller, G. Cohen, M. Hudson, Jr., and E. Rosen, *U.S. Regulation of the International Securities Markets* (1999)

Reprinted from *U.S. Regulation of the International Securities Markets* with the permission of Prentice Hall Law & Business.

G. Haberman, "Capital requirements of commercial and investment banks: contrasts in regulation," Federal Reserve Bank of New York Quarterly Review, Autumn 1987

Reprinted with permission from G. Haberman; reprinted with permission from Federal Reserve Bank; and reprinted with permission from Federal Reserve Bank of New York Quarterly Review.

S. Henderson, "Should Swap Termination Payments Be One-way or Two-way," International Financial Law Review (October 1990), 27-32

This article first appears in the October 1990 issue of International Financial Law Review. Copyright Euromoney Publications PLC, London, England.

J. Hull, *Introduction to Futures and Options Markets*, copyright © 1991

Reprinted by permission of Prentice-Hall, Inc., Englewood Cliffs, N.J.

M. D. Levi, *International Finance* (1990)

Reproduced with permission of McGraw-Hill, Inc.

R. Litan, "Nightmare in Basle," The International Economy, November/December 1992

Reprinted with permission by The International Economy magazine, November/December 1992, Washington, D.C.

T. Prime, *International Bonds and Certificates of Deposit* 45-54 (1991)

Reprinted by permission by Butterworth-Heinemann Ltd.; and reprinted by permission of T. Prime.

S. Radelet and J. Sachs, "The East Asian Financial Crisis: Diagnosis, Remedies, Prospects" Brookings Papers on Economic Activity 1:1998.

Reprinted by permission of the Brookings Institute.

H. Scott, "Supervision of International Banking Post-BCCI," 8 Georgia State University Law Review 487 (1992)

Reprinted by permission.

R. Smyth, "Bank of England Blueprint for LSE Settlement System," International Financial Law Review (October 1993), 21-23

This article first appears in the October 1993 issue of International Financial Law Review. Copyright Euromoney Publications PLC, London, England.

D. Sneider, "Financial Services Reform in Japan," International Securities Regulation Report 6 (February 6, 1993)

Reprinted with permission from International Securities Regulation Report. Copyright © 1994 by LRP Publications, 580 Village Boulevard, Suite 140, West Palm Beach, FL 33409. All rights reserved. For more information on International Securities Regulation Report, please call 1-407-687-1220, ext. 716.

I. Swary and B. Topf, *Global Financial Deregulation: Commercial Banking at the Crossroads* (1992)

Reprinted by permission of Blackwell Publishers.

E. Symons and J. White, *Banking Law*, 3rd Edition (1991), 806-9

Reprinted with permission of the West Publishing Corporation.

M. Warren, "The Investment Services Directive: The 'North Sea Alliance' Victory over 'Club Med'," International Securities Regulation Report 6 (January 12, 1993)

Reprinted with permission from International Securities Regulation Report. Copyright © 1994 by LRP Publications, 580 Village Boulevard, Suite 140, West Palm Beach, FL 33409. All rights reserved. For more information on International Securities Regulation Report, please call 1-407-687-1220, ext. 716.

J. Willoughby, "Exchange or Die", Institutional Investor, November (1998).

Reprinted with permission of Institutional Investor.

SUMMARY OF CONTENTS

*   There are four infrastructure chapters—capital, foreign exchange, the payment system and clearance and settlement—covering subjects that are important to international finance generally, not just to the Part of the book in which they happen to appear. We take them up when needed.

TABLE OF CONTENTS

---

[*]   There are four infrastructure chapters—capital, foreign exchange, the payment system and clearance and settlement—covering subjects that are important to international finance generally, not just to the Part of the book in which they happen to appear. We take them up when needed.

INTERNATIONAL FINANCE

TRANSACTIONS, POLICY, AND REGULATION

*

CHAPTER ONE

INTRODUCTION

This book examines international banking and securities transactions and their regulation. It begins with the major national markets of the United States, Europe, and Japan, then turns to the offshore markets. We also consider major areas of international regulation and policy, such as capital adequacy and clearance and settlement.

The first chapter reviews the transactions, markets, long-term trends, and basic concepts and language of international finance. The excerpts offer several different perspectives on the subject, that of the scholar (in Dufey and Chung and in Bryant) and the practitioner (Maughan). The material about the currency crisis in Korea in 1997-98 illustrates the impact of globalization and shows why it is important to understand the concepts of international finance.

Many financial words of art appear in the material often without explanation. Do not be surprised if many words are new and hard to understand. We include a glossary at the end of the book.

A. THE DEFINITION OF AN INTERNATIONAL FINANCIAL TRANSACTION

International financial transactions are the subject of this book. But what is a "financial" transaction? What makes it international? To answer the first question, this book adopts an approach from the field of finance that identifies three types of transactions. The first is payment, the method of transferring value from one party to another, and includes exchange transactions in which one currency is exchanged for another. This has been described as "the movement of financial claims over space." The second type is credit, which involves "the exchange of funds over time." According to G. Dufey and T. Chung, International Financial Markets: A Survey, 3 (R. Kuhn ed. 1990),

> Savers, whose income temporarily exceeds their use of funds, make the additional output they have created available to borrowers who have a shortage of funds because they commit resources to real assets (either consumer durables, productive assets in the form of business investment, or government projects) in excess of their current income. Credit markets also aid in distributing risks among participants in

this savings and investment process. By generating various types of financial claims, these markets permit savers and borrowers to "fine tune" the combination of risks they are willing to bear.

The creditor has the right to repayment of the principal at an agreed rate of interest. The third type is the equity transaction, in which the saver/investor's right to payment depends on the performance of the issuer of the security. "Derivative" transactions are based on, or derived from, these three types of transactions. This book does not systematically examine transactions involving control over real assets, commonly referred to as foreign direct investment.

1. INTERNATIONAL TRANSACTIONS

Several factors make a financial transaction international. The following sections offer a general definition and then elaborate on key elements of that definition, types of market participants and countries.

a. A GENERAL DEFINITION

Dufey and Chung provide a useful starting point with their definition of international credit markets.

G. DUFEY AND T. CHUNG, INTERNATIONAL FINANCIAL MARKETS: A SURVEY

International Finance and Investing
3-29 (R. Kuhn ed. 1990) (Dufey and Chung).

A CLASSIFICATION OF INTERNATIONAL CREDIT MARKETS

We begin by introducing a simple conceptual scheme for classifying international credit markets. (See Figure 1.) Essentially it is based on two dimensions: *how* (through which financial channel) and *where* (in which governmental jurisdiction) funds are transferred from savers to borrowers.

Institutional Structure

The first dimension represents the *channel,* or the institutional structure of market participants through which funds are moved.

Resources can be transferred from savers to borrowers through two channels: (1) *financial intermediaries* that attract funds from savers by issuing their own claims and, in turn, lend the funds to those who invest in real assets; and (2) organized *securities markets* in which savers and borrowers can link up directly (savers can purchase securities issued by ultimate borrowers). The organizational pattern of such markets is determined either by convention, the explicit agreement of the participating private entities, by government regulation, or both.

FIGURE 1

International Credit Markets: A Schematic Presentation

Credit Channel	National	International	
	Domestic	Foreign	"Euro"
Financial Intermediaries			
Securities Markets			
	"Internal"		"External"

. . .

Jurisdictions

The other dimension concerns the *jurisdiction* in which financial resources are transferred. Most credit transactions take place in domestic financial markets. However, many financial markets have extensive links abroad: domestic investors purchase foreign securities and may invest funds in foreign financial institutions. Conversely, domestic banks may lend to foreign residents, and foreign residents may issue securities in the national market or deposit funds with resident financial intermediaries. These are the traditional "foreign" markets for international financial transactions.

The significant aspect of such traditional foreign lending and borrowing is that all transactions are expected to abide by the rules, customs, and institutional arrangements prevailing in the national market concerned. Most important, all these transactions are directly subject to public policy, governing transactions with nonresidents ("foreign transactions") in a particular market. To illustrate, when savers purchase securities in a foreign market, they do so according to the rules, market practices, and regulatory precepts governing such transactions in that particular market. The same applies to those who invest their funds with financial intermediaries abroad.

Likewise, borrowers from abroad who wish to issue securities in a national market must follow the rules and regulations of that market. Here we encounter an important phenomenon that is crucial to understanding international markets: the rules governing the access of foreign borrowers to national markets tend to be discriminatory and restrictive. The same is true with respect to financial intermediaries. The borrower who approaches a foreign financial institution for a loan obtains funds at rates and conditions imposed by the financial institutions of the foreign country, and he is directly affected by the authorities, policy on lending to foreign residents.

During the 1960s, market mechanisms removed international (and to a certain extent even national) borrowing and lending from the jurisdiction of national authorities. This was accomplished by locating the market for credit denominated in a particular currency *outside* the country where that currency is legal tender, i.e., into a jurisdiction offering a more hospitable regulatory climate for such transactions. For example, markets for dollar-denominated loans, deposits, and securities in jurisdictions other than the United States to a large extent avoid U.S. banking and securities regulations. We refer to these markets as *Euromarkets* or more properly as *external* or *offshore markets* to indicate that they are not part of the domestic (or national) financial system. Thus, the essence of this classification is the nature of regulation. Differences in interest rates, practices, and regulations that exist between domestic and external markets arise primarily from the extent to which regulatory constraints are different.

Structural Summary

Today, virtually all major capital markets, including those of the United States, exhibit the three-tiered structure depicted in Figure 1:

- *Domestic Market.* Usually with unique procedures and institutions stemming from historical and regulatory determinants.

- *Foreign Market.* Attached to the domestic market, where nonresidents supply and take funds, but always under the specific rules established for foreign participants in the national market.

- *External or "Offshore" Market.* Located in a different political jurisdiction and only linked by the currency used to denominate the financial claims to the national market.

The various external markets have more features in common with each other than with their respective national markets. Therefore, they are properly discussed as a common, integrated market where claims denominated in different currencies are exchanged and are referred to as Euromarkets.

THE OFFSHORE MARKETS

As pointed out . . . , different national markets are separated by regulation, whereby the regulation and control of the relative money supply (e.g., the currency) represents only a relatively minor aspect of that segmentation. In contrast, the Euromarkets are quite homogeneous, which is why many observers treat them as one market, using the term in singular form. These markets are fairly big and therefore important in and of themselves for both users and providers of funds. In addition, it is largely via the offshore market that national markets have been integrated, which justifies in a fashion the use of the term *global* financial market. Again, however, it is important to distinguish between intermediated markets and securities markets. The first category refers to the Eurocurrency market for bank deposits and bank loans. In contrast, securities include the Eurobond, note, and commercial paper markets.

While similar in principle, the reasons that explain the intermediated Eurocurrency market differ somewhat from those that explain segmented markets for fixed-income securities. Indeed, each could exist without the other. Recognizing these determinants is not only important from the point of view of understanding markets, but also with respect to the analysis of market imperfections that allow arbitrage transactions. Indeed, much of what is known as financial innovation is based on an exploitation of variations in offshore-onshore differences in terms of interest rates and financial contract provisions.

The Catalyst of Regulations

Beginning in the early 1960s, the external market for bank deposits and assets came into existence because banks operating domestically (a category that includes foreign-owned banks) are burdened with costly regulations. These regulations include reserve requirements, the cost of deposit insurance schemes, taxes, and other factors. By the same token, regulations and political pressures that force banks to book assets that are inferior from a risk-return point of view make financial intermediaries in national markets less competitive. Thus, *costs* have forced the shift of deposits and bank assets from national markets to "books" offshore.

Ralph Bryant refined this definition of "international" by explicitly adding claims on domestic residents in foreign currency. He did so in the context of analyzing the statistics that reported banks' international credit about 15 years ago. He argued then that conventional measures of banks' international loans were inadequate. His calculations for 1982 and 1983 are given in the following two tables. He defines international according to the currency of the transaction as well as the parties' residence. In the following tables, bank loans (assets or claims) with an "international characteristic" consist of claims

- on foreign residents in foreign currency,

- on foreign residents in the bank's home currency, and

- on domestic residents in foreign currency.

These appear in columns 1, 2, and 3 of Table A and are aggregated in Table B. Column 3 reports claims on domestic residents in foreign currency. The statistics in Table A are unusual because they also include traditional domestic assets (column 4) and allow a comparison of those domestic assets with international assets.

R. BRYANT, INTERNATIONAL FINANCIAL INTERMEDIATION

26 (1987)

Table A. *Assets (including Interbank Claims) Reported by Banking Offices in Fifteen Industrial Countries and Eight Offshore Banking Centers, December 31, 1982*

Billions of U.S. dollars at end–1982 exchange rates unless otherwise indicated

	Assets with one or more international characteristic			Traditional domestic assets (claims on home residents denominated in home currency)	Total assets (gross size of banks' balance sheets)	Subtotal of assets with some international characteristic	
	Claims on foreign residents denominated in foreign currencies	Claims on foreign residents denominated in home currencies	Claims on home residents denominated in foreign currencies			Amount	Percent of total balance sheet
Country or group of countries	(1)	(2)	(3)	(4)	(5) (1 + 2 + 3 + 4)	(6) (1 + 2 + 3)	(7) [(6 + 5) x 100]
A. Five major European banking centers	716	160	242	1,957	3,075	1,118	36
United Kingdom	437	26	183	248	893	646	72
Germany	19	64	2	1,054	1,140	86	8
France	124	24	40	466	654	188	29
Switzerland (excluding trustee accounts)	33	38	5	184	260	76	29
Luxembourg	102	8	12	6	128	122	96
B. Seven other European countries	177	29	69	826	1,101	275	25
Austria	20	8	8	106	141	35	25
Belgium	61	5	22	42	130	88	68
Denmark	5	*	2	25	33	7	22
Ireland	3	*	3	14	19	5	28
Italy	33	1	18	495	547	53	10
Netherlands	49	13	8	97	168	72	42
Sweden	6	1	9	48	63	16	25
C. Twelve European countries (BIS reporters) (A + B)	893	188	311	2,783	4,176	1,392	33
D. Japan	66	25	87	1,437	1,615	178	11
E. Canada	37	2	26	171	236	65	27
F. United States	8	356	*	1,745	2,109	363	17
G. Fifteen industrial reporting countries (C + D + E + F)	1,003	571	425	6,136	8,135	1,999	25
H. Eight offshore banking centers	499	9	69	82	660	577	87
Singapore	80	2	28	18	128	109	86
Hong Kong	56	2	28	47	133	86	65
Bahrain	45	5	8	4	62	58	94
Lebanon	4	*	12		16	6	60
Bahamas	132	*	*	2	134	132	98
Cayman Islands	128	...	*	...	128	128	100
Panama	44	...	3	...	47	47	100
Netherlands Antilles	11		*	1	12	11	89
I. Swiss trustee accounts	93		...	...	93	93	100
J. Grand total (G + H + I)	1,593	583	494	6,218	8,887	2,669	30

The final column shows international as a share of total assets. As you will see later in this Chapter, it is likely that the international share of all assets has risen since then. For this section, please concentrate on the data for Japan, the U.K., and the U.S. You can find an update of these data at the end of the Notes and Questions for this section.

Table B. *International Assets Reported by Banking Offices in Main BIS Reporting Countries, by Nationality of Ownership, December 1983*

Billions of U.S. dollars at end–1983 exchange rates

Parent country	Type of international asset					Total international assets of offices in all reporting countries
	Claims on related offices	Claims on other nonaffiliated banks	Claims on nonbanks	Claims on official monetary institutions	CDS	
United States	234	213	180	1	2	631
Japan	120	194	133	2	3	451
France	24	104	56	5	*	190
United Kingdom	19	82	65	3	2	171
Germany	11	70	62	1	*	144
Canada	22	29	37	*	1	89
Italy	2	57	20	*	1	80
Switzerland	13	36	20	2	5	77
Netherlands	5	36	21	*	n.a.	62
Belgium	2	18	18	--	n.a.	38
Luxembourg	*	3	2	--	n.a.	5
Sweden	1	6	11	*	n.a.	18
Denmark	2	5	2	--	n.a.	9
Other BIS reporting countries	2	4	5	*	*	12
Consortium Banks	2	21	19	1	*	43
Other developed countries	3	9	11	*	*	23
Middle East	2	11	5	*	*	18
Latin America	9	3	9	--	*	21
Eastern Europe	--	3	2	3	n.a.	8
Others	7	19	12	*	1	40
Unallocated	--	3	4	--	--	6
Total	480	925	695	21	16	2,136

In 1997, the market share of foreign banks in the Group of Ten countries, measured by their share of total bank assets in the country, ranged from lows of 1.6% in Sweden, 4.3% in France, and 4.9% in Japan to highs of 20.7% in the U.S., 36.3% in Belgium, and 52.1% in the U.K. This share had been growing. A. Berger, R. DeYoung, H. Genay, and G. Udell, *Globalization of Financial Institutions: Evidence from Cross-Border Banking Performance* (2000) ("Berger") at 103.

Notes and Questions

1. According to Dufey and Chung, a banking transaction is international if it involves a foreign resident in the domestic (or national) banking market or involves offshore markets. A loan by a U.S. bank to a foreign resident, or a deposit from a foreign bank to a U.S. bank, both involving cross-border movement of funds, is an international transaction

in the U.S. domestic market. Consider the following for Citibank, a U.S. bank with a New York headquarters:

  a. Suppose Citibank (New York) made a Deutschemark loan to a U.S. company. Dufey and Chung would presumably classify this as a "euro-loan" and therefore an international transaction. But their classification is not certain because no foreign resident is involved and the lender and borrower are subject to the regulations of their home country.

  b. Suppose Citibank's U.K. branch or U.K. subsidiary made a sterling loan to a resident of the U.K. According to Dufey and Chung, this is not an international transaction. Do you agree with this aspect of their definition?

2. Dufey and Chung define a securities transaction as international according to the same criteria. A sale of securities of a U.S. corporation to a foreign resident, or a sale of the securities of a foreign corporation to a U.S. resident, would be international securities transactions involving the U.S. domestic market. Please consider the following:

  a. If a Japanese company issued securities in Tokyo, and they were bought in Tokyo by a U.S. citizen residing in Tokyo, Dufey and Chung would not classify this as an international transaction. Do you agree with this aspect of their definition?

3. Compare Bryant's definition of international banking transaction with the Dufey and Chung definition. Bryant's explicitly includes foreign currency lending to residents. Which do you prefer? Should any factors in addition to currency and residence be included in a comprehensive definition?

4. For simplicity, focus on Japan, the U.K., and the U.S. in Table A.

  a. The relative importance of international lending for banks based in the three countries varies. As a share of total lending by banks in the country in 1982, international lending was 11% for Japan, 17% for banks in the U.S., and 72% for banks in the UK. What would explain these differences?

  b. The international business of banks in the three countries varies by currency and clientele. Banks in Japan loaned mostly to residents in foreign currency; those in the U.S. loaned almost entirely in dollars to non-residents; and those in the UK loaned largely in non-Sterling currencies to non-residents. A closer reading of the table will refine this sketch. What would account for the differences?

5. Look carefully at the distribution of international assets found in Table B. Consider the role of banks headquartered in the Group of Five (G–5) countries: France, Germany, Japan, the U.K., and the U.S.

  a. What do you learn about the international business of the banks in the countries?

b.   Why do banks in the U.K. dominate in the first table but not in the second table?

6.   Note that banks are important takers of credit from other banks. What accounts for their role on both sides of the transaction?

7.   By September 2000, the positions shown in Bryant's 1982 and 1983 tables had changed significantly. The most striking changes were the relative decline in the role of U.S. banks and the major shift in the business of banks in Japan, which now mainly lend in yen to non-residents, something they did little of in 1982. What could account for these changes? The following tables correspond to Bryant's and the total is for all reporting countries. As you read them, note the major changes that have occurred.

Table A. Assets Reported by Banks Located in Selected Countries
(U.S. $ billions, end-June 2001)

Claims on:	(1)	(2)	(3)
Banks in:	Foreign residents in: Foreign currency	Domestic currency	Domestic residents, in foreign currency
UK	1,918.5	209.2	586.0
Japan	734.2	439.9	141.0
USA	77.4	990.5	--
Total	7,018.3	3,893.7	1,462.6

Table B. International Assets of Banks in Selected Countries
by Nationality of Ownership
(U.S. $ billions, end-June 2001)

	International Assets	
Banks based in:	Total	With Related Offices
France	1,040.6	243.7
Germany	2,358.7	534.3
Japan	1,585.1	416.5
UK	837.2	152.2
US	1,391.8	677.1
Total	11,775.4	3,449.9

Source: Bank for International Settlements, *International Banking and Financial Market Developments*, Tables 2A, 2C, 4A, and 8 (Basel, Dec. 2001).

8. Banks operating in their home country have a competitive advantage over foreign banks operating there, but this general statement conceals the fact that foreign banks from one country—the U.S.—are more efficient than even domestic banks in several developed countries, according to a study of domestic and foreign banks in France, Germany,

Spain, the U.K., and the U.S. Berger showed that in France, Germany, and Spain domestic banks were more profitable (by a relative measure of profit efficiency that they devised) than foreign banks from most other countries but not banks from the U.S. In France, U.S. banks reported profitability significantly higher than domestic banks at a 5% level. The authors conclude that the U.S. banks may derive a competitive advantage from their global operations that offsets the home advantage of the banks based in these countries. But the findings may be limited to these more developed countries. In many emerging markets, foreign banks from many countries have won a large and growing market share. Researchers at the International Monetary Fund compared the assets of banks owned more than 50% by foreigners to the assets of all banks in certain countries of Asia (Korea, Malaysia, Thailand), Central Europe (the Czech Republic, Hungary, Poland), and Latin America (Argentina, Brazil, Chile, Colombia, Mexico, Peru, Venezuela). The study reported that foreign control of bank assets was mainly below 10% in 1994 but rose substantially by 1999, in most cases to over 40%. In almost all countries, the foreign banks' return on equity was significantly higher than that of domestic banks, many of which showed losses. D. Mathieson and G. Schinasi, *International Capital Markets* (September 2000) at 153 and 166.

b. MARKET PARTICIPANTS

At this point, it should be clear that the markets for international finance include a variety of participants. It is useful to clarify these. The suppliers of funds are often referred to as savers and may be depositors or investors, depending on the transaction. The users of funds may be borrowers or issuers, depending on the transaction.

Financial intermediaries come between the savers and users. Traditionally, banks intermediate between savers (as depositors) and users (as borrowers) of funds. Banks as principals have continuing obligations to depositors and bear credit risk. This distinguishes them from securities companies, which help savers (investors) and users (issuers) transact business. The saver invests in the user by buying its securities. The securities company does not normally have to hold bonds or shares very long and has no continuing obligation to the investor or the issuer. The investor bears the risks of the issuer's performance. Banking and securities transactions are at the core of international finance.

c. THE ROLE OF COUNTRIES IN INTERNATIONAL FINANCE

Countries play a role in the market too. Bryant's tables reveal a profound difference between countries that serve as financial centers and those that do not. The international component of banks' assets (in Table A, Column 7) is much higher in Switzerland and the offshore banking centers, compared to countries that are not financial centers, such as Canada, Germany, France, or many other European countries. The latter group of countries have financial systems that are much more domestically oriented than the former group. In addition, the differences between host and home countries is revealed by comparing Bryant's Table A and Table B. The former group hosts banks that have their headquarters in many other countries called the home country. The governments of these host and home countries can become an important force in international finance by setting standards that govern market participants.

In all countries, government policy is important to savers and users of funds. The existence or even the threat of a damaging economic policy, an interventionist executive, high tax rates, price controls (including interest rate controls), exchange controls, a weak legal system, and political instability all affect investors' willingness to put their funds at risk in the country. The home/host distinction is relevant here. When, for example, investors are citizens of a high risk country, their special knowledge of that country can lead to massive capital flight.

d. MULTILATERAL INSTITUTIONS AND INTERNATIONAL FINANCE

In addition to the market participants and countries are a third set of institutions called multilateral because they are created and controlled by national governments. For international finance, two important institutions are the International Monetary Fund (IMF) and the World Bank, both based in Washington, D.C.. The Allied powers established both in 1944 by treaty to help stabilize post-war economies and rebuild Europe. The IMF, a multilateral institution controlled by the U.S. and other industrial countries, was set up to help member countries maintain the agreed exchange rates (see Chapter 6). The World Bank began as the International Bank for Reconstruction and Development (IBRD) to help Europe rebuild after the war.

For several decades, both agencies conservatively expanded their operations from post-War Europe to developing countries as colonies gained independence. Originally, the IMF loaned short-term to give countries time to adjust their balance of payments and the World Bank loaned long-term to government projects.

Their operations expanded in the 1970s, after the oil shock, in the 1980s as countries needed general purpose funds to adjust the structure of their economies, and again in the 1990s when the collapse of the Soviet Union brought demand from new states and countries in Eastern Europe and the former Soviet Union. Both agencies were funded by their shareholders, though the World Bank borrowed on international markets on the strength of its members' capital commitments. The major industrial countries controlled both agencies through weighted voting, the U.S. initially controlling about a third of the votes alone and well over 50% when combined with a few other countries, such as the U.K. and France at first, plus Germany and Japan later. Most other countries pooled their votes to form regional blocs that would elect an executive director. The size of the U.S. vote gradually eroded as membership boomed. Even so, the president of the IMF was traditionally French and the president of the World Bank was traditionally American. By the early 1990s, both agencies deployed around the world thousands of highly skilled people drawn from almost all member countries. For an analysis of the changing role of the IMF, see M. Bordo and H. James, *The International Monetary Fund: Its Present Role in Historical Perspective* (June 2000).

Notes and Questions

1. How might it matter to the various players, such as national governments, regulators, companies, and banks themselves, that a financial transaction is international rather than domestic?

B. INTERNATIONAL FINANCIAL MARKETS: TYPES AND TRENDS

Over several decades, international financial markets evolved as the structure of finance and international conditions changed. This section examines these trends.

1. THE LONG-TERM SHIFT OF FINANCIAL MARKETS FROM DOMESTIC TO INTERNATIONAL TO GLOBAL

Deryck Maughan, then president of Salomon Brothers and now co-chairman and co-CEO of Salomon Smith Barney, outlined the shift from domestic to international to global markets.

D. MAUGHAN, GLOBAL CAPITAL MARKETS AND THE IMPLICATIONS FOR FINANCIAL INSTITUTIONS
Talk Given at Harvard Law School (Sept. 20, 1993) (Maughan).

The world's economies, capital markets and financial institutions are connected today as never before.

Was this ordained? Only in part. Are the consequences fully understood? No. How will governments respond to further erosion of their economic sovereignty? Not clear. And how will we, denizens of Wall Street, respond? Variously.

. . .

National capital markets: For thirty years after the Second World War the international monetary system conceived by Keynes and White held up remarkably well. The key concepts were free trade, fixed but flexible exchange rates, and development finance—promoted in turn by the GATT, the IMF and the World Bank.

By and large this was a time of steady growth and low inflation, the era of demand management and the Phillips Curve. Credit markets were highly regulated. Interest rates were subject to government regulation, rather than being set by market forces. Capital markets were poorly developed and essentially national in character and purpose. Exhibit 1 shows the changing relationships among the world's capital markets, with the dots representing the national markets. Prior to 1973, financial markets were independent of one another, ringed by exchange controls and limited by regulations governing financial product innovation and market access.

International capital markets: The strains inherent in this ordered world became apparent in the late 1960s and culminated in President Nixon's devaluation of the dollar in 1971 and declaration that it was no longer convertible into gold. By 1973, the efforts to fix exchange rates between the dollar, the pound, the mark and the yen were abandoned, leading to generalized floating exchange rates, where the demand and supply for currencies established their price. We faced oil shocks, stagflation and interest rates at 20%. The policy consensus fractured, with disagreement on whether it was better to move forward under fixed or floating rates. In this period we also witnessed the rapid development of a large—and largely unregulated—off-shore capital market: the Euromarket. National capital and credit markets were now linked—not directly, but linked nonetheless. There were no reserve requirements for the banks and no SEC for the investment banks. London became the home for literally hundreds of banks and securities companies from all parts of the world, partly due to its favorable location, straddling the time zones of Tokyo and New York, and partly due to regulations which allowed this off-shore market to exist.

Global markets: We have not lacked for drama these ten years past. From the Plaza Accord in 1985 to the rupture of the European monetary system last year; from the bursting of Japan's bubble to the leveraged excesses in our own markets; from the Berlin Wall to Tiananmen Square, and a whole new group of countries looking to the West and its markets for capital. From 1985 on, in country after country, interest rates have been deregulated, capital markets liberated and foreign institutions granted increased access to hitherto protected markets. The essential point for today, however, is that the international system has become a multinational system, a global system where capital flows directly and in growing quantities from one economy to another.

Maughan illustrated his analysis with the following chart:

Capital Markets Evolution

	National	International	Global
Period	1945 - 73	1973 - 84	1985 - ?
System	Bretton Woods	Generalized Floating	G7/EC
Exchange Rates	Fixed	Floating	Hybrid
Exchange Controls	Yes	Hybrid	No
Market Access	No	Limited	Yes
Derivatives	No	Limited	Yes
Deregulation	No	Partial	Yes

Tracking the trend toward globalization statistically over several decades turned out to be very difficult with no overall measure for all financial flows (see Section 7 below). International trade flows grew five time faster than GDP from 1970 to 1990, and international finance grew even faster. But high international financial flows do not in themselves reveal how much financial systems are integrated. Statistical trends in international banking and securities markets reveal themselves better at a lower level of aggregation. One sees dramatic growth in the markets for foreign exchange, loans, bonds, and equities, and derivatives based on them. As you read the following sections, note how the relative importance of various instruments changed since the mid-1980s.

Notes and Questions

1. Review Maughan's discussion of the evolution of financial markets. Is there a significant difference between the "international" and "global" phases described in the text and his chart?

2. Consider the relevance of the two phases for regulation and government policy toward international finance.

   a. The shift to international allowed the players to escape domestic regulation. A major debate exists about the ability of national regulators to shape behavior to desired ends. Some say regulators are always at least one jump behind the protean markets. Others say regulation profoundly shapes market behavior, since it can change the cost structure of an activity. Would you expect the governments of the largest countries -- U.S., Japan, Germany -- to be powerless in this shift to international? Would they have gained from it in any ways?

b. The shift to global markets, according to Maughan, results from deregulation and liberalization. This does not mean governments of the largest countries no longer have a regulatory function, rather that they play less of a direct or command role and more of an indirect role affecting market behavior. To affect interest rates, for example, they no longer instruct banks to fix the rates at a given level. Instead, they try to affect the forces of supply and demand that determine interest rates. What would you expect the consequences of this new indirect approach to government policy to be for international financial markets? Would the euromarkets disappear or diminish in importance relative to domestic markets?

c. How would you expect these shifts to affect relations among regulators from different countries? Maughan says that globalization links domestic markets and that a liberal policy regime governs. Would you expect regulators to withdraw from the markets as a result? If you would not, what are the important national interests that would prompt them to remain active. What sort of activity would you expect? Would you expect national regulators to cooperate or compete more now than in the past?

2. FOREIGN EXCHANGE MARKETS

From the 1960s, governments of industrial countries and, more gradually, developing countries, lowered barriers to the cross-border flow of funds that had been segregating domestic financial markets. Dufey and Chung explain the importance of this:

DUFEY AND CHUNG

[O]ffshore banks must be able to clear payments in the respective national payment system, since at the beginning and end of every offshore deposit, and at the beginning and end of every loan, a payment must be made through the clearing system of the country where the respective currency is legal tender. Technically speaking, this system requires the existence of *nonresident convertibility* as a necessary, but not sufficient, condition for the existence of an offshore banking market. Without it, offshore transactions can only happen on a brokered basis by matching placers and takers of funds. In addition, transactors must have some freedom from exchange controls, because all offshore deposits and loans are international transactions from a legal point of view.

The statistics reveal the explosion of foreign exchange markets even since the mid-1980s. They consistently and substantially outstripped the growth of either world GDP or trade. For example, the nominal growth of worldwide foreign exchange trading from 1992 to 1995 was 48%. Daily turnover exceeded $1 trillion.

3. MARKETS FOR INDIRECT FINANCE: INTERNATIONAL BANK LENDING

International lending by banks exploded in the 1970s. According to the Bank for International Settlements, lending rose from $8.8 billion in 1972 to $103.6 billion 10 years later. It reached $349.7 billion in 1996 and continued to grow after that (see Section 7 below). Bank loans are indirect in the sense that the banks take deposits from savers and lend on to the users. The banks, as principals in the transaction, come between the ultimates savers and users. They intermediate the funds.

Banks engaged in international lending, as intermediaries, for centuries, usually financing trade and sometimes lending to sovereigns. The explosion of indirect lending in the 1970s took the form largely of syndicated loans, in which banks formed a group or syndicate that loaned very large sums to governments and multinational companies. Syndicated loans are discussed in Chapter 9.

4. MARKETS FOR DIRECT FINANCE: INTERNATIONAL BONDS

"We cannot show you the central place, the debt or stock exchange where international bonds are traded," noted Maughan. "Rather, it is a network of dealers connected by modern technology." The market for these bonds originally grew in response to government policy in many countries, as described by Dufey and Chung.

DUFEY AND CHUNG

With respect to the Eurobond market, the set of market imperfections responsible for its existence is based essentially on a regulatory dichotomy: foreign borrowers are prevented from issuing securities in national markets in various ways. (Sometimes these restrictions also pertain to domestic corporate issuers, especially when government preempts the domestic market.) On the other hand, the regulations that might prevent domestic investors from purchasing foreign securities are either less rigid or unenforceable.

. . .

Medium-term, fixed-income obligations of well-known entities denominated in strong currencies (essentially U.S. dollars, the currencies of the DM bloc, and the Japanese yen) represent the ideal vehicle for this investment clientele. Such securities are issued and largely placed *outside* the respective countries where these currencies are means of payment. They are therefore free from withholding taxes and assure anonymity to the holder because they are invariably issued in bearer form. And, while the Eurobond market has attracted a fair share of institutional investors, the market is to a great extent dominated by the behavior of individual investors. Indeed, with the wave of liberalization of major—and even not so major—national markets in the first half of the 1980s, many institutional investors pursuing active portfolio strategies have shifted their purchases back into the national markets, where they find securities with better liquidity.

———

International bond markets grew from merely $5.2 billion during 1967 to $708.8 billion in 1996. Displaced in the 1970s by the growth of intermediated lending, international bond markets expanded relatively again after the 1982 debt crisis. Including both bonds issued by foreign residents and eurobonds, the market for bond issues doubled between 1993 and 1999 to $2.6 trillion. See Berger at 7.

Since the mid-1980s, the line between debt and equity started to blur. For example, the supply of, and demand for, convertible bonds and bonds with warrants giving a right to equity of the issuer, grew in the 1980s. Japanese tax policy and financial regulations encouraged this growth.

In the late 1990s, corporate bonds routinely reached jumbo proportions. In 1999, for example, $1.4 trillion in international bonds were issued. In June 2000, Deutsche Telecom issued eight bonds that totaled $14.6 billion. M. Peterson, *Heyday of the Capital Markets*, Euromoney (September 2000) at 305. This was part of a long-term rising trend in corporate debt. U.S. non-financial firms, for example, had debt that was 28% of U.S. gross domestic product in 1960. By 1999, the ratio was 45%. C. Osler and G. Hong, *Rapidly Rising Corporate Debt: Are firms Now Vulnerable to an Economic Slowdown?* Federal Reserve Bank of New York Current Issues in Economics and Finance (June 2000).

Investors are worldwide. U.S. investors, for example, have found international bond markets increasingly important to them. Foreign investors in U.S. securities grew in importance relative to U.S. GDP. From 1993 to 2000, foreign ownership grew from 18% to 36% of U.S. treasuries and from 11% to 17% of U.S. corporate bonds. D. Mathieson and G. Schinasi, *International Capital Markets: Developments, Prospects, and Key Policy Issues*, Sept. 2000, at 10. A concern for the future was what would happen in financial markets when the volume of U.S. treasuries declined as the federal government reduced its debt. R. Garver, *Fed Chief: Wall St. to find Alternative to Treasuries*, American Banker, Apr. 30, 2001.

5. MARKETS FOR DIRECT FINANCE: CROSS-BORDER EQUITIES

Compared to the international markets for loans and bonds, the market for cross-border equities began to grow dramatically and achieve significance only in the mid-1980s. Investment managers actively began to seek differences in the valuation of similar companies listed and traded in various countries or of the same issuing company cross-listed in several countries. Investors sought to diversify their risk across countries. Accurate data about foreign ownership of shares varied by country. For the U.S. markets, foreign investors' share was relatively low: in 2000, they owned only 7% of U.S. equities, according to D. Mathieson and G. Schinasi, *International Capital Markets: Developments, Prospects, and Key Policy Issues*, Sept. 2000, at 10.

Accurate data about cross-border equity trading are particularly difficult to find. From 1987 to 1994 cross-border equity trading was reported in terms of flows. The amounts are recorded in Table 1 below. The table distinguishes between flows that are "gross" or "net." These two words have many meanings in finance. The IMF explained in a letter to the authors that:

a. Foreign equity investment has two main conduits:

   1. The purchase or sale of an equity security on a stock exchange local to the issuing company for the benefit of a non-resident investor. ... A UK fund manager's purchase of IBM stock in New York would be defined as a cross-border transaction.

   2. The purchase or sale of a foreign equity on a stock exchange local to the investor. A UK fund manager's sale of IBM stock via SEAQ International in London would be recorded as a cross-exchange transaction.

b. A distinction is made between the value of foreign equity trading and the value of new money flows into foreign equities....

   1. Foreign equity trading, or gross equity flows, are the sum of all purchases and all sales of foreign equity.

   2. New money inflows, or net equity investment, is the difference between the purchases and the sales of foreign equity.

Table 1: Cross-Border Equity Trading

	1987	1989	1990	1991	1992	1993	1994
	(Gross issues in billions of U.S. dollars)						
Cross equity flows	1,377.8	1,562.6	1,390.9	1,322.5	1,404.9	2,266.1	2,550.0
Cross-exchange trading	508.6	582.9	873.9	779.1	968.7	1,547.5	2,000.0
Net equity flows	16.4	86.6	3.2	100.6	53.7	196.3	119.6
Cross-border mergers and acquisitions	70.9	117.5	128.4	83.7	91.0	95.1	156.2

Source: International Monetary Fund, International Capital Markets: Developments, Prospects, and Policy Issues 189 (Aug. 1995).
[1]Data for 1994 are estimates.

Unfortunately, these data are difficult to identify and collect. The IMF stopped using this classification after 1994. Since then, it has reported only net purchases of domestic securities by non-residents and of foreign securities by residents in each of a few major industrial countries. Using a different measure (in constant dollars), the BIS estimated that international equity issues grew 40% in just two years between 1996 and 1998. Berger at 7.

6. MARKETS FOR DIRECT FINANCE: DERIVATIVES

The growth in derivative products has been perhaps the most remarkable feature of international markets in recent years," according to Herring and Litan. Derivative markets allow parties to take positions on the future value of many financial commodities, including interest rates and exchange rates. This in turn allows investors to hedge or speculate with great particularity by isolating, pricing, and managing risk across many financial markets. Some instruments are listed and traded on organized exchanges; these are for futures on interest rates, currencies, and stock indexes, and for many options. Other derivatives, such as interest and currency swaps, are created and traded over the counter.

These markets have grown rapidly since the late 1980s so that now nominal values are in the trillions of dollars. Exchange-traded derivatives exceeded $12 trillion in 1997, for example, and over the counter derivatives amounted to even more. The international component of derivative markets is difficult to identify, but both investors and instruments are often global. The huge nominal amounts combined with several other factors to make government officials around the world skeptical about the impact of the markets on countries' economies. Investors are often able to take positions using relatively little of their own money. The actual risk is difficult to quantify. Price movements in the derivatives markets may affect prices in the underlying markets for credit or currencies. Some policy makers fear that derivative markets destabilize other financial markets and increase systemic risk.

7. THE LONG-TERM SHIFT OF FINANCIAL MARKETS FROM INDIRECT TO DIRECT

Over many decades, indirect lending by banks declined relative to direct finance. Herring and Litan report that "the rate of growth of international bank lending has been eclipsed in the past decade by the growth in international issues of securities and in derivative instruments."

In the late 1970s, international bankers based particularly in New York had started to forecast the decline of their traditional deposit and loan business. Bankers Trust Company acted on this, selling many of its branches and setting out to become a leader in fee earning rather than asset based services. Its strategy paid off in increased profitability and by the late 1980s it was often cited as a leader in capital market operations worldwide. Many other banks followed. The troubles they encountered in the mid-1990s were a direct outcome of this earlier strategic change. Bankers Trust, for example, reported a 64% decline in its income for the fourth quarter of 1994. Four years later, it was acquired by Deutsche Bank of Germany.

Maughan, describing the shift to capital markets in the U.S., explains that the trend is due, at least in part, to an increasing emphasis on performance and diversification.

MAUGHAN

There has been a dramatic decline in the role of banks and thrifts as financial intermediaries in the United States. Their share of assets has declined from 56% in 1975 to 35% today. Pension funds and mutual funds are the big gainers over this period, from 16% to 35%. Deregulation has intensified competition in what has been a highly segmented financial system. Loans have been turned into securities—commercial paper, high-grade bonds, high-yield bonds, collateralized mortgage obligations, and so on. Deposits . . . migrated to lower cost, performance-oriented asset management vehicles. Ten years ago, Fidelity had $20 billion under management; today $235 billion. Technology will continue to pose a real threat to bricks-and-mortar distribution systems. Banks have responded by diversifying into investment banking, asset management, and, in Europe, insurance. But the point here is simply that loans today are just another financial product. And two-thirds of America's financial assets are now held by institutions that primarily buy securities..

[D]ebt securities as a [share of all] debt and credit in the United States. . . . account for 65% of this $15 trillion market, up from 45% of a much smaller market 15 years ago.

. . .

Performance & Diversification

Performance is [a related] trend. A lot of people start with government yield curves, what government bonds yield at different maturities. . . . [A]t 10 years, you can invest in Japan for a 4 1/4% yield, the United States at 5 3/8%, Germany 6 1/8%, UK 7 1/8%, Italy 9 3/4%. Which do you select? We have a balance sheet of about $180 billion at Salomon Brothers. About half of that balance sheet is resident outside the United States. So we make this decision every day. We track the correlations between these markets, to assess their degree of independence and whether there is indeed diversification of risk or the risks simply build one on another. Through diversification we seek higher risk-adjusted returns.

It might be argued that as markets continue to be open, the free flow of capital will force convergence of returns across all markets. . . . [But] important differences in the yield curves persist. Markets, we have to say, are still significantly domestic. Not everyone is a global investor. Our argument is not that we have a single pool of capital but that markets are now importantly connected, interact, and that the national markets exist within a global system.

———

Aggregate data that allow one to compare precisely the evolution of various international markets for financial instruments over many decades do not exist. For almost 30 years up to the mid-1990s, the Organization for Economic Cooperation and Development reported statistics for funds raised on international loan and bond markets, changing the series once, after 1982. Table 2 shows that in the early 1980s international loan markets were larger even than bond markets. Both were much larger than equity offers, for which five years of data have been added. These offers are similar to, but not quite the same as, funds raised. One problem for those who hunt and gather statistics is that the line between direct and indirect markets has blurred. You will see later in this book, for example, that participations in syndicated loans started as indirect finance but by the mid-1990s many were traded, putting them into the direct markets.

Table 2: Funds Raised on International Markets, 1967-1996
in billions US dollars

INSTRUMENT	1967	1972	1977	1982	1987	1992	1996
Loans	-	8.8	34.2	103.6	122.9	124.6	349.7
Of which:	-						
Syndicated Euro-loans		8.8	34.2	90.8	80.3	116.2	345.2
Bonds	**5.2**	**10.9**	**34.8**	**75.5**	**180.8**	**333.7**	**708.8**
Distribution:							
Euro-bonds	2.2	6.5	18.7	50.3	140.5	276.1	589.8
Foreign bonds	3.0	4.4	16.1	25.2	40.3	57.6	119.0
Type:							
Floating-rate notes	-	-	2.2	15.35	13.0	43.6	165.7
Straight bonds	5.1	9.5	31.1	7.2	121.3	265.4	464.4
Convertibles	-	1.1	1.2	2.6	18.2	5.2	25.6
With equity warrants	-	.1	.1	.5	24.8	15.7	8.8
Equity offers	-	-	-	-	**20.4**	**25.3**	n.a.
Total	**5.2**	**19.7**	**69.0**	**179.1**	**324.1**	**483.6**	

Source: Organization for Economic Co-operation and Development, Table F.T-O.a, "International Capital Markets Statistics" (1996), OECD Financial Market Trends (November 1997), and International Monetary Fund, International Capital Markets: Developments, Prospects, and Policy Issues 189 (Aug. 1995). Time series changes after 1982.

The Bank for International Settlements also collected data about international financial markets, using slightly different terms and grouping the markets in somewhat different ways. For some instruments, the BIS tables give amounts outstanding on a specific date. This is called the stock of funds and is reported in "Stock end-2001" in Table 3. For example, on December 31, 2001, investors held $243.1 billion of commercial paper issued in international markets. You can calculate the value of outstanding commercial paper a year earlier by deducting the net issues ($26.9 billion) in 2001 from the stock at the end of 2001. It is instructive to compare the stock of funds raised on international markets with its domestic counterpart. Domestic data are available for the end of September 2001. As of that date, the stock of bonds and notes raised on international markets was $6.7 trillion, or 27% of the $24.8 trillion on domestic markets. See BIS Quarterly Review, *International Banking and Financial Market Developments*, March 2002 at A79.

The BIS also reports the flow of funds during a period of time, such as from January 1, 2001 through December 31, 2001. These flows take different forms. New issues, also called gross issues, report flows of new funds in the market from savers to users, with no offsetting flows the other way. Reducing gross issues by repayments gives net issues. Net issues in year 2 equal the stock of funds at the end of year 2 less the stock of funds at the end of year 1. Table 3 shows net issues and new issues from 1994 to 2001. Announced issues are just that: announcements culled from the press about transactions in a market. An issue could be announced without being drawn in whole or part, so announcements give a less reliable picture of the actual flow of funds.

The tables suggest the fluctuating relative importance of each instrument. The causes, in addition to structural changes, are complicated economic factors having to do with existing and expected inflation rates, exchange rates, fiscal policy (since governments are big borrowers), and demand in the real economy, all major macro-economic variables.

Looking forward in 2000, a comprehensive comparative study reported the following (Berger at 64):

First, the finding . . . that foreign banks are less efficient on average than domestic banks suggests that efficiency considerations may limit the global consolidation of the financial services industry. Thus, domestically-based institutions would continue to play a large role in the provision of financial services. Second, our finding that some banking organizations can operate in foreign countries at or above the efficiency levels of domestic banks suggests that additional global consolidation of financial markets may be in the offing. Third, our finding that banking organizations from some countries, particularly the U.S., are better able to operate efficiently across borders suggests that financial institutions from these countries may capture disproportionate shares of international financial services business in the future. Fourth, if future research finds that U.S. banks derive their apparent efficiency advantages from U.S. regulatory/supervisory

Table 3: Funds Raised on International Markets, 1994-2001
in billions US dollars

Instruments	Net Issues						Stock-end 2001
	1994	1997	1998	1999	2000	2001	
Money Market	3.2	19.8	9.8	66.4	122.0	-79.3	397.5
Of which:							
Commercial Paper	0.5	7.9	22.2	44.3	76.8	26.9	243.1
Bonds & Notes	168.0	545.6	668.7	1148.8	1016.2	1150.4	6852.0
Of which:							
Floating rate	53.5	185.3	173.0	333.1	333.2	306.1	1745.2
Straight fixed	132.7	333.4	479.6	784.5	674.5	808.5	4833.7
Convertibles	4.8	43.6	31.4	34.9	14.4	37.0	261.2
Warrants	-23.0	-16.7	-15.3	-3.8	-6.0	-1.2	9.9
	New Issues						
Syndicated credit*	250.4	1136.3	902.2	957.1	1460.3	1434.4	—
Money Market	197.2	515.8	551.9	679.7	844.8	1042.7	s.a.
Of which:							
Commercial Paper	38.4	350.3	380.6	490.8	625.6	767.7	
Bonds & Notes	385.7	962.9	1076.2	1577.1	1767.2	1964.2	s.a.
Of which:							
Floating rate	78.7	265.2	247.8	442.7	557.0	571.81	
Straight fixed	273.9	663.6	796.9	1091.9	1163.8	1340.2	
Convertibles	22.3	31.0	30.6	41.7	44.6	50.3	
Warrants	10.8	3.1	0.9	0.8	2.4	1.9	
Equity	—	118.4	125.7	215.8	313.8	179.0	—
Total	833.3	2733.4	2656.0	3434.8	4386.1	4620.3	—

Source: *BIS Quarterly Review, International Banking and Financial Market Developments*, February 1995 - March 2001; 1994, tables 8, 9, 12; 1996-1997, tables 8, 11a, 11b; 1998 tables 10, 13a, 13b, 18; 1999 tables 10, 13a, 13b, 17; 2000-2001 tables 10, 13a, 13b, 18
— = not available   s.a. = see above   * = announced

conditions (e.g., easy geographic mobility) rather than from U.S. market conditions (e.g., a well developed securities market), then one might predict cross-border efficiency gains from similar liberalizations in other nations such as the Single Market Programme in the EU. . . . Because we base our conclusions on empirical results generated over a relatively short period of time, for a relatively short list of countries, and for a relatively small number of foreign banks, we make them cautiously . . . .

Notes and Questions

1. Be sure you understand the terms used in the tables and the text, such as international bonds, euronotes, floating rate notes, cross-border equity, and syndicated loans. What are the important differences among the instruments in the way they allocate risk?

2. Compare international finance through lending by banks (intermediated credit) with that through the securities markets. How significant are they in relation to each other? What would explain their relative importance?

3. The data about the relative importance of intermediated credit and of direct credit and equity investments through securities markets are difficult to compare because those for credit usually report the stock of funds and those for equity report flows. Data for banks are net of repayments, while those for bonds may be gross. (Check the Glossary for the meaning of these terms.) If it is so difficult to get basic data about the overall dimensions of major financial markets, what would be the effect on regulation of international finance??

4. In the 19th century, financial markets had also been international. Banks loaned to borrowers around the world and investors, particularly in Europe, bought the bonds of issuers from many countries, including the U.S., Latin America, and Asia. A study asked if the financial world today is really more integrated than it was 100 years ago, and concluded that the world was less integrated before World War I. Compared, however, to the earlier era, financial instability is now lower. M. Bordo, B. Eichengreen, and D. Irwin, *Is Globalization Today Really Different than Globalization a Hundred Years Ago?* June 1999.

C. COSTS AND BENEFITS OF THE INTERNATIONALIZATION OF FINANCE

A debate about whether the internationalization of finance is good or bad rages worldwide. No one contests the notion that internationalization and the opportunities for innovation that accompany it give investors much greater latitude to manage their risks. The argument is about whether the costs of this trend exceed the benefits. In the following excerpt, Maughan identifies some of the broader consequences of the trend.

MAUGHAN

Development Finance

Let us assume for the moment that the system of free trade and global capital prevails. What does it mean for countries that need development finance? Markets are not politically correct. Markets make their own choices. Markets seek the highest risk-adjusted return to capital. Will markets fund the development of sub-Saharan Africa? We doubt it. Markets will sift through the perceived opportunities and make their own choices. Capital is finite. Capital is rationed. More private capital will flow to China in the next five years than Russia. How about Argentina or Poland? Argentina can come to the market right now. Poland does not have the same opportunities. Which would you invest in—India or Brazil? Vietnam is attracting non-American capital; Angola gets very little of anyone's capital. So while we believe in markets as allocators of resources, we have to understand their requirements, and limits. There is still an important role for governments to support countries that do not have access to the capital markets.

Macroeconomic Management

What does the development of global capital markets mean for the ability of governments to manage their economies? How effective are fiscal, monetary and exchange rate policies in pursuit of employment and inflation objectives?

Fiscal policy: Governments find it difficult to increase tax rates and the majority of their spending is non-discretionary. Health and welfare benefits are largely provided on demand. There is a structural deficit in most developed societies. It is not as easy as was once thought to increase spending or cut taxes and create jobs. So fiscal policy as a tool for national economic managers is severely constrained.

Exchange rate policy: It is often said that the prime function of exchange rate policy relates to the balance of payments and specifically the trade account. Aggregate demand includes exports and imports, not just domestic consumption and investment. The exchange rate certainly affects the price of tradable goods and services. But our view is the weight of the argument runs the other way, that is to say capital flows largely determine exchange rates and trade flows adjust accordingly. The numbers: In 1992, $800 billion a day was traded on the foreign exchange market; that is sixty times the volume of world trade in goods.

Monetary policy: It seems to us that global capital flows make monetary targeting more problematic because foreign capital is flowing in and out of the national system. We no longer have a closed system as defined by the national money supply. Similarly, interest rates are responding to the total flow of capital, not just the domestic flow of capital. With international capital mobility, attempts to maintain fixed exchange rates and coordinated monetary policies are subject to the ratification of the capital markets. And there lies the tale of monetary union in Europe. The ERM crises of September 1992 and July 1993 demonstrated the limitations faced by national policy makers in their ability to set interest rates and exchange rates in defiance of what markets believed was sustainable.

The comparative study of cross-border banking by Berger looked for possible costs and benefits of globalization. Much quantitative research about efficiency was inconclusive because of methodological and data problems (Berger at 25-26). The authors speculated that globalization could increase systemic risk by spreading a crisis from one country to another, but noted that it could also mitigate systemic risk by permitting diversification (Berger at 37). The increasing scale of banks that accompanies globalization allows the larger issue and trading of securities by institutional customers of the banks (Berger at 44). On the other hand, scale may reduce national governments' ability to manage monetary policy, since large banks appear to be less sensitive to central banks' interest rate policies than small banks (Berger at 49).

Notes and Questions

1. To what extent do the consequences of internationalization described by Maughan result in costs or benefits?

    a. Maughan describes markets that are ruthless in their evaluation of investment opportunities. Is this a cost or benefit of internationalization?

    b. Is the apparent diminution of a national government's control over its financial system desirable?

D. THE IMPACT OF INTERNATIONALIZATION: THE CASE OF KOREA IN 1997

In 1997, as a financial crisis transformed the Asian miracle into what appeared to be a disaster, many people became acutely aware of the extent to which countries had opened themselves to the vagaries of global financial markets. This vulnerability is revealed in the crisis that hit Korea.

Finance's global imperative reached Korea more slowly than many other countries. But in the 1990s, Korea opened to international capital flows. Lenders and investors rushed to take advantage of the country's booming economy and prospects. Indeed, when crisis hit in 1997, Korea boasted the eleventh largest output in the world.

Korea's performance made it part of the East Asian miracle. Having grown a spectacular 7.7% each year from 1985 to 1995, Korea's per capita income of $9,700 placed among the top 25 countries worldwide. Trade accounted for much of its growth, and exports -- almost all manufactures -- were 33% of GDP in 1995. With over 95% of the population literate, the workforce was well equipped for global markets. Domestic investment was very high and growing: 32% of GDP in 1980 and 37% in 1995. Domestic savings grew to finance most of this, accounting for 25% of GDP in 1980 and 36% in 1995. See World Bank, *World Development Report 1997*. Many people knew that Korea's financial system was weak and that powerful business groups played a major role in the economy, but a common view before the 1997 crisis was that the economy was strong enough to accommodate these problems so that the government, elected in 1993, could deal with them gradually.

By 1997, Koreans tapped many sources of international finance, as described in Tables 3 and 4. A full range of instruments was deployed: short, medium, and long maturities included deposits with banks, notes, loans, and bonds. Derivatives and other off-balance-sheet contingent liabilities like back-up facilities grew in use. Foreign banks were the largest providers of funds. From December 1993 to July 1997, foreign banks' loans to Koreans grew from $45.2 billion to $116.8 billion, while their liabilities (such as dollar deposits from Koreans) remained much lower. Outstanding international debt securities issued by Korean nationals rose from $15.2 to $48.9 billion. Korean banks were the largest group of direct recipients and Korean companies the second largest, though the banks loaned much of the funds they received on to the companies, still in the foreign currencies. Borrowers took the funds through units in Korea and outside; Korean banks, for example, borrowed dollars through their Seoul offices and through branches and subsidiaries located in London, Hong Kong, and other financial centers. Foreign banks in Korea funded loans to companies in Korea by borrowing from headquarters or sister banks outside Korea.

By comparison, domestic financing grew more slowly (see Table 3). Bank loans, made in won, grew from $149.3 to $277.3 billion from 1993 to 1995, then declined to $185 billion in 1996. Debt securities, in won, rose from $185.1 in 1994 to $233.3 billion in June 1997. The market capitalization of the Korean stock exchange fluctuated. In the mid-1990s, the size and activity of Korea's stock market was appropriate to its per capita income, according to the International Finance Corporation. In 1995, for example, Korea's stock market ranked 16th in the world by market capitalization, 9th by trading (just ahead of Canada), and 10th by the number of listed domestic companies (just ahead of Germany). Listed companies were relatively small, so Korea placed only 33rd in this ranking. See IFC, Emerging Stock Markets Factbooks 1996, Korea, 170-

**Table 4. Foreign and Domestic Financing for Korea
December 1993 - June 1997**
(\$ billions, amount outstanding at end of period unless noted)

Item	12/93	12/94	12/95	12/96	6/97
Foreign currency loans by banks: BIS reporting banks' external positions with Korea:					
Assets	45.2	61.0	83.3	108.8	116.8
Liabilities	15.2	20.5	25.1	30.0	36.6
of which: with non-bank Korean borrowers					
Assets	10.6	13.5	17.9	23.9	26.2
Liabilities	1.5	2.3	3.6	3.5	3.1
Syndicated lending: Announced international syndicated credit to Koreans (not outstanding)	3.7	4.1	3.1	5.9	11.2
International debt securities					
Issued by Korean residents	13.9	18.2	26.7	42.5	47.2
of which:					
International money market instruments	na	na	na	4.4	2.4
International bonds and notes	13.9	18.2	18.4	38.1	44.8
Issued by Korean nationals	15.2	19.9	28.2	44.5	48.9
of which, by issuer:					
Financial institutions	na	na	5.0	14.8	14.1
Governments and state institutions	na	na	12.1	15.5	19.2
Corporate issuers	na	na	11.1	14.1	15.6
of which, by type of instrument:					
International money market instruments	na	na	na	4.9	2.6
International bonds and notes	19.9	26.9	28.0	39.6	46.2
Domestic (won) bank credit (\$ equivalent)	196.0	237.5	277.3	185.2	na
Domestic debt securities (\$ equivalent)					
Private	na	149.3	186.0	195.1	189.3
Public	na	35.8	41.3	43.9	44.0
Stock market capitalization (\$ equivalent)	139.4	191.8	182.0	138.8	na

Sources: Bank for International Settlements, *International Banking and Financial Market Developments (Basel, various issues)*, IMF, *International Financial Statistics Yearbook* (1997), International Finance Corporation, *Emerging Markets Statistical Factbook* (1996 and 1997).
na = not available.

73. The full role of foreign portfolio investors, who were allowed in very gradually, is not known.

According to the BIS, at the end of June 1997, banks had $103.4 billion in cross border claims in all currencies and in non-Won local claims against borrowers in Korea. Of this, Korean banks owed $67.3 billion and the non-bank private sector owed $31.7 billion. Most – $70.2 billion was for less than one year. Bank for International Settlements, *The Maturity, Sectoral and Nationality Distribution of International Bank Lending*, Basel, January 1998, Table 1.

The crisis that drained Korea in late 1997 first gathered force in Southeast Asia during the summer. Thailand, then Indonesia and Malaysia, suffered from massive outflows of funds as their currencies plunged against the dollar and other major currencies. Through the International Monetary Fund, the world's leading economies organized support in the form of short-term loans conditioned on changes in national policy that were expected to strengthen the recipient's economy. Turning to Korea, investors saw a slowing economy with many structural problems, feared being caught in a repeat of the Southeast Asian debacle, and rushed to withdraw their funds.

The collapse of the won marked and increased the depth of the crisis. For several years, the won traded around 800 to the dollar, then declined to around 900 in early 1997. Over a few weeks starting in mid-October, the won fell almost 10% against the dollar. When it fell another 10% in one day, November 19, the Korean government suspended trading in the won and stopped efforts to support it with the country's dwindling reserves of dollars, other hard currencies, and gold. The IMF negotiated a $55 billion aid package that was quickly revealed to be inadequate and the won fell more. By late January 1998, a dollar bought over 1700 won.

In a letter dated November 24, 1999 to the Managing Director of the IMF, Korea's central bank governor and finance minister promised to continue the structural changes underway. They agreed to detailed policies, setting dates for specific benchmarks. By late 2000, Korea led the region in corporate restructurings. International Monetary Fund, "IMF Concludes Article IV Consultation with Korea," Public Information Notice No. 99/115 (Dec. 29, 1999); S. Fidler, *IMF Urges Asia to Speed Up Corporate Reform*, Financial Times, Dec. 5, 2000; and F. Gimbel, *Bank Loans to Emerging Asia Jump*, Financial Times, Dec. 7, 2000.

Korea's recovery took time. Growth was negative in 1998. Indeed, the 10,000 bankruptcies during January to March 1998 almost equaled the 11,570 bankruptcies in the entire 1996. In May 1998, the stock market reached an eleven year low. The government and the IMF revised their agreement in 1998 and again in 1999. In 1998, the government set up the Korea Asset Management Corporation (KAMC), modeled on the U.S. Resolution Trust Corporation and funded by a huge bond issue.

KAMC bought banks' bad loans at a discount. The government closed merchant banks and required others to increase their capital to world standards that year. It pursued recapitalization plans for all 12 commercial banks. The government reorganized deposit insurance funds and consolidated into one agency the supervision of all financial institutions. In January 1999, for example, the government chose a consortium of U.S. investors to buy 51% of a top local Korean commercial bank; the government itself would own the other 49%. Similar efforts were underway to restructure Korea's corporate sector. In all, government support amounted to 14% of GDP, the country's output, in 1998.

In 1999, the economy turned around so dramatically that it grew about 9% and posted strong growth into 2002. Annual inflation was below 1%. Personal consumption led this growth, and investment followed. Macroeconomic policies supported the turnabout. Structural change took place grudgingly, however. Analysts reported that basic business practices were not changing. For example, affiliates were acquiring many of the companies that were being closed. The five largest chaebol became even more dominant, measured by their share of GDP, during the several years of restructuring. The government tried to show that they were not too big to fail by forcing the bankrupt Daewoo group, the second largest of the chaebol, to restructure and sell units even to foreign firms under the threat of receivership. As a result, many observers questioned whether Korea's recovery would last. See C. Adams, D. Mathieson, G. Schinasi, and B. Chadha *International Capital Markets: Developments, Prospects, and Key Policy Issues* (September 1998); J. Lowenstein, "Korea: Can't Change -- Won't Change," Euromoney 106 (September 1998); and J. Larkin, "U.S. Consortium Wins Race to Buy Korea First Bank," Financial Times, January 2-3, 1999; S. Irvine, "The Great Universe is Torn Asunder," Euromoney 358 (September 1999); R. Lee, "Seoul in New Push to Clear Daewoo Debts," Financial Times, January 7, 2000.

Notes and Questions

1. Countries have long histories of domestic financial crises in which lenders and investors fuel large price rises in assets of various sorts (real estate is a typical case), only to see the bubble burst and their investments badly eroded or erased. How would the role played by international finance in the Korean crisis make it different from domestic crises? In addressing this question, consider the causes of the crisis, its effect, and possible solutions to it.

2. To avoid similar crises in the future, should Korea reimpose capital controls?

INTERNATIONAL ASPECTS OF MAJOR DOMESTIC MARKETS

Part I presents the international aspects of the world's major domestic financial markets, the United States (Chapters 2 and 3), the European Union (Chapters 5 and 7), and Japan (Chapter 8). We focus on banking and securities markets. The international aspects of these markets involve cross-border transactions. For example, for United States domestic banking markets, this part covers the entry and operation of foreign banks serving U.S. customers and U.S. banks serving foreign customers. For U.S. securities markets, the international aspects involve foreign issuers selling securities to U.S. investors and U.S. issuers selling securities to investors outside the United States. One important theme is the difficulty of applying a pure national treatment standard to foreign firms.

For the European Union, our primary interest is the operation of the internal market and the rules for the conduct of banking and securities within the union. The creation of the European Economic and Monetary Union (EMU), and the advent of the euro, are events of enormous importance to international finance. EMU will likely lead to further integration and expansion of European markets.

For Japan, the theme is the effect of the Big Bang reforms of financial markets, with particular focus on the problem of troubled financial institutions. The gyrations in the Japanese markets have created enormous opportunities and risks for foreign financial institutions.

CHAPTER TWO

INTERNATIONAL ASPECTS OF U.S. SECURITIES REGULATION

This Chapter begins with some background data on the degree to which the U.S. capital market is internationalized and then examines how the United States regulates (1) the distribution and trading of securities issued by foreign companies in the United States and (2) the distribution outside the United States of securities issued by U.S. and foreign companies to U.S investors. This requires some basic understanding of securities regulation in general.

The traditional goal of securities regulation, investor protection, may have to be tempered in a "global market" by (1) the desire of U.S. investors to invest and trade in foreign securities, (2) the reality that they may do so outside the United States, and (3) the importance to the United States of maintaining the world's leading domestic capital market, which requires openness to foreign issuers.

Our focus is on the regulation of the securities markets, primary and secondary, rather than on the firms participating in these markets. Institutional regulation, however, will be the major focus for banking. This difference is driven by the nature of the primary regulatory concerns, investor protection in securities markets and safety and soundness of banks.

A. INTERNATIONALIZATION OF U.S. SECURITIES MARKETS

In 1987, a major study of the Securities and Exchange Commission (SEC) examined the internationalization of the U.S. securities markets. Some key excerpts follow.

U.S. SECURITIES AND EXCHANGE COMMISSION, INTERNALIZA-
TION OF THE SECURITIES MARKETS
II-11 to II-24, II-62 to II-90 (1987).

C. Unique and Influential Role of U.S. Securities Markets

The U.S. capital markets' influence on other markets—both foreign and international—appears to have been substantial. In general, the U.S. regulatory system has allowed financial innovation to take place—both in the U.S. domestic securities market and in the dollar sector of the Eurobond market. This has facilitated the operational efficiency of our securities markets and international capital mobility. The rapid maturation of the other securities markets, however, presents new challenges and opportunities resulting from increased competition for new issues placement and in secondary market trading in both domestic and international issues.

At the end of 1986 the market capitalization of U.S. equities totaled $2.6 trillion or about 43 percent of the world's stock market capitalization. This is down from 56 percent just two years ago. As seen in Table II-2, the next largest, Japan's, was about two-thirds the size of the U.S. The appreciation of the yen relative to the U.S. dollar and the strong growth of the Japanese stock market have both contributed to the rapid growth in the capitalization of the Japanese equities market. The equity capitalization of most other major markets has been growing faster (measured in U.S. dollars) than the U.S. market.

. . .

Table II-2

MARKET CAPITALIZATION OF WORLD'S STOCK MARKETS
(US $ Billions)

Country	1978	1980	1982	1984	1985	1986
United States	$ 870	$1,391	$1,481	$1,714	$2,160	$2,556
Japan	327	357	410	617	909	1,746
United Kingdom	118	190	182	219	328	440
Germany	83	71	69	78	179	246
Canada	67	113	105	116	147	166
France	45	53	29	40	79	150
Italy	10	25	20	23	65	141
Switzerland	41	46	41	43	90	132
Australia	27	60	41	52	63	78
Netherlands	22	25	22	31	52	73
All Others	75	141	125	133	172	267
TOTAL	$1,685	$2,472	$2,525	$3,066	$4,244	$5,995

Note: Data are estimates of exchange-listed stocks with market value of investment companies excluded. U.S. data includes NASDAQ stocks. Data excludes foreign corporations, except for the NASDAQ portion of the U.S. market during the years 1978 to 1982.

Source: SEC Monthly Statistical Review (various issues)
NASDAQ Fact Book (various issues)

A broader view of the size and depth of the U.S. securities markets is given in Table II-3 which shows the amount of new debt and equity capital raised by governments, private non-financial enterprises, financial institutions and foreign issuers. In 1986, all issuers raised $812 billion in capital through securities issued in the U.S. In Japan, the next largest market, issuers raised slightly more than one-half this amount, $438 billion. Ten years ago the proportions were roughly the same with issuers raising $206 billion in the U.S. and $89 billion in Japan.

Table II-3

GROSS NEW ISSUES IN THE CAPITAL MARKETS
OF TEN MAJOR COUNTRIES: 1986

		Percent of Total			
	Total U.S. $ Billions	Central State Gov't.	Private Enter-prises[1]	Financial Institu-tions[2]	Foreign Issues
United States	$812	63%	18%	18%	1%
Japan	438	43	12	44	1
Italy	126	77	13	10	0
Germany	126	30	5	65	0
France	68	34	31	35	0
United Kingdom	33	63	23	11	2
Switzerland	34	4	11	15	69
Canada[3]	57	58	---	---	0
Australia[4]	28	90	6	4	0
Netherlands	12	51	6	41	1

*Insignificant (less than 1%)
1. This category includes all non-financial business.
2. This category includes both government and privately-owned institutions.
3. The "Private Enterprises" and "Financial Institutions" figures are combined for Canada totaling 42 percent.
4. Table shows 1985 data for Australia.

Sources: OECD Financial Statistics; Bank of Canada Review, March 1987; Year Book Australia, 1986; Reserve Bank of Australia Bulletin, March 1987; Directorate of Economic and Policy Analysis

The dominant position of the U.S. securities markets can be explained, in part, by the size of our gross national product which is double and even triple that of the other leading economies of the world.

.   .   .

The U.S. securities markets and its regulation appear to have influenced the shape of other markets. Many securities instruments were first introduced in the U.S. securities market and are now being introduced around the world. U.S. securities firms maintain a sizable presence in most international financial centers.

.   .   .

A considerable dynamic for change was initiated in the U.S. in the early 1970s with the gradual deregulation of brokerage commission rates on stock exchange transactions. When legislation passed in 1975 completed the process, the U.S. securities industry moved into a much more competitive era. Other countries, such as Canada, started to reduce commission rates on large orders fairly soon thereafter. The process of unfixing commission rates was not completed until 1983 in Canada, 1984 in Australia and 1986 in the United Kingdom.

The quotation and transaction systems which have become an important market medium in the U.S. are being used increasingly in other markets such as Japan, the United Kingdom and Singapore. In addition, automated execution systems for small orders which were introduced in U.S. stock markets in response to the deregulation of commission rates are now being offered in other markets around the world.

.   .   .

The regulatory climate in the U.S. has permitted our securities markets to become a leader in financial innovation. New financial instruments are now being introduced in foreign markets with increasing frequency. Trading of standardized options began in the U.S. in 1973.

.   .   .

The U.S. securities markets are also unique in their regulations governing disclosure, insiders and intermediaries, accompanied by a flexibility that has permitted competition and innovation. The U.S. prohibits insider trading and has vigorous enforcement. U.S. regulation also requires the purchasers of corporate securities to register their ownership (conducted almost entirely by transfer agents and brokers). In many countries the bearer form of securities issuance is practiced, especially for bonds.

Regulation of new issue and periodic disclosure in the U.S. places considerable emphasis on extensive financial reporting. The disclosure program, including related procedures and potential legal liabilities may, however, serve as a disincentive to the issuance of foreign bonds and equity securities in the U.S. capital market. U.S. regulation emphasizes full disclosure rather than merit regulation which seems to play a much larger role in some other capital markets. Recent modifications to the disclosure program have placed more emphasis on the continuous reporting of corporate issuers. In the U.S. broker-dealers are also closely regulated regarding trading practices, customer protections and financial solvency. The supervision of broker-dealers and trading markets is primarily conducted by self-regulatory organizations ("SROs") such as the exchanges and the NASD under the oversight of the SEC.

. . .

I.   Foreign Stock Listings and International Stock Trading

Listing on a foreign exchange may broaden an issuer's shareholder base and, in some markets, it is necessary in order for domestic institutions to purchase the company's shares. For example, in France local insurance companies may be prohibited from purchasing shares that are not listed on a French bourse. With respect to certain markets, changes in accounting standards and disclosure requirements have made foreign listings more attractive. This apparently has been a factor in increasing the interest of foreign listings on the Tokyo Stock Exchange.

U.S. exchanges have also undertaken initiatives to increase the number of foreign listed companies. The American and New York Stock Exchanges in June 1987 received approval from the Commission to revise their listing standards. Some foreign corporations apparently had been reluctant to list on U.S. exchanges due to differences in listing standards in the U.S. and their home country. Now certain listing standards may be waived by the American and New York Stock Exchanges if those standards conflict with the laws and practices found in the home market of a foreign corporation. The rule revisions afford U.S. exchanges a better opportunity to compete on an international basis and may provide U.S. investors with greater access to foreign securities.

As of December 1986, 512 foreign corporations had their securities listed on the London Stock Exchange. At the same time 59 foreign companies were listed on the New York Stock Exchange ("NYSE"), approximately one-third of which are Canadian corporations. At the Tokyo Stock Exchange, 52 foreign firms were listed at year-end 1986 compared to only 21 firms at year-end 1985.

. . .

Table II-14

DOMESTIC AND FOREIGN LISTED COMPANIES
ON MAJOR STOCK EXCHANGES
(Year-End)

Exchange	Domestic Listings 1985	Domestic Listings 1986	Foreign Listings 1985	Foreign Listings 1986	Total Listings 1985	Total Listings 1986
American	731	747	51	49	783	796
Amsterdam	232	267	242	242	474	509
Australia[1]	1,069	1,162	26	31	1,095	1,193
Brussels	192	191	144	140	336	331
Copenhagen	243	274	6	7	249	281
Germany[1]	451	492	177	181	628	673
London	2,116	2,101	500	512	2,616	2,613
Luxembourg	N/A	253	N/A	168	N/A	421
Milan	147	184	0	0	147	184
New York	1,487	1,516	54	59	1,541	1,575
Paris	489	874	189	226	687	1,100
Singapore	122	122	194	195	316	317
Tokyo	1,476	1,499	21	52	1,497	1,551
Toronto	912	1,034	54	51	966	1,085
Zurich	131	145	184	194	315	339

1. Reflects data for the Association of Australian and German stock exchanges
which include all exchanges in their respective countries.

N.A.—Not available

Source: The London Stock Exchange Quarterly, The London Stock Exchange
(various issues)

Table II-14 shows the extent of foreign stock listings on fourteen of the world's major stock exchanges at year-end 1986. With the exception of Milan, each of the exchanges had at least one non-domestic listing. The London Stock Exchange has the greatest number of U.S. companies listed on an exchange outside of the U.S. and the highest number of foreign listings of any market. U.S. equity listings on the London Stock Exchange have increased from 73 in 1975 to 199 in 1986. For the three Benelux countries, 44 percent of the listed corporations are foreign companies, while the comparable figure for the Zurich Stock Exchange is 59 percent.

Trading of foreign shares has increased on many exchanges. On the London Stock Exchange, for example, trading activity in foreign equities has averaged approximately $507 million per day since Big-Bang. Prior to October 27, 1986, this figure may have been as low as $24 million per day. At the Tokyo Stock Exchange, between 1973 and 1984, annual trading in foreign equities averaged less than two million shares. In 1985, annual volume in foreign equities increased to 131 million, while trading during the first six months of 1986 equaled 185 million shares.

Trading in foreign equity issues has also increased on the NYSE, from 804 million shares in 1984 to 1.2 billion shares in 1986. As a percent of total NYSE share volume, however, the amount attributable to foreign issues remained fairly constant during this period at approximately 3.5 percent.

.   .   .

J. Internationalization of Portfolio Investment Flows

U.S. investors have increased their purchases of foreign stocks since the elimination of the interest equalization tax. In 1975 U.S. investors bought $1.7 billion in foreign stocks (see Table II-16). By 1986 U.S. purchases of foreign stocks totaled a record $51.7 billion. In a similar dramatic fashion, U.S. investors have increased their purchases of foreign debt securities from $8.7 billion in 1975 to $169.8 billion in 1986. Though U.S. investors sell their holdings of foreign stocks and bonds in adjusting their portfolios, the net capital flow from U.S. transactions in foreign securities has been outbound in every year since 1975. In 1975 U.S. investors purchased $6.3 billion more in foreign securities than they sold. In 1986 net purchases of foreign securities by U.S. investors amounted to $4.5 billion.

.   .   .

Table II-16

INTERNATIONAL TRANSACTIONS IN U.S. AND FOREIGN CORPORATE STOCKS AND DEBT SECURITIES

(U.S. $ Millions)

Corporate Stocks

	Foreign Activity in U.S. Stocks			U.S. Activity in Foreign Stocks		
Year	Purchases	Sales	Net Capital Flow	Purchases	Sales	Net Capital Flow
1975	15,355	10,678	4,677	1,730	1,542	-188
1980	40,298	34,870	5,428	10,044	7,897	-2,147
1981	40,686	34,856	5,830	9,586	9,339	-247
1982	41,881	37,981	3,900	8,504	7,163	-1,341
1983	69,770	64,360	5,410	17,046	13,281	-3,765
1984	59,834	62,814	-2,980	15,917	14,816	-1,101
1985	81,995	77,054	4,941	24,803	20,861	-3,942
1986	148,134	129,436	18,698	51,744	50,292	-1,452

All Debt Securities[1]

	Foreign Activities in U.S. Debt Securities			U.S. Activity in Foreign Debt Securities		
Year	Purchases	Sales	Net Capital Flow	Purchases	Sales	Net Capital Flow
1975	14,306	11,545	2,761	8,720	2,383	-6,337
1980	66,595	56,262	10,333	18,090	17,090	-1,000
1981	85,763	65,677	20,086	23,013	17,553	-5,460
1982	117,632	98,863	18,769	33,809	27,167	-6,642
1983	153,680	147,351	6,329	39,572	36,333	-3,239
1984	275,634	241,237	34,397	59,948	56,017	-3,931
1985	585,174	541,042	44,132	85,214	81,216	-3,998
1986	1,176,027	1,100,951	75,076	169,798	166,700	-3,098

1. Data includes both corporate and governmental debt issues.
Source: U.S. Treasury Bulletin (various issues)

Foreign investors' purchases of U.S. stocks and bonds has mirrored the growth of U.S. corporations' presence in overseas markets. Foreigners purchased $15.4 billion of U.S. stocks and $14.3 billion of U.S. debt securities in 1975. In 1986 foreign investors' purchases had increased to $148.1 billion of U.S. stocks and $1.2 trillion of U.S. debt instruments. The net capital flow from their purchases and sales of all U.S. securities has been inbound to the U.S. every year since 1975, increasing from $7.4 billion in 1975 to $93.7 billion in 1986.

Foreign activity in U.S. equity and debt securities reached record highs in 1986. Nevertheless, foreign activity in U.S. debt securities (primarily U.S. Treasury issues) is substantially greater than in U.S. equities. During 1986, 89 percent of the foreign activity in U.S. securities was attributable to transactions in debt securities. The most active foreign participants in the secondary market for U.S. debt securities are investors from Japan and the United Kingdom. Investors from these two countries accounted for 50 percent of the total foreign activity in U.S. debt securities during 1986.

. . .

Total U.S. activity in foreign securities (purchases and sales) also reached a record high in 1986 of $438.5 billion and represents a two-fold increase from 1985's record of $212 billion. As with foreign activity in U.S. securities, U.S. investors' trading in both foreign stocks and bonds reached record levels in 1986.

U.S. activity in foreign securities has traditionally been concentrated in the debt and equity issues of the United Kingdom and Japan. The equity markets of Japan and the United Kingdom are, respectively, the second and third largest in the world. During 1986, U.S. transactions in the debt and equity securities of these two countries accounted for 67 percent of the total activity by U.S. investors in foreign debt and equity issues.

.   .   .

K. Impact of Internationalization on U.S. Markets

There has been an international presence in the U.S. securities markets for at least a century. Strong investment ties have existed among the United Kingdom, Canada, and the U.S. and, more recently, the U.S., Japan and Western Europe. As noted above, there has been a dramatic increase in foreign portfolio investments in the U.S. and in U.S. investments in foreign securities markets. Part of the increase in U.S. portfolio investments in foreign markets reflects the trend in recent years for U.S. investors to purchase mutual funds and closed-end funds investing in foreign securities markets. These funds provide U.S. investors with another avenue into foreign securities markets as well as the diversification typically associated with mutual funds. The number of global mutual funds has increased from 21 in December 1983 to 59 in December 1986 (see Table II-18). The value of international fund sales also grew from $1.5 billion in 1984 to $7.6 billion during 1986. In addition to these global funds, there are about twelve U.S. exchange-listed closed-end country funds investing in the securities of the emerging markets of Korea, Taiwan and Mexico as well as the developed markets such as France, Australia, Germany and Japan.

.   .   .

Table II-18

OVERVIEW OF GLOBAL MUTUAL FUNDS
(U.S. $ Billions)

Year	Number of Funds	Global Fund Assets	Global Fund Sales
1983	21	$ 3.5	$ NA
1984	30	5.2	1.5
1985	42	7.9	1.8
1986	59	$15.9	$ 7.6

Source: Investment Company Institute

An increase in U.S. demand for foreign securities is also evidenced by the number of foreign companies with securities traded through NASDAQ or on exchanges in the form of ADRs.

Between 1982 and 1986 the number of ADRs traded through NASDAQ or on a stock exchange increased from 85 to 110. Most ADRs are traded through NASDAQ. In addition, there are several hundred more ADRs traded over-the-counter outside of NASDAQ. There also has been a substantial increase in the total number of ADR shares. Ten years ago there were roughly 150 million such shares outstanding in the U.S. In 1986, there were 2.4 billion shares outstanding; this represents a 16-fold increase over the past decade.

Despite the growth of foreign stocks traded through ADRs there has been a decline in the number of foreign securities listed on U.S. exchanges. In 1976 there were 175 foreign bond issues listed on U.S. exchanges. Ten years later there were 105 issues (see Table II-19). The number of foreign stocks (including ADRs) listed on U.S. exchanges increased only slightly from 115 in 1976 to 123 in 1986. The U.S. stock markets have not kept pace with other stock markets around the world in attracting foreign listings. As noted earlier, the Commission recently approved modifications to the American and NYSE listing standards. This may facilitate foreign listings in the U.S.

The U.S. domestic market has not kept pace with the trend toward internationalization in terms of the amount of capital raised in the U.S. securities market by foreigners. Throughout the last ten years, Yankee securities (foreign issues of stocks and bonds in the U.S.) registered with the SEC have remained generally in the four to six billion dollar range. Also, the number of foreign equity issues traded on U.S. exchanges has remained fairly constant. In 1977 there were 116 such issues. Ten years later there were 123. Foreign bonds traded on the U.S. exchanges have declined from 175 in 1977 to 105 in 1986.

A closer look at the Yankee securities markets shows how U.S. participation in the internationalization process has been uneven. The annual issuance of foreign securities registered with the SEC has not kept pace with the growth in international markets in debt and equity securities. While the issuance of foreign securities in the U.S. has not declined in nominal terms, it has declined in relative terms. In 1977 registered public offerings of foreign issues in the U.S. represented 13 percent of the dollar volume of our public new issues market (see Table II-20). In 1986 that portion dropped to three percent.

.   .   .

Table II-19

DOMESTIC AND FOREIGN SECURITIES
LISTED ON U.S. EXCHANGES
(Number of Issues)

	Equity		Bonds		Total	
Year	Domestic	Foreign	Domestic	Foreign	Domestic	Foreign
1976	3,746	116	2,923	175	6,669	291
1977	3,559	115	---	---	3,771	---
1978	3,459	106	2,961	177	6,420	283
1979	3,377	96	3,190	174	6,567	270
1980	3,557	99	3,350	157	6,907	256
1981	3,498	103	3,405	148	6,903	251
1982	3,530	103	3,579	134	7,109	237
1983	3,484	111	3,831	128	7,315	239
1984	3,421	114	4,043	121	7,464	235
1985	3,374	113	4,215	117	7,589	230
1986	3,360	123	4,002	105	7,362	228

Source: Directorate of Economic and Policy Analysis
          Securities and Exchange Commission

Table II-20

DOMESTIC CORPORATE FOREIGN ISSUES REGISTERED AND OFFERED IN THE U.S.

(1977-1986)

		Foreign Issues	
Year	Domestic and Foreign Issues Combined ($billions)	Total ($billions)	Percent of Domestic and Foreign Combined
1977	$ 36.5	$4.7	13%
1978	32.9	4.4	13
1979	40.4	5.2	13
1980	67.4	4.3	6
1981	67.7	4.4	6
1982	74.6	2.5	3
1983	104.0	4.1	4
1984	89.2	4.3	5
1985	132.9	5.6	4
1986	228.4	6.4	3

Note: The U.S. issues are corporate debt and business equity issues. The foreign issues also include government debt offerings. Cash offerings are included while secondary and exchange offerings are excluded. Also note that the OECD figures on foreign new issues in the U.S. reported in Table 8 differ somewhat from those in this table. The difference is accounted for by the OECD including certain private placements and exempt offerings while under-reporting registered issues in some years.

Source: Directorate of Economic and Policy Analysis
Securities and Exchange Commission

Canada is by far the most frequent user of the Yankee securities market. Canadian disclosure and accounting standards are similar to those of the U.S., making it easier for Canadian entities to raise capital in the U.S. Canadian issuers accounted for roughly half of all foreign debt and equity offerings during the ten-year period ending in 1986 (see Table II-21). With regard to corporate debt offerings, Japan had the next highest number (9) after Canada (36). With regard to equity offerings, Bermuda with 29 was second to Canada with 277. For government debt, Sweden (13 issues) was next after Canada (70 issues) over this ten-year period.

Another aspect of the Yankee securities markets is the extent of secondary market trading in foreign securities. Table II-22 shows the number of ADRs registered for trading in the U.S. The number registered has fluctuated considerably over the last ten years but generally increased in the last three years. In 1981 there were 106 ADRs newly registered with the Commission. In 1982 only 45 were registered. The number rose to 288 registrations in 1985 then dropped to 204 in 1986. Many of these ADRs, however, are the registrations of additional shares of issues already traded in the U.S. Some of the ADR registrations represent the introduction of new foreign issues into the U.S. market. The leading sources of ADRs over the last 10 years have been Australia (308 registrations), the

United Kingdom (174), Japan (149), and South Africa (142) (see Table II-21).

. . .

Table II-21

FOREIGN SECURITIES REGISTERED IN THE U.S. BY ISSUER'S COUNTRY OF ORIGIN:
1977-1986 COMBINED
(Number of Registrations)

	Corporate Debt	Corporate/ Business Equity	Govern- ment Debt	ADRs	Total
Africa, Middle East					
South Africa	1	3	---	142	146
Israel	3	21	9	3	36
All Others	---	---	---	4	4
Asia					
Japan	9	10	6	149	174
Hong Kong	---	2	---	69	71
Singapore	---	---	---	25	25
All Others	---	1	3	7	11
Caribbean, Central and South America					
Bermuda	1	29	---	8	38
Netherlands Antilles	1	11	---	2	14
Bahamas	---	11	---	1	12
All Others	1	21	3	3	28
Europe, Australia					
Australia	4	3	4	308	319
United Kingdom	2	23	1	174	200
Sweden	1	5	13	19	38
W. Germany	---	---	---	34	34
France	---	4	11	16	31
All Others	6	35	41	51	133
North America					
Canada	36	277	70	9	392
Mexico	1	3	2	8	14
	66	459	163	1,032	1,720

Source: Directorate of Economic and Policy Analysis
          Securities and Exchange Commission

Table II-22

**TYPES OF FOREIGN SECURITIES REGISTERED
WITH THE SEC: 1977-1986**
(Number of Issues)

	Corporate Debt	Corporate/ Business Equity	Government Debt	ADRs	Total
1977	1	22	34	35	92
1978	2	21	19	31	73
1979	4	29	18	58	109
1980	8	49	9	66	132
1981	15	48	26	106	195
1982	6	32	17	45	100
1983	12	84	15	60	171
1984	3	44	9	139	195
1985	6	80	5	288	379
1986	9	50	11	204	274

Source: Directorate of Economic and Policy Analysis
          Securities and Exchange Commission

Another example of the impact of internationalization on U.S. corporations is the extent to which they now conduct overseas bond financing. U.S. corporations raised $5.8 billion through international bonds and $41.9 billion in registered domestic bond offerings in 1980. The international bonds represented 12 percent of the total $47.7 billion raised in the two markets. By 1986 international bond financing rose to $44 billion while domestic registered bond financing was $157 billion. Thus in 1986 international bonds rose to 22 percent of the total capital raised in these two markets by U.S. issuers.

L. Future Prospects

The internationalization of the world's securities markets presents new challenges and opportunities for the U.S. securities markets and its regulators. In recent years the international financial landscape has changed in response to economic, institutional, technological, and regulatory forces. While the future cannot be predicted with any degree of certainty, it does appear that the securities markets are likely to maintain their global character in the years ahead.

During the 1980's the world's capital markets became more interdependent. At the same time, the securities markets assumed a larger role in the international capital market. This was due in part to favorable economic conditions and regulatory liberalizations, such as the elimination of exchange controls in Japan and the United Kingdom, that contributed to the expansion of both domestic and international securities markets around the world. Technology also played a role in this process. In a very real sense, the world is getting smaller due to improvements in technology and reduced information costs.

The U.S. markets have played a large role in shaping global trends in securities. In particular, the U.S. markets are highly competitive and innovative. They remain the largest, most sophisticated in the world with the widest range of financial products available to market participants.

The U.S. regulatory structure also appears to have had an impact on other major capital markets around the world. The reductions in transactions costs associated with the deregulation of commission rates in the U.S. exerted pressure on other markets. The benefits that result from vigorous competition have not gone unnoticed in other financial centers. Regulatory restructuring is now occurring in the capital markets of, among others, the United Kingdom, Canada, Japan, and France.

Looking back, the 1960's may be characterized as the decade when the internationalization of the securities markets began its latest phase. The 1970's may be viewed as the decade when the U.S. securities markets entered into a major restructuring, some of which resulted from the Securities Acts Amendments of 1975. This restructuring, the increased competition, and the financial innovation in the U.S. during this decade helped influence the character and pace of regulatory changes in other securities markets.

The 1980's may be viewed as a decade of rapid growth for international transactions in securities and a time when many other financial centers undertook major restructuring of their markets. Regulatory liberalization resulted in increased competition in domestic financial markets and permitted greater foreign participation which accelerated the process of internationalization. The 1990s may present opportunities for further growth and integration of international securities markets and the challenge to develop a global regulatory framework that preserves the efficiencies associated with international capital mobility.

Updated Information

The SEC study is quite outdated. The following tables give more current information.

Table A below gives equity market capitalization data for certain years from 1988-1999 and should be compared with the data in Table II-2 in the SEC study, *supra*.

Table A
Global Equity Markets Capitalization
($ Billions)

COUNTRY	1988	1990	1992	1993	1994	1997	1999
United States	2,780	3,107	4,506	5,216	5,105	12,885	16,641
Japan	3,789	2,822	2,319	2,906	3,592	2,217	4,455
United Kingdom	711	858	928	1,199	1,158	1,996	2,855
Canada	447	462	443	601	580	997	789
Germany	251	355	347	461	499	825	1,432
France	223	304	350	455	452	676	1,502
Italy	135	149	124	144	186	345	728
G-7 Nations	8,336	8,057	9,017	10,983	11,572	19,941	28,402
All Other Nations	1,470	1,548	1,888	3,078	3,266	1,706	6,603
WORLD	9,806	9,605	10,905	14,061	14,838	21,647	35,005

Source: F.I.B.V.

Table B below gives listing and trading information on foreign companies for the twelve largest stock markets and should be compared with the data in Tables II-14 and II-19 in the SEC study, supra.

Table B
Foreign Companies on the Twelve Largest Stock Markets[1]

Market	1999 Average[2] Daily Turnover (Millions of $U.S.)	Foreign Turn-over as % of Average Daily Turn-over	Number of Foreign Companies			1999 Foreign Listings as % of Total
			1986	1990	1999	
NYSE	24,507	7.7%	59	96	406	13.4%
NASDAQ (R)[3]	28,677	3.3%	244	256	429	9.8%
London (R)	9,313	57.4%	584	613	448	19.7%
Tokyo	4,590	0.0%	52	125	43	2.2%
Taiwan	2,503	0.2%	0	0	0	0.0%
Germany	4,250	11.3%	181	234	234	27.5%
Switzerland (R)	1,539	4.9%	194	240	173	42.0%
Korea	2,009	0.0%	0	0	0	0.0%
Paris	2,109	1.2%	195	226	176	15.4%
Osaka	591	0.0%	0	0	0	0.0%
Italy	1,477	0.6%	0	0	6	2.2%
Toronto	979	0.2%	51	66	47	3.2%

[1] Size measured by 1994 Turnover.

[2] Average in total turnover divided by 365.

[3] Exchanges designated R include in turnover all transactions subject to supervision by their market authority, whereas other exchanges only include transactions which pass through their trading systems or take place on their floors. Source: F.I.B.V.

As a point of comparison, foreign companies were delisting from the Tokyo Stock Exchange in 1990-1998 due to lack of investor interest and the general fall of activity accompanying the plunge of the Nikkei.

In addition to the organized U.S. markets such as the NYSE, NASDAQ, and the American Stock Exchange, foreign stocks are traded in the U.S. in more informal markets. The Over-the-Counter Bulletin Board (OTCBB) is an inter-dealer quotation system, limited to two update quotations per day, established by the NASD in 1988. At the end of 1994, 4,700 domestic issues, 400 ADRs and 186 foreign securities were quoted on the system. The average daily dollar value of foreign stocks traded (including ADRs) was $98.4 million. In addition, there are the Pink Sheets, twice daily quotations of stocks published by the National Quotation Bureau. The Pink Sheets are principally a listing of stocks, with the names and telephone numbers of market makers. In 1994, 440 ADRs and over 7,600 foreign securities traded through the Pink Sheets, with an average daily dollar value of $136.2 million. The combined daily dollar value of trading of foreign stocks on OTCBB and the Pink Sheets was $234.6 million. This compares with $320 million on NASDAQ and $1,063 million on NYSE. J. Cochrane, J. Shapiro and J. Tobin, Foreign Equities and U.S. Investors: Breaking Down the Barriers Separating Supply and Demand 11-13 (NYSE Working Paper No. 95-04, 1995).

Charts C, D and E below give data on U.S. ownership of foreign equities and should be compared with the data in Table II-16 in the SEC study, *supra*.

Chart C

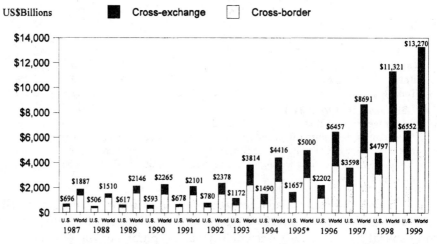

International Trading of Equities

Source: Cross-Border Capital
Cross-Border Capital, U.S. Treasury Bulletin and NYSE estimates

NYSE
New York
Stock Exchange, Inc.

Chart D

Holdings of Non-U.S. Equities in the United States

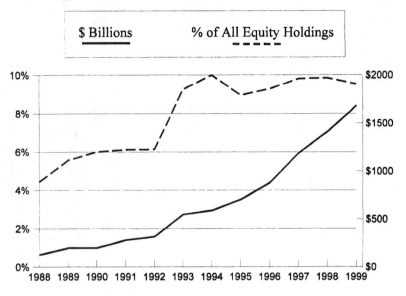

NYSE
New York
Stock Exchange, Inc.

Source: "Flow of Funds Accounts," Board of Governors of the Federal Reserve System

    As Cochrane notes, J. Cochrane, Assessing and Evaluating the Current
Directions of Transnational Listings 15 (NYSE Working Paper No. 93-03,
1993): "International trading takes two forms: cross-border trading
(investors trading a stock in a foreign country but in that stock's 'home
market'--e.g., a customer in Paris buying Exxon on the NYSE) and cross-
exchange trading (investors trading a 'foreign' stock away from its 'home
market'--e.g., an insurance company in Osaka selling Exxon on the Tokyo
Stock Exchange or a British unit trust buying Daimler Benz in London)."

Chart E
Purchases and Sales of Foreign Stock in U.S. Markets

AMEX-Listed   Nasdaq Issues   NYSE-Listed

1987	1988	1989	1990	1991	1992	1993	1994	1995	1996	1997	1998	1999
$213	$142	$196	$229	$267	$348	$604	$711	$810	$1034	$1472	$1699	$2313

NYSE
New York
Stock Exchange, Inc.

Table F below shows the market value of foreign holdings of certain U.S. long-term securities. By 2000, compared to 1974, the percent of equity and Treasury debt foreign owned more than doubled, while corporate and municipal debt increased over thirteen times.

Table F
**Market value of foreign holdings of U.S. long-term securities, by type
of security, selected years, 1974-2000[1]**

Year	Total outstanding	Foreign owned	Percent foreign owned
		Corporate entity	
1974	663	25	3.8
1978	1,012	48	4.7
1984	1,899	105	5.5
1989	4,212	275	6.5
1994	7,183	398	5.5
2000	23,038	1,711	7.4
		Corporate and municipal debt	
1974	458	n.a.	n.a.
1978	680	7	1.0
1984	1,149	31	2.7
1989	2,400	190	7.9
1994	3,342	276	8.3
2000	5,404	712	13.2
		Marketable U.S. Treasury securities	
1974	163	24	14.7
1978	326	39	12.0
1984	873	118	13.5
1989	1,599	333	20.8
1994	2,392	464	19.4
2000	2,508	885	35.3

[1] In billions of dollars, except as noted
NOTE: For 2000, data are as of March 31; for all other years, December 31. n.a.
Not available.
SOURCE: Data on amount of outstanding for all categories, except marketable
Treasury securities are from Federal Reserve Statistical Release Z.1, *Flow of
Funds Accounts of the United States.* Amount outstanding of marketable Treasury
securities, which excludes Treasury bills, from the Bureau of Public Debt,
Monthly Statement of the Public Debt of the United States.

Notes and Questions

1.   The purchases of U.S. government debt by foreigners is particularly important.   Foreign investors' share of the U.S. government bond
market has grown substantially over the last 20 years, from a 20% share
in 1980 to 40% ($1.3 trillion) in 2000. Net foreign purchases of Treasury
securities in 1997 amounted to a record $252 billion, or more than the net
$38.2 billion-worth of issues that year.   In effect, foreigners financed the
U.S. deficit.   Domestic investors were net sellers during the same period.
In 1997, foreigners held 38% or $1.3 trillion of the $3.4 trillion outstand-

ing. Investors from the United Kingdom and Japan accounted for one-half of the foreign share. Federal Reserve Bank of New York, 4 Current Issues 2 (May 1998).

2. How internationalized are U.S. securities markets? Have the markets become more internationalized since 1986?

3. Why should the United States care whether or not its securities markets are internationalized?

4. The pattern of share ownership in the United States has changed significantly since the 1980's. The percentage of direct household holdings of all corporate stock has decreased from 68 to 41 percent, whereas indirect household holdings through trusts and estates, life insurance companies, private pension funds and mutual funds, increased from 16 to 28 percent. While the market has become more institutional, direct holdings are still quite significant, and thus protection of individual investors remains an important policy issue. NYSE, *Share Ownership 2000* (2000).

B.   THE BASIC SECURITIES LAW FRAMEWORK

The following description relies heavily on G. Palm and D. Walkovik, United States: A Special Guide to Securities Regulation Around the World, International Financial Law Review 62-84 (Supp. July 1990). We have summarized and updated this excellent work.

1. GENERAL RULES

Securities Statutes

In general, six federal statutes govern the distribution of U.S. securities: the Securities Act of 1933, the Securities Exchange Act of 1934, the Public Utility Holding Company Act of 1935, the Trust Indenture Act of 1939, the Investment Advisers Act of 1940, and the Investment Company Act of 1940. With the exception of the Public Utility Holding Company Act, these statutes are applicable to foreign securities as well. Responsibility for the administration and enforcement of these statutes rests in the Securities and Exchange Commission (SEC), an independent agency empowered to adopt regulations and perform quasi-judicial functions.

Securities Act Registration

Under the Securities Act of 1933, an issuer must register with the SEC before making a public offering. Upon filing, the SEC determines, normally within two to five days, whether the registration statement will be reviewed. As a general rule, first-time offerings are reviewed, a process that takes four to six weeks. During that time, securities may be offered orally or through a preliminary prospectus, but may not be sold. This restriction acts to limit the issuer's promotional activity. Upon satisfactory review and upon request by the issuer, the SEC will declare the registration effective and authorize the sale of securities. Even after effectiveness, stringent standards prohibit distribution of materials similar to a prospectus if unaccompanied by a copy of the registered prospectus.

Conventional Offerings. Two types of registrations are generally available: registration of conventional offerings and shelf registration. In a conventional offering, the securities are expected to be offered soon after filing and the filed statement relates directly to this imminent offering. The offering price and other related terms, such as the underwriting syndicate, discounts, and offering commissions can be filed as an amendment at the same time the issuer asks the SEC to declare the registration effective. Alternatively, the registration may be declared effective without the information, as long as the issuer files a later prospectus.

Shelf Registration. In contrast, shelf registration provides the issuer with greater flexibility and enables it to respond quickly to market conditions by allowing advance registration of securities expected to be sold within a two-year period. As with registration of conventional offerings, a registration statement and a prospectus is filed with the SEC and after possible review and upon request by the issuer are made effective. Securities can be sold any time within the two-year period following effectiveness but must be accompanied by a supplement prospectus enumerating the specific terms of the offering and noting any developments in the issuer's status. For the non-U.S. issuer, the SEC imposes the additional requirement that updated financial statements, dating not more than six months, be kept on file with the SEC. Though these financial statements need not be audited, the requirement, nevertheless, may cause "black out" periods during which securities may not be offered.

Form F-1 Registration

Requirements. The principal forms used by non-Canadian foreign private issuers in registering with the SEC are Forms F-1, F-2, F-3, relating to capital raising and F-4, relating to business combinations. Many of the items of the forms incorporate by reference provisions of Regulation S-K which contains standard instructions for filing forms under the Securities Act and Exchange Act. The requirements of Form F-1, used by first-time non-Canadian issuers, include the following:

- Information regarding the terms of the securities, the terms of the offering, the plan of distribution of the securities and the use of proceeds.

- A description of the business of the issuer, including (i) a discussion of the general development of the business over the past five years; (ii) principal products produced and services rendered and the principal markets for and methods of distribution of such products and services; (iii) a breakdown of total revenues during the past three years by categories of activity and into geographical markets, with a narrative discussion of material differences between relative contributions to operating profit as compared to relative contributions to revenues; and (iv) special characteristics of the registrant's operations or industry which may have a material impact on future financial performance, and any material country risks unlikely to be known by investors, including dependence upon a few major customers or suppliers, governmental regulation, expiration of material contracts or rights, unusual competitive conditions, cyclicality of the industry and anticipated raw material or energy shortages. Additional disclosures required of electric or gas utilities, companies with oil or gas operations, banks and insurance companies are set out in industry guides adopted by the SEC. Additional information is required of registrants which have not received revenues from operations during each of the three preceding years.

- A brief description of the location and general character of the principal plants, mines and other materially important physical properties of the registrant. In the case of an extractive enterprise, material information as to production, reserves, locations, development and the nature of the registrant's interests is to be given. (Generally, only proven oil or gas reserves and proven or probable other reserves may be disclosed.)

- Selected financial data for each of the last five years, including revenues, income, assets and long-term obligations.

- A management's discussion of the registrant's financial condition, changes in financial condition and results of operations for each year for which financial statements are presented (three years), including information as to trends, commitments and material events and uncertainties relating to liquidity, capital resources and results of operations.

- Prescribed information as to material pending legal proceedings, control of the registrant by a parent or others and 10 per cent shareholders, the nature of any trading market for the securities registered, exchange controls and other governmental, legal or charter limitations affecting non-resident holders of the registrant's securities, withholding or similar taxes to which US holders would be subject under the laws of the country in which the registrant is organised, the directors and executive officers of the registrant and the aggregate compensation paid to them as a group for services in the last year, outstanding options to purchase from the registrant securities of the class being registered, and information otherwise made public as to the interest of management or controlling shareholders and certain associated persons in material transactions with the registrant.

- A description of the securities to be registered.

- Audited balance sheets as of the end of each of the two most recent fiscal years and audited statements of income and changes in financial position for each of the three most recent fiscal years. Regulation S-X sets forth the form and content of and requirements for financial statements required by the US securities laws and SEC rules.

   (i) If the last audited balance sheet is dated more than six months prior to the effective date of the registration statement, interim unaudited financial statements are required. This requirement has had a significant impact on the ability of non-US issuers which publicly release financial statements on a semi-annual basis only. In view of the time required to prepare such financial statements, this requirement has had the effect of creating 'blackout periods' during which the public capital markets in the US have been unavailable to such issuers. Our firm has proposals pending before the SEC to alleviate these problems, in part by adding a grace period to the existing rules which would take into account time necessary to prepare.

   (ii) Generally, the statements must be presented in the currency of the registrant's country.

   (iii) The statements must disclose an informational content substantially similar to statements which comply with US generally accepted accounting principles (GAAP) and Regulation S-X.

   (iv) The statements may be prepared according to US GAAP or, alternatively, according to an identified comprehensive body of accounting principles together with a discussion and quantification of material variations from US GAAP and Regulation S-X in the accounting principles, practices and methods used in preparing the financial statements.

   (v) In contrast to ongoing Exchange Act reporting requirements, the statements and notes are required to include supplementary information required by US GAAP and Regulation S-X, such as business segment and pension information, unless the securities registered are to be offered only upon exercise of rights granted pro rata to all existing security holders of a class, pursuant to a dividend or interest reinvestment plan or upon the conversion of outstanding convertible securities or the exercise of outstanding warrants (all of which are referred to herein as offerings to existing security holders).

Other Requirements. Preparation of the financial statement is likely to incur substantial expense and requires that the issuer retain expert accounting and legal services. Accuracy and exercise of "due diligence" by all persons involved in the process are imperative, since the SEC requires signatures from the principal executive, financial and accounting officers, a majority of its board of directors, and its authorized U.S. representatives. Moreover, liability for false or misleading statements flows to the issuer, its directors, certain officers, its U.S. representatives, and the underwriters. With the exception of the issuer, a person will be exempted from liability if that person can show that despite reasonable diligence, it could reasonably believe and did believe that the statement was accurate.

Financial Statements

Financial statements of non-U.S. issuers must also comply with U.S. GAAP standards or with an identified body of accounting procedures coupled with an explanation of material differences with the U.S. GAAP. The SEC also requires that notes to the financial statement include a breakdown of revenues, operating profits, and assets by industry and geographical segments. Moreover, the SEC imposes a stringent requirement of independence in the use of accounting firms. No profession of the firm may hold material interests in the issuer's securities or have held any position or performed any service "incompatible with the audit function." These statements must be updated every six months, a requirement that can prove burdensome to some non-U.S. issuers. Compliance with state "blue sky" or securities laws can also prove burdensome.

Private Placements

In the case of non-public and limited offerings, known as "private placements," Section 4(2) and Regulation D provide exemptions from the registration requirements of the Securities Act. The exemptions have proved useful to non-U.S. issuers desiring limited U.S. distribution of securities also being offered abroad.

Section 4(2). Section 4(2) exempts from registration "transactions by an issuer not involving any public offering" made in the U.S. or to U.S. nationals. The rationale behind the exemption provision is that purchasers of offerings falling under Section 4(2) do not require the protection provided by the Securities Act registration requirement. To fall under the Section 4(2) exemption, however, the offering must meet the following requirement:

- There must be a limited number of offerees and purchasers with a possible exception for large institutional investors.
- No general promotion is allowed.
- Information provided to or known by offerees and purchasers must be comparable to that provided through the registration process to

the extent that they are material to the transaction. U.S. GAAP standards need not be met.

- Offerees and purchasers must be able to evaluate the investment.

- The transaction must be designed to prevent resale and distribution by purchasers in a way that would have disqualified the initial offering from exemption under Section 4(2). The limitation is not applicable to sales to non-U.S. persons.

- When the private placement offering is made in conjunction with a public offering abroad, the transactions must be designed to restrict the U.S. offerings to private placements.

Regulation D. Regulation D acts as a safe harbor rule for all transactions that meet the requirements of Rule 506, and by reference, the Section 4(2) exemption. To fall under the safe harbor protection of Rule 506, the following requirement must be met:

- Issuer must reasonably believe or there must actually be no more than 35 U.S. persons, other than "accredited investors," that are purchasers of the securities. Accredited investors include institutional investors, directors and officers of the issuer, and persons meeting certain minimum net worth standards.

- Purchasers who are not accredited investors must be provided with information comparable to that provided in a registration statement, made aware of and additional information provided to accredited investors, furnished with such information upon request, and given an opportunity to verify information provided.

- There must be no general promotion.

- Issuer must adopt reasonable measures to ensure that purchasers are not buying to resell. Reasonable measures include direct inquiries, written disclosure to the purchaser on the limits to distribution of the security, and placing legends to this effect on the securities.

Although Rule 506 is most often used for investors who are natural persons, the majority of non-public transactions with institutional investors entail Section 4(2).

Exchange Act Registration and Reporting

The Exchange Act of 1934 requires registration under the '33 Act of securities listed on U.S. stock exchanges or quoted on NASDAQ and provides ongoing disclosure requirements for all securities registered under the Securities Act of 1933 (suspended for any year where the securities are held by less than 300 U.S. residents).

For non-Canadian non-U.S. private issuers the relevant forms are Form 20-F and Form 6-K. Form 20-F contains financial information similar to that disclosed in Form F-1 under the Securities Act and must be filed within six months of the close of the fiscal year of the issuer.

Form 6-K requires the issuer to provide the SEC with any information made public by the regulations of its own country, filed with and made public by a non-U.S. stock exchange, or provided to its security holders. Such information is not considered "filed" and thus is not subject to the liability provisions of the Exchange Act for false or misleading documents filed with the SEC. If a foreign company simply cross-lists without issuing new shares (a Level 2 offering), Form 20-F requires only partial reconciliation of the issuer's financial statement with U.S. GAAP (item 17) rather than the full reconciliation requirement for the raising of capital (a Level 3 offering)(item 18).

Liability. Liabilities for false and misleading information under the Securities Act and Exchange Act are imposed on a wide range of persons. Under Section 11(a) of the Securities Act, the issuer, any persons who signed the registration statement, and directors, underwriters, accountants, and other experts who prepared or certified the registration statement can incur civil liabilities. With the exception of the issuer, a person will be exempt from liability if that person can show that despite reasonable diligence, it could reasonably believe and did believe that the statement was accurate and that there were no omissions rendering the statement misleading.   Sections 11(b) and (c) sets the standard of reasonableness as that required by a prudent man in the management of his own property. Recovery for Section 11 violations are, in general, limited to the difference between the price paid for the security and the market value at the time of suit or the price at which the security was sold before the suit. Section 12 provides additional grounds for recovery. Any person who sold the security by oral communication or prospectus can be held liable to the purchaser.

Section 18(a) of the Exchange Act similarly holds issuers and related persons liable if the security's purchase or sales price was affected the purchaser's reliance on a false or misleading statement. Even where the false statement is not misleading, the issuer may be liable through Section 10(b) and Rule 10b-5 thereunder for statements made knowingly and recklessly. As under the Securities Act, a controlling person of any person held liable is jointly and severally liable, under Section 20(a) , unless that controlling person can show that he did not know and did not have reasonable grounds to know of the liable person's alleged acts.

The "Aircraft Carrier" Proposal

On November 3, 1998, the SEC proposed a wide range of changes to the rules currently governing the distribution of securities, for example various rules restricting communications with prospective buyers before registration is effective. SEC Release No. 33-7606; 34-40632; IC-23519. The revisions generally leave disclosure requirements intact. The SEC's proposals are motivated, in part, by attracting a greater volume of transactions to the U.S. public market through registration and thus reducing reliance on use of Rule 144A. Generally, the proposal would greatly reduce restrictions on distribution of securities for large seasoned issuers—those reporting to the SEC for one year and having either a public float of $75 million and $1 million U.S. average trading volume ("ADTV"), or a public float of $250 million.

Another objective of the SEC was to increase information available to investors in securities issued under shelf registration. For example, the Commission has proposed that investors receive a term sheet or preliminary prospectus prior to agreeing a to buy securities. Many issuers have objected to these new requirements and believe that the net effect of the Commission's proposals may be to increase restrictions on distribution for shelf-filers. It does not appear, at present, that the "Aircraft Carrier" proposal will be implemented.

Selective Disclosure

Effective October 23, 2000, the SEC adopted a controversial rule, Regulation FD, preventing selective disclosure by companies of material non-public information. Release No. 33-7881, August 15, 2000. This was designed by the SEC to fill the gap in insider trading law created by the Supreme Court's decision in *Dirks v. Securities and Exchange Commission*, 463 U.S. 646 (1983) which held that it would not be a breach of fiduciary duty for a company to divulge material non-public information to analysts unless the company received a benefit. Without such benefit, the analyst's tippees would not violate Rule 10b-5 by trading on such information. While lawyers still advised their clients after *Dirks* not to disclose such information since a benefit might be found, the SEC thought more had to be done, hence Regulation FD.

The SEC toned down the Regulation from its proposed form due to a hostile industry reception. As adopted, there is no private liability, e.g. under 10b-5, for violating the Regulation; it is enforced solely by the SEC. It only covers reckless violations and communications by "senior officials." It does not apply to disclosures in connection with registered offerings, and does not prohibit confidential communications. There was preliminary evidence that the Regulation was limiting issuer communications with analysts, J. Junewicz, *The SEC Raises the Stakes in Issues-Analyst Communications*, 33 Securities and Commodities Regulation 237 (November 2000), and that the information discontinuities it has created had increased volatility in equity markets, J. Chaffin, *Disclosure rule attracts flak*, Financial Times, April7/9, 2001. A survey of the Securities Industry Association showed that 72% of the respondents thought the quality of disclosures has been poorer after the adoption of Regulation FD. A Beard, *New disclosure rules come under attack*, Financial Times, May 18, 2001.

Two later studies have found no increase in volatility. V. Eleswarapu, R. Thompson and K. Venkataraman, *The Impact of Regulation Fair Disclosure: Trading Costs and Information Asymmetry* (Draft of October 2001) and F. Heflin, K.R. Subramanyam and Y. Zhang, *Regulation FD and the Financial Information Environment* (Working Paper 2001). The former study also found no increase in trading costs following the introduction of Regulation FD, suggesting that there was no increase in information asymmetry or the exploitation of inside information. See also S. Sunder, *Investor Access to Conference Call Disclosures: Impact of Regulation Fair Disclosure on Information Asymmetry* (Draft January 2002) for similar findings.

Continuous Disclosure

Harvey Pitt, who took over as SEC Chairman in the new Bush Administration in 2002, has indicated his interest in having more continuous rather than periodic disclosure. The SEC has already taken some modest steps along this line. It has proposed to shorten the filing deadlines for large public companies from 45 to 30 calendar days after period end for quarterly reports and from 90 to 60 calendar days after fiscal year end for annual reports, Exchange Act Release No. 33-8089 (April 12, 2002). Furthermore, Section 4 of H.R. 3763, 107th Cong. 2nd. Sess., which passed the House on April 24, 2002, proposes that the Commission devise a system for the disclosure of corporate information on "a rapid and essentially contemporaneous basis." Real time disclosure will be greatly facilitated by automated data collection techniques by corporations and the use of the internet to distribute such information. See R. Litan and P. Wallison, *The GAAP Gap, Corporate Disclosure in the Internet Age* (2000).

2. SPECIAL RULES FOR FOREIGN PRIVATE ISSUERS

Accommodation to foreign issuers started early in the SEC's history when foreign issuers were exempted in 1935 from the proxy rules (section 14) and the short-swing profits rules (section 16) of the '34 Act. The proxy rules gives shareholders rights in the governance of the issuer, while the short-swing profit rules prevent insiders or 10% shareholders from selling stock within six months of a purchase or purchasing within six months of a sale. How would you compare possible justifications for these exemptions with those for the 1994 relaxations GAAP reconciliation rules? Are the justifications for the 1935 exemptions still applicable today?

The SEC makes important regulatory accommodations for "foreign private issuers." To qualify, a company must meet either a shareholder or business contacts test. Rule 405 under the Securities Act of 1933, Rule 3b-4 under the Securities Exchange Act of 1934. The shareholder test requires that 50% of the company's outstanding voting securities are held by U.S. residents. The business contacts test requires that (a) a majority of the company's executive officers or directors be U.S. citizens or residents, (b) more than 50% of the company's assets are located in the United States, or (c) the company's business is administered principally in the U.S.   See S. Kinsey, *Foreign Private Issuers*, Securities and Commodities Regulation 79 (April 25, 2001).

a.   INTERNATIONAL DISCLOSURE STANDARDS

In September 1998, the International Organization of Securities Commissioners (IOSCO) issued a consultation document for comment entitled *International Disclosure Standards for Cross-Border Offerings and Initial Listings by Foreign Issuers.*   IOSCO formulated a common prospectus that would be used for cross-border offerings and initial listings. The proposal does not include financial statements; work in this area is left to the International Accounting Standards project. IOSCO sought harmonization for international securities transactions.   The proposal is organized in two parts.   Part I contains information that would be disclosed in a standardized way in all jurisdictions; it includes information that any jurisdiction would already require, e.g. business overview, risk factors etc., and describes such information in general terms.   Part II deals with "disclosure issues outside the scope of the standards," such as materiality, projections and forward looking information, indemnification of directors and officers, and derivatives and market risk." This Part formulates no harmonized standards; instead, it discusses differences among countries on the issues. On September 28, 1999, the SEC adopted a complete revision of Form 20-F which contains the basic disclosure requirements applicable to foreign private issuers based on the IOSCO proposals. Release Nos. 33-7745 (September 28, 1999). This change effects no real relaxation in standards for foreign issuers since the IOSCO proposals basically mimicked existing U.S. requirements.   See M. Joseph, *How to meet the SEC's new form 20-F rules*, International Financial Law Review 14 (February 2001).   How promising is this IOSCO approach?

b.   THE RULE 12g3-2(b) EXEMPTION

The Rule 12g3-2(b) exemption establishes special rules for continuous reporting by foreign issuers. Foreign companies with total assets over $5 million and a class of equity held by at least 500 shareholders, of which 300 reside in the United States, are subject to the reporting requirements of the Exchange Act of 1934. Rule 12g3-2(b) of the 1934 Act, first adopted in 1967, exempted non-U.S. companies from the reporting requirements of the Exchange Act so long as they do not make public offerings in the United States or list their shares on a U.S. securities exchange (including the New York Stock Exchange and NASDAQ), provided that the companies furnish the SEC with copies of material information made public in their local jurisdictions or sent to foreign investors in their securities (home country reports). The SEC described the reason for this exemption as follows:

[A] distinction is made between foreign issuers that voluntarily enter the United States securities markets and those companies whose securities are traded in the United States without any significant voluntary acts or encouragement by the issuer. Currently, this distinction is accomplished by deeming all foreign companies having either securities listed on a United States exchange or having made a public offering of securities registered under the Securities Act as having voluntarily entered the United States market. Other foreign companies whose securities are traded in the United States through no direct acts of the issuers are deemed not to have taken any voluntary acts to enter the United States markets.

Integrated Disclosure System for Foreign Private Issuers, Securities Act Release No. 6360, [1981-1982 Transfer Binder] Fed. Sec. L. Rep. (CCH) ¶ 83,054, at 84,643 (Nov. 20, 1981).

E. Greene, D. Braverman and S. Sperber, *Hegemony or Deference: U.S. Disclosure Requirements in the International Capital Markets*, 50 Business Lawyer 413, 426-429 (1995) cite three additional factors for the adoption of the Rule: (1) that the SEC was relatively satisfied in 1967 with the level of information being disclosed by non-U.S. companies in their home markets; (2) there was no reason to believe a significant U.S. shareholder base would develop for issuers relying on the rule (the exemption assumes added importance in light of Regulation D, and Rule 144A and Regulation S discussed infra); and (3) the world's capital markets were not nearly as integrated as they are today.

The Rule originally discriminated between the trading of foreign securities on organized stock markets like NYSE where securities must be registered and are fully subject to the 1934 Act reporting requirements, and stock traded through other means, as through NASDAQ, OTCBB and the Pink Sheets, where the Rule 12g3-2(b) exemption applied. In 1983, the SEC revised the Rule by terminating the exemption for foreign issuers quoted on NASDAQ; however, the SEC grandfathered indefinitely securities of foreign issuers who were in compliance with the terms of the exemption and listed on NASDAQ as of October 6, 1983. Exchange Act Release No. 20264, 48 Federal Register 46,736 (October 6, 1983). The exemption continued to apply to stock traded on OTCBB and the Pink Sheets.

J. Cochrane, J. Shapiro and J. Tobin, Foreign Equities and U.S. Investors: Breaking Down the Barriers Separating Supply and Demand 11 (NYSE Working Paper No. 95-04, 1995) reported that some of the companies traded on the OTCBB and Pink Sheets did not appear, as of December 31, 1994, on either the SEC's list of companies reporting under the '34 Act, or the September 1995 list of companies exempt from such reporting under Rule 12g3-2(b). While it is possible that these companies were not required to file for an exemption, for example they may not have the minimum number of U.S. shareholders to trigger the '34 Act, it is also possible that they were not in compliance, and that the SEC had not sought to enforce such compliance.

In March 1997, the SEC required that securities traded on OTCBB be registered under §12 of the '34 Act, as of April 1, 1998. While the Commission acknowledged the transparency benefits (dissemination of price information) of trading foreign issues on OTCBB, as compared with the Pink Sheets, which only provide for non-firm quotations updated twice daily, it believed transparent trading in unregistered stock was inconsistent with the full disclosure rationale of the securities laws. SEC Release No. 34-38456 (March 31, 1997). Since 1999 the pink sheets moved online into real time and market makers publish their bids and offers.

c. THE RELAXATION OF OTHER RULES

In April 1994, the SEC relaxed some registration and reporting requirements for U.S. public offerings by foreign issuers, 59 Fed. Reg. 21645 (April 26, 1994). The new SEC rules extend the availability of the short-form F-3 registration statement by bringing the eligibility criteria in line with those for domestic companies. A Form S-3 ordinarily contains information regarding the security being registered and the plan of distribution; all financial and other information is simply incorporated by reference to the issuer's annual report on Form 20-F and other reports filed with the SEC. The new requirements are: (1) at least one previous filing of an annual report on Form 20-F; (2) periodic reports filed with the SEC for at least 12 months (reduced from 36 months); and (3) public float of $75 million (reduced from $300 million). In addition, foreign issuers are now permitted to use the universal shelf registration procedure previously available only to U.S. issuers. This form of shelf registration enables an issuer to use a single registration statement to register an aggregate amount of different classes of securities, e.g. debt and equity, without allocation among the classes.

In January 1997, 62 Federal Register 520 (January 3, 1997), the SEC adopted a new Regulation M which significantly eases restrictions on trading new issues during their distribution. Actively traded equities, those with an average daily trading volume of $1 million or more and a public float of at least $150 million, would be exempted from any restrictions. One commenter states that this "would effectively result in the worldwide implementation of pricing and stabilizing activities conducted on the basis of home-country regulation and practice subject to the general anti-fraud requirements of the U.S. securities laws [which remain applicable]." D. Brandon and G. Reiter, *Regulators Move to Harmonize Capital Markets Rules*, International Financial Law Review 53, 54 (June 1996). It appears that these domestic reforms were in part motivated to bring U.S. rules more into line with those in other major markets, thereby facilitating "global" offerings. We look at this type of reform again in Chapter 12, Eurobonds and Global Bonds.

Finally, on October 19, 1999, the SEC adopted a number of exemptions to tender offer rules and registration requirements which should make it easier for foreign issuers and bidders to engage in transactions with U.S. security holders of non-U.S. companies. Release No. 33-7759 (October 22, 1999).

Notes and Questions

1. What are the major problems encountered by foreign companies in issuing securities in the U.S. market through a public offering or through a private placement?

The advantages to a foreign company of having a listing on an organized exchange such as the NYSE are: (1) more access to capital; (2) diversification of equity base from home country thereby giving more flexibility in raising funds in the U.S.; (3) enhancement of international image from association with a prestigious stock exchange; (4) ability to represent compliance with rigorous U.S. disclosure standards; (5) increased liquidity from increased trading; (6) potential use of U.S. stock to make acquisitions; and (7) cultivation of investors from customer base (relevant to retail firms). J. Hicks, *The Listing of Daimler-Benz A.G. Securities on the NYSE: Conflicting Interests and Regulatory Policies*, 37 German Yearbook of International Law 360, 365-368 (1994); J. Fanto and R. Karmel, *A Report on the Attitudes of Foreign Companies Regarding a U.S. Listing,* NYSE Working Paper 97-01 (March 1997). See also G. A. Karolyi, *What Happens to Stocks that List Shares Abroad? A Survey of the Evidence and its Managerial Implications*, NYSE Working Paper 96-04 (September 1996), which found evidence for the view that foreign listings increased overall liquidity, particularly for foreign companies listing on the NYSE. This study also found that "the stock's exposure to domestic market risk is significantly reduced and is associated with only a small increase in global market risk and foreign exchange risk, resulting in a net reduction in the cost of equity capital of 114 basis points on average". (Executive Summary). See also, C. Doidge, G. A. Karolyi and R. Stultz, *Why are Foreign Firms Listed in the U.S. Worth More?,* NBER Working Paper 8538 (October 2001) finding that foreign companies listed in the U.S. have higher valuations, 37% more for exchange-listed firms. The authors attribute this to the U.S. regulatory regime which limits the ability of controlling shareholders to extract value from a firm.

W. Reese and M. Weisbach, *Protection of Minority Shareholder Interests, Cross-listings in the United States and Subsequent Equity Offerings*, NBER working Paper 8164 (March 2001) find that firms from civil law countries (weak minority shareholder protection), after cross-listing in the U.S., place the majority of their subsequent equity issues outside the U.S., whereas firms from common law countries (strong minority shareholder protection) place subsequent issues in the U.S. The authors state "[t]his empirical finding is consistent with a view that firms with strong protection at home tend to cross-list in order to access U.S. investors and/or markets, while firms from countries with weak shareholder protection will cross-list for the purpose of voluntarily bonding themselves to U.S. securities and market regulations, allowing them to raise capital more easily at home and elsewhere outside the U.S.," p. 26.

2.   How significant is the adoption of IOSCO international disclosure standards by the SEC? Is this the first step toward harmonization of the world's disclosure rules? Countries have taken different approaches to implementing IOSCO rules. Whereas the U.S. and Switzerland apply the rules only to foreign issuers–they are optional, foreign issuers can use U.S. or IOSCO rules–Singapore and Mexico have adopted the rules for both foreign and domestic issuers.   S. Wolff, *Implementation of International Disclosure Standards*, 22 University of Pennsylvania Journal of International Economic Law 91 (2001). The EU must reconcile the use of IOSCO rules with its own harmonization approach, see Chapter 5. Would such harmonization be a good thing?

3.   Regulation 12g3-2(b) was adopted in 1967 based on assumptions that are largely no longer true. Should the Regulation be repealed with the effect that all foreign issues trading in the U.S. would be subject to registration and reporting requirements? If unregistered securities with home country reports (and some with none) can be traded outside the exchanges, why not let them be traded on the exchanges with more liquidity and protection for investors?

4.   Regulation FD, as proposed, would have applied to foreign as well as domestic issuers. The effect would be for SEC policies to govern how foreign issuers (most of which have foreign listings) made disclosures to analysts in their own markets.   Foreign regulators, like many commentators, believed that the proposal could delay the timely release of information to the market in order to avoid selective disclosure. Some countries, however, like the U.K., have policies requiring issuers to promptly disclose material information even in the absence of insider trading.   I. Taylor, S. Orton and S. Parkes, *Selective Disclosure by Companies to Analysts,* Journal of International Financial Markets 174 (2001). As adopted, Regulation FD excluded foreign private issuers. Do you think such exclusion was justified? See M. Fox, *Regulation FD and Foreign Issuers: Globalization's Strains and Opportunities,* 41 Va. J. Int'l L. 653 (2001).

5.   Is there ever any justification for having more onerous or different registration requirements for foreign as compared to U.S. issuers? In a May 8, 2001 letter, outgoing acting SEC Chairman Laura Unger sent a letter to Frank Wolf, Chairman of the U.S. House Appropriations subcommittee that regulates the SEC, indicating that the SEC will require overseas companies to disclose if they are doing business in any countries where U.S. sanctions apply, e.g., Iran, Sudan, Libya. Unger said: "[o]ur aim is to make available to investors additional information

about situations in which the material proceeds of an offering could–however indirectly–benefit countries, governments, or entities that, as a matter of U.S. foreign policy, are off-limits to U.S. companies." E. Alden, *SEC seeks closer watch on overseas groups*, Financial Times, May 11, 2001. Do you agree with this? Wolf was apparently furious that PetroChina, a Chinese national oil company, was able to get a New York listing in 2000 when it was selling oil to Sudan.

6. Do you agree with the Commission's decision to force OTCBB traded stock to be registered with the result that unregistered stock may only be traded in the pink sheets? As of May 2001, 970 ADRs traded on the pink sheets as compared with 540 ADRs on the NYSE or NASDAQ. The pink sheet companies include Nestlé, Nintendo, and Volkswagen, large foreign companies that have not listed here. ADRs account for only 5% of the companies on the pink sheets but they represent half of the dollar volume.

7. The SEC is currently investigating how shares of initial public offerings are allocated to investors, and has indicated that allocation based on future quid pro quos, e.g. future underwriting business or large commissions on future trades, or promises to hold and buy in the after-market, may violate antifraud and antimanipulation rules. S. Pulliam and R. Smith, *Seeking IPO Shares, Investors Offer to Buy More in After-Market,* Wall St. Journal, December 6, 2000. K. Kranhold, *Deals and Deal Makers,* Wall St. Journal, December 13, 2000. Assuming the SEC were to regulate IPO allocations, should it exempt foreign issuers? The SEC and the New York Attorney General are engaged in an investigation of the independence of research analysts. The issue primarily concerns whether investment advice given by analysts to investors (buy side) is influenced by investment banking relationships with issuers (sell side). It may also concern whether public advice is consistent with proprietary decisions, e.g. touting a stock publicly but selling it for the firm's own account. C. Gasparino and S. Paltrow, *SEC Joins Pack, Opens Inquiry into Analysts,* Wall Street Journal, April 26, 2002. Assuming the SEC were to regulate research analysts, should it exempt foreign analysts?

8. The National Securities Markets Improvement Act of 1996 (Section 102) exempts "covered securities," which includes exchange-traded securities, from state Blue Sky law registration requirements.

C.   GAAP RECONCILIATION

1. DAIMLER BENZ CASE

In addition to the stringent disclosure requirements of U.S. securities laws, the need to reconcile financial statements with U.S. generally accepted accounting principles (GAAP) has been a major obstacle to foreign companies listing on U.S. exchanges. Reconciliation can be not only time consuming and costly, but conceptually difficult as well. Fundamental categories or concepts in GAAP may not have obvious counterparts in the foreign system.

Differences Between German and GAAP Standards

During the early 1990s, a number of German companies, including Daimler-Benz, attempted to get the SEC to waive the GAAP reconciliation requirements. Despite over two years of negotiations, the SEC ultimately rejected the German request for a waiver, noting a number of fundamental incompatibilities between the German accounting system and the GAAP. Two of those key differences were the treatment of hidden reserves and segment reporting. German accounting standards allow the maintenance of hidden or "silent" reserves, from which the firm's reported earnings are increased and decreased on discretion. The hidden reserve system enables German firms to moderate differences in reported earned income during lean and prosperous years. For example, in 1994 Daimler-Benz reported a DM 600 million profit under the German accounting system which translated to a DM 1 billion in profit under U.S. GAAP. Moreover, German accounting standards do not require the reporting of operating profits, assets, and other accounts by individual business segments.

Negotiated Resolution

Independent negotiations in 1993 with Daimler-Benz, however, proved more successful. Specifically, Daimler-Benz and the SEC came to an understanding on four issues: disclosure of reserves, provisions for contingencies, segment reporting, and the presentation of historical financial information. Daimler-Benz agreed to disclose all hidden reserves and to list provisions for contingencies as special stockholders' equity rather than as liabilities. In return, the SEC agreed to recognize Daimler-Benz's existing corporate units for purposes of segment reporting and agreed to accept three years of GAAP reconciled financial statements rather than the normal requisite five years.

Item 4 of Form 20-F. Disclosure requirements under Form 20-F's Item 4 and Item 9 also presented some difficulties. Item 4 requires the disclosure of stockholders holding more than 10% of the voting stock and disclosure of the amount of stocks owned by the firm's officers. The difficulty in applying Item 4 disclosure requirements stems from the fact that German stock often takes the form of bearer shares and are not registered as in the U.S. A literal reading of Item 4 makes its disclosure requirement applicable only "[i]f the registrant's outstanding voting securities are in registered form" and would thus exempt disclosure of stock being held as bearer shares. However, under Germany's bearer share system, stockholders with more than 25% of a firm's shares are required to notify the firm. Whether this notification subjects the owners of those shares to Item 4 disclosure requirements is not clear. Ultimately, Daimler-Benz concluded that the purpose of restricting Item 4 disclosure requirements to registered shares was to limit corporate responsibility to those shares of which it had knowledge. In recognition of this purpose and to avoid possible liability under Rule 10b-5 for omission of material information, Daimler-Benz elected to disclose information on the two shareholders holding 25% or more of the firm's stocks. Daimler-Benz also disclosed information on a third shareholder on the basis of its belief that the shareholder held more than 10% of its stock.

In addition to disclosing the names of the appropriate stockholders, Daimler-Benz went one step further by disclosing information on future events likely to affect the stock ownership proportions. For example, Daimler-Benz was scheduled to merge with one of it's major shareholders and some of its stock was to be transferred in payment. A second major shareholder had indicated intentions to reduce its holdings. In both cases, Daimler chose to disclose the information, reasoning that such disclosure was similar to disclosure under Schedule 13D of planned dispositions of securities by shareholders with 5% or more of the stocks.

Item 9 of Form 20-F. The multinational nature of Daimler-Benz's business presented problems under Item 9 of Form 20-F. Item 9 requires a "Management Discussion and Analysis of Financial Condition and Results of Operations."   Normally, such a discussion consists of information on pricing, unit sales, and other conventional data showing general trends in a firm's operations. In Daimler-Benz's case, the analysis had to take into account foreign exchange translations, the effect of GAAP adjustments, and other considerations unique to its status as a multinational German corporation. In both cases, Daimler-Benz chose to include separate disclosure statements. The foreign exchange disclosure statement explained the impact and risks of foreign exchange along with Daimler-Benz's strategy in handling that risk. The GAAP disclosure statement explained how the financial data, as reconciled to GAAP standards, affected each of Daimler-Benz's business segments. In addition to addressing foreign exchange and GAAP adjustment, Daimler-Benz had to differentiate its four business segments and specify the earnings contribution of each, which it did in the conventional numerical form along with an explanation of those numbers.

Response of Other German Firms

A number of German firms have followed Daimler-Benz in entering the U.S. capital market. In November 1996, Deutsche Telekom became the second German company to obtain a NYSE listing in connection with its privatization through a $11.59 billion worldwide distribution of its stock. Also Veba, Germany's leading industrial conglomerate, began filing its accounts according to U.S. GAAP in 1996, a key preliminary step to obtaining a listing. However, the general reluctance of German firms to seek a listing indicates a concern with GAAP reconciliation even as somewhat relaxed by the SEC. They may fear that greater disclosure and less conservative accounting will expose them to increased pressure from disgruntled investors. German accounting standards reportedly smooth out earnings, understating both good or bad results. Another factor may be less interest of German companies in being listed anywhere, Germany or the United States. A NYSE listing was not a magic bullet for Daimler-Benz. In 1995, it had the biggest losses in its history. However, in 1996 it was back in the black by about $1.65 billion. In October 1998 Daimler-Benz merged with Chrysler Corp. to form DaimlerChrysler.

In November 2000, DaimlerChrysler was faced with another major problem of a U.S. listing, liability under U.S. securities laws. Tracinda Corporation, controlled by Kirk Kerkorian, DaimlerChrysler's third largest shareholder, sued the corporation for $8 billion in damages, claiming senior executives of Daimler-Benz knowingly deceived the board and shareholders of Chrysler by presenting the deal as a "merger of equals" whereas in reality the intent was to make Chrysler a division of the new company. T. Burt, *DaimlerChrysler faces $8bn claim over alleged fraud,* Financial Times, November 28, 2000.

In addition to the problems Daimler-Benz had in complying with SEC rules, banks had even more problems. For example, Deutsche Bank which owns a substantial portion of many German companies, including 12% of DaimlerChrysler, would have to incorporate the financial statements (under GAAP rules) of many of those companies into its own. J. Hicks, *The Listing of Daimler-Benz A.G. Securities on the NYSE: Conflicting Interests and Regulatory Policies*, 37 German Yearbook of International Law 360, 369 (1994). See also L. Radebaugh, G. Gebhardt and S. Gray, *Foreign Stock Exchange Listings: A Case Study of Daimler-Benz*, 6 Journal of International Financial Management 2 (1995). In November 1998, Deutsche Bank bought one of the largest U.S. banks, Bankers Trust and began actively to consider listing its shares in the U.S. It did so in October 2001. Perhaps to accomplish this, it earlier announced plans to move $28.3 billion of its stakes in German companies into newly formed fund management subsidiaries.

German officials have been very critical of the United States position on the necessity for U.S. GAAP reconciliation to obtain a listing. Herbert Biener, Ministerialrat at the German Justice Ministry and the senior civil servant for accounting has stated:

> In 1991 in Germany, 578 foreign enterprises were listed on stock exchanges. Although they publish only their original financial statements without reconciliation to German accounting standards, damages to investors have not been reported. A deficiency of comparability of financial statements is therefore no reason for denying mutual recognition. There is no doubt that improved comparability is helpful but, in a market economy, this issue can be solved by competition. If investors prefer enterprises

to give comparable information, competitors will consider whether in this case additional information should be used to influence the market price of their securities.

H. Beiner, *What Is the Future of Mutual Recognition of Financial Statements and Is Comparability Really Necessary*, 3 The European Accounting Review 335, 341 (1994). It seems that choice of accounting rules can indeed influence the price of a stock. C. Leuz and R. Verrecchia, *The Economic Consequences of Increased Disclosure,* 38 J. of Accounting Research 91 (2001) find that German firms which switch from German to U.S. GAAP or International Accounting Standards have lower bid-asked spreads and higher trading volume, indicating investors believe that the switch has reduced information asymmetry.

2. INTERNATIONAL ACCOUNTING STANDARDS

In April 1994, the SEC eased the GAAP reconciliation requirements for foreign issuers by permitting foreign issuers to file a cash flow statement prepared in accordance with International Accounting Standard (IAS) no. 7 without reconciliation to U.S. GAAP. First-time foreign issuers are now only required to reconcile their past two years financial statements (reduced from five years). Some other more minor reconciliation changes were also made. The Commission has also accepted further use of IAS standards in lieu of GAAP reconciliation with respect to hyperinflationary accounting, 59 Federal Register 65628 (1994) and certain business combinations, 59 Federal Register 65637 (1994).

In July 1995, the International Organization of Securities Commissions (IOSCO) and the International Accounting Standards Committee (IASC) announced a program to develop a set of accounting standards for companies seeking a listing in global markets and for the raising of cross-border capital. This project resulted in the formulation of 12 standards and was completed in December 1998. IOSCO has endorsed the standards, as has the Bank for International Settlements, but it is up to individual countries to adopt them. They are already accepted by the London Stock Exchange and almost all other European exchanges. IOSCO endorsed these standards in May 2000, but envisioned that regions like the EU or individual countries could require reconciliations to local standards or additional disclosures. BNA, World Securities Law Report (June 2000). The EU has announced plans for common EU standards based on the IASC standards by 2005. For general background on international accounting standards, see M. Iqbal, T. Melcher and A. Elmallah, *International Accounting: A Global Perspective* (1997).

The SEC has generally encouraged this development while reserving judgment as to whether it will allow such standards to be used in lieu of U.S. GAAP. The primary concern has been that IASC have a mechanism to provide ongoing interpretations of the type available in the United States through the Financial Accounting Standards Board (FASB).

Another is that the standards measure up to U.S. standards. A FASB study found 255 variations between U.S. accepted accounting practices and international standards, many of which were significant. FASB, *The IASC-U.S. Comparison Project* (1997). Finally, both the SEC and FASB have insisted that IASC be structured in such a way as to be independent from political and industry pressure. On February 16, 2000, the SEC issued a Concept Release on International Accounting Standards, Release Nos. 33-7801, 34-42430 (IAS Release) which sought to determine under what conditions it should accept financial statements of foreign private issuers using IAS. The IAS Release continued to call attention to significant differences between U.S. GAAP and IAS, as well as the fact that IASC standards were more general and less detailed than U.S. rules. The Release expressed concern that IAS rules could be implemented differently in different jurisdictions and sought ways to reduce the development of diverging interpretations of IASC standards. It seems to the authors, however, that divergence in implementation of a common accounting standard would be preferable to maintaining several national standards.

The SEC's concern with IASC's governance appeared over. Outgoing SEC Chairman Levitt headed a nominating Committee to select 19 Trustees who, in turn, appoint Members of the IASC Board, the Standing Interpretations Committee, and a new Standards Advisory Council. The Trustees have now been chosen, and the chairman is former Federal Reserve Board Chairman Paul Volcker, the world's most respected person in international finance, and the other trustees are extremely distinguished. A respected European, Sir David Tweedle, has been selected as the Chairman of the IASC Board.

The favorable environment to U.S. allowance of IAS standards in some form was significantly altered by the Enron-Andersen scandal of 2001-2002. This has led to the prospect of more rather than less U.S. control over accounting standards for companies with significant U.S. investors. For example, H.R. 3763, 107th Congress, 2nd Sess., which passed the House on April 24, 2002, would establish a new five-member oversight body with a non-accounting majority that would certify any accountant wishing to audit a public company and that would have disciplinary powers over industry participants. In addition, the legislation would require the SEC to promulgate new rules on periodic disclosures with respect to off-balance sheet transactions and affiliate transaction. And the SEC has also indicated its own heightened concern with U.S. accounting standards, proposing that Management's Discussion and Analysis (MD&A) in annual reports, registration statements and proxy and information statements include disclosure of critical accounting policies. SEC, Press Release, April 30, 2002.

Those favoring U.S. allowance of IAS have tried to turn Enron to their advantage. For example, Tweedle and Volcker have stressed the independence of the IASC Board from industry pressure as compared with FASB. M. Peel, *Volcker urges global body for accounts,* Financial Times, February 14, 2002.   And Frederik Bolkestein, the European Union Commissioner in charge of financial services and tax issues, has touted the virtues of IAS in light of the failure of U.S. GAAP to stop Enron's off-books transactions.   Bolkestein claims the more general rules of IAS compared to the detailed approach of U.S. GAAP is less likely to be circumvented. P. Meller, *International Auditing rules Urged on U.S.,* New York Times, February 22, 2002.

Notes and Questions

1. The requirement for U.S. GAAP reconciliation is based largely on the asserted need for U.S. investors to be able to compare the performance of foreign and U.S. firms. Some finance researchers believe national accounting results can be compared through a "universal translator," a valuation model under which accounting numbers produced under alternative national systems could be translated into consistent measures of firm value. R. Frankel and C. Lee, *Accounting Diversity and International Valuation* (NYSE Working Paper No. 96-01, 1996).

2. Is the solution to reconciliation adoption of international accounting standards? Should international standards apply only to international transactions, or domestic ones as well?

3. The SEC Release envisions three ways in which IAS might be implemented in the U.S. First, the U.S. might implement selected IASC standards, and then follow up with others based on review of the effect of the initial step. Second, it could rely on IASC standards for recognition and measurement principles but require U.S. GAAP and SEC supplemental disclosure requirements for footnote disclosures and the level of detail in line items in financial statements.   Or third it could accept IASC entirely.

In its endorsement of the IASC standards, IOSCO stated that national regulators should be able to supplement the IOSCO standards: "Those supplemental treatments are: reconciliation: requiring reconciliation of certain items to show the effect of applying a different accounting method, in contrast with the method applied under IASC standards; disclosure: requiring additional disclosures, either in the presentation of the financial statements or in the footnotes; and interpretation: specifying use of a particular alternative provided in an IASC standard, or a particular interpretation in cases where the IASC standard is unclear or silent. In addition, as part of national or regional specific requirements, waivers may be envisaged of particular aspects of an IASC standard, without requiring that the effect of the accounting method used be reconciled to the effect of applying the IASC method. The use of waivers should be restricted to exceptional circumstances such as issues identified by a domestic regulator when a specific IASC standard is contrary to domestic or regional regulation." Do you think these supplemental treatments will cause problems?

4. If the U.S. were to allow IAS standards, should they be required for all companies, U.S. and domestic? This would seem an unlikely result given the general preference of regulators for U.S. standards and the difficulties of a massive conversion. It is thus much more likely that IAS standards will be optional. If they are optional, should domestic as well as foreign firms have the option? If the option is only given to foreign firms, there would be issues concerning the competitive effects of such a system, i.e. domestic firms might be at a competitive disadvantage. If the option is given only to foreign firms, who should enforce such IAS standards? It seems likely that the SEC would insist on a major enforcement role for securities sold to U.S. investors under IAS standards. If national bodies generally enforced IAS rules, particularly given their generality, wouldn't this result in uneven application of such rules? See R. Dye and S. Sunder, *Why Not Allow FASB and IASB Standards to Compete in the U.S.?,* 15 Accounting Horizons 257 (September 2001).

D. OPENING UP U.S. SECURITIES MARKETS

In recent years the SEC has taken various initiatives to make it easier for foreign companies to issue securities in the U.S. market. Rule 144A has liberalized private placement rules. The Multijurisdictional Disclosure rules (MJDS) have made it easier for Canadian companies to issue publicly traded securities in the U.S., and the ADR system has facilitated issuance and trading in foreign securities. We now turn to each of these developments

1. RULE 144A AND PRIVATE PLACEMENTS

Global Capital Market

In April of 1990, the SEC adopted Rule 144A which made resales of securities that were not fungible with securities trading in public markets and that were sold only to Qualified Institutional Buyers (QIB) exempt from the registration requirements of the 1933 Act. While applicable to both domestic and foreign issuers, its adoption was driven by the concerns of foreign issuers and the U.S.'s failure to take full advantage of this trend toward globalization.

The reluctance of foreign issuers to enter the U.S. market was due in part to the stringent registration requirements of U.S. securities laws. The Securities Act requires the registration of any securities to be issued under a public offering. An exemption exists, under §4(2) of the Securities Act, for private offerings. The exemption, however, is limited to those private placements intended for investment rather than resale and requires a two year holding period. This illiquidity requires users to pay a premium to investors that generally can be avoided by issuing in markets other than the U.S.

Advantages of Rule 144A

Rule 144A attempts to remedy the situation by extending the private placement exemption to the resale of securities, thereby increasing liquidity and decreasing the premium. Under Rule 144A, the issuer need only provide, at the purchaser's request, some minimal level of financial information, an obligation considerably less burdensome than the disclosure requirements of registration. Even this minimal level of disclosure is waived where the issuer already files reports under the Exchange Act or, as a foreign issuer, files home country reports under Rule 12g3-2(b). Moreover, the information need not comply with GAAP accounting standards.

Besides its lenient registration and disclosure requirements, the Rule 144A market offers other advantages such as speed and efficiency. While a public offering takes 8-15 weeks to consummate, a Rule 144A offering can be completed in 6-8 weeks. Preparations for a Rule 144A offering are so quick that "overnight" deals have become possible.

Requirements of Rule 144A

Resale. The main requirements under Rule 144A are that the resale must be of a non-fungible security to qualified institutional buyers (QIBs). Any resales of securities on an offshore market qualify. Primary offerings can also benefit from Rule 144A if such offering is exempt from registration under §4(2) or Regulation D of the Securities Act and is made through an underwriter. The benefit accrues from the fact that subsequent purchasers of the securities are covered by Rule 144A even if the securities are purchased from the underwriter with an intent to resell.

Fungibility. To meet the non-fungibility requirements of Rule 144A, the security must not be exchangeable with the same class of stock as that listed on an exchange or on the NASDAQ. The requirement insures that Rule 144A issued stock does not compete with stock offered through the normal public offering process. In determining whether securities are of the same class, the following guidelines apply:

- Common equity securities are of the same class if the terms, right and privileges are largely similar.
- Preferred equity securities are of the same class if the terms covering dividends, accumulation, voting rights, liquidation preference, participation, convertibility, call, and redemption are largely similar.
- Debt securities are of the same class if terms covering interest rate, maturity, redemption, subordination, call, and convertibility are largely similar.

However, because fungibility is determined at the time of issuance, issuers are able to by-pass this limitation on convertibility. By listing the securities on the exchanges or on NASDAQ *after* the Rule 144A offering, issuers are able to offer convertible stock that nevertheless meets the fungibility requirement at the time of issuance.

Qualified Institutional Buyer. The requirement that the purchaser be a QIB insures that only those with the most sophisticated knowledge of the securities market are not under the protection of the Securities Act registration and disclosure requirements. To qualify as a QIB, the firm must own and invest a minimum of $100 million in securities or must be owned by firms or individuals all of whom qualify as QIBs. The minimum investment for broker-dealers is $10 million, but less if it acts as an agent for QIBS on a non-discretionary basis. If the firm is a bank or a thrift, it must have a net worth of $25 million. A QIB can only make purchases for itself or for another QIB.

The seller's responsibility in meeting the QIB requirement is fulfilled if the seller upon reasonable reliance determines that the purchaser is a QIB. Reliance is reasonable where the seller uses information available in publicly disclosed financial statements, documents filed with the SEC or other U.S. or foreign regulatory agency, "recognized security manuals," or a certification document from the executive officer of the purchasing company.

Notice. Rule 144A requires that the purchaser be given notice of the seller's reliance on Rule 144A. The seller has met its requirement if it has taken "reasonable steps" to give notice.

Impact on Foreign Issuers and Private Placement

Although Rule 144A is equally applicable to the securities of domestic and foreign firms, its greatest impact has been in the market for foreign securities. Within one year of Rule 144A's adoption, foreign firms were responsible for one-third of the $16.7 billion in issuance of Rule 144A stock. Their representation in 144A stock issuance was substantially greater than in either the traditional private or public bond markets where they comprised only 16% and 7% of the offerings respectively. By 1997, 30% of all foreign transactions were Rule 144A deals. For many foreign firms hoping to eventually make a full public offering in the U.S., Rule 144A is a ideal way to ease into the U.S. market.

The effect of Rule 144A on the private placements market has been tremendous. In 1997, the private placements market grew by approximately 74% with Rule 144A issuance constituting 74% of total private placements. At the same time, the traditional private placement market has remained distinct from the Rule144A market. Insurance companies, which constitute 98% of private placement buyers, are not interested in greater liquidity for their securities and are unwilling to forego higher yields for that liquidity. The very reason traditional buyers like insurance companies have purchased private placement securities has been to hold rather than sell.

PORTAL

Rule 144A's success, however, has not come by the anticipated route. The architects of Rule 144A had envisioned the creation of a liquid secondary market through the PORTAL (Private Offering, Resale and Trading Through Automated Linkages) exchange system. Its computer network would post quotations, accessible by personal computers or at designated PORTAL stations by firms previously qualified as QIBs. Clearance and settlement of trade transactions would be handled by PORTAL depositories such as The Depository Trust Company for US securities and CEDEL for non-US securities.

However, though PORTAL had the backing of both NASD and the SEC, it has not been fully utilized, due in part to burdensome trading restrictions. A complete overhaul in 1993 did little to increase use of the system. Investment banks making markets in Rule 144A securities have been the preferred substitute. Rule 144A private placements have increasingly come to resemble public offerings, with non-negotiable, public-style covenants, prospectus-like documentation and a public rating system. The SEC fears that the circumvention of the PORTAL system is creating a quasi-public market with much of the benefits of the public market without the burdens and checks of registration and disclosure.

Quasi-Public or Private Placement

While Rule 144A is generally seen as a success, a minority of critics question whether the increasingly quasi-public character of Rule 144A issuance is positive or negative. For example, when Goldman Sachs, as the first underwriter for a Rule 144A offering, placed $100 million of 10-year unsecured senior notes for British Aerospace (BAe), some analysts claimed the transaction was a failure. The deal required the issuer to pay 115 basis points more than treasury bills compared to a public offering spread over treasuries of 85-95 but included public style bond covenants. The difference between the Rule 144A and public offering spread in the Bae deal of 30 (115-85) has now narrowed to 5-10.

Notes and Questions

1. What are the basic provisions of Rule 144A? What is the role of PORTAL?

2. Investment companies, e.g. mutual funds, which have a 10% statutory restriction on investing in illiquid securities, generally regard 144A securities as illiquid—they do, however, have the legal discretion to classify them as liquid. Many Rule 144A offerings are two part transactions where a foreign issuer both issues shares on a foreign public market and through the U.S. private placement market. This suggests that the investor may get liquidity on the foreign market. Amendments to Rule 144A include as QIBs both insurance company separate accounts

(if the insurance company is a QIB) and bank collective and master trusts for pension and other employee benefit plans. The ultimate purchaser must qualify, where sales are made to an adviser or other fiduciary, on behalf of another account.

3.   The SEC has exempted Rule 144A securities issued by foreigners from the anti-manipulation rules, Rules 10b-6, 10b-7, and 10b-8, which are designed to prevent issuers, underwriters and other participants in a securities offering in the United States, from supporting the price of the securities. Securities and Exchange Commission, Securities Releases Nos. 33-7028, 34-33138, 58 Federal Register 60326 (1993). What is the justification for granting such exemptions to foreign issuers?

4.   Since its inception a number of changes, approved by the SEC, have been made in the PORTAL system. Participants (brokers, dealers and investors) can qualify a prospective investor as a QIB rather than having the determination made by NASD. Sales of securities can be made to any investor as long as the sale is in compliance with some exemption, not restricted to Rule 144A. Use of PORTAL's automatic clearance and settlement facilities is no longer compulsory, and may be made through depositories other than the Depository Trust Company (clearance and settlement issues are dealt with in Chapter 15). The quotation system has also become more flexible. State Street Boston Corporation, 6 The Global Navigator, Nov. 1994, at 4.

5.   What could be done to make Rule 144A more attractive?

2.   THE MJDS APPROACH

We now turn to another technique to open up the U.S. market—generally permitting foreign issuers to use their home country disclosure rules subject to the requirement that accounts be reconciled to U.S. GAAP.

Basic Approach

Foreign issuers find it burdensome to meet the various securities regulations of multiple countries. The SEC has responded in part with the multijurisdictional disclosure system (MJDS), adopted in 1991 for qualified securities transactions by Canadian issuers, 58 Federal Register 30036 (1991). The large number of Canadian firms issuing registered securities in the United States and the similarities between U.S. and Canadian securities regulation made Canada an obvious first choice. The Commission has chosen not to extend this approach to other countries.

Registration. The MJDS is designed to facilitate securities offerings in multiple markets by subjecting the issuer to the regulations of only one jurisdiction. Specifically, qualified Canadian issuers may use disclosure documents filed with the appropriate Canadian agency in registering with the Commission and in meeting the periodic disclosure requirements. As originally adopted MJDS filings did not require financial statements to be reconciled with U.S. GAAP standards, as long as they met Canada's equivalent but as explained below that approach was changed in 1993 —reconciliation is now required. Except for rights offerings, compliance with U.S. independent auditing standards apply for audits beginning with the first year the issuer files under MJDS. For prior periods, compliance with Canadian independence standards is sufficient. Moreover, the filed documents are usually not reviewed by the Commission in reliance on the Canadian review process and are made effective immediately. If a simultaneous offering is not being made in Canada, registration does not become effective in the United States until the completion of review by the Canadian authorities.

Prospectus. The MJDS issuer generally uses the same prospectus with its U.S. investors as used with its home jurisdiction Canadian investors. The prospectus, however, must specifically warn its investors of the possibility of tax consequences and the potential need to pursue legal remedies in the issuer's home jurisdiction. Any information that need be disclosed in the U.S. but not in its home jurisdiction can be filed with the Commission and disclosed by reference only in the prospectus or registration. Conversely, information that need be disclosed in the home jurisdiction but not in the U.S. can be filed with the Commission rather than directly included in the prospectus or registration. The information, however, must be available upon request by the shareholder.

Liability. Liability under U.S. civil law and antifraud statutes apply to securities issued under the MJDS. A registration, however, will not be considered misleading or fraudulent simply because it does not contain information required for traditional registrations, because the registration requirements of Canada substitute for U.S. requirements. As long as the issuer complies with Canadian standards, as construed by Canadian authorities, the issuer is in compliance with U.S. regulations as well and suffers no liability for undisclosed information not required to be disclosed under Canadian law.

Additional Requirements

Securities Act. To take advantage of MJDS exemptions, Canadian firms must have a minimum history of three years filing with a Canadian securities agency and have a specified minimum market value and/or public float. Issuers must be "substantial" as defined by the Commission. For convertible investment grade securities, the value of an issuer's equity must be at least $180 million and the value of their public float at least $75 million to meet the "substantial" requirement. To be considered an investment grade security, it must be rated within the top four ratings of a nationally recognized statistical rating organization (NRSRO). For all other securities, the minimum value for equity shares is $360 million and the minimum public float is $75 million.

The issuer must be a "foreign private issuer," as defined by the Commission or a Canadian crown corporation owned directly or indirectly by the Canadian government. A foreign private issuer is defined in Rule 3b-4 of the Exchange Act and Rule 405 of the Securities Act to include all foreign issuers other than (1) foreign governments, and (2) foreign issuers that have more than 50 percent of their outstanding voting securities held of record by U.S. residents and that also have: U.S. citizens or residents making up a majority of their executive officers and directors; more than 50 percent of their assets located in the United States; or their business administered principally in the United States. While technically a company with all of its business operations and most of its shareholders in Nigeria could qualify to use MJDS if it were incorporated in Canada and was a foreign private issuer, in practice this would not be allowed. Only "real" Canadian companies can use MJDS.

While registration under the MJDS allows Canadian issuers to use disclosure documents prepared in accordance to Canadian regulations and renders inapplicable U.S. standards on the preparation of prospectuses, other U.S. requirements relating to the distribution of securities remain intact. For example, U.S. requirements on the delivery of the prospectus, safe harbor provisions on advertisements, and rules on the publication of opinions and recommendations still apply. Also, because Canadian law does not require disclosure on indemnification provisions regarding directors, officers, and controlling persons, MJDS issuers must supplement their registration with such information.

Exchange Act. Section 15(d) of the Exchange Act requires periodic reporting by issuers registered under the Securities Act that meet certain threshold requirements in terms of assets and number of U.S. resident shareholders. It also requires periodic reporting by issuers whose securities are listed on a stock exchange or on the NASDAQ. In both situations, Canadian issuers using the MJDS can generally satisfy continuous reporting requirements by filing home country reports under Rule 12g3-2(b).

State Securities Registration

The North American Securities Administrators Association (NASAA), encompassing U.S., as well as Canadian and Mexican, securities regulators has attempted to reconcile state law with the MJDS system. After endorsing the MJDS in 1989, completing a survey of various state law, and consulting state agencies, it proposed a four point amendment to the Uniform Securities Act (1956). First, it called for the reconciliation of state review periods with Canada's seven day review system. It also asked states to accept the MJDS Form F-7 as a substitute for state forms exempting registration for rights offerings. Third, it called for the acceptance of Canadian accounting standards for financial statements as allowed under the MJDS. Lastly, it asked states to exempt secondary sales of securities for which a registration was effective with the Commission through Forms F-8, F-9, or F-10 from additional registration. Many states have adopted these recommendations.

Notes and Questions

1. How would you compare the objectives of MJDS with those of Rule 144A?

2. In principle, MJDS allows Canadian issuers to comply with U.S. securities laws by filing their home-country disclosure documents. What important qualifications are there to this principle, and are these qualifications justified?

3. There have been recent reports that the SEC is seeking to abolish MJDS. The official justifications are (1) that this represents an anomalous bilateral arrangement given the new thrust to develop harmonized international standards represented by SEC endorsement of IOSCO disclosure rules and the likely endorsement of IAS and (2) that it has proven unfeasible to extend MJDS to other countries like the U.K. Some feel the real reason is the SEC's lack of confidence in Canadian enforcement of its rules. Edward Alden, *Canadians Mobilise Over Loss of MJDS,* Financial Times (December 1, 1999). Do any of these reasons justify ending MJDS?

a.   U.S. GAAP RECONCILIATION

In 1993, the SEC made some important changes in MJDS. In April, the Commission required that Canadian financial information be reconciled with U.S. GAAP, 58 Fed. Reg. 35367 (1993). This was based, in part, on the result of a study of the effect of different accounting rules on the statement of income and equity between the U.S. GAAP and foreign GAAP of several countries including Canada, Division of Corporate Finance, SEC, Survey of Financial Statement Reconciliations by Foreign Registrants (1993). The following results were found for Canada:

CANADA

Number of Registrants

291

BASIS OF ACCOUNTING PRESENTATION

Two hundred sixty-nine registrants presented financial statements in accordance with GAAP in their home jurisdiction.

Twenty-two registrants presented financial statements in accordance with U.S. GAAP.

RECONCILIATION DATA

Ninety reported no material reconciling differences.[3]

RECONCILIATION VARIANCES—INCOME

Income Under U.S. GAAP Greater Than Income Under Foreign GAAP	Number of Registrants	Variance Range Percent of Foreign GAAP
More than 100%	2	101.63% - 109.91%
50.01% to 100%	3	57.80% - 62.19%
25.01% to 50%	4	25.78% - 40.08%
10.01% to 25%	8	11.49% - 21.92%
0.01% to 10%	35	0.06% - 7.91%

Income Under U.S. GAAP Less Than Income Under Foreign GAAP	Number of Registrants	Variance Range Percent of Foreign GAAP
More than 100%	1	(638,900.00)%[4]- (116.39)%
50.01% to 100%	1	(82.46)% - (52.32)%
25.01% to 50%	1	(50.00)% - (28.09)%
10.01% to 25%	3	(24.86)% - (10.01)%
0.01% to 10%	18	(7.44)% - (0.03)%

[3] Some registrants reported no material reconciling differences in shareholders' equity but provided a reconciliation for material variances in income. Likewise, some registrants reported no material reconciling income statement differences but provided a reconciliation for material variances in balance sheet items. . . .

[4] Three registrants reported income variances in excess of 1000%, seven reported variances between 500% and 1000% and two reported variances between 200% and 500%. The 638,900% variance is primarily attributable to a large reconciling item compared to an extremely small net income amount. Excluding this variance, the largest percentage would have been 17,835%.

RECONCILIATION VARIANCES—EQUITY

Equity Under U.S. GAAP Greater Than Equity Under Foreign GAAP	Number of Registrants	Variance Range Percent of Foreign GAAP
More than 100%	1	259.04%
50.01% to 100%	1	59.35%
25.01% to 50%	1	34.57%
10.01% to 25%	3	13.70% -22.14%
0.01% to 10%	18	0.36% - 7.24%

Equity Under U.S. GAAP Less Than Equity Under Foreign GAAP	Number of Registrants	Variance Range Percent of Foreign GAAP
More than 100%	9	(1,757.89)% - (101.03)%
50.01% to 100%	10	(99.56)% - (51.23)%
25.01% to 50%	15	(48.95)% - (25.37)%
10.01% to 25%	22	(20.35)% - (10.03)%
0.01% to 10%	39	(8.87)% - (0.01)%

. . .

Notes and Questions

1. Did these results justify a U.S. GAAP reconciliation requirement under MJDS?

2. As of mid-1995, after three and one-half years of existence, MJDS had not been widely used by Canadian issuers; there were only 95 filings under the 1933 Act by 66 Canadian issuers. On the other hand, in 1999 Canadian firms accounted for 38% of the 1,116 international offering in the U.S. but this data includes privately placed as well as public distributions that would make use of MJDS. Some of the reasons for the relatively low use of MJDS seem to be: (1) issuers prefer to use the Regulation S exemption in combination with Rule 144A (this technique is discussed at the end of the Chapter); (2) the need for GAAP reconciliation; (3) the fear of prospective 10b-5 liability; (4) the inability, as in Canada, to have investors pay for securities by installment sale, due to U.S. margin rules preventing the extension of credit in excess of 50 percent in the public offering of securities; (5) necessity to comply with state blue sky laws; and (6) the refusal of the SEC (until 1994) to recognize Canadian rating agencies in connection with the investment grade rating requirement for debt or preferred stock.

3. Should MJDS be further liberalized and extended to other countries? Is it relevant in considering this question that the London Stock Exchange (and the U.K.), which competes with U.S. stock exchanges for listings, see Chapter 14, will accept either compliance with international accounting standards, or with U.K. or U.S. GAAP standards. M. Brown et al., *The Approach of Full Multinational Compliance:*

Registered Public Offerings in Many Jurisdictions, in Global Offerings of Securities 20 (M. Brown and A. Paley eds., 1994) (Global Offerings).

Most securities offered in Europe use U.K. disclosure standards. If the U.S. were to accept U.K. disclosure standards, including U.K. or IASC accounting standards, as an alternative to U.S. standards, it would greatly reduce the barriers to foreign issuers of distributing securities in the United States. U.K. standards are generally quite close to U.S. standards. M. Fallone, *Comparing Disclosure Requirements in the United States with those Found in the United Kingdom,* Third Year Paper at Harvard Law School (1999). Of course, it wouldn't go very far to extend this right only to U.K. companies the way the current MJDS extends only to Canadian companies; one would want to allow any foreign issuer to use U.K. disclosure standards. Would this pose different issues than restricting the right to U.K. companies?

If MJDS were liberalized and extended to other countries, or if U.S. requirements for foreign issuers were further relaxed, would it be fair to subject domestic issuers to higher standards than foreign issuers?

4. S. Choi and A. Guzman have recommended the adoption of "portable reciprocity," a regime under which a firm would be able to choose the law of any country under which it issued its securities and under which the securities traded.   There would be no territorial constraints, so that a U.S., German or Japanese firm could issue securities in the U.S. under Japanese law, or any other law. The authors contend that investors would apply appropriate discounts to the legal regime, e.g. more discounts for regimes with less disclosure, and issuers could trade off less disclosure for lower prices. *Portable Reciprocity: Rethinking The International Reach of Securities Regulation,* 71 Southern California Law Review 903 (1998). What do you think of this proposal? Isn't it highly unlikely that the SEC would allow individuals to buy securities distributed under the law of a country with a low level of required disclosure?   For a very similar proposal, see R. Romano, *Empowering Investors: A Market Approach to Securities Regulation,* 107 Yale Law Journal 2359 (1998) and R. Romano, *The Need for Competition in International Securities Regulation,* Yale ICF Working Paper No. 00-49 (June 30, 2001).

5. An alternative suggestion would expand the MJDS approach and allow foreign issuers to rely on home country disclosure when foreign markets were "efficient." "Efficiency would be a reflection of certain characteristics of both the company and its home market. The main criteria could be the following: (i) minimum disclosure requirements, (ii) minimum periodic reporting requirements, (iii) satisfactory rules aimed at preventing market manipulation and ensuring market transparency, and (iv) minimum market capitalization and trading volume requirements.   It is thought that a company meeting minimum capitalization and trading volume requirements implies a significant

following of the company's stock by analysts." E. Greene, D. Braverman and S. Sperber, *Hegemony or Deference: U.S. Disclosure Requirements in the International Capital Markets*, 50 Business Lawyer 413, 438 (1995). At the same time, Reg. 12g3-2(b) would be narrowed to truly involuntary entry. It would not be available to companies that sponsor Level 1 ADR programs or conduct private placements under Rule 144A. *Id.*, at 443. What do you think of this proposal?

3. THE USE OF ADRs

Overview of ADR

American Depository Receipts (ADR) are the primary method by which U.S. investors hold foreign securities other than Canadian securities. The depository, usually a bank or a trust company, holds the actual stock certificate of the foreign security, and investors hold a negotiable instrument representing their interests. ADRs are priced in dollars even though the underlying securities are priced in foreign currencies. They also provide for the payment of dividends in dollars and the reporting by the depositary in English of significant corporate actions. In addition, ADRs are cleared and settled through the U.S. clearing and settlement process. The depositary charges a fee for these services.

It is far from clear, however, that ADRs are attractive to securities dealers and institutional investors, who may think the services provided by the depositary are too expensive. These professionals may themselves be able to more cheaply convert foreign currency dividends into dollars and to keep track of corporate actions. And foreign clearing and settlement systems in major markets may be even more efficient than systems in the U.S. We examine this issue in Chapter 15. These professionals might well prefer a mechanism to trade the exact same underlying security in different markets.

Establishing an ADR Facility

An ADR facility can be established in one of two forms—as a sponsored or as an unsponsored facility.

Sponsored. A sponsored facility is one created jointly by the issuer and the depositary through the execution of a deposit agreement and a Form F-6 registration statement. The facility is maintained through income generated from dividend payment fees paid by the issuer and deposit and withdrawal fees paid by the investors. As part of the deposit agreement, the depositary notifies investors of shareholder meetings and disseminates information provided by the issuer.

Unsponsored. An unsponsored facility is one that is established independent of the issuer, though issuers are normally solicited for letters of non-objection. Market interest for the issuer's securities serves as the impetus and the depositary usually serves as the sponsor of a new facility. While issuer participation is not necessary in establishing an unsponsored facility, its cooperation may be necessary. If the issuer is not exempt from reporting under the Exchange Act, the issuer must apply for the 12g3-2(b) exemption. Only then can the depositary file a Form F-6 for the ADR. The facility is maintained through income generated from deposit and withdrawal fees, conversion fees, and other payments by investors. Because the issuer does not financially support the facility's maintenance, there is no obligation on the part of the depositary to report corporate actions.

While both sponsored and unsponsored facilities are in existence, there is increasing pressure for ADR facilities to be sponsored by the issuer. The NYSE and the Amex, for example, will not list ADRs that are unsponsored and the NASDAQ highly recommends the same. Over-the-counter markets such as the Pink Sheets and the Bulletin Board continue to accept unsponsored ADRs.

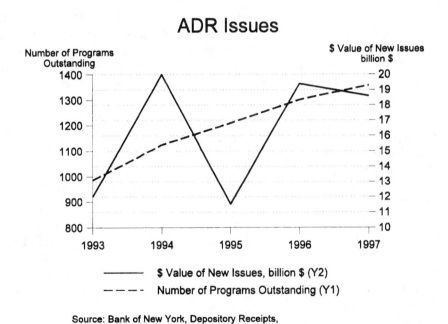

ADR Issues

Source: Bank of New York, Depository Receipts,
1997 Year-End Market Survey

Securities Act and Exchange Act

Securities Act. The registration requirement of the Securities Act is applicable to both the deposited security itself and the ADRs in evidence of that security. For example, when an issuer makes a public offering of its securities, both the ADRs and the deposited securities must be registered with the Commission. It is also possible to have a transaction in which the deposited security need not be registered but the issued ADR must be. Foreign securities purchased in the secondary markets may be deposited in an ADR facility without incurring an obligation to register them. When ADRs are issued for those deposited shares, however, the ADRs must be registered as they constitute a public offering.

To register an ADR with the Commission, the depositary signs Form F-6 in place of the issuer. For sponsored facilities, the issuer, a majority of it board, its principal officer, and U.S. representative must also sign. In order to qualify for use of Form F-6 in registered ADRs, the issuer must be registered under the Securities Act or exempt from such. The issuer must also be or be in the process of becoming a reporting issuer under the Exchange Act. An issuer is exempt from the reporting requirements through Rule 12g3-2(b) if information it files abroad meets certain requirements. Lastly, to qualify for use of Form F-6, investors must be able to freely exchange their ADRs for the deposited securities.

Once an issuer meets the requirements for use of Form F-6, it must comply with a limited number of disclosure requirements as mandated by Form F-6. The disclosure requirement includes a prospectus describing the ADRs registered, a notice that information on the issuer is available, and an outline of the fees imposed on the ADRs. Most of this disclosure is provided directly on the ADR certificate.

Exchange Act. The establishment of an ADR facility will not in and of itself subject the issuer to reporting requirements under the Exchange Act. However, if the ADRS are listed on an exchange or the NASDAQ, they become subject to the Exchange Act and must file Form 20-F and other documents required by laws of the issuer's home jurisdiction. ADRs traded in OTC markets need not provide periodic reports if they issuers maintain a Rule 12g3-2(b) exemption.

Sponsored ADRs are often referred to as being Level I, II or III. Level I refers to ADRs traded in the OTC; most ADRs are traded in this form. Level II refers to ADRs listed on an exchange that do not, like Level III, involve a new issue of shares to raise capital. ADRs may also be used for private placements as under Rule 144A.

The chart above shows the activity of ADRs in the 1990s. This data indicates that new ADR issues in the U.S. have flattened out despite an unprecedented bull market. In 1998, the volume of new ADRs coming to market fell to $10 billion, a 40% drop from 1997, largely as a result of U.S. investor interest in the booming U.S. equity market to the exclusion of foreign issues. *Mixed Results for ADRs as issuance slows down,* Financial Times (March 23, 1999). But the value of ADR issuance rebounded to over $21.2 billion in 1999, a new record. Business Wire (December 16, 1999) reporting on Citibank's Year-End Review.

Notes and Questions

1. Joseph Velli of the Bank of New York, an expert on ADRs, gives various reasons for foreign companies establishing ADR programs, including: (1) foreign companies can increase their share value if the U.S. puts a higher price/earnings ratio on their stock than their home markets; and (2) U.S. investors can buy the shares more cheaply and conveniently in the U.S. than abroad. In connection with the second point, he points out that ADRs avoid foreign custody fees (a global custodian holding the stock abroad could charge 10-40 basis points per year), provide better foreign exchange rates on dividends (the depositary converts to dollars in bulk), and avoids inefficient foreign settlement systems. J. Velli, *American Depositary Receipts: An Overview*, 17 Fordham International Law Journal S38 (1994).

2. What is an ADR? Compare it to a "normal" security. What is the difference between a sponsored and unsponsored ADR? Unsponsored ADRs are becoming obsolete. Very few new ones are being established.

3. Why might ADRs be attractive to foreign issuers and U.S. investors?

4. The F-6 registration statement provides no information about the issuer, only the terms of the ADR arrangement. So the creation of an ADR facility does not by itself trigger the need for a '33 Act issuer registration statement. Exchange listed ADRs, as is the case for other listed securities, are subject to periodic reporting under the '34 Act. If the issue is unlisted, the 12g3-2(b) exemption is available. Is there a registration loophole?

5. Another type of depositary receipt, global depositary receipts or global depositary shares (GDRs or GDSs) have emerged since 1990. These are depositary receipts issued in connection with non-U.S. offerings of foreign securities which are often listed on a foreign stock exchange. When GDRs are issued in combined offerings, both abroad and in the U.S., the U.S. receipts are referred to as either ADRs or GDRs.

6. The NYSE has considered the creation of a facility for trading the shares of non-U.S. companies in their local currencies under U.S. clearing and settlement rules on the theory that the "repackaging" advantages of ADRs are not worth the fees charged to investors.

7. After the 1998 Daimler-Benz merger with Chrysler, the new DaimlerChrysler stock (DCX) traded in ordinary common stock form rather than as ADRs (the form in which Daimler-Benz had previously traded). Indeed, DCX now trades on 22 exchanges around the world with the same instrument, albeit in different currencies. It is referred to as a global registered share (GRS). Most notably, DCX trades on the NYSE in dollars and on the Frankfurt Stock Exchange in euros. Dividends will be paid once a year in dollars to U.S. registered shareholders and in euros to German-registered shareholders. Trades are cleared through a

bilateral link between the U.S. and German clearing systems, more fully described in Chapter 15. U.S. holders can elect, however, to receive dividends in dollars, at a cost. See N. Brumm, *DaimlerChrysler paves the way for new listing structure,* International Financial Law Review, U.S. Capital Markets Report 62 (December 1999) and G. Karolyi, *DaimlerChrysler AG, The First Truly Global Share,* Working Paper (September 1999). As of May 2000, only two companies, Celanese AG, also a German company and UBS, the Swiss bank, have obtained a GRS listing on the NYSE, but when Deutsche Bank listed on the NYSE in October 2001, it chose to do so through a GRS. Given the fact that most German companies issue shares in bearer form, and that NYSE listings required registered shares, German companies seeking to list shares rather than ADRs must convert their share from bearer to registered form, a complex process. It is examined in depth by M. Gruson, *Global Shares of German Corporations and Their Dual Listings on the Frankfurt and New York Stock Exchanges,* 22 U. Pa. J. of Int'l Economic Law 185 (2001).

What explains so little interest in GRS's? Brumm, supra, discusses some obstacles. First, the GRS requires a clearing link between the U.S. and the issuer's home country but many such bilateral links exist. Second, it requires that the shares be issued in registered form (since the U.S. demand this) rather than in bearer form. In many jurisdictions, shares are accustomed to trade in bearer form. Brumm suggests this can be dealt with by converting from bearer to registered form when shares are sold by German investors on the NYSE and back again when sold by U.S. investors on the Frankfurt Exchange, but this would add some cost. Third, a major problem seems to be countries like England which prohibit the transfer of shares on a share registry maintained outside of the issuer's home jurisdiction. Such a requirement is imposed in order to assure stamp taxes are collected on share transfers. Apparently, the ADR form may also be more flexible in some cases. One of the reasons Novartis opted for ADR form was because Swiss stock exchange rule prevent its splitting its share price to a level comparable to its U.S. peers. With an ADR, it can obtain a split in the U.S. by merely adjusting the ratio of conversion of ADRs to shares. W. Hall, *Global shares face a long uphill battle,* Financial Times, May 31, 2000. The costs of establishing a GRS program are quite expensive compared to ADRs. A. Beard, *Global shares a let-down for Daimler Chrysler,* Financial Times, April 30, 2001.

Karolyi, supra, points to the low trading volume in DaimlerChrysler, which could also explain the reluctance of other companies to use the GRS, although low volume could be explained by factors other than the ADR v. GRS decision. Trading volume has also been low for UBS compared with the expected volume for ADRs, Hall, supra.

8. H. Jackson & E. Pan, *Regulatory Competition in International Securities Markets: Evidence from Europe in 1999 - Part II* Business

Lawyer, May 2001, observe that there is a declining importance of the ADR market in the United States for foreign issuers with active home markets, in particular European issuers. They show that for the 10 ADR European issues in 1995, ADR shares at the end of that year were 123%, indicating that home shares flowed into the United States after the issue. From 1995-1999, shares of these issues continued to flow in. In comparison, for the 6 European issues in 1998, only 59% of the shares issued remained in ADR form at the end of the year; these shares moved back to the home market. And in 1999, these shares continued to flow out of the United States. The authors posit that institutional investors do not want to trade shares in ADR form in the U.S. but prefer to trade on the more active and deeper home market. For shares from countries with less active home markets, however, such as those from Latin America, trading in ADR form in the United states is preferred. Thus, the overall growth in ADR trading previously observed is due largely to shares from these relatively less active home markets.

E. ISSUING SECURITIES ABROAD

Holdings of foreign equities by U.S. investors increased from $100 billion in 1988 to over $1.5 trillion in 1999. The general concern is that off-shore distributions to U.S. investors could be used to circumvent U.S. law. The piece below describes Regulation S of the SEC, 55 Federal Register 18306 (1990), which deals with the issuance of securities abroad.

1. THE REGULATION S FRAMEWORK

M. STEINBERG AND D. LANSDALE, REGULATION S AND RULE 144A: CREATING A WORKABLE FICTION IN AN EXPANDING SECURITIES MARKET
29 International Lawyer 41, 47-57 (1995).

A. POLICY UNDERLYING REGULATION S

. . .

In Regulation S the SEC embraced a territorial approach to the extraterritorial application of the Securities Act. This approach is based on the notion that the registration requirements of the Securities Act are intended to protect the U.S. capital markets and all investors in such markets, whether U.S. or foreign nationals. Regulation S represents a change in emphasis, from attempting to protect U.S. persons irrespective of where they are located, to protecting the integrity of the U.S. capital markets. For registration purposes, the Commission decided to rely upon the laws in the jurisdictions in which the transactions occur rather than the U.S.

Securities Act. The Commission stated: "The territorial approach recognizes the primacy of the laws in which a market is located. As investors choose their markets, they choose the laws and regulations applicable in such markets."

. . .

B. THE REGULATION S REGULATORY FRAMEWORK-- GENERAL PRINCIPLES

Regulation S comprises four rules: Rules 901, 902, 903, and 904. Rule 901 contains a general statement that reflects the SEC's new territorial approach. Rule 901(a) states that only offers and sales of securities inside the United States are subject to section 5.

. . .

The primary inquiry under the new regulatory scheme, as stated in Rule 901, is whether the offer and sale of securities occurs "outside the United States." If the offer and sale are outside the United States within the meaning of Rule 901, the registration provisions of section 5 are not applicable; if the offer or sale occurs within the United States, the registration provisions (absent the perfection of an exemption) are applicable. However, determining whether an offer and sale have occurred outside the United States is not necessarily an easy matter to resolve.

The SEC provides that whether an offer and sale are made outside the United States is to be determined on an ad hoc basis. To clarify when an offer and sale will be considered outside the United States, Regulation S provides two nonexclusive safe-harbor provisions in Rules 903 and 904. If the offer and sale satisfy the conditions of either of the safe-harbor provisions, such transaction will be deemed to have occurred outside the United States and outside the reach of section 5. Since perfecting a safe harbor provides an issuer assurance that the registration provisions of the Securities Act will not apply, the remaining discussion of Regulation S focuses on the safe-harbor provisions.

C. REGULATION S--SAFE HARBORS

Regulation S comprises two safe-harbor provisions: (1) an issuer safe harbor (Rule 903) and (2) a safe harbor for resales (Rule 904) [We only look at the issuer safe harbor]. All offers and sales, whether made in reliance on the issuer or the resale safe harbor, must satisfy two general conditions. In addition, the issuer must satisfy specific conditions that are set out in each safe-harbor provision.

1. *General Conditions*

The general conditions applicable to all offers and sales, whether based on the issuer or resale safe harbor, are that: (1) the offer or sale is made in an "offshore transaction"; and (2) no "direct selling efforts" take place in the United States in connection with the distribution or resale of the securities. To engage in an offshore transaction there can be no offer or sale to a person in the United States and either of two additional requirements must be satisfied. The first of the alternative requirements is that the buyer is outside the United States, or the seller reasonably believes that the buyer is outside of the United States, at the time the buy order is originated.

. . .

The second alternative means of satisfying the offshore-transaction requirement is to execute the transaction on a designated offshore securities market. However, if the seller or its agent knows that the transaction has been prearranged with a buyer in the United States, the second alternative will not be satisfied.

The second general condition that must be satisfied in order for an offer and sale to be considered outside the United States is that there be no direct selling efforts in the United States. For purposes of the issuer safe harbor, neither the issuer, distributors, nor their respective affiliates may engage in direct selling efforts in the United States. Failure to adhere to this condition will result in loss of the safe harbor for all participants in the offering.

Directed selling efforts are defined as any activity that could reasonably be expected to have the effect of conditioning the market in the United States for any of the securities being offered in reliance on Regulation S. Specifically, placing advertisements with television or radio stations reaching the United States or in publications with a general circulation in the United States, mailing printed material to U.S. investors, or conducting promotional seminars in the United States are considered direct selling efforts. Rule 902(b), however, excludes certain types of advertising from the definition of direct selling efforts. These exceptions include advertisements that are required under either U.S. or foreign law and "tombstone" advertisements placed in publications that have less than 20 percent of their total circulation in the United States.

. . .

2. *Issuer Safe Harbor--Rule 903*

The issuer safe harbor is applicable not only to the actual issuer, but also to the issuer's distributors, their respective affiliates, and persons acting on behalf of the foregoing. The safe harbor may be utilized by both U.S. and foreign issuers offering securities outside the United States. Similar to the regimen prevailing under Release 4708 and SEC no-action letters issued in connection therewith, the conditions that must be satisfied to meet the issuer safe harbor differ depending on the type of securities being offered. For purposes of Regulation S, the SEC separates securities into three categories: Category I, Category II, and Category III. The categorization of securities is based on the likelihood that the securities will flow back to the United States. As the probability that the securities will flow back to the United States increases, the procedural requirements necessary to avoid registration become more difficult. Under the Regulation S regulatory scheme, Category I securities are subject to the least regulatory restraints and Category III securities to the most.

Category I securities are securities of "foreign issuers" for which there is no "substantial U.S. market interest," * securities offered and sold in "overseas directed offerings," securities backed by the full faith and credit of a "foreign government," and securities sold pursuant to certain employee benefit plans. Because the SEC concluded that these securities were the least likely to flow back to the United States, it put only minimal procedural requirements upon them. Accordingly, to satisfy the issuer safe harbor, an issuer of Category I securities need only satisfy the general conditions described above: (1) an offshore transaction; and (2) no direct selling efforts in the United States.

. . .

Offerings falling within the second issuer safe harbor, Category II, are those by foreign and U.S. companies that are subject to the Exchange Act's reporting requirements as well as offerings of debt securities by nonreporting foreign issuers. To qualify for the Category II issuer safe harbor the issuer must satisfy not only the general conditions, but must also comply with certain selling restrictions.

Two types of selling restrictions apply to offerings of securities falling within Category II: (1) "transactional restrictions" and (2) "offering restrictions." The transactional restrictions prohibit offers and sales of such securities in the United States or to a "U.S. person" during a restricted period lasting forty days.

---

* Substantial U.S. market interest exists when the United States constitutes the largest market for the trading of the security or when more than 20 percent of the security is traded in the U.S. when less than 55 percent of the trading took place in a single foreign country. Rule 902(j). Eds.

.   .   .

In addition, the issuer and its entire distribution syndicate must adhere to certain "offering restrictions" (which basically are procedures) to meet the Category II and Category III issuer safe harbors.

.   .   .

Generally, as currently formulated, the procedures require that all distributors agree in writing that all offers and sales during the applicable restricted period be made only in accordance with a Regulation S safe harbor or pursuant to registration under the Securities Act or an exemption therefrom. Furthermore, the issuer, distributors, and their respective affiliates must include statements in all offering materials that the securities have not been registered under the Securities Act and may not be offered or sold in the United States or to U.S. persons unless the securities are registered or an exemption from registration is perfected.

The final safe-harbor category, Category III, applies to all securities not within Categories I or II. This category includes offerings of nonreporting U.S. issuers and equity securities of nonreporting foreign issuers when there is a substantial U.S. market interest in such securities. The SEC imposes the most rigorous restrictions on offerings falling within this category due to the Commission's position that these securities have the highest probability of flowing back to the United States.

As is the case in the first two categories of securities, the general conditions that the offer and sale be made in an offshore transaction and that there be no direct selling efforts in the United States or to a U.S. person are applicable to Category III securities. Moreover, the offering restrictions relating to Category II offerings discussed above also are applicable to offerings under Category III. However, the transactional restrictions applicable to Category III offerings are more demanding than those required under Category II.

The transactional restrictions applicable to Category III offerings are somewhat similar to the restrictions existing under Release 4708 prior to the promulgation of Regulation S. Due to the Commission's belief that debt offerings of Category III securities are less likely to flow back to the United States, the SEC imposes less stringent transactional restrictions upon them than it does upon equity securities.

Debt securities offered pursuant to Category III are subject to a forty-day restricted period.*

     .   .   .

During this period the securities may not be sold to U.S. persons or for the account (or benefit) of U.S. persons. As was the procedure under Release 4708, the debt securities must be represented by a temporary global security, which is not exchangeable for definitive securities until the forty-day restricted period has expired. When the global security is exchanged for the definitive security, certification must be effected that a non-U.S. person owns the security or that a U.S. person purchased securities in a transaction that was exempt from the registration requirements of the Securities Act.   If a distributor or other person receiving a selling concession sells prior to the expiration of the forty-day restricted period, it must send a "confirmation or other notice" to the purchaser stating that the purchaser is subject to the same restrictions on offers and sales that apply to the distributor.

    The transactional restrictions applicable to equity offerings under the third issuer safe harbor--Category III--are even more demanding than the restrictions applicable to debt securities in the same category. Rule 903(c)(3)(iii) prohibits equity securities offered under Category III from being sold to a U.S. person or for the account (or benefit) of a U.S. person for a period of one year. Furthermore, the purchaser of the security must certify that it is not a U.S. person and is not acquiring the securities for the account (or benefit) of any U.S. person.   In addition, the purchaser must agree to resell only if it adheres to one of three conditions, namely, that such resale is made in accordance with Regulation S, pursuant to a registration statement, or under an exemption from registration. If a U.S. issuer is utilizing the Category III safe harbor, it must place a legend on the securities offered stating that all transfers are prohibited except as set forth above. Finally, the issuer is required, either by contract or pursuant to a provision in its bylaws, articles, or charter, to refuse to register any transfer not in accordance with the foregoing.

2. REGULATION S REFORMS FOR U.S. COMPANIES ISSUING SECURITIES ABROAD

    The SEC has been concerned with possible abuses of the Regulation S exemption particularly in cases where U.S. issuers seek to escape registration by sham offerings to foreign investors abroad (where the economic investment risk never shifts to the foreign owners) followed by flowback into the U.S. after the expiration of the restrictive period, if any.

---

* For equity securities, securities issued by reporting issuers have a 40 day holding period and securities issued by non-reporting issuers have a one year holding period, eds.

Securities and Exchange Commission, Problematic Practices Under Regulation S, Interpretive Release No. 33-7190 (June 27, 1995). The SEC has also been concerned about "short selling and other hedging transactions such as option writing, equity swaps, or other type of derivative transactions where purchasers transfer the benefits and burdens of ownership back to the United States market during the restricted period." *Id*. at 5. These concerns suggest that it may be futile, or at best extremely difficult, in the modern financial world to erect barriers between markets.

In 1996, the SEC adopted rules about "Periodic Reporting of Unregistered Equity Sales," to address some of the concerns described above. 61 Federal Register (October 18, 1996). U.S. companies issuing shares to foreign investors under Regulation S must now report this activity to the SEC (and, thereby, the public) within 15 days. This insures that the market will know about such distributions before the expiration of the normal 40 day restriction on flowback. Such reporting, it is hoped, will reduce the possibility of selling such issues abroad at a steep discount from the U.S. price (due to the avoidance of registration costs and the absence of knowledge on the part of existing investors that their shares are being diluted through the offshore offering). Foreign investors purchasing at a discount should now expect the U.S. price to fall before they can resell their shares in the U.S. market. M. Hendrickson, *SEC Adopts Reporting Rules in Attempt to Curb Reg S Abuses*, Securities Industry News (October 28, 1996). The SEC also relaxed domestic disclosure rules regarding reporting requirements concerning financial statements of acquired and to be acquired businesses in order to reduce the incentive of using Regulation S offerings to escape such reporting. 61 Federal Register 54509 (October 18, 1996).

The SEC, however, remained concerned with abuses of Regulation S to distribute unregistered U.S. equity securities abroad. On February 25, 1998, it adopted modifications to Regulation S providing that such securities will be classified as "restricted securities" within the meaning of Rule 144, and their restricted holding periods increased from 40 to one year. In addition, certain certification and legending requirements are imposed on the sales of restricted equity securities by reporting as well as non-reporting issuers. In effect, the treatment of offshore sales for the covered issuers will be aligned with that for domestic private placements. 63 Federal Register 9632 (February 25, 1998).

The new modifications apply to issuance by U.S. issuers abroad even where there is no substantial U.S. market interest in the securities. Does this make sense? The SEC originally proposed that the new rules would also apply to foreign equity securities whose primary market is the U.S., e.g. equity securities mainly traded in the United States, which may then flowback into the United States. 62 Federal Register 9258 (February 28, 1997) but did not include this proposal in its final Rule.

3. DIRECTED SELLING

In October 1997, the SEC adopted a new rule establishing safe harbors to facilitate U.S. press access to offshore press activities. The safe harbors would clarify the conditions under which journalists may be provided with access to offshore press conferences, offshore meetings and press materials released offshore, without an issuer losing the Regulation S exemption from registration requirements due to engaging in "directed selling efforts." 62 Federal Register 53948 (October 17, 1997). Congress had directed the SEC to address this issue in Section 109 of the National Securities Markets Improvements Act of 1996.

How does the use of the Internet affect the issue of the use of "directed selling efforts" under Regulation S? Suppose a British firm places a prospectus on its Internet home page for an offering (unregistered in the U.S.) principally targeted at U.K. investors. If a U.S. investor accesses the site, could the British firm be in violation of U.S. registration requirements? The SEC has taken the position that the offering would not violate registration requirements if the Web site on which the securities are offered includes a prominent disclaimer making it clear that the offer is directed only to countries other than the United States and the Web site offeror implements procedures that are reasonably designed to guard against sales to U.S. persons in the offshore offering, e.g. by ascertaining the purchaser's residence. Statement of the Commission Regarding Use of Internet Web Sites To Offer Securities, Solicit Securities Transactions, or Advertise Investment Services Offshore, III. B, Release Nos. 33-7516, 34-39779 (March 23, 1998).

The SEC has taken a more restrictive approach where the offshore offering is made by a U.S. issuer. This flows from its more general concern with the abuse of Regulation S by U.S. offerors. In this case, the SEC not only requires the general precautions for foreign issuers described above but also requires that the U.S. issuer implement "password-type" procedures that are reasonably designed to ensure that only non-U.S. persons can obtain access to the offer. This would require that prospective purchasers demonstrate that they are not U.S. persons before obtaining the password to the site. Id., at IV. B. What do you think of the SEC's approach?

4. REGULATION S - RULE 144A OFFERINGS

Regulation S can be used in conjunction with Rule 144A to sell foreign securities in the United States. Securities subject to Reg. S resale restrictions (Categories II and III) can be sold immediately to U.S. qualifying investors under Rule 144A. Regulation S restrictions must be complied with for all unregistered securities issued abroad. Thus, even if an issuer has a 12g3-2(b) exemption (files home country reports), the foreign issue cannot be generally traded by U.S. investors in the U.S.

(flowback) until the restriction periods expire. Thus, while unregistered foreign securities can eventually generally trade in the United States through the Pink Sheets, they cannot do so until they are "seasoned" abroad. This permits material information about the securities to be reflected in their prices before the securities are bought by U.S. persons, either in the U.S. or abroad. In short, U.S. investors can trade in unregistered stocks, either here or abroad, but only after the seasoning period (for Category II and III securities).

When Rule 144A offerings through ADRs in the United States (whether by U.S. or foreign issuers) are made alongside the issuance of the same securities abroad as GDRs, pursuant to Regulation S, the fact of the Rule 144A offering is certainly material to the U.S. investors, given that the wider offering may improve the liquidity of the issue.

This creates two important issues. First, the SEC has been concerned that the parallel offerings would risk improper "leakage" of the restricted ADRs traded by sophisticated investors to U.S. investors trading GDRs in the United States. Why should the SEC care? If U.S. public investors can trade GDR securities, which are functionally identical to the ADRs, why shouldn't they be able to trade the ADRs as well? To minimize leakage, the SEC issued an interpretive letter in April 1993 requiring that (1) the unrestricted depositary receipts be distinguished by separate names (e.g. GDR as opposed to ADR) and different CUSIP numbers; (2) that deposits into and withdrawal from the restricted depositary facility, e.g. PORTAL, require the owner to agree to specified restrictions on transfer; and (3) that depositors into the unrestricted facility, e.g. DTC, certify that they are not an affiliate or acting on behalf of the issuer of the underlying securities. In addition, the Commission staff also required that the Form F-6 registration of the foreign issued securities should not be effective until 40 days after the completion of the foreign offering. M. Brown, E. Greene, and A. Paley, *Avoiding the Applicability of the Most Burdensome Requirements, in* Global Offerings 120, 121.

A second issue arises under Regulation S, as to whether disclosure of the offshore offering to the U.S. investors would violate the prohibition on directed selling efforts. The SEC, as part of its April 1994 reforms, adopted a new Rule 135(c) safe harbor permitting the issuer to publicly announce certain information concerning the securities offered outside the U.S., but not the name of the underwriters or placement agents. The safe harbor is only available to issuers filing periodic reports under the '34 Act or, in the case of foreign issuers, enjoying a Rule 12g3-2(b) exemption. 59 Federal Register 21644 (1994).

5. REGULATION S - A REFORM PROPOSAL

In *Internationalization of Primary Public Securities Markets,* 63 J. of Law and Contemporary Problems 71 (2000), H. Scott posits that it would be desirable for issuers in public primary securities markets to be able to

issue securities to investors worldwide using one set of optimal
distribution procedures and disclosure documents, and one set of liability
standards and enforcement remedies. The article points out that this
state of affairs is currently not possible because the United States
conditions public issuance in its territory—and to some significant extent
to U.S. investors outside its territory—on compliance with its unique set
of distribution procedures, disclosure requirements, and enforcement rules.

Harmonization of world rules is not the answer to this problem.
There is no reason to assume that the world would choose an optimal
level of disclosure, particularly because the United States will push for
world rules that are closely equivalent to its own. Moreover, there is
substantial doubt as to whether worldwide agreement can be reached on
the issue of disclosure, let alone distribution and enforcement rules. Nor
is mutual recognition the answer. The approach creates basic inequities
for domestic issuers and has not worked well in the European Union,
which has the advantage of supranational institutions, despite much
fanfare about the single passport. Broader versions of mutual recognition,
such as portable reciprocity, under which issuers could issue securities
anywhere under any law founder on problems of enforcement.

The Article proposes instead the establishment of an offshore free
zone. This would require that the United States, like other countries,
permit its investors to participate in the offshore market for primary
distributions of foreign issuers free of restrictions other than minimum
disclosure requirements. Regulation S would be substantially repealed.
In addition, foreign issues could be directly advertised in the U.S. on the
theory that investors are entitled to know about offshore opportunities.
One major benefit of this approach is that it would permit the use of
common distribution procedures. For some refinements of this proposal,
see Internationalization of Primary Public Securities Markets Revisited,
in Capital Markets in the Age of the Euro: Cross-Border Transactions,
Listed Companies and Regulation, eds. K Hopt, E. Wymeersch and G.
Ferrarini (forthcoming Kluwer 2002).

Notes and Questions

1. What are the justifications for generally applying U.S. law on an
extraterritorial basis? Is this justified by the need to protect U.S.
investors abroad, or in the United States (given the possibilities of
flowback)? What do you think of Professor Scott's proposal? Note that
European countries do not presently restrict offshore purchases of their
residents, but this may change with the implementation of new
prospectus proposals see Chapter 5.

2. Regulation S defines when securities issued abroad will be exempt
from the registration requirements of the '33 Act. What considerations
are taken into account in making this determination?

3.   What are the general conditions for a Regulation S exemption, and how do they take into account the concerns about granting an exemption?

4.   Regulation S restrictions are premised on the need for seasoning to protect U.S. investors. Do you agree with this?

5.   Given the availability of Rule 144A and the ability of U.S. investors to buy Category I securities (most European issuers which trade mainly in their home market) in the secondary market immediately after the underwriting is complete, is there any real need for the reform contemplated by Professor Scott? If primary distributions were made through auctions on electronic exchanges abroad, could they be sold to U.S. residents? How likely are auctions to be used for primary distributions?

6.   The NYSE has proposed exempting "world class" foreign companies, defined as those with revenue of $5 billion, and market capitalization of $2 billion, or average weekly trading volume outside the United States of at least $1 million or 200,000 shares from GAAP reconciliation, permitting them instead to submit their independently home audited financial statements, as long as they included a written explanation of any material differences between home country and U.S. accounting practices. J. Cochrane, *Are U.S. Regulatory Requirements for Foreign Firms Appropriate*, 17 Fordham International Law Journal 558 (1994). What do you think of this proposal? Under Section 105 of the National Securities Market Improvement Act of 1996 the SEC now has explicit authority to exempt securities of large companies from normal registration requirements.

7.   Consider the implications of the case of *Roby v. Corporation of Lloyd's*, 996 F.2d 1353 (2d Cir. 1993) where the court refused to invalidate under U.S. securities laws an agreement between a U.S. "Name" (an investor) and a Member Agent of Lloyd's (a London insurance market) that all disputes would be decided in England under English law. The court based its decision on the reasoning in *Shearson/American Express v. McMahon*, 482 U.S. 220 (1987) enforcing an arbitration clause against an attack under section 10(b) of the 1934 Act on the grounds that arbitration could adequately preserve the substantive rights granted under the Act. The Second Circuit in *Roby* reasoned that English law provided U.S. investors with the reasonable equivalent of U.S. securities' law protections. The court concluded: "While we do not doubt that the United States securities laws would provide the Roby Names with a...greater chance of success due to lighter scienter and causation requirements, we are convinced there are ample and just remedies under English law." 996 F.2d at 1366.

Suppose issuers of securities in the United States, whether domestic or foreign, inserted English forum and choice of law clauses in their prospectuses and share certificates. Would this protect them from liability under U.S. securities laws? Should it? See D. Hall, *Note, No Way Out: An Argument Against Permitting Parties to Opt Out of U.S. Securities Laws in International Transactions*, 97 Colum. L. Rev. 57 (1997).

8. This Chapter has not dealt with issues concerning the enforcement of U.S. anti-fraud rules in connection with the sales of foreign securities to U.S. investors. A key part of the enforcement system are Memoranda of Understanding (MOUs) and Mutual Legal Assistance Treaties (MLATs) entered into between the United States and other countries. These agreements authorize foreign assistance in the investigations and prosecutions of securities fraud. See *International Securities Law Enforcement: Recent Advances in Assistance and Cooperation*, 27 Vanderbilt Journal of Transnational Law 635 (1994). Nor has the Chapter dealt with the issue of when foreign broker-dealers must incorporate and register in the United States. See C. Gittleman, J. Moran and E. Don-Siemon, *SEC loosens regulation of foreign broker dealers,* International Financial Law Review 11 (1997).

Links to Other Chapters

This is our first look at domestic regulation of the international aspects of securities markets. Later, we will be able to compare the U.S. approach with that of the European Union (Chapter 5) and Japan (Chapter 8). In addition, we will focus later on how U.S. regulation of U.S. stock markets affects competition between U.S. and foreign markets (Chapter 14). We will also be able to appreciate in more depth how important clearance and settlement is to the attraction of U.S. markets, a subject we touched upon in this Chapter with respect to ADRs (Chapters 15 and 20). Finally, bear in mind that one big advantage of investing in U.S. markets is that the securities are dollar denominated. As we shall see, foreign exchange considerations are a big factor in investment decisions (Chapter 6).

CHAPTER THREE

INTERNATIONAL ASPECTS OF U.S. BANKING REGULATION

This Chapter deals with the international aspects of U.S. banking regulation. It begins with some background on the importance of foreign banks in the United States, and the basic features of U.S. regulation of all banks. Major changes have been made in these features by the enactment in November 1999 of the Gramm-Leach-Bliley Act: Financial Modernization Legislation of 1999 (GLB) which liberalized various restrictions on banking activities. The material then examines the two key statutes dealing with foreign banks, the International Banking Act of 1978 (IBA) and the Foreign Bank Supervision Act of 1991 which amended the IBA. The latter statute was in large part prompted by the 1991 failure of the Bank of Commerce and Credit International (BCCI). An Appendix to this Chapter contains the IBA, as amended, together with Regulation K of the Federal Reserve Board that implements its provisions. Regulation K was thoroughly revised in October 2001. A major theme throughout is the difficulty of applying a simple "national treatment" standard to foreign banks.

A. THE IMPORTANCE OF FOREIGN BANKS

Foreign banks operate in the United States in various ways. They may operate without a U.S. office, on strictly a *cross-border* basis. Thus, the foreign bank make take deposits of U.S. depositors at an office outside the United States, or make loans from its foreign office to U.S. borrowers. A foreign bank may establish a presence in the United States by four means.

First, foreign banks can operate through *branches* by establishing a domestic office of the foreign bank in the United States. The office can be chartered by the federal government through the Office of the Comptroller of the Currency (OCC), an agency within the Department of the Treasury, or by a state. Branch offices are part and parcel of the foreign bank. A branch is entitled to do normal banking, including taking deposits and making loans. Its powers are generally any banking business permitted to a state or federal bank. Section 1(a) of the IBA, 12 U.S.C. §3101(3), defines a branch as an office which receives deposits. However, as indicated below, offices receiving deposits from non-U.S. citizens or residents are treated as agencies.

Secondly, foreign banks may operate through *subsidiaries*. The foreign bank may own a subsidiary bank (de novo or through acquisition) in the United States. The U.S. bank subsidiary may be chartered by the OCC or a state. Typically, the U.S. bank is a subsidiary of a foreign bank, rather than a subsidiary of a separate bank holding company (BHC) which owns both the foreign and U.S. bank. Most foreign countries do not have the BHC form.

Third, the foreign bank may operate through a*gencies*. These are U.S. offices of the foreign bank that can make loans and receive foreign deposits or maintain credit balances. As with branches and subsidiaries, agencies may be federal or state chartered. New York permits its agencies to take domestic deposits over $100 thousand. While treated as agencies under New York law, they are treated as branches under federal law because they take domestic deposits.

Fourth, foreign banks can establish *representative offices*, federal or state-chartered, that do not actually do business in the United States, in the sense that they do not make loans or take deposits. They drum up business for their foreign offices which make the loans and take the deposits. They function as international loan production offices (LPOs).

This Chapter concentrates on branches and subsidiaries as these are the most important form of operation of foreign banks. As of June 1999, foreign banks maintained 299 U.S. branch offices and 93 U.S. bank subsidiaries. See Table A below. All entities of foreign banks held $1.22 trillion in assets, approximately 22% of total U.S. banking assets ($4.3 trillion), and $279.1 billion in commercial loans, approximately 25.4% of the U.S. total. Table A also shows the distribution of offices, assets and loans among branches, agencies and subsidiaries.

Table A
Total Assets and Commercial Loans[1] of U.S. Offices of Foreign Banks
June 30, 1993 and December 31, 1999 ($ Billions)

	1993			1999		
	Number of Offices	Assets	Loans	Number of Offices	Assets	Loans
Agencies	200	96.4	53.5	75	40.9	22.5
Branches	376	596.8	155.7	299	862.5	182.5
Total Agencies and Branches	576	693.2	209.2	374	903.5	205.0
Bank Subsidiaries	90	174.1	63.3	93	324.8	74.1
Total Foreign	666	867.3	272.5	467	1,228.3	279.1
Total U.S.	11,822	3,973.0	1,017.5	9,055	6,450.1	1,100.5
Ratio of Foreign to All U.S. banks	5.8%	21.8%	26.9%	5.2%	19.0%	25.4%

1. Commercial, industrial, and commercial real estate loans.
Source: Federal Reserve Board

In 1992, Japanese banks alone had $402.1 billion in assets, or 10.6% of all U.S. banking assets and over 50% of foreign bank assets. But Japanese market share fell significantly after 1993, due to the ongoing decline of the Japanese economy and the fragility of the Japanese banks. As of December 31, 1999, Japanese banks held only 3.4% of all U.S. banking assets and 17.7% of foreign bank assets. One result of the Japanese decline was the sale of Japanese owned banks in the United States, such as the sale of United California Bank by UFJ Holdings to BNP Paribas, a French bank, in 2001.

As we shall see, branches and agencies of foreign banks can be chartered by the states or federal government. At year-end 1999, 242 of the total 299 branches were state chartered and held 91.5% of all the assets of branches of foreign banks.

Between 1972 and 1990, the number of foreign banks operating in the United States increased from 77 to 600, and their assets grew at an annual rate of 20 percent. After 1990, growth slowed and the number of offices declined. Key factors in this long period of growth were the expansion of foreign businesses in the United States which could be served by their foreign bankers. Also, rising federal deficits increased the United States' demand for capital—including foreign capital—while large trade deficits created a surplus of dollars abroad. These dollars were often deposited in foreign banks and were then reinvested by them in loans to U.S. borrowers. U.S. General Accounting Office, *Foreign Banks, Assessing Their Role in the U.S. Banking System* 13-15 (1996).

How important are foreign banks to the U.S. economy? Their 25.4% market share of business loans would seem to indicate that they are very important. However, it is worth noting that most of their lending is financed by U.S. borrowing. For example, if one looks at U.S. branches and agencies of Japanese banks in 1992, their $61.1 billion of lending, $21.1 billion to U.S. non-banks and $41.1 billion to banks, was mainly financed by borrowings from U.S. banks, $51.6 billion.

As the following Table indicates,* it is unclear whether foreign branches and agencies of foreign banks are net suppliers of funds to the U.S. market.

Table B
Sources and Uses of Funds in
Foreign Branches, Agencies and Shell Branches,
December 1994 (Dollars in Billions)

Sources/uses of funds	Funds Raised	Funds Used	Difference
Transactions with customers-U.S. addresses	$357	$475	-$118
Transactions with customers-Non U.S. addresses	340	190	150
Transactions with customers-location unknown	162	218	-56
Transactions with parent and related depositories	184	160	160

Source: Call Report Data

As Table B shows, foreign branches and agencies supplied $118 billion more to U.S. addresses (presumably U.S. borrowers) than they raised from U.S. sources. By contrast funds raised from abroad (non-U.S. addresses) exceeded funds used by $150 billion. However, given the large amount of unknown transactions, one cannot be sure that foreign branches and agencies were, in fact, net providers of funds to the U.S. economy.

---

* U.S. General Accounting Office, Foreign Banks: Assessing Their Role in the U.S. Banking System 37 (1996).

It appears that foreign banks in the United States have lower profit rates than their domestic counterparts due to less efficient operations and higher cost of funds (due to more heavy reliance on wholesale funding). R. DeYoung and D. Nolle, *Foreign-Owned Banks in the United States: Earning Market Share or Buying It?*, 28 Journal of Money, Credit, and Banking 622 (1996).

Of the largest ten banking organizations in the world, as of the end of 1998, only two were American, Citigroup and Bank of America Corp., ranking third and fourth respectively. Deutsche Bank was the biggest bank in the world with $735 billion in total assets. American Banker (August 5, 1999).

B.   BASIC FEATURES OF U.S. REGULATORY SYSTEM

The U.S. bank regulatory system, like securities regulation, is quite complicated and is an entire field of study by itself. See H. Jackson and E. Symons, Jr., *Regulation of Financial Institutions* (1999). There follows a brief description of the major features of this system.

1. *Safety and soundness regulation.* This type of regulation is intended to prevent banks from failing through controlling risks, and ensuring adequate capital. Failure avoids deposit insurance pay-outs and systemic risk (chain reaction of bank failures through interbank deposit linkage or payment settlement systems, or imitative runs).

2. *Deposit Insurance.* The U.S. insures deposits of up to $100,000. This may minimize bank runs, and be a form of creditor protection, but raises a moral hazard issue: since creditors are insured, they do not police bank risk. The insurance fund (BIF) is normally funded by bank paid premiums, but in the 1980's this funding was insufficient due to thrift and banking failures, and has had to be greatly subsidized (over $200 billion) by federal government expenditures. There is now a system of so-called risk-based insurance premiums where the premiums are determined by capital adequacy and supervisory rating.

3. *Dual Banking System.* Banks are chartered by both states, and the federal government through the Office of the Comptroller of the Currency (OCC). National bank powers are regulated by OCC, while state bank powers are regulated by the states, subject to federal limits. National banks are regulated for safety and soundness by OCC, insured state banks by states and their "primary" federal regulator (the Federal Reserve Board (FRB) if the bank is a Fed member, the Federal Deposit Insurance Corporation (FDIC) if it is not). Uninsured state chartered banks are only regulated by the states, but there are very few. The dual system comes out of a federalist tradition: unwillingness to concentrate too much power in the national government. The multiplicity of federal regulators has largely resulted from historical factors no longer present,

and is retained due to bureaucratic turf protection and distrust of centralized power.

4. *Activities Regulation.* Until the enactment of GLB in 1999, all large banking organizations operated through bank holding company (BHC) form; public shareholders own the BHC not bank. This was principally because some activities could be performed through BHCs that could not be performed through banks or bank subsidiaries. BHCs are regulated by the FRB. Banks generally had more limited powers than BHCs. BHCs could do activities "closely related to banking," under § (4)(c)(8) of the Bank Holding Company Act (BHCA). While BHC powers were more expansive than "banking," neither BHCs nor banks could generally engage in life insurance, commercial activities, or certain securities activities. The theory underlying the more restrictive regime for bank as compared with BHC activities was that there was less risk to the bank when activities were done through the BHC (in the BHC itself or in a non-bank subsidiary of the BHC) since BHC losses do not directly hit bank capital. Parallel with BHC power limitations, insurance, commercial and securities firms could not own banks. BHCs, in the view of the Fed, were supposed to serve as a "source of strength" for banks—be ready to inject capital if bank subsidiaries needed it. Thus, they must be adequately capitalized. All formations of BHCs or acquisitions of banks by BHCs were reviewed by FRB.

Under new Section 4(k) of the BHCA, GLB permits a BHC, all of whose subsidiary banks are "well-capitalized" and "well-managed," to become a financial service holding company (FHC) through which it can engage in a full range of financial activities, including insurance, securities and merchant banking (investment in companies, including purely commercial companies, for resale). In statutory terms a FHC is permitted to engage in activities which are "financial in nature." Certain of these financial activities, such as a full range of securities activities, are defined in the statute. FHCs can also engage in additional financial activities, activities "incidental to such financial activities," or "complementary to a financial activity," as determined by the Fed with the agreement of the Secretary of the Treasury. Further, GLB allows a 10-year to 15-year grandfathering for the nonfinancial activities of predominantly financial companies (85% of whose gross revenue is financial) that become FHCs by acquiring banks. As of March 13, 2000, 117 bank holding companies had switched to FHC form. As of November 2000, 435 companies have become financial holding companies, including foreign banks like Credit Suisse and UBS, but some important U.S. financial firms like Bank One and Merrill Lynch had not. B. Rehm, *Reform Law Leaves Some Doubters*, American Banker, November 8, 2000.

GLB also expands the power of well-capitalized and well-managed national banks to engage in financial activities through subsidiaries. These are the same financial activities permitted for FHCs with three exceptions: (1) certain underwriting of insurance and annuities, (2) real estate investment or development, and (3) merchant banking (this can be permitted in 2004 if the Fed and Treasury so agree). In the case of banks, activities beyond those specified in the statute (which are the same as for FHCs) are determined by the Treasury with the agreement of the Fed. The total investment of a national bank in all financial subsidiaries is limited to the lesser of 45% of the bank's total assets or $50 billion (which is adjusted periodically by an index). As of October 2000, the Office of the Comptroller of the Currency had approved 60 financial subsidiaries pursuant to GLB.

As of February 2001, 500 FHCs had been formed including 20 or so by foreign banking organizations. Only a small number of large FHCs have purchased securities firms since enactment of GLB; rather FHCs have mainly been used to free holding companies from restrictions placed on existing securities affiliates, i.e. limit on underwriting and dealing to 25 percent of securities affiliate revenue. No FHC has acquired a large insurance company since the Citi-Travelers merger prior to enactment of GLB. Charles Schwab acquired U.S. Trust and Met Life acquired a small commercial bank. L. Meyer, Implementing the Gramm-Leach-Bliley Act: One Year Later, Federal Reserve Board (February 15, 2001).

This liberalization of activities restrictions brings the U.S. in line with other countries. A 1997 study indicated that of the 15 European Union countries, Canada, Japan, Switzerland and the United States, only Japan and the United States limited the financial activities of banking organizations. J. Barth, D. Nolle, and T. Rice, *Commercial Banking Structure, Regulation and Performance: An International Comparison*, Office of the Comptroller of the Currency, Economics Working Paper (February 1997). However, other countries provide more unlimited choice to banking organizations about whether to engage in financial activities in the holding company or bank.

5. *Limited Interstate Banking*. Until the passage of the Interstate Banking and Branching Efficiency Act of 1994 (IBBEA), under the Douglas Amendment to the BHCA, BHCs could not acquire a bank outside their home state (state in which they took the most deposits) unless the state in which the target bank was located permitted the acquisition. By 1994, most states, and all large states, had permitted such acquisitions under various conditions. Under IBBEA, interstate acquisitions, as of September 29, 1995, no longer require state authorization. However, states may require that the acquired bank be in existence for some minimum time not to exceed five years (five year aging), and may require the acquirer to comply with various state antitrust and community reinvestment laws (CRA). The federal law also imposes concentration limits. An acquiring company cannot control more than 10 percent of total U.S. deposits or 30 percent of deposits in a particular state without the state's approval. The state may, however, set

even more stringent anti-concentration requirements as long as they do not discriminate against out-of-state acquisitions.

The IBBEA repealed the blanket federal restrictions on interstate branching that existed under the McFadden Act since 1927. As of June 1, 1997, interstate branching through mergers was permitted between states unless the states "opt out," and interstate branching through de novo branching was prohibited unless the states "opt in." As of February 1996, only one state, Texas, had opted out of the merger provisions and 22 had opted-in to the de novo provisions. Many of the states (host states) have opted-in on a reciprocal basis--only allowing banks to branch in that are located in states which permit banks from the host state to branch in. States may impose conditions on interstate branching arising through interstate mergers (the acquired bank's branches become interstate branches of the acquirer), like those for acquisitions, e.g. five year aging and antitrust and community reinvestment laws. Concentration ratio requirements quite similar to those for acquisitions also apply.

6. The Community Reinvestment Act (CRA) of 1977 requires federal banking agencies to encourage banks to meet the credit needs of their local communities (including low and moderate income neighborhoods) consistent with safety and soundness considerations. Communities are the areas contiguous to bank offices.

CRA performance is taken into account by banking regulators whenever a banking organization applies for permission to open a new branch or make an acquisition. Interest groups have used this requirement to file extensive protests against applications based on banks' alleged shortcomings in fulfilling their CRA obligations under the general assessment factors. These protests can lead to hearings and significant costly delays in approving applications.

The Clinton Administration (and bank regulators) sought to put more teeth in CRA. New "objective" standards for measuring CRA performance became effective on July 1, 1995. See Regulation BB of the Federal Reserve Board, 12 C.F.R. §§228.1- §§228.51 and appendices A and B.

C.   REGULATION OF FOREIGN BANKS

The following material deals with some key areas of regulation of foreign banks: systemic risk, safety and soundness, deposit insurance, permissible activities for financial holding companies and banks, and interstate banking. The important provisions of the key statute, the IBA as amended, and the implementing Regulation K of the Federal Reserve Board, are at the end of the Chapter in the form of a Statutory Supplement. Problems of regulation differ depending on whether one is considering branches or subsidiaries. Of course, branches and subsidiaries are not the only forms in which banks operate abroad. They can also operate purely cross-border without a corporate presence in a host country, as when a bank in London solicits U.S. residents to place funds with the London bank. Banks may also operate abroad through agencies and representative offices. But branches and subsidiaries are the most important forms of operation, and are concentrated on here.

1. SYSTEMIC RISK

Avoidance of systemic risk is usually cited as the major objective of bank regulation. Within the international system, it is principally the concern of the host country, although the collapse of a banking system in one country can spill over to other countries, as well. The concern with systemic risk only arises, of course, when a bank fails, but this can occur even with the best supervisory control system. We next explore the nature of systemic risk and how it works with respect to subsidiaries and branches of foreign banks.

a. THE CHAIN REACTION PROBLEM

Systemic risk involves a chain reaction of bank failures which can occur for three principal reasons. First, it can result from the linkage of interbank deposits. This was a major concern when Continental Illinois Bank, a Chicago bank, almost failed in the mid-1980s. Continental held sizable deposits of other banks; in many cases the amount of the deposits substantially exceeded the capital of the depositor banks. These banks generally held such sizable deposits because they cleared payments, for example, checks or wire transfers, through Continental. If Continental had failed, those banks would have failed as well. Section 308 of the FDIC Improvement Act of 1991 gives the Federal Reserve Board powers to deal with this problem. It permits the Board to limit the credit extended by an insured depository institution to another depository institution. This may be feasible with respect to placements by one bank with another since the amount of credit extended is fixed for a given term. A study of bilateral credit exposures arising from overnight federal funds transactions finds that the contagion effect of a large bank failure would be minimal. It found that aggregate assets at subsequently failing banks would never be expected to exceed 1% of total commercial banking assets when loss rates are kept to historically observed levels. Craig Furfine, *Interbank Exposures: Quantifying the Risk of Contagion*, BIS Working Paper (June 22, 1999).

The study only measured federal funds exposures. It is more difficult to identify and control exposures with respect to interbank clearing accounts where the amount of credit extended is a function of payments traffic. For example, Bank *A* may be credited by its correspondent Bank *B* for an incoming wire transfer of $10 million. Bank *A* is thus a creditor of Bank *B* for this amount. If Bank *B* were to fail, Bank *A* is seriously exposed. It will be quite difficult, without serious changes in the payment system (for example, forcing banks to make and receive all payments through Federal Reserve rather than correspondent accounts), to limit these types of exposures.

Second, a chain reaction of bank failures can occur through payment system linkage. If one bank fails to settle its position in a net settlement system for large value payments, for example, the Clearing House Interbank Payments System (CHIPS) in the United States, other banks which do not get paid may in turn fail. This risk has been substantially limited by CHIPS credit limits, loss-sharing, and collateral requirements, but could still materialize if two large banks, at the maximum of their permissible net debit positions, were to fail. This problem is explored at length in Chapter 10.

Finally, a chain reaction of bank failures can occur through imitative runs. When one bank fails, depositors in other banks, particularly those that are uninsured, may assume that their banks may also fail and so withdraw their funds, exposing these banks to a liquidity crisis and ultimately to failure. This is largely a result of lack of information in the market about the specific causes of the failure of the first bank.

There have been few attempts to measure systemic risk. G. De Nicolo and M. Kwast, *Systemic Risk and Financial Consolidation,* Working Paper (June 19, 2001) finds a significant interdependency between the stock prices of the large banking organizations. This may reflect actual interlinks between the organizations or correlated exposures to financial market changes. For a general review of the literature on systemic risk, see O. De Bandt and P. Hartmann, *Systemic Risk: A Survey,* European Central Bank Working Paper No. 35 (November 2000).

Fear of systemic risk is widely accepted as the primary rational for bank regulation yet some believe that bank regulation itself increases systemic risk by creating moral hazard through government guarantees and bailouts. G. Kaufman and K. Scott, *Does Bank Regulation Retard or Contribute to Systemic Risk,* Stanford Law School, Olin Program in Law and Economics, Working Paper No. 211 (December 2000).

b.. SUBSIDIARIES

When a foreign bank operates in a host country through a subsidiary, the host country can protect itself against systemic risk by subjecting the subsidiary to the same rules as other domestic banks. For example, the host country can control the level of deposits the subsidiary takes from other banks or limit the positions it incurs in net settlement payment systems in the same way as it does for domestic banks. Imitative runs could be a major concern to a host country since the failure of any domestic bank, even one that is foreign owned, could cause imitative runs on other domestic banks. Thus, there were reportedly imitative runs on other foreign banks in Hong Kong when Bank of Credit and Commerce International's (BCCI's) subsidiary in that country was closed in 1991 in connection with the worldwide collapse of BCCI. It is much less likely that the failure of the foreign parent will cause a run on host-country banks. While there is some evidence that there was a deposit loss at First American, a U.S. bank subsidiary of BCCI, after the failure of BCCI, it is unclear whether this was caused by the BCCI failure or an independent problem of bad loans. In any event, there were no runs on First American or other non-BCCI domestic banks.

If the failure of a foreign-owned bank would likely cause a chain reaction of bank failures, the host country could use its lender-of-last-resort power to keep the bank afloat. The host-country central bank would be lending to a domestic bank in its own currency—the fact of foreign ownership should not be a major obstacle to central bank support.

c. BRANCHES

When a foreign bank operates in a host country through a branch, it is more difficult for the host country to deal with the systemic risk problem, particularly as it may manifest itself in the payment system. Branches of foreign banks may be less able than domestic banks to fund settlement obligations quickly in host-country money markets, and their home-country markets could be closed. On the other hand, linkage of interbank deposits should not be a significant problem since domestic banks generally will not clear local currency payments through branches of foreign banks. In addition, imitative runs on domestic banks are less likely to be caused by the failure of a foreign bank; depositors in domestic banks are unlikely to believe their own banks are in trouble just because a foreign bank has failed. The major concern is the payment system.

Unlike the case of the failure of a foreign-owned subsidiary, the failure of the foreign bank itself, along with its host-country branch offices, raises significant lender-of-last-resort issues for the United States. The foreign bank may have to be kept afloat by its own central bank through loans in the home-country currency. But the United States will have no assurance that the home-country central bank will do so. While the Federal Reserve could, in principle, itself extend credit in dollars to the foreign bank, it will be reluctant to do so. Such lending might expose it, and ultimately U.S. taxpayers, to losses. This will be hard to justify when support could have come instead from the home-country central bank.

The host country is likely to take measures to avoid becoming a lender-of-last-resort to a foreign bank. First, it may limit the participation of branches of foreign banks in host-country payment systems. The Banque de France, for example, does not allow foreign banks to participate directly in Sagittaire, its net settlement system for clearing international funds transfers. And it is perhaps not an accident that it was only in 1997 that Deutsche Bank became the first foreign bank settling participant in CHIPS. Second, the host country may specially limit the settlement positions of branches of foreign banks in their payment systems or require that these positions be fully collateralized.

It appears that the BCCI banks in Luxembourg and the Caymans and their branches, subsidiaries, and agencies (including the U.S. agencies) cleared a significant amount of their dollar payments through Bank of America, but there is no indication that this resulted in any settlement problems for Bank of America or other CHIPS participants. Perhaps this is partly explained by the fact that the Federal Reserve had advance information of the timing of the closure of the BCCI banks. This information was apparently used to help insure that Bank of America and other U.S. banks were not left exposed when the BCCI banks were closed. For example, Bank of America could have managed BCCI payments in a manner that would assure that payments out never exceeded payments in by an amount greater than the collected balances of the BCCI banks. A system for insuring advance warning might be an important way of controlling systemic risk. *See* H. Scott, *Supervision of International Banking Post-BCCI*, 8 Georgia State University Law Review 487 (1992).

2. SAFETY AND SOUNDNESS

Maintaining safety and soundness is a key policy objective of host countries which affects their supervision of foreign banks. This type of regulation is designed to avoid bank failures, which cause deposit insurance pay-outs and systemic risk. Host countries generally have less concern with maintaining the safety and soundness of foreign banks operating through subsidiaries than they do in the case of branches because they regulate subsidiaries more fully. Branches, on the other hand, which are part and parcel of the foreign bank, are mainly regulated by home countries.

a. DETERMINATION OF THE "HOME COUNTRY"

Since the adequacy of home-country supervision may be an issue for a host country with respect to subsidiaries, and is clearly an issue in the case of branches, identifying the home country for this purpose is essential. This can be done without much difficulty if two conditions hold: (1) there is one foreign bank parent located in one foreign country, and (2) the principal operations of the bank are carried on in that same country. For example, Deutsche Bank, the ultimate parent of all Deutsche Bank foreign subsidiaries, is located in Germany, and the principal operations of Deutsche Bank, as measured by total assets, are in Germany as well. Neither of these conditions was met, however, in the case of BCCI, with somewhat disastrous results.

BCCI was organized as follows. BCCI Holdings, a Luxembourg holding company, was at the top of the corporate pyramid. This entity, in turn, owned two principal banks, BCCI S.A., incorporated in Luxembourg, and BCCI Overseas, incorporated in the Cayman Islands. These banks had subsidiaries and branches in various countries; for example, the Luxembourg bank had over twenty branches in the United Kingdom and a subsidiary in Canada. There were two foreign bank parents rather than one, and neither bank's principal operations were in the country of incorporation, namely Luxembourg or the Cayman Islands.

Why did this cause problems? The fact that there were two foreign bank parents meant that two countries rather than one were responsible for the safety and soundness of the banking organization as a whole; thus, there was no overall consolidated supervision of the banking organization. In principle, this problem might have been cured if Luxembourg had authority to regulate the entire operations of the bank holding company, BCCI Holdings, but this was not the case. The problem might also have been cured if there had been an international agreement that there could only be one ultimate bank parent, that is, that one of the banks had to become a subsidiary of the other, but this was also not the case.

Where two home countries are responsible, neither country is in the position to determine the safety and soundness of the entire operation, and matters can easily fall between the cracks. Where multiple regulators are responsible for the safety and soundness of a bank, no one is really accountable. Further, since the principal operations of the banking organization were in neither country, the supervisors in these countries had a limited ability to make judgments about the safety and soundness of their two banks. Perhaps in such cases the home country should be the country of principal operations, which would probably be the United Kingdom in the case of BCCI. The problem was further compounded by the fact that supervision in the Caymans, and to a lesser extent in Luxembourg, was rather weak.

b.   SUBSIDIARIES

When a foreign bank operates through a subsidiary, the subsidiary is fully subject to the safety and soundness regime of the host country. The host country can ensure the safety and soundness of the foreign subsidiary through the same techniques it applies to domestic banks, such as capital requirements, examinations or audits, and loan limits. The host country will not necessarily be concerned with the safety and soundness of the foreign parent of the host-country subsidiary. The bankruptcy of the parent may result in a transfer of the ownership of the subsidiary, but it will not necessarily affect the safety and soundness of the subsidiary. The subsidiary can continue to operate even though its parent is bankrupt. This was true in the BCCI case where subsidiary U.S. banks, like the First American banks, continued to operate even though the BCCI bank owners were in insolvency proceedings.

But some countries, most notably the United States, are concerned with the safety and soundness of the foreign parents of host-country subsidiaries. This concern is based on the source of strength doctrine. Under this doctrine, the host country looks to the foreign parent to supply capital to the subsidiary if the subsidiary becomes weak. The basic idea is that the strength of the parent determines whether it will be able to save its subsidiary from difficulty by injecting additional capital. In addition, the host country may be concerned that a weak foreign parent may try to loot a local subsidiary through nonmarket value affiliate transactions, for example, purchasing its assets at below market prices.*

The safety and soundness of the foreign parent is not, however, within the regulatory control of the host country. Thus, for example, the safety and soundness of a U.K. banking parent of a U.S. bank is largely determined by the United Kingdom, not the United States. The United Kingdom determines the capital requirements, auditing and examination standards, and loan limits of its banks. And if one of its banks gets into trouble, the United Kingdom determines whether and how to rescue it. And if the foreign parent is not a bank, it may be entirely unregulated by the home country.

c. BRANCHES

When a foreign bank operates abroad through a branch, the host country is more at the mercy of the home country. The branch is but an office of a bank located in another country. If the foreign bank fails, so do its branches abroad. The viability of the branches is largely determined by the efficacy of supervision by the bank's home country. Host countries again may get some comfort from the fact that the bank's home country subscribes to the Basel Accord, but here the weaknesses of the Basel approach are more serious since the failure of the foreign bank leads directly to the failure of its branches, rather than just depriving the host country of a source of strength as is the case with subsidiaries.

It may be tempting to conclude that host countries would be better off if they forced foreign banks to operate in their countries through subsidiaries rather than branches, but this would be incorrect, principally for two reasons. First, many host countries would prefer that local deposits be backed by the entire capital of the bank, which is the case with branch deposits, rather than the capital of the local subsidiary, the case with subsidiary deposits. Although the host country may have less control over the capital adequacy of the entire bank than it does over the subsidiary, the amount of capital is likely to be much larger. Also, many

---

* The Hong Kong subsidiary of BCCI was closed on July 8, 1991, shortly after its parent holding company, BCCI Holdings (Luxembourg) SA, was declared insolvent. The Hong Kong subsidiary's insolvency had been largely caused by the discovery of over $268 million in unrecorded liabilities, some of which were due to other failed BCCI entities. A subsidiary may also be imperiled by loans made to failed affiliates.

host countries, particularly smaller or less developed ones, may prefer to rely on home-country supervision rather than their own.   Second, and quite important, branches of foreign banks are more competitive than their subsidiaries in host-country markets.   This is largely because the loan capacity of the branch in the host country is a function of the bank's worldwide capital; that capacity would be much less if it were a function of the capital of a host-country subsidiary.

d.   THE BASEL CONCORDAT

The BCCI case raised major issues about the allocation of regulation authority among various jurisdictions.   This has been partially dealt with through an international agreement, the Basel Concordat of the Bank for International Settlements (BIS).   The BIS, created in 1930 to manage German reparations, is a bank whose depositors are limited to central banks.   A significant portion of the world's foreign exchange reserves are held on deposit with the BIS.   The BIS serves as a forum for cooperation among central banks and bank supervisors.   The Board of Directors are all drawn from the Group of Ten countries (Belgium, Canada, France, Germany, Italy, Japan, the Netherlands, Sweden, Switzerland, the United Kingdom and the United States).   The Basel Committee on Banking Supervision is the key forum within BIS for international banking regulation.   This Committee formulated minimum standards for the supervision of foreign banks, through promulgation of a Concordat.

BASEL COMMITTEE ON BANKING SUPERVISION, MINIMUM STANDARDS FOR THE SUPERVISION OF INTERNATIONAL BANKING GROUPS AND THEIR CROSS-BORDER ESTABLISHMENTS
(July 1992).

The following four minimum standards are to be applied by individual supervisory authorities in their own assessment of their relations with supervisory authorities in other countries. In particular, a host-country authority, into whose jurisdiction a bank or banking group is seeking to expand, is called upon to determine whether that bank or banking group's home-country supervisory authority has the necessary capabilities to meet these minimum standards. In making this determination, host-country authorities should review the other authority's statutory powers, past experience in their relations, and the scope of the other authority's administrative practices. Some authorities may initially need to make either statutory or administrative changes in order to comply with these new standards; therefore, in cases where an authority fails to meet one or more of these standards, recognition should be given to the extent to which the authority is actively working to establish the necessary capabilities to permit it to meet all aspects of these minimum standards.

1. *All international banking groups and international banks should be supervised by a home-country authority that capably performs—consolidated supervision*

As a condition for the creation and maintenance of cross-border banking establishments, a host-country authority should assure itself that the relevant bank and, if different, the banking group is subject to the authority of a supervisor with the practical capability of performing consolidated supervision.   To meet this minimum standard, the home-country supervisory authority should (a) receive consolidated financial and prudential information on the bank's or banking group's global operations, have the reliability of this information confirmed to its own satisfaction through on-site examination or other means, and assess the information as it may bear on the safety and soundness of the bank or banking group, (b) have the capability to prevent corporate affiliations or structures that either undermine efforts to maintain consolidated financial information or otherwise hinder effective supervision of the bank or banking group, and (c) have the capability to prevent the bank or banking group from creating foreign banking establishments in particular jurisdictions.

2. *The creation of a cross-border banking establishment should receive the prior consent of both the host-country supervisory authority and the bank's and, if different, banking group's home-country supervisory authority*

Consent by a host-country authority for the inward creation of a cross-border banking establishment should only be considered if the appropriate home-country authorities have first given their consent to the bank or banking group's outward expansion. Outward consent by a home-country authority should always be made contingent upon the subsequent receipt of inward consent from the host authority. Thus, in the absence of consent by both the host-country authority and the bank's home-country authority and, if different, the banking group's home-country authority, cross-border expansion will not be permitted. As a matter of procedure, a host-country authority should seek to assure itself that consent has been given by the supervisory authority directly responsible for the entity seeking to create an establishment;   this authority, in turn, should assure itself that consent is given by the next higher tier supervisory authority, if any, which may perform consolidated supervision with respect to the entity as part of a banking group....

3. *Supervisory authorities should possess the right to gather information from the cross-border banking establishments of the banks or banking groups for which they are the home-country supervisor*

As a condition for giving either inward or outward consent for the creation of a cross-border banking establishment, a supervisory authority should establish an understanding with the other authority that they may each gather information to the extent necessary for effective home-country supervision, either through on-site examination or by other means satisfactory to the recipient, from the cross-border establishments located in one another's jurisdictions of banks or banking groups chartered or incorporated in their respective jurisdictions. Thus, consent for inward expansion by a prospective host-country authority should generally be contingent upon there being such an understanding, with the foreign bank's or banking group's home-country authority, that each authority may gather such information from their respective bank's and banking group's foreign establishments. Similarly, consent for outward expansion by the home-country authority should generally be contingent upon there being such an understanding with the host-country authority. Through such bilateral arrangements, all home-country authorities should be able to improve their ability to review the financial condition of their banks' and banking groups' cross-border banking establishments.

4. *If a host-country authority determines that any one of the foregoing minimum standards is not met to its satisfaction, that authority could impose restrictive measures necessary to satisfy its prudential concerns consistent with these minimum standards, including the prohibition of the creation of banking establishments*

In considering whether to consent to the creation of a banking establishment by a foreign bank or foreign banking group, or in reviewing any other proposal by a foreign bank or banking group which requires its consent, a host-country authority should determine whether the bank or banking group is subject to consolidated supervision by an authority that has—or is actively working to establish—the necessary capabilities to meet these minimum standards. First, the host-country authority should determine whether the bank or banking group is chartered or incorporated in a jurisdiction with which the host-country authority has a mutual understanding for the gathering of information from cross-border establishments. Secondly, the host-country authority should determine whether consent for outward expansion has been given by the appropriate home-country authorities. Thirdly, the host-country authority should determine whether the bank and, if different, the banking group is supervised by a home-country authority which has the practical capability of performing consolidated supervision.

If these minimum standards are not met with respect to a particular bank or banking group, and the relevant home-country authorities are unwilling or unable to initiate the effort to take measures to meet these standards, the host-country authority should prevent the creation in its jurisdiction of any cross-border establishments by that bank or banking group. However, in its sole discretion, the host-country authority may alternatively choose to permit the creation of establishments by such a bank or banking group, subject to whatever prudential restrictions on the scope and nature of the establishment's operations which the host-country authority deems necessary and appropriate to address its prudential concerns, provided that the host-country authority itself also accepts the responsibility to perform adequate supervision of the bank's or banking group's local establishments on a "stand-alone" consolidated basis.

Thus, if a bank or banking group is not subject to the level of supervision and supervisory co-operation required by these minimum standards, and the relevant supervisory authority is not actively working to establish the necessary capabilities, that bank or banking group will only be permitted to expand its operations into jurisdictions whose authorities are adhering to these minimum standards if the host-country authority itself accepts the responsibility to perform supervision of the bank or banking group's local establishments consistent with these minimum standards.

e.   U.S. LEGISLATION

1. International Banking Act of 1978.

The United States has also dealt with the problem of the safety and soundness of foreign banks through domestic legislation. In the United States, in the 1970s, the Federal Reserve became alarmed at the fact that no federal framework existed for supervision and regulation of foreign banks operating in the United States through branches. The International Banking Act of 1978 (the "IBA") represented the first comprehensive piece of federal legislation aimed at regulating the activities of foreign banks which do business in the United States. The IBA and certain provisions of FIRICA (Financial Institutions Regulatory and Interest Control Act of 1978) represented the response of Congress to a growing concern over the increase in foreign bank activity in the United States and the effect of these operations on the domestic banking industry.

Prior to the passage of IBA, foreign banks doing business in the United States were regulated solely by the state(s) in which they operated. This meant that Federal laws restricting domestic banks, such as federal limits on interstate banking and reserve requirements, did not apply to these banks. Additionally, foreign banks were free from federal restrictions on nonbanking activities unless they acquired a controlling interest in a domestic bank. Many thought that foreign banks had been given a competitive advantage over their domestic rivals. The IBA and certain provisions of FIRICA attempted to address this problem by extending certain federal regulations applicable to domestic entities to foreign banks and by establishing the principle of parity of treatment between foreign and domestic banks in like circumstances.

The IBA accomplished this by giving foreign banks the option of establishing an agency or branch in the United States pursuant to federal, as well as state, authority. Section 4(a) of the IBA provides that a foreign bank which "engages directly in a banking business outside the United States" may establish, with the approval of the Comptroller, one or more federal branches or agencies in any state in which it is not operating a state branch or agency, provided that the laws of such state do not prohibit the establishment of an agency or branch by a foreign bank.

Unless otherwise specified, the operations of a foreign bank at a federal agency or branch are to be conducted with the same rights and privileges applicable to a national bank at the same location and are subject to the same duties, restrictions, penalties, liabilities, conditions and limitations that would apply under the National Bank Act to a national bank doing business at the same location. Federal agencies are not required to obtain FDIC insurance, since the Act does not allow them to accept deposits. Furthermore, federal agencies and branches are not required to become members of the Federal Reserve System.

The IBA contained several provisions designed to reflect the legal and operational differences created by the fact that federal agencies and branches, unlike national banks, will not be separately incorporated entities. For example, loan limitations and other restrictions usually expressed, in the case of a national bank, as a percentage of the bank's capital stock and surplus, are considered, when applied to a federal branch or agency, to refer to the dollar equivalent of the capital stock and surplus of the foreign bank as a whole. Additionally, federal agencies and branches must satisfy capitalization requirements by means of deposit arrangements. The IBA provided that for these arrangements, the sum of the deposited assets for each federal agency or branch *may not be less* than the *greater* of (i) "that amount of capital (but not surplus) which would be required" of a national bank being organized at the same location or (ii) 5 percent of the total liabilities of the agency or branch (including acceptances, but excluding accrued expenses and amounts due and other liabilities to offices, branches, agencies, and subsidiaries of the foreign bank). These deposit requirements may be more burdensome than comparable requirements under state law with respect to state agencies and branches. *See* Section 4(g) of IBA. For an interesting study of the IBA, *see* P. Skigen and J. Fitzsimmons, *The Impact of the International Banking Act of 1978 on Foreign Banks and Their Domestic and Foreign Affiliates*, 35 Business Lawyer 55 (1979).

2. The Foreign Bank Supervision Enhancement Act of 1991

In 1991, in the wake of the BCCI scandal, Congress passed legislation greatly strengthening U.S. Government scrutiny of and power over foreign banks. Title II of the legislation contains the Foreign Bank Supervision Enhancement Act of 1991 (FBSEA), designed to strengthen federal supervision, regulation, and examination of foreign bank operations in the United States.

With FBSEA, the U.S. attempted to upgrade the quality and transparency of international banking supervision by retaining its own regulatory power in the event overseas home country supervision or information available on a particular foreign bank was deemed inadequate. For a number of years the Fed had been agreeable to the principles of "consolidated bank supervision" and "home country" supervisory control as employed in the 1983 Basel Revised Concordat on Consolidated Bank Supervision (this preceded the version of 1992 discussed above). However, issues surrounding the BCCI episode made clear that significant gaps in the Concordat's consolidated supervision principles still existed. Further it was seen by the Fed that the *host* country regulators needed to maintain authority to evaluate the quality and the effectiveness of the *home* country's application of the Concordat's consolidated supervisory practices. The Fed also felt that the host country regulators needed to be aware of the nature and reliability of the information available on the foreign bank, its parent, and its affiliates before deferring to the supervisory and regulatory authority of the home country.

FBSEA prohibits a foreign bank from establishing a branch, an agency, or acquiring ownership or control of a commercial lending company without the prior consent of the Federal Reserve, regardless of whether the branch or agency is chartered under state or federal law. This means that a foreign bank can no longer avoid U.S. Government scrutiny by obtaining a state charter for its branch or agency, which is what most foreign banks had done prior to FBSEA.

Furthermore, the Fed cannot approve a foreign branch, agency, or acquisition of a lending company unless the foreign bank conducts business outside the United States and is "subject to comprehensive supervision and regulation on a consolidated basis" by its home country authorities. Additionally, the foreign bank must provide the Fed with information necessary to assess the application.

Additionally, FBSEA amended the Bank Holding Company Act of 1956 (BHCA) to allow the Fed to consider the "managerial resources"—the competence, experience, and integrity of the officers, directors, and shareholders—and "financial resources" of the foreign bank when deciding whether to approve a foreign bank's application to form a U.S. subsidiary. In many bank failures (including BCCI), the lack of quality and integrity of bank management and the insufficiency of bank financial resources are significant contributing causes.

FBSEA also establishes additional discretionary standards that the Fed may take into account when assessing an application. These include the consent of the home country supervisor, the nature of the cooperative relationship of the Fed and the home country regulator as to sharing of material information, various assurances of the foreign bank, compliance with U.S. laws, needs of the community, and the relative size of the bank in its home country. Additionally, the Fed may impose conditions on its approval as it deems necessary (for example, cessation or restriction of certain activities). All of these judgments by the Fed may have particular importance when a foreign bank seeks to acquire a U.S. bank. See J. Norton and C. Olive, *A By-product of the Globalization Process: The Rise of Cross-Border Bank Mergers and Acquisitions—The U.S. Regulatory Framework,* 56 The Business Lawyer 591 (2001).

FBSEA places the ultimate regulatory sanction of an organizational "death sentence" (termination) in the hands of the Fed. After notice and opportunity for a hearing, the Fed may order a foreign bank operating a state branch, or agency, or commercial lending company to cease operations. In order for the Fed to take such action, the foreign bank must not be subject to "comprehensive supervision or regulation on a consolidated basis" by its home country authorities. In addition, there must be reason to believe that the foreign bank has violated the law or engages in "unsafe or unsound banking practice." Consequently, continued operation in the United States would not be within the public interest or purposes of the IBA, the Bank Holding Company Act of 1956, or the FDICA. Furthermore, the Fed may also recommend to the OCC that the license of any federal branch or federal agency be eliminated if the Fed has reason to believe that such foreign bank or any affiliate has engaged in conduct for which the activities of any state branch or agency may be terminated as set forth above.

If it determines that expeditious action is necessary in order to protect the public interest, the Fed can also issue a termination order without a hearing. Unless the Fed lengthens the period, an order becomes effective within a 120-day period beginning on the date the order is issued. Foreign banks ordered to end business in the United States must follow federal and state law regarding closure or dissolution of such offices. The Fed or the OCC is authorized to invoke the aid of a U.S. district court to obtain a judicial mandate requiring compliance with the order, if any office or subsidiary refuses to comply with a termination order. Also, within thirty days after an order is released, a foreign bank can obtain review of a termination order in the United States court of appeals for any circuit in which the bank branch is located or in the United States Court of Appeals for the District of Columbia Circuit.

FBSEA effectively eliminated current competitive advantages that may have been available to state branches and agencies by imposing new limitations on their activities. For example, a foreign bank state branch may not conduct business that a federal branch is prohibited from conducting unless the activity is within "sound banking practice." If the foreign bank branch is insured, it cannot engage in any activity that poses "significant risk" to the FDIC fund. Also, state branches and agencies are subject to the same limitations, with respect to loans made to a single borrower, as are applicable to federal branches and federal agencies under the IBA.

Under FBSEA, the Fed was given authority to examine all U.S. branches of foreign banks (without preempting the examination authority of the other federal and state regulators). The Fed is required to examine each branch or agency of a foreign bank, each commercial lending company or bank controlled by one or more foreign banks or one or more foreign companies that control a foreign bank, and any other office or affiliate of a foreign bank conducting business in any state. Each branch or agency of a foreign bank must be subject to an on-site examination at least once during each twelve-month period (beginning on the date the most recent examination of such branch or agency ended). The Fed, the OCC, and the FDIC are mandated to coordinate their examinations with each other and with appropriate state regulators, to the extent that such coordination is possible. For more information on the FBSEA, *see* D. Gail, J. Norton, and M. O'Neal, *The Foreign Bank Supervision Enhancement Act of 1991: 'Expanding the Umbrella of Supervisory Regulation,'* 26 International Lawyer 993 (1992).

f. THE DAIWA CASE: SAFETY AND SOUNDNESS TESTED

A trader, Mr. Toshihide Iguchi, at the New York state-chartered branch of Daiwa Bank, as of 1995 one of the 10 largest Japanese banks and the 19th largest bank in the world, lost $1.1 billion from trading U.S. treasuries at its principal New York branch between 1984 and 1995 and apparently concealed the losses from management until July 1995. Daiwa operated two state-chartered branches in New York City and 12 other branches and agencies in the United States. In addition, Daiwa owned a New York state-chartered bank, Daiwa Trust Company.

The losses were not reflected in the books and records of the bank or in its financial statements, and were concealed through liquidations of securities held in the bank's custody accounts and falsification of its custody records. When management discovered the losses in July 1995, they did not promptly report them to U.S. bank regulators (Federal Reserve and New York State Banking Department). These regulators only learned of the losses on September 18, 1995. In addition, it appears that in 1992 and 1993 Daiwa management falsely assured Federal Reserve Board examiners that trading and custody had been split (this reduces the possibility of concealed losses) whereas they had not and actually remained under the control of Mr. Iguchi. These assurances were given as a result of Fed examinations which were mandated under FBSEA. It also appears that the Japanese Ministry of Finance (MOF) knew of the branch losses in August 1995 and did not inform the U.S. regulators (ironically, when the Fed learned of the losses it waited four days before reporting them to New York officials). Daiwa further announced in October 1995 losses of approximately $97 million in its insured bank subsidiary, a trust company, due to trading activities, at least some of which were unauthorized, between 1984-1987. These losses were concealed by transferring them to offshore facilities. Daiwa had more than a sufficient amount of capital to absorb these losses without any threat to its solvency.

As a result, Daiwa's branch license and other U.S. banking operations were terminated by consent orders effective February 2, 1996. Board of Governors of the Federal Reserve System, Federal Deposit Insurance Corporation and New York State Banking Department, Joint Statement (Nov. 1995). Daiwa also faced U.S. criminal charges, brought on November 2, 1996, for defrauding regulators and obstructing justice. If convicted, it might have had to pay up to $1.3 billion in fines. American Banker, Nov. 1995. On February 28, 1996, Daiwa entered into a plea bargain under which it pled guilty and was fined $340 million. Daiwa stated that its decision to conceal the losses resulted from the advice of MOF which was concerned about the effect a disclosure would have on the already fragile Japanese financial system. *Daiwa Bank Pleads Guilty to Conspiring to Hide Loss*, Wall Street Journal, Feb. 29, 1996.

Criminal charges were also filed against Iguchi and Mr. Tsuda, the branch manager, and both pled guilty. Iguchi received a four year prison sentence and a $2.6 million fine. Tsuda was sentenced to two months in prison, one year of supervised release to be served in Japan and a $100,000 fine. F. McMorris and M. Rappoport, *Daiwa Bank Ex-Trader Gets 4 Years, Fine,* Wall St. Journal (December 17, 1996). See also Alan Greenspan, Chairman, Board of Governors of the Federal Reserve System, Statement Before the Subcommittee on Financial Institutions and Consumer Credit of the Committee on Banking and Financial Services, U.S. House of Representatives (Dec. 5, 1995), *in* 82 Federal Reserve Bulletin 133 (1996).

On January 29, 1996, Daiwa announced that it had sold $3 billion in U.S. assets to Sumitomo Bank Ltd, and transferred $1 billion of its remaining assets to head office in Japan. In addition, Daiwa sold Sumitomo the rights to its U.S. operations for $65 million. Other Japanese banks have experienced difficulties with U.S. regulators. In August 1996, a U.S. subsidiary of Long-Term Credit Bank of Japan (LTCB) was fined $1 million by the New York State Banking Department after the discovery of irregularities in the company's reporting (it had booked purchases of Federal National Mortgage Association notes as repurchase agreements rather than outright purchases in contravention of its internal rules, and misreported the trades to officials). G. Baker, *Japanese bank fined $1m in US,* Financial Times (August 15, 1996). On February 13, 1997, the Federal Reserve Board and the New York State Banking Department issued a joint Cease and Desist Order against the Asahi Bank, and the Board imposed a $5 million fine, as a result of two bank executives reading confidential documents stored by regulators at the bank in sealed boxes. Federal Reserve Press Release (February 13, 1997). In October 1998, Daiwa announced it was closing all of its foreign branches and would liquidate its overseas subsidiaries due to its inability to meet international capital standards.

Daiwa has also faced problems in Japan. Most recently, in September 2000, a Japanese court ordered the executives and former executives of Daiwa to pay $775 million to the bank for the losses caused by the New York branch management. This is the highest damage award in the history of Japan. BNA, Banking Report (October 2, 2000).

Notes and Questions

1. What did BCCI teach us about the problems of insuring the safety and soundness of foreign bank owners of U.S. banks? A major part of the BCCI problem was worthless affiliate assets, e.g. one branch was owed a worthless asset by another branch. This was made possible to some extent by the lack of consolidated supervision. A branch (Branch A) with a worthless asset, a bad loan to a third party, could transfer the asset to another branch (Branch B) in exchange for a note from Branch B in the amount of the asset. A supervisor of Branch A would not know that the Branch B note was worthless insofar as Branch B was now saddled with a worthless asset. This might be avoided if the same supervisor was looking simultaneously at the books of both branches. However, notice that even one supervisor could be deceived if it did not examine all the entities of the bank at the same time. Non-simultaneous examinations would permit a bank to rotate its good assets to whatever unit of the bank was being examined at any particular time, and then rotate them out when the exam was finished. How does effective consolidated supervision, as now required under IBA, work? See Regulation K, 12 C.F.R. § 211.24(c). Does it solve the safety and soundness problem?

A key consideration for the Federal Reserve in approving foreign branch applications is whether the home country has subscribed to and enforces international capital standards, the content of which we examine in Chapter 4.

2. Is the adequacy of foreign safety and soundness regulation more or less important with respect to branches or subsidiaries of foreign banks? The U.S. has tried to deal with this issue by imposing stricter entry requirements on branches of foreign banks. Do you agree with this approach? The OCC has authorized foreign banks to establish operating

subsidiaries of branches which are allowed to engage in any activity in a branch subsidiary as they could engage in a subsidiary of the national bank, Office of the Comptroller of the Currency, Final Rule, 66 Federal Register 49093 (September 26, 2001), as corrected 66 Federal Register 62914 (December 4, 2001). Does this affect the validity of the basic branch versus subsidiary distinction in considering safety and soundness?

3. Are the new U.S. standards protectionist?   R. Bhala, *Tragedy, Irony, and Protectionism After BCCI: A Three-Act Play Starring Maharajah Bank*, 48 SMU Law Review 11 (1994), thought so. He pointed to the high transaction costs for foreign bank entry into the United States. As of April 1993, almost two and a half years after FBSEA was enacted, only three foreign bank applications had been approved by the Fed. A voluminous amount of information about the foreign regulatory system must be compiled (accompanied by much higher legal fees), and Bhala reported that foreign banks often withdrew applications after incessant questioning and requests for documentary material. A great amount of time is consumed in "name checks," to check into the character of every officer, director and principal shareholder, and to make sure that none of the individuals is fronting for someone else (as was the case in BCCI). Reviews for federal branches must be conducted by both the Fed and the OCC.

In March 1993, the Fed streamlined its procedures by imposing time deadlines for the various steps in the application process. A GAO Report found that as of January 29, 1996, "the Federal Reserve has received 96 applications from foreign banks seeking to establish offices or bank subsidiaries under FBSEA.   The Federal Reserve had approved 45 applications [15 for branches], had returned or applicant banks had withdrawn 23, and 28 were under review." The approved applications represented banks from 23 countries.   Processing foreign bank applications took more than a year on average. *GAO Applauds Fed on Implementation of Foreign Bank Law*, 15 Banking Policy Report 10, 12-13 (November 4, 1996) (excerpts from GAO Report).

In considering the issue of whether U.S. policy could be motivated by protectionist considerations is it relevant that the largest U.S. banking organization Citicorp only ranked 28th in the world in 1995 with $255 billion in assets? The biggest was Deutsche Bank with $502 billion; eight of the top ten were Japanese. *The Top 200 World Banking Companies,* American Banker (August 5, 1996).

The Federal Reserve Board has generally applied the effective consolidated supervision requirement to representative offices of foreign banks even though they do not take deposits, although such a standard is not mandated by IBA. In the first case of an application by a bank from the Russian Federation to establish a representative office, the Fed did not apply the standard. Promstroybank of Russia, Federal Reserve System Order Approving Establishment of a Representative Office (April

8, 1996). Does this indicate that banks from different countries may be subject to different standards depending on the political importance of the country?

Many foreign banks are publicly owned and thereby enjoy state subsidies. Within the European Union, such subsidies have been limited but are still the subject of controversy. See e.g. A. Jack, *EU set for tough line on Crédit Lyonnais rescue,* Financial Times (September 25, 1996). Even privately owned foreign banks may benefit by stronger safety net arrangements than provided by the United States. See Chapter 4's discussion of the Japanese safety net. Would this justify some measure of U.S. protectionism?

4. Under the GLB Act, the Federal Reserve Board has become the umbrella regulator, responsible for the overall safety and soundness of bank holding companies and the new financial service holding companies. The Federal Reserve assesses the holding company on a consolidated or group-wide basis with the objective of ensuring that the "holding company does not threaten the viability of the depository institution subsidiaries." Letter from Richard Spillenkothen, Framework for Financial Holding Company Supervision (August 15, 2000), at 2. Holding company regulation has mainly been justified on the grounds that the holding company should serve as a source of strength for the banks, i.e. be able to inject capital if needed. The Fed has emphasized that it does not intend to apply bank-like supervision to the non-banking entities of holding companies, or replace supervision by primary bank regulators. Id., at 3. This has relieved concerns of foreign banks and their regulators that the Fed might be intruding into their own supervision of foreign banks and their holding companies.

5. Much of safety and soundness regulation in the United States is done through the examination process. In recent years, this has focused on making sure regulators understand the nature of the risks banks run. Examiners evaluate credit, market, liquidity, operational, legal and reputational risk. These are particularly of concern for so-called large complex banking organizations, LCBOs. The concentration of assets in LCBOs has increased in recent years. The share of total assets of the ten largest banking organizations has risen from 26 percent in 1989 to 49 percent in 1999. In LCBO examinations the emphasis seems to have moved away from transaction testing, e.g. looking at individual loan files, to evaluating the organizations' own systems for risk management. As we shall see in Chapter 4, this is consistent with new approaches to assuring capital adequacy, the models-based approach. Where foreign LCBOs are concerned, the U.S. must rely on foreign management and foreign supervisors, as well as local management, in making judgments about the adequacy of risk management. L. DeFerrari and D. Palmer, *Supervision of Large Complex Banking Organizations*, Federal Reserve Bulletin 47 (February 2001).

6.   Under IBA §7(e) foreign bank offices in the United States may be terminated if the foreign bank is not subject to comprehensive and consolidated supervision by its home country.   Pursuant to §7(e)(7), the Fed has adopted extensive criteria to evaluate the operation of a foreign bank that is not subject to the required supervision abroad.   Regulation K, §211.30.   A bank that does not meet these criteria would be in danger of having its U.S. operations terminated.   These criteria are "soft" versions of the comprehensive and consolidated supervision requirement. For example, the Fed wants to know the "proportion" of assets and liabilities that are located or booked in the home country, presumably because this reduces the costs of non-consolidated supervision.   Should the criteria for termination be softer than the criteria for entry?

7.   Do you think the U.S. response to Daiwa, or the subsequent cases, was appropriate?   Should host country regulators be involved in insuring the safety and soundness of branches of foreign banks?   Under the 1991 FBSEA legislation, the Fed is charged with examining branches of foreign banks.   Would your answer be affected by whether the home country supervisor examines or requires audits of foreign branches?   The Japanese did neither before the Daiwa affair.   MOF announced in December 1995 that overseas branches of Japanese banks would be encouraged to obtain external audits and that the Bank of Japan would inspect branches in New York and London.   This was in accord with Federal Reserve Board policy announced in November 1996 requiring foreign bank branches with poor management ratings to hire independent accountants to perform audits.   J. Seiberg, *Fed Requires External Audits for Poorly Run Foreign Branches*, American Banker (November 18, 1996).

8.   As we shall see in Chapter 8, Japanese banks were in very bad shape in the late 1990's.   Some believed that many of the largest banks were actually insolvent if bad loan losses were fully written off.   Given the oft-expressed Japanese policy since the Occupation of never permitting banks to fail, this insolvency was not a major concern; indeed as we shall see in Chapter 4, it permitted Japanese banks to be competitive with lower levels of capital than their U.S. rivals.   As Chapter 8 will develop more fully, reforms of the Japanese financial system may relax the iron clad guarantee.   Indeed, Moody's downgraded the credit rating of four Japanese banks as a result of concerns with such a change.   G. Robinson, *Japan's banks near danger zone as 'Big Bang' looms,* Financial Times (January 28, 1997).   Given the significant presence of Japanese banks in the United States, should the U.S. be concerned with this change, and if so, how should it respond?

9.   The U.S. has tried to deal with the safety and soundness issue by ring fencing the assets of branches of foreign banks in the event the foreign bank fails (this was done with respect to the agencies of BCCI). Do you agree with this approach?   L. Bebchuk and A. Guzmán, *An Economic Analysis of Transnational Bankruptcies*, Discussion Paper No.

180, John M. Olin Center for Law, Economics, and Business (February 1996) found that a territorial rule, as contrasted with a universal (one jurisdiction) rule, not only incurs ex-post uncertainty costs of multiple adjudications and raises fairness issues among creditors, but may also distort ex-ante borrowing decisions. "By borrowing strategically, firms with existing debt are able to use such territorialist legislation to confer senior status on new creditors, who will therefore offer an interest rate discount. This will come at the expense of old creditors who are already committed to a particular interest rate. Firms will, in some cases, not to invest in the country offering the greatest return on investment, accepting a lower return in exchange for a lower interest rate on loans." Id., at 3-4. The authors also found that countries can benefit from territorialism by attracting investment.

10. The dual chartering system for U.S. branches of foreign banks used to permit states to have lower safety and soundness standards for allowing a foreign bank to establish a branch than those used by the federal government. Given the insurance by the FDIC of deposits at both types of branches, states could externalize the potential costs of their more lax policies. This risk has been substantially reduced by reducing the latitude for state policy. Now all foreign banks must comply with Basel capital standards, and the Federal Reserve reviews all branch applications. However, the rationale for such incursions into the dual banking system seems undermined to some extent by the decision to abolish insurance for deposits in branches of foreign banks.

11. In 2001, the Federal Reserve Board promulgated Regulation W which revises the rules for inter-affiliate transactions between a U.S. bank and its affiliates pursuant to the GLB Act, 66 Federal Register 33649 (June 25, 2001); 66 Federal Register 24186 (May 11, 2001). It does not apply to transactions between a U.S. branch and any affiliate not engaged in newly authorized activities under GLB. Nor does it apply to transactions between the foreign bank's non-U.S. banking offices and its U.S. affiliates. It does apply to transactions between U.S. branches of foreign banks and certain U.S. affiliates (those engaged in GLB activities).

3. FEDERAL DEPOSIT INSURANCE

A third key area of concern to the United States is deposit insurance. Prior to the adoption of the IBA in 1978, the deposits of foreign bank branches were not required to be insured by the FDIC and the FDIC would not insure them. IBA completely reversed course. Section 6(a) of IBA prohibited a foreign bank from establishing a Federal branch which receives "deposits" of less than $100,000 unless the branch obtained FDIC insurance or the Comptroller determined by order or regulation that the branch was not engaged in "domestic retail deposit activities." With regard to state branches, section 6(b) of the Act provided that no foreign bank could establish, and after September 17, 1979 no foreign bank could operate, a state branch in any state in which the deposits of a state bank would be required to be insured unless (i) the branch does not accept deposits of less than $100,000, (ii) the branch has obtained FDIC insurance, or (iii) the FDIC determines by order or regulation that the branch is not engaged in "domestic retail deposit activities."

Foreign banks with insured branches were required to pledge assets equal to 10 percent of the average of the insured branch's liabilities. Qualifying assets consisted of a variety of interest-bearing obligations issued by banks, corporations, governmental entities and certain international organizations. In addition, the FDIC imposed an asset maintenance test on insured branches requiring insured branches to maintain eligible assets (generally safe and liquid) payable in United States dollars in an amount at least equal in book value to the amount of the branch's liabilities.

All but a very few branches of foreign banks remained uninsured after the enactment of IBA by limiting their deposits to over $100,000. If foreign banks had chosen the insurance option for their banks, they would have had to pay for the insurance by contributions to the FDIC fund, a cost that would largely be passed on to depositors in the form of lower interest. Large depositors were more interested in having higher interest rates that having the first $100,000 of their deposits insured.

The deposit insurance rules were significantly changed in 1991 with the enactment of the FDIC Improvement Act (FDICIA) and the basic rules were established that we have today. Foreign banks can no longer take insured deposits (deposits under $100,000) through branches, they must now do so through subsidiaries. Existing insured branches, of which there were only 52, were grandfathered.

Section 6 of IBA was further amended in 1994 to deal with policies of the regulatory agencies allowing uninsured branches, in certain instances, to take initial deposits of under $100,000. Under previous FDIC regulation, 12 C.F.R. §346.4 (1995), there were five categories of deposits under $100,000 that could be accepted: business, U.S. government, international organizations, funds received from certain instruments, e.g. cashier's checks issued by the branch, and deposits of non-citizens who are not U.S. residents at the time of deposit. In addition, there was a de minimis exemption for 5% of branch deposits (for deposits that could not benefit from a specified exemption). The de minimis exemption has now been cut by the new legislation to 1% and Section 6(b)(2) of the IBA suggests some "Specific Factors" that should inform the formulation of more narrow specified exemptions. The FDIC adopted regulations to implement the new legislation, 61 Federal Register 5671 (1996). The major change from past regulation is a limitation of the corporate deposit exemption to firms with more than $1 million of gross revenue. Studies show that the actual amount of deposits under $100 thousand in uninsured branches of foreign banks is trivial. 60 Federal Register 36074, 36075 (1995).

The following piece gives some perspective on deposit insurance issues connected to how the United States deals with bank insolvencies, with particular attention to the BCCI case.

H. SCOTT, SUPERVISION OF INTERNATIONAL BANKING POST-BCCI ("Scott")

8 Georgia State University Law Review 487 (1992).

.   .   .

III. Depositor Protection

One of the principal concerns of a host country is the protection of depositors against losses in the case of bank failure. I will examine this concern as it applies to branches and agencies of foreign banks and then briefly deal with the much simpler case of subsidiaries.

A. Branches and Agencies

Depositors, rightly or wrongly, have come to expect protection, and the failure to honor this expectation carries substantial political risk for incumbent politicians. In my view, depositors are unlikely to differentiate between losing funds in domestic branches of foreign banks and losing funds in domestic banks and will seek to hold politicians responsible in both cases. This political concern mainly involves domestic rather than foreign depositors, although some foreign depositors may be citizens of the host country, for example, a U.S. citizen living abroad, or may have an affiliation with residents in the host country, for example, a foreign subsidiary of a U.S. corporation.

Some countries protect depositors in branches of foreign banks through providing deposit insurance. As previously discussed, until the passage of the FDIC Improvement Act of 1991, the United States required "retail" branches of foreign banks, those taking deposits under $100,000, to be insured; now, such branches are prospectively prohibited. Some other major industrialized countries such as Germany and the United Kingdom insure deposits in branches of foreign banks, while others such as Japan do not. The provision of deposit insurance to depositors in branches of foreign banks creates a major problem for the host-country insurer since its insurance exposure is dependent on the efficacy of home-country regulation and on supervision of the bank. But even if the host country does not insure deposits in branches of foreign banks, it will still be concerned with the potential losses to uninsured branch depositors—particularly domestic depositors—that might arise from the failure of a foreign bank.

One way for the host country to limit insurance fund or depositor losses is to require branches of foreign banks to pledge readily marketable assets and to maintain the value of assets at a certain level in excess of liabilities, a "quasi-capital" requirement. These requirements would help to insure that if the foreign bank failed, sufficient branch assets would be available to the host-country authorities to cover losses. Federally-licensed and many state-licensed branches of foreign banks are subject to such requirements in the United States.

This approach is based on an important but questionable assumption—that the host-country authorities have or should have the legal power to seize branch assets and to control their disposition in the event of the failure of the foreign bank. If the home-country receiver asserts a claim to the assets of the entire bank, including the assets of foreign branches, the host country may not be able to dispose of the assets of the branch, at least not without causing conflict with the home-country receiver. This kind of problem has arisen in the BCCI litigation in the United States and abroad.

While BCCI did not have branches in the United States, the Luxembourg bank operated uninsured state-licensed agencies in New York and Los Angeles at the time of its failure in July 1991. Agencies, like branches, make loans and other investments and are offices of a bank. Both New York and California agencies can take deposits from foreign individuals and companies, and maintain credit balances for any borrower, that is, credit a borrower's account with loan proceeds. In addition, New York agencies can take domestic corporate deposits of $100,000 or greater. While agencies in both states are legally prohibited from taking deposits from individual U.S. citizens or residents, it appears the BCCI agencies did so anyway.

When BCCI failed, its U.S. agencies failed with it. The U.S. assets of the failed BCCI banks, estimated at $550 million, consisted only in minor part of the agencies' assets. Far more important were their alleged stockholdings in several U.S. banks, including First American, and clearing accounts at the Bank of America and some other banks. Claims against U.S. assets included somewhat less than $20 million owed by the agencies to third parties (non-BCCI entities), as well as a $200 million fine which the Federal Reserve Board sought to levy against BCCI for illegally acquiring certain U.S. banks. There was also the prospect of additional fines as a result of criminal prosecutions by federal and state authorities.

In a bankruptcy proceeding in the U.S. District Court, Southern District of New York, which was dealing with BCCI's United States assets, the liquidators of the Luxembourg holding company and the two subsidiary banks obtained, on August 2, 1991, a temporary restraining order (TRO) against any claims to BCCI's U.S. assets, including the assets of the agencies. The TRO was based on section 304 of the U.S. Bankruptcy Code that permits a court to enjoin the pursuit of claims against the U.S. assets of a bankrupt entity on the theory that the claims should be brought as part of a foreign proceeding, in this case, the insolvency proceedings in Luxembourg and the Cayman Islands.

On October 15, 1991, the foreign liquidators agreed to a consent order entered by the bankruptcy court that permitted the California and New York state regulators of the BCCI agencies to remove the agency assets from the bankruptcy court and to take control of them pursuant to ongoing state liquidation proceedings. The consent order further provided that the foreign liquidators would assert no claims to the agency assets in the state proceedings and that any surplus remaining after the liquidation of the assets and satisfaction of estimated claims on the agencies would be remitted to the bankruptcy court.

The consent order also dealt with another group of BCCI assets, deposits in BankAmerica International (BAI), Bank of America's New York Edge Act subsidiary, that served as a clearing bank for the two BCCI banks. BAI had interpleaded these assets, and they had become subject to the jurisdiction of the bankruptcy court. Under the terms of the consent order, the Luxembourg bank's deposits in BAI (SA accounts) were removed from the bankruptcy court's jurisdiction. The foreign liquidators further agreed not to assert claims to the SA accounts unless they failed to become subject to the New York state liquidation proceeding. Other BCCI assets, such as the alleged stock interests in various United States banks, remained subject to the jurisdiction of the bankruptcy court and to the operation of the section 304 TRO.

On December 19, 1991, the BCCI liquidators agreed to plead guilty to various federal and state criminal charges brought against the BCCI banks. These charges included a federal indictment alleging that BCCI secretly acquired control over several U.S. banks. Under the settlement, $275 million in U.S. assets will be used to pay off U.S. creditors of the agencies, to pay part of the outstanding fines, and to increase the capital of U.S. banks illegally owned by BCCI. The $275 million balance of the $550 million in U.S. assets will be turned over to the consolidated bankruptcy proceedings in Luxembourg and the Caymans. On January 23, 1992, the U.S. District Court, Southern District of New York, which had jurisdiction over the bankruptcy proceedings, refused to upset the settlement on the grounds that it could not interfere with the federal prosecution, and on January 24, 1992, the settlement was approved by the U.S. District Court for the District of Columbia over the objections of various creditors.

The net effect of the United States proceedings, pending further appeals, was that $275 million in U.S. assets was not consolidated with the worldwide receivership assets of the BCCI banks in the Luxembourg and Caymans proceedings and thus was not available to creditors of those banks. Also, it appears that the U.S. creditors of the BCCI agencies will receive full payment of their claims.

Certain conclusions can be drawn about these proceedings. As a threshold matter, it is unclear whether assets of agencies or branches of foreign banks are at all subject to the jurisdiction of the U.S. bankruptcy court; assets of failed banks clearly are not. This uncertainty might partly account for the willingness of the BCCI liquidators to have agreed to the bankruptcy consent order of October 15, 1991. In addition, it appears that U.S. assets of failed foreign banks can be cut off from claims by foreign liquidators through the use of host-country criminal prosecutions.

If U.S. or other country assets of failed foreign banks are not fully consolidated in home-country foreign insolvency proceedings—what is called the "ring fence" approach—and such assets are substantial, the ability of a foreign receiver to reorganize a failed bank will be severely limited. While this was not a practical alternative in the BCCI case—earlier efforts to reorganize the bank with an infusion of capital from Abu Dhabi foundered—it could be a problem in future bankruptcies of multinational banks. Indeed, the possible need to reorganize a failed company is a significant rationale for the U.S. Bankruptcy Code's section 304 proceeding. In fact, it was this concern that was behind the decision of U.S. authorities to assert jurisdiction over the London branch assets of Franklin National Bank when that bank was in danger of failing in 1974. The fact that the U.S. authorities had control over all of Franklin's assets was an important factor in their ability to sell the troubled bank to European American Bank.

The failure to consolidate may also result in the inability of non-U.S. creditors to obtain the same pro rata share of all of the bank's assets that they would have obtained if the assets were consolidated. While the creditors of BCCI's U.S. agencies will be fully paid off, creditors in the foreign insolvency proceedings are expected to recover only thirty to forty percent of their claims. This is a somewhat arbitrary result.

Apart from the difficulties of preferring some creditors of a bank at the expense of others, the assets of an agency or branch of a foreign bank may have little to do with their actual business activities. It appears that the BCCI banks shifted assets among branches to avoid detection of insolvency. The difficulty of sorting out assets between various offices of a bank illustrates the need for a consolidated bankruptcy proceeding. A further complication arises insofar as the host country asserts jurisdiction over assets of a failed foreign bank that are within its jurisdiction but are not assets of the entities, an agency or branch, operating in its country. For example, part of the U.S. assets of the BCCI banks reportedly consisted of $85 million of deposits of the Tokyo branch of BCCI Luxembourg. There is no clear rationale for using these assets to satisfy claims of U.S.

creditors of U.S. agencies or to make capital infusions into U.S. banks allegedly owned by BCCI, rather than using them to satisfy the claims of Japanese creditors against the Tokyo branch or the claims of worldwide creditors against the Luxembourg bank.

The strongest argument for the host country preserving the assets of a branch or agency of a failed foreign bank for local creditors is that the host country is at risk for the supervisory failures of the home country. This rationale is much stronger when the host country insures local depositors than when it merely seeks to protect their interests as in the case of the U.S. agencies of BCCI. The insurance commitment represents a potential exposure for the taxpayers of the host country. In my view, the claims of uninsured depositors should be fully consolidated with other claims to the worldwide assets of a failed bank. In addition, I do not believe that local assets should be subject to a ring fence just because the host country brings criminal actions against a failed bank. This creates a loophole to consolidation that can be easily exploited by a host country. Moreover, if criminal prosecution is the key to jurisdiction over assets, what if there are prosecutions in several countries? If the Japanese had criminally prosecuted BCCI, why should the United States rather than Japan use all of the U.S. assets (particularly those of the Tokyo branch) to satisfy the criminal fines?

One might consider another approach to the deposit insurance problem: deposits in a branch of a foreign bank could be covered under the deposit protection scheme of its home country and the home country could be given jurisdiction over the worldwide assets of any failed bank. This would have the advantage of having the insuring country bear the risk for its own supervisory shortcomings and preserve the unity of the bankruptcy of the bank. But this approach raises problems of its own.

First and foremost, there is the issue of consumer confusion. Imagine a potential depositor winding his way through Wall Street, or perhaps even Atlanta, past the offices of various banks, including those of branches of foreign banks. A deposit in each domestic bank would be insured similarly under the United States deposit insurance scheme, but a deposit at each of the branches of foreign banks would be insured differently, according to the various schemes in place in the home countries of these banks. Even with full disclosure of the terms of such insurance, as to level of coverage, the degree of risk sharing by depositors, the types of deposits covered, and the speed and convenience of payouts, the consumer may be left with substantial confusion.* These are sophisticated and complicated

---

* It could be argued that the rational consumer would also want information about how the deposit insurance "system" works in practice. For example, does the foreign country ever liquidate failed banks, or does it routinely bail them out through capital infusions or central bank loans? But these issues are equally important where deposits in branches of foreign banks are

matters. In theory, this issue might be addressed by some harmonization of deposit insurance schemes through an international agreement, but this is not realistically achievable, in my judgment, in the foreseeable future.

Secondly, there is the ultimate question of whether the home-country insurance fund obligation will actually be honored—this issue has not been free from doubt even in the United States. It would certainly be a major concern for host countries where the bank's home country had a history of economic difficulty.

B. The Need for International Solutions

An international agreement is seriously needed in this area. At the outset, there should be agreement as to what to do when the local entity of the failed foreign bank is not insured. In my view, there is a strong case for home-country bankruptcy jurisdiction for all uninsured claims, including those of government authorities. Also, agreement is needed as to whether host countries should have any claim to jurisdiction over assets other than those of the local entity of the failed bank, for example, clearing accounts of the foreign bank. Again, in my judgment, these assets should be part of the home-country bankruptcy proceeding.

While host countries may be able to ring fence all local assets through brute force, this may be done at the expense of engendering conflict with home-country receivers, as well as foreign creditors, which in some cases may be government authorities. Further, host countries that prefer a ring fence in a case where they are in surplus—host-country assets exceed local claims (the U.S. with respect to BCCI)—may prefer consolidation when they are in deficit. In the context of an international agreement, countries could define their general and long-term interests rather than responding to the exigencies of a particular case.

1. There are two principal approaches to the deposit insurance issue: (1) host-country deposit insurance and host-country bankruptcy jurisdiction over the assets of insured branches or other insured entities of failed foreign banks, and (2) home-country deposit insurance and home-country bankruptcy jurisdiction over the worldwide assets of failed foreign banks. While each approach has its own problems, I think the former is probably more realistic. However, this choice should be settled by international agreement.

The United States has chosen a third path: not permitting insured retail branches of foreign banks. I think this is ill-advised for the reasons previously stated. It deprives depositors and their insurers

---

insured by the host country. Deposits in excess of host-country insured amounts may be protected to a greater or lesser degree depending on the bailout policies of the home country.

of the backing of the worldwide capital of strong foreign banks. These creditors can now only look to the capital of U.S. subsidiaries. Also, this approach limits the competitiveness of foreign banks in U.S. markets. Foreign banks with retail deposit funding will have less lending capacity since they are forced to lend off the capital of subsidiaries rather than worldwide capital. This is not in the interest of potential U.S. borrowers.

C. Subsidiaries

Subsidiaries raise no major problems with respect to depositor protection. Subsidiaries are supervised and insured by the host country, and the host country has jurisdiction over the bankruptcy of its own domestic banks whether or not they are owned by foreign banks. As in the BCCI case, various claims may be asserted against the failed bank's interest in its foreign subsidiaries. For example, there are claims against BCCI's interests in various United States banks allegedly owned by BCCI, but these claims only concern ownership of the banks, not their supervision or solvency.

On December 20, 1995, the Luxembourg court in charge of the BCCI bankruptcy, cleared a worldwide settlement for creditors. The debts of the bank, originally estimated at $14 billion, were reduced to $10 billion through lengthy negotiations. Assets, initially estimated at somewhat over $1 billion, stood at $3.3 billion (as of April 1996) as a result of a contribution of $1.8 billion from the government of Abu Dhabi, the principal shareholder, $243 million received from the United States, and more than $400 million from Sheikh Khalid bin Mahfouz of Saudi Arabia (a settlement of claims against him by the liquidators). Assets were further increased in 1998 by a settlement with the BCCI accounting firms for $125 million and an additional $70 million contribution from Abu Dhabi. The case was finally settled in September 1998 for around 60 percent of claims. Additional recoveries may come from actions filed by liquidators. In March 2001, the House of Lords decided that the liquidators could bring a $1 billion claim against the Bank of England for negligent supervision. *Three Rivers District Council v. Governor and Company of the Bank of England* [2001] UKHL/16.

Notes and Questions

1. How was deposit insurance dealt with prior to 1978, by IBA after 1978, and by the amendments to IBA in 1991? Which of the three approaches is preferable? Some countries like Germany insure worldwide deposits. Should the U.S. allow retail or wholesale branches to operate in the U.S. covered by foreign insurance schemes?

2. Under the 1991 reforms, foreign banks under §6 of IBA can only take   retail   deposits   (less   than $100,000)   through   insured

subsidiaries—there can be no new insured retail branches. Did this reform make sense?

3. Under the Federal-Depositor Preference Law, amending the Federal Deposit Insurance Act, 12 U.S.C. §1821(d)(11), depositors' claims against failed banks are given a preference. This allows the FDIC as subrogee of insured deposits, as well as uninsured deposits, to be paid before other creditors. Deposits in foreign branches of U.S. banks (deposits only payable abroad) are not given such a preference. The rationale for the exclusion is that such deposits are not generally insured, but uninsured U.S. deposits (over $100,000) are preferred. However, such depositors do bear the cost of insurance (as passed on by banks) on their insured deposits. Of course, inclusion of foreign deposits in the preference would decrease the recovery of the FDIC. Do you think foreign deposits should be excluded from the preference? See C. Curtis, *The Status of Foreign Deposits Under the Federal Depositor-Preference Law*, 21 U. of Pennsylvania J. of International Economic Law 237 (2000).

4. The U.S. is currently considering some basic reforms of its deposit insurance system, including indexation of insurance coverage levels to rates of inflation, fuller authority to charge risk-based premiums and new ways of calculating target levels of Fund reserves. BNA Banking Report, *FDIC Recommends Broad Overhaul in Reform of Deposit Insurance System* (March 9, 2001).

4. PERMISSIBLE ACTIVITIES

Under §8(a) of the IBA, a foreign bank with a branch, agency or commercial lending company in the United States is subject to the BHCA and, therefore, absent grandfathering or exemption. must restrict its activities to those "closely related" to banking under §4(c)(8) of the BHCA. The definition of foreign bank is very broad and includes the foreign subsidiaries and affiliates of a foreign bank. The IBA's restrictions on the activities of a foreign bank can be far-reaching, applying to the domestic and foreign activities of its nonbanking, as well as its banking, affiliates.

At the time Congress passed the IBA, many foreign financial institutions owned more than 5 percent of the voting shares of nonbanking companies or were engaging, either directly or through their affiliates, in nonbanking activities in the United States. In order to avoid imposing an undue burden on those institutions, the Act grandfathered certain investments and activities.

a. GRANDFATHERING

Section 8(c) of IBA permits a foreign bank or company to continue, after December 31, 1985, to engage in those nonbanking activities in the United States in which it was lawfully engaged either directly or through an affiliate on July 26, 1978, and to engage directly or through an affiliate in nonbanking activities in the United States which were covered by an application filed on or before July 26, 1978. The Federal Reserve Board, however, can terminate the authority to continue such nonbanking activities after December 31, 1985, if it determines that such action is necessary to prevent undue concentration of resources, decreased or unfair competition, conflicts of interest or unsound banking practices in the United States.

In addition, a foreign bank or company may retain ownership or control of any voting shares (and where necessary to prevent dilution of its voting interest, may acquire additional voting shares) of a nonbanking company provided that (i) the foreign bank or company owns, controls or holds with power to vote more than 5 percent of the voting shares of the nonbanking company; (ii) the activities engaged in by the nonbanking company are securities activities; (iii) the majority of the voting shares of the nonbanking company have been owned since July 26, 1978 by a company or group of companies organized under the laws of the United States or any state; and (iv) no foreign bank or group of banks owns or controls, directly or indirectly, 45 percent or more of the voting shares of the nonbanking company.

b.   EXEMPTIONS

Section 2(h)(2) of the BHCA, originally enacted as part of IBA and then later amended, exempts from the activity restrictions of the BHCA investments by foreign bank holding companies in certain foreign corporations principally engaged in business outside the United States (the "2(h) exemption"). It provides:

(2) Except as provided in paragraph (3) the prohibitions of section 4 of this chapter [on nonbanking activities and direct or indirect ownership or control of the voting shares of nonbanking companies] shall not apply to shares of any company organized under the laws of a foreign country (or to *shares held by such company in any company engaged in the same general line of business as the investor company* or in a business related to the business of the investor company) that is principally engaged in business outside the United States if such shares are held or acquired by a bank holding company organized under the laws of a foreign country that is principally engaged in the banking business outside the United States. For the purpose of this subsection, the term "section 2(h)(2) company" means any company whose shares are held pursuant to this paragraph.

(3) Nothing in paragraph (2) authorizes a section 2(h)(2) company to engage in (or acquire or hold more than 5 percent of the outstanding shares of any class or voting securities of a company engaged in) any banking, securities, insurance, or other financial activities, as defined by the Board in the United States. This paragraph does not prohibit a section 2(h)(2) company from holding

shares that were lawfully acquired before August 10, 1987...(Emphasis added).

The 2(h)(2) exemption is required because foreign banking organizations commonly engage in a wide range of financial, and even commercial activities. If the BHCA were fully applicable to foreign banks with subsidiaries in the U.S., the foreign bank parent, or its affiliates, could only engage in activities that were "closely related to banking," in or *outside* the U.S. This would effectively preclude foreign banks from doing banking in the United States.

The statutory 2(h)(2) exemption is fleshed out by Regulation K, 12 C.F.R. §211.23(f), which provides that a "qualified foreign banking organization" (QFBO) can engage in virtually any activity outside the U.S. A subsidiary of a QFBO can engage in any activity in the United States that it engages in abroad except for certain financial activities, including insurance and securities. These financial activities can only be engaged in with Board approval, which will not be given if domestic bank holding companies cannot engage in the same activity.

There is a second exemption from the activities exemption in Section 4(c)(9) of the BHCA. It provides that the Federal Reserve Board may exempt a foreign company from the BHCA activities restrictions if the Fed determines this to be in the public interest. This exemption has rarely been used.

c.   GLB PROCEDURES

The need for grandfathering and exemptions from activities restrictions has been substantially alleviated by GLB which allows foreign banks, like U.S. bank holding companies, to become FHCs with a wider range of permissible activities. As previously noted, GLB permits a well-capitalized and well-managed U.S. BHC to become a financial service holding company (FHC) through which it can engage in a full range of financial activities, including insurance, securities and merchant banking (investment in companies, including purely commercial companies, for resale).

Under GLB, if a foreign bank is a BHC in the United States because it owns a subsidiary bank in the United States, its subsidiaries must comply with the same "well capitalized" and "well managed" requirements as must the subsidiaries of U.S. based BHCs. If, however, the foreign bank operates in the U.S. through branches and wishes to become a FHC, GLB requires that "the Board shall apply comparable capital and management standards...giving due regard to the principle of national treatment and competitive opportunity." Section 4(l)(3) of the BHCA, as amended. Rigid application of the "well-capitalized" standard to foreign banks could prevent them from becoming FHCs. A well-capitalized bank must maintain leverage capital (capital/total assets) of 5%, Tier I risk-based capital of at least 6% and total risk-based capital of at least 10%. These standards, as we shall see in Chapter 4, are substantially higher than international capital standards.

On January 25, 2000, 65 Federal Register 3785, as amended on March 21, 2000, 65 Federal Register 15053, the Federal Reserve Board adopted an interim rule applying the 6% Tier I and 10% total risk-based standards to foreign banks from countries whose home-country supervisors have adopted Basel capital standards. However, the proposed leverage ratio (capital over total assets unadjusted for risk) was 3% rather than the normal 5%. The Board thought a lower standard was appropriate given that foreign banks hold both banking and nonbanking operations under the foreign bank, domestic bank holding companies (as opposed to banks) which also hold banking and nonbanking operations are subject to a minimum leverage ratio of 4% (or in some instances 3%), and that many countries do not impose a leverage ratio. Banks from countries that have not adopted Basel standards must obtain from the Board a determination that their capital is comparable to the capital that would be required of a U.S. bank.

If a foreign bank becomes a FHC, its IBA activity grandfather rights are terminated. If a foreign bank is unable to qualify as a FHC, it may not engage in the expanded set of new financial activities, but all of its previously authorized activities are grandfathered. However, giving due regard to the principles of national treatment and competitive equality, the Fed may impose the same prudential restrictions on such grandfathered activities as apply to those activities when engaged in by FHCs.

The European Commission complained about the leverage requirement, pointing to the fact that it went beyond agreed international capital standards. The Fed argued that U.S. banks are subject to a higher leverage requirement, 5 percent as compared with 3 percent, and that foreign banks below 3% may still qualify as FHCs if they can show "comparable" capital strength to a well capitalized U.S. bank. Indeed, the Fed stated that it had approved FHC status for two European banks with leverage ratios below 3%. Letter from Federal Reserve Board Governor Lawrence Meyer to John Mogg, Director-General, Directorate-General, Internal Market and Financial Services, European Commission (April 17, 2000). The letter was an important statement of the Fed's view of national treatment. Meyer stated: "The principle of national treatment requires that foreign banks operating in the United States meet standards that are at least comparable to those we apply to our own banks. The comparability requirement set out in the Act is an outgrowth of this principle. In implementing the comparability requirement, the Board adopted a flexible approach."

In adopting its Final Rule, the Fed dropped the leverage requirement entirely, bending to the pressure from foreign banks, as well as many in

Congress. Instead, a bank's leverage ratio has been added to the list of factors the Board may look at in determining whether a foreign bank has adequate capital. In addition, the Board changed its approach on the application of the "well managed" standards. The interim rule had required each U.S. branch of the foreign bank to be well-managed, while the Final Rule looks at such branches in the aggregate. Board of Governors of the Federal Reserve System, Press Release, December 21, 2000.

d. GLB AND MERCHANT BANKING

GLB permits FHCs to engage in merchant banking (which can involve the ownership of purely commercial companies) as well as in financial activities, such as insurance and securities. In principle, merchant banking only involves holding shares for investment and resale and does not involve operational control over companies in which the FHC has an investment. But it is very hard to draw lines in this area. Thus GLB, under new BHCA Section 4(k)(4)(H) allows ownership of shares that are "held for a period of time to enable the sale or disposition thereof on a reasonable basis consistent with the financial viability of the activities" and provides that the FHC "not routinely manage or operate" companies in which it has invested "except as may be necessary to obtain a reasonable return on investment upon resale or disposition."

The Federal Reserve Board and the Secretary of the Treasury issued a final rule (the Rule) fleshing out the GLB merchant banking authority, 66 Federal Register 8466 (January 31, 2001). The Rule defines a "merchant banking investment" as an investment by a FHC in a nonfinancial entity. Before a FHC may engage in merchant banking, it must be affiliated with either a securities firm, or insurance firm and an investment adviser that advises an insurance company. Merchant banking investments must be made through a subsidiary other than a depository institution, but a foreign bank is not a depository for this purpose. However, a U.S. branch of a foreign bank is a depository.

Three mechanisms can be used for merchant banking investments: portfolio investment, a private equity fund controlled by the FHC or a private equity fund not controlled by the FHC. A FHC may routinely operate and manage its portfolio companies in private equity funds not controlled by the FHC, but not otherwise. The Rule further provides that in most cases merchant banking investments may be held for only 10 years, and 15 years if the investment is made through a qualifying private equity fund. A FHC may not cross-market products or services between a portfolio company and a depository institution, following the provisions of GLB.

The Fed has also issued a rule on merchant banking capital, 67 Federal Register 3784 (January 25, 2002). It provides for deductions from capital for certain merchant banking investments. The proposal applies to banks and their holding companies and would apply to equity investments made under the new merchant banking authority under GLB and to equity in non-financial companies under most other authority. However, investments by SBIC (many existing private equity are organized in this form) are exempt and subject to standard capital rules. The rule imposes a capital charge that increases in steps as the level of concentration in equity investments increases, ranging from an 8% Tier I capital deduction for investments up to 15 percent of an organization's Tier I capital, to a 25 percent charge for investments over 25% of Tier I capital.

The GLB permits the Fed to impose additional requirements or restrictions on relationships or transactions between branches of foreign banks and their U.S. affiliates for a variety of reasons, e.g. to prevent evasions of law, to avoid significant risk, or unfair competition. However, such requirements and restrictions cannot be applied to relationships or transactions between the foreign bank itself and a U.S. affiliate. The Fed has proposed a comprehensive revision of all its affiliate rules, including those applicable to FHCs, 66 Federal Register 24186 (May 11, 2001).

Notes and Questions

1.   Some countries have foreign banks that can engage in almost any activity (universal banks) and other countries permit non-bank affiliates of the bank to engage in these activities. How does IBA and Regulation K handle the problem of the non-U.S. activities of foreign bank holding companies? How does it handle activities within the U.S.? To what extent can a simple national treatment standard be applied to activities of foreign banks?

The Federal Reserve Board originally proposed amending Regulation J to

> ...eliminate from the first prong of the QFBO test (*i.e.* that more than half its worldwide business be banking), the requirement that all banking activities be conducted within the bank ownership chain. Thus, a FBO that had substantial life insurance activities outside of the banking chain would have been able to count such activities as 'banking' in calculating whether the majority of its worldwide activities are banking, but not when calculating whether the majority of its banking business is outside of the United States.

> The Final Rule does not adopt the 1997 Proposal. The Fed believes that, in light of GLBA, elimination of the banking chain requirement would permit a foreign insurance group that owned a foreign bank and qualified as a financial holding company (FHC) to make commercial and industrial investments in the United States beyond those permissible under either the insurance or merchant banking authority, even though a domestic insurance company with FHC status could not make such investments. Therefore, the existing QFBO test was maintained.

The Final Rule adds a new provision to the existing QFBO test, however, that would permit FBOs that would meet the QFBO test if banking activities outside the bank ownership chain are counted (limited QFBO), to be eligible for the exemptions afforded a QFBO, other than the exemption that permits certain foreign companies in which the limited QFBO has an interest to engage in activities in the United States. In order to be considered a limited QFBO, the organization must include a foreign bank that itself could meet the current QFBO test. This foreign bank could utilize all exemptions available to a QFBO. L Kaplan and E. Schadé, *Final Amendment to Regulation K, Part II, 21* Banking & Financial Services Policy Report, 4. (March, 2002)

2.   Why was the United States more liberal in allowing foreign bank holding companies to engage in commercial activity in the United States, e.g. manufacturing, than in financial activity? Could a U.S. bank holding company take advantage of the better than national treatment given to foreign bank holding companies by just reincorporating the holding company abroad?

3.   Earlier reform proposals, before GLB, would have required foreign banks to mimic the structure of U.S. banks by organizing their U.S. banking and securities activities in separate subsidiaries of a U.S. bank holding company. That is, it would have prohibited foreign banks seeking to take advantage of the new securities powers from engaging in banking through direct branches of the foreign bank. Would that have been a good idea?   See H. Scott, *Shackling Foreign Banks is Bad Policy,* American Banker, April 30, 1991.

4.   Under §8 of IBA, a foreign bank could engage in any securities activities that it was engaged in 1978, and even add to them, but it lost this authority if the foreign bank becomes a bank holding company by acquiring a U.S. bank. Many German and Swiss banks were in this position. This will no longer be a problem, of course, if the foreign bank becomes a FHC since FHCs can engage in a full range of securities activities. In fact, many foreign banks had solved this problem even before the passage of GLB through the use of a so-called §20 subsidiary. Under Federal Reserve Board interpretation of §20 of Glass-Steagall, a bank could affiliate with a securities firm as long as the firm was not "engaged principally" in prohibited securities activities like underwriting (brokering was not prohibited at all), i.e. such prohibited activities were no more than 25% of the securities affiliate's gross revenue. Several large banks, including some foreign banks, created securities affiliates that used the large amounts of gross revenue generated by government bond dealing (another non-prohibited activity) to shelter prohibited activity like underwriting.

Deutsche Bank was a prime exploiter of §20. In 1992, when Deutsche Bank acquired Morgan Grenfell, a U.K. securities firm with a U.S. subsidiary, C.J. Lawrence, Inc., a government bond dealer, it merged

Lawrence, together with two grandfathered securities subsidiaries, Deutsche Bank Capital Corp. and Deutsche Bank Government Securities, into a new Section 20 subsidiary. Having transferred its grandfathered securities activities to the Section 20 subsidiary, Deutsche Bank was in the position to acquire Bankers Trust in 1998.

5.   Does it make sense to require foreign banks which operate in the United States only through branches and not subsidiaries to be "well-capitalized" and "well-managed" before they can own securities, insurance or merchant banking affiliates in the United States? Under GLB, a U.S. bank holding company which is not "well-capitalized" or "well-managed" can become a FHC as long as its subsidiary banks are "well-capitalized" and "well-managed."

6.   What do you think of the restrictions in the Rule on merchant banking activity? Without such restrictions would banks have been basically free to engage in commerce? If so, would that have been a good idea? Can General Motors acquire a bank through the merchant banking route? If not, does it make sense to have a system in which FHCs own commercial firms but commercial firms cannot own banks? In considering this question, note that the effect of requiring that there be a capital charge on investment of FHCs in merchant banking is to substantially increase the capital requirements of FHCs with such investments.

7.   Under GLB, the statutory definition of financial activity includes any activity that the Federal Reserve Board has determined under Regulation K to be usual in connection with the transaction of banking or other financial operations *abroad*. See 12 C.F.R. §221.4(b) in the Appendix. This list includes, in §211.10(a) (10), "data processing" without qualification. Currently, under Regulation Y, U.S. bank holding companies are only able to engage in data processing for third parties in the U.S. to the extent of 30% of total data processing revenues, 12 C.F.R. §225.28(b)(14). Does this mean Microsoft could acquire a bank and qualify as a FHC? GLB was widely reported to have removed the barriers between banking and finance but to have preserved the barriers between finance and commerce. Indeed, many of the key players, such as Congressman Leach, the ex Chairman of the House Banking Committee, publicly supported the reforms on the basis that commerce and finance would be kept separate. And the Federal Reserve actively opposed the combination. Indeed, the proposed banking reforms of President Bush, embodied in H.R. 1505, 102nd Cong. (1991), which explicitly allowed commercial firms to own bank holding companies, were rejected by many for the very reason that it allowed commerce to be combined with banking, and reform efforts since that time have avoided such combination.

8.   In 1997, the Comptroller of the Currency (OCC) permitted the Zions First National Bank of Salt Lake City, Utah to engage in underwriting of municipal bonds through an operating subsidiary. 1997

OCC Letter LEXIS 127 (December 11, 1997).   The Comptroller's Operating Subsidiary Rule, 12 C.F.R. §5.34 (d)(1) provides that a national bank operating subsidiary may engage in "activities that are part of or incidental to the business of banking." The Comptroller observed that the bank would restrict underwriting to less than 25% of its total revenue thus complying with Section 20. Under GLB, national banks can use operating subsidiaries to own securities firms but insurance underwriting and merchant banking (at least until 2004) must be done through the FHC. What is the rationale for this distinction? Is it convincing?

9. Although GLB seems to give the Fed the upper hand over the OCC in limiting the non-financial activities of holding companies, the OCC still tries to find ways to permit such activities in national banks or their subsidiaries. Thus, the OCC has approved banks holding stock in commercial companies if such holdings hedged their position on equity swaps, under which the bank agrees to pay a counterparty the appreciation on a stock portfolio in exchange for a specified fee. The OCC justified this approval as "incidental to banking" since banks can engage in such activities under the National Bank Act, 12 U.S.C. §24 (Seventh) and swaps are considered banking products under GLB. This has triggered a controversy between the House Banking Committee and the OCC. See Letter from Congressman Leach to Jerry Hawke, Comptroller of the Currency, September 18, 2000; Letter from Hawke to Leach, September 8, 2000; and Letter from Leach to Hawke (with Staff Memorandum), December 18, 2000. Banks had formerly hedged such transactions in holding company affiliates but this is more costly than directly hedging in the bank.

5. INTERSTATE BANKING AND FOREIGN BANKS

Section 104 of the IBBEA, amending §5 of the IBA, permits a foreign bank to establish and operate a federal or state branch to the same extent as is permissible for a national or state bank whose "home state" (defined in §5(c)) is the same as that of the foreign bank. The branch may be a direct branch of the foreign bank, §5(a), or a branch of its U.S. subsidiary, if any, §5(d). Special rules apply to §5(a) applications.

In reviewing a §5(a) branch application, the regulators must apply a two-step process. *Step 1.* The foreign bank must satisfy the same standards applicable to the initial establishment of U.S. offices by a foreign bank as provided by FBSEA. In this regard, the regulators in consultation with the Secretary of Treasury, must determine that the foreign bank's financial resources, including capital, are "equivalent" to those required by a domestic bank to branch interstate. The regulators may require, under §5(a)(6), a foreign bank to establish a U.S. bank subsidiary if they cannot verify capital equivalence.

Step 2. The regulators must then apply to a foreign bank's interstate branching application the same standards applicable to an application by a domestic bank, including CRA compliance, if applicable. It is unclear whether CRA requirements apply to the establishment of a new wholesale uninsured branch. It would, however, apply if a branch to which CRA does apply is acquired by a foreign bank, even if such branch is subsequently converted to a wholesale branch, §5(a)(8).

IBBEA grandfathers the existing branches of foreign banks, i.e. their legitimacy is exempt from the two-step review outlined above. §5(b).

Notes and Questions

1. With respect to interstate banking through subsidiaries, IBBEA has eliminated the thorny problems that existed in applying the old Douglas Amendment regime to foreign banks. As FSBEA indicates foreign bank acquisitions of U.S. banks may have to be evaluated differently than purely domestic transactions, but no differences in treatment are necessary for interstate acquisitions.

Under the prior interstate regime, host states could discriminate among states in allowing out-of-state BHCs to make acquisitions in their states. Thus, Massachusetts could, under the Douglas Amendment, permit a Rhode Island but not a New York based BHC to acquire a Massachusetts bank. Northeast Bancorp, Inc. v. Board of Governors of the Federal Reserve System, 472 U.S. 159 (1985). Some states used this authority to discriminate against foreign bank acquisitions in their states. Under IBBEA, this no longer appears possible.

2. (a) As described in the reading, foreign banks can establish direct branches of the foreign bank or branches of a U.S. subsidiary of the foreign bank. How does one determine a foreign bank's home state?

Section 104(d) of IBBEA modified the existing definition of a foreign bank's home state under Section 5(c) of IBA. IBA continues to provide that a foreign bank that has any combination of operations in more than one state can choose one of those states as a home state. But it also provides for the first time that if a foreign bank has U.S. banking operations in only one state, that state is the foreign bank's home state for purposes of interstate branching. The Board has adopted an amendment to Regulation K implementing that change, 61 Federal Register 24439 (1996).

The determination of a bank's home state was extremely important before the rules on interstate banking were liberalized. Under old §5 of IBA, a foreign bank could only acquire a U.S. bank in a state (host state) other than its home state if the host state generally permitted U.S. banks from the foreign bank's home state to make the acquisition. However, since interstate acquisitions have been completely liberalized, the home state determination no longer seems important for that purpose.

The concept of home state may have new importance in the branching context. Many states who have opted-in to de novo branching have done so on a reciprocal basis. Thus, Virginia has said any bank can branch into Virginia if the bank's home state permits Virginia banks to branch into its state. Thus, a New York bank could branch into Virginia if New York permitted Virginia banks to branch into New York. There is a substantial question of whether state de novo reciprocity statutes conform to the IBBEA requirements. Under section 103, states must opt-in for all "out-of-state" banks. Arguably a reciprocity statute which allows entry for banks from some states but not others is prohibited by such requirement.

Assuming such statutes are permissible, the issue arises as to how to treat foreign banks. If the foreign bank were to branch in from a U.S. subsidiary, the issue would be relatively simple. If the U.S. subsidiary were in a state that qualified for entry under a reciprocity statute, it could come in just like any other bank from its state. However, if the foreign bank sought to establish a direct branch in a state with a de novo reciprocity statute, it might well be necessary to determine the foreign bank's U.S. home state. Thus, only foreign banks with home states that qualified for entry under a reciprocity statute would be permitted to enter; otherwise foreign banks would have interstate branching advantages. There is nothing under federal law requiring this result--this kind of question was probably not anticipated in the legislation. But host states adopting reciprocity statutes might well restrict their market to foreign banks from qualifying home states.

Suppose a state opted in to de novo branching without requiring reciprocity but sought to exclude all foreign banks from branching into the state. Would this be permissible. On the one hand, the state could point to §4(a)(1) that permits it to exclude all branches of foreign banks. On the other hand, §103 of IBBEA (as discussed above) requires an opt-in for all "out-of state" banks. Even if a general opt-in could be conditioned on reciprocity, the statute clearly prohibits a host state from specifically discriminating among states, e.g. permitting Massachusetts but not New York banks to enter. However, one could still argue that "out-of-state" refers only to another state of the United States, not a foreign country, and that a host state could opt-in to de novo branching for U.S. but not foreign banks. These issues remain unresolved.

In testing your understanding of these concepts ask yourself the following questions:

(i) The IBBEA 1994 requires that one determine the "home state" of a foreign bank for purposes of applying the branching law. Suppose IBJ, a Japanese bank, has New York and California subsidiary national banks and direct wholesale uninsured branches in Illinois and New York. What is its home state? Under amended Regulation J, 211.22 (a), each subsidiary could have its own home state. New Regulation J also implements new procedures for changing one's home state, 211.22 (b). Address the following questions regarding amended Regulation J.

(ii) If the California subsidiary wanted to open a de novo branch in Texas, and Texas affirmatively permitted (opt-in) out-of-state banks to branch in, without requiring reciprocity, would the California subsidiary be able to take advantage of this permission?

(iii) Suppose the Texas de novo opt-in statute had a reciprocity requirement, so that only banks from states that allowed Texas banks to branch in could branch into Texas. Further assume that California did not allow Texas banks to branch in but New York did. Could IBJ's California bank subsidiary branch into Texas?

(iv) Under the same set of facts, assuming reciprocity requirements are permitted, could IBJ open a direct branch in Texas?

(v) Could Texas ban all direct branches of foreign banks while permitting through opt-in (without reciprocity) all de novo branches of U.S. banks (including those that are foreign owned)?

(b) Why should there be a two-step procedure for new direct branches of a foreign bank outside its home state? Aren't the concerns addressed in Step 1 dealt with at the time the foreign bank established its home state branch? Does this put foreign banks at a disadvantage relative to U.S. banks establishing interstate branches? The Senate version of IBBEA would have forced foreign banks to establish new branches through a U.S. subsidiary thereby prohibiting new direct branches of the foreign bank. The European Union objected to the Senate approach as not providing national treatment. Would the Senate approach have been preferable?

(c) Should CRA obligations be applicable to the establishment of all branches, direct or indirect, insured or uninsured, of foreign banks? Currently, CRA only applies to insured retail branches and not uninsured wholesale branches.

D. THE GATS

This Chapter has focused on U.S. attempts to regulate foreign banks doing business in the United States through its power to condition access to its markets. This power has been affected by the GATS.

The 1994 General Agreement on Trade in Services (GATS) resulted from the Uruguay Round of trade negotiations which closed in December 1993. The Uruguay Round produced a new structure, the World Trade Organization (WTO), as well as the agreement on services. Special provisions of GATS apply to financial services. The core principle of GATS, expressed in Article II, is unconditional most-favored-nation (MFN) treatment: each service or service supplier from a member country must be treated no less favorably than any other foreign service or service supplier.

The paper which follows deals with the agreement on financial services. It makes reference to the OECD, the Organization for Economic Co-operation and Development. This multilateral was founded as the Organization for European Economic Cooperation after World War II to administer U.S. aid under the Marshall Plan. It was transformed into the OECD in 1961, based in Paris, to offer a forum through which its 29 members, the world's leading economic powers that are part of the broad western alliance, can promote world trade and development.[*]

S. KEY, FINANCIAL SERVICES IN THE URUGUAY ROUND AND THE WTO
Group of Thirty, Occasional Paper 54 (1997)

The General Agreement on Trade in Services (GATS), which was negotiated in the Uruguay Round, marks the first time that services have been covered by a global trade agreement. The GATS brings trade in services into a multilateral framework of rules and disciplines broadly comparable to that provided for trade in goods by the General Agreement on Tariffs and Trade (GATT), originally negotiated in 1947. The overall goal of multilateral trade negotiations is to support economic growth and development by reducing or eliminating barriers to trade, thereby promoting competitive and efficient markets.

.   .   .

The Uruguay Round Agenda

When the agenda for the Uruguay Round was being negotiated in the mid-1980s, the U.S. government, partly in response to an initiative by the U.S. financial services industry, was the primary advocate for including financial and other services. After prolonged negotiations culminating in the Punta de Este ministerial meeting in September 1986, services became part of the agenda in a complicated series of tradeoffs that shaped the Uruguay Round. In effect, industrial countries agreed to strengthen the multilateral framework of rules and disciplines by including textiles and agriculture and, in return, developing countries agreed to the inclusion of services, trade-

---

[*] The current members of OECD (with accession dates in parentheses) are: Australia (1971), Austria (1961), Belgium (1961), Canada (1961), Czech Republic (1995), Denmark (1961), Finland (1969), France (1961), Germany (1961), Greece (1961), Hungary (1996), Iceland (1961), Ireland (1961), Italy (1961), Japan (1964), Korea (1996), Luxembourg (1961), Mexico (1994), The Netherlands (1961), New Zealand (1973), Norway (1961), Poland (1996), Portugal (1961), Spain (1961), Sweden (1961), Switzerland (1961), Turkey (1961), United Kingdom (1961), and the United States (1961).

related intellectual property rights (TRIPS), and trade-related investment measures (TRIMS).

The U.S. financial services industry expected that a multilateral negotiation with simultaneous bargaining across a wide range of goods and services sectors would provide opportunities for tradeoffs that would lead to significant market opening for financial services by a number of the more advanced developing countries, often referred to as emerging market economies. A hypothetical example used by the U.S. industry was that emerging market economies might be willing to make binding commitments to lift restrictions on the provision of financial services by foreign firms in return, explicitly or implicitly, for concessions by the major industrial countries in other sectors such as textiles. However, as will be discussed later in this paper, such tradeoffs between financial services and other sectors did not occur.

Free Riders

The financial services negotiations—like those for other major service sectors such as basic telecommunications, maritime transport, and audiovisual services—proved to be very difficult. As the Uruguay Round drew to a close in December 1993, the hoped-for commitments to market opening had still not materialized. For financial services, some of the most significant problems involved foreign direct investment—for example, the refusal by some emerging market economies to make commitments to allow foreign financial firms to hold majority-ownership positions in domestic firms.

Although the United States and the European Community shared the goal of obtaining strong commitments to market opening in financial services from emerging market economies, their approaches differed. The European Community's priority was putting in place a multilateral agreement that included binding commitments for financial services, even if some of the initial commitments were weak. By contrast, the United States gave priority to obtaining strong initial commitments and was unwilling to allow emerging market economies to become so-called free riders.

The free rider problem arises because the GATS—like the GATT—is based on the most-favored-nation (MFN) principle, which precludes discrimination among foreign countries. (Literally, no foreign country can be accorded treatment less favorable than that accorded to the most favored foreign nation.) This makes it possible for a country that does not offer strong commitments to market opening to become a free rider. That is, without opening its own market, its service providers have the opportunity to benefit from the openness provided by other countries.

The U.S. government took the position that, unless improvements were made in the commitments being offered by a number of emerging market economies, it would make only a limited commitment for banking and securities in the GATS. That is, the United States would guarantee market access and national treatment *only* for *existing* operations of foreign financial firms. The United States would then take a broad MFN exemption that would leave open the possibility of discriminating among countries with regard to new entry or operations. Thus, without violating the GATS, the United States could prohibit future entry into the U.S. market for firms whose home countries were not sufficiently open to U.S. financial market firms; for firms already established in the United States, expansion into new activities or new locations could be prohibited.

In the final hours of the Uruguay Round, negotiations between the United States and the European Community resulted in the extension of the financial services negotiations for eighteen months. The new deadline was June 30, 1995, six months beyond the establishment of the WTO and the entry into force of the GATS and other Uruguay Round agreements. Although the United States took a broad MFN exemption for banking and securities, the compromise provided that MFN exemptions would be suspended pending the results of the extended negotiations. Financial services thus became one of several sectors for which negotiations were extended at the close of the Uruguay Round—the others were basic telecommunications, maritime transport, and movement of natural persons.

The Interim Agreement on Financial Services

Some offers were improved during the extended financial services negotiations. However, just prior to the deadline, the United States announced that the market opening being offered by a number of countries was still not sufficient and that it would make a binding commitment only for existing operations of foreign financial firms and take a broad MFN exemption with regard to new entry and operations. To avoid losing what had been accomplished in the negotiations up to that point, the European Community then took the lead in trying to preserve the commitments that had already been offered by other countries. The result—the so-called interim agreement on financial services—was that other countries agreed to maintain their existing MFN-based offers through the end of 1997 despite the minimal commitment and broad MFN exemption that had been taken by the United States.

Financial services negotiations resumed once again in Geneva in April 1997, with an agreed deadline of mid-December. In July, the United States submitted an MFN-based offer with strong commitments that was expressly conditioned on the strength of the commitments to be offered by other countries. As of this writing (October 1997), offers from most emerging market economies have not yet been submitted.

Liberalization in the GATS in Perspective

In the financial services negotiations in the Uruguay Round and the WTO, the main focus has been on liberalization involving the reduction or removal of *discriminatory* barriers and other barriers that, in economic terms, have a similar effect.   The former discriminate against foreign services and service providers vis-à-vis their domestic counterparts with regard to entry and operation in a host-country market; the latter, while not overtly discriminatory, are also used to keep foreign services and service providers from entering the market.

A host country might, for example, discriminate against foreign financial firms by refusing to grant licenses to their branches or subsidiaries, imposing limitations on their aggregate market share, or prohibiting them from engaging in certain activities that are permissible for their domestic counterparts. A country might also impose certain other restrictions, such as economic needs tests or quantitative limits on the total number of new banking licenses, that may, at least on their face, appear to be nondiscriminatory; however, their practical effect is usually similar to that of the more overtly discriminatory barriers. To deal both with discriminatory barriers to entry and operation and with other barriers to entry, the GATS uses the widely accepted principles of "national treatment" and "market access," which are discussed in the following chapter.

Another major type of liberalization involves nonquantitative and nondiscriminatory structural barriers.   Such barriers arise from aspects of national regulatory systems that do not discriminate between foreign and domestic services and service suppliers. For example, fundamental differences among nations in rules for permissible activities for banks or the types of products that may be offered can create significant barriers to trade. Even if they are nondiscriminatory, a country's rules may be so much more restrictive than those in other major countries that they create market distortions and inefficiencies.

Removing such barriers goes far beyond ensuring that foreign services and service suppliers can enter a host-country market as currently structured and enjoy equality of competitive opportunities vis-à-vis their domestic counterparts. Instead, it represents an effort to create maximum potential competitive opportunities in a host-country market, often referred to as "international contestibility of markets." Achieving such opportunities would require liberalization and reform of domestic regulatory structures, including, for example, competition policy, which covers the actions of private parties. Such liberalization would necessarily involve some degree of convergence of national regulatory systems, either de facto or through negotiated harmonization. The European Community's internal market program represents the most far-reaching effort to date to remove nondiscriminatory structural barriers among a group of nations.

However, that effort, in addition to being predicated on political agreement on goals for economic liberalization, is being carried out in the context of the unique supranational legislative, judicial, and administrative structure of the European Community.

The GATS addresses certain types of nonquantitative and nondiscriminatory structural barriers. For example, it imposes a general "transparency" obligation on WTO members to publish all measures of general application—including statutes, regulations, and administrative decisions—that are relevant to trade in services. It also requires countries to apply domestic regulations in a "reasonable, objective and impartial manner" to avoid undermining commitments to market access and national treatment. Moreover, countries must have in place appropriate legal procedures to review administrative decisions affecting trade in services. The GATS mandates further work to develop disciplines to ensure that domestic licensing requirements or technical standards do not constitute unnecessary barriers to trade in services. Meanwhile, countries must refrain from adopting rules or standards that are so burdensome, restrictive of trade, or lacking in transparency that they undermine their commitments to market access and national treatment.

The GATS deals with additional nondiscriminatory structural barriers in provisions applicable only to specific sectors. The most far-reaching example is the establishment of procompetitive regulatory principles in the telecommunications sector. For financial services, nondiscriminatory structural barriers are addressed simply by a "best efforts" commitment made by most of the OECD countries to remove or eliminate any significant adverse effects.

Besides liberalization to promote competitive and efficient markets, another important policy goal of international trade in financial services is ensuring adequate prudential regulation and supervision of financial firms. Current work toward achieving this goal—and thereby to promote the stability of the international monetary and financial system—involves two major efforts, both of which, with leadership from the Group of Seven (G-7), have become a high priority on the international economic agenda. One is enhancement of cooperation and coordination among supervisors in different countries and among supervisors of different types of financial institutions; the other is establishment of strong prudential standards and effective supervisory structures in emerging market economies.

When the idea of including financial services in the Uruguay Round was first proposed, financial regulators were concerned about the possibility of a trade agreement interfering with their ability to regulate and supervise financial institutions. They made it clear that inclusion of financial services in the GATS would be unacceptable without a specific exception for prudential regulation and supervision. As a result, the GATS contains a so-called prudential carve-out to ensure that the opening of markets that the agreement is intended to achieve will not jeopardize prudential regulation and supervision. Now, it is taken for granted by everyone involved that such a provision is necessary whenever financial services are included in an international trade or investment agreement. For example, a prudential carve-out is contained in the North American Free Trade Agreement (NAFTA) and the Multilateral Agreement on Investment (MAI) currently being negotiated at the Organisation for Economic Co-operation and Development (OECD).

.   .   .

II. The GATS and Financial Services

Most of the restrictions facing foreign services and service suppliers described in the introductory chapter—discriminatory barriers to entry and operation, barriers that have a similar effect in restricting entry, and nonquantitative and nondiscriminatory structural barriers—are regulatory barriers. The main exception comprises certain barriers to entry that are more akin to quantitative restrictions applied to trade in goods. For services, tariffs are not an issue.

Thus a global negotiation on trade in services necessarily had to address regulatory barriers at the outset. Unlike most goods, services—and financial services in particular—tend to be highly regulated domestically, the regulations usually apply to producers rather than to output, and the output itself is often intangible. In addition, providing services often requires proximity of producers and customers. For example, in the financial sector, as already mentioned, foreign direct investment plays a major role in the international provision of services.

The result was that many of the most complicated and difficult types of issues were telescoped into the first global negotiation on services. Such an effort was unprecedented. In the goods sector, early negotiations dealt almost exclusively with tariffs and quantitative restrictions. The process of dealing with barriers that result form domestic policies evolved over several decades—beginning primarily with the focus in the 1970s on production subsidies, product standards, and government procurement. In the 1990s, the potential scope of the multilateral trading system has been further broadened—although, at present, without a mandate to negotiate—by establishment of the WTO Committee on Trade and the Environment and working groups on the relationship between trade and competition policy and between trade and investment.

National Treatment and Market Access

The GATS, as already noted, relies on the principles of national treatment and market access to reduce or eliminate discriminatory barriers to entry and operation and barriers that, in economic terms, have a similar effect in restricting entry.

The GATS uses a generally accepted definition of national treatment, that is, it requires a host country to treat foreign services or service suppliers no less favorably than "like" domestic services or service suppliers. Use of the broad term "treatment no less favorable" has the effect of requiring both de jure and de facto national treatment. Moreover, it does not require precisely identical treatment of domestic and foreign services and service suppliers. The GATS goes beyond previous usage in clarifying this point: It explicitly states that national treatment could comprise formally identical or formally different treatment provided that the "conditions of competition" are not modified in favor of domestic services or service suppliers.

In theory, market access would be defined as the right to enter a host-country market in whatever form a service supplier chooses. Under this definition, a foreign service supplier could decide to eschew establishment in a local market and instead provide its services across borders to host-country customers; alternatively, the foreign service supplier could choose to invest locally, de novo or by acquisition, and operate through a commercial presence in the host country. The specific type of legal entity—such as a branch or a subsidiary—would be chosen by the investor. A right of entry to a host-country market could not, of course, be absolute, since the foreign financial service provider would need to meet prudential and other applicable regulatory standards.

However, in contrast to its handling of the concept of national treatment, the GATS does not attempt to define market access. Instead, the GATS provides a list of restrictive measures, primarily quantitative, that are typically used to deny entry to a host-country market to foreign services or service suppliers. These barriers include limitations, in the form of numerical quotas or economic needs tests, on the number of service suppliers or their total assets and limitations on foreign ownership of domestic firms. The barriers listed also include restrictions on the type of legal entity through which a service may be supplied, for example, requiring establishment of a subsidiary as opposed to a branch.

The line between barriers that restrict market access and those that deny national treatment in the GATS is not always clear. On the one hand, the definition of national treatment is *not* limited to discrimination that occurs *after* a foreign service provider has established operations in a host country. On the other hand, the list of measures restricting market access includes some barriers to entry—such as restrictions on ownership positions in local firms by foreign service providers—that are overtly discriminatory and thus would also be a denial of national treatment under the GATS.

In general, it is difficult to realize fully the benefits of liberalization of trade in financial and other services without free cross-border movement of capital.   The GATS therefore contains certain provisions aimed at ensuring that a country does not apply restrictions on payments and transfers that would undermine its commitments to market access and national treatment.   The provisions refer to and are consistent with the IMF's responsibilities in this area; consideration is currently being given to strengthening the IMF Articles of Agreement to include formal responsibility for capital account convertibility.

Structure of the GATS

The GATS, which is part of the Agreement Establishing the World Trade Organization, has two major components.   The first consists of a so-called framework agreement, which establishes overall rules and disciplines for trade in services, together with various annexes, including one dealing with issues specific to financial services.   The second consists of each country's schedule for specific commitments and list of MFN exemptions.

For financial services, there is a unique additional element, namely, the Understanding on Commitments in Financial Services. The Understanding provides an alternative approach to scheduling commitments that was used by most of the OECD countries to supplement the requirements of the framework agreement.   In legal terms, the Understanding is incorporated by reference into the GATS through the schedules of commitments of the countries that use it. Commitments scheduled under the Understanding are extended to all members of the WTO, regardless of whether the members scheduled commitments under the framework or the Understanding.

The expression "financial services agreement" is widely used to refer to the GATS as it applies to financial services, although in fact, a separate agreement for financial services does not exist.   Table 1 highlights some of the principal features of the GATS that are relevant for financial services.   Outside the GATS, other provisions of the WTO Agreement—in particular, the strengthened dispute settlement mechanism that was an important achievement of the Uruguay Round—are also relevant for financial services, as are various ministerial declarations and decisions.

Table 1.
Highlights of the GATS:
Financial Services

Framework agreement

Modes of supply
    Cross-border provision of services
    Consumption abroad
    Establishment of a commercial presence
    Temporary presence of natural persons

General obligations
    Most-favored-nation treatment
    Transparency

Specific commitments
    Market access
    National treatment

Financial services annex

Prudential carve-out

Financial services expertise in dispute
    settlement

Recognition of prudential measures

Coverage and definition of financial services

Schedules of commitments

Hybrid list approach

Negative list approach for countries using the
    Understanding on Commitments in
    Financial Services

Scheduling by mode of supply

---

a. Alternative approach to scheduling
    commitments used by most of the
    OECD countries.

Because of the special characteristics and sensitivity of the financial sector—in particular, the role of financial firms and markets in financing the real economy, the role of banks in monetary and payments systems, and the phenomenon of systemic risk—finance ministry officials in the United States and other countries insisted that financial services negotiations required financial as well as trade expertise. Accordingly, although trade officials retained overall responsibility, finance officials played a major role in the financial services negotiations for those countries that were the most active participants. Thus, while the GATS framework agreement and the structure of the schedules of commitments were negotiated by trade officials, the Annex on Financial Services, the Understanding on Commitments in Financial Services, and the contents of the schedules of commitments for financial services were negotiated primarily by finance officials. Possible effects of the separateness of the financial services negotiations are discussed later in this paper.

.   .   .

General Obligations: MFN and Transparency

Two major "general obligations" of the GATS are the MFN principle and "transparency," which were discussed in the introduction. A country is required to honor a general obligation for *all* services sectors regardless of whether it has included a particular sector in its schedule of commitments. However, subject to certain conditions, the GATS allows a country to take exemptions from the general MFN obligation. The United States, as discussed earlier, took a broad MFN exemption for financial services. No exemptions are permitted from the transparency requirement.

Specific Commitments: Market Access and National Treatment

In the GATS, market access and national treatment are "specific commitments" as opposed to general obligations. As a result, national treatment and market access do not apply across-the-board to all services sectors; instead, they apply only to sectors, subsectors, or activities that are listed in a country's schedule of commitments. The use of specific commitments for market access and national treatment instead of general obligations applicable to all services sectors is widely regarded as a structural weakness of the GATS. This weakness is usually discussed in terms of the associated scheduling techniques—the so-called "hybrid list" approach used in the GATS and the "negative list" approach that had been advocated by the United States.

Table 2.
Negative Lists and GATS Hybrid Lists;
Applicability of Market Access and National Treatment

Scheduling technique	Approach	Coverage of unlisted sectors/ subsectors/activities/measures
Negative list	General obligations of market access and national treatment apply to all services sectors except for nonconforming measures listed	Market access and national treatment apply
GATS hybrid list Positive list of sectors/subsectors/ activities	Commitments to market access and national treatment undertaken only for sectors/subsectors/ activities	Market access and national treatment do not apply
Negative list of limitations	For each sector/subsector/ activity listed, market access and national treatment apply except for nonconforming measures listed or for "unbound" modes of supply	Market access and national treatment apply only within listed sector/subsector/ activity

Negative versus Hybrid Lists.   If market access and national treatment were general obligations applicable to all services sectors, a negative list of exceptions or "top-down" approach could be used for scheduling.   Under this approach, all "nonconforming measure"—that is, measures that do not conform to the principles of market access and national treatment—must be listed as limitations in a country's schedule of commitments. As a result, for all sectors, market access and national treatment apply to all measures *not* listed in a country's schedule (see table 2). For example, in the banking subsector, if a country prohibited branches of foreign banks from taking domestic deposits and wished to continue to do so without violating its GATS obligations, it would need to inscribe that limitation in its schedule. The only nonconforming measures that would not need to be listed are those covered by specific public policy exceptions such as national security or, in the case of financial services, prudential regulation and supervision.

Beginning in mid-1989, the United States, with initial support from the European Community, pushed hard for a negative list approach in the GATS. However, this initiative faced strong opposition from emerging market economies and other developing countries fearful of undertaking general obligations that would be binding across all services sectors subject only to specified exceptions. These countries also noted that they did not have the administrative resources and the research capability necessary to determine the exceptions they would want to take under a negative list approach.

They pointed out that the so-called "positive lists"—where the only commitments being made are explicitly listed—would be much easier to construct and urged use of such a "bottom-up" approach. Although discussions continued for more than a year, developing countries remained adamantly opposed to general obligations and negative lists. With time seemingly running out—the Uruguay Round was supposed to terminate in December 1990—the Untied States agreed to accept a hybrid approach for scheduling as a compromise.

The Hybrid list approach used in the GATS relies on both positive and negative lists (see table 2). It requires a positive list of sectors or subsectors; that is, commitments to market access and national treatment are undertaken only for sectors or subsectors listed. However, for financial services, some countries used such narrow subsectors—for example, "acceptance of deposits and other repayable funds from the public"—that the portions of their schedules devoted to financial services are, in effect, detailed lists of activities. *Within* each sector, subsector, or activity, a negative list approach is used; that is, limitations on market access and national treatment must be listed. Such limitations include nonconforming measures, as is customary under a negative list approach. However, the practice under the GATS is to schedule commitments separately for each mode of supply, which means that the limitations may also include one of more modes of supply. For example, by entering the term "unbound," a country could avoid making any commitments for an entire mode of supply.

It is, of course, technically possible to construct a negative list and a hybrid list that produce the same result in terms of reduction or removal of restrictions on market access and national treatment. However, for trade in services, the two approaches are qualitatively different. Most important, negative lists provide an inventory of all remaining barriers in all sectors and are therefore much more transparent than hybrid lists, under which no accounting of barriers is provided for unlisted sectors or for "unbound" modes of supply. As a result, negative lists can facilitate future liberalization, both in international negotiations and in the domestic political process. Moreover, negative lists make possible—and are normally accompanied by—an across-the-board "standstill" obligation, which precludes new measures inconsistent with market access and national treatment in all sectors. In addition, negative lists can significantly affect the dynamics of the negotiations by putting a burden on countries to inscribe exceptions to liberalization in their schedules, since "silence" means adherence to market access and national treatment in all sectors. Because of these advantages, negative lists are used in the OECD framework of obligations and in the NAFTA, where market access and national treatment are, in effect, general obligations.

Absence of a Standstill. The absence of a standstill is another major weakness in the structure of the GATS. Although an across-the-board standstill obligation applicable to all sectors requires a negative list approach, a standstill could nevertheless be superimposed on the hybrid list approach in the sense that it would apply to the sectors, subsectors, or activities listed in a country's schedule of commitments. Within each listed sector, subsector, or activity, the only permissible limitations would be *existing* nonconforming measures; entire modes of supply could not be excluded. However, during the negotiations, emerging market economies and other developing countries made clear that a services agreement that included a standstill provision would be unacceptable to them. As a result, the GATS allows a country to introduce new barriers to market access and national treatment and continue to benefit form the openness provided by other parties to the agreement.

In the absence of a standstill, some countries scheduled commitments in financial services that are more restrictive than measures currently in force. Suppose, for example, a host country currently allows foreign banks to have 60 percent ownership positions in domestic financial firms. By making a binding commitment guaranteeing an ownership position of only 40 percent, the country retains the option of restricting foreign ownership positions to that level. Indeed, one emerging market country made clear its intention—subsequently enacted into law—to require divestiture of *existing* majority-ownership positions by foreign insurance companies. Such a measure violated the principle of "grandfathering" existing operations and activities. This principle, which is also referred to as guaranteeing the retention of "acquired rights," is often accepted as a basis for national policies dealing with foreign direct investment in the financial sector.

Commitments beyond Market Access and National Treatment. The GATS provides an opportunity for countries to make additional commitments that go beyond market access and national treatment. Accordingly, besides the columns for market access and national treatment, the schedules contain a column entitled "additional commitments" for liberalization involving nonquantitative and nondiscriminatory structural barriers. To date, this column has been used mainly for the procompetitive regulatory principles agreed in the telecommunications sector. For financial services, the additional commitments column has almost never been used. However, if, for example, Japan decides to incorporate into its GATS financial services schedule the commitments it made in bilateral U.S.-Japan agreements covering insurance and other financial services, it might prefer to list those commitments in the column for additional commitments, since they address barriers that are technically, not denials of market access or national treatment.

Special Provision for Financial Services

The Annex on Financial Services and the Understanding on Commitments in Financial Services, already mentioned, contain provisions specific to financial services. These provisions emerged from a text originally developed by an informal group of finance officials from Canada, the European Community, Japan, Sweden, Switzerland, and the United States. This group had initially gathered to discuss how financial services should be handled in the GATS and was known as the "Fu Lung group" after the restaurant where its first meeting was held in September 1989.

In 1990, the Fu Lung group was broadened to include selected Asian, Eastern European, and Latin American countries, with the result that the interests of nearly 40 countries were represented. However, upon completion of a text for a proposed financial services annex in the autumn of 1990, the emerging market economies, led by Mexico, suddenly and unexpectedly withdrew. In December 1990 at the beginning of the ministerial meeting in Brussels that was supposed to conclude the Uruguay Round, a slightly revised version of the Fu Lung text—the so-called "four-country text"—was formally submitted by Canada, Japan, Sweden, and Switzerland to the committee overseeing the Uruguay Round negotiations.

Trade negotiators used two ideas from the Fu Lung text to strengthen the GATS framework agreement. First, they expanded the scope of the general obligation of transparency to include administrative measures in addition to statutes and regulations. Second, they clarified the definition of national treatment to emphasize the importance of the conditions of competition, regardless of whether treatment of foreign services or service suppliers is formally identical to or formally different from that of domestic services or service suppliers.

Provisions on which only the industrial countries could agree, which had formed an optional second section of the Fu Lung text, became the Understanding on Commitments in Financial Services. The remaining provisions of the Fu Lung text became the Annex on Financial Services. Initially, finance officials from the United States had envisaged the Fu Lung text as a financial services agreement separate from the GATS framework agreement. However, the idea of a separate agreement for financial services was unacceptable to trade officials, both in the United States and other countries. It was also opposed by finance officials in some countries and by the U.S. financial services industry.

Understanding on Commitments in Financial Services

For the financial services schedules of the countries that use it, the Understanding on Commitments in Financial Services addresses the structural weaknesses of the GATS and thus offers an approach that would have been desirable, but was not achievable, in the framework agreement.   Countries that choose to schedule commitments in accordance with the Understanding undertake commitments to market access and national treatment—under the framework agreement as supplemented by the Understanding—for all financial services subsectors and use a negative list approach to scheduling. The Understanding also contains a standstill, thereby limiting exceptions to existing nonconforming measures. Countries using the Understanding retained mode of supply as a scheduling technique. Although a standstill would normally preclude taking an exception for a mode of supply, countries using the Understanding retained the flexibility to conform their commitments regarding temporary entry of natural persons to those set forth in their so-called horizontal commitments applicable to all services sectors.

As regards market access, the Understanding supplements the framework agreement's list of prohibited measures by setting forth a broad commitment to the right of establishment or expansion of a commercial presence. However, the Understanding's provision regarding cross-border services is designed to facilitate a narrower commitment for this mode of supply, reflecting in part the concerns of financial regulators in a number of countries. For example, the U.S. Securities and Exchange Commission (SEC) does not allow soliciting from abroad for securities that are not registered in the United States or, absent an exemption, for mutual funds not registered in the United States. As regards national treatment, the Understanding relies on the definition in the framework agreement, but clarifies its application in the financial services sector with regard to both payment and clearing systems and self-regulatory bodies.

For nonquantitative and nondiscriminatory structural barriers, the Understanding includes a "best-efforts" undertaking to remove or limit any significant adverse effect. It also states that this understanding does not endorse reverse discrimination against domestic service providers. The Understanding deals separately with one type of nondiscriminatory structural barrier, namely, barriers to the provision of new services. The Understanding requires each host country to allow an office of a foreign financial firm to offer "any new financial service," defined as a financial service already being supplied in another country but not in the host country. The purpose of this provision, which was strongly supported by the U.S. financial services industry, is to allow innovative products introduced by financial institution in their home countries—and approved by the relevant home-country authorities—also to be introduced by their offices in other countries. However, the scope of the provision appears to be relatively narrow.

Annex on Financial Services

The prudential carve-out mentioned in the introduction to this paper is contained in the Annex on Financial Services. Other provision in the Annex deal with dispute settlement, recognition of prudential measures in other countries, and the coverage and definition of financial services.

Prudential Carve-Out.   The prudential carve-out for domestic regulation permits a country to take prudential measures "for the protection of investors, depositors, policy holders or persons to whom a fiduciary duty is owed," or "to ensure the integrity and stability of the financial system" regardless of any other provisions of the GATS. This provision may not, however, be used to avoid a country's obligations and commitments under the agreement.

Disagreement over whether a particular national measure falls within the prudential carve-out is subject to WTO dispute settlement procedures and thus, if necessary, to a determination by a dispute settlement panel.   However, most regulators do not appear to be particularly concerned about this possibility.   For one thing, if a country is concerned that a particular measure might not be generally accepted as prudential in the future, it could list the measure as an exception in its initial schedule of commitments.   Indeed, some countries may have been too cautious in this regard.   That is, they may have taken exceptions for measures that are clearly prudential, for example, requirements for applications by foreign financial firms to set up host-country offices.   For another, if a prudential issue reaches dispute settlement, the panel will have appropriate financial services expertise, as discussed below.   In addition, only governments—not private parties—may bring claims to dispute settlement, and, absent a truly egregious action, governments may prefer to respect each other's ability to determine which rules are prudential.

Dispute Settlement.   Ensuring financial services expertise in the handling of disputes involving financial services was another issue of particular concern to financial services regulators.   Indeed, at one point, financial official from the major industrial countries were pushing the idea of a separate body for settlement of disputes involving financial services, an idea that trade officials found unacceptable.   Ultimately, the concerns of financial officials were addressed by inserting a requirement in the Annex that dispute settlement panels on prudential issues and other financial matters must have the expertise necessary to deal with "the specific financial service under dispute."   This standard is more narrowly drawn than the general standard applicable to the GATS, which requires panels to have the "necessary expertise relevant to the specific services sectors which the dispute concerns."

Another aspect of dispute settlement of concern to financial officials was the possibility of cross-sector retaliation against financial services.   Such retaliation would involve a suspension by one country of concessions for financial service providers from an offending country in accordance with a ruling by a dispute settlement panel involving a controversy in a different sector.   Because of concern that such retaliation could disrupt the smooth functioning of the financial system, some finance officials advocated an asymmetric provision whereby retaliation in another sector would be allowed for disputes involving financial services but not the reverse. The approach that was adopted in the new WTO dispute settlement mechanism requires that a country first seek to retaliate with respect to the sector in which the violation was found. If that is not practical or effective, the party may retaliate in other sectors covered by the same agreement—for example, in the case of GATS, other services sectors. As a final resort, a party is allowed to retaliate in any sector covered by any Uruguay Round agreement, for example, in a services sector for a goods dispute, or vice-versa.

Recognition of Prudential Measures. The Annex allows a country to recognize prudential measures of selected other countries—either unilaterally or through a negotiated arrangement or agreement—without such a step being challenged by excluded countries as a denial of MFN treatment. A country must, however, be willing to accord similar recognition to measures of other countries that meet the same standards. Despite the prudential carve-out, finance officials from the industrial countries considered this provision necessary to ensure that arrangements such as the multijurisdictional disclosure systems (MJDS) adopted by the U.S. Securities and Exchange Commission (SEC) and by securities regulators in Ontario and Québec would be immune from MFN challenges under the GATS. In effect, the recognition provision in the Annex elaborates on the application to the financial services sector of a "mutual recognition" provision in the framework agreement that allows a country to recognize standards or licensing or certification requirements of selected countries without being subject to the MFN obligation of the GATS.

Coverage and Definition of Financial Services. The Annex defines a financial service as any service of a financial nature offered by a financial service supplier of a WTO member and provides a nonexclusive list of financial services. If a firm supplies any one of the listed services, it falls within the GATS definition of a financial service supplier and can benefit from the GATS regime for financial services. The list is product-based, that is, it enumerates various types of banking and other financial services as well as insurance and insurance-related services. It includes instruments such as derivatives and appears to be sufficiently broad to encompass new instruments. The definitions section of the Annex also clarifies that the exclusion from GATS coverage for services supplied in the exercise of governmental authority applies to activities of central banks or monetary authorities in pursuit of monetary or exchange rate policies.

In December 1997, a final agreement was reached, and the United States joined in, removing the broad most-favored nation exemption it had previously taken. The Asian financial crisis contributed to this result, since many of the countries resisting market opening, like South Korea, now had less choice if they wanted IMF assistance. Reaching an agreement does not, of course, mean that markets are open. It only means that the 102 countries involved have all made commitments of various kinds. In November 2001, the WTO members authorized a new round of trade negotiations, the so-called Doha round, which will once again include financial services.

Notes and Questions

1. If the U.S. had failed to reach any multilateral agreement, it would have been left with its own unilateral policies or bilateral agreements such as the one with Japan. Up until the present, the U.S. has largely had an open market (although we have seen there are many conditions placed on that openness) which grants unconditional national treatment (and sometimes even better than national treatment). However, there have been proposals to change this policy.

The Fair Trade in Financial Services Act of 1995 (H.R. 19) (FTFS) sponsored by Mr. Leach, the Chairman of the House Banking and Financial Services Committee took the following approach.

It defined "national treatment" as granting "the same competitive opportunities (including effective market access) in such country as are available to the foreign country's domestic banking, securities, or insurance organizations in like circumstances."

The bill required the Secretary of the Treasury to determine whether possible denial of national treatment by a foreign country may be having a significant adverse affect on U.S. financial institutions, and enumerates the following factors the Secretary should consider in reaching this conclusion with respect to banking:

(A) The extent of United States trade with and investment in the foreign country, the size of the foreign country's markets for the financial services involved, and the extent to which United States banking organizations operate or seek to operate in those markets.

(B) The importance of operations by United States banking organizations in the foreign country to the export of goods and services by United States firms to such country.

(C) The extent to which the foreign country provides in advance to United States banking organizations a written draft of any measure of general application that the country proposes to adopt, such as regulations, guidelines, or other policies regarding new products and services, in order to allow an opportunity for such organizations to comment on the measure and for such comments to be taken into account by the foreign country.

(D) The extent to which the foreign country-

(i) Makes available, in writing, to United States banking organizations the foreign country's requirements for completing any application relating to the provision of financial services by any such organization;

(ii) Applies published objective standards and criteria in evaluating any such application from any United States banking organization; and

(iii) Renders administrative decisions relating to any such application within a reasonable period of time.

Once the Secretary determined that another country failed to grant national treatment, he was required to open negotiations (or any process called for by bilateral or multilateral treaties, if applicable) with the country to ensure such treatment, absent giving a notice to the Congress that negotiations would be unlikely to lead to progress or would impair the economic interests of the United States.

The Secretary could also recommend to federal bank regulators, after consultation with other key cabinet officials and those regulators, that pending applications by institutions from the offending country be suspended or denied (sanctions), if he determined that such action would assist the United States in its negotiations or if the country has not adhered to any negotiated agreement. Regulators were required to act in accord with the Secretary's recommendation unless a written finding was made that such action would have a serious adverse effect on the U.S. financial or payment system, or would interfere with a foreign bank acquiring a failed U.S. bank.

Existing operations of foreign banks would not have been affected. In addition, under a "reciprocal grandfather exemption," sanctions could not be applied to a U.S. subsidiary of foreign bank, established before December 31, 1994, if the foreign bank's country explicitly provided, as of that date, national treatment to bank subsidiaries of U.S. banks (and their subsidiaries) in that country.

What do you think of the FTFS national treatment standard as compared with other more traditional definitions, such as de jure national treatment, which bans formal discriminatory barriers, e.g. prohibiting foreign banks from taking retail deposits in a country, or de facto national treatment, which looks at whether there is actual as compared to formal discrimination? How would the U.S. fare if other countries were to apply the FTFS standard to the U.S.?

2. Is it more difficult to negotiate removal of regulatory barriers than to reduce tariffs due to the lack of a price mechanism for regulation?

There were no cross-sector negotiations in GATS. Why do you think this was the case and was it a good approach?

3. Under the GATS, the U.S. has agreed to preserve its open markets. In exchange, it has received commitments from other countries to increase the openness of their markets, but the opening in emerging markets falls far short of that in the United States. Is this a good deal? Did it overcome the free rider problem that originally led the U.S. to take a broad MFN exemption?

4. One very significant aspect of the GATS is that many countries agreed to bind existing levels of trade liberalization. This means that these countries cannot in the future unilaterally adopt new restrictive measures. One of the last minute issues in the December 1997 negotiations was whether Japan would bind in the GATS the commitments it had made in bilateral financial service agreements with the United States, which it agreed to do. See S. Key, *GATS 2000: Issues For The Financial Services Negotiations,* Draft of May 23, 2000 (Key). Thus, the achievements of GATS cannot simply be measured by determining the degree to which additional liberalization was achieved.

5. The GATS requires WTO members not to impose restrictions on capital transactions or associated payments or transfers that would be inconsistent with specific liberalization commitments, subject to a balance-of-payments safeguard which permits temporary restrictions. GATS art. XII. See Key supra. As we shall see in Chapter 22, the use of capital controls has become more popular in the wake of the Asian crisis. Are the imposition of such controls inconsistent with liberalization of trade in financial services? Some commentators who advocate such controls, have urged that WTO, with its free-trade bias, may not be the appropriate forum for negotiating freer trade in financial services. A. Steinherr and E. Perée, *How Strong is the Case for Free Trade in Financial Services? Walking the Tightrope between Domestic Stability and International Shocks,* 22 World Economy 1221 (1999).

E. U.S. BANKS ABROAD

The United States has an interest in controlling the activities of U.S. banks abroad. Obviously, bank solvency can be affected by foreign as well as domestic losses. Subpart A of Regulation K governs the activities of U.S. banks and bank holding companies abroad. A few important points about this regime. First, foreign branches of U.S. banks are given some powers abroad that they do not have at home, §211.3 (not in Supplement), in order to be able to compete with domestic banks. In some countries only banks can engage in certain activities, as compared with affiliates. Thus, it would not avail U.S. banks abroad if U.S. regulators would only allow the activities to be conducted in the holding company.

Second, there are a range of vehicles through which U.S. banks can carry on activities abroad, §211.5, for example, through branches, non-banking subsidiaries of the holding company, banking subsidiaries of the holding company or banking subsidiaries of the domestic bank. Complicated rules determine which vehicle can conduct which activities, but the rules are generally consistent with the principle of allocating activities regarded as more risky or less traditional to the vehicle whose losses would have less direct impact on the domestic bank. The risk order (most risk first) would be: (1) branch; (2) domestic bank subsidiaries; and (3) foreign bank or non-bank subsidiaries of the holding company. Under the proposed amendments to Regulation J, 62 Federal Register 68424 (December 31, 1997), the authority of well capitalized U.S. banking organizations to engage in equity securities underwriting and dealing outside the United States would be expanded.

Third, there are procedures for obtaining consent from the Federal Reserve Board to engage in various activities abroad. The Board now grants a "general consent" to strongly capitalized and well-managed banking organizations to make aggregate investments abroad in a 12-month period up to certain percentages of their capital without prior notice or application in certain defined investments. If investments do not fall within general consent, specific notice and application procedures must be followed. 60 Federal Register 67050 (1995).

Note

Should the United States assume the mantle of global regulator? Consider the case in which Manhattan District Attorney, Robert M. Morgenthau, successfully prosecuted three Venezuelans for scheming to defraud other Venezuelans of millions of dollars. The only connection with the United States is that the scheme involved use of the U.S. payment system through the sending of dollar wire transfers and payment of dollar checks. No one in the U.S. was injured by the fraud. See W. Glaberson, *Morgenthau's Prosecution of Venezuelans Raises Eyebrows*, N.Y. Times, February 13, 1997; New York Daily News, April 11, 1997.

Links to Other Chapters

This Chapter examines U.S. regulation of the international aspects of its banking markets. We look at how the European Union approaches this matter in Chapter 5 and how the Japanese do so in Chapter 8. The idea and importance of capital adequacy for international banks was dealt with in this Chapter, but our next Chapter gets into the details. Much of the concern over bank failure is related to systemic risk. A big area of systemic risk is in the payments system which we examine in depth in Chapter 10. Also, to a great extent, the current concern with the risks of derivatives, dealt with in Chapters 16 and 17, is based on a fear of bank failure, and systemic risk. Vehicles for international cooperation are discussed in many of these chapters.

STATUTORY SUPPLEMENT TO CHAPTER THREE
International Banking Act of 1978, as amended
12 U.S.C. §3101 et. seq.

Short title; definitions and rules of construction

SEC. 1(a) This Act may be cited as the "International Banking Act of 1978"

(b) For the purposes of this Act

(1) "agency" means any office or any place of business of a foreign bank located in any State of the United States at which credit balances are maintained incidental to or arising out of the exercise of banking powers, checks are paid, or money is lent but at which deposits may not be accepted from citizens or residents of the United States;

(2) "Board" means the Board of Governors of the Federal Reserve System;

(3) "branch" means any office or any place of business of a foreign bank located in any State of the United States at which deposits are received;

(4) "Comptroller" means the Comptroller of the Currency;

(5) "Federal agency" means an agency of a foreign bank established and operating under section 4 of this Act;

(6) "Federal branch" means a branch of a foreign bank established and operating under section 4 of this Act;

(7) "foreign bank" means any company organized under the laws of a foreign country, a territory of the United States, Puerto Rico, Guam, American Samoa, or the Virgin Islands, which engages in the business of banking, or any subsidiary or affiliate, organized under such laws, of any such company. For the purposes of this Act the term "foreign bank" includes, without limitation, foreign commercial banks, foreign merchant banks and other foreign institutions that engage in banking activities usual in connection with the business of banking in the countries where such foreign institutions are organized or operating;

(8) "foreign country" means any country other than the United States, and includes any colony, dependency, or possession of any such country;

(9) "commercial lending company" means any institution, other than a bank or an organization operating under section 25 of the Federal Reserve Act, organized under the laws of any State of the United States, or the District of Columbia which maintains credit balances incidental to or arising out of the exercise of banking powers and engages in the business of making commercial loans;

(10) "State" means any State of the United States or the District of Columbia;

(11) "State agency" means an agency of a foreign bank established and operating under the laws of any State;

(12) "State branch" means a branch of a foreign bank established and operating under the laws of any State;

(13) the terms "affiliate," "bank," "bank holding company," "company," "control" and "subsidiary" have the same meanings assigned to those terms in the Bank Holding Company Act of 1956, and the terms "controlled" and "controlling" shall be construed consistently with the term "control" as defined in section 2 of the Bank Holding Company Act of 1956;

(14) "consolidated" means consolidated in accordance with generally accepted accounting principles in the United States consistently applied; and

(15) the term "representative office" means any office of a foreign bank which is located in any State and is not a Federal branch, Federal agency, State branch, or State agency;

(16) the term "office" means any branch, agency, or representative office; and

.   .   .

Establishment of Federal branches
and agencies by foreign bank
Approval of Comptroller

SEC. 4(a) ESTABLISHMENT AND OPERATION OF FEDERAL BRANCHES AND AGENCIES.—

(1) INITIAL FEDERAL BRANCH OR AGENCY.—Except as provided in section 5, a foreign bank which engages directly in a banking business outside the United States may, with the approval of the Comptroller, establish one or more Federal branches or agencies in any State in which (1) it is not operating a branch or agency pursuant to State law and (2) the establishment of a branch or agency, as the case may be, by a foreign bank is not prohibited by State law.

(2) BOARD CONDITIONS REQUIRED TO BE INCLUDED.—In considering any application for approval under this subsection, the Comptroller of the Currency shall include any condition imposed by the Board under section 7(d)(5) as a condition for the approval of such application by the agency.

(b) RULES AND REGULATIONS; RIGHTS AND PRIVILEGES; DUTIES AND LIABILITIES; EXCEPTIONS.—In establishing and operating a Federal branch or agency, a foreign bank shall be subject to such rules, regulations, and orders as the Comptroller considers appropriate to carry out this section, which shall include provisions for service of process and maintenance of branch and agency accounts separate from those of the parent bank.   Except as otherwise specifically provided in this Act or in rules, regulations, or orders adopted by the Comptroller under this section, operations of a foreign bank at a Federal branch or agency shall be conducted with the same rights and privileges as a national bank at the same location and shall be subject to all the same duties, restrictions, penalties, liabilities, conditions, and limitations that would apply under the National Bank Act to a national bank doing business at the same location except that (1) any limitation or restriction based on the capital stock and surplus of a national bank shall be deemed to refer, as applied to a Federal branch or agency, to the dollar equivalent of the capital stock and surplus of the foreign bank and if the foreign bank has more than one Federal branch or agency the business transacted by all such branches and agencies shall be aggregated in determining compliance with the limitation; (2) a Federal branch or agency shall not be required to become a member bank, as that term is defined in section 1 of the Federal Reserve Act; and (3) a Federal agency shall not be required to become an insured bank as that term is defined in section 3(h) of the Federal Deposit Insurance Act.   The Comptroller of the Currency shall coordinate examinations of Federal branches and agencies of foreign banks with examinations conducted by the Board under section 7(c)(1) and, to the extent possible, shall participate in any simultaneous examinations of the United States operations of a foreign bank requested by the Board under such section.

(c) APPLICATION TO ESTABLISH FEDERAL BRANCH OR AGENCY; MATTERS CONSIDERED.–In acting on any application to establish a federal branch or agency, the Comptroller shall take into account the effects of the proposal on competition in the domestic and foreign commerce of the United States, the financial and managerial resources and future prospects of the applicant foreign bank and the branch or agency, and the convenience and needs of the community to be served.

(d) RECEIPT OF DEPOSITS AND EXERCISING OF FIDUCIARY POWERS AT FEDERAL AGENCY PROHIBITED.–Notwithstanding any other provision of this section, a foreign bank shall not receive deposits or exercise fiduciary powers at any Federal agency.   A foreign bank may, however, maintain at a Federal agency for the account of others credit balances incidental to, or arising out of, the exercise of its lawful powers.

(e) MAINTENANCE OF FEDERAL BRANCH AND FEDERAL AGENCY IN SAME STATE PROHIBITED.–No foreign bank may maintain both a Federal branch and a Federal agency in the same state.

(f) CONVERSION OF FOREIGN BANK BRANCH, AGENCY OR COMMERCIAL LENDING COMPANY INTO FEDERAL BRANCH OR AGENCY, APPROVAL OF COMPTROLLER.–Any branch or agency operated by a foreign bank in a State pursuant to State law and any commercial lending company controlled by a foreign bank may be converted into a Federal branch or agency with the approval of the Comptroller. In the event of any conversion pursuant to this subsection, all of the liabilities of such foreign bank previously payable at the State branch or agency, or all of the liabilities of the commercial lending company, shall thereafter be payable by such foreign bank at the branch or agency established under this subsection.

(g) DEPOSIT REQUIREMENTS; ASSET REQUIREMENTS.–(1) upon the opening of a Federal branch or agency in any State and thereafter, a foreign bank, in addition to any deposit requirements imposed under section 6 of this Act, shall keep on deposit, in accordance with such rules and regulations as the Comptroller may prescribe, with a member bank designated by such foreign bank, dollar deposits or investment securities of the type that may be held by national banks for their own accounts pursuant to paragraph "Seventh" of section 5136 of the Revised Statutes, as amended, in an amount as hereinafter set forth. Such depository bank shall be located in the State where such branch or agency is located and shall be approved by the Comptroller if it is a national bank and by the Board of Governors of the Federal Reserve System if it is a State Bank.

(2) The aggregate amount of deposited investment securities (calculated on the basis of principal amount or market value, whichever is lower) and dollar deposits for each branch or agency established and operating under this section shall be not less than the greater of (1) that amount of capital (but not surplus) which would be required of a national bank being organized at this location, or (2) 5 per centum of the total liabilities of such branch or agency, including acceptances, but excluding (A) accrued expenses, and (B) amounts due and other liabilities to offices, branches, agencies, and subsidiaries of such foreign bank. The Comptroller may require that the assets deposited pursuant to this subsection shall be maintained in such amounts as he may from time to time deem necessary or desirable, for the maintenance of a sound financial condition, the protection of depositors, and the public interest, but such additional amount shall in no event be greater than would be required to conform to generally accepted banking practices as manifested by banks in the area in which the branch or agency is located.

(3) The deposit shall be maintained with any such member bank pursuant to a deposit agreement in such form and containing such limitations and conditions as the Comptroller may prescribe. So long as it continues business in the ordinary course such foreign bank shall, however, be permitted to collect income on the securities and funds so deposited and from time to time examine and exchange such securities.

(4) Subject to such conditions and requirements as may be prescribed by the Comptroller, each foreign bank shall hold in each

State in which it has a Federal branch or agency, assets of such types and in such amount as the Comptroller may prescribe by general or specific regulation or ruling as necessary or desirable for the maintenance of a sound financial condition, the protection of depositors, creditors and the public interest. In determining compliance with any such prescribed asset requirements, the Comptroller shall give credit to (A) assets required to be maintained pursuant to paragraphs (1) and (2) of this subsection (B) reserves required to be maintained pursuant to section 7(a) of this Act, and (C) assets pledged, and surety bonds payable, to the Federal Deposit Insurance Corporation to secure the payment of domestic deposits. The Comptroller may prescribe different asset requirements for branches or agencies in different States, in order to ensure competitive equality of Federal branches and agencies with State branches and agencies and domestic banks in those States.

(h) ESTABLISHMENT OF ADDITIONAL BRANCHES OR AGENCIES; APPROVAL OF COMPTROLLER.—ADDITIONAL BRANCHES OR AGENCIES.—

(1) APPROVAL OF AGENCY REQUIRED.—A foreign bank with a Federal branch or agency operating in any State may (A) with the prior approval of the Comptroller establish and operate additional branches or agencies in the State in which such branch or agency is located on the same terms and conditions and subject to the same limitations and restrictions as are applicable to the establishment of branches by a national bank if the principal office of such national bank were located at the same place as the initial branch or agency in such State of such foreign bank and (B) change the designation of its initial branch or agency to any other branch or agency subject to the same limitations and restrictions as are applicable to a change in the designation of the principal office of a national bank if such principal office were located at the same place as such initial branch or agency.

(2) NOTICE TO AND COMMENT BY BOARD.—The Comptroller of the Currency shall provide the Board with notice and an opportunity for comment on any application to establish an additional Federal branch or Federal Agency under this subsection.

(i) TERMINATION OF AUTHORITY TO OPERATE FEDERAL BRANCH OR AGENCY.—Authority to operate a Federal branch or agency shall terminate when the parent foreign bank voluntarily relinquishes it or when such parent foreign bank is dissolved or its authority or existence is otherwise terminated or canceled in the country of its organization. If (1) at any time the Comptroller is of the opinion or has reasonable cause to believe that such foreign bank has violated or failed to comply with any of the provisions of this section or any of the rules, regulations, or orders of the Comptroller made pursuant to this section, or (2) a conservator is appointed for such foreign bank or a similar proceeding is initiated in the foreign bank's country of organization, the Comptroller shall have the power, after opportunity for hearing, to revoke the foreign bank's authority to operate a Federal branch or agency. The Comptroller may, in his discretion, deny such opportunity for hearing if he determines such denial to be in the public interest. The Comptroller may restore any such authority upon due proof of compliance with the provisions of this section and the rules, regulations, or orders of the Comptroller made pursuant to this section.

(j) RECEIVERSHIP OVER ASSETS OF FOREIGN BANK IN UNITED STATES.—(1) Whenever the Comptroller revokes a foreign bank's authority to operate a Federal branch or agency or whenever any creditor of any such foreign bank shall have obtained a judgment against it arising out of a transaction with a Federal branch or agency in any court of record of the United States or any State of the United States and made application, accompanied by a certificate from the clerk of the court stating that such judgment has been rendered and has remained unpaid for the space of thirty days, or whenever the Comptroller shall become satisfied that such foreign bank is insolvent, he may, after due consideration of its affairs, in any such case, appoint a receiver who shall take possession of all the property and assets of such foreign bank in the United States and exercise the same rights, privileges, powers, and authority with respect thereto as are now exercised by receivers of national banks appointed by the Comptroller.

(2) In any receivership proceeding ordered pursuant to this subsection (j), whenever there has been paid to each and every depositor and creditor of such foreign bank whose claim or claims shall have been proved or allowed, the full amount of such claims arising out of transactions had by them with any branch or agency of such foreign bank located in any State of the United States, except (A) claims that would not represent an enforceable legal obligation against such branch or agency if such branch or agency were a separate legal entity, and (B) amounts due and other liabilities to other offices or branches or agencies of, and wholly owned (except for a nominal number of directors' shares) subsidiaries of, such foreign bank, and all expenses of the receivership, the Comptroller or the Federal Deposit Insurance Corporation, where that Corporation has been appointed receiver of the foreign bank, shall turn over the remainder, if any, of the assets and proceeds of such foreign bank to the head office of such foreign bank, or to the duly appointed domiciliary liquidator or receiver of such foreign bank.

Interstate banking by foreign banks

SEC. 5(a) INTERSTATE BRANCHING AND AGENCY OPERATIONS.—

(1) FEDERAL BRANCH OR AGENCY.—Subject to the provisions of this Act and with the prior written approval by the Board and the Comptroller of the Currency of an application, a foreign bank may establish and operate a Federal branch or agency in any State

outside the home State of such foreign bank to the extent that the establishment and operation of such branch would be permitted under section 5155(g) of the Revised Statutes or section 44 of the Federal Deposit Insurance Act if the foreign bank were a national bank whose home State is the same State as the home State of the foreign bank.

(2) STATE BRANCH OR AGENCY.–Subject to the provisions of this Act and with the prior written approval by the Board and the appropriate State bank supervisor of an application, a foreign bank may establish and operate a State branch or agency in any State outside the home State of such foreign bank to the extent that such establishment and operation would be permitted under section 18(d)(4) or 44 of the Federal Deposit Insurance Act if the foreign bank were a State bank whose home State is the same State as the home State of the foreign bank.

(3) CRITERIA FOR DETERMINATION.–In approving an application under paragraph (1) or (2), the Board and (in the case of an application under paragraph (1)) the Comptroller of the Currency–

(A) shall apply the standards applicable to the establishment of a foreign bank office in the United States under section 7(d);

(B) may not approve an application unless the Board and (in the case of an application under paragraph (1)) the Comptroller of the Currency–

(i) determine that the foreign bank's financial resources, including the capital level of the bank, are equivalent to those required for a domestic bank to be approved for branching under section 5155 of the Revised Statutes and section 44 of the Federal Deposit Insurance Act; and

(ii) consult with the Secretary of the Treasury regarding capital equivalency; and

(C) shall apply the same requirements and conditions to which an application for an interstate merger transaction is subject under paragraphs (1), (3), and (4) of section 44(b) of the Federal Deposit Insurance Act.

(4) OPERATION.–Subsections (c) and (d)(2) of section 44 of the Federal Deposit Insurance Act shall apply with respect to each branch and agency of a foreign bank which is established and operated pursuant to an application approved under this subsection in the same manner and to the same extent such provisions of such section apply to a domestic branch of a national or State bank (as such terms are defined in section 3 of such Act) which resulted from a merger transaction under such section 44.

(5) EXCLUSIVE AUTHORITY FOR ADDITIONAL BRANCHES.–Except as provided in this section, a foreign bank may not, directly or indirectly,

acquire, establish, or operate a branch or agency in any State other than the home State of such bank.

(6) REQUIREMENT FOR A SEPARATE SUBSIDIARY.—If the Board or the Comptroller of the Currency, taking into account differing regulatory or accounting standards, finds that adherence by a foreign bank to capital requirements equivalent to those imposed under section 5155 of the Revised Statutes and section 44 of the Federal Deposit Insurance Act could be verified only if the banking activities of such bank in the United States are carried out in a domestic banking subsidiary within the United States, the Board and (in the case of an application under paragraph (1)) the Comptroller of the Currency may approve an application under paragraph (1) or (2) subject to a requirement that the foreign bank or company controlling the foreign bank establish a domestic banking subsidiary in the United States.

(7) ADDITIONAL AUTHORITY FOR INTERSTATE BRANCHES AND AGENCIES OF FOREIGN BANKS, UPGRADES OF CERTAIN FOREIGN BANK AGENCIES AND BRANCHES.—Notwithstanding paragraphs (1) and (2), a foreign bank may—

(A) with the approval of the Board and the Comptroller of the Currency, establish and operate a Federal branch or Federal agency or, with the approval of the Board and the appropriate State bank supervisor, a State branch or State agency in any State outside the foreign bank's home State if—

(i) the establishment and operation of such branch or agency is permitted by the State in which the branch or agency is to be established; and

(ii) in the case of a Federal or State branch, the branch receives only such deposits as would be permitted for a corporation organized under section 25A of the Federal Reserve Act; or

(B) with the approval of the Board and the relevant licensing authority (the Comptroller in the case of a Federal branch or the appropriate State supervisor in the case of a State branch), upgrade an agency, or a branch of the type referred to in subparagraph (A)(ii), located in a State outside the foreign bank's home State, into a Federal or State branch if—

(i) the establishment and operation of such branch is permitted by such State; and

(ii) such agency or branch—

(I) was in operation in such State on the day before September 29, 1994; or

(II) has been in operation in such State for a period of time that meets the State's minimum age requirement permitted under section 44(a)(5) of the Federal Deposit Insurance Act.

(8) CONTINUING REQUIREMENT FOR MEETING COMMUNITY CREDIT NEEDS AFTER INITIAL INTERSTATE ENTRY BY ACQUISITION.—

(A) IN GENERAL.—If a foreign bank acquires a bank or a branch of a bank, in a State in which the foreign bank does not maintain a branch, and such acquired bank is, or is part of, a regulated financial institution (as defined in section 803 of the Community Reinvestment Act of 1977), the Community Reinvestment Act of 1977 shall continue to apply to each branch of the foreign bank which results from the acquisition as if such branch were a regulated financial institution.

(B) EXCEPTION FOR BRANCH THAT RECEIVES ONLY DEPOSITS PERMISSIBLE FOR AN EDGE ACT CORPORATION.—Paragraph (1) shall not apply to any branch that receives only such deposits as are permissible for a corporation organized under section 25A of the Federal Reserve Act to receive.

(9) HOME STATE OF DOMESTIC BANK DEFINED.—For purposes of this subsection, the term 'home State' means—

(A) with respect to a national bank, the State in which the main office of the bank is located; and

(B) with respect to a State bank, the State by which the bank is chartered.

(b) CONTINUANCE OF LAWFUL INTERSTATE BANKING OPERATIONS PREVIOUSLY COMMENCED.—Unless its authority to do so is lawfully revoked otherwise than pursuant to this section, a foreign bank, notwithstanding any restriction or limitation imposed under subsection (a) of this section, may establish and operate, outside its home State, any State branch, State agency, or bank or commercial lending company subsidiary which commenced lawful operation or for which an application to commence business had been lawfully filed with the appropriate State or Federal authority, as the case may be, on or before July 27, 1978. Notwithstanding subsection (a), a foreign bank may continue to operate, after the enactment of the Riegle-Neal Interstate Banking and Branching Efficiency Act of 1994, any Federal branch, State branch, Federal agency, State agency, or commercial lending company subsidiary which such bank was operating on the day before the date of the enactment of such Act to the extent the branch agency, or subsidiary continues, after the enactment of such Act, to engage in operations which were lawful under the laws in effect on the day before such date.

(c) DETERMINATION OF HOME STATE OF FOREIGN BANK.—For the purposes of this section—

(1) in the case of a foreign bank that has any branch, agency, subsidiary commercial lending company, or subsidiary bank in more than 1 State, the home State of the foreign bank is the 1 State of

such States which is selected to be the home State by the foreign bank or, in default of any such selection, by the Board; and

(2) in the case of a foreign bank that does not have a branch, agency, subsidiary commercial lending company, or subsidiary bank in more than 1 State, the home State of the foreign bank is the State in which the foreign bank has a branch, agency, subsidiary commercial lending company, or subsidiary bank.

(d) CLARIFICATION OF BRANCHING RULES IN THE CASE OF A FOREIGN BANK WITH A DOMESTIC BANK SUBSIDIARY.—In the case of a foreign bank that has a domestic bank subsidiary within the United States—

(1) the fact that such bank controls a domestic bank shall not affect the authority of the foreign bank to establish Federal and State branches or agencies to the extent permitted under subsection (a); and

(2) the fact that the domestic bank is controlled by a foreign bank which has Federal or State branches or agencies in States other than the home State of such domestic bank shall not affect the authority of the domestic bank to establish branches outside the home State of the domestic bank to the extent permitted under section 5155(g) of the Revised Statutes or section 18(d)(4) or 44 of the Federal Deposit Insurance Act, as the case may be.

Insurance of Deposits

SEC. 6(a) OBJECTIVE.—In implementing this section, the Comptroller and the Federal Deposit Insurance Corporation shall each, by affording equal competitive opportunities to foreign and United States banking organizations in their United States operations, ensure that foreign banking organizations do not receive an unfair competitive advantage over United States banking organizations.

(b) DEPOSITS OF LESS THAN $100,000.—No foreign bank may establish or operate a Federal branch which received deposits of less than $100,000 unless the branch is an insured branch as defined in section 3(s) of the Federal Deposit Insurance Act, or unless the Comptroller determines by order or regulation that the branch is not engaged in domestic retail deposit activities requiring deposit insurance protection, taking account of the size and nature of depositors and deposit accounts.

(c) DEPOSITS REQUIRED TO BE INSURED UNDER STATE LAW.

(1) After September 17, 1978, no foreign bank may establish a branch, and after one year following such date no foreign bank may operate a branch, in any State in which the deposits of a bank organized and existing under the laws of that State would be required to be insured, unless the branch is an insured branch as defined in section 3(s) of the Federal Deposit Insurance Act, or unless the branch will not thereafter accept deposits of less than $100,000, or unless the Federal Deposit Insurance Corporation determines by

order or regulation that the branch is not engaged in domestic retail deposit activities requiring deposit insurance protection, taking account of the size and nature of depositors and deposit accounts.

(2) Notwithstanding the previous paragraph, a branch of a foreign bank in operation on September 17, 1978 which has applied for Federal deposit insurance pursuant to section 5 of the Federal Deposit Insurance Act by September 17, 1979, and has not had such application denied, may continue to accept domestic retail deposits until January 31, 1980.

(d) RETAIL DEPOSIT-TAKING BY FOREIGN BANKS.

(1) IN GENERAL.–After the date of enactment of this subsection, notwithstanding any other provision of this Act or any provision of the Federal Deposit Insurance Act, in order to accept or maintain domestic retail deposit accounts having balances of less than $100,000, and requiring deposit insurance protection, a foreign bank shall–

(A) establish 1 or more banking subsidiaries in the United States for that purpose; and

(B) obtain Federal deposit insurance for any such subsidiary in accordance with the Federal Deposit Insurance Act.

(2) EXCEPTION.–Domestic retail deposit accounts with balances of less than $100,000 that require deposit insurance protection may be accepted or maintained in a branch of a foreign bank only if such branch was an insured branch on the date of the enactment of this subsection.

(3) INSURED BANKS IN U.S. TERRITORIES.–For purposes of this subsection, the term *"foreign bank"* does not include any bank organized under the laws of any territory of the United States, Puerto Rico, Guam, American Samoa, or the Virgin Islands the deposits of which are insured by the Federal Deposit Insurance Corporation pursuant to the Federal Deposit Insurance Act.

Authority of Federal Reserve System

SEC. 7(a) BANK RESERVES.–(1)(A) Except as provided in paragraph (2) of this subsection, subsections (a), (b), (c), (d), (f), (g), (i), (j), (k), and the second sentence of subsection (e) of section 19 of the Federal Reserve Act shall apply to every Federal branch and Federal agency of a foreign bank in the same manner and to the same extent as if the Federal branch or Federal agency were a member bank as that term is defined in section 1 of the Federal Reserve Act; but the Board either by general or specific regulation or ruling may waive the minimum and maximum reserve ratios prescribed under section 19 of the Federal Reserve Act and may prescribe any ratio not more than 22 per centum, for any obligation of any such Federal branch or Federal agency that the Board may deem reasonable and appropriate, taking into consideration the character of business conducted by such institutions and the need to maintain vigorous and fair competition between and among such institutions and member banks. The Board may impose reserve requirements on Federal branches and Federal agencies in such graduated manner as it deems reasonable and appropriate.

(B) After consultation and in cooperation with the State bank supervisory authorities, the Board may make applicable to any State branch or State agency any requirement made applicable to, or which the Board has authority to impose upon, any Federal branch or agency under subparagraph (A) of this paragraph.

(2) A branch or agency shall be subject to this subsection only if (A) its parent foreign bank has total worldwide consolidated bank assets in excess of $1,000,000,000; (B) its parent foreign bank is controlled by a foreign company which owns or controls foreign banks that in the aggregate have total worldwide consolidated bank assets in excess of $1,000,000,000; or (C) its parent foreign bank is controlled by a group of foreign companies that own or control foreign banks that in the aggregate have total worldwide consolidated bank assets in excess of $1,000,000,000.

(b) Examination of branches and agencies by board.—Section 13 of the Federal Reserve Act is amended by adding at the end thereof the following new paragraph:

"Subject to such restrictions, limitations, and regulations as may be imposed by the Board of Governors of the Federal Reserve System, each Federal Reserve bank may receive deposits from, discount paper endorsed by, and make advances to any branch or agency of a foreign bank in the same manner and to the same extent that it may exercise such powers with respect to a member bank if such branch or agency is maintaining reserves with such Reserve bank pursuant to section 7 of the International Banking Act of 1978. In exercising any such powers with respect to any such branch or agency, each Federal Reserve bank shall give due regard to account balances being maintained by such branch or agency with such Reserve bank and the proportion of the assets of such branch or agency being held as reserves under section 7 of the International Banking Act of 1978. For the purposes of this paragraph, the terms 'branch', 'agency', and 'foreign bank' shall have the same meanings assigned to them in section 1 of the International Banking Act of 1978."

(C) AUTHORITY OF BOARD TO CONDUCT AND COORDINATE EXAMINATIONS.—

(1) FOREIGN BANK EXAMINATIONS AND REPORTING.—

(A) IN GENERAL.—The Board may examine each branch or agency of a foreign bank, each commercial lending company or bank controlled by 1 or more foreign banks or 1 or more foreign companies that control a foreign bank, and other office or affiliate of a foreign bank conducting business in any State.

(B) COORDINATION OF EXAMINATIONS.–

(i) IN GENERAL.–The Board shall coordinate examinations under this paragraph with the Comptroller of the Currency, the Federal Deposit Insurance Corporation, and appropriate State bank supervisors to the extent such coordination is possible.

(ii) SIMULTANEOUS EXAMINATIONS.–The Board may request simultaneous examinations of each office of a foreign bank and each affiliate of such bank operating in the United States.

(iii) AVOIDANCE OF DUPLICATION.–In exercising its authority under this paragraph, the Board shall take all reasonable measures to reduce burden and avoid unnecessary duplication of examinations.

(C) ANNUAL ON-SITE EXAMINATION.–Each Federal branch or agency, and each State branch or agency, of a foreign bank shall be subject to on-site examination by an appropriate Federal banking agency or State bank supervisor as frequently as would a national bank or a State bank, respectively, by the appropriate Federal banking agency.

(D) COST OF EXAMINATIONS.–The Cost of any examination under subparagraph (A) shall be assessed against and collected from the foreign bank, as the case may be, only to the same extent that fees are collected by the Board for examination of any State member bank.

(2) REPORTING REQUIREMENTS.–Each branch or agency of a foreign bank, other than a Federal branch or agency, shall be subject to paragraph 20 and the provision requiring the reports of condition contained in paragraph 6 of section 9 of the Federal Reserve Act (12 U.S.C. 335 and 324) to the same extent and in the same manner as if the branch or agency were a State member bank. In addition to any requirements imposed under section 4 of this Act, each Federal branch and agency shall be subject to subparagraph (a) of section 11 of the Federal Reserve Act (12 U.S.C. 248 (a)) and to paragraph 5 of section 21 of the Federal Reserve Act (12 U.S.C. 483) to the same extent and in the same manner as if it were a member bank.

(d) ESTABLISHMENT OF FOREIGN BANK OFFICES IN THE UNITED STATES.–

(1) PRIOR APPROVAL REQUIRED.–No foreign bank may establish a branch or an agency, or acquire ownership or control of a commercial lending company, without the prior approval of the Board.

(2) REQUIRED STANDARDS FOR APPROVAL.–The Board may not approve an application under paragraph (1) unless it determines that–

(A) the foreign bank engages directly in the business of banking outside of the United States and is subject to comprehensive supervision or regulation on a consolidated basis by the appropriate authorities in its home country; and

(B) the foreign bank has furnished to the Board the information it needs to adequately assess the application.

(3) STANDARDS FOR APPROVAL.–In acting on any application under paragraph (1), the Board may take into account–

(A) whether the appropriate authorities in the home country of the foreign bank have consented to the proposed establishment of a branch, agency or commercial lending company in the United States by the foreign bank;

(B) the financial and managerial resources of the foreign bank, including the bank's experience and capacity to engage in international banking;

(C) whether the foreign bank has provided the Board with adequate assurances that the bank will make available to the Board such information on the operations or activities of the foreign bank and any affiliate of the bank that the Board deems necessary to determine and enforce compliance with this Act, the Bank Holding Company Act of 1956, and other applicable Federal law; and

(D) whether the foreign bank and the United States affiliates of the bank are in compliance with applicable United States law.

(4) FACTOR.–In acting on an application under paragraph (1), the Board shall not make the size of the foreign bank the sole determinant factor, and may take into account the needs of the community as well as the length of operation of the foreign bank and its relative size in its home country. Nothing in this paragraph shall affect the ability of the Board to order a State branch, agency, or commercial lending company subsidiary to terminate its activities in the United States pursuant to any standard set forth in this Act.

(5) ESTABLISHMENT OF CONDITIONS.–Consistent with the standards for approval in paragraph (2), the Board may impose such conditions on its approval under this subsection as it deems necessary.

(6) EXCEPTION–

(A) IN GENERAL.–If the Board is unable to find, under paragraph (2), that a foreign bank is subject to comprehensive supervision or regulation on a consolidated basis by the appropriate authorities in its home country, the Board may nevertheless approve an application by such foreign bank under paragraph (1) if–

(i) the appropriate authorities in the home country of the foreign bank are actively working to establish arrangements for the consolidated supervision of such bank; and

(ii) the appropriate authorities in the home country of the foreign bank are not making demonstrable progress in establishing arrangements for the comprehensive supervision or regulation of such foreign bank on a consolidated basis;

(B) OTHER CONSIDERATIONS.–In deciding whether to use its discretion under subparagraph (A), the Board shall also consider whether the foreign bank has adopted and implements procedures to combat money laundering. The Board may also take into account whether the home country of the foreign bank is developing a legal regime to address money laundering or is participating in multilateral efforts to combat money laundering.

(C) ADDITIONAL CONSIDERATIONS.–In approving an application under this paragraph, the Board, after requesting and taking into consideration the views of the appropriate State bank supervisor or the Comptroller of the Currency, as the case may be, may impose such conditions or restrictions relating to the activities or business operations of the proposed branch, agency, or commercial lending company subsidiary, including restrictions on sources of funding, as are considered appropriate. The Board shall coordinate with the appropriate State bank supervisor or the Comptroller of the Currency, as appropriate, in the implementation of such conditions or restrictions.

(D) MODIFICATION OF CONDITIONS.–Any condition or restriction imposed by the Board in connection with the approval of an application under authority of this paragraph may be modified or withdrawn.

(7) TIME PERIOD FOR BOARD ACTION.–

(A) FINAL ACTIONS.–The Board shall take final action on any application under paragraph (1) not later than 180 days after receipt of the application, except that the Board may extend for an additional 180 days the period within which to take final action on such application after providing notice of, and the reasons for, the extension to the applicant foreign bank and any appropriate State bank supervisor or the Comptroller of the Currency, as appropriate.

(B) FAILURE TO SUBMIT INFORMATION.–The Board may deny any application if it does not receive information requested from the applicant foreign bank or appropriate authorities in the home country of the foreign bank in sufficient time to permit the Board to evaluate such information adequately within the time periods for final action set forth in subparagraph (A).

(C) WAIVER.–A foreign bank may waive the applicability of this paragraph with respect to any application under paragraph (1).

(e) TERMINATION OF FOREIGN BANK OFFICES IN THE UNITED STATES.–

(1) STANDARDS FOR TERMINATION.–The Board, after notice and opportunity for hearing and notice to any appropriate State bank

supervisor, may order a foreign bank that operates a State branch or agency or commercial lending company subsidiary in the United States to terminate the activities of such branch, agency, or subsidiary if the Board finds that—

(A) the foreign bank is not subject to comprehensive supervision or regulation on a consolidated basis by the appropriate authorities in its home country; or

(B)(i) there is reasonable cause to believe that such foreign bank, or any affiliate of such foreign bank, has committed a violation of law or engaged in an unsafe or unsound banking practice in the United States; and

(ii) as a result of such violation or practice the continued operation of the foreign bank's branch, agency or commercial lending company subsidiary in the United States would not be consistent with the public interest or with the purposes of this Act, the Bank Holding Company Act of 1956, or the Federal Deposit Insurance Act.

However, in making findings under this paragraph, the Board shall not make size the sole determinant factor, and may take into account the needs of the community as well as the length of operation of the foreign bank and its relative size in its home country. Nothing in this paragraph shall affect the ability of the Board to order a State branch agency, or commercial lending company subsidiary to terminate its activities in the United States pursuant to any standard set forth in this Act.

(2) DISCRETION TO DENY HEARING.—The Board may issue an order under paragraph (1) without providing for an opportunity for a hearing if the Board determines that expeditious action is necessary in order to protect the public interest.

(3) EFFECTIVE DATE OF TERMINATION ORDER.—An order issued under paragraph (1) shall take effect before the end of the 120-day period beginning on the date such order is issued unless the Board extends such period.

(4) COMPLIANCE WITH STATE AND FEDERAL LAW.—Any foreign bank required to terminate activities conducted at offices or subsidiaries in the United States pursuant to this subsection shall comply with the requirements of applicable Federal and State law with respect to procedures for the closure or dissolution of such offices or subsidiaries.

(5) RECOMMENDATION TO AGENCY FOR TERMINATION OF A FEDERAL BRANCH OR AGENCY.—The Board may transmit to the Comptroller of the Currency a recommendation that the license of any Federal branch or Federal agency of a foreign bank be terminated in accordance with section 4(i) if the Board has reasonable cause to believe that such foreign bank or any affiliate of such foreign bank

has engaged in conduct for which the activities of any State branch or agency may be terminated under paragraph (1).

(6) ENFORCEMENT OF ORDERS.–

(A) IN GENERAL.–In the case of contumacy of any office or subsidiary of the foreign bank against which–

(i) the Board has issued an order under paragraph (1); or

(ii) the Comptroller of the Currency has issued an order under section 4(i), or a refusal by such office or subsidiary to comply with such order, the Board or the Comptroller of the Currency may invoke the aid of the district court of the United States within the jurisdiction of which the office or subsidiary is located.

(B) COURT ORDER.–Any court referred to in subparagraph (A) may issue an order requiring compliance with an order referred to in subparagraph (A).

(7) CRITERIA RELATING TO FOREIGN SUPERVISION.–Not later than 1 year after the date of enactment of this subsection, the Board, in consultation with the Secretary of the Treasury, shall develop and publish criteria to be used in evaluating the operation of any foreign bank in the United States that the board has determined is not subject to comprehensive supervision or regulation on a consolidated basis. In developing such criteria, the Board shall allow reasonable opportunity for public review and comment.

(f) JUDICIAL REVIEW.–

(1) JURISDICTION OF UNITED STATES COURT OF APPEALS.–Any foreign bank–

(A) whose application under subsection (d) or section 10(a) has been disapproved by the Board;

(B) against which the Board has issued an order under subsection (e) or section 10(b); or

(C) against which the Comptroller of the Currency has issued an order under section 4(i) of this Act.

may obtain a review of such order in the United States court of appeals for any circuit in which such foreign bank operates a branch, agency, or commercial lending company that has been required by such order to terminate its activities, or in the United States Court of Appeals for the District of Columbia Circuit, by filing a petition for review in the court before the end of the 30-day period beginning on the date the order was issued.

(2) SCOPE OF JUDICIAL REVIEW.–Section 706 of title 5, United States Code (other than paragraph (2)(F) of such section) shall apply with respect to any application or action under subsection (d) or (e).

(g) CONSULTATION WITH STATE BANK SUPERVISOR.–The Board shall request and consider any views of the appropriate State bank supervisor with respect to any application or action under subsection (d) or (e).

(h) Limitations in Powers of State Branches and Agencies.—

(1) In general.—After the end of the 1-year period beginning on the date of enactment of the Federal Deposit Insurance Corporation Improvement Act of 1991, a State branch or State agency may not engage in any type of activity that is not permissible for a Federal branch unless—

(A) the Board has determined that such activity is consistent with sound banking practice; and

(B) in the case of an insured branch, the Federal Deposit Insurance Corporation has determined that the activity would pose no significant risk to the deposit insurance fund.

(2) Single borrower lending limit.—A State branch or State agency shall be subject to the same limitations with respect to loans made to a single borrower as are applicable to a Federal branch or Federal agency under section 4(b).

(3) Other authority not affected.—This section does not limit the authority of the Board or any State supervisory authority to impose more stringent restrictions.

(i) Proceedings Relating to Conviction for Money Laundering Offenses.—

(1) Notice of intention to issue order.—If the Board finds or receives written notice from the Attorney General that—

(A) any foreign bank which operates a State agency, a State branch which is not an insured branch, or a State commercial lending company subsidiary;

(B) any State agency;

(C) any State branch which is not an insured branch; or

(D) any State commercial lending subsidiary,

has been found guilty of any money laundering offense, the Board shall issue a notice to the agency, branch, or subsidiary of the Board's intention to commence a termination proceeding under subsection (e).

(2) Definitions.—For purposes of this subsection—

(A) Insured branch.—The term "insured branch" has the meaning given such term in section 3(s) of the Federal Deposit Insurance Act.

(B) Money laundering offense defined.—The term "money laundering offense" means any criminal offense under section 1956 or 1957 of title 18, United States Code, or under section 5322 of title 31, United States Code.

(j) Study on Equivalence of Foreign Bank Capital.—Not later than 180 days after enactment of this subsection, the Board and the

Secretary of the Treasury shall jointly submit to the Committee on Banking, Housing, and Urban Affairs of the Senate and the Committee on Banking, Finance and Urban Affairs of the House of Representatives a report—

(1) analyzing the capital standards contained in the framework for measurement of capital adequacy established by the Supervisory Committee of the Bank for International Settlements, foreign regulatory capital standards that apply to foreign banks conducting banking operations in the United States, and the relationship of the Base and foreign standards to risk-based capital and leverage requirements for United States banks; and

(2) establishing guidelines for the adjustments to be used by the Board in converting data on the capital of such foreign banks to the equivalent risk-based capital and leverage requirements for United States banks for purposes of determining whether a foreign bank's capital level is equivalent to that imposed on United States banks for purposes of determinations under section 7 of the International Banking Act of 1978 and sections 3 and 4 of the Bank Holding Company Act of 1956.

An update shall be prepared annually explaining any changes in the analysis under paragraph (1) and resulting changes in the guidelines pursuant to paragraph (2).

(k) MANAGEMENT OF SHELL BRANCHES.—

(1) TRANSACTIONS PROHIBITED.—A branch or agency of a foreign bank shall not manage, through an office of the foreign bank which is located outside the United States and is managed or controlled by such branch or agency, any type of activity that a bank organized under the laws of the United States, any State, or the District of Columbia is not permitted to manage at any branch or subsidiary of such bank which is located outside the United States.

(2) REGULATIONS.—Any regulations promulgated to carry out this section—

(A) shall be promulgated in accordance with section 13; and

(B) shall be uniform, to the extent practicable.

(2) EFFECTIVE DATE.—The amendment made by paragraph (1) shall become effective at the end of the 180-day period beginning on the date of enactment of this Act.

Nonbanking activities of foreign banks
Applicability of Bank Holding Company Acts

SEC. 8(A) APPLICABILITY OF BANK HOLDING COMPANY ACTS.—Except as otherwise provided in this section (1) any foreign bank that maintains a branch or agency in a State, (2) any foreign bank or foreign company controlling a foreign bank that controls a commercial lending company organized under State law, and (3) any company of which any foreign bank or company referred to in (1) and (2) is a subsidiary shall be subject to the provisions of the Bank Holding Company Act of 1956 [12 U.S.C. 1841 et seq.], and to section 1850 of this title and chapter 22 of this title [12 U.S.C.] [sections 105 and 106 of the Bank Holding Company Act Amendments of 1970] in the same manner and to the same extent that bank holding companies are subject to such provisions.

Ownership or control of shares of nonbanking companies for certain period

(b) OWNERSHIP OR CONTROL OF SHARES OF NONBANKING COMPANIES FOR CERTAIN PERIOD.—Until December 31, 1985, a foreign bank or other company to which subsection (a) of this section applies on September 17, 1978, may retain direct or indirect ownership or control of any voting shares of any nonbanking company in the United States that it owned, controlled, or held with power to vote on September 17, 1978, or engage in any nonbanking activities in the United States in which it was engaged on such date.

(c) ENGAGEMENT IN NONBANKING ACTIVITIES AFTER CERTAIN PERIOD.—

(1) After December 31, 1985, a foreign bank or other company to which subsection (a) of this section applies on September 17, 1978, or on the date of the establishment of a branch in a State an application for which was filed on or before July 26, 1978 may continue to engage in nonbanking activities in the United States in which directly or through an affiliate it was lawfully engaged on July 26, 1978 (or on a date subsequent to July 26, 1978, in the case of activities carried on as the result of the direct or indirect acquisition, pursuant to a binding written contract entered into on or before July 26, 1978, of another company engaged in such activities at the time of acquisition), and may engage directly or through an affiliate in nonbanking activities in the United States which are covered by an application to engage in such activities which was filed on or before July 26, 1978; except that the Board by order, after opportunity for hearing, may terminate the authority conferred by this subsection on any such foreign bank or company to engage directly or through an affiliate in any activity otherwise permitted by this subsection if it determines having due regard to the purposes of this chapter [12 U.S.C.] and the Bank Holding Company Act of 1956 [12 U.S.C. 1841 et seq.], that such action is necessary to prevent undue concentration of resources, decreased or unfair competition, conflicts of interest, or unsound banking practices in the United States. Notwithstanding subsection (a) of this section, a foreign bank or company referred to in this subsection may retain ownership or control of any voting shares (or, where necessary to prevent dilution of its voting interest, acquire additional voting shares) of any domestically-controlled affiliate covered in 1978 which since July 26, 1978, has engaged in the business of underwriting, distributing, or otherwise buying or

selling stocks, bonds, and other securities in the United States, notwithstanding that such affiliate acquired after July 26, 1978, an interest in, or any or all of the assets of, a going concern, or commences to engage in any new activity or activities. Except in the case of affiliates described in the preceding sentence, nothing in this subsection shall be construed to authorize any foreign bank or company referred to in this subsection, or any affiliate thereof, to engage in activities authorized by this subsection through the acquisition, pursuant to a contract entered into after July 26, 1978, of any interest in or the assets of a going concern engaged in such activities. Any foreign bank or company that is authorized to engage in any activity pursuant to this subsection but, as a result of action of the Board, is required to terminate such activity may retain the ownership of control of shares in any company carrying on such activity for a period of two years from the date on which its authority was so terminated by the Board. As used in this subsection, the term "affiliate" shall mean any company more than 5 per centum of whose voting shares is directly or indirectly owned or controlled or held with power to vote by the specified foreign bank or company and the term "domestically controlled affiliate covered in 1978" shall mean an affiliate organized under the laws of the United States or any State thereof if (i) no foreign bank or group of foreign banks acting in concert owns or controls, directly or indirectly, 45 per centum or more of its voting shares, and (ii) no more than 20 per centum of the number of directors as established from time to time to constitute the whole board of directors and 20 per centum of the executive officers of such affiliate are persons affiliated with any such foreign bank. For the purpose of the preceding sentence, the term "persons affiliated with any such foreign bank" shall mean (A) any person who is or was an employee officer, agent, or director of such foreign bank or who otherwise has or had such a relationship with such foreign bank that would lead such person to represent the interests of such foreign bank, and (B) in the case of any director of such domestically controlled affiliate covered in 1978, any person in favor of whose election as a director votes were cast by less than two-thirds of all shares voting in connection with such election other than shares owned or controlled, directly or indirectly, by any such foreign bank.

(2) TERMINATION OF CERTAIN NONBANKING ACTIVITIES.–The authority conferred by this subsection on a foreign bank or other company shall terminate 2 years after the date on which such foreign bank or other company becomes a "bank holding company" as defined in section 2(a) of the Bank Holding Company Act of 1956 (12 U.S.C. 1841(a)); except that the Board may, upon application of such foreign bank or other company, extend the 2-year period for not more than one year at a time, if, in its judgment, such an extension would not be detrimental to the public interest, but no such extensions shall exceed 3 years in the aggregate.

(d) CONSTRUCTION OF TERMS.—Nothing in this section shall be construed to define a branch or agency of a foreign bank or a commercial lending company controlled by a foreign bank or foreign company that controls a foreign bank as a "bank" for the purposes of any provisions of the Bank Holding Company Act of 1956 [12 U.S.C. 1841 et seq.], or section 1850 of [12 U.S.C.] [section 105 of the Bank Holding Company Act Amendments of 1970], except that any such branch, agency or commercial lending subsidiary shall be deemed a "bank" or "banking subsidiary", as the case may be, for the purposes of applying the prohibitions of chapter 22 of [12 U.S.C.] [section 106 of the Bank Holding Company Act Amendments of 1970] and the exemptions provided in sections 4(c)(1), 4(c)(2), 4(c)(3), and 4(c)(4) of the Bank Holding Company Act of 1956 (12 U.S.C. 1843(c)(1),(2),(3), and 4)) to any foreign bank or other company to which subsection (a) of this section applies.

(e) Section 2(h) of the Bank Holding Company Act of 1956 is amended (1) by striking out "(h) The" and inserting in lieu thereof "(h)(1) Except as provided by paragraph (2), the," (2) by striking out the proviso, and (3) by inserting at the end thereof the following:

"(2) The prohibitions of section 4 of this Act shall not apply to shares of any company organized under the laws of a foreign country (or to shares held by such company in any company engaged in the same general line of business of the investor company) that is principally engaged in business outside the United States if such shares are held or acquired by a bank holding company organized under the laws of a foreign country that is principally engaged in the banking business outside the United States, except that (1) such exempt foreign company (A) may engage in or hold shares of a company engaged in the business of underwriting, selling or distributing securities in the United States only to the extent that a bank holding company may do so under this Act and under regulations or orders issued by the Board under this Act, and (B) may engage in the United States in any banking or financial operations or types of activities permitted under section 4(c)(8) or in any order or regulation issued by the Board under such section only with the Board's prior approval under that section, and (2) no domestic office or subsidiary of a bank holding company or subsidiary thereof holding shares of such company may extend credit to a domestic office or subsidiary of such exempt company on terms more favorable than those afforded similar borrowers in the United States."

(3) TERMINATION OF GRANDFATHERED RIGHTS.—

(A) IN GENERAL.—If any foreign bank or foreign company files a declaration under section 4(l)(1)(C) of the Bank Holding Company Act of 1956, any authority conferred by this subsection on any foreign bank or company to engage in any activity that the Board has determined to be permissible for financial holding companies under section 4(k) of such Act shall terminate immediately.

(B) RESTRICTIONS AND REQUIREMENTS AUTHORIZED.–If a foreign bank or company that engages, directly or through an affiliate pursuant to paragraph (1), in an activity that the Board has determined to be permissible for financial holding companies under section 4(k) of the Bank Holding Company Act of 1956 has not filed a declaration with the Board of its status as a financial holding company under such section by the end of the 2-year period beginning on the date of the enactment of the Gramm-Leach-Bliley Act, the Board, giving due regard to the principle of national treatment and equality of competitive opportunity, may impose such restrictions and requirements on the conduct of such activities by such foreign bank or company as are comparable to those imposed on a financial holding company organized under the laws of the United States, including a requirement to conduct such activities in compliance with any prudential safeguards established under section 114 of the Gramm-Leach-Bliley Act.

. . .

REGULATION K OF THE FEDERAL RESERVE BOARD (1999)
12 C.F.R. §211.1 et. seq.

SUBPART A–INTERNATIONAL OPERATIONS OF UNITED STATES BANKING ORGANIZATIONS

§ 211.1   Authority purpose, and scope.

(a) Authority. This subpart is issued by the Board of Governors of the Federal Reserve System (Board) under the authority of the Federal Reserve Act (FRA) (12 U.S.C.221 et seq.); the Bank Holding Company Act of 1956 (BHC ct) (12 U.S.C.1841 et seq.); and the International Banking Act of 1978 (IBA) (12 .S.C.3101 et seq.).

(b) Purpose.   This subpart sets out rules governing the international and foreign activities of U.S. banking organizations, including procedures for establishing foreign branches and Edge and agreement corporations to engage in international banking, and for investments in foreign organizations.

(c) Scope. This subpart applies to:

(1) Member banks with respect to their foreign branches and investments in foreign banks under section 25 of the FRA (12 U.S.C. 601-604a);[1] and

(2) Corporations organized under section 25A of the FRA (12 U.S.C.611-631) (Edge corporations);

(3) Corporations having an agreement or undertaking with the Board under section 25 of the FRA (12 U.S.C.601-604a) (agreement corporations); and

(4) Bank holding companies with respect to the exemption from the nonbanking prohibitions of the BHC Act afforded by section 4(c)(13) of that act (12 U.S.C.1843(c)(13)).

§ 211.2 Definitions.

Unless otherwise specified, for purposes of this subpart:

(a) An affiliate of an organization means:

(1) Any entity of which the organization is a direct or indirect subsidiary; or

(2) Any direct or indirect subsidiary of the organization or such entity.

(b) Capital Adequacy Guidelines means the "Capital Adequacy Guidelines for State Member Banks: Risk-Based Measure" (12 CFR part 208, app. A) or the "Capital Adequacy Guidelines for Bank Holding Companies: Risk-Based Measure" (12 CFR part 225, app. A).

(c) Capital and surplus means, unless otherwise provided in this part:

(1) For organizations subject to the Capital Adequacy Guidelines:

(i) Tier 1 and tier 2 capital included in an organization's risk-based capital (under the Capital Adequacy Guidelines); and

(ii) The balance of allowance for loan and lease losses not included in an organization's tier 2 capital for calculation of risk-based capital, based on the organization's most recent consolidated Report of Condition and Income.

(d) Directly or indirectly, when used in reference to activities or investments of an organization, means activities or investments of the organization or of any subsidiary of the organization.

(e) Eligible country means any country:

(1) For which an allocated transfer risk reserve is required pursuant to § 211.43 of this part and that has restructured its sovereign debt held by foreign creditors; and

---

[1] Section 25 of the FRA (12 U.S.C. 601-604a), which refers to national banking associations, also applies to state member banks of the Federal Reserve System by virtue of section 9 of the FRA (12 U.S.C. 321).

(2) Any other country that the Board deems to be eligible.

(f) An Edge corporation is <u>engaged in banking</u> if it is ordinarily engaged in the business of accepting deposits in the United States from nonaffiliated persons.

(g) <u>Engaged in business</u> or <u>engaged in activities</u> in the United States means maintaining and operating an office (other than a representative office) or subsidiary in the United States.

(h) <u>Equity</u> means an ownership interest in an organization, whether through:

(1) Voting or nonvoting shares;

(2) General or limited partnership interests;

(3) Any other form of interest conferring ownership rights, including warrants, debt, or any other interests that are convertible into shares or other ownership rights in the organization; or

(4) Loans that provide rights to participate in the profits of an organization, unless the investor receives a determination that such loans should not be considered equity in the circumstances of the particular investment.

(i) <u>Foreign</u> or <u>foreign country</u> refers to one or more foreign nations, and includes the overseas territories, dependencies, and insular possessions of those nations and of the United States, and the Commonwealth of Puerto Rico.

(j) <u>Foreign bank</u> means an organization that:

(1) Is organized under the laws of a foreign country;

(2) Engages in the business of banking;

(3) Is recognized as a bank by the bank supervisory or monetary authority of the country of its organization or principal banking operations;

(4) Receives deposits to a substantial extent in the regular course of its business; and

(5) Has the power to accept demand deposits.

(k) <u>Foreign branch</u> means an office of an organization (other than a representative office) that is located outside the country in which the organization is legally established and at which a banking or financing business is conducted.

(l) <u>Foreign person</u> means an office or establishment located outside the United States, or an individual residing outside the United States.

(m) <u>Investment</u> means:

(1) The ownership or control of equity;

(2) Binding commitments to acquire equity;

(3) Contributions to the capital and surplus of an organization; or

(4) The holding of an organization's subordinated debt when the investor and the investor's affiliates hold more than 5 percent of the equity of the organization.

(n) <u>Investment grade</u> means a security that is rated in one of the four highest rating categories by:

(1) Two or more NRSROs; or

(2) One NRSRO if the security has been rated by only one NRSRO.

(o) <u>Investor</u> means an Edge corporation, agreement corporation, bank holding company, or member bank.

(p) <u>Joint venture</u> means an organization that has 20 percent or more of its voting shares held directly or indirectly by the investor or by an affiliate of the investor under any authority, but which is not a subsidiary of the investor or of an affiliate of the investor.

(q) <u>Loans and extensions of credit</u> means all direct and indirect advances of funds to a person made on the basis of any obligation of that person to repay the funds.

(r) <u>NRSRO</u> means a nationally recognized statistical rating organization as designated by the Securities and Exchange Commission.

(s) <u>Organization</u> means a corporation, government, partnership, association, or any other entity.

(t) <u>Person</u> means an individual or an organization.

(u) <u>Portfolio investment</u> means an investment in an organization other than a subsidiary or joint venture.

(v) <u>Representative office</u> means an office that:

(1) Engages solely in representational and administrative functions (such as soliciting new business or acting as liaison between the organization's head office and customers in the United States); and

(2) Does not have authority to make any business decision (other than decisions relating to its premises or personnel) for the account of the organization it represents, including contracting for any deposit or deposit-like liability on behalf of the organization.

(w) <u>Subsidiary</u> means an organization that has more than 50 percent of its voting shares held directly or indirectly, or that otherwise is controlled or capable of being controlled, by the investor or an affiliate of the investor under any authority. Among other circumstances, an investor is considered to control an organization if:

(1) The investor or an affiliate is a general partner of the organization; or

(2) The investor and its affiliates directly or indirectly own or control more than 50 percent of the equity of the organization.

(x) <u>Tier 1 capital</u> has the same meaning as provided under the Capital Adequacy Guidelines.

(y) <u>Well capitalized</u> means:

(1) In relation to a parent member or insured bank, that the standards set out in section 208.43(b)(1) of Regulation H (12 CFR 208.43(b)(1)) are satisfied;

(2) In relation to a bank holding company, that the standards set out in section 225.2(r)(1) of Regulation Y (12 CFR 225.2(r)(1)) are satisfied; and

(3) In relation to an Edge or agreement corporation, that it has tier 1 and total risk-based capital ratios of 6.0 and 10.0 percent, respectively, or greater.

(z) <u>Well managed</u> means that the Edge or agreement corporation, any parent insured bank, and the bank holding company received a composite rating of 1 or 2, and at least a satisfactory rating for management if such a rating is given, at their most recent examination or review.

§ 211.3 Foreign branches of U.S. banking organizations.

(a) <u>General</u>. (1) <u>Definition of banking organization</u>. For purposes of this section, a <u>banking organization</u> is defined as a member bank and its affiliates.

(2) A banking organization is considered to be operating a branch in a foreign country if it has an affiliate that is a member bank, Edge or agreement corporation, or foreign bank that operates an office (other than a representative office) in that country.

(3) For purposes of this subpart, a foreign office of an operating subsidiary of a member bank shall be treated as a foreign branch of the member bank and may engage only in activities permissible for a branch of a member bank.

(4) At any time upon notice, the Board may modify or suspend branching authority conferred by this section with respect to any banking organization.

(b) (1) <u>Establishment of foreign branches</u>. (i) Foreign branches may be established by any member bank having capital and surplus of $1,000,000 or more, an Edge corporation, an agreement corporation, any subsidiary the shares of which are held directly by the member bank, or any other subsidiary held pursuant to this subpart.

(ii) The Board grants its general consent under section 25 of the FRA (12 U.S.C.601-604a) for a member bank to establish a branch in the Commonwealth of Puerto Rico and the overseas territories, dependencies, and insular possessions of the United States.

(2) <u>Prior notice</u>. Unless otherwise provided in this section, the establishment of a foreign branch requires 30 days' prior written notice to the Board.

(3) <u>Branching into additional foreign countries</u>. After giving the Board 12 business days prior written notice, a banking organization that operates branches in two or more foreign countries may establish a branch in an additional foreign country.

(4) <u>Additional branches within a foreign country</u>. No prior notice is required to establish additional branches in any foreign country where the banking organization operates one or more branches.

(5) <u>Branching by nonbanking affiliates</u>. No prior notice is required for a nonbanking affiliate of a banking organization (i.e., an organization that is not a member bank, an Edge or agreement corporation, or foreign bank) to establish branches within a foreign country or in additional foreign countries.

(6) <u>Expiration of branching authority</u>. Authority to establish branches, when granted following prior written notice to the Board, shall expire one year from the earliest date on which the authority could have been exercised, unless extended by the Board.

(c) <u>Reporting</u>. Any banking organization that opens, closes, or relocates a branch shall report such change in a manner prescribed by the Board.

(d) <u>Reserves of foreign branches of member banks</u>. Member banks shall maintain reserves against foreign branch deposits when required by Regulation D (12 CFR part 204).

(e) <u>Conditional Approval; Access to Information</u>. The Board may impose such conditions on authority granted by it under this section as it deems necessary, and may require termination of any activities conducted under authority of this section if a member bank is unable to provide information on its activities or those of its affiliates that the Board deems necessary to determine and enforce compliance with U.S. banking laws.

§ 211.4 Permissible activities and investments of foreign branches of member banks.

(a) <u>Permissible Activities and Investments</u>. In addition to its general banking powers, and to the extent consistent with its charter, a foreign branch of a member bank may engage in the following activities and make the following investments, so far as is usual in connection with the business of banking in the country where it transacts business:

(1) <u>Guarantees</u>. Guarantee debts, or otherwise agree to make payments on the occurrence of readily ascertainable events (including, but not limited to, nonpayment of taxes, rentals, customs duties, or costs of transport, and loss or nonconformance of shipping documents) if the guarantee or agreement specifies a maximum

monetary liability; however, except to the extent that the member bank is fully secured, it may not have liabilities outstanding for any person on account of such guarantees or agreements which, when aggregated with other unsecured obligations of the same person, exceed the limit contained in section 5200(a)(1) of the Revised Statutes (12 U.S.C.84) for loans and extensions of credit;

(2) <u>Government obligations</u>. (i) Underwrite, distribute, buy, sell, and hold obligations of:

(A) The national government of the country where the branch is located and any political subdivision of that country;

(B) An agency or instrumentality of the national government of the country where the branch is located where such obligations are supported by the taxing authority, guarantee, or full faith and credit of that government;

(C) The national government or political subdivision of any country, where such obligations are rated investment grade; and

(D) An agency or instrumentality of any national government where such obligations are rated investment grade and are supported by the taxing authority, guarantee or full faith and credit of that government.

(ii) No member bank, under authority of this paragraph (a)(2), may hold ,or be under commitment with respect to, such obligations for its own account in relation to any one country in an amount exceeding the greater of:

(A) 10 percent of its tier 1 capital; or

(B) 10 percent of the total deposits of the bank's branches in that country on the preceding year-end call report date (or the date of acquisition of the branch, in the case of a branch that has not been so reported);

(3) <u>Other investments</u>. (i) Invest in:

(A) The securities of the central bank, clearinghouses, governmental entities other than those authorized under paragraph (a)(2) of this section, and government-sponsored development banks of the country where the foreign branch is located;

(B) Other debt securities eligible to meet local reserve or similar requirements; and

(C) Shares of automated electronic-payments networks, professional societies, schools, and the like necessary to the business of the branch;

(ii) The total investments of a bank's branches in a country under this paragraph (3) (exclusive of securities held as required by the law of that country or as authorized under section 5136 of the Revised Statutes (12 U.S.C.24, Seventh)) may not exceed 1 percent of the total deposits of the bank's branches in that country on the preceding year-end call report date (or on the date of acquisition of the branch, in the case of a branch that has not been so reported);

(4) <u>Real estate loans</u>.   Take liens or other encumbrances on foreign real estate in connection with its extensions of credit, whether or not of first priority and whether or not the real estate has been improved;

(5) <u>Insurance</u>. Act as insurance agent or broker;

(6) <u>Employee benefits program</u>. Pay to an employee of the branch, as part of an employee benefits program, a greater rate of interest than that paid to other depositors of the branch;

(7) <u>Repurchase agreements</u>. Engage in repurchase agreements involving securities and commodities that are the functional equivalents of extensions of credit;

(8) <u>Investment in subsidiaries</u>. With the Board's prior approval, acquire all of the shares of a company (except where local law requires other investors to hold directors' qualifying shares or similar types of instruments) that engages solely in activities:

(i) In which the member bank is permitted to engage; or

(ii) That are incidental to the activities of the foreign branch.

(b) <u>Other activities</u>. With the Board's prior approval, engage in other activities that the Board determines are usual in connection with the transaction of the business of banking in the places where the member bank's branches transact business.

.   .   .

§ 211.8 Investments and activities abroad.

(a) <u>General policy</u>. Activities abroad, whether conducted directly or indirectly, shall be confined to activities of a banking or financial nature and those that are necessary to carry on such activities. In doing so, investors[2] shall at all times act in accordance with high standards of banking or financial prudence, having due regard for diversification of risks, suitable liquidity, and adequacy of capital. Subject to these considerations and the other provisions of this section, it is the Board's policy to allow activities abroad to be organized and operated as best meets corporate policies.

(b) <u>Direct investments by member banks</u>. A member bank's direct investments under section 25 of the FRA (12 U.S.C.601 et seq.) shall be limited to:

---

[2] For purposes of this section and §§ 211.9 and 211.10 of this part, a direct subsidiary of a member bank is deemed to be an investor.

(1) Foreign banks;

(2) Domestic or foreign organizations formed for the sole purpose of holding shares of a foreign bank;

(3) Foreign organizations formed for the sole purpose of performing nominee, fiduciary, or other banking services incidental to the activities of a foreign branch or foreign bank affiliate of the member bank; and

(4) Subsidiaries established pursuant to § 211.4 (a)(8) of this part.

(c) Eligible investments. Subject to the limitations set out in paragraphs (b) and (d) of this section, an investor may, directly or indirectly:

(1) Investment in subsidiary. Invest in a subsidiary that engages solely in activities listed in § 211.10 of this part, or in such other activities as the Board has determined in the circumstances of a particular case are permissible; provided that, in the case of an acquisition of a going concern, existing activities that are not otherwise permissible for a subsidiary may account for not more than 5 percent of either the consolidated assets or consolidated revenues of the acquired organization;

(2) Investment in joint venture. Invest in a joint venture; provided that, unless otherwise permitted by the Board, not more than 10 percent of the joint venture's consolidated assets or consolidated revenues are attributable to activities not listed in § 211.10 of this part; and

(3) Portfolio investments. Make portfolio investments in an organization, provided that:

(i) Individual investment limits. The total direct and indirect portfolio investments by the investor and its affiliates in an organization engaged in activities that are not permissible for joint ventures, when combined with all other shares in the organization held under any other authority, do not exceed:

(A) 40 percent of the total equity of the organization; or

(B) 19.9 percent of the organization 's voting shares.

(ii) Loans and extensions of credit. Any loans and extensions of credit made by an investor or its affiliates to the organization are on substantially the same terms, including interest rates and collateral, as those prevailing at the same time for comparable transactions between the investor or its affiliates and nonaffiliated persons; and

(iii) Protecting shareholder rights. Nothing in this paragraph (c)(3) shall prohibit an investor from otherwise exercising rights it may have as shareholder to protect the value of its investment, so long as the exercise of such rights does not result in the investor's direct or indirect control of the organization.

(d) <u>Investment limit</u>. In calculating the amount that may be invested in any organization under this section and §§ 211.9 and 211.10 of this part, there shall be included any unpaid amount for which the investor is liable and any investments in the same organization held by affiliates under any authority.

(e) <u>Divestiture</u>. An investor shall dispose of an investment promptly (unless the Board authorizes retention) if:

(1) The organization invested in:

(i) Engages in impermissible activities to an extent not permitted under paragraph (c) of this section; or

(ii) Engages directly or indirectly in other business in the United States that is not permitted to an Edge corporation in the United States; provided that an investor may:

(A) Retain portfolio investments in companies that derive no more than 10 percent of their total revenue from activities in the United States; and

(B) Hold up to 5 percent of the shares of a foreign company that engages directly or indirectly in business in the United States that is not permitted to an Edge corporation; or

(2) After notice and opportunity for hearing, the investor is advised by the Board that such investment is inappropriate under the FRA, the BHC Act, or this subpart.

(f) <u>Debts previously contracted</u>. Shares or other ownership interests acquired to prevent a loss upon a debt previously contracted in good faith are not subject to the limitations or procedures of this section; provided that such interests shall be disposed of promptly but in no event later than two years after their acquisition, unless the Board authorizes retention for a longer period.

(g) <u>Investments made through debt-for-equity conversions</u>.

(1) <u>Permissible investments</u>. A bank holding company may make investments through the conversion of sovereign-or private-debt obligations of an eligible country, either through direct exchange of the debt obligations for the investment, or by a payment for the debt in local currency, the proceeds of which, including an additional cash investment not exceeding in the aggregate more than 10 percent of the fair value of the debt obligations being converted as part of such investment, are used to purchase the following investments:

(i) <u>Public-sector companies</u>. A bank holding company may acquire up to and including 100 percent of the shares of (or other ownership interests in) any foreign company located in an eligible country, if the shares are acquired from the government of the eligible country or from its agencies or instrumentalities.

(ii) <u>Private-sector companies</u>. A bank holding company may acquire up to and including 40 percent of the shares, including voting shares, of (or other ownership interests in) any other foreign company located in an eligible country subject to the following conditions:

(A) A bank holding company may acquire more than 25 percent of the voting shares of the foreign company only if another shareholder or group of shareholders unaffiliated with the bank holding company holds a larger block of voting shares of the company;

(B) The bank holding company and its affiliates may not lend or otherwise extend credit to the foreign company in amounts greater than 50 percent of the total loans and extensions of credit to the foreign company; and

(C) The bank holding company's representation on the board of directors or on management committees of the foreign company may be no more than proportional to its shareholding in the foreign company.

(2) <u>Investments by bank subsidiary of bank holding company</u>. Upon application, the Board may permit an indirect investment to be made pursuant to this paragraph (g) through an insured bank subsidiary of the bank holding company, where the bank holding company demonstrates that such ownership is consistent with the purposes of the FRA. In granting its consent, the Board may impose such conditions as it deems necessary or appropriate to prevent adverse effects, including prohibiting loans from the bank to the company in which the investment is made.

(3) <u>Divestiture</u>. (i) <u>Time limits for divestiture</u>. A bank holding company shall divest the shares of, or other ownership interests in, any company acquired pursuant to this paragraph (g) within the longer of:

(A) Ten years from the date of acquisition of the investment, except that the Board may extend such period if, in the Board's judgment, such an extension would not be detrimental to the public interest; or

(B) Two years from the date on which the bank holding company is permitted to repatriate in full the investment in the foreign company.

(ii) <u>Maximum Retention Period</u>. Notwithstanding the provisions of paragraph (g)(3)(i) of this section:

(A) Divestiture shall occur within 15 years of the date of acquisition of the shares of, or other ownership interests in, any company acquired pursuant to this paragraph (g); and

(B) A bank holding company may retain such shares or ownership interests if such retention is otherwise permissible at the time required for divestiture.

(iii) <u>Report to Board</u>. The bank holding company shall report to the Board on its plans for divesting an investment made under this paragraph (g) two years prior to the final date for divestiture, in a manner to be prescribed by the Board.

(iv) <u>Other conditions requiring divestiture</u>. All investments made pursuant to this paragraph (g) are subject to paragraph (e) of this section requiring prompt divestiture (unless the Board upon application authorizes retention), if the company invested in engages in impermissible business in the United States that exceeds in the aggregate 10 percent of the company's consolidated assets or revenues calculated on an annual basis; provided that such company may not engage in activities in the United States that consist of banking or financial operations (as defined in § 211.23((f)(5)(iii)(B)) of this part, or types of activities permitted by regulation or order under section 4(c)(8)of the BHC Act (12 U.S.C.1843(c)(8)), except under regulations of the Board or with the prior approval of the Board.

(4) <u>Investment procedures</u>. (i) <u>General consent</u>. Subject to the other limitations of this paragraph (g), the Board grants its general consent for investments made under this paragraph (g) if the total amount invested does not exceed the greater of $25 million or 1 percent of the tier 1 capital of the investor.

(ii) All other investments shall be made in accordance with the procedures of § 211.9 (f) and (g) of this part, requiring prior notice or specific consent.

(5) <u>Conditions</u>. (i) <u>Name</u>. Any company acquired pursuant to this paragraph (g) shall not bear a name similar to the name of the acquiring bank holding company or any of its affiliates.

(ii) <u>Confidentiality</u>. Neither the bank holding company nor its affiliates shall provide to any company acquired pursuant to this paragraph (g) any confidential business information or other information concerning customers that are engaged in the same or related lines of business as the company.

.   .   .

SUBPART B—FOREIGN BANKING ORGANIZATIONS

§ 211.20 Authority, purpose, and scope.

(a) <u>Authority</u>. This subpart is issued by the Board of Governors of the Federal Reserve System (Board) under the authority of the Bank Holding Company Act of 1956 (BHC Act) (12 U.S.C.1841 et seq.) and the International Banking Act of 1978 (IBA) (12 U.S.C.3101 et seq.).

(b) <u>Purpose and scope</u>. This subpart is in furtherance of the purposes of the BHC Act and the IBA. It applies to foreign banks and foreign banking organizations with respect to:

(1) The limitations on interstate banking under section 5 of the IBA (12 U.S.C.3103);

(2) The exemptions from the nonbanking prohibitions of the BHC Act and the IBA afforded by sections 2(h)and 4(c)(9)of the BHC Act (12 U.S.C.1841(h), 1843(c)(9));

(3) Board approval of the establishment of an office of a foreign bank in the United States under sections 7(d)and 10(a)of the IBA (12 U.S.C.3105(d), 3107(a));

(4) The termination by the Board of a foreign bank's representative office, state branch, state agency, or commercial lending company subsidiary under sections 7(e) and 10(b) of the IBA (12 U.S.C. 3105(e), 3107(b)), and the transmission of a recommendation to the Comptroller to terminate a federal branch or federal agency under section 7(e)(5) of the IBA (12 U.S.C. 3105(e)(5));

(5) The examination of an office or affiliate of a foreign bank in the United States as provided in sections 7(c) and 10(c) of the IBA (12 U.S.C. 3105(c), 3107(c));

(6) The disclosure of supervisory information to a foreign supervisor under section 15 of the IBA (12 U.S.C. 3109);

(7) The limitations on loans to one borrower by state branches and state agencies of a foreign bank under section 7(h)(2) of the IBA (12 U.S.C. 3105(h)(2));

(8) The limitation of a state branch and a state agency to conducting only activities that are permissible for a federal branch under section (7)(h)(1) of the IBA (12 U.S.C.3105(h)(1)); and

(9) The deposit insurance requirement for retail deposit taking by a foreign bank under section 6 of the IBA (12 U.S.C.3104).

(10) The management of shell branches (12 U.S.C.3105(k)).

(c) <u>Additional requirements</u>. Compliance by a foreign bank with the requirements of this subpart and the laws administered and enforced by the Board does not relieve the foreign bank of responsibility to comply with the laws and regulations administered by the licensing authority.

§ 211.21 Definitions.

The definitions contained in §§ 211.1 and 211.2 apply to this subpart, except as a term is otherwise defined in this section:

(a) <u>Affiliate</u> of a foreign bank or of a parent of a foreign bank means any company that controls, is controlled by, or is under common control with, the foreign bank or the parent of the foreign bank.

(b) <u>Agency</u> means any place of business of a foreign bank, located in any state, at which credit balances are maintained, checks are paid, money is lent, or, to the extent not prohibited by state or federal law, deposits are accepted from a person or entity that is not a citizen or resident of the United States. Obligations shall not be considered credit balances unless they are:

(1) Incidental to, or arise out of the exercise of, other lawful banking powers;

(2) To serve a specific purpose;

(3) Not solicited from the general public;

(4) Not used to pay routine operating expenses in the United States such as salaries, rent, or taxes;

(5) Withdrawn within a reasonable period of time after the specific purpose for which they were placed has been accomplished; and

(6) Drawn upon in a manner reasonable in relation to the size and nature of the account.

(c) (1) Appropriate Federal Reserve Bank means, unless the Board designates a different Federal Reserve Bank:

(i) For a foreign banking organization, the Reserve Bank assigned to the foreign banking organization in § 225.3 (b)(2) of Regulation Y (12 CFR 225.3(b)(2));

(ii) For a foreign bank that is not a foreign banking organization and proposes to establish an office, an Edge corporation, or an agreement corporation, the Reserve Bank of the Federal Reserve District in which the foreign bank proposes to establish such office or corporation; and

(iii) In all other cases, the Reserve Bank designated by the Board.

(2) The appropriate Federal Reserve Bank need not be the Reserve Bank of the Federal Reserve District in which the foreign bank's home state is located.

(d) Banking subsidiary, with respect to a specified foreign bank, means a bank that is a subsidiary as the terms bank and subsidiary are defined in section 2 of the BHC Act (12 U.S.C.1841).

(e) Branch means any place of business of a foreign bank, located in any state, at which deposits are received, and that is not an agency, as that term is defined in paragraph (b) of this section.

(f) Change the status of an office means to convert a representative office into a branch or agency, or an agency or limited branch into a branch, but does not include renewal of the license of an existing office.

(g) Commercial lending company means any organization, other than a bank or an organization operating under section 25 of the Federal Reserve Act (FRA) (12 U.S.C.601-604a), organized under the laws of any state, that maintains credit balances permissible for an agency, and engages in the business of making commercial loans. Commercial lending company includes any company chartered under article XII of the banking law of the State of New York.

(h) <u>Comptroller</u> means the Office of the Comptroller of the Currency.

(i) <u>Control</u> has the same meaning as in section 2(a) of the BHC Act (12 U.S.C.1841(a)), and the terms <u>controlled</u> and <u>controlling</u> shall be construed consistently with the term <u>control</u>.

(j) <u>Domestic branch</u> means any place of business of a foreign bank, located in any state, that may accept domestic deposits and deposits that are incidental to or for the purpose of carrying out transactions in foreign countries.

(k) A foreign bank <u>engages directly in the business of banking outside the United States</u> if the foreign bank engages directly in banking activities usual in connection with the business of banking in the countries where it is organized or operating.

(l) To <u>establish</u> means:

(1) To open and conduct business through an office;

(2) To acquire directly, through merger, consolidation, or similar transaction with another foreign bank, the operations of an office that is open and conducting business;

(3) To acquire an office through the acquisition of a foreign bank subsidiary that will cease to operate in the same corporate form following the acquisition;

(4) To change the status of an office; or

(5) To relocate an office from one state to another.

(m) <u>Federal agency</u>, <u>federal branch</u>, <u>state agency</u>, and <u>state branch</u> have the same meanings as in section 1 of the IBA (12 U.S.C.3101).

(n) <u>Foreign bank</u> means an organization that is organized under the laws of a foreign country and that engages directly in the business of banking outside the United States. The term <u>foreign bank</u> does not include a central bank of a foreign country that does not engage or seek to engage in a commercial banking business in the United States through an office.

(o) <u>Foreign banking organization</u> means

(1) a foreign bank, as defined in section 1(b)(7) of the IBA (12 U.S.C. 3101(7)), that:

(i) Operates a branch, agency, or commercial lending company subsidiary in the United States;

(ii) Controls a bank in the United States; or

(iii) Controls an Edge corporation acquired after March 5, 1987; and

(2) Any company of which the foreign bank is a subsidiary.

(p) <u>Home country</u>, with respect to a foreign bank, means the country in which the foreign bank is chartered or incorporated.

(q) <u>Home country supervisor</u>, with respect to a foreign bank, means the governmental entity or entities in the foreign bank's home country with responsibility for the supervision and regulation of the foreign bank.

(r) <u>Licensing authority</u> means:

(1) The relevant state supervisor, with respect to an application to establish a state branch, state agency, commercial lending company or representative office of a foreign bank; or

(2) The Comptroller, with respect to an application to establish a federal branch or federal agency.

(s) <u>Limited branch</u> means a branch of a foreign bank that receives only such deposits as would be permitted for a corporation organized under section 25A of the Federal Reserve Act.

(t) <u>Office</u> or <u>office of a foreign bank</u> means any branch, agency, representative office, or commercial lending company subsidiary of a foreign bank in the United States.

(u) A <u>parent</u> of a foreign bank means a company of which the foreign bank is a subsidiary. An <u>immediate parent</u> of a foreign bank is a company of which the foreign bank is a direct subsidiary. An <u>ultimate parent</u> of a foreign bank is a parent of the foreign bank that is not the subsidiary of any other company.

(v) <u>Regional administrative office</u> means a representative office that:

(1) Is established by a foreign bank that operates two or more branches, agencies, commercial lending companies, or banks in the United States;

(2) Is located in the same city as one or more of the foreign bank's branches, agencies, commercial lending companies, or banks in the United States;

(3) Manages, supervises, or coordinates the operations of the foreign bank or its affiliates, if any, in a particular geographic area that includes the United States or a region thereof, including by exercising credit approval authority in that area pursuant to written standards, credit policies, and procedures established by the foreign bank; and

(4) Does not solicit business from actual or potential customers of the foreign bank or its affiliates.

(w) <u>Relevant state supervisor</u> means the state entity that is authorized to supervise and regulate a state branch, state agency, commercial lending company, or representative office.

(x) <u>Representative office</u> means any office of a foreign bank which is located in any state and is not a Federal branch, Federal agency, State branch, State agency, or commercial lending company subsidiary.

(y) <u>State</u> means any state of the United States or the District of Columbia.

(z) <u>Subsidiary</u> means any organization that:

(1) Has 25 percent or more of its voting shares directly or indirectly owned, controlled, or held with the power to vote by a company, including a foreign bank or foreign banking organization; or

(2) Is otherwise controlled, or capable of being controlled, by a foreign bank or foreign banking organization.

§ 211.22 Interstate banking operations of foreign banking organizations.

(a) <u>Determination of home state</u>. (1) A foreign bank that, as of December 10, 1997, had declared a home state or had a home state determined pursuant to the law and regulations in effect prior to that date shall have that state as its home state.

(2) A foreign bank that has any branches, agencies, commercial lending company subsidiaries, or subsidiary banks in one state, and has no such offices or subsidiaries in any other states, shall have as its home state the state in which such offices or subsidiaries are located.

(b) <u>Change of home state</u>. (1) <u>Prior notice</u>. A foreign bank may change its home state once, if it files 30 days' prior notice of the proposed change with the Board.

(2) <u>Application to change home state</u>. (i) A foreign bank, in addition to changing its home state by filing prior notice under paragraph (b)(1) of this section, may apply to the Board to change its home state, upon showing that a national bank or state-chartered bank with the same home state as the foreign bank would be permitted to change its home state to the new home state proposed by the foreign bank.

(ii) A foreign bank may apply to the Board for such permission one or more times.

(iii) In determining whether to grant the request of a foreign bank to change its home state, the Board shall consider whether the proposed change is consistent with competitive equity between foreign and domestic banks.

(3) <u>Effect of change in home state</u>. The home state of a foreign bank and any change in its home state by a foreign bank shall not affect which Federal Reserve Bank or Reserve Banks supervise the operations of the foreign bank, and shall not affect the obligation of the foreign bank to file required reports and applications with the appropriate Federal Reserve Bank.

(4) <u>Conforming branches to new home state</u>. Upon any change in home state by a foreign bank under paragraph (b)(1) or (b)(2) of

this section, the domestic branches of the foreign bank established in reliance on any previous home state of the foreign bank shall be conformed to those which a foreign bank with the new home state could permissibly establish or operate as of the date of such change.

(c) <u>Prohibition against interstate deposit production offices</u>. A covered interstate branch of a foreign bank may not be used as a deposit production office in accordance with the provisions in § 208.7 of Regulation H (12 CFR 208.7).

§ 211.23 Nonbanking activities of foreign banking organizations.

(a) <u>Qualifying foreign banking organizations</u>. Unless specifically made eligible for the exemptions by the Board, a foreign banking organization shall qualify for the exemptions afforded by this section only if, disregarding its United States banking, more than half of its worldwide business is banking; and more than half of its banking business is outside the United States.[3] In order to qualify, a foreign banking organization shall:

(1) Meet at least two of the following requirements:

(i) Banking assets held outside the United States exceed total worldwide nonbanking assets;

(ii) Revenues derived from the business of banking outside the United States exceed total revenues derived from its worldwide nonbanking business; or

(iii) Net income derived from the business of banking outside the United States exceeds total net income derived from its worldwide nonbanking business; and

(2) Meet at least two of the following requirements:

(i) Banking assets held outside the United States exceed banking assets held in the United States;

(ii) Revenues derived from the business of banking outside the United States exceed revenues derived from the business of banking in the United States; or

(iii) Net income derived from the business of banking outside the United States exceeds net income derived from the business of banking in the United States.

(b) <u>Determining assets, revenues, and net income</u>. (1)(i) For purposes of paragraph (a) of this section, the total assets, revenues, and net income of an organization may be determined on a consolidated or combined basis.

---

[3] None of the assets, revenues, or net income, whether held or derived directly or indirectly, of a subsidiary bank, branch, agency, commercial lending company, or other company engaged in the business of banking in the United States (including any territory of the United States, Puerto Rico, Guam, American Samoa, or the Virgin Islands) shall be considered held or derived from the business of banking "outside the United States".

(ii) The foreign banking organization shall include assets, revenues, and net income of companies in which it owns 50 percent or more of the voting shares when determining total assets, revenues, and net income.

(iii) The foreign banking organization may include assets, revenues, and net income of companies in which it owns 25 percent or more of the voting shares, if all such companies within the organization are included.

(2) Assets devoted to, or revenues or net income derived from, activities listed in section 211.10(a) shall be considered banking assets, or revenues or net income derived from the banking business, when conducted within the foreign banking organization by a foreign bank or its subsidiaries.

(c) <u>Limited exemptions available to foreign banking organizations in certain circumstances</u> The following shall apply where a foreign bank meets the requirements of paragraph (a) but its ultimate parent does not:

(1) Such foreign bank shall be entitled to the exemptions available to a qualifying foreign banking organization if its ultimate parent meets the requirements set forth in (a)(2) and could meet the requirements in (a)(1) but for the requirement in (b)(2) that activities must be conducted by the foreign bank or its subsidiaries in order to be considered derived from the banking business;

(2) An ultimate parent as described in (c)(1) shall be eligible for the exemptions available to a qualifying foreign banking organization except for those provided in section 211.23(f)(5)(iii).

(d) <u>Loss of eligibility for exemptions</u>.   (1) <u>Failure to meet qualifying test</u>. A foreign banking organization that qualified under paragraph (a) or (c) of this section shall cease to be eligible for the exemptions of this section if it fails to meet the requirements of paragraphs (a) or (c) of this section for two consecutive years, as reflected in its annual reports (FR Y-7) filed with the Board.

(2) <u>Continuing activities and investments</u>. (i) A foreign banking organization that ceases to be eligible for the exemptions of this section may continue to engage in activities or retain investments commenced or acquired prior to the end of the first fiscal year for which its annual report reflects nonconformance with paragraph (a) or (c) of this section.

(ii) <u>Termination or divestiture</u>.   Activities commenced or investments made after that date shall be terminated or divested within three months of the filing of the second annual report, or at such time as the Board may determine upon request by the foreign banking organization to extend the period, unless the Board grants consent to continue the activity or retain the investment under paragraph (e) of this section.

(3) <u>Request for specific determination of eligibility</u>. (i) A foreign banking organization that ceases to qualify under paragraph (a) or (c) of this section, or an affiliate of such foreign banking organization, that requests a specific determination of eligibility under paragraph (e) of this section may, prior to the Board's determination on eligibility, continue to engage in activities and make investments under the provisions of paragraphs (f)(1), (2), (3), and (4) of this section.

(ii) The Board may grant consent for the foreign banking organization or its affiliate to make investments under paragraph (f)(5) of this section.

(e) <u>Specific determination of eligibility for organizations that do not qualify for the exemptions</u>. (1) <u>Application</u>. (i) A foreign organization that is not a foreign banking organization or a foreign banking organization that does not qualify under paragraph (a) or (c) of this section for some or all of the exemptions afforded by this section, or that has lost its eligibility for the exemptions under paragraph (d) of this section, may apply to the Board for a specific determination of eligibility for some or all of the exemptions.

(ii) A foreign banking organization may apply for a specific determination prior to the time it ceases to be eligible for the exemptions afforded by this section.

(2) <u>Factors considered by Board</u>. In determining whether eligibility for the exemptions would be consistent with the purposes of the BHC Act and in the public interest, the Board shall consider:

(i) The history and the financial and managerial resources of the foreign organization or foreign banking organization;

(ii) The amount of its business in the United States;

(iii) The amount, type, and location of its nonbanking activities, including whether such activities may be conducted by U.S. banks or bank holding companies;

(iv) Whether eligibility of the foreign organization or foreign banking organization would result in undue concentration of resources, decreased or unfair competition, conflicts of interests, or unsound banking practices; and

(v) The extent to which the foreign banking organization is subject to comprehensive supervision or regulation on a consolidated basis or the foreign organization is subject to oversight by regulatory authorities in its home country.

(3) <u>Conditions and limitations</u>. The Board may impose any conditions and limitations on a determination of eligibility, including requirements to cease activities or dispose of investments.

(4) <u>Eligibility not granted</u>. Determinations of eligibility generally would not be granted where a majority of the business of the foreign

organization or foreign banking organization derives from commercial or industrial activities.

(f) <u>Permissible activities and investments</u>. A foreign banking organization that qualifies under paragraph (a) of this section may:

(1) Engage in activities of any kind outside the United States;

(2) Engage directly in activities in the United States that are incidental to its activities outside the United States;

(3) Own or control voting shares of any company that is not engaged, directly or indirectly, in any activities in the United States, other than those that are incidental to the international or foreign business of such company;

(4) Own or control voting shares of any company in a fiduciary capacity under circumstances that would entitle such shareholding to an exemption under section 4(c)(4) of the BHC Act (12 U.S.C.1843(c)(4)) if the shares were held or acquired by a bank;

(5) Own or control voting shares of a foreign company that is engaged directly or indirectly in business in the United States other than that which is incidental to its international or foreign business, subject to the following limitations:

(i) More than 50 percent of the foreign company's consolidated assets shall be located, and consolidated revenues derived from, outside the United States; provided that, if the foreign company fails to meet the requirements of this paragraph (f)(5)(i) for two consecutive years (as reflected in annual reports (FR Y-7) filed with the Board by the foreign banking organization), the foreign company shall be divested or its activities terminated within one year of the filing of the second consecutive annual report that reflects nonconformance with the requirements of this paragraph (f)(5)(i), unless the Board grants consent to retain the investment under paragraph (g) of this section;

(ii) The foreign company shall not directly underwrite, sell, or distribute, nor own or control more than 10 percent of the voting shares of a company that underwrites, sells, or distributes securities in the United States, except to the extent permitted bank holding companies;

(iii) If the foreign company is a subsidiary of the foreign banking organization, the foreign company must be, or must control, an operating company, and its direct or indirect activities in the United States shall be subject to the following limitations:

(A) The foreign company's activities in the United States shall be the same kind of activities, or related to the activities, engaged in directly or indirectly by the foreign company abroad, as measured by the "establishment" categories of the Standard Industrial Classification (SIC). An activity in the United States shall be considered related to an activity outside the United States if it consists of supply, distribution, or sales in furtherance of the activity;

(B) The foreign company may engage in activities in the United States that consist of banking, securities, insurance, or other financial operations, or types of activities permitted by regulation or order under section 4(c)(8) of the BHC Act (12 U.S.C.1843(c)(8)), only under regulations of the Board or with the prior approval of the Board, subject to the following;

(1) Activities within Division H (Finance, Insurance, and Real Estate) of the SIC shall be considered banking or financial operations for this purpose, with the exception of acting as operators of nonresidential buildings (SIC 6512), operators of apartment buildings (SIC 6513), operators of dwellings other than apartment buildings (SIC 6514), and operators of residential mobile home sites (SIC 6515); and operating title abstract offices (SIC 6541); and

(2) The following activities shall be considered financial activities and may be engaged in only with the approval of the Board under paragraph (g) of this section: credit reporting services (SIC 7323); computer and data processing services (SIC 7371, 7372, 7373, 7374, 7375, 7376, 7377, 7378, and 7379); armored car services (SIC 7381); management consulting (SIC 8732, 8741, 8742, and 8748); certain rental and leasing activities (SIC 4741, 7352, 7353, 7359, 7513, 7514, 7515,and 7519); accounting, auditing, and bookkeeping services (SIC 8721); courier services (SIC 4215 and 4513);and arrangement of passenger transportation (SIC 4724, 4725, and 4729).

(g) Exemptions under section 4(c)(9) of the BHC Act. A foreign banking organization that is of the opinion that other activities or investments may, in particular circumstances, meet the conditions for an exemption under section 4(c)(9) of the BHC Act (12 U.S.C. 1843(c)(9)) may apply to the Board for such a determination by submitting to the appropriate Federal Reserve Bank a letter setting forth the basis for that opinion.

(h) Reports. The foreign banking organization shall report in a manner prescribed by the Board any direct activities in the United States by a foreign subsidiary of the foreign banking organization and the acquisition of all shares of companies engaged, directly or indirectly, in activities in the United States that were acquired under the authority of this section.

(i) Availability of information. If any information required under this section is unknown and not reasonably available to the foreign banking organization (either because obtaining it would involve unreasonable effort or expense, or because it rests exclusively within the knowledge of a company that is not controlled by the organization) the organization shall:

(1) Give such information on the subject as it possesses or can reasonably acquire, together with the sources thereof; and

(2) Include a statement showing that unreasonable effort or expense would be involved, or indicating that the company whose shares were acquired is not controlled by the organization, and stating the result of a request for information.

§ 211.24 Approval of offices of foreign banks; procedures for applications; standards for approval; representative office activities and standards for approval; preservation of existing authority.

(a) <u>Board approval of offices of foreign banks.</u> (1) <u>Prior Board approval of branches, agencies, commercial lending companies, or representative offices of foreign banks</u>. (i) Except as otherwise provided in paragraphs (a)(2) and (a)(3) of this section, a foreign bank shall obtain the approval of the Board before it:

(A) Establishes a branch, agency, commercial lending company subsidiary, or representative office in the United States; or

(B) Acquires ownership or control of a commercial lending company subsidiary.

(2) <u>Prior notice for certain offices</u>. (i) After providing 45 days' prior written notice to the Board, a foreign bank may establish:

(A) An additional office (other than a domestic branch outside the home state of the foreign bank established pursuant to section 5(a)(3) of the IBA (12 U.S.C.3103(a)(3))), provided that the Board has previously determined the foreign bank to be subject to comprehensive supervision or regulation on a consolidated basis by its home country supervisor (<u>comprehensive consolidated supervision or CCS</u>); or

(B) A representative office, if:

(1) The Board has not yet determined the foreign bank to be subject to consolidated comprehensive supervision, but the foreign bank is subject to the BHC Act, either directly or through section 8(a) of the IBA (12 U.S.C.3106(a)); or

(2) The Board previously has approved an application by the foreign bank to establish a branch or agency pursuant to the standard set forth in paragraph (c)(1)(iii) of this section; or

(3) The Board previously has approved an application by the foreign bank to establish a representative office.

(ii) The Board may waive the 45-day notice period if it finds that immediate action is required by the circumstances presented. The notice period shall commence at the time the notice is received by the appropriate Federal Reserve Bank. The Board may suspend the period or require Board approval prior to the establishment of such office if the notification raises significant policy or supervisory concerns.

(3) <u>General consent for certain representative offices</u>. (i) The Board grants its general consent for a foreign bank that is subject to the BHC Act, either directly or through section 8(a) of the IBA (12 U.S.C. 3106(a)), to establish:

(A) A representative office, but only if the Board has previously determined that the foreign bank proposing to establish a representative office is subject to consolidated comprehensive supervision;

(B) A regional administrative office; or

(C) An office that solely engages in limited administrative functions (such as separately maintaining back-office support systems) that:

(1) Are clearly defined;

(2) Are performed in connection with the U.S.banking activities of the foreign bank; and

(3) Do not involve contact or liaison with customers or potential customers, beyond incidental contact with existing customers relating to administrative matters (such as verification or correction of account information).

(4) <u>Suspension of general consent or prior notice procedures</u>. The Board may, at any time, upon notice, modify or suspend the prior notice and general consent procedures in paragraphs (a)(2) and (3) of this section for any foreign bank with respect to the establishment by such foreign bank of any U.S. office of such foreign bank.

(5) <u>Temporary Offices</u>. The Board may, in its discretion, determine that a foreign bank has not established an office if the foreign bank temporarily operates at one or more additional locations in the same city of an existing branch or agency due to renovations, an expansion of activities, a merger or consolidation of the operations of affiliated foreign banks or companies, or other similar circumstances. The foreign bank must provide reasonable advance notice of its intent temporarily to utilize additional locations, and the Board may impose such conditions in connection with its determination as it deems necessary.

(6) <u>After-the-fact Board approval</u>. Where a foreign bank proposes to establish an office in the United States through the acquisition of, or merger or consolidation with, another foreign bank with an office in the United States, the Board may, in its discretion, allow the acquisition, merger, or consolidation to proceed before an application to establish the office has been filed or acted upon under this section if:

(i) The foreign bank or banks resulting from the acquisition, merger, or consolidation, will not directly or indirectly own or control more than 5 percent of any class of the voting securities of, or control, a U.S. bank;

(ii) The Board is given reasonable advance notice of the proposed acquisition, merger, or consolidation; and

(iii) Prior to consummation of the acquisition, merger, or consolidation, each foreign bank, as appropriate, commits in writing either:

(A) To comply with the procedures for an application under this section within a reasonable period of time; to engage in no new lines of business, or otherwise to expand its U.S. activities until the disposition of the application; and to abide by the Board's decision on the application, including, if necessary, a decision to terminate the activities of any such U.S. office, as the Board or the Comptroller may require; or

(B) Promptly to wind-down and close any office, the establishment of which would have required an application under this section; and to engage in no new lines of business or otherwise to expand its U.S. activities prior to the closure of such office.

(7) Notice of change in ownership or control or conversion of existing office or establishment of representative office under general-consent authority. A foreign bank with a U.S. office shall notify the Board in writing within 10 days of the occurrence of any of the following events:

(i) A change in the foreign bank's ownership or control, where the foreign bank is acquired or controlled by another foreign bank or company and the acquired foreign bank with a U.S. office continues to operate in the same corporate form as prior to the change in ownership or control;

(ii) The conversion of a branch to an agency or representative office; an agency to a representative office; or a branch or agency from a federal to a state license, or a state to a federal license; or

(iii) The establishment of a representative office under general-consent authority.

(8) Transactions subject to approval under Regulation Y. Subpart B of Regulation Y (12 CFR 225.11-225.17) governs the acquisition by a foreign banking organization of direct or indirect ownership or control of any voting securities of a bank or bank holding company in the United States if the acquisition results in the foreign banking organization's ownership or control of more than 5 percent of any class of voting securities of a U.S. bank or bank holding company, including through acquisition of a foreign bank or foreign banking organization that owns or controls more than 5 percent of any class of the voting securities of a U.S.bank or bank holding company.

(b) Procedures for application. (1) Filing application. An application for the Board's approval pursuant to this section shall be filed in the manner prescribed by the Board.

(2) Publication requirement. (i) Newspaper notice. Except with respect to a proposed transaction where more extensive notice is required by statute or as otherwise provided in paragraphs (b)(2)(ii) and (iii) of this section, an applicant under this section shall publish a notice in a newspaper of general circulation in the community in which the applicant proposes to engage in business.

(ii) Contents of notice. The newspaper notice shall:

(A) State that an application is being filed as of the date of the newspaper notice; and

(B) Provide the name of the applicant, the subject matter of the application, the place where comments should be sent, and the date by which comments are due, pursuant to paragraph (b)(3) of this section.

(iii) Copy of notice with application. The applicant shall furnish with its application to the Board a copy of the newspaper notice, the date of its publication, and the name and address of the newspaper in which it was published.

(iv) Exception. The Board may modify the publication requirement of paragraphs (b)(2)(i) and (ii) of this section in appropriate circumstances.

(v) Federal branch or federal agency. In the case of an application to establish a federal branch or federal agency, compliance with the publication procedures of the Comptroller shall satisfy the publication requirement of this section. Comments regarding the application should be sent to the Board and the Comptroller.

(3) Written comments. (i) Within 30 days after publication, as required in paragraph (b)(2) of this section, any person may submit to the Board written comments and data on an application.

(ii) The Board may extend the 30-day comment period if the Board determines that additional relevant information is likely to be provided by interested persons, or if other extenuating circumstances exist.

(4) Board action on application. (i) Time limits. (A) The Board shall act on an application from a foreign bank to establish a branch, agency, or commercial lending company subsidiary within 180 calendar days after the receipt of the application.

(B) The Board may extend for an additional 180 calendar days the period within which to take final action, after providing notice of and reasons for the extension to the applicant and the licensing authority.

(C) The time periods set forth in this paragraph (b)(4)(i) may be waived by the applicant.

(ii) Additional information. The Board may request any information in addition to that supplied in the application when the Board believes that the information is necessary for its decision, and may deny an application if it does not receive the information requested from the applicant or its home country supervisor in sufficient time to permit adequate evaluation of the information within the time periods set forth in paragraph (b)(4)(i) of this section.

(5) Coordination with other regulators. Upon receipt of an application by a foreign bank under this section, the Board shall promptly notify, consult with, and consider the views of the licensing authority.

(c) Standards for approval of U.S. offices of foreign banks. (1) Mandatory standards. (i) General. As specified in section 7(d) of the IBA (12 U.S.C. 3105(d)), the Board may not approve an application to establish a branch or an agency, or to establish or acquire ownership or control of a commercial lending company, unless it determines that:

(A) Each of the foreign bank and any parent foreign bank engages directly in the business of banking outside the United States and, except as provided in paragraph (c)(1)(iii) of this section, is subject to comprehensive supervision or regulation on a consolidated basis by its home country supervisor; and

(B) The foreign bank has furnished to the Board the information that the Board requires in order to assess the application adequately.

(ii) Basis for determining comprehensive consolidated supervision. In determining whether a foreign bank and any parent foreign bank is subject to comprehensive consolidated supervision, the Board shall determine whether the foreign bank is supervised or regulated in such a manner that its home country supervisor receives sufficient information on the worldwide operations of the foreign bank (including the relationships of the bank to any affiliate) to assess the foreign bank's overall financial condition and compliance with law and regulation. In making such a determination, the Board shall assess, among other factors, the extent to which the home country supervisor:

(A) Ensures that the foreign bank has adequate procedures for monitoring and controlling its activities worldwide;

(B) Obtains information on the condition of the foreign bank and its subsidiaries and offices outside the home country through regular reports of examination, audit reports, or otherwise;

(C) Obtains information on the dealings and relationship between the foreign bank and its affiliates, both foreign and domestic;

(D) Receives from the foreign bank financial reports that are consolidated on a worldwide basis, or comparable information that permits analysis of the foreign bank's financial condition on a worldwide, consolidated basis;

(E) Evaluates prudential standards, such as capital adequacy and risk asset exposure, on a worldwide basis.

(iii) <u>Determination of comprehensive consolidated supervision not required in certain circumstances</u>. (A) If the Board is unable to find, under paragraph (c)(1)(i) of this section, that a foreign bank is subject to comprehensive consolidated supervision, the Board may, nevertheless, approve an application by the foreign bank if:

(1) The home country supervisor is actively working to establish arrangements for the consolidated supervision of such bank; and

(2) All other factors are consistent with approval.

(B) In deciding whether to use its discretion under this paragraph (c)(1)(iii), the Board also shall consider whether the foreign bank has adopted and implemented procedures to combat money laundering. The Board also may take into account whether the home country supervisor is developing a legal regime to address money laundering or is participating in multilateral efforts to combat money laundering. In approving an application under this paragraph (c)(1)(iii), the Board, after requesting and taking into consideration the views of the licensing authority, may impose any conditions or restrictions relating to the activities or business operations of the proposed branch, agency, or commercial lending company subsidiary, including restrictions on sources of funding. The Board shall coordinate with the licensing authority in the implementation of such conditions or restrictions.

(2) <u>Additional standards</u>. In acting on any application under this subpart, the Board may take into account:

(i) <u>Consent of home country supervisor</u>. Whether the home country supervisor of the foreign bank has consented to the proposed establishment of the branch, agency, or commercial lending company subsidiary;

(ii) <u>Financial resources</u>. The financial resources of the foreign bank (including the foreign bank's capital position, projected capital position, profitability, level of indebtedness, and future prospects) and the condition of any U.S. office of the foreign bank;

(iii) <u>Managerial resources</u>. The managerial resources of the foreign bank, including the competence, experience, and integrity of the officers and directors; the integrity of its principal shareholders; management's experience and capacity to engage in international banking; and the record of the foreign bank and its management of complying with laws and regulations, and of fulfilling any commitments to, and any conditions imposed by, the Board in connection with any prior application;

(iv) <u>Sharing information with supervisors</u>. Whether the foreign bank's home country supervisor and the home country supervisor of any parent of the foreign bank share material information regarding the operations of the foreign bank with other supervisory authorities;

(v) <u>Assurances to Board</u>. (A) Whether the foreign bank has provided the Board with adequate assurances that information will be made available to the Board on the operations or activities of the foreign bank and any of its affiliates that the Board deems necessary to determine and enforce compliance with the IBA, the BHC Act, and other applicable federal banking statutes.

(B) These assurances shall include a statement from the foreign bank describing the laws that would restrict the foreign bank or any of its parents from providing information to the Board;

(vi) <u>Measures for prevention of money laundering</u>. Whether the foreign bank has adopted and implemented procedures to combat money laundering, whether there is a legal regime in place in the home country to address money laundering, and whether the home country is participating in multilateral efforts to combat money laundering;

(vii) <u>Compliance with U.S. law</u>. Whether the foreign bank and its U.S. affiliates are in compliance with applicable U.S. law, and whether the applicant has established adequate controls and procedures in each of its offices to ensure continuing compliance with U.S. law, including controls directed to detection of money laundering and other unsafe or unsound banking practices; and

(viii) The needs of the community and the history of operation of the foreign bank and its relative size in its home country, provided that the size of the foreign bank is not the sole factor in determining whether an office of a foreign bank should be approved.

(3) <u>Additional standards for certain interstate applications</u>. (i) As specified in section 5(a)(3) of the IBA (12 U.S.C. 3103(a)(3)), the Board may not approve an application by a foreign bank to establish a branch, other than a limited branch, outside the home state of the foreign bank under section 5(a)(1) or (2) of the IBA (12 U.S.C. 3103(a)(1), (2)) unless the Board:

(A) Determines that the foreign bank's financial resources including the capital level of the bank, are equivalent to those required for a domestic bank to be approved for branching under section 5155 of the Revised Statutes (12 U.S.C. 36) and section 44 of the Federal Deposit Insurance Act (FDIA) (12 U.S.C. 1831u);

(B) Consults with the Department of the Treasury regarding capital equivalency;

(C) Applies the standards specified in section 7(d) of the IBA (12 U.S.C. 3105(d)) and this paragraph (c); and

(D) Applies the same requirements and conditions to which an application by a domestic bank for an interstate merger is subject under section 44(b)(1), (3), and (4) of the FDIA (12 U.S.C.1831u(b)(1), (3), (4)); and

(ii) As specified in section 5(a)(7) of the IBA (12 U.S.C. 3103(a)(7)), the Board may not approve an application to establish a branch through a change in status of an agency or limited branch outside the foreign bank 's home state unless:

(A) The establishment and operation of such branch is permitted by such state; and

(B) Such agency or branch has been in operation in such state for a period of time that meets the state's minimum age requirement permitted under section 44(a)(5) of the Federal Deposit Insurance Act.

(4) Board conditions on approval. The Board may impose any conditions on its approval as it deems necessary, including a condition which may permit future termination by the Board of any activities or, in the case of a federal branch or a federal agency, by the Comptroller, based on the inability of the foreign bank to provide information on its activities or those of its affiliates that the Board deems necessary to determine and enforce compliance with U.S.banking laws.

(d) Representative offices. (1) Permissible activities. A representative office may engage in:

(i) Representational and administrative functions. Representational and administrative functions in connection with the banking activities of the foreign bank, which may include soliciting new business for the foreign bank; conducting research; acting as liaison between the foreign bank's head office and customers in the United States; performing preliminary and servicing steps in connection with lending;[4] or performing back-office functions; but shall not include contracting for any deposit or deposit-like liability, lending money, or engaging in any other banking activity for the foreign bank;

(ii) Credit approvals under certain circumstances. Making credit decisions if the foreign bank also operates one or more branches or agencies in the United States, the loans approved at the representative office are made by a U.S. office of the bank, and the loan proceeds are not disbursed in the representative office; and

(iii) Other functions. Other functions for or on behalf of the foreign bank or its affiliates, such as operating as a regional administrative office of the foreign bank, but only to the extent that these other functions are not banking activities and are not prohibited by applicable federal or state law, or by ruling or order of the Board.

(2) Standards for approval of representative offices. As specified in section 10(a)(2) of the IBA (12 U.S.C.3107(a)(2)), in acting on the application of a foreign bank to establish a representative office, the Board shall take into account, to the extent it deems appropriate, the standards for approval set out in paragraph (c) of this section. The

---

[4] *See* 12 C.F.R.§ 250.141((h) for activities that constitute preliminary and servicing steps.

standard regarding supervision by the foreign bank's home country supervisor (as set out in paragraph (c)(1)(i)(A) of this section) will be met, in the case of a representative office application, if the Board makes a finding that the applicant bank is subject to a supervisory framework that is consistent with the activities of the proposed representative office, taking into account the nature of such activities and the operating record of the applicant.

(3) <u>Special-purpose foreign government-owned banks</u>. A foreign government-owned organization engaged in banking activities in its home country that are not commercial in nature may apply to the Board for a determination that the organization is not a foreign bank for purposes of this section. A written request setting forth the basis for such a determination may be submitted to the Reserve Bank of the District in which the foreign organization's representative office is located in the United States, or to the Board, in the case of a proposed establishment of a representative office. The Board shall review and act upon each request on a case-by-case basis.

(4) <u>Additional requirements</u>. The Board may impose any additional requirements that it determines to be necessary to carry out the purposes of the IBA.

(e) <u>Preservation of existing authority</u>. Nothing in this subpart shall be construed to relieve any foreign bank or foreign banking organization from any otherwise applicable requirement of federal or state law, including any applicable licensing requirement.

(f) <u>Reports of crimes and suspected crimes</u>. Except for a federal branch or a federal agency or a state branch that is insured by the Federal Deposit Insurance Corporation (FDIC), a branch, agency, or representative office of a foreign bank operating in the United States shall file a suspicious activity report in accordance with the provisions of section 208.62 of Regulation H (12 CFR 208.62).

(g) <u>Management of shell branches</u>.

(1) A state-licensed branch or agency shall not manage, through an office of the foreign bank which is located outside the United States and is managed or controlled by such state-licensed branch or agency, any type of activity that a bank organized under the laws of the United States or any state is not permitted to manage at any branch or subsidiary of such bank which is located outside the United States.

(2) For purposes of this subsection, an office of a foreign bank located outside the United States is "managed or controlled" by a state-licensed branch or agency if a majority of the responsibility for business decisions, including but not limited to decisions with regard to lending or asset management or funding or liability management, or the responsibility for record keeping in respect of assets or liabilities for that non-U.S. office, resides at the state-licensed branch or agency.

(3) The types of activities that a state-licensed branch or agency may manage through an office located outside the United States that it manage or controls include the types of activities authorized to a U.S.bank by state or federal charters, regulations issued by chartering or regulatory authorities, and other U.S.banking laws, including the Federal Reserve Act, and the implementing regulations, but U.S. procedural or quantitative requirements that may be applicable to the conduct of such activities by U.S. banks shall not apply.

(h) <u>Government securities sales practices</u>. An uninsured state-licensed branch or agency of a foreign bank that is required to give notice to the Board under section 15C of the Securities Exchange Act of 1934 (15 USC 78o-5) and the Department of the Treasury rules under section 15C (17 CFR 400.1(d)and part 401) shall be subject to the provisions of 12 CFR 208.37 to the same extent as a state member bank that is required to give such notice.

(i) <u>Protection of customer information</u>. An uninsured state-licensed branch or agency of a foreign bank shall comply with the Interagency Guidelines Establishing Standards for Safeguarding Customer Information prescribed pursuant to sections 501 and 505 of the Gramm-Leach Bliley Act (15 USC 6801 and 6805), set forth in appendix D-2 to part 208 of this chapter.

§ 211.25 Termination of offices of foreign banks.

(a) <u>Grounds for termination</u>. (1) <u>General</u>. Under sections 7(e) and 10(b) of the IBA (12 U.S.C.3105 (d), 3107(b)), the Board may order a foreign bank to terminate the activities of its representative office, state branch, state agency, or commercial lending company subsidiary if the Board finds that:

(i) The foreign bank is not subject to comprehensive consolidated supervision in accordance with section 211.24(c)(1), and the home country supervisor is not making demonstrable progress in establishing arrangements for the consolidated supervision of the foreign bank; or

(ii) Both of the following criteria are met:

(A) There is reasonable cause to believe that the foreign bank, or any of its affiliates, has committed a violation of law or engaged in an unsafe or unsound banking practice in the United States; and

(B) As a result of such violation or practice, the continued operation of the foreign bank's representative office, state branch, state agency, or commercial lending company subsidiary would not be consistent with the public interest, or with the purposes of the IBA, the BHC Act, or the FDIA.

(2) <u>Additional ground</u>. The Board also may enforce any condition imposed in connection with an order issued under section 211.24.

(b) <u>Factor</u>. In making its findings under this section, the Board may take into account the needs of the community, the history of operation of the foreign bank, and its relative size in its home country, provided that the size of the foreign bank shall not be the sole determining factor in a decision to terminate an office.

(c) <u>Consultation with relevant state supervisor</u>. Except in the case of termination pursuant to the expedited procedure in paragraph (d)(3) of this section, the Board shall request and consider the views of the relevant state supervisor before issuing an order terminating the activities of a state branch, state agency, representative office, or commercial lending company subsidiary under this section.

(d) <u>Termination procedures</u>. (1) <u>Notice and hearing</u>. Except as otherwise provided in paragraph (d)(3) of this section, an order issued under paragraph (a)(1) of this section shall be issued only after notice to the relevant state supervisor and the foreign bank and after an opportunity for a hearing.

(2) <u>Procedures for hearing</u>. Hearings under this section shall be conducted pursuant to the Board's Rules of Practice for Hearings (12 CFR part 263).

(3) <u>Expedited procedure</u>. The Board may act without providing an opportunity for a hearing, if it determines that expeditious action is necessary in order to protect the public interest. When the Board finds that it is necessary to act without providing an opportunity for a hearing, the Board, solely in its discretion, may:

(i) Provide the foreign bank that is the subject of the termination order with notice of the intended termination order;

(ii) Grant the foreign bank an opportunity to present a written submission opposing issuance of the order; or

(iii) Take any other action designed to provide the foreign bank with notice and an opportunity to present its views concerning the order.

(e) <u>Termination of federal branch or federal agency</u>. The Board may transmit to the Comptroller a recommendation that the license of a federal branch or federal agency be terminated if the Board has reasonable cause to believe that the foreign bank or any affiliate of the foreign bank has engaged in conduct for which the activities of a state branch or state agency may be terminated pursuant to this section.

(f) <u>Voluntary termination</u>. A foreign bank shall notify the Board at least 30 days prior to terminating the activities of any office. Notice pursuant to this paragraph (f) is in addition to, and does not satisfy, any other federal or state requirements relating to the termination of an office or the requirement for prior notice of the closing of a branch, pursuant to section 39 of the FDIA (12 U.S.C.1831p).

§ 211.26 Examination of offices and affiliates of foreign banks.

(a) <u>Conduct of examinations</u>--(1) <u>Examination of branches, agencies, commercial lending companies, and affiliates</u>. The Board may examine:

(i) Any branch or agency of a foreign bank;

(ii) Any commercial lending company or bank controlled by one or more foreign banks, or one or more foreign companies that control a foreign bank; and

(iii) Any other office or affiliate of a foreign bank conducting business in any state.

(2) <u>Examination of representative offices</u>. The Board may examine any representative office in the manner and with the frequency it deems appropriate.

(b) <u>Coordination of examinations</u>. To the extent possible, the Board shall coordinate its examinations of the U.S. offices and U.S. affiliates of a foreign bank with the licensing authority and, in the case of an insured branch, the Federal Deposit Insurance Corporation (FDIC), including through simultaneous examinations of the U.S. offices and U.S. affiliates of a foreign bank.

(c) <u>Frequency of on-site examination</u>--(1) <u>General</u>. Each branch or agency of a foreign bank shall be examined on-site at least once during each 12-month period (beginning on the date the most recent examination of the office ended) by –

(i) The Board;

(ii) The FDIC, if the branch of the foreign bank accepts or maintains insured deposits;

(iii) The Comptroller, if the branch or agency of the foreign bank is licensed by the Comptroller; or

(iv) The state supervisor, if the office of the foreign bank is licensed or chartered by the state.

(2) <u>18-month cycle for certain small institutions</u>--(i) <u>Mandatory standards</u>. The Board may conduct a full-scope, on-site examination at least once during each 18-month period, rather than each 12-month period as required in paragraph (c)(1) of this section, if the branch or agency –

(A) Has total assets of $250 million or less;

(B) Has received a composite ROCA supervisory rating (which rates risk management, operational controls, compliance, and asset quality) of 1 or 2 at its most recent examination;

(C) Satisfies the requirement of either the following paragraph (c)(2)(i)(C)(1) or (2):

(1) The foreign bank's most recently reported capital adequacy position consists of, or is equivalent to, tier 1 and total risk-based

capital ratios of at least 6 percent and 10 percent, respectively, on a consolidated basis; or

(2) The branch or agency has maintained on a daily basis, over the past three quarters, eligible assets in an amount not less than 108 percent of the preceding quarter's average third-party liabilities (determined consistent with applicable federal and state law) and sufficient liquidity is currently available to meet its obligations to third parties;

(D) Is not subject to a formal enforcement action or order by the Board, FDIC, or OCC; and

(E) Has not experienced a change in control during the preceding 12-month period in which a full-scope, on-site examination would have been required but for this section.

(ii) Discretionary standards. In determining whether a branch or agency of a foreign bank that meets the standards of paragraph (c)(2)(i) of this section should not be eligible for an 18-month examination cycle pursuant to this paragraph (c)(2), the Board may consider additional factors, including whether –

(A) Any of the individual components of the ROCA supervisory rating of a branch or agency of a foreign bank is rated "3" or worse;

(B) The results of any off-site surveillance indicate a deterioration in the condition of the office;

(C) The size, relative importance, and role of a particular office when reviewed in the context of the foreign bank's entire U.S. operations otherwise necessitate an annual examination; and

(D) The condition of the foreign bank gives rise to such a need.

(3) Authority to conduct more frequent examinations. Nothing in paragraphs (c)(1) and (2) of this section limits the authority of the Board to examine any U.S. branch or agency of a foreign bank as frequently as it deems necessary.

§ 211.27 Disclosure of supervisory information to foreign supervisors.

(a) Disclosure by Board. The Board may disclose information obtained in the course of exercising its supervisory or examination authority to a foreign bank regulatory or supervisory authority, if the Board determines that disclosure is appropriate for bank supervisory or regulatory purposes and will not prejudice the interests of the United States.

(b) Confidentiality. Before making any disclosure of information pursuant to paragraph (a) of this section, the Board shall obtain, to the extent necessary, the agreement of the foreign bank regulatory or supervisory authority to maintain the confidentiality of such information to the extent possible under applicable law.

§ 211.28 Provisions applicable to branches and agencies: limitation on loans to one borrower.

(a) <u>Limitation on loans to one borrower</u>. Except as provided in paragraph (b) of this section, the total loans and extensions of credit by all the state branches and state agencies of a foreign bank outstanding to a single borrower at one time shall be aggregated with the total loans and extensions of credit by all federal branches and federal agencies of the same foreign bank outstanding to such borrower at the time; and shall be subject to the limitations and other provisions of section 5200 of the Revised Statutes (12 U.S.C.84), and the regulations promulgated thereunder, in the same manner that extensions of credit by a federal branch or federal agency are subject to section 4(b) of the IBA (12 U.S.C.3102(b)) as if such state branches and state agencies were federal branches and federal agencies.

(b) <u>Preexisting loans and extensions of credit</u>. Any loans or extensions of credit to a single borrower that were originated prior to December 19, 1991, by a state branch or state agency of the same foreign bank and that, when aggregated with loans and extensions of credit by all other branches and agencies of the foreign bank, exceed the limits set forth in paragraph (a) of this section, may be brought into compliance with such limitations through routine repayment, provided that any new loans or extensions of credit (including renewals of existing unfunded credit lines, or extensions of the maturities of existing loans) to the same borrower shall comply with the limits set forth in paragraph (a) of this section.

§ 211.29 Applications by state branches and state agencies to conduct activities not permissible for federal branches.

(a) <u>Scope</u>. A state branch or state agency shall file with the Board a prior written application for permission to engage in or continue to engage in any type of activity that:

(1) Is not permissible for a federal branch, pursuant to statute, regulation, official bulletin or circular, or order or interpretation issued in writing by the Comptroller; or

(2) Is rendered impermissible due to a subsequent change in statute, regulation, official bulletin or circular, written order or interpretation, or decision of a court of competent jurisdiction.

(b) <u>Exceptions</u>. No application shall be required by a state branch or state agency to conduct any activity that is otherwise permissible under applicable state and federal law or regulation and that:

(1) Has been determined by the FDIC, pursuant to 12 CFR 362.4(c)(3)(i)-(3)(ii)(A), not to present a significant risk to the affected deposit insurance fund;

(2) Is permissible for a federal branch, but the Comptroller imposes a quantitative limitation on the conduct of such activity by the federal branch;

(3) Is conducted as agent rather than as principal, provided that the activity is one that could be conducted by a state-chartered bank headquartered in the same state in which the branch or agency is licensed; or

(4) Any other activity that the Board has determined may be conducted by any state branch or state agency of a foreign bank without further application to the Board.

(c) Contents of application. An application submitted pursuant to paragraph (a) of this section shall be in letter form and shall contain the following information:

(1) A brief description of the activity, including the manner in which it will be conducted, and an estimate of the expected dollar volume associated with the activity;

(2) An analysis of the impact of the proposed activity on the condition of the U.S. operations of the foreign bank in general, and of the branch or agency in particular, including a copy, if available, of any feasibility study, management plan, financial projections, business plan, or similar document concerning the conduct of the activity;

(3) A resolution by the applicant's board of directors or, if a resolution is not required pursuant to the applicant's organizational documents, evidence of approval by senior management, authorizing the conduct of such activity and the filing of this application;

(4) If the activity is to be conducted by a state branch insured by the FDIC, statements by the applicant:

(i) Of whether or not it is in compliance with 12 CFR 346.19 (Pledge of Assets) and 12 CFR 346.20 (Asset Maintenance);

(ii) That it has complied with all requirements of the FDIC concerning an application to conduct the activity and the status of the application, including a copy of the FDIC's disposition of such application, if available; and

(iii) Explaining why the activity will pose no significant risk to the deposit insurance fund; and

(5) Any other information that the Reserve Bank deems appropriate.

(d) Factors considered in determination. (1) The Board shall consider the following factors in determining whether a proposed activity is consistent with sound banking practice:

(i) The types of risks, if any, the activity poses to the U.S. operations of the foreign banking organization in general, and the branch or agency in particular;

(ii) If the activity poses any such risks, the magnitude of each risk; and

(iii) If a risk is not de minimis, the actual or proposed procedures to control and minimize the risk.

(2) Each of the factors set forth in paragraph (d)(1) of this section shall be evaluated in light of the financial condition of the foreign bank in general and the branch or agency in particular and the volume of the activity.

(e) Application procedures. Applications pursuant to this section shall be filed with the appropriate Federal Reserve Bank. An application shall not be deemed complete until it contains all the information requested by the Reserve Bank and has been accepted. Approval of such an application may be conditioned on the applicant's agreement to conduct the activity subject to specific conditions or limitations.

(f) Divestiture or cessation. (1) If an application for permission to continue to conduct an activity is not approved by the Board or, if applicable, the FDIC, the applicant shall submit a detailed written plan of divestiture or cessation of the activity to the appropriate Federal Reserve Bank within 60 days of the disapproval.

(i) The divestiture or cessation plan shall describe in detail the manner in which the applicant will divest itself of or cease the activity, and shall include a projected timetable describing how long the divestiture or cessation is expected to take.

(ii) Divestiture or cessation shall be complete within one year from the date of the disapproval, or within such shorter period of time as the Board shall direct.

(2) If a foreign bank operating a state branch or state agency chooses not to apply to the Board for permission to continue to conduct an activity that is not permissible for a federal branch, or which is rendered impermissible due to a subsequent change in statute, regulation, official bulletin or circular, written order or interpretation, or decision of a court of competent jurisdiction, the foreign bank shall submit a written plan of divestiture or cessation, in conformance with paragraph (f)(1) of this section within 60 days of the effective date of this part or of such change or decision.

§ 211.30 Criteria for evaluating U.S. operations of foreign banks not subject to consolidated supervision.

(a) Development and publication of criteria. Pursuant to the Foreign Bank Supervision Enhancement Act, Pub.L.102-242, 105 Stat.2286 (1991), the Board shall develop and publish criteria to be used in evaluating the operations of any foreign bank in the United States that the Board has determined is not subject to comprehensive consolidated supervision.

(b) <u>Criteria considered by Board</u>. Following a determination by the Board that, having taken into account the standards set forth in § 211.24 (c)(1), a foreign bank is not subject to CCS, the Board shall consider the following criteria in determining whether the foreign bank's U.S. operations should be permitted to continue and, if so, whether any supervisory constraints should be placed upon the bank in connection with those operations:

(1) The proportion of the foreign bank's total assets and total liabilities that are located or booked in its home country, as well as the distribution and location of its assets and liabilities that are located or booked elsewhere;

(2) The extent to which the operations and assets of the foreign bank and any affiliates are subject to supervision by its home country supervisor;

(3) Whether the home country supervisor of such foreign bank is actively working to establish arrangements for comprehensive consolidated supervision of the bank, and whether demonstrable progress is being made;

(4) Whether the foreign bank has effective and reliable systems of internal controls and management information and reporting, which enable its management properly to oversee its worldwide operations;

(5) Whether the foreign bank 's home country supervisor has any objection to the bank continuing to operate in the United States;

(6) Whether the foreign bank's home country supervisor and the home country supervisor of any parent of the foreign bank share material information regarding the operations of the foreign bank with other supervisory authorities;

(7) The relationship of the U.S. operations to the other operations of the foreign bank, including whether the foreign bank maintains funds in its U.S. offices that are in excess of amounts due to its U.S. offices from the foreign bank's non-U.S. offices;

(8) The soundness of the foreign bank's overall financial condition;

(9) The managerial resources of the foreign bank, including the competence, experience, and integrity of the officers and directors, and the integrity of its principal shareholders;

(10) The scope and frequency of external audits of the foreign bank;

(11) The operating record of the foreign bank generally and its role in the banking system in its home country;

(12) The foreign bank's record of compliance with relevant laws, as well as the adequacy of its anti-money-laundering controls and procedures, in respect of its worldwide operations;

(13) The operating record of the U.S. offices of the foreign bank;

(14) The views and recommendations of the Comptroller or the relevant state supervisors in those states in which the foreign bank has operations, as appropriate;

(15) Whether the foreign bank, if requested, has provided the Board with adequate assurances that such information will be made available on the operations or activities of the foreign bank and any of its affiliates as the Board deems necessary to determine and enforce compliance with the IBA, the BHC Act, and other U.S.banking statutes; and

(16) Any other information relevant to the safety and soundness of the U.S. operations of the foreign bank.

(c) Restrictions on U.S. operations. (1) Terms of agreement. Any foreign bank that the Board determines is not subject to CCS may be required to enter into an agreement to conduct its U.S. operations subject to such restrictions as the Board, having considered the criteria set forth in paragraph (b) of this section, determines to be appropriate in order to ensure the safety and soundness of its U.S. operations.

(2) Failure to enter into or comply with agreement. A foreign bank that is required by the Board to enter into an agreement pursuant to paragraph (c)(1) of this section and either fails to do so, or fails to comply with the terms of such agreement, may be subject to:

(i) Enforcement action, in order to ensure safe and sound banking operations, under 12 U.S.C.1818; or

(ii) Termination or a recommendation for termination of its U.S. operations, under § 211.25 ((a) and (e) and section (7)(e) of the IBA (12 U.S.C.3105(e)).

CHAPTER FOUR

INFRASTRUCTURE: CAPITAL ADEQUACY

Over twenty years ago, financial regulators in developed countries started to coordinate their activities, prompted a dramatic growth in banks' international and cross-border activities. Banks from many countries were opening offices and lending to borrowers outside their home country. The oil price rises of the early 1970s had catapulted banks into a new job, recycling the deposits of oil surplus countries by lending to others in deficit. Regulators were concerned.

This Chapter reviews the remarkable story of how regulators from many countries cooperated to address those concerns. After devising ways to allocate among themselves responsibility for banks with cross-border operations, regulators turned to substantive policy. Capital adequacy rules were seen as a critical tool. Because rules for credit risk and position or market risk differ so much, we examine them separately.

SECTION I

CAPITAL ADEQUACY FOR CREDIT RISK

This section considers the relevance of capital, the key elements of the Basel Accord, the Accord's performance so far, and proposals to amend or replace it. The Accord took shape under the wing of the Bank for International Settlements (the BIS), which is described in Chapter 3. The capital adequacy standards for credit risk discussed in this section apply to banks.

A.   THE BACKGROUND OF THE ACCORD

In 1976 the BIS, concerned about the need to coordinate banking supervision in member countries, set up the Committee on Banking Regulations and Supervisory Practices as a standing committee of the central bank governors of the Group of Ten (G10) countries. Eventually called the Basel Committee on Banking Supervision, its members are from Belgium, Canada, France, Germany, Italy, Japan, Luxembourg, the Netherlands, Spain, Sweden, Switzerland, the United Kingdom, and the United States. Each sends a representative of its central bank and bank supervisor.

The Basel Committee has no authority to bind member countries. At first, the committee was a forum in which regulators of banks in industrialized countries could coordinate their activities. Gradually its reach extended to coordination with regulators of other financial institutions. The committee, supported by a secretariat based in Basel, studies issues and recommends action to the Committee of G10 Governors. By the late 1990s, it met quarterly, convened annual conferences of bank supervisors from over 100 countries, proposed ways to strengthen coordination, developed principles to guide regulators around the world, worked with supervisors of other financial institutions (such as securities regulators) and supervisors within a region (such as the European Union), and generally served as the nerve center for communications and common action.

The first activities of the Basel Committee coordinated procedures, not substantive rules. In 1976, its Basel Concordat allocated responsibility among home and host supervisors of banks with offices in more than one country or doing cross-border business. It modified the Concordat in 1983 to ensure that every international bank would be subject to consolidated supervision by one regulator. That is, one supervisor would have an overview of all the bank's activities, anywhere in the world. In theory, no bank would slip between gaps among national regulators. Much of this and the following paragraphs is drawn from P. Cooke, Bank Capital Adequacy (1991).

The rules on capital convergence marked the entry of the Basel Committee into the arena of substantive rules. Since even the G10 countries' rules about bank regulation varied widely and the variations affected competition among banks in international markets, any attempt to align the rules could affect banks' profits and operations. The committee was treading on sensitive ground. On the other hand, after cutting margins, profits, and capital to compete for business from the mid-1970s on, banks in G10 countries were on the ropes in 1982 when many developing countries effectively defaulted on their debt to international banks and the ensuing crisis highlighted the need for collective regulatory action. Within a few years, new banking activities off balance sheet (or, non-lending operations) required a more sophisticated approach to capital adequacy.

UK and US regulators led the way with an initiative in 1986 to relate capital requirements to the risk of the asset. This departed from the practice of using a fixed percentage of the value of the asset regardless of its risk. Regulators of other industrial countries joined. In July 1988, the committee accepted an 8% minimum capital rule with the following elements, as described by Peter Cooke:

THE KEY ELEMENTS OF THE CAPITAL CONVERGENCE FRAMEWORK

■ capital definition

- capital is split between Tier 1 or core elements (equity and disclosed reserves) and Tier 2 or supplementary elements (undisclosed reserves, asset revaluation reserves, general provisions, hybrid debt/equity instruments and subordinated term debt). Some practitioners choose to distinguish between Upper Tier 2 (perpetual debt) and Lower Tier 2 (dated debt). The inclusion of the individual Tier 2 elements is at national discretion.

- deductions from capital cover goodwill, investments in unconsolidated financial subsidiaries and, at national discretion, holdings of other banks' capital.

- Tier 2 elements are only eligible up to 100% of Tier 1; subordinated debt must not exceed 50% of Tier 1; and general provisions are limited to 1.25% of risk assets.

■ risk asset weightings

- for on-balance sheet assets five basic scales of risk weightings are applied (0%, 10%, 20%, 50% and 100%). The main categories are central governments, public sector entities, banks and non-bank corporates and for the first three of these certain distinctions are made between OECD and non-OECD counterparties.

- for off-balance sheet items a system of credit conversion factors is used. These include such categories as commitments and contingencies. The conversion factors are applied to the nominal principal amount of exposure to produce a credit equivalent amount which in turn is weighted according to the category of the counterparty. Interest rate and foreign exchange rate contracts are treated similarly but with adjustments to take into account their particular nature.

■ target ratio and timetables

- the Basel guidelines envisage that banks should build up gradually to the 8% minimum standard by the end of 1992 (of which at least 50% must be in Tier 1 capital). An interim standard of 7.25% was set to be reached by end 1990.

- in building up from the interim to the full target ratio the balance between Tier 1 and Tier 2 and the amounts of subordinated debt and general provisions allowed in Tier 2 are gradually reduced.

These rules applied to banks with international operations, but countries could choose to apply them to all banks. This was important for the EU, which, as it worked toward the single internal market, was preparing its own rules on capital adequacy for banks in the EU. These consisted of two directives, one on Own Funds (89/299/EEC) and the other on Solvency (89/647/EEC). As it framed the rules, the Basel Committee coordinated closely with the European Commission.

By 2002, proposals were being debated for a Basel Accord II that would revise the original standards for credit risk. The Basel Committee was quite explicit at the time that the rules only applied to credit risk. After completing these rules, it turned its attention to setting capital standards for other types of risk, such as interest risk, exchange risk, and market risk, which is examined in the second part of the Chapter.

Notes and Questions

1. Capital cushions against the risk of loss from loans and affects competition. Governments regulate the capital of banks, but it is not immediately obvious that they have to do so. One goal is to protect depositors, but creditors could protect themselves by not using banks with capital they find inadequate. Why would governments not rely on this market discipline?

2. Capital/asset ratios are seen as a very powerful tool of regulation. Consider a simple ratio, such as 1/20, which many regulators applied before the Basel Accord. By setting this ratio, the regulators limit the assets of the bank to 20 times its capital. A bank with $5 million in capital could only lend $100 million. The ratio limits the ability of banks to expand credit (as we will see in Chapter 9), which could augment inflation.

   a. Regulators also want capital to cushion against bad loans. But many failed banks appear to have adequate or even high capital just before they collapse. Why would this be the case?

   b. Banks generally prefer to want the capital/asset ratio to be smaller (e.g., 1/40) rather than larger (1/20). Assume that every $100 in loans gives a bank $1 in profit. How would the two capital asset ratios affect the bank's profitability? Why would a bank not simply raise more capital to comply with the 1/20 ratio?

3. What, if anything, is wrong with a simple capital/asset ratio? What would be the impact if banks from country X followed a 1/20 rule and those from country Y a 1/40 rule?

B. THE BASEL ACCORD

Each country that chose to adopt the Accord had to implement it through national regulations. In the United States, the Federal Reserve Board issued one set of regulations for state banks and another for bank holding companies. The Fed had been a leading and early proponent of the Accord, working with the Bank of England to push regulators in other countries to accept it.

The following excerpts from the Fed's guidelines for state banks give some more background about the Accord. You should consider the nature of this Accord. Whose is it? What does it require? How do the parties to the Accord enforce it?

1. GENERAL ELEMENTS AND THE DEFINITION OF CAPITAL

FEDERAL RESERVE SYSTEM, RISK-BASED CAPITAL GUIDELINES
12 CFR 208 app. A (1999).

I. OVERVIEW

The Board of Governors of the Federal Reserve System has adopted a risk-based capital measure to assist in the assessment of the capital adequacy of state member banks.[1] The principal objectives of this measure are to (i) make regulatory capital requirements more sensitive to differences in risk profiles among banks; (ii) factor off-balance-sheet exposures into the assessment of capital adequacy; (iii) minimize disincentives to holding liquid, low-risk assets; and (iv) achieve greater consistency in the evaluation of the capital adequacy of major banks throughout the world.[2]

The risk-based capital guidelines include both a definition of capital and a framework for calculating weighted-risk assets by assigning assets and off-balance-sheet items to broad risk categories. A bank's risk-based capital ratio is calculated by dividing its qualifying capital (the numerator of the ratio) by its weighted-risk assets (the denominator).[3] The definition of "qualifying capital" is outlined below in section II, and the procedures for calculating weighted-risk assets are discussed in section III. Attachment I

---

[1] Supervisory ratios that relate capital to total assets for state member banks are outlined in appendix B of this part [at 3-1950] and in appendix B to part 225 of the Federal Reserve's Regulation Y, 12 CFR 225 [at 3-1940].

[2] The risk-based capital measure is based upon a framework developed jointly by supervisory authorities from the countries represented on the Basel Committee on Banking Regulations and Supervisory Practices (Basel Supervisors' Committee) and endorsed by the Group of Ten Central Bank Governors. The framework is described in a paper prepared by the BSC entitled "International Convergence of Capital Measurement," July 1988.

[3] Banks will initially be expected to utilize period-end amounts in calculating their risk-based capital ratios. When necessary and appropriate, ratios based on average balances may also be calculated on a case-by-case basis. Moreover, to the extent banks have data on average balances that can be used to calculate risk-based ratios, the Federal Reserve will take such data into account.

illustrates a sample calculation of weighted-risk assets and the risk-based capital ratio.

In addition, when certain banks that engage in trading activities calculate their risk-based capital ratio under this appendix A, they must also refer to appendix E of this part, which incorporates capital charges for certain market risks into the risk-based capital ratio. When calculating their risk-based capital ratio under this appendix A, such banks are required to refer to appendix E of this part for supplemental rules to determine qualifying and excess capital, calculate risk-weighted assets, calculate market-risk-equivalent assets, and calculate risk-based capital ratios adjusted for market risk.

.   .   .

The risk-based guidelines apply to all state member banks on a consolidated basis. They are to be used in the examination and supervisory process as well as in the analysis of applications acted upon by the Federal Reserve. Thus, in considering an application filed by a state member bank, the Federal Reserve will take into account the bank's risk-based capital ratio, the reasonableness of its capital plans, and the degree of progress it has demonstrated toward meeting the ... risk-based capital standards.

The risk-based capital ratio focuses principally on broad categories of credit risk, although the framework for assigning assets and off-balance-sheet items to risk categories does incorporate elements of transfer risk, as well as limited instances of interest-rate and market risk. The framework incorporates risks arising from traditional banking activities as well as risks arising from nontraditional activities. The risk-based ratio does not, however, incorporate other factors that can affect an institution's financial condition. These factors include overall interest-rate exposure; liquidity, funding, and market risks; the quality and level of earnings; investment, loan portfolio, and other concentrations of credit; certain risks arising from nontraditional activities; the quality of loans and investments; the effectiveness of loan and investment policies; and management's overall ability to monitor and control financial and operating risks, including the risks presented by concentrations of credit and nontraditional activities.

In addition to evaluating capital ratios, an overall assessment of capital adequacy must take account of those factors, including, in particular, the level and severity of problem and classified assets as well as a bank's exposure to declines in the economic value of its capital due to changes in interest rates. For this reason, the final supervisory judgment on a bank's capital adequacy may differ significantly from conclusions that might be drawn solely from the level of its risk-based capital ratio.

The risk-based capital guidelines establish *minimum* ratios of capital to weighted-risk assets. In light of the considerations just discussed, banks generally are expected to operate well above the minimum risk-based ratios. In particular, banks contemplating significant expansion proposals are expected to maintain strong capital levels, substantially above the minimum ratios and should not allow significant diminution of financial strength below these strong levels to fund their expansion plans. Institutions with high or inordinate levels of risk are also expected to operate well above minimum capital standards. In all cases, institutions should hold capital commensurate with the level and nature of the risks to which they are exposed. Banks that do not meet the minimum risk-based standard, or that are otherwise considered to be inadequately capitalized, are expected to develop and implement plans acceptable to the Federal Reserve for achieving adequate levels of capital within a reasonable period of time.

The Board will monitor the implementation and effects of these guidelines in relation to domestic and international developments in the banking industry. When necessary and appropriate, the Board will consider the need to modify the guidelines in light of any significant changes in the economy, financial markets, banking practices, or other relevant factors.

The extent to which regulators become involved in the activities of a bank vary with the strength of the bank's capital. The Federal Deposit Insurance Corporation Improvement Act of 1991 (FDICIA) designated five levels of capital. Well capitalized banks had 10% or more risk-weighted capital, 5% in Tier 1, and were minimally supervised. Adequately capitalized banks had 8-10% capital, 4-5% in Tier 1, and were monitored more often. Undercapitalized banks, with 3-6% capital and 3-4% in Tier 1, were required to develop a recovery plan and limit growth. Significantly undercapitalized banks, with less than 3% capital, had to recapitalize and their transactions with affiliates and payments on deposits were restricted. Finally, critically undercapitalized banks, with a book value net worth (less goodwill) of below 2% of assets, were to be sold or closed quickly. The following Attachments are from the guidelines.

ATTACHMENT I
Sample Calculation of Risk–Based Capital Ratio
for State Member Banks

Example of a bank with $6,000 in total capital and the following assets and off-balance sheet items:

Balance Sheet Assets

Cash	$ 5,000
U.S. Treasuries	20,000
Balances at domestic banks	5,000
Loans secured by first liens on 1-4 family residential properties	5,000
Loans to private corporations	65,000
Total Balance Sheet Assets	$100,000

Off-Balance Sheet Items

Standby letters of credit ("SLCs") backing general obligation debt issues of U.S. municipalities ("GOs")	$ 10,000
Long-term legally binding commitments to private corporations	20,000
Total Off-Balance Sheet Items	$ 30,000

This bank's total capital to total assets (leverage) ratio would be:
($6,000/$100,000) = 6.00%.

To compute the bank's weighted risk assets:

1. Compute the credit equivalent amount of each off-balance sheet ("OBS") item.

OBS Item	Face Value		Conversion Factor		Credit Equivalent Amount
SLCs backing municipal GOs	$10,000	×	1.00	=	$10,000
Long-term commitments to private corporations	$20,000	×	0.50	=	$10,000

2. Multiply each balance sheet asset and the credit equivalent amount of each OBS item by the appropriate risk weight.

0% Category

Cash	$ 5,000				
U.S. Treasuries	20,000				
	$25,000	×	0	=	0

20% Category

Balances at domestic banks	$ 5,000				
Credit equivalent amounts of SLCs backing GOs of U.S. municipalities	10,000				
	$15,000	×	0.20	=	$ 3,000

50% Category

Loans secured by first liens on 1-4 family residential properties	$ 5,000	×	0.50	=	$ 2,500

100% Category

Loans to private corporations	$65,000				
Credit equivalent amounts of long-term commitments to private corporations	10,000				
	$75,000	×	1.00	=	$75,000
Total Risk-Weighted Assets					$80,500

This bank's ratio of total capital to weighted risk assets (risk-based capital ratio) would be:
($6,000/$80,500) = 7.45%

ATTACHMENT II

Summary Definition of Qualifying Capital for State Member Banks Using the Year-end 1992 Standards

Components	Minimum Requirements After Transition Period
Core Capital (tier 1)	Must equal or exceed 4% of weighted risk assets
Common stockholders' equity	No limit
Qualifying non-cumulative perpetual preferred stock	No limit; banks should avoid undue reliance on preferred stock in tier 1
Minority interest in equity accounts of consolidated subsidiaries	Banks should avoid using minority interests to introduce elements not otherwise qualifying for tier 1 capital
Less: Goodwill and other intangible assets to be deducted [but see note 1]	
Supplementary Capital (tier 2)	Total of tier 2 limited to 100% of tier 1
Allowance for loan and lease losses	Limited to 1.25% of weighted risk assets[2]
Perpetual preferred stock	No limit within tier 2
Hybrid capital instruments and equity contract notes	No limit within tier 2
Subordinated debt and intermediate-term preferred stock (original weighted average maturity of 5 years or more)	Subordinated debt and intermediate-term preferred stock are limited to 50% of Tier 1;[3] amortized for capital purposes as they approach maturity
Revaluation reserves (equity and building)	Not included [until 10/98, when up to 45% of pretax net unrealized holding gains on available for sale equity securities (measured as the excess of fair value over historical cost) was allowed in tier 2 capital]
Deductions (from sum of tier 1 and tier 2)	On a case-by-case basis or as a matter of policy after formal rulemaking
Investments in unconsolidated subsidiaries	
Reciprocal holdings of banking organizations' capital securities	
Other deductions (such as other subsidiaries or joint ventures) as determined by supervisory authority	
Total Capital (tier 1 + tier 2–Deductions)	Must equal or exceed 8% of weighted risk assets

1. All goodwill, except previously grandfathered goodwill approved in supervisory mergers, is deducted immediately. [From August 1998, marketable mortgage and nonmortgage servicing assets and purchased credit card relationships are not deducted, but their amount in capital may not exceed 100% of tier 1 capital.]
2. Amounts in excess of limitations are permitted but do not qualify as capital.
3. Amounts in excess of limitations are permitted but do not qualify as capital.
4. A proportionately greater amount may be deducted from Tier 1 capital if the risks associated with the subsidiary so warrant.

Notes and Questions

1. Countries differed so much in their definitions that it was essential to define capital. A capital/asset ratio without an agreed definition of capital would be a rubber yardstick. The basic idea used to define capital in the Accord was that some forms of capital meet losses better than other forms. Consider the components of Tier I capital (in Attachment II). What do they have in common? Why are they included in Tier I rather than Tier II?

    a. For example, "qualifying non-cumulative perpetual preferred stock" means that holders cannot receive missed dividends later, despite their priority over common stock holders in the payment of dividends. The stock need not be retired by the issuer. Why would this be classified in Tier I rather than Tier II?

    b. Goodwill, which some countries include in capital, is deducted from Tier I capital because it is hard to value and may not be worth anything in a crisis.

2. Tier II capital is less residual than Tier I. How do its components differ from Tier I capital?

    a. The inclusion of loan loss reserves in Tier II capital was the subject of a major debate among the countries. Although all eventually agreed to cap the loan loss reserves that could be treated as capital, some governments decided, and were permitted, to accept a higher limit than that adopted by the U.S. Why cannot all loan loss reserves be part of Tier II capital?

    b. Revaluation reserves also attracted great debate among the countries. What are they? The Accord permitted regulators to allow as Tier II capital up to 45% of unrealized appreciation of a bank's assets. Some governments, including Japan's, did so from the start. Why would any country permit this? Alternatively, why would any country prohibit this treatment? The U.S. did so until 1998, when it permitted certain unrealized gains on equity securities to be calculated as Tier II capital. When U.S. bank regulators proposed in 1997 to adopt this provision, "only 21 institutions hold investments with unrealized gains large enough to comprise a significant proportion of their risk-based capital." See O. Domis, *FDIC Would Let Unrealized Gains Count Toward Tier 2 Risk Capital*, American Banker, September 17, 1997.

3. Why is Tier II limited to 100% of Tier I capital?

4. The 4% + 4% = 8% ratios were compromises from common experience in the 1980s revealed in a study made in 1987. By 1996, some regulators were wondering if the ratios are too low.

5. While the Basel Accord specifies that it applies only to international banks, many countries including the U.S. decided to apply the standards to all banks. Is this appropriate?

6. Banks continue to search for a hybrid instrument that is enough like equity to qualify as Tier 1 capital but sufficiently like a bond to let the issuer deduct payments it makes to investors as interest (dividends would not be deductible). In October 1996, the Fed classified as Tier I capital new instruments called trust-preferred securities, a type of preferred stock designed to meet the Tier I standards and also to resemble bonds, with which they compete. See G. Zukerman, *Bonds Face New Rival: Preferred*, The Wall Street Journal, December 2, 1996. Banks issued $40 billion of trust preferred securities after that because of the lower cost. According to one regulator, 'The trick is to use a mirror. It has to look like debt to the investor and like equity to the supervisor." G. Graham, *Banking Industry Divided on Safety Net Rules*, Financial Times, Apr. 6, 1998. One estimate was that U.K. banks could reduce their funding costs 60% by issuing Tier I instruments on which interest payments were tax deductible. G. Graham, *Harassed Regulators Try To Draw the Line*, Financial Times, Apr. 6, 1998. BIS regulators, fearing a proliferation of securities like these, agreed in October 1998 to a common definition for acceptable new capital instruments of this sort and limited them to 15% of Tier I capital. BIS Press Release, *Instruments Eligible for Inclusion in Tier 1 Capital*, Oct. 30, 1998. In early 2000, Barclays Bank issued a euro 850 million tier one Reserve Capital Instrument. It is perpetual. Documents are those used for eurobonds. If any interest payment is not made, Barclays will issue, to the bondholders, new shares in the amount of the unpaid interest. This is designed to meet the requirement that any preferred shares be cumulative. M. Peterson, *Barclays' Tier-One Invention Takes to the Air*, Euromoney (May 2000) at 26.

7. A problem for banks occurred when their capital was in a currency other than that of their loans. Japanese banks, for example, suffered when dollar loans were supported by yen-denominated capital and the yen depreciated against the dollar. Their capital base eroded because of changing foreign exchange rates. A solution was to raise capital on international markets. In early 1998, Sumitomo Bank raised funds in the US market, in dollars, to counteract the exchange rate effect. G. Tett, *Sumitomo Bank To Launch $1bn Securities Issue*, Financial Times, Feb. 3, 1998.

8. In addition to the risk-weight capital rules, federal regulators apply a simple rule that Tier 1 capital must equal 3% of the assets of the highest-rated banks and a higher multiple, which they proposed in October 1997 to set at 4% for all other banks. See 62 Federal Register October 27, 1997 at 98. The Federal Reserve Board made the rule final for bank holding companies in June 1998. See Federal Reserve Press

Release, June 1, 1998. The capital ratios provide the basis for zones for prompt corrective action, as described in Chapter 3. Special rules for U.S. branches of foreign banks required them to hold 5% of their liabilities in capital equivalency deposits. In 2002, U.S. regulators were changing the rule to set the branches' capital using risk weights, and reduce the minimum from $3million to $2 million. This reduced the capital burden for 52 banks' U.S. branches, freeing about $1.6 billion. G. Silverman, *U.S. Regulators Ease Rules for Some Foreign Banks*, Financial Times, Mar. 5, 2002.

9. Risk-taking varies with the level of capital. Under-capitalized banks and well-capitalized banks "take more risk than banks with 'intermediate' capital position. Under-capitalized banks take more risk because if the gamble pays off the bank will become stronger and if not, the FDIC will bear the cost if the bank is bankrupt. Well-capitalized banks are more profitable and can accept more risk given their capital. Graphing capital levels against risk levels, then, shows a U-shaped curve. P. Calem and R. Rob, *The Impact of Capital-Based Regulation on Bank Risk-Taking*, 8 Journal of Financial Intermediation 317, 319 (1999).

2. RISK-WEIGHTING

The Accord shifted capital adequacy measures away from the simple ratios (such as 1/20) used in many countries at the time. It introduced risk-weighting. The Fed guidelines set out the risk weights in Attachment III, which follows.

ATTACHMENT III
Summary of Risk Weights and Risk Categories for State Member Banks

Category 1: Zero percent

1. Cash (domestic and foreign) held in the bank or in transit
2. Balances due from Federal Reserve Banks (including Federal Reserve Bank stock) and central banks in other OECD countries
3. Direct claims on, and the portions of claims that are unconditionally guaranteed by, the U.S. Treasury and U.S. Government agencies[1] and the central governments of other OECD countries, and local currency claims on, and the portions of local currency claims that are unconditionally guaranteed by, the central governments of non-OECD countries (including the

---

[1] For the purpose of calculating the risk-based capital ratio, a U.S. Government agency is defined as an instrumentality of the U.S. Government whose obligations are fully and explicitly guaranteed as to the timely payment of principal and interest by the full faith and credit of the U.S. Government.

central banks of non-OECD countries), to the extent that the bank has liabilities booked in that currency

4. Gold bullion held in the bank's vaults or in another's vaults on an allocated basis, to the extent offset by gold bullion liabilities

5. Claims collateralized by cash on deposit in the bank or by securities issued or guaranteed by OECD central governments or U.S. government agencies for which a positive margin of collateral is maintained on a daily basis, fully taking into account any change in the bank's exposure to the obligor or counterparty under a claim in relation to the market value of the collateral held in support of that claim

Category 2: 20 percent

1. Cash items in the process of collection

2. All claims (long- or short-term) on, and the portions of claims (long- or short-term) that are guaranteed by, U.S. depository institutions and OECD banks

3. Short-term claims (remaining maturity of one year or less) on, and the portions of short-term claims that are guaranteed by, non-OECD banks

4. The portions of claims that are conditionally guaranteed by the central governments of OECD countries and U.S. Government agencies, and the portions of local currency claims that are conditionally guaranteed by the central governments of non-OECD countries, to the extent that the bank has liabilities booked in that currency

5. Claims on, and the portions of claims that are guaranteed by U.S. government-sponsored agencies[2]

6. General obligation claims on, and the portions of claims that are guaranteed by the full faith and credit of, local governments and political subdivisions of the U.S. and other OECD local governments

7. Claims on, and the portions of claims that are guaranteed by, official multilateral lending institutions or regional development banks

8. The portions of claims that are collateralized[3] by cash on deposit in the bank or by securities issued or guaranteed by the U.S. Treasury, the central governments of other OECD coun-

---

[2] For the purpose of calculating the risk-based capital ratio, a U.S. Government-sponsored agency is defined as an agency originally established or chartered to serve public purposes specified by the U.S. Congress but whose obligations are not *explicitly* guaranteed by the full faith and credit of the U.S. Government.

[3] The extent of collateralization is determined by current market value.

tries, and U.S. government agencies that do not qualify for the zero percent risk-weight category, or that are collateralized by securities issued or guaranteed by U.S. government sponsored agencies.

9.   The portions of claims that are collateralized by securities issued by official multilateral lending institutions or regional development banks

10.   Certain privately-issued securities representing indirect ownership of mortgage-backed U.S. Government agency or U.S. Government-sponsored agency securities

11.   Investments in shares of a fund whose portfolio is permitted to hold only securities that would qualify for the zero or 20 percent risk categories

Category 3: 50 Percent

1.   Loans fully secured by first liens on one- to four-family residential properties on multi-family residential properties that have been made in accordance with prudent underwriting standards, that are performing in accordance with their original terms, that are not past due or in nonaccrual status, and that meet other qualifying criteria, and certain privately-issued mortgage-backed securities representing indirect ownership of such loans. (Loans made for speculative purposes are excluded.)

2.   Revenue bonds or similar claims that are obligations of U.S. state or local governments, or other OECD local governments, but for which the government entity is committed to repay the debt only out of revenues from the facilities financed

3.   Credit equivalent amounts of interest rate and foreign exchange rate related contracts, except for those assigned to a lower risk category

Category 4: 100 Percent

1.   All other claims on private obligors.

2.   Claims on, or guaranteed by, non-OECD foreign banks with a remaining maturity exceeding one year

3.   Claims on, or guaranteed by, non-OECD central governments that are not included in item 3 of Category 1 or item 4 of Category 2; all claims on non-OECD state or local governments

4.   Obligations issued by U.S. state or local governments, or other OECD local governments (including industrial development authorities and similar entities), repayable solely by a private party or enterprise

5.   Premises, plant, and equipment; other fixed assets; and other real estate owned

6.   Investments in any unconsolidated subsidiaries, joint ventures, or associated companies—if not deducted from capital

7.   Instruments issued by other banking organizations that qualify as capital—if not deducted from capital

8.   Claims on commercial firms owned by a government.

9.   All other assets, including any intangible assets that are not deducted from capital.

Notes and Questions

1.   The basic idea of risk weighting assets is that less risky assets require less capital to protect against loss than do riskier assets. The challenge for the drafters of the Accord was to classify assets correctly.

2.   Examine the components of each category. They were the subject of great debate as the Accord was drafted. Note that the members of the OECD are Australia, Austria, Belgium, Canada, the Czech Republic,* Denmark, Finland, France, Germany, Greece, Hungary,* Iceland, Ireland, Italy, Japan, Korea,* Luxembourg, Mexico,* the Netherlands, New Zealand, Norway, Poland,* Portugal, Spain, Sweden, Switzerland, Turkey, the United Kingdom and the United States (* indicates membership after 1993).

a.   What is the idea of each of the agreed classifications?

b.   Do the items in each component make sense? For example, why do family home mortgages carry one weight and fully collateralized private loans another? Would these weightings distinguish between a U.S. bank's loans to a Mexican bank and a Malaysian bank? Should they? What would your opinion be if you discovered that Malaysian banks were as strong or stronger than Mexican banks?

c.   Some fine tuning took place. In 1996, the U.S. considered assigning a zero weight to loans secured by government securities or cash. In 1997, regulators proposed rules that would apply the risk-weight standards to asset-backed securities. See A. Yonan, Jr., *Fed Board Proposes New Rules for Banks*, The Wall Street Journal, August 22, 1997.

3.   In April 1998, the BIS agreed to change the risk weight for loans to OECD securities firms subject to supervision and regulation, particularly for risk-based capital, "comparable to" that for the banks. Until then, the weight was 100%. The change reduced the weight to 20%. See Basel Committee on Banking Supervision, Amendment to the Capital Accord, April 1998. In September 2001, The Basel Committee announced that if an OECD supervisor allows banks to assign a risk weight from zero to 10% for credit to domestic public sector entities (other than central banks), foreign supervisors can let their banks do the same for credit to

those entities. Otherwise, the foreign banks would have to hold capital for a 20% risk weight. Basel Committee Newsletter No. 2 (September 2001).

4. The BIS also proposed "to accept novation for on-balance-sheet netting as a means of reducing gross exposures to a single net amount." It also accepted that banks could net their loans to, and deposits from, the same counterparty if that netting was enforceable, the term of the deposit was no shorter than the loan, they were in the same currency, and the bank monitored the exposure. Basel Committee on Banking Supervision, Consultative Paper on On-Balance-Sheet Netting, April 7, 1998.

5. During the mid-1990s, dissatisfaction with the Basel Accord's credit risk standards mounted. A study by the Federal Reserve Bank of Boston said that capital ratios did not help regulators identify problem banks. By late 1996, the Chairman and Vice Chairman of the Federal Reserve System were both suggesting that the credit risk standards were too simplistic. The rules failed to distinguish among types of loans to private sector borrowers, for example. Banks were engaging in "regulatory capital arbitrage." A simple example is their investments in US government debt rather than loans to private sector firms. More complex forms of risk capital arbitrage involved securitization, which is discussed in a later chapter. They could "restructure traditional balance-sheet positions (through the use, for example, of securitization and credit derivatives) so as to effectively place the positions within lower regulatory 'risk-weight buckets' (including the zero risk-weight bucket) . . . ." J. Mingo, *Policy Implications of the Fed's Study of Large Bank Credit Risk Models*, 17 Banking Policy Report 8 (1998). A bank could retain the entire credit risk of a transaction against a much smaller volume of assets that would require less capital. See D. Jones, *Emerging Problems with the Basel Capital Accord: Regulatory Capital Arbitrage and Related Issues*, 24 Journal of Banking & Finance 35 (2000).

6. To what extent should national regulators add stricter capital requirements? Banks with subprime lending programs needed to set aside much more capital than would otherwise be required, according to U.S. supervisors in 2001. Subprime borrowers "have weakened credit histories that include payment delinquencies, and possibly more severe problems such as charge-offs, judgments, and bankruptcies." The higher risk inherent in these programs meant that an institutions should hold capital 1.5 to 3 times higher than that required for similar assets that were not subprime. This guidance applies to pools of such assets, not isolated loans. It would not apply if the loans are well secured and the borrowers only slightly below prime. On the other hand, the supervisors recognized that in some cases the capital might have to reach even 100% of the loans outstanding. The extent of additional capital would be up to the bank examiner. OCC, Board of Governors of the Federal Reserve

System, FDIC, and Office of Thrift Supervision, *Expanded Guidance for Subprime Lending Programs,* Jan. 31, 2001.

7. Overall, how good is this technique of risk weighting? One observer said "Ideally, I would like to see the entire risk weighting system completely scrapped, except to allow for some weighting of off-balance sheet risks in computing the required capital ratio." See R. Litan, *Nightmare in Basel*, The International Economy, Nov.-Dec. 1992, at 7. Do you agree with his evaluation? One study found that the relative risk of different traditional groups of loans (such as real estate, commercial, and consumer loans) varies as time passes and, in some conditions, that loans to governments may be more risky than loans to private sector borrowers. The latter point raises the question of whether a zero risk weight for loans to national governments is appropriate. See L. Hooks, Group of Thirty, Capital, Asset Risk and Bank Failure (1994).

3. THE TREATMENT OF OFF–BALANCE SHEET ITEMS

Before the Basel Accord, capital adequacy referred to the level of capital relative to loans and other assets carried on the bank's balance sheet. During the early 1980s, however, commercial banks sought more business for which they could charge fees without generating liabilities or assets. See the discussion in Chapter 1. Some of the largest international banks began to grapple with the question of how to measure the risk associated with these non-traditional services. Capital for over-the-counter derivatives, such as swaps, is discussed in Chapter 17.

Regulators agreed on the solution in Attachment IV, which follows. The reading gives the basic elements. To learn about other matters, such as credit conversions for derivative contracts, such as interest rate and foreign exchange futures, see the guidelines.

ATTACHMENT IV
Credit-Conversion Factors for Off–Balance Sheet Items for State Member Banks

100 Percent Conversion Factor

1. Direct credit substitutes. (These include general guarantees of indebtedness and all guarantee-type instruments, including standby letters of credit backing the financial obligations of other parties.)

2. Risk participations in bankers acceptances and direct credit substitutes, such as standby letters of credit.

3. Sale and repurchase agreements and assets sold with recourse that are not included on the balance sheet.

4. Forward agreements to purchase assets, including financing facilities, on which drawdown is certain.

5. Securities lent for which the bank is at risk.

50 Percent Conversion Factor

1. Transaction-related contingencies. (These include bid bonds, performance bonds, warranties, and standby letters of credit backing the nonfinancial performance of other parties.)
2. Unused portions of commitments with an original maturity exceeding one year, including underwriting commitments and commercial credit lines.
3. Revolving underwriting facilities (RUFs), note issuance facilities (NIFs), and similar arrangements.

20 Percent Conversion Factor

Short-term, self-liquidating trade-related contingencies, including commercial letters of credit.

Zero Percent Conversion Factor

Unused portions of commitments with an original maturity of one year or less, or which are unconditionally cancellable at any time, provided a separate credit decision is made before each drawing.

Notes and Questions

1. Off-balance sheet items are obligations of banks that may or may not be called, such as bank guarantees. These contingent liabilities depend on some action or event for the bank to pay. Check the items listed in Attachment IV to identify their contingent nature.

2. Banks always had off-balance sheet activity, but its growth was strong in the early 1980s before the Accord. Then banks' assets were subject to capital ratios, but off-balance sheet (OBS) items were not. How would this affect the growth of contingent liabilities in the early 1980s? Analysts disagree about the extent to which banks turn to OBS transactions to avoid capital requirements. See J. Jagtiani, A. Saunders, and G. Udel, *The Effect of Bank Capital Requirements on Bank Off-balance Sheet Financial Innovations*, 19 Journal of Banking and Finance 647 (1995).

3. Regulators were concerned about OBS volumes. For example, by 1990 the nine largest U.S. banks had $2 trillion in swaps alone, but as Chapter 17 shows, this nominal value far exceeded the value at risk. It is difficult to measure the banks' true exposure. This uncertainty prompted regulators to convert OBS items to assets, which can be valued more readily, then weigh them by risk.

a. The basic idea behind each conversion factor is that the more an item is likely to be called and the greater the risk that the counterparty will be unable to pay, the closer it is to an asset and the higher should be the conversion factor. Examine each conversion factor: what is its logic?

b.   The standard risk weights are used once the item is converted. Does this make sense?

4.   Work through the treatment of a $1000 standby letter of credit for financial obligations and a $1,000 commercial letter of credit. Assume two different recipients, a private party and the World Bank, a multilateral agency. What capital is required in each of the four cases?

5.   New capital rules for securitized assets held by banks have been proposed by the Basel Committee and U.S. federal banking agencies starting in 2000. The Basel Committee issued a new working paper in October 2001 that would be consistent with its proposals for Basel II. Chapter 13 discusses securitization. Banks can pool loans they made and transfer ownership, with rights to income, to investors in the bonds that securitize the loans. To the extent the banks no longer own the loans, they no longer need to hold capital against them. But if the banks may be responsible for the performance of the loans, the loans are not completely off the books. Of course, banks can also invest in securitized assets. So banks may be exposed to risk both as originators of the assets and investors in them. The proposed revisions assign a risk-based charge to positions in securitized transactions using credit ratings to measure the risk.   They define various kinds of recourse and treat them more consistently.   The proposals are similar to those made by the Basel Committee in January 2001 (see Section C below). See Joint Release, Board of Governors of the Federal Reserve system, Federal Deposit Insurance Corporation, Office of the Comptroller of the Currency, and Office of Thrift Supervision, *Agencies Propose Revision of Risk-Based Capital Rules' Treatment of Recourse and Direct-Credit Substitutes*, Feb. 17, 2000; D. Pruzin, *Basel Panel Asset Securitization Paper Proposes Setting Capital Requirements*, 77 International News 654, Oct. 22, 2001.

C.   THE PERFORMANCE OF THE BASEL ACCORD

1.   THE TRANSITION TO FULL STANDARDS

The Accord provided for a phased transition to the new rules. Banks would have to meet a modest standard initially, then a more stringent one by the end of 1990. Almost immediately, banks began to adjust. By some accounts, many U.S. banks were ready early.   Problems in Japan's financial markets, described in Chapter 8, undermined the effort of banks there to adjust on schedule. By the end of 1992, most international banks in major industrial countries reported at least nominal compliance with Basel's rule, some just barely and others by a large margin.

The Accord was adopted country by country. Provisions were not identical since some governments set standards for their banks higher than those of the Accord. One study of the U.S., the U.K., and Japan concluded that the U.K. definition of Tier II capital was most liberal and the Japanese risk weighting most lenient. See M. Hall, *Capital-Adequacy Assessment, in* 1 Global Risk Based Capital Regulations: Capital Adequacy 171 (C. Stone and A. Zissu eds., 1994). Even within the European Community, EC members adopted different rules. For example, for commercial mortgages, banks in Denmark, Germany, and Greece were allowed to provide only half the capital required of banks in the other member countries. See S. London, *EU May Change Banks' Property Loan Rules*, Financial Times, Nov. 17, 1994.

Countries continued to join even after 1992. In August 1994, for example, Brazil's Central Bank adopted the Basel Accord.

Notes and Questions

1. Why would a country want to adopt the Accord? What might prevent it from doing so?

2. THE ACCORD AND THE CREDIT CRUNCH

As the Basel Accord became final in 1992, a slowdown in bank lending seemed to be creating or intensifying a recession in the U.S. and other industrial countries. The Accord contributed to the slowdown, according to its critics.

The major problem was that the Accord encouraged banks to invest in government bonds, with zero risk weight and therefore no capital cost, rather than lend to commercial and consumer borrowers subject to as much as 8% capital. One author concluded that a bank would have to pay 56 basis points more to fund a loan than the bond, because of the Accord (R. Litan, *Nightmare in Basel*, The International Economy, Nov.-Dec. 1992, at 7):

> Consider the typical U.S. bank that, at this writing, pays about three percent for deposits and an average of roughly ten percent for long-term (uninsured) debt and equity. With a zero risk weight on government bonds, the cost of funding an investment in such bonds solely with deposits is just three percent. In contrast, the typical bank must fund a 100–percent risk-weighted investment in riskier commercial loans with 8 percent capital and 92 percent deposits, at a weighted cost of 3.56 percent.

Litan argued that over a recent six month period banks had invested $50 billion more in government bonds and $20 billion less in commercial and industrial loans, the first time in almost 30 years that banks' investments in government bonds exceeded their C&I loans. This was, he said, particularly bad as the country was coming out of the recession. Others added that as banks' capital shrinks during a recession the banks must reduce their lending, exacerbating the downturn. J. Plender, *Taming Wild Money*, Financial Times, Oct. 20, 1998.

The many studies of the capital rules and credit crunch after Litan wrote drew no simple causal relationship. See S. Sharpe, *Bank Capitalization, Regulation, and the Credit Crunch: A Critical Review of the Research Findings* (Federal Reserve Board Finance and Economics Discussion Series No. 95-20, 1995). Indeed, the case that capital rules have limited impact has been made by analysts in the Federal Reserve System. One study concluded that banks not subject to formal action by their regulator do not quickly shrink their assets to satisfy capital requirements and that when they do reduce assets it is through the sale of existing assets rather than by cutting off existing customers. See J. Peek and E. Rosengren, *Bank Regulation and the Credit Crunch*, 19 Journal of Banking and Finance 679 (1995). Another study found that between 1989 and 1992, regulators "scrutinized lending standards and loan holdings more rigorously causing banks to ration credit... [which] resulted in banks reducing their holdings of loans and increasing their holdings of government securities." J Wagster, *The Basel Accord of 1988 and the International Credit Crunch of 1989-1992*, Aug. 9, 1996. A more serious challenge took the view that capital adequacy regulation was not binding on banks because the market forced them to hold more capital. For example, an analyst found that during the 1980s, before Basel, U.S. banks with low capital would bring themselves up to the average well before government policy changed. After policy changes, banks with low capital would not raise their capital faster than well-capitalized banks. A. Ashcraft, *Do Tougher Bank Capital Requirements Matter? New Evidence from the Eighties*, July 23, 2002.

In the mid-1990s, concern shifted from a credit crunch to the danger of "unwise" lending prompted by excessive levels of capital. According to one report, the top ten banks in Germany, Japan, and France had ratios over 9%, in Italy over 11%, and in the U.K. and the U.S. over 12%. One effect was that banks stepped up their acquisitions of other banks. See *Those Damned Dominoes*, The Economist, Mar. 4, 1995, at 78; and *Too Much of a Good Thing?*, The Economist, May 27, 1995, at 67.

Japan's banks, however, seemed to contribute to a credit crunch in the mid- and late-1990s. They found their lending constrained by the capital adequacy rules at a time when some argued that more lending could help the country pull out of its recession. This is discussed later in this chapter.

Notes and Questions

1. Are possible macroeconomic effects of the Accord appropriately the concern of those who framed and implement it? How easy do you suppose it is to amend the Accord?

2. The macroeconomy could affect banks' ability to comply with the Basel Standard. During 1994, rising interest rates led to the fall in the value of bonds held by banks as capital. In the U.S., FASB 115 required banks to mark to current value bonds held as available for sale. If the bonds were part of Tier I capital, should the banks mark down the value of the Tier I capital if the bonds price fell? FASB said yes. In November 1994, U.S. bank regulators decided not to require banks to calculate unrealized gains and losses in valuing Tier I securities. The Office of the Comptroller of the Currency treated these securities as permanent in nature and feared big swings in their value. See Comptroller of the Currency News Release 94-119 (Nov. 9, 1994) and BNA's Banking Report 690 (Nov. 14, 1994).

3. Toward a More Level International Playing Field

A second goal of the Accord was to level the playing field so that no government could give its banks a competitive advantage over other countries' banks by setting low capital adequacy rules. Did it succeed? The early returns raise grave doubts. As you read about the following critique, ask yourself about the implicit standard of performance expected from the Accord. How much can be appropriately asked?

a. LIMITS OF THE ACCORD: THE US AND JAPAN

Analysis of the competitive effect of the Accord across many countries is thwarted by the many factors that shape international competition. A comparison of Japan and the United States revealed the power of these factors in H. Scott and S. Iwahara, *In Search of a Level Playing Field: The Implementation of the Basel Capital Accord in Japan and the United States* 1-11 (Group of Thirty Occasional Paper No. 46, 1994) (Scott and Iwahara). They argued that comparative advantage, the home economy, and government safety nets had a much greater effect on competitive advantage among banks than did capital ratios.   Japanese banks benefitted because Japan enforced the rules less strictly and because U.S. banks were subject to leverage and other capital ratios. U.S. banks benefitted, relative to Japanese, in other ways. For example, U.S. bank holding companies, subject to less stringent versions of the Basel rules than banks themselves, were able to raise capital more cheaply than their bank and downstream it to the bank as equity, which could not be done in Japan. U.S. banks also benefitted because their more sophisticated capital market reduced capital costs, while tax, and accounting rules permitted the use of gains on appreciated securities as capital. Scott and Iwahara concluded that differences in accounting and tax rules, and bank regulations, led to a "distortion . . . so massive as to render comparability impossible."

A difference in capital costs does affect competition among banks, giving the more leveraged bank an advantage. Scott and Iwahara used this illustration:

> Take two banks, Bank A and Bank B. They face a 7 percent market rate of interest for marginal increases in the cost of funding; they operate in the same markets and are equally creditworthy. Bank A has a 4 percent capital requirement, that is capital must equal 4 percent of total assets, and Bank B has a 6 percent requirement. Here, capital refers to equity.
>
> The total cost for Bank A in making new loans is
>
> $$.07 \times .96 + .0C \times .04 = .0672 + .0004C,$$
>
> where C is the cost of capital; and the total cost for Bank B in making new loans is
>
> $$.07 \times .94 + .0C \times .06 = .0658 + .0006C.$$
>
> Where the cost of capital exceeds the marginal interest rate (7 percent in the example), Bank A, the more leveraged bank, has a cheaper cost of funds. If, for example, the cost of capital for both banks were 10 percent, the cost of funds for Bank A would be 7.12 percent (6.72 + 0.40), as compared with Bank B's 7.18 percent (6.58 + 0.60). Since equity is almost always costlier than debt because equity is more risky and receives less favorable tax treatment, Bank A will enjoy a competitive advantage over Bank B. Bank A can charge borrowers a lower rate of interest and make the same spread (profit) as Bank B. For example, Bank A can make a 2 percent spread by charging a borrower 9.12 percent, whereas Bank B must charge 9.18 percent to make the same spread. In addition, capital requirements affect the total lending capacity of banks. Bank A, with a 4 percent capital requirement, can lend twenty-five times its capital; Bank B, with a 6 percent requirement, can lend only 16.66 times its capital.

Bank A's creditors might insist on higher rates of interest than Bank B's creditors, unless the government regulating Bank A provides a safety net, through insurance, bailout policies, and lender of last resort facilities, that is better than that for Bank B. The authors found that Japan's safety net for banks was more comprehensive than that in the U.S. For decades, for example, the Japanese government policy was that no bank should fail, while in the U.S. many banks failed each year. Looking for evidence that this affected the capital ratios, they found in 1993 that the capital on the books of the 10 largest Japanese banks was substantially lower than that of the top 10 U.S. banks: 9.67% and 13.60% of assets for Japanese and U.S. banks, respectively. The authors concluded that the value of Japan's safety net, reduced by the greater cost of regulation in Japan, created a net subsidy for Japanese banks.

The 8% minimum ratio set by Basel may reduce the gap in nominal capital ratios between banks from different countries but it probably does not reduce the real ratio. According to Scott and Iwahara,

> Real capital is the market value of assets minus the market value of liabilities. If the market (debt suppliers, in particular) believes it is sufficient for Japanese banks to hold 2 percent real capital, it may be inefficient for Japanese banks to hold higher levels, given their put on government capital (the guarantee). They will have a substantial incentive to keep real capital at 2 percent while complying with the nominal 8 percent Basel requirement. This can be done simply by not fully writing off bad loans.

> The market and the availability of government guarantees will tend to determine the real capital ratios of banks, as well as the differential in required capital ratios among banks in different countries. Governments may alter this tendency by trying to ensure that real capital ratios are identical to Basel nominal ratios, but different governments may do more or less. Indeed, if the United States were to try to make its banks hold 8 percent real capital, and the Japanese were content to have their banks hold 2 percent real capital, the impact of the 8 percent minimum would be to widen the difference . . . .

The 8% minimum could also perversely increase the capital differential, rather than decrease it, if the marginal cost of capital rises as a bank raises higher levels of capital. A U.S. bank might pay more to maintain a 3% differential (e.g. 11% to Japan's 8%) than a 5% differential at lower levels (e.g., 7% to 2%).

b.   THE EFFECT OF THE JAPANESE BANKING CRISIS

Since the early 1990s, Japan's banks and financial system generally have faced a deepening crisis. Many of the biggest banks were forced to merge with each other or with smaller banks on the verge of failure. Minimal domestic growth and steep declines in the value of real estate and publicly traded shares eroded the quality of the banks' assets to the point that problem loans were a large share of the loan portfolios. A political crisis ended the decades long tenure of the dominant party and no effective political leader emerged in its place. Confronted with government proposals to bail out crisis-ridden financial firms, such as mortgage lenders, the Parliament divided and taxpayers became visibly angry. Chapter 8 describes this in more detail.

During the early 1990s, the Government of Japan reiterated its policy that no bank will fail. Nevertheless, international credit rating agencies down-graded the ratings for many Japanese banks. When Moody's did so in December 1996, for example, it explained that the banks had substantial problem loans, that the government's policy was merely ad hoc, and that the banks would suffer substantially if financial sector reform took place in the manner then being discussed. As a result, Japanese banks paid a premium for funds in international markets, which persisted and then rose at the end of 1997 with the Asian financial crisis. The price of Japanese bank stocks fell.   Indeed, the Japanese government was expected to pay a premium on its bonds in the future. At the end of 1995, the BIS capital ratio of the six largest Japanese banks ranged from 8.36 to 9.40. See *The Top 200 World Banking Companies*, American Banker, August 5, 1996.

From late 1997, observers argued that many big Japanese banks probably held negative capital. The government indicated it was willing to let banks fail. As their banks' condition eroded, the government considered allowing the banks' capital to fall below the 8% ratio set by the Basel Accord. Yet by late 2001, Japanese banks reported capital of 11% of risk weighted assets. They could do so because the regulators allowed them to include as capital deferred tax assets (potential tax credits over the next five years) and public funds (preferred shares held by the government that the banks are expected to repay later). Big Japanese banks hold over 50% Tier 1 capital in these two forms, compared to 10% for US and European banks. P. Dvorak, Japan's Banks Face Debate On What Counts as Capital, The Wall Street Journal, November 20, 2001.

c. CAPITAL RATIOS OF MAJOR EUROPEAN BANKS

In 1993, at the same time as the data given above for the U.S. and Japan, European banks reported capital ratios averaging 10.12%, higher than those of Japanese banks (9.67%), but substantially below the U.S. average (13.60%). Four French banks — Credit Lyonnais, Credit Agricole, Societe Generale, and Banque National de Paris — had lower ratios than the Japanese average. State-owned until recently, they too appear to have benefitted from a safety net.

Notes and Questions

1. Be sure you understand the analysis of the bailout differential. What is the nature of the governments' guarantees? If a strong guarantee exists, why have capital at all? Will forcing Japan to adopt a 10% capital standard equalize competition?

2. The Scott/Iwahara article suggests that the 8% ratio is unnecessarily high if the bailout policy is in place. Yet the Japanese premium suggests their analysis is wrong. Do these recent developments in Japan undermine or confirm the Scott/Iwahara argument about the effect of the bailout policy on capital? What explains the premium?

3. Immediately before the Accord, many American and British bankers believed that banks from France and Japan had a great competitive advantage because of their high leverage. Both French and Japanese banks accepted very low rates in international lending, arguably made possible by their low capital requirements. In their discussion of

the 8% minimum ratios, are the authors undermined by the relative withdrawal of French and Japanese banks from international markets after capital requirements rose in the late 1980s?

4. A formal argument that capital adequacy rules must reflect the government's bank bail out policy appears in V. Acharya, *Is the International Convergence of Capital Adequacy Regulation Desirable?* (April 20, 2000) (Acharya). The author concludes "That in the presence of international operations by banks, a uniform capital adequacy regulation across regimes with differing rescue policies not only destabilizes the regime for which the capital adequacy regulation is inconsistent with its rescue policy, but also has a systemic effect on the other regimes, destabilizing the global economy as a whole." (Acharya at 1). The problem is that the country with "a greater forbearance in its rescue policy sustains a greater moral hazard and should compensate for this by requiring tighter capital adequacy." But convergence of capital requirements undermines this (Acharya at 32). He proposes as a solution that banks operate overseas through subsidiaries rather than branches, so the host can subject the local subsidiary to the host's supervisory rules and separate it from the home's rules.

5. The authors say that "differences in comparative advantage, economic fundamentals or government support levels" determine competitive advantage among banks. What if any conditions would give capital adequacy regulations a significant impact on competition?

6. Do bank capital standards now adequately deal with credit risk? Given the limitations of the Basel Accord, is the Fed correct in concluding that sophisticated banks should not be allowed to use their own internal models to calculate capital for credit risk? If only one or two banks had sophisticated internal models, why should they not be permitted to rely on them rather than the Accord?

7. If regulators are unwilling to let banks use their own internal credit models, should the regulators improve the Basel Accord? If so, what improvements would you recommend?

4. THE BASEL COMMITTEE'S 2001 PROPOSAL TO AMEND THE ACCORD

The Basel Committee sought since early 1999 to amend the Accord. Initially, regulators from Germany and the U.S. brought discussions to a halt by deadlocking over Germany's call for lower risk weights for loans secured by commercial mortgages, which Germany said had a very low default rate. See G. Graham, *US-German Animosity Stalls Progress on Bank Capital Talks*, Financial Times, May 13, 1999. A set of proposals issued in June 1999 identified weaknesses in the original Accord, but decided to build on it rather than scrap it. The Committee specifically rejected the use of internal credit models as too uncertain. Basel

Committee on Banking Supervision, *A New Capital Adequacy Framework* (June 1999). These proposals generated great criticism.

The Committee issued much more comprehensive proposals on January 16, 2001 and said that it hoped the new Accord would be completed by the end of 2001 and begin to be implemented in 2004. In June 2001, however, the Committee promised to revise this proposal and delay implementation to 2005 because of the many adverse comments. By December 2001, the Committee said it would examine the impact of its proposals on banks in detail. It seemed likely to issue its new proposals in mid-2002 and the rules even after 2005. The Committee published an overview paper, another paper with the detailed rules that countries would be expected to issue, and seven supporting documents giving technical details. The Committee suggested that implementing countries apply the rules to all banks. In the U.S., however, regulators questioned whether this would happen there, since they had recently proposed simple rules for non-complex institutions. See *Simplified Capital Framework for Non-Complex Institutions*, Federal Register, Nov. 3, 2000.

The Committee presented three pillars of bank capital regulation, all essential. These are summarized in a joint paper by the Board of Governors of the Federal Reserve System, Federal Deposit Insurance Corporation, and Office of the Comptroller of the Currency, Summary of the Basel Committee's *The New Basel Capital Accord*, Jan. 2001 ("U.S. Joint Paper"), at 2:

> The first pillar of the new Accord is the minimum regulatory capital charge. The Pillar 1 capital requirement includes both the standardized approach, updated since the 1988 Accord, and the new IRB approaches (foundation and advanced). . . . [T]his first pillar is likely to be the focal point for industry comment . . . .
>
> Pillar 2 is supervisory review. It is "intended to ensure not only that banks have adequate capital to support all the risks in their business, but also to encourage banks to develop and use better risk management techniques in monitoring and managing these risks." This pillar encourages supervisors to assess banks' internal approaches to capital allocation and internal assessments of capital adequacy, and, subject to national discretion, provides an opportunity for the supervisor to indicate where such approaches do not appear sufficient. Pillar 2 should also be seen as a way to focus supervisors on other means of addressing risks in a bank's portfolio, such as improving overall risk management techniques and internal controls.
>
> The third pillar recognizes that market discipline has the potential to reinforce capital regulation and other supervisory efforts to ensure the safety and soundness of the banking system. Thus, the Committee is proposing a wide range of disclosure initiatives,

which are designed to make the risk and capital positions of a bank more transparent. As a bank begins to use the more advanced methodologies, such as the IRB approach, the new Accord will require a significant increase in the level of disclosure. In essence, the tradeoff for greater reliance on a bank's own assessment of capital adequacy is greater transparency.

The Committee elaborated on Pillar 3 in a paper issued September 2001. The paper focused on disclosure and the assessment of risk exposure. Banking Committee, *Working Paper on Pillar 3--Market Discipline*, September 2001. The following sections describe the main elements in Pillar 1.

a. THE STANDARDIZED APPROACH

The Committee proposed to replace the four original risk weight categories with a more complex set, which it called the *standardized approach*. It would allow banks to use external credit assessments by rating agencies to weight the risk of loans to borrowers in certain classes. The Committee used Standard & Poor's classifications as an example and said that other rating agencies could also be used if they met standards for such criteria as objectivity, independence, and transparency. The Committee recognized that the rating agencies had a mixed track record identifying high risk companies, and were slow to change ratings.

For *sovereigns* and central banks, only the highest rated (AAA to AA-) would win a zero risk weight. The Committee suggested a 20% risk weight for sovereigns rated A+ to A-, 50% for BBB+ to BBB-, 100% for BB+ to B-, and 150% for those below B-. Supervisors could use country risk scores published by export credit agencies that accepted a methodology set by the OECD in 1999. The Committee had special rules for claims on non-central government public sector entities and multilateral development banks like the Asian Development Bank.

For loans to *banks*, the Committee offered two options. One was to give the bank a risk weight that was one category less favorable than that of the sovereign of the bank's home country (e.g., if the sovereign was weighted 20%, the bank would be 50%), up to 100%. The second option was to use ratings by a qualifying rating agency. Most banks would be weighted 50%, but AAA to AA- banks would be 20%, BB+ to B- would be 100%, and below B- 150%. For credits of 3 months or less, the rates would be reduced one step, subject to a floor of 20%. Claims on *securities firms* would receive the same treatment if the firms were comparably regulated and subject to the new Basel Rules.

For loans to *corporate borrowers*, those rated AAA to AA- would be weighted 20%, A+ to A- 50%, BBB+ to BB- 100%, and below BB- 150%.

Unrated borrowers would be weighted 100%, except that the weight would be 50% for the second option in loans to banks. The Committee set weights for asset securitization based on external ratings of the securities.

The Committee proposed to extend the Accord to bank holding companies and banking groups, consolidating all banking activities.

Off-balance sheet items would be treated as before, except that the conversion factor for business commitments (i) originally a year or less would be 20% generally and 0% if unconditionally cancellable and (ii) over one year, 50%. Moreover, banks lending securities or using them as collateral prompt a 100% conversion factor.

The rating agencies, called External Credit Assessment Institutions, were to be evaluated by national supervisors against criteria set by the Committee.

The Committee set rules for assessing the impact on capital require-ments of techniques to mitigate credit risk, such as use of collateral, derivatives, guarantees, and netting. For collateral, for example, a "comprehensive approach" provided for haircuts off the market value, some set by supervisors and others by the bank itself. A "simple approach" would follow risk weights set according to factors listed by the Committee. In September 2001, however, the Committee abandoned this approach. It shifted the matter to Pillar 2, requiring supervisors to evaluate the residual risk of collateral, guarantees, and credit derivatives. Basel Committee Newsletter No. 2 (September 2001).

The Committee left loans secured by residential property with a 50% weight and those secured by commercial property at 100%. It decided not to take the maturity of a loan into account when assessing risk.

b.   THE INTERNAL RATINGS-BASED APPROACH

An alternative to the standardized approach was the *internal ratings-based (IRB) approach* for sophisticated banks. The supervisor would assess the breadth and quality of the bank's own system for rating credit risk of individual loans. The Committee offered guidelines for supervisors allowing the IRB approach. Bank supervisors would need to check the number of gradations of risk, the link between the rating scale and measurable loss (e.g., does the bank's internal rating scale take recovery rates into account), the range of risk factors, the clarity of criteria, and the usefulness of historical data. The BIS had earlier released papers describing best practices for managing and disclosing credit risk. In January 2001, as described in the U.S. Joint Paper, at 3:

> The IRB approach represents a fundamental shift in the Commit-tee's thinking on regulatory capital. It builds on internal credit risk rating practices of banks used by some institutions to estimate the amount of capital they believe necessary to support their economic risks. In recent years, as a result of technological

and financial innovations and the growth of the securities markets, leading banking institutions throughout the world have improved their measurement and management of credit risks. These developments have encouraged the supervisory authorities to devote greater attention to developing more risk-sensitive regulatory capital requirements, particularly for large, complex banking organizations.

Banks must meet an extensive set of eligibility standards or "minimum requirements" in order to use the IRB approach. Because the requirements are qualitative measures, national supervisors will need to evaluate compliance with them to determine which banks may apply the new framework. The requirements vary by both the type of exposure and whether the bank intends to use the simpler "foundation" IRB framework or the more advanced IRB framework. A small sample of the minimum requirements includes:

- The bank has a risk rating system that can differentiate borrowers and facilities into groupings that are of similar levels of credit risk and across all levels of risk.

- There should be a meaningful distribution of exposure across grades with no excessive concentrations in any one grade.

- Borrower risk ratings must be assigned before there is a commitment to lend and must be reviewed periodically by an independent source.

- The board of directors and senior management have a responsibility to oversee all material aspects of the IRB framework, including rating and probability of default (PD) estimation processes, frequency and content of risk rating management reports, documentation of risk rating determinations, and evaluation of control functions.

- A one-year PD estimate for each grade must be provided as a minimum input.

- Banks must collect and store historical data on borrower defaults, rating decisions, rating histories, rating migration, information used to assign ratings, PD estimate histories, key borrower characteristics, and facility information.

As mentioned above, the requirements that a bank must meet are partially dependent upon which of the two IRB approaches a bank will use. The first methodology, called the "foundation" approach, requires few direct inputs by banks and provides several supervisory parameters that, in many cases, carry over from those proposed for the standardized approach. The second approach, the "advanced" approach, allows banks much greater use of their internal assessments in calculating their regulatory capital requirements. This flexibility is subject to the constraints of prudential regulation, current banking practices and capabilities, and the need for sufficiently compatible standards among countries to maintain competitive equality among banks world-wide. [For example, the foundation approach assumes loans to banks, sovereigns, and corporates have an average maturity of 3 years, but the advanced approach allows the bank to calculate remaining maturities and link them to risk weights.]

There are four key inputs that are needed under IRB, for both the foundation and advanced approaches. The first element is the probability of default (PD) of a borrower; the bank is required to provide the PD in both the foundation and the advanced ap-proaches. The second piece is the estimated loss severity [a rate for each transaction], known as the loss given default (LGD). The final two elements are the amount at risk in the event of default or exposure at default (EAD) and the facility's remaining maturity (M).   LGD, EAD and M are provided by supervisors in the foundation approach, but in the advanced approach banks are expected to provide them (subject to supervisory review and validation). For each exposure, the risk weight is a function of PD, LGD, and M.

The IRB approach envisions internal rating systems that are two-dimensional. One dimension focuses on the borrower's financial capacity and PD estimates that quantify the likelihood of default by the borrower, independent of the structure of the facility. The other dimension takes into account transaction-specific factors such as terms, structure, and collateral. These characteristics would determine the second dimension, i.e., the LGD. Implicit in this treatment is the assumption that when a borrower defaults on one obligation, it will generally default on all its obligations. (This assumption is relaxed with the IRB treatment of retail portfolios.) Calculating the capital charge under the IRB approach involves several steps. The first of these steps is the breakdown of the bank's portfolio into six categories: corporate, retail, bank, sovereign, equity, and project finance. The IRB rules differ to varying degrees across these portfolios. As a result, the IRB charge is calculated by category, with the PD, LGD, and EAD inputs potentially differing across these categories. Supervisory approval is needed before banks can use the IRB approach for any of the six categories. The minimum requirements described above also differ somewhat across these six types of exposure. The IRB approaches are most developed for portfolios of exposures to banks, corporates, and sovereigns.

Another important step is the determination by the bank of the PDs for its loan grading categories in both the foundation and advanced IRB approaches. The PD of an exposure is the one-year PD associated with the borrower grade, subject to a floor of 0.03% (except for sovereign exposures, which are exempt from the 0.03% floor).   The determination of PDs for borrowers supported by guarantees or credit derivatives is more complex. Banks under the advanced approach would use their internal assessments of the degree of risk transfer within supervisory defined parameters, while those under the foundation approach would use the framework set forth in the credit risk mitigation section. Overall, the PD must be "grounded in historical experience and empirical evidence," while being "forward looking" and "conservative." A reference definition of default has been developed for use in PD estimation and internal data collection of realized defaults.

Once the PD has been established, a second credit risk dimension -- loss severity or LGD – must be determined. [This is a measure of the expected average loss per unit of exposure if the counterparty defaults. It varies by type of exposure.] Under the foundation approach, the bank simply matches the collateral characteristics of the exposure to a specified list of LGDs, expressed as a proportion of the credit exposure. If the collateral type is not specified in the Accord, the exposure is considered unsecured and receives the corresponding LGD. If banks can meet the requirements for using their own LGD estimates, they can implement the advanced approach. Then, for each facility the effective maturity, M, must be determined. To limit burden, under the foundation IRB approach each facility's M is assumed to equal three years. The Committee is considering several options for the advanced approach, of which the most developed would involve basing M on each facility's remaining contractual maturity.

After the bank determines the PDs and LGDs for all applicable exposures, those combinations can be mapped into regulatory risk weights. The risk weights are calibrated to include coverage for both expected and unexpected losses. Unexpected loss is a probability-based assessment of the losses that would occur under severe stress conditions. The risk weights are expressed as a continuous function, which provides maximum risk sensitivity and flexibility in accommodating diverse bank risk rating systems.

The capital charge is determined by multiplying the risk weight by the amount expected to be outstanding at the time of default, known as the EAD, and by 8%. If a bank has a high degree of single-borrower or single-group credit risk concentrations (a "nongranular" portfolio) within its non-retail credit portfolios, the bank would be required to increase the regulatory capital minimum by the granularity adjustment which is specified in the proposal. The adjustment would be a reduction in capital for a bank with a relatively low degree of single-borrower risk.

A final step in this process involves the ongoing review by the supervisors of the systems used to develop the IRB capital charge. Periodically, supervisors will need to validate these systems and review the internal controls that provide the foundation for the IRB approach. In addition, supervisors will also have to consider, under Pillar 2, whether the amount of capital generated by the IRB approach is commensurate with the bank's risk profile.

In the following year, the Committee expanded and refined the IRB Approach. For example, it explained how the IRB approach would work for credit risk in financing for projects, income producing real estate, and commodities. Basel Committee, *Working Paper on the Internal Ratings Based Approach to Specialized Lending Exposures*, October 2001.

d.   CRITICISM OF THE JANUARY 2001 PROPOSAL

One of the most inclusive responses to the Basel Committee's January 2001 Proposal came from the Shadow Financial Regulatory Committee (SFRC), which consisted of U.S.-based scholars in law, finance, and economics. The SFRC argued that, given the weak state of knowledge and practice, no single formula could "provide a credible and robust measure of capital adequacy." SFRC, Statement No. 169, *The Basel Committee's Revised Capital Accord Proposal*, Feb. 26, 2001 at 1. The increased complexity and delays in drafting demonstrate the "basic flaw" in the regulators' doomed efforts to keep up with the evolving complexity of the market. The greater discretion given banks and regulators, coupled with the lack of consensus about even basic matters like how to measure probability of loan default with historical data, undercut the claim for a global standard and offered new opportunities for risk arbitrage. Risk measurement will become even more arbitrary; no cogent justification exists for setting all operational risk weight at 20%, for example. Greater reliance on ratings will probably "degrade the quality of information" in the ratings, as the rating agencies are pressed to relax their standards. Overall, the proposal's complexity is unnecessary and harmful.

Others argued that rather than creating a level playing field with common rules, the 2001 Proposals would make things worse. Applying the four methodologies–the Basel 1988 rules, the standardized approach, a foundation IRB, and an advanced IRB–together would generate great confusion. Peterson at 51. By applying the rules only to banks, as Basel does, and not to securities firms, the Proposal adds to the competitive inequality between the two groups. J. Mackintosh, *Call to Soften Rules on Capital*, Financial Times, Apr. 10, 2001.

Critics focused on the problems of the standardized approach and the internal ratings-based approach. Criticism of the standardized approach surfaced immediately after it appeared. According to the critics, it:

(1) Still relied on risk weights that failed to differentiate enough among types of credit quality, were arbitrary. For example, one analyst calculated a range of "appropriate" capital given the performance of differently rated issuers and found a low of 1.4% for

AAA issuers up to a high of 17% for those below B-. This contrasts with the range of 1.6% to 12% for the standardized approach. That is, AAA corporate assets are weighted 20%, and .20 x the 8% capital ratio is 1.6%, while for assets below BB- the 150% weight would generate 1.50 x 8% or 12% required capital. See H. Jackson, *The Role of Credit Rating Agencies in the Establishment of Capital Standards for Financial Institutions in a Global Economy* (2000)). They were also inconsistent (for example, borrowers with the same external ratings get different risk weights from Basel if they are corporations, foreign governments, or agencies, and if the credit is a loan or securitized, *Bankers Snub Changes to Basel Accord, Particularly Use of External Rating Systems*, 74 Banking Report (Apr. 10, 2000) at 672).

(2) Ignored the effect on risk of a bank's overall portfolio.

(3) Created two tiers of required capital unnecessarily.

(4) Relied too much on private rating agencies. Even in the U.S. most banks held portfolios in which only a small portion of loans was rated by agencies and rating agencies played a much smaller role even in the public markets of many other industrial countries. A conflict of interest existed because the issuers pay the rating agencies' fees.

(5) Used ratings differently from the way the agencies designed them to be used, which would give the wrong incentives. Later, the Enron collapse prompted the rating agencies to reconsider their methods, notably the slow speed with which they modified ratings. J.Wiggins and P. Spiegel, *Enron's Fall May Spark Credit Rating Rethink*, Financial Times, January 19-20, 2002.

The IRB approach attracted criticism on many counts. Definitions and parameters the Committee selected were incomplete, inadequate or wrong. They were wrong to assume that either banks or their regulators could implement this approach soon. Very few could. On the other hand, if many could, the impact would hurt the economy. The Basel Committee micro-managed the scope and application of the IRB Approach. Finally, the Approach did not let banks employ their own internal credit models. The following paragraphs elaborate each of these points.

Incomplete, inadequate, or wrong parameters for IRB. The 2001 Proposal has many important undecided elements. One example is the key issue of the maturity of the credit. While the 2001 Proposal assumes each credit's effective maturity is 3 years for the Foundation IRB Approach, it did not yet recommend principles to set maturity for a bank using the Advanced IRB approach. Off-balance sheet operations by big banks are usually significant, so this is a big gap. See Basel Committee, *The Internal Ratings-Based Approach*, Jan. 2001 at 24-25.

Basic definitions and parameters specified in the 2001 Proposal are often inadequate, according to critics. Several examples follow.

a. The concept of loss is narrow. Hirtle *et al.* identify two approaches to defining loss. B. Hirtle, M. Levonian, M. Saidenberg, Stefan Walter, and D. Wright, *Using Credit Risk Models for Regulatory Capital: Issues and Options*, Federal Reserve Bank of New York Economic Policy Review, Mar. 2001, at 19 (Hirtle 2001). One, used by Basel, is to define loss as default. This is the Default Mode. A second, used now by banks and much more nuanced, is to define loss as either default or a reduction in credit quality, as when a loan become more risky and must be shifted to a lower credit category that would require a higher return. A bank that cannot receive that return has a loss. This is the Multistate Mode. By using a simple default/no default concept of loss for each credit classification, the 2001 Proposal does not take into account losses that arise as credits migrate from one category to another.

b. The time horizon for loss is short. Hirtle 2001 identifies three approaches to setting a time horizon. One looks at a single year as the period in which to estimate the risk of loss. This is the industry practice, according to Hirtle, and is used by the 2001 Proposal. Other periods, usually longer, could be set, however. Finally, a bank might set the time horizon as the remaining life of each loan. This would most accurately reflect the length of exposure for most commercial banks.

c. By relying on the internal ratings of banks, the Proposal fails to confront the inadequacies of those systems as used by even the biggest banks. Some parameters do not reflect reality. For example, both the IRB approach and the common practice among banks assume that every bank operates independently and that herd behavior does not exist. (M. Peterson, *Basel Gives Banks the Whip Hand*, Euromoney, Mar. 2001 at 48 (Peterson)).

d. The parameters are general, not tailored to the needs of different jurisdictions. Any set of rules that is proposed for adoption by many countries must be alert to the way differences in local law and financial practice would affect the implementation of the proposed rules. The 2001 Proposals do not understand and incorporate the relation between banks' internal ratings and their home's laws for bankruptcy and accounting.

Weak implementation by banks and regulators. The Committee was wrong, say critics, to leave it to the discretion of national regulators to decide whether to let a bank adopt the IRB Approach. Few if any banks or regulators can implement it. In May 2001, a member of the Fed said that no U.S. banks would then qualify to use the advanced IRB approach. Meyer, *Fed Will Insist on High Standards for Basel Accord's Internal Ratings Option*, 76 BNA Banking Report 888, May 21, 2001. By 2004, possibly 60 to 80 would qualify to use either IRB approach according to another source. Financial supervisors in many countries, even including Germany, lack the sophistication to evaluate the banks using the IRB Approach. One danger is that regulatory competition, and patriotic fervor, might lead them to allow their biggest banks to use internal models even if the banks also lacked sophistication. Peterson at 51.51.

Costly. The January 2001 Proposals could raise the volume of regulatory capital needed by 30% to 40% above levels at the time. Anja Helk, *Bankers Balk at Basel II*, Euromoney, August 2001 at 52.

Harmful economic impact. If many banks could implement the IRB approach, the impact might hurt the economy. The 2001 Proposal would be pro-cyclical, encouraging more lending when the economy is strong and discouraging lending when weak. This would also hurt the creditors. Peterson at 51. The German government warned that it would oppose the January 2001 proposals because they would limit lending to small and medium sized businesses that depend largely on banks for funds. H. Simonian, P. Ehrlich, and J. Willman, *Germans Warn Over Banking Capital Rules,* Financial Times, November 1, 2001. Regulatory capital costs to banks might increase 30%-40%. A. Helk, *Backers Balk at Basel II*, Euromoney August 2001, at 52.

Micro-management. Overall the Basel Committee micro-managed the scope and application of the IRB Approach. This is particularly, and deliberately, true for the Foundation IRB Approach, which in the early years, at least, would apply to most if not all banks in this group. For almost every step it describes, the 2001 Proposal sets out how a bank is to implement the rule. It decides the six categories banks must use to group credits in their portfolio (sovereign, corporate, etc.). It sets a one year probability of default for each borrower grade, then sets a 0.03% floor (excepting sovereign credits). When estimating its expected loss given default (LGD), a bank with the Foundation IRB approach was told the rates to use. For instance, it would have to assume a 50% LGD for senior corporate claims lacking collateral. When collateral existed, the Committee specified the methodologies to calculate LGD. A bank eligible to use the Advanced IRB approach could make its own estimates, but few would qualify. When estimating exposure at default (EAD), a bank using the Foundation IRB approach was told to convert off-balance sheet exposures with uncertain drawdowns at 75% of the undrawn amount, for example.

No internal models. The 2001 proposal did not let banks employ their own internal credit models. The Internal Ratings-Based Approach of Basel differs from letting banks use their own internal models to determine capital for credit risk. Basel's IRB Approach rejects analysis of the credit risk of the portfolio as a whole, which is key to the internal models for credit risk that banks use today. The idea is that price movements of securities in the portfolio are correlated to different degrees. A diversified portfolio would have less risk than one less diversified.

e.   WHY NOT LET BANKS USE THEIR OWN INTERNAL CREDIT MODELS?

Regulators could, either as an alternative to the Basel 2001 Proposal or in addition to it, let banks use their own internal models for credit risk, as regulators now provide for market risk (see the next Section of this chapter). The bank would determine the value at risk (VAR) in its own loan portfolio and hold enough capital to cover that risk. A credit risk model is designed to predict the probability of default and the likely recovery of assets after a default. A portfolio is risky if there is a significant likelihood that actual losses will substantially exceed expected losses. D. Jones and J. Mingo, *Industry Practices in Credit Risk Modeling and Internal Capital Allocations: Implications for a Models-Based Regulatory Capital Standard*, 4 Federal Reserve Bank of New York Economic Policy Review 53 (1998).

Banks employ different methods—or credit risk models—to estimate the probability that actual loan losses will exceed loan loss provisions. The top-down method is often used for consumer and small business loans. It relies on the volatility of charge-offs historically for the type of loan rather than individual loans. For example, banks have data for many years showing the default rate on portfolios of consumer loans through all phases of the economic cycle. This experience will allow the bank to determine the probability of default for its own portfolio. The bottom-up method, generally used for large corporate credit, quantifies credit risk for each loan and, adjusting for correlations among them, aggregates the credit risk of each loan to measure the credit risk of the entire portfolio. See W. Treacy and M. Carey, *Credit Risk Rating Systems at Large US Banks*, Journal of Banking & Finance 167 (2000).

A bottom-up credit model has three common elements, according to Hirtle 2001. One defines key concepts, such as loss and the time horizon within which that loss would occur. The IRB Approach does this, as described above. The second calculates distributions of future loss from an analysis of each credit, as the IRB Approach does. The third element assesses the behavior of the overall portfolio, estimating variance in, and correlation of, credit exposures, valuations, and the transitions of credits from one credit category to another. The IRB Approach does not do this.

Regulators reject the internal models approach, particularly this third element, for credit risk because significant difficulties now exist, they say, in model construction, data availability, and model validation procedures. The Fed reached this conclusion after a study of industry practice with internal credit models. The authors of Hirtle 2001, all employees of the Federal Reserve System, do not actually criticize the Fed Task Force, but reach conclusions that differ in significant ways, as described in the following paragraphs.   See Federal Reserve System Task Force on Internal Credit Risk Models, *Credit Risk Models at Major U.S. Banking Institutions: Current State of the Art and Implications for Assessments of Capital Adequacy* (May 1998) ("Fed Task Force").

The limits of existing techniques were severe, according to the Fed. The definition of credit loss was an example. Most banks used a simple default/no-default definition that failed to capture the extent of actual loss given default. Bank models often treated as equal the loss rate and volatility for very different types of loans. For identical types of credit, one bank would estimate risk at ten times the rate of another bank because of modeling assumptions. Banks' modeling assumptions were often inconsistent. Some, for example, assumed that the draw-down rates of committed credit lines were independent of changes in the customer's credit quality, even though experience showed that customers drew increasingly on their credit lines as their creditworthiness worsened. The planning horizon was generally much too short. Most banks applied a time horizon of only one year in the belief that the bank could "mitigate its credit exposure" within that time. Some regulators thought this process would often take more than a year. Hirtle 2001 at 23, however, was prepared to accept a one year time horizon if the bank used a multistate concept of loss, which would incorporate the risk of defaults beyond one year through down grading during that year.

Limited data were a major problem. Model building relied on many assumptions and general estimates because data were not available to estimate precise parameters for "the joint probability distribution of the relevant risk factors." Most loans were not marked to market. Default events were infrequent. So analysts used simplifying assumptions and proxy data. Model validation was hindered by the lack of data that would allow a bank, when testing the predictions of its model after the fact (called "back-testing"), to compare the losses on loans in its portfolio with those in portfolios outside the bank's sample.

The standards to evaluate existing models were not obvious to the Fed Task Force. It turned to the Market Risk amendment to the Basel Accord (see Section II of this Chapter). These standards required "that a risk measurement model be (a) analytically sound, (b) subject to period back-testing and stress testing, and (c) well integrated into the bank's management decision making process." Fed Task Force at 34. Internal models for credit risk failed each test, according to the Task Force, after it reviewed the models used by US banks to evaluate the credit risk of medium-sized and large borrowers. Hirtle 2001 at 29, however, proposed that the regulator's job would be to provide conceptual standards for validation rather than specify the specific techniques, and let the banks try to meet the standards. Regulators could, for example, give "sound-practice guidance" for management of the models (e.g., a test that the bank actually used the model to manage its businesses) and a "quantitative testing to detect systematic biases in model result."

While conceding that similar problems existed with internal models used for market risk, for the credit risk the problems were "much more acute. At most large banks, the size of the loan portfolio and the length of its relevant planning horizon are many time larger than those of the trading account." Where market risk models typically employed a horizon of a few days, credit risk models generally relied on a time frame of one year or more.   The longer holding period, coupled with the higher confidence intervals used in credit risk models, presented problems to model-builders in assessing the accuracy of their models. "Errors in measuring risks for the banking book are more likely to affect assessment of the institution's overall financial health." Fed Task Force at 42. In contrast to the market risk models that are run daily, the credit risk internal models to estimate new a PDF of future losses need only be used periodically, perhaps every 30 days now and at most weekly in the future.

Later Fed studies of large banks confirmed these conclusions. A Fed study of 45 large U.S. banks' credit-risk models concluded that 'the great majority of the 50 largest holding company rating systems are not really well-prepared to support the most advanced credit-risk modeling techniques.' J. Seiberg, *Fed Study: Bank Risk Models Too Weak for Setting Capital*, American Banker, Nov. 18, 1998. The Basel Committee reached the same conclusions in its report, *Credit Risk Modelling: Current Practices and Applications*, in April 1999. See also *BIS Finds Divergent Practices in Banks' Assignment of Internal Credit Ratings*, 13 Swaps Monitor 4 (January 17, 2000) at 1.

If regulators were to rely on internal models to set regulatory capital for credit risk, they could take several approaches. One approach would be to set the parameters of acceptable models. The regulator might, for example, set a maximum target default rate that is the same for all banks.

A second approach would be to set conceptual guidelines rather than parameters. Conceptual standards for model structure would require the bank, for example, to address probabilities for transition among credit categories (e.g., by saying that a model would have to address correlations across borrowers but not specifying the method), uncertainty in credit exposure (e.g., saying the model must take account of random variation), and the uncertainty in credit migration (e.g., saying the model must explicitly take into account the volatility in market credit spreads and their correlations). Hirtle 2001, at 25-26.

A third approach would be to let each bank design its own model, using its own parameters and principles, but then test the model's performance. This is called the precommitment approach. Banks would estimate in advance of a period of time the capital they would need to offset their credit risk during that period. If their estimate fell short of the capital they actually needed during the period, the regulators would fine them. There are several problems with this approach. Regulators might be constrained from imposing a fine that could put the bank's solvency in jeopardy. A bank already in trouble might not be deterred by the possibility of a fine. Both the internal models and precommitment approaches are drawn from techniques developed for risk in securities markets, the subject of Section II. See J. Seiberg, *The Fed Considers Sweeping Changes in Risk-Based Capital Requirements*, American Banker, December 13, 1996.

If the IRB approach is too complex and directive, and banks are not able to use internal models yet, perhaps regulators should turn to the financial markets to help discipline the banks. This was the proposal of the Shadow Committee.

f.   THE USE OF SUBORDINATED DEBT

The Shadow Committee offered a proposal that would apply an explicit market discipline to banks by having investors in subordinated debt police the banks that issued it. The Shadow Committee argued that subordinated debt is superior to equity. A bank in trouble takes higher risks because its shareholders have an incentive to gamble, with little more to lose if the gamble fails and a profit if it pays off. Holders of subordinated debt have no such upside. They will reap only the yield on the debt, so they have an incentive to discourage risky strategies by banks in trouble. As the issuer's risk rises, the holders will demand a higher yield. Banks with less risky portfolios will have strong incentives to disclose this to investors in order to keep down the cost of funds.

But the Shadow Committee believes that subordinated debt must be limited in several ways if it is to serve as capital. To ensure that it is subordinate to all other liabilities, it cannot receive any benefit from an FDIC rescue of the bank. It must have a minimum remaining maturity of one year to ensure that capital is available when needed. The subordinated debt can only be redeemed by issuing more subordinated debt to make sure that it does not disappear as a bank encounters troubles, and redemption requires regulatory approval if the bank is undercapitalized. It should be sold in denominations exceeding $100,000 to ensure that investors are sophisticated and understand the debt is not insured. The regulator must be able to instruct the bank to stop paying principal and interest on the subordinated debt if the bank's capital falls below designated levels.

The requirement that large banks issue subordinated debt equal to at least 2% of their assets and off-balance sheet liabilities links regulation to market signals explicitly. The designers want to remove regulators' discretion in order to end what they see as the pernicious practice of regulatory forbearance, which allows troubled banks to delay difficult reforms. Formal guidelines would link market price signals to existing requirements that regulators strictly supervise and even close banks as their capital weakens. So when the yields on a bank's subordinated debt reach junk levels (BBB or lower) and remain there for 3 months, the regulators would have to examine the bank, raise the cost of deposit insurance, require a strategy to recover, and limit payments to depositors and investors, as well as the growth of the bank's assets. Regulators would have to monitor the yield on each bank's subordinated debt. When trading in the debt is minimal, banks should make frequent offerings.

Support for this proposal was not universal. One quantitative study concluded that while regulators have no clear informational advantage over bond markets, the market signals would only be useful if they supplemented regulators' data or reduced their cost. Deyoung, Flannery, Lang, and Soresca, *The Information Content of Bank Exam Ratings and Subordinate Debt Prices*, 33 Journal of Money, Credit, and Banking, 900 (2001). A theoretical analysis led to the conclusion that this would not happen. Sub debt had few advantages over equity, and was sometimes inferior, since equity prices conveyed at least the same information as sub-debt. M. Levonian, *Subordinated Debt and the Quality of Market Discipline in Banking,* May 2001. Attacking proposals to rely on sub debt was an article by Bert Ely, *Sub Debt—Silver Bullet or a Big Dud?*, 5:2 Financial Regulator 32, Sep. 2000. According to the author, it rested on several false premises:

- the untested belief that supervisors would be embarrassed into action by market signals about risky sub debt, when they do not even now lack information about banks' risk;

- that equity signals were less effective than those of subordinated debt;

- that sub debt holders have no upside potential, despite the fact that a speculator in a troubled bank's discounted debt is betting that the market value of that debt will rise;

- that diversification of risk through government deposit insurance is inferior to a bank's nearly exclusive reliance on its own capital; and

- that one-size-fits-all will work for sub debt rules when it does not work in the Basel Accord.

According to the U.S. Treasury and the Federal Reserve, mandatory subordinated debt could encourage market discipline but additional evidence was needed to answer practical questions for implementation. *The Feasibility and Desirability of Mandatory Subordinated Debt* (December 2000) study reviewed the existing market and evaluated many proposals to use sub debt, including that of the Shadow Committee. One question was whether the sub debt market was big enough, in number of instruments, issuers, and investors, to let it play the disciplinary role. Illiquidity in normal times, let alone in crisis, could undermine its signaling effect. The study found a deep corporate bond market, with over $1 trillion in issues a year. But banks and BHCs issued only about $9 billion in subordinated debt each year from 1995-1999. The 50 largest BHCs issued about 4 times each year. The 20 largest issuers averaged issues of $200 million each. While the large issues had standard terms, issues smaller than $75 million did not. Trading took place in a dealer market among largely institutional investors. The secondary markets was highly liquid except in times of stress like the Russian default in August 1998. About 15 of the top 20 issuers had enough qualifying subordinated debt outstanding to reach the 2% ceiling permitted by the capital adequacy rules in effect. So the sub debt market was not deep and liquid compared to the market for all commercial bonds,, but it had a foundation on which to grow.

The Treasury and Fed found evidence that the banks' decisions to issue and the issuance spreads were sensitive enough for subordinated debt to improve direct market discipline. During a period of bank distress in 1988-91, the weaker banks had been less likely to issue subordinated debt. Secondary market spreads were risk sensitive, but could also be driven by such things as shortages or surpluses of the issue, or market illiquidity. Even so, the agencies found evidence that the market could exert an indirect discipline as well. Bank supervisors follow these spreads to monitor the banks; the OCC has done so for the 25 largest BHCs since 1993. One question was whether equity data give a better and earlier warning than bond data. The jury was not yet in. It did appear, however, that requiring banks to issue new sub debt regularly would be useful because a few studies found that new debt issues reveal new information, improving transparency and disclosure. Another issue was whether sub-debt would be superior to the regulators' evaluation of credit risk. An empirical comparison of capital ratios and sub-debt spread found insignificant differences in their ability to predict changes in the supervisors' ratings (called CAMEL ratings) of banks. D. Levanoft and L. Wall, *Sub-Debt Yield Spreads or Bank Risk Measures*, Federal Reserve Bank of Atlanta Working Paper 2001-11 (May 2001).

For mandatory subordinated debt to be a useful tool, policy makers would have to resolve five basic issues. The jury was still out on the appropriate resolution of these issues, however.

- Should the rules apply to the bank or the BHC? To all banks, or only large ones? Very little work has been done to assess "the combined risks of large organizations that provide both bank and traditionally non-bank activities." Spreads on BHC sub debt, by including both activities, might give indistinct signals about the bank. The Fed/Treasury study described a "'switching rule' that would require subordinated debt issuance at the depository level if depository institution assets fell below a given proportion . . . of total holding company assets." The switching point would be arbitrary.

- What amount of subordinated debt should be required? About half the proposals reviewed by the study recommended a mandatory 2% of risk-weighted assets, but the rest recommended from 4%to 6%. The lower recommendations tended to see sub debt as a tool for indirect market discipline imposed by the supervisors and thought equity was a good substitute for sub debt. The higher recommendations took the opposite view. Costs were not seen as a problem.

- What type of subordinated debt should qualify? Unresolved questions existed about whether the debt should be publicly-traded, with only standard terms (for comparability), and subject to maturity restrictions.

- How close should be the link between market signals and insolvency procedures? A hard-wired link would remove discretion from the deposit insurer and close banks that might otherwise be salvaged.

- Should banks be required to issue subordinated debt at regular intervals? If not, they could try to by-pass markets in hard times. If so, they might have to pay excessively high fees in illiquid markets.

For this reason, the Treasury/Fed study concluded that more analysis is needed before legislation can be drafted.

The Shadow Committee responded that the Treasury/Fed arguments actually supported the Committee's proposal. To get the additional data the Treasury/Fed wants, regulators should implement the proposal and then track it through difficult times. Requiring issuance in hard times is "precisely the . . . time when such debt should be issued" because that is when the market's information becomes important to regulators. As regulators follow the market's response, they can fine tune the rule. SFRC, Statement No. 168, *Requiring Large Banks to Issue Subordinated Debt*, Feb. 26, 2001 at 1.

Notes and Questions

1. The European Union began to revise its capital rules for credit risk, largely following the BIS. The EU's rules would be legislative, and apply to banks and securities companies. *EU Capital Adequacy to Mirror New Basel Capital Accord, EC Announces,* BNA Banking Report (January 29, 2001) at 157; and New Capital Adequacy Standards Proposed for Banks, Investment Firms, BNA World Securities Law Report (Feb. 1, 2001) at 3. The EU decided to wait for the Basel II proposals to evolve before implementing its own rules.

2. Is the BIS proposal to amend the Basel Accord a significant change for the better? According to a U.S. supervisor, "The $64,000 question is: Does the industry think that this degree of complexity—which we think is probably necessary if you are going to fine-tune the rule—is an approach they are comfortable with?" R. Garver, *Basel Capital Proposal May Turn Off Banks*, American Banker, Jan. 19, 2001. More specifically,

a. Does it reduce the problems of credit allocation and regulatory capital arbitrage?

b. Does it increase the likelihood that capital adequacy rules will be applied consistently across countries?

c. Are its uses of rating agencies sufficiently flexible? For example, both Moody's and Standard & Poor's will rate companies higher than their home government. P. Beaumont, *Credit Risk Becomes the Key to Judging Investments*, Financial Times, July 12, 2002.

3. Do you agree with the proposal to rely much more on subordinated debt for capital adequacy? What are the strengths and weaknesses of the proposal?

4. At the same time the Basel Committee released the New Accord proposals about credit risk, it released a consultative document on *Principles for the Management and Supervision of Interest Rate Risk* (Jan. 2001). This explicitly did not set rules, but left it to national supervisors to decide how to monitor and respond to interest rate risk within the broad framework of the principles.

5. A move away from complexity is found in a proposal by U.S. supervisors to simplify capital adequacy regulation for small banks. The problem, according to the banks, however, is that the new rules would force them to hold more capital than before and incur substantial costs retooling their own programs and risk-management systems. L. Daigle, *Capital Proposal Has More Pain Than Gain, Small Banks Say,* American Banker, Feb. 8, 2001.

SECTION II

CAPITAL ADEQUACY FOR MARKET RISK

Diversity confounds agreement on capital standards for the non-credit risks of issuing and trading securities, called market or position risk. Players, interests, and national approaches are at odds. Banks and securities companies compete, so regulators of both types of firms play a role.

National and multinational rules apply. At the national level, securities regulators setting capital standards include independent agencies such as the U.S. Securities and Exchange Commission (SEC), units in finance ministries as in Japan, or even departments of central banks. At the multilateral level, three organizations are trying to draft common standards for their members. For members of the European Union, the European Commission issued the Capital Adequacy Directive (CAD) for investment firms and credit institutions in March 1993. The Basel Committee on Banking Supervision issued its consultative proposal for the prudential supervision of international banks' netting, market risks, and interest rate risk in April 1993, supplemented the proposal in April 1995 and issued the final amendment to the Accord in January 1996. The International Organization of Securities Commissions (IOSCO) tried to issue common capital standards for its members but the effort collapsed in late 1992. In May 1995, the Basel Committee and IOSCO issued joint proposals for capital standards for derivatives operations. Each is alert to the need to cooperate with the others.

This section examines the problems of finding a common standard for market risk in equities. It raises two basic questions. First, what is the appropriate approach for calculating position risk? Second, since the function of capital for position risk differs greatly from that for bank credit, can a common ground be found for the capital needs of securities firms and banks operating in the securities markets? Some countries have standards for their broker-dealers that differ greatly from those for banks. Others relied on the Basel Accord for both. If one standard is set for securities companies and another for banks, which standard applies to a bank's securities subsidiaries or sister companies through a holding company? What of universal banks that carry out their own securities operations? The CAD resolved these issues for members of the European Union, generating dismay in the United Kingdom. The rest of the world has not resolved them.

This section sketches the range of risks faced by securities operations, then describes governmental direct regulation of position risk: the building block approach of the Basel Committee (and the CAD) and the comprehensive approach, used in the United States. A note compares these two approaches with the more complex portfolio approach used in the U.K. before the Basel Standard took effect. We ask how these approaches affect capital requirements for portfolio risk and examine the implications independently of whether a bank or non-bank holds the portfolio. We then turn to a very different approach: regulatory reliance on the internal risk management systems of the financial firms, called models-based regulation. We briefly note other risks of securities operations that may call for capital charges. Then we raise the thorny issue: How should regulators apply capital standards for position risk to banks and securities companies? Note throughout the material that position risk and market risk are used to mean the same thing.

As you read the materials, bear in mind that since regulators have not agreed on a common global standard for securities operations, there are many different rules or proposals.   For simplicity, we make some assumptions. When CAD and the Standard differ, countries adopt the stricter. National securities regulations will continue to govern non-bank securities firms outside the European Union. The discussion will focus on three types of big players:

a. U.S. securities companies are an example of non-bank securities firms, probably the most important example. U.K. securities companies are a second example.

b. Some banks take positions for their own account; German universal banks are among the best known.

c. Finally, at least in the U.S., a bank holding company (BHC), its bank, and any banking affiliates are now subject to the Basel Standard. A BHC's securities subsidiaries, however, are subject to SEC rules. Consolidated accounting would seem difficult.

While Basel applies only to banks, CAD applies to banks and securities companies. While the Accord really addressed only credit risk, the Basel Standard and CAD address a range of risks, including position risk, counterparty risk, foreign exchange risk, and others. For simplicity, we only address position risk and that only for equity positions. The following chart describes the different rules to which firms and banks from various countries are subject.

Equity Position Risk Rules

Firms with Positions	Sample Country	Comprehensive National SEC	EC CAD	Basel Standards	Portfolio National UK
Universal bank	Germany		X	X	
Securities firm	USA	X			
Securities firm	UK		X		X (past)
BHC	USA			X	
BHC securities subsidiary	USA	X			

A. RISKS ASSOCIATED WITH SECURITIES OPERATIONS

Regulators now try to tailor their capital standards to the different types of non-credit risk. The U.S. Government Accounting Office explains the common differences and the way a few countries approach them. As you read, consider the ways in which the risks and responses differ from those you encountered in the Basel Accord.

U.S. GOVERNMENT ACCOUNTING OFFICE, SECURITIES MARKETS: CHALLENGES TO HARMONIZING INTERNATIONAL CAPITAL STANDARDS REMAIN

12-62 (1992).

Securities firms and banks doing securities business risk their capital in complex trading strategies involving securities, futures, currencies, and interest rate swap instruments in the international securities markets. Securities activities are subject to a variety of risks. The type and amount of risk depends on the nature and extent of the securities firms' and banks' activities. The most important of these risks are market risk and counterparty risk. To a lesser extent, securities firms and banks doing a securities business may also face other types of risk, such as the risk of reduced revenues and foreign exchange risk.

Market risk, also called "position risk," is the risk of an adverse movement in a security's price. For example, the market value of a security purchased by a firm may fall before it can be resold.[5] In the case of an equity security, or stock, concerns about the financial performance of the corporate issuer may lead to a decline in the price of the security. In the case of a debt security, or bond, the nonpayment of principal or interest by the issuer, or a change in interest rates, may lead to a subsequent decline in the value of the security.

Counterparty risk, also called "settlement" risk, is the risk that a firm's trading partner will be either unwilling or unable to meet its contractual obligation. For example, a buyer may contract to purchase a security from a second-party seller and then commit to selling the security to a third party. The original buyer would then be exposed to the risk that the original seller may default and not deliver the security.

Other risk may include the risk to a firm associated with such factors as reduced net revenues, an increased administrative burden, or fraud. For example, a decrease in a firm's transaction volume may result in reduced income, while expenses remain constant or increase. Similarly, an unexpected increase in a firm's business may result in a heavier administrative burden that could lead to recordkeeping

---

[5] Alternatively, if a securities firm has a "short" position in a security (i.e., it has contracted to sell a security it does not own and must buy it before the contracted sale date), the market risk is that the price of the security may increase.

problems and, in turn, delays in completing transactions, called settlement delays.

Securities activities are also subject to other kinds of risks, such as foreign exchange risk. Foreign exchange risk is the risk that the value of a financial instrument will change due to currency fluctuations.

Systemic risk is the risk that a disturbance could severely impair the workings of the financial system and, at the extreme, cause a complete breakdown in it. For example, the collapse of securities prices could lead to the default of one or more large securities firms. Because of financial interrelationships, this could lead to further defaults of securities firms and banks. A series of such defaults could extend into the banking system and cause a disruption in the flow of payments in the settlement of financial transactions throughout the world. Shocks could be transmitted from one domestic market to other domestic markets. Such a breakdown in capital markets could disrupt the process of saving and investment, undermine the long-term confidence of private investors, and disrupt the normal course of economic transactions.

Capital Standards Protect Against Risks

The efficient functioning of financial markets requires that members of the financial community have confidence in each other's ability to transact business. This understanding means that each member of the financial community must have, among other things, adequate capital. Because of the high degree of interdependence among firms in the securities industry—where securities firms often buy and sell securities from one another and have contractual commitments with their counterparts—the failure of one firm to meet its obligation to another could affect the financial viability of other firms.

In general, capital standards are designed to protect customers and to ensure a viable financial system by diminishing the chance of a series of interrelated defaults because of risks in securities markets. Capital standards specify the minimum amount of capital a securities firm or a bank doing securities business should maintain and are often based on the nature and scope of its financial activities. This capital should be sufficient to pay customers, counterparties, and creditors.

.   .   .

How Capital Is Regulated in Securities Markets

Each country has different arrangements for regulating capital. The biggest difference among countries occurs in their treatment of securities and banking activities. In "universal" banking countries, securities business is generally done within banks, and typically one capital standard is applied to both securities and banking activities.

In "nonuniversal" banking countries such as the United States, securities firms and banks are separately regulated and subject to distinctly different capital standards.

Another difference among national capital standards is that the objectives of the standards can differ among countries. For example, in the United States the primary emphasis is on providing sufficient liquid assets to meet liabilities, including customer liabilities, and fostering confidence in the securities industry and the financial system; in Japan the emphasis is on preventing a firm's failure or protecting the financial system.

On an average day, firms and banks doing an international securities business hold billions of dollars in capital . . . .

In the United States, SEC is the primary regulator of securities firm capital, but the Federal Reserve System (FRS) and the Department of the Treasury also have a role. SEC oversees capital through a strategy of self-regulation. It creates and revises capital standards as well as oversees self-regulatory organizations, such as NYSE, that have primary responsibility for enforcing the compliance of their member firms with the standards. Although firms created under section 20 of the 1933 Glass–Steagall Act—i.e., securities subsidiaries of bank holding companies—must comply with SEC's capital standards, FRS sets other capital levels and approves capital plans for holding companies that own Section 20 companies. FRS requires that firm capital meet securities industry norms, which in turn are well above SEC minimum capital requirements. The Department of the Treasury has rule-making authority for firms registered as government securities dealers, while the securities regulators carry out oversight and enforcement activities.

In general, the capital levels of large U.S. securities firms exceed minimum requirements. . . .[T]he 10 largest U.S. securities firms have capital levels many times the minimum requirement on any given day. There are a variety of reasons why securities firms operate with capital levels in excess of minimum requirements, including (1) the firm needs to conduct large underwritings or other activities that occur periodically, and (2) the firm uses its capital level as a marketing tool to attract both individual and institutional investors.

Country Capital Standards Differ

International securities market participants are subject to a wide variety of country-specific capital standards.

. . .

For example, some countries value securities at current market prices ("mark to market"), while other countries value them at their original cost. Further, some countries have settlement risk requirements so that the risk of nonperformance in a timely manner is covered within the capital standards, while other countries do not.

Also, some countries set differential capital standards according to the type of business done, while other countries use uniform minimum standards for all types of securities businesses.

.   .   .

If securities firms or banks doing securities business fail, any remaining capital can be used to pay off customers, creditors, and counterparties. If securities firms or banks doing securities business fail when their capital falls to minimum capital standards, the failures are more likely to have adverse consequences for customers, creditors, and counterparties in countries with low minimum standards. Firms and banks that fail with higher minimum capital are more likely to meet their obligations. Poorly capitalized firms and banks that cannot meet their obligations may also cause financial difficulty for other securities firms, banks, clearing systems,[9] and hence securities markets. Widespread failure of these firms and banks may thus, in turn, cause other firms and banks to fail in markets with higher capital standards and result in a ripple effect across international financial markets.

Differing country capital standards may also have competitive effects both within a country where securities firms and banks compete for the same securities business or among countries. For example, if banks have more stringent capital standards than those imposed on competing securities firms within the same country, then banks may be at a competitive disadvantage because of the costs associated with holding the higher capital amounts. For the same reason, countries with higher capital standards could be at a competitive disadvantage to countries with lower capital standards. Alternatively, countries with higher standards might be competitively advantaged if they are viewed as safer places to do business than countries with lower capital standards.

Integrating Securities and Banking Capital Standards

Although securities activities of bank holding companies in the United States, other than government or municipal securities activity, have generally been limited to Section 20 firms—securities subsidiaries of bank holding companies—foreign banks and the foreign operations of U.S. banks, are heavily involved in securities activities. The Basel Committee . . . international capital standards for [banks' credit risk] . . differ from the capital standards traditionally applied to securities activities. For example, securities firms are generally required to value their securities at current market values, while banks generally use cost or lower of cost or market. U.S. banks have the

---

[9] Clearing systems capture trade data and guarantee that the trade will settle once the data match. Settlement is the final stage of the process when funds and/or financial instruments are exchanged between parties through the clearing organization.

option of valuing the securities in their trading portfolios at lower of cost or market, or marking the securities to market. U.S. banks value their investment portfolios at cost.   In general, securities firms' standards are designed to provide that the firms have sufficient liquid assets to meet their obligations, while bank standards are designed to ensure that banks remain solvent. Both banks and securities firms are concerned that if securities activities of banks are subject to capital standards different from those of securities firms, the one with the lower standard will have a competitive advantage. Resolving any differences in capital standards is a formidable task, however, because of the differences in operations of banks and securities firms and the resulting variance in the oversight methods securities regulators and bank supervisors use.

Regulators view risks differently for banks and securities firms. Because bank asset turnover is slow and securities firm asset turnover is relatively high, bank risk changes more slowly than securities firm risk. Banks have traditionally invested most of their funds in long-term illiquid assets, such as loans to customers. These funds come from highly liquid customer deposits as well as borrowings and the banks' own capital. Banks have traditionally held these assets to maturity. As a result, bank regulators focus on credit risk as the most important and predominant risk.

Because of their high asset turnover, securities firms must be able to absorb the effect of changing market values of their portfolios as they occur. Consequently, securities regulators emphasize valuing securities positions at market prices—and take a deduction on the market value of the securities position—to provide a margin of safety against potential losses that can be incurred as a result of market fluctuations. Securities regulators place little or no value on illiquid assets.   Securities firms holding large concentrated securities positions are more vulnerable to sudden market movements than diversified banks because a large portion of securities firms' net worth can be lost quickly.

Notes and Questions

1.   Governments regulate the capital adequacy of firms with securities business for several reasons described in the text.   Some emphasize customer protection. Others emphasize systemic stability. How would you expect these differing goals to affect capital standards?

2.   Do you agree that the business of securities firms and commercial banks differs so much that they require different capital standards? The reading describes the general approach of regulators to the possibility a security company would fail. What are the operational implications of this approach?   How does it compare to the approach of bank regulators? Why?

3.   Do you agree with the following assertion that securities firms may not need capital standards at all? It comes from The Economist, Oct. 5, 1991, at 92.

> Securities firms are not banks, whose failure can involve support from central banks or taxpayers. They are, it is sometimes argued, more like manufacturers, whose failure can damage creditors and customers but not enough to justify nannying supervision. Imposing capital standards on securities firms puts costs on both issuers and investors; raising them would reduce the price differential that has led those in search of capital increasingly to prefer securities to bank loans. High mandatory capital ratios might keep some securities firms out of the market.

B.   CAPITAL ADEQUACY AND POSITION RISK.

Among the very different approaches to capital adequacy for position risk are those, described in this section, taken by BIS bank regulators (and EU financial regulators) and the SEC. This section gives evaluations of these approaches, then presents regulation through internal models.

1.   POSITION RISK AND THE BUILDING BLOCK APPROACH

The Basel Committee designated two approaches to capital adequacy for market risk, one the building block approach discussed in this Section, and the other relying on the internal models of large financial firms (discussed in section 3 below). The Basel Standard was presented as a proposal at the end of April 1993, elaborated in April 1995 and, after negative comment, issued as an amendment to the 1988 Accord in January 1996. The Basel Committee expressed the hope that it could be extended beyond banks to securities firms. See The Basel Committee on Banking Supervision, The Supervisory Treatment of Market Risks (1993); Planned Supplement to the Capital Accord to Incorporate Market Risks (1995); and Amendment to the Capital Accord to Incorporate Market Risks (1996). We refer to the last as the "Basel Standard."

The Basel Building Block Standard set formulas to compute capital for a bank's "trading book," against whose current market value the capital is charged. The trading book includes a "bank's proprietary positions in financial instruments" held to benefit "in the short term from actual or expected differences between their buying and selling prices," to hedge other trading book items, for short-term sale, or "to execute a trade with a customer." The capital charges for debt and equity would substitute for the credit risk weights now applied by the Basel Accord. Non-trading book items remained subject to the Basel Accord.

The building blocks are the separate calculations of general position risk and specific position risk for securities in the trading book. The distinction between specific and general risks is basic in finance theory and practice. Specific risk refers to the risks associated with the issuer itself. General risks are those not associated with an issuer, such as changes in the market or economy. For equity position risk, the standard applies to long and short positions in all instruments... Long and short positions in the same issue may be reported on a net basis.

. . .

The minimum capital standard for equities is expressed in terms of two separately calculated charges for the "specific risk" of holding a long or short position in an individual equity and for the "general market risk" of holding a long or short position in the market as a whole. Specific risk is defined as the bank's gross equity positions (i.e., the sum of all long equity positions and of all short equity positions) and general market risk as the difference between the sum of the longs and the sum of the shorts (i.e., the overall net position in an equity market). The long or short position in the market must be calculated on a market-by-market basis, i.e., a separate calculation has to be carried out for each national market in which the bank holds equities.

The capital charge for *specific* risk will be 8%, unless the portfolio is both liquid and well-diversified, in which case the charge will be 4%. Given the different characteristics of national markets in terms of marketability and concentration, national authorities will have discretion to determine the criteria for liquid and diversified portfolios. The *general market risk* charge will be 8%. Basel Standard, *supra*, at 19.

The Standard permits countries to use a "comprehensive approach" like that of the SEC (see below) if they demonstrate the effect is at least as stringent as that of the Standard.

The basic formula was 8+8 (specific + general risk), but for "liquid and marketable stock" it would be 4+8 at the discretion of the national regulator. The Basel Committee illustrated the methodology as follows:

Equities

Illustration of x plus y methodology

Under the proposed two-part calculation described in Section 3 there would be separate requirements for the position in each individual equity (i.e. the gross position) and for the net position in the market as a whole. The table below illustrates how the system would work for a range of hypothetical portfolios, assuming a capital charge of 4% for the gross positions and 8% for the net positions.

Sum of long positions	Sum of short positions	Gross position (sum of cols. 1 & 2)	Specific risk: 4% of gross	Net position (difference between cols. 1 & 2)	General risk: 8% of net	Capital required (gross + net)
100	0	100	4	100	8	12
100	25	125	5	75	6	11
100	50	150	6	50	4	10
100	75	175	7	25	2	9
100	100	200	8	0	0	8
75	100	175	7	25	2	9
50	100	150	6	50	4	10
25	100	125	5	75	6	11
0	100	100	4	100	8	12

After much debate and delay, the European Commission issued its Capital Adequacy Directive (CAD) for investment companies and other credit institutions in March 1993 (93/6/EEC). This complemented the Investment Services Directive 93/22/EEC of May 10, 1993 discussed in Chapter 5.

The CAD sets capital adequacy rules for several kinds of risk in the firms' trading book, including position risk (Annex I). The CAD defines key terms, sets rules for initial capital that vary according to the investment firms' services, specifies the "own funds" or capital firms need to provide against risk, and requires consolidated supervision and reporting. Institutions must mark their trading book to market daily. The CAD's Building Block approach to market risk is essentially the same as the Basel approach. The major differences are that its specific risk requirements are 4% and, for diversified liquid portfolios, 2%, rather than the 8% and 4% of Basel.

The CAD required members to implement its rules by the end of 1996. Germany did not meet this deadline, even though most other EU members had done so, including the U.K. The German approach before it adopted the Building Block approach reflected the fact that Germany has universal banks, which both accept deposits like commercial banks and engage in the securities business. The German capital adequacy rules simply said that securities held for trading were subject to the general standard for capital adequacy set out by the German version of the Basel Accord if the financial intermediary is a bank, as most are. German rules were silent on whether long and short positions should be netted. They did not allow subordinated debt. Capital was not marked to market. Germany was facing infringement proceedings before the European Court of Justice when, in late 1997, it did adopt implementing law. The EC suspended the proceedings. See International Securities Market Association, *Implemen-*

tation of the Investment Services Directive, Capital Adequacy Directive, and Third Insurance Directives, Progress Report No. 3, December 19, 1997.

The International Organization of Securities Commissions (IOSCO) represents most countries with stock exchanges. Managed by an executive committee and a small secretariat based in Montreal, Canada, IOSCO works through two committees: the Technical Committee, most of whose members are industrial countries, and the Emerging Markets Committee. Its working groups, acting by consensus, give members advisory opinions. Implementation varies widely among member countries. See T. Ito and D. Folkerts-Landau, *International Capital Markets*, Annex IV, International Monetary Fund, 1996.

From early 1992, the Basel Committee and the Technical Committee of IOSCO had jointly searched for common rules. The goal was harmony in approach to banks and securities firms. The Technical Committee accepted Basel's building block method. The Basel group, for its part, agreed to differentiate between specific and general risk in their approach to position risk. But in late 1992, Richard Breeden -- chairman of the U.S. SEC and chairman of the IOSCO Technical Committee -- announced his implacable opposition to the building block approach. Supported by some other countries like Japan, he stopped IOSCO's three-year effort. Breeden argued that the approach was "highly unsafe." R. Peston and T. Corrigan, *Breeden Opposes IOSCO Capital Standard*, Financial Times, Oct. 28, 1992. During 1993, the initiative for global harmonization shifted from IOSCO to the Basel Committee as IOSCO pulled back. But by mid-1996, the two groups announced plans to work closely together in the future. They announced eight major principles, very general. 66 BNA Banking Report 956 (1996).

Notes and Questions

1. Take care to think through the differences between general and specific risk. The SEC Comprehensive Approach described below makes no clear distinction between the two, in part because it was devised before the concepts were popularized and the costs of changing would be high for regulators and financial firms.

2. The Basel Standard governs position taking by German universal banks. What is the logic of this standard? Whom does it try to protect? Does it seem to be designed to protect against all possible losses or something less than 100%? Why distinguish between general and specific risk?

3. How does the Basel Standard calculate general risk for equity? Suppose a universal bank's assets consist of $100 in long equity positions and $85 in short equity positions and its liabilities are $140. What is its required capital?

     a. The first step in the calculation is to net the long and short positions in each security, then add all securities that are net long and all that are net short. Long and short positions are referred to throughout this section of the Chapter. Long means the investor holds the stock now. The risk is that the value of the stock will decline. Short means the investor must deliver stock at a set price on a future date but the investor does not own the stock at the time of the sale. The investor must buy the stock to deliver it. The risk is that the price of the stock will rise. For example, a short investor sells 100 IBM shares today at $100/share and promises to deliver them on April 1, when he will receive $100/share for them. He does not own those shares now. When he buys, if the price has fallen (e.g. to $75/share), he makes $25 a share. If it rises above $100, he loses. This is a short forward position. One could also sell short, for delivery at settlement (3 days later in the U.S.). If a firm holds IBM long (e.g. 200 shares) and short (e.g., 100), it nets the two for 100 net long. The numbers in the hypothetical report net long and net short positions in individual securities.

b. Work through the hypothetical to apply the general risk rule. It requires capital equal to 8% of the net position in the market. With these facts, the overall net position is the larger net position ($100) less the smaller net position ($85), or $15. Eight percent of $15 is $1.2 capital for general risk.

1. Why allow a net short position to offset a net long position?

2. Why require 8% capital?

3. Why is $15 the general or market risk?

4. Richard Breeden, when chairman of the SEC, said that during the 1987 market crash airline equities fell much more than railroad equities. Does this affect your view of the usefulness of the Basel rule for general risk?

c. How does the Basel Standard calculate the capital needed for specific risk for equity? Work through the hypothetical, assuming the portfolio is highly liquid and diversified (or marketable). The rule for specific risk is that the bank must hold capital equal to 8% of the overall gross position or only 4% if the portfolio is highly liquid and diversified. To get the overall gross position, one adds the net long position ($100) and the net short position ($85), giving $185. Four percent of $185 is $7.4.

1. Why add net long and net short positions?

2. Why distinguish between highly liquid and other positions?

3. What would account for the divergence in the specific risk ratios of the CAD (4% generally and 2% for highly liquid and diversified) and the Basel Standard (8% and 4%)?

d. The capital needed for the hypothetical portfolio is $1.2 for general risk plus $7.4 for specific risk, or $8.6 total. The following table summarizes the rules and the calculations. The bracketed material calculates specific risk for a portfolio that is not highly liquid and diversified.

Basel Rules for Position Risk

General Risk: 8% of Net Position in the Market	General Risk	Specific Risk
	Larger	Net
Specific Risk: 8% of	Net (100)	Longs
Overall Gross Position	- Smaller	+Net
or	Net (85)	Shorts
4% if Highly Liquid and	= $15	= $185 Gross
Diversified	X 8%	X 4% [x 8%]
	= $1.2 Cap	= $7.4 [=$14.8]
	Total Cap	= $8.6 [=$16.4]

2. THE COMPREHENSIVE APPROACH TO POSITION RISK: THE U.S.

The SEC sets net capital requirements for brokers and dealers. The main element of the SEC rule is its emphasis on customer protection over continuity of intermediaries. The SEC protects the liquidation value of the firm rather than its value as a going concern. It requires liquid capital and reduces its value for possible fluctuations in price through a haircut. The following summary is from an article written before changes in 1992, which are noted after it.

G. HABERMAN, CAPITAL REQUIREMENTS OF COMMERCIAL AND INVESTMENT BANKS: CONTRASTS IN REGULATION

Federal Reserve Bank of New York Quarterly Review, Autumn 1987, at 1-10.

Securities and Exchange Commission Uniform Net Capital Rule for Brokers and Dealers

The SEC first adopted a capital rule in 1944 to establish a standard of financial responsibility for registered brokers and dealers. The most recent comprehensive update of the rule was implemented in 1982. Firms that provide retail brokerage services and that underwrite or deal in corporate or municipal securities must abide by the rule.

The capital rule . . . seeks to ensure that liquid assets, adjusted for trading risk, exceed senior liabilities by a required margin of safety. A broker-dealer should be able to liquidate quickly and to satisfy the claims of its customers without recourse to formal bankruptcy proceedings. The test is a two-step procedure: first, a determination of the amount of net capital available to meet a firm's capital requirement, and second, a determination of the capital requirement (that is, the margin of safety). Net capital is total capital reduced by various charges and by haircuts that measure trading risk. A firm may choose either the basic or the alternative requirement. (See Figure 1.)

Figure 1
SEC Net Capital Computation

Total capital:	Equity Allowable subordinated debt Allowable credits
Less deductions:	(Illiquid assets) (Unsecured receivables) (Charges for aged credit exposure) (Market risk haircuts)
	Compared to
→Net capital requirement:	6⅔ percent aggregate indebtedness, or 2 percent aggregate debit items
Excess capital:	Net capital less the requirement

. . .

Total Capital

Total capital equals net worth plus subordinated liabilities and is augmented by allowable credits. It is determined by generally accepted accounting principles on a mark-to-market basis. To be counted as capital, subordinated debt must have a minimum term of one year and may not be prepayable without the prior written approval of the broker-dealer's examining authority (New York Stock Exchange or NASD). Subordinated debt may be in the form of either borrowed cash or borrowed securities, the latter serving as collateral for "secured demand notes." The rule also allows two forms of temporarily borrowed capital. Broker-dealers are permitted to obtain temporary subordinations not exceeding 45 days in maturity as often as three times a year to capitalize underwriting and extraordinary activities. A firm may also have a revolving subordinated loan agreement providing for prepayment within a year.

Broker-dealers are prohibited from distributing equity capital (for example, through dividends or unsecured loans to owners) if doing so would reduce the firm's net capital below warning levels. Supervisory authorities set warning levels somewhat higher than the minimum requirement; for example, one is 120 percent of the basic requirement.

Capital charges: Total capital is reduced by nonallowable assets and various special charges. An asset is considered nonallowable if it cannot be immediately or quickly converted into cash. This definition applies to fixed and intangible assets, investments and unsecured receivables from affiliates and subsidiaries, most other unsecured receivables, and nonmarketable securities.

. . .

Haircuts: The rule recognizes that the prices of marketable assets and liabilities may move adversely during liquidation, thereby reducing net capital available to cover a firm's obligations. The deduction for price risk in the firm's proprietary positions, haircuts, are percentages of the market value of security and forward positions held by the broker-dealer. As a measure of price risk, haircut factors vary in accordance with the type and remaining maturity of securities held or sold short.

For government and high-grade corporate debt, some forms of hedging serve to reduce haircuts. Moreover, within the several maturity subcategories into which government, high-grade corporate and municipal debt securities are grouped, short positions serve to offset long positions fully. Forward contracts receive the haircuts applicable to their underlying securities. Futures and options positions are also explicitly treated. The rule specifies additional haircut charges where the broker-dealer has an undue concentration in securities of a single issuer. For broker-dealers choosing the alternative method of calculating required capital, lower haircut percentages may be taken on certain securities positions, including undue concentration and underwriting commitments.

. . .

Capital requirement: Net capital must exceed a minimum absolute dollar level and one of two standards that relate to the size of a broker-dealer's business.

The basic method requires that net capital exceed 6 2/3 percent of aggregate indebtedness, which includes all liabilities less those specifically exempted. In essence, aggregate indebtedness is any liability not adequately collateralized, secured, or otherwise directly offset by an asset of the broker-dealer. It also includes contingent, off-balance sheet obligations.

. . .

The alternative method requires that net capital exceed two percent of aggregate debit items computed in accordance with the Reserve Formula under the Customer Protection Rule. These debit items are the gross debit balances of particular asset accounts and generally represent good quality customer receivables. The rule uses these debit items as a proxy for the size of customer-related business. For small broker-dealers whose business is heavily retail-oriented, these aggregate debit items can represent a majority of a firm's assets. However, for most large broker-dealers who are not heavily retail-oriented, these debit items usually constitute less than 25 percent of total assets.

————————

In 1992, the SEC amended the net capital rule (see 57 Federal Register 56986). Haircuts for equity would be a deduction of

> 15 percent of the market value of the greater of the long or short positions and to the extent the market value of the lesser of the long or short positions exceeds 25 percent of the market value of the greater of the long or short positions, the percentage deduction on such excess shall be 15 percent of the market value of such excess.

The haircut is a discount intended to offset market risk. The size of the haircut for equity, and those for debt instruments, originally reflected the discounts that banks at the time used when they loaned to broker-dealers against securities used as collateral. The shift in 1992 suggests that the SEC had begun to relate the size of the haircut to the historic volatility of each security type over one month, which was the target to wind down the broker-dealer. R. Dale, *The Capital Adequacy Regulation of US Broker-Dealers: A Comparative Analysis — Part I,* 3 Journal of Financial Regulation and Compliance 11 (1995).

The SEC considered narrowing the scope of the comprehensive approach in the late 1990s. In December 1997, the SEC proposed to adopt a standard similar to the BIS building block method to calculate capital for market risk on interest bearing instruments. The firm would be required to determine the general risk and specific risk of its portfolio. See SEC Proposed Net Capital Rule, 17 CFR Part 240 (Release No. 34-39455). This proposal did not become final, however. In October 1998, the SEC adopted "Broker-Dealer Lite," a rule allowing dealers to carry out over-the-counter derivatives operations in subsidiaries that would be subject to minimal capital rules. See Schulte Roth & Zabel LLP, Bank Regulatory Report, v. 7, no. 6, Oct. 1998, at 1. The rules for equity positions, however, remained unchanged.

Many countries other than the U.S. used the comprehensive approach, although the parameters vary greatly. The countries included Japan (10% haircut for liquid stocks), Australia (15%), Hong Kong (40%) and, before CAD, France and Italy (20%). Holland required a 30% haircut if stocks were illiquid. Some countries allow no offset of long and short positions. See E. Dimson and P. Marsh, The Debate on International Capital Requirements (The City Research Project, London Business School, 1994) (Dimson and Marsh).

Notes and Questions

1.   To see how the U.S. sets capital standards for equity held by security companies, use the same hypothetical from the previous section: a company's assets consist of $100 in long equity positions and $85 in short equity positions and its liabilities are $140. What is its total capital, applying the comprehensive approach? Its net capital? In working through the hypothetical, use 6 ⅔% of aggregate debt to determine required net capital. The hypothetical does not include customer receivables.

   a.   The first step in the SEC's calculation is to determine net worth. Net the long and short positions in each security, then add all securities that are net long and all that are net short (already done in the hypothetical). The net worth of the company is its assets ($100 net longs plus $85 net shorts) minus its liabilities ($140), or $45.

   b.   Next, the haircut is given. The haircut is 15% of the larger position ($100 net longs) or $15 and 15% of the smaller position reduced by one-quarter of the larger position ($85 less $100/4 or $25), or $9. The total haircut is $15 plus $9, or $24, and is subtracted from the $45 total capital, or net worth, giving $21 in net capital.

   c.   Minimum capital is 6⅔% of liabilities ($140), or $9. The company's net capital ($21) minus minimum capital ($9) gives excess capital ($12).

   d.   The following table presents the calculation:

U.S. Security Company

1.	Total Capital		$45
2.	less Haircut:		-24
	Larger (longs): 100 * 15%	= $15	
	Smaller (shorts): [85 - (100/4)] * 15%	= $ 9	
3.	= Net Capital		$21
4.	Minimum cap. = 6⅔% of Liabilities ($140)	=	9
5.	Excess capital	=	$12

2.   In the abstract, what is the purpose of this rule? Who is being protected? How much protection is being sought?

   a.   What is the haircut and the idea behind it? Why reduce net worth by about 15% of market positions? What is the logic of the haircut on the long positions?

   b.   How does this approach compare to the Building Block approach? Why not distinguish between general and specific risk?

   c.   What is the logic of the haircut on the smaller (short) positions? Why not subject short positions (generally the smaller net position) to capital requirements as stringent as those for long positions? The SEC excludes them from any capital requirements if they are below 25% of the long positions. It subjects them to capital requirements as they increase relative to long positions. What are the strengths and weaknesses of this rule?

3. Do either the building block approach or the comprehensive approach make sense? The following sections present alternatives.

3. A COMPARISON OF THE BUILDING BLOCK AND COMPREHENSIVE APPROACHES TO THE PORTFOLIO APPROACH

A third way to regulate capital adequacy for position risk is the portfolio approach. It lowers capital requirements as a portfolio of securities becomes increasingly balanced in long and short positions and increasingly diversified. The approach was applied by the U.K. Securities and Futures Authority before the UK applied the Building Block Approach. Rather than give the equations that embody the rules, we summarize the major elements as described in Dimson and Marsh. As you read, compare the portfolio approach to the comprehensive approach and the building block method.

In the U.K., capital requirements for a portfolio were calculated by netting long and short positions in the same stock, which hedges market risk, and by determining the extent to which the portfolio is diversified. The portfolio theory on which this approach is based has been frequently tested and refined since the early 1950s. A key element is that the risk or variance of an equity portfolio is a function of each security's share in the portfolio and the relationship between returns on each security in the portfolio, called the residual risk. This means that in addition to the risk of the individual security (its beta or, in the language of Basel and CAD, its specific risk) and of the market (general risk in Basel and CAD), there is the residual risk of the portfolio itself. The relationship is complicated to estimate when many securities are in the portfolio. Since there can be millions of parameters for a portfolio of 2000 stocks, it is costly for firms to apply the academic theory in full. So UK regulators simplified assumptions about the relation of each security's returns to all others and about the specific risk of each security, reducing the parameters drastically.

UK regulators required sufficient capital to absorb losses during the period in which a portfolio would be at risk as the investor trades out of a position. They set the position risk ratio (PRR), which determines the capital required for the position, so that the probability of insufficient capital is low over that period. For very liquid stocks, the regulators assumed it will take 1 week to trade out and required a confidence interval of 95 percent. This means the capital prescribed by the PRR should be adequate to absorb all but 5% of the variance in price that is likely -- based on past performance -- over the week. The period for less liquid securities was 2 weeks and for the least liquid was 3 weeks.

For the most liquid portfolio of UK equities, capital was a function of two items. One was the variance of market returns over a 1 week period. This affected the risk of the position (during the trade out) and therefore the capital that was required. Using historical performance, the regulators set the variance of market returns as the equivalent for one week of 18.7% per annum. The second was the variance of average residual returns (i.e., the residual risk) adjusted for diversification. The more diversified the portfolio, the lower the allowance for residual risk; a very diversified portfolio would effectively eliminate residual risk. Capital would then be a function of the market returns alone. Regulators set the variance for average residual returns as the equivalent for one week of 21.5% per annum. Note that the UK regulators did not use a historical estimate of betas, which they assumed were 1, the same for each security. The resulting capital was a percentage that was applied to the net trading book.

UK regulators adjusted for different national equity markets and allowed for diversification by country for portfolios of designated U.K., U.S., and Japanese securities.

How would each approach -- comprehensive, building block, and portfolio -- apply to actual portfolios of stock? Would one be more effective than the others? Dimson and Marsh tested each approach on 58 UK equity portfolios held at various times between December 1986 and September 1988 and managed by 16 securities firms making markets in the UK. The portfolios varied widely by value, number of shares, long and short positions, industry, liquidity, size of issuer, and concentration.

To learn how well each approach set capital requirements that would absorb "unanticipated changes in the value of the trading books," Dimson and Marsh compared each PRR with the volatility of the return on each book over the past 5 years. The following charts show the results. The vertical axis shows volatility, in terms of the monthly standard deviations of returns on each trading book as a share of the book's gross value. The horizontal axis (PRR) shows the required capital as a share of the book's gross value. The results for each of the 58 trading books are reported. See Dimson and Marsh, *supra*, at 29.

1. US Comprehensive Approach (Panel A): The capital required by this approach ranges between 12% and 14% of the gross value of the book (see the horizontal axis), regardless of the historical volatility of the portfolio.

2. Basel 4+8 Building Block Approach (Panel B): This approach requires capital ranging from 4% to 12% of the book's value. Generally the less volatile the book the less the required capital, though the distribution is not tight.

3. UK Simplified Portfolio Approach (Panel C): The capital required by this approach ranges from just below 2% for positions with low variability to about 7% for the position with the highest variability.

The distribution is tighter than the Basel approach, indicating a closer relation between historical volatility and required capital. This approach requires less capital than Basel.

Figure 1: Volatility vs PRR for 58 Books Under Alternative Approaches

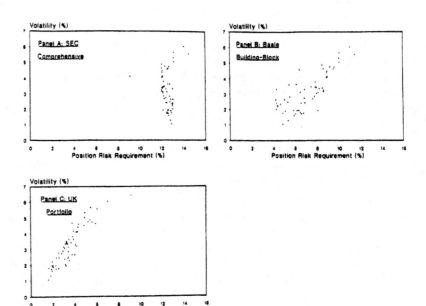

The Portfolio Approach emerges, in the view of the authors, as the most appropriate for position risk. The Comprehensive Approach requires a lot of capital and takes no account of the volatility of the positions. The Building Block Approach adjusts for volatility, but requires more capital than the Portfolio Approach. But how does one know if the higher or lower rate for capital works better for position risk? The authors tested this in various ways and concluded that the portfolio approach most closely approximated the past volatility of the stock.

In 1996, Dimson and Marsh published a similar study that tested a broader set of regulatory approaches in periods of financial stress, such as the 1987 collapse. Their new findings confirmed the original study, showing that the comprehensive approach required the highest amount of capital as a share of the gross value of a trading book in periods of downward stress on equity markets. The building block approach acquired the second highest capital levels. A simple portfolio approach and another approach based on estimations from historical risk vied for the lowest rates, depending on the confidence level. See E. Dimson and P. Marsh, *Stress Tests of Capital Requirements*, October 1996.

Notes and Questions

1. In the abstract, which approach seems most appropriate to determine capital adequacy for equity positions? What are your assumptions about the purpose of capital adequacy rules?

2. The key difference between the comprehensive approach of the SEC, the Building Block approach, and the portfolio approach of the UK is the treatment of liquid, diversified portfolios. The SEC only takes diversification into account when increasing the haircut for very concentrated security portfolios. The Building Block approach simply defines a portfolio as liquid and diversified or not and prescribes two different levels of capital for specific risk. The UK had three categories of liquidity and a sliding scale for diversification. Did the UK solve the problems of oversimplification in the Building Block approach? Should the Building Block approach be changed to be more sensitive to liquidity and diversification? If so, should it follow the UK approach?

3. The portfolio approach used by the UK prescribed that capital should be adequate to absorb 95% of the variance in price that was likely -- based on past performance -- over the week in which the portfolio was being wound down. That is, the UK explicitly recognized that the capital would not be adequate in 5% of the cases. Neither the Building Block Approach nor the Comprehensive Approach does this. Should they do so? Is there such a thing as too much required capital? If so, what is the basis for deciding how much is too much? Some critics of the PRR set by the UK portfolio approach say it is set imprudently low. According to the GAO (op. cit., chapter 2):

> An SEC analysis of a hypothetical portfolio of unrelated buy and sell positions of highly liquid securities suggests that a 2-percent standard is too low because, in contrast to the U.S. standard, it would not have preserved enough capital to cover price moves during the 1987 and 1989 markets breaks. UK Securities and Investment Board officials [said] that an actual test of portfolios of equities indicated that 2 percent accurately covers the risks in diversified portfolios. SEC officials [said] that no agreement exists on the best model of portfolio diversification.

Dimson and Marsh say that "prudence," at least as used by the critics, is subjective and costly. They estimate that, compared to the portfolio approach, the costs to the system of the building block approach are double and those of the comprehensive approach six times higher. Who would bear these costs? Which of the perspectives do you find more compelling? Why?

4. Suppose Dimson and Marsh had used the parameters set by CAD for the liquid diversified portfolio. How would this have affected the scatter graph for the building block approach? Why did they not use it?

5. What do these tests tell you about the apparent purpose of each approach? Are the regulators motivated by the same concerns? Are they regulating to address the same risks or the same levels of risk?

4. INTERNAL MODELS-BASED REGULATION OF CAPITAL

The inadequacies of the standardized methods led regulators to try a very different approach, one relying on the financial institution's own system of risk analysis to set the appropriate level of capital. Regulators acknowledged that the inadequacies of the Comprehensive and Building Block approaches included:

- treating each part of the portfolio separately rather than examining the overall risk given the correlation between the various instruments.

- not recognizing that some markets can be more or less volatile than each other. The Japanese stock market had been more volatile than the U.K. market recently. Critics said that regulators should not require financial firms to equate the risk of price changes in the two markets.

- requiring much more capital for the same trading book than a portfolio approach, which is costly for banks and creates a disincentive for them to create their own sophisticated internal systems to measure risk.

The U.K. portfolio approach oversimplified in order to standardize the analysis.

The Basel Committee let sophisticated well-run banks use their own models if the models met minimum standards set by Basel and were subject to regular tests. The goal was to "preserve the integrity and flexibility of banks' internal models against the need to ensure a minimum level of prudence, transparency, and consistency of the capital requirement across banks." See Basel Standard, *supra*, at 4. The amendments to the Basel Accord would take effect at the end of 1997.

a. TYPES OF INTERNAL MODELS USED BY BANKS

Many banks already estimated their trading book's value at risk (VAR). VAR is the amount in the potential one-day profit and loss distribution above which any greater loss due to general market movements over a given holding period has only a 1 percent (or at most 5 percent) probability of occurring. P. Kupiec, Techniques for Verifying the Accuracy of Risk Measurement Models 2 (Federal Reserve Board Finance and Economics Discussion Series No. 95-24, 1995) (Kupiec, May 1995).

Banks used two kinds of internal tests: covariance and historical simulation,

(i) Covariance analysis uses summary statistics, calculated from historic data on price volatilities and correlations within and between markets, to estimate likely potential losses.   Price changes are assumed to be normally distributed....   The confidence level is calculated by reference to the standard deviation of past percentage price changes multiplied by a scaling factor."   For example, a bank could estimate at a 99% confidence level the likely volatility of the index for each equity market represented in its portfolio and the correlations between them.   P. Johnson, *Risk Measurement and Capital Requirements for Banks*, 35 Bank of England Quarterly Bulletin 180 (1995) (Johnson).   A problem is that in practice distributions have fatter tails, meaning that price movements are more extreme than in the normal distribution.   This prompts the use of the second internal test.

(ii) Historical simulation draws from the bank's trading book over the past one or two years the essential elements (since not all securities existed) "to calculate the changes in the value of the book that would have been experienced had it been held throughout the period."   The bank calculates "the 99% confidence interval *without* assuming that the price changes are normally distributed by computing the loss which was not exceeded on 99% of occasions."   See Johnson.

Covariance calculates the confidence level of 95% or 99% using a not entirely realistic assumption that price changes are normally distributed. Historical simulation observes the confidence level, but using simulated data.

A few banks applied these tests to their entire trading portfolio, but the majority tested their book in components (e.g., equities, government bonds, foreign exchange) without integrating the entire book.   The Basel Committee wanted banks to integrate their tests, but set no timetable.

b.   THE BASEL COMMITTEE'S RULES FOR INTERNAL MODELS

The Basel Committee set minimum standards for the use of internal models.   First, supervisors would determine the bank's qualifications. Unqualified banks would be subject to the building block method.   To qualify, the bank needed:

- an active independent risk control unit;
- actively involved directors and senior managers;
- a model closely integrated in daily risk management;
- regular stress tests for exceptional plausible conditions;
- thorough compliance procedures; and

- regular internal review by the bank's internal audit unit.

Second, the model had to include prescribed parameters. The following are required for equity positions (those for other positions are similar):

1. compute value at risk daily;

2. use risk factors corresponding at least to each equity market in which the bank has a significant position, and even better to market sectors (such as by industry), and ideally also to individual stocks in which the bank's positions are concentrated;

3. use a 99th percentile confidence interval;

4. use a one year historical observation period;

5. calculate value at risk assuming a minimum instantaneous price shock equivalent to a 10 trading-day move in prices (called the holding period);

6. recognize empirical correlations within and across broad risk categories (but the supervisor must be satisfied with the system and it must be adjusted if market prices change materially);

7. set the capital charge as the higher of (i) the previous day's value-at-risk or (ii) three times the average of the daily value-at-risk of the preceding sixty business days. The multiplication factor of three is applied because, said the Basel Committee, models for one day do not capture the impact of cumulative charges over an extended period of time. Modeling oversimplifies, volatilities and correlations change abruptly, VAR estimates use end-of-day positions and miss intra-day trading risk, and models miss exceptional circumstances. So Basel multiplies the VAR by three (or more) to adjust for these shortcomings.

Third, the model had to be back-tested regularly and subject to a "plus factor" if the test reveals weaknesses. Back-testing compares the model's risk measure (looking forward in time) with the actual daily changes in portfolio value (after they occur). The bank counts the number of times the model's risk measures exceeded actual trading outcomes: did the 99th percentile actually cover 99% of the trading results? The Basel Committee requires the bank to calculate the number of times trading outcomes were not covered by the risk measures -- the "exceptions" -- over the twelve months before the trading day. Banks must test and account for exceptions quarterly. Since many different models with different parameters are used, regulators want to know if the bank's model accurately predicts losses.

The basic problem with back-testing is that no agreed method exists and when a model fails in a test, there is no way to know if the model or the test was faulty. The portfolio used by the model to predict likely loss over the next day is never the actual portfolio throughout the day.

Trading during the day changes the portfolio and commissions earned change the income on the actual portfolio from that in the model's portfolio.

The Basel Committee tried to solve this problem by probability analysis. It estimated the probability that the prediction of an accurate model would be wrongly classified as an exception and that the prediction of an inaccurate model would not appear as an exception. Based on these estimates it decided that when back-testing of 250 trading days (12 months) revealed:

- 10 or more exceptions (the red zone), the supervisor would assume the bank's model had a problem, investigate the problem, and raise the "plus factor" by one (e.g., from 3 to 4).

- 5-9 exceptions (the yellow zone), the bank would have to prove to the supervisor that the model is sound (e.g., low probability events occurred) and the supervisor might raise the plus factor by a fraction of one).

- 4 or fewer exceptions (the green zone) would require no action by the supervisor.

The "plus factor" meant that instead of multiplying the VAR by 3, the bank would have to multiply it by 3 plus some additional amount. A plus factor of 1 makes the multiple 4.

Fourth, banks still had to estimate specific risk. A bank with a model that takes "little or no account of specific risk," which the Basel Committee says is common today, must continue to use the standardized building block approach to specific risk. Banks with models that did account for specific risk were initially subject to a floor for specific risk: the charge had to be at least 50% of the standardized approach because no industry consensus had emerged. In 1997, the Committee removed this requirement. A bank that could demonstrate through backtesting that its specific risk model was effective could rely on that model. However, a bank that could not demonstrate effectiveness would have to multiply the specific risk calculation of its model by a factor of 4.

c. CRITICS OF THE BASEL APPROACH

Critics of the Basel Committee's approach emphasize its short-term perspective and related costs. P. Kupiec and J. O'Brien, *The Use of Bank Trading Risk Models for Regulatory Capital Purposes* (Federal Reserve Board Finance and Economics Discussion Series No. 95-11, 1995). According to Kupiec and O'Brien, at i,

Bank internal models are not capable of measuring risk exposures over the relatively lengthy time interval of regulatory interest. Long-horizon risk exposure estimates are compromised by statistical complications surrounding time aggregation of trading portfolio returns and because operational risk measurement models do not adequately capture large options risks, nor do these risk estimates recognize the endogeneity of a bank's risk exposures. ... Verification problems plague an internal models approach. When capital requirements are based on estimates of low probability potential loss events, there is no reliable procedure ... to validate a bank's reported risk estimate. These results suggest that an internal models approach for setting market risk capital requirements may be less than ideal if the accuracy of risk exposure estimates and the potential for independent verification are valued aspects of the regulatory capital system.

As a result, the Basel Committee is forced to rely on a heavy handed multiplier of 3 to 4 times the VAR.

The Basel Committee's members respond that "conditioning supervisory standards on a clear framework, though limited and imperfect, is ... preferable to a purely judgmental standard or one with no incentive features whatsoever." Basel Committee on Banking Supervision, Supervisory Framework for the Use of "Back-testing" in Conjunction with the Internal Models Approach to Market Risk Capital Requirements 5 (1996). In December 1996, the Committee explicitly decided not to drop or change the multiplier. In 1997, researchers from several member central banks reported on their efforts to collect and analyze data on aggregate market risk, which was important because in many conditions of stress market players would be affected by each other. The researchers acknowledged that they lacked the methodology to measure aggregate market risk. They noted that Value at Risk analysis could not indicate whether an exposure would generate a profit or loss and proposed other approaches. See Bank for International Settlements, *The Measurement of Aggregate Market Risk* (Basel 1997).

d. IMPLEMENTATION OF THE MARKET RISK RULES

To implement the Basel Internal Models Approach in the European Union, the EC proposed CAD II. Bickering between Germany and the U.K. delayed political agreement until late December 1997. The resulting proposal, once released, was to be implemented generally within 24 months but permitted a long transition period, to 2006, for commodities traders. It was also less strict in its rules for calculating capital needed for equity positions and in the uses of Tier 3 capital. Clifford Chance, *CAD II Moves Forward,* European Financial Markets Newsletter, December 1997/January 1998.

In August 1996, U.S. bank regulators amended their capital standards with measures for market risk based largely on the approach recommended by the Basel Committee. The new rules applied to "any bank or bank holding company ... regulated by the Board, the OCC, or the FDIC, with significant exposure to market risk...," meaning that the sum of trading assets and liabilities was at least 10% of its assets or $1 billion. By late December 1997, this was about 20 banks. See B. McConnell,

Capital Rule Eased for Banks Reserving Against Trading Loss, American Banker, December 26, 1997. The "covered positions" (i.e., covered by the rule) include those in the trading account and also foreign exchange and commodity positions whether or not in the trading account. Capital must support exposure to market fluctuations of interest rates, equity prices, foreign exchange rates, and commodity prices, and to specific risk of debt and equity positions.

Every day, a bank would calculate its market risk, using an internal model acceptable to the regulators. Key parameters are a 99% (one-tailed) confidence level to estimate maximum loss and a 10 day movement in rate and prices to estimate price shock, a one-year historical observation period, and an updating of the model at least every 3 months. Cross-correlations among risk categories, calculated from historical data, may be used. Every quarter, the bank must backtest, comparing daily VAR measures for one-day price movements against its actual daily net trading profit or loss for each of the past 250 business days. If backtesting revealed over five days in which VAR fell short of losses, the multiplication factor would rise above three to a total of four in the case of ten days.

The specific risk of a bank's debt and equity positions (in its trading account) may be calculated as part of the bank's internal model or using the standardized approach described by the Basel Committee. Equity, for example, carries a charge of 8% of gross positions in each national market or 4% if the portfolio is liquid and well-diversified. A bank may use an internal model approved by its regulator. The U.S. initially followed the BIS rule that if the model generated a capital charge below 50% of the standardized approach, the charge must be raised to the 50%. Shortly after the BIS changed this rule in 1997, the U.S. adopted the change. The model may correlate the specific risk of debt and equity positions or calculate them separately.

The regulators decided that the rule would "not include the proposed standardized approach for measuring general market risk." They explained that an institution with significant exposure to market risk "can most accurately measure that risk using detailed information" it has about its own portfolio. They promised to continue to examine the techniques being used and modify these rules as the technology changed.

The market risk rules prompted the regulators to modify the credit risk rules. Covered positions were "no longer subject to a credit risk capital charge." See Federal Reserve Press Release, August 29, 1996.

Bankers Trust became the first bank to apply the BIS rules through its own model in May 1997. See G. Graham, *Bankers Trust Adopts Own Risk Model,* Financial Times, May 2, 1997. The U.S. bank Morgan Guaranty had released its internal model for quantifying market risk long before that, in October 1994. Morgan quantified market risk for portfolios of 400 securities in 22 industrialized countries, applying both market data of correlation and volatility and a methodology to estimate value-at-risk.

The bank offers these data daily through its World Web site. See M. Phelan, Probability and Statistics Applied to the Practice of Financial Risk Management: The Case of JP Morgan's RiskMetrics(TM) 2 (The Wharton Financial Institutions Center Working Paper No. 95-19, 1995). However, both the BT and Morgan models failed to predict actual losses on 5 days during the third quarter of 1998 due to extreme volatility associated with the collapse of the Long-Term Capital Management hedge fund. L. Moyer, *Morgan, Bankers Trust Say Risk Models Broke Down*, American Banker, Nov. 19, 1998.

The technical complexity of VAR raises the question of how well many banks will apply it, suggesting a new danger, model implementation risk. An intriguing study gave leading vendors of risk management systems the same portfolio and the same model, RiskMetrics(TM), then analyzed the VAR results. The portfolio consisted of bonds, notes, interest rate swaps, forwards, caps and floors, and FX spot, forwards, and options. The authors found and tried to explain variance in the results among different vendors. The least variance was for the simplest of instruments, FX forwards and, for some elements of risk, government bonds. Large variance occurred in the analysis of risk for interest rate swaps, FX options, and interest rate caps and floors. No two implementations produced precisely similar VAR for the same instrument. The authors found that users of the system exercise discretion over important variables even though the software would seem to determine the outcome. They concluded that it would be naive and possibly dangerous to treat the systems as "deterministic black boxes." C. Marshall and M. Siegel, *Value at Risk: Implementing a Risk Measurement Standard*, July 1996. An econometric analysis found circumstances in which risk-averse banks could actually increase the variability of their portfolios by switching to VaR for regulatory capital, a perverse effect. G. Alexander and A. Baptiste, *A VaR Constrained Mean-Variance Model: Implications for Portfolio Selection and the Basle Capital Accord*, July 6, 2001.

Banks do supplement their risk analysis with stress testing, as required by Basel. A study of 43 major commercial and investment banks in ten of the G-10 countries revealed that all used stress tests to uncover market risk missed by statistical analysis, which is most likely when historical data about prices are inadequate. However, while 100% used stress tests to communicate the firm's risk profile to senior managers, only 19% used them to allocate capital. Only 25% of the banks used the tests for the interaction of market risk and credit risk, such as counterparty default risk. The tests vary widely. I. Fender, M. Gibson, and P. Mosser, *An International Survey of Stress Tests*, in Federal Reserve Bank of New York Current Issues in Economics and Finance, November 2001.

Note on the Precommitment Approach

An alternative to the Basel Internal Models Approach, or at least a prescription for supervisor action when internal models prove to be inadequate, is found in P. Kupiec and J. O'Brien, *A Pre-Commitment Approach to Capital Requirements for Market Risk* (Federal Reserve Board Finance and Economics Discussion Series No. 95-36, 1996). The authors argue that a bank should commit in advance to a "maximum loss exposure" over a set future period and allocate capital to meet that exposure. The regulator's level of risk coverage prescribes appropriate levels and applies penalties, such as fines, if the actual losses exceed the commitment. Advocates maintain that the precommitment approach solves the problems of back-testing by circumventing it and gives banks great flexibility. A. Daripa and S. Varoto, Value at Risk and Precommitment: Approaches to Market Risk Regulation, in Federal Reserve Bank of New York Economic Policy Review, v. 4, no. 3, Oct. 1998, at 137.

The Fed began testing the precommitment approach in 1996. In 1997, the New York Clearing House Association reported that 10 banks had tested the method over the period of one quarter and found that each set aside enough capital using it. This led them to conclude that the precommitment approach is a viable alternative to internal models. See J. Seiberg, *Pre-commitment System for Market-Risk Capital Said to Succeed in Test,* American Banker, March 3, 1997, and J. Considine, *Pilot Exercise--Pre-Commitment Approach to Market Risk*, in Federal Reserve Bank of New York Economic Policy Review, v. 4, no. 3, Oct. 1998, at 131.

Fixing the penalty was identified as the main remaining issue. Banks argued that requiring disclosure that the model failed was a sufficient penalty. Regulators were concerned that a "one-size-fits-all" penalty would not be adequate, compelling them to tailor penalties to each bank. This would be exceedingly difficult for them as outsiders, since they would need to know "the bank's cost of capital and . . . its individual investment opportunities." P. Parkinson, *Commentary*, in Federal Reserve Bank of New York Economic Policy Review, v. 4, no. 3, Oct. 1998, at 155 ("Parkinson").

A critic of the precommitment approach, a member of the Managing Board of Germany's central bank, argued that supervisors cannot and should not rely on banks to assess their risks themselves. The banks' experience in the Asian currency crisis was one example of their serious limits. Regulation should be preventive and apply consistent sanctions. The precommitment approach, however, applies after the bank has shown it failed to maintain adequate capital. Fining a bankrupt bank is too late. K. Engelen, *The Basel Capital Accord*, The International Economy (March/April 1998) at 33.

Perhaps a marriage of the internal models and precommitment approaches would combine their virtues and eliminate their deficiencies.

One suggestion was that the precommitment penalty should be to require the bank to use the internal models approach. Another was to use a multiple of VAR as a floor for the precommitment. See Parkinson.

Notes and Questions

1. The premise of the Basel Internal Models Approach is that individual banks are much more capable and motivated than regulators to manage the risk of their trading books. Does this premise make sense? Why use internal models?

   a. Does this approach resolve the problems Dimson and Marsh found in the Comprehensive and Building Block methods?

   b. Does the Basel approach provide sufficient regulatory safeguards to protect against the uncertainties of internal models? For example, the multiplication factor of three for the capital charge, and the "plus factor" if back testing reveals problems with the model, are designed to address the short-term perspective of the models. Do they accomplish their goal efficiently?

2. The Basel Internal Models Approach introduces new problems, such as the ineffectiveness of back-testing and the inability of banks to integrate their entire trading book. Do these outweigh its benefits?

3. The Long Term Capital Management hedge fund collapsed in August 1998 partly because the long historical parallel movement of rates on public and private bonds ended. LTCM's sophisticated models did not recognize this change and LTCM bet, incorrectly, that the rates would converge. Many commentators note that the big problems for investors follow basic discontinuities in historical relationships. Does this problem mean regulators should not rely on internal models?

4. Do you agree with the response to their critics by the Basel Committee that the imperfect framework of the Basel Internal Models Approach is better than the existing approaches used by regulators?

5. Why not simply use the precommitment approach instead of the imperfect framework of the Basel Internal Models Approach? Why not simply let the markets regulate the position takers?

6. In the U.S., merchant banking was one of the new activities that the Gramm-Leach-Bliley Act opened up to banks, through financial holding companies. Venture capital, previously permitted by exceptions, was one activity that the Fed believed would augment banks' risks. The Fed proposed in March 2000 to require FHCs to hold capital equal to 50% of their venture capital equity investments. The OCC disputed the need for this special rule. In its view venture capital need not create excess risk if well managed. J. Sapsford, *Fed to Make Banks Boost Capital To Cover Venture-Investing Risks*, Wall Street Journal, Mar. 14, 2000; G. Silverman, *Fed Rule on Banks' Capital Under Fire,* Financial Times, Apr. 10, 2000.

C.   OTHER RISKS AND CAPITAL FOR NON-CREDIT RISKS

1.   OTHER SECURITIES RISKS ADDRESSED BY CAPITAL ADEQUACY RULES

Capital standards exist or are being proposed for risks, other than position risk, in the securities business. The CAD set capital adequacy rules for several other kinds of risk in the firms' trading book, including settlement and counter-party risk (Annex II), foreign exchange risk (Annex III), the risk of a material change in business (Annex IV), and large exposures (Annex VI). Some of these capital requirements are cumulative and supplement capital required for other purposes, such as non-trading business.

For foreign exchange risk, the CAD "requires that once the firm's overall net foreign exchange position exceeds 2% of its own funds, capital must be provided to cover the excess." The Regulation of Market Risk 36 (Price Waterhouse 1994). The capital standard, 8% of the excess, applies to almost all of a firm's exposure, including its trading book. The Basel Standard offers "a measure for the net open position in each currency and two methods for estimating foreign exchange risk in a portfolio of positions." See International Monetary Fund, International Capital Markets Part II: Systemic Issues in International Finance 36 (1993) (IMF).

Settlement risks also attract capital standards. We discuss payments and clearance and settlement later in this book. The CAD sets capital standards for settlement risk. The Basel Standard includes capital adequacy standards for bilateral netting if the arrangements can be enforced when a default occurs.

Capital standards are also set by the CAD for underwriting and large positions. Underwriters may very briefly hold many of a firm's shares as a normal part of business; the CAD increases the capital charges against the underwriter's net position in a security as the number of working days the position is held grows. The CAD also sets special capital requirements when the financial institution holds securities issued by one customer that are 25% or more of the institution's own funds. The capital charge rises as the amount rises above 25% and as the number of days in excess grows.

International regulators are also concerned about interest rate risk, which is "the risk that changes in market interest rates might adversely affect an institution's financial condition," according to the Glossary of the Basel Standard. They proposed "a measure of the sensitivity of banks' on- and off-balance-sheet positions to fluctuations in interest rates. Although this risk measure would not attract a capital charge, it was designed to alert regulators of possible excessive exposures to interest rate risk." See IMF, *supra*, at 36. U.S. bank regulators proposed a similar measure that would carry capital costs. In 1996, however, the Basel Committee decided not to pursue a common approach to interest rate risk. U.S. regulators, as a substitute, issued guidelines to help banks manage the risk.

Note on Capital for Operational Risk

According to the U.S. Joint Paper, at 6, one of the most significant changes in the new Basel Accord was the proposal for an operational risk charge.

> It is expected to represent, on average, 20% of the minimum regulatory capital charge. The framework is based upon the following operational risk definition: "the risk of direct or indirect loss resulting from inadequate or failed internal processes, people and systems or from external events." Although the focus of operational risk is on the Pillar 1 capital charge, it also brings in elements of Pillar 2 (strong control environment) and Pillar 3 (disclosure).

> The Committee is proposing a spectrum of approaches, which represent a continuum of increasing sophistication and risk sensitivity. The Basic Indicator Approach is the simplest of the three approaches to determine an operational risk charge. It allocates operational risk capital using a single indicator as a proxy for an institution's overall operational risk exposure. The current proposal would require banks to hold capital equal to a fixed percentage of its gross income. The Committee expects only the least sophisticated institutions to use this method.

> To the extent that banks can demonstrate to supervisors an increased sophistication and precision in their measurement, management and control of operational risk, they would move along the spectrum to a more advanced approach, the Standardized Approach. Under this approach, supervisors establish standardized business lines (e.g., asset management), standardized broad indicators (e.g., total funds under management), and standardized loss factors (the beta) per business line. Within each business line, the capital charge will be calculated by multiplying the bank's relevant broad indicator measurement by the relevant beta factor. The total capital charge for operational risk would be the sum of the business line charges.

> The most complex approach presented by the Committee as a current option is the Internal Measurement Approach. This approach, unlike the first two approaches, allows banks more direct input into calculating the operational risk capital charge. For standardized business lines banks would provide the following: an exposure indicator (EI), which is a proxy for the size or amount of risk of each business line; a parameter representing the probability of a loss event (PE); and a parameter representing the loss given that event (LGE). The product of EI*PE*LGE produces an expected loss (EL) for each business line/risk type

combination. Regulators provide a standardized factor (gamma) per business line that translates the EL into a capital charge.

There are still a number of open issues related to operational risk and much work is needed to finalize the proposals, particularly the Internal Measurement Approach. The Committee has recognized this and is encouraging greater industry input in the development of an operational risk capital charge. In particular, there is currently only limited data to support the various operational risk charges. Additionally, more work is needed on defining loss types and loss events, risk categories, and business types. As part of this, the Committee will also have to look closely at the betas associated with the Standardized Approach to ensure that they appropriately reflect the risk associated with the individual business lines.

When banks objected to the high cost of capital for operational risk, the Committee reduced the anticipated share from 20% of all capital to 12%. D. Hendricks, Revising the Basel Accord, Talk given at Harvard Law School, October 22, 2001.

The Committee proceeded with papers specifying ten principles that should govern banks' policies toward operational risk and studying the banks' actual practice mitigating operational risk. The principles concerned the role of the board of directors, senior management, and information flows within the bank to develop an appropriate risk management environment. They concerned risk management itself: identifying, measuring, monitoring, and controlling operational risk. They broadly described the role of supervisors and, through disclosure, the market. Basel Committee, *Sound Practices for the Management and Supervision of Operational Risk*, December 2001.

The study of bank practice identified seven types of operational risk: internal fraud, external fraud, employment practices and workplace safety, damage to physical assets, business disruption and system failures, plus execution, delivery, and process management, and finally clients, products and business services. It asked 30 banks in 11 countries to report their experience with operational risk, from 1998-2000, in eight banking activities: corporate finance, trading and sales, retail banking, commercial banking, payment and settlement, agency and custody services, asset management, and retail brokerage. Acknowledging that the data are sketchy enough to be narrowly interpreted, the Committee reported the value of losses in each category. Execution, delivery, and process management was the single largest operational risk, accounting for 35% of all losses. Clients, products, and business services were second, with 28%, while fraud accounted for 31%, of which 11% was internal and 20% external. Among the eight service lines, retail banking reported 39% of all losses, commercial banking 23%, and trading and sales 19%. It was too soon, however, to draw conclusions about capital adequacy for operational risk. Basel Committee, *The Quantitative Impact Study for Operational Risk: Overview of Individual Loss Data and Lessons Learned*, Table 4, January 2002. The study did not identify legal risk separately.

Legal risk is a form of operational risk. A preliminary paper about legal risk, prepared as part of a study of capital adequacy regulation by the Program on International Financial Systems at Harvard Law School, found the concept hard to define but concluded that legal risk refers to losses that depend on how the law allocates risk between financial institutions and other transactors or the government. A review of a sample of court cases concluded that data from court sources are hard to define. It concluded that insurance for legal risk is dependable for "non-major repetitive claims," but not for major losses such as the World Trade Center. In short, legal risk is difficult to define, insure against, or securitize. Under these circumstances, setting capital to guard against legal risk is largely a matter of guesswork. This conclusion could probably be extended to much of operational risk. H. Scott, Legal Risk: *The Operational Risk Problem in Microcosm*, draft paper delivered at the Federal Reserve Bank of Boston, Nov. 16, 2001.

Basel may misdefine operational risk. One can think of operational risk as all risk remaining after one removes financial risk (e.g., credit risk, position risk, and foreign exchange risk), in one view. This non-financial risk has two components. One is business risk, that for some reason a firm's revenues will fall short of costs. Basel ignores this risk, which is very important for most firms. The other is non-business or event risk, that something unanticipated will happen to cripple the firm (e.g., loss of a major law suit). Event risk is Basel's operational risk. The problem is that these events are so hard to predict that capital may not be the right form of protection. A. Kuritzkes, *Operational Risk*, draft paper delivered at Harvard Law School, December 10, 2001.

2. THE DEFINITION OF CAPITAL FOR NON-CREDIT RISK

National and multilateral capital standards identify the acceptable components of a firm's capital. The CAD bases its definition on the Council's 1989 Own Funds Directive, which specifies two tiers of capital. Elements include paid up share capital, accumulated reserves, and revaluation reserves. National regulators may permit an alternative definition solely for market risk (Annex V). The CAD provides, for non-credit risk, what is often called Tier III. The main component is subordinated debt. The notion is that this shorter-term instrument is acceptable as capital for position risk, which is short-term, while longer-term instruments are needed as capital for credit risk.

The CAD requires that subordinated loan capital have an initial maturity of at least two years, be fully paid and, unless national regulators approve, subject to no early repayment arrangements other than that the debtor is being wound up. No servicing of principal or interest is permitted if to do so would put the firm's capital below 100% of total capital required for non-credit risk. CAD sets a ceiling for subordinated debt of 60% of the total capital required for position risk. National authorities may permit 67% if they decide it is "prudentially adequate" and may permit 71% if a firm's capital excludes illiquid assets (Annex V).

The Basel Standard recognizes that the volatility of trading positions requires a source of capital more flexible than that provided in the 1988 Accord. Despite their preference to keep the definition in the Basel Accord, the authors want their approach to extend to securities firms. They add a third tier of capital for market risks. Subordinated debt can be part of this third tier if it has the characteristics defined by CAD, with a stricter lock-in clause: no servicing is permitted if it would put the firm's required capital below 120%. This subordinated debt, which differs from that permitted by the Basel Accord, could not exceed 71% of total capital required for position risk; the remainder would be Tier I capital.

The Basel Standard provides a rule for the use of subordinated debt that differs somewhat from the CAD rule, because Basel is designed for banks.

Notes and Questions

1. A key element in the CAD and Basel Standard is the trading book (see Note to Section B.1. above, for example). Tier III capital can be used against the trading book and Tier I capital can be dedicated to it. Capital for the trading book is supposed to perform a different function from that for banks' credit risk. Is the trading book concept practical? Banks could easily shift instruments from one book to another. Suppose a bank's trading book collapsed but its commercial banking operations were sound. In practice, might a bank refuse to service Tier III subordinated debt if it could do so without jeopardizing its commercial operations?

D. THE SEARCH FOR A COMMON TREATMENT OF BANKS, THEIR AFFILIATES, AND UNAFFILIATED SECURITIES COMPANIES

Governments, at least those outside the European Union, may continue to apply different capital standards to banks and securities firms. This raises a question about the level playing field. A similar question may be raised for banks that organize their securities operations in different ways.

Now, at least four types of organizations compete in the international equity market: securities companies, banks that carry out their own securities activities (the German universal banks are an example), banks that operate through subsidiaries (as in France), and the banks with sister companies commonly owned by a holding company (as with U.S. banks).

Assume that the rules for banks' positions were stricter than those for securities companies. Banks would have an incentive to trade through an affiliated securities company if they could. Those banks that could not do so would be at a competitive disadvantage, not only with securities firms but with other banks.

Regulators have tried to come to grips with these competitive issues and with enforcement problems by requiring groups to consolidate their accounts to determine capital adequacy. In the U.S., the securities subsidiary of a Financial Holding Company is subject to the SEC rules for position risk. The FHC is subject to the Basel rules, but the Federal Reserve Board requires the FHC to consolidate the securities subsidiary when determining FHC capital requirements. In Europe, the CAD, with other directives, requires consolidation when an investment firm or credit institution is the parent of another investment company or credit institution and where a holding company is the parent of an investment company or credit institution. A country's regulators can, according to Price Waterhouse at 79, exempt firms that:

(i) deduct their holding in subsidiaries from base capital before determining the short-term subordinated debt headroom;

(ii) satisfy the capital requirements on a solo basis;

(iii) have systems in place to monitor and control capital and funding resources; and

(iv) can properly monitor their large exposures on a group basis.

The Tripartite Group of Bank, Securities, and Insurance Regulators, which included members of the Basel Committee and IOSCO, published The Supervision of Financial Conglomerates (1995) (the Tripartite Report). Their report explored many basic supervisory problems and suggested solutions. Excerpts of their Executive Summary follow:

The Tripartite Group agreed that, for its purposes, the term "financial conglomerate" would be used to refer to "any group of companies under common control whose exclusive or predominant activities consist of providing significant services in at least two different financial sectors (banking, securities, insurance)". ...

Among the issues discussed were the overall approach to the supervision of financial conglomerates; the assessment of capital adequacy and ways of preventing double gearing; contagion, in particular the effect of intra-group exposures; large exposures at group level; problems in applying a suitability test to shareholders and a fitness and propriety test to managers; transparency of group structures; the exchange of prudential information between supervisors responsible for different entities within a conglomerate; rights of access to information about non-regulated entities; supervisory arbitrage; and mixed conglomerates. ...

The Tripartite Group agreed that supervision of financial conglomerates cannot be effective if individual components of a group are supervised on a purely solo basis. ...

Banks, insurance companies and securities firms are subject to different prudential requirements, and accordingly supervisors face a difficult problem in determining whether there is adequate capital coverage. The Tripartite Group discussed this issue in some depth and concluded that the desired group-wide perspective can be achieved either by adopting a consolidated type of supervision, or by a "solo-plus" approach to supervision. For the purposes of this report, the following working definitions were agreed upon:

- **Consolidated supervision** - This supervisory approach focuses on the parent or holding company, although individual entities may (and the Tripartite Group advocates that they should) continue to be supervised on a solo basis according to the capital requirements of their respective regulators). In order to determine whether the group as a whole has adequate capital, the assets and liabilities of individual companies are consolidated; capital requirements are applied to the consolidated entity at the parent company level; and the result is compared with the parent's (or group's) capital.

- **Solo-plus supervision** - This supervisory approach focuses on individual group entities. Individual entities are supervised on a solo basis according to the capital requirements of their respective regulators. The solo supervision of individual entities is complemented by a general qualitative assessment of the group as a whole and, usually, by a quantitative group-wide assessment of the adequacy of capital. There are several ways in which this quantitative assessment can be carried out (see below).

Recognising the different starting points of the solo-plus and consolidated supervision approaches, the Tripartite Group discussed a range of techniques available to supervisors for making a quantitative assessment of capital adequacy in a financial conglomerate. The Group recognised the value of accounting-based consolidation (involving a comparison, on a single set of valuation principles, of total consolidated group assets and liabilities, and the application at parent level of capital adequacy rules to the consolidated figures) as an appropriate technique for assessing capital adequacy in **homogeneous groups**. This is the technique commonly used by bank supervisors in respect of banking groups; under European legislation, it is also a technique applied to groups made up of banks and securities companies.

As a means of applying accounting-based consolidation in respect of **heterogeneous groups**, the Tripartite Group considered a technique referred to as "**block capital adequacy**," which envisages the classification and aggregation of assets and liabilities according to the type of risk involved (rather than according to the institution to which they pertain), and the development of harmonised standards for assessing a conglomerate's capital requirement.   However, this technique was not thought to be a practical possibility for heterogeneous groups in the immediately foreseeable future.

Instead, the Tripartite Group concluded that three techniques - the "**building-block prudential approach**" (which takes as its basis the consolidated accounts at the level of the parent company), a simple form of **risk-based aggregation** and **risk-based deduction** - are all capable of providing an accurate insight into the risks and capital coverage. It is suggested that these three techniques might form the basis of a set of minimum ground rules for the assessment of capital adequacy in financial conglomerates and that some form of mutual recognition of their acceptability would be eminently desirable. The Group also agreed that "**total deduction**" might be recognised as a fourth technique, which deals effectively and conservatively with double gearing but one which does not in itself seek to provide a full picture of the risks being carried by the conglomerate. The type and structure of the conglomerate in question may determine which of these four techniques is most appropriate for supervisory use.

Detailed consideration was given to the way in which supervisors should regard a parent institution's participation of less than 100% in a financial subsidiary for the purposes of assessing group capital adequacy. It was agreed that simple minority shareholdings over which the group has neither control nor significant influence (i.e. less than 20% of the shares or voting rights owned) should not be taken into account for group capital adequacy purposes.   They would normally simply be regarded as portfolio investments and would be treated by the parent's supervisor in accordance with the relevant solo rules. Only in exceptional circumstances would supervisors expect to integrate such share holdings in an assessment of capital adequacy from a group perspective.

Where the group has what is deemed to be a "significant influence" (i.e. ownership of between 20% and 50% of the shares or voting rights) over a subsidiary undertaking, a pro-rata approach is advocated with regard to the inclusion of capital in the group-wide assessment.

A major barrier to consolidated management is that "the cost . . . discouraged firms from adopting consolidated risk management." C. Cumming and B. Hirtle, *The Challenges of Risk Management in Diversified Financial Companies*, FRBNY Economic Policy Review, Mar. 2001, at 1.

E. A REVIEW OF THE MARKET RISK CAPITAL ADEQUACY RULES

The different approaches to regulating capital adequacy for position risk are likely to co-exist for some time. The disparity in approach could significantly shape competition in the international market. CAD appears to have resolved the issues, though the British launched a counter-attack that included the work of Dimson and Marsh, who argued for a change in CAD before it was implemented. The following questions and notes focus on aspects of this.

Notes and Questions

1.   The market risk approaches now apply in different ways to various types of firms and banks from different countries. This should have a competitive effect. How would the SEC, CAD, and Basel Standard position risk rules affect competition among U.S. securities companies, U.K. securities firms, German universal banks, and U.S. Financial Holding Companies' securities subsidiaries? Assume that Germany has not yet implemented the Basel Standard for internal models. Also assume that where two rules apply to one firm, the stricter rule governs. What can any type of firm do to escape if it is hurt competitively?

2.   To succeed, the overall building block approaches must marry capital adequacy regulations for banks operating in securities markets and commercial banking markets, combining the building block approach, the use of subordinated debt as Tier III capital, the trading book, and consolidation.

a.   Is this an effective solution from a prudential point of view?

b.   What would account for the CAD solution? British firms and scholars object increasingly to it, suggesting that Britain lost an important contest. Who was the winner? Why?

3.   Some people argue that CAD's approach to position risk is so beset with problems that it should be amended quickly. One authority on international financial law suggested three possible directions to take changing CAD. Professor Richard Dale identified the following options. See R. Dale, The Regulation of Investment Firms in the European Union, Paper Prepared for the ESRC Single Market Programme Conference, University of Exeter 8-11 (Sept. 1994):

a.   Separate banking and securities activities by institution. Because their systemic impact can be so much more severe than that of the securities companies, banks should not be allowed to take on position risk by trading. Their deposit base requires protection. Securities firms need no special protection. No institution should carry on both businesses.

b. Allow bank to engage in securities business, but apply capital standards to the banks' securities business that reflect the banks' systemic role. These capital standards would be more stringent than those applied to securities firms.

c. Follow CAD but require banks to structure their trading so that their deposit base cannot be affected by the performance of the trading activities.

Would any of these modifications to CAD be useful and appropriate?

Links To Other Chapters

Capital rules drive much of international finance. They are very important to the behavior of financial intermediaries in markets for banking (Chapters 3 and 8), securities (Chapters 2 and 8), and derivatives (Chapters 16 and 17). Capital adequacy standards have slowed banks' lending activities and increased their off-balance sheet transactions (Chapter 13) in Europe, Japan, and the U.S. and in other offshore markets (Chapter 9). By so doing, the rules promoted the massive growth in securitization (see Chapter 13). Capital rules limit banks in the payments system (Chapter 10). We return to these issues repeatedly in the book.

CHAPTER FIVE

THE EUROPEAN UNION: THE SINGLE MARKET IN FINANCIAL SERVICES

This Chapter examines the operation of the European Union's (EU) internal market in financial services. It begins with some background material on the European Union and its general program to create an internal market free of trading barriers. It then focuses more specifically on securities and banking markets. A key principle underlying the market reforms is mutual recognition.

A. INTRODUCTION

S. KEY, MUTUAL RECOGNITION: INTEGRATION OF THE FINANCIAL SECTOR IN THE EUROPEAN COMMUNITY
75 Federal Reserve Bulletin 591 (1989).

DEVELOPMENT OF THE INTERNAL MARKET PROGRAM

In the early 1980s, concern was widespread within the European Community that the EC countries were recovering very slowly, compared with the United States and Japan, from the recessions of the late 1970s and were being outstripped by the United States and Japan in new high-technology industries. The conventional wisdom was that, even though tariff barriers among the member states had been dismantled more than a decade earlier, nontariff barriers and market fragmentation within the Community were major impediments to EC economic growth. Partly because of this view, in the first half of the 1980s new initiatives were proposed to reactivate the process of European integration. Perhaps the most far-reaching of these proposals was the draft treaty establishing a European Union that the European Parliament adopted in early 1984. This treaty had no chance of ratification by the member states; but it encouraged the heads of the EC member states, who had previously renewed their commitment in general terms to the goals set forth in the 1957 Treaty of Rome, to take concrete action toward completion of the internal market.[1]

. . .

The 1985 White Paper

By mid-1985, the Commission had prepared a white paper, *Completing the Internal Market,* which the European Council subsequently adopted as the basis for the EC internal market program. The white paper identified 300 pieces of legislation (later revised to 279) that the Community would have to enact to remove restrictions or to harmonize laws of member states. It also set forth a timetable for the enactment of each proposal that called for the entire program to be in place by the end of 1992 (see the box "Forms of EC legislation").

The white paper also announced a new strategy regarding the harmonization of national laws and regulations. In place of the previous, unsuccessful attempt to achieve complete harmonization of standards at the Community level, the Commission adopted an approach involving harmonization of only essential laws and regulations (such as those affecting health and safety) for both goods and services. Under the Commission's new approach, the harmonization of essential standards provides the basis for *mutual recognition* by the member states of the equivalence and validity of each other's laws, regulations, and administrative practices that have not been harmonized at the EC level.

The Single European Act

Both the white paper's goal of implementing the internal market by the end of 1992 and the principle of mutual recognition were included in provisions of the Single European Act, a 1986 agreement

---

[1] The treaty that established the European Economic Community (EEC), which is one of three European Communities established under three separate treaties, is generally known as the Treaty of Rome. The European Coal and Steel Community was established by a 1951 Paris treaty, and the European Atomic Energy Community was established by another Rome treaty in 1957. The term *European Community* is commonly used to refer to all three European Communities; the EC institutions are common to all three Communities.

among the EC member states that amended the Treaty of Rome.[5] Although the act ... does not use the term *mutual recognition,* it provides that the Council "may decide that the provisions in force in a Member State must be recognized as being equivalent to those applied by another Member State."

A major purpose of the Single European Act, which became effective in July 1987, was to make EC decision making more efficient and thereby to facilitate the completion of the internal market. To this end, the Single European Act replaced unanimous voting with "qualified majority voting" for the Council's adoption of most harmonization measures necessary to achieve the internal market. Under qualified majority voting, the number of votes that each member state exercises in the Council is weighted roughly according to its population. Fifty-four votes (out of a total of seventy-six) are required to adopt legislation. Fiscal measures, such as the harmonization of taxes, however, still require unanimous approval of the Council.

Other institutional provisions of the Single European Act were designed to strengthen the role of the European Parliament in EC decision making; however, the Parliament's role remains primarily consultative rather than legislative. Under the new "cooperation procedure," which applies to most measures involving harmonization, the Commission and the Council must take into account amendments that the Parliament proposes. However, the Commission retains considerable power because a parliamentary amendment that the Commission does not support requires the Council's unanimous approval. If the Parliament rejects a measure in its entirety, the Council may enact it only by unanimous vote (see the box "The 'cooperation procedure'").

.   .   .

CREATION OF A "EUROPEAN FINANCIAL AREA"

An important part of the EC program to complete the internal market is the creation of a "European Financial Area," which involves eliminating restrictions on the movement of capital among the member states and establishing a framework for a Community wide market for financial services.

Forms of EC legislation

EC legislation can be in the form of regulations or of directives. A *regulation* is binding in its entirety and is directly applicable

---

[5] The member states of the European Community are Belgium, Denmark, France, Germany, Greece, Ireland, Italy, Luxembourg, the Netherlands, Portugal, Spain, and the United Kingdom. [Austria, Finland and Sweden joined in 1995 bringing the total member countries to 15, eds]

throughout the Community without any implementing legislation by the member states. By contrast, a *directive* is addressed to the member states, which are obligated to ensure that the result set forth in the directive is achieved but have discretion as to the details of implementation.

Most of the EC internal market legislation is in the form of directives. Each directive specifies a date by which member states must conform their national laws to the provisions of the directive; typically the states have two years to do so. Therefore, to complete the internal market by the end of 1992, directives would need to be enacted by the Community by the end of 1990.

If a member state does not conform its laws in accordance with an EC directive, not only the EC Commission but also in many cases an individual or a company may take legal action against the member state. An individual or a company may invoke rights under EC law in national courts under the principle of "direct effects," which was developed by the European Court of Justice and has become an important mechanism for ensuring implementation of EC legislation.

Institutions of the European Community

The *Commission* is the executive branch of the European Community and has responsibility for proposing legislation and for ensuring implementation of EC law by the member states. Commissioners are appointed by agreement among the governments of the member states for four-year terms.

The *Council of Ministers,* which consists of representatives of the governments of the member states, is the decision making body and enacts legislation proposed by the Commission. The presidency of the Council rotates among member states every six months. Participants at Council meetings change on the basis of the subject being considered. For example, if banking legislation is being considered, the Council participants are the economic and finance ministers. The "European Council" consists of the heads of state or government and meets semiannually.

The *European Parliament,* which is elected directly by the citizens of the member states, has an extremely limited legislative function. It does, however, have the final approval over the EC budget and over applications for membership in the Community and, with regard to other matters, a consultative role in Council decisions.

The *European Court of Justice* consists of thirteen judges appointed by agreement among the governments of the member states for six-year terms. In general, the Court has original jurisdiction in cases in which the Commission or another Community institution is a party. Other actions are brought in national courts but are referred to the European Court of Justice for preliminary rulings on matters of EC law; such rulings are binding on the national courts. (An EC Court of First Instance was created in 1988 to hear actions brought against Community institutions by EC staff or by private parties in certain technical areas; the European Court of Justice has appellate jurisdiction in such cases.)

The "cooperation procedure"

The cooperation procedure, which is used only for measures that may be adopted by a qualified majority of the Council, involves two readings of the legislation by the European Parliament. When the EC Commission submits a proposal to the Council, the proposal is also sent to the Parliament for a first reading. After obtaining Parliament's opinion and receiving any revisions proposed by the Commission, the Council adopts a "common position." The Council must then submit its common position to Parliament for a second reading.

If the Parliament *accepts* the proposal (or fails to act within three months), the Council must adopt the measure in accordance with its common position.

If the Parliament *rejects* the Council's common position, the Council may adopt the proposal only by a unanimous vote.

If the Parliament *proposes amendments,* within one month the Commission must reexamine the proposal and submit to the Council a revised proposal that either incorporates the Parliament's amendments or justifies their omission. The Council may adopt the Commission's revised proposal by a qualified majority. Unanimity is required for the Council to adopt Parliamentary amendments that were not accepted by the Commission or otherwise to amend the Commission's revised proposal. If the Council does not adopt the revised proposal within three months, the proposal is deemed not to have been adopted.

.   .   .

THE CONCEPT OF MUTUAL RECOGNITION

The goal of the internal market program for the financial sector is to create a single, unified market by removing barriers to the provision of services across borders, to the establishment of branches or subsidiaries of EC financial institutions throughout the Community, and to transactions in securities on Community stock exchanges. In determining the best method of achieving these goals, the Community must decide what principles should be used to establish a regulatory, supervisory, and tax structure that would both facilitate the integration of Community financial markets and satisfy the public policy interests of the member states with regard to safety and soundness, monetary policy, market stability, and consumer and investor protection.

The starting point for the Community was the principle of *nondiscrimination,* a term that in this context refers to the prohibition of discrimination between domestic and foreign residents based on nationality.   (By contrast, in the context of trade and capital movements, *nondiscrimination* usually refers to the prohibition of discrimination among foreign residents of different nationalities; the concept is similar to that of a most-favored-nation clause, that is, benefits of any liberalization must be extended to all foreign countries on a nondiscriminatory basis.)   Although the right of establishment and the right to provide services in other member states without being subject to any restrictions based on nationality were set forth in the Treaty of Rome, legislative action by the Community and decisions of the European Court of Justice have been necessary to give practical effect to these rights.

Nondiscrimination by an EC member state amounts to offering national treatment to individuals and firms from other member states. Under a policy of national treatment, foreign firms have the same opportunities for establishment and the same powers with respect to their host-country operations that their domestic counterparts have; similarly, foreign firms operating in a host country are subject to the same obligations as their domestic counterparts.   The OECD's National Treatment Instrument defines national treatment as treatment under host-country "laws, regulations, and administrative practices ... no less favorable than that accorded in like situations to domestic enterprises."   The expression "no less favorable" appears to allow for the possibility that exact national treatment cannot always be achieved and that any adjustments should be resolved in favor of the foreign firm; the wording is not meant to endorse an overall policy of "better than national treatment." The principal purpose of a policy of national treatment is to promote competitive equality between domestic and foreign banking institutions by allowing them to compete on a "level playing field" within the host country.

If the European Community had adopted national treatment as an approach to financial integration, the result would have been a level playing field for foreign and domestic institutions within each national market.   But, even though each country's rules would have been applied on a nondiscriminatory basis, twelve separate markets with different rules in each would still have existed.   Moreover, although national treatment removes barriers to the provision of services by ensuring fair treatment for entry and operation within a country, it does not by itself address two important issues: the extent to which multinational cooperation or agreement is necessary to regulate and supervise financial activities conducted internationally and the de facto barriers created by the lack of multinational harmonization of regulatory structures.   The Community's program attempts to deal with these issues.

One approach, which, as noted previously, the Community originally used with regard to products, is to require member states to modify their differing national laws and regulations in order to implement comprehensive, uniform standards established by the Community.   This approach of complete harmonization was abandoned as involving too much detailed legislation at the Community level and as totally impractical to achieve within any reasonable period.

The Community's solution was to adopt the approach of mutual recognition. This approach requires each country to recognize the laws, regulations, and administrative practices of other member states as equivalent to its own and thereby precludes the use of differences in national rules to restrict access. The concept of mutual recognition goes well beyond that of national treatment. Under a policy of mutual recognition, some member states in effect agree to offer treatment that is more favorable than national treatment to firms from other member states.

Mutual recognition cannot simply be decreed among a group of countries with widely divergent legal systems, statutory provisions, and regulatory and supervisory practices. Mutual recognition of rules that differ as to what a country regards as essential elements and characteristics would be politically unacceptable. As a result, a crucial prerequisite for mutual recognition is the harmonization of essential rules. If member states consider certain rules essential but cannot reach agreement on initial harmonization, they may agree explicitly to exclude such rules from mutual recognition and home-country control until agreement can be reached.

In the financial sector, the process of harmonization involves identifying the rules that are essential for ensuring the safety and soundness of financial institutions and the rules that are essential for the protection of depositors, other consumers of financial services, and investors. It also involves determining how detailed the harmonization of these rules must be. For example, one question is whether specifying that the major shareholders of a financial institution must be determined to be "suitable" by home-country authorities is sufficient or whether more specific criteria are needed.

Home-Country Control

A corollary of mutual recognition is home-country control. If national laws, regulations, and supervisory practices that have not been harmonized at the EC level are to be accorded mutual recognition, home-country rules and supervisory practices must be accepted as controlling the operations of branches and the cross-border provision of services by financial institutions. However, the principle of home-country control adopted by the Community is not absolute. In accordance with judgments of the European Court of Justice and with EC directives, the host country retains the right to regulate branches or the cross-border provision of services to the extent that doing so is necessary to protect the public interest.

In practice, the division of responsibility between home-and host-country regulators may be rather complicated. In general, the EC directives that have been proposed or adopted in the area of financial services provide for home-country control for initial authorization and for ongoing prudential supervision. However, various aspects of the day-to-day conduct of business could be subject to host-country control on a national treatment basis under, for example, consumer protection laws that are necessary to protect the public interest but have not been harmonized by the Community. In some directives, such host-country control is strictly limited or is prohibited either because the extent of harmonization of investor protection rules at the EC level is considered sufficient (as in the cases of securities prospectuses and unit trusts) or because the wholesale customers covered by the directive are deemed not to require host-country protection (as in the case of cross-border nonlife insurance services). As a result, under the EC directives on securities markets, a company headquartered in Greece and listed on the Greek stock exchange could, for example, be listed on the London stock exchange under Greek rules that satisfied the EC minimum standards but provided prospective British investors with less information than that required of a U.K. firm.

The European Court of Justice has already played a major role in establishing a public interest test for host-country regulation and in determining whether that criterion has been met, and it will undoubtedly continue to do so. In the case of banking, the public interest of the host state appears to be particularly strong because of the role of banks in the credit, monetary, and payments systems and because banks are within the so-called safety net of deposit insurance and of lending of last resort by the monetary authorities. Rather than relying on the overall public interest exception to home-country control, the Second Banking Directive includes explicit exceptions for rules relating to the conduct of host-country monetary policy. In line with the Revised Basel Concordat, an exception to the principle of home-country control is also provided for the supervision of liquidity. In practice, of course, questions are likely to arise as to whether particular restrictions are truly necessary for purposes of monetary policy and whether particular regulations are addressed toward liquidity or solvency.

. . .

Regulatory Convergence

The EC approach of mutual recognition could result, at least in the short run, in competitive inequalities and fragmentation of markets. With regard to financial services, however, the Community assumes that over the longer run market forces will create pressure on governments that will lead to a convergence of additional national rules and practices that have not been harmonized at the EC level. Pressures for regulatory convergence within the Community would arise both from the absence of restrictions on capital movements and from the regulatory advantages enjoyed by branches of banks and of investment firms from other member states and also by the head offices of such banks and investment firms in providing services across borders.

In the financial sector, the Community is using the principle of mutual recognition as a pragmatic tool that, together with market forces, is expected to result in a more unified, less restrictive regulatory structure. The process is interactive: mutual recognition requires initial harmonization, and additional harmonization results from mutual recognition. In adopting the approach of mutual recognition in the financial area, the Community is in effect using trade in financial services as a lever to arbitrage the regulatory policies of the member states.

Regulatory convergence is particularly likely to occur with regard to bank powers because the Community has reached a theoretical consensus on what activities are permissible for banks. In effect, the member states have agreed upon a goal for regulatory convergence. Banks permitted by their home country to engage in any of the activities listed in the Second Banking Directive are specifically permitted to engage in such activities anywhere in the Community through a branch or through cross-border provision of services. As a result, although the Community has not required governments to give their banks the powers on the list, it has created a situation in which regulatory convergence toward the EC list of activities as a result of market forces seems almost inevitable. Other areas, particularly if the model for convergence has not been specified in advance, could be more complicated.

.   .   .

Supranational Structure of the Community

In considering mutual recognition as the approach to financial integration within the Community and its relevance in contexts beyond the Community, one must remember that the member states have agreed to use it as a tool to achieve an integrated market in the context of a structure that, though not a federation, is a rather powerful supranational structure to which the member states have already transferred a significant degree of sovereignty. The customs union with its common external commercial policy is the basis of the internal market, but the internal market is much more than a customs union. It involves a supranational legislative process under which supranational rules ensuring the free movement of goods, persons, services, and capital are adopted and the harmonization of basic laws, regulations, and practices at a supranational level can be achieved. Moreover, a member state is obligated to implement or enforce all EC rules, including those it opposed in the Community legislative process. Community law is accepted as prevailing over national law, and both judgments and preliminary rulings of the

European Court of Justice based on Community law are binding and enforceable in the member states. (The principle of supremacy of Community law was not explicitly stated in the Treaty of Rome, but it has been confirmed by the European Court of Justice in judgments interpreting provisions of the treaty.)

The European Community is also more than a single, unified market. Other aspects of the Community addressed either by the original Treaty of Rome or by the Single European Act include social policy, economic and social cohesion, research and development, the environment, and economic and monetary union. The Single European Act also refers to the goal of a "European Union," although there is considerable disagreement within the Community as to what such a union would entail.

These institutional and political characteristics of the European Community are extremely important in considering whether the approach the Community is using for internal financial integration is applicable to removing barriers and achieving a more integrated regulatory structure for financial services and markets beyond the Community.   A basic question is how much multinational harmonization would be required and the extent to which sovereignty might need to be surrendered to use the principle of mutual recognition more broadly among nations.

B.   SECURITIES MARKETS

The EU has focused its efforts in securities markets on facilitating the distribution and trading of securities on a Union-wide basis, rather than having twelve separate markets. This has led to Union-wide disclosure standards and the removal of prohibitions on the Union-wide operation of securities firms.

1. DISCLOSURE: THE OLD REGIME

M. WARREN, REGULATORY HARMONY IN THE EUROPEAN COMMUNITIES: THE COMMON MARKET PROSPECTUS
26 Brooklyn Journal International Law 19 (1990).

.   .   .

The EC has adopted or proposed a number of directives that have contributed to the development of a supranational securities law for the common market. These directives actually include both company law and securities law directives because both classes of directives have embraced a mandatory disclosure philosophy. Accordingly, it is difficult to separate them into discrete categories.   Those measures most commonly referred to as securities law directives, include the Admissions Directive, the Listing Particulars Directive, the Interim Reports Directive, the POP Directive, the Mutual Funds Directive, the Investment Services Directive, and the Insider Trading Directive. These seven directives clearly represent the core of an emergent European securities code. Of these, the Listing Particulars Directive, as amended, and the POP Directive are the most significant in the regulation of multijurisdictional securities offerings.

A. *The Listing Particulars Directive*

The Listing Particulars Directive, which was adopted in 1980 and may be referred to as the Information Directive, further develops the EC's "philosophy of disclosure" in the regulation of securities. This directive strongly influenced the United States Securities and Exchange Commission (SEC) in its development of United States disclosure forms for foreign issuers. Unlike national legislation in most of the individual member states, which traditionally required that extensive disclosure be made only to regulatory or self-regulatory bodies, the EC's policy requires disclosure to the general public. The purposes of this directive, as expressed in its preamble, are to provide equivalent protection for investors throughout the common market, to facilitate cross-border exchange listings, and to promote greater interpenetration of national securities markets within the EC. The Listing Particulars Directive requires that an information sheet, termed "listing particulars," in compliance with the directive's disclosure requirements and a prescribed format, be filed and approved in connection with the admission of securities to listing on any securities exchange in the EC. According to the directive, in its implementing legislation each member state must designate a "competent authority" to scrutinize listing particulars to determine whether they satisfy the common disclosure standards imposed by it. Subsequent to approval, the listing particulars must be published for the benefit of investors. For the first time, a multinational disclosure regime, with common disclosure standards and a prescribed format, was to be established by this directive; ultimately it should enable investors and securities analysts, both within and outside the EC, to make investment decisions based on relatively comparable information.

1. The Disclosure Scheme

The layout and detailed disclosure requirements of the Listing Particulars Directive are set forth in Schedule A, for equity securities and Schedule B, for debt securities. The areas of disclosure include, *inter alia,* information concerning: 1) those parties responsible for preparing the listing particulars and for auditing the financial statements; 2) the securities and the listing application; 3) the capitalization of the issuer; 4) the issuer's principal business activities, including a breakdown of net turnover by category of activity and geographical markets for the previous three years, its material contracts, patents, and licenses, legal proceedings, employees and investment policies; 5) the issuer's assets and liabilities, financial position, and profits and losses; 6) the issuer's administration management, and supervision, including remuneration, unusual transactions, and equity interests; and 7) recent developments and prospects of the issuer, including recent trends in production, sales, orders, inventories, costs, and selling prices, as well as prospects for the current year. The information is to be presented in an "easily analyzable and comprehensible" form. Competent authorities are permitted to exempt certain required information if it is deemed to be of "minor importance" or if disclosure would be "contrary to the public interest" or "seriously detrimental to the issuer." Significantly, the issuer must also include all other information, based on the particular nature of the issuer and the securities, which "is necessary to enable investors and their investment advisers to make an informed assessment of the assets and liabilities, financial position, profits and losses, and prospects of the issuer and of the rights attaching to such securities." The mandatory disclosure required by this directive is not limited to "filling out a form," but instead extends to all material information relating to the securities to be listed on an EC exchange.

The listing particulars, following their review and approval by the competent authority of the member state, must be published in a widely-distributed newspaper in the member state or in the form of a free brochure made available to the public. Publication must be made within a reasonable period before the effective date on which the securities are officially listed. This directive does not require the delivery of the listing particulars to investors either prior to, at the time of, or subsequent to, their purchase of securities. This regulatory gap is closed in substantial part by the POP Directive, which requires publication of a prospectus prior to a public offering of securities. Civil and criminal sanctions for compliance failures under either directive, however, are left to the discretion of the individual member states. The Listing Particulars Directive does provide for cooperation among competent authorities of the various member states to facilitate simultaneous or roughly contemporaneous listings based on a coordinated text.

2. Mutual Recognition

Member states retain considerable flexibility in adopting more stringent or additional disclosure requirements. As previously stated, the first step of the EC's legislative strategy was to establish common minimum standards to ensure a given level of protection for the EC's securities markets. The EC properly recognized that it could not immediately preempt the entire field of securities regulation, despite the primacy of EC law in areas covered by the Treaty of Rome. An important second step was taken by the EC in 1987, when the Council of Ministers approved the Mutual Recognition Directive, which amended the Listing Particulars Directive. The amendment states that once approved by a competent authority in a member state, listing particulars must be recognized as such by all other member states without further approval by their competent authorities and without any additional information generally required by any of those member states. Where more stringent, additional disclosure requirements are applicable to listing particulars in the member state where recognition is sought, these requirements must be disregarded. Consequently, such a member state finds itself in the untenable position of imposing more disclosure requirements and greater regulatory costs on its own domestic issuers, which may pose less of an investment risk than foreign issuers from less-regulated member states. The domestic pressure to reduce this regulatory disequilibrium is likely to result in lowering the stricter state's disclosure regimen to the common denominator established by the directive.

Nevertheless, the Mutual Recognition Directive does undertake to reduce opportunities for forum shopping. It provides that where an issuer seeks to list its securities simultaneously or within a short interval in two or more member states, including the member state where its registered office is located, then the issuer must first secure approval of its home state's competent authority pursuant to its home state's laws. The issuer could still engage in regulatory arbitrage by listing only outside its home state, but this is less likely to occur given the typically wider acceptance and liquidity of its securities in its own domestic market. This course remains possible, however, especially as trading markets centralize and as off-exchange trading volumes increase.

The Mutual Recognition Directive has greater authority than merely extending mutual recognition to listing particulars—as listing particulars—in all member states after approval by a competent authority in any member state. The directive also extends mutual recognition—as listing particulars—to public offer prospectuses used in the sale of listed securities in other member states. Presently, this mutual-recognition requirement is limited to circumstances in which a listing is sought on exchanges in two or more member states and when another member state has approved the prospectus, in accordance with the Listing Particulars Directive, within three months of the further application. A proposed amendment to the Mutual Recognition Directive, however, will extend the mutual recognition requirement to all public offer prospectuses that have been approved by the competent authority in any member state, regardless of whether the securities have been listed previously on a member state's exchange. As amended, the Listing Particulars Directive is designed to integrate the disclosure requirements applicable to the public offer and sale of both listed and unlisted securities. The EC's policy, which is reflected by the directive, is to establish a heretofore

nonexistent integrated disclosure system for the listing and
distribution of securities in the member states.

. . .

B. The Public Offer Prospectus Directive

The POP Directive was adopted by the Council of Ministers in
1989 after almost a decade of controversial and secretive
negotiations. The development of this directive ranks among the
EC's most difficult journeys on the path to regulatory harmony. When
originally proposed in 1980, the POP Directive faced major
opposition. Questions were raised whether 1) a uniform disclosure
policy was necessary; 2) the directive should exclude small and
medium-sized enterprises; 3) it should exclude Eurobonds and
Euroequities; and 4) the POP Directive should incorporate the
principle of mutual recognition.[80] In order to secure its adoption,
major compromises were reached that have substantially reduced the
scope and effect of this directive. Nevertheless, it represents a

---

[80] At the time the *POP Directive* was proposed, the United Kingdom Law Society's
Standing Committee on Company Law (Law Society), in response to an inquiry from
the United Kingdom Department of Trade and Industry, stated that the directive was
not necessary. The Law Society's Standing Committee on Company Law, Memorandum on the Draft Directive on Prospectuses for Unlisted Securities (1981) (unpublished
memorandum) (Law Society Memorandum).

> We do not consider that there is any need for a [d]irective, and indeed we would
> consider that the introduction of such a directive would be highly detrimental in the
> United Kingdom in that it would at the least increase the cost to smaller
> companies of raising money by the issue of securities without a corresponding
> increase in the protection of investors.

Id. at 5. The Law Society was also opposed to the requirement in the original proposal
that all prospectuses be subject to review and approval by a competent authority. Id.
at 6.

> This is clearly too great a task for any competent authority [that] does not have
> the opportunity to be involved throughout the process of the prospectus'
> preparation. It is hard enough for the most experienced legal and accountancy
> advisers and merchant banks when engaged actively in the preparation of a
> prospectus to satisfy themselves that adequate inquiries are made to ensure that
> there are no material omissions from a prospectus.

Id. at 7. In addition, the committee viewed prior governmental scrutiny or "vetting" as
potentially misleading to investors:

> If a system of qualitative vetting [was] introduced, this would cast a heavy
> responsibility on the persons carrying out the process. While it would be possible
> to exclude legal liability by appropriate provision in our domestic law, there would
> still be a tendency for the investing public to believe, even if words of disclaimer
> were included in the document itself, that the fact that it had been through the
> vetting process was to some extent a guarantee that there were no material
> omissions and that the contents of the document were true and based on full
> enquiry.

Id. at 8-9. The Law Society's position was accepted and, as adopted, the *POP
Directive* does not require prior scrutiny of prospectuses for unlisted securities....
Prospectuses that have not been subjected to prior scrutiny, however, will not be
entitled to mutual recognition.

major achievement by the EC in the establishment of regional regulatory harmony for multijurisdictional securities offerings.

The POP Directive's underlying policies complement those of the Listing Particulars Directive, which was adopted ten years earlier. The POP Directive is intended to protect investors by providing information necessary to assess the risks of investment in securities, to reinforce confidence in securities, to contribute to the correct functioning, and the development of, securities markets, and to establish an equivalent level of securities disclosure among the member states.   The directive undertakes to harmonize the disclosure standards of the member states for public offerings of securities, regardless of whether the securities are to be listed on an exchange.   By imposing prospectus requirements similar to those required of listing particulars, this directive eliminates disclosure disparities that may have been a disincentive to listing on an exchange.   It also further develops the EC's integrated disclosure system in which prospectuses and listing particulars ultimately may be used almost interchangeably throughout the common market.

Before the adoption of the POP Directive, EC law did not require the publication of a prospectus before a public offering of securities. As stated previously, the Listing Particulars Directive requires publication of an information sheet within a reasonable time before the securities are listed on an EC exchange.   Currently, if the securities to be listed were also the subject of a public offering, the member state's non-EC law governed whether a prospectus was required, as well as the prospectus' contents and publication. Once the POP Directive is implemented by national legislation in each of the member states, however, this will no longer be the case. The directive requires that all public offerings of securities within the EC be subject to the publication of a prospectus by the offeror on or before the time the offering is made. Thus, the POP Directive should result in the creation of a "common market prospectus."

1. The Disclosure Scheme

The POP Directive establishes a common market prospectus by imposing a prospectus requirement for securities that are to be listed and for those that are not.   This is accomplished by the establishment of two regimes. First, to create a regime for public offerings of securities that are to be listed on an exchange, it forces the Listing Particulars Directive to serve two roles. In addition to providing the disclosure format for listing particulars, the Listing Particulars Directive is harnessed by the POP Directive to serve as the disclosure format for a public offer prospectus.   The POP Directive simply incorporates by reference the disclosure requirements of the Listing Particulars Directive for public offerings of securities that are to be listed on an EC exchange. With respect to these securities, the directive provides that the contents and procedures for scrutiny and distribution of the prospectus should be determined by the Listing Particulars Directive "subject to adaptations appropriate to the circumstances of a public offer." The POP Directive thus establishes a dual function for listing particulars: they are to serve 1) as an initial information sheet for the secondary market where the securities trade; and 2) as a prospectus for the public offering of those securities.

Second, the POP Directive establishes a prospectus regime of its own for the public offering of securities that will not be listed on an EC exchange. Although the disclosure requirements are less detailed in this instance, they reflect the same basic standards set forth in the Listing Particulars Directive. For securities that are not to be listed, the following categories of disclosure are established for transferable equity-related and debt securities: the persons responsible for the prospectus; the terms of the offer; the nature of the securities; withholding taxes; underwriting arrangements; transfer restrictions and preemptive rights; the issuer's capitalization; the issuer's business activities; the issuer's material contracts, patents, and licenses; legal proceedings; the issuer's annual and interim financial statements; the auditors; management and the issuer's business trends and prospects for the current year. In addition to specific categories of disclosure, the POP Directive, in a manner similar to that of the Listing Particulars Directive, requires disclosure of all other information, based on the particular nature of the issuer and the securities that may be necessary to enable investors to make an informed assessment of the investment. Prior scrutiny of the prospectus for listed securities is required by reference to the Listing Particulars Directive, but prospectuses for unlisted securities must only be delivered to the appropriate member state authority before its publication. Prior scrutiny and approval by a competent authority, however, is a critical precondition to mutual recognition within the EC.

2. The Exclusions From Coverage

The mandatory disclosure regimes imposed by the POP Directive for public offerings of both listed and unlisted securities serve to upgrade and harmonize disclosure standards in the EC. The exclusions set forth in the directive, however, may result in a mandatory disclosure system with very limited application to securities offerings in the common market.

. . .

The exemptions for private placements, small offerings, minimum purchase offerings, exchange offers, employee offerings, and Eurosecurities come very close to swallowing the disclosure rule. With the exclusion of Eurosecurities, a term that includes both equities and bonds, many regulators are given pause by the question, "what is left?" These exemptions cause one to seriously question the potential for successful implementation of the disclosure goals set forth in the recitals. The POP Directive appears to constitute a mandatory disclosure scheme in search of an issuer.

In fairness to the drafters, it must be conceded that the exigencies of any effort to harmonize the preexisting regulatory policies of twelve sovereign states required considerable compromise. The lobbying efforts of the International Primary Market Association (IPMA), finding its strongest ally in United Kingdom regulators fearful of losing the market that its members control, were difficult to resist. The Commission also proved an ally because of the time pressures of the 1992 deadline and its desire to move on to other equally or more difficult measures, like the proposed Investment Services Directive. The paranoia generated by the IPMA, as well as the general backlash in the United Kingdom to the perceived excesses in the implementation of its Financial Services Act, was more than enough to transform the directive into political rhetoric.

From the beginning, an all-pervasive fear of the Eurobond market taking flight to Zurich or elsewhere outside the EC dictated opposition to the POP Directive.

·   ·   ·

This "party line" deliberately underestimated the numerous factors that established London as the primary base of operations for the Eurosecurities market. London's preeminent position has largely proved immune from regulatory arbitrage. After all, it has been, and remains, the most highly regulated jurisdiction in the EC in terms of mandated disclosure for public offerings of securities. London's attractiveness as the world's primary international securities market stems from its time zone, language, professional expertise and skilled work force, advanced technological infrastructure, cultural adaptability, quality of life, and political stability. Further, one writer has concluded that London's international market has profited the most from "the globalization of insecurities." Contrary to the IPMA position, it is unlikely that international investment firms, having made huge capital investments to secure positions there, would readily abandon London for another city outside the common market.

·   ·   ·

Once it became clear to the IPMA and other opponents of the POP Directive that a Eurobond exemption could be secured, the goal was expanded to include Euroequities as well. Precisely when this expansion occurred is difficult to determine, but the success achieved in securing the exclusion of Euroequities from the POP Directive was surprising even to the Eurobond industry.   The goal and its achievement were predicated largely on the desire for *laissez faire* flexibility, rather than established practice. As one investment banker described it, "we do not want regulation today [that] may hurt us five years from now," despite an acknowledgment that equities involve considerably more investment risk than the investment grade debt typically sold in the Euromarkets. Most experts recognize that a decision to buy equities is much more complex than one to buy bonds given the absence of benchmarks for comparison. Another investment banker described the distinction this way:

> You cannot just say what is the yield, what is the spread to Treasuries, or what is the yield on comparable paper in the secondary market? Is it generous or is it tight? It is much less mathematically mechanical because you need to read each unique story.

In practice Euroequity offerings had initially followed United States disclosure standards, but the relaxed regulatory environment in Europe gradually led to a diminution in the level of disclosure. It now appears that these disclosure practices will not be improved as a result of the POP Directive.

Efforts were made to preserve at least minimal coverage of Eurobonds and Euroequities under the directive. During the working party discussions on the draft directive, informal suggestions were made both for a reduced disclosure scheme for Euroequities and Eurobonds and for a shelf-registration scheme. Another suggestion proffered was to permit prospectuses for these securities to be filed and published after the sale. These proposals received little positive response and, accordingly, were rejected before ever being reduced to print for circulation among regulators and other interested parties.

The POP Directive, as finally adopted, did not exclude Eurobonds and Euroequities altogether. An accord was reached that will require a two-step analysis to determine whether a transactional exemption is available. The first step turns on whether the securities satisfy the terms of the definition provided in the directive. Both Eurobonds and Euroequities are subsumed by the term "Eurosecurities," which is defined by the POP Directive:

> [Eurosecurities] shall mean transferable securities which:
> — are to be underwritten and distributed by a syndicate at least two of the members of which have their registered offices in different [s]tates, and
> — are offered on a significant scale in one or more [s]tates other than that of the issuer's registered office, and
> — may be subscribed for or initially acquired only through a credit institution or other financial institution.

Once the threshold definitional criteria are satisfied, the second step in determination of the exemption must be made. The directive excludes Eurosecurities unless "a generalized campaign of advertising or canvassing was employed." The drafters were unable to reach a consensus as to what is meant by the terms "generalized campaign," "advertising," or "canvassing." Because these terms are undefined in the final version of the directive, numerous questions remain regarding the scope of the exclusion and the degree of regulatory harmony that will be achieved. Even a cursory examination of these terms reveals serious difficulties that are likely to plague the implementation of this directive.

The POP Directive's use of the term "generalized campaign" poses an interesting dilemma. The term must refer to some variant of the term "public offering," because the directive does not apply to securities offerings that are not "public offerings." Unfortunately, the drafters of the POP Directive were unable to reach any agreement on a definition of the term, "public offering."[155] This occasioned their resort to the term, "generalized campaign"; but it is used only in connection with the Eurosecurities exclusion. The exclusion for "[E]urosecurities not subject to a generalized campaign" implies that these offerings actually would constitute public offerings otherwise covered by the directive. If this were not true, the exclusion would have been unnecessary. Accordingly, it would appear that Eurosecurities offerings, as defined by the POP Directive, are public offerings regardless of whether a generalized campaign is employed. Nevertheless, the directive excludes from coverage only those public offerings of Eurosecurities in which no generalized campaign is undertaken. Although this is a plausible construction, the drafters presumably had no answer to the issue of whether Eurosecurities offerings were public or nonpublic offerings. The "party line" discussed above seems to have produced considerable confusion.

.   .   .

---

[155]

.   .   .

Because offerings of securities directly to the general public have occurred only rarely in continental Europe, the public offering concept, as understood in the United States, Canada, and the United Kingdom, is not well developed in the Common Market. Interview with Frank Dangeard, Sullivan & Cromwell, in London, Eng. (Dec. 20, 1988). For example, it is common practice for financial institutions to acquire substantial blocs of newly-issued securities and immediately resell them to their existing clients. Interview with Andrew Peck, Linklaters & Paines, in London, Eng. (Nov. 8, 1988). Despite the institution's role as a conduit for the public distribution of securities, this practice is not generally viewed as a public offering requiring prior publication of a prospectus. Id. Issuers and their investment firms apparently turn out the lights following the offer and sale of securities to institutional customers, darkening from view the large volume of immediate resales to those institutions' retail customers. The several steps in the distribution process are separated, rather than integrated, to deny, rather than confirm, the public offering that has been concluded. The end investor is the phantom of Europe's primary market for securities. The public offering concept is poorly developed; the statutory underwriter is virtually unknown.

3. Mutual Recognition

The mutual recognition provision of the POP Directive complements the mutual recognition amendment to the Listing Particulars Directive, which was previously discussed. A primary policy underlying the mutual recognition doctrine is that investors throughout the common market should be given equivalent protection. Because prospectuses for securities to be listed are subject to the stricter regime under the Listing Particulars Directive, the POP Directive authorizes member states to permit prospectuses for unlisted securities to be prepared in conformity with the Listing Particulars Directive. This facilitates greater equivalence than the widely-variant prospectuses for unlisted securities prepared only on the basis of the general standards set forth in the POP Directive. As a result, all prospectuses, whether for listed or unlisted securities, which are adopted and prepared in conformity with the Listing Particulars Directive, and approved after prior scrutiny by a competent authority, must be given full recognition throughout the EC as public offer prospectuses. Certain limitations are set forth in the POP Directive, but these should not seriously undermine the mutual recognition requirement.

The most important limitation in the POP Directive's mutual recognition provision is the contemporaneity requirement. Public offerings must be conducted either simultaneously or within a short interval of each other. Member states must be given advance notice and may impose translation requirements. Lastly, member states may require additional information specific to its particular market and relating to income tax consequences, paying agents, and notices to investors to be included in the prospectus. Member states, however, cannot require any other additional disclosures and cannot condition use of the prospectus upon first obtaining local approval. After adoption of the proposed revision of the Listing Particulars Directive's mutual recognition amendment, public offer prospectuses and listing particulars approved by a competent authority in a single member state will be entitled to interchangeable mutual recognition in other member states.

. . .

2. DISCLOSURE: THE NEW REGIME

The mutual recognition system has not worked particularly well. A 1998 report of the U.K. Treasury, *Public Offers of Securities*, finds that there have been very few cross-border securities offers in the EU despite the promise of the Directives. Indeed, it appears that the 1999 Deutsche Telekom distribution was the first and last European-wide public offering. The obstacles to such offers are the need to make translations of the prospectus, and the need to include information specific to a country, such as paying agents, the income tax system and the method of notification of investors (together with the cost of the legal advice to determine this). And with listed securities, host states impose additional requirements despite the provisions of the Listing Directive. This spurred initiatives to change the system. *Financial Services: Implementing the Framework for Financial Markets: Action Plan* (1999).

The U.K. Treasury also averts to another possible cause of the low usage of the Directives, even in connection with initial public offers: that large companies list their securities on one exchange in a member state and let investors come to the exchange. The very premise of the mutual recognition regime, that public offers need to be distributed in several territories, may be wrong. As long as investors (or their representatives) can buy the issue somewhere within the EU, there may be no need to offer the security in multiple territories. A single market could be achieved by simply insuring that member states not apply their rules to their own investors extraterritorially (as does the United States). In the EU, member states have never applied securities laws extraterritorially, so this has never been a problem. See also H. Scott, *Internationalization of Primary Public Securities Markets,* 63 Law and Contemporary Problems 71, 82 (2000)

One additional reason for the low usage of the cross-border directives may be the wide scope for private placements within the EU and the relative ease of the resale of privately distributed securities to public investors. Many countries have broad exemptions from disclosure requirements for sales to sophisticated investors or market professionals, in addition to the "eurosecurities" exemption.

In July 2000, the European Union's Economic and Finance Ministers (ECOFIN) requested that the so-called Wise Men Committee, chaired by Alexandre Lamfalussy, recommend regulatory changes that could improve the functioning of European securities markets. This resulted in the *Final Report of The Committee of Wise Men on The Regulation of European Securities Markets* (February 15, 2001). The Report's basic recommendation was that two new regulatory bodies be created, the European Securities Regulators Committee (CESR) and the European Securities Committee (ESC), to regulate securities markets on an EU wide basis. The ESC will act both in an advisory and regulatory capacity. It will have the key power of implementing Commission directives. This will achieve a key objective of the Lamfalussy Committee, to create a more flexible law-making process. The CESR will advise the Commission and ESC on preparing implementing measures. It will supplant the Forum of European Securities Commissions (FESCO) which has formulated proposals for reforms in the past. See G. Wittich, *Implementing the Lamfalussy Report: The Contribution of Europe's Securities Regulators*, Journal of International Financial Markets 209 (2001). It is not altogether clear how these two new bodies will divide responsibilities. The European Parliament approved this new procedure in February 2002 subject to various "democratic safeguards."   The Commission has agreed with Parliament to accept "sunset clauses" in financial legislation that will enable the Parliament to review the new procedure after four years, and all draft implementing measures, including regulations, will be subject to a three month period in which Parliament can review the proposals.   P.Norman, *Financial reforms proposals win backing*, Financial Times, February 6, 2002.

In terms of substantive measures, the Lamfalussy Committee said the following priority issues needed to be addressed by no later than the end of 2003:   (1) a single prospectus for issuers, with a mandatory shelf registration system; (2) modernization of listing requirements and introduction of a clear distinction between admission to listing and trading; (3) generalization of the home country principal for wholesale markets; (4) modernization and expansion of investment rules for investment funds and pension funds; (5) adoption of International Accounting Standards; and (6) a single passport for a recognized stock market on the basis of the home country principle.

The first proposal envisioned a significant change in the existing disclosure regime and has resulted in an important new proposed directive. On May 30, 2001, the European Commission issued a proposal for a new Directive on a common prospectus to be required when securities are offered to the public in primary markets or admitted for trading in secondary markets, COM(2001) 280 final (Common Prospectus Proposal or CPP). This proposal requires a common prospectus, whose details will be specified by the Commission upon advice of a Securities Committee, Art. 6(1), for any primary public offering, Art. 3(1).   The prospectus cannot be published until approved by the home country, Art. 11(1). Article 13 of the proposal contains rules on advertising. Article 13(1) provides: "Advertisements, notices, posters shall be communicated in advance to the competent authority of the home Member State which shall check them before publication against the principles contained in this Article [that advertisements be fair, accurate and consistent with that contained in the prospectus]. The documents shall state that a prospectus will be published and indicate where investors will be able to obtain it." The EU disclosure requirements are to be in accordance with the information requirements set out by IOSCO in Part I of their International Disclosure Standards for cross-border offerings and initial listings. Enforcement of the EU rules will generally be left to the home country, Art. 19. When the host country finds irregularities in an offer, it must refer the matter to the home country. The host country is, however, entitled to act, after informing the home country, if measures taken by the home country prove inadequate or violations of laws and regulations persist.

As discussed above, under the current EU regime, so-called "eurosecurities," not subject to "a generalized campaign of advertising or canvassing," are exempt from any EU disclosure requirements. Eurosecurities are securities (1) underwritten and distributed by a syndicate at least two of the members of which have their registered offices in different states (*multiple state underwriters*); (2) offered on a significant scale in one or more states other than that of the issuer's registered office (*distribution in state other than the issuer's*); and (3) subscribed for or initially acquired through a credit institution or other financial institution (*sold to financial institutions*).

What is advertising and canvassing has been left to various host state requirements. For example, Germany provides that the "canvassing" prohibition only applies to door-to-door sales, and not apparently calls to clients, while the Netherlands provides that an investor may be approached by a financial institution as long as this is not done systematically by way of a general campaign.

Thus, under the existing EU securities regulation regime, a multiple state bank syndicate, including Deutsche Bank and Barclays, could sell the securities of a German issuer to various banks in London and Germany, who might purchase them for, or immediately resell them to, retail investors throughout the EU, as long as the retail investors were not procured by a generalized advertising or canvassing campaign, the latter requirement being subject to the interpretation of host states (where the investors are). Such securities would, however, be subject to national laws, in the example the laws of England and Germany. But these laws generally provide for disclosure exemptions for offers to sophisticated investors like financial institutions, and, unlike U.S. law, would not generally integrate financial institution resales to investors into the initial offering.

Under the CPP, offshore sales in the EU may be significantly more restricted than at present. It is true that sales to financial institutions would be outside the scope of the proposal since these sales would not be defined as public offerings, Art. 3(2)(a), Art. 2(1)(c). In a sense the "eurosecurities" exemption has been widened by dropping the requirements for multiple state underwriters and distribution outside the state of the issuer, in line with the new broader exemption for sophisticated investors. However, more importantly, any advertising of such issues would be reviewed for content by the home Member State and would subject issuers to the Common Prospectus requirement. Issuers would continue to be free to sell securities under their own "international style" disclosure documents in London to financial institutions who could pass them on or resell them to retail investors, but no advertising of such offerings could be made. The power to define permissible advertising would be taken away from host Member States. German retail investors could still participate in London offerings through a financial institution, but they would be much less likely to know about them. This has the effect of making the offshore public market less accessible.

The CPP also incorporates a concept of shelf registration for seasoned issuers and expedited registration for new issuers, based on prior work by FESCO, *A "European Passport" for Issuers,* A Report for the EU Commission (December 2000). As in the United States, only new information about newly offered securities would have to be disclosed. Unlike the U.S. system, however, no universal shelf registration statement describing various securities that might be issued and different distribution procedures that might be employed, would be required.

The CPP addresses another issue that has hampered the development of a single internal securities market, the language problem. Currently, disclosure documents must be distributed in the local language, thus requiring significant translation costs and potential liabilities due to discrepancies in meaning between various language versions. Article 7 of the CPP provides that the prospectus shall "be drawn up in a language accepted by the competent authority in the home Member State." Article 16 then states: "Where an offer is made. . . in more than one Member State, the prospectus. . .shall. . .be made available in a language customary in the sphere of finance and which is generally accepted by the competent authority of the host Member State. In such case, the competent authority of the host Member State may only require that the summary note be translated into its domestic language."

The EU proposal raises some interpretative questions. If a French company prepares a prospectus in French, must the U.K. accept it or can it require that the entire prospectus be translated into English? This would seem to turn on whether French is a language "customary in the sphere of finance" and whether French is "generally accepted" by the U.K. In practice English is the only customary language in the sphere of international finance, but will the French accept that? If French is customary, could the English still reject it on the grounds that it is not "generally accepted" in the U.K., whatever that means? There may be significant political pressure for local authorities to insist that prospectuses, and not just summaries, be available in the local language.

The EU Commission has also put forward a consultation paper on ongoing reporting obligations that it proposes be required of all companies listed on an exchange, a protean '34 U.S. Act initiative. *Towards an EU Regime on Transparency Obligations of Issuers Whose Securities are Admitted to Trading on a Regulated Market,* Consultation Document of the Internal Market Directorate General, July 11, 2001. The paper proposes that companies must file quarterly reports and requires companies "to inform the public without delay of all new information which is not of public knowledge and necessary to enable investors to make an informed assessment of its assets and liabilities, financial position, profit and losses, prospects and rights attaching to its securities, which may lead to substantial movements in the prices of its securities."

The proposal for quarterly reports has met with significant opposition. Many commentators thought this should be left to issuer discretion and would create "short-termism" among companies. In addition, the need for quarterly reports was questioned given existing requirements in many countries that material information should be provided to the market as soon as possible. European Commission, Internal Market Directorate General, *Summary of Replies Received to the Consultation Document of 11 July 2001* (2001). This proposal takes on added interest given statements by the new SEC Chairman Harvey Pitt that the U.S. needs to adopt a system in which new material information is more promptly disclosed to the market.

Notes and Questions

1. The general idea behind the Listing Particulars and POP Directives is relatively clear—it is to create a single EU market for multijurisdictional securities offerings. This can be done by having a single set of disclosure documents with which securities can be offered in any EU country.

The Listings Particulars Directive provides that disclosures required for listing on one EU exchange must be accepted by other EU exchanges. Information required by the Directive must be filed and approved before stock can be listed on any exchange. After the disclosures are approved, they are published.

There are also minimum standards that must be observed by any exchange, under the Listing Conditions Directive (not referred to in the Warren article). All listed firms must meet certain minimum requirements with respect to size, earnings, and public float. Why is it necessary to have minimum listing requirements? In the U.S. listing requirements are left to individual exchanges.

The POP provides that any securities offered to the public must have a POP, and that a POP approved in one jurisdiction can be used in another. What does POP add to what was already required under the Listings Particulars Directive?

The home country system could theoretically lead to less disclosure for investors when securities were offered by companies in countries with low disclosure requirements. This does not seem to have happened because issuers have complied with standards familiar to international investors. Thus, in the case of a Danish public offering in the U.K., the issuer would comply with the higher U.K. disclosure requirements since the lower level of Danish disclosure would not be acceptable. C. Rovinescu and G. Thieffry, *Cross-Border Marketing*, D3 (1995) (unpublished paper delivered at Oxford Law Colloquium on The Future for the Global Securities Market - Legal and Regulatory Aspects, Oxford Colloquium). Similarly, French issues abroad follow "international" rather than lower French standards. W. Smith, *The French View of Cross-Border Securities Offerings*, L13-14 (1995) (unpublished paper delivered at Oxford Colloquium).

2. How does mutual recognition work? If you are a French company can you list first on the Luxembourg Exchange and then the French to take advantage of the less rigorous Luxembourg disclosure rules? POP provides that you must list first in the country of your registered office if you are listing there at all. Could you forum shop by locating your registered office in whatever jurisdiction you want? Until quite recently the answer to this question was clearly no because countries required firms to have their registered office in the country where the "direction" of the company came from, usually corporate headquarters. But these country requirements were invalidated to some degree in *Centros Ltd v. Erhvervs-og Selskabsstyrelsen* [Danish Companies Board], Case C-212/97, European Court of Justice (March 9, 1999). If a stock is approved for listing on the Athens Stock Exchange, must it also be approved for listing on the Frankfurt Exchange?

3. Note that there is no common enforcement system; no EU SEC. If a prospectus complying with Luxembourg law is being distributed in France, who is supposed to enforce compliance with Luxembourg law? For a general review of EU disclosure rules, see E. Wymeersch, *The EU Directives on Financial Disclosure*, European Financial Services Law, Feb. 1996, at 34.

4. How would you compare the EU approach to the U.S.'s MJDS initiative?

5. "Eurosecurities" are securities which (1) are underwritten and distributed by a syndicate at least two of the members of which have their registered offices in different states (*multiple state underwriters*); (2) are offered on a significant scale in one or more states other than that of the issuer's registered office (*distribution in state other than issuer's*); and (3) may be subscribed for or initially acquired only through a credit institution or other financial institution (*sold to banks*). Eurosecurities are exempted from the EU disclosure requirements if they are not subject to "a generalized campaign of advertising or canvassing." Does that mean that they are subject to no disclosure requirements?

Suppose a German company wants to issue bonds underwritten by a bank syndicate, including Deutsche Bank and Barclays, to be sold initially to various banks in London. Is this issue exempt from EU disclosure requirements? Would it matter if the bank buyers immediately sold the bonds to individual investors?

Professor Warren obviously disagrees with the exemption. Is he right?

6. The "eurosecurities" exemption has been implemented in different form in different member states. For example, Germany has said that the "canvassing" prohibition only applies to door-to-door sales, and not

apparently to calls to clients. The Netherlands has said that a retail investor may be approached by a financial institution as long as this is not done systematically by way of a general campaign. Neither Germany or the Netherlands has limited the "eurosecurities" exemption to particular types of securities, whereas Belgium has limited it to Eurobonds. N.R. van de Vijver, *Euro-securities: Regulatory Aspects*, Securities and Capital Markets Law Report, May 1994, at 15. Is it desirable or permissible for an EC Directive on financial services to be implemented differently in different countries?

7.   What do you think of the new EU CPP? Do you think it is necessary, given the offshore alternative? Do you agree with the advertising rules and the idea of having prospectuses only in English? How about the EU version of shelf registration. Do you agree with the contemplated approach to ongoing reporting?

8.   A significant boost to the development of EU capital markets may come from the adoption of the Euro. This is discussed in Chapter 7. Another boost may come from a German tax-reform plan which would free companies from capital gains taxes on the sale of their industrial holdings as of 2002. The high capital-gains tax has discouraged many German financial institutions from selling their holdings in other public companies. C. Rhoads, *New Tax Law Will Transform Germany Inc.,* Financial Times, July 17, 2000.

9.   The Commission has endorsed the use of IASC accounting standards by 2005 and has thus refrained from trying to promulgate EU accounting standards, BNA, World Securities Law Report (June 2000). Two European stock exchanges, EASDAQ and EURO.NM require their listed companies to reconcile their financial statements to U.S. GAAP or IAS.

10.   The Commission has also proposed a Council Directive of 30 May 2001 on insider trading and market manipulation, COM(2001) 281 fin. Inside information, defined as "information which has not been made public of a precise nature relating to one or more issuers of financial instruments. . .which if it were made public, would be likely to have a significant effect on the price of those financial instruments." Article 1.1. Enforcement of measures to prohibit the exploitation of inside information is left to individual Member States. In addition, the Commission continues to implement a takeover regulation, an effort it began in 1995. Its latest proposal, Common Position of the Council of 19 June 2000 on the proposed 13th Directive concerning takeover bids, O.J. E.C. 2001 C23/1-14, January 24, 2001, was rejected by the Parliament, largely under the urging of Germany, in July 2001 on an extraordinary 273-273 vote. BNA, World Securities Law Report 3 (July 2001). For the substance of parliamentary concerns, see Legislative Resolution of the European Parliament, Takeover Bids, Minutes of December 13, 2000. The major issues are whether there should be a mandatory bid for minority

shares and the extent to which target board can adopt defensive measures.

3. PROVISION OF SERVICES

The EU disclosure requirements deal with securities sold within the EU. Another important element of the single market program is the institutions providing securities services. The Investment Services Directive aims at facilitating the operation of such institutions throughout the Union. Key provisions of the Directive are in an Appendix to this Chapter.

M. WARREN, THE INVESTMENT SERVICES DIRECTIVE: THE "NORTH SEA ALLIANCE" VICTORY OVER "CLUB MED"
6 International Securities Regulation Report 6 (1993).

Last June's breakthrough on the sweeping EC Investment Services Directive marked a decisive victory for the so-called "North Sea Alliance" of free-market oriented European Community countries over the protectionist "Club Med" group (France, Italy, Spain, Portugal, Greece, and Belgium). And among the alliance countries—the United Kingdom, Germany, Ireland, Luxembourg, and the Netherlands—the United Kingdom is the victor with the most spoils.

The breakthrough enabled the EC Council of Ministers to adopt a common position on the ISD on Nov. 24. Its primary purposes are to provide:

- Common minimum authorization (licensing) requirements among the member states.
- Mutual recognition of the license granted in the "home state" by all other member states (or "host states").
- Common minimum financial soundness or "prudential rules."
- Certain guiding principles for adoption of "conduct of business" rules.
- Direct access to domestic stock exchanges for both outside investment firms and banks.
- Investor freedom to trade in either regulated markets or in less-regulated off-exchange markets.
- Minimum transparency rules for regulated exchange markets.

The directive should lead ultimately to a rough equivalency among the 12 member states as to authorization standards, financial soundness rules, and conduct of business principles.

Moreover, the directive's mutual recognition provision, providing in effect a single license, should greatly facilitate EC-wide operations for investment firms and, hence, significant integration of the EC's securities markets. The extent of this integration, while hardly creating a true, single market, should serve as a powerful catalyst for the eventual development of a supranational market system in the EC.

This analysis, however, examines three controversial provisions of the ISD—access to stock exchanges, off-market vs. on-market trading, and transparency rules—and how they will affect European securities markets. It also examines certain competitive advantages that EC banks will enjoy in the securities field as a result of the Council's decision to delay ISD implementation until 1996.

Access to Stock Exchanges

One of the directive's most contested provisions provides expanded access for both investment firms and banks, with home state authorization, by allowing them to become members of the regulated markets of the host states. If the host state's regulated market has numerical limitations on membership, the host state is required to abolish or to adjust them to meet demand. Investment firms and banks are entitled, through a branch or a host state subsidiary, to become members of, or have access to, regulated markets and clearance and settlement systems of the host state.

The six member states whose laws do not currently allow market membership for banks, but only for their specialized subsidiaries, are allowed to deny access until Dec. 31, 1996, and Spain, Greece, and Portugal are permitted to extend that period until Dec. 31, 1999.

These extensions of time accommodate somewhat the Club Med's understandable opposition to Germany's desire for direct bank access to the domestic stock markets of other member states (which explains why Germany joined the North Sea Alliance in the first place). Prior to the compromise, the Club Med group insisted that member states should be allowed to require all banks to incorporate (and capitalize) separate investment firm subsidiaries as a pre-condition to accessing their domestic stock markets.

Off-Market vs. On-Market Trading

The Club Med insisted that the directive embody the notion of "concentration," which in its French conception means that shares in French companies held by French residents must be traded in the French stock market. The United Kingdom refused to buy this and, with the backing of the North Sea group, accepted only a watered-down version.

The directive permits a member state to require that securities transactions be carried out on a "regulated market," as opposed to an off-market, assuming four conditions are met: (1) The investor must be a resident of that member state; and (2) must not have exercised the right granted by the directive to opt for an off-exchange market ("explicit authorization" may be required by the host state); (3) the transaction is carried out by the investment firm through its main office or a branch (or under its freedom to provide services) in that member state; and (4) the securities traded are actually listed on a "regulated market" in that member state.

(The ISD defines a "regulated market" as (1) a regularly functioning securities market that is (2) formally designated by its home state and in compliance with home state regulations, (3) with traded securities satisfying certain listing requirements, and is (4) a market that requires compliance with the directive's reporting and transparency requirements.)

The Club Med, led by France, insisted on a concentration requirement as a way to ban lightly regulated, mainly quote-driven and off-exchange markets, including London's SEAQ International and the Eurobond markets, in favor of the more tightly regulated exchange-based, order-driven markets on the Continent.

The Club Med argued that this was necessary to protect widows, orphans, and retail investors, to which one critic replied: "How touching. The simple truth is that southern Europeans want to protect their exchanges from competition." In particular, the Paris bourse has already lost a third of its business in French shares, estimated at $250 million a day, to SEAQ International, which quotes prices in more than 650 international stocks and has cornered roughly 90 percent of international or cross-border securities transactions.

One commentator recently observed that the "reluctance on the part of the Paris market to encourage off-exchange trading at the expense of highly regulated retail exchange markets is related to the apprehension among Europe's exchanges that London's SEAQ International will run them out of business even sooner under the ISD's passport system."

Many have proposed that a two-tier market system would be the best alternative, permitting retail trades to flow through traditional exchange-based markets with their stricter disclosure rules, monitoring functions, and transparency requirements, while permitting wholesale trades by institutional investors and dealers to be handled by more loosely regulated off-exchange markets. The compromise proposed by the Dutch, providing for an investor's right to opt out of a regulated market in favor of an off-market, is likely to harden into a two-tiered system.

Most observers have dreamed about an electronically linked trading system in which the shares of all major EC companies would be listed and traded on all 12 member state exchanges, with equal access and equal protection for all investors. The compromise, at least for the time being, allows SEAQ International to remain as a 13th market for professional traders, co-existing with the exchange-based markets of the member states.

Transparency

Not unrelated to the concentration notion, and equally controversial, is the directive's creation of minimum transparency rules for the regulated exchange markets of the member states. The Club Med argued that stringent transparency rules were critical to ensuring an adequate level of investor protection and to reducing risks of distortion between competitive markets. The North Sea group, especially the British, argued that limited secrecy regarding trading transactions was essential to the protection of market makers and other financial intermediaries.

The directive now reflects a compromise between the two clubs. It requires (1) publication at the market opening of the weighted average price, the high and low prices, and the volume during the preceding trading day; and (2) after a two-hour calculation period, publication of the weighted average price and the high and low price (not volume) after a one-hour delay, to be updated every 20 minutes to the close. Assuming a 9 a.m. opening, the weighted average traded price, plus the high and low prices, for the period 9 a.m. to 11 a.m. would be published at 12 p.m., and updated every 20 minutes thereafter to cover a two-hour period on a one-hour delayed basis.

Moreover, the directive permits member states to except large blocks and illiquid securities. In stark contrast to the U.S. markets' real-time reporting standards, the directive's market transparency standards are remarkably opaque.

. . .

On July 24, 2001, the Commission issued a consultative document on extensive revisions to the Investment Services Directive, Revision of the Investment Services Directive—Open consultation of interested parties, Document 1, *Overview of Proposed Adjustments to the Investment Services Directive (ISD Revisions)*. Among the proposals would be an expanded list of investment services to include investment advice and commodity derivatives, a redefinition of the dividing line between organized markets and investment firms engaging in order-matching services, a revision of the definition of regulated market for the purpose of deciding how offerings on such a market should be regulated, a definition of professional investors who would fall outside of mandatory conduct of business rules, and provision for a more harmonized set of conduct of business rules.

In April 2002, an open hearing was held on revision of the Directive, Memorandum from the Commission, April 24, 2002. The most contentious issue had to do with "off-exchange" trading through an ATS (similar issues plague the U.S. Market). The Commission stated that a solution would consist of:

1. clarifying conditions under which market participants can be expected to have access to ATS or internalising systems which display limit orders better than competing trading venues;

2. strengthening obligations on providers of investment services to ensure that orders are executed in the way most beneficial to the customer ("best execution" obligation"). This would be a means of bringing about effective linkage between different types of market and

of ensuring that orders are only fulfilled internally within banks where this delivers demonstratable benefits for clients:

3. clarifying the obligations of banks or investment firms when they receive orders from clients. Should banks be required to display such orders to the wider market if the order represents an improvement on best prevailing bids or offers in the marketplace?

Notes and Questions

1. The main purpose of the Investment Services Directive (ISD) is to authorize a securities firm that offers certain services (on an agreed list) in its home state, to also offer them through branches in any other EU country. In particular, it allows a firm access to stock exchange membership outside of its home country. ISD came into effect on January 1, 1996. As of that date only seven of the EU's fifteen states (Belgium, Denmark, Ireland, Luxembourg, the Netherlands, Sweden and the United Kingdom) had implemented ISD in national legislation.

As we shall see, banks were first given the authority to offer securities services on a cross-border basis through branches in the Second Banking Directive (SBD). The delay in implementing the Investment Services Directive gave a theoretical advantage to universal banks; but universal banks must also now meet Basel type capital standards. ISD was implemented, along with CAD, in 1996. For a general review of ISD, see M. Warren, *The European Union's Investment Services Directive*, 15 University of Pennsylvania Journal of International Business Law 181 (1994). The ISD, like the SBD, requires firms seeking to engage in cross-border services to notify home and host authorities. This raises the issue as to when such services are actually being provided cross-border or only in the home country. For example, if securities are issued in the home country by a firm from that country is the service cross-border if investors from another country invest? See C. Abrams, *The Investment Services Directive - Who Should Be the Principal Regulator of Cross-Border Services?*, European Financial Services Law (1995). This issue is examined at more length for banking in C1 of this Chapter.

2. Do states have an interest in the safety and soundness of securities firms? If so, how will a host state satisfy itself that an out-of-state firm is safe and sound? See ISD, art. 3 and 10. How can you reconcile Article 11 with a mutual recognition, home country control approach? A further problem exists as to when a host country can apply conduct of business rules to a cross-border transaction. The ISD revisions would exempt professional investors from conduct of business rules. The proposed definition of professional investors excludes institutions but does not exclude sophisticated or wealthy investors. Do you agree with this approach?

3. To what extent can European securities firms choose their home states? Could a German firm faced with heavy regulation in Germany shift its home state to Luxembourg? See ISD, arts. 1(6), 3(2) and 6.

4. As Warren observes, the Club Med countries were against allowing banks (as opposed to their affiliates) to have direct membership on exchanges, but they lost out to the North Sea Alliance. See ISD or art. 15. Why was Club Med against this? Under Article 15(3), Belgium, France and Italy could wait until December 31, 1996, and Greece, Spain and Portugal until the end of 1999, to implement this change. You should also note a related provision in Article 15(4) which provides that states (home and host) must allow out-of-state investment firms to obtain electronic access (screens) to regulated markets, i.e. French brokers must be given the opportunity to conduct trades on SEAQ. How does this fit within the mutual recognition framework?

5. Club Med took the position that most securities trading should only be allowed on "regulated markets" (defined in Article 1(13)). Is this merely protectionist, or can it be based on investor protection concerns? How does Article 14 solve this problem? Assuming SEAQ International (London's stock exchange for foreign securities) is not a "regulated market" can the French prevent French investors from trading on SEAQ? Under the ISD Revisions "regulated markets" like stock exchanges would be subject to higher regulation than other markets. Regulated markets would be basically defined as those trading publicly offered securities and publicly traded derivatives.

6. Could the Paris Bourse, assuming it was a regulated market, offer Dutch brokers the possibility of trading on the Bourse through a screen-based trading system installed in the Netherlands, or could the Dutch prevent this under Article 15(5)? The Dutch did initially claim such power but abandoned this position after vociferous complaints from other Member States. Financial Times, *The ISD in action: liberalization like this who needs protectionism*, Financial Regulation Report (March 1996). For a thorough review of how ISD has been implemented in the Member States see E. Wymeersch, *Implementation of the ISD and CAD in the National Legal System*, paper presented at the Conference on European Investment Markets, University of Genoa (October 1996). See also, M. Tison, *The Investment Services Directive and its Implementation in the EU Member States,* University of Ghent, Financial Law Institute, Working Paper 1999-17 (November 1999).

7. Club Med was in favor of market transparency, and would have required that the price and volume of all trades, including large block trades, be reported quickly after completion. This is the trading rule on the Paris Bourse but not on SEAQ, the London Stock Exchange (it is also the rule on the NYSE). What are the pros and cons of this approach? How does Article 21 resolve this issue? Can SEAQ be a regulated market under ISD?

8. The EU Commission believes that the most widespread difficulty encountered in the operation of the ISD passport are the powers left to host countries over conduct of business, advertising and some custody rules, see Article 11. The Commission believes these matters can be left to home country control with respect to professional investors. Commission Communication COM (XX) 2000: The application of conduct of business rules under Article 11 of the ISD. The fact that Member States can restrict advertising (as well as other aspects in the provision of cross-border services, see the discussion of the common good in banking below) is recognized to be at odds with the Commission's Directive on electronic commerce, Directive 2000/31/EC, June 8, 2000, which is generally trying to promote electronic commerce. See Communication from the Commission to the Council and the European Parliament, *E-Commerce and Financial Services* COM (2001).

9. The UCITS ("undertakings for collective investments in transferable securities" or mutual funds as referred to in the United States) Directive 85/611 of December 20, 1985, 1985 O.J. (L 375), as amended by Directive 88/220 of March 22, 1988, 1988 O.J. (L 100), harmonizes national rules on the authorization, supervision, structure, activities and disclosure obligations of mutual funds. A single license granted by the UCITS' home state permits the UCITS to be marketed throughout the EU. In most cases the home state is responsible for compliance, however, host state marketing rules apply. L. Garzanti, *Single Market-Making: EC Regulation of Securities Markets*, 14 Company Lawyer 43 (1992).

The UCITS Directive came into force in most Member States in 1989. A Bank of England survey of 25 firms reported that the Directive had a limited impact on facilitating cross-border funds within the EU. *The Developing Single Market in Financial Services*, 34 Bank of England Quarterly Bulletin 341, 345 (1994). This is the same conclusion reached in a study of Lipper Analytical Services, a U.S. based mutual fund group. It found that only 38% of the 5,436 UCITS are marketed outside the country of domicile of their promoters. The rest are "round-trippers," incorporated in a low tax jurisdiction such as Dublin or Luxembourg and then marketed exclusively in the domicile of the promoters. N. Cohen, *EU Collective Investment Scheme Laws "A Failure"*, Financial Times, Oct. 28, 1994.

In May 2000, the Commission proposed to amend the UCITS directives by proposing to remove barriers to the cross-border marketing of the funds by widening the range of assets in which they can invest. Currently they can only invest in listed stocks and bonds, and not in money market instruments, financial derivatives or "fund of funds." In addition, it would allow fund management companies to operate throughout the EU under s single passport and widen the range of activities in which they can engage. COM (2000) 331, May 30, 2000. These directives were adopted on December 4, 2001.

10. Should there be a European or EU Securities Commission or a European or EU Financial Service regulator responsible for both securities and banking? In considering this question, note that some countries in the EU, Sweden, Denmark, Norway and the United Kingdom, already have single financial regulators. On the other hand, the U.S. has multiple federal regulators, e.g. Federal Reserve, FDIC, and SEC. Will the call of the Wise Men for a European Securities regulator lead to such a system?

As we discuss later in this Chapter, there is currently no single European banking regulatory agency; the European Central Bank is not a supervisor, it is only responsible for monetary policy. As for securities regulation in the EU, this is left to individual states. There is, however, an organization to foster cooperation between states on a European level (it includes 17 countries, broader than EU), called the Forum of European Securities Commissions (FESCO), created in 1997. It is currently working on minimum standards for granting recognition as a "regulated market" under ISD.

There is a serious question whether the legal authority exists under the Rome Treaty to create either a EU securities or financial services regulator. One author claims that there might be authority under Article 308 which provides that the Council acting unanimously on a proposal from the Commission, after consultation with the European Parliament, can take actions which "prove necessary" to "obtain one of the objectives of the Community" where the Treaty has not provided such powers. However, under case law interpreting Article 308, it is quite unclear that Article 308 would support such a move. See Giles Thieffry, *Toward a European Securities Commission,* International Financial Law Review 14 (October 1999).

C.   BANKING MARKETS

In the banking area, the EU approach focuses on facilitating the Union-wide operation of banks while at the same time protecting depositors. Some overall data on banking in the European Union based on A. Belaisch, L. Kodres, J. Levy and A. Ubide, *Euro-Area Banking at the Crossroads,* IMF Working Paper WP/01/28, March 2001 (the Paper), provides some context.

To begin with Europe is still more banking dominated than the United States. Bank loans to Euro area countries (Austria, Belgium, Finland, France, Germany, Ireland, Italy, Luxembourg, the Netherlands, Portugal and Spain in the Paper) are 100 percent of GDP, twice the ratio in the United States and about the same as Japan. Germany has by far the biggest number of credit institutions, 3000 as compared with the next largest country France with half that many. Consolidation in banking has accelerated rapidly. More than half of the 30 biggest euro-area banks are the result of recent mergers and the average size of the top five banks as of 1999 (Deutsche Bank, BNP Paribas, ABN-Amro, Hypervereinsbank and Crédit Agricole) has doubled since 1995. Loan markets are fairly concentrated in some countries like Belgium where the top 5 banks make 98% of the loans or France where they make 77%. By any measure, Germany has the least concentrated markets.

Foreign banks' market share in the Euro are is 12.7%. It is 4.3% in Germany and 9.8% in France. Unfortunately, the Paper does not give comparable data for the U.K. but the banking system of the U.K. is fairly concentrated and highly international.

1. THE SECOND BANKING DIRECTIVE

a. OVERVIEW

M. GRUSON AND W. FEURING, A EUROPEAN COMMUNITY BANKING LAW: THE SECOND BANKING AND RELATED DIRECTIVES, IN THE SINGLE MARKET AND THE LAW OF BANKING
19-34 (R. Cranston ed., 1991).

The Second Council Directive on the Co-ordination of Laws, Regulations and Administrative Provisions Relating to the Taking-up and Pursuit of the Business of Credit Institutions and Amending Directive 77/780/EEC (the "Second Directive") is the centrepiece of a new banking law unfolding in the European Community. This Directive obliges the Member States of the Community to implement its provisions into their national banking regimes by means of conforming their national banking laws and practices (as to the required results to be achieved) by 1 January 1993. The Second Directive will cause fundamental changes in the legal framework of the banking business in the Community, and will profoundly affect both the way in which banks will be doing business in the Community and the way in which non-Community banks can enter the European market.

. . .

THE SECOND DIRECTIVE

Institutional coverage

The Second Directive applies to "credit institutions." A credit institution is defined as an "undertaking whose business is to receive deposits or other repayable funds from the public and to grant credits for its own account." According to the Second Directive, credit institutions that are authorised and supervised as credit institutions by the competent authorities of their Home Member States[10] will benefit from mutual—i.e. Community-wide—recognition of their banking licences with respect to the activities enumerated in the Annex to the Second Directive (the "Annex") and for which they are licensed in the Home Member State. This means that the following entities or activities do not benefit from mutual recognition:

(a) entities that are not authorised and supervised as credit institutions, i.e. a deposit-taking institution, by a Member State, even though they are engaged in some of the activities set forth in the Annex (for example, if a company engages only in financial leasing, and as such is not authorised and supervised by the Home Member State as a credit institution, it is not a credit institution under the Second Directive, although financial leasing is an activity listed in the Annex); and

(b) entities that engage in activities not included in the Annex, even though they are authorised and supervised as credit institutions by a Member State.

Subsidiaries established in Community countries by non-Community persons under a licence for credit institutions are credit institutions benefitting from the principle of mutual recognition. In other words, non-Community ownership or control of a credit institution does not destroy the mutual recognition of the licence of the credit institution. Community branches of non-Community credit institutions are not authorised as credit institutions by a Member State and therefore do not benefit from mutual recognition.

.   .   .

The licence

The objective of the Second Directive is to create a truly Community-wide internal market for banking services.   "Credit institutions" authorised in the Home Member State will be entitled in each of the other Member States: (i) to establish branches; and (ii) to offer their services freely to individuals and businesses, in each case without the need for any further authorisation by the Host Member State.   Community credit institutions will be entitled to operate in this way under their Home Member State licences, which will be a Community-wide "single banking licence."

Thus, the Second Directive does not create a "Community" banking licence; but it decrees that each Member State's banking

---

[10] "Home Member State" of a credit institution as used in this chapter means that Member State of the Community where the credit institution has been licensed as a credit institution. "Host Member State" of a credit institution, as used in this chapter, means the Member State where a credit institution licensed as such in another Member State carries out activities or operates a branch.

licence shall be valid throughout the Community. The principle proposed by the Second Directive is one of "mutual recognition": each Member State recognises the banking licences of the other Member States. This principle differs radically from the concept of "national treatment," which merely entitles a foreign bank to the same treatment as a domestic bank. The principle of mutual recognition gives credit institutions in one Member State access to all Member States, and creates a Community-wide inter-Member State banking market.

The recognition of the Home Member licence required by the Second Directive is limited to certain specified banking activities or powers: the Home Member State licence is valid in other Member States only with respect to those specified banking activities that are enumerated in the Annex to the Second Directive. The Annex defines the scope of the principle of mutual recognition. Each Member State will have the duty to ensure that at least the activities listed in the Annex may be pursued in its territory by any credit institution authorised and supervised by the authorities of its Home Member State, either through the establishment of a branch or by way of the provision of services across the Member State border. However, the principle of mutual recognition extends only to a branch of a credit institution and not to a subsidiary credit institution, because a subsidiary cannot operate under the parent's licence. A subsidiary, being a separate entity, is required to have its own licence before it can engage in banking activities.

A credit institution licensed in a Member State may provide services throughout the Community with respect to banking activities that meet the following cumulative criteria: (i) the Home Member State licence must permit the pursuit of such activity, or in other words, must give the credit institutions the power to conduct such activity; and (ii) the activity must be set forth in the Annex.

As a consequence, any credit institution authorised as such in its Home Member State may exercise in the Host Member State activities that meet such criteria even if the same activities are not permitted to similar credit institutions of the Host Member State. For instance, if a bank is authorised by its Home Member State licence to participate in securities issues, it is permitted to do so anywhere in the Community, since participation in securities issues is an activity listed in the Annex. On the other hand, if the Home Member State licence does not authorise participation in securities issues, a credit institution may not engage in this activity in a Host Member State even if credit institutions licensed in the Host Member State are entitled to engage in this activity. If the Home Member State licence permits travel agency services, a credit institution still cannot conduct this activity in a Host Member State by virtue of the Second Directive, because travel agency services are not included in the Annex.

The banking powers permitted by the banking licence of a Member State may fall short of the powers enumerated in the Annex. In that case, credit institutions from other Member States may provide services in that Host Member State that credit institutions licensed in that particular Host Member State are not permitted to provide. A probable consequence of the Second Directive is that the powers permitted to banks in all Member States will soon include all the powers set forth in the Annex. The Second Directive will bring about an indirect harmonisation of law, if only by virtue of self-interest of the Member States.

Mutual recognition permits a Community credit institution to provide its services anywhere in the Community, irrespective of where it is licensed. However, the Second Directive forestalls "forum shopping" by obtaining a banking licence in a less restrictive Member State. It states that the principle of mutual recognition requires that Member States do not grant an authorisation or withdraw an existing authorisation where factors such as the credit institution's activities programme and the geographical distribution of activities actually carried on "make it quite clear" that the credit institution has opted for the legal system of one Member State for the purpose of evading the stricter standards in force in another Member State in which it intends to carry on, or if already authorised, where it is actually carrying on, the greater part of its activities.[35] Such power to refuse or withdraw an authorisation is only given to *Home* Member States. Host Member States do not have the power to refuse or withdraw an authorisation to operate a branch of a credit institution from another Member State. This provision will prevent the creation of a "banking Delaware" in the Community.

The Annex to the Second Directive sets forth the activities "integral to banking" that currently, in the opinion of the Commission, constitute the core of the traditional banking services in the Community:

1. acceptance of deposits and other repayable funds from the public;

2. lending, including, *inter alia,* consumer and mortgage credit, factoring with or without recourse, and financing of commercial transactions including forfaiting;

3. financial leasing;

4. money transmission services;

5. issuing and administering means of payment (e.g. credit cards, traveler's' cheques and bankers' drafts);

---

[35] Second Directive, 8th "whereas" clause. Member States must require that the head office of a credit institution is situated in the same Member State as the registered office, and a credit institution is deemed situated in the Member State where it has its registered office. Id.

6. guarantees and commitments;

7. trading for own account or for account of customers in

    (a) money market instruments (cheques, bills, CDS, etc.),

    (b) foreign exchange,

    (c) financial futures and options,

    (d) exchange and interest rate instruments,

    (e) transferable securities;

8. participation in share issues and the provision of services related to such issues;

9. advice to undertakings on capital structure, industrial strategy and related questions, and advice and services relating to mergers and the purchase of undertakings;

10.   money broking;

11.   portfolio management and advice;

12.   safekeeping and administration of securities;

13.   credit reference services;

14.   safe custody services.

The Annex is based on the liberal "universal banking" model; it does not distinguish between investment banking and commercial banking, and does not embrace the philosophy of the US Glass-Steagall Act, which in the US prohibits commercial banks from the underwriting of and dealing in corporate debt or equity securities and from being affiliated with companies engaged in such business. Thus, the Annex permits a wide range of securities powers.

The Commission recommends that the Annex be updated under the flexible procedure so that it can respond to the development of new banking services. The Commission obviously wishes to avoid repeating the experience of US banking law, which does not easily respond to changing market environments.

Branch establishment

Under the Second Directive, a Member State may not require a credit institution already authorised in another Member State to obtain a licence before it is permitted to establish a branch in its territory.

A credit institution wishing to establish a branch in another Member State need only inform the authorities of its Home Member State of its intention to set up a branch in the Host Member State. This notification must be accompanied by certain information concerning the credit institution and the branch, in particular the programme of operations and the structural organisation of the branch. The Home Member State authorities must communicate this information, and information on the amount of own funds and the

Solvency Ratio of the credit institution, to the authorities of the prospective Host Member State within three months. The only measure that can be taken against the establishment of the branch is a refusal by the Home Member State authorities to inform the Host Member State. This measure may be taken if the Home Member State authorities have reason to doubt the adequacy of the credit institution's organisational structure or its financial situation. The Home Member State must give reasons for such refusal, which is subject to a right of appeal to the courts of the Home Member State.

The Second Directive abolishes the initial endowment capital that is currently required by the majority of Member States for the authorisation of branches of credit institutions already authorised in other Member States.

Allocation of supervision

The Second Directive is based on the principle of "home country control," under which each credit institution will generally be supervised by the authorities of its Home Member State, even in regard to activities carried out across the borders of, or through a branch located in, another Member State. There are only a few exceptions to that rule.

As a result of insufficient harmonisation of liquidity standards and insufficient co-ordination in the implementation of monetary policy in the Community within the framework of the European Monetary System, the Second Directive proposes that, as an exception to the principle of home country control, the Host Member State, pending further co-ordination, will retain primary responsibility for the supervision of liquidity of the branches of credit institutions and exclusive responsibility for the implementation of monetary policy. These measures, however, must not embody discriminatory or restrictive treatment based on the fact that the credit institution is authorised in another Member State.

Although the activities of a credit institution's branches in a Host Member State will generally be supervised by the authorities of the Home Member State according to the rules of the Host Member State, those branches still have to comply with the legal provisions in force in the Host Member State which have been "adopted in the interest of the general good." It remains to be seen whether Member States will use this provision to make inroads against the rule of Home Member State supervision.

. . .

Investments in the non-bank entities

In order to control potential risks to the financial stability of credit institutions arising out of investments in non-banking corporations, the Second Directive contains provisions on investments in non-credit and non-financial institutions. These investments ("participations") require particular attention, because they may affect the financial stability of the investing credit institution. Participations in a subsidiary may affect the soundness of the credit institution if the former runs into financial difficulties ("contagion risk") and equity participations constitute a long-term freezing of the assets of the investing credit institution.

The Second Directive requires harmonisation of the differing standards of the Member States regarding equity participations by credit institutions by limiting credit institutions in the following two respects, if they wish to acquire or maintain participations in non-credit or non-financial institutions:

(a) a credit institution may not hold a qualifying (10 per cent or more) holding of an amount greater than 15 per cent of its own funds in an undertaking that is neither a credit institution nor a financial institution; and

(b) the total value of such qualifying holdings may not exceed 60 per cent of own funds of the credit institution.

These limits do not apply to shares held only (i) temporarily during a financial rescue or restructuring operation, (ii) during the normal course of the underwriting process, or (iii) in the institution's own name on behalf of others.

The limits mentioned above may be exceeded in exceptional circumstances. However, in that case the supervisory authorities of the Home Member State of the credit institution exceeding its limits must require such credit institution to increase its own funds or to take other equivalent measures. Compliance with these limits shall be ensured by the authorities of the Home Member State by means of supervision on a consolidated basis in accordance with the Directive on Consolidated Supervision. The authorities of the Home Member State need not apply these limits if they require that 100 per cent of the amounts by which a credit institution's qualifying holdings exceed those limits must be covered by own funds and that the latter shall not be included in the calculation of the solvency ratio.

As a formal matter, the SBD has been superseded by Directive 2000/12/EC of the European Parliament and the Council, March 20, 2000, which codifies the SBD along with other legislation relating to banking, e.g. the Capital Adequacy Directive. The substance of the SBD was not changed.

b. NOTIFICATION

The SBD allows banks to provide cross-border banking services, as well as branch services, as determined by the home state (subject to the agreed list). Article 20 requires that "any credit institution wishing to exercise the freedom to provide services by carrying on its activities within the territory of another Member State for the first time shall notify the competent authorities of the host Member State of the activities on the list in the Annex which it intends to carry on." Banks must also notify their home country authorities of their intention to offer cross-border services and receive approval to do so from the home country.

The notification requirement has raised difficult issues of interpretation with respect to what is a cross-border service. Provision of safe custody services, i.e. the renting of a safe deposit box, is on the Annex list. Would a German bank renting such deposit boxes for a yearly fee to citizens of all EC states have to notify each state of this service? Suppose it had offered the same service in the past for a monthly fee? Suppose the German bank's local EC branches solicit customers for the service, must the German bank still provide a notice? See D. George, *Cross-Border Banking Business and the Second Banking Directive: Legal Uncertainty Resulting from the Notification Requirement*, International Banking and Financial Law, Sept. 1994 at 373. There appears to be a very uneven practice among banks in different countries in supplying notifications. In 1993-94, U.K. and German authorities respectively received 123 and 116 notifications from their own institutions compared with Italy and Spain which respectively received 5 and 3 notifications. And in the same period, Belgium received 144 notifications from foreign institutions as compared with the U.K. and Germany which respectively received 59 and 49 notifications. K. Lannoo, *The Single Market in Banking: A First Assessment*, Butterworths Journal of International Banking and Financial Law, Nov. 1995, at 485, 487 (Lannoo). It would seem difficult to attribute this data to actual patterns of services. For example, it seems doubtful that Spanish banks are only offering cross-border services at 2.6% the rate of German banks.

The Commission has issued an Interpretative Communication covering when notification of a cross-border service is required, No. C209/04 (O.J. 10.71.97) (1997 Communication). It provides that notification will not be required unless "the place of provision of what may be termed the 'characteristic performance' of the service, i.e. the essential supply for which payment is due," is carried out in the territory of another Member State. Temporarily visiting another state to carry on an activity preceding the supply of a service, e.g. a survey of property prior to granting a loan, or to conclude a contract for the service would not involve "characteristic performance," and thus would not require a notice. Nor would engaging in cross-border advertising, whether general or targeted require a notice.

A further issue is raised as to whether a given service is being offered on a cross-border basis or through a branch. Some host states take the view that there is a branch establishment whenever services are provided on a regular basis in their territory. A branch (unlike a cross-border service provider) has the duty to provide statistical information and to pay levies in the host country, and will also be subject to EU deposit insurance requirements as set forth in C2 of this Chapter. Id. at 486.

Notes and Questions

1. The SBD applies to credit institutions, "undertakings whose business is to receive deposits or other repayable funds from the public and to grant credits for its own account." Why not cover institutions providing either function?

2. The SBD provides that a bank incorporated in one state (home state) can offer in another state (host state) any service it can offer in its home state (that is on an agreed list) and will be supervised by the home state authorities. Does this mean a German bank could offer a type of deposit account or life insurance in France even if French banks were not authorized by French law to do so?

3. What if a Greek bank could not do financial leasing in Greece but wanted to do so in Germany even though German banks could not offer the service in Germany. What could it do? Gruson and Feuring, text at note 35, refer to the 8th "whereas" clause in SBD. It provides:

> Whereas the principles of mutual recognition and of home Member State control require the competent authorities of each Member State not to grant authorization or to withdraw it where factors such as the activities programme, the geographical distribution or the activities actually carried on make it quite clear that a credit institution has opted for the legal system of one Member State for the purpose of evading the stricter standards in force in another Member State in which it intends to carry on or carries on the greater part of its activities; whereas, for the purposes of this Directive, a credit institution shall be deemed to be situated in the Member State in which it has its registered office; whereas the Member States must require that the head office be situated in the same Member State as the registered office;

In July 1993 the Commission proposed that the SBD be amended to provide that "the head office of a financial undertaking must be in the same Member State as its registered office and that in which the authorization [license] is being required." COM(93) 363 final—SYN 468 (1993 O.J. (C229/10)) (1993 Proposals). When the European Parliament considered this proposal in March 1994, the Parliament suggested replacing the term "head office" with "central administration, where the most important decision making bodies are established." The Commission supported the idea, but the Council of Ministers rejected it. On its second reading in October 1994, the Parliament supported another alternative to "head office": "where the undertaking's governing bodies are established." This was ultimately resolved by returning to the Commission's 1993 proposals, European Parliament and Council Directive 95/26/EC (L168/7, 18.7.95). Article 3 of the SBD has been amended to provide that:

Each Member State shall require that:

— any credit institution which is a legal person and which, under its national law has a registered office, have its head office in the same Member State as its registered office,

— any other credit institution have its head office in the Member State which issued its authorization and in which it actually carries on its business.

The term "head office" is additionally important because it determines the "home country" for purposes of supervision, as well as for permissible activities (subject to the agreed list).

Could the Greek bank offer the service in Greece through a branch of a Spanish bank subsidiary, employing a "roundtrip" strategy?

c.   THE GENERAL GOOD

In 1992, France prohibited a French subsidiary of Barclays from transferring interest on unit trust accounts (mutual funds) to a demand deposit account as an evasion of the French prohibition on paying interest on demand deposit accounts. According to the then-Finance Minister Socialist Michael Sapin, remunerated checking accounts would increase the cost of credit and force banks to charge for checking. According to Sapin, checking charges would have the biggest impact on poorer customers for whom checking services were free. Barclay's offered this service in the U.K. and "acceptance of deposits and other repayable funds from the public" was on the agreed list of services. Under SBD would France be able to prohibit a branch of Barclays from offering the service? Would this fall into the monetary policy exception to mutual recognition?

As Gruson and Feuring point out, host states can adopt measures "in the interest of the general good." These measures must be equally applicable to domestic and foreign entities. Such a "safeguard" clause has been common in various EU directives based on mutual recognition. The European Court of Justice, in its landmark decision in *Cassis de Dijon*, Case 120/78, 1979 E.C.R. 649, held that such clauses did not allow host states to set their own technical or qualitative standards for imported goods where the home states (member states of origin) had already set essential minimum standards. But EU case law may be departing from this approach by allowing host state "general good" requirements that apply *de jure* and *de facto* to domestic as well as foreign firms. See G. Hertig, *Imperfect Mutual Recognition for EC Financial Services*, 14 International Review of Law and Economics 177 (1994). Should France be able to require all banks, including branches of EC banks, to make disclosures about how interest rates are calculated on loans to retail borrowers?

Mortgage loans have been a focal point for "general good" issues. U.K. building societies offer variable rate mortgages which are not acceptable in Belgium which regulates mortgage rates strictly. German banks offer long-term mortgages that prohibit early repayment; this restriction violates consumer protection laws in France and Belgium. Lannoo at 488.

The Commission's 1997 Communication points to six criteria, based in case law, for determining the general good: (1) the measure must not be discriminatory; (2) the measure must not impose higher requirements than those of a Harmonization Directive covering the subject; (3) the measure must have a general good objective; (4) the general good objective must not already be safeguarded in the country of origin; (5) the measure must be capable of guaranteeing that the objective will be met; and (6) the measure does not go beyond what is necessary to achieve the objective pursued. The last criterion, "proportionality," may often be the hardest to satisfy.

d. CROSS-BORDER SUPERVISION

The SBD leaves supervision to home countries. The home country must supervise banking groups, and a 1992 Council Directive, 92/30/EEC (OJ L110/52, 28.4.92) established the principle of consolidated supervision of the various entities within a banking group. EU banks are subject to common supervisory standards, such as capital requirements, single exposure limits, limitations on investments in non-financial institutions etc. And EU supervisors are in close touch through various supervisors' committees. The Banking Advisory Committee (BAC) is attached to the European Commission and comprises high level representatives of Member States' supervisory authorities, finance ministries and central banks. The BAC's primary role is to assist the Commission in formulating legislation and to give advice on regulation and supervision.

In October 1998 the Banking Supervision Committee (BSC) of the European System of Central Banks was set up to assist the European Central Bank (ECB) in formulating macro-economic policy. The oldest group is the Groupe de Contact (GDC) which is not formally attached to any institution. It is composed of mid-management banking supervisors from EU countries who are involved in the day-to-day supervision of banks. Group members are in regular contact and exchange confidential information on individual cases relevant to banking supervision. European Commission, Internal Market Directorate General, *Institutional Arrangements for the Regulation and Supervision of the Financial Sector,* January 2000. In addition, countries haven entered into bilateral Memoranda of Understanding (MOU) establishing cooperative procedures, see e.g. the French-German MOU. Does this solve the potential BCCI problem?

The Commission has adopted a new Directive, that has been pending consideration since 1985, providing that when a credit institution with branches in other Member States fails, the insolvency (winding up) process will be subject to a single bankruptcy proceeding in the home state of the failed institution. This is consistent with the home country supervision principle. 2335 Council - ECOFIN, Press Release, March 12, 2001.

The actual conduct of banking supervision in the member states is done by different institutions. In some countries, it is done by the central bank, e.g. the Banca d'Italia in Italy, in other countries by a banking supervisory agency, e.g. Bundesaufsichtsamt für das Kreditwesen in Germany, the Ministry of Finance, e.g. Austria, or a consolidated supervisory agency with responsibility for all financial institutions, e.g. the Financial Supervisory Agency (FSA) in the United Kingdom.

The FSA was created in May 1997, when the new Labor government in the U.K. announced a total restructuring of the regulatory regime for financial services, the most radical feature of which was to combine banking supervision and securities regulation under an enlarged Securities and Investments Board (SIB) called the Financial Supervisory Authority (FSA). The plan was implemented in 1998. Banking supervision had previously been conducted by the Bank of England. Another major part of the reform was to fold existing self-regulatory organizations (SROs) into the FSA. The rationale for the change is the existence of universal banking under which financial firms engage in both securities and banking activities. See *Financial Regulatory Reform in the U.K.,* 16 International Banking and Financial Law 47 (1997). The FSA has a MOU with the Bank of England, entered into in 1997, which makes it clear that the Bank is responsible for the overall stability of the financial system, including monetary policy, whereas the FSA is responsible for the authorization, supervision and regulation of financial institutions. Other countries are beginning to follow this model. Germany announced a similar plan on the heels of the announcement that Allianz, a leading German insurer, was to acquire Dresdner bank. The German plan, unlike the FSA, did not eliminate the existing separate regulators of banking, securities and insurance, but would combine them within one central body. H. Simonian, *Germany aims for unified finance market supervision,* Financial Times, April 12, 2001. Germany passed a law to this effect on March 22, 2002, BNA Banking Report, April 15, 2002. The FSA seeks to use a consistent approach to controlling risks of various kinds across the entire range of financial institutions. FSA, *A New Regulator for the New Millenium,* January 2000.

A long-standing debate has gone on about whether the central bank should have supervisory power on a EU wide basis because of the possible connection between supervision and monetary policy or whether some other supervisory body should be created. Not surprisingly, the European Central Bank has taken the position that it should be entrusted with this role. European Central Bank, *The Role of Central Banks in Prudential*

Supervision, March 22, 2001. Preservation of a supervisory role for the central bank is seemingly inconsistent with consolidation of supervision along the lines of the FSA model because of the unlikelihood that the central bank would become the supervisor of non-banking firms.

In April 2001, the European Commission proposed a new Directive to deal with financial conglomerates, COM(2001) 213 final, April 24, 2001. The proposal seeks to eliminate some inconsistencies in existing Directives applicable to what the Commission calls homogeneous financial groups, e.g. banking or insurance groups. In addition, it seeks to insure that regulation of different sectors, e.g. banking, is not undermined by financial conglomerate. Specifically, it seeks to insure that the same capital is not used to support different regulated institutions. It does not seek to regulate capital at the holding company level (as in the United States). The proposal also seeks to address supervisory concerns about intra-group transactions and risk exposures built on three pillars: effective internal management systems, reporting requirements to supervisors and effective enforcement. It does not seek to impose quantitative limits on such transactions (as in the United States). In addition, it envisions new mechanisms of cooperation among existing supervisors. It would appear that this approach is somewhat at odds with the consolidation approach of the FSA within the U.K. The Commission seeks to preserve and coordinate separate sectoral regulation, whereas the FSA seeks to consolidate regulation in one supervisor.

As we shall see in Chapter 7, European Monetary Union (EMU) began to be implemented on January 1, 1999. Supervision of banking institutions remained with local supervisors and was not moved to the ECB. The IMF believes that the advent of EMU may greatly accelerate cross-border banking in Europe. If this occurs, the IMF questions whether national supervision can remain viable, and suggests it should be replaced with supervision at the European Union level through the ECB. R. Chote, *IMF warns European banks over euro,* Financial Times, September 23, 1997. The Maastricht Treaty gives ECB a limited role in supervision.

The Treaty entrusts the ESCB with contributing "to the smooth conduct of policies pursued by the competent authorities relating to prudential supervision of credit institutions and the stability of the financial system, Article 105(5) EC Treaty and Article 3.3 ESCB Statute. Further, the ECOFIN Council may entrust the ECB with "specific tasks concerning policies relating to the prudential supervision of credit institutions...." Could this be the basis of ECB becoming the EU banking supervisor? Should the ECB become the EU banking supervisor? See R. Smits, *Banking Supervision in the monetary union,* 1 Journal of International Banking Regulation 122 (1999); C. Hadjiemmanuil and M. Andenas, *Banking Supervision and European Monetary Union,* 1 Journal of International Banking Regulation 84 (1999); and T. Padoa-Schioppa, *EMU and Banking Supervision*, 2 International Finance 295 (1999).

Howard Davies, the head of the U.K.'s FSA opposes giving supervisory authority to the ECB. He contends that "concentrating banking supervision in the ECB, or indeed anywhere else, would almost certainly be quite the wrong way to go, at a time when the boundaries between banking and other regulation are becoming blurred." H. Davies, *Euro-regulation*, 1 The Journal of International Banking Regulation 113, 116 (1999).

In April, 2002 the United Kingdom and Germany proposed that banking supervision in the EU be handled by a forum of member state finance authorities, including the ECB and central banks, the ECB continued to advocate the role for itself alone. 78 BNA Banking Report 755 (April 29, 2002).

Notes and Questions

1. How would the United Kingdom protect itself against a shaky Luxembourg bank's branch taking U.K. deposits (the BCCI problem)?

2. Although the SBD has been in force in the majority of member states since January 1993, and its geographical scope was extended to cover most EFTA countries from January 1994, the Bank of England has reported, based on a survey of 25 firms, that the SBD has had limited impact. Most increased competition was either from existing players in the domestic market or non-banks. Banks have not used the single passport to establish de novo branches in other EU states; future expansion has rather been by acquisition. The major use of the directive has been for banks to convert existing subsidiaries into branches to permit a more efficient allocation of capital. *The Developing Single Market in Financial Services*, 34 Bank of England Quarterly Bulletin 341, 344 (1994). These findings differ somewhat from those of a study of the European Commission, *Impact on Services, Credit Institutions and Banking,* The Single Market Review, Subseries II: Volume 3 (1997). This study found that from 1992-1995 cross-border branches increased by 179, 32 of which represented conversion of existing subsidiaries, Table 4.15, at p. 55. One would assume that 179 is a rather small number considering the total number of branches (domestic plus cross-border) in the EU. The study concludes that there was more significant activity from cross-border mergers and acquisitions, id. at 64. However, it also indicated that overall cross-border financial activity increased by a small amount from 1992-1997, id. at 51.

3. A significant issue for the single market in banking concerns subsidies for state-owned banks that could give such banks competitive advantages. EU competition rules come into play in trying to control such subsidies. For example, when France in July 1995 injected $9.37 billion into Crédit Lyonnais to rescue it from failing, the Commission extracted

some promises from France to limit future aid and to reduce by 35 percent the presence of the bank outside France, including a sale of a substantial part of its 900 office banking network. *Rescue at Crédit Lyonnais*, Financial Times, July 27, 1995.

In 1999, the state aid focus was on the German Landesbanks. In July, the Commission forced the Westdeutsche Landesbank (WestLB) to repay its owner, the regional government of North-Rhine Westphalia, $834 million, representing the value of a state housing agency that the government had transferred to the bank in 1992 at no cost. The Landesbanks (banks owned by various regional governments) which do more than a third of Germany's banking business, receive guarantees of their assets from their government owners allowing them to obtain AAA credit ratings, thus putting them at a competitive advantage. *Germany's Landesbanks set for the moment of truth,* Financial Times, July 8, 1999. When the Landesbanks failed to devise a satisfactory plan for repayment, the Commission referred the case to the European Court of Justice where it is now pending, The Economist, April 15, 2000. In February 2001, WestLB proposed setting up a subsidiary that would take over competitive activities such as corporate lending and investment banking. WestLB proposed giving its subsidiary a "comfort letter" that looks like a guarantee. The Commission has said this is a step in the right direction but not enough. *Co-operative Spirit,* The Economist, February 17, 2001.

Government ownership of banks is pervasive. R. La Porta, F. Lopez-de-Silanes and A. Shleifer, *Government Ownership of Banks,* National Bureau of Economic Research, Working Paper 7620 (March 2000), found that average ownership by governments of their 10 largest banks was 41.74 percent. While the U.K. was at zero, France, Germany and Italy were respectively at 17.26, 36.36 and 35.95 percent. The authors found that government ownership of banks is associated with slower subsequent financial development, lower subsequent growth of per capital income and with lower productivity.

4. There is a concern that the single market in banking may be partially undermined by government policies preventing cross-border acquisitions. In June 1999, the Portuguese government vetoed a link-up between Spain's Banco Santander Central Hispano (BSCH) and Mundial Confiança (MC), Portugal's third largest financial group. The Commission challenged the Portuguese action on the grounds that it constituted a violation of freedom of establishment as guaranteed by the Treaty of Rome having found that the veto could not be justified on prudential grounds. Portugal then backed down to some extent, allowing BSCH to gain control of two of the MC's subsidiary banks but requiring BSCH to transfer a third bank to Caixa Geral de Depositos (CGD), a state-owned bank. *Portuguese banking plays the end game,* Retail Banker International, January 28, 2000. A signal that protectionism may be

waning is the acquisition in April 2000 of the French bank Crédit Commercial de France by the U.K. based HSBC, the world's second largest banking organization after Citigroup.

H. SCOTT, RECIPROCITY AND THE SECOND BANKING DIRECTIVE, IN THE SINGLE MARKET AND THE LAW OF BANKING
85-91 (R. Cranston ed., 1991).

The European Economic Community (EC) adopted its Second Banking Directive on 15 December 1989. Article 9 of this Directive incorporates a reciprocity requirement requiring other countries to give certain specified treatment to EC banks as a condition for banks from these countries taking advantage of the Directive's liberal rules for providing banking services within the EC.

Article 9(3) provides that if the Commission determines "that a third country is not granting Community credit institutions effective market access comparable to that granted by the Community to credit institutions from that third country", the Council may authorise the Commission to open up negotiations to obtain such "comparable competitive opportunities" for EC credit institutions.

Article 9(4) provides that negotiations may also be opened by the Commission on its own, without Council authorisation, whenever it appears to the Commission "that Community credit institutions in a third country do not receive national treatment offering the same competitive opportunities as are available to domestic credit institutions and that the conditions of effective market access are not fulfilled." Furthermore, such a determination may also lead to Member States being required to close their markets to "acquisition of holdings by direct or indirect parent undertakings governed by the laws of the third country in question."

Article 9(4) also provides that such acquisition bans cannot apply to acquisitions that have already been made or to future acquisitions of entities already authorised to operate in the EC. Existing authorised institutions from third countries are thus grandfathered, and are treated on a par with EC institutions.

In short, lack of effective market access for EC institutions can lead to negotiations, whereas lack of national treatment and effective market access can lead to either negotiations or prospective entry bans. There is considerable ambiguity about the use of the word "and." If the "and" is conjunctive, then two findings would be required for an entry ban: lack of national treatment, and effective market access. This holds out the possibility that EC institutions might have effective market access in a country even where there was a lack of national treatment. On the other hand, if the "and" is disjunctive, the EC could impose an entry ban where there was national treatment but no effective market access.

.   .   .

Note

The EU Schedule of Commitments under the GATS, entered into in 1997, precludes use of the SBD reciprocity requirements against countries that tabled their own MFN Commitments (which now includes the U.S.). Once the GATS is actually adopted by such countries (through their treaty approval processes), the reciprocity requirement will be "history."

2. DEPOSIT INSURANCE

R. DALE, DEPOSIT INSURANCE: POLICY CLASH OVER EC AND US REFORMS

13-16 (May 1993) (unpublished paper presented at London School of Economics).

In 1986 the EC Commission issued a recommendation to the effect that all member states should put in place some form of deposit insurance, although there was no specification of minimum (or maximum) coverage. At this time the EC favoured a territorial approach for national schemes, apparently on the grounds that this would ensure competitive equity for banks operating within any given jurisdiction.

In June 1992 the EC followed its earlier recommendation with a proposal for a Council Directive on deposit guarantee schemes. This was amended in December 1992 and again in March 1993. The stated objectives are to provide some degree of consumer protection while also strengthening systemic stability ("the costs of a run on the banking system may outweigh the costs of imposing a deposit protection check scheme"). The major elements of the proposal can be summarised as follows:

(1) A key principle—representing a reversal of the 1986 recommendation—is that branch depositors should be protected by the home member state, i.e. where the bank has its head office. The stated rationale for this approach is that it locates responsibility for deposit protection in the jurisdiction that also has supervisory responsibility.

(2) The proposal establishes a minimum level of deposit protection in all member states, both with regard to the size of protected deposits and the kinds of deposit to be protected. The minimum size of a protected deposit is set at 15,000 ECU, except that where a member state chooses to adopt a 90% pay-out option (involving an element of coinsurance) the minimum size of the protected deposit is ECU 16,500. Inter-bank deposits and subordinated debt are specifically

excluded from insurance coverage, while debt securities and bearer instruments may be excluded.

(3) There is an optional "top-up" provision which allows branches to join a host country deposit insurance scheme. This enables the branch to offer the same level of protection accorded to local banks operating under the host scheme, in cases where the host scheme is more generous than the home scheme. Furthermore, the revised proposal includes a "no export" clause, whereby branches will not be permitted to offer deposit protection in excess of the "host" country, in cases where the home scheme is more generous than the host scheme.

(4) There are no harmonisation requirements relating to the maximum insurance coverage, which is left to the discretion of member states, nor to funding arrangements or the pricing of deposit insurance. Furthermore, schemes may be administered by either the private or public sector.

When assessed in the light of the previous discussion there appear to be serious problems with the EC's general approach to harmonisation of deposit insurance schemes.

In the first place the proposal represents an awkward compromise between existing national schemes that have quite different objectives. This is most clearly evident in the option accorded to national authorities to incorporate an element of co-insurance, involving depositors in losses of up to 10% of their protected deposits. The co-insurance option appears to be designed to accommodate schemes (such as Germany's) which offer virtually full protection in the interests of systemic stability as well as schemes (notably the UK's) whose main purpose is to protect consumers. However, as pointed out above, co-insurance is unsuited to a deposit protection regime intended to prevent bank runs. The Brussels proposal, instead of establishing clear EC policy priorities, permits the co-existence of rival national schemes with conflicting aims.

To the extent that the EC initiative on deposit insurance is intended to contribute to systemic stability, there is a further difficulty. On the one hand, the EC proposal openly acknowledges the moral hazard dangers of deposit protection and, indeed, cites recent US banking instability as an example of what can happen when deposit protection is excessive. On the other hand, the proposal contains no provisions dealing with the problem of moral hazard—a matter that is by implication left entirely to the discretion of national authorities. In particular, deposit protection can be open-ended (as in Germany) over and above the required minimum level and there are no requirements on the pricing of deposit insurance. Therefore, while the US is responding actively to its own experience of excessive risk-taking associated with 100% de facto deposit protection (above) the EC appears to be largely ignoring these lessons.

In so far as the EC proposal is concerned with eliminating potential competitive distortions, more problems arise. To begin with the key question of funding and pricing of deposit insurance is left largely to the discretion of national authorities. Furthermore, the optional top-up scheme and the "no export" clause ((3) above) are designed to create a level playing field within each national jurisdiction but do so at the cost of creating uneven deposit insurance coverage between member states and between different offices of the same bank. It is paradoxical that in a single European financial market competitive equality should be so overtly sacrificed at the inter-jurisdictional level in an attempt to ensure competitive equality within each Member State's territory.

More generally, the latitude allowed under the harmonisation proposal means that schemes to which banks operating within the EC are subject may vary in the following key respects:

(1) Some schemes will apply the Directive's minimum insurance coverage, others will be more generous.

(2) Some schemes will require insured depositors to absorb up to 10% of deposit losses, others will exclude such coinsurance.

(3) Some bank branches may choose to top up the home country's deposit insurance to the level of the host country's scheme (where higher). Other banks may decline this option.

(4) The coverage of certain categories of wholesale depositor, as well as various categories of financial instrument will vary between schemes.

(5) Branches of banks originating from outside the EC may be subject to the home-country scheme or the host-country scheme.

The authors of the EC proposed Directive are confident that this diversity is workable since a variety of schemes already co-exist within member states. However, the EC proposal makes no allowance for the fact that European regulators have generally preferred to bail out failing banks rather than rely on deposit insurance arrangements. To the extent that this attitude persists, the deposit insurance Directive will be largely redundant. But if there is a change of approach and banks are permitted to fail, then confusion caused by a multiplicity of schemes could prompt calls for full harmonisation of insurance schemes.

Finally, for reasons explained in the previous section, a proposal that focuses exclusively on deposit insurance while neglecting other aspects of the official safety net, cannot be expected to achieve either systemic stability or competitive equity.

The general conclusion, therefore, is that the EC proposal on deposit insurance is either too far-reaching or too limited in scope. It is too far-reaching in that national authorities are being required to adapt their own schemes to a complex common formula which professes to be aimed at financial stabilisation and consumer protection, but which does not appear to make a significant contribution to either. And it is too limited in scope because if these goals are to be achieved a much more radical harmonisation initiative is called for, embracing issues such as moral hazard and procedures for handling failed banks.

————————

The ceilings for some key countries are:

Current Deposit Guarantee Ceilings, Selected Countries (euros)[1]

Country	Ceiling
Germany	Virtually unlimited[2]
Italy	103,291[3]
Japan	60,853
United States	85,708
France	60,980
U.K.	22,222[4]
Spain	20,000

Source: Bank for International Settlements, *70th Annual Report*, June 5, 2000, Table VII.6
1. As of end-1998
2. 30% of a private bank's equity capital
3. 100% of first Lit 200mm
4. 90% of protected deposits, maximum euro equivalent of £20,000

Notes and Questions

1.   The Council of the European Union issued a Common Position On the Proposal For A Directive On Deposit-Guarantee Schemes on October 25, 1993 which went into effect on January 1, 1995. Directive 94/19/EC of the European Parliament and of the Council, OJ 1994, L 135/5, May 30, 1994. It differs in some respects from the earlier proposal described by Professor Dale. First, the deposit minimum is ECU 20,000 although states whose current coverage is below that level, need only provide 15,000 worth of coverage until December 31, 1999. Second, home states are only prohibited until December 31, 1999 from insuring above the host state maximum. The limitation will be reassessed at that time. Also, certain deposits are excluded from the scheme, for example deposits of other banks or large corporations.

In its May 13, 1997 judgment in C-233/94, Federal Republic of Germany v. European Parliament and the Council of the European Union,

ECR 1997, I-2405, the European Court of Justice rejected a German challenge to the Deposit-Guarantee Directive. The Germans brought the case because the Directive prevented Germany until the end of 1999 from providing unlimited insurance to its foreign branches. See A. Landsmeer and M. Van Empel, *The Directive on deposit-guarantee schemes and the directive on investor compensation schemes in view of Case C-233/94,* European Financial Services Law 143 (July/August 1998).

2. In the United States, until 1991, depositors in U.S. branches of foreign banks that took retail deposits had to be insured by the United States. After 1991, retail deposit branches are prospectively prohibited—foreign banks must take retail deposits through subsidiaries. The United States abolished retail insured branches of foreign banks largely out of concern that it—the host state—might have to pay for the supervisory failures of a foreign country. Why didn't the EU follow the same approach?

3. The EU scheme prevents home states from providing insurance above the level of host states—the "no export" clause. Do you agree that such a limitation is necessary for an even playing field? The EU scheme permits branches of out-of-state EU banks, whose insurance is below the level of a host state, to join the host state deposit scheme in order to "top-up" their insurance to the level of the host state. Germany currently has unlimited insurance coverage for deposits. How do you think it feels about the no export and top-up provisions? Will out-of-state banks from low insurance countries want to top-up?

The Future of the Single Market

This Chapter has concentrated on the European Union as a single market. For the most part, this entails a picture of a firm doing business throughout the various domestic markets within the EU, e.g. a U.K. bank opening a German branch. With respect to some financial services, banks and securities firms must seek out customers in local markets, but this is generally not true for wholesale services. For example, German corporations can put their money, in whatever currency, in a U.K. bank located in the U.K. or borrow money from a U.K. bank located in the U.K. Or, a German institutional investor could trade in German stocks listed on the London Stock Exchange through a U.K. broker. And even with respect to retail services, location near the customer is less and less important, given electronic distribution of services (e.g. credit cards).

So, another key element of the picture is competition between countries to become European, or perhaps even worldwide, financial centers providing financial services. London is now the European center of such services by various measures, e.g. proportion of non-resident deposits and claims, number of foreign banks, share of foreign exchange trading, although its share is falling. H. Rose, International Banking Developments and London's Position as an International Banking Centre

(City Research Project, July 1994).   Indeed, in 1994 Deutsche Bank, Germany's largest bank, located its investment banking activities in London rather than Frankfurt.   This followed its earlier acquisition of Morgan Grenfell, a U.K. investment bank.   However, Germany, particularly with respect to capital markets, is hoping to attract business to Frankfurt, away from London and other financial centers.   *Bowing Smartly to the Inevitable*, Euromoney Capital Reports, July 1994, at 76.

Links to Other Chapters

The EU has adopted an internal mutual recognition approach in the banking and securities areas that goes considerably beyond the U.S.'s and Japan's willingness to defer to the regulatory regimes of other countries (Chapters 2, 3 and 7).   This reflects the degree of political union.   The EU does not apply the mutual recognition approach to non-EU countries; indeed regulation of financial institutions from non-EU countries is left up to each EU country.   Capital adequacy standards for banks and securities firms, CAD, dealt with in the last Chapter, underpins the "single passport" approach.   The integration of the internal market is looked upon as part of the greater financial integration contemplated by Maastricht, examined in the next Chapter.

Offshore markets in "eurosecurities" particularly Eurobonds, are looked at extensively in Chapter 12, and the role of European stock exchanges in worldwide competition is covered in Chapter 14 on Stock Exchange Competition.   We will also look again in that Chapter at the Club Med proposals whose essential aim was to limit stock market competition.

APPENDIX

Council Directive 93/22/EEC of May 10, 1993 on Investment Services in the Securities Field, 1993 O.J. (L 141/27).

TITLE I

Definitions and scope

Article 1

For the purposes of this Directive:

1. *investment service* shall mean any of the services listed in Section A of the Annex relating to any of the instruments listed in Section B of the Annex that are provided for a third party;

2. *investment firm* shall mean any legal person the regular occupation or business of which is the provision of investment services for third parties on a professional basis.

For the purposes of this Directive, Member States may include as investment firms undertakings which are not legal persons if:

— their legal status ensures a level of protection for third parties' interests equivalent to that afforded by legal persons, and

— they are subject to equivalent prudential supervision appropriate to their legal form.

.   .   .

6. *home Member State* shall mean:

(a) where the investment firm is a natural person, the Member State in which his head office is situated;

(b) where the investment firm is a legal person, the Member State in which its registered office is situated or, if under its national law it has no registered office, the Member State in which its head office is situated;

(c) in the case of a market, the Member State in which the registered office of the body which provides trading facilities is situated or, if under its national law it has no registered office, the Member State in which that body's head office is situated;

.   .   .

13.   *regulated market* shall mean a market for the instruments listed in Section B of the Annex which:

— appears on the list provided for in Article 16 drawn up by the Member State which is the home Member State as defined in Article 1(6)(c),

— functions regularly,

— is characterized by the fact that regulations issued or approved by the competent authorities define the conditions for the operation of the market, the conditions for access to the market and, where Directive 79/279/EEC is applicable, the conditions governing admission to listing imposed in that Directive and, where that Directive is not applicable, the conditions that must be satisfied by a financial instrument before it can effectively be dealt in on the market,

— requires compliance with all the reporting and transparency requirements laid down pursuant to Articles 20 and 21;

.   .   .

Article 3

.   .   .

3. Without prejudice to other conditions of general application laid down by national law, the competent authorities shall not grant authorization unless:

— an investment firm has sufficient initial capital in accordance with the rules laid down in Directive 93-6-EEC having regard to the nature of the investment service in question,

— the persons who effectively direct the business of an investment firm are of sufficiently good repute and are sufficiently experienced.

The direction of a firm's business must be decided by at least two persons meeting the above conditions. Where an appropriate arrangement ensures that the same result will be achieved, however, particularly in the cases provided for in the last indent of the third subparagraph of Article 1(2), the competent authorities may grant authorization to investment firms which are natural persons or, taking account of the nature and volume of their activities, to investment firms which are legal persons where such firms are managed by single natural persons in accordance with their articles of association and national laws.

.   .   .

Article 6

The competent authorities of the other Member State involved shall be consulted beforehand on the authorization of any investment firm which is:

— a subsidiary of an investment firm or credit institution authorized in another Member State,

— a subsidiary of the parent undertaking of an investment firm or credit institution authorized in another Member State, or

— controlled by the same natural or legal persons as control an investment firm or credit institution authorized in another Member State.

TITLE III

Relations with third countries

Article 7

. . .

3. Initially no later than six months before this Directive is brought into effect and thereafter periodically the Commission shall draw up a report examining the treatment accorded to Community investment firms in third countries, in the terms referred to in paragraphs 4 and 5, as regards establishment, the carrying on of investment services activities and the acquisition of holdings in third-country investment firms. The Commission shall submit those reports to the Council together with any appropriate proposals.

4. Whenever it appears to the Commission, either on the basis of the reports provided for in paragraph 3 or on the basis of other information, that a third country does not grant Community investment firms effective market access comparable to that granted by the Community to investment firms from that third country; the Commission may submit proposals to the Council for an appropriate mandate for negotiation with a view to obtaining comparable competitive opportunities for Community investment firms. The Council shall act by a qualified majority.

5. Whenever it appears to the Commission, either on the basis of the reports referred to in paragraph 3 or on the basis of other information, that Community investment firms in a third country are not granted national treatment affording the same competitive opportunities as are available to domestic investment firms and that the conditions of effective market access are not fulfilled, the Commission may initiate negotiations in order to remedy the situation.

In the circumstances described in the first subparagraph it may also be decided, at any time and in addition to the initiation of negotiations, in accordance with the procedure to be laid down in the

Directive by which the Council will set up the committee referred to in paragraph 1, that the competent authorities of the Member States must limit or suspend their decisions regarding requests pending or future requests for authorization and the acquisition of holdings by direct or indirect parent undertakings governed by the law of the third country in question. The duration of such measures may not exceed three months.

Before the end of that three-month period and in the light of the results of the negotiations the Council may, acting on a proposal from the Commission, decide by a qualified majority whether the measures shall be continued.

Such limitations or suspensions may not be applied to the setting up of subsidiaries by investment firms duly authorized in the Community or by their subsidiaries, or to the acquisition of holdings in Community investment firms by such firms or subsidiaries.

TITLE IV

Operating conditions

. . .

Article 10

Each home Member State shall draw up prudential rules which investment firms shall observe at all times. In particular, such rules shall require that each investment firm:

- have sound administrative and accounting procedures, control and safeguard arrangements for electronic data processing, and adequate internal control mechanisms including, in particular, rules for personal transactions by its employees,

- make adequate arrangements for instruments belonging to investors with a view to safeguarding the latter's ownership rights, especially in the event of the investment firm's instruments for its own account except with the investors' express consent,

- make adequate arrangements for funds belonging to investors with a view to safeguarding the latter's rights and, except in the case of credit institutions, preventing the investment firm's using investors' funds for its own account,

- arrange for records to be kept of transactions executed which shall at least be sufficient to enable the home Member State's authorities to monitor compliance with the prudential rules which they are responsible for applying; such records shall be retained for periods to be laid down by the competent authorities,

— be structured and organized in such a way as to minimize the risk of clients' interests being prejudiced by conflicts of interest between the firm and its clients or between one of its clients and another. Nevertheless, where a branch is set up the organizational arrangements may not conflict with the rules of conduct laid down by the host Member State to cover conflicts of interest.

Article 11

1. Member States shall draw up rules of conduct which investment firms shall observe at all times. Such rules must implement at least the principles set out in the following indents and must be applied in such a way as to take account of the professional nature of the person for whom the service is provided. The Member States shall also apply these rules where appropriate to the non-core services listed in Section C of the Annex. These principles shall ensure that an investment firm:

— acts honestly and fairly in conducting its business activities in the best interests of its clients and the integrity of the market,

— acts with due skill, care and diligence, in the best interests of its clients and the integrity of the market,

— has and employs effectively the resources and procedures that are necessary for the proper performance of its business activities,

— seeks from its clients information regarding their financial situations, investment experience and objectives as regards the services requested,

— makes adequate disclosure of relevant material information in its dealings with its clients,

— tries to avoid conflicts of interests and, when they cannot be avoided, ensures that its clients are fairly treated, and

— complies with all regulatory requirements applicable to the conduct of its business activities so as to promote the best interests of its clients and the integrity of the market.

2. Without prejudice to any decisions to be taken in the context of the harmonization of the rules of conduct, their implementation and the supervision of compliance with them shall remain the responsibility of the Member State in which a service is provided.

3. Where an investment firm executes an order, for the purposes of applying the rules referred to in paragraph 1 the professional nature of the investor shall be assessed with respect to the investor from whom the order originates, regardless of whether the order was placed directly by the investor himself or indirectly through an investment firm providing the service referred to in Section A(1)(a) of the Annex.

. . .

TITLE V

The right of establishment and the freedom to provide services

Article 14

1. Member States shall ensure that investment services and the other services listed in Section C of the Annex may be provided within their territories ... either by the establishment of a branch or under the freedom to provide services by any investment firm authorized and supervised by the competent authorities of another Member State in accordance with this Directive, provided that such services are covered by the authorization.

2. Member States may not make the establishment of a branch or the provision of services referred to in paragraph 1 subject to any authorization requirement, to any requirement to provide endowment capital or to any other measure having equivalent effect.

3. A Member State may require that transactions relating to the services referred to in paragraph 1 must, where they satisfy all the following criteria, be carried out on a regulated market:

— the investor must be habitually resident or established in that Member State,

— the investment firm must carry out such transactions through a main establishment, through a branch situated in that Member State or under the freedom to provide services in that Member State,

— the transaction must involve a instrument dealt in on a regulated market in that Member State.

4. Where a Member State applies paragraph 3 it shall give investors habitually resident or established in that Member State the right not to comply with the obligation imposed in paragraph 3 and have the transactions referred to in paragraph 3 carried out away from a regulated market. Member States may make the exercise of this right subject to express authorization, taking into account investors' differing needs for protection and in particular the ability of professional and institutional investors to act in their own best interests. It must in any case be possible for such authorization to be given in conditions that do not jeopardize the prompt execution of investors' orders.

5. The Commission shall report on the operation of paragraphs 3 and 4 not later than 31 December 1998 and shall, if appropriate, propose amendments thereto.

Article 15

1. Without prejudice to the exercise of the right of establishment or the freedom to provide services referred to in Article 14, host Member States shall ensure that investment firms which are authorized by the competent authorities of their home Member States to provide the services referred to in Section A(1)(b) and (2) of the Annex can, either directly or indirectly, become members of or have access to the regulated markets in their host Member States where similar services are provided and also become members of or have access to the clearing and settlement systems which are provided for the members of such regulated markets there.

Member States shall abolish any national rules or laws or rules of regulated markets which limit the number of persons allowed access thereto. If, by virtue of its legal structure or its technical capacity, access to a regulated market is limited, the Member State concerned shall ensure that its structure and capacity are regularly adjusted.

2. Membership of or access to a regulated market shall be conditional on investment firms' complying with capital adequacy requirements and home Member States' supervising such compliance in accordance with Directive 93-6-EEC.

Host Member States shall be entitled to impose additional capital requirements only in respect of matters not covered by that Directive.

Access to a regulated market, admission to membership thereof and continued access or membership shall be subject to compliance with the rules of the regulated market in relation to the constitution and administration of the regulated market and to compliance with the rules relating to transactions on the market, with the professional standards imposed on staff operating on and in conjunction with the market, and with the rules and procedures for clearing and settlement. The detailed arrangements for implementing these rules and procedures may be adapted as appropriate, *inter alia* to ensure fulfilment of the ensuing obligations, provided, however, that Article 28 is complied with.

3. In order to meet the obligation imposed in paragraph 1, host Member States shall offer the investment firms referred to in that paragraph the choice of becoming members of or of having access to their regulated markets either:

— directly, by setting up branches in the host Member States, or

— indirectly, by setting up subsidiaries in the host Member States or by acquiring firms in the host Member States that are already members of their regulated markets or already have access thereto.

However, those Member States which, when this Directive is adopted, apply laws which do not permit credit institutions to become members of or have access to regulated markets unless they have specialized subsidiaries may continue until 31 December 1996 to apply the same obligation in a non-discriminatory way to credit institutions from other Member States for purposes of access to those regulated markets.

The Kingdom of Spain, the Hellenic Republic and the Portuguese Republic may extend that period until 31 December 1999. One year before that date the Commission shall draw up a report, taking into account the experience acquired in applying this Article and shall if appropriate, submit a proposal. The Council may, acting by qualified majority on the basis of that proposal, decide to review those arrangements.

4. Subject to paragraphs 1, 2 and 3, where the regulated market of the host Member State operates without any requirement for a physical presence the investment firms referred to in paragraph 1 may become members of or have access to it on the same basis without having to be established in the host Member State. In order to enable their investment firms to become members of or have access to host Member States' regulated markets in accordance with this paragraph home Member States shall allow those host Member States' regulated markets to provide appropriate facilities within the home Member States' territories.

5. This Article shall not affect the Member States' right to authorize or prohibit the creation of new markets within their territories.

.   .   .

Article 21

1. In order to enable investors to assess at any time the terms of a transaction they are considering and to verify afterwards the conditions in which it has been carried out, each competent authority shall, for each of the regulated markets which it has entered on the list provided for in Article 16, take measures to provide investors with the information referred to in paragraph 2. In accordance with the requirements imposed in paragraph 2, the competent authorities shall determine the form in which and the precise time within which the information is to be provided, as well as the means by which it is to be made available, having regard to the nature, size and needs of the market concerned and of the investors operating on that market.

2. The competent authorities shall require for each instrument at least:

(a) publication at the start of each day's trading on the market of the weighted average price, the highest and the lowest prices and the volume dealt in on the regulated market in question for the whole of the preceding day's trading;

(b) in addition, for continuous order-driven and quote-driven markets, publication:

- at the end of each hour's trading on the market, of the weighted average price and the volume dealt in on the regulated market in question for a six-hour trading period ending so as to leave two hours' trading on the market before publication, and

- every 20 minutes, of the weighted average price and the highest and lowest prices on the regulated market in question for a two-hour trading period ending so as to leave one hour's trading on the market before publication.

Where investors have prior access to information on the prices and quantities for which transactions may be undertaken:

(i) such information shall be available at all times during market trading hours;

(ii) the terms announced for a given price and quantity shall be terms on which it is possible for an investor to carry out such a transaction.

The competent authorities may delay or suspend publication where that proves to be justified by exceptional market conditions or, in the case of small markets, to preserve the anonymity of firms and investors. The competent authorities may apply special provisions in the case of exceptional transactions that are very large in scale compared with average transactions in the security in question on that market and in the case of highly illiquid securities defined by means of objective criteria and made public. The competent authorities may also apply more flexible provisions, particularly as regards publication deadlines, for transactions concerning bonds and other forms of securitized debt.

3. In the field governed by this Article each Member State may adopt or maintain more stringent provisions or additional provisions with regard to the substance and form in which information must be made available to investors concerning transactions carried out on regulated markets of which it is the home Member State, provided that those provisions apply regardless of the Member State in which the issuer of the financial instrument is located or of the Member State on the regulated market of which the instrument was listed for the first time.

4. The Commission shall report on the application of this Article no later than 31 December 1997; the Council may, on a proposal from the Commission, decide by a qualified majority to amend this Article.

.   .   .

Article 31

No later than 1 July 1995 Member States shall adopt the laws, regulations and administrative provisions necessary for them to comply with this Directive.

These provisions shall enter into force no later than 31 December 1995. The Member States shall forthwith inform the Commission thereof.

When Member States adopt the provisions referred to in the first paragraph they shall include a reference to this Directive or accompany them with such a reference on the occasion of their official publication. The manner in which such references are to be made shall be laid down by the Member States.

.   .   .

ANNEX

SECTION A

Services

1. (a) Reception and transmission, on behalf of investors, of orders in relation to one or more of the instruments listed in Section B.

(b) Execution of such orders other than for own account.

2. Dealing in any of the instruments listed in Section B for own account.

3. Managing portfolios of investments in accordance with mandates given by investors on a discriminatory, client-by-client basis where such portfolios include one or more of the instruments listed in Section B.

4. Underwriting in respect of issues of any of the instruments listed in Section B and—or the placing of such issues.

SECTION B

Instruments

1. (a) Transferable securities.

(b) Units in collective investment undertakings.

2. Money-market instruments.

3. Financial-futures contracts, including equivalent cash-settled instruments.

4. Forward interest-rate agreements (FRAs).

5. Interest-rate, currency and equity swaps.

6. Options to acquire or dispose of any instruments falling within this section of the Annex, including equivalent cash-settled

instruments. This category includes in particular options on currency and on interest rates.

SECTION C

Non-core services

1. Safekeeping and administration in relation to one or more of the instruments listed in Section B.

2. Safe custody services.

3. Granting credits or loans to an investor to allow him to carry out a transaction in one or more of the instruments listed in Section B, where the firm granting the credit or loan is involved in the transaction.

4. Advice to undertakings on capital structure, industrial strategy and related matters and advice and service relating to mergers and the purchase of undertakings.

5. Services related to underwriting.

6. Investment advice concerning one or more of the instruments listed in Section B.

7. Foreign-exchange service where these are connected with the provision of investment services.

CHAPTER SIX

INFRASTRUCTURE:
FOREIGN EXCHANGE
REGIMES

The European Community's attempts to build a monetary union brought its member governments face to face with the awesome power of the world's foreign exchange markets. The encounters may have seriously damaged economies in Europe and elsewhere. This Chapter explores the variety of complex regimes that exist to organize foreign exchange markets. The next Chapter examines the European Economic and Monetary Union (EMU).

To this end, the Chapter examines the interplay between exchange rate regimes, government policy, and foreign exchange markets. We present the basics of fixed and floating exchange rate systems, consider the way spot and forward exchange markets work, and examine the logic of interest rate parity. This will hopefully serve as useful background to an understanding of the EMU discussed in the next chapter.

A. BASIC TYPES OF EXCHANGE RATE SYSTEMS

An exchange rate gives the prices at which two currencies are sold for each other. Different systems determine these prices. Four types of systems during the last century tended toward either flexible rates set by supply and demand or rates fixed by governments. The first, the gold standard, existed for decades until it ended with World War I. The second was called the gold exchange standard. It operated from the mid-1920s to the early 1930s. The third foreign exchange regime followed World War II and was known as the Bretton Woods system. It was based on the U.S. dollar and gold and lasted to 1973. The fourth system, which followed, was one of floating rates. Before discussing the individual regimes, this chapter briefly analyzes the concept of a country's balance of payments, a recurring topic throughout.

The balance of payments of a nation is simply an accounting statement of its transactions with the rest of the world during a certain period of time. A country's exchange rate affects its balance of payments and its balance of payments affects the currency's strength against other currencies. As the statement measures flows, it reflects only changes in assets and liabilities, not absolute levels of these elements. Payment inflows, from non-residents, are recorded as a "plus." Outflows, to non-residents, are expressed as a "minus." For example, exports are registered as a plus because they reflect payments flowing into the country from the sale of goods.

The balance of payments consists of three accounts, the current account, the capital account, and the official reserves. The current account measures trade in goods, services, and gifts between nations. It primarily includes exports and imports of goods, measuring the "balance of trade." This trade balance is in surplus when exports exceed imports and in deficit when imports exceed exports. For 1997 the United States had a current account balance deficit of $155 billion, owing to a substantial trade imbalance. See U.S. Commerce Department, *Survey of Current Business* 21 (January 1999). A surplus in the current account is associated with a strengthening of a country's exchange rate and a deficit with a falling exchange rate. For example, exports from the U.S. are denominated in dollars. Payment for them means that a foreigner must buy dollars and sell the foreign currency. This tends to strengthen the dollar in certain exchange regimes. When imports exceed exports, however, the process is reversed and the dollar weakens.

The capital account records international movements of financial assets and liabilities, such as loans and equity investments. In recent years, this account has helped offset the current account deficit in the U.S. balance of payments, as capital inflows into the U.S. grew relative to outflows. Any difference between the current account and capital account is made up by the official reserves which are the country's official holdings of gold and hard currencies (other than its own). These holdings increase if the current and capital accounts together are in surplus and decrease if the accounts are in deficit. Management of the official reserves is a key consideration in the way some countries manipulate their exchange rates. For example when a government supports its currency, it sells its holdings of official reserves to pay for the cost of "propping up the currency."

As you read about the four exchange rate systems, please recall that the balance of payments is used by many economists to forecast the direction in which a country's currency is headed.

1. FIXED RATE SYSTEMS: THE GOLD STANDARD

The gold standard that existed around the world prior to World War I was heavily dependant on the British pound. However, the effect of the war upon Britain caused it to abandon the gold standard temporarily.

Since the pound had financed most of the world payments, Britain's wartime decision seriously reduced confidence in the gold standard. The gold exchange standard which emerged from World War I differed from its predecessor. The dollar and the franc emerged as dominant reserve assets. Prices and costs were no longer flexible. The UK abandoned the gold standard in 1931. *See* A. Buckley, *Multinational Finance* (1996).

The basic mechanics underlying the gold standard nevertheless merit consideration in light of recent efforts to return to this type of regime. In theory, the gold standard system required very little government intervention. Levi described it:

M. LEVI, INTERNATIONAL FINANCE
476–80 (2d ed. 1990) (Levi).

Under a gold standard each country stands ready to convert its paper or fiat money into gold at a fixed price. This fixing of the price of gold fixes exchange rates between paper monies. For example, if the U.S. Federal Reserve (the "Fed") agrees to buy and sell gold at $40 per ounce, and the Bank of England agrees to £20 per ounce, the exchange rate between the pound and dollar in the form of paper currency or commercial bank deposits will be $2/£. If the exchange rate is not $2/£, the foreign exchange market will not balance because it will be used for converting one currency into the other, but not vice versa. For example, if the exchange rate in the foreign exchange market is $1.60/£, the market will be used for converting dollars into pounds, but not for converting pounds into dollars. This is because it is cheaper for people buying dollars with pounds to buy gold from the Bank of England, ship the gold to the U.S., and sell it to the Federal Reserve for dollars.

.   .   .

Price Adjustment under the Gold Standard

The price-level adjustment mechanism under the gold standard is known as the price-specie adjustment mechanism, where "specie" is just another word for precious metal...In order to explain the mechanism, let us continue to assume that gold is $40/oz. in the U.S. and £20/oz. in Britain and that at the resulting exchange rate of $2/£, Britain is buying more from the U.S. than the U.S. is buying from Britain. That is, let us assume that Britain has a balance-of-payments deficit with the U.S. The price-specie adjustment mechanism explains how the British deficit and the U.S. surplus are corrected in the following manner.

With Britain buying more from the U.S. than the U.S. is buying from Britain, there is an excess supply of pounds. With flexible exchange rates this will reduce the value of the pound below $2/£, but with a gold standard this will not happen because nobody will sell pounds in the foreign exchange market for less than $2. Rather, as soon as the pound dips even slightly below $2, people will sell pounds to the Bank of England in return for gold, ship the gold to the U.S., and sell the gold to the Federal Reserve for dollars. This gives people $2 for each pound. Therefore, the result of the British balance-of-payments deficit is the movement of gold from the Bank of England to the U.S. Federal Reserve.

The movement of gold from Britain, the deficit country, to the U.S., the surplus country, has effects on both countries' money supplies. This is because in standing ready to exchange gold for paper money at a fixed price, central banks have to make sure they have sufficient gold on hand for those occasions when many people wish to return paper money for gold. Prudent banking requires that a minimum ratio of gold reserves to paper money be held, and indeed, this used to be mandated in many countries, including the U.S., which required that the dollar be backed by at least 25 percent in gold reserves. The maintenance of a minimum reserve ratio means that as the Bank of England loses gold it is forced to reduce the amount of its paper money in circulation. At the same time, the increase in the Federal Reserve gold reserves allows it to put more paper money into circulation.

In the minds of the eighteenth-century classical economists who described the working of the gold standard, the fall in the money supply in the deficit country would cause a general fall in prices. At the same time, the increase in the money supply in the surplus country (in the world we are describing, one country's deficit in the other country's surplus) would cause a general increase in prices. With prices falling in the deficit country, Britain, and increasing in the surplus country, the U.S., there is a decline in British prices versus U.S. prices. This makes British exports more competitive in the U.S., helping them increase. At the same time, U.S. goods in Britain become less competitive than Britain's own import substitutes, so that British imports decline. With British exports increasing and imports decreasing, Britain's deficit declines. Indeed, until the deficit has been completely eliminated there will be an excess supply of pounds, the sale of pounds to the Bank of England, the shipment of gold to the U.S., a decrease in the British money supply, an increase in the U.S. money supply, increasing competitiveness of British products at home and abroad, and a continued reduction in the British deficit.

The price-specie adjustment mechanism works not only via changes in relative prices *between* countries, but also via changes in relative prices *within* each country. In the deficit country, for example, the prices of nontraded goods will decline, but the prices of goods which enter international trade will remain unchanged.

. . .

Unfortunately for the effectiveness of the price-specie adjustment mechanism of the gold standard, governments were often tempted to abandon the required reserve ratio between gold and paper money when the maintenance of that ratio ran counter to other objectives. ...

The policy of not allowing a change in reserves to change the supply of money is known as sterilization or neutralization policy. As goals of full employment became common in the twentieth century, many countries abandoned their effort to maintain the required reserve ratio and focused on their local economic ills.

———————

So in practice, limited government intervention in a gold standard regime was a myth. Kenneth Dam has argued that the gold standard was essentially a "sterling standard" where the Bank of England was the banker to the world, keeping everything in equilibrium. See K. Dam *The Rules of the Game* (1982) at 6. Dam also reports that during this period central banks worked against the automatic forces in more years than they permitted them to work.

The question remains whether the gold standard could have worked. Some economists, most notably Robert Triffin, have said that it was not feasible. Basically Triffin suggests that deficits from gold outflows cannot be self-correcting, because prices cannot fall. See Levi at 479-80. Triffin's theory, known as *Triffin's Dilemma*, posits that under a gold standard a country is forced into choosing between economic growth (spending from reserves) and credibility (maintaining appropriate reserves to ensure confidence).

Despite this, a number of twentieth-century economists and politicians have favored a return to the gold standard. What appeals to the adherents of this view is the discipline that the gold standard placed on the expansion of the money supply and the resulting check this placed on inflation.

2. FIXED RATE SYSTEMS: THE BRETTON WOODS DOLLAR STANDARD

As World War II was ending, financial leaders from many Allied countries met in Bretton Woods, New Hampshire, where they agreed to a new regime. The U.S. dollar, then the world's strongest currency, would be fixed to gold. The U.S. government promised to give any holder of dollars gold at the rate of $35 for an ounce of gold. Other countries tied their exchange rates to the U.S. dollar at agreed rates that could fluctuate around it in a narrow band. To maintain these par values, the countries agreed to sell their currency if it approached the upper limit or to buy their currency at the lower limit with their foreign exchange reserves (mainly gold and dollars at first).

The International Monetary Fund, which was established at Bretton Woods, could make funds available to a deficit country if the country adopted agreed policies to improve their economic situation. Devaluation was discouraged but not outlawed. The new system of fixed rates was a gold exchange and U.S. dollar standard embodied in the 1944 IMF treaty. The U.S. was not obligated to maintain a one-to-one ratio of dollars to gold, however; it held reserves at a level that gave people confidence it could meet any demand for gold. Since the dollar was used for international transactions and since governments held dollars as reserves, demand for gold in exchange for dollars was relatively low. But by the time the system broke down in the early 1970s, U.S. reserves were so low that confidence had evaporated. By then, most non-communist countries had signed the treaty.

The dollar standard assumes a price adjustment mechanism. Levi describes this, assuming that private demand sets the dollar/pound exchange rate within the allowed range. If private demand for pounds increases, the Bank of England will supply more by buying dollars and the U.K. money supply will rise. The competitiveness of British goods will fall and imports will rise. As demand for pounds falls, the dollar/pound rate is restored within the allowed range. He continues (Levi, at 29-37):

> The need to reduce the value of a currency in a country experiencing deficits and declining reserves depends on the ability of the central bank to borrow additional reserves. There are arrangements between central banks for exchanging currency reserves, and there are many lines for borrowing from international institutions such as the International Monetary Fund....Another factor making exchange-rate forecasting under fixed rates difficult is the difference in the need to react to surpluses and deficits. Countries that are facing a deficit and losing reserves will eventually be forced into a devaluation because their reserves and ability to borrow will eventually be gone. On the other hand, the countries enjoying surpluses will be under no pressure to revalue their currencies and may instead allow reserves to keep growing. This represents one of the major problems with the gold-exchange and dollar standards, namely that the responsibility for adjustment, whether this be via a change in the exchange rate or via an automatic change in money supplies and prices, falls on deficit countries more heavily than on surplus countries.

Fixed exchange rates work only as long as countries in the system maintain competitiveness and are able to coordinate their economic policies, according to P. Sercu and R. Uppal in *International Financial Markets and the Firm* (1995). They write:

> [N]ote that the UK could not possibly have 100 percent inflation and still maintain the exchange rate if its trading partners have near-zero inflation: with a stable exchange rate, the UK's exporters would have to quit foreign markets, and British firms selling in the UK would likewise be wiped out by foreign producers. In short, fixed rates require similar inflation rates across countries, which, in turn, require coordination of economic policy. There was very little policy coordination in the period

following World War II, however, and this ultimately led to the demise of the fixed-rate system.

Notes and Questions

1.   What is the function of an exchange rate system or regime? What is a regime such as the gold standard supposed to do? Are these functions important?

2.   What is a fixed rate system?   How is it supposed to work? Suppose Germany exports more to the U.K. than it imports from the U.K. Since the trade flows between them are not in balance, how are the two countries supposed to adjust?

3.   Kenneth Dam entitled his book "The Rules of the Game," suggesting that exchange regimes have a regulatory role. But no treaties bound the members of the classical gold standard. What are the rules of a fixed rate regime? Who would enforce them? Distinguish between the classical gold standard and the Bretton Woods system.

3. FLOATING RATE REGIMES—AN OVERVIEW

The Bretton Woods regime expired in 1973 when major industrial countries said they would let foreign exchange markets determine the value of their currencies. The U.S. government said it would no longer support the dollar's value. The EC decided to float members' currencies together against the dollar. The EC float could be seen as "merely a decision by Germany to float against the dollar, with the other countries pegging their currencies on the German mark to form a mark area. However, the dictates of European integration required that the decision be presented as a European Economic Community initiative." Dam at 191.

While supply and demand were supposed to set currency prices, each country could intervene in the market for its own currency to maintain order. During the early Reagan years, the U.S. remained passive while Japan and Europe set targets. By the mid–1980s, the U.S. had decided to intervene in markets so as to devalue the dollar against other currencies, notably the Yen. The willingness to manage the float has persisted since then.

Over the next two decades there evolved a mixture of exchange rate regimes.   Major trading countries try to manage the value of their currency. They intervene in the currency markets, buying or selling their currency to change its price. They use macroeconomic fiscal and monetary policies.   They jawbone, making public announcements to encourage market players to act differently. Finance ministers meet periodically in efforts to coordinate or realign their currencies.

B. TYPES OF FLOATING RATE SYSTEMS

The IMF classifies exchange rate systems in a way designed to take account of the variation and complexity that now characterize regimes around the globe. It classifies countries on the basis of their actual (rather than officially announced) exchange rate regime, ranked by degree of flexibility and the monetary policy the country follows in relation to the chosen regime. The following categories and brief descriptions come from Johnson at 36-37 and are ordered from the most rigid arrangements to the most flexible regimes. B. Johnson, *et al.*, International Monetary Fund, *Exchange Rate Arrangements and Currency Convertibility: Developments and Issues*, (1999) at 32-37 (IMF in 1999). An extended discussion of the European Monetary System is included because its experience in the 1990s has been very important to the evolution of foreign exchange markets and set the foundations for EMU.

1. EXCHANGE ARRANGEMENTS WITH NO SEPARATE LEGAL TENDER

According to the IMF in 1999:

> The currency of another country circulates as the sole legal tender or the member belongs to a monetary or currency union in which the same legal tender is shared by members of the union. Adopting such regimes is a form of ultimate sacrifice for surrendering monetary control where no scope is left for national monetary authorities to conduct independent monetary policy.

As of the end of 1997, the IMF identified 26 countries in this group. Of these, 14 were members of the CFA franc zone, which used a common currency, and another 6 were in a similar zone in the Caribbean. Of the remainder, Kiribati used the Australian dollar, San Marino used the Italian lira, and four used the U.S. dollar. Of these six, Panama had the largest economy.

Dollarization, in which the U.S. dollar serves as the substitute, is a common form of this practice. Several Latin American countries moved to accept the dollar. Ecuador and El Salvador adopted it in 2000, joining Panama, which used the dollar for decades. In Argentina, which used the dollar as a second currency for many years, the central bank suggested in January 1999 that the U.S. dollar become the sole currency of the country. Mexico continues to debate whether to adopt the dollar as its national currency. Note that a partial, informal dollarization has been common in former Socialist countries, which allowed the dollar to serve as a second currency. Vietnam, for example, permitted the use of the dollar for domestic transactions until 2000. This is different from complete reliance on a foreign currency.

The effect of dollarization is to forego all monetary independence. The reason is to ensure that local politics do not lead to inflationary monetary policies. A country that issues currency receives income from doing so. A person who takes cash from a bank gives the bank a deposit in exchange. The bank gets the cash from the central bank and pays for the cash by transferring a deposit to the central bank. The central bank pays no interest on the deposit, which is a payment, and can invest the funds, keeping the income. The income is known as seigniorage. Under dollarization the government loses the benefits of seigniorage, which is the return to the central bank of holding reserves against the local currency In so doing, an Argentina would lose the benefits of seigniorage. If Argentina were to use the U.S. dollar, the seigniorage goes to the government of the U.S., not Argentina. Suppose, however, that government economic policy so lacks credibility that people are fleeing the local currency. Dollarization might restore credibility by demonstrating the government's commitment to stability. This might bring gains in welfare that offset the cost of seigniorage. See R. Chang and A. Velasco, *Dollarization: Analytical Issues*, National Bureau of Economic Research (March 2002).

An Argentina would become even more exposed to U.S. monetary policy, over which it could have no control. It could not act as a lender of last resort to its own banks, because their accounts would be in U.S. dollars. The populace could react hostilely to the loss of the local currency as a national symbol.

Critics attack the claims made for dollarization. It does not promote greater trade with the United States, according to one study. They say it turns over a key tool for managing a country's economy, especially considering that the U.S. Federal Reserve does not directly consider the effects of rate changes based on other countries that have adopted the dollar. According to one study, "neither theory nor evidence suggests that removing all scope for an independent monetary policy will necessarily accelerate the pace of reform." B. Eichengreen, *When to Dollarize*, 34 Journal of Money, Credit, and Banking, 1 (February 2002). In a study of Panama's use of the dollar, the authors concluded that on the one hand dollarization does not guarantee fiscal discipline, does not help eliminate currency risk, slows GDP growth, and might slightly increase its volatility. On the other hand, however, dollarized economies tend to do very well against inflation and may even reduce the impact of external confidence shocks, although not external real shocks. *See* M. Klein, Dollarization and Trade, National Bureau of Economic Research Working Paper 8879 (April 2002); J. Kahn, *U.S. and IMF Welcome Salvador's Adoption of Dollar*, The New York Times, Nov. 25, 2000 at B2; S. Edwards, *Dollarization and Economic Performance: An Empirical Investigation,* NBER Working Paper 8274, May 2001; I. Goldfajn and G. Olivares, *Full Dollarization: The Case of Panama*, published in LCSPR, Economic Management Group, *The Choice of Currency Arrangements in Latin America and the Caribbean.*

2. CURRENCY BOARD ARRANGEMENTS

According to the IMF in 1999:

A monetary regime based on an implicit legislative commitment to exchange domestic currency for a specified foreign currency at a fixed exchange rate, combined with restrictions on the issuing authority to ensure the fulfillment of its legal obligation. This implies that domestic currency be issued only against foreign exchange and that new issues are fully backed by foreign assets, eliminating traditional central bank functions such as monetary control and the lender of last resort and leaving little scope for discretionary monetary policy; some flexibility may still be afforded depending on how strict the rules of the boards are established.

The IMF identified eight countries in 2000 that used currency boards: Djibouti (since 1949), Brunei (1967), Hong Kong (1983), Argentina (1991), Estonia (1992), Lithuania (1994), Bulgaria (1997), and Bosnia (1997). M. Mussa, P. Masson, A. Swoboda, E. Jadresic, P. Mauro, and A. Berg, *Exchange Rate Regimes in an Increasingly Integrated World Economy* (2000) (IMF 2000).

A currency board directly relates the domestic money supply to the country's foreign exchange reserves by supplying or redeeming central bank liabilities at a fixed rate. The currency board effectively removes from the central bank the power to manage reserves and the money supply. The idea of a currency board is that the monetary authority has no discretion. The board fixes an exchange rate, against the dollar, for example. It promises to redeem or provide its currency at that rate. The money supply rises and falls automatically and the country undertakes not to interfere with those changes. For example, in Indonesia, the Rupiah/$ rate went from 2,400 in June 1997 to 14,800 in January 1998, then recovered to 9,300 in late February. At that point, President Suharto proposed to adopt a currency board and set the Rupiah/$ at 5,000. The IMF and President Clinton tried to dissuade him.

By its nature, a currency board with ample reserves should not be subject to speculative attacks. Yet Hong Kong's board came under attack in October 1997. One explanation was that the board was not unambiguously seen as willing to carry out its promise to redeem or provide currency at the given rate. The board had begun to act like a central bank, setting interest rate targets for monetary policy. To counter the market perceptions, the board accepted liability for losses Hong Kong banks might suffer on their substantial dollar assets if the rate changed. Its credibility as a passive implementer was restored. K. Kasa, *Why Attack a Currency Board*, Nov. 26, 1999.

Argentina abandoned its 1:1 peg of the peso to the U.S. dollar in 2001. It acted as the country's economy collapsed and the government defaulted on its debt (see Chapter 21). Advocates of currency boards accused the government of failing to implement the rules, noting that the country's foreign reserves fluctuated from 83% of domestic money to 193% in 2001. To make the transition, the government first announced it would switch to a basket of U.S. dollars (50%) and euros (50%). Late in the year, the government introduced the "argentino" to pay State employees and pensioners, at the rate of one argentino to one peso. But the argentino had no fixed rate to the dollar, against which it would devalue. Many observers expected major devaluation. S. Hanke, *Peso Peg: Done Wisely, but Not Too Well?* New York Times, Feb. 10, 2002, and D. Altman, *Argentina Pins Its Hopes on 3rd 'Floating' Currency*, New York Times, Dec. 28, 2001.

3. OTHER CONVENTIONAL FIXED PEG ARRANGEMENTS

According to the IMF in 1999:

The country pegs its currency (formally or de facto) at a fixed rate to a major currency or a basket of currencies, where a weighted composite is formed from the currencies of major trading or financial partners and currency weights reflect the geographical distribution of trade, services, or capital flows. In a conventional fixed pegged arrangement the exchange rate fluctuates within a narrow margin of at most +/-1 percent around a central rate...The monetary authority stands ready to maintain the fixed parity through intervention, limiting the degree of monetary policy discretion; the degree of flexibility is greater relative to currency board arrangements...in that traditional central banking functions are, although limited, still possible, and the monetary authority can adjust the level of the exchange rate, although infrequently.

The IMF identified, as of the end of 1997, 38 countries pegged to a single currency (of which the largest were Egypt and Nigeria) and another 16 pegged to a composite of other currencies (Kuwait and Pakistan were the largest economies in this subset).

Many smaller or non-industrial countries fix or peg their exchange rates against the currency of one or more major trading partners, then adjust as their costs change relative to the partners' costs. Pakistan, for example, might fix the Rupee against a basket of other currencies, dominated by the U.S. dollar and the Japanese Yen. If inflation in Pakistan outstrips that in its partner countries, the Government might devalue by announcing a lower fixed rate of exchange for the Rupee. The central bank would intervene in financial markets to maintain the new rates or use direct rules. Other countries that peg only against a single currency, such as the dollar, include The Bahamas, Egypt, Iran, and Iraq.

4. PEGGED EXCHANGE RATES WITHIN BANDS

According to the IMF in 1999:

The value of the currency is maintained within margins of fluctuations around a formal or de facto fixed peg that are wider than the +/-1 percent around a central rate. It also includes the arrangements of the countries in the exchange rate mechanism (ERM) of the European Monetary System (EMS) (replaced with ERM-II on January 1, 1999). There is some limited degree of monetary policy discretion, with the degree of discretion depending on the band width.

At the end of 1997, in addition to the cooperative arrangement of the European Monetary System described below, 14 other countries were in this group. They included several of the larger developing countries, such as Brazil, China, Ukraine, and Vietnam.

The European Monetary System. The best example of this type of exchange rate regime is the European Monetary System (EMS), which was called the snake when it began in 1972. The organization of the EMS and its interaction with onslaughts by the currency markets in the early 1990s proved to be significant for the evolution of foreign exchange regimes and governments' policies toward them. This section explains the EMS and the speculative attacks.

The purpose of the EMS was to keep the exchange rates of the countries in the European common market within a narrow band of each other, in order to promote trade and speed economic integration. In 1979, the snake became the EMS. It was built around a basket of currencies, each with a fixed amount that gave it a weight in the basket, called the European Currency Unit (ECU). The fixed amount of each member currency was set by agreement roughly in line with the relative size of the member's economy in the EU. Every five years the amounts were reviewed and could be changed to reflect changes in the underlying economy. The members could also, by unanimous action, agree to change the weights at other times, such as when the U.K. joined the EMS in 1990. Then, for example, the amounts of each currency were those set out in Table B.

Table B
Composition of the ECU

Currency	Amount[a]	Weight[b]
Belgian franc	3.431	8.1
French franc	1.332	19.3
Lira	151.8	9.8
Dutch guilder	0.2198	9.4
Deutschmark	0.6242	30.2
Danish krone	0.1976	2.5
Irish punt	0.008552	1.1
Peseta	6.885	5.3
Drachma	1.44	0.7
Sterling	0.08784	12.8
Escudo	1.04741	0.8
		100.0

[a] These amounts have applied since September 1989.
[b] Weights based on exchange rates on 12 October 1990. This date has been chosen at random. The weights in the ECU will of course change as the exchange rates for the component currencies are determined by forces of supply and demand.

Source: 30 Bank of England Quarterly Bulletin 479 (1990).

The weight of each currency in the ECU was determined by multiplying its rate in the market at any time by its amount in the ECU. Anyone could make the calculation. The EU did it every day by calculating the value of each currency's amount in U.S. dollars and adding them to get the dollar value of the ECU. For example, on the day the U.K. joined, one could determine the dollar value of the ECU by calculating the dollar value of 3.431 Belgian francs, 1.332 French francs, 151.8 Lira, 0.2198 Dutch guilders, 0.6242 Deutschmark, and so forth, then adding them all to calculate the dollar value of the ECU. From this, one could determine the weight of each currency in the ECU. For example, 0.6242 Deutschmark had a weight of 30.2% of the ECU (see Table B).

While the amount of each currency in the ECU was fixed by agreement, the weight of each currency in the ECU would fluctuate as its value changed in foreign exchange markets. Countries were to maintain the stability of their currencies against the ECU, however. When the amounts of each currency were fixed by agreement, their central rates against the ECU were known as of that time, of course. When the U.K. joined, for example, the central rates of each currency were those given in Table C. From these central rates against the ECU, one could determine the central cross-rates of each currency against all other currencies in the ECU basket.

Table C
Central rates of EMS currencies against
the ECU since 8 October 1990

Units of national currency per ECU

Belgian/Luxembourg franc	42.4032
Danish krone	7.84195
French franc	6.89509
Deutschemark	2.05586
Irish punt	0.767417
Lira	1538.24
Dutch guilder	2.31643
Peseta	133.631
Sterling	0.696904
Drachma	205.311
Escudo	178.735

Source: 30 Bank of England Quarterly Bulletin 479 (1990).

The Exchange Rate Mechanism allowed each currency to float within an agreed range around its central cross-rate with each of the other currencies. When the U.K. joined, each long-term member had to keep its currency within a band 2 1/4% above and below each other currency. Each newcomer—the U.K., Spain, and Portugal—had to keep its currency within a 6% band above and below the central cross-rates. For example, on 8 October 1990, the cross-rates between Sterling and the Deutschemark were as follows:

£ and DM Cross-Rates in the Exchange Rate Mechanism:
Upper Limit, Central Rate, and Lower Limit
on 8 October 1990

	DM 100 = £	£1 = DM
Upper limit	35.997	3.132
Central Rate	33.8984	2.95
Lower limit	31.928	2.778

Source: 30 Bank of England Quarterly Bulletin, Table A.

When a currency gets to the edge of the band with another currency, the governments are supposed to intervene. At the top edge, the central bank buys other currencies with its own. At the bottom edge, the central bank sells other currencies and buys its own. Consider what happens as the value of one pound sterling reaches DM 3.132 or DM 2.2778. At both points, note the obligation of the central bank of each country. If one Pound rises to DM 3.132, then the German and UK governments both sell pounds and buy DM. If the Pound falls to DM 2.778, both the German and UK governments buy pounds and sell DM.

The governments may intervene other than by buying and selling currency. They may change interest rates, in order to attract or discourage cross-border flows of funds that affect the exchange rates. They may use monetary or even fiscal policy to affect the rates. They may seek to change their currency's cross-rate, but this is seen as a last resort.

When the U.K. joined the EMS in 1990, the Governor of the Bank of England spoke enthusiastically about the benefits membership would give the U.K. His reasoning was that the mere act of joining would force Great Britain to focus on their battle against inflation in order to sustain growth in the long run. As the Governor put it in 30 Bank of England Quarterly Bulletin at 483 (1990):

> I believe that ERM membership will reinforce our counter-inflationary strategy. In addition, it will help our economy to converge with the economies of our Community partners; and will help business by bringing greater exchange rate stability against other European currencies, and possibly more widely, and thus a better environment in which to plan and invest . . . .

> But, as I have said many times before in anticipation of our joining, the ERM is *not* a panacea. Its benefits will have to be worked for, most of all by maintaining a *firm anti-inflation policy*.

Britain withdrew from the EMS on September 16, 1992, the victim of a market whose participants believed, despite repeated assertions of commitment by the British government, that the U.K. could do nothing to prevent an inevitable devaluation of the pound. These events underscored the fragility of the EMS.

An underlying question ever since has been whether devaluation was due to massive speculation or to fundamental economics. Economists have not agreed.

The case for speculation as the cause of the 1992 crisis. Those who argue that the markets overwhelmed the ERM central banks recount the events in the currency market in the months before the UK withdrew. In June, Danish voters had rejected a referendum to ratify the Maastricht treaty for economic and monetary union of EC members. The treaty, which was eventually signed December 1992, set a timetable and criteria for economic convergence that would permit monetary union. We turn to Maastricht later in this book. The Danish vote cast doubt on Europe's commitment to convergence and hence even the ERM. Polls in August suggested that in the referendum set for September 20, 1992, the French could also reject the treaty.

Events over the summer of 1992 reinforced the market's doubts. Some EC economies continued to be stronger than others, suggesting that the weaker economies would have to devalue their currencies. Germany raised interest rates in mid-July, attracting foreign funds, as the US lowered its interest rates, leading investors to shift to more lucrative markets such as Germany's. By early September, the dollar was at an historic low against the DM. Meanwhile, the DM strengthened against other ERM currencies.

Italy was most vulnerable, politically unable to reduce the high inflation caused by a large public sector deficit. Speculation against the lira led Italy to devalue 7% on September 12, 1992, despite massive intervention by European central banks to support the lira. Foreign exchange traders decided "the emperor had no clothes,"* meaning that the central banks supporting the ERM lacked the power to make it hold.

After September 12, the UK was the next target. Sterling was very near the bottom of the band against the DM. The new prime minister, John Major, facing an election the next spring, had incurred a large fiscal deficit and allowed interest rates to fall in order to stimulate the recession-ridden economy. Raising interest rates or devaluing the pound were not politically acceptable. Elsewhere in the ERM, other members raised their interest rates, Germany announced it would very slightly lower its interest rates and the Spanish peseta fell from the top of the band to the bottom.

On September 16, a tidal wave of position-taking against Sterling swept the markets. Companies and institutional investors with Sterling assets tried to hedge in the foreign exchange markets. Thousands of speculators bet on devaluation. The Bank of England, armed with reserves of $40 billion, and the central banks of Germany and France bought Sterling and sold DM, but Sterling hit the lower ERM limit mid-morning. The Bank of England raised short-term interest rates from 10% to 12% at 11 am, then to 15% at 2 pm. At 4 pm, having spent $15 billion of its reserves, the Bank of England stopped buying Sterling and at 7:45 pm took it out of the ERM and let it devalue.

In this story, huge powerful markets react convulsively to events and swamp any efforts by governments to support a currency. Another view is that the governments' policies failed because they were crippled by flaws in fundamental economics. By implication, the policies would not have failed if economic fundamentals were strong. This is a major debate in international finance about the power of national governments.

The case for fundamental economics as the cause of the 1992 crisis. A longer perspective emphasizes the persistent underlying differences in economic policy and performance among the ERM countries and between them and countries outside the bloc, particularly the US.

Inflation rates in countries like the UK, Italy, Spain, and Portugal were persistently higher than in Germany, Belgium, and the Netherlands

---

* S. Hansell, *Taming the Trillion-Dollar Monster*, Institutional Investor International Dec. 1992, at 47 (Hansell). Much of this account is from Hansell and International Monetary Fund, World Economic Outlook Interim Assessment 1-6 (1993) (IMF).

over several years. The ERM prevented the currencies from adjusting enough to reflect the different inflation rates. Given inflation from 1987 to 1992, for example, the Italian lira should have devalued 18% against the DM but had not. The pound should have, but had not, devalued 10% against the DM since the UK joined the ERM in 1990. Conditions in the countries in 1992 suggested the divergence would widen. High fiscal deficits in Portugal, Spain, and Italy continued to far outstrip those elsewhere in the ERM.

Germany's monetary policy goals differed dramatically from those of its closest ERM partners. Germany financed its integration of East Germany by borrowing and in the process ran large fiscal deficits. Anticipating inflation, the Bundesbank, its central bank, raised interest rates to tighten monetary policy. As interest rates rose, currencies of other countries, including those in the ERM, were exchanged for DM, raising the value of the DM against those currencies. Germany's neighbors faced slowing economies and feared that if they raised interest rates to keep their currency strong, they would worsen their recessions. Despite their pleas, the Bundesbank was unwilling to relax its tight money policy, citing a deep fear of inflation among Germans since hyper-inflation devastated the country after World War I.

The weak US economy in 1992, an election year, was being urged to grow by easy monetary policy and lowering interest rates. This reduced demand for the dollar and encouraged a shift to stronger currencies like the DM, raising their value even more.

Differentials in long-term interest rates between the stronger and weaker ERM countries persisted over many years even though short-term differentials narrowed. This suggested to some analysts that despite expectations that ERM would hold in the short-term, financial markets expected inflation rates to diverge significantly in the long run. This implied the markets saw a need to realign the ERM in the medium term.

In this view, efforts to maintain the ERM were doomed by the fundamentals of divergent economic policy and performance over many years. The September 1992 collapse under market pressure was just the next logical step in the story. ERM could have realigned the currencies before September and avoided the crisis. One could not conclude from this that government efforts to support ERM currencies with sound economies would have failed. Indeed, ERM members repulsed speculative pressure on the franc and Danish krone later in 1992. The Danish, French, and German fundamentals converged enough for speculators in the markets to lose their bets that the franc and krone could be forced to devalue against the DM. IMF economists argued that early adjustment of the fundamentals would allow a regime like the ERM to persist.

Testing the two explanations of the crisis was difficult but important. If the speculative attacks themselves created the imbalances, then one could conclude that the EMS and probably the convergence required for monetary union were doomed because of their vulnerability. In a statistical analysis of all speculative attacks on OECD countries since 1969, Eichengreen, Rose, and Wyplosz identified prior macroeconomic problems preceding speculative attacks on currencies not in the ERM, but failed to identify them in the attacks on the ERM. While the authors did not conclude that the speculators created the ERM crises, their study suggests that effect. B. Eichengreen, A. Rose, and C. Wyplosz, National Bureau of Economic Research, Inc., Speculative Attacks on Pegged Exchange Rates: An Empirical Exploration with Special Reference to the European Monetary System (1994). A later study concluded that intervention is more effective when the parameters of the band being defended are not clear to the market. Intervention is less effective when, as with the ERM, the band's dimensions are certain. K. Koedijk, B. Mizrach, P. Stork, and C. de Vries, New Evidence on the Effectiveness of Foreign Exchange Market Intervention (1995).

During the summer of 1995, however, 12 central banks, including Germany, Japan, and the US, intervened successfully to reverse the long slide of the dollar against the DM and yen. Here the fundamentals in Japan helped the central bankers.

The markets were not mollified by the 1992 changes in the EMS. Spain and Portugal were forced to devalue their currencies further within the ERM during May 1993. In July, Belgium, Denmark, and France came under attack. On July 30 the French franc fell below its ERM floor rate several times but returned as central banks intervened. Other countries defended their own currencies, but the market doubted Germany's willingness to lower interest rates enough to save the EMS. Then on August 2, the eight countries in the EMS agreed to widen the margins for currency fluctuations to 15% from 2.25% or 6%. Germany and the Netherlands agreed to keep the 2.25% band for their two currencies.

After the 1993 crisis, the wide band remained in place to 1998 and EMS countries clustered within it. The stronger ones moved into the 2.25% band, which came also to include France, Denmark, Belgium, and Ireland, Others were weaker. In March 1995, the Spanish peseta devalued 7% against the central rate and Portugal's escudo devalued 3.5%.

It appeared that strict compliance with the ERM rules harmed a country's trade and growth. While Germany and France were in recession, the U.K. economy began to grow after it withdrew from EMS. Wages actually fell and inflation was relatively low. The trade balance improved. Sterling began to recover on exchange markets. A British financial specialist opined that "Leaving the ERM was unquestionably a good thing ... It freed us from being dragged further down by the continent's recession and allowed growth to begin." Within the ERM, the countries whose rates devalued saw their exports surge within the EU, while exports from France and Germany grew much more slowly. The

European Commission, however, rejected France's request that the EU protect the stronger countries from the "competitive devaluations" of the weaker. The EC found no evidence the stronger actually suffered. See G. Tett, A. Fisher, and A. Hill, *When Strength Is a Weakness*, Financial Times, Aug. 9, 1995; and L. Barber, *Protection against EU Currency Swings is Rejected*, Financial Times, Nov. 1, 1995.

In October 1996, Finland and Italy rejoined ERM, Italy at a central rate of Lira 990 to the DM. By early 1997, the U.K., Sweden, and Greece remained outside. The U.K. and Sweden floated.

After the 1992-93 crises, the use of the DM as a reserve currency declined 4.5%, according to the Bundesbank. See *Monthly Report*, April 1997, at 27.

A possible synthesis of the two explanations. Eichengreen argued in 2000 that both rationales are needed to explain the power of the attacks in 1992. For many of the countries under attack, his analysis found fundamental economic problems in current account variables such as export growth and the current deficit. Italy's problems included excessive short-term debt, on the capital account. Portugal and Ireland, however, suffered speculative attacks not justified by their fundamentals. B. Eichengreen, *The EMS Crisis in Retrospect* (2000) (Eichengreen).

The EMS collective peg, had it been cooperatively managed, should have been more stable than a currency pegged unilaterally, in the view of some. Members could assist one another and had reason to do so. The criticism is that in September 1992 cooperation failed. According to John Major, even Germany was prepared to realign the ERM but France refused for non-economic reasons because to do so would reveal that the franc was not an equal partner to the DM. The French government sought a *Franc fort*, or strong Franc, to justify its co-leadership of Europe. Eichengreen at 30.

The EMS crisis was the first in a series of exchange crises during the 1990s, according to Eichengreen, that took place as the countries deregulated their domestic financial systems and opened their capital accounts. All these crises are explained by both weak domestic fundamentals and speculative financial movements. The countries included Mexico in 1994, and those in East and Southeast Asia in 1997. Later chapters of this textbook discuss these crises.

5. CRAWLING PEGS

According to the IMF in 1999:

The currency is adjusted periodically in small amounts at a fixed, preannounced rate or in response to changes in selective quantitative indicators (past inflation differentials vis-a-vis major trading partners, differentials between the target inflation and expected inflation in major trading partners, and so forth). The rate of crawl can be set to generate inflation adjusted changes in the currency's value ("backward looking"), or at a preannounced fixed rate below the projected inflation differentials ("forward looking"). Maintaining a credible crawling peg imposes constraints on monetary policy in a similar manner as a fixed peg system.

At the end of 1997, only 7 countries were in this group, including three smaller Latin American countries, and Turkey.

6. EXCHANGE RATES WITHIN CRAWLING BANDS

According to the IMF in 1999:

> The currency is maintained within certain fluctuation margins around a central rate that is adjusted periodically at a fixed preannounced rate or in response to changes in selective quantitative indicators. The degree of flexibility of the exchange rate is a function of the width of the band, with bands chosen to be either symmetric around a crawling central parity or to widen gradually with an asymmetric choice of the crawl of upper and lower bands (in the latter case, there is no preannouncement of a central rate). The commitment to maintain the exchange rate within the band continues to impose constraints on monetary policy, with the degree of policy independence being a function of the band width.

This group included 11 countries in 1997, such as Russia, Israel, and several countries in Eastern Europe and South America.

7. MANAGED FLOATING WITH NO PREANNOUNCED PATH FOR THE EXCHANGE RATE

According to the IMF in 1999:

> The monetary authority influences the movements of the exchange rate through active intervention in the foreign exchange market without specifying or precommitting to a preannounced path for the exchange rate. Indicators for managing the rate are broadly judgmental, including for example, the balance of payments position, international reserves, parallel market developments, and the adjustments may not be automatic.

The IMF identified 23 countries in this group, including many from Eastern Europe and the former Soviet Union, a few African countries, and Singapore.

8. INDEPENDENT FLOATING

According to the IMF in 1999:

> The exchange rate is market determined, with any foreign exchange intervention aimed at moderating the rate of change and preventing undue fluctuations in the exchange rate, rather than at

establishing a level for it. In these regimes, monetary policy is in principle independent of exchange rate policy.

As many as 44 countries are in this category. Most OECD countries that are not part of EMU float independently. In addition, many countries float in Africa and Asia, particularly those that are English speaking (e.g., Ghana and India, respectively), as do a few countries in Latin America, such as Peru.

9. OVERALL TRENDS

The major trend in exchange rate regimes has been to flexible arrangements. Between 1976 and 1996, the use of flexible arrangements grew substantially while pegs declined, according to an IMF study (see IMF *World Economic Outlook*, October 1997, at 79). Independently floating regimes grew from 1 country in 1976 to 36 in 1996, while other floating arrangements grew from 10 to 29. Pegs to the US dollar fell from 42 to 19, pegs to the French franc held steady at 13, pegs to other single currencies fell from 7 to 5, and pegs to composite currencies fell from 24 to 20. Part of the growth occurred as IMF membership grew with the collapse of the Soviet Union. Part, however, was by choice, as member countries opted for more liberal regimes. The cost of managing a pegged rate became too high with the external shocks and higher variability of currencies in major economies. See IMF *Survey*, November 17, 1997, at 357. The dramatic changes included a big shift by industrial countries from pegged or managed floating regimes to those with more flexibility and by developing and emerging countries from pegged to managed floating. Johnson at 27.

It is useful to distinguish among the regimes of several different types of countries. The three big currency blocks are the U.S. dollar, the Japanese Yen, and the euro. Their rates float. Over the last two decades, these rates (or those of their predecessors) suffered from large short term volatility and medium term swings. Pressure exists for the countries to try major initiatives to stabilize their rates. Other industrial countries, medium-sized, have different regimes and concerns. Many pegged their currencies to their main trading partner but some, such as Canada, floated successfully. For them, their exchange rate is of major importance, so their monetary policy is a crucial tool. Finally, many emerging markets adopted much less flexible foreign exchange regimes.

Despite the attempt to classify exchange rate regimes, their complexity is apparent, especially because some countries set official rates largely unrelated to the supply and demand for their currency. A Central American country reportedly wrote the exchange rate into its constitution. People use their official markets when they have no choice; for example, they must convert their investment officially in order to repatriate earnings. Some countries set different rates for different types of transactions; perhaps one high rate for currency to buy consumer goods and another lower rate to buy capital goods. These official rates promptly generate black or grey markets in the currency that operate parallel to the official market and the government loses more leverage over exchange rates.

Notes and Questions

1. How does the floating rate system work? What economic factors would you expect to shape supply and demand for a currency?

2. How would countries adjust if their trade is not in balance? Suppose that Germany exports more to Britain than it imports from Britain and that there are no other offsetting flows. What happens next? How does this compare with adjustment in the fixed rate regime?

3. What are the rules for the floating rate regimes described? Is there an appropriate role for government intervention if market forces are supposed to dominate?

4. Why would any government want to interfere with the process of adjustment in a pure fixed regime (as opposed to its applied form in, for example, Bretton Woods)? In a pure floating regime? Suppose Germany, exporting more to Britain, or the UK, in deficit, wanted to interfere with the adjustment process. What could they do? What intervention mechanisms might not interfere with adjustment?

5. Would a currency board have been a good idea for Indonesia in 1997, when then Presidents Suharto and Clinton took differing views? If you believe not, what do you make of the fact that Hong Kong has used a currency board for years, and Argentina and other countries used boards during crises? Can you think of a reason why wealthy politically powerful people in a country like Indonesia might have wanted a currency board with an overvalued currency?

6. What is the Exchange Rate Mechanism in the European Monetary System? How is a member's exchange rate set? How does the member's exchange rate fluctuate?

   a. If one pound rises to DM 3.132, then the German and UK governments both sell pounds and buy DM. How would this concerted action reduce the pound/DM rate below the ceiling?

   b. If the pound falls to DM 2.778, both the German and UK governments buy pounds and sell DM. How would this concerted action raise the pound/DM rate above the floor?

Are the governments of Germany and the UK equally well positioned to intervene in the markets in either case? If not, does the EMS provide a fool-proof adjustment mechanism?

7. How effective has the EMS been as an exchange regime? Evaluate the British solution. Could the other members have done the same with the same results? Did they effectively do it in August 1993?

8. Should the U.S. share seigniorage with countries that adopt the U.S. dollar? How? Should the U.S. share seigniorage with countries like Panama that now use the U.S. dollar, or only with countries that opt for the dollar in the future?

a. Consider a recent bill proposed in the Senate, the International Monetary Stabilization Act. The US would share seigniorage with foreign governments that dollarize their economies. The Treasury Department opposed such a move. See, S. Fidler, *US Treasury Opposes Bill on Dollarization*, Financial Times, July 26, 2000, at 4. Who do you think is correct? The bill did not reach the floor of the Senate, but the issues remain.

9. The latest example of currency markets overwhelming governmental efforts to manage exchange rates is the Asian currency crisis of 1997-98 (see Chapter 1) and its aftermath, as the crisis spread to other continents. In early 1999, for example, Brazil left its peg to the US dollar and saw the value of its currency collapse. This prompted some analysts to announce the demise of pegged currency regimes. Their major criticism was that countries wait too long to change the peg despite significant changes in their economy relative to the rest of the world. Several proposals were offered to fix the system.

a. The seven leading industrial countries (the G-7) should follow the example of the EMS by setting a wide range (perhaps 15% on each side of agreed cross-rates) within which their currencies could fluctuate and committing to intervene if any of the seven currencies reached the limit. Intervention would include central bank purchases or sales of the currency as well as appropriate changes in monetary policy. Emerging markets could link to a trade-weighted basket of G-7 currencies. See F. Bergsten, How to Target Exchange Rates, Financial Times, Sep. 20, 1998.

b. The G-7 should cooperate in three ways, according to the French government. This would involve

i) closer exchange rate surveillance by the IMF, which would report regularly whether rate levels and changes accurately reflected underlying economic changes;

ii) closer coordination of macro-economic policies among the G-7, particularly to respond to shocks in the world economy; and

iii) creating a "framework for monetary relations with emerging markets."

In the French view, Europe must cooperate closely with Japan and the US to stabilize euro, yen, and dollar rates. See P. Norman, *France Proposes Forex Stability Plan*, Financial Times, Feb. 9, 1999.

c. Keynes' proposal for a World Central Bank should be revived, in the view of the director of the Trilateral Institute in Japan, S. Saito,

Point of View: Time to Contemplate a World Central Bank, Apr. 18, 2001.

d.   The ASEAN plus 3 countries agreed to a $1 billion currency swap arrangement for use during currency crises in members.   The Association of Southeast Asian Nations, with 10 members, was joined by China, Japan, and Korea.   The swaps would be available to any signatory country with a short-term liquidity crisis.   It was not clear if users would be subject to any conditions; Japan reportedly wanted only the first 10% to be without conditions and the rest to comply with IMF conditions.   One view was that a credible arrangement had to have a minimum of $75 billion.   C. Cockerill, *It's All Just a Drop in the Ocean*, Euromoney, May 2001, at 85.

Would any of these suggestions, or some combination of them, resolve the problems in the world's foreign exchange markets?

10. It may not matter whether a small economy uses a fixed or floating regime.   A study of 5 small open economies (Czech Republic, Greece, Hungary, Israel, Poland) "found no empirical evidence that the pressures on exchange rates, interest rates and stock markets were primarily influenced by the exchange rate regime in place." Z. Darvas and G. Szapary, *Financial Contagion in Five Small Open Economies: Does the Exchange Rate Regime Really Matter?* Another study, this one of East Asian economies, concluded that "average differences in macroeconomic performance under pegging and floating in the region were relatively modest." R. Moreno, *Pegging and Macroeconomic Performance in East Asia*, Dec. 2000.

C.   CAPITAL CONTROLS AND FOREIGN EXCHANGE REGIMES

One way governments tried to counter the financial and economic impact of foreign exchange markets was to control the movement of capital into and out of their country.   In the period after World War II, many countries—industrial, developing, and socialist—turned to capital controls. They hoped that these controls would give freer rein to domestic monetary policy, prevent the inflationary effects of financial inflows, prevent domestic savers and financial intermediaries from misreading foreign exchange risk (assuming that the exchange rate was managed rather than set by the market) or speculating against the currency, and repress the domestic financial system to keep the cost of funds low for the government and domestic firms.   The goal was to segregate domestic and international financial markets. See A. Ariyoshi, K. Habermeier, B. Laurens, I. Otker-Robe, J. Canales-Kriljenko, and A. Kirilenko, *Capital Control: Country Experiences with Their Use and Liberalization* (2000) ("Ariyoshi"), another IMF study.

The two main types of capital controls are direct controls, relying on administrative action, and indirect controls, relying on the market.   Direct controls generally set quantitative limits on the cross-border movement of funds and rely on banks to enforce them. Anyone who wants to import or export capital can only do so with permission from the exchange authorities working through the banks. Indirect controls distinguish among types of foreign exchange transactions, applying differential taxes, multiple exchange rates, or compulsory deposits to those transactions that are favored or not. Ariyoshi at 7.

The controls may be used in conjunction with the managed foreign exchange regimes described above. Countries that peg their currency, for example, may rely on capital controls. On the other hand, floating rate regimes are not compatible with capital controls, nor are regimes tied to another currency, such as dollarization or currency boards.

The effectiveness of capital controls seems to vary over the short- and long-run. Controls seem to moderate the impact of short-term capital inflows initially, but are hard to maintain for very long, particularly when the country has a sophisticated financial system, as in Brazil or Chile. When capital outflows grow, controls may delay domestic adjustments. Controls imposed on outflows during a financial crisis receive mixed reviews. Malaysia seemed to have benefitted from focused capital controls that allowed the domestic economy some breathing space to recover from the 1997 financial crisis described in Chapter 21. Extensive capital controls imposed in Romania, Russia, and Venezuela, however, reduced access to foreign capital. Long-standing capital controls in India and China may have helped reduce their vulnerability to regional crises in the late 1990s, but so did other domestic economic policies. A study of 160 currency crises in 69 developing countries from 1975-97, controlling for "macroeconomic, political, and institutional characteristics," concluded that capital controls do not insulate economies from currency problems; rather they appear to increase the vulnerability of economies to speculative attack." R. Glick, and M. Hutchison, *Capital Controls and Exchange Rate Instability in Developing Economies*, Dec. 2000. A big debate about the transition from capital controls is whether it should be rapid or deliberate. Despite speedy decontrols in some countries, many observers seem to believe that countries should decontrol gradually while they build their domestic financial systems. See Ariyoshi, 31.

Notes and Questions

1. How would capital controls affect cross-border and offshore financial transactions and activities? For example, would Citibank's bank subsidiary in Bombay, India be likely to want India to remove its exchange controls? How would capital controls in South Africa be likely to affect the development of the Johannesburg Stock Exchange and the exchanges of neighboring countries? Would Swiss banks, on balance, want all countries to abolish their capital controls? Would a major Swiss reinsurer want this?

2. Developing countries with large economies, such as China and India, have apparently used capital controls to insulate themselves from the vagaries of international capital flows. Why would a country like Indonesia, with a population of almost 200 million and a diversifying economy, reject capital controls as ineffective?

D. THE DEBATE ABOUT THE 1990S' FOREIGN EXCHANGE REGIME

By the late 1980s, people referred to the international monetary non-system. They observed that no agreement existed among the world's nations about how to share responsibilities to correct significant balance of payments disequilibria. Although the dollar still served as the reserve currency, its strength eroded steadily against currencies like the yen and the Deutschmark. Indeed, some people saw currency blocs emerging: the DM (or ECU) in Europe, the yen in Asia Pacific, and the dollar in the Western Hemisphere.

Critics of this "non-system" argued that the G-7, though key players, had no duties to manage exchange rates and regularly placed their domestic economic goals above international ones. Japan, for example, was reported to spend $35 billion to slow the yen appreciation against the dollar over 15 months starting January 1993. The government feared an even stronger yen would reduce exports and raise imports, hurting the domestic economy. Though the G-7 and other governments set exchange rate targets, they were so broad and soft as to be irrelevant in practice. Noting that exchange rate fluctuations since the mid-1970s were large and frequent, compared to the Bretton Woods era, the critics asserted that the instability hurt the world's real economies and trade in particular by increasing the uncertainty in cross-border business. This in turn encouraged protectionism. For an interesting discussion, see Y. Kashiwagi, *Future of the International Monetary System and the Role of the IMF*, and K. Ohno, *The Case for a New System in* Bretton Woods: Looking to the Future, (Bretton Woods Commission ed., July 1994).

Proponents of a new system urged a shift from the classical regimes. One proposal built on the European Monetary System. It would define zones in which currencies could fluctuate without government intervention, specify governments' duties when a currency reached the edge of a band, and provide rules for realignment. See P. Kenen, *Ways to Reform Exchange-Rate Arrangements*, in Bretton Woods Commission. A second proposal would set target rates to reflect economic fundamentals, realign the targets continuously as the fundamentals shifted, allow relatively broad bands (say 10% above or below the target rate), and even allow currencies to move outside those bands temporarily. A more ambitious version would have the G-7 follow a blueprint for economic policy coordination to meet agreed current account targets, assisted by a permanent secretariat (possibly in the IMF). See C. Bergsten and J. Williamson, *Is the Time Ripe for Target Zones or the Blueprint?* in Bretton Woods Commission. Even the managing director of the International Monetary Fund called for currencies to be pegged against central values or kept within target ranges.

The problem for these proposals was that many people believed the "non-system" was not particularly bad. In their view, exchange rates had been relatively stable from 1987 Changing fundamentals justified the decline in the dollar after that time. See M. Wolf, *In Praise of the International Monetary Non-System*, Financial Times, March 28 1994. One leading scholar argued that it was a mistake to see countries as being forced to choose between fixed rates or a completely floating system. In his view, different regimes are appropriate for different countries or for the same country at different times. Very large countries may find floating best because it gives them some control over their monetary policy, while small open countries or those with a history of hyperinflation may prefer fixed regimes since they lack effective control over monetary policy. Many countries could, however, prefer the middle ground of some partial float. Examples include those trying to end high inflation, with an overvalued peg, or with a large neighbor with which they are tightly linked. J. Frankel, *No Single Currency Regime is Right for All Countries or At All Times*, National Bureau of Economic Research, September 1999.

E. FOREIGN EXCHANGE MARKETS

Foreign exchange markets include cash, spot, forward, swap, futures, and options. Here we focus on the spot and forward markets. Elsewhere in the book we treat derivatives markets. The cash market transfers bank notes at both a retail level, for users such as travelers, and a wholesale level among banks. It is relatively small.

Daily worldwide foreign exchange turnover in traditional markets (spot, forward and forex swaps) grew from $590 billion in 1989 to $1.5 trillion, then fell to $1.2 trillion in 2001 with the introduction of the euro and on-line trading, described below. The rate of growth measured in nominal dollars was already slowing: 26% in 1995-98, compared to 48% from 1992-95 and 42% from 1989-92. Part of the slowdown reflected the increased strength of the dollar against other currencies. Transactions increasingly took place in two locations: London (26% of all activity in 1989 and 31% in 2001) and New York (16% in 1989 and 2001). The shares of other centers by 2001 were: Tokyo - 9% (down from 15% in 1989), Singapore - 6%, Hong Kong 4%, Zurich - 4%, and Frankfurt - 5%. Most transactions – by 2001, 90% – involved the US dollar, though trading of "exotic" currencies, such as those of emerging markets, increased. In most countries, the spot market dominated, but its share of all FX trading had declined worldwide from about 60% in 1989 to 32% in 2001; in the remainder, the share of forex swaps was five time larger than forwards in 2001.

In addition to the traditional markets, daily turnover in currency derivatives (mainly options) was $60 billion and OTC interest rate derivatives (mainly swaps) was $489 billion by 2001 See Bank for International Settlements, *Triennial Central Bank Survey of Foreign Exchange and Derivatives Markets Activity in 2001* (Oct. 19, 1998), and *Turnover on Foreign Exchange Markets Tumbles*, financial Times, May 13, 2001.

The IMF sketched the market structure:

M. GOLDSTEIN, INTERNATIONAL CAPITAL MARKETS, PART I
International Monetary Fund, 25–26 (1993) ("Goldstein")

Foreign exchange transactions are organized at two levels: the wholesale (often called "interbank") market in which dealers trade with each other and with the central banks, and the retail market, which comprises customer transactions. Brokers and dealers participate in both markets, as do some central banks. The distinction between the retail and wholesale markets has become further blurred as some of the larger customers have gained access to the wholesale market through automated trading systems and direct communication links with a large number of dealing banks and financial institutions. The essential difference between dealers and customers is that the latter generally initiate most of their trades whereas dealers also buy and sell foreign currencies in response to orders received from their clients.

The wholesale market is an over-the-counter (OTC) market with no central clearinghouse or exchange. Foreign exchange market activity is dominated by transactions among dealers.

. . .

But the share of wholesale transactions in total net turnover [revenue] is decreasing. In the United Kingdom, the share of wholesale trade declined from 91 percent in 1986 to 77 percent in 1992.

The dominance of wholesale transactions reflects dealers' position-taking activity; however, most banks have internal controls … limiting the size of their open positions. In addition, each retail transaction gives rise to a greater number of wholesale transactions. The limits on open positions, especially overnight positions, mean that dealers will generally try to offset the exposures that result from retail trades. If the bank cannot find another customer interested in undertaking exactly the reverse of the original transaction on the same day, it generally tries to close the position by trading on the wholesale market. If another bank is willing to undertake the reverse transaction, this generates a 1:1 ratio between wholesale orders and retail orders; otherwise, offsetting the original trade would require two or more wholesale transactions. More wholesale transactions are often required to cover an exposure involving forward, swap, or derivatives contracts, particularly if the bank is exposed to changes in a nondollar exchange rate.

The foreign exchange market is dominated by the dealing banks, many of which specialize in making markets in particular currencies—that is, posting public bid and ask prices. For example, the 1993 survey of activity in the United States found that 83 percent of total gross turnover was accounted for by market makers .... Similarly, ... the ten largest dealing banks accounted for 41 percent of total activity . ...

[T]he broker's role in the wholesale market is to match buyers and sellers of foreign exchange, in return for a commission that is usually specified as a percentage of the volume of the transaction. This role is important, owing to the large number of dealing banks .... Larger banks ... dispense with brokers and maintain close working relationships directly with the market-makers in order to have access to timely quotes.   ... [B]rokers' share of trading ... has declined [with the] introduction and increased use of automated dealing systems.

1. THE SPOT FOREIGN EXCHANGE MARKET

The spot foreign exchange market is where currency can be bought or sold for immediate delivery, usually two days following the transaction. The price at which the currency is quoted is known as the "spot rate."

The foreign exchange market is the largest financial market in the world. It is an informal organization of the larger commercial banks and a number of foreign exchange brokers for buying and selling foreign currencies. The spot markets are extremely efficient. Spreads between buying and selling prices can be smaller than a tenth of a percent of the value of a contract. This is about one-fortieth of the spread international travelers pay to exchange currency notes.

This efficiency is also seen in the tremendous speed with which exchange rates respond to the continuous flow of information on the market. The participants are linked together by telephone, Telex, and a satellite communications network called the Society for Worldwide International Financial Telecommunications, SWIFT. Owing to the speed of communications, significant events have almost immediate impact everywhere in the world despite the huge distances separating market participants. In fact, in some of the major foreign exchange players in London, New York, and Tokyo maintain 24 hour operations. This is why the foreign exchange market is as efficient as a conventional stock or commodity market housed under a common roof.

The banks and foreign exchange brokers, in all countries, collectively establish exchange rates. Each dealer gets a sense of where the market is headed and takes positions to buy or sell on the basis of these assumptions and corresponding to orders received from customers. The feel for the market in each currency, as well as the goal of trying to balance the books, is what determines the position the banker is willing to take. If it is determined that the bank's exposure in euros should be balanced and, further, customers wish to sell euros, the bank will enter the market to sell euros.

Once the amount of buying or selling of a currency has been decided, the banker will contact other foreign exchange dealers to "ask for the market." The banker does not reveal whether he wants to buy or sell, but rather might inquire, "What's your market in euros?" This means he is asking for the price at which the other party is willing to buy and sell euros for U.S. dollars. The reason for the veil of secrecy is that the stakes are incredibly high. A mere difference in quotation of the fourth decimal place of a price can mean thousands of dollars on a large order.

If the banker who has been called wants to sell euros, he will quote on the side that is felt to be cheap for euros, given this banker's sense of the market. For example, if the banker believes that other banks are selling euros at \$1.1328/euro he or she might quote \$1.1326/euro as the selling price to attract business. The banker actually quotes both the buying and selling price. Having considered the two-way price, the caller will state whether he desires to buy or sell euros and the amount. Once the rate has been quoted, custom requires that it must be honored regardless of the decision of the caller and the amount that is involved. The caller has about 1 minute to decide and it is permissible to change the rate after this time. While it is only exchange rates between banks that are settled in the spot market, exchange rates paid by banks' clients are based on these interbank rates. Banks charge their customers slightly more than the going selling or ask rate, and pay their customers slightly less than the buying or bid rate.

With so many participants in the market, it is difficult to comprehend that each currency actually clears, or rather, supply equals demand. To help the markets clear, banks sometimes use foreign exchange brokers as intermediaries to find sellers when banks want to buy currencies and buyers when banks want to sell.

The method for conducting business with brokers is different from that of banks dealing with each other. A bank calls a broker and states how much foreign currency it wants to buy or sell and the rate at which it is willing to transact. This means that it will not ask for a two-way market but will offer to buy or sell at a set rate for a certain amount. The broker will announce to other banks what rates and amounts are available, always showing the best quotes to the potential counterparties. If the two sides of the market are equivalent so that a bank will meet the exchange rate demanded by another bank, a trade will be struck. Until an agreement has been met, neither of the two parties are aware of the identity of the other. Once the contract is created, the broker provides the names of the two banks and receives a fee from each of them. This fee makes dealing through brokers more costly than direct exchange, encouraging larger institutions to try to make a market between themselves before turning to a broker.

The spot markets in Canada, Britain, and many other countries are, like the United States, loose organizations of banks and brokers. In France, Germany, and the Scandinavian countries, the procedure is more formal, with bank representatives, including an official of the central bank, meeting daily in the same room. Contracts are exchanged directly, however an informal market does co-exist where many of the transactions take place. The formal meeting provides official settlement exchange rates for certain types of transactions. Much of this section is drawn from Levi at 29-37.

Notes and Questions

1. Assume you are advising a U.S. multinational company. The company regularly and in large volumes exports goods to France and buys French products. It holds at least $1 million in French bank accounts and liquid French securities. The company also trades with and invests in the U.K. It is a time when the euro is under pressure and it seems likely that the euro will devalue further against the pound.

   a. The company can use the spot market to protect itself. The US MNC is concerned about its accounts in US dollars, not euros or sterling. If it wants to protect itself against a further decline in the euro, it will move to dollars, withdrawing the funds from the bank account and exchanging into dollars.

   b. A shift to dollars would be hedging by the MNC. If the MNC draws from its euro account to buy pounds, it is speculating.

   c. The effect of the company's actions on the euro/£ exchange rate would be to push the euro down against the pound.

2. In 1992, electronic foreign exchange brokerage services were introduced. Within the next two years, at least four competing services appeared. Two leading providers were Reuters and Electronic Broking System. Electronic broking allowed banks' dealers, particularly in smaller banks, to by-pass the brokers and offer buy or sell orders directly to other banks' dealers. Trades are anonymous and prices transparent, unlike trades with brokers. By 1996, electronic broking accounted for over 33% of all spot transactions and over 50% of yen-dollar spot transactions in Tokyo. See T. Ito and D. Folkerts-Landau, *International Capital Markets*, International Monetary Fund 126-9 (1996) (Ito and Folkerts-Landau).

3. Two different views of the way dealers price are inventory control and private information. The first assumes that much trading occurs as dealers hedge; they modify prices to affect their positions. This is sometimes called hot-potato trading, as an end-user's transaction passes through many dealers. The second assumes that some dealers, better informed than others by virtue of their trading activity, use this information to price transactions. The important point is that in both views, order flow affects prices. See Ito and Folkerts-Landau.

4. Leading international banks, handling 30% of FX business, established a central clearing bank linking national systems to provide instantaneous settlement. By late 2001, it had over 70 banks, and the leading central banks, as members. Called the CSL Bank (for Continuous Linked Settlement), it will match and settle trades in five hours. It will be housed in London but regulated by the Fed. A. Skorecki, Forex System That Takes the Waiting out of Wanting, Financial Times, Jan. 4, 2002. See Chapter 10 for information about the payment system.

5. Recently the foreign exchange markets have been suffering from liquidity problems. For example on February 28, 2000 the euro fell 5 percent against the yen as the market was trying to handle a modest sale of euros. The reason for this problem are the rise of electronic matching systems, which do not need market makers to provide liquidity and a vacuum created by hedge funds leaving the foreign exchange markets for more profitable equity markets. Despite these problems, banks are pushing forward with high technology platforms which give clients online access to quotes from several rival banks. See C. Swann, *Healthy Facade Conceals Frustrations*, Financial Times, June 2, 2000 at I, VI. In fact, multi-bank internet platforms have begun to give clients access to bid-offer prices from a range of banks--which will not have similar access to each other's prices. Two competing systems have started. Currenex is based in California and backed by Shell and Nokia, while FXConnect is backed by State Street Bank. They serve institutional customers. In late 2001, some estimates put on-line currency trading at 10-12% of all FX trading and estimated their market share could rise to 30% to 40%. See *E Pluribus Unum*, Euromoney, October 2000, at 89, and D. Cameron, *Currenex to Form Exchange*, Financial Times, Nov.26, 2001.

2. THE FORWARD MARKET

In the forward market the parties contract today to deliver "currency at a specified date in the future, at a price agreed upon today." See Levi 50. Forward exchange quotations are common in the most heavily traded currencies. Banks will give each other quotations only for rather short periods, such as 30–days, 90–days, and 180–days. Banks tailor contract periods for their customers from two days to several years. The longer contracts carry greater spreads between the buy and sell prices because as maturity increases the market thins, making it more difficult for banks to offset their positions.

Two types of forward contracts prevail, according to the IMF. See Goldstein 29:

Forward contracts are concluded either in isolation (so-called outright forward purchases or sales) or in combination with a spot or another forward contract in what is referred to as a swap. An outright forward contract is an agreement to exchange specified amounts of one currency for another at some date beyond the spot value date and at an exchange rate specified in the contract. Forward contracts generally come in standard maturities of one month, two months, and so on. Outright forward contracts are not generally concluded between dealers but are common transactions in retail business: they can be closely matched to the customer's needs by being written with nonstandardized quantities and with customer-specific value dates and delivery locations.

Most forward contracts are written as part of a swap arrangement, the simplest form of which matches an exchange of one currency for another on the current spot value date and a reverse exchange on a forward basis. Since the two foreign exchange transactions are made at preset exchange rates, there is no exchange risk in this transaction, but considerable counterparty risk can be involved as one transaction is not made until the contract matures. Swaps are highly flexible instruments that provide a means of hedging against specific maturity exposures in foreign countries or of moving an exposure forward or back in time.

. . .

Swaps are most commonly entered into by banks and other financial institutions. For example, in the United Kingdom in 1992, only 12 percent of retail business was accounted for by swaps involving nonfinancial customers. Swaps accounted for 41 percent of the total gross market turnover but only 34 percent of retail turnover. On the other hand, outright forward contracts are more often entered into by customers than dealers. For the United Kingdom, 12 percent of customer business (about evenly split between financial customers and nonfinancial customers) was in outright forward contracts compared with only 6 percent for the market as a whole.

Swaps and forwards are mainly short-term, seven days or less.

Notes and Questions

1. Be sure you understand the basic terms and players. What is forward exchange? Who are the major intermediaries?

2. To say that one currency (such as the pound) is at a forward premium against another (the euro) means that the pound spot rate for euros is below the pound forward rate. Markets expect the pound to increase in value against the euro. The euro is at a forward discount.

3. Return to the hypothetical in Question 1 in the section following spot markets. Assume that the French unit must pay the British unit 1 million pounds three months from now.

    a. The MNC could use the outright forward market to protect itself by having its French unit buy pounds forward now in order to lock in the rate.

b.   This would be hedging. Not to use the forward market would be speculative.

c.   The effect of the MNC's action on the euro/£ rate would be to reduce demand for the euro, increase demand for sterling, and push down the euro against the pound.

F.   PURCHASING POWER PARITY AND INTEREST RATE PARITY

Among the economic forces shaping foreign exchange movements, two of the most well known are purchasing power parity and interest rate parity.

Purchasing power parity applies to markets for goods and derives from the law of one price, which holds that "goods priced in different currencies should have the same price when one currency is translated into the other using the spot exchange rate prevailing at the time ...." See C. Kester and T. Luehrman, Case Problems in International Finance 38 (1993) (Kester and Luehrman). If the prices differ, arbitrageurs will buy the cheaper to sell elsewhere until the price differential is erased or else demand for the more expensive good drops, forcing its price down.

Purchasing power parity extends "the law of one price to prices of a basket of goods. In its absolute form, PPP says that the dollar price of a basket of goods in the U.S. is the pound price of the basket in Britain, multiplied by the exchange rate of dollars per pound." See Levi 121. The spot rate equates national price levels. "In its relative form, PPP says that the rate of change of the exchange rate is equal to the difference between inflation rates." See Levi 121.

Economists testing this theorem empirically achieved only weak results.

Interest rate parity extends PPP to financial securities. Kester and Luehrman explain below, using DM before the currency was replaced by the euro.

KESTER AND LUEHRMAN, 39–40.

INTEREST RATE PARITY

The *interest rate parity* (IRP) condition stipulates that the forward premium or discount for one currency relative to another should be equal to the ratio of nominal interest rates on securities of equal risk denominated in the two currencies in question.

Notationally, the relationship can be expressed as[***]:

$$\frac{F}{S} = \frac{(1 + R_F)}{(1 + R_D)} \quad \text{or alternatively} \quad F = S\frac{(1 + R_F)}{(1 + R_D)}$$

where F = the forward exchange rate for a given time interval
          S = the current spot exchange rate
         R_F = the nominal interest rate on a security with a maturity equal to that of the forward exchange rate and denominated in a foreign currency, expressed as a decimal fraction
        R_D = the nominal interest rate on a security of equivalent maturity and denominated in the domestic currency, also expressed as a decimal fraction

If this condition does not hold, then it will be possible to engage in covered interest arbitrage: a series of transactions that will provide a riskless profit. For example, if the yield on 1–year deutsche mark government bonds is 4 percent and the yield on 1–year U.S. Treasury notes is 8 percent, the deutsche mark should be trading at a 1–year forward premium to the dollar of 3.7% = [(1.04/1.08) – 1] × 100. Suppose the deutsche mark/dollar spot exchange rate was 1.8000. IRP would imply a 1–year forward rate of 1.8(1.04/1.08) = 1.7333. If, instead, the deutsche mark were trading in the 1–year forward market at 1.75, a riskless profit could be earned by buying what was cheap and selling what was dear, all the time remaining in a "square" position (i.e., being neither long nor short of deutsche marks or dollars). The arbitrage would work as follows:

1. Borrow deutsche marks today for 1 year at 4 percent.
2. Convert the borrowed deutsche marks to dollars in the spot market at an exchange rate of DM 1.8/$.
3. Invest the dollars for 1 year at 8 percent.
4. Buy deutsche marks forward 1 year at DM1.75/$.

If an arbitrageur borrowed, say, DM10 million in step 1, received $5,555,556 upon immediate conversion in the spot market, and received $6,000,000 after investing the dollars for one year at 8%, his or her future profit would be $57,143, regardless of what happened to the deutsche mark/dollar exchange rate during the intervening year. This can be determined by calculating the dollar size of the forward contract the arbitrageur would have to execute in order to repay the borrowed deutsche mark principal plus interest 1 year later: DM10,400,000/1.75 = $5,942,857. The difference between this sized forward contract and the $6 million proceeds from the dollar investment yields the riskless profit of $57,143. Note that the arbitrageur could achieve this without any equity commitment of his or her own. As many

---

[***] If interest rates are expressed on a continuously compounding basis, IRP can be approximated as $(F - S)/S = R_F - R_D$. This says that the forward premium or discount on a currency should equal the difference between interest rates.

arbitrageurs acted to exploit this opportunity, exchange rates and interest rates would be modified through the forces of supply and demand until they conformed to the IRP condition shown above.

———————

Empirical tests of interest rate parity support the theorem. Kester and Luehrman, for example, identified "potential covered interest arbitrage opportunities between the yen and the dollar from January 1976 to November 1985." They plotted "forward premia and discounts on the yen against the national differences in interest rates" and found "close conformity" after accounting for transaction costs. They found few opportunities for riskless profit, suggesting interest rate parity between the yen and the dollar. But they noted that currencies with less active markets might not have arbitrageurs able to borrow, lend, or cover forward in sufficient volume to achieve interest parity.

IRP works most clearly between currencies in offshore markets and, absent exchange controls, between offshore and onshore markets in the same currency. But most analysts find it does not hold well when one compares the difference between nominal interest rates and anticipated exchange rate changes. Nor do they find evidence of real interest rate parity, in which differences in nominal interest rates offset anticipated differences in inflation rates. R. Herring and R. Litan, Financial Regulation in the Global Economy (1994). An IMF review concluded in 1994 that PPP works as a guide to long-term exchange rate behavior but not for the short- and medium-term. Prices are often slow to change. Trade flows may be costly and time-consuming to change. Traded goods are not perfectly substitutable. The IMF study proposed a "macroeconomic balance approach" as an alternative. This would determine if a currency is over- or under-valued by relating the real exchange rate (that is, after adjusting for price differences between countries) to real domestic demand (a basic concept of macroeconomics). The goal is to identify the real exchange rate at which aggregate domestic and foreign demand are both in balance in the medium term. Needless to say, this calculation has a theoretical appeal and is very hard to compute. P. Clark, L. Bartolini, T. Bayoumi, and S. Symansky, Exchange Rates and Economic Fundamentals, A Framework for Analysis 115 (International Monetary Fund Occasional Paper, 1994). More recent studies do not even find evidence of strong PPP over the long run, though they do find weaker PPP. See C. Engel, Long-Run PPP May Not Hold After All, Nat'l Bur. of Econ. Research (1996) and A. Taylor, International Capital Mobility in History: Purchasing-Power Parity in the Long Run, Nat'l Bur. of Econ. Research (1996).

Prompted by an Economist survey using the price of a Big Mac in various countries to test relative exchange rates, one researcher found a rapid convergence to "relative Big Mac parity" and that deviations from that parity predict changes in exchange rates. With certain adjustments, the author associated a 10% undervaluation of hamburgers with a 3.5% appreciation in the currency over the next year. See R. Cumby, *Forecasting Exchange Rates and Relative Prices with the Hamburger Standard: Is What You Want What You Get with McParity?* Nat'l Bur. Of Econ. Research (1996).

Notes and Questions

1. Work through the illustrations of the interest parity condition to be sure you understand the principles. In the abstract, what is the relation between domestic interest rates and the value of a currency? What are the key relative cost elements that determine returns on securities?

2. Using the hypothetical in Question 1 in the section following spot markets:

(a) Assume the MNC described above faces these market conditions:

the spot exchange rate is euro 1.605 = £ 1 (or £ 0.623 = euro 1) and the three month forward rate is euro 1.612 = £ 1 (or £ 0.620 = euro 1); and domestic interest rates (annualized for a three month instrument) are 15% in the E.U. and 9% in the U.K.

Applying the interest rate parity theorem, should the MNC do nothing, borrow £10 million to invest in French securities for three months, or borrow euro 20 million to invest in U.K. securities?

(b) Assume most private market players expect the euro to devalue 10% against sterling within 6 months. How would their behavior in the forward markets affect the spot rates?

(c) How would your answer be affected by the following statement by Levi at 157?

"The amount of adjustment in the interest rates vis-a-vis spot or forward exchange rates depends on the 'thinness' of the markets. The spot exchange market and the securities markets are generally more active than the forward market. It is likely, therefore, that a large part of the adjustment toward interest parity will take place in the forward rate. ... We can therefore think of the forward premium as being determined by the interest differential."

3. One consequence of IRP was that investors from country A who bought bonds denominated in country B's currency might not find hedging as relevant as if they had invested in equity denominated in the B's currency. By buying the bonds, they were taking on both interest rate and currency risk. There should be a one to one trade-off between the cost of a foreign exchange future and the interest differential. Under what circumstances might this general rule not apply?

4. Assume you are the legal adviser for the underwriter of a five year Rupiah bond issued by a private borrower in Indonesia in 1996. Indonesia's central bank manages the value of the Rupiah against a basket of currencies dominated by the US dollar. It has devalued in small percentages a few time and fought off speculative attacks successfully several times over the last 10-15 years. Your client hopes to attract dollar-based investors as well as those in Indonesia. How would you advise your client to structure the transaction to deal with the FX risk of the dollar-based investors?

Links to Other Chapters

Foreign exchange regimes link to all other chapters in this book. The foreign exchange markets are part of the cross-border aspects of U.S. securities and banking (Chapters 2 and 3). Foreign exchange risk is a subject for capital adequacy (Chapter 4). While less of an issue for the EU internal market, foreign exchange regimes are a critical part of the European Monetary Union (Chapters 5 and 7). Japan's management of the yen's rate against other currencies drove much of government policy toward cross-border financial operations (Chapter 8).

International instruments and euromarket often exist because of foreign exchange markets (Chapters 9 and 12). Investors in asset securitizations may face foreign exchange risk (Chapter 13). Stock exchanges compete using currency differences (Chapter 14). Futures, options, and swaps exist in part to mitigate foreign exchange risk (Chapters 16 and 17) and mutual funds bear foreign exchange risk when they venture abroad (Chapter 18). Systems for payments and clearance and settlement must deal with problems, such as delays, created by foreign exchange markets.

Foreign exchange risk drives much cross-border investment in emerging markets (Chapters 19 and 20) and prompts investors to flee emerging markets en masse, creating crises (Chapters 21 and 22).

CHAPTER SEVEN

EUROPE'S ECONOMIC AND MONETARY UNION

The advent of the Economic and Monetary Union (EMU) in Europe is one of the major structural events in international finance over at least the last quarter century. Its potential impact radiates from foreign exchange markets, which it immediately affects, to markets for banking, bonds, equity, and derivatives.

This Chapter first describes the original plan for the organization of EMU and the stages to achieve union by January 1, 1999, as set out in the Maastricht Treaty. It then presents evaluations of the costs and benefits of monetary union in Europe. The Chapter presents the steps countries took toward convergence, to bring their economies to roughly similar levels of performance and align certain economic policies, laws, and institutions. Finally, the Chapter raises key issues about how the union has worked after January 1, 1999. The new euro coins and notes were introduced on schedule in the first two months of 2002.

A. THE DESIGN OF THE EUROPEAN MONETARY UNION

On January 1, 1999, eleven countries in the European Union began the third stage of the Economic and Monetary Union. They were Austria, Belgium, Germany, Finland, France, Ireland, Italy, Luxembourg, Netherlands, Portugal, and Spain. Two other countries—Denmark and the U.K.—had also qualified but decided not to join just yet. In October 2000, the Danish voters rejected entry into EMU. Sweden had not made its central bank sufficiently independent and Greece had not met the quantitative criteria to qualify. But in early 2000, the EU decided that Greece was ready to join, which it did in January 2001.

The following section describes the ground rules set by treaty to achieve monetary union in Europe and the key stages in the transition to union.

1. THE MAASTRICHT TREATY

EC member governments meeting December 1992 in Maastricht, the Netherlands, agreed to a treaty that would carry them to economic and monetary union in seven years. Their decision grew from recommendations made in 1989 by the Delors Committee. The plan included locking the currencies of each country permanently, following a single monetary policy, and using a single currency managed by the European Central Bank (ECB) in a European System of Central Banks (ESCB).

The treaty envisioned an evolution toward monetary union through three stages. In the first, through 1993, EU governments would try to coordinate their economic policies so that their economies could begin to converge, complete the Single Market (see Chapter 5), and adopt a stronger common competition policy. In Stage 2, from 1994 through 1998, EU countries would push their economies to converge toward common inflation rates, long-term interest rates, government deficits, and currency fluctuations within the European Exchange Rate Mechanism. The Treaty set numeric goals for each of these and provided that countries that met the targets would qualify for membership in Stage 3. The Treaty created the European Monetary Institute as a precursor to the European Central Bank, which was to be set up in mid-1998. The design of Stage 3 is described in the following article by the Bank of England.

THE MAASTRICHT AGREEMENT ON ECONOMIC AND MONETARY UNION
32 Bank of England Quarterly Bulletin 64 (1992).

Key features of Stage 3

Stage 3 will start with the irrevocable locking of exchange rates between participating currencies and with the assumption by the ECB and ESCB of their full powers under the Treaty. They will be responsible for issuing and managing the single currency—the ECU [the Euro]—that will replace national currencies in due course. The basket definition of the ECU will cease to apply when the locking of exchange rates takes place, but the single currency is unlikely to replace national currencies until some time, possibly up to several years, after that. At that time, the national central banks will issue the single currency, subject to ECB authorisation.

The primary objectives and basic tasks of the ESCB and ECB are laid down in Article 105 of the Treaty and Chapter 2 of the ESCB Statute; and the System's structure, operations, governance, and accountability in Articles 106–8 and 109a and b of the Treaty and Chapters III–VI of the Statute. Their primary objective will be to maintain price stability. They will also be required to support the 'general economic policies in the Community', without prejudice to the price stability objective. Their actions will be required to be in accordance with the principles of an open market economy, favouring an efficient allocation of resources.

The ESCB will have as its main tasks the formulation and execution of the single monetary policy, the holding and management of participating member states' official foreign exchange reserves, promotion of the smooth operation of payments systems, and contribution to 'the smooth conduct of policies pursued by the competent authorities relating to the prudential supervision of credit institutions and the stability of the financial system.' This mandate will imply pooling of national responsibility for monetary policy through participation in the Governing Council of the ECB. National central bank governors from participating states will be members of that Council, along with a full time Executive Board appointed by the Heads of State or Government of member states. Members of the Executive Board will have non-renewable eight-year terms. The terms of office of national central bank governors will be at least five years.

No specific *operational* role in prudential supervision is given to the ECB, but the ECOFIN Council will have power to confer specific tasks relating to policies on prudential supervision on the ECB in due course. Such a step would need to be based on a proposal from the Commission, and would require the assent of the European Parliament, and unanimity of all member states in the ECOFIN Council. Furthermore, the ECB and national central banks are empowered to provide clearing and payments facilities, and the ECB will be able to issue regulations on those activities within the Community and with third countries (Statute Article 22). Although the Treaty does not give the ECB an operational role in supervision, the ECB will inevitably be involved in major policy decisions in that area, as in other areas affecting monetary policy, and it would be able to supply liquidity to the banking system through its power 'to conduct credit operations with credit institutions and other market participants, with the lending being based on adequate collateral', subject to its other objectives and responsibilities (Statute Article 18.1, 2nd tiret). National central banks can maintain their existing role in prudential supervision, where they have one.

In the pursuit of their objectives and tasks under the Treaty, the ECB and national central banks are required to be free from all outside interference. Staff of the institutions and members of their decision-making bodies will be required not to seek or take instructions from any outside body, including Community bodies and national governments, and these bodies will undertake not to seek to influence the ECB or national central banks in the performance of their tasks.

Careful thought was given to the question how as powerful an institution as the ECB could be made accountable without detracting unduly from its policy independence. It was recognised that severe organisational and procedural difficulties would be encountered if the ECB were to be made directly accountable to twelve national governments and twelve parliaments individually. Accountability to governments is therefore to be secured through the ECOFIN Council, whose

President can participate (but not vote) in meetings of the ECB's Governing Council and submit motions for its consideration; and which may invite the President of the ECB to discuss with it matters relating to ECB tasks and objectives. The ECOFIN Council will also be empowered to amend certain parts of the ESCB Statute, although not those relating to its independence or principal objectives and tasks. The ECB must address an annual report on monetary policy to the European Parliament, the ECOFIN Council, the Commission and the European Council (of Heads of State or Government); and the ECB's President will be required to present the report to the ECOFIN Council and the European Parliament, which may debate it. The ECB President and other members of its Executive Board can be requested to attend hearings of competent committees of the European Parliament. Central bank governors will be free to attend national parliamentary committees in their national capacity or as a representative of the Governing Council of the ECB, although it is possible that they could not be required to do so in the latter capacity.

. . . Responsibility for the choice of exchange rate system (or regime) for the ECU (the single currency) against non-EC currencies in Stage 3, and the central ECU rate within the system, should remain essentially with the ECOFIN Council (Article 109 paragraph 1). It was also agreed that Ministers may, in the absence of a formal system for the exchange rate, 'formulate general orientations' for exchange rate policy *vis-á-vis* non-EC currencies (Article 109, paragraph 2). But the choice of system and central rates would have to be after consultation with the ECB, in an endeavour to reach consensus consistent with the price stability objective: any policy orientations would have to be without prejudice to that objective. Only experience can show how these arrangements will turn out in practice, but the agreed provisions clearly require that exchange rate policy is consistent with the non-inflationary monetary policy of EMU, and that the ECB will have a strong consultative role in this process. Day-to-day exchange rate operations will be the responsibility of the ECB, exercised in a manner consistent with the provisions on exchange rate policy. The ECB will be provided with a strategic sum—initially up to ECU50 billion—of foreign currency reserves for the conduct of exchange-market intervention (Statute Article 30.1).

Some key aspects of the role and operations of the ESCB were left mainly open for later decision. The precise division of labour between the ECB and national central banks in the execution of monetary policy will be for decision nearer the time, but it was agreed that the ECB would 'to the extent deemed possible and appropriate' conduct its operations through the national central banks (Statute Article 12.1, third paragraph), it being accepted that 'the national central banks are an integral part of the ESCB and shall act in accordance with the guidelines and instructions of the ECB' (Statute Article 14.3).

. . .

Fiscal policy provisions

The . . . Treaty contains a number of provisions that strengthen the process of fiscal surveillance begun in Stage 1 and introduce constraints in the size of fiscal deficits and their financing. From an early stage there was agreement on the three basic fiscal principles of 'no excessive fiscal deficits', 'no monetary financing' and 'no bailouts', but considerable debate developed about how these should be defined, and how they might be implemented in practice. In the event, agreement was reached on provisions that prohibit the ECB or national central banks from providing credit facilities to government or to Community institutions or other public sector bodies, and from purchasing debt instruments *directly* from them (Article 104). There are also provisions that will prevent the Community and governments of member states assuming the financial commitments of other governments or public authorities in the Community (Article 104b), as a necessary condition for the exercise of effective market discipline on national fiscal policy; and to set up more formal procedures of surveillance over fiscal policy, including numerical triggers designed to prompt a Commission investigation into the fiscal policy of member states (Article 104c). In extreme cases, if the ECOFIN Council concludes that policy is grossly in error, there is provision for sanctions on member states failing to correct excessive deficits (Article 104c, paragraph 11), including the imposition of fines.

Other aspects of macroeconomic policy in Stage 3 were left for decision by national governments, subject only to some extension of the kind of general consultation which is already practiced as part of economic surveillance under Stage 1 arrangements.

. . . The central bank governors of countries not joining Stage 3 would become members of an ECB *General* Council, which would take over the residual functions of the EMI, including in particular the administration of the EMCF and the monitoring of the EMS or a successor exchange rate arrangement governing relations between the single currency and the currencies of member states that do not join Stage 3. It is envisaged that there will be a continuation of arrangements for stabilising exchange rates within the Community in the event that some countries do not join Stage 3.

2. THE PROS AND CONS OF MONETARY UNION

As early as 1969, EC heads of state wanted to coordinate monetary policy. Twenty years later, a committee chaired by Jacques Delors proposed an Economic and Monetary Union (EMU). The committee described the expected costs and benefits of EMU, which are reported in the following article. Several critiques of monetary union are summarized after the article.

H. CARRÉ AND K. JOHNSON, PROGRESS
TOWARD A EUROPEAN MONETARY UNION

Federal Reserve Bulletin, Oct. 1991, at 769-76.

. . .

According to Robert A. Mundell's seminal contribution to the literature on "optimum currency areas," the judgment on the formation of a monetary area depends on balancing two factors:

1. Monetary union, especially with a single currency, provides benefits by eliminating transaction costs and the uncertainty associated with exchange rate variability.

2. If labor and capital cannot move freely among the regions of the union, adjustment to some kinds of economic shocks, without changes in the nominal exchange rates of the regions, will lead to unemployment and lost output.

On this basis, the overall cost-benefit balance of EMU may be uncertain because labor mobility in the Community is limited and is bound to remain limited at least for a time. Direct examination of the criteria for an optimum currency area for the EC member countries suggests that regional problems are likely. Compared with the U.S. economy, the EC member states show significantly lower labor mobility; have experienced to a greater degree economic shocks that have affected the constituent regions asymmetrically; and, as a result, have relied far more on adjustment of real exchange rates across regions.

The analysis of the costs and benefits of monetary union has been extended to include other considerations. In particular, some analysts have argued that the openness and the industrial diversification of the economies concerned are important criteria that need to be taken into account. The larger the volume of interregional trade, the greater are the cost savings stemming from a monetary union that links the regions. Changes in exchange rates to help sustain economic performance are less critical in a diversified industrial economy, with more intra-industry trade, than in a more specialized economy. In addition, recent developments in the theory of economic growth point to dynamic gains, potentially much greater than the direct gains associated with the elimination of transaction costs and more stable exchange rates. These gains would result from an improvement in the business climate that leads to a self-reinforcing cycle of stronger growth.

. . .

In 1990, the EC Commission staff published its evaluation of the potential benefits and costs of forming an economic and monetary union. On balance, the Commission staff found that EMU benefits are likely to outweigh the costs (see the following text).

The Main Benefits and Costs of EMU

The Commission of the European Communities recently completed an analysis of the main benefits and costs of forming EMU. The following statement, which is quoted from that study, groups the benefits and costs under five headings.

(i) *Efficiency and Growth.* Elimination of exchange rate uncertainty and transaction costs, and further refinements to the single market are sure to yield gains in efficiency. Through improving the risk-adjusted rate of return on capital and the business climate more generally there are good chances that a credible commitment to achieving EMU in the not-too- distant future will help further strengthen the trend of investment and growth.

(ii) *Price Stability.* This is a generally accepted objective, and beneficial economically in its own right. The problem is that of attaining price stability at least cost, and then maintaining it. The Community has the opportunity of being able to build its monetary union on the basis of the reputation for monetary stability of its least inflationary Member States. Given the paramount importance of credibility and expectations in winning the continuous fight against inflation at least cost, this is a great advantage.

(iii) *Public Finance.* A new framework of incentives and constraints will condition national budgetary policies, for which the key-words will be autonomy (to respond to country-specific problems), discipline (to avoid excessive deficits) and coordination (to assure an appropriate overall policy-mix in the Community). EMU will also bring valuable gains for many countries' national budgets through reductions in interest rates, as inflation and exchange risk premiums are eliminated. These benefits will very probably outweigh the loss of seigniorage revenue to be experienced by some countries.

(iv) *Adjusting to Economic Shocks.* The main potential cost of EMU is that represented by the loss of monetary and exchange rate policy as an instrument of economic adjustment at the national level. This loss should not be exaggerated since exchange rate changes by the Community in relation to the rest of the world will remain possible, whereas within the EMS the nominal exchange rate instrument is already largely abandoned, and EMU will reduce the incidence of country-specific shocks. Relative real labour costs will still be able to change; budgetary policies at national and Community levels will also absorb shocks and aid adjustment, and the external current account constraint will disappear.

Moreover, model simulations suggest that with EMU, compared to other regimes, the Community would have been able to absorb the major economic shocks of the last two decades with less disturbance in terms of the rate of inflation and, to some extent also, the level of real activity. This is of renewed relevance, given that the Gulf crisis of summer 1990 once again subjects the Community to a potentially damaging economic shock.

(v) *The International System.* With the ECU becoming a major international currency, there will be advantages for the Community as banks and enterprises conduct more of their international business in their own currency; moreover the monetary authorities will be able to economize in external reserves and achieve some international seigniorage gains. EMU will also mean that the Community will be better placed, through its unity, to secure its interests in international coordination processes and negotiate for a balanced multipolar system.

————

By many measures, the economies and financial markets of the countries that would make up EMU, when combined, came close to or sometimes exceeded either of the world's two largest economies, Japan or the U.S. This would give the Union the economies of scale necessary to succeed. See the following table.

A Comparison of EMU, Japanese, and U.S. Financial Markets (1995, in $ trillions unless otherwise stated)			
Indicator	EMU	Japan	U.S.
GDP	$ 6,804	$ 5,114	$ 7,354
Reserves less gold	$ 0.3	$ 0.2	$ 0.1
Stock market capitalization	$ 2,119	$ 3,667	$ 6,858
Public debt securities	$ 3,910	$ 3,450	$ 6,712
Private debt securities	$ 3,984	$ 1,876	$ 4,295
Bank assets	$11,972	$ 7,382	$ 5,000

Bonds, equities, bank assets
    Total:
    As % of GDP:
	$11,971
	310%
		$16,375
		320%
			$22,865
			315%

Population (mns)	286	125	263

Source: R. Cooper, *Key Currencies After the euro,* 22 World Economy 1, Jan. 1999.

After the treaty was published, Martin Feldstein, a Harvard economics professor who chaired President Reagan's Council of Economic Advisers, challenged the idea that EMU was a worthwhile goal. See M. Feldstein, *The Case Against EMU*, The Economist, June 13, 1992, at 19. We summarize Feldstein's argument in the following points:

First, the benefits do not outweigh the costs under EMU. "A move to a single currency is economically justified if the gains (lower transactions costs and an expanded financial market) ... outweigh the losses (the loss of domestic interest rates and the nominal exchange rate as policy tools)."

Second, a common currency will not enhance trade within the EU and may actually diminish it. Eliminating currency fluctuations within Europe is not necessary to facilitate trade because trading companies can hedge in increasingly efficient markets with low transactions costs. The US and Japan have seen their trade grow in periods of high currency variability.

Third, member countries will no longer be able to use monetary policy to manage domestic interest rates and the exchange rates. So a UK exporter to France competing with a US exporter could no longer benefit from a devaluation of sterling against the dollar when British costs but not EMU-wide costs would have justified a devaluation. The only way for the UK to adjust is by lowering wages and prices. Big differences among member countries will persist because their economies differ a lot (in products and imports) and big cultural differences reduce the mobility of labor, which would be a useful safety valve if a member country or region's economy was weak.

Fourth, the big US market and its common currency, the dollar, do not make a good model because the US also has a common fiscal policy. When a US region's economy turns down, its residents pay less tax and receive more transfers from the federal government. This helps the region recover. Europe's taxes are local and national, not EU-wide.

Fifth, EMU does not guarantee an EU-wide anti-inflationary policy. The Bundesbank forces that policy on many of its neighbors already. The institutional arrangements for the central bank allow politics to play an important role in decision-making, and many people see the European central bank as a device to reduce the power of the Bundesbank by making it share its power with other EMU members.

Sixth, while EMU's economic costs exceed its benefits, it sends a very important signal that political union is underway. This political function would justify EMU in a way that its economic effect does not.

Countering Feldstein was a group of European economists, who argued that "EMU is full of calculated risk. But so is the status quo ...." See P. De Grauwe, et al, *In reply to Feldstein*, The Economist, July 4, 1992, at 67. They said the transaction costs of hedging are big for smaller firms, devaluation is often ineffective and inflationary, and countries' economies would converge over time. The US has to have a federal tax because labor is so mobile that workers would move to escape taxes applied only at the state level, but Europe's national tax systems are more effective than any for the entire EU because labor mobility is low in Europe. They believed that the European central bank would be even more independent than the Bundesbank because the ECB's powers could only be changed by treaty, while the Bundesbank's powers could be changed by a majority vote in the German legislature. Finally, writing in mid-1992, they pointed to the success of the ERM and the convergence of many EU economies.

The loss of national control over monetary and foreign exchange policy may not be serious. Labor mobility is probably less of an issue than Feldstein suggested, according to some. Labor mobility may be low now as much because incentives to move are low as because barriers are high. Mobility should increase as economies integrate and English becomes more widespread, but the speed of these changes cannot be predicted now. B. Eichengreen, *European Monetary Unification: A Tour d'Horizon,* 14:3 Oxford Review of Economic Policy 24, 26-7 (1998) (Eichengreen).

"The *singleness* of monetary policy, administered centrally by the ECB, and the *multiplicity* of fiscal policies, run separately for each participant...could create...problems," according to Charles Taylor in 1997. Both fiscal and monetary policy can affect aggregate demand in the economy and inflation. The ECB is obliged to maintain price stability, but fiscal policy in which one or more member countries ran large deficits could destabilize prices. If one member country pursued such an expansionary policy, that could have an expansionary effect on other members. Greater integration would bring greater spillover. If the ECB responded by raising real interests, the entire union would be hit, hurting investment and long run growth. C. Taylor, "The Separation of Monetary and Fiscal Policy in Stage Three of EMU," in L. Gormley, C. Hadjiemmanuil, I. Harden, eds., *European Economic and Monetary Union: The Institutional Framework* (1997) at 171 (Taylor 1997). On the other hand, automatic transfer from a federal (EU) budget to a country with high unemployment could create moral hazard if strong conditions did not accompany the transfer. Eichengreen at 30.

The different financial structures of member countries would augment the differential impact of ECB monetary policy. "A given change in the short-term interest rates...is likely to have a larger effect on lending rates and credit conditions in an economy with a liberalised banking system and much lending at variable rates, as in the UK, than in one where banks are still relatively cartelised and lending is typically at fixed rates, as in Germany." Taylor 1997 at 176.

As the euro becomes a reserve currency, it would displace the US dollar and, to some extent, the yen. The euro area would benefit, to the cost of the US. Indeed, as much as 20% of the stock of dollar assets held by non-residents of the US could be converted into euro holdings, forcing the dollar to depreciate. See R. Portes and H. Rey, *The Emergence of the euro as an International Currency*, National Bureau of Economic Research (1998). But it will take a long time for the euro to become a reserve currency, according to Eichengreen, because the euro and its managers must prove themselves.

Another analysis of the costs and benefits of EMU distinguished between the macroeconomic effects and the impact at the level of firms. At the macro level, EMU should lower transaction costs by about 0.2% to 0.5% of GDP each year, but the costs of conversion could equal the savings in the early years. By eliminating exchange rates variation among the member states, EMU takes away disruptive volatility from arbitrary speculation (a benefit of EMU) but also removes a tool to manage the macroeconomy (a cost). The ECB is expected to pursue policies that keep inflation low (a benefit). But since the Bundesbank had done so long before Stage 3, pulling many other countries with it, EMU will mainly help member countries with a history of higher inflation. If the ECB is less effective than the Bundesbank, the benefit will be less. Since the ECB must conduct its open market operations in the securities of member governments, rather than European federal debt, it can select which governments' debt to hold. How the ECB uses this power will affect its success. It could discipline profligate governments by not buying their paper, forcing up interest rates to help keep lower inflation. Or it could buy their paper and withhold the discipline. D. Carrie, The Pros and Cons of EMU (1997).

At the level of firms, Carrie argued, businesses will gain from lower costs of managing cash (since currency exchange costs inside Stage 3 countries would be eliminated), less currency risk (since that risk would not exist within Europe), and bigger, more integrated markets. Hedging is not a full substitute for currency union because no hedge is perfect and small and medium-sized firms often lack the management capacity to hedge well. So the currency union would be on balance beneficial.

Of course, it cost firm money to convert. EU bankers estimated in 1995 that the changeover would cost their industry 2% of annual operating costs each year for three to four years. See Federation Bancaire de l'Union Europeenne, Survey on the Introduction of the Single Currency: A First Contribution on the Practical Aspects (1995).

Notes and Questions

1. What do you see as the major costs and benefits of monetary union? Review the major policies, such as fixing exchange rates, creating the euro, and setting membership at eleven. Note that fiscal policy remains with the member governments, who issue their own debt (subject to ceilings described below). Monetary policy is set by the European Central Bank and implemented by the national central banks, who retain

no discretion as to policy. The ECB determines, for example, which markets for government debt are those in which the national central banks will engage in open market operations, buying and selling securities to affect supply and demand.

2. Feldstein, and many others, see the political goals of monetary union in Europe as much more compelling than the economic goals. What would account for the political goals? Do you agree with Feldstein?

B.   THE TRANSITION: GETTING TO STAGE 3

The treaty came into force November 1, 1993, despite opposition and even court challenges in several countries.

1. CONVERGENCE

In 1992, few EU countries met the convergence criteria for inflation, deficits, debt, exchange rates, and long-term interest rates. The story did not change in the years immediately following. From 1993 into 1997, since it appeared that many countries would not meet the convergence criteria on schedule, the EU confronted and rejected several modified paths to monetary union. A push for broad membership began in 1996. Several countries reduced their deficits by special actions that could not be repeated later, despite strong criticism from other countries.

The political map changed in May and June 1997. The Conservative government in the U.K. lost a national election to a "new" Labor government led by Tony Blair.   In contrast to the outgoing prime minister, who had campaigned against joining Stage 3, Prime Minister Blair supported EMU and expected the U.K. to become a member, though most probably not in 1999. In France, the conservative government lost in national elections to the Socialists, who required the support of the Communists to govern. The new government had campaigned against the slow growth and high unemployment caused by strict adherence to policies that would allow France to qualify for Stage 3. It continued, however, to support French membership in January 1, 1999. Even in late 1997, it appeared that Germany itself would not meet the fiscal criteria to qualify for membership in 1999 without radical and fast change. Kohl's government proposed suggested solutions that made Germans wonder if the Chancellor would accept harmful policies that would weaken Germany's economy in order to realize his dream of monetary union.

The EU settled several outstanding issues in mid-1997. In June, EU leaders agreed on a stability and growth pact, promising to coordinate economic policy but committing little new money to support employment. This is discussed below in Part C. Gradually, for eleven countries the key indicators converged, so that even by mid-1997 it appeared that all but Greece would qualify. The EMI confirmed this in March 1998 and during a meeting May 1-3, 1998 the heads of state officially set the membership in Stage 3 even though several countries barely qualified by some criteria.

Some critics argued that the indicators did not really measure convergence among the economies. They said that these macroeconomic indicators were very limited and that the EU needs measures of social factors to gauge convergence. For example, a stereotype of Germany has its people giving very high priority to stability and low inflation, while one of France has its people preferring to improve living standards. In this view, unless these underlying social factors become more common across the Stage 3 countries, the economies have not really converged.

2. THE MONETARY INSTITUTIONS FOR STAGES 2 AND 3

The European Central Bank was created during the summer of 1998, replacing the European Monetary Institute (EMI), which had officially opened January 1, 1994 at the start of Stage 3. The main jobs for EMI were to prepare for the European System of Central Banks and help coordinate monetary policy among the central banks of EMU countries.

France and Germany engaged in a tug-of-war over who would head the ECB, which tested the credibility of EMU in financial markets. They failed to appoint the president until the last minute. They also forced the appointee—Wim Duisenberg of the Netherlands, favored by Germany—to promise to step down "voluntarily" after 4 years, at which time the French choice—Jean-Claude Trichet, of France—would succeed him. Duisenberg announced on February 8, 2002, that he would be stepping down in July 2003. Trichet's succession has been put in doubt by his entanglement in a criminal investigation of the collapse and bailout of Crédit Lyonnais in the early 1990s.

During the rest of 1998, the ECB prepared to take over monetary policy and operations from the national central banks on January 1, 1999. The Ecofin Council appointed ECB's executive board in May 1998. The six board members were leaders in European finance. They included Christian Noyer, a French civil servant, Otmar Issing, a German central banker, and Tommaso Padoa-Schioppa, formerly head of Italy's securities commission and vice chairman of the Bank of Italy. By December 31, 1998, the ECB completed the legislation needed for the ECB to work. Before that, the treaty was interpreted to allow the ECB to direct the national central banks to make necessary preparations. See R. Smits, The European Central Bank: Institutional Aspects (1997) at 128-9.

The assumption that the ECB would fulfill its mandate was questioned by many people. Formal and political power is distributed in a way that weakens the power of the ECB technocrats. Since ECB represented eleven countries rather than merely Germany, and its 6 Executive Board members were outnumbered on the Governing Council by 11 national central bank (NCB) representatives, the ECB might be less likely to pursue price stability than the Bundesbank had been. The ECB staff of only 700 people is outnumbered by the 60,000 people in the NCBs, who could brief their representatives on the Governing Board to represent national rather than EMU interests. This makes the ESCB a coalition of central banks rather than a unified organization, according to D. Gros, *EMU and Capital Markets: Big Bang or Glacier?*, 1 International Finance 3, 12 (1998) (Gros). The ECB, moreover, lacks the full authority of a central bank to set foreign exchange policy. It is subject to the Council of Ministers (the Ecofin Council) on issues involving basic foreign exchange policy, such as whether to take part in target zones with other major currencies like the dollar and yen, though the Council requires a unanimous vote to exercise this power.

3. THE SHIFT FROM MULTIPLE CURRENCIES TO ONE

To shift to the euro from the currencies of Stage 3, members made three decisions. Decision 1 was that the value of the euro against the dollar (and therefore other non-Stage 3 currencies) would equal the dollar value of the Ecu on December 31, 1998 and be set by foreign exchange markets after that. This was decided by Article 1091(4) of the treaty as interpreted by the European Council.

Decision 2 was the value of the currencies of the countries in Stage 3 against each other (setting cross-rates) and was officially announced on May 2, 1998 by the European Council of the EU in the *Joint Communique on the Determination of the Irrevocable Conversion Rates for the euro*. A cross rate is the rate of one currency against another, e.g. the DM against the French franc. Cross rates are important in Stage 3 because the rates affect the terms of trade among the members. If one national currency unit of the DM was the equivalent in euro of three French francs, then French goods would be less costly to buyers in Germany than if the DM was the equivalent of only 2 francs. The 1-to-3 cross rate would promote the sale of French goods to Germany and undercut the sale of German goods in France. It would take a long time for costs in the two countries to adjust to this imbalance.

The cross rates had to be in place on January 1, 1999 when the currencies acquired irrevocable rates (called conversion factors) against the euro and therefore against each other. The EU decided that the fixed cross rates would be the official cross rates of the currencies in the Ecu, called the bilateral central rates. For example, from January 1, 1999, one DM would equal 3.35386 French francs and one French franc would equal DM 0.298163. The EU announced the cross rates in May 1998 to give the markets time to adjust and to promote stable foreign exchange markets during the transition.

Decision 3, on December 31, 1998, fixed the conversion factor of each old currency against the euro when it came into existence on January 1,

1999. That is, from 1999 on, the DM should have a fixed conversion factor of 1.95583 to a euro (see the table).

Irrevocable Rates of Each Stage 3 Currency against the euro, set December 31, 1998	
Stage 3 Member and Currency	**Rate against one euro**
GERMANY (DEM)	1.95583
BELGIUM/LUXEMB. (BEF/LUF)	40.3399
SPAIN (ESP)	166.386
FRANCE (FRF)	6.55957
IRELAND (IEP)	0.787564
ITALY (ITL)	1,936.27
NETHERL. (NLG)	2.20371
AUSTRIA (ATS)	13.7603
PORTUGAL (PTE)	200.482
FINLAND (IM)	5.94573

Source: Council Regulation (EC) No. 2866/98 of 31 December 1998, Official Journal of the European Communities 31 December 1998, L359/1

On December 31, 1998 the ECB calculated the final value of the Ecu, in dollars, using the dollar market rates of each currency against the Ecu that day. Since 1 Ecu equaled 1 euro, this final Ecu/$ rate became the official euro/$ rate. Also from that day on, the cross-rates for all currencies of countries entering Stage 3 were their official bilateral cross rates, described above. The ECB also calculated the irrevocable rates of each stage 3 currency against the euro (see the table).

When markets opened on January 4, 1999, the market set the rate of one euro to $1.17. By the Big Mac test, the euro was 13% overvalued. A Big Mac hamburger cost an average of $2.98 in the 11 European countries in early January, compared to only $2.63 in the US, according to *Food for Thought*, Economist, Jan. 9, 1999, at 68. In any case, the euro fell against the dollar to below $0.90 in May 2000. Initially, investors worried about the weakness of the German economy and mounting tension between the German government and the ECB. Oskar Lafontaine, the outspoken finance minister, forcibly argued that the ECB should ease its monetary finance minister quit, markets took heart and the euro rose immediately to $1.10. But from then on, the euro fell against the dollar, the pound, and even more against the yen. In part, weak economic performance by Germany and the government's direct involvement in the economy continued to be major concerns. In part, market sentiment soured on the euro. By September 2000, the euro had fallen to less than $.90 and the ECB raised interest rates by 0.25 percentage point with little impact on the euro's value, and reached a low of $.82 by October. So far in 2002, the euro has made somewhat of a recovery, standing at $.87 on February 19, but it is still substantially below its opening 1999 value of $1.17. Contrary to most expectations, the euro has become a "weak" currency.

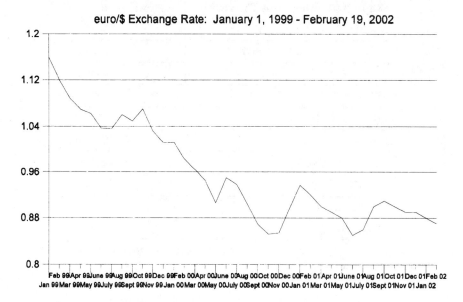

euro/$ Exchange Rate: January 1, 1999 - February 19, 2002

Notes and Questions

1. Will the ECB be independent and effective?

2. Is it wise to define the ECB's sole goal as price stability? Why would this have been done? What is the effect of the governance structure for the ESCB? Would you expect the ECB to be stronger or weaker than Germany's Bundesbank?

3. How significant is it that the value of the euro has been weak as against the dollar? The standard explanation for the weak euro was the economic growth differential between Europe and the U.S.; however, the euro fell even while European stock markets outperformed those in the U.S. See D. Cohen and O. Loisel, *Why was the euro weak? Markets and Policies*, Centre for Economic Policy Research, Working Paper No. 2633, December 2000. Can the euro survive in the long term if it remains a "weak" currency? In May 2001, the ECB cut interest rates although inflation seemed to be rising, raising the question of whether it was

sacrificing price stability in response to concerns over the weak euro or demands by the United States that it needed to stimulate economic growth.

C.   STAGE 3: HOW DOES IT WORK?

Once Stage 3 was achieved, from January 1, 1999, the important question became how it would work. Stage 3 was itself transitional, and EMI set a schedule for its further evolution into 2002. This is set out below. Several matters directly involve international financial markets. These include the impact of EMU on systems for payments, clearance, and settlement, financial markets, government accounts, fiscal and monetary policy, continuity of contracts, and the UK as a financial center. Each topic is discussed below. Finally, this section raises the question of whether Stage 3 will survive.

1. FROM 1999 TO 2002: EMI'S SCHEDULE

The transition from national currencies to the euro would be gradual. In May 1995, the EMI published the *Green Paper on the Practical Arrangements for the Introduction of the Single Currency,* (the Green Paper) and in November 1995, after discussing the Green Paper with many affected groups in the public and private sector, the EMI published *The Changeover to the Single Currency* (The Changeover). The EMI called the period before Stage 3 "Phase A." The Changeover identified several key periods:

a. *At the starting date of Stage 3* (January 1, 1999), the euro started to be used in scriptural, non-cash form but national banknotes remained the only banknotes with legal tender status. The ESCB started conducting its single monetary policy in the European currency. Financial markets largely changed over to the euro on January 1, 1999 or soon after. However, most private individuals and most enterprises continue to operate in the national monetary units. This is "Phase B," from 1999-2001.

b. *At the latest three years after the start of Stage 3* (January 1, 2002) the ESCB will start issuing euro banknotes and start exchanging the national banknotes and coins against the euro. At the end of the period, all economic agents, including the public sector, will have completed the changeover to the euro ["Phase C," January 1- June 30, 2002]. The introduction of euro notes and cash was on schedule, and took place in the first two months of 2002. The chart below, from G. Yeowart, *How to get ready for the euro*, International Financial Law Review 17 (December 2001) set out the dates until which commercial and national central banks will replace legacy notes and coins for euros:

Time limits for exchanging legacy coins

State	Commercial banks	National central banks	
	Notes/coins	Notes	Coins
Austria	*	unlimited	unlimited
Belgium	12/31/2002	unlimited	end of 2004
Finland	*	10 years	10 years
France	6/30/2002	10 years	3 years
Germany	*	unlimited	unlimited
Greece	*	10 years	2 years
Italy	*	10 years	10 years
Ireland	*	unlimited	unlimited
Luxembourg	6/30/2002	unlimited	end of 2004
Netherlands	12/31/2002	1/1/2032	1/1/2007
Portugal	6/30/2002	20 years	end of 2002
Spain	6/30/2002	unlimited	unlimited

* At least until March 1, 2002, afterwards to be decided individually by banks.

c. *Six months after the first day of introduction of the European banknotes and coins* (July 1, 2002) the changeover to the euro will have been completed for all operations and all agents. National banknotes and coins, which will gradually disappear from circulation, will lose their legal tender status and the euro ones will become the only banknotes and coins to have the status of legal tender within the European currency area. The distribution process was completed in early 2002.

2. FINANCIAL MATTERS

a. THE SEQUENCE IN SWITCHING TO THE EURO

At the start of Stage 3, the euro became the currency for the accounts of the ESCB and national central banks, and for the ESCB's conduct of monetary policy and foreign exchange operations. The euro also became the currency of new public bond issues, although investors could settle in national currencies. Until the euro became the sole EMU currency, the euro and national currencies of EMU member countries co-existed, with the national currencies as perfect substitutes for the euro. The national central banks, as part of the ESCB, recorded all their transactions in euro, but permitted financial institutions, national treasuries, and other public and private parties dealing with the central bank to transact in the national currency.

For non-cash transactions in the private sector, the euro quickly came to dominate inter-bank and foreign exchange markets. About 90% of all financial transactions were non-cash, so this was important. Over Conversion Weekend, the weekend of January 1, 1999, the euro became the currency for interbank payments, securities traded on European exchanges as well as dividends and coupons on them, and outstanding government debt and new issues, so professional traders could operate in euro. Major multinational corporations changed over quickly. As expected, consumers and small businesses were the slowest to change.

The official reason that it would take up to three and one-half years for cash transactions to change to the euro was logistical. Old banknotes and coins had to be replaced by the new ones. The EMI estimated that "at the end of 1994 "more than 12 billion banknotes and 70 billion coins, with a weight of more than 300,000 tons, were in circulation in the EU Member States." See The Changeover 36. Retooling automated teller machines, teller assist systems, and coin-operated machines would take time. The public had to be educated. The dual operating systems for banks during this time would be complicated.

Since EMU would not initially include all EU or EMS members, a new exchange rate mechanism (ERM) was set up on January 1, 1999 to replace the EMS. Membership was voluntary. Denmark and Greece chose to join, while Sweden and the UK stayed out. The ECB and central banks of non-euro EU countries defined the operating procedures. The EU prescribed a mechanism based on central rates with the euro and with fluctuations of 15% above or below that rate. So the euro would form the core currency, around which currencies of the non-Stage 3 members of EMS could fluctuate.

b. LENDER OF LAST RESORT

It is not clear how the lender-of-last-resort function will be discharged under EMU. This subject is raised in Article 18 of the Statute of the ECB, which merely provides:

18.1 In order to achieve the objectives of the ESCB and to carry out its tasks, the ECB and the national central banks may...conduct credit operations with credit institutions and other market participants, with lending being based on adequate collateral.

18.2 The ECB shall establish general principles for...credit operations carried out by itself or the national central banks, including for the announcement of conditions under which they stand ready to enter into such transactions.

A banking and financial crisis could demand more from the EMU institutions than they are able to deliver. They would have to provide liquidity quickly and lead organized work-outs. The ECB is limited in providing liquidity because it is must take "full and instantaneous collateral" from a bank seeking credit from it. To receive a loan from the ECB, an illiquid bank can give the ECB good collateral, defined as Tier 1 or Tier 2 assets. An insolvent bank cannot give good collateral because it has no capital, so it cannot receive a loan from the ECB. But because bank supervision is separated from the ECB and dispersed across the eleven member countries, the ECB will lack systematic information about troubled banks. The ECB must rely on the bank's national central bank to determine if collateral is good and, more broadly, if the bank is merely illiquid. The NCB can shift the cost of a bailout to the ECB (and so to all Stage 3 countries) by deciding that questionable Tier 1 or 2 assets are in fact good. Of course, the ECB is aware of this. If it is unable to evaluate assets offered as collateral, it may be unable to provide liquidity quickly at the crucial time. More generally, its sole mandate, to minimize inflation, could lead the ECB to withhold liquidity to banks during a crisis. So the ECB cannot be counted on to act as lender of last resort in a way the Bundesbank would have, earlier. See Begg at 37. More generally, "If several European banks are simultaneously hit by a default anywhere in the world, a very plausible occurrence, who is responsible for coordinating the orderly workout?" D. Begg, P. De Grauwe, F. Giavazzi, H. Uhlig, and C. Wyplosz, *The ECB: Safe at Any Speed?* (1998) (Begg), at 39. ECB is not responsible for bank supervision, although it liaises with national bank supervisors. See European Central Bank, Annual Report (1999) at 98.

Notes and Questions

1. Within EMU, should the ECB or the national central banks, or both, serve as lenders-of-last-resort to insolvent banks? One view is that the home-country central bank should be the lender-of-last resort, and not the ECB, because supervision remains at the home level. See D. Schoenmaker, "Banking Supervision and Lender-of-Last-Resort in EMU," in *European Economic and Monetary Union: The Institutional Framework,* M. Andenas, L. Gormley, C. Hadjiemmanuil, and I. Harden, eds. (1997).

2. Due to the adoption of the euro, national central banks will lose their ability to earn seignorage. This is the profit a central bank makes by issuing currency, on which it pays no interest, in exchange for bank deposits which it can invest to make interest. Member states will share seignorage earnings of the ECB, but only based on their share of ECB capital, which is determined by a country's share in EU population and GDP, an index that does not track foregone seignorage. Germany was a big loser on seignorage (due to the strong demand for DM currency), losing 41.1 billion euros, while France gained 23.5 billion euros. H. Feist, *The Enlargement of the European Union and the Redistribution of*

Seignorage Wealth, CESifo Working Paper No. 408, January 2001. It is also interesting to note that there will be an additional seignorage windfall of about $15 billion, due to the fact that it is estimated that this amount of legacy currencies will not be traded in for euros.

c.   IMPACT ON FINANCIAL MARKETS

Stage 3 immediately affected the cost and pricing of goods and services.   Not all businesses could pass their conversion costs on to customers. Banks were not allowed to levy fees when converting accounts to EMU. Retailers could pass most of their costs on to customers. Both national governments and the EU picked up some of the costs of training and public education. The consulting firm BCG estimated that banks would lose $5 billion in revenues each year after EMU was in place because FX business associated with the national currencies would disappear. So it came as no surprise when the Bank of England found overall FX turnover in London did fall 5%-10% in 1999 and turnover in other EU foreign exchange markets fell 15%-30%. Bank of England, *Practical Issues Arising from the euro*, December 1999, at 33.

There is much speculation about whether Stage 3 will lead to more integration among the markets of Stage 3 countries than has previously been achieved by the Single Market initiatives, e.g. the Second Banking Directive and the Investment Services Directive.   The following paragraphs describe changes by types of financial institutions, pricing mechanisms, and other conventions, in anticipation of, and after, January 1, 1999.

EU banks, which had begun to merge to achieve scale even before Stage 3, speeded up the trend afterwards. Banks struggled to recover from their loss of foreign exchange business within the eleven countries. Tiering in the interbank market increased, as credit risk replaced country and currency risk as the dominant concern. Bank of England, *Practical Issues Arising from the euro,* December 1999, at 28.

In government bond markets, all instruments redenominated to euro immediately. The markets continued in Stage 3 to vary by country, since each national government can issue bonds subject to the constraints of the Stability Pact on debt ratios (see below). The risk of each issue varies according to the risk associated with each country's government. Thus a German government bond is lower risk than one issued by the Italian government. Although each government continues to have the authority to tax, it cannot create money to repay its debt.   In this way, the government's debt in euro is like debt in a foreign currency, which is usually rated lower than debt in the home currency. Some private issuers of euro securities could even receive higher credit ratings than their governments. See Bank of England, *Practical Issues Arising from the Introduction of the euro*, Issue No. 7, pp. 62-64 (March 12, 1998); OECD,

Impact of the euro on Financial Markets, Financial Market Trends, no. 72, at 21, Feb. 1999.

In the first 18 months, yields on EU government bonds initially moved closer together, then started to diverge. From May to June 2000, Italian government bonds' premium over German government bonds (or gap) moved from 28 basis points to 37 b.p., for example. Reasons included Italy's much larger government debt relative to GNP, the declining supply of German bonds as the fiscal deficit fell, and the shift by investors into U.S., Japanese, and German bonds as interest rates rose worldwide. One question was whether if this trend continued it would affect the monetary union. A gap of 37 b.p. might not be large, but if it grew to several 100 b.p. it would signal a divergence in the economies within the union. The markets' diagnosis might be that the economies were failing to integrate as expected. An union under stress for other reasons might become even more fragile.

Corporate bond markets in 1999, as expected, became broader and deeper as institutional investors sought greater diversity and many companies began to issue in euro. Issuance of corporate bonds in euro were 130 billion euro, exceeding the value of bonds issued in dollars. While dollar issues exceeded euro issues in 2000, it is clear that the euro has strengthened the EU corporate bond markets. Much of the growth has been fueled by increased holding of euro denominated bonds by euroland rather than foreign investors. C. Detken and P. Hartmann, *The euro and International Capital Markets,* 3 International Finance 54 (2000).

Exchanges for stock and derivatives immediately quoted in euro. The exchanges increased cooperative efforts among themselves.

Pricing mechanisms were needed for instruments in the new currency. For medium and long-term instruments, normally a security would be priced off a reference rate provided by an instrument that was very low risk and traded in a liquid market. In the U.S., treasury securities serve as benchmarks. The benchmark for euro issues was still being established in early 2000. In long-term markets, German government long-term bonds were the logical benchmark, as trade in German issues vastly outnumbered trade in French government issues. In long-term instruments, a consistent spread began to appear between German securities and others. In medium-term markets, however, some French securities performed better as benchmarks than their German counterparts. Bank of England, *Practical Issues Arising from the euro,* December 1999, at 39.

In the interbank market for euro deposits, a mechanism was needed to set a short term rate for banks in all member countries. Bank trade associations designed an interbank offer rate for the euro, to be called EURIBOR. The European Banking Federation announced plans to calculate this rate from quotes given daily by a large panel of banks in each euro member country. The Federation published "a new euro area-wide overnight effective rate" using "actual rates at which trades take place in the money market, weighted by volume. . . ." See Bank of England, *Practical Issues Arising from the Introduction of the euro*, March 1998 at 100 ("Practical Issues March 1998).

At a technical level major changes took place in the conventions in these markets. Each national financial market had many conventions to resolve practical issues for trading and settling transactions in foreign exchange, securities, and money. The topics included the number of days in a year (360 or 365), the number of days to settle a trade, the expression of prices in decimals or fractions, and coupon frequency (annual or semi-annual). These were needed because, when the euro replaced each national currency, it became impossible to know from a security denominated in euro which nation's conventions applied. Many international security associations cooperated to design new conventions. C. Dammers, *Markets Move to euro Conventions*, International Financial Law Review 15-18 (December 1997).

Notes and Questions

1. Will the success of EMU be conditioned on the degree of integration in financial markets? Integration would seem to depend, in part, on whether the use of a common currency will lead to more cross-border investment. For most European countries, less than 10% of total financial assets are claims on foreign companies or governments. An important constraint on cross-border investment is national rules limiting foreign investments of pension funds and insurance companies. For example, France put a 5% ceiling on foreign assets.

2. Who will win and lose if further integration of capital markets is achieved?

3. Will the use of a common currency and the creation of the ECB have a substantial impact on the integration of banking markets? Who will win and lose if further integration of banking markets is achieved?

3. FISCAL AND MONETARY POLICY, AND THE STABILITY PACT

Fiscal policy remained a tool of the national governments. Germany sought to limit the use of this tool. At the Dublin summit in December 1996, EU leaders agreed to a "stability pact." Any country that ran a fiscal deficit greater than 3% of GDP for longer than 10 months would have to make a non-interest bearing deposit with the EC and, if it did not remedy the problem within two years, would have to pay a fine (if voted by two-thirds of the Stage 3 members of the European Council) of 0.2% of GDP, plus 0.1% of GDP for each year the deficit exceeded 3%, up to a total of 0.5% in fines. Less severe sanctions would require the country to publish more information before issuing government securities or reduce loans to the country by the European Investment Bank. A country with a decline in GDP of over 2% within the past four quarters could be exempted from penalties by the Council of Ministers. See *Resolution of the European Council*, No. 1467/97, June 7, 1997, O.J. No. L 209, 2-8-1997; *Regulation of the European Council*, No. 1466/97 , July 7, 1997, O.J. No. L 209, 2-9-1997.

Economists criticized this pact as so inflexible that it could create serious damage in a major recession. Rarely during the last 30 years had a county reported a 2% decline in GDP over four quarters, so rarely could a country expect to receive an exemption. Countries would be too limited when using deficit financing as a tool of fiscal policy to restore economic growth. During the 1993 recession, member government deficits had averaged 6% and were high in countries like France (5.8%), Belgium (6.6%), and the UK (7.7%). See Taylor 1997 at 179. If countries anticipated the ceiling, they would hold the deficit much lower than 3% to give themselves flexibility in a recession. This could keep their fiscal policy too tight and impede economic growth. On the other hand, many countries had barely met the 3% limit to qualify for membership in Stage 3. They would probably hover near the 3% limit for some time, leaving them no room for further deficit if the economy went into recession. If the 3% limit prevented effective macroeconomic responses, the political reaction, critics feared, would undermine EMU.

The problem with proposed solutions was that they could introduce too much flexibility. This had been a concern for some time. In 1995, former president of France Valery Giscard d'Estaing said the rules on budget deficits should be flexible enough to adjust for recessionary fiscal policy. Officials in the EU, Germany, and France immediately denounced his suggestion. In 1997, Taylor suggested that the deficit be calculated as a five year rolling average to take account of cyclical factors. To induce a country to lower its deficit, he recommended that in addition to the fines, which served as a stick, the other member governments offer a carrot in the form of a low cost loan that would help the country adjust. Indeed, he suggested that the members create a ministerial council for fiscal and monetary matters that would substitute for Ecofin. This would shift the decisions to specialists.

During 1999, the ECB warned that several member countries were adopting policies that would push their deficits to the 3% ceiling. By the end of 2000, however, members were well below the 3% ceiling. Excluding receipts from UMTS (telecommunications licensing fees), only five countries (Germany, France, Italy, Austria, and Portugal) showed a deficit above 0.5% GDP. Portugal was the top, at 1.7%. European Central Bank, *Annual Report 2000* (ECB 2000), p. 46. However, in 2002, the Commission was forecasting a 2.7 percent deficit in Germany, and some economists said it would be nearer to 3 percent. Financial Times, Jan. 29, 2002. Germany succeeded in avoiding a warning from the

Council in exchange for new commitments to bring its budget into line. Similar action was taken with Portugal. P. Norma, *Protagonists each claim satisfaction from accord,* Financial Times, Feb. 13, 2002.

Proposals to reduce the problems posed by the Stability Pact included structural change and a new instrument. One idea was to create one European agency that would issue debt for the governments of all 11 member countries. The governments would no longer do so. V. Boland and E. Tucker, *De Silguy Proposal May Confound Sceptics*, Financial Times, Aug. 4, 1999. The other idea was for the EU to set an overall ceiling for the deficit of all EMU members, issue permits to each member to incur a share of that deficit, and then allow members to trade the permits. Countries that needed to incur a larger deficit than permitted would buy some portion of the permit given to another member country. See A. Casella, *Tradable Deficit Permits: Efficient Implementation of the Stability Pact in the European Monetary Union*, National Bureau of Economic Research, Inc. Working Paper 7278, Aug. 1999. For an interesting collection of essays on the Stability Pact, see *The Stability and Growth Pact, the Architecture of Fiscal Policy in EMU*, A. Brumila, B. Bat and D. Franco, eds. (2001).

4. LEGAL MATTERS

There were two key legal issues involved in the conversion to the euro from national currencies. One establishes the euro as legal tender. The second determines the impact on contracts denominated in national currencies. Both of these issues have been dealt with in two important regulations that appear in the appendix to this chapter.

a. EURO AS LEGAL TENDER

From January 1, 1999 - December 31, 2001 (Phase B), the currency of the participating Member States was the euro, but national currencies continued to exist as alternative denominations of the euro. Article 8 (1)-(3) of the May 3 Regulation indicates that cashless payments could be made either in euros or national currencies at the euro conversion rate. This, in effect, meant that both the euro and national currencies constituted legal tender. From January 1, 2002 and thereafter (Phase C), national currencies disappeared and only the euro was legal tender. May 3 Regulation, Article 14.

b. CONTINUITY OF CONTRACT

When the euro was substituted for national currencies, the issue arose as to whether a development of such magnitude might allow existing contracts denominated in national currencies to be voided on the grounds of frustration or force majeure. Under U.K. law, the doctrine of frustration applies where performance of the contract has become physically or legally impossible (i.e. the subject-matter of the contract no longer exists, or performance has become illegal), or where performance will no longer achieve the commercial object of the contract and will instead result in a "radically different" outcome. Generally, if the event which allegedly frustrates a contract is foreseeable, a court will not find a contract frustrated. However, where an event was foreseeable, but both parties assumed it would not transpire, and had no intent that their contract continue if it did, a court might still apply the doctrine. Financial Law Panel, *Economic and Monetary Union: Continuity of Contracts in English Law* (1998).

Article 3 of the 235 Regulation provides for the continuity of contracts under EMU by providing:

> The introduction of the euro shall not have the effect of altering any term of a legal instrument or of discharging or excusing performance under any legal instrument, nor give a party the right unilaterally to alter or terminate such an instrument. This provision is subject to anything which parties may have agreed.

Trade associations designed solutions to problems that their members could encounter. Over 1,100 securities firms signed the International Securities and Derivatives Association (ISDA) *EMU Protocol* of May 6, 1998. It provided that "an event associated with economic and monetary union . . . will not have the effect of altering any term of, or discharging or excusing performance" or "give a party the right unilaterally to alter or terminate" an agreement or transaction. Parties could override this provision in writing by expressly referring to the protocol or EMU. A major problem was the disappearance of price sources on January 1, 1999. For example, a franc floating rate loan outstanding in 1998 would use PIBOR (Paris interbank offering rate) as the reference rate and rely on a Reuters screen for PIBOR. But PIBOR would disappear with Stage 3. The *Protocol* specified what would happen if such a price source disappeared. If no successor rate appeared, several other possible sources were given, including the use of Euribor.

Notes and Questions

1. The May 3 Regulation gives participating governments the option of redenominating existing national currency-denominated government debt into euros during Phase B even though such redenomination is not compulsory until Phase C. All governments did so. Suppose the conversion rate for french franc/euro is 5.31415 FF = 1 euro, and that one holds bonds with a FF par value of 100. The new euro denominated bonds would have a par value of 18.8177 euro. What problems might such redenomination create? Suppose an individual owned 6 of these euro bonds, and the French government renominalized these bonds by issuing one euro denominated bond with a face value of 100 euros, leaving a stub amount of 12.9062 euros ((18.8177 x 6) - 100)). What would be done with

the stub?   If the government redeemed the stub, what would the redemption price be?

2.   Suppose the FF government bonds have a fixed rate of 7% and the euro interest rate for debt of equivalent maturity is 6% at the beginning of Phase B.   Would the French government want to redenominate its bonds?   Who would win and who would lose if it did so?

3.   Suppose French consumers have borrowed from banks at 12% fixed rates.   Can their debt be redenominated in Phase B?   See May 3 Regulation, Article 8 (4), in the Appendix.   How about in Phase C? Assuming this debt is redenominated in Phase C, and the euro interest rate for bank debt of equivalent maturity is 6%, who would win or lose from the redenomination?   Should something be done to mitigate the consequences?

Consider the following from W. Fowler, *Practical Arrangements for the Introduction of the Single Currency - The English Legal Issues*, Butterworths Journal of International Banking and Financial Law, Dec. 1995, at 536.

There are concerns about the treatment of contractual parties who have committed themselves to fixed interest contracts based on the prevailing rates for a particular national currency of obligation and who find that, following the conversion of that currency into the single currency, the contractual rate of interest by which they are bound is considerably higher than that which then prevails in the market for interest payable on new obligations denominated in the single currency.   Clearly, this will work to the advantage or disadvantage of the parties, depending on whether they are lenders or borrowers.   The English legal issues raised by such a scenario seem to be unproblematic; it is unlikely that the doctrine of frustration would operate in such circumstances to release a contractual party from the consequences of what proves to be a bad bargain and it is also unlikely that English law would interfere with fixed rate contracts merely because one party claims to have been disadvantaged by the introduction of the single currency.

It has been suggested that consumers who are parties to fixed interest contracts where the contractual rate of interest proves to be higher than the then prevailing market rate might be treated differently and that legislation should perhaps be introduced which permits such consumers to prepay their loans.   This is an issue of policy rather than a legal issue.   In any event, levels of interest rates in Europe are such that any differential is likely to be relatively small and it is to be hoped that the convergence of economic conditions throughout the European Union will operate to reduce the practical significance of this issue by further removing marked differentials between the interest rates payable on national currencies.

4. Suppose there is a 7 year "diff" swap, entered into 1996, in which Party A pays lira libor and Party B pays peseta libor (see Chapter 17, B(3)). Can Italy and Spain redenominate this contract into euros at the outset of Phase B? What would be the impact on the parties? Could either party claim frustration and terminate the contract? If not, should they be able to make such a claim? Note that ISDA's 1998 amendments to its swaps Master Agreement, the EMU Protocol, accepts continuity as a default provision. Annex 1. It could have recommended the opposite, i.e. that parties contract for non-continuity. Why did it take this position?

5. Will contracts denominated in french francs but governed by U.K. law, e.g. eurobonds, be subject to claims of frustration?

c.   RECOGNITION OF THE CHANGE IN NON-EU JURISDICTIONS

One of the concerns most troubling to EU bankers was whether contracts governed by the law of non-EU states would recognize that the changeover was not an event permitting termination. When the law of a non-EU state (such as New York) governs a contract, said one legal commentator, one must establish:

- whether the single currency will be recognized by the law of the non-member state as replacing the existing national currency of the relevant member state;

- whether the contract will be treated under that law as non-revocable following the introduction of the single currency; and

- whether there are any grounds on which it might be claimed under that law that a money obligation ought to be revalued or devalued to allow for any depreciation or appreciation in the purchasing power of the money in which the debt was originally denominated.

See G. Yeowart, *Legal Repercussions of a Single European Currency*, International Financial Law Review (December 1995). Bankers urged the EU Commission to coordinate with other major governments and to establish a commission to review such contracts. On July 29, 1997, New York enacted a law which closely parallels the EU regulations on frustration, so as to protect contracts governed by New York law against frustration claims. New York General Obligations Law, §5-1602 (1)(a) provides:

> If a subject or medium of payment of a contract, security or instruments is a currency that has been substituted or replaced by the euro, the euro will be a commercially reasonable substitute and substantial equivalent that may be either: (i) used in determining the value of such currency; or (ii) tendered, in each case of the conversion rate specified in, and otherwise calculated in accordance with, the regulations adopted by the council of the European Union.

Section 5-1602(2) of the New York law provides that the introduction of the euro does not trigger the application of doctrines such as frustration and impossibility:

None of: (a) the introduction of the euro; (b) the tendering of euros in connection with any obligation in compliance with paragraph (a) or (b) [dealing with the Ecu] of subdivision one of this section; (c) the determining of the value of any obligation in compliance with paragraph (a) or (b) of subdivision one of this section; or (d) the calculating or determining of the subject of the medium of payment of a contract, security or instrument with reference to interest rate or other basis [that?] has been substituted or replaced due to the introduction of the euro and that is a commercially reasonable substitute and substantial equivalent, shall either have the effect of discharging or excusing performance under any contract, security or instrument, or give a party the right to unilaterally alter or terminate any contract, security or instrument.

Notes and Questions

1. Suppose there is a floating rate loan in French Francs that is redenominated in euros. The loan calls for interest at PIBOR which, after redenomination, is interpreted by the lender as referring to PIBOR for euro. Will this new interest rate stand up? Is it clear that the rate would always be a "commercially reasonable substitute and substantial equivalent"?

2. How would this issue be dealt with under Article 3 of the 235 Regulation (see Appendix)? See M. Gruson, *The Introduction of the euro and Its Implications for Obligations Denominated in Currencies Replaced by the euro,* 21 Fordham International Law Journal 65, 100-107 (1997).

5. THE ROLE OF THE UK IN STAGE 3

The UK government said in October 1997 that the country would not join Stage 3 during the term of parliament that could end as late as May 2002. Elections are now scheduled for mid-2001. At the end of 1999, the Bank of England assessed the market share of the City in the euro markets. It reported that 18% of cross border payments through TARGET were made via CHAPS, the UK system. London's share of all turnover in foreign exchange markets was 32%, compared to 5% for Germany and 4% for France (and 18% for the US). Of the short-term interest rate contracts in euro traded on the three major European derivatives exchanges, over 90% is traded on LIFFE. London's share of all underwritten Eurobonds, in euro, rose from 48% in the first quarter of 1999 to 58% in the third quarter. See Bank of England, Practical Issues Arising from the euro, Dec. 1999, at 10-11.

The government had anticipated the effects on the UK of the shift across the channel to Stage 3 and encouraged UK banks and firms to prepare. The UK changed its Ecu treasury note issues to euro notes in January 1998, using the Ecu (at the rate of 1 Ecu for 1 euro), and paid in euro the interest and principal due after January 1, 1999.

Many UK firms were insulated from the initial impact of Stage 3, but some felt it immediately. UK exporters to Stage 3 countries had to transact business in euro with powerful buyers, such as large German companies. Large UK retailers, like Marks and Spencer, began to accept euro checks in their stores. The inter-bank rate for the euro-euro, called euro-LIBOR, is set by the British Bankers Association, using a standard panel of 16 banks.

By not being an initial member of Stage 3, the UK would benefit and also suffer. It would not be subject to rules designed to coordinate fiscal policy and it could pursue its own monetary policy, using its own tools. UK banks would not have to meet ECB reserve requirements, though they would have to maintain two clearing systems, one for sterling and the other for euro. The UK would be outside decisions about monetary policy made for the euro. Since the ECB would be in Frankfurt deciding monetary policy and using the securities that are its tools of indirect monetary policy, some observers thought that bond dealers would move to Frankfurt to be in close proximity to the ECB.

Despite the delay, many people expected the UK to join Stage 3 very soon after 2002. It could do so at any point, having met the convergence criteria in March 1998. The government would hold a referendum and, assuming popular support, would take 24 to 30 months to integrate with other members, then 6 more months to phase in the euro cash. The Bank of England was actively preparing for the transition.

Notes and Questions

1. Was it a good idea for the UK to postpone deciding whether to join Stage 3? How could one of three leading financial centers in the world, one based in Europe, stay outside the major new currency bloc for Europe? Can the U.K. preserve its financial center role if it stays outside the euro? See D. Lascelles, *Financial Centers under Threat*, Journal of International Financial Markets 193 (2000).

2. Would there be a need for a euro-eurocurrency market? Will the euro-eurocurrency market become as important in the medium term as the combined eurocurrency markets for the national currencies of the members of the eleven countries entering Stage 3? Is London well placed to capture a large share of that market, if it develops?

6. INTERNATIONAL IMPACT: THE EURO AS AN INTERNATIONAL CURRENCY

There are various predictions about how the advent of the euro will affect the international currency status—as part of transactions and official reserves—of the euro versus the dollar. Fred Bergsten, in *The Import of the euro on Exchange Rates and International Policy Cooperation* (Paper, March 17-18, 1997), sets out the current share in global finance of the dollar, DM, all EU currencies and the Yen in the table below.

Currency Shares in Global Finance, 1995
(in percent)

	Dollar	DM	All EU[41]	Yen
Official Foreign Exchange Reserves	64.1	15.9	21.2	7.5
(of which, Developing Countries)	(63.5)	(15.6)	(21.9)	(8.3)
Foreign Holdings of Bank Deposits	47.5	18.4	42.5	4.2
International Security Issues (1990-95)	38.8	n.a.	40.6	20.6
Developing Countries Debt	50.0	n.a.	16.1	18.0
Denomination of World Exports (1992)	47.6	15.3	33.5	4.8
Foreign Exchange Market Turnover	42	19	28[42]	12
All International Private Assets[43]	37.9	15.5	32.0	12.4
(excluding intra-EU holdings)	(50)	n.a.	(10)	(18)

[41] Includes intra-EU holdings so considerably overstates consolidated EU position (and hence understates dollar and yen positions), except in final line.
[42] Includes only DM, sterling and French franc.
[43] Includes international bonds, cross-border bank liabilities to non-banks, euro currency liabilities to domestic non-banks and euronotes.

Sources: F. Bergsten, The Import of the euro on Exchange Rates and International Policy Cooperation. (Paper, March 17-18, 1997), p. 52.

Bergsten argues that there are five central considerations for the role the euro will play as an international currency: (1) the size of the underlying economy and its global trade; (2) the economy's independence from external constraints; (3) avoidance of exchange controls; (4) the breadth of its capital markets; and (5) the strength and stability of the economy and its external position. On the first two criteria, he argues that the EU is slightly superior to the United States. In 1996, EU GDP was $8.4 trillion compared with $7.2 trillion in the U.S., and the volume of EU trade (exports plus imports) was $1.9 trillion compared with theU.S. total of $1.7 trillion. Bergsten contends that there is a potential for the euro and the dollar to have equal roles as an international currency, with the Yen as the third weaker partner. The effect would be to divert from $500 billion to $1 trillion of reserves now held in dollars to euro-denominated instruments. See C. Bergsten, *America and Europe: Clash of the Titans?* 78:2 Foreign Affairs 20, March/April 1999.

Not all commentators agree with this forecast. For example, R. Cooper, Key Currencies After the euro, 22:1 World Economy, Jan. 1999, argues that the euro will not replace the dollar because markets for dollar assets are much bigger, more liquid, familiar, and proven to investors than for euro assets, particularly for short-term instruments. R. McCauley, *The euro and the Dollar*, BIS Working Paper No. 50, concludes that the dollar role in global finance may be enhanced by EMU. He believes that the euro will generally carry more weight as an international money than the mark carries but less weight than the sum of the euro's constituent currencies now plays.

The first analysis of the euro's international role was made as of June 1999, too early in the life of the new currency to be very useful. The ECB compared the role of the euro in early 1999 with the role of the 11 members' currencies in a comparable period in 1998. It found that in 1999 reserves held in euro, as a share of all reserves, declined compared to 1998 but did not report the size of the decline. It occurred mainly because EMU members needed less reserves than in the past. The ECB also examined the currency composition of the stock of debt securities issued by non-residents of the EMU countries at the end of 1997 and June 30, 1999. It found a very slight increase—25% to 27%— in the portion denominated in euros, offset by a decline in the share of yen. The ECB could not give data showing the use of the euro for payment or pricing. See European Central Bank, *Monthly Bulletin*, Aug. 1999, at 31.

A further measure was the extent to which other countries used the euro as part of their foreign exchange regime. The ECB found that the euro was at least a partial peg for the exchange regime in many countries in Eastern Europe, in other European countries that were not part of EMU, and in some developing countries, mainly in Africa.

Notes and Questions

1. Note that one of the key factors in whether the euro will become the partner of the dollar in international finance is whether or not the EMU countries' financial markets will be integrated enough to provide a euro financial market with the same depth and breadth as the dollar financial market.

2. Is it altogether clear that EMU countries will want a truly internationalized euro? What are the costs and benefits to the euro countries of the euro becoming an international currency?

3. How likely is the euro to become a reserve currency equal to or

surpassing the dollar? How would the declining rate of the euro against the dollar affect this?

4. How will the United States view euro competition in global finance? What will be the effect on U.S. trade? What will be the effect on the ability of the United States to be the leader of the world?

7. WILL STAGE 3 SURVIVE?

A key question is whether a member that wants to withdraw from the monetary union could do so without serious damage to itself or the other members. This depended on the scenario for withdrawal. The question is important because the Treaty did not contemplate failure.

The following article examines this question, assuming that Italy desires to withdraw. The argument preceding the excerpt is that the Stability Pact could fail to rein in governments with high deficits, and that other countries, such as Germany, could object. Nationalistic feelings could drive a wedge among members. Markets could suspect that a country, such as Italy, might withdraw and issue a currency weaker than the euro, the new lira. Private transactors could shift from bank accounts in Italy to accounts in a stronger country, such as Germany, causing a run on Italian banks. Professor Scott believed there was at least a 10% chance that EMU would break up. He noted that the Treaty left in place many institutions, such as national central banks and national payments systems. Their existence would make it easier to withdraw.

H. SCOTT, "WHEN THE EURO FALLS APART"
1 International Finance 207 (1998)

V. Key Economic and Legal Break-up Problems

Any break-up of the euro would entail sacrifice of some of the benefits claimed for instituting the euro in the first place. Benefits to transactors generally, such as the transaction cost savings of using a single currency and the elimination of exchange-rate volatility between EMU members, would be given up, and the promise of curtailing inflation in withdrawing countries would have to be sacrificed. However, one of the benefits of EMU, increased integration of capital and banking markets, might well survive the return to more national currencies.

The break-up of the euro would not merely return countries and markets to the status quo ante prior to the adoption of the euro. Two key new problems would have to be faced: the difficulty re-establishing a national currency and legal uncertainty attending the re-denomination of existing contracts in a new currency.

A. Re-establishing National Currencies

If the euro falls apart, countries will want to replace the euro with their own national currencies. The difficulties of the replacement process will depend on whether the euro survives for some countries or whether it dissolves entirely.

i. Partial break-up

Assume that Italy leaves EMU and desires to re-establish the lira while the other ten EMU countries continue to use the euro. Italy could well experience substantial difficulties in re-establishing the lira as the national currency and these difficulties would exist whether the break-up occurs before or after the disappearance of the existing lira. This paper focuses initially on the case where Italy seeks to replace the euro with the new lira after the existing lira has gone out of existence, that is, after 2002.

One's initial reaction to this situation might be that Gresham's law would permit Italy to replace the euro, assuming the new lira was worth less against the dollar or other external currencies than was the euro. The new lira would be the 'bad money' driving the euro out of Italy. This is unlikely to happen for a number of reasons. [Scott argues that economists no longer believe that Gresham's law is accurate.]. . .

Italy could try to force exchanges of existing euro cash or bank accounts in Italy for Italian lira, but such forced exchanges would seem extremely problematic. What would be the rationale for forcing Italians to give up euros for new lira, as compared to dollars for new lira? Both dollars and euro would remain as major international currencies. How would such forced exchanges be accomplished?

As for cash, Italy could seal its borders for some short period and order that all euros in Italy be surrendered for new lira (a typical measure where monetary unions suffer total break-up), or in the short term require all euros held by Italian citizens (or even foreigners in Italy) to be stamped with a new lira symbol. But people would hold euro cash back and take it out of Italy as soon as the borders were reopened. Further, the moment the borders were reopened the preferred euro currency would come flowing back into Italy.

As for bank accounts, Italy could order all euro bank accounts of Italian citizens to be re-denominated into the new lira, but what would this accomplish? It would not ensure that such accounts remained in new lira. Depositors would take their losses and get into some other currency outside Italy as soon as possible. This result could only be forestalled by imposition of foreign-exchange controls for some substantial period of time, again isolating Italy financially and economically from the rest of Europe.

Once the euro becomes the currency of Italy, it may prove very difficult for Italy to re-establish the lira and thereby get control of its own monetary policy. Italy may become 'euroized' in the same way that countries in Latin America have become dollarized. Transactors will want to hold euros because they are likely to be more valuable than lira, and dual pricing of euros and the new lira will allow transactors to contract and pay in euros. This problem might be less severe if Italy sought to exit from EMU before 2002, when the existing lira was still in circulation and before the euro was fully established as a currency. On the other hand, withdrawal from EMU might signal such an inflationary future that Italians and others would try to exit from lira holdings as quickly as possible.

There is very little experience with how a country deals with breaking away from a monetary union where the currency of the union survives. Cohen (1993) reviewed the history of six monetary unions, three of which still exist: Belgium-Luxembourg (1922), CFA Franc Zone (1959) and the East Caribbean Currency Area (1965). The three monetary unions that broke up, did so entirely: East African Community (1967-1977), Latin Monetary Union (1865-World War I) and Scandinavian Monetary Union (1873-World War I, although the latter two took some years to effect the final break-up. Garber and Spencer (1994) did an extensive study of the break-up of the Austro-Hungarian Monetary Union, which spanned the 1867-1919 period, again where there was an entire break-up as the former empire was split into several new states. They also describe the Czechoslovakian break-up of 1993 which was also a complete break-up, as both the Czech and Slovak Republics together abandoned the old Czechoslovak crown.

The break-up of the rouble of the Soviet Union was a partial break-up, since Russia and some former Soviet republics retained the rouble, while other former republics, Estonia, Latvia, Lithuania, the Ukraine and the Kyrgyz Republic, adopted their own currencies. But the scenario was the reverse from the one envisioned in our hypotheticals. Russia was rapidly inflating and the breakaway states, and their citizens, wanted more stable currencies. They were happy to see the rouble go. It is possible that a country could pull out of EMU to re-establish a national currency that was stronger than the euro. If this were to occur, such country would not have difficulty doing so.

ii. Complete break-up

Complete break-up makes it easier for the withdrawing countries, even those whose new currencies would be perceived as 'weak', to re-establish national currencies. However attractive the common currency might be compared to the new national currencies, it will disappear. This is not to say that such a process will be easy. If national currencies are replaced over a period of time, some of the problems of partial break-up could well exist for those countries going first. The experience with the Austro-Hungarian break-up demonstrates that countries must generally close their borders for some period of time to stamp old currencies or swap old currencies for new ones. and such border closings will not be totally effective.

In a complete break-up, each country will set a conversion rate for euros into new national currencies. If, based on the new conversion rates, the euro will have more real value (in terms of purchasing power) in one country rather than another, transactors will try to exchange the euro in those countries where it will have more value. This will lead to hold backs from exchange in countries where new currencies will be relatively less valuable and movement of currencies to countries with better value. For example, if an Italian thought he could get more real value by exchanging cures in Germany, he would hold back from exchanging euros in Italy. If the last country to make a conversion, say Germany, has a strong new currency, it may find that a large portion of outstanding euros will be held back from exchanges in other countries for later exchange in Germany. This could result in inflationary pressures as the last converting country is forced to expand the currency money supply. These problems, however, are temporary, and can be greatly minimized by a degree of coordinated action.

iii. The need for collective action

This paper argues that a partial withdrawal from a continuing monetary union is unlikely because a withdrawing country would find it exceedingly difficult to re-establish control over its money supply. If Italy, in our example, could not achieve this objective through withdrawal, it would have little incentive to withdraw. It would have to coordinate its withdrawal with the other countries in a way that would permit it to establish its own currency. This would require a high degree of cooperation from the remaining countries. Indeed, the only sure way this could be accomplished would be relatively simultaneously to adopt a new euro for the remaining countries and a new lira for Italy.

Suppose that EMU countries wished to expel Italy from EMU. It is unclear how this could be accomplished without Italy's cooperation. Without the use of force by the other members, Italy could just stay and accumulate higher deficits. Again, expulsion might only be accomplished by simultaneously adopting a new euro and a new lira, again necessitating cooperation among all of the member states.

B. Continuity of Contract

The second significant break-up problem concerns the enforceability of re-denominated contracts between debtors of withdrawing countries and their creditors, particularly foreign creditors. Before examining this question in the context of a euro break-up, it is useful to recall how this issue has been handled in the adoption of the euro.

i. Euro adoption

The issue in adopting the euro was whether courts would enforce contracts that were issued in national currencies that are subsequently re-denominated in euros. As previously stated, this will be an immediate issue for government bonds which are to be re-denominated on 1 January 1999.

Rather than rely on general principles of law dealing with this issue, the EU in 1997 promulgated the so-called 235 Regulation which provides in Article 3:

> The introduction of the euro shall not have the effect of altering any term of a legal instrument or of discharging or excusing

performance under any legal instrument, nor give a party the right unilaterally to alter or terminate such an instrument. This provision is subject to anything which parties may have agreed.

The effect of this provision, which is effective in the entire European Union, not just in the EMU participant countries, is to ensure that euro contracts are enforceable, if there is no agreement to the contrary. Also, there can be no legal issue within the EU as to whether contracts can be re-denominated from national currencies to the euro, as this is clearly provided for in the Regulation of 3 May 1998.

Of course, European law was not automatically operative outside the EU, and thus there was an issue of whether non-EU countries would enforce the re-denominated contracts. Several jurisdictions have adopted laws dealing with this question. For example, on 29 July 1997, New York enacted such a law. New York General Obligations Law, 5-1602 (I)(a) provides that contracts can be re-denominated in euros:

> If a subject or medium of payment of a contract, security or instruments is a currency that has been substituted or replaced by the euro, the euro will be a commercially reasonable substitute and substantial equivalent that may be either: (i) used in determining the value of such currency; or (ii) tendered, in each case of the conversion rate specified in, and otherwise calculated in accordance with, the regulations adopted by the council of the European Union.

Section 5-1602(2) of the New York law provides that the introduction of the euro does not trigger the application of doctrines such as frustration and impossibility:

> None of: (a) the introduction of the euro; (b) the tendering of euros in connection with any obligation in compliance with paragraph (a) or (b)[dealing with the Ecu] of subdivision one of this section; (c) the determining of the value of any obligation in compliance with paragraph (a) or (b) of subdivision one of this section; or (d) the calculating or determining of the subject of the medium of payment of a contract, security or instrument with reference to interest rate or other basis that has been substituted or replaced due to the introduction of the euro and that is a commercially reasonable substitute and substantial equivalent, shall either have the effect of discharging or excusing performance under any contract, security or instrument, or give a party the right to unilaterally alter or terminate any contract, security or instrument.

The New York law, as well as the law of other US jurisdictions that have addressed this problem, such as Illinois and California, are one-way streets. They ensure continuity going from national currencies to the euro. They do not generally deal with changes of currencies or particularly with the possibility of going from the euro to national currencies.

ii. Replacement of the euro with national currencies

If Italy, or any other EMU member, were to withdraw from EMU and redenominate euro-denominated contracts, such as government bonds, loans or commercial contracts, with the new lira or other new national currency, the courts of the re-denominating country would almost certainly enforce that re-denomination – they would be bound to do so by the laws providing for the re-denomination. The issue would be much more complicated if the re-denomination were put at issue in a foreign court.

Foreign courts would normally determine whether the re-denomination was effective by reference to *lex monetae*, the law of the currency issuer (Mann 1959; Nussbaum 1950). Thus, when Germany replaced the Mark with the Reichsmark in the 1920s, courts of other countries enforced re-denominated contracts because they resolved the matter under German law, the *lex monetae*. However, this default principle is not easily applied to national currency re-denomination of euro contracts. What is the *lex monetae*? If Italy re-denominated euro contracts, Italy is the issuer of the replacement currency, the new lira, but may not be regarded as the issuer of the replaced currency, the euro. Where a monetary union is involved, all of the participating countries are joint issuers of a currency under a common legal arrangement and EU law could be regarded as the *lex monetae*. As Mann argues, *lex monetae* would be of no avail in such a case for the 'very question is which of two competing laws of the currency shall prevail' (Mann 1959, p. 261). Note that if reference was made to EU law as lex monetae, the Italian re-denomination would be ineffective. Whatever Italy did, EU law would continue to provide that all contracts issued in Italy, once denominated in euros, would continue to be denominated in euros.

Mann argues that in such a case, courts should apply the proper law of the contract, that is apply the law specified in the contract. For many obligations, for example Italian government bonds, this would be Italian law. Under Italian law, government bonds issued in Italy are 'titoli del debito publico' – public debt securities which are assumed to be governed by Italian law. On the other hand, Italian government bonds issued outside of Italy can provide for Italian or foreign law. This is provided for in Article 9 on 'Issuance of government bonds in foreign currency'[5] of Decree Law No. 149 of 20 May 1993. In practice, however, all present issues of Italian debt are subject to Italian law. This means that under the proper law of the contract approach, courts would uphold the re-denomination of Italian bonds. However, with respect to other obligations, such as private debt, foreign law might apply if it were specified in the contract. If no explicit choice of law is made in the contract, the foreign court would apply its own conflict of

---

[5]This includes bonds issued in lira outside Italy.

law rules – the rules the foreign court uses to decide what law applies to a contract where no explicit choice has been made in the contract itself. This could lead the court to the law of Italy or a foreign law.

Would foreign law, if applicable, such as the law of the United States or Germany, enforce the re-denomination or provide instead that the contracts must be honoured in euros or are breached if not honoured in euros? This is far from clear given the lack of precedents. There are no court cases involving the withdrawal of a country from a surviving monetary union. If foreign law would apply to a substantial number of outstanding contracts, there could be severe economic disruption attending a partial withdrawal as parties seek to resolve the legal uncertainties.

If EMU broke up entirely, the legal problems would also be severe. Although the *lex monetae* could no longer be that of the EU, given the end of the euro, it would be unclear whether the *lex monetae* was the law of one or the other of the exiting states. All of the EMU countries would be re-denominating contracts, and conflicts could easily arise among the terms of their re- denomination laws. For example, suppose Germany provided that any debt obligations of a German creditor, e.g. loans by German banks, were to be re-denominated in new Deutschmarks, while Italy provided that all loans of Italian debtors, including loans from German banks, were to be re-denominated in new lira. Similar problems were experienced when Germany was divided into two states in 1948 (Mann 1959, p. 268). Again, the solution could only be to decide the proper law of the contract, with the attendant uncertainties of that determination.

iii. The need for collective action

The economic disruptions that result from the uncertain effectiveness of re-denominated contracts would give EMU participants, the greater EU and, indeed, other important economic powers, incentives to address collectively the legal problems of withdrawal from the cure by enacting clarifying legislation, much as they did when adopting the euro. Herdegen (1998) reaches the same conclusion. Such incentives would exist whether or not one contemplates a partial or complete break-up. As part of their collective process, countries would no doubt address the losses creditors might experience as a result of re-denomination, particularly with respect to government bonds.

Notes and Questions

1. Why do neither the Maastricht Treaty nor the implementing laws and regulations set up a process to permit an orderly dismantling of the union?

2. Will the euro fall apart? What would be the impact of a substantial decline in the value of the euro against the dollar, such as to $0.70?

3.   You are advising a potential investor in new bonds to be issued by a company in one of the euroland countries. Assume the investor believes there is a significant chance that the euro would fall apart. What provisions, if any, would you recommend be included in the bond?

4.   If the euro does fall apart, can the EU go back to the situation that preceded it, including the single market and ERM, or will the break up of EMU mean the break up of the EU?

Links to Other Chapters

While issues about EMU link directly to the preceding chapters about the EU single market and foreign exchange regimes (Chapters 5 and 6), they also tie in to other chapters. As Stage 3 member currencies shift to the euro, and euro-DM, -francs, and other currencies give way to the euro-euro, changes will take place in the eurocurrency markets (Chapters 9 and 12), stock exchange competition across Europe (Chapter 14), markets for futures, options, and swaps (Chapters 16 and 17), and portfolio investment (Chapters 18 and 20). Infrastructure is affected. Capital adequacy rules are affected by EU rules (Chapter 4). The monetary union needed to design its own payments system (Chapter 10), while clearance and settlement systems will change (Chapter 15).

APPENDIX

EU Regulations Governing Conversion

Passed under Article 235 of the Treaty of Rome, Council Regulation (EC) No. 1103/97 (the "235 Regulation"), O.J. No. L 162, 19/06/1997, came into force on June 20, 1997, and applies to all EU member states, regardless of their plans to participate in the euro. Articles 1-3 of this Regulation provide as follows:

Article 1

For the purpose of this Regulation:

'legal instruments' shall mean legislative and statutory provisions, acts of administration, judicial decisions, contracts, unilateral legal acts, payment instruments other than banknotes and coins, and other instruments with legal effect,

'participating Member States' shall mean those Member States which adopt the single currency in accordance with the Treaty,

'conversion rates' shall mean the irrevocably fixed conversion rates which the Council adopts in accordance with the first sentence of Article 1091 (4) of the Treaty,

'national currency units' shall mean the units of the currencies of participating Member States, as those units are defined on the day before the start of the third stage of Economic and Monetary Union,

'euro unit' shall mean the unit of the single currency as defined in the Regulation on the introduction of the euro which will enter into force at the starting date of the third stage of Economic and Monetary Union.

Article 2

1. Every reference in a legal instrument to the ECU, as referred to in Article 109g of the Treaty and as defined in Regulation (EC) No 3320/94, shall be replaced by a reference to the euro at a rate of one euro to one ECU. References in a legal instrument to the ECU without such a definition shall be presumed, such presumption being rebuttable taking into account the intentions of the parties, to be references to the ECU as referred to in Article 109g of the Treaty and as defined in Regulation (EC) No 3320/94.

2. Regulation (EC) No 3320/94 is hereby repealed.

3. This Article shall apply as from 1 January 1999 in accordance with the decision pursuant to Article 109j (4) of the Treaty.

Article 3

The introduction of the euro shall not have the effect of altering any term of a legal instrument or of discharging or excusing performance under any legal instrument, nor give a party the right unilaterally to alter or terminate such an instrument. This provision is subject to anything which parties may have agreed.

The second regulation, based on Article 1091(4) of the Treaty of Rome, was issued by the Council on May 3, 1998 (the "May 3 Regulation"), No. 974/98, O.J. No. L 139/1, 11/05/98. It provides as follows:

PART I

Definitions

For the purpose of this Regulation:

'participating Member States' shall mean Belgium, Germany, Spain, France, Ireland, Italy, Luxembourg, Netherlands, Austria, Portugal and Finland,

'legal instruments' shall mean legislative and statutory provisions, acts of administration, judicial decisions, contracts, unilateral legal acts, payment instruments other than bank-notes and coins, and other instruments with legal effect,

'conversion rate' shall mean the irrevocably fixed conversion rate adopted for the currency of each participating Member State by the Council according to the first sentence of Article 1091(4) of the Treaty,

'euro unit' shall mean the currency unit as referred to in the second sentence of Article 2,

'national currency units' shall mean the units of the currencies of participating Member States, as those units are defined on the day before the start of the third stage of Economic and Monetary Union,

'transitional period' shall mean the period beginning on 1 January 1999 and ending on 31 December 2001,

'redenominate' shall mean changing the unit in which the amount of outstanding debt is stated from a national currency unit to the euro unit, as defined in Article 2, but which does not have through the act of redenomination the effect of altering any other term of the debt, this being a matter subject to relevant national law.

PART II

Substitution of the euro for the Currencies of the Participating Member States

Article 2

As from 1 January 1999 the currency of the participating Member States shall be the euro. The currency unit shall be one euro. One euro shall be divided into one hundred cents.

Article 3

The euro shall be substituted for the currency of each participating Member State at the conversion rate.

Article 4

The euro shall be the unit of account of the European Central Bank (ECB) and of the central banks of the participating Member States.

PART III

Transitional Provisions

Article 5

Articles 6, 7, 8 and 9 shall apply during the transitional period.

Article 6

1. The euro shall also be divided into the national currency units according to the conversion rates. Any subdivision thereof shall be maintained. Subject to the provisions of this Regulation the monetary law of the participating Member States shall continue to apply.

2. Where in a legal instrument reference is made to a national currency unit, this reference shall be as valid as if reference were made to the euro unit according to the conversion rates.

Article 7

The substitution of the euro for the currency of each participating Member State shall not in itself have the effect of altering the denomination of legal instruments in existence on the date of substitution.

Article 8

1. Acts to be performed under legal instruments stipulating the use of or denominated in a national currency unit shall be performed in that national currency unit. Acts to be performed under legal instruments stipulating the use of or denominated in the euro unit shall be performed in that unit.

2. The provisions of paragraph 1 are subject to anything which parties may have agreed.

3. Notwithstanding the provisions of paragraph 1, any amount denominated either in the euro unit or in the national currency unit

of a given participating Member State and payable within that Member State by crediting an account of the creditor, can be paid by the debtor either in the euro unit or in that national currency unit. The amount shall be credited to the account of the creditor in the denomination of his account, with any conversion being effected at the conversion rates.

4. Notwithstanding the provisions of paragraph 1, each participating Member State may take measures which may be necessary in order to:

- redenominate in the euro unit outstanding debt issued by that Member state's general government, as defined in the European System of integrated accounts, denominated in its national currency unit and issued under its own law. If a Member State has taken such a measure, issuers may redenominate in the euro unit debt denominated in that Member State's national currency unit unless redenomination is expressly excluded by the terms of the contract; this provision shall apply to debt issued by the general government of a Member State as well as to bonds and other forms of securitized debt negotiable in the capital markets, and to money market instruments, issued by other debtors,

- enable the change of the unit of account of their operating procedures from a national currency unit to the euro unit by:

  (a) markets for the regular exchange, clearing and settlement of any instrument listed in section B of the Annex to Council Directive 93/22/EEC of 10 May 1993 on investment services listed in the securities field and of commodities; and

  (b) systems for the regular exchange, clearing and settlement of payments.

5. Provisions other than those of paragraph 4 imposing the use of the euro unit may only be adopted by the participating Member States in accordance with any time-frame laid down by Community legislation.

6. National legal provisions of participating Member States which permit or impose netting, set-off or techniques with similar effects shall apply to monetary obligations, irrespective of their currency denomination, if that denomination is in the euro unit or in a national currency unit, with any conversion being effected at the conversion rates.

Article 9

Banknotes and coins denominated in a national currency unit shall retain their status as legal tender within their territorial limits as of the day before the entry into force of this Regulation.

PART IV

Euro Banknotes and Coins

Article 10

As from 1 January 2002, the ECB and the central banks of the participating Member States shall put into circulation banknotes denominated in euros. Without prejudice to Article 15, these banknotes denominated in euros shall be the only banknotes which have the status of legal tender on all these Member States.

Article 11

As from 1 January 2002, the participating Member States shall issue coins denominated in euros or in cents and complying with the denominations and technical specifications which the Council may lay down in accordance with the second sentence of Article 105a (2) of the Treaty. Without prejudice to Article 15, these coins shall be the only coins which have the status of legal tender in all these Member States. Except for the issuing authority and for those persons specifically designated by the national legislation of the issuing Member State, no party shall be obliged to accept more than 50 coins in any single payment.

Article 12

Participating Member States shall ensure adequate sanctions against counterfeiting and falsification of euro banknotes and coins.

PART V

Final Provisions

Article 13

Articles 14, 15 and 16 shall apply as from the end of the transitional period.

Article 14

Where in legal instruments existing at the end of the transitional period reference is made to the national currency units, these references shall be read as references to the euro unit according to the respective conversion rates. The rounding rules laid down in Regulation (EC) No 1103/97 shall apply.

Article 15

1. Banknotes and coins denominated in a national currency unit as referred to in Article 6 (1) shall remain legal tender within their territorial limits until six months after the end of the transitional period at the latest; this period may be shortened by national law.

2. Each participating Member State may, for a period of up to six months after the end of the transitional period, lay down rules for the use of the banknotes and coins denominated in its national currency unit as referred to in Article 6 (1) and take any measures necessary to facilitate their withdrawal.

Article 16

In accordance with the laws or practices of participating Member States, the respective issuers of banknotes and coins shall continue to accept, against euros at the conversion rate, the banknotes and coins previously issued by them.

PART VI

Entry Into Force

Article 17

This Regulation shall enter into force on 1 January 1999.

This Regulation shall be binding in its entirety and directly applicable in all Member States, in accordance with the Treaty, subject to Protocols No 11 and No 12 and Article 109k (1).

CHAPTER EIGHT

JAPANESE BANKING AND SECURITIES MARKETS: INTERNATIONAL ASPECTS

On November 8, 1996, Prime Minister Hashimoto of Japan set a major new goal for his government, to create a financial market comparable to those of New York and London by the year 2001. He planned to "transform the financial administration into a more transparent one based on the market mechanism" and "vitalize the Tokyo market through structural reform." His goal was quickly dubbed Japan's "Big Bang," a reference to the U.K. big bang, a set of major regulatory and structural changes rapidly made in Britain's financial system in 1986.

Japan's Big Bang espoused the principles of "free, fair, and global." It would create a free financial market mechanism, transparent and credible, subject to internationally accepted laws, supervision, and accounting standards. The Prime Minister forecast painful changes. He directed government officials to begin work immediately. His plan won the support of a large part of the voting public, itself disenchanted with the system, and his party, which governed with less than a full majority in the Diet. The plan took the financial community by surprise. The changes, whether or not they succeeded, were expected to have major implications for international financial markets as well as cross-border flows to and from Japan.

The Big Bang apparently rejected the unique Japanese financial system that had worked so well until the late 1980s. For decades after World War II, Japan's financial system had mobilized savings to fuel the country's remarkable economic recovery and then miracle growth. Financial firms, guided by the Ministry of Finance (MOF) and the Bank of Japan (BOJ), its central bank, channeled funds at low rates to high value-added manufacturers, whose exports contributed to the country's ever stronger trade balance. Savers, consumers, and workers bore the cost of this system. To Western observers, the system looked very different from those they knew.

After decades of remarkable growth, the early 1990s brought the collapse of Japan's stock market, a weak domestic economy, a mountain of bad debts held by the banks, and the end of the almost 40 years of government by the Liberal Democratic Party (LDP). Briefly replaced by a loose coalition amid strong public dissatisfaction with the country's political economy, the remaining members of the splintered LDP allied in 1994 with long-time rivals to jointly reclaim control of the government. Few saw the coalition as stable. For the financial system, the question seemed to be whether it could survive without fundamental change. Cross-border financial flows and offshore operations seemed to add pressure for change that a weakened government might not be able to avoid. Prime Minister Hashimoto's Big Bang appeared to offer that basic change. Change was welcomed because the economy was performing poorly.

Five years later, the Finance Minister of Japan, Kiichi Miyazawa, announced that the government's finances were nearing a "catastrophic situation." Speaking in March 2001, he was referring to the huge government debt. The same week, the governor of the Bank of Japan told Parliament that "We should look squarely at the reasons why we could not make the economic recovery a certainty, despite the full measure of financial and fiscal measures we took in the last 20 years."

A month later, at the end of April 2001, a new prime minister took office. Junichiro Koizumi, a third generation Diet member known as a maverick and an outsider, took office riding a wave of popularity in the ranks of the LDP that swamped the traditional factions. Having promised structural reform of the economy and reform of his party during the campaign to head the LDP, Koizumi's, task was to lead the discredited LDP to victory in the summer elections. He appointed some younger politicians as ministers, which was in itself a gesture toward reform, although his finance minister, Masajuro Shiokawa, was 79 and new to finance. But almost a year after he took office, many were questioning his ability to institute fundamental reforms.

Section I of this Chapter concerns banks and Section II concerns securities markets. Both parts describe the system existing into the early 1990s as the basis against which to evaluate the Big Bang proposals, described later in each part.

SECTION I

BANKS

Over the decades since the end of World War II, the task of Japan's banking system shifted from helping the nation recover to meeting the needs of an increasingly integrated world economy. To analyze the Big Bang, one must understand the system it was trying to change. This section sketches Japan's banking system first during the post-War period into the 1970s, then identifies the major structural changes underway during the 1970s and 1980s, and finally raises the issues that confront Japanese banking in the early 21st century.

A. HISTORY

1. THE OLD REGIME: JAPAN'S BANKING SYSTEM TO THE 1970S

The major characteristics of Japanese banking after the war were the power of financial regulators, the segmentation of both the financial system and banking, the limited role of market forces pricing credit, and the close relations between leading banks and groups of manufacturing and service firms, called keiretsu.

a. STRONG CONTROL BY FINANCIAL AUTHORITIES

Japan's financial system is conventionally seen as a major tool in the country's fast strong growth, both from the time Japan opened to the West in the Meiji restoration, beginning in the 1860s, and during its remarkable recovery after the devastation of World War II. The Meiji period saw a massive overhaul of Japanese institutions that adapted Western models to Japan's culture and politics. The government played an active role mobilizing resources. When the post-war occupation ended, Japan found itself with a large, highly educated labor force, but an extreme shortage of capital and raw materials. To promote investments and exports, the government used several financial tools. Direct funding at rates subsidized by the public sector was one tool, but incentives and informal directives played a bigger role. Tax and other policies promoted savings and investment. The government used interest rate ceilings and foreign exchange controls to promote industries and companies it believed could compete internationally. It insulated industries from foreign competition.

At the center were the Ministry of Finance (MOF) and the Bank of Japan (BOJ). BOJ, the nation's central bank, controlled the money supply and credit. Both held great informal control over financial firms. In the early decades, BOJ was able to guide bank lending because it supplied liquidity to banks starved for deposits. Its role as lender of last resort gave it additional informal power to dictate conditions to banks despite its lack of a clear legal basis for intervention. MOF set policy for, and regulated, all sectors of the financial system. For decades, MOF exercised substantial power over financial firms. It combined fiscal, policy making, and supervisory functions. Financial legislation delegated broad regulatory powers to MOF, which asserted further power to interpret the general laws in detail. Not surprisingly, financial firms adopted the practice of consulting with MOF before taking any major action, such as opening new branches, major changes in business operations, or mergers with other banks. Through this informal administrative guidance MOF exercised substantial power that went far beyond its formal powers.

During this period, the government pursued a no-fail policy for banks to give depositors confidence. From the end of World War II into the mid-1990s, only one bank failed in Japan. In the U.S., by comparison, one or two hundred failed in one year alone. Japan relied instead on the convoy system, in which a healthy bank would merge with a failed bank, assuring the full value of deposits. See M. Speigel, *Bank Charter Value and the Viability of the Japanese Convoy System*, Dec. 1999.

Later changes in policy are described in Section B(3).

b. SEGMENTATION OF FINANCIAL INSTITUTIONS

The government deliberately segmented Japan's financial sector. Every type of institution -- such as a commercial bank, trust bank, or securities firm -- had a function, including a way to fund itself, and these functions should not overlap.

Separation of banks and securities firms. Banks and securities firms were separated from the end of World War II, though not before. Article 65 of the Securities and Exchange Law, enacted at the behest of the Occupation, was based on the Glass-Steagall Act of the United States. It prohibited banks from engaging in securities business. Though Article 65 permitted banks to invest and participate in the underwriting of Japanese National, Municipal and Government guaranteed bonds, administrative guidance prohibited the banks from underwriting government bonds. Commercial paper was not considered a security but a discounted bill, so a compromise allowed both banks and securities firms to handle commercial paper. Unlike the Glass-Steagall, Article 65 did not limit banks from acquiring securities and equities for investment purposes.

Despite Article 65, indirect finance dominated Japanese finance. Protected from competition from commercial banks, several large securities firms grew to dominate their sector, surrounded by many small securities companies. But their role in the financial sector was limited. During the period 1980-84, 89% of all financial flows was indirect, with only 11 % direct. This heavy reliance on banks led to debt/equity ratio levels as high as 4:1 (compared to 1:1 in the U.S.).

Separation of commercial banking functions by maturity of credit and type of activity. Different types of firms provided different commercial banking services. Some primarily intermediated deposits (including ordinary banks, sogo banks, and shinkin banks) and others offered trust accounts and financial debentures to fund long-term loans (long-term credit banks and trust banks). Other segments financed small- and medium-sized enterprises and agriculture.

Long- and short-term financing was segmented. Specialized long-term credit institutions, such as the three long-term credit banks and the trust banks, lent long. Administrative guidance supported this by setting maximum maturities at which banks could raise funds, in the absence of formal legal provisions. Long-term credit banks, given their monopoly in obtaining long-term funding, dominated long-term lending.

The strict separation of banking and trust business was enforced largely through administrative guidance. The trust banks managed few individual assets, focusing instead on joint management through such instruments as money and loan trusts. The trust banks, while providing some commercial banking products, concentrated on managing funds entrusted to them.

Other specialized banks had even more distinctly defined products and roles. They included hundreds of banks and credit associations for small business; a network of agricultural credit cooperatives under the umbrella of a central cooperative bank that invested their very large surplus in money markets; government financial institutions, such as an export-import bank; and a postal savings system that held a very large share of private savings because of an exemption from withholding tax. Each specialized bank had clearly defined customer bases and roles.

Foreign banks, with little access to domestic business, were relegated to the margins of the system and concentrated on foreign exchange and on serving subsidiaries of foreign firms. The Bank of Tokyo specialized in foreign exchange and non-yen finance.

Commercial banks included the city and regional banks. The most important were the 12 city banks, located in major cities. Commercial banks, banned from both the securities and long-term credit markets, collected deposits and extended short-term credit. The city banks focused on wholesale banking by maintaining a close relationship with the larger blue chip companies and serving their needs both domestically and abroad. With high corporate demand during this period, the city banks were cash poor despite their branches across the major Japanese population centers. They bought funds in the interbank market because they could not rely entirely on deposits and were prevented by regulation from raising long-term funds. Japanese banks could not engage in insurance or real estate activities.

The 64 regional banks, though limited to a specific locality, could grow because they, unlike the city banks, had an abundant base of funds from retail depositors. The regional banks served small local and regional firms, raised funds through a large natural deposit base, and often lent those funds through the interbank market to the liquidity-starved city banks. The regional banks served a vital need in the interbank market as large suppliers of funds to the large cash-starved city banks.

Specialization and segmentation prohibited or restricted access to designated markets, allowing only special institutions to enter. Each type of banking institutions was strictly limited to its product and range of activities. With inter-group competition almost nonexistent, competition within each group was intense.

Later changes in policy are described in Section B(1)(a).

c. REGULATION ON INTEREST RATES

From the early post-War era, maintaining below market interest rates for depositors and key producers was a key government policy. A dual system of regulated and market interest rates developed. In two markets, supply and demand set rates: the short-term money markets and bond trading. The interbank market between the city banks and other financial institutions developed to deal with the maldistribution of funds. These two markets were very small, compared to their relative size in other industrial countries, though after 1975 the interbank market became a center for wholesale banking.

Regulated rates, set by discussion among interested parties including the government, included deposit rates, short and long-term prime rates used by financial intermediaries in the interbank market, and subscriber's yields on public funds. The Bank of Japan set and precisely controlled deposit rates. The government allowed short-term lending rates to fluctuate within an upper and lower limit. After 1975, the government gradually loosened or eliminated the laws and administrative guidance for interest rates, so that they were not important by the mid-1990s.

Direct subsidies were less common. Government financial institutions supplied long-term funds at lending rates considerably below those of private institutions. BOJ gave preferential export finance to reduce funding costs and target key industries and companies.

A key element was foreign exchange controls on international transactions. By limiting the access of domestic savers to offshore financial markets, the government ensured that cross-border financial flows did not undercut its management of domestic rates. The Foreign Exchange Law set a barrier to cross-border flows of funds and institutions, in and out of Japan. It gave only banks designated by MOF as Foreign

Exchange Banks the authority to engage in FX transactions. They were required to make comprehensive reports to MOF, which monitored the flows and used its approval powers to constrain the flows. Major amendments to the FEL took place over the decades, as for example when Japan joined the OECD and again in 1980. But it was still necessary to notify MOF of many transactions and MOF used this to examine proposed transactions in advance. Retail cross-border transactions were controlled up to the Big Bang. These controls were relaxed in 1980 and the Big Bang.

d. KEIRETSU RELATIONSHIPS BETWEEN BANKS AND FIRMS

The Meiji period of industrialization was characterized by the concentration of power and control in interlocking corporate groups called *zaibatsu*. This form of conglomerate built on traditional Japanese values of tradition and loyalty to create increasingly large and complex business groups. The occupation forces broke up the zaibatsu, but they did not prevent a looser form of cooperation among banks and firms in *keiretsu*, groups of Japanese companies in various lines of business, including banks, formed by cross-shareholdings. Group members held each others' shares, coordinated their business strategies, and shared staff.

The practice grew after 1970 to protect Japanese firms from foreign control when Japan entered the OECD. If group members held over 50% of issued shares, no foreign investor could buy control. Indeed, roughly 65% of equity in companies listed on the Tokyo Stock Exchange was held in an interlocking fashion by firms in the same keiretsu or with a similar close relationship. Later, when banks issued equity to meet the Basel Accord standards in the period from 1984-90, for example, associated companies bought most, according to C. Milhaupt, *Managing the Market: The Ministry of Finance and Securities Regulation in Japan*, 30 Stanford Journal of International Law 423 (1994).

A bank in a keiretsu was the "main bank" for the group's firms. For example, many city banks, direct descendants of Zaibatsu banks, as the main banks for a particular conglomerate group had nearly exclusive long-term relationships with major Japanese companies in their group. Main bank relationships also extended to firms outside groups, as they do in many countries. The common practice was for a firm to offer its main bank any major business before it accepted the services of another bank. The main bank, supported by other group members, helped a member in trouble. While many banks may lend to keiretsu firms, the main bank was the largest creditor and played a pivotal role. Main banks had great power even though the Anti-Monopoly Law permitted them to hold no more than 5% of any commercial firm's shares and prohibited Bank Holding Companies.

Keiretsu came in many different combinations and degrees of cohesion, with member firms sometimes working closely to coordinate their activities and in other cases merely using their relationship to facilitate isolated transactions that would benefit from joint action.

For a more limited view, that keiretsu relationships merely reflected the banks' insider trading on borrowers' shares and, in the first half of the 20th century, that banks were not the major source of funds for businesses, see M. Ramseyer, *Does Corporate Governance Converge? The A-Contextual Logic to the Japanese Keiretsu*, unpublished paper, Nov. 26, 1997, and Y. Miwa and M. Ramseyer, *Banks and Economic Growth: Implications from Japanese History*, Aug. 2000.

Later changes in keiretsu relationships are described in the following Section.

2. STRUCTURAL CHANGES TO THE EARLY 1990S

The Japanese economy ended its high-growth period and moved into a new era of slower growth in the mid-1970s, hurt by the Nixon shock (the suspension of convertibility of the dollar to gold which led to a large-scale revaluation of the yen) and the oil crises. The slowdown upset the balance which the Japanese government had tried to maintain for nearly three decades. As a result of these changes and the worldwide movement toward deregulation, the rigid Japanese banking structure began to change very slowly.

a. CHANGES IN THE FLOW OF FUNDS

The flow of funds to various sectors of the economy changed dramatically. Corporate demand for loans fell as domestic economic growth slowed. Large companies became important suppliers of funds along with households, which already had unusably high savings rates compared to most other countries. In this borrower's market, cash rich Japanese firms became less dependent on their bankers and the importance of long-term relationships and corporate loyalty diminished. Companies turned to equity markets, which boomed after 1985.

Japanese banks widened the scope of their activities as a result. Commercial banks, with falling loan demand and interest margins, sought fee earning services such as foreign exchange and securities trading, mortgage lending, credit cards, and even investment banking activities (security underwriting, mergers and acquisition business). Long-term credit banks, with declining demand for long-term loans, began to transform themselves into investment banks and looked to overseas markets. Regional banks entered national and even international markets. They set up a nationwide automatic teller machine (ATM) network and courted large, blue chip firms that were once the exclusive preserve of the city banks.

b.   ISSUANCE OF JGB AND SECURITIES OPERATIONS BY BANKS

After the oil shock in the mid-1970s pushed Japan into recession, the public sector deficits grew. The government funded them by issuing bonds to a captive market, Japanese financial institutions and banks in particular.   To facilitate the purchase of government bonds, the government eased regulations governing their sale. Banks agreed to buy the bonds on the promise that they would be permitted to expand their activities. At first trading was moribund because the bonds were issued at below-market rates, but gradually the secondary market in JGBs developed. Over time, short-term markets began to develop and interest rate controls relaxed. The market grew fast. During the 1960s and the early 1970s, the public sector took about 20% of total funds raised. By the late 1970s, it took about 50%.

The government delivered the *quid pro quo*. It relaxed Article 65 of the Security and Exchange Law. During the early 1980s, the government allowed Japanese banks to underwrite and deal in government bonds, render investment advice, and engage in futures activities for their own account and customers. Nevertheless, the contribution of non-interest income remained modest. Through a remarkable arrangement called the Three Bureaus Agreement, banks were allowed to underwrite bonds offshore even though they could not do so at home. M. Tanaka explained how Japanese regulations affected these operations of Japanese banks.

M. TANAKA, JAPANESE REGULATIONS CONCERNING JAPANESE BANK OPERATIONS IN FOREIGN COUNTRIES
Talk Delivered at Harvard Law School 15-18 (May 5, 1992) ("Tanaka")

A major debate occurred during the early 1980s with regard to applicability of Article 65 of the Securities and Exchange Law, which separates banking and securities businesses, to European subsidiaries of Japanese banks and securities companies. The background of this debate was competitive disadvantage allegedly incurred by those subsidiaries against European financial institutions which engage in "universal banking." Eventually permission was granted for those European subsidiaries of the banks to conduct securities business, but no written official document can be found to this effect.

While the foreign subsidiaries of the banks started securities business, it remains essentially unknown to what extent they may expand the scope of their securities business. As there is no definitive Japanese legal authority which prohibits such companies from conducting a full range of securities business, it has been the position of the banks that those subsidiaries should be allowed to engage in the type of securities businesses permitted under the local laws and regulations.

On the other hand, the Ministry, being under the pressure from the Japanese securities industry, has been citing the *spirit* of Article 65 in issuing oral administrative guidances.

One example of such a guidance is called "Three Bureaus' Agreement." It is simply an agreement reached among the Banking Bureau, the International Banking Bureau and the Securities Bureau of the Ministry of Finance with regard to the business of underwriting securities by foreign local companies owned by Japanese banks. Even no circular exists on this issue. What is believed to contain the contents of the agreement is an internal memorandum of the MOF's Banking Bureau, although no seal, an equivalent of a signature, is placed on the memo. The memo reads as follows:

"1. In cases where a foreign local company of a Japanese bank participates in a syndicate of underwriting managers, on the occasion of issuance of a foreign bond by a Japanese company, the Japanese bank shall pay high respect to the experience and the role of the securities companies to date, and be cautious so that no violation arises with respect to the provisions of Article 65 of the Securities and Exchange Law."

"2. In order to implement the purpose of the above thoroughly, an arrangement, an order and so on of the names of companies in a prospectus and tombstone ad shall be given a careful attention."

This is interpreted to mean essentially that a foreign securities subsidiary of a Japanese bank is not allowed to become a lead manager when a Japanese company issues a bond overseas. Currently a regulatory action named "Review of Various Regulations and Practices" is underway, and the Three Bureaus' Agreement is the subject of the review. But, the review process seems to be proceeding not from a legal standpoint, but in search for compromise among interested parties.

The Three Bureaus Agreement was phased out in the mid-1990s.

c.   INTERNATIONALIZATION AND GRADUAL LIBERALIZATION

Japan's government began to relax the strict barriers to its banks offshore activities when the country, to join the OECD in 1970, had to comply with OECD policies to liberalize capital flows. The country's shift from balance of payments deficit to surplus at about the same time brought growing foreign pressure to open. Falling domestic demand prompted Japan's banks to turn abroad, too. This trend was further accelerated by revisions of the Foreign Exchange and Foreign Trade Control law in 1980, by which cross-border transaction became fully liberalized in principle.

The strong yen led the U.S. and Japan to agree that they should manage their relative exchange rates. In the 1985 Plaza Accord, the G-7 countries -- but particularly the U.S. and Japan -- agreed to intervene in a massive and coordinated way to realign exchange rates. The effect was to double the yen's value in dollars to about ¥130. The US-Japan Yen/Dollar Committee monitored the relative exchange rates from then on.

For many years until the mid-1980s, MOF allowed Japanese banks to open only one or two foreign branches or subsidiaries each year. The quantitative limit forced banks to think carefully about the strategy behind their overseas expansion over a long period of time. The limit fell as Japan's balance of payments improved dramatically in the 1980s.

In 1992, Tanaka explained how the Japanese government supervised the operations of Japanese banks in foreign countries (Tanaka at 18):

> The MOF supervises banks' subsidiaries indirectly via reports from the banks. The "Ordinance On Reports Of Foreign Exchange Transactions Etc." requires banks to submit a certain form of report concerning a foreign subsidiary's management condition on an annual basis.

> The MOF inspectors also conduct indirect supervision by grading the bank's investment in a foreign subsidiary. The financial position of a subsidiary is examined and discussions take place between the inspector and the bank's official during the examination period.

> An on-site examination of a foreign subsidiary is not conducted, but informal hearings from senior management of those subsidiaries are frequently conducted by MOF officials traveling abroad.

> During the 1980s, the Japanese banks rapidly expanded their foreign franchise. It may not be too far from the truth to say that the Japanese Banking Law, when enacted in 1981, did not expect such a wave of rapid internationalization of Japanese banks. As a result, the Ministry of Finance was placed in the awkward situation of having to regulate banks' international activities without evident legal authorities. The MOF turned to the objectives of the Banking Law and strived to attain its mission making full use of traditional regulatory process of administrative guidance.

By the 1980s Japanese banks had emerged as a driving force in international markets outside Japan. Their sheer size, the growing strength of the yen, and the country's burgeoning foreign reserves gave them a clout in foreign and offshore markets matched by few others. By the mid-1980s, the ten largest banks in the world were Japanese. Japanese banks accounted for over 50% of the growth in banks' international assets. In 1989, they held almost 40% of international bank assets. They were large net borrowers in the interbank Eurocurrency market and the largest issuer of Euro-CDs. Competing banks from other countries complained that Japanese banks penetrated foreign markets by concentrating on market share rather than profit margins, focused on long-term plans rather than short-term results, and benefitted from protected markets at home.

At the apex of their international power, in the late 1980s, 41 Japanese banks had established 272 branches abroad, as well as 194 subsidiaries, and 396 representative offices, a massive overseas presence. While located throughout the world, the largest share (about 70%) was in the United States, with an especially strong presence in California. Five of the eleven largest banks in California were Japanese-owned. In addition to domestic business, they served more than 1,000 subsidiaries of Japanese firms and the sizable Japanese population in California. Commercial and industrial loans to US residents reached $60 billion. US offices of Japanese banks were large net borrowers in the domestic interbank market. Sumitomo Bank invested US$500m for a limited interest in Goldman Sachs, the US investment banking partnership. As a condition for approval of the deal, Sumitomo Bank received no voting rights in return for its investment. Their offshore business gave Japanese banks experience in securities dealing, experience that would be invaluable when Article 65 was relaxed.

3. FOREIGN BANKS' ENTRY AND ACTIVITIES IN JAPAN

The limited role of foreign banks in Japan provoked their home country governments to accuse Japan of unfair treatment. As you read the following material, ask yourself how much of the foreign banks' low market share was likely to be the result of Japanese government protectionism and how much due to business practices.

a.   FOREIGN BANKS' MARKET PENETRATION

For years, foreign banks played a marginal role in Japan's financial system, with a market share hovering around 2% of total bank assets. The following material describes their limited penetration and the reasons for it.

I. SWARY AND B. TOPF, GLOBAL FINANCIAL DEREGULATION: COMMERCIAL BANKING AT THE CROSSROADS
180–92 (1992) (Swary and Topf).

Foreign banks in Japan play a relatively limited role. With no natural customer base, restricted access to yen funding, and handicapped by cultural differences, the bulk of their business is in foreign exchange and other related areas.

.   .   .

Only eight banks were represented in Japan before World War Two; by 1968 the number had only grown to sixteen. In that year international pressure on Japan to liberalize the licensing of foreign banks began to bear fruit, resulting in the number of foreign banks with branches in Japan increasing to 50 by 1978, and 82 by 1989. [During the 1980s, the foreign banks' share of all banks' assets fell from 1.9% to 1.4%.] . . .

An additional 124 banks maintained representative offices in Japan by 1987. In July 1985, permission was granted to foreign banks to open trust banks and by 1986 eight such autonomous trust banks were established.

Foreign banks in Japan lack a natural yen deposit base, because foreign institutions lack branch networks. As foreign banks engage to a certain degree in wholesale banking, they tend to depend on corporate bonds and short-term financial markets. However, foreign banks are prevented from issuing bank bonds, and therefore have been dependent on the money market and yen swap market for yen funds, and on borrowed funds (primarily from their head offices and the Euromarkets) for foreign currency denominated funds.... In November 1984, they were allowed to deal in government bonds.

Foreign banks in Japan have always been very active in the Tokyo foreign exchange market, in trade financing, and letters of credit. ... These services have probably been the main reason that many Japanese corporations have maintained a relationship with foreign banks.

The entry of foreign banks into the trust banking business is seen as potentially very profitable. With the development of a freer market in asset management, many foreign banks believe that their experience in overseas funds management will enable them to capture a significant market share. Given the vast pool of assets in Japan, such potential fees would be very attractive.

By the end of 1993, there were 90 foreign commercial banks in Japan, of which 20 were American, and 9 trust banks, of which 6 were American. See 1994 National Treatment Study 334. At the end of 1994, all foreign banks' assets in Japan were 2.6% of the assets of all banks in Japan.

b.   THE REGULATION OF FOREIGN BANKS' IN JAPAN TO THE EARLY 1990s

"Formally, foreign banks operating in Japan operate under the same laws and guidelines as domestic banks. In practice, however, the treatment of foreign banks is determined by the treatment accorded Japan's banks in the country of origin," according to Swary and Topf, 97-98. This section describes the rules and practice up to the early 1990s.

E. SYMONS, JR. AND J. WHITE, 3 BANKING LAW
806–09 (1991).

The Bank Law of 1981 took effect on April 1, 1982. The Law includes a chapter entitled "Foreign Bank Branch" (Chapter 7). The chapter's six provisions are founded upon the stated principles that foreign bank branches are to be treated equally to domestic commercial banks and that as much "administrative guidance" as possible is to be expressly spelled out in the statute.

So far, the Bank Law has not changed the fact that branching is the only viable means of entry into Japan beyond a representative office. The Law requires that each foreign bank branch receive an individual license from the Finance Minister. Therefore, a foreign bank cannot be granted one license which, without more, comprehensively permits the bank to establish two or more branches. [Art. 47, para. 1]. The Law treats each branch established as an independent "bank." [Art. 47, para. 2]. A license is granted to an applicant bank after the examination of its application by the M.O.F. in light of criteria set forth in the statute.

. . . There has never been a "bank" created under the new Bank Law. In fact, no new Japanese commercial bank has been created since World War II, and a foreign "bank," as opposed to "branch," has never been created in Japan. The reason is the view that Japan is overbanked. . . . Consequently, establishing a subsidiary is not a realistic way for a foreign bank to enter the Japanese banking market.

Acquisition of part or even all of the shares of a presently licensed and operating bank is another logical alternative to de novo entry. However, this method does not have many of the advantages of branching. First, Japanese corporate law allows the use of bylaws to prohibit cumulative voting. (The Commercial Code: Art. 256–3, para. 1). Consequently, acquisition of a small percentage of voting shares cannot guarantee a voice in management. Second, the Anti–Monopoly Law requires the permission of the Fair Trade Commission before a financial institution can acquire more than a 5 percent interest in any domestic corporation (Art. 11). Third, a foreign investor that wishes to obtain more than 10 percent of the outstanding shares of a domestic company must give advance notice to the pertinent authorities and sometimes must procure special approval. (The Foreign Exchange Law: Art. 26, para. 3). Fourth, and most important, is the "interlocking stockholding" phenomenon, wherein bank shareholders usually maintain a business relationship with a bank. Should the bank become the target of a takeover, these so-called "stable shareholders" would show a marked inclination not to dispose of their shares.

Another consideration in entering the banking business in Japan is that the "business of banking" does not cover the broad area of activities in which foreign bankers might wish to engage. (The Bank Law: Art. 10). The business of banking is a much narrower concept in

Japan than in the United Kingdom or West Germany, or even than in the United States. For example trust business is in principle reserved exclusively to trust banks. As a legal entity trust banks are identical to commercial banks. They are both "banks" under the Bank Law. As a matter of form trust banks have obtained special approval to operate both trust business and traditional banking business at the same time. What has divided "banks" into two categories—those whose business is orthodox banking and those who devote themselves to trust operations and long-term lending—has been "administrative guidance."

. . .

Relative scarcity of Japanese depository funds for foreign bank branches is mainly due to the lack of branches. As noted above, each branch must acquire an additional license. The result is that 90 percent of foreign bank branches are located in the central business districts of Tokyo and Osaka. Foreign bank branches are not present in any form in the neighborhoods where most retail banking is done.

Additional foreign banks' funds come from the conversion of dollars to Yen on the foreign exchange market. The net conversion into Yen is limited within a certain prescribed amount (swap limit). Although this regulation applies to all authorized foreign exchange banks, considerably larger limits are allocated to foreign bank branches than to domestic banks because, for foreign bank branches, deposits are insufficient to meet their needs for Yen funds. Foreign banks also rely on Yen credits (borrowings) from Japanese financial institutions as a source of funds. There is no restriction today on these credits.

Other means used by foreign banks to raise Yen funds are issuance of negotiable certificates of deposit (NCD), and participation in the "call market," "bills discount market" and "Gensaki market." In each case foreign banks are treated more favorably than domestic banks. NCD's may be issued up to 30 percent of the Yen loan balance of a foreign bank, consisting of loan and securities assets, while a Japanese bank's limit is 50 percent of *its net worth*. Foreign banks also can freely participate in both the "call market" and the "bills discount market." They can raise Yen funds there without any limit, whereas domestic banks are often "guided" by the Bank of Japan which regards excessive dependence on these markets as unsound.... The "Gensaki market," where swap transactions of securities take place, is also completely open to foreign banks. On the other hand domestic city banks are given "guidance" from the B.O.J. on the maximum amount of securities selling used to raise funds. The B.O.J.'s lending facility is also available on favorable terms, although in general its use is strictly limited.

The majority of the Yen funds raised by foreign banks are allocated to commercial loans. Loans are subject to "regulation of large lot loans" and "window guidance." Under the "regulation of large lot loans," credit extension to one debtor may not exceed certain prescribed limits. (The Bank Law: Art. 13, para. 1). The limit for a commercial bank is 20 percent of its net worth (capital plus reserve funds). Foreign banks are exempt from this regulation for the five year period following the effective date of the Bank Law of 1981. "Window guidance," on the other hand, is not based upon a statutory or an administrative power. It is conducted by persuasion through the private business relationship between the B.O.J. and the Japanese financial institutions. The main function of the guidance is to control increases in bank lendings, particularly at a time of monetary restraint. The Japanese domestic banks are subject to detailed guidance and required to maintain strict compliance. Except for the period from 1973 to 1974 when the worldwide oil crisis occurred, foreign banks have never come under this guidance system.

c.   FOREIGN GOVERNMENT PRESSURE ON JAPAN

Since the 1970s, U.S.-Japanese trade has been contentious. U.S. exporters argued that Japan set high barriers and the Japanese, noting that the U.S. was not devoid of protectionist policies, replied that the trade problems were due to the weak U.S. economy and U.S. firms' failure to master Japanese business practices, consumer needs, or even the language. U.S. banks in Japan prevented the contention from spreading to them in the 1970s. They recognized that their small but lucrative share of the Japanese market derived from foreign banks' monopoly over lending in foreign currencies to local borrowers. Unfortunately for them, this ended with the foreign exchange law of 1979. Trade in services, including banking, was the subject of debate between the Japanese and U.S. governments. The two governments began a series of bilateral meetings in 1983 and started to coordinate management of the yen/dollar exchange rate in 1985, forming the US-Japan Yen/Dollar Committee. The UK-Japan and German-Japan Financial Consultations also played a role in liberalization. The Clinton Administration, taking office in 1993, announced its plan to open Japanese financial markets substantially. Its initiative led to the Financial Services Agreement of 1995, discussed later in this Chapter. U.S. financial firms in Japan played an important role in the negotiations.

The criticisms routinely raised the problems caused by administrative guidance. "A chronic complaint of U.S. financial institutions operating in Japan is the lack of transparency in Japan's regulatory environment," reported the U.S. Treasury in its 1994 National Treatment Study (at 346) of the policy of other governments toward U.S. financial firms in their countries. Administrative guidance was particularly strong in matters of economic and industrial policy, where government bureaucrats "organize the bargains," while politicians do so in social and regional matters. See S. Vogel, *Japan's Financial System*, 7 Governance, July 1994 at 220. According to Symons and White, administrative guidance makes it "foolish to venture into the Japanese banking market without a resident expert as a guide." They continue:

> Any foreigner attempting to do business in Japan has, almost without exception, encountered a wall of ambiguity with respect to the laws governing the market. The reason lies in the complex way the Japanese government and commerce interact to create the commercial regulatory scheme. Japanese laws grant a great deal of discretion to the authorities who regulate commerce. As a result, actual regulatory policies and practice develop "flexibly" and are embodied in a complicated web of regulations, guidelines, interpretations and decisions, both published and unpublished. This complex web is called "administrative guidance" ("Gyosei-shido").

> This style of administration has often caused substantial difficulties for foreign banks, even those that have long engaged in banking activities in Japan. For example, a bank's main office may issue an order to its Tokyo branch based upon the published rules but its Tokyo branch may find it impermissible to carry out the order after holding lengthy person-to-person negotiations with an official of the Ministry of Finance (M.O.F.). This makes it difficult for foreign banks to plan accurately and with assurance. This ambiguity of rules accompanied by an "administrative guidance" system has recently become a main issue in negotiations between the United States and Japan concerning international commerce. Although under the policy of "internationalization of the Japanese financial market" the M.O.F. has tried to spell out some of the specifics of administrative guidance as clearly as possible, it is unlikely that this can suffice to westernize the Japanese way of governing commerce. This is largely because of the legal and social ethos that underlies all of Japanese business.

In 1990, the Treasury had said:

> Although there has been some improvement in their ability to transmit their views to responsible officials since 1986, foreign firms still experience difficulty on occasion in gaining access to Ministry of Finance and industry consultations influencing their operations. This was a particular problem in the formation of the Tokyo International Financial Futures Exchange, where foreign firms had little input in the decision process and were only informed of important specifics on the eve of the exchange's formation. Foreign participants are not included in the official advisory councils, which advise the Ministry of Finance on proposed structural and regulatory changes of central interest to both domestic and foreign financial firms. There are occasionally, however, informal Ministry of Finance study groups where a foreign firm may be included. One of these is the MOF/BOJ study group on money markets, operating since 1989, with three foreign firm members on it.

A second major complaint concerned the effect of the keiretsu. As restrictions on entry by foreign banks fell, foreign bankers nevertheless complained that barriers existed in the structure of Japanese industry. High stock prices deterred even friendly acquisitions. Cross-shareholding limited the portion of shares of any bank traded in the market.

The Big Bang, supplementing the US-Japan Financial Services Agreement of 1995 removed many of the special problems faced by foreign banks in Japan (see the next section). But Japan continued to limit foreign banks' presence to branches.

Questions

1. Is the argument that administrative guidance is a serious barrier to foreign banking operations in Japan convincing? What is the likely economic and political function of administrative guidance in Japan?

B.   ISSUES FROM THE 1990S ON

By the end of the 1990s, Japan's government was trying to change its banking system radically. The following sections describe the Big Bang's reform of segmentation (underway since 1992) and its other reforms, the full dimensions and possible solutions to the bad loan problem of the banks, and the dispersion of powers of the MOF and BOJ.

1.   BASIC STRUCTURE OF BIG BANG

By late 1996, the government's ability to act according to the old rules seemed to have eroded to the point of no return. High fiscal deficits, rising from 3% of GDP in 1993 to 5% in 1996, inhibited the free use of government funds to bail out insolvent banks. A radical change seemed necessary.

The Big Bang, if fully implemented, would change Japanese banking in important ways. The following two sections describe first the basic changes in segmentation, then other major changes.

a.   REFORMING FINANCIAL SYSTEM SEGMENTATION

The Prime Minister and supporting committees identified the following:

- entry would be promoted, so barriers between city, trust, and long-term banks would fall (firewalls would be retained but changed), banks could open branches without authorities' approval, and non-bank banks would operate within a sound regulatory system;

- banks and securities firms could engage in each others' businesses;

- the monopoly of foreign exchange banks would end, so other banks, securities firms, and trading firms could do foreign exchange business; and

- holding companies would be permitted for firms with assets up to ¥ 15 trillion ($123 billion), which would exclude the large City banks and the Big Four securities companies.

By mid-1998, most of the Big Bang had been enacted as legislation and was taking effect. The Foreign Exchange Control Act was amended to make most transactions subject to reporting only after they took place. Bank retail customers could open foreign currency accounts at the regular retail counters. The Anti-Monopoly Act was amended to allow non-financial holding companies. Amendments to allow financial holding companies were anticipated during 1998. Banks received some securities powers (see Section II of this Chapter).

Domestic and foreign banks looked for opportunities. Fuji Bank considered creating a bank holding company. Troubled banks became objects of possible acquisition. Bankers Trust Company of the U.S. considered equity links with Nippon Credit Bank. As described below, NCB had major problems and had withdrawn from foreign markets as a result. Even non-banks considered their options.

The government had started earlier to eliminate financial market segmentation with the Financial Reform Act of 1992.

D. SNEIDER, FINANCIAL SERVICES REFORM IN JAPAN
International Securities Regulation Report, Feb. 6, 1993, at 6.

In June 1992, Japan's Diet enacted sweeping legislation aimed at increasing competition among different segments of the financial services industry. The Financial Reform Act ... amended the Securities and Exchange Law, the Banking Law, and other statutes. The two most significant reforms give banks permission to establish securities subsidiaries similar in function to the so-called "Section 20 affiliates" in the United States and give securities companies and other financial institutions permission to establish trust bank subsidiaries.

The basic approach of the Financial Reform Act is to impose relatively few statutory restrictions on the newly permitted subsidiaries while granting broad regulatory discretion to the Ministry of Finance (MOF) to apply additional limitations. This should enable the MOF to carefully adjust the pace and scope of change according to how quickly affected financial institutions are able to adjust to the new competitive environment. Indeed, while the Financial Reform Act has transformed the landscape of Japan's financial services industry, it is likely to be implemented in such a gradual manner that the impact of the reform will not be felt fully for many years to come.

Securities Activities by Banks

The Financial Reform Act establishes for the Japanese securities industry a framework similar to that now existing in the United States: Bank groups will be able to compete with securities firms in most lines of business by continuing to conduct certain securities activities in the bank itself and by engaging in other activities through newly permitted securities subsidiaries.

At the same time, however, banks will be handicapped in several important respects: The licenses granted initially to the new subsidiaries will limit their activities primarily to corporate bond underwriting and dealing as well as activities that banks can currently engage in directly; firewall restrictions will be imposed between banks and their securities subsidiaries; and new securities licenses will be issued only on a selective basis. The MOF has stated that it will not consider easing its initial regulations for at least two to three years.

The statutory basis for the new subsidiaries is an amendment to the Securities and Exchange Law's Article 65—often referred to as Japan's Glass–Steagall Act—that allows the MOF to grant securities business licenses to majority-owned subsidiaries of banks and other financial institutions to be specified by ordinance ("securities subsidiaries"). Although acquiring an existing securities firm is a theoretical option, the MOF has made it clear that acquisitions will not be approved except in a "rescue" context.

1. Scope of Activities. Banks in Japan may directly engage in underwriting and dealing of government bonds as well as instruments newly designated as securities under the Securities and Exchange Law as a result of the Financial Reform Act. The latter include such instruments as commercial paper and asset-backed securities. Banks also will be permitted to handle private placements of any security.

Although the Financial Reform Act formally expanded the securities powers of banks—for example, by making commercial paper a "security"—in practice it did little to expand the scope of their direct securities activities.

The only explicit statutory restriction on the scope of activities of securities subsidiaries relates to equity brokerage. Here, the Financial Reform Act provides that "for the time being" the MOF shall not grant to any securities subsidiary a license to engage in that activity and that, if an existing securities firm is acquired by a bank, the MOF may terminate the firm's stock brokerage license. This provision is intended to protect medium- and small-size brokers in particular, which are largely dependent on stock brokerage commissions for their revenue.

In addition to the restriction on equity brokerage, the MOF announced in a Dec. 17 release that it will exercise its licensing authority to exclude securities subsidiaries from engaging initially in the following activities: underwriting, dealing, and brokerage of stocks; brokerage of stock index futures and options; and dealing and brokerage of equity-related products such as convertible bonds and bonds with warrants. In effect, the principal initial reward to the banking industry is access to the straight corporate bond market. . . .

2. Firewall Restrictions. As with the restrictions on the scope of activities, firewall restrictions will be implemented primarily through regulation. As a matter of statute, the Securities and Exchange Law and the Banking Law expressly prohibit the following with respect to banks and their securities subsidiaries (as well as with respect to new banks and their securities company parents):

- Dual employment of officers or employees in the bank and securities affiliate.

- Transactions between the bank and the securities affiliate that are not entered into on an arm's-length basis.

- Transactions by the securities affiliate with a customer of the bank that are tied to an extension of credit to the customer by the bank.

The Financial Reform Act authorized the MOF to stipulate by ordinance more detailed restrictions deemed necessary to implement the foregoing principles or to otherwise protect investors or the soundness of banks. In its Dec. 17 release, the MOF announced that forthcoming regulations will include the following firewall restrictions:

(a) "Main Bank" Firewall. A securities subsidiary will not be allowed to act as lead manager in a securities offering by any issuer with which its parent bank has a "main bank" relationship unless the issuer has net assets of ¥500 billion ($4 billion) or more. Such a relationship will be deemed to exist if the bank is acting as the issuer's bond trustee (or so-called commissioned company) for the issue or so acted in a majority of the issuer's recent bond offerings. The ¥500 billion net asset test leaves unrestricted underwriting for approximately the 34 largest issuers whose outstanding debt securities currently constitute more than 40 percent, by volume, of the bond market.

In a related move, the MOF announced the five-year phase-out of the so-called Three Bureaus' Guidance, which prevents offshore securities subsidiaries of Japanese banks from lead managing foreign bond offerings by Japanese issuers.

(b) Joint Visits. Joint visits to customers by representatives of a bank and its securities subsidiary will be prohibited in principle unless requested by the customer.

(c) Confidential Information. Exchanges of non-public information concerning a customer or an issuer between a bank and its securities subsidiary will be prohibited unless consented to in writing.

(d) Exchange of Personnel. A securities subsidiary will be expected to raise to 50 percent within five years the ratio of directly recruited employees, as opposed to transferees from its parent bank. Additional restrictions will limit the ability of persons who have served as officers or directors of the securities subsidiary to return to positions of responsibility at its parent bank.

(e) Shared Facilities.   The headquarters offices of a bank and its securities subsidiary may not be in the same building. Other restrictions will be imposed on sharing branches, dealing rooms, and computer facilities.

(f) Additional Restrictions.   The following will also be subject to restrictions: the percentage of revenues that a securities subsidiary may derive from transactions with its parent bank; underwriting by a securities subsidiary of securities issued by its parent bank; tie-in sales; sales to a bank of securities underwritten by its securities subsidiary; and bank financing of customer purchases of securities underwritten by its securities subsidiary. In addition, the use of proceeds must be disclosed if an offering underwritten by a securities subsidiary is intended to refinance a debt to its parent bank.

3. Selective Licensing. Consistent with a Diet resolution attached to the Financial Reform Act, the MOF has stated its intention to control the number and timing of licenses granted to securities subsidiaries in order to maintain an appropriate competitive balance between the securities and banking industries and among different segments of the banking industry. Japan's three long-term credit banks, seven trust banks, and two central cooperative banks are being given a head start of at least one year on the 10 city banks whose extensive retail branch networks are thought to provide an advantage. The MOF is also expected to grant securities licenses only to a limited number of the eligible institutions in any segment, such as to the stronger two of the three long-term credit banks.

New Trust Banks

The Financial Reform Act, for the first time, permits securities firms to establish commercial bank or trust bank subsidiaries and also permits other financial institutions to set up trust banks. Since Japan's major securities firms are not thought to have an interest in retail banking, they are expected to establish only trust bank subsidiaries which, in addition to trust banking activities, may conduct commercial banking activities such as foreign exchange, swaps, and lending. It is likely that only two or three securities firms will be permitted to establish trust banks initially. Similar to the case of securities subsidiaries, at first only the long-term credit banks, the central cooperative banks, and the Bank of Tokyo will be eligible to establish trust bank subsidiaries, and only several of them will in fact obtain permission.

Like securities subsidiaries, the new trust banks will be restricted both in terms of scope of activity and firewalls. Most significantly, the new firms will be excluded initially from engaging in the most profitable segments of the trust banking business, including loan trusts (a form of savings instrument) and pension trusts (which manage corporate pension funds). Permitted activities include property trusts, such as land trusts, and certain designated money trusts, such as securities investment trusts and fund trusts, which are expected to be a strategic focus of securities firms' subsidiaries.

Options for Foreign Financial Institutions

The Financial Reform Act offers relatively few benefits to foreign financial institutions because special dispensation previously enabled them to operate both securities and banking entities, and in some cases trust banks, in

Japan.   The MOF allowed foreign banks to establish 50 percent-owned securities affiliates in the 1980s and foreign securities firms to establish bank branches of 50 percent-owned bank affiliates beginning in 1991.

Under the new law, foreign banks seeking to enter the Japanese securities industry will have three options: apply as in the past for a securities license for the Japanese branch of a non-Japanese securities affiliate, but limit the affiliation to 50 percent; do the same, but increase the affiliation to more than 50 percent; or establish a domestic Japanese securities subsidiary.

In the past, the second and third options were not available because the law required foreign firms to enter the Japanese market through Japanese branches of 50 percent or less foreign affiliates licensed under the Foreign Securities Companies Law.   Despite the change in law, the advantages of majority ownership or of entering through a domestic subsidiary rather than an offshore company are unclear.

For foreign financial institutions that already operate securities and banking operations in Japan, the Financial Reform Act offers the option of increasing the affiliation of the two entities from 50 percent.   However, because it is highly unlikely that new firewall restrictions will be imposed between the two entities so long as their affiliation is limited to 50 percent, there may be a significant advantage to maintaining the status quo.   Some firewall restrictions currently exist between the banking and securities affiliates of foreign institutions, but they are far more limited than the new rules proposed.

During the six months ending September 1994, the security subsidiaries of Japanese commercial banks underwrote 7% of domestic straight bonds and 5% of corporate bond issues. These units included no subsidiaries of the city banks. The finance ministry waited until October 1994 to authorize the first five city banks' subsidiaries (Letter from Thomson Corporation Japan, DEAL WATCH screen service).

On February 12, 1995, the U.S. Secretary of the Treasury and the Ambassador of Japan to the United States signed a Financial Services Agreement. Much of it concerned securities markets and is described in Section II of this Chapter. The part most relevant to banking markets in Japan concerned the transparency of regulation. Major elements included:

a.   Japan would publish standards for licensing, explain adverse licensing decisions to applicants, make compliance with administrative guidance voluntary, put oral administrative guidance in writing upon request, and publicize items of guidance that are common to "a multiple number of persons"

b.   The Japanese government will "strongly request" local groups advising it about financial services to allow foreign participation. Foreign financial service suppliers can join relevant Japanese trade associations and be treated in the same manner as Japanese members.

c. Foreigners will receive "meaningful and fair opportunities to be informed of, comment on, and exchange views with officials" about measures concerning financial services in Japan.

In December 1996, the Japanese and U.S. governments signed an agreement to open Japan's insurance markets, in which foreign firms had a 3-4% market share. Japan agreed to deregulate automobile and fire insurance pricing by July 1998 and, 2½ years later, reduce barriers to Japanese insurers investing in the protected markets for foreign firms. Before this, Japanese industry associations had set casualty insurance prices. D. Hamilton, *U.S. and Japan End Insurance dispute With Tokyo Conceding to Demands*, Wall Street Journal, Dec. 16, 1996.

By early 2001, Japan's insurance industry was in the middle of major change. The crisis erupted in the insurance industry in early 1997, when the nation's sixteenth largest insurer, Nissan Mutual Life Insurance Company, collapsed. In the next few years, the exposure of life insurance companies became clear. The barrier between life and non-life insurance was gone. Foreign insurance firms had entered, some to help failing firms. Two of the 10 largest life insurance companies, Chiyoda and Kyoei, had gone bankrupt, along with others. American International Group (AIG) offered to acquire Chiyoda in early 2001. Still others had merged. The government indicated that it could not provide to insurance firms the kind of support that it had given banks. After September 11, Taisei Fire and Marine Life Insurance failed, only the second non-life company to fail after World War II, and the ratings of other Japanese non-life firms fell. The fifth largest insurer threatened to fail. The public doubted that the regulatory solvency ratios for insurers were adequate. The Oriental Economist, *Insuring the Insurers*, Nov. 2000, and S. Strom, *Another Japanese Insurer Sets Record for Bankruptcy*, New York Times, Oct. 21, 2000; *Lust for Life*, The Economist, Oct. 28, 2000; K. Hijino, *AIG Poised to Acquire Troubled Chiyoda Mutual*, Financial Times, Jan. 21, 2001; K. Hijino and J. Croft, *Japanese Insurer Collapses*, Financial Times, Nov. 23, 2001; K. Hijino, *Japanese Life Assurers on Shaky Foundations*, Financial Times, Mar. 13, 2002.

Questions

1. Why was it necessary to end segmentation? Are the changes made to reduce segmentation by the Financial Reform Act and the Big Bang significant?

2. Did the decision to end the Three Bureaus Agreement indicate that MOF was losing control over offshore activities of banks?

3. What is the role of offshore markets in this restructuring? Would it be fair to say they were the primary cause?

b. OTHER BIG BANG REFORMS

Big Bang also took aim at other special features of Japanese banking. The Prime Minister vowed further changes:

- disclosure would be thorough and substantial, including consolidated accounts;

- rule violations would be actively punished;

- accounting would meet international standards; and

- supervision would meet international standards, including prompt corrective action, and cooperation with supervisors elsewhere would be commonplace.

The market reacted in various ways. Almost immediately, Moody's decided to downgrade several Japanese banks' ratings because of the Big Bang. Moody's said that Japanese policy "was shifting from one of protection and forbearance to one of resolution via liquidation, which may expose creditors to risk." G. Robinson, *Japan Bank Shares Plunge*, Financial Times, Jan. 28, 1997.

These policy changes gradually took effect. Big Bang had called for a policy of prompt corrective action that would penalize banks automatically if their capital fell too low. The crisis, however, led authorities to delay by a year enforcing this policy against smaller banks. In addition, banks could include property assets as reserves from April 1, 1998. See Analytica Japan, *Japan's Big Bang -- A Critical Review*, December 12, 1997; *Crunch Time?*, The Economist, January 24, 1998 at 70; J. Sapsford and B. Spindle, *Japan's Bank Overhaul Seems Solid*, Wall Street Journal, January 27, 1998. Similarly, the Big Bang planned to end protection for all depositors and substitute protection by the Deposit Insurance Corporation (DIC) for retail deposits, up to a ceiling. In 1999, the government decided to delay implementing this reform by a year, then postponed it still further. M. Nakamoto, *Japan Delays Financial Reform Law*, Financial Times, Dec. 30-31, 1999. Domestic confidence in the banking system had not been restored, despite measures to strengthen the DIC that added much greater financial resources and power to collect and investigate abuses, in anticipation of more failures. See C. Milhaupt, *Japan's Experience with Deposit Insurance and Failing Banks: Implications for Financial Regulatory Design?*, 17 Monetary and Economic Studies 21, Aug. 1999.

Coupled with the policies to end the bad debt problems, described below, the Big Bang helped Japanese banks recover some by late 1999. The major banks, having reported losses for the previous three years, reported modest profits for the six months ending September 30, 1999. As concrete policies were announced, the Japan premium, in international financial markets, fell and then disappeared. See G. Tett, *Improving Fortunes for Japan's Banks*, Financial Times, Sep. 23, 1999; J. Peek and

E. Rosengren, *Determinants of the Japan Premium: Actions Speak Louder than Words,* Sep. 9, 1999.

Questions

1. How significant would the proposed changes be for Japanese banks, if they were implemented? Is Big Bang enough?

2. Please see the earlier discussion of administrative guidance. Do the measures for banks that were adopted in the Financial Services Agreement of 1995 address the concerns about guidance?

3. How would the changes affect cross-border banking flows into and out of Japan?

   a. What are the implications of Big Bang for foreign banks in Japan?

   b. How big a threat to Japanese banks will foreign banks become?

4. Will Big Bang significantly affect international markets?

5. What would be the implications of the changes for systemic risk? Should U.S. regulators be concerned about the effect on U.S. banking markets? If so, what should they do?

6. Is Big Bang happening too quickly or slowly?

2. BAD LOAN PROBLEMS

The full extent of the financial crises of the early 1990s revealed itself slowly, in part because neither the banks nor the government announced it. It is useful to follow the revelations chronologically, since the process itself contributed to public dissatisfaction with the way the crises were handled. This section follows the sequence of crises, revelations, and responses by the banks to show the process.

a. SOURCE AND SIZE OF THE PROBLEMS

In 1992, Japan's finance minister acknowledged publicly that the nation's banks carried a dangerously high level of nonperforming loans. The immediate cause was the steep collapse of stock and real property values, whose spectacular price rises the banks had helped to finance in the 1980s. The stock market collapse is discussed in more detail in Section II. The ensuing recession pushed more borrowers into bankruptcy, so that the value of bankruptcies in both 1991 and 1992 was eight times the 1989 value. A well known rating agency for international banks reported that if loan loss provisions were "at the right level" the Japanese banks would lose all existing capital except their hidden reserves on securities. Japan's banks placed as the least profitable in the world. See J. Gapper, *Japanese Banks' Loan Woes*, Financial Times, Dec. 20, 1993.

Not surprisingly, credit rating agencies like Moody's lowered the ratings of Japan's largest banks.

As the crisis progressively worsened, the city banks wrote off mainly undisclosed bad debt. Most of the funds for write-offs were from the sale of stock the banks owned, tapping the hidden reserves. The banks generally sold the stock, earned a profit, and bought back the stock. Sectoral collapse pushed the crisis deeper. Over the summer of 1995, the bankruptcy of seven housing loan companies called *jusen* precipitated the first run on Japanese banks since the end of World War II, forcing the Bank of Japan to provide liquidity. Some observers saw this as the beginning of the end of consensus; the jusen problems arose from the "regulatory cartel" of public and private sector entities but could not be solved by that cartel. C. Milhaupt and G. Miller, *Regulatory Failure and the Collapse of Japan's Home Mortgage Lending Industry: A Legal and Economic Analysis*, 22 Law and Policy 245 (2000).

Both the government and banks revised the bad debt numbers upward so regularly that they destroyed confidence in any set of figures. In early 1993, some observers guessed that bad loans held by the 21 largest banks were probably ¥30 trillion (roughly $300 billion), twice as high as the publicly announced figure of 4.1% of all loans. See R. Thomson, *Japan's Banks Under Heavy Pressure*, Financial Times, Mar. 24, 1993. By November 1998, Standard & Poor's estimated that the bad loans could be twice as high the government's estimate of $726 billion (¥87 trillion). A government audit at the end of March 1998 found $427 billion (¥427 trillion) of bad loans in the 17 largest banks alone and concluded that they had underestimated the bad debt by $80 billion. G. Tett, *Stock Market Rally Suggests New Dawn for Japan's Banks*, Financial Times, Nov. 19, 1998; *More Problem Debts Found in Audit* of Japanese Banks, New York Times, Dec. 26, 1998 (no author); G. Tett, *Japan's Banks 'Up to $80bn Adrift Over Risky Loans,'* Financial Times, Nov. 26, 1998.

The big banks began to write off more bad debt and declare losses. Sumitomo Bank declared a loss in 1994/5, something no bank had done since World War II. Others followed suit, each year. See W. Dawkins, *Barclays Chief Urges Loan Rethink at Japanese Banks*, Financial Times, Feb. 16, 1996. As a result, Moody's downgraded many major Japanese banks, including Sumitomo. The banks experimented with partial solutions from 1997 on. These included securitizing bad debt, writing off more than before, cutting staff, closing foreign operations, selling equity assets, overhauling their operations, cutting even the size of their board of directors, and merging. Mitsui Trust and Chuo Trust prepared to merge, for example. See *And It Finally Came to Tears*, The Economist, November 29, 1997, at 78; S. WuDunn, *Tokyo Tries to Calm Fears on Bad Loans,* New York Times, January 13, 1998; G. Tett, *Sumitomo and Daiwa Report Large Losses*, Financial Times, May 22, 1998; *Moody's Drops*

Ratings on Japanese Banks, New York Times May 28, 1998; and *Bank Mergers Give Tokyo Hope*, Financial Times, Jan. 22, 1999 (no author).

To replace their lost capital, banks raised funds at home and abroad. In Japan, they issued subordinated debt that one study found funded about half of their capital losses from 1990-1995. The main buyers were the banks' affiliated financial and non-financial firms. See A. Horiuchi and K. Shimizu, *The Deterioration of Banks' Balance Sheets in Japan: Risk-Taking and Recapitalization*, 1996. The very low prices of bank stock in Japan had eliminated domestic equity markets as a source for recapitalization. Japanese banks' average share price fell 44% in 1996 and another 11% in January 1997. Life insurance companies began to sell their shares in banks. G. Robinson, *Japan's Banks Near Danger Zone as 'Big Bang' Looms*, Financial Times, Jan. 28, 1997. The prices began to rise when the government announced its bailout plans in mid-1998.

Some banks turned abroad but foreign markets imposed premiums on Japanese banks, reaching a reported 50 to 100 basis points by January 1998. Although the premium fell to below 1 bp by 2000, it rose to 11 bp in mid-January 2001 before falling slightly. The big banks' return on equity was only 1.5%, compared to 8% for big German banks, 15% for U.S. banks, and 21% for U.K. banks. Prospects were particularly bad if the Japanese stock market declined and the ¥/$ rate fell much further. An analyst at Deutsche Bank found that 5 of the largest banks would hold capital below the 8% Basel rule if the Nikkei Index fell to 17,000 and the dollar rose to ¥130. Foreigners' distrust of the Japanese banks' reported exposure persisted. Foreign investors began to doubt that the Government would bail out banks in trouble. See *Good Money After Bad*, The Economist, Aug. 31, 1996, J. Sapsford, *U.S. Brokers Polish Up Japanese Bank Stocks*, Wall Street Journal, Sep. 25, 1996, and R. Steiner, *Raging Dollar Threatens Tokyo's Banks*, Wall Street Journal, Feb. 13, 1997; S. Strom, *Western Banks Raise Premium on Japan Loans*, New York Times, Jan. 31, 2001.

As Japanese banks' access to international funding markets eroded, so did their share of international lending markets: in 1989, Japanese banks held almost 40% of international bank assets, but their share dropped to 25% by 1996. The government expected that the number of Japanese banks operating abroad would fall from 80 to 40 "soon." G. Tett, *Japan Banks Abroad May Fall by Half*, Financial Times, Oct. 27, 1998; G. Tett, *Daiwa Is to Close Overseas Branches*, Financial Times, Oct. 26, 1998; A. Pollack, *Japanese Banks Cutting Back on U.S. Presence*, New York Times, July 10, 1998.

Foreign financial institutions became interested in acquiring Japanese firms in the late 1990s. The Fleet Financial Group, the ninth largest U.S. bank, negotiated the purchase of a lending unit from Sanwa Bank in 1998. Prudential Insurance (US) and Mitsui Trust & Banking set up an asset management joint venture in July 1998. T. O'Brien, *Fleet Reported About* to Buy Unit of Sanwa, New York Times, Nov. 20, 1998; G. Robinson, *Why Troubled Japan Lures Foreign Groups*, Financial Times, July 16, 1998. GE Capital Services bought a securities unit from the failed Long Term Credit Bank.

These problems helped to erode some foundations of the keiretsu system. As firms' performance and dividends weakened in the continuing recession, insurance company shareholders faced a choice. They could either sell their stakes or actively try to improve companies' performance. Activism would repudiate the mutual agreement of keiretsu members not to interfere in each other's internal management and would not be consistent with the role of a passive institutional investor. Banks began to consider selling their shares in keiretsu members in 1995 and were doing so by 1997. See *Japan Inc. Frays at the Edges*, The Economist, June 3, 1995, at 158. In November 1997, faced with the imminent collapse of Yamaichi Securities Company (see Section II of this Chapter), the president of Fuji Bank said "Let me make this clear....My responsibility is to uphold the credibility of Fuji Bank, and the priority is always Fuji. Every decision I make will be based on this -- not on any responsibility to rescue [someone else]." G. Tett, *A Commitment Problem for Fuji*, Financial Times, November 22-23, 1997.

Notes and Questions

1. What is the source of the banking crisis?

2. How would the steep decline in stock prices affect Japanese banks' capital? How would the crises affect the big banks' international operations?

3. How would the declining interest rates affect Japanese savers? In the 1980s, a yen deposit equal to $50,000 would earn $2,500. By 1996, it would earn only $125. See S. WuDunn, *The Heavy Burden of Low Rates*, New York Times, Oct. 11, 1996. How would it affect Japanese investment in foreign securities, such as U.S. treasury bonds? Suppose the ¥/$ exchange rate was managed, so that interest rate parity did not work smoothly. What would you think of a strategy of borrowing in Japan, exchanging Yen for dollars, and investing in U.S. government bonds?

b.   EARLY RESPONSES TO THE CRISIS BY THE GOVERNMENT

For much of the 1990s, the government did not address the bad loan problem head on. This section describes its actions during this period.

Disguise the extent of the problem. At first, the LDP Government took steps to disguise the extent of the problem at individual banks and for banks as a group. Rather than force a rapid write-off of the bad debts, the government had initially encouraged banks to help ailing companies and promoted a cooperative agency that would buy problem loans from the banks. It allowed banks not to classify as non-performing any loans which they had "restructured" by substantially reducing the interest rate. Banks could deduct from taxes the lost interest. Trust banks, previously obliged to report only interest actually received, were allowed to book as received unpaid interest not more than six months overdue. See R. Thomson, *Japan's Banks Under Heavy Pressure*, Financial Times, Mar. 24, 1993 and R. Thomson, *Japanese Banks Put Off Facing Up to Bad Loans*, Financial Times, May 14, 1993.

Banks transfer bad loans to get tax benefits. The Cooperative Credit Purchasing Company (CCPC) was established in 1992, with a ten year life, by Japanese banks acting jointly. The banks cannot deduct provisions for their bad loans from income for tax purposes, but they can deduct losses. A bank sells the CCPC bad loans, along with the collateral, usually worth no more than 70% of the loan principal when the loan is made. CCPC values the collateral and pays the bank that value, financed by a loan from the bank. The bank continues to manage the loan and the collateral. If the collateral is sold for less than its transfer price to CCPC, the bank makes up the difference. CCPC made its first big loan purchases, with face values of ¥ 683 billion, in the weeks before the end of the banks' fiscal year in 1993. BOJ announced the transfers. During the year ending March 1994, the CCPC handled 1,891 transactions with a face value of ¥3.8 trillion, a price of ¥1.8 trillion, and a discount of 53.7%. By January 1995, the CCPC had bought ¥7.3 trillion, paying ¥3.3 trillion ($36.2 billion). CCPC initially sold very little of the collateral it acquired. In early 1995, it began to auction property held as collateral. W. Dawkins, *CCPC Starts Property Auctions*, Financial Times, Mar. 14, 1995. See IMF International Capital Markets 80 (September 1994). W. Dawkins, *Slow Progress on Japan Bank Debts*, Financial Times, Jan. 6, 1995.

Expansionary monetary policy to reduce banks' interest costs. The Bank of Japan let its rediscount rate fall to 1.75% by late 1993. Explained as a way to stimulate growth, this dropped the cost of funds to the banks which, because their lending rates did not fall proportionately, became more profitable. BOJ continued to lower the rate through 1995 to 0.5%, a rate lower than that in any other OECD country since World War II, allowing the banks' to generate increases in operating earnings as large as 50% in a year. They could write off bad loans against these higher earnings.

Let banks earn their way out, not write off bad loans quickly. Into the mid-1990s, BOJ and MOF proposed different ways to solve the bad debt problem. BOJ urged more liberal policies to allow banks to securitize their bad loans, writing off the losses. The governor reportedly wanted stronger banks to write off as much as possible, but the finance minister wanted all banks to follow the ministry's guidelines for gradual write-offs and refrain from securitization. R. Thomson, *Japan Learns the American Way*, Financial Times, Dec. 9, 1993. MOF allowed banks to enter lines of business previously closed to them, at home and abroad. Abroad, for example, commercial banks led underwritings of 29 straight international bonds issued by Japanese companies from April to September 1993; Japanese securities companies led only 17. *One Mountain Conquered*, The Economist, Oct. 23, 1993, at 93.

Inject government funds. Protection of uninsured depositors became an object of political debate in January 1995. A month earlier BOJ, to forestall runs by depositors and close bankrupt institutions, helped depositors in two failed credit unions that had invested in property development in the 1980s. BOJ, Sumitomo Bank, and the National Federation of Credit Co-operatives would fund the lifeboat effort. Since neither credit union threatened the stability of Japan's financial system, public debate centered on whether politicians pressed BOJ to act.

In a bailout, the basic question is who will bear the cost. MOF proposed in the mid-1990s that all players should pay. The exposed banks would bear the cost of write-offs and a much higher fee for deposit insurance. Some bank employees would be laid off and some senior managers would contribute from their own savings. Depositors would receive very low interest to keep the banks' cost of funds low. Borrowers would pay enough to maintain the banks' operating revenues for writing off the loans. And the public would pay through the government budget and tax benefits to banks building provisions against bad debts. Even the huge Postal Savings System was suggested as a possible funder. The basic question was whether MOF had the political capability to distribute costs broadly. Parliament opposed the government's proposal to contribute over $6 billion toward writing off the bad housing loans in early 1995 and the opposition successfully fought a bailout in early 1996.

The government's increasingly public direct involvement generated a nationwide debate about the use of public money to bail out the banks. MOF floated several plans to deal with the *jusen*, each drawing serious criticism in the press and Parliament. MOF promised not to use public funds to resolve the banks' bad debt problems with non-banks. However, in mid-1996, the Diet approved the liquidation of the seven *jusen* that had failed. Institutional investors would lose $53 billion and the Government would absorb $6 billion. The Jusen Resolution Organization, set up to manage the *jusen*, failed to place one in bankruptcy in November 1996. *Japanese Banks: Wobbly*, The Economist, Nov. 9, 1996.

c. POLICY TOWARD THE BAD LOANS IN THE LATE 1990s AND EARLY 2000s

In June 1998, Prime Minister Hashimoto promised President Clinton in a highly publicized telephone conversation that Japan would speed up its reform of the banking system. The leaders' shared concern was the damage a weak yen could wreak on many Asian countries. As elaborated by the finance ministers of the two countries in a press release dated June 17, 1998, Japan would:

1. Dispose of bad assets more aggressively. The accumulated bad assets need to be removed from the books of financial institutions and to be liquidated to restore confidence and lending activity. The Japanese Government will ensure that Japanese banks sell off bad assets and will put in place the legal and institutional measures necessary to sell the collateral underlying bad loans.

2. Rapidly restructure financial institutions. The "convoy" system will be abandoned. We will take aggressive measures to restructure the financial system and institutions in accordance with the market mechanism. The use of public funds to financial institutions to avoid systemic risks will be conditioned stringently so as to induce restructuring.

3. Improve transparency and disclosure. Recognizing the importance of transparency and disclosure in improving capital market efficiency and reducing uncertainty, Japanese banks will be required to disclose the full extent of nonperforming loans on a consolidated basis, based on world-class accounting and disclosure standards by end of March 1999.

4. Strengthen banking supervision and prudential standards. Government oversight and supervision of the financial sector will be improved to ensure that prudent standards are being met and to thereby promote confidence in the system. The new Financial Supervisory Agency will receive appropriate enforcement powers and more examiners.

The government announced in early 1998 that it would set up a huge fund to solve the banking crisis. During the year, the size doubled. Initially, in January, the government said it would spend ¥30 trillion ($250 billion), ¥13 trillion to recapitalize the banks and ¥17 trillion to pay depositors in failed banks. But this was inadequate. The law passed in October allocated ¥63 trillion or over 10% of GDP: ¥20 trillion to protect depositors in bankrupt banks, ¥18 trillion to regenerate nationalized banks and set up a bridge bank that would acquire and dispose of non-performing debt, and ¥25 trillion to invest (probably as preferred shares) in viable banks with capital ratios over 8%. By the end of March 1999, 8 City Banks, IBJ, 5 Trust Banks, and a Regional Bank had received public capital injections of ¥7.5 trillion. Of this, 75% took the form of convertible preferred shares, 17% subordinated debt, and 8% nonconvertible preferred shares (for two City Banks only). The average yield was 1.09%. *Japanese Banks: Still Mired in the Mud,* Economist, Nov. 28, 1998; C. Adams, D. Mathieson, G. Schinasi, *International Capital Markets: Developments, Prospects, and Key Policy Issues, Annex II*, Sept. 1999, at 136.

To raise the funds needed for this infusion, the government planned to issue ¥10 trillion in bonds and guarantee ¥53 trillion in borrowing by BOJ and private financial institutions. It had originally planned to borrow from the Post Office Savings Bank, but seems to have dropped that idea.

In addition, various government agencies planned to lend to Japanese companies needing funds or to encourage banks to lend to them. BOJ, for example, planned to lend at subsidized rates to banks against corporate bonds as collateral.   G. Tett, *Financial Socialism, Japanese Style*, Financial Times, Nov. 16, 1998.

Stimulate economic growth while restructuring the banks.   Japan's economy had been in recession for a year by the end of 1998 and its unemployment rate, over 4%, was in stark contrast to decades of minuscule unemployment.   Since 1997, bank lending fell progressively, leading some to fear a severe credit crunch.   J. Sapsford, *Japanese Banks To Get Tax Break On Bad-Loan Sales*, Wall Street Journal, June 2, 1998. The yen fell dramatically to about ¥140 to the dollar, then recouped as the U.S. and Japanese governments intervened and held at around ¥110 by early 1999.   Although the economy did expand in early 2000, by late 2000 Japan contemplated deflation and recession.

The government's macroeconomic options were limited.   Lowering interest rates would not induce growth because rates were already almost negative.   BOJ's rediscount rate was below 1% for much of the late 1990s and early 2000s.   In March 2001, as consumer prices dropped for the second year in a row, and as imports rose and exports fell, BOJ accepted a zero-rate policy.   Lenders would soon be paying borrowers to borrow. BOJ had been increasing the money supply slowly during the 1990s.   At least one observer urged the government to go further, arguing that the central bank should simply create money with which to buy the banks' bad loans.   Money creation could help reverse the deflationary trend in the economy.   See J. Sachs, *Danger in Flogging Japan*, Financial Times, April 24, 1998. See D. Ibison and R. Wolffe, *Bank of Japan Brings Back Zero Interest Rate,* Financial Times, Mar. 20, 2001.

Fiscal stimulus was limited by the very large government debt, brought on by earlier stimulus policies.   For example, in August 1998, the government proposed to cut taxes by the equivalent of $41 billion and raise spending by $69 billion.   Then in early 1999, the government decided to issue an extra $1.2 trillion in Japanese Government Bonds over five years.   A substantial amount would fund the government's support to ailing banks.   These bond issues would increase the government's debt by 60% and give Japan the highest ratio of government debt to GNP in the industrial world. Yields on JGBs quickly trebled to 2% and were expected to reach as high as 5%. In late 1999, BOJ began to buy government bonds from an account managed by the MOF's Trust Fund bureau.   When the bond issue proved to be inadequate, the government sought other sources. It asked banks to lend its local governments up to ¥8 trillion.   It may have hoped to discourage the local governments from taxing banks, but the governor of Tokyo did so anyway, to meet funding shortfalls due to the recession and the growing cost of debt caused by the national government's borrowing. The finance ministry expected the debt to rise another 33% over the next four years.   Over 60% of the central government's budget (after transfers to regions) serviced this debt, a ratio more than twice as high as the closest OECD government.   This led Koizumi to propose to limit new issues of government bonds to ¥30 trillion ($240 billion) a year, roughly the value issued in 2000-01. G. Tett, *Japan Set to Issue Extra $1.228bn of Bonds*, Financial Times, Jan. 22, 1999; E. Luce, *Japan Set to be World's Top Borrower*, Financial Times, Feb. 9, 1999; M. Nakamoto and N. Nakamae, *BOJ Under Pressure to Buy More Bonds*, Financial Times, Feb. 9, 1999; G. Tett and A. Ostrovsky, *Japanese Yields Test Their Upper Limits*, Financial Times, Feb. 8, 1999; G. Tett, *BOJ Changes Policy and Buys Bonds*, Financial Times, Nov. 6, 1999; G. Tett, *Tokyo in Plea to Bankers on Loan Plans*, Financial Times, Feb. 4, 2000; G. Tett, *Japan Bankers Reel in Wake of 'Ishihara Shock,'* Financial Times, February 9, 2000; G. Tett, *Japan Sees Surge in Debt Even if Economy Recovers*, Financial Times, February 3, 2000; D. Asher, *Japan's National Debt, Demography, and Pensions* (Aug. 1999); G. Tett, *BoJ Grapples with Spectre of Deflation*, Financial Times, Nov. 1, 2000; G. Tett, *Call for Tokyo to Limit Bond Issuance*, Financial Times, Apr. 12, 2001.

The restructuring of the largest banks moved forward. Bank of Tokyo-Mitsubishi Bank had already formed. Dai-Ichi Kangyo Bank, Industrial Bank of Japan (IBJ), and Fuji Bank formed as Mizuho Bank in September 2000 and became the largest in the world, measured by asset and capital. It reorganized, simplifying business lines, but the impediments to success were great.   For example, the old managements persisted after the merger. Some bank analyst believed that Mizuho had failed to address its bad debt problem. The formal opening of a unified Mizuho Bank on April 1, 2002 was followed by weeks of paralysis when computer systems failed to integrate. Payments disappeared, ATMs across the country failed to work, the web site displayed customers' accounts and pin numbers, and many accounts had double deductions. K. Rafferty, *Big, Bold, But . . .* , Euromoney, Dec. 2000 at 30; d. Ibison, *Mizuho Fiasco Leaves Confidence at a Low*, Financial Times, Apr. 8, 2002; *Undispensable*, The Economist, Apr. 27, 2002. Sumitomo Bank and Sakura Bank merged April 1, 2001 into the Sumitomo Mitsui Banking Corp. (SMBC), creating the second largest bank in the world. Sanwa, Tokai, and Toyo Trust and Banking would merge January 15, 2002 to become UFJ Holding Inc. UFJ planned to integrate systems, close branches, and cut jobs. They all explained that they needed a stronger capital base, because of problem loans and to invest in information technology.   S. Brady, *Japan's New Leviathans*, Euromoney 1999 at 48.   In late 2000, Japan's minister for reform, Hideyuki Aizawa, said that he expected more mergers. G. Tett, *Reform Chief Urges Greater Consolidation*, Financial Times, Sep. 22, 2000; *Sanwa, Tokai to Expedite Merger*, Asahi Shimbun, Apr. 26. 2001.

The keiretsu system eroded further because of the bank restructuring. For example, in November 1999, Nissan Motor, IBJ, and Fuji Bank announced that they would sell their cross shareholdings in each other. The government had already urged foreign investors to bid, even hostilely, for groups or their members. See P. Abrahams and G. Tett, *The Circle is Broken*, Financial Times, Nov. 9, 1999; G. Tett and P. Montagnon, *Tokyo to Welcome Hostile Foreign Bids*, Financial Times, June 23, 1999.

Force recognition of bad debts, helping viable banks with government funds. Rather than limp along trying to disguise the problem, the government decided in 1997 to force banks to account for bad loans accurately and write them off, while at the same time improving the institutions needed to help them do so. New laws made it easier for banks to sell collateral held against bad loans, provided a framework for companies that would enforce claims against collateral, simplified court procedures involving claims on collateral, and prohibited courts from permitting debtors to delay enforcement of the claims.

The Deposit Insurance Corporation (DIC) was strengthened. Financial resources grew as premiums increased five times and the government injected funds. DIC gained power to collect and investigate abuses, in anticipation of more failures. A new intermediary to take banks' bad loans, called the Resolution and Collection Bank, was created in 1996 as a subsidiary of the DIC. In late 1998, the Resolution and Collection Organization (RCO) was created from the RCB, modeled on the U.S. Resolution Trust Corporation. RCO could buy nonperforming loans from failed and solvent banks. It would follow new procedures to streamline the process. The DIC and RCO reported to the Minister of State for Financial Reconstruction. His commission held a mandate that lasted until 2001. See C. Milhaupt, *Japan's Experience with Deposit Insurance and Failing Banks: Implications for Financial Regulatory Design?*, Draft Paper, Nov. 30, 1998. By 2000, the government estimated that public funds of ¥70 trillion ($640 bn, which is 14% of GDP) were available to protect depositors. IMF, Annex 1, *Progress in Financial and Corporate Restructuring in Japan*, International Capital Markets, May 2000 at 194.

A concerted effort to help viable banks recover took place at the end of the 1998/99 accounting year. On March 30, the DIC provided (in yen) $64 billion. The next day, the banks set aside $77 billion against what the DIC said was all their bad debt plus a reserve against future bad loans. The size of the set-aside was based on the findings of on-site examinations. Inspection teams of about 10 people visited each bank for at least two months. Banks relied on government help to different extents. Sumitomo wrote off the most in bad loans (about $9 billion), but relied on DIC funds for only 50%. Fuji Bank wrote off about $5.8 billion but received $8.2 billion from DIC. Of the 9 city banks, only Bank of Tokyo-Mitsubishi refused to take part. The DIC required each bank to restructure, for example eliminating some directors, and rethink their strategy. All the main banks decided to strengthen their retail business. Much could be done; for example, none yet even had links to the internet.

The DIC provided the funds in return for preferred shares in the banks that it could convert into common at their market price. This was an incentive for banks to perform well. If the price of common fell, the government would receive more common stock and have greater voting power than if the common price rose. Indeed, by early April 1999, banks' shares had risen 65% from their low six months earlier. S. WuDunn, *The Banking System and the Sword,* New York Times, Apr. 7, 1999; A. Adelson, *Putting a Braver Face on Japan's Bad Loans*, New York Times, May 2, 1999.

The government argued in favor of letting banks forgive borrowers that could recover. It amended the tax law to encourage banks to sell their bad loans at discounts. Until that change, banks had to pay a "gift tax" on the difference between the face value and sale price of the loan. It set reserve ratios for the two worst categories of bad loans. It did not do so for "questionable" loans because most of the banks' bad loans were in this category and the amount needed would be too high. Setting these reserve ratios could take a year. One estimate put the banks' sales of non-performing loans at $40 billion, at prices averaging 10% of face value, since 1996. Large Japanese firms were asking banks to forgive their very big debts and the rate of debt forgiveness accelerated from 1998 on. In November 2000, several banks bought preferred shares in Daiei, Inc., a discount retail chain. In December 2000, banks forgave ¥430bn ($3.8bn) in bad debt owed by the general contractor Kumagai Gumi. Almost 25% of this was forgiven by Shinsei Bank, the successor to LTCB. See R. Feldman, *Japan Economics: Leading Horses to Water*, Morgan Stanley Dean Witter (Oct. 14, 1998); A. Adelson, *Putting a Braver Face on Japan's Bad Loans*, New York Times, May 2, 1999; S. Strom, *Big Japan Contractor Asks Banks to Forgive Billions in Debts,* New York Times, May 25, 2000; K. Hijino, *Japan's Banks Drop Y430bn of Kumagai Debt*, Financial Times, Dec. 29, 2000; S. Strom, *Japan's Banks Pressed by Troubled Corporate Clients*, New York Times, Nov. 25, 2000.

Government sought to reorganize the corporate sector by allowing bankruptcies to increase and reforming corporate law. From January to June 2000, the debt owed by bankrupt firms rose 50% above the same period a year before to a record of ¥10.9 trillion ($101bn at that time). M. Nakamoto and B. Rahman, *Failed Japanese Company Debt Hits Record*, Financial Times, Oct. 17, 2000. One of the biggest department stores, Sogo, went bankrupt in July 2000.

Efforts by banks to hide their bad debts prompted increasingly severe reactions by the government. Japan's bank supervisor, for example, suspended the banking license of Credit Suisse First Boston, a foreign bank, for helping Japanese banks make complex bond transactions to disguise losses and evade inspection. In 1994, CSFB had offered a service to Japanese banks by "touting a document entitled 'Restructuring an Investment Portfolio.'" In formal financial language, it explained exactly how Credit Suisse could offer its Japanese clients ways to conceal losses on their balance sheet. CSFB offered "dozens of plans." "A Japanese bank holding a bad loan, for example, could 'sell' the loan to a subsidiary at its face value, record the 'profit,' and then lend money to the same subsidiary to cover up the subsidiary's actual loss. Since there was no consolidated accounting, any losses went unrecorded." G. Tett and N. Nakamae, *Tokyo Turns Against Its 'Friendly' Foreign Banks*, Financial Times, May 21, 1999. The FSA reinstated CSFB's license at the end of December 2000, then barely two months later a Tokyo district court convicted Credit Suisse Financial Products of violating the securities law and obstructing an FSA investigation by trying to hide relevant documents. The court fined CSFP about $333,000 and sentenced its former branch manager, Shinji Yamada, to four months in jail. N. Nakamae, P. Abrahams, and W. Hall, *Credit Suisse Arm Loses Japan Banking License*, Financial Times, July 30, 1999; P. Abrahams, N. Nakamae, and D. Ibison, *Japan Moves on Credit Suisse in UK*, Financial Times, Dec. 9, 1999; M. Tanikawa, *Tokyo Court Moves Harshly Against a Credit Suisse Unit*, New York Times, Mar. 9, 2001.

CSFB had attracted attention in other countries around this time. In 1999, CSFB was investigated for a role in laundering money on behalf of a prime minister in the Ukraine. The Ukraine government reopened the case in 2001 after an IMF investigator found no evidence of corruption. C. Clover, *Swiss Banks Named in Ukraine Probe*, Financial Times, Aug. 13, 1999; C. Clover, *Ukraine Reopens Case of Bank Reserves 'Misuse,'* Financial Times, Apr. 6, 2001. In 1999, CSFB was investigated for its part in a scheme to launder billions of dollars, including food aid to Russia. D. Randall, *Banking Scandal Engulfs Europe*, The Independent (London), Aug. 29, 1999. In 2001, India banned CSFB from trading there because of its involvement in a scheme to rig share prices that led to a collapse of the stock market there. K. Merchant and C. Pretzlik, *India Stops CSFB Broking After Equities-Rigging Probe*, Financial Times, Apr. 20, 2001. In 2001, US regulators investigated leading securities firms, including CSFB, for violating anti-trust laws in allocating IPOs. They started their probe in depth by investigating 6 CSFB employees. CSFB became one of 10 securities firms named as a defendant in a class action suit alleging anti-competitive activities, based on the regulators' investigations. J. Labate and J. Chaffin, *CSFB Staff Face Public Offering Probe*, Financial Times, May 19, 2001; J. Chaffin and J. Labate, *Law Firm Launches IPO Suit Against 10 Banks*, Financial Times, May 15, 2001. CSFB denied improper behavior in these matters. It gave its position on some of them at a hearing before the U.S. House Banking and Financial Institutions Committee in 2000. *Panels II and III of a Hearing of the House Banking and Financial Institutions Committee on the IMF, World*

Bank and Other Int'l Financial Institutions, Federal News Service, Mar. 23, 2000.

Other foreign and Japanese banks caught the Japanese bank supervisor's eye. Lehman Brothers was investigated, Deutsche Bank was reprimanded and banned from trading OTC derivatives for six months, and Citibank (with Merrill Lynch) was implicated in a scandal. Foreign bankers argued that the services were tacitly approved by the government at the time and that they were being made "scapegoats for the government's mismanagement." Other foreign bankers said they had chosen not to provide this service because it was not ethical. G. Tett and N. Nakamae, *Japanese Watchdog Launches Inquiry into CSFB's Business,* Financial Times, Jan. 28, 1999. Criminal charges were lodged against the senior executives of Long Term Credit Bank.

From March 1993 to March 2000, non-performing loans grew steadily from less than 1% of total loans to almost 15%. Banks built their reserves from 30% of NPLs in 1993 to 60% by 1998, but then let reserves fall to 40% by 2000. The most they wrote off annually was 20% of NPLs (1995-1997), but write-offs fell to 12% of NPLs by 2000. The Oriental Economist, *Non-Performing Loans Continue to Mount*, Sep. 2000 at 9. Over the 8 years to 1999, the 17 biggest banks wrote off ¥51 trillion of bad loans. *Japanese Banks Write Off $472bn Worth of Bad Loans*, Financial Times, Feb. 2, 2000; D. Ibison, *Tokyo to Take Action on Non-Performing Loans*, Financial Times, Feb. 21, 2001.

A collapse in asset prices in Japan in 2000 rekindled the fear that the banks once more faced a crisis. By January 2000, land prices had fallen for 8 years, 12% in 1999 alone. A year later, the Nikkei fell to the lowest level in 16 years. Some analysts concluded that when the Nikkei hit 13,000 or another index, the Topix, fell to 1,300, most banks would lose all their unrealized gains. It was their view that most Japanese banks had by then lost all hidden gains. The markets' collapse made Japanese banks still more reluctant to sell bad loans at a discount, and their sale of assets slowed. The minister for financial affairs, Mr. Yanagisawa, said that by March 2002 banks should be rid of all bad debt. But the cost of carrying bad loans was low, for banks, because the interest rate was so low. M. Nakamoto, *Eight-Year Fall in Japan Land Prices*, Financial Times, Aug. 5-6, 2000; D. Ibison, *Japanese Banks' Bad-Loan Strategy Hit by Indices Falls*, New York Times, Mar. 1, 2001; G. Tett, *Japan Sees Decline in Asset Sales*, Financial Times, Nov. 7, 2000; R. Katz, *The 'Anesthesia Option'*, Oriental Economist 9, March 2001; J. Fiorillo, *Japan's Banking Policies Have Been Dismal*, Oriental Economist 9, Jan. 2001.

By mid-2001, the debate was over how to classify loans as bad. The FSA, following US practice, reported at the end of March 2001 "bad" loans of ¥ 33 trillion ($264 billion) but did not include in this number "doubtful" loans of ¥117 trillion ($936 billion). The FSA said that only about ¥14 trillion ($112 billion) of the doubtful or "carefully monitored" loans were bad.   The opposition party argued that the two should be combined because Japanese banks' finances were much less transparent than U.S. banks and the economic downturn argued against hoping that recovery would improve the banks' balance sheets.   Combining the two would suggest bad loans of ¥150 trillion ($1.2 trillion), about 25% of GDP. The opposition's "concerns are shared by many bank analysts and the Bank of Japan."   G. Tett, *Japan's Bad Loans Put at $1,200bn by Opposition*, Financial Times, April 20, 2001.

Soon after Koizumi's government took office in April 2001, the 16 largest banks reported at the end of their fiscal year on March 31 that they had written off ¥4.28 trillion ($34 billion). They had responded to the previous government's "emergency economic measures package" that called on them to remove from their balance sheets, over 2 to 3 years, ¥11.7 trillion ($93.6 billion) of the ¥18.03 trillion then assumed to be bad loans. The Resolution Collection Corporation (successor to the RCO) had bought about ¥17 trillion in bad loans from all banks since its founding, but sold very few. Instead, it held and managed them. This approach reportedly dampened the property market further. The RCC was subject to a rule that it lose no money when selling the loans. The average price it offered banks was 10% of the face value of the loan. Banks were reluctant to sell when the loss was so great and so the acquisitions of non-performing loans by RCC slowed in 2001.   See M. Negishi, *Doubts Linger Over Loan Disposal*, The Japan Times Online, Apr. 7, 2001; G. Tett, *Japan's Bankers Should Learn From the Swedes*, Financial Times, Apr. 2, 2001.

By early 2002, Japanese banks' NPLs were ¥42 trillion ($320 billion), according to the government, 8% of GDP. The number was probably much higher according to many observers who believed the FSA had returned to a policy of letting the banks not report the full extent of their NPLs. Since some banks expected the government would buy NPLs at a subsidized rate, they preferred to hold rather than sell and take losses. In the nine years ending March 2001, the government reported that the banks had written off ¥72 trillion of bad loans. D. Pilling, *Japan's Bad Banks*, Financial Times, Jan. 29, 2002.

Let weak banks fail. For 50 years, MOF promoted a convoy system: all banks -- weak and strong -- would move together. The industry would solve its problems together.   In 1999, the government said it must officially abandon the convoy system. This had begun in 1995. Mergers were creating a few super-banks that vastly outstripped the next tier of City Banks. Compared to the weak banks, the stronger banks were able to write off or securitize more bad loans by selling them at a discount. Observers asked if the old system was unraveling. In November 1996, the Government allowed Hanwa Bank, a small regional bank, to go into bankruptcy and be liquidated rather than find a stronger bank into which it could merge. The Government was willing to let Hanwa staff lose their jobs. In February 1997, markets attached a premium to debentures issued by the 17th largest bank, Nippon Credit Bank, which was rumored about to collapse. The bank's share price had fallen 60% in 3 months. *Japanese Banks: Sayonara?*, The Economist, Feb. 15, 1997.

Faced with the possible collapse of a major bank, in February 1997 the finance minister announced that the government would support the 20 largest banks "if they faced difficulties in disposing of non-performing loans." G. Robinson, *Reassurance for Japanese Banks*, Financial Times, Feb. 11, 1997. In March, the government decided to buy $3.1 billion in land held as collateral for bad debts owed to the banks. To reassure foreign hosts to Japanese banks, the government encouraged troubled Japanese banks to withdraw from activities overseas. But the announced support rang hollow when Hokkaido Takushoku Bank, the tenth largest, was allowed to collapse in November 1997. The government had failed in its effort to find a merger partner for the bank. Instead, it arranged the transfer of the failed bank's assets to a regional bank. See S. Strom, *Bailing Out of the Bailout Game,* New York Times, November 18, 1997. This came on the heels of the collapse of securities companies described in Section II of this Chapter.

Nationalize important failing banks. The government decided that the Deposit Insurance Corporation (DIC) would take ownership of the Long Term Credit Bank in October 1998 and Nippon Credit Bank in December 1998. At both banks, liabilities far outstripped assets; LTCB was in the red by almost $3 billion. LTCB was the tenth largest bank measured by assets. It reported loans of ¥14.6 bn nominal value, debentures of ¥9.1bn, deposits of ¥3.1bn, and debt of ¥4.7bn (including ¥3.4bn due to the BOJ).

For LTCB, DIC apparently paid a nominal ¥1 per share, so investors bore substantial losses. BOJ loaned over $20 billion so LTCB's business could continue smoothly. The DIC guaranteed the banks' liabilities, including not only deposits but also very substantial bond obligations and derivatives. According to A. Riles, *The Transnational Appeal of Formalism: The Case of Japan's Netting Law*, unpublished article (1999) at 30:

> . . . [T]he Ministry of Finance and the Bank of Japan jointly summoned representatives from each of the banks which held outstanding swap contracts with LTCB. They assured these counterparties—first privately, and later, at the urging of the foreign banks, in public statements—that the government would assume all of the bank's outstanding obligations with termination dates of within three years. On this basis, MOF and BOJ official jointly and emphatically asked the counterparties not to declare a situation of default requiring close-out netting, as was their prerogative to do under the terms of the Master Agreement in the LTCB Case.

About 850 borrowers from LTCB saw their loans transferred to RCO. They were expected to go bankrupt. It was not clear how these loans were priced. Other troubled borrowers would not be closed, but neither would they be forgiven any of their debts.

DIC started immediately to dismember the banks, selling viable units to other domestic and foreign banks or nonbanks. GE Capital, for example, first bought LTCB's equipment and auto leasing unit for $6.9 billion and later bought LTCB's U.S. assets for $11 billion. In September 1999, a group of US investors, including Citigroup, under the leadership of Ripplewood, a U.S. equity fund, acquired the rest of LTCB, valued at ¥11 trillion ($106 bn). They paid over $1 bn. The government removed ¥5 trillion in bad loans, added loan loss reserves, would inject up to ¥300 billion, and buy collateral backing the LTCB loans if its value fell over 20% in 3 years. LTCB was renamed Shinsei Bank. N. Nakamae and P. Abrahams, *US Group Set to Buy LTCB*, Financial Times, Sep. 28, 1999.

Other nationalized banks were sold to groups that included foreign investors. Japan's Softbank Corporation led a group that bought Nippon Credit Bank. This was interesting because Softbank is not a commercial bank but rather an investor in internet businesses. Softbank took 48.8% of the shares of the new bank, called Aozora, with Orix, a leasing company, and Tokio Fire and Marine, an insurer, as its main partners. Small portions were held by foreign groups, including Cerberus (a private investor in equity), Chase Manhattan Bank, and UBS of Switzerland. The government provided Aozora $30 billion, of which $27.5bn was a cash injection, and promised to let the new bank return loans whose value fell 20% or more over the next three years. Aozora's start was plagued by bad debts, unhappy customers, and the suicide in September 2000 of its new president, who was himself not a banker. M. Nakamoto, *Tokyo Sweetens Controversial NCB Sale with Extra $29bn*, Financial Times, Aug. 26/27, 2000; G. Tett and A. Harney, *Bank Chief's Suicide Shatters Aozora's Credibility*, Financial Times, Sep. 22, 2000. The Asia Recovery Fund, managed by a U.S. corporate turnaround group, bought two smaller regional banks, Kofuku for ¥30bn and Tokyo Sowa for ¥35bn ($332mn at the time). The government had spent ¥70bn to clean up Tokyo Sowa, including reserves equal to about 20% of the bank's loan portfolio. G. Tett, *WL Ross buys Tokyo Sowa for Y35bn*, Financial Times, June 28, 2000; S. Strom, *Japan Sells Tokyo Sowa Bank to an Investment Fund,* New York Times, June 28, 2000.

The cost of LTCB to DIC was not known to the public. One estimate, before the sale, of ¥1 trillion was based on ¥157bn of equity less hidden losses on securities (¥436bn) and other reserves (¥735bn). In addition, the government had a contingent liability to buy back loans valued at up to ¥450bn ($4.2bn at the time) in the next three years. E. Terazono, *Shinsei Mulls Requests Over Debt Waivers*, Financial Times, June 13, 2000.

DIC funded its acquisitions from the ¥18 trillion set aside for this purpose in the ¥63 trillion support package. The BOJ was to lend DIC ¥6.7 trillion, of which 36% was assumed to be for LTCB. The DIC would receive funds from the government, its own bonds issued with a government guarantee (starting after July 1999 to avoid competing with many other government bond issues), premiums from member banks, and revenues from the sale of bad loans and viable units of LTCB (and others like it).

To compare the ¥63 trillion, consider that the total assets of 146 banks in Japan (including their trust accounts) were ¥1,034 trillion. The nine city banks held 43%, 64 first tier regional banks 19%, 63 second tier regional banks 7%, 7 trust banks 23%, and 3 long term credit banks 8%. The sources for this section include G. Tett, *Japan Reassures Markets as LTCB is Nationalised,* Financial Times, Oct. 24-25, 1998; Bloomberg News, *Acting Quickly, Japan Seizes a 2d Big and Failing Bank*, New York Times, Dec. 14, 1998; and communication of authors with Morgan Stanley Dean Witter, Japan of March 4, 1999.

In May 2001, the Koizumi government indicated that one or two more banks might have to be nationalized. Daiwa and Chuo-Mitsui were identified in the press as particularly weak. G. Tett and D. Ibison, *Tokyo 'May Need To Take Over Banks*, Financial Times, May 25, 2001.

Reform prudential rules. The government would force the remaining banks to follow appropriate safety and soundness rules. It would help these banks recapitalize by injecting capital, but the banks had to meet standards set by the government for management, loan quality, and internal systems. Basic reform of prudential supervision took place in October 1998. It reflected proposals by the September 1995 report by the Financial System Stabilization Committee (a senior group advising the MOF) to impose tighter supervisory powers:

- allow authorities to close insolvent financial institutions immediately,
- allow regulators to liquidate insolvent banks,
- ensure that financial institutions abide by the loan limits and other rules,
- raise premiums for the deposit insurer and allow it to borrow more,
- ban thrift executives from borrowers' boards,
- disclose banks' bad loans accurately, and
- allow the use of public funds to stabilize weak banks.

See A. Pollack, *Japan Panel Urges Reform of Nation's Bank System*, New York Times, Nov. 28, 1995; G. Baker, *Calls for Greater Supervision*, Financial Times, Sept. 28, 1995; J. Sapsford, *Panel to Unveil Reforms for Japan's Banks*, Wall Street Journal, Sept. 25, 1995.

d. THE SUFFICIENCY OF THE REFORMS

The underlying question was whether these reforms would be sufficient to let the financial system recover. One line of reasoning was that the problems originally grew because of the weakness of Japan's prudential rules and safety net. Undercapitalized banks were unable to lend to help end the recession. H. Akiyoshi, *Financial Fragility and Recent Developments in the Japanese Safety Net*, Social Science Japan Journal, 23 (1999); and T. Bayoumi, *The Morning After: Explaining the Slowdown in Japanese Growth in the 1990s*, National Bureau of Economic Research Working Paper 7350, Sep. 1999. By addressing these problems, the reforms, including the Big Bang, would shrink the role of banks in the economy and allow it to recover. T. Hoshi and A. Kashyap, *The Japanese Banking Crisis: Where Did It Come From and How Will It End?*, NBER Working Paper 7250, July 1999.

A different line of thinking led others to conclude that more needed to be done. Meetings between US and Japanese government and financial sector leaders, in July 1998, June 1999, September 2000, and December 2001, led by Harvard Law School's Program on International Financial Systems, identified the following concerns that remained if the market was to help solve the crisis:

a. Macroeconomic problems in Japan could have a serious impact on the financial system.

b. Disclosure and accounting rules had to meet international standards and be fully enforced, a continuing concern.

c. Better legal mechanisms, including loan-loss rules and surveillance of lending, were needed for banks to dispose of bad assets soon, since non-performing assets had serious microeconomic effects.

d. Financial regulators had to be independent and well staffed.

e. The government solved the bad debt problem by incurring huge deficits itself, but it needed to address the macroeconomic and microeconomic consequences quickly.

f. For the equity market to replace the banking market, major reforms were needed, including a more rapid unwinding of cross-shareholding.

Doubts about the effectiveness of bank reform grew from late 2000, but the press reported in February 2001 that the FSA, BOJ, and Keidanren (representing business interests) had reached an understanding that would result in "a broad set of financial and structural reforms to clean up the banks and their borrowers. . . ." In this view, the good sign was the willingness of the business association to admit that banks needed to write off all bad loans (without a capital injection from the government), even if it hurt the corporate sector. But perhaps this initiative was doomed. Soon after, a senior official in the finance ministry said that it was "respectable" to lend more rather than write off loans, and that writing off raised the specter of a domino effect of failure in the corporate sector that would damage financial institutions as well. A powerful LDP leader urged the government to use public pension funds to support the declining stock market and asked banks not to unwind their cross-shareholdings. *Bank Reform in Japan-Seriously?*, The Economist, Feb. 24, 2001; M. Nakaoto, *Japan's Pressing Economic Problems Spark Fresh Case of Policy Paralysis*, Financial Times, Feb. 28, 2001; *In With the Old*, The Economist, Jan. 6, 2001.

The Koizumi government gave priority to reducing government deficits and reducing the role of government-owned corporations and financial institutions. To conserve political capital, it did not press banks to reduce their NPLs, moving away from the goal it announced at the end of June 2001 that it would "get rid of the banks' non-performing loans . . . ." G. Tett, *Tokyo Outlines Reform Timetable*, May 9, 2001.

Unlimited deposit insurance ended April 1, 2002, a year after the original date. Time deposits became insured only up to ¥10 million (about $75,000). A year later, current deposits would have the same limit. In the months before this, pressure grew for the government to delay implementation. People foresaw a major outflow of funds from banks, arguing that given the uncertainty about the banks' balance sheets, depositors would shift their funds elsewhere, such as to the Post Office Savings System. Those most outspoken for delay were politicians who opposed reforms generally. With its credibility at issue, however, the Koizumi government held firm.

The FSA and the general public seemed to think that the government had the systems in place to manage any banking crisis and that the country had the resources. After all, Japanese workers saved 55% of their disposable income. Further delays in strengthening the banks, however, risked prolonging the credit drought. The very low interest rates allowed margins so fine that Japanese banks could not even pay the costs of administering the loans. By the end of March 2002, banks were offering interest of 0.001% on savings accounts, down from the 0.02% they had been paying. While U.S. savers would double their money in 30 years, Japanese savers would take 69,315 years Rolling over NPLs meant that new stronger borrowers could not borrow from the banks. D. Pilling, *Japan's Bad Banks*, Financial Times, Jan. 29, 2002; K. Belson, *Jitters in Japan for Savers and Banks*, New York Times, Jan. 23, 2002; K. Belson, *Two Japanese Banks Lower an Interest Rate to 0.001%*, Financial Times, Mar. 30, 2002.

Also at the end of the fiscal year, the banks had to mark to market the securities they held. A declining stock market would cause a large decline in capital that could damage any remaining confidence in the banks. Then the Nikkei 225 index started to rise in early February 2002 and closed 20% higher at the end of March, largely because the government banned short sales of stock. Short sellers had to buy shares to cover their positions, raising demand. Critics found the move a flagrant intervention to manipulate the market at the end of the fiscal year, with short-lived benefits. D. Ibison, *Japanese Banking Shares Flatter to Deceive*, Financial Times, Apr. 1, 2002.

The Koizumi government, finally, considered a second large infusion of funds into the stronger banks, much as had been done in 1998. As the government had done before, it could also nationalize weaker banks. K. Belson, *Tokyo Weighs Pouring More Public Money Into Banks*, New York Times, Dec. 29, 2001.

By the end of 2001, the government reported a fourth recession in a decade. Although it was forecast to be the worst in 20 years, growth appeared on the horizon in mid-2002. The Bank of Japan had begun buying more government bonds to inflate the economy, and the government offered more fiscal stimulus, but the turnaround seemed to be export-led. The Yen had fallen further against the dollar. K. Belson, *Japan's Revised Forecast Sees Deepest Slump in 2 Decades*, New York Times, Nov. 10, 2001; K. Belson, *The Bank of Japan Moves to Halt Economic Slide*, New York Times, Dec. 20, 2001; D. Ibison, *Yen on Slide as Japan Confirms New Recession*, Financial Times, Dec. 8-9, 2001.

Questions

1. Why was it necessary in 1997 to change government policy toward the banks' bad debt problem? Is the new policy, as it evolved into 1999, a good one?

    a. Why would the government have offered banks incentives to restructure their bad loans rather than encourage them to write them off in the early 1990s?

    b. How did Japan deal with the bad debts of foreign banks in Japan?

    c. How well has the government resolved issues concerning form and pricing of government investment, size of the government share of a bank's equity, conditions imposed on the banks, and what the banks should do with the bad loans?

    d. Why is there strong public opposition to the use of government funds to help the banks? What does this set of solutions tell you about the likelihood that the financial system is changing fundamentally?

2. Will the changes in prudential regulation substantially reduce the likelihood of serious bad loans problems in the future?

    a. How will prompt corrective action affect Japanese banks in the near term?

    b. Is the full disclosure required by Big Bang a good idea for Japanese banks?

c.   What will be the effect of removing supervision from the MOF, as described below?

3.   What will be the effect on world financial markets of: the Japanese government's nationalization of big banks? The declining market share of Japanese banks abroad? The techniques used by Japan to resolve the bad debt crisis?

4.   What policy should the Koizumi government adopt toward the banks' non-performing loans?

3.   DISPERSION OF POWERS OF FINANCIAL AUTHORITY

MOF and BOJ power seemed under threat even in the early 1990s with the enactment of Administrative Procedure Law No. 88 of 1993, the first general statute governing administrative procedure in Japan. The APL specifically addressed administrative guidance. It instructed regulators not to exceed, at all, the scope of their duties as set by the relevant law and to rely on voluntary compliance, not threats. Regulators should make the rules clear to the concerned party and, if requested, give their directions in writing unless to do so would be very inconvenient. When more than one person was concerned, the regulator was to apply standard rules and, unless to do so would be very inconvenient, publicize them.

MOF's efforts to preserve its domain were weakened by scandals in late 1997 and early 1998. Leading banks were accused of bribing MOF and central bank officials, with lavish entertainment and gifts. Their headquarters were raided. Former senior MOF officials were arraigned. Two committed suicide just before their hearings. In the wake of these scandals, the finance minister and his political aides quit in January 1998. This allowed the appointment of a new minister from outside MOF; indeed, he had earlier been a prosecutor in Tokyo. The governor of the BOJ resigned when even the central bank was tarred by scandal. See S. WuDunn, *Japan Names Outsider as Finance Minister*, New York Times, January 31, 1998.

The scandals had an international dimension as well. A consequence of the Japanese government's non-inspection of overseas offices of its banks was the Daiwa Bank scandal that emerged in late September 1995, described in Chapter 3. Other foreign scandals emerged. In 1996, the New York State Banking Department fined the Long-Term Credit Bank $1 million for improper securities lending. The regulators found weak internal controls and practices that violated the law and warned other large Japanese banks to tighten their controls.

Proposals to reform MOF intensified in 1995. Responding to public criticism, the ministry censured several senior officials and let others, including the vice minister, resign during the year. The Japanese and foreign financial press questioned the capability of MOF. In February

1996, the Prime Minister launched a study of proposals to break up MOF. In March 1997, the cabinet approved a proposal to create a new supervisory agency independent of MOF and reporting directly to the prime minister to license financial firms, close insolvent ones, and control the deposit insurance corporation. MOF would draft legislation and advise about collapsing firms. See W. Dawkins, Independent Agency to Police Japanese Financial Sector, Financial Times, Feb. 27, 1997.

The new Financial Supervisory Agency took over MOF's regulatory power in July 1998. The FSA licenses, inspects, and supervises banks, securities companies, and insurance companies. Its staff came from MOF and the Securities and Exchange Surveillance Council. MOF would make policy and draft financial legislation. The law did not regulate the flow of personnel between the two agencies. The FSA reports directly to the Prime Minister's Commission for Financial Reconstruction. By January 2001, the FSA shared with MOF responsibility to manage and resolve financial crises and oversight of the Deposit Insurance Corporation.

The Commission for Financial Reconstruction has cabinet status and was created in October 1998 to oversee and regulate private financial institutions. The Commission, whose five members require Parliamentary approval, would be MOF's equal. The Commission controls the ¥63 trillion fund established by the government. In making those funds available, it requires recipient banks to accept enough to write off bad loans and hidden losses on equity portfolios. Unfortunately, the "FSA remains notoriously overworked, understaffed, and undertrained for the challenges that it now faces." R. Feldman, *Japan Economics: Leading Horses to Water*, Morgan Stanley Dean Witter (Oct. 14, 1998) at 2. See G. Tett, *Signs of Cheer Point to End of Debt Nightmare*, Financial Times, Feb. 16, 1999; M. Hall, *Financial Reform in Japan: Redefining the Role of the Ministry of Finance*, 13 Journal of International Banking Law 171 (May 1998) ("Hall").

The Financial Services Agency (also called the FSA) took over responsibility on January 1, 2001 for banking, securities, insurance, and other financial activities. It merged the Financial Services Agency and the Commission for Financial Reconstruction. Its leader was also the first head of the old FSA, Hakuo Yanagisawa. Although he had a good reputation from his earlier stint as head, Yanagisawa had less political clout than in the past, according to some. He maintained a strong reputation among foreign financial institutions until early 2002, when they began to accuse the FSA of not revealing the full size of banks' problem loans. *New Regulator Established to Oversee Financial Services*, World Securities Law Report 3, July 2000; In With the Old, The Economist, Jan. 6, 2001; D. Pilling, *Minister's Halo Slips as Japan is Seen as Timid Over Bad Loans,* Financial Times, Apr. 25, 2002.

Turnover in senior personnel of the regulator emerged as a concern in late 1999. The first head was replaced in October 1999 with Michio Ochi, previously the head of the Economic Planning Agency. Then Ochi had to resign in February 2000 after suggesting in a meeting with bankers that they should contact him if his Commission's staff was too strict with them. Perhaps some CFR staffer had leaked Ochi's remarks. The public was not prepared to treat the banks with any special leniency. Ochi's successor left office in July 2000 for failing to reveal gifts from a bank and others. G. Tett, *Japanese Minister Forced to Quit After Bank Reform Gaffe*, Financial Times, Feb. 26-27, 2000, G. Tett, *Japan's Top Bank Regulator Forced to Quit Over Scandal*, Financial Times, July 31, 2000.

The move to increase the Bank of Japan's independence took effect April 1, 1998. Monetary policy would be set by a board consisting of 3 from BOJ and 6 outsiders. The board would elect the chairman, who was expected to be the BOJ governor. MOF would no longer be able to remove BOJ officials or force delays in implementing BOJ policy, but BOJ was required to coordinate policy with MOF and MOF would be able to approve the central bank's budget. See J. Sapsford, *Bank of Japan Lacks Autonomy Under Reform Plan*, Wall Street Journal Feb. 7, 1997; W. Dawkins and R. Lambert, *Bank of Japan Set to Win Greater Self-rule*, Financial Times, Feb. 6, 1997; J. Sapsford, *Japan's Parliament Shifts Regulation of Financial Markets to a New Agency*, Wall Street Journal, June 17, 1997; and Hall.

MOF retained control of the postal savings system, long an important part of the Japanese financial system. The system rose to prominence around 1980 when personal deposits shifted to it. Postal savings deposits offered anonymous ten-year, high-yielding, fixed-interest deposits free of withholding tax. These competed favorably with the regulated low interest deposits offered by banks.

In the late 1990s, the future of postal savings was a major unresolved issue. These funds, still benefitting from special tax treatment and not having to pay for deposit insurance since the system was governmental, amounted to almost 20% of personal financial assets. The MOF managed the ¥400 trillion in postal savings, investing them in many government activities. Critics charged that the system helped the LDP buy votes and conceal bad loans. See Analytica Japan, *Japan's Big Bang -- A Critical Review*, December 12, 1997; S. Strom, *Crusader Takes On the Postal Piggy Bank*, New York Times, November 18, 1997.

The postal savings system created problems for interest rate deregulation. Its rates were still not fully determined by the market. If interest rates for small deposits were fully liberalized, the system would be forced to offer depositors higher rates. Because the system's share of savings was so large, the government could not afford the increased cost but was unwilling to give up its direction over the use of postal savings funds.

In January 2001, the government announced its plan to drastically reduce the number of ministries immediately and cut the staff of the civil service 25% over ten years. The move, which also increased the power of the prime minister, was to reduce the bureaucrats' power to make government policy. D. Ibison, *Tokyo in Shake-Up of Bureaucracy*, Financial Times, Jan. 6-7, 2001.

SECTION II

JAPANESE SECURITIES MARKETS

Japanese securities markets, long quiet, soared in the late 1980s, crashed in 1989, then stagnated. From 1986 to 1990, total equity and bond issues by Japanese firms, at home and abroad, grew more than 4.5 times to Yen 28 trillion, of which 41% was external. Japanese investors, issuers, and financial firms played an increasingly important role in foreign and international markets during the 1980s. In 1991, the volume on the Tokyo Stock Exchange fell 65%. The late 1989 crash virtually closed the markets in the second quarter of 1990 and new issuers were prohibited, then curtailed. Over the next decade, the market stagnated, despite occasional surges suggesting recovery. Then a steady fall returned the stock market in early 2001 to the lowest level since 1985.

Japan was a major source of capital to the world, and the most important buyer of U.S. government debt, for decades. The crisis in the 1990s muted this role.

This Section describes government policy, the securities markets, and cross-border operations in the period leading up to 1995. It then describes the changes embodied in the U.S.-Japan Financial Services Agreement of 1995 and the Big Bang. As you read, contrast the policies through 1994 with those that followed. How big a change did the later policies make? Why have they not solved the problems in Japan's domestic capital markets and restored its role in international markets?

A. JAPAN'S SECURITIES MARKETS TO THE EARLY 1990s

The readings identify the major features of Japanese securities markets over the past decades. These features were strong in the post-war decades, only gradually eroding in the run up to the late 1990s, when they came under severe attack. This Section describes the era before the mid-1990s. The features included the following:

Functional firms specialized

Banking markets were bigger than securities markets

Capital account surpluses and high domestic savings rates created large pools of investable funds

MOF played a big role, subjecting markets to many direct government controls

Industry associations limited and protected securities companies

FX laws "protected" the Yen in cross-border transactions

Financial innovation was limited by the view that MOF should authorize any new instrument

Keiretsu relationships were important

Securities companies were concentrated in the Big 4, while many much smaller securities firms existed

Failure and loss was cushioned

The Securities Bureau of the Ministry of Finance until 1998 regulated Japanese securities markets. It supervised securities companies, securities finance companies, stock exchanges, central depository and delivery organizations, investment trust management companies, foreign securities firms, and banks doing securities business. The Securities Bureau administered primary and secondary markets in stocks, yen and foreign currency bonds. The Securities and Exchange Surveillance Commission (SESC) was created in July 1992, after scandals in the securities markets suggested that the finance ministry should not be both regulator and advocate of the industry. The SESC could investigate and, through other agencies, prosecute and cannot levy fines. It was part of the finance ministry and relied on staff seconded from the ministry and other agencies. It was, however, independent of MOF's Securities Bureau and tended to be less responsive to the special interests of the securities industry. It was less powerful than the U.S. S.E.C. See 1994 National Treatment Study 351. These bureaus shifted to the new umbrella regulatory agency in the Prime Minister's office in 1998.

One analyst described MOF's dominant policy into the early 1990s as, rather than regulating markets, instead protecting the securities industry, relying on the Big 4 to help frame policy, supply information, and implement policy. In practice, MOF rather than courts interpreted the law because, with shareholders friendly, shareholder suits were rare to unknown. C. Milhaupt, *Managing the Market: The Ministry of Finance and Securities Regulation in Japan*, 30 Stanford Journal of International Law 423 (1994). By 1995, MOF's policy was under attack.

SWARY AND TOPF, at 180–92

The stock exchanges had been relegated to a marginal role by frequent speculative cycles and suggestions of unsound practices (such as insider trading and manipulation). However, in the past decade the volume and extent of trading have grown tremendously, undoubtedly marking a turning point in the role of the exchanges both as a source of funding for companies and as a venue for investment by the public. Indeed, the Tokyo Stock Exchange is presently the world's largest. ...

The privatization of government firms through flotations on the exchange has contributed to this rapid growth. In fact, the market value of one such firm, Nippon Telephone and Telegraph (in 1988, the largest firm in the world by market value), was greater than that of *all* listed West German industrials combined. Clearly, the TSE has become a major factor in Japanese financial markets, both as a venue for raising capital and as an investment alternative for individuals and institutional fund managers. It now presents increased competition for Japan's banks.

The bond market in Japan, including the huge government bond market, while enormous in size, ($1,980 billion at year-end 1989, 19 percent of the global bond market) is overwhelmingly dominated by public sector debt, 64 percent of the total. Bonds issued by private non-financial corporations constitute a marginal part of the bond market (7.7 percent).

. . . Since banks are banned from the securities markets, security companies have filled this vacuum. There are 224 such firms in Japan, with an overwhelming concentration of influence and market share in the so called "big four"—Nomura, Daiwa, Nikko and Yamaichi. While dominating the securities industry in Japan, these firms have also acquired considerable worldwide influence. And as the barriers among financial institutions in Japan are reduced, they will undoubtedly come into more direct competition with the banking industry. For example, in January 1980, security companies began selling small denomination certificates of participation in bond trusts. The trusts, known as Chukoku funds since they invest primarily in medium term government bonds, are essentially similar to Money Market Mutual Funds in the United States. The ability of security firms to offer a close substitute to a bank deposit represented a significant blurring of the line between the security business and banking. In fact, the volume of such funds grew rapidly until 1987, when the deregulation of deposit interest rates slowed and eventually reversed their growth.

The short-term money market in Japan is extremely underdeveloped compared with those of other major industrialized countries. Whereas the volume of outstanding short-term debt in the United States in 1985 was equivalent to 40 percent of GNP, in Japan the figure was only 8 percent. Moreover, the market continues to be highly regulated and controlled, and most reforms enacted in recent years have been largely the result of foreign pressure.

Until 1980, the short-term market consisted of just two instruments: call money (available in maturities of up to seven days and used for settling bank reserve positions); and the bill discount market (in maturities from one to four months and used for transferring liquidity among financial institutions). Access to both instruments is extremely curtailed by the Bank of Japan (BOX), which also controls the interest rates according to its monetary objectives. The first "free" short-term market, in which interest rates were able to respond to supply and demand, was the Gensaki or collateralized loan market (security repurchase agreement) established in 1970. In addition to having market-sensitive rates, the Gensaki is open to a wider range of participants. Individuals, however, cannot enter the market, and city bank activities are subject to various restrictions. Since 1984, three short-term market instruments have been created: short-term government bonds with a maturity of six months were introduced in February 1986; bonds with a three-month maturity began to be issued in September 1989; and yen-denominated bankers' acceptances were brought forth in June 1985.

Moreover, the combination of domestic demand and foreign pressure has resulted in a number of financial innovations in recent years, including yen CDS in 1984, and the introduction of foreign commercial paper in 1987. Nevertheless, the market is still encumbered by a wide range of restrictions due to both pressure from special interest groups and characteristic Japanese conservatism and caution in introducing change. The BOX influences the money market by its leverage over the brokers, known as Tanshi, through whom many money market transactions must be channeled. These brokers are traditionally ex-BOX officials, and as a matter of course consult the BOX as to the calibration of crucial money market interest rates. Nevertheless, present trends clearly indicate that a freer, more integrated market is evolving.

B. FOREIGN ACCESS TO SECURITIES MARKETS IN JAPAN

Into the early 1990s, it was "remarkable how little non-residents have directly used Japanese financial markets to tap surplus domestic savings," say Takeda and Turner at 67. They cited several points of comparison in the early 1990s. One was the low relative turnover of equity issued by foreigners compared to all equity: 1% or less on the Tokyo Stock Exchange, compared to almost 49% on the London Stock Exchange, 7% on the New York Stock Exchange, 3% on NASDAQ, 3% on the Paris Bourse, and 2% on the German exchanges. Foreign bond issues were low in Japan. Foreign investors were scarce: in Japan, their purchases and sales of securities as a share of all domestic securities transactions barely reached one quarter of foreign investors' share of US securities transactions in the mid-1980s before falling to one-tenth in 1991. Foreign holdings of Japanese shares barely exceeded 5%. Foreign holdings of government bonds outstanding rose from 5% in 1988 to 11% in 1991, compared to 40% in Germany, 20% in the US and France, and 11% in the UK in 1990.

By 1996-97, Japan's relative position was even weaker. Turnover of foreign issuers' equity, compared to total turnover, was 0.2%, as against 58% for the LSE, 8% in the NYSE, and 4% in NASDAQ. See London Stock Exchange, F Tables. Foreign listings on the TSE, having peaked in 1991 at 127, were 67 in 1996, compared to 293 and 305 on the NYSE. The companies withdrew because, they said, costs were high, administration was a burden, and trading very limited. Daily trading volume had peaked in 1987 at 2.76 million shares and fallen to 200,000 shares in 1993. E. Terazono, *More Foreign Companies to Delist from Tokyo SE*, Financial Times, July 23, 1993; M. Gonzalez, *Four U.S. Firms Delist Their Shares on Tokyo Bourse*, Wall Street Journal, Mar. 27, 1995. Foreign ownership of all equities on the Tokyo exchange peaked in 1984 at 8.8% of market value, fell to 3.5% in 1988 as price/ earnings ratios became unacceptably high, hovered between 4% and 5% to 1991, then grew to 9% in 1995, a new record. Yamaichi Research Institute, Foreign Investors Hit New High on Tokyo Stock Exchange (1995). By 1995, the net positive investment of foreigners exactly offset the net disinvestment of domestic investors. From 1993 to 1996, total turnover on the TSE was flat and since turnover on the other large exchanges grew, the TSE's relative position slipped, from 33% of NYSE turnover in 1993 to 23% in 1996, and from 90% of the LSE's turnover to 62% in the same period.

After 1997, portfolio investment gradually returned to Japan. Residents' net outflows diminished and non-residents net inflows started to grow again, showing a very slight positive net inflow overall. By late 1998, foreign fund managers reported a growing interest in Japanese securities. In 2000, foreign investors were sometimes net importers of funds into the country, and at other times net exporters. Their market share was low compared to other countries. Foreigners held less than 10% of the bonds issued by the Japanese Government, compared to 30% in the US, and 50% in Europe. B. Rahan, *Foreign Investors Flock Back to Japan*, Financial Times, Sep. 13, 2000. C. Kentouris, *Japan's New Regs a Stymie Foreign Investment*, Securities Industry News, Jan. 22, 2001.

Notes and Questions

1. Do you agree with Takeda and Turner that non-residents' limited direct use of Japanese financial markets is remarkable?

2. Cross-holding of shares by members of a group has been described as impeding foreign investors. A side effect of cross-holding was to make it difficult for foreign investors to weigh the industries when they built a portfolio of Japanese shares: buying bank shares would indirectly involve the investor in the industries the bank invested in through its affiliates. Goldman Sachs devised an index to solve this problem, cutting the weight indexes normally gave banks in half, to 11% of a portfolio, and raising the weights of other industries. See *A Japanese Cross-Holding Puzzle*, The Economist, Oct. 5, 1996.

1. REGULATION OF NON-RESIDENT ISSUERS IN JAPAN

a. REGULATION TO THE EARLY 1990s

The following comparison of Japanese and U.S. securities law was done in the early 1990s. It provides a base against which to see the subsequent evolution of Japanese law. As you read this portion of Shimada's article, consider the nature of the government's involvement. In what ways does this differ from the U.S.? The following notes identify important subsequent changes.

Y. SHIMADA, A COMPARISON OF SECURITIES REGULATION IN JAPAN AND THE UNITED STATES

29 Columbia Journal of Transnational Law 319, 354–57 (1991) (Shimada).

A. *Japan's Foreign Exchange and Foreign Trade Control Law*

In the United States, international securities offerings are regulated under the statutory framework of the Securities Act. In Japan, international securities offerings are regulated under the statutory framework of not only the 1948 Act, but also the Foreign Exchange and Foreign Trade Control Law (the FECL), a statute that has no counterpart in the United States. Because of the dual statutory frameworks of the 1948 Act and the FECL, legal issues frequently arise in Japan as to whether international securities offerings are subject to the 1948 Act's registration and prospectus delivery requirements, in addition to the FECL's notification or licensing requirements. [The FECL requires that issuers of certain international securities offerings notify or obtain a license from the MOF.] In addition, issuers of certain international securities offerings are required to satisfy certain eligibility criteria. By contrast, in the United States, securities offerings, including international securities offerings, are subject to the Securities Act's registration and prospectus delivery requirements only to the extent that they fall within the extraterritorial scope of the Securities Act.

International securities fall into primarily two categories: (1) Euro-securities, which are offered in Europe usually through an international syndicate of banks and securities companies and sold mostly, and sometimes exclusively, in countries other than the home country of the issuer, and (2) foreign securities, which are offered in a country other than the home country of the issuer primarily through banks and securities companies located in the country where the offering is to be made, distributed in ways that are similar to offerings by domestic issuers in such country and usually denominated in the currency of such country. Because the international new issue market for debt securities is larger than that for equity securities, this part focuses on two types of Eurobonds (Euroyen and Eurodollar bonds) and three types of foreign bonds (Yankee, Samurai and Shogun bonds). The FECL requires MOF notification for issuance by Japanese resident issuers of Euroyen, Eurodollar and Yankee bonds even though these generally fall outside the extraterritorial scope of the 1948 Act and are thereby exempt from the registration and prospectus delivery requirements thereof. Such issuers must also satisfy certain eligibility requirements. Samurai and Shogun bond offerings, on the other hand, trigger both the MOF notification requirements of the FECL and the registration and prospectus delivery requirements of the 1948 Act. In addition, non-resident issuers of Samurai, Shogun and Euroyen bonds in Japan must meet certain eligibility requirements.

. . .

B. Official Notification Under the FECL

The FECL regulates securities offerings in Japan by non-resident issuers, securities offerings outside Japan by Japanese resident issuers, and offerings in Japan by Japanese resident issuers of securities payable outside Japan or denominated in a currency other than the yen by requiring issuers to file an official notification with the MOF through The Bank of Japan. Any issuer required to file official notifications with the MOF under the FECL is prohibited from issuing or offering for subscription its securities until the expiration of a twenty-day period [which he MOF may shorten,] commencing from the date on which the MOF formally accepts the notification. If the MOF does not formally accept the notification filing, the issuer cannot commence the offering. In practice, the MOF does not accept official notification filings unless the issuer has met certain eligibility requirements.[224]

The MOF generally will not accept the filing of an official notification unless the issuer has engaged in discussions with it prior to the filing. During these discussions, the terms and conditions of the filing and any restrictions placed thereon are modified if necessary to meet the MOF's recommendations for changes. After the MOF informally approves the offering, the official notification is formally filed. At this stage, the filing is almost always accepted. On the other hand, if the MOF has not informally approved the offering, the filing of the official notification will probably not be accepted, thereby effectively prohibiting the issuer from issuing or offering for subscription its securities.

A period of time preceding formal acceptance, the "prescreening process," is therefore essential for international securities offerings which trigger the FECL's

In addition, the MOF has formal authority under the FECL to intervene and order a change in the terms and arrangements of an offering or a suspension of the offering itself if the MOF deems that one of four outcomes would result without its intervention. These four outcomes are: (1) negative effects on international money markets; (2) negative effects on Japan's money or capital markets; (3) negative effects on certain industrial sectors of Japan; or (4) an interference in the performance of Japan's duties under its treaties or other international agreements or a disruption of international peace and security.

In Japan, any non-resident issuer is required to file an official notification with the MOF before issuing or offering for subscription its securities in Japan. This requirement arises regardless of the securities' currency of denomination or whether an exemption from registration is available under the 1948 Act.

Accordingly, the FECL requires non-resident issuers of Samurai and Shogun bonds in Japan to notify the MOF and to undergo a twenty-day waiting period during which the MOF, and sometimes The Bank of Japan at the MOF's direction, review the offering.[230] The decision to issue Samurai and Shogun bonds is normally made during discussions held between the MOF and the participating underwriters on behalf of the issuers.[231] Only non-resident issuers in Japan that have met certain eligibility criteria are considered during these discussions. Only after the MOF and the issuer have agreed to the terms of the offering does the issuer file an official notification with the MOF. Because the official notification is filed after the MOF has

notification requirements. During the prescreening process, the International Finance Section of the MOF, which administers the FECL, may consult with the Securities and Banking Bureaus of the MOF, and with various banking and securities trade associations whose members may be affected by the approved offering. The objective of such discussions is to ensure that no portion of the Japanese financial system will be adversely affected by the proposed offering. The prescreening process is also essential for international securities offerings that trigger the licensing requirements of the FECL.

A concern of the MOF and The Bank of Japan is that substantial proceeds arising from issues of Samurai bonds may affect the exchange rate of the yen. Because Samurai proceeds flow overseas when they are converted to the national currency of the issuer, an oversupply of yen abroad in conjunction with increased demand for foreign currencies in Japan would, according to standard economic theory, weaken the yen on world foreign currency markets.

The four largest securities companies in Japan dominate the Samurai bond market, and typically, each submits to the MOF a list ranking, in order or preference, those clients who wish to issue Samurai bonds. If any particular offering is opposed by the MOF, the securities companies eliminate it from the list. Each fiscal quarter, these securities companies engage in discussions amongst themselves to arrive at a joint master list compiled on the basis of the various eligibility criteria. If the securities companies cannot reach agreement, the MOF intervenes to arbitrate. This interplay between the MOF and the underwriter(s) eliminates the issuer as an active participant in the approval process and delegates its role to an observer awaiting the outcome of stricter domestic negotiations.

already informally approved the offering, the filing of the official notification is generally a procedural formality.

For offerings in Japan by non-resident issuers, the MOF's basic policy has been to disapprove securities offerings if the securities involved are not of a type that Japanese resident issuers may generally issue. For example, if a Japanese resident issuer is barred from privately placing four-year floating rate, U.S. dollar-denominated bonds in Japan, a non-resident issuer will likewise be barred from issuing such securities in Japan, even if that issuance forms only a small percentage of a larger global offering. However, this basic policy has been subject to modification on a case-by-case basis.

The MOF generally will not approve an offering of Samurai or Shogun bonds unless the issuer has met certain eligibility criteria. Separate criteria exist for corporate and sovereign issuers. Corporate issuers with net assets totaling less than ¥600 billion must either have an A rating or better from one of the rating companies or satisfy other financial criteria. Corporate issuers with net assets totaling more than ¥600 billion need not meet any financial criteria nor have obtained any minimum rating. Ineligible corporate issuers are permitted to issue Samurai or Shogun bonds if guaranteed by an eligible parent company. Sovereign issuers engaged in a public offering that have previously issued bonds need not meet any rating or financial criteria, while those that have not previously issued any bonds must have an A rating or better in order to be eligible.

In Japan, any non-resident issuer of yen-denominated securities is required to obtain a license from the MOF before issuing and selling the securities abroad. In addition, these issuers are required to file reports with the MOF on a monthly basis disclosing the specific terms of any yen-denominated securities issued during each month. These requirements apply to issuers issuing or offering for subscription Euroyen bonds in the Euromarkets[268] and Yankee bonds denominated in yen and issued in the United States. The MOF typically grants this license on the condition that the yen-denominated securities issued outside Japan not be sold to Japanese resident investors for a

---

Non-resident issuers of Euroyen bonds in Japan used to be required to satisfy eligibility criteria. With the opening of Euroyen bond market in April 1977, the MOF limited the number of issuers permitted to offer Euroyen bonds. The MOF justified this limitation on the ground that increased yen holdings outside of Japan would lessen control over monetary policy and render the Japanese economy more susceptible to adverse economic events and conditions in other countries. "[Too rapid establishment of a free Euroyen market may have adverse effects on Japanese fiscal and monetary policies, exchange rates, and Japan's domestic financial systems. . . . [Gradually the rules were relaxed.] After June 1985 the MOF permitted the issuance of the following types of Euroyen bonds by Japanese resident and non- resident issuers as well as straight Euroyen bonds: dual currency bonds; floating rate notes; zero coupon bonds; deep discount bonds; and currency conversion bonds. For example, U.S. resident issuers have raised yen in the Euroyen market and converted their yen proceeds into U.S. dollars via currency swaps . . . ."

ninety-day period following the date on which the securities were originally issued abroad.

The MOF will generally not grant licenses unless the issuer or the yen-denominated securities themselves have been assigned a specific rating by at least one rating agency recognized by the MOF. Thus, any non-resident issuer is eligible to issue Euroyen bonds and yen-denominated Yankee bonds, so long as either the issuer or the bonds have been assigned a rating from a recognized rating agency.

. . .

When any non-resident issuer raises capital by offering securities in Japan or by issuing yen-denominated securities outside of Japan, not only must the issuer either notify or obtain a license from the MOF, but it must also meet certain eligibility criteria specified by the MOF. In addition, when a securities offering takes place in Japan, the MOF requires registration under the 1948 Act unless an exemption from registration is available. The result of this regulatory framework is that the MOF is able to exercise greater control than the SEC over the capital markets and the flow of capital in and out of Japan and the United States, respectively.

b. REGULATION FROM THE MID-1990s

Since Shimada wrote, MOF relaxed some of the rules for foreign issuers, often in response to the Financial Services Agreement of 1995. It created a comprehensive system of notification for non-resident issuers to issue bonds repeatedly over a 12 month period with ex post notice after the initial approval from MOF (a form of shelf registration). MOF streamlined filing requirements and promised a response from MOF within 5 business days of filing. MOF eliminated the minimum rating requirements and substituted permission for financial covenants in place of required covenants, along with a requirement that even listed issuers disclose risk information (this applied to all issuers, not merely foreigners). MOF abolished the 90-day seasoning period for Euroyen bonds by non-resident non-governmental issuers, effective January 1, 1996. It reduced the period only to 40 days for resident issuers for reasons having to do with tax law. Sovereign Euroyen bonds had ceased being subject to the rule in 1993. CS First Boston, Financial Deregulation in Japan Current Issues (1995) (CS First Boston) and H. Ozawa, *Tokyo Report*, Butterworths Journal of International Banking and Financial Law, June and Oct. 1995, at 281.

By mid-1995, retail purchases of foreign yen bonds were substantial. The Japanese housewife was said to be displacing the Belgian dentist. An Italian government issue in May 1995 attracted 50,000 retail buyers. A major motive was the very low rates payable on domestic yen bonds. Monthly retail sales of foreign bonds by the Big 4 rose from Yen 1 billion in April 1995 to Yen 5.5 billion in September. E. Terazono and R. Lapper, *Home 'Ministries of Finance' buy Euroyen*, Financial Times, June 19, 1995; E. Terazono, *Japanese Investors Take Bonuses Abroad*, Financial Times, Dec. 23-24, 1995.

Barriers for foreign issuers continued, however, in the view of U.S. firms. The commercial code required a company seeking to list its securities to file all documents in Japanese and set the par value of its share at ¥50,000 ($473 at the time). A. Harney and B. Rahan, *Barriers to Tokyo Listings Attacked*, Financial Times, June 20, 2000.

Note on the Samurai Bond Market

Yen denominated bonds issued in Japan by non-residents (Samurai bonds) were dominated historically by multilateral institutions like the Asian Development Bank and sovereign issuers. The number of issues was 461 from 1970–90, growing precipitously from only 18 in 1986 to 76 in 1990.

In the mid-1990s, Samurai bond issues exploded, roughly doubling from ¥1.6 trillion ($17 billion) to ¥3.9 trillion ($36 billion) from 1995 to 1996. For the first time in years, Samurai issues exceeded the volume of yen denominated eurobonds. Part of this growth reflected the easing of rules described in Note 1 below. For example, Packer and Reynolds estimated that about 23% of the growth was attributable to the changes in rating requirements, which suggested to them that access to lower rated issues was not the major factor driving growth. Issuers were also attracted by the low interest rate in Japan, according to Sugiyama, along with their ability to issue more complex securities than had been previously permitted. They could, for example, issue bonds with interest paid in foreign currency and principal repaid in Yen. They could issue asset backed bonds.

Citibank became the first foreign commercial bank to issue Samurai bonds in April 1997, after Japan ended the rules that limited debenture issuance to long-term credit banks and foreign exchange banks. Citibank had an advantage over Japanese banks, which could only sell these bonds to institutional investors, while foreign banks could sell to retail investors as well. Issuance was more flexible and attractive than in the past because issuers could obtain permission for a one year period to issue bonds without notifying MOF in advance. See F. Packer and Reynolds, *The Samurai Bond Market*, 3:8 Federal Reserve Bank of New York Current Issues in Economics and Finance, June 1997; and Y. Sugiyama, *The Growth of the Samurai Bond Market*, Butterworths Journal of International Banking and Financial Law, June 1997 at 270.

The number and volume of Samurai bonds, issued in yen by foreigners, rose steadily in 1998/99 and 1999/2000. In each fiscal year, foreigners issued yen bonds worth $5.3 billion. A. Van Duyn and R. Bream, *Japan: Land of the Rising Bond Issuance,* Financial Times, June 2, 2000.

Notes and Questions

1. How have Japanese policies responded to the potential problems foreigners could cause? What have been the trends?

2. Why did foreigners not tap the Japanese markets so much before 1996/7? How important were regulatory factors? How important were economic factors?

2. FOREIGN SECURITIES FIRMS IN JAPAN

a. RECENT HISTORY

From the mid-1980s, foreign securities firms were gradually allowed to play an expanding role in Japan. Pressure from foreign governments, notably the US and UK, helped them win a broader range of activities. They could take part in syndicates to underwrite government bonds from 1984. Each foreign securities firm was initially allowed to take 0.07% of an issue (with a total foreign share of 2.5%), then in 1998 1% each (with a total of 8%). The next year, several were allowed to lead manage the issue. By the end of the 1980s, 48 foreign securities firms were in Japan, up from 12 in 1984. Of these 48, 25 held regular membership in the Tokyo Stock Exchange. See Swary and Topf, 95.

b. FOREIGN SECURITIES FIRMS IN THE 1990s

Licensing for securities firms is regulated by the Securities and Exchange Law (SEL), which requires a firm to have MOF's explicit approval for each type of activity it offers: dealing, brokerage, underwriting, and distribution. In March 1994, 129 of the 220 Japanese securities companies held licenses to carry on the full range of securities business. The four largest firms had substantial capital (almost $4 billion combined). (Much of the basic data in this and the following paragraphs is drawn from 1994 National Treatment Study.)

The number of licensed foreign firms in Japan declined from 53 in 1990 to 48 in 1994; another 92 foreign firms had representative offices. No foreign firm had a securities subsidiary, despite the finance ministry's statement in 1986 that it would consider applications. Until the mid-1980s, the main business of foreign securities companies was to intermediate inflows and outflows of cross-border securities. In the late 1980s, foreign firms started to compete more in domestic markets. They won about 12% of total Japanese Government Bond auctions in 1993, doubling their 1992 share. They were active in equity trading; their share of turnover on the Tokyo Stock Exchange rose from 6% in 1989 to 20% in 1992, then retreated to 18% in 1993. U.S. firms were active in derivative markets: 9 were members of the Tokyo International Financial Futures Exchange (TIFFE).

After several years in which a number of foreign securities firms made record profits in Japan, while their Japanese counterparts reported serious problems, the foreign firms became less interested in operating in Japan. In 1992, for example, foreign branch profits fell by 70% to $112 million. A study by the Japan Center for International Finance reported that foreign financial firms did not expect Tokyo to displace London or New York to become the world's pre-eminent financial center. Ten percent of foreign brokers were leaving or cutting back. In 1993, for instance, Salomon Brothers Asia was reducing its staff from 600 to 510 and reducing its branches from 2 to 1. Merrill Lynch Japan closed half of its 6 retail branches and moved its Asia chief to Hong Kong, which was closer to most of its Asian clientele. The U.K. National Westminster Bank subsidiary sold its TSE membership. Tokyo costs were exorbitant: the monthly rent for executive homes ranged from $15,000 to $60,000. But by 1997, as the yen and the economy weakened, the tide had turned. Tokyo office rents were substantially lower than Hong Kong or Singapore. Demand for foreign firms' services had risen: assets they managed rose from only $12 billion in 1993 to $90 billion in 1997. By mid-1997, even though Barclays and Lehman Brothers were scaling back, the number of foreign brokerage firms had risen to 53. See R. Steiner, *Tokyo Regains Its Place as a Finance Hub*, Wall Street Journal, May 29, 1997.

Foreign securities firms took an increasing share of the Japanese market. In October and November 1997, the U.S. securities firms of Morgan Stanley and Merrill Lynch captured the two highest shares of trading. Faced with this embarrassment, the Big Three Japanese firms announced that they would no longer publish their market shares. See G. Tett, *Japanese Business Traditions Yield to Big Bang*, Financial Times, December 12, 1997. In 1998, increased foreign competition further eroded the earnings of the Big Three. P. Abrahams, *Competition Hits Japan's Brokers*, Jul. 26, 1998.

Foreign securities firms fell afoul of the crackdown by Japanese regulators in the late 1990s. Several securities firms were penalized: the UK firm Schroders failed to report obligations in its asset management business for five years; Deutsche Securities helped some companies hide losses during the Asian financial crisis; BNP Paribas Securities made improper trades; and WestLB Securities Pacific also broke the law. The government threatened in April 2000 to stop using Goldman Sachs because it said the firm violated conflict of interest standards. G. Tett and N. Nakarae, *Schroders Admits Breaching Japanese Regulations*, Financial Times, Jan. 23-24, 1999; G. Tett, *Deutsche Securities Faces*

Japanese Ire, Financial Times, May 16, 2000; G. Tett and C. Pretzlik, *Goldman Seeks to Repair Relations with Japan*, Financial Times, April 25, 2000; E. Terazono, *Japan Penalises BNP Paribas Securities*, Financial Times, June 10/11, 2000; D. Ibison, *FSA Investigates NSSB in Japan*, Financial Times, Jan. 19, 2001.

3. FOREIGN SECURITIES FIRMS AND THE CORPORATE BOND MARKET

This section describes the evolution of policies toward Japan's corporate bond market from the early 1990s, when it began to open to foreign firms. According to Brian Wallace Semkow, *Foreign Financial Institutions in Japan: Legal and Financial Barriers and Opportunities, Part 2*, Butterworths Journal of International Banking and Financial Law, Mar. 1993, at 127:

> Foreign securities firms are beginning to make inroads into the underwriting market for corporate bonds. In December 1991, Morgan Stanley was appointed as the first securities firm to co-lead a domestic bond issue for a Japanese borrower, Nippon Telegraph and Telephone, the shares of which were not permitted to be owned by foreigners until August 1992. NTT chose Morgan Stanley in part because the bond issue was the first in Japan under which the underwriters would use a negotiated fixed-price offering method common in North America and Europe, whereby the issuer and the underwriter determine the terms of the offering in light of market conditions. It is hoped that this approach would become more prevalent in Japan, as it would encourage transparency and stimulate the secondary market for corporate bonds; the prevailing practice of corporate bond underwriters is to offer the highest prices to the issuer, and sell the bonds at varying discounts on the secondary market, making up the difference with high [fixed] commission rates of 1.2 percent of the face value of the bond.

The Securities Industry Association, a U.S. trade group, said that in 1992 four U.S. securities firms were among the top 20 highest capitalized firms in Japan and three U.S. firms "took the top three spots in operating income generated in Japan." The SIA pointed out that U.S. securities firms lead managed barely 3% of Japanese corporate bond issues worth $36 billion that year. The reasons, according to the SIA, were:

> lack of transparency in securities regulation, which reinforces the monopoly position of the "Big Four" Japanese securities firms;

> administrative guidance and outdated regulations [such as "unnecessary involvement of a commission bank, stringent eligibility standards," and costly procedures] which govern the issuance process; and

> impediments to issuing and placing new and innovative products ["of the 25 financial products typically available in New York and London,

only 12 are allowed in Tokyo"] which address the needs of issuers and investors.

The "long-standing relationship between Japanese issuers and underwriters shut out foreign firms." See Securities Industry Association, Accessing the Japanese Corporate Bond Market (1993).

The U.S. Treasury concurred. It reported in its 1994 National Treatment Study 356-58:

Underwriting Corporate Securities Issues

Despite persistent efforts and growing domestic client bases, foreign securities firms are rarely able to secure more than a minimal share in corporate underwriting syndicates. The yen-based corporate bond and equity new issue markets are essentially locked up by the Big Four Japanese underwriters. No foreign securities firm has ever lead-managed a nongovernment domestic corporate bond or equity issue in Japan, even though U.S. securities firms have excelled in underwriting yen issues in the Euroyen and nondollar corporate securities markets in other major financial centers. Moreover, U.S. securities firms have participated in the lead management of only six issues in total, but in each case a Japanese partner acted as co-lead. All six issues were for NTT, a quasi-government telecommunications company. This situation is anomalous when viewed against foreign firms' share of secondary market trading in Japan and their leading positions in underwriting offshore bond and equity issues.

The minimal presence of foreign underwriters in lead-managing corporate bond and equity issues in Japan stems in large part from a number of regulations and industry practices endorsed by the Finance Ministry that govern who can issue corporate securities in Japan, the types and structures of products that may be issued, and the amounts and types of products that institutional investors may purchase. These regulations and practices include the following:

- Through the use of administrative guidelines, MOF sets minimum rating requirements and other financial criteria (such as minimum net worth) for corporate bond issuers. These restrictions narrow the pool of eligible issuers and limit business opportunities for U.S. securities companies. Minimum rating and net worth requirements have been relaxed in recent years, but restrictions remain. These regulations prevent smaller firms from participating in the capital markets and have the effect of preserving their business for Japanese banks.

- A combination of regulations and informal guidance frustrates, and often prevents, securities firms in Japan from introducing new securities products and services, and in many cases from marketing securities products that are widely available in other major financial markets. The relatively narrow definition of a "security" under Article 2 of the Securities and Exchange Law is a principal obstacle in this regard. New securities instruments are prohibited "in principle" unless specifically approved by the Finance Ministry, on a case-by case basis, and in some cases, on a transaction-by-transaction basis. The list of permissible securities under Article 2 has been expanded somewhat in recent years, but until any new product -- except those explicitly excluded for prudential reasons -- can be introduced in principle, this limitation will remain a significant barrier to foreign securities firms with a competitive advantage in offering innovative new products. For example, the SEL permits only those equity derivatives instruments that are traded on a regulated exchange, thus restricting the ability of U.S. firms (as well as Japanese securities firms) to meet their clients' needs by providing specifically structured, non-exchange traded derivative instruments to institutional investors, although some OTC bonds can be sold. The prior reporting/prior approval framework of the Foreign Exchange and Trade Control Law is another barrier when the new product has a currency exchange component or involves a cross-border trade. Foreign firms have also questioned the need for multiple personal visits to various MOF bureaus to gain new product approval, as well as the general lack of transparency in the approval process. U.S. firms also have expressed concern that MOF consults with Japanese competitors, indirectly via the JSDA, in the course of reviewing new product applications by foreign firms. Many U.S. securities firms view these constraints as an explicit attempt by Finance Ministry officials to keep foreign securities firms at a competitive disadvantage by denying them the opportunity to market in Japan their most competitive skills.

- The development of an asset-backed securities market in Japan has been limited. It is a market that is of considerable importance to U.S. securities firms, which excel at underwriting these kinds of instruments.

- Despite gradual liberalization and commitments to further reform, MOF continues to limit the types of corporate bonds that may be issued in Japan and regulates their interest rate structures.

- MOF administrative guidelines set limits on the amounts and kinds of investments that life insurance companies and mutual funds may make in various financial instruments, albeit they are free to make investments pursuant to MOF's investment framework. These restrictions hamper distribution capacity for foreign securities first by limiting the kinds of products they may market to Japan's leading institutional investors.

• A "10,000-share rule" limiting the number of shares that can be placed with a single investor, individual or institutional, was imposed by the Japan Securities Dealers Association (JSDA) in the wake of the securities scandals in the summer of 1991, in order to reinforce new legal prohibitions on loss compensation. (Preferential allocation of new public offerings had been one means by which Japanese securities companies compensated favored customers for poor performance of their existing securities portfolios.) A broad range of exceptions to the 10,000-share rule are granted, but foreign firms view the rule as impeding their ability to distribute shares to their (mainly institutional) clients. (Note: A separate "30 percent rule" imposed by the JSDA, which limited the distribution share of each securities house in the syndicate and was listed as a concern in the 1990 report, was eliminated in July 1992.)

The U.S.-Japan Financial Services Agreement of 1995 addressed these concerns in Part IV on Securities. The two governments stated that regulation of securities activities should be minimal and for prudential purposes only. Japan confirmed that "any instrument will constitute a security to the extent that it satisfies the definition of a 'security' ... in Article 2 of the SEL" and that no one needed the government's acknowledgment, before issue, that an instrument is a security. If asked, however, the government would respond expeditiously. The government confirmed that certain new instruments were within the definition, including certain types of asset backed securities, foreign closed-end funds, bonds with debt warrants, and others, though it did not mention equity derivatives. Japan agreed to deregulate investment guidelines for investment trust management companies, to review the limits on the number of shares that could be sold to any one buyer in a primary issue and to "invite" stock exchanges not to limit distribution of newly listed shares. As to corporate bond issues, it said:

(7) Additional Liberalization of Corporate Bond Issues

a.   The Government of Japan also intends to take the following measures:

i.   assure that no restriction is imposed on the maturity structure of corporate bonds issued in Japan or offshore;

ii. steadily promote diversification in structures, including interest rate structures, of corporate bonds issued in Japan by residents or non-residents; and,

iii. concerning the minimum rating requirements and financial criteria on all domestic issues by Japanese residents, fundamentally review and, after public hearing, announce a relaxation program, by the end of March 1995, including possible elimination of the minimum rating requirements in a reasonable transitional period, at a maximum within one year after the announcement.

The Agreement specified criteria by which to evaluate progress in implementing it. The parties disclaimed any plan to apply the measures slavishly. For corporate securities, the agreed criteria were:

(3) Securities Activities

a. change and rate of change, from one reporting period to the next, in the percentage, by value, of new corporate issues in Japan and in the U.S. underwritten by foreign firms and underwritten by foreign firms as lead or co-lead managers;

b. diversification of securities products and product types issued and sold in Japan;

c. the variety of maturity and interest rate structures in use in the Japanese corporate bond market; and

d. implementation of the procedural measures relating to the clarification and expansion of the definition of a security.

New issues on the corporate bond market had collapsed in 1991, falling from ¥ 9.3 trillion in 1990 to ¥ 3.3 trillion, then started a steady recovery to ¥ 6.6 trillion in 1996. The potential for further growth was there, according to some, because Japanese companies relied so much on indirect finance (about 50% of funds came from banks), compared to U.S. firms (only about 20%). But the market was still not sophisticated, nor was trading active. In August 1996, for example, an AAA rated issuer got a 2.6% coupon and an AA rated issuer got 2.7%. Turnover was only three times market capitalization in 1995. Clearance and settlement was slow; it could take a month to register ownership formally. It was difficult to compare the relative values of JBGs and corporate bonds; MOF did not want comparison. A 20% withholding tax applied to domestic bonds. In 1997, only about $50 billion were issued, contrasted with total domestic financial assets of $18 trillion. C. Smith, *Japan Inc.'s Burgeoning Bond Market*, Institutional Investor, Feb. 1997 at 63; J. Sapsford, *New Rules Roil Japan Bond Underwriting*, Wall Street Journal, June 11, 1997.

Japan carried out almost all the steps promised in the Financial Services Agreement of 1995 by the end of 1996. MOF reconfirmed that it did not restrict the maturity structure of corporate bonds issued onshore. In March 1995, it eliminated minimum rating and financial requirements for domestic issuers. It restated its promise to promote corporate bond diversification, but had not acted by October 1995. It allowed foreign securities firms to issue yen CP with a guarantee from their parent. For equity, it reconfirmed stock distribution rules for institutional investors, but had not yet reviewed the 10,000-unit stock distribution rule of the Japan Securities Dealers' Association. See CS First Boston.

Foreign financial firms did not rest content, however. A major concern was that notice and pre-notice requirements not be used to assert a governmental power to approve. Transparency of rules and their application still required work. Mergers and acquisitions remained very low for a variety of reasons, including legal barriers to mergers of Japanese companies with foreign ones and to dismissing employees in the merged company. The lack of a viable OTC market hindered mergers where the newly restructured company could not qualify for a listing on the TSE. See T. Porte and W. Erb, *Traditional Obstacles to M&A Activity in Japan*, in Final Report of the Symposium on Building the Financial System of the 21st Century: An Agenda for Japan and the United States (1998) at 154.

Notes and Questions

1. The Financial Services Agreement addressed other concerns of foreign firms as well. These included the management of pension funds (which had $1 trillion in assets) and the investment trust business (mutual funds). While much of the treaty consisted of commitments by the government of Japan, the U.S. government also agreed to act in some cases. For securities, the U.S. undertook to try to eliminate redundancy between the U.S. and Japanese broker-dealer exams and to try to coordinate state and federal registration requirements better. Why would the Japanese securities markets command so much more attention in the Agreement than Japanese banking, especially given the relative performance of foreigners in each?

2. What would account for the performance of foreign securities firms in Japan, compared to the Japanese firms? Note that entry is not an issue. Why would this be so? Why would entry be more of an issue for banking?

3. Does the Financial Services Agreement resolve the problems foreign securities firms faced in corporate bond issuance? Why? Are domestic underwriting practices an appropriate topic for intergovernmental discussion? A few years after early 1995, would you expect to see foreign securities firms playing a much greater role in this market, even without the Big Bang? Why? What is the idea of the performance indicators?

4. Review the evolution of the securities laws toward foreign issuers and firms in Japan since 1990. Is Japan opening its securities markets primarily because of outside pressure or in response to domestic forces?

C. THE JAPANESE ROLE IN FOREIGN AND INTERNATIONAL SECURITIES MARKETS

Japan's role in foreign and international securities markets shifted during the 1990s. Japanese investors moved abroad as Japanese issuers slowed their activity. Overall, Japanese purchases of securities in foreign and international markets rose from $69 billion in 1995 to $89 billion in 1996. By 1996, Japanese institutional investors were looking abroad actively because of the very low domestic interest rate, the poor performance of domestic securities markets, and a rising $/¥ rate that made the dollar look safe. Japanese trust banks managed portfolios with almost 30% of all Japanese-owned foreign securities. Trust banks' foreign securities were 8.3% of total assets in 1995 and 9.1% in 1996. Some trust banks raised their ceilings for overseas investments to as much as 20% of total portfolios. Life insurance firms, which hold about 20% of all Japanese-owned foreign securities, could not meet their obligation to pay policy holders 3-4% each year if they relied on investments in JGBs yielding only 2.4% p.a., so they too turned abroad. The insurers' holdings of foreign securities rose from 6.9% of total assets in 1995 to 8.1% in 1996. Even the Post Office Savings Bank began to invest abroad. Japanese investors became significant holders of US government bonds, once again. See R. Steiner, *Japanese Are Still Hungry for U.S. Bonds*, Wall Street Journal, Dec. 16, 1996; R. Lapper, *Japanese Investors Look Abroad Again,* Financial Times, Dec. 13, 1996; S. Pullam and G. Zuckerman, *Japanese Role Could Hurt U.S. Market*, Wall Street Journal, Dec. 11, 1996; and F. Packer and E. Reynolds, *The Samurai Bond Market*, 8:3 Federal Reserve Bank of New York, Current Issues in Economics and Finance, June 1997.

Japanese companies' issuance of offshore securities, especially bonds, declined to the mid-1990s. Protracted slow growth, very low domestic interest rates, and a weakening yen all played a role. Having accounted for 38% of all issues in 1989, they raised only 2.5% in the first 3 quarters of 1996 and 5.6% in the first three of 1997. Much of the growth in earlier years took the form of equity related bonds giving the holder a warrant to buy equity in the issuer at a later time (see table). At home, most of the growth in issues was convertible bonds, but annual domestic issues by Japanese corporations during the 1980s rarely reached half the volume of their foreign issues.

The attraction of offshore markets in early years was clear: issuance costs were lower offshore (1.943% of principal, on average) than in Japan (2.334%), according to Takeda and Turner at 78. Higher issue costs included fees for trustees and agents in Japan and a three day delay in passing the proceeds to the issuer in Japan. It also cost more to prepare and comply with the terms of the loans in Japan. Unlike offshore issues, those in Japan were subject to limits on dividends, took much longer to register, and were limited by type of instrument. Even the cost of

External Bond Issues
In billions of US dollars, Selected Years

	1985	1990	1991	1993	1994	1995	1996
TOTAL *of which:*	147.2	222.9	297.1	481.0	428.6	467.3	708.8
Japanese issues *of which:*	21.6	55.4	70.7	61.0	38.6	38.8	42.3
Fixed rate.........	11.4	20.2	37.6	34.3	19.2	20.9	23.0
Floating rate....	2.3	8.0	1.7	5.4	6.5	8.5	3.3
Convertible.......	4.8	6.5	2.7	5.0	3.9	3.4	8.0
Equity warrants	1.1	20.2	28.6	16.0	8.4	5.4	7.7

Source: OECD *Financial Market Trends*

swapping from foreign currency into yen did not make an offshore issue more costly.

Japan's economic and financial problems, however, took their toll on Japanese issuers abroad. In November 1998, Moody's downgraded JGBs in November 1998. The economic and financial recovery did not go far enough, according to Moody's. It put Japanese yen debt under review in early 2000. Moody's did not say that it expected Japan to default on yen debt. Rather, it was concerned that the relative growth of debt in Japan might undermine the country's economic recovery, which would in turn make it hard for the government to reduce the debt. In September 2000, Moody's downgraded JGBs to AA2, two steps below the top rating, then downgraded them again to AA3, and raised the prospect of a rating (A2), below Botswana, in 2002. Standard & Poor's, and Fitch, followed suit. With the prospect of government debt equaling 149% of GDP in late 2003 and over 200% by 2010, rating agencies saw the risk of inflation and default. G. Tett, *Moody's Raises Hackles in Japan*, Financial Times, Feb. 18, 2000; G. Tett, Japan's Debt Downgraded by US Agency, Financial Times, Sep. 9/10, 2000; M. Williams, P. Dvorak, and G. Zuckerman, *S&P Lowers Japan's Domestic and Foreign Credit Rating*, Wall Street Journal, Feb. 23, 2001; M. Wolf, *How to Avert a Ratings Disaster*, Financial Times, Mar. 27, 2002.

1. THE REGULATION OF OFFSHORE SECURITIES OPERATIONS

The regulatory framework has been no less complex and illusive for securities than for banking abroad.

a. REGULATION TO THE EARLY 1990s

The system of written law and practice by the early 1990s is captured by Shimada, at 319, 350–4, 357–60, 363. Subsequent important changes to these rules are briefly described in the materials below.

All Japanese residents issuing or offering any securities outside Japan had to notify the MOF in advance according to the FECL. MOF's acceptance depended on the issuer's compliance with eligibility rules. According to Shimada, "Market participants have suggested that the MOF's policy has been to promote . . . eligibility criteria comparable to those which Japanese resident issuers must meet when issuing bonds in the Japanese markets in order to avoid encouraging them to offer bonds overseas." The requirements set thresholds for ratings and net assets that varied according to the security type, currency (yen or otherwise), and the existence of a guarantee by a bank or parent. Sometimes issues also had to meet requirements for a domestic issue.

Shimada concluded his study as follows:

> The securities statutes and the regulations promulgated thereunder in both Japan and the United States are similar. However, the manner in which international securities offerings are regulated and the extent to which regulatory control is exercised are quite different. Although the Japanese system of securities regulation was borrowed from the United States, the spirit of the U.S. regulatory system was not. To a certain extent, the differences between the two countries result from the unique Japanese system of administrative guidance. Unlike the SEC, the MOF informally pressures issuers and securities companies involved in international securities offerings to act in ways that further the administrative goals of the MOF.

> In the United States, when either a resident or non-resident issuer raises capital by offering securities in the United States or abroad, the SEC requires registration under the Securities Act if the offering falls within the extraterritorial reach of the Securities Act and an exemption from registration is not available under the Securities Act. SEC "approval" is never required. On the other hand, in Japan, issuers and securities companies often engage in informal discussions with the MOF before the start of any international securities offering to ensure MOF approval under the FECL and the 1948 Act. Whenever any Japanese resident issuer raises capital by offering securities abroad, MOF notification and MOF acceptance of such notification is required.

---

b.   A CASE STUDY: EUROYEN BONDS

The Euroyen bond market gives a glimpse of how government policies affected offshore fund raising by Japanese and other issuers. One reason the Euroyen bond market developed was the lack of a full range of domestic alternatives. The long-term credit banks used their monopoly on long-term securities to prevent even the government from issuing five-year bonds. Issuers and investors had to go off-shore. The source of this Daiwa Europe, LTD., Euroyen Bonds, Euromoney Guide to Financing 15 (1991).

The European Investment Bank issued the first Euroyen bond in 1977. Four types of issuers came to use the market: surpranationals and sovereigns, Japanese corporations, other corporations, and non-Japanese banks. All required the permission of MOF to make a new issue; they sought it through the issuers lead manager. Japanese investors were the main buyers, but they could not do so in the first 90 days of issue because of Japanese law, so the issue would have "a short first coupon linked to Libor (London Interbank Offered Rate), so that a European-based financial institution can park the securities; when the 90 days are up, the institution will sell the bonds to a pre-chosen investor in Japan." The Japanese investors tended not to trade, but to hold to maturity.

The Japanese government gradually deregulated the Euroyen bond market. In the following chronology, Daiwa Europe reported the sequence:

May 1977   Daiwa launches first Euroyen issue, a ¥CD10 bn deal with a seven-year maturity.

Dec 1984   Issuance of unsecured bonds by foreign corporates, state and local governments and government agencies allowed.
Foreign securities companies allowed to act as lead managers
Lead management and co-management restrictions lifted for foreign dealers
Resident corporates allowed to issue Euroyen bonds

April 1985 Abolition of 20% withholding tax payable by foreign investors on bonds issued by Japanese companies

June 1985   Zero coupon and dual currency issues allowed
Non–Japanese borrowers permitted to issue floating rate notes

April 1986 180–day lock-up period reduced to 90–days

June 1986   Foreign banks allowed to issue Euroyen bonds

April 1987 Issues with four-year maturities allowed

June 1989   Most other restrictions lifted. Issuance in yen permitted under Euro- medium term note programmes

----

c.   REGULATORY CHANGES IN THE 1990s

Rules governing offshore securities activities have changed since the Shimada and Euroyen articles. MOF introduced a comprehensive system of notification for the offshore issuance of securities by residents and yen securities by non-residents. It confirmed that it would not restrict the maturity structure or set financial criteria for corporate bonds issued by residents offshore. MOF reduced the 90-day seasoning requirement for resident issuers' Euroyen bonds to 40 days.

2. THE FINANCIAL SERVICES AGREEMENT OF 1995 AND CROSS-BORDER CAPITAL FLOWS

Article V of the Financial Services Agreement of 1995 between Japan and the U.S. addressed cross-border capital transactions. As you review the promises made by the government of Japan, ask whether the changes, if they occur, indicate a fundamental shift in the government's policy toward cross-border outflows.

In Article V, the government of Japan agreed to introduce a new advance approval system allowing manufacturing firms to deposit funds abroad for portfolio investments of at least Y100 million equivalent offshore and report only afterwards. Non-financial corporations and individuals could "directly invest, without solicitation," in securities derivatives listed on overseas exchanges. Corporate investors meeting certain standards could invest for their own accounts in financial futures and options listed abroad, without separate approval or notice. Securities companies, insurance companies, and investment trust companies would no longer be required to get advance approval to trade for their own account in currency spot options listed abroad. In paragraphs (3) and (4), the government made the following declarations:

(3) Liberalization of Securities Issued Offshore by Residents

a. The Government of Japan intends to introduce by the end of March 1995 a new comprehensive notification system for securities issued offshore by resident issuers. Under this system, an issuer may issue securities in one or more transactions over a period of one year subject only to ex post reporting, provided that the issuer requests an exemption from the standard notification requirement from the Ministry of Finance at the outset of the one-year period.

b. The comprehensive notification under this new system will be effective within five business days of the receipt by the Ministry of Finance of the request, except in extraordinary administrative circumstances. Such a request need include only the name of the issuer (address, type of industry, and nationality). If available, the following items may also be included, but only for informational purposes:

-   agent for issuer
-   planned total amount of issues
-   kinds of planned securities issues
-   rating
-   use of raised funds
-   parties concerned (lead manager, fiscal agent, etc.)

c. In addition, and related to the above, the Government of Japan intends to:

i.   assure that no restriction is imposed on the maturity structure of corporate bonds issued offshore by residents;

ii.   impose no restrictions on securities structures, including interest rate structures, of corporate bonds issued offshore by residents;

iii.   eliminate the minimum rating requirement on all offshore bond issues by residents in the case that deregulation on domestic issues is put into place; and,

iv.   confirm that no financial criteria will be imposed on resident companies issuing bonds offshore.

(4) Liberalization of Seasoning Requirements

a.   The Government of Japan intends to:

i.   announce by the end of March 1995 a program to abolish the current 90-day offshore seasoning period on non-sovereign Euroyen bond issues by non residents with the timing to coincide with the deregulation of the minimum ratings requirement for domestic bond issues, in accordance with the timetable in paragraph (7)a.iii. of Section IV; and,

ii.   study whether the offshore seasoning period on Euroyen bond issues by residents could be relaxed considering such factors as the situation of the domestic market.

The agreed measures of implementation for Article V of the Financial Services Agreement were:

(4) Cross-Border Capital Transactions

a.   change and rate of change, from one reporting period to the next, in:

i.   the number of resident and non-resident Euroyen market issues;

ii.   the number of non-resident securities issues in the Japanese market;

iii.   the number of comprehensive approvals granted to establish overseas deposit accounts in excess of the 100 million yen ceiling; and,

iv.   the percentage, by value, of Euroyen issues underwritten by foreign firms and underwritten by foreign firms as lead or co-lead managers.

b.   the variety of maturity, interest rate, and other structures in the Euroyen market; and,

c.   the extent to which prior approval/notification requirements are effectively changed.

By the end of 1996, Japan had implemented almost all that it promised to do in the agreement.

Notes and Questions

1. Does the fact that Japan would sign the Financial Services Agreement of 1995 mean its financial system has radically altered since 1980? If not, would the agreed policies lead to basic change?

2. How would MOF policies affect the foreign and offshore operations of Japanese securities firms? Would their impact be significant? Compare the rules before and after 1994.

   a. What is the impact of restrictions on domestic securities markets? For example, how would the absence of a full range of long-term domestic bonds affect the pricing of credit in general?

   b. Does government policy help or hurt the competitive position of Japanese securities firms abroad? For example, recall the discussion of Article 65 and the Three Bureaus guidance in the first section of this Chapter. What was the purpose of this policy and how would it affect the securities companies abroad? What are the implications of its abolition? The government regulates commissions at home. What would be the effect of these rules on securities companies' operations abroad? What other competitive effects would you expect from the government's policies?

   c. On balance, does their Japanese base help or hinder Japanese securities companies competing in international markets? Consider regulatory and other factors.

   d. Rules of this sort often protect one group or another. Whom do these rules protect?

3. How do MOF's policies affect operations abroad by others than securities firms? What is the impact of rules governing investment flows out of Japan? Why should MOF control all this? Do these rules discriminate against foreign securities companies that want to bring Japanese investors to financial markets outside Japan?

4. How would the Administrative Procedures Law, described in Section I, affect the practices described by Shimada? For example, the APL makes it illegal for MOF to impose eligibility rules on residents notifying it of issue. Would you expect MOF's practice to stop?

5. One result of more restrictive regulations at home was that firms innovated in offshore markets instead. Japanese firms developed their skills in program trading or the use of derivatives, for example, offshore and refrained from applying those skills in Japan. Thus Nomura Securities Company, the largest in Japan, became a leader in program trading in New York, but left program trading in Japan to foreign firms. Indeed, a partial explanation for the long deep fall in the Tokyo stock

market was that program trading and other derivatives exacerbated the collapse. U.S. securities companies in Japan were condemned for their role. Given Japanese policy toward program trading and off-shore operations at home, what would be the rationale for allowing Nomura to take such an important role abroad?

D. THE STOCK MARKET CRISIS AND THE GOVERNMENT'S RESPONSE

The serious problems in Japan's stock market began in 1989. Japan was not alone at the time, but its problems persisted after other countries' markets recovered. The collapse of stock and property markets wiped out $6 trillion in value by 1994, according to one estimate. The period from 1987 to 1990 became known as the bubble economy. Economic activity and property values had soared because the Japanese government adopted an interest rate policy that would comply with its promise to the U.S. government to let the yen rise against the dollar in order to reduce Japan's trade surplus. People borrowed to invest in both productive and speculative assets. In late 1989, Japan's government tried to slow market excesses by raising interest rates. The market's tumble began. See J. Sterngold, "The $6 Trillion Hole in Japan's Pocket," New York Times, January 21, 1994.

Over the decade, the government proposed a range of solutions to the crisis, from macroeconomic policy to efforts to make the markets more efficient to getting government pension funds to invest, to changes in the law that might encourage more trading. Price keeping operations (PKO) and the moratorium on new equity underwriting for listed shares continued into 1995. Late in 1997, the government decided to reduce taxes, which lifted the Nikkei. As reports that speculators were short selling in anticipation that share prices would fall, the government restricted short sales effective October 1998. Investors could not sell borrowed stock if the price of the stock was falling. Hedge funds could no longer easily short the Japanese market, previously a popular pastime. J. Martinson, *Hedge Funds Unnerved by Short-Selling*, Financial Times, Oct. 23, 1998; G. Tett, *Anger over Japan's New Curbs on 'Short-Selling,'* Financial Times, Oct. 23, 1998. In 1998, the government proposed to create an investor protection fund that would help customers of bankrupt securities companies. Protection was needed because Japan, alone among industrial countries, did not require securities firms to segregate their accounts from those of their customers. All securities firms were to contribute to the $360 million fund, but foreign firms objected because they saw an unlimited liability. Also in 1998, a leading Japanese business group proposed that the government buy 10% of outstanding traded shares. A weak stimulus was considered in early 2001. The BOJ, having raised interest rates to 0.25% in August 2000, was forced to trim them to 0.15%, and consider a zero rate.

The Nikkei 225 average fluctuated between 14,000 and 24,000 after 1993, before falling back to the 1985 level in 2001. In late 1995, weakness in bank and insurance stock prices depressed the index. It rose to almost 21,000 in mid-1997, then fell to below 15,000, and rose again (as U.S. indices fell) to 24,000 in 1999, only to drop to 19,000 in mid-2000. In the mid-1990s, Japanese investors blamed foreign institutional investors who were pulling out their money. But changes were also taking place at home. Japanese institutional investors started to increase their relative investment abroad. The convoy system seemed to be falling apart. The practice had been for stronger firms to gear their performance to weaker firms. Share prices for companies in stronger sectors and stronger companies within a sector diverged from those of weaker sectors and firms. The market was pricing securities with closer attention to the performance and the prospects of the individual issuer.

The securities markets picked up in 1999, only to fall again in 2000. Propelling the growth were high tech and internet sectors, not industrial firms. Individual investors returned. Investment trusts became popular with rich investors, and Nomura reported that its fund was surpassing Fidelity's. It appeared that investment trust managers might be trading simply to increase their commissions, however. Mergers and acquisitions were more than double the 1998 level. Low interest rates revived the Samurai bond market, though not to its mid-1990s level. B. Spindle and R. Guth, *Finally, Japan's Market Is Way Up, Thanks To Banks and Internet,* Wall Street Journal, Dec. 29, 1999; N. Nakamae, *Individual Investors Double Trading Activity in Japanese Stock Markets*, Financial Times, Jan. 12, 2000; N. Nakamae, Investors put ¥500bn into Nomura Fund, Financial Times, Feb. 2, 2000; N. Nakamae, *Nomura Posts Profit as Brokers Bounce Back*, Financial Times, Oct. 23, 1999; N. Nakamae, *Brokers Set to Pay Price for Return to Old Habits*, Financial Times, Dec. 9, 1999; N. Nakamae, *Japan's Low Rates Revive Samurais*, Financial Times, Dec. 23, 1999; M. Nakamoto, *No Longer Taboo*, Financial Times, Aug. 25, 1999.

Foreigners helped fuel the rise in 1999. Domestic fears about the weak economy and political balance undermined the market in 2000. Demand from M&A activity slowed in 2000 to less than half the rate of 1999, suggesting that corporate restructuring had faltered. Possibly companies lacked a sense of urgency, but managers were also reluctant to fire employees. Sales of cross-held stocks created over-supply. According to one estimate, companies and banks sold ¥2 trillion ($17bn) of cross-shareholdings in the first quarter of 2001. B. Rahman, *Japan Moves to End 'Horror Show,'* Financial Times, Feb. 12, 2001; D. Ibison, M&A Activity in Japan Shows Sharp Decline, Financial Times, Oct. 20,

2000; K. Rafferty, *Some Signs of an Urge to Merge*, Euromoney, Oct. 2000 at 82.

In the 1990s, Japanese securities companies suffered from very weak performance and saw their ratings fall. The brief market recovery in 1999 buoyed the companies but its decline in 2000 left them still exposed to foreign securities firms. Compared to foreign securities firms, those in Japan reported very low returns on equity. Nomura, for example, had a 5% target ROE and only 0.15% ROE in 1993, compared to a 20% target for most US securities companies. During the 1990s, the financial condition of most Japanese firms progressively worsened. At home, low trading, big declines in fees from corporate bond underwriting, and competition from foreign securities firms all contributed. International operations did little to alleviate the weak domestic performance. Overseas, the overall share of Japanese securities companies in eurobond markets was estimated to be high, but their share in national markets such as the US market was low. By 1998, even Nomura found its overseas operations undermined its performance, since its US division lost money in mortgage-backed operations and its trading in Russian securities was caught in the Russian default that year. This was a serious problem for Nomura because its international revenues had grown from 33% of all revenues in 1996 to 50% in 1998. Estimates even in the mid-1990s were that capital at many of the firms was inadequate. The most severely hit were lower tier firms, which the MOF was trying to protect. Interest rates cuts helped the firms, but soon interest rates were so low that further cuts were not practical. See C. Smith, *Where Does the Japanese Securities Industry Go from Here?*, Institutional Investor, Dec. 1995, at 72; *4 Big Brokers in Japan Lift Profits From Lows of '94*, New York Times, Oct. 24, 1995; R. Seiner, *Winding Down the MOF*, Institutional Investor, June 1996 at 65; G. Tett, *Big Bang Hits Japanese Brokers*, Financial Times, May 16-17, 1998; G. Tett, *Nomura Set to Report Large Overseas Loss*, Financial Times, Oct. 20, 1998; and G. Tett, *Young, Gifted and Back to the Wall at Nomura Securities*, Financial Times, February 10, 1999.

Ties to gangsters became a serious issue for securities firms. In early 1997, Nomura Securities admitted having made illegal payments to gangsters for investment losses. MOF fined Nomura and prohibited certain lucrative activities as a penalty. The police arrested the former president, Ryuataro Sakamaki, after he admitted having met with one of the gangsters. Later Nomura was excluded from underwriting certain government bond issues, a penalty that was estimated to lower the firm's profits by about 15%.

The rapid rise in interest rates payable on JGBs in early 1999, as the government began massive new issues, prompted a new attack on market transparency. Large investors traded the bonds in secret at non-market prices to avoid revealing losses. The investor would sell JGBs at above market rates and accept unlisted bonds (eg., issued by local governments) at low prices. The sellers included tax exempt agencies like the postal savings system. In December, the Japan Securities Dealers Association had ended a rule that prohibited transactions at prices 2% or more off the market price. Nomura estimated 5% off all transactions. G. Tett and N. Nakamae, *Secret Japan Bond Deals Fuel Fears Over Losses,* Financial Times, Feb. 10, 1999.

The November 1997 collapse of Yamaichi Securities Company, then the smallest of the Big Four, was the most spectacular of several collapses. As the oldest Japanese security company, it was in its 100th year. Its employees made up 10% of the industry workforce. When it failed, Yamaichi had nominal capital of ¥516 ($4 billion) and liabilities of ¥3.5 trillion ($27.1 billion), and it managed ¥23 trillion in trust funds. An initial review after it closed suggested that its assets were ¥3.6 trillion ($27.9 billion), but this amount was not final. The firm's problems had been growing since the early 1990s. Yamaichi was revealed to have hidden ¥260 billion ($2 billion) in losses off its books beginning in 1991, a practice known as *tobashi*. Its operating profit per employee were 1.6% of those at Nomura. Yamaichi's chairman, until he resigned in August 1997, was indicted for paying off a corporate blackmailer (*sokayia*). Yamaichi's chairman was also implicated in complex schemes to reimburse some corporate clients for their trading losses, which was no longer legal. Fuji Bank, a member of the keiretsu that included Yamaichi, had refused to lend since December 1996 because it was denied access to Yamaichi's books. By mid-1997, creditors and depositors knew Yamaichi was in trouble. As they declined to roll over large short term loans or withdrew their deposits, Yamaichi became illiquid. Fuji refused to bail out the securities company just before the collapse. When Yamaichi was declared bankrupt in June 1999, the Bank of Japan refused to bear the loss on the ¥489 billion ($4 billion) loan BOJ had made to the securities company at the request of the government. It demanded that the finance ministry repay BOJ. See G. Tett, *The Day Japan Let a Flagship Go Under*, Financial Times, January 14, 1998; A. Horvat, *And Then There Were Three*, Euromoney, January 1998 at 58; and G. Tett, *Bankrupt Yamaichi Provokes Debt Dispute*, Financial Times, June 3, 1999.

Yamaichi's collapse was the largest business failure in Japan. Several other smaller securities firms soon followed it into the void. BOJ supplied excess liquidity amounting to ¥3.7 trillion, then loaned directly to banks, in order to keep the financial system afloat.

MOF knew since at least 1991 that Yamaichi hid losses, according to the testimony of a former MOF regulator before the Diet's committee of inquiry. The firm first shifted the losses first to clients' accounts, then its own offshore affiliates. Despite its knowledge, MOF was in no position to bail out Yamaichi. It just closed Hokkaido Takushoku Bank, the tenth largest bank, and Sanyo Securities, the seventh largest securities firm.

But the problem for MOF was even more serious. Former senior MOF employees were being prosecuted for accepting bribes in the form of lavish entertainment. Indeed, several committed suicide rather than face trial. MOF was politically discredited. See N. Shirouzu, *Ex-Regulator Knew of Losses At Yamaichi*, Wall Street Journal, February 5, 1998; S. WuDunn, *Finance Scandal in Japan Takes a Nasty Turn,* New York Times, February 20, 1998.

Two new exchanges for small cap companies opened, but both suffered from illiquidity and volatility. In December 1999, TSE launched Mothers, an exchange for venture companies, but trading was very weak. Several scandals led TSE to tighten listing rules for that market. In June 2000, NASDAQ and Softbank Corp. launched NASDAQ-Japan, an electronic stock trading market mainly for small-cap issues. Softbank is a Japanese firm that invests in internet companies. Investors in Japan get online data about issuers and prices, in Japanese, and execute trades online. Initial trading hours are 9-11am and 12:30-3:10pm, but would be round the clock within a year. The JSDA's JASDAQ, which opened in 1991, remains small and illiquid. JSDA announced that it would ally with NASDAQ to help Japanese investors invest abroad. A. Nusbaum, *Electronic Trading to Open Up the World to Japan's Investors,* Financial Times, June 16, 1999; N. Nakamae, *US and Japanese Securities Bodies to Link*, Aug. 26, 1999; Associated Press, *Japan Nasdaq To Start in June*, Mar. 15, 2000; A. Harney, *Tokyo Market Tightens its Listing Rules*, Financial Times, Nov. 10, 2000.

On the horizon were even more serious problems for Japan's securities markets. Underfunded corporate pension plans threatened the financial well being of the companies. In 1997, for example, 27 traded companies reported funding shortfalls equal to 19% of their equity. They reported because their shares were also traded on US exchanges. People feared the problem was much more widespread. Participants in the Harvard symposium in mid-1999 agreed that public as well as private pension systems were considerably underfunded. Moreover, many Japanese employees and self-employed workers were not participating in mandatory social pension schemes. The view was that good government policies implemented quickly could solve these problems, given the vast Japanese savings. But as Japan's population aged, pension claims would rise and the shortfalls would become acute. Life insurance companies posed a different problem. Their anticipated switch from mutual to public ownership would increase listed shares, but the companies themselves seemed to be very weak financially, even on the point of bankruptcy. They too needed to be restructured. A major problem was that early policies guaranteed owners returns at rates that exceeded yields on the insurers' portfolios now. The industry's compensation fund, when it finally reached its full size in 2008, would be smaller than the losses sustained by one medium sized insurer that regulators suspended in 1999.

See J. Lowenstein, *Life, But Not As We Know It,* Euromoney (Oct. 1998) at 53; C. Smith, *From Weakness to Weakness*, Institutional Investor (Nov. 1998) at 101; Passing the Buck, The Economist Dec. 4, 1999.

With elections due in July 2001, in March the LDP proposed an emergency package to stop the sliding stock market and boost the real estate market. The package would do so primarily by stimulating retail investment through tax and other means. It proposed to reduce taxes on dividends (particularly those paid to individuals), long term capital gains, property purchases, and inherited stocks. It also prepared for a private fund to buy shares without a government guarantee, reducing the supply of cross-held shares banks are selling to fund write-offs of NPLs. The government would ask banks to dispose of NPLs faster and ask BOJ to ease monetary policy, set a target for inflation ("price stability"), and buy JGBs. Not used were several tools, including economic or market stimulus. The package did not propose extra government spending to prop the banks, the construction industry, or the stock market (such as having the government buy stock itself or guarantee a fund that would buy stock), unlike the past. Observers said the government was admitting, despite divisions in the LDP, the failure of a decade of stimulus totaling ¥128 trillion ($1,075bn). The government proposed no specific measures to encourage or force banks to dispose of their NPLs faster. It did not amend the law to encourage companies to buy back their shares (concerns existed that this would encourage insider trading). To many observers, the measures fell short of promised drastic change, but some thought that the tax changes could bring householders into equity markets. In any event, before the proposals took effect, they would have to be approved by the three-party coalition, the tax commission, and Parliament. G. Tett, *Business Chiefs Urge Japan to Buy Up to 10% of Stock Market*, Financial Times, Dec. 9, 1998; G. Tett, *Foreign Brokers Threaten to Boycott Protection Fund*, Financial Times, Oct. 21, 1998; M. Tanikawa, *Stocks in Japan at 15-Year Low*, New York Times, March 2, 2001; D. Ibison and C. Swann, *Japan Plans Package to Spur Growth*, Financial ties, March 3/4, 2001; D. Ibison and B. Rahman, *Japan's Politicians at Odds Over Market Support Measures,* Financial Times, Jan. 18, 2001; Reuters, *Japan Proposes Emergency Steps to Try to Stop Plunge in Stocks,* New York Times, Mar. 10, 2000; D. Ibison, *Japanese Package Falls Short*, Financial Times, Mar. 9, 2001; B. Rahman, *Japan Unveils Half-hearted Economic Package*, Financial Times, Mar. 9, 2001.

The actions of the Koizumi government, which took office after the elections, are described at the end of the next section.

Notes and Questions

1. What do the government's proposals and actions reveal about the extent to which the special features of Japan's securities markets were changing?

2.   Compare the relative market share and performance of U.S. securities firms in Japan and Japanese firms in the U.S.A. How have U.S. securities firms performed in Japan? Compare the relative market shares of banks and securities companies in the U.S. and Japan. What does it tell you?

3.   Compare the relative weight given competition and prudential issues by government policy in Japan and the U.S. Is the weight the same for banking and securities markets? What explains the differences?

4.   How well does the LDP proposal address the problems in Japan's securities markets? What more is needed?

E.   THE BIG BANG AND JAPAN'S SECURITIES MARKETS

"This isn't a gimmick. ... This is the last opportunity to revitalize the Tokyo market," said a senior official of MOF just after the Prime Minister's announcement of the Big Bang. See J. Sapsford, *Japan Proposes Financial Market Reform*, Wall Street Journal, November 12, 1996.

The elements of the Big Bang designed for the securities markets also fell under the rubric of free, fair, and global. They were announced by the government, then embellished through proposals by the Securities and Exchange Council and the Financial System Research Council in June 1997. In addition to those described for banking, the elements included:

- ending fixed commissions and deregulating other fees (starting in April 1998 for large issues and freeing completely within the following twelve months);

- ending product restrictions;

- liberalizing asset management regulation (eg., register rather than license suppliers and disclose better);

- easier entry and exit, including by non-securities firms as discount brokers;

- ending restrictions on a variety of instruments (eg., asset-backed securities or stock options), exchange, and OTC operations;

- entry of banks, through subsidiaries;

- the own-risk principle;

- ending government price-keeping operations, which propped up prices by asking state-owned enterprises and private firms to buy shares in down markets;

- permitting electronically-processed data filing and disclosure;

- thorough and substantial disclosure;

- transparent regulation;

- active punishment for violation of rules;
- a legal system to support financial innovation, including derivatives;
- ending the 20% ceiling on pension fund investments in equities and requiring them to disclose the market values of their positions;
- promoting mutual funds by, for example, allowing banks and others to distribute them and letting mutual funds as well as pension funds to invest in unlisted securities;
- ending the Foreign Exchange Law in April 1998, replacing the need for permission with simplified reporting after the fact, and allowing securities firms and others to do foreign exchange business, investors to order from foreign securities firms directly, and individuals and corporations to open bank accounts and hold assets abroad, and generally ending constraints on domestic and cross-border FX operations;
- harmonizing Japanese accounting with international standards; and
- reviewing, in order to rationalize, all tax rules for fairness, neutrality, and simplicity, which includes ending the tax on securities transactions, double taxation of dividends, and withholding taxes on JGBs and other public sector bonds.

The government started to implement parts of the Big Bang quickly. Almost immediately, securities houses were allowed to offer customers much more flexible cash management accounts. Unlisted and unregistered equities could be traded and held by investment trusts. The limits on the business of banks' securities subsidiaries were lifted. The securities' firms trust bank subsidiaries could provide all but pension trusts. Exemptions from the Anti-Monopoly Law were revoked for many types of cartels. Trading of stock options in individual companies was allowed on the TSE and OSE and began in July 1997. See Analytica Japan, *Japan's Big Bang*, December 12, 1997 at 30 as the source for this and the next three paragraphs.

In 1998, the government passed more implementing legislation. It clarified banks' powers to provide equity based derivatives. Fixed commissions were ended on transactions over ¥50 million ($435,000) and brokers began to offer clients discounts up to 50%. Notice of securitization to individual debtors was to be replaced by public notice, making securitization much easier. The ¥10 million minimum investment for commodity futures was abolished. Markets responded. New issues in the corporate bond market were 56% more in 1997 than 1996. See G. Tett, *Japan's Brokers Hint At Price War After Big Bang*, Financial Times,

March 27, 1998; G. Tett, Japanese *Corporate Bonds Boom as Banks Cut Lending*, Financial Times, June 1, 1998.

In 1999, securities firms were allowed to engage in most activities by simply registering with MOF, whose discretion in granting a license was be limited to high risk activities like OTC derivative trading. All restrictions on issuance of corporate bonds and commercial paper by non-bank financial institutions ended. Securities firms could offer asset management services and banks could sell OTC investment trust funds. Mutual funds, rather than simply contractual investment trusts, could be offered and offers could be private as well as public. Loopholes making consolidated accounting difficult were closed. Financial holding companies were encouraged. Withholding tax ended for payments to foreign holders of JGBs. Fixed commission ended for any commissions on securities transactions under ¥50 million on October 1, 1999. Securities firms and trust banks could compete through subsidiaries. Banks could issue straight bonds. Insurance firms could carry on banking and securities businesses and securities firms and banks could provide insurance.

To promote securities markets in late 2000, however, the government tried to modify tax law. The finance ministry wanted to offer tax breaks to foreign investors in JGBs. The government delayed reforming the capital gains tax. The proposal was to replace the flat fee on any sale, regardless of its profitability, with a rate on the gain. G. Tett, *Japan to Delay Tax Reform After Stocks Fall*, Financial Times, Oct. 19, 2000.

In the future, a financial services act would consolidate the laws regulating insurers, banks, and securities companies. No specific deadline was set for when securities had to be marked to market, but the need to do so was recognized. Indeed, mark-to-market accounting had applied to banks' and securities firms' trading of derivatives since 1996. See M. Simada, *New Accounting and Disclosure Requirements for Derivative Transactions*, Butterworths Journal of Banking and Financial Law, September 1997, at 392.

Financial firms responded. A small Japanese securities firm in the OTC market (and therefore not subject to rules as strict as those governing exchange operations) quickly halved its commission fees. The exchanges eased their listing requirements and lengthened their trading hours for large lots. Securities firms started to restructure. Nikko, the third largest, decentralized its international activities to London, relying more on non-Japanese staff. It expected to reduce its equity business in Japan. Nomura appointed a young president who had spent most of his career in the U.S. and Europe. Securities firms and banks started to cooperate. Sumitomo Bank and Daiwa Securities decided to form a joint venture for wholesale securities, derivatives, and asset management. Other cooperative ventures included Nomura and IBJ, and Nikko Securities and Salomon Smith Barney. Japanese insurers decided to enter the securities markets as well. See G. Tett, *Nikko Shake-Up Will*

Transfer Global Operations to London, Financial Times, October 8, 1997; P. Abrahams and T. Corrigan, *Sumitomo and Daiwa Seek Joint Venture Partners*, Financial Times, August 29, 1998; and P. Abrahams, *Daiwa and Sumitomo Follow Rivals' Lead*, Financial Times, Jul. 29, 1998; G. Tett, *Japanese Insurer Plans Move Into Securities*, Financial Times, Mar. 12, 1998.

Old relationships changed. Shareholders began to sue managers. After the Sumitomo Corporation revealed substantial losses in 1996 from investments in copper, shareholders sued the company. Shareholders of Nomura sued its former executives for their relations with the gangsters. Keiretsu relationships loosened. The keiretsu became weakened by mergers and foreign investors acquiring Japanese firms. Some firms turned to foreign financial advisors for help with mergers that would undermine keiretsu ties. Mergers and acquisitions in Japan boomed, rising from 600 in 1996 to 1,600 in 2000. Nomura considered selling its holdings in some big Japanese companies. Keiretsu firms lost their traditional advantage in bond markets. As recently as 1997, yields on their bonds were substantially less than those on bonds issued by non-keiretsu members. By mid-1999, the situation had reversed. Yields on keiretsu bonds substantially exceeded those of non-keiretsu. Keiretsu membership no longer lowered risk. The Japan Fair Trade Commission began a study of restrictions on cross-shareholding, including the 5% limit on banks' ownership of non-financial firms and the treatment of foreign firms. The Justice Ministry had already begun to review the commercial code to help smaller high tech start-ups. G. Tett, *Nomura Ponders Sale of Japanese Equity Stakes*, Financial Times, February 3, 1999; G. Tett, Western Institutions Have Their Eyes On Rich Pickings, Financial Times, Dec. 17, 1999; F. Packer, *Credit Risk in Japan's Corporate Bond Market*, Federal Reserve Bank of New York, 5 Current Issues in Economics and Finance (Nov. 1999); *Restrictions on Share Ownership to be Reviewed, Possibly Loosened,* The Bureau of National Affairs 10, Feb. 2001; *Justice Ministry Begins Revision of 50-Year Old Commercial Code,* World Securities Law Report 3, Oct. 2000; C. Cockerill, *Foreign Banks Seize Their Chance*, Euromoney, Mar. 2001, at 66.

Not all the old habits disappeared, however. In mid-1999, the Japanese Securities Dealers' Association penalized 5 securities firms for price adjustment. These trades at non-market prices allowed investors to conceal trading losses when government bond prices fell. JSDA also admonished 18 other securities firms. N. Nakamae, *Japanese Securities Houses Reprimanded*, Financial Times, July 1, 1999. Only in 2000 did the government try to dismantle techniques that foreign and domestic investors used to avoid withholding tax on government bonds. The Bank of Japan registers government bonds and withholds tax due from foreigners. Although nominees are not permitted by law in Japan, Japanese brokers and dealers, who are exempt from withholding tax, held many foreign investors' bonds as the registered owner. The BOJ let the Japanese firms do this only during one three-month payment period, but it allowed the brokers to roll over the investment by selling the foreigners' bonds after the quarterly cycle and using the payment to acquire bonds that, because they were new, would be exempt, briefly, from withholding tax. Domestic investors went a step further, trading hand written receipts to avoid registration and tax. In 2000, the finance ministry made serious efforts to stop the charades, provoking threats that foreign investors would withdraw. The FSA disciplined Nomura for breaking the law, by banning its asset management unit from overseas investment advice for two months, the most severe penalty imposed by FSA on a Japanese broker. N. Nakamae, *Japan Warned that Tax Law May Hit Government Bonds*, Financial Times, June 2000; D. Ibison, *Regulator Penalises Nomura*, Financial Times, December 29, 2000.

Foreign firms took a new look at Japan's financial markets. Several cut their fees. Foreign fund managers began to eye the $2 trillion pension fund market. Foreign asset managers vastly increased their share of Japanese securities from under 2% in 1994 to 13% in 1999, only to see it drop to 9% in 2000 as Japanese banks offered mutual funds and reclaimed market share. Merrill Lynch opened retail offices in Japan, using ex-employees of Yamaichi, having rejected an offer to buy a majority stake in the company before it failed. Merrill forecast that it would take 3 years for the new operations to turn a profit. Alliances included Morgan Stanley and Sanwa Bank, in retail asset management, and Lazard with Daiwa for cross-border mergers and acquisitions. Morgan Stanley raised $2bn to $3bn for a fund to invest in real estate globally, much in Japan, and had invested about $3 billion in problem loans over the past few years. Fidelity was authorized to act as a broker and sell mutual funds through Japanese banks. American Express applied for a broker's license. Other foreign investment advisers expanded their activities. The U.S. financial conglomerate Citigroup invested $1.6 billion to acquire 25% of Japan's third largest broker, Nikko Securities Company, announced in June 1998. Nikko created a joint venture with Salomon Smith Barney, a subsidiary of Citigroup. One article reported eight leading banks, funds, and financial groups from four foreign countries teaming up with leading Japanese financial banks, brokers, and insurance companies that would sell securities in Japan. Finally, foreign insurers expanded, through joint ventures or by acquiring staff of defunct Japanese firms like Yamaichi. These foreign firms were seen as a major competitive threat to the leading Japanese financial firms. See R. Radin, *Big Bangs and Whimpers: The Future of Japan's Administrative State*, Feb. 14, 1997 ("Radin"); P. Truell, *Travelers Deal With Nikko Set for Today,* New York Times, June 1, 1998; S. WuDunn, *Japan Braces for Arrival of Big Bang*, New York Times, June 4, 1998; C. Smith, *Merrill Tackles Japan -- With Difficulty*, Institutional Investor (Jan. 1999) at 120; J. Authers, *AmexCo Aims for Japanese Brokerage Arm,* Financial Times, Nov. 19, 1998; G.

Tett, *Morgan Stanley Links Up With Japan's Sanwa Bank*, Financial Times, Aug. 25, 1999; A. Hill, *Lazard In Link With Daiwa To Advise Japanese*, Financial Times, Nov. 29, 1999; T. Ewing and B. Spindle, *Nasdaq Plans Stock Market Based in Japan*, Wall Street Journal, June 15, 1999; C. Smith, *Can the Upstarts Topple the Giants?*, Institutional Investor, Sep. 1999, at 112; N. Nakamae, P. Abrahams, and G. Tett, *Citicorp, Nikko Plan Further Deals*, Financial Times, Mar. 27, 2000; G. Tett, *Japan's Banks Share of Mutual Funds Signals Domestic Rebound*, Financial Times, Sep. 22, 2000.

The U.S. government welcomed the Big Bang. A senior official in the Treasury urged that it be implemented quickly so that Japan's economy could grow faster. Indeed, in March 1997, LDP leaders wanted to complete the Big Bang by 1998, three years early. Nevertheless, in March 1998, some LDP ministers suggested that the government should draw on funds in the postal savings system to support prices in the stock market, raising questions about the political commitment to Big Bang. See G. Tett and B. Hutton, *Politicians' Intervention Call Rallies Tokyo Market*, Financial Times, March 3, 1998. The government prepared a $128 billion stimulus program for the economy.

Opinions about the likely effect of Big Bang diverged. Some observers of Japan saw it as more of the same. For example, "Japanese bureaucrats and politicians, including the elite at the Ministry of Finance, continue to be in deep denial. They do not comprehend the extent of reforms necessary to restore the nation to economic health." See E. Lincoln, *Japan's Financial Mess*, 77 Foreign Affairs no. 3 (May/June 1998) at 58. He asserted that Japan has not rejected its old habits. The Bank of Japan largely financed Yamaichi Securities for 6 months before it failed and arranged for two banks to acquire the operations of Hokkaido Takushoku Bank. Government money supports weak banks in several ways. The government will buy preferred shares and subordinated bonds to recapitalize them. Government-controlled postal savings and pension funds are investing in weak banks. As to the reforms of Big Bang, Lincoln did not believe that Japanese companies would be prepared to disclose information needed for a market-oriented financial system like that of the US to work in Japan.

Other foreign observers saw Big Bang as a sea change for the financial system of Japan, while recognizing that even more change would be needed. In a talk given at the Japanese Law Research Conference, April 4-5, 1998, Robin Radin said

> Less than one and a half years following its launch, and less than nine months since any detailed plan for its implementation was issued, the Big Bang has come to be associated with dramatic changes in the financial marketplace, disorder and competitive upheaval in all financial service sectors, panic and confusion in governmental ranks,

and a reign of prosecutorial terror targeting the pillars of the old financial establishment.

After citing many examples of fundamentally new behavior, he continued:

Complementing these manifestations of unprecedented change in the competitive and institutional environment of finance, there is evidence of a radical shift in the prevailing standards of financial business and regulatory behavior. . . . [Among many examples,] the public has been treated to the shocking spectacle of phalanxes of prosecutors marching en masse into the Ministry of Finance and the Bank of Japan to ransack the offices of officials for evidence of criminal activity. . . .

In Radin's view, the Big Bang "defies the conventional assumptions regarding Japanese bureaucratic behavior." He continued

First, the plan is uniquely comprehensive, targeting the rebuilding of an entire institutional infrastructure affecting not only financial regulation but taxation, clearing and settlement systems, civil procedure, judicial administration, alternative dispute resolution, and corporate governance. . . . Second, rather than attempting to redefine the boundaries of competition among domestic players, the plan is affirmatively driven by the goal of creating a market whose functions meet or exceed international competitive standards. . . . Third, the plan and its implementation has been driven by the personal leadership of individual MOF officials . . . acting in collaboration with the Hashimoto administration, not some anonymous group planning process. Fourth, and most exceptionally, the plan contemplates a reduction in the scope of function and power of the bureaus that have worked hardest to bring about its implementation. . . .

More would be needed, according to Radin and others, for the Big Bang to succeed in the long run. For example, a vigorous bond market required the end of certain withholding taxes. Consumers and investors needed access to efficient civil dispute resolution mechanisms and enough judges and lawyers to support them. Investors needed a better system of corporate governance. Companies should shift to internal management that emphasized shareholder value, and profitability in particular, consolidating all entities in a group.

In early 2002, Japan's capital markets looked weak. The Nikkei Average was around 10,000. Japanese investors were buying foreign bonds in massive amounts. Foreign investors held only a small portion of shares outstanding. International rating agencies were lowering their ratings the government's yen bonds. Foreign listings continued to drop. Many foreign securities companies were scaling back. Merrill Lynch closed 75% of its retail offices, Morgan Stanley closed all, and Charles Schwab, a leading U.S. discount broker, closed a venture. *Japanese Investors Flock to Purchase Foreign Bonds*, Financial Times, Oct. 8. 2001; K. Belson, *Moody's Lowers Debt Rating On Government Credit in Yen,*

New York Times, Dec. 5, 2001; J. Brooke, *Bad News Keeps Coming for Japanese Economy*, New York Times, Jan. 10, 2002; K. Belson, *Morgan Stanley Ends Small-Investor Push in Japan*, New York Times, Nov. 14, 2001; K. Belson, Charles Schwab Will Close Its Online Venture in Japan, New York Times, Dec. 8, 2001.

A major problem, beyond the recession, was that investors did not trust the stock market. Retail investors believed the post-bubble years showed the market was rigged against them. Loopholes in the disclosure laws for consolidated reporting still let firms conceal losses, supported by the FSA. In January 2000 the government had decided not to require companies to consolidate their tax accounting as planned in 2001. The market for corporate control had not developed; even owners who acquired a large portion of a company's stock in the public markets found they had bought no voice in its decisions. The government was reported to be intervening in the stock market to prevent share prices from falling so low that banks would become obviously insolvent. M. Toda, *Recommendation for the Revitalization of Japanese Corporations*, May 1999; G. Tett, *Japan Postpones Company Tax Reform*, Financial Times, Jan. 13, 2000; *Final Report*, Symposium on Building the Financial System of the 21st Century: An Agenda for Japan & the United States, 2001; B. Rahman and K. Hijono, *Japan Suspected of Stock Market Intervention, Financial Times*, Feb. 22, 2002.

Beyond the immediate concerns, however, was a bigger one. The Japanese economy appeared to be segmented. On one side was a viable export sector that would profit from the declining yen and seemed to be helping the economy start to grow again. On the other hand, Japan had a very weak domestic sector that was not recovering. Many agreed that Japan needed to shift from a financial system based on banks to one based on capital markets. But asset prices continued to fall. Perhaps it was not possible to shift to capital markets while asset prices declined. See D. Pilling, *Japan Survey Tells Tale of Two Economies*, Financial Times, Apr. 2, 2002; R. Guth, M. Phillips, C. Hutzler, *As the Yen Keeps Dropping, A New View of Japan Emerges*, Wall Street Journal, Apr. 24, 2002.

Notes and Questions

1. Evaluate the elements of the Big Bang. If most or all are achieved roughly within the Prime Minister's schedule, how fundamental would the changes be to the financial system? What would be the effect on cross-border flows of funds, securities, and operations of financial institutions?

2. How likely is the Big Bang to succeed? Do you find the Lincoln or Radin analysis more compelling?

3. If the Big Bang succeeds (at least by creating a free, fair, and global system), how would the new financial system look to Japanese and foreign banks and securities firms, retail Japanese investors, the U.S.

government, and Singapore? What indicators would you look for, two years after the Big Bang was announced, to show it was on track?

4. Is the Big Bang likely to be just another example of the convergence of national financial systems? What special features might a free, fair, and global system have in Japan?

Links To Other Chapters

Japan's government and financial institutions are very important players in international finance. They and many of the issues raised in this Chapter surface throughout this book.

In foreign exchange markets, the government's role extends beyond the policies described in this Chapter. In the 1980s, the US and Japanese governments tried to raise the Yen/$ exchange rate and the Bank of Japan tried to offset the deflationary effects by easing the money supply with lower interest rates. This added to liquidity that fueled the bubble. See Chapter 6.

Japanese policies affect the capital adequacy of its financial institutions (see Chapter 4), which in turn affect their performance in international markets and the growth of those markets. The bailout policy in Japan appears to affect its banks' need for capital profoundly, even after the Basel Accord. This policy, and the resulting low capital ratios in the late 1970s and early 1980s encouraged Japanese banks to lend substantially to developing countries through syndicated eurocredits (Chapter 8).

The Japanese and U.S. approaches to financial policy contrast sharply. See Chapters 2 and 3.

Japan's approach to innovation has a significant effect on the growth of international financial markets. It affected the eurobond market's performance (Chapter 12), securitization (Chapter 13), and the futures and options markets (Chapter 16).

The offshore markets offer a way for Japanese financial institutions to escape from stringent domestic regulation. But it is not clear the escape is very far. Japanese influence over its firms' activities in markets outside Japan seems broader than the U.S. government's; see its policy toward Yen eurobonds. Japanese policy is possibly more effective than the U.S. government's; see the reading on asset freezes (Chapter 11).

The performance of Japan's financial system affects its banks and securities companies in international markets. In the mid–1980s, they seemed omnipresent. In the 1990s, they withdrew. One sees their limited role in the Telmex global ADR offering (Chapter 20).

PART II

INSTRUMENTS AND OFFSHORE MARKETS

Part II deals with instruments and offshore markets. These subjects are linked because many of the instruments of interest are offered offshore. In offshore markets, the transactors, as well as the currencies transacted in, are usually foreign to the local market. For example, London and Hong Kong are centers for transactions in dollars between many non-British or non-Hong Kong institutions. These markets exist largely because of restrictions in domestic markets, as well as time zone and expertise advantages in offshore markets such as London. A major question in this part is whether the London market will continue to flourish given the advent of EMU and the relaxation of domestic restrictions.

This part begins with the traditional "euromarkets" for deposits and loans (Chapters 9 and 11), and bonds (Chapter 12). We also discuss in Chapter 12 how global securities, involving coordinated use of several major domestic markets, may displace offshore markets.

Newer types of financial instruments are offered in both domestic and offshore markets, such as securitized debt (Chapter 13) and derivatives. The materials on derivatives focus on futures and options traded on exchanges around the world (Chapter 16), and swaps which are entered into off exchanges, largely in offshore markets (Chapter 17). Derivatives have had tremendous growth in recent years, and the Barings crisis shows why regulation of instruments traded on exchanges is important.

For equity worldwide, the primary focus is on competition for listings among the world's stock exchanges (Chapter 14). This chapter poses the question as to whether there is convergence in trading systems and whether this augurs in an era of consolidation of the world's stock exchanges. The market for offshore mutual funds is profoundly segmented as between the United States and the rest of the world (Chapter 18). U.S. investors do not invest in foreign funds and foreigners do not invest in U.S. funds.

CHAPTER NINE

EURODOLLAR DEPOSITS AND SYNDICATED LOANS

Mystery shrouds the origins of the eurocurrency markets, the major part of the offshore markets. One story, set in the period immediately after World War II, has Soviet firms holding dollars propose to banks based outside the U.S. that they hold the dollars as deposits to avoid the risk that the U.S. might confiscate the funds.

For over twenty-five years, the euromarkets have played a significant part in international finance. This Chapter begins with an explanation of what a eurodollar is, given when the market's role first became apparent. For recent information about the interbank market that makes up much of the eurocurrency market, see the article in the first chapter.

We then turn to the loan syndication market. It is a market for medium-term loans by groups of banks who fund their loans from deposits in the eurocurrency market. This is the first opportunity to examine the key elements of a sample contract.

A. INTRODUCTION TO THE EUROCURRENCY MARKET

M. FRIEDMAN, THE EURO–DOLLAR MARKET: SOME FIRST PRINCIPLES
The Morgan Guaranty Survey, Oct. 1969, at 4-14.

The Euro-dollar market is the latest example of the mystifying quality of money creation to even the most sophisticated bankers, let alone other businessmen. Recently, I heard a high official of an international financial organization discuss the Euro-dollar market before a collection of high-powered international bankers. He estimated that Euro-dollar deposits totaled some $30 billion. He was then asked: "What is the source of these deposits?" His answer was: partly, U.S. balance-of-payments deficits; partly, dollar reserves of non-U.S. central banks; partly, the proceeds from the sale of Euro-dollar bonds.

This answer is almost complete nonsense. Balance-of-payments deficits do provide foreigners with claims on U.S. dollars. But there is nothing to assure that such claims will be held in the form of Euro-dollars. In any event, U.S. deficits, worldwide, have totaled less than $9 billion for the past five years, on a liquidity basis. Dollar holdings of non-U.S. central banks have fallen during the period of rapid rise in Euro-dollar deposits but by less than $5 billion. The dollars paid for Euro-bonds had themselves to come from somewhere and do not constitute an independent source. No matter how you try, you cannot get $30 billion from these sources. The answer given is precisely parallel to saying that the source of the $400 billion of deposits in U.S. banks (or for that matter the much larger total of all outstanding short-term claims) is the $60 billion of Federal Reserve credit outstanding.

The correct answer for both Euro-dollars and liabilities of U.S. banks is that their major source is a bookkeeper's pen.[1] The purpose of this article is to explain this statement. The purpose is purely expository. I shall restrict myself essentially to principle and shall not attempt either an empirical evaluation of the Euro-dollar market or a normative judgment of its desirability.

Another striking example of the confusion about Euro-dollars is the discussion, in even the most sophisticated financial papers, of the use of the Euro-dollar market by U.S. commercial banks "to evade tight money," as it is generally phrased. U.S. banks, one reads in a leading financial paper, "have been willing to pay extremely high interest rates ... to borrow back huge sums of U.S. dollars that have piled up abroad." The image conveyed is that of piles of dollar bills being bundled up and shipped across the ocean on planes and ships—the way New York literally did drain gold from Europe in the bad—or good—old days at times of financial panic. Yet, the more dollars U.S. banks "borrow back" the more Euro-dollar deposits go up! How come? The answer is that it is purely figurative language to speak of "piled up" dollars being "borrowed back." Again, the bookkeeper's pen is at work.

What are Euro-dollars?

Just what are Euro-dollars? They are deposit liabilities, denominated in dollars, of banks outside the United States. Engaged in Euro-dollar business, for example, are foreign commercial banks such as the Bank of London and South America, Ltd., merchant banks such as Morgan Grenfell and Co., Ltd., and many of the foreign branches of U.S. commercial banks. Funds placed with these institutions may be owned by anyone—U.S. or foreign residents or citizens, individuals or corporations or governments. Euro-dollars

---

[1] The similarity between credit creation in the U.S. fractional reserve banking system and in the Euro-dollar market has of course often been noted.

have two basic characteristics: first, they are short-term obligations to pay dollars; second, they are obligations of banking offices located outside the U.S. In principle, there is no hard and fast line between Euro-dollars and other dollar-denominated claims on non-U.S. institutions—just as there is none between claims in the U.S. that we call "money" and other short-term claims. The precise line drawn in practice depends on the exact interpretation given to "short-term" and to "banks." Nothing essential in this article is affected by the precise point at which the line is drawn.

A homely parallel to Euro-dollars is to be found in the dollar deposit liabilities of bank offices located in the city of Chicago—which could similarly be called "Chicago dollars." Like Euro-dollars, "Chicago dollars" consist of obligations to pay dollars by a collection of banking offices located in a particular geographic area. Again, like Euro-dollars, they may be owned by anyone—residents or nonresidents of the geographic area in question.

The location of the banks is important primarily because it affects the regulations under which the banks operate and hence the way that they can do business. Those Chicago banks that are members of the Federal Reserve System must comply with the System's requirements about reserves, maximum interest rates payable on deposits, and so on; and in addition, of course, with the requirements of the Comptroller of the Currency if they are national banks, and of the Illinois State Banking Commission if they are state banks.

Euro-dollar banks are subject to the regulations of the relevant banking authorities in the country in which they operate. In practice, however, such banks have been subject neither to required reserves on Euro-dollar deposits nor to maximum ceilings on the rates of interest they are permitted to pay on such deposits.

Regulation and Euro-dollars

The difference in regulation has played a key role in the development of the Euro-dollar market. No doubt there were minor precursors, but the initial substantial Euro-dollar deposits in the post-World War II period originated with the Russians, who wanted dollar balances but recalled that their dollar holdings in the U.S. had been impounded by the Alien Property Custodian in World War II. Hence they wanted dollar claims not subject to U.S. governmental control.

The most important regulation that has stimulated the development of the Euro-dollar market has been Regulation Q, under which the Federal Reserve has fixed maximum interest rates that member banks could pay on time deposits. Whenever these ceilings become effective, Euro-dollar deposits, paying a higher interest rate, became more attractive than U.S. deposits, and the Euro-dollar market expanded. U.S. banks then borrowed from the Euro-dollar market to replace the withdrawn time deposits.

A third major force has been the direct and indirect exchange controls imposed by the U.S. for "balance-of-payments" purposes the interest-equalization tax, the "voluntary" controls on bank lending abroad and on foreign investment, and, finally, the compulsory controls instituted by President Johnson in January 1968. Without Regulation Q and the exchange controls—all of which, in my opinion, are both unnecessary and undesirable—the Euro-dollar market, though it might still have existed, would not have reached anything like its present dimensions.

Fractional reserves

Euro-dollar deposits like "Chicago deposits" are in principle obligations to pay literal dollars—i.e., currency (or coin), all of which consists, at present, of government-issued fiat (Federal Reserve notes, U.S. notes, a few other similar issues, and fractional coinage). In practice, even Chicago banks are called on to discharge only an insignificant part of their deposit obligations by paying out currency. Euro-dollar banks are called on to discharge a negligible part in this form. Deposit obligations are typically discharged by providing a credit or deposit at another bank—as when you draw a check on your bank which the recipient "deposits" in his.

To meet their obligations to pay cash, banks keep a "reserve" of cash on hand. But, of course, since they are continuously receiving as well as paying cash and since in any interval they will be called on to redeem only a small fraction of their obligations in cash, they need on the average keep only a very small part of their assets in cash for this purpose. For Chicago banks, this cash serves also to meet legal reserve requirements. For Euro-dollar banks, the amount of literal cash they hold is negligible.

To meet their obligations to provide a credit at another bank, when a check or similar instrument is used, banks keep deposits at other banks. For Chicago banks, these deposits (which in addition to facilitating the transfer of funds between banks serve to meet legal reserve requirements) are held primarily at Federal Reserve banks. In addition, however, Chicago banks may also keep balances at correspondent banks in other cities.

Like cash, deposits at other banks need be only a small fraction of assets. Banks are continuously receiving funds from other banks, as well as transferring funds to them, so they need reserves only to provide for temporary discrepancies between payments and receipts or sudden unanticipated demands. For Chicago banks, such "prudential" reserves are clearly far smaller than the reserves that they are legally required to keep.

Euro-dollar banks are not subject to legal reserve requirements, but, like Chicago banks, they must keep a prudential reserve in order to be prepared to meet withdrawals of deposits when they are demanded or when they mature. An individual bank will regard as a prudential reserve readily realizable funds both in the Euro-dollar market itself (e.g., Euro-dollar call money) and in the U.S. But for the Euro-dollar system as a whole, Euro-dollar funds cancel, and the prudential reserves available to meet demands for U.S. dollars consist entirely of deposits at banks in New York or other cities in the U.S. and U.S. money market assets that can be liquidated promptly without loss.

The amount of prudential reserves that a Euro-dollar bank will wish to hold—like the amount that a Chicago bank will wish to hold—will depend on its particular mix of demand and time obligations. Time deposits generally require smaller reserves than demand deposits—and in some instances almost zero reserves if the bank can match closely the maturities of its dollar-denominated liabilities and its dollar-denominated loans and investments. Although a precise estimate is difficult to make because of the incompleteness and ambiguity of the available data, prudential reserves of Euro-dollar institutions are clearly a small fraction of total dollar-denominated obligations.

This point—that Euro-dollar institutions, like Chicago banks, are part of a fractional reserve banking system—is the key to understanding the Euro-dollar market. The failure to recognize it is the chief source of misunderstanding about the Euro-dollar market. Most journalistic discussions of the Euro-dollar market proceed as if a Euro-dollar bank held a dollar in the form of cash or of deposits at a U.S. bank corresponding to each dollar of deposit liability. That is the source of such images as "piling up," "borrowing back," "withdrawing," etc. But of course this is not the case. If it were, a Euro-dollar bank could hardly afford to pay 10% or more on its deposit liabilities.

A hypothetical example

A Euro-dollar bank typically has total dollar assets roughly equal to its dollar liabilities. But these assets are not in currency or bank deposits. In highly simplified form, the balance sheet of such a bank—or the part of the balance sheet corresponding to its Euro-dollar operations—must look something like that shown in the adjoining column (the numbers in this and later balance sheets are solely for illustrative purposes).

It is the earnings on the $9,500,000 of loans and investments that enable it to pay interest on the $10,000,000 of deposits.

Where did the $10,000,000 of deposits come from? One can say that $700,000 (cash assets minus due to other banks) came from "primary deposits," i.e., is the counterpart to a literal deposit of cash or transfer of funds from other banks. The other $9,300,000 is "created" by the magic of fractional reserve banking—this is the bookkeeper's pen at work.

EURO-DOLLAR BANK H OF LONDON

Assets		Liabilities	
Cash Assets*	$1,000,000	Deposits	$10,000,000
Dollar-denominated loans	7,000,000	Due to other banks	300,000
Dollar-denominated bonds	2,500,000	Capital accounts	200,000
Total assets	$10,500,000	Total liabilities	$10,500,000

* Includes U.S. currency, deposits in N.Y. and other banks, and other assets immediately realizable in U.S. funds.

Let us look at the process more closely. Suppose an Arab Sheik opens up a new deposit account in London at Bank H (H for hypothetical) by depositing a check for $1,000,000 drawn on the Sheik's demand deposit account at the head office of, say, Morgan Guaranty Trust Company. Let us suppose that Bank H also keeps its N.Y. account at Morgan Guaranty and also as demand deposits. At the first stage, this will add $1,000,000 to the deposit liabilities of Bank H, and the same amount to its assets in the form of deposits due from New York banks. At Morgan Guaranty, the transfer of deposits from the Sheik to Bank H will cause no change in total deposit liabilities.

But Bank H now has excess funds available to lend. It has been keeping cash assets equal to 10% of deposits—not because it was required to do so but because it deemed it prudent to do so. It now has cash equal to 18% (2/11) of deposits. Because of the $1,000,000 of new deposits from the Sheik, it will want to add, say, $100,000 to its balance in New York. This leaves Bank H with $900,000 available to add to its loans and investments. Assume that it makes a loan of $900,000 to, say, UK Ltd., a British corporation engaged in trade with the U.S., giving corporation UK Ltd. a check on Morgan Guaranty. Bank H's balance sheet will now look as follows after the check has cleared:

Assets		Liabilities	
Cash assets	$1,100,000	Deposits	$11,000,000
Dollar-denominated loans	7,900,000	Due to other banks	300,000
Dollar-denominated bonds	2,500,000	Capital accounts	200,000
Total assets	$11,500,000	Total liabilities	$11,500,000

We now must ask what UK Ltd. does with the $900,000 check. To cut short and simplify the process, let us assume that UK Ltd. incurred the loan because it had been repeatedly troubled by a shortage of funds in New York and wanted to maintain a higher average level of bank balances in New York. Further assume that it also keeps its account at Morgan Guaranty, so that it simply deposits the check in its demand deposit account.

This particular cycle is therefore terminated and we can examine its effect. First, the position of Morgan Guaranty is fundamentally unchanged; it had a deposit liability of $1,000,000 to the Sheik. It now has a deposit liability of $100,000 to Bank H and one of $900,000 to UK Ltd.

Second, the calculated money supply of the U.S. and the demand deposit component thereof are unchanged. That money supply excludes from "adjusted demand deposits" the deposits of U.S. commercial banks at other U.S. commercial banks but it includes deposits of both foreign banks and other foreigners. Therefore, the Sheik's deposit was included before. The deposits of Bank H and UK Ltd. are included now.

Third, the example was set up so that the money supply owned by residents of the U.S. is also unchanged. As a practical matter, the financial statistics gathered and published by the Federal Reserve do not contain sufficient data to permit calculation of the U.S.-owned money supply—a total which would exclude from the money supply as now calculated currency and deposits at U.S. banks owned by nonresidents and include dollar deposits at non-U.S. banks owned by residents. But the hypothetical transactions clearly leave this total unaffected.

Fourth, Euro-dollar deposits are $1,000,000 higher.

However, fifth, the total world supply of dollars held by nonbanks—dollars in the U.S. plus dollars outside the U.S.—is $900,000 not $1,000,000 higher. The reason is that interbank deposits are now higher by $100,000, thanks to the additional deposits of Bank H at Morgan Guaranty. This amount of deposits was formerly an asset of a nonbank (the Arab Sheik); now it is an asset of Bank H. In this way, Bank H has created $900,000 of Euro-dollar deposits. The other $100,000 of Euro-dollar deposits has been transferred from the U.S. to the Euro-dollar area.

Sixth, the balance of payments of the U.S. is unaffected, whether calculated on a liquidity basis or on an official settlements basis. On a liquidity basis, the Arab Sheik's transfer is recorded as a reduction of $1,000,000 in short-term liquid claims on the U.S. but the increased deposits of Bank H and UK Ltd. at Morgan Guaranty are a precisely offsetting increase. On an official settlements basis, the series of transactions has not affected the dollar holdings of any central bank or official institution.[4]

Clearly, there is no meaningful sense in which we can say that the $900,000 of created Euro-dollar deposits is derived from a U.S. balance-of-payments deficit, or from dollars held by central banks, or from the proceeds of Euro-dollar bond sales.

Some complications

Many complications of this example are possible. They will change the numbers but not in any way the essential principles. But it may help to consider one or two.

(a) Suppose UK Ltd. used the dollar loan to purchase timber from Russia, and Russia wished to hold the proceeds as a dollar deposit at, say, Bank R in London. Then, another round is started—precisely like

---

[4] It is interesting to contrast these effects with those that would have occurred if we substitute a Chicago bank for Bank H of London, i.e., suppose that the Arab Sheik had transferred his funds to a Chicago Bank, say, Continental Illinois, and Continental Illinois had made the loan to UK Ltd., which UK Ltd. again added to its balances at Morgan Guaranty. To simplify matters, assume that the reserve requirements for Continental Illinois and Morgan Guaranty are the same flat 10% that we assumed Bank H of London kept in the form of cash assets (because, let us say, all deposit changes consist of the appropriate mix of demand and time deposits).

First, the position of Morgan Guaranty is now fundamentally changed. Continental Illinois keeps its reserves as deposits at the Federal Reserve Bank of Chicago, not at Morgan Guaranty. Hence it will deposit its net claim of $100,000 on Morgan Guaranty at the Chicago Fed to meet the reserves required for the Sheik's deposit. This will result in a reduction of $100,000 in Morgan Guaranty's reserve balance at the New York Fed. Its deposits have gone down only $100,000 (thanks to the $900,000 deposit by UK Ltd.) so that if it had no excess reserves before it now has deficient reserves. This will set in train a multiple contraction of deposits at Morgan Guaranty and other banks which will end when the $1,000,000 gain in deposits by Continental Illinois is completely offset by a $1,000,000 decline in deposits at Morgan Guaranty and other banks.

Second, the calculated money supply of the U.S. and the demand deposit component thereof are still unchanged.

However, third, the money supply owned by the residents of the U.S. is reduced by the $900,000 increase in the deposits of UK Ltd.

Fourth, there is no change in Euro-dollar deposits.

Fifth, there is no change in the total world supply of dollars.

Sixth, the balance of payments of the U.S. is affected if it is calculated on a liquidity basis but not if it is calculated on an official settlements basis. On a liquidity basis, the deficit would be increased by $900,000 because the loan by Continental Illinois to UK Ltd. would be recorded as a capital outflow but UK Ltd.'s deposit at Morgan Guaranty would be regarded as an increase in U.S. liquid liabilities to foreigners, which are treated as financing the deficit. This enlargement of the deficit on a liquidity basis is highly misleading. It suggests, of course, a worsening of the U.S. payments problem, whereas in fact all that is involved is a worsening of the statistics. The additional dollars that UK Ltd. has in its demand deposit account cannot meaningfully be regarded as a potential claim on U.S. reserve assets. UK Ltd. not only needs them for transactions purposes; it must regard them as tied or matched to its own dollar indebtedness. On an official settlements basis, the series of transactions does not affect the dollar holdings of any central bank or official institution.

the one that began when the Sheik transferred funds from Morgan Guaranty to Bank H. Bank R now has $900,000 extra deposit liabilities, matched by $900,000 extra deposits in New York. If it also follows the practice of maintaining cash assets equal to 10% of deposits, it can make a dollar loan of $810,000. If the recipient of the loan keeps it as a demand deposit at Morgan Guaranty, or transfers it to someone who does, the process comes to an end. The result is that total Euro-dollar deposits are up by $1,900,000. Of that total, $1,710,000 is held by nonbanks, with the other $190,000 being additional deposits of banks (the $100,000 extra of Bank H at Morgan Guaranty plus the $90,000 extra of Bank R at Morgan Guaranty).

If the recipient of the loan transfers it to someone who wants to hold it as a Euro-dollar deposit at a third bank, the process continues on its merry way. If, in the extreme, at every stage, the whole of the proceeds of the loan were to end up as Euro-dollar deposits, it is obvious that the total increase in Euro-dollar deposits would be: 1,000,000 + 900,000 + 810,000 + 729,000 + ... = 10,000,000. At the end of the process, Euro-dollar deposits would be $10,000,000 higher; deposits of Euro-dollar banks at N.Y. banks, $1,000,000 higher; and the total world supply of dollars held by nonbanks, $9,000,000 higher.

This example perhaps makes it clear why bankers in the Euro-dollar market keep insisting that they do not "create" dollars but only transfer them, and why they sincerely believe that all Euro-dollars come from the U.S. To each banker separately in the chain described, his additional Euro-dollar deposit came in the form of a check on Morgan Guaranty Trust Company of New York! How are the bankers to know that the $10,000,000 of checks on Morgan Guaranty all constitute repeated claims on the same initial $1,000,000 of deposits? Appearances are deceiving.

This example (involving successive loan extensions by a series of banks) brings out the difference between two concepts that have produced much confusion: Euro-dollar creation and the Euro-dollar multiplier. In both the simple example and the example involving successive loan extensions, the fraction of Euro-dollars outstanding that has been created is nine-tenths, or, put differently, 10 Euro-dollars exist for every U.S. dollar held as a cash asset in New York by Euro-dollar banks. However, in the simple example, the Euro-dollar multiplier (the ratio of the increase in Euro-dollar deposits to the initial "primary" deposit) is unity; in the second example, it is 10. That is, in the simple example, the total amount of Euro-dollars goes up by $1 for every $1 of U.S. deposits initially transferred to Euro-dollar banks; in the second example, it goes up by $10 for every $1 of U.S. deposits initially transferred. The difference is that in the simple example there is maximum "leakage" from the Euro-dollar system; in the second example, zero "leakage."

The distinction between Euro-dollar creation and the Euro-dollar multiplier makes it clear why there is a definite limit to the amount of Euro-dollars that can be created no matter how low are the prudential reserves that banks hold. For example, if Euro-dollar banks held zero prudential reserves—as it is sometimes claimed that they do against time deposits—100% of the outstanding deposits would be created deposits and the potential multiplier would be infinite. Yet the actual multiplier would be close to unity because only a small part of the funds acquired by borrowers from Euro-dollar banks would end up as additional time deposits in such banks.[5]

(b) Suppose Bank H does not have sufficient demand for dollar loans to use profitably the whole $900,000 of excess dollar funds. Suppose, simultaneously, it is experiencing a heavy demand for sterling loans. It might go to the Bank of England and use the $900,000 to buy sterling. Bank of England deposits at Morgan Guaranty would now go up. But since the Bank of England typically holds its deposits at the New York Federal Reserve Bank, the funds would fairly quickly disappear from Morgan Guaranty's books and show up instead on the Fed's. This, in the first instance, would reduce the reserves of Morgan Guaranty and thus threaten to produce much more extensive monetary effects than any of our other examples. However, the Bank of England typically holds most of its dollar reserves as Treasury bills or the equivalent, not as noninterest earning deposits at the Fed. It would therefore instruct the Fed to buy, say, bills for its account. This would restore the reserves to the banking system and, except for details, we would be back to where we were in the other examples.

The key points

Needless to say, this is far from a comprehensive survey of all the possible complications. But perhaps it suffices to show that the complications do not affect the fundamental points brought out by the simple example, namely:

1. Euro-dollars, like "Chicago dollars," are mostly the product of the bookkeeper's pen—that is, the result of fractional reserve banking.

2. The amount of Euro-dollars outstanding, like the amount of "Chicago dollars," depends on the desire of owners of wealth to hold the liabilities of the corresponding group of banks.

3. The ultimate increase in the amount of Euro-dollars from an initial transfer of deposits from other banks to Euro-dollar banks depends on:

(a) The amount of their dollar assets Euro-dollar banks choose to hold in the form of cash assets in the U.S., and

---

[5] This is precisely comparable to the situation of savings and loan associations and mutual savings banks in the U.S.

(b) The "leakages" from the system—i.e., the final disposition of the funds borrowed from Euro-dollar banks (or acquired by the sale of bonds or other investments to them). The larger the fraction of such funds held as Euro-dollar deposits, the larger the increase in Euro-dollars in total.

4. The existence of the Euro-dollar market increases the total amount of dollar balances available to be held by nonbanks throughout the world for any given amount of money (currency plus deposits at Federal Reserve Banks) created by the Federal Reserve System. It does so by permitting a greater pyramiding on this base by the use of deposits at U.S. banks as prudential reserves for Euro-dollar deposits.

5. The existence of the Euro-dollar market may also create a greater demand for dollars to be held by making dollar balances available in a more convenient form. The net effect of the Euro-dollar market on our balance-of-payments problem (as distinct from our statistical position) depends on whether demand is raised more or less than supply.

My own conjecture—which is based on much too little evidence for me to have much confidence in it—is that demand is raised less than supply and hence that the growth of the Euro-dollar market has on the whole made our balance-of-payments problem more difficult.

6. Whether my conjecture on this score is right or wrong, the Euro-dollar market has almost surely raised the world's nominal money supply (expressed in dollar equivalents) and has thus made the world price level (expressed in dollar equivalents) higher than it would otherwise be. Alternatively, if it is desired to define the money supply exclusive of Euro-dollar deposits, the same effect can be described in terms of a rise in the velocity of the world's money supply. However, this effect, while clear in direction, must be extremely small in magnitude.

Use of Euro-dollars by U.S. banks

Let us now turn from this general question of the source of Euro-dollars to the special issue raised at the outset: the effect of Regulation O and "tight money" on the use of the Euro-dollar market by U.S. banks.

To set the stage, let us suppose, in the framework of our simple example, that Euro-dollar Bank H of London loans the $900,000 excess funds that it has as a result of the initial deposit by the Arab Sheik to the head office of Morgan Guaranty, i.e., gives Morgan Guaranty (New York) a check for $900,000 on itself in return for an I.O.U. from Morgan Guaranty. This kind of borrowing from foreign banks is one of the means by which American banks have blunted the impact of CD losses. The combined effect will be to leave total liabilities of Morgan Guaranty unchanged but to alter their composition: deposit liabilities are now down $900,000 (instead of the $1,000,000 deposit liability it formerly had to the Sheik it now has a deposit liability of $100,000 to Bank H) and other liabilities ("funds borrowed from foreign banks") are up $900,000.

Until very recently, such a change in the form of a bank's liabilities—from deposits to borrowings—had an important effect on its reserve position. Specifically, it freed reserves. With $1,000,000 of demand deposit liabilities to the Arab Sheik, Morgan Guaranty was required to keep in cash or as deposits at the Federal Reserve Bank of New York $175,000 (or $60,000 if, as is more realistic, the Sheik kept his $1,000,000 in the form of a time deposit). With the shift of the funds to Bank H, however, and completion of the $900,000 loan by Bank H to Morgan Guaranty, Morgan Guaranty's reserve requirements at the Fed fell appreciably. Before the issuance of new regulations that became effective on September 4 of this year, Morgan Guaranty was not required to keep any reserve for the liability in the form of the I.O.U. Its only obligation was to keep $17,500 corresponding to the demand deposit of Bank H. The change in the form of its liabilities would therefore have reduced its reserve requirements by $157,500 (or by $42,500 for a time deposit) without any change in its total liabilities or its total assets, or in the composition of its assets; hence it would have had this much more available to lend.

What the Fed did effective September 4 was to make borrowings subject to reserve requirements as well. Morgan Guaranty must now keep a reserve against the I.O.U., the exact percentage depending on the total amount of borrowings by Morgan Guaranty from foreign banks.[6] The new regulations make it impossible to generalize about reserve effects. A U.S. bank losing deposits to a Euro-bank and then recouping funds by giving its I.O.U. may or may not have additional amounts available to lend as a result of transactions of the kind described.

If Bank H made the loan to Chase instead of to Morgan Guaranty, the latter would lose reserves and Chase would gain them. To Chase, it would look as if it were getting additional funds from abroad, but to both together, the effect would be the same as before—the possible release of required reserves with no change in available reserves.

The bookkeeping character of these transactions, and how they can be stimulated, can perhaps be seen more clearly if we introduce an additional feature of the actual Euro-dollar market, which was not essential heretofore, namely, the role of overseas branches of U.S. banks. In addition, for realism, we shall express our example in terms of time deposits.

---

[6] The required reserve is 3% of such borrowings so long as they do not exceed 4% of total deposits subject to reserves. On borrowings in excess of that level the required reserve is 10%.

Let us start from scratch and consider the head office of Morgan Guaranty in New York and its London branch. Let us look at hypothetical initial balance sheets of both. We shall treat the London branch as if it had just started and had neither assets nor liabilities, and shall restrict the balance sheet for the head office to the part relevant to its CD operations. This set of circumstances gives us the following situation:

NEW YORK HEAD OFFICE

Assets		Liabilities	
Deposits at F.R. Bank of NY	$6,000,000	Time certificates of deposit	$100,000,000
Other cash assets	4,000,000		
Loans	76,000,000		
Bonds	14,000,000		
Total assets	$100,000,000	Total liabilities	$100,000,000

(Note: Required reserves, $6,000,000)

LONDON OFFICE

Assets	Liabilities
$0	$0

Now suppose a foreign corporation (perhaps the Arab Sheik's oil company) which holds a long-term maturing CD of $10,000,000 at Morgan Guaranty refuses to renew it because the 6 1/4% interest it is receiving seems too low. Morgan Guaranty agrees that the return should be greater, but explains it is prohibited by law from paying more. It notes, however, that its London branch is not. Accordingly, the corporation acquires a time deposit at the London office for $10,000,000 "by depositing" the check for $10,000,000 on the New York office it receives in return for the maturing CD—or, more realistically, by transfers on the books in New York and London. Let us look at the balance sheets:

NEW YORK HEAD OFFICE

Assets		Liabilities	
Deposits at F.R. Bank of NY	$6,000,000	Time certificates of deposits	$90,000,000
Other cash assets	4,000,000		
Loans	76,000,000		
Bonds	14,000,000	Due to London branch	10,000,000
Total assets	$100,000,000	Total liabilities	$100,000,000

LONDON OFFICE

Assets		Liabilities	
Due from N.Y. office	$10,000,000	Time certificates of deposit	$10,000,000

Clearly, if we consolidate the branch and the head office, the books are completely unchanged. Yet these bookkeeping transactions: (1) enabled Morgan Guaranty to pay a rate in London higher than 6-1/4% on some certificates of deposit; and (2) reduced its required reserves by $600,000 prior to the recent modification of Regulation M. The reduction in required reserves arose because until recently U.S. banks were not required to keep a reserve against liabilities to their foreign branches. With the amendment of Regulation M, any further reduction of reserves by this route has been eliminated since the Fed now requires a reserve of 10% on the amount due to branch offices in excess of the amount due on average during May.

Hypocrisy and window dressing

This example has been expressed in terms of a *foreign* corporation because the story is a bit more complicated for a U.S. corporation, though the end result is the same. First, a U.S. corporation that transfers its funds from a certificate of deposit at a U.S. bank to a deposit at a bank abroad—whether a foreign bank or an overseas branch of a U.S. bank—is deemed by the Department of Commerce to have made a foreign investment. It may do so only if it is within its quota under the direct control over foreign investment with which we are still unfortunately saddled. Second, under pressure from the Fed, commercial banks will not facilitate direct transfers by U.S. corporations—indeed, many will not accept time deposits from U.S. corporations at their overseas branches, whether their own customers or not, unless the corporation can demonstrate that the deposit is being made for an "international" purpose. However, precisely the same results can be accomplished by a U.S. holder of a CD making a deposit in a foreign bank and the foreign bank in turn making a deposit in, or a loan to, the overseas branch of a U.S. bank. As always, this kind of moral suasion does not prevent profitable transactions. It simply produces hypocrisy and window dressing—in this case, by unnecessarily giving business to competitors of U.S. banks!

The final effect is precisely the same as in the simple example of the foreign corporation. That example shows, in highly simplified form, the main way U.S. banks have used the Euro-dollar market and explains why it is that the more they "borrow" or "bring back" from the Euro-dollar market, the higher Euro-dollar deposits mount. In our example, borrowing went up $10,000,000 and so did deposits.

From January 1, 1969 to July 31, 1969 CD deposit liabilities of U.S. banks went down $9.3 billion, and U.S. banks' indebtedness to their own overseas branches went up $8.6 billion. The closeness of these two numbers is not coincidental.

These bookkeeping operations have affected the statistics far more than the realities. The run-off in CD's in the U.S., and the accompanying decline in total commercial bank deposits (which the Fed uses as its "bank credit proxy") have been interpreted as signs of extreme monetary tightness. Money has been tight, but these figures greatly overstate the degree of tightness. The holders of CD's on U.S. banks who replaced them by Euro-dollar deposits did not have their liquidity squeezed. The banks that substituted "due to branches" for "due to depositors on time certificates of deposit" did not have their lending power reduced. The Fed's insistence on keeping Regulation Q ceilings at levels below market rates has simply imposed enormous structural adjustments and shifts of funds on the commercial banking system for no social gain whatsoever.

Correcting a misunderstanding

A column that appeared in a leading financial paper just prior to the Fed's revision of reserve requirements encapsules the widespread misunderstanding about the Euro-dollar market. The Euro-dollar market, the column noted, has: " ... ballooned as U.S. banks have discovered that they can ease the squeeze placed on them by the Federal Reserve Board by borrowing back these foreign-deposited dollars that were pumped out largely through U.S. balance-of-payments deficits. Of this pool of $30 billion, U.S. banks as of last week had soaked up $1.3 billion ...

"Thanks to this system, it takes only seconds to transmit money—and money troubles between the U.S. and Europe ... The Federal Reserve's pending proposal to make Euro-dollar borrowing more costly to U.S. banks might make their future demands a shade less voracious, but this doesn't reduce concern about whether there will be strains in repaying the massive amounts already borrowed."

Strains there may be, but they will reflect features of the Euro-dollar market other than those stressed by this newspaper comment. The use of the Euro-dollar market by commercial banks to offset the decline in CD's was primarily a bookkeeping operation. The reverse process a rise in CD's and a matching decline in Euro-dollar borrowings will also require little more than a bookkeeping operation.

Notes and Questions

1. Be sure you understand the definition of a eurodollar. How is a eurodollar different from a domestic dollar?

2. Would you expect that a bank would have to book and manage offshore accounts in the same place?

3. Consider the relation between interest rates in the eurocurrency and domestic deposit markets. The following chart compares the two rates in on deposits in U.S. dollars and Deutsche Marks from 1982 to 1996.

Deutsche Mark Rates

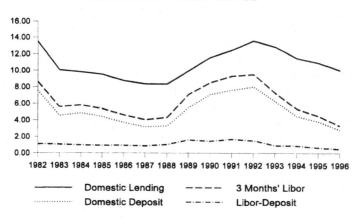

U.S. Dollar Rates

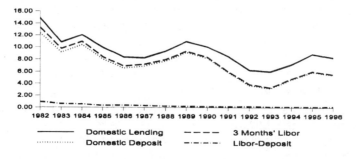

a. What relation would you expect to see between the London Interbank Deposit Rate (LIBOR) and domestic deposit rates. What accounts for this relationship?

b. What trends do you see in the Dollar rates and in the DM rates? What might explain these trends?

c. Since the eurocurrency markets are unregulated, why are not the interest rates on the various eurocurrencies closely correlated?

d. Why would a bank raise eurodollars rather than U.S. dollars, which have a lower interest rate?

4. Milton Friedman described how various U.S. regulations contributed to the growth of the eurodollar market. Many of these regulations are of historical interest only, including Regulation Q, which put a ceiling on interest payable on deposits, and the foreign exchange controls (the voluntary foreign credit restraint program and the limits on overseas foreign direct investment). Why would the eurodollar market for banking persist after the regulations ended?

5. Various countries have established special arrangements that allow banks to accept deposits from foreigners without making them subject to at least some domestic banking regulations. The U.S. permits U.S. banks to operate international banking facilities that do not impose reserve requirements on foreign depositors. The goal was to allow banks in the U.S. to compete with financial centers. In fact, however, the IBFs have not seriously challenged offshore financial centers like London or Singapore. The U.S. feared that domestic funds might move to the IBFs, so it imposed complex rules to prevent such a shift. The rules muted demand.

6. In the first decades of the euromarkets' existence, national governments were very concerned about their existence and rapid growth. What reasons might account for their concern? If governments were concerned about the domestic impact of offshore markets, what could they do about the problems they saw? These markets are offshore, by definition. How much power do governments have to affect activities in offshore markets? Do all governments have equal power? Would the following increase or decrease the US government's ability to regulate offshore activities:

a. US bank dominance of the eurocurrency markets.

b. European financial markets' weakness relative to US markets.

c. The US dollar as the reserve currency.

Later in this Chapter we see clauses in eurocredit agreements designed to specify what the parties do if governments close the euromarket. An example of such a thrust occurred in 1979, when a member of the US Congress offered a Eurocurrency Market Control Bill to impose reserve requirements on eurocurrency holdings of banks with offices in the US and try to force other governments to do the same for banks in their countries. The law was not passed. Were efforts of this sort ever credible? If so, why was the eurodollar market's growth never curtailed?

B. THE GROWTH OF THE MARKET FOR SYNDICATED EURODOLLAR LOANS

DEVELOPMENTS IN THE INTERNATIONAL SYNDICATED LOAN MARKET IN THE 1980s

30 Bank of England Quarterly Bulletin 71 (1990).

General overview

At the beginning of the 1980s, the market for international syndicated loans was already well established and business was buoyant. New credit facilities worth almost $83 billion were announced in 1980, and a further $101 billion were announced in the following year. Many major international banks were heavily involved in extending loans to borrowers from the less developed countries (LDCs) and newly industrialising economies (NIEs) in the period 1976–82. Some of the assumptions which underlay the banks' policy of portfolio diversification through more overseas lending were, however, increasingly being questioned, particularly in relation to loans extended to state entities in the LDCs. With the intensification of the debt crisis resulting from the decision by Mexico to suspend interest payments to its creditors in August 1982, the euroloan market entered a phrase of sharp contraction. Activity reached a nadir in 1985, when the value of new international syndicated loans amounted to only $19 billion. In contrast, in the capital markets, gross eurobond issues increased from $74 billion in 1982 to $163 billion in 1985. Thus the decline in the use of the syndicated loan as a vehicle for international financial flows was very clearly associated with the process of securitisation which was then having a major impact on financial markets. This phenomenon was related to an increased investor preference for tradable claims and the desire of some borrowers—notably major industrial companies—to exploit the fact that their creditworthiness relative to the banking sector had improved markedly, so giving them an incentive to issue securities directly to end investors.

Since the last quarter of 1986, however, the market for syndicated loans, both international and domestic, has once more experienced high levels of activity, although the composition of borrowers has changed significantly from that at the beginning of the decade. This resurgence has been attributable to three salient factors:

- the desire of corporate institutions in the developed countries to restructure their existing lines of credit into more flexible financing arrangements, such as multiple-option facilities (see below);

- the growth in debt-financed takeovers and management buyouts, reflecting, in part, the reduction in the cost of debt finance resulting from the decline in inflation from the early 1980s; and

- more generally, the competitive funding opportunities that this sector offers to second-tier corporate borrowers which do not possess a sufficiently high credit rating to obtain access to the eurobond market and utilise interest rate swaps at favourable rates.

.   .   .

Conditions in the syndicated loan market, 1980–89

Until 1985, borrowers from the LDCs and the NIEs generally accounted for a more substantial share of the international syndicated loan market than did borrowers from the major OECD countries (see Chart 2 and Table A). The recovery in volumes which has taken place since the end of 1986, however, almost entirely reflects greater activity by borrowers from the major industrial economies. In recent years there has also been a change in the importance of industrial borrowers generally relative to sovereign borrowers, although the former has always represented the single most important group of borrowers since 1980. Borrowing by central governments and other government departments accounted for approximately 20% of all credits in the early 1980s. After 1982, this proportion declined significantly and is now around 5% of the overall market: governments of LDCs have, in many cases, been excluded from the market altogether, and those of the industrial countries have increasingly turned their attention to bond financing and the euronote sector, where they have been able to obtain finer rates and pursue more precise debt management policies. For example, the Kingdoms of Belgium, Spain and Sweden developed large commercial paper or medium-term note programmes either in the US domestic market or in the euromarket. In contrast, credit facilities arranged on behalf of industrial borrowers have represented over 45% of all syndicated loans in every year since 1982, reaching 88% of all announcements in 1988 and 81% in 1989. US dollar denominated credits have always formed the most significant component of the total market; in every year since 1980 dollar facilities accounted for more than 60% of all international syndicated loans.

Chart 2
Announcements of international syndicated loans, 1972-89

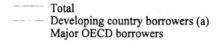

——— Total
— · — Developing country borrowers (a)
——— Major OECD borrowers

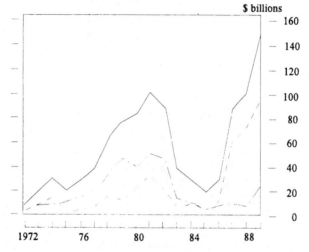

Source: Bank of England ICMS Database.

(a) Includes less developed countries, newly industrialising economies and oil producing countries.

Table A
International syndicated credits: borrowers, by region
$ billions

	1980	1981	1982	1983	1984	1985	1986	1987	1988	1989(x)
Major OECD countries	20.5	33.2	22.6	8.2	9.9	5.1	11.6	61.4	72.8	98.7
Minor OECD countries	19.4	15.7	18.4	13.6	6.2	4.4	6.5	14.9	18.3	23.9
Eastern Europe	2.8	1.1	0.5	0.5	2.2	3.6	2.3	1.9	1.2	2.2
International institutions	0.6	0.4	----	1.2	0.1	----	0.4	0.4	0.1	0.1
Less developed countries	15.0	22.5	19.7	5.1	4.0	1.5	3.7	6.5	6.2	15.0
Newly industrializing economies	11.1	14.7	11.8	3.5	3.5	3.0	1.1	1.1	1.5	3.7
Oil producing countries	13.0	12.9	13.8	5.5	3.8	1.2	3.3	2.0	1.6	5.3
Other	0.4	0.4	1.4	0.4	0.4	0.2	0.7	0.5	0.1	0.1
Total	82.8	100.9	88.2	38.0	30.1	19.0	29.6	88.7	101.8	149.0

Source: Bank of England ICMS database.
(x) Provisional

Table B
International syndicated credits: breakdown by type of borrower
$ billions

	1980	1981	1982	1983	1984	1985	1986	1987	1988	1989(a)
Industrial borrowers	48.5	65.1	53.3	22.0	17.1	8.5	15.2	67.8	89.4	120.6
Banks and financial institutions	16.9	18.9	16.9	5.0	9.0	8.2	9.0	15.0	8.9	21.1
Central banks	----	----	1.1	1.9	0.3	0.5	1.5	1.0	1.1	1.2
Central government	14.2	14.4	16.0	8.8	3.6	1.6	3.7	4.0	1.5	4.5
Other government	3.2	2.5	0.9	0.3	0.1	0.2	0.2	0.9	0.9	1.6
Total	82.8	100.9	88.2	38.0	30.1	19.0	29.6	88.7	101.8	149.0

Source: Bank of England ICMS database (a) Provisional.

Chart 3
Spreads[(a)] on major OECD and less developed country loans

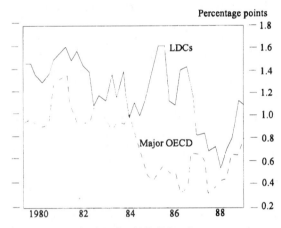

Source: Bank of England ICMS Database.

(a) Three-quarterly moving average.

Margins[1] on international syndicated loans for major OECD borrowers underwent a general but not continuous decline from 1982 to the first half of 1988 (see Chart 3). The fall in average margins which took place after 1983 can be attributed to two main factors. First, with the onset of the debt crisis many prime corporate borrowers

---

[1] International syndicated loans are generally priced with reference to the Labor benchmark, although other bases such as the Paris Interbank offered rate (Pibor), the US prime rate or various CD rates are also used. As well as being influenced by market conditions, the margin that is charged above that will essentially be a function of country and credit risk.

turned to the various securities markets to service their financing requirements. In particular, the growth of the eurocommercial paper and floating-rate note markets provided borrowers with alternative sources of short-term and floating-rate funding. The banks were therefore obliged to compete more aggressively for international and wholesale business as well as turning their attention to off-balance-sheet financing. Second, the major international banks became involved in arranging standby credit facilities designed to support the commercial paper activities of industrial companies or provide short-term cash advances for working capital purposes. As such loan facilities are not intended to be fully drawn upon in normal circumstances, the margins attached to them are comparatively low and the facility fee represents a more important element in the overall pricing. For almost all of the period from 1982 to 1988, the average margin on loans for borrowers from the major OECD countries was below that incurred by borrowers from the LDCs.

More recently, however, average margins have increased for both borrowers from the major OECD countries and those from LDCs, although they remain below the levels seen at the beginning of the decade. The new capital adequacy rules introduced under the auspices of the Bank for International Settlements represent one factor that should cause banks to negotiate higher margins. The increase in spreads may also be attributed to a change in the composition of loan facilities which have been arranged in recent quarters. For example, high margin business in the form of loans to finance acquisitions has become a greater component of the total market. The strength of potential competition among banks in the syndicated loan market, however, acts as a countervailing force, limiting the extent to which spreads may rise.

Market attributes

The demand for international syndicated credit facilities, which predominantly reflects private sector funding requirements, results from the fact that the syndicated loan market, or more generally the banking sector, is able to perform certain essential functions more satisfactorily than securities-based capital markets. The main advantages of a syndicated loan facility are:

- a credit facility provides the borrower with a stable source of funds—of particular value in the event that other capital markets are subject to some form of disruption;
- the syndicated loan sector generally allows borrowers to raise larger sums than they would be able to obtain through either the eurobond or the equity markets in the short term;
- the ability to arrange deals quickly and discreetly, which may be of value with certain transactions such as takeovers;

- the capacity to provide commitments to lend which can be canceled relatively easily; it would be difficult to cancel borrowing in the securities markets without reducing investor confidence.

To some extent these advantages are relative rather than absolute. For example, the US domestic commercial paper market and the ECP market can offer a wide range of borrowers access to short-term funds, albeit on an uncommitted basis, and the medium-term note market can be regarded as a form of contingent bond financing. As dealers in these markets will only place notes on a 'best efforts' basis, such programmes do not offer the certainty of committed bank lines. For prime industrial corporate borrowers and well-regarded sovereign borrowers, this does not present a major problem as they will be able to place their paper and bonds at more competitive rates than they could obtain funding in the bank market under normal circumstances. But for a wide spectrum of companies, particularly in Western Europe where the domestic CP markets are less well developed than in the United States and an established 'below investment grade' bond market has not as yet emerged, the stability and certainty of banking relationships continue to be attractive.

Multiple-option facilities

A multiple-option facility (MOF) is the general name for a number of credit and money-market fund-raising mechanisms which are documented in a single agreement and are administered by a single agent on behalf of a syndicate of banks. The MOF is typically based upon a committed revolving credit and incorporates other arrangements which allow the borrower to obtain finance on an uncommitted basis, such as tender panels for multicurrency cash advances and bankers' acceptances or facilities allowing for the issue of commercial paper or some other form of note. Such facilities therefore represent a more convenient packaging of existing banking services rather than a fundamental innovation; instead of managing a series of bilateral banking relationships, the corporate treasurer can arrange a significant part of his company's funding through one agent. Under normal circumstances borrowers will obtain funding through a tender panel mechanism or by issuing short-term promissory notes, and will achieve finer rates than they would have to pay if they were to make drawings upon the committed credit component of their MOF. For many major companies the MOF has represented a rationalisation of existing banking services, rather than a net increase in bank intermediation. Moreover, available evidence suggests that drawings made under these facilities are generally modest when compared with the total value of funds that could potentially be obtained under the uncommitted portions.

. . .

As many major companies, both in the United Kingdom and elsewhere, have now acquired MOFs, the demand for such arrangements will increasingly come from second-tier corporate borrowers, for whom various eurocurrency options are less relevant. The implementation of the Basel capital convergence agreement by the United Kingdom and other countries should make banks more reluctant to participate in MOFs at the aggressively-priced margins which were common in the early part of 1988. Some banks may, however, choose to participate in this lower return business in order to establish or retain long-term relationships with customers. Moreover, the more cautious attitude which some bankers have adopted towards high yield mezzanine debt and leveraged transactions could result in a desire to reweight portfolios more towards lower-geared companies wishing to have access to funds for general corporate purposes.

The syndication process

The syndicated loan market is able to provide a broad spectrum of borrowers with funding for a wide range of projects. Loans can vary in size from small club deals, where three or four relationship banks can participate in transactions for as little as £10 million, to very large acquisition or project-related credits worth in excess of a billion pounds. For example, Eurotunnel obtained two syndicated loans in the third quarter of 1987 with a combined value of £5 billion, where the syndicate comprised approximately 160 banks. . . .

The syndication process commences when either a borrower approaches a bank and invites it to become a syndicate arranger or when the bank itself approaches a corporate borrower which it believes to be seeking funds. The arranger, or in some cases the arrangers, once mandated will then set about co-ordinating a consortium of banks who are prepared to lend money given an initial set of terms. The borrower's relationship banks will usually form the basis of the syndicate and further invitations may be extended according to the size, complexity and the pricing of the loan as well as the desire of the borrower to increase the range of its banking relationships.

Eventually, the arranger or lead-manager may find itself at the apex of a whole hierarchy of institutions, who may accept positions as co-lead managers, managers, co-managers or just participant banks, depending on the amount of money that they are prepared to lend or commit and the input that they have in the syndication process. The larger the credit, the more complex the structure. The lead-management role itself is occasionally undertaken by the treasury department of the company seeking to raise the loan.

The arranger may either undertake the syndication on a 'best efforts basis' or, if the borrower is prepared to pay an appropriate fee, put together an underwriting group to give the borrower a guarantee of committed finance. If the latter route is adopted, the syndication process will take place in two phases. The underwriting group will come together in the primary syndication and then subsequently their commitments may be reduced during a secondary syndication, when new banks will be invited into the consortium. If the terms of the loan are considered attractive or the borrower is well-regarded by the market, the loan may well be oversubscribed. In this case the arranger may either invite the borrower to increase the size of the total credit or the banks may find that the amounts they have committed are scaled down *pro rata.* The completion of a transaction is often evidenced by the publication of a notice, generally referred to as a 'tombstone', in the financial press.

As well as earning a margin over Libor (or any other benchmark) when the loan is drawn, banks in the syndicate will receive various fees. The arranger and other banks in the lead management team, who may be responsible for various aspects of documentation, will generally receive some form of front-end management fee. Other participants will usually expect to receive a participation fee for agreeing to join the facility; the actual size of the fee will vary with the size of the commitment. Once the credit is established, members of the syndicate will often receive an annual facility or commitment fee, again proportional to their commitments. Loan documents may sometimes incorporate a penalty clause, whereby the borrower agrees to pay a fee or give some consideration to the lenders in the event that it pre-pays its debts prior to the specified term.

Merger and acquisition related lending

The stock market crash of October 1987 led to speculation that new merger and acquisition activity would decline significantly, reflecting the perceived difficulties of raising new equity finance. The continued buoyancy of company profits within the major industrial economies during 1988, together with the depressed state of many companies' stock market valuations, however, provided a considerable stimulus to new acquisitions. In many cases the syndicated loan has been the vehicle through which such takeovers have been financed. As mentioned above, the banking sector, through consortium loans, allows borrowers to raise larger sums than they are able to obtain through either the eurobond or the equity market over the short term, and to do so quickly. Moreover, borrowers may subsequently refinance such debt by utilising other markets.

. . .

Merger-related business can provide banks with two major forms of income: fees from giving advice on the mechanics of mounting a takeover (or defence) and interest charges and other fees from participating in any financing package arranged on behalf of the acquirer. While there is some debate on the subject of exactly how generous are the returns on merger and acquisition business, the greater emphasis which many banks have placed on this type of activity since the beginning of 1988 indicates that it has been perceived as a welcome source of income. . . .

Mezzanine debt

Another development which has received considerable attention during the last two years has been the growing use of mezzanine or subordinated debt. This instrument has generally been associated with the current wave of corporate restructuring that is taking place in Western Europe and North America, particularly in connection with leveraged buyouts, where companies are acquired with borrowed funds which result in the acquirer assuming a relatively high gearing ratio. Mezzanine funding can take a number of different forms and refers to the issue of any form of subordinated debt claim. In the United States, mezzanine debt often takes the form of 'below investment grade' bonds, while in Europe it is generally some form of bank debt with equity warrants attached. Although mezzanine debt is usually associated with financing acquisitions and buyouts, it could have other applications, such as certain forms of project finance, where the actual project involved is particularly cash-generative.

Announcements of international syndicated credits and international banking flows

Data on announcements of syndicated loans can yield useful information on a number of issues, such as the degree of competition within particular sectors of the banking market, the extent to which companies in certain countries are restructuring their financial commitments and the growth of new loan products (mezzanine finance, multiple-option facilities). It has also been suggested that announcements of new international syndicated credits could be used as a leading indicator of bank lending to non-banks. The arrangement of credit facilities, however, represents the establishment of commitments to lend and, therefore, it is not always possible to make direct inferences about the value of actual drawings; trends evident in the international syndicated loan market are not necessarily reflected in cross-border flows. A recent study at the Bank using univariate time series techniques came to the conclusion that there was only a weak statistical relationship between announcements of new international syndicated credits and international banking flows. The difficulty in relating the two data sets also arises from the fact that the Bank of England's data on international syndicated loans do not include facilities with a maturity of less than one year; moreover, data on international banking flows will also incorporate drawings upon bilateral lines of credit.

. . .

Secondary market

Another major development since the early 1980s has been the increasing tendency for banks to trade credit participations in the secondary market. While there are few statistics on the total size of the secondary market, the LDC debt problem and more recently the growth in LBOs have encouraged banks to adjust the balance of their loan portfolios. The recent Basel agreement on capital adequacy has presented many banks with the choice of increasing capital or removing assets from their balance sheets; many appear to have chosen to adopt the latter option to some degree, using loan transfers or securitisation to effect the reduction. There are three main methods by which loan participations may be transferred: novation, assignment and subparticipation. Novation involves the replacement of one legal agreement with another, thus extinguishing the contractual relationship between the original creditor and the debtor; assignment and subparticipation are non-recourse funding arrangements which do not normally involve the borrower as they operate in parallel with, rather than instead of, the original loan. This heightened emphasis on marketability could result in the syndicated loan market assuming some of the characteristics of the FRN market. The existence of a well-developed market in participations in syndicated loans results in banks developing many of the same skills that are required to operate successfully in the bond market, namely the ability to market debt claims and to establish a major network of potential investors. This could be regarded as part of a more general process in the euromarkets, where in recent years innovation and securitisation have led to the gradual dissolving of the boundaries between money, credit and capital markets. The existence of an established market in loans or loan participations also raises some interesting issues for bank supervisors. After consultation with the markets, the Bank issued a Notice in February 1989 (BSD/1989/1) which sets out the Bank's supervisory policy on the treatment of loan transfers involving banks.

Conclusion

Over the last three years, the international syndicated loan market has clearly demonstrated its ability to mobilise substantial volumes of funds on behalf of a variety of different borrowers. The strength of investment spending over the past three years and the buoyant levels of merger and acquisition activity in recent years have generally provided international financial markets with a major stimulus on the demand side. In particular, acquisition-related lending has come to represent a major component of the overall market for international syndicated credits. More recently, there have been some indications that borrowers from the less developed countries are making greater use of the market in specific contexts. The market has also shown its ability to meet the increasingly complex needs of major corporate borrowers. While the demand for syndicated loans may fluctuate over time, this sector is likely to remain a significant and durable component of international financing.

Note on the Market in the 1990s and Beyond

The market for syndicated eurocurrency loans grew dramatically from 1991 to 1995, leveled in 1996, became a borrowers' market, and then, when Russia defaulted on its debt in mid-1998, became a lenders' market. The Tables at the end of this note describe the growth into 1997, after which point the time series ends. In the mid-1990s, much of the growth refinanced outstanding loans or financed acquisitions, infrastructure projects, or the restructuring of national industries, such as telecommunications. By 1999 and through 2000, jumbo loans to fund mergers and acquisitions dominated the market, squeezing out the ordinary corporate loans and accounting for most new lending. In 2000, a syndicated loan of $30 billion, the largest ever, supported the hostile takeover of Mannesmann A.G. by Vodaphone. M&A financings brought the syndicated loan market together with the eurobond market. Banks could easily raise large amounts in the loan market relatively short term as they hurried to finance the M&A transaction, then refinance longer term in the eurobond market. R. Bream, *Surge in M&A Comes to the Rescue*, Financial Times, May 19, 2001. The Vodaphone funding did just this. Borrowers were generally based in countries of the OECD, whose membership expanded during this period (see Chapter 4). Emerging markets accounted for very little, barely $12 billion in 2000. Though the U.S. dollar continued to dominate, its share declined as the role of Sterling and the French franc grew.

Lead managers came from industrial countries. Studies of the top ten lead managers in 1991 and 1998 ranked them by volume of loans arranged. They revealed that U.S. banks accounted for 6 of the top ten in 1991 and 4 in 1998. Two U.K. banks were in the top ten in 1991 and three made the list in 1998. Others hailed from Switzerland, Germany, and the Netherlands. Despite the huge size of Japanese banks, only one placed among the top ten lead managers in 1991 and none placed in 1998. By 1999, ten banks lead managed 80% of the syndicated loans in Europe. See J. Evans, *U.S. Banks Remain Tops in Syndication*, American Banker, Jan. 9, 1992; C. Spink, *Jumps in the Cycle*, Euromoney, Aug. 1996, at 69; M. Peterson, The Relationship Starts to Change, Euromoney (November 1998) at 64 (Peterson); and J. Dyson, *Big Banks Learn to Flex Their Muscles,* Euromoney, July 1999, at 140 (Dyson).

The lenders market that emerged in 1998 reflected several trends. Major borrowers from many emerging markets, including sovereign governments, seemed much riskier following the Asian financial crisis and its contagious spread to other regions. The Russian default drew the line

Table 1. Announced International Syndicated Loans (US$ bns)
Source: Capital DATA; BIS

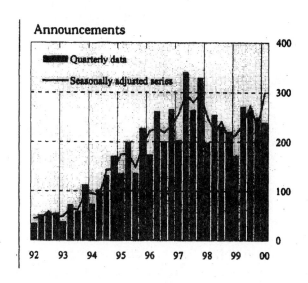

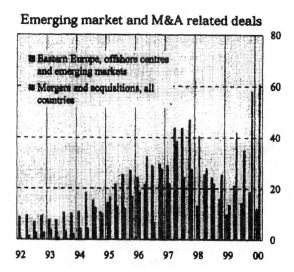

Table 2. Spreads on euro-credits[1]

Basis points

	1991	1993	1994	1995	1996	1-9 1997
OECD area	80	79	59	43	50	57
Non-OECD	74	100	107	108	99	115
General average	79	81	64	50	56	65

1. Weighted average of spreads applied to euro-loans signed during the period. Tax-sparing loans as well as facilities classified under "Other debt facilities" are excluded.
Source: OECD/ Financial Market Trends, Oct. 1994 at p.67, Nov. 1996 at p.140, and Nov. 1997 at 120.

for banks around the world. The number of lenders in the market fell precipitously when Japanese banks pulled out of the market, reducing the supply of funds by 20%, according to Peterson. As a result, spreads widened and the "market-flex" clause became common for U.S. banks, at least. When they arranged loans, rather than promise the borrower a spread, the banks began to offer only provisional prices and retain the right to increase the price if the market was not receptive to the original one. Many borrowers in emerging markets accepted the market-flex clause, but those in Europe, and banks there, objected to the clause because it removed pricing certainty. See Peterson at 65. In addition, as banks merged, the new bank was often not able to take on a credit exposure to a single borrower that equaled the sum of the exposure of the merging banks. This also reduced demand for syndicated eurocredit paper. See Dyson at 141. This shift to a lenders market allowed Citigroup in 2001 to reveal that it would limit new loan syndications to existing customers whose other business with the group generated adequate income from fees. A. Leibowitz, *Citi May Limit Syndications to Its Existing Customers*, American Banker, Feb. 7, 2001.

The secondary market that developed for syndicated eurocredits in the 1980s expanded. In December 1996, leading banks formed the Loan Market Association, whose purpose was to encourage corporate and governmental borrowers, particularly in developing and transition countries, to let their paper trade in secondary markets. The LMA would draft legal language and design methods to settle the transactions. It argued that the increased liquidity would lower the cost of funds for the borrowers. See G. Gapper, *Banks Seek to Set Up Secondary Market for Debt*, Financial Times, Dec. 17, 1996. Some of the growing liquidity in the secondary market during the 1990s might have been due to special conditions. For example, in liquidity in 1998 might have been occurred, in part, because the Japanese banks were unloading their portfolios to fund problem loans at home. See Dyson at 142. By 2000, the LMA estimated a secondary market of $30 billion in Europe and over $150 billion in the U.S. Institutional investors were a small but growing source of demand in Europe, perhaps less than 5%, but accounted for over 40% of all investors in the U.S. secondary market. B. Beasley-Murray, *Reality Hits Mad Merger Pricing*, Euromoney, July 2000, at 122; R. Bream, *Institutions Move In On Leveraged Loans*, Financial Times, Nov. 17, 2000.

Table 3. Average maturity of recorded euro-credits

Years/months

	1991	1993	1994	1995	1996	1-9 1997
OECD area	5/1	4/3	5/0	5/4	5/4	5/0
Non-OECD[1]	7/7	5/5	5/9	5/1	5/0	5/2
General average	5/5	4/5	5/1	5/3	5/4	5/0

1. Developing countries only.
Source: OECD/ Financial Market Trends, Oct. 1994 at p.68, Nov. 1996 at p.141, and Nov. 1997 at 121.

Table 4. Medium-term international bank loans by borrowing country[1]

$ billion

	1991	1993	1994	1995	1996	1-9 1997
Borrowers						
OECD area	87.8	116.4	212.5	329.4	311.8	245.2
Non-OECD	27.6	20.0	23.4	40.8	33.4	43.7
International development institutions	0.6	0.3	0.3	-	-	0.1
Total	**116.0**	**136.7**	**236.2**	**370.2**	**345.2**	**289.0**

1. Covers the aggregate of foreign and euro medium-term bank loans, excluding loan renegotiations.
Source: OECD/ Financial Market Trends, Oct. 1994 at p.69, Nov. 1996 at p.141, and Nov. 1997 at 121.

From the early 1990s, as the tables show, spreads fell and maturities for OECD borrowers contracted, then lengthened again. Spreads narrowed to as low as 11.5 BP. Aggressive competition squeezed profits.

Banks turned increasingly to developing countries and countries in transition. Hungary's central bank raised $350 million for five years at a spread of 20 basis points over LIBOR. Countries like Kazakstan and Namibia debuted in the market. Worried regulators were reminded of the events leading to the 1982 crisis. They questioned whether lenders had adequate information about borrowers. See O. De Senerpont Domis, *Concerns Mounting Over Risks in Booming Syndication Market*, American Banker, Jan. 29, 1997; N. Povey, *The Banks Learn How to Say No,* Euromoney, July 1997 at 123. In the late 1990s, the lenders market brought wider spreads. See Dyson at 141.

Table 5. Currency distribution of international bank loans[1]

Per cent

	1991	1993	1994	1995	1996	1-9 1997
US dollar	84.5	81.0	80.7	76.8	74.7	72.4
Pound sterling	4.2	2.2	8.6	11.7	12.5	18.3
Deutschmark	2.1	3.2	1.1	4.1	4.2	3.3
ECU	3.9	6.4	3.9	3.8	0.2	0.3
French franc	n.a.	1.9	1.6	1.5	4.8	0.4
Japanese yen	1.1	0.7	0.2	0.2	0.2	0.1
Swiss franc	0.6	0.4	0.1	0.1	0.5	1.4
Other	3.6	4.2	3.8	1.8	2.9	3.8
Total	100.0	100.0	100.0	100.0	100.0	100.0
Memorandum item:						
Total in US$ billion equivalent	117.7	140.2	243.1	378.6	355.1	303.2

1.   Foreign and international bank loans, excluding loan renegotiations. Currencies of denomination converted into US dollar at constant (end-1990) exchange rates.
Source: OECD/ Financial Market Trends, Oct. 1994 at p.69, Nov. 1996 at p.142, and Nov. 197 at p. 121.

Notes and Questions

1. Be sure you understand the definition of a syndicated eurocurrency loan (eurocredit).

2. Who are the parties to a eurocredit? Note that this market expanded during an era of strong lending to borrowers based in developing countries.

3. Compared to a standard bank loan, what are the special features of a eurocredit? How do they work? Why are they possible? How do these features help the parties?

C.   THE ALLOCATION OF RISK AMONG THE PARTIES TO A EUROCREDIT

The standard contract for a eurocredit describes who will bear various risks. Some clauses are common to many types of loans. Others, more peculiar to a eurocredit, are the subject of this section.

The clauses come from a sample Revolving Credit Agreement by Anthony Gooch and Linda Klein. The authors, whose practice includes this field, wrote a hypothetical agreement for State–Owned Company to borrow U.S. $250 million for 5 years. The agreement is dated April 15, 1991. The funds are for working capital. The guarantor is the borrower's home government, the Republic of Somewhere. The managers are Big Bank. S.A. (a French bank), Bigger Bank PLC (a British bank), and Biggest Bank, N.A. (a U.S. bank). The eurodollar agent is Infallible Agent Bank and the swing-line agent is Biggest Bank, N.A. The lenders are The Banks Named Herein, often called participating banks in the market.

This is a multi-option revolving credit facility. Within the $250 million limit, the borrower can draw funds priced either as a eurocurrency loan based on LIBOR or as the swing-line loan based on the U.S. prime rate, which is the rate the banks charge their best customers. The authors explain:

> When a borrower may require funds on short notice, the swing-line option is a common alternative in Eurodollar facilities, under which LIBOR-based advances generally require at least three business days' advance notice so that the lenders can make their funding arrangements in the London interbank market. The swing-line option also serves as a stop gap if the lenders cannot fund a desired advance in the London market.

For these services, the borrower agrees to pay interest described below and several fees. A 1% commitment fee is paid annually on the unused part of each commitment. A 1/4% facility fee is paid annually on the full commitment, used or not. The management fee, paid at signing, is 1% of the total commitments (in this case, $250 million). Each year both the agents receive $10,000. All payments are made either by or to the eurodollar agent or the swing-line agent, as appropriate.

Sovereign immunity is waived. New York law governs this agreement, although many eurocredits are governed by U.K. law.

These agreements are normally quite long, suggesting the drafters are paid by the weight of the document. Here we excerpt parts of the agreement that are specially relevant for eurodollar loans. Some clauses concern the relation between the borrowers and the lenders, others the relation between managers, agents, and the participating banks.

As you read the clauses, ask how each allocates risk and responsibility among the parties. Assume that in mid-1996, a government-owned

Korean firm negotiates a $250 million 5 year eurocredit with the terms described in this sample agreement: advances of 1,3, or 6 months and a 1⅛% spread. Lenders include banks from Europe, Japan, and the U.S. A major U.S. bank lead manages. Consider also the consequences of this allocation for the parties and the financial system. Are there some aspects of these agreements that should concern national regulators?

1. THE BASIC TERMS OF THE LOAN

a. ADVANCES AND REPAYMENT

A. GOOCH AND L. KLEIN, LOAN DOCUMENTATION
(2nd ed. 1991)("Gooch and Klein").

"Advance" means any Eurodollar Advance or Swing–Line Advance.

"Commitment," with respect to any Bank at any time means the amount designated as such and set forth opposite the name of that Bank on the signature pages hereof, subject to reduction as provided herein.

2.1.   *Commitment to Lend.* (a) On the terms and subject to the conditions set forth herein, each Bank shall make Advances hereunder through its Lending Branch to the Borrower from time to time in an aggregate principal amount at any one time outstanding not exceeding that Bank's Commitment. Failure by any Bank to make an Advance to the Borrower shall not relieve any other Bank of its obligations hereunder. No Bank shall have any responsibility for any failure by any other Bank to fulfill its obligations hereunder.

2.2.   *Term.* The *"Term"* of each Advance shall mean the period beginning with the applicable Disbursement Date and, (i) in the case of a Eurodollar Advance, ending on the day numerically corresponding to that Disbursement Date in the first, third or sixth month thereafter (subject to Subsection 7.1(b)), and (ii) in the case of a Swing–Line Advance, ending on a day not later than the seventh day after that Disbursement Date (subject to Subsection 7.1(c)), in each case as specified by the Borrower in accordance with Section 2.3.

2.3.   *Notice of Intention and Commitment to Borrow.* (a) The Borrower may request Eurodollar Advances hereunder by delivering to the Eurodollar Agent a notice substantially in the form set forth in Exhibit D, with all blank spaces appropriately completed in compliance with Subsection 2.3(d), not later than 1:00 p.m. (London time) on the third Banking Day before the day on which the Borrower wishes to make the borrowing.

(b) The Borrower may request Swing–Line Advances hereunder by giving the Swing–Line Agent notice by telephone and confirming it immediately by a written notice substantially in the form set forth in Exhibit E, with all blank spaces appropriately completed in compliance with Subsection 2.3(d), hand-delivered or sent by telex or facsimile transmission and received not later than 9:30 a.m. (New York City time) on the day on which the Borrower wishes to make the borrowing.

The aggregate principal amount of Eurodollar Advances to be made on a Disbursement Date must be $50,000,000 or a higher integral multiple of $5,000,000. The aggregate principal amount of all Advances to be made on a Disbursement Date shall be an amount which, when taken together with all other Advances outstanding on that Disbursement Date (excluding any Advances to be repaid from the proceeds of Advances to be made on that date), does not exceed the Total Commitment.

2.4. *Disbursements.* (a) The Eurodollar Agent shall promptly advise each Bank by telex or facsimile transmission of the contents of each request for Eurodollar Advances hereunder, and the amount of the Eurodollar Advance to be made by that Bank on that date, which shall be that Bank's Pro Rata Share of the aggregate principal amount of all the Eurodollar Advances to be made on that date determined on the basis of the respective Commitments of the Banks, subject to such rounding as the Eurodollar Agent may determine. Except as otherwise expressly provided in Subsection 2.4(b), by 10:00 a.m. (New York City time) on each Disbursement Date, each Bank shall, subject to the conditions set forth herein, make available to the Eurodollar Agent the amount so specified, in funds settled through the New York Clearing House Interbank Payments System or such other same-day funds as the Eurodollar Agent may at the time determine to be customary for the settlement in New York City of international banking transactions denominated in Dollars, by deposit to the Eurodollar Agent's account specified in or pursuant to Section 7.1. Subject to the conditions set forth herein, and except as otherwise expressly provided in Subsection 2.4(b), the Eurodollar Agent shall, on that Disbursement Date, credit the funds so received to the account specified by the Borrower pursuant to Subsection 2.3(d).

' (b) Any Bank that is obligated to make a new Advance hereunder on a day on which the Borrower is obligated to repay an outstanding Advance of that Bank shall apply the proceeds of its new Advance to make the repayment, and only an amount equal to the excess (if any) of the amount being so borrowed from that Bank over the amount being so repaid to that Bank shall be made available by that Bank to the relevant Agent and remitted by that Agent to the Borrower.

(c) The Swing–Line Agent shall, by 10:30 a.m. (New York City time) on each Disbursement Date for Swing–Line Advances, advise each Bank by telephone of the contents of the request for the Advances and the amount of the Swing–Line Advance to be made by that Bank on that date, which shall be that Bank's Pro Rata Share of the aggregate principal amount of all the Swing–Line Advances to be made on that date determined on the basis of the respective Commitments of the Banks, subject to such rounding as the Swing–Line Agent may determine, and shall confirm such advice immediately by written notice. By 12:30 p.m. (New York City time) on the Disbursement Date, each Bank shall, subject to the conditions set forth herein, make available to the Swing–Line Agent the amount so specified, in immediately available funds, by deposit to the Swing–Line Agent's account specified in or pursuant to Section 7.1. Subject to the conditions set forth herein, and except as otherwise expressly provided in Subsection 2.4(b), the Swing–Line Agent shall, on the Disbursement Date, credit the funds so received to the account specified by the Borrower pursuant to Subsection 2.3(d).

3.1. *Repayment.* Except as otherwise expressly provided herein, the Borrower shall repay each Advance on the last day of its Term.

3.2. *No Prepayment of Eurodollar Advances.* Except as provided in Section 3.4 and Section 3.5, the Borrower may not prepay Eurodollar Advances.

16.3. *Currency.* (a) If any expense required to be reimbursed pursuant to Article 15 is originally incurred in a currency other than Dollars, the Borrower shall nonetheless make reimbursement of that expense in Dollars, in an amount equal to the amount in Dollars that would have been required for the person that incurred that expense to have purchased, in accordance with normal banking procedures, the sum paid in that other currency (after any premium and costs of exchange) on the day that expense was originally incurred. Any interest accruing thereon pursuant to Section 4.2 shall be computed on the basis of the Dollar amount.

(b) Each reference in this Agreement to Dollars is of the essence. The obligation of the Borrower in respect of any amount due under this Agreement or the Notes shall, notwithstanding any payment in any other currency (whether pursuant to a judgment or otherwise), be discharged only to the extent of the amount in Dollars that the person entitled to receive that payment may, in accordance with normal banking procedures, purchase with the sum paid in the other currency (after any premium and costs of exchange) on the Banking Day immediately following the day on which that person receives that payment. If the amount in Dollars that may be so purchased for any reason falls short of the amount originally due, the Borrower shall pay such additional amount, in Dollars, as is necessary to compensate for the shortfall. Any obligation of the Borrower not discharged by that payment shall, to the fullest extent permitted by applicable law, be due as a separate and independent obligation and until discharged as provided herein, shall continue in full force and effect.

Questions

1. Work through the procedure for making the loans. Why is this called a revolving credit agreement?

2. Who bears the risk of exchange rate fluctuations between the dollar and the currency of Somewhere? How would you determine who is best able to bear this risk? What information would you need to know about each party?

b. INTEREST RATE DETERMINATION

GOOCH AND KLEIN

"Federal Funds Rate," for any day, means the rate of interest (expressed as an annual rate) set forth for that day (or, if that day is not a New York Banking Day, the next preceding New York Banking Day) (i) in the daily statistical release of the Federal Reserve Bank of New York entitled "Composite 3:30 p.m. Quotations for U.S. Government Securities" opposite the heading "Federal Funds/Effective Rate" or (ii) if that publication ceases to be published, in any successor to that publication or, if neither that publication nor any successor publication is available, in another publication selected by the Swing–Line Agent reasonably and in good faith for the purpose of giving effect to the intent of the parties, as the rate for overnight borrowing between banks in Dollars in immediately available funds.

"LIBOR," with respect to any Eurodollar Advance, means the rate of interest (expressed as an annual rate) determined by the Eurodollar Agent to be the arithmetic mean (rounded up to the nearest one sixteenth of one percent (1/16%)) of the respective rates of interest communicated to the Eurodollar Agent by the several Reference Banks as the rates at which each of them would offer a deposit in Dollars for a period coextensive with the Term of the Advance in the amount of $5,000,000 (or, if that amount is not representative of the normal amount for a single deposit transaction in that currency in that market at the time, such other amount as is representative thereof), to major banks in the London interbank market at approximately 11:00 a.m. (London time) on the second London Banking Day before the commencement of the Term of that Advance; *provided, however,* that if any of the Reference Banks fails so to communicate a rate, LIBOR shall be determined on the basis of the rate or rates communicated to the Eurodollar Agent by the remaining Reference Bank or Reference Banks.

"Margin" means one and one eighth percent (1 1/8%).

"Reference Bank" means each of the respective principal London offices of Biggest Bank, N.A., Average Quoter Bank Plc and Small & Obscure Banking Company, and *"Reference Banks"* means those offices collectively.

"Swing–Line Rate" means, for any day, the greater of (i) the rate of interest publicly announced by the Swing–Line Agent in New York City as its prime or base rate in effect for that day and (ii) the sum of one eighth of one percent (1/8%) and the Federal Funds Rate for that day.

4.1. *Basic Rate.* (a) Except as otherwise expressly provided in Section 4.2, interest shall accrue on each Advance during its Term, from and including the first day of that Term, to but excluding the last day thereof, at a rate per annum equal, (i) in the case of Eurodollar Advances, to the sum of the Margin and LIBOR for that Advance and, (ii) in the case of Swing–Line Advances, to the Swing–Line Rate as in effect on each day during that period.

Questions

1. Be sure you understand the floating interest rate. How does it work? Why have it?

2. What accounts for the difference between interest rate determination for the eurodollar advances and the swing-line advances?

3. Who bears the risk that the lender's cost of funds will change? Why is this done? During the negotiations for the hypothetical loan described at the start of this section C, what could the borrower propose to reduce the impact on it of a big rise in LIBOR (eg., from 6% to 18%)?

4. The move to the European Monetary Union and the Euro created a problem for banks: how would they determine the benchmark interbank offer rate (to be called Euribor)? Euribor would replace national interbank rates, like FIBOR (Frankfort) in Germany. But Euribor's benchmark banks would include banks from other countries than Germany, some of which would presumably have lower credit ratings than the German banks and therefore raise the benchmark above what it would have been if only German banks contributed to it. In December 1997, the European Banking Federation issued rules. A panel of 64 qualified banks would include 4 from countries outside EMU and 60 from inside it. Banks were to meet strict size standards. Each country would have a maximum number of banks that could participate on the panel; if any country had more banks qualified to be panelists than its quota, the banks would rotate membership. See G. Graham, *Banks Settle Dispute on Euribor Rate*, Financial Times, December 16, 1997.

5. Suppose that the reference banks chosen for the hypothetical loan in 1996 were Japanese banks in London. How would this choice affect the borrower? Could the borrower have protected against the risk that the cost of funds to these reference banks might rise above the cost of funds to other banks?

6. Suppose the borrower of the hypothetical loan takes a 6 month advance at 10% LIBOR and LIBOR rates fall to 6% in month 2. The borrower cannot take advantage of declining rates. How could it redesign the contract to allow it to shorten an advance in these circumstances?

7. Clause 3 prohibits prepayment. Some agreements permit prepayment but add a "broken funding indemnity clause" that obligates the borrower to pay lenders for any losses they incur due to early

payment. The problem is that the banks would "need to liquidate or redeploy the deposits they took to fund the loan for the interest period concerned." See L. Buchheit, *How to Negotiate the Broken Funding Indemnity Clause*, International Financial Law Review, Apr. 1994, at 20. If interest rates fell after the period began, the bank would not earn as much on the new investment and might even lose money. The indemnity clause assumes that banks match their floating rate loans with deposits to fund them. But some banks deliberately mismatch, taking a view on the direction of interest rates. Should the indemnity be contingent on whether the bank actually links the loan to deposits? How can the bank prove its method of funding? If rates move up instead of down, should the bank pay the borrower in case of prepayment?

8. Borrowers in many developing countries defaulted on their eurocredit payments when LIBOR rose to about 20% in the early 1980s. Many had borrowed years earlier when LIBOR was 6%. The countries' foreign exchange earnings were a function of international commodity prices, which did not rise with the interest rate.

    a. Since both lenders and borrowers knew the source of the countries' hard currency at the time of the loan, was this a credible allocation of risk?

    b. What alternatives would there be to allocating risk this way?

c.   EVENTS OF DEFAULT: THE CROSS DEFAULT CLAUSE

GOOCH AND KLEIN

12.1   *Events of Default.* If one or more of the following events of default (each an "*Event of Default*") occurs and is continuing, the Eurodollar Agent and the Banks shall be entitled to the remedies set forth in Section 12.2.

(d) The Borrower or any Subsidiary (i) fails to pay any of its Indebtedness as and when it becomes payable or (ii) fails to perform or observe any covenant or agreement to be performed or observed by it contained in any other agreement or in any instrument evidencing any of its Indebtedness and, as a result of that failure, any other party to that agreement or instrument is entitled to exercise, and has not irrevocably waived, the right to accelerate the maturity of any amount owing thereunder.

(e) The Guarantor (i) fails to pay any of its External Indebtedness as and when it becomes payable or (ii) fails to perform or observe any covenant or agreement to be performed or observed by it contained in any agreement or instrument evidencing any of its External Indebtedness if, as a result of that failure, any other party to that agreement or instrument is entitled to exercise, and has not irrevocably waived, the right to accelerate the maturity of any amount owing thereunder; *provided, however,* that a failure to pay External

Indebtedness shall not constitute an Event of Default under this Subsection if (i) the overdue amounts in the aggregate do not exceed $10,000,000 or the equivalent of that amount in another currency or currencies, (ii) the obligation to pay the overdue amounts has not resulted from acceleration and (iii) the failure is remedied on or before the thirtieth day after it occurs; and *provided further, however,* that a failure to perform any such other covenant or agreement shall not constitute an Event of Default under this Subsection if (i) the aggregate principal amount of External Indebtedness subject to acceleration as a result of all such failures at the time does not exceed $250,000,000 or the equivalent of that amount in another currency or currencies and (ii) the failure is remedied on or before the thirtieth day after it occurs.

12.2. *Default Remedies.* (a) If any Event of Default occurs and is continuing, the Eurodollar Agent shall, upon the request of Majority Banks, by notice to the Borrower and the Guarantor, (i) declare the obligations of each Bank hereunder to be terminated, whereupon those obligations shall terminate, and (ii) declare all amounts payable hereunder or under the Notes by the Borrower that would otherwise be due after the date of termination to be immediately due and payable, whereupon all those amounts shall become immediately due and payable, all without diligence, presentment, demand of payment, protest or notice of any kind, which are expressly waived by the Borrower and the Guarantor;

(b) Each Bank is acting hereunder individually. Nothing herein, and no action taken by any Agent, Bank or Manager, shall be construed to constitute them or any of them a partnership, an association, any other entity or a joint venture. Without limiting the generality of the foregoing, each Agent, Bank and Manager shall be entitled to act independently, whether by court action or otherwise, to enforce or protect its rights under this Agreement and the Notes, subject, in the case of each Bank, to the provisions of Section 12.2(a) regarding any declaration that any unmatured obligations of the Borrower hereunder or under the Notes shall be immediately due and payable upon the occurrence of an Event of Default.

12.3. *Right of Set off.* If any amount payable by the Borrower or the Guarantor hereunder is not paid as and when due, each of the Borrower and the Guarantor authorizes each Bank and each Affiliate of each Bank to proceed, to the fullest extent permitted by applicable law, without prior notice, by right of set off, banker's lien, counterclaim or otherwise, against any assets of the Borrower or the Guarantor in any currency that may at any time be in the possession of that Bank or Affiliate, at any branch or office, to the full extent of all amounts payable to the Banks hereunder. Any Bank that so proceeds or that has an Affiliate that so proceeds shall forthwith give notice to the Agents of any action taken by that Bank or Affiliate pursuant to this Section.

"External Indebtedness," with respect to any Person, means any Indebtedness of that Person (i) that is or may by its terms become payable in any currency other than the lawful currency of the Republic of Somewhere or (ii) that is payable to any Person resident in, organized under the laws of or having its principal office outside the Republic of Somewhere.

Questions

1. Why have the cross-default clause?

2. Under what circumstances would the cross-default clause be effectively unavailable to the lenders? Suppose that (a) the borrower failed to service another loan on schedule because the country's foreign exchange reserves had fallen below its short-term foreign debt, (b) the central bank was not willing to make dollars available to domestic borrowers seeking to repay their foreign loans, and all of the agreements for the country's substantial foreign debt had cross default clauses.

3. How effective would the cross-default clause in this agreement be?

4. What happens if the lenders disagree?

5. What could the Korean lender have proposed in the hypothetical loan during negotiations in 1996?

d. ADVERSE CHANGE

GOOCH AND KLEIN

(c) If the Eurodollar Agent, after consultation with the Banks to the extent practicable, determines at any time that (i) it would not be possible to determine LIBOR for a period of one, three or six months as provided herein or (ii) LIBOR as so determined would not adequately reflect the costs to Majority Banks of funding Eurodollar Advances for that period in the London interbank market, the Eurodollar Agent shall forthwith give notice of that determination to the Borrower and the Banks, whereupon the obligations of the Banks to make Eurodollar Advances to the Borrower for a Term equal to the period or periods specified in that notice shall be suspended until the Eurodollar Agent gives notice to the Borrower and the Banks that the circumstances that gave rise to that determination no longer exist.

3.4. *Special Prepayment.* (a) If the Borrower gives notice to the Agents pursuant to Subsection 6.1(a) that it will be required to withhold or deduct Indemnifiable Taxes from a payment to any Bank under this Agreement, the Borrower may elect to terminate the Commitment of that Bank and prepay all outstanding Advances of that Bank on any Banking Day selected by the Borrower by giving notice to the Eurodollar Agent (which shall promptly advise each Bank thereof) not later than the fifth Banking Day before the Banking Day so selected; *provided, however,* that the prepayment date may not be more than five

Banking Days before the effective date of the requirement to so withhold or deduct Indemnifiable Taxes; and *provided further, however,* that the Borrower shall not prepay Advances or terminate any Commitment pursuant to this Section if, more than ten Banking Days before the scheduled prepayment date, the withholding or deduction of Indemnifiable Taxes ceases to be required.

6.1.   *Withholding; Gross–Up.* (a) Each payment by the Borrower or the Guarantor under this Agreement or the Notes shall be made without withholding on account of any Taxes; *provided, however,* that, if any Taxes are required so to be withheld, the Borrower or the Guarantor (as the case may be) shall give notice to that effect to the Agents, make the necessary withholding and make timely payment of the amount withheld to the appropriate governmental authority. If any Taxes so withheld are Indemnifiable Taxes, the Borrower or the Guarantor (as the case may be) shall forthwith pay any additional amount that may be necessary to ensure that the net amount actually received by each Agent, Bank or Manager (as the case may be) free and clear of Indemnifiable Taxes is equal to the amount that the Agent, Bank or Manager would have received had no Indemnifiable Taxes been withheld. All Taxes so withheld shall be paid before penalties attach thereto or interest accrues thereon. If any such penalties or interest nonetheless become due, the Borrower or the Guarantor (as the case may be) shall make prompt payment thereof to the appropriate governmental authority. If any Agent, Bank or Manager pays any amount in respect of Indemnifiable Taxes on any payment due from the Borrower or the Guarantor hereunder, or penalties or interest thereon, the Borrower or the Guarantor (as the case may be) shall reimburse that Agent, Bank or Manager in Dollars for that payment on demand. If the Borrower or the Guarantor pays any such Taxes or penalties or interest thereon, it shall deliver official tax receipts evidencing the payment or certified copies thereof to the Eurodollar Agent not later than the thirtieth day after payment.

(b) If any Bank gives notice to the Agents of increased costs pursuant to Section 15.4, the Borrower may elect to terminate the Commitment of that Bank and prepay all outstanding Advances of that Bank on any Banking Day by giving notice to the Eurodollar Agent (which shall promptly advise each Bank thereof) not later than the fifth Banking Day before the Banking Day so specified.

15.4.   *Increased Costs.* The Borrower shall reimburse each Bank in Dollars on demand for all costs incurred and reductions in amounts received or receivable, as determined by that Bank, that are attributable to that Bank's Advances or the performance by that Bank of its obligations under this Agreement and that occur by reason of the promulgation of any law, regulation or treaty or any change therein or in the application or interpretation thereof or by reason of compliance by that Bank with any direction, requirement or request (whether or not having the force of law) of any governmental authority, including, without limitation, any such cost or reduction resulting from (i) the imposition or amendment of any tax other than (A) any tax measured by the net income of that Bank or its Lending Branch and imposed by the jurisdiction in which that Bank's principal office or Lending Branch is situated and (B) any Taxes (any such cost or reduction occurring by reason of the imposition or amendment of any tax referred to in clauses (A) and (B) of this Section being expressly excluded from the coverage of this Section), (ii) the imposition or amendment of any reserve, special deposit or similar requirement against assets of, liabilities of, deposits with or for the account of, or loans by, that Bank or (iii) the imposition or amendment of any capital requirements or provisions relating to capital adequacy that have the effect of reducing the rate of return on such Bank's or the relevant Lending Branch's capital as a consequence of its Advances or its obligations hereunder to a level below that which it could have achieved but for such adoption, change or compliance. If a Bank has sold one or more participations in its Advances, costs incurred and reductions in amounts receivable by the participants shall be deemed to be attributable to the relevant Advances for purposes of this Section; *provided, however,* that the Borrower shall not be required to reimburse any Bank for an amount greater than the amount that would have been due if that Bank had not sold participations in its Advances.

3.5.   *Illegality.* If any Bank determines at any time that any law, regulation or treaty or any change therein or in the interpretation or application thereof makes or will make it unlawful for the Bank to fulfill its commitment in accordance with Section 2.1, to maintain an Advance or to claim or receive any amount payable to it hereunder, the Bank shall give notice of that determination to the Borrower, with copies to the Agents, whereupon the obligations of that Bank hereunder shall terminate and the Bank's Commitment shall be reduced to zero. The Borrower shall repay the Advances of that Bank in full at the end of their respective Terms; *provided, however,* that, if the affected Bank certifies to the Borrower that earlier repayment is necessary in order to enable that Bank to comply with the relevant law, regulation or treaty and specifies an earlier date for repayment, the Borrower shall make repayment on the earlier date so specified. Repayment pursuant to this Section shall be made without premium but together with interest accrued on the Advances being repaid to the date of repayment and all other amounts then payable to the relevant Bank by the Borrower hereunder.

Notes and Questions

1. Why make the borrower liable for these changes? Are these credible allocations of risk?

2. Using the hypothetical described at the beginning of this Section C, suppose that in 1999 a Japanese participating bank was required to increase its bad loan provisions generally. It tells the Korean borrower

to pay the bank's share of that increase. Must the firm pay or terminate the loan? If so, should the contract have been drafted differently?

3. Clause (c) above is one form of the disaster clause. The notion is that when banks make eurocredits they must be able to fund at LIBOR. If they cannot because of events in the market, they should be able to withdraw from their obligation to lend and the borrower should repay. Consider an alternative. Would it be better to give the lenders the right to seek other funding sources and change the pricing of the loan appropriately? The borrower could prepay and withdraw. What if only a few participating banks must pay a premium to raise funds because the market considers them higher risk than the others? This tiering often happens in the interbank market. Should they be protected? What if lower tier (higher risk) banks form the majority of the lenders?

4. The original motive for the illegality clause was to protect banks if their home governments closed the eurocurrency market by regulation. After over twenty years, however, few now expect the euromarkets to be closed. Does this clause still have a purpose? Should it be removed from standard contracts? Some clauses broaden their scope by referring to government policies with or without the force of law. Is this appropriate?

2. ALLOCATION OF RISK AMONG MANAGERS, AGENTS, AND PARTICIPATING BANKS

Since many banks lend but only a few deal directly with the borrower and guarantor, the banks provide in the eurocredit agreement for their own responsibilities and risks, on the one hand, and for circumstances in which they must act jointly. The following clauses describe a standard solution. As you read them, consider the balance that is achieved between individual and joint responsibility. What would account for this?

GOOCH AND KLEIN

WHEREAS the Borrower proposes to borrow from the Banks, and the Banks, severally but not jointly, propose to lend to the Borrower, an aggregate amount of up to $250,000,000 at any one time outstanding, the parties agree as follows.

14.2. *Exculpation.* The Agents and the Managers and their respective directors, officers, employees and agents shall have no responsibility for (i) the truth of any representation or warranty made by the Borrower or the Guarantor in this Agreement or any other document delivered in connection with this Agreement, (ii) the validity or enforceability of this Agreement or any such document, (iii) any failure of the Borrower or the Guarantor to fulfill any of its respective obligations under this Agreement or any such document or (iv) any action taken or omitted to be taken in connection with this Agreement or the Notes, absent gross negligence or willful misconduct. Each Agent shall be entitled to rely in good faith on any communication or document believed by it to be genuine and to have been sent or signed by the proper person or persons and on the opinions and statements of any legal counsel or other professional advisors selected by it and shall not be liable to any other person for any consequence of any such reliance.

14.3. *Information about the Borrower and the Guarantor.* (a) Each Bank has investigated and evaluated, and shall continue to investigate and evaluate, the creditworthiness of the Borrower and the Guarantor and such other issues and information as it has judged appropriate and prudent in connection with its commitment to lend hereunder and the making of its Advances. Except as expressly provided herein, neither Agent shall have any duty to provide any Bank with any credit or other information with respect to the Borrower or the Guarantor, whether that information comes into its possession before or after the disbursement of any Advance.

(b) The Eurodollar Agent shall promptly (i) advise each Bank upon receipt of all the documents referred to in Section 8.1, (ii) advise each Bank upon its receipt of any documents requested in accordance with Section 8.2, (iii) forward to each Bank all Notes received by it for that Bank and (iv) forward to each Bank copies of any documents delivered to the Eurodollar Agent in accordance with Section 6.1. The Eurodollar Agent shall, as soon as practicable, forward to each Bank copies of the documents received pursuant to Section 8.1 and Section 8.2. Each Agent shall promptly transmit to each Bank each notice or other document received by that Agent from the Borrower or the Guarantor addressed to, or calling for action by, that Bank.

14.4. *Duties in Respect of Events of Default.* Neither Agent shall be under any obligation to inquire as to the performance by the Borrower or the Guarantor of its respective obligations under this Agreement or the Notes; *provided, however,* that each Agent shall give prompt notice to each Bank of any Default or Event of Default of which it receives actual notice in its capacity as an Agent hereunder.

14.5. *Other Dealings with the Borrower and the Guarantor.* The Agents and the Managers and their respective Affiliates may, without liability to account to any Bank therefor, make loans to, accept deposits from, and generally engage in any kind of business with, the Borrower and the Guarantor as though the Agents were not the Agents and the Managers were not the Managers hereunder.

14.7. *Covenant to Reimburse.* Each Bank shall reimburse each Agent (to the extent not reimbursed by the Borrower or the Guarantor) on demand for that Bank's Pro Rata Share of all expenses incurred by that Agent in the exercise of its responsibilities hereunder, including, without limitation, the reasonable fees and expenses of legal and other professional advisors.

"Majority Banks" means, at any time when no Advance is outstanding, Banks whose Commitments total more than fifty percent

(50%) of the Total Commitment and, at any time when any Advance is outstanding, Banks maintaining Advances representing more than fifty percent (50%) of the aggregate principal amount of the Advances outstanding at that time.

13.2.   *Sharing of Payments*. (a) Except as provided in Subsection 13.2(b), if any Bank obtains payment of any amount payable hereunder from the Borrower or the Guarantor other than pursuant to Section 3.3, Section 3.4 or Section 3.5 or by distribution by an Agent pursuant to Section 13.1, whether by exercising a right of set off or counterclaim or otherwise, with the result that it receives a greater proportion of the interest on or principal of its Advances than any other Bank receives in respect of its Advances, the Bank receiving such proportionately greater share shall promptly purchase from the other Banks such participations in the Eurodollar Advances or Swing–Line Advances, as the case may be, maintained by those other Banks as may be necessary to cause the purchasing Bank to share the excess amount obtained by it ratably with the other Banks; *provided, however,* that, if all or any portion of the amount so obtained by the purchasing Bank is thereafter recovered from that Bank, the related participating purchases under this Subsection shall be rescinded and the purchase price restored to the extent of the recovery, with such adjustments of interest as shall be equitable.

(b) If a Bank obtains a payment of the kind described in Subsection 13.2(a) as a result of a judgment in or settlement of any action or proceeding maintained by that Bank in any court, that Bank shall not be required to share the amount so obtained with any Bank which had a legal right to, but did not, join in that action or proceeding.

Questions

1.   What do the managers do for the participating banks? Could any bank do this?

2.   What standard of care to participating banks does the agreement set for the managers? Should the standard be one of arm's length or fiduciary relations? Should it vary by function? For example, what standard should apply to the information about the borrower that the managers give participating banks before the agreement is signed? Suppose employees of the managing bank's subsidiary in the borrowing country know that the borrowing public company's profits have been high over the last few years because of close but largely secret family ties between the country's prime minister and the company's president. Suppose that they also know that the prime minister's political base is weak and he is in serious danger of losing office. Should the managing bank be obliged to reveal this information to other participating banks? What if those banks have no commercial relations with the country? The few cases to examine these questions conclude that "the relationship between the arranger and the syndicate banks was a 'classic example' of

a situation where a duty of care did arise." See S. Sequeira, *Syndicated Loans - Let the Arranger Beware,* Butterworths Journal of International Banking and Financial Law, Mar. 1997, at 117. The facts giving rise to this statement were that the arranger of a syndicate had told prospective participants that it would inform them of the terms of a crucial insurance policy guaranteeing part of the loan. The syndicate members alleged that the arranging bank failed to disclose the terms and they sustained losses when the insurance was not adequate to meet the defaulted amount. The court found a duty of care in tort and that the contractual limitations on the arranger's liability were not enough to exclude this liability for acts before the contract was made. The author concluded that "although loan documents will continue to contain clauses [exonerating]... the arranger and agent from liability, ... the arranger [must] ... exercise sufficient care [preparing]... the information memorandum ...." Id at 118.

3. The fiduciary obligations of participating banks to the borrower arose in the U.K. in 2000. Deutsche Bank took a small participation (8%) in a syndicated loan to United Pan-Europe Holdings NV (UPC) in 1997, then with an affiliate took over 50% of each of two syndicated loans to UPC in 1998. As a participant, Deutsche Bank received confidential financial and business information from UPC that described the borrower's strategy and capabilities. In 1999, UPC sought to acquire a German company in its industry, telecommunications. Deutsche Bank at first seemed to offer to invest in the acquisition, but ultimately also bid on the target and won. UPC sued in the UK, arguing that Deutsche Bank broke its contractual obligation to treat confidentially the information it received as a syndicated lender and that the bank also breached its fiduciary duty to the borrower. UPC asked the court to enjoin the bank from selling the company and, instead, to transfer the company to UPC, upon payment of the purchase price on the theory that Deutsche Bank held the company under a constructive trust. The lower court declined to enjoin sale through the trial, but was reversed on appeal. The appellate court first found a possible contractual obligation: there was "at least an arguable case that . . . the value of the [confidential] information was not restricted to what UPC's bid might be but extended to . . . wider considerations" such as the way UPC's business strategy would affect its approach to the bid. The appellate court also found that Deutsche Bank "was under some fiduciary duty to UPC, the scope of which could only be determined at the trial." A fiduciary, said the court, "has undertaken to act for or on behalf of another in a particular matter in circumstances which give rise to a relationship of trust and confidence." The duty of loyalty would arise "from the key banking relationship . . . between UPC and DB, the mutual trust and confidence without which it could not properly operate and the requirement . . . that UPC pass to DB confidential information . . . on a regular basis." *United Pan-Europe Communications N.V. v. Deutsche Bank AG,* 2000 WL 699349 (CA), [2000] 2 B.C.L.C. 461, paras 35 and 37. In

a challenge to this decision, Alan Berg argued that "a bank which participates in a syndicated loan cannot sensibly be said to have undertaken 'to act for or on behalf' of the borrower." The lender's interests differ from the borrower's. "Deutsche Bank was contractually entitled to use the information it its own interests and contrary to those of UPC." A. Berg, *UK Court Ruling Imposes Fiduciary Duties on Capital Markets*, International Financial Law Review, July 2000, at 25, 27.

Links to Other Chapters

The eurocredit market illustrates the difficulty national governments face when they try to regulate the activities of their financial institutions in global markets. The different national responses emerge in the readings on the U.S. and Japanese banking markets (Chapters 3 and 8). One source of difficulty is the existence of financial centers (Chapter 1). One result is the reliance by financial intermediaries on private contracts to resolve many issues that the law of any one nation might resolve.

This is the first chapter to examine a market for a specific financial instrument. We also encounter markets for eurobonds and global bonds (Chapter 12), mortgage backed securities (Chapter 13), euro-Yen interest rate futures and options on those futures (Chapter 16), diff swaps (Chapter 17), and ADRs for equity (Chapter 20). Several of these chapters permit analysis at the level of the contract itself.

Syndication, the organizing mechanism for eurocredits, reappears in somewhat different form in bond underwriting (Chapter 12) and global equity offerings (Chapter 20).

The development of secondary markets for eurocredit participations was an early step toward international securitization (Chapter 13).

Developing countries, which played such an important role in the eurocredit market, do so again in the global market for ADRs (Chapter 20).

CHAPTER TEN

INFRASTRUCTURE: THE PAYMENT SYSTEM

Broadly speaking, the payment system is comprised of the institutions and technologies used for one party to transfer value to another. In modern economies, value is transferred by cash or through claims on banks. Claims on banks may be transferred by a variety of devices, including checks, credit cards and wire transfers. Our focus in this Chapter is on large value transfers through wire transfers, as these are the most important payments in international financial transactions. Each major country has its own large value systems, but the dollar systems have a significant international as well as domestic importance, due to the importance of the use of the dollar as a reserve currency and the size of the eurodollar market. Thus, the U.S. large value transfer systems play a key role in international financial transactions.

This Chapter first examines the operation of the U.S. large value transfer systems, Fedwire and CHIPS, in terms of how they operate, the risks they pose, and current efforts to control those risks. Readers should be aware that the CHIPS system underwent fundamental changes in January 2001, in order to further reduce risks. These changes will be taken up in part B2 of this Chapter. The Chapter then turns to "Herstatt risk" and some aspects of cross-border and offshore payment systems. It concludes with an examination of the money laundering problem.

A.   THE USE OF THE U.S. PAYMENT SYSTEM FOR INTERNATIONAL TRANSACTIONS

H. SCOTT, WHERE ARE THE DOLLARS?— OFFSHORE FUNDS TRANSFERS[*]

3 Banking and Finance Law Review 243, 252-263 (1989).

.   .   .

There are numerous methods of making dollar payments in the United States, such as by cash, credit card, paper (cheque or draft), or electronic means (wire transfer).   I shall concentrate on wire transfers, the form of payment used for large dollar transfers. Payments by "wire transfer" are transmitted through banks or other depository institutions.   "Wire transfer" is a generic term to describe a transaction in which the drawer, which may be an individual, corporation or a bank, instructs his bank (by telephone, computer, or written instruction) to debit his account and transfer funds to the account of a payee.   The payee receives payment in the form of a credit to his account.

There are three means by which wire transfers can be made: (1) in-house or correspondent transfer; (2) Fedwire; or (3) CHIPS. This section discusses the use of these methods for purely domestic transactions, and then shows how they may be used to transfer dollars from and to parties holding accounts with banks located outside the United States.

---

[*]   Some of the information in this article has been updated, eds.

IN-HOUSE WIRE TRANSFER

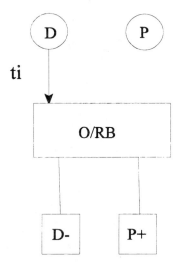

D   = Drawer
P   = Payee
O/RB = Originating/Receiving Bank
ti   = Transfer Instruction

Note: Payees generally receive
advices from their banks of credits
entered on transfer instructions.

(i) *In-House and Correspondent Transfers*

If the drawer (the party originating the transfer) and the payee (the beneficiary of the transfer) hold accounts at the same bank, the bank of account merely makes a book transfer by debiting the account of the drawer and crediting the account of the payee. The entire transaction is handled on the books of one bank and is therefore referred to as an in-house transfer.

If the accounts of the parties are with different banks, correspondent transfers may be used to effect the payment and settle accounts between the originating bank (the bank holding the drawer's account) and the receiving bank (the bank holding the payee's account).

CORRESPONDENT WIRE TRANSFER-I

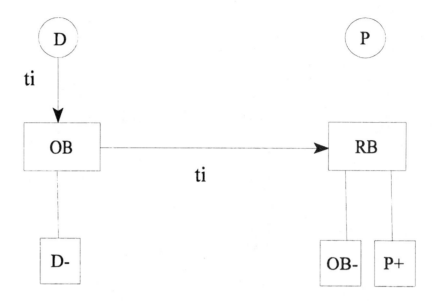

D   = Drawer
P   = Payee
OB = Originating Bank
RB = Receiving Bank
ti = Transfer Instruction

The originating bank, having debited the drawer's account on a payment instruction, may use a communication system, such as a telex, to instruct the receiving bank to credit the account of the payee. Settlement between the banks can be effected by the receiving bank charging the correspondent account of the originating bank held at the receiving bank. This requires the originating bank to hold a balance sufficient to cover the payment with the receiving bank.

Alternatively, the receiving bank ("RB") may hold an account with the originating bank ("OB"). In that event, a rolling settlement takes place. OB debits its customer and credits the RB account, a type of in-house transfer. RB, in turn, credits its customer's account. No balances need to be maintained by RB with OB.

CORRESPONDENT WIRE TRANSFER-II

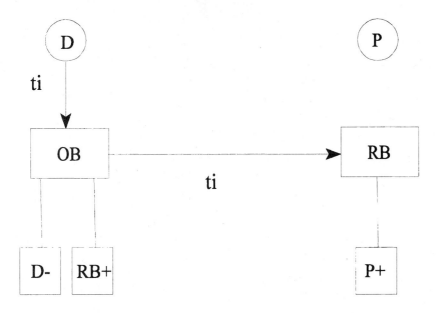

D   = Drawer
P   = Payee
OB = Originating Bank
RB = Receiving Bank
ti   = Transfer Instruction

In the event that OB and RB do not hold accounts with each other, OB may make use of a correspondent to transfer the funds to RB. One possibility is to use an intermediary bank ("IB") which holds an account of both OB and RB. In this case, OB debits the drawer's account, IB debits the OB account and credits the RB account, and RB, having been notified by IB of its credit for the benefit of the payee, credits the payee's account. This transaction would require OB to hold a sufficient balance at IB to cover the payment.

CORRESPONDENT WIRE TRANSFER-III W/ INTERMEDIARY

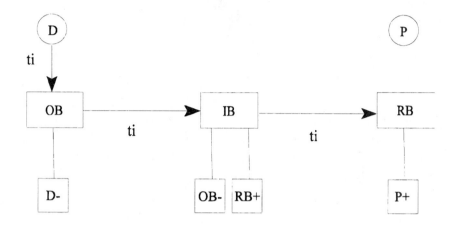

```
D   = Drawer
P   = Payee
OB  = Originating Bank
RB  = Receiving Bank
IB  =   Intermediary Bank
ti  = Transfer Instruction
```

There are many variations on the theme of correspondent transfers. Another possibility is that IB-X holds an account with OB and also holds the account of RB. In that event, a rolling settlement can take place through account entries. OB debits the drawer and credits IB-X, IB-X credits RB, and RB credits the payee. In this case, there is no need for banks to maintain balances with each other.

CORRESPONDENT WIRE TRANSFER-IV
W/ INTERMEDIARY

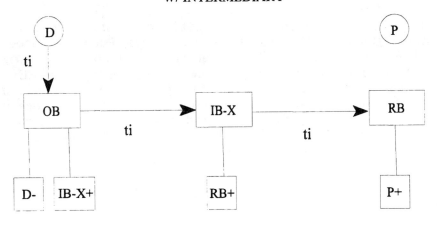

D = Drawer
P = Payee
OB = Originating Bank
RB = Receiving Bank
IB-X = Intermediary Bank
ti = Transfer Instruction

In-house and correspondent transfers in the United States may be used by foreigners to transfer dollars to United States or foreign payees. Suppose a London drawer ("LD") wants to transfer dollars from his London bank ("LOB") to a payee ("NYP") which holds an account at a New York bank ("NYRB"). If LOB and NYRB both hold dollar accounts at the same New York bank ("NYIB"), LOB debits LD, NYIB debits LOB and credits NYRB, and NYRB credits NYP. This is an in-house transfer at NYIB, which is a correspondent of both LOB and NYRB.

Now suppose LD wants to transfer dollars from its LOB account to a London payee ("LP") who banks with another London bank ("LRB"). If LOB and LRB both hold dollar accounts with NYIB, the transaction is the same as above, except that LRB, after receiving the credit from NYIB, credits LP on its books in London. Again, there may be many variations on this theme, but as long as interlinked accounts exist between LOB and LRB, provided by correspondents, a correspondent transfer may be used. No data are collected on the overall use of in-house or correspondent transfers in the United States payment system, but the dollar amounts and number of transactions must be substantial given the fact that correspondent balances at United States banks exceed $31 billion.[1]

(ii) *Fedwire*

Fedwire is a communication and settlement system owned by the twelve United States Federal Reserve Banks. Fedwire is used as follows. Having debited the drawer on the payment instruction, the originating bank instructs its Federal Reserve Bank ("FRB") to transfer the funds to the account of the payee at the receiving bank. If FRB holds the accounts of both the originating and receiving banks, it debits the former and credits the latter, and notifies the receiving bank of the credit. The receiving bank then credits the account of the payee.

FEDWIRE TRANSFER

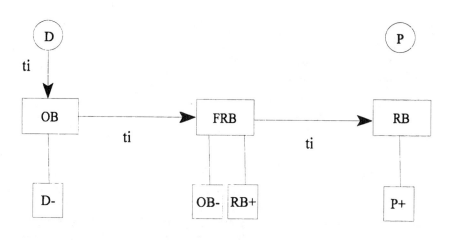

D   = Drawer
P   = Payee
OB = Originating Bank

RB   = Receiving Bank
FRB = Federal Reserve Bank
ti   = Transfer Instruction

Assumption
OB and RB are located in the same Federal Reserve District

If the receiving bank holds its account with a different Reserve Bank, FRB-R (the receiving bank's reserve bank), FRB-O (the originating bank's Reserve Bank) debits the originating bank and communicates the instruction to FRB-R. FRB-R credits the account

---

[1] 74 Federal Reserve Bulletin A 19 (1988), lines 49 and 50. This aggregates demand balances held by domestic banks, $24.4 billion, and foreign banks, $7.2 billion, at large weekly reporting United States commercial banks, as of October 28, 1987.

of the receiving bank and notifies the receiving bank of the credit. The receiving bank then credits the account of the payee. The two Reserve Banks then settle their own accounts.

Fedwires are often more convenient than correspondent transfers because a large number of United States banks maintain Federal Reserve accounts. In 1995, there were approximately 4,000 reserve accounts. The Federal Reserve Banks, taken together, serve the IB role. Since in most cases the Fed will hold both the OB and RB accounts, there is no need to look for private intermediaries in each transaction. Fedwire can be used in connection with correspondent transfers. If the receiving bank does not hold a Fedwire account, the originating bank can send a Fedwire to the receiving bank's correspondent, that holds a Fed account, for further credit to the receiving bank and its customer.

Fedwire can also be used for transactions involving overseas customers. If LD wants to transfer funds from LOB to NYP at NYRB, and LOB holds an account with its New York correspondent bank ("NYCB1"), LOB debits LD, NYCBI debits LOB and sends a Fedwire to NYRB for NYP. The Fed debits NYCB1 and credits NYRB, and NYRB credits NYP. If the transfer were for LP at LRB, and LRB held an account with its New York correspondent ("NYCB2"), NYCB1 would send the Fedwire to NYCB2. NYCB2 would credit LRB, and LRB would credit LP on its books in London. Thus, New York correspondents serve as intermediaries between the two London banks and use Fedwire as a means for communicating the funds transfer and settling their accounts.

(iii) *CHIPS*

The Clearing House Interbank Payments System ("CHIPS") is owned and operated by the New York Clearing House Association, an organization composed of the major New York City banks.

. . .

CHIPS is a communications and net settlement system for payments by and to two classes of participant banks located in New York City: "settling" and "non-settling" participants. All participants ... can send payment instructions during the day to each other through a central CHIPS switch linked to their own terminals and computers.

. . .

A CHIPS transfer works as follows. Bank OB, a CHIPS participant, sends a payment instruction, on behalf of Customer D, through the CHIPS computer and switching system to Bank RSB (a "settling" receiving bank). The instruction tells Bank RSB to credit the account of Customer P.

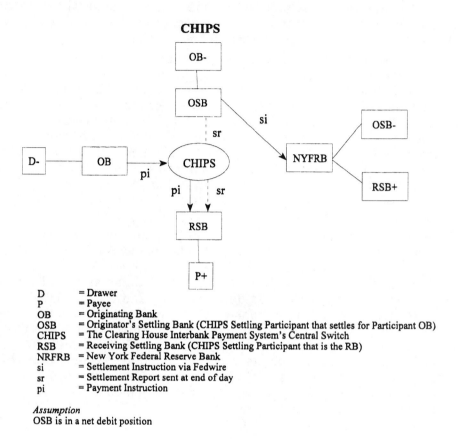

CHIPS

D	= Drawer	
P	= Payee	
OB	= Originating Bank	
OSB	= Originator's Settling Bank (CHIPS Settling Participant that settles for Participant OB)	
CHIPS	= The Clearing House Interbank Payment System's Central Switch	
RSB	= Receiving Settling Bank (CHIPS Settling Participant that is the RB)	
NRFRB	= New York Federal Reserve Bank	
si	= Settlement Instruction via Fedwire	
sr	= Settlement Report sent at end of day	
pi	= Payment Instruction	

Assumption
OSB is in a net debit position

. . .

CHIPS is regularly used for transactions involving foreign banks. Rather than use Fedwire, LOB's New York correspondent NYCBI can send a CHIPS transfer to NYRB for NYP or to the New York correspondent of LRB, NYCB2, for credit to LRB, and ultimately LP. It is estimated that 90 per cent of CHIPS payment instructions are in connection with foreign transactions.

CHIPS is often used in connection with correspondent transfers to effect payments, particularly where foreign banks are involved. An originating bank may telex its correspondent to transfer funds to a payee at a receiving bank. The originating bank and its correspondent will settle through a debit to the account of the originating bank with the correspondent. But the correspondent then uses CHIPS to transfer funds to the payee at the receiving bank.

. . .

G. JUNCKER, B. SUMMERS AND F. YOUNG, A PRIMER ON THE SETTLEMENT OF PAYMENTS IN THE UNITED STATES
77 Federal Reserve Bulletin 847 (1991).

In recent years, the soundness of the U.S. payment system, which can be measured by the certainty that payments will settle on schedule, has become a key public policy issue. Payment, or the transmission of an instruction to transfer value that results from a transaction in the economy, and settlement, or the final and unconditional transfer of the value specified in a payment instruction, need not, and in fact generally do not, occur simultaneously. Therefore, the recipient of a payment may face some uncertainty about receiving value even though a payment has been made to him or her. Efforts to reduce the gap of time between payment and settlement, or to ensure ultimate settlement of the payment, contribute to the integrity of the payment system and the efficiency of a market economy.

Four developments have led to the increased public policy attention to payment system integrity and settlement in the United States. First, the daily value of payments has increased significantly because of increased economic activity, growing sophistication and turnover of financial products, and opportunity costs associated with holding non-interest-earning demand deposits. Second, participants in the payment system have become increasingly aware of the credit and liquidity risks associated with clearing and settling payments. Third, the payment process has become more complex because of technological advances and increased emphasis on the efficient processing of payments and their underlying transactions. Finally, new settlement techniques involving netting are being increasingly employed to reduce liquidity requirements and to control risk.

.   .   .

PAYMENT AND SETTLEMENT

In a modern economy, payment obligations are discharged through the transfer of an accepted monetary asset. In earlier times, the monetary asset could take the form of a commodity, such as gold or silver. Today, most sovereign nations issue fiat money denominated in a national currency unit. Fiat money serves as a store of value and a medium of exchange because it has the public's confidence.

In the United States, the deposits held with banks by their customers, along with bank deposits held with the Federal Reserve, are the monetary assets most frequently used to discharge payment obligations. Accordingly, banks and the banking system are integral to the payment process. In important ways, the safety of the banking system is itself tied to the integrity of the payment system.

A large proportion of economic obligations are discharged primarily through the transfer of demand deposit claims on banks' books.

Because a bank can fail, its depositors may bear some default and liquidity risk as a result of their decision to hold bank balances. Banks face no risk in holding deposits directly with the Federal Reserve, however, since a central bank—reflecting its governmental status—is immune from liquidity or credit problems. Thus, balances held with the Federal Reserve, which are referred to as "central bank money," have special significance when used by commercial banks to settle their payments. Settlement in central bank money is universally acceptable because the resulting deposit claim is free of default and liquidity risk.

Banks and the Federal Reserve together provide the settlement infrastructure for the nation's payment system. Commercial banks hold accounts through which the general public's payments are recorded and settled. The many thousands of payments that bank customers make each day result in transfers of balances between banks and therefore affect banks' positions with each other and with the central bank. Of course, banks also make their own payments in connection with carrying out the business of banking. These add to, and are often major sources of, large daily payment flows among banks. Banks can settle these interbank payments through accounts that they hold with each other or through accounts that they hold with a correspondent bank. However, many interbank payments, especially large-value payments, are made through the transfer of balances on the books of the Federal Reserve.

When a bank receives a payment on behalf of its customer, the account holder obtains a deposit claim. If the bank receiving the payment is satisfied that the payment will settle, the bank may make funds available to its customer, that is, it will allow the customer to withdraw, or typically to retransfer, the funds. When a bank makes funds available to its customers before settlement, it is exposed to credit risk because an account holder may withdraw funds and, if settlement does not occur, the bank may not be able to recover the funds. Banks sometimes guarantee the unconditional use of funds to their customers based on the receipt of payments before settlement. In this case, the bank is providing a credit service as well as a payment service to its customer by assuming the risk that settlement may not occur as scheduled. When settlement occurs at the same time the payment is made, however, settlement risk is eliminated for the bank and its customer.

THE WAY PAYMENTS ARE MADE

. . .

Two electronic funds transfer systems—Fedwire, operated by the Federal Reserve Banks, and the Clearing House Interbank Payment System (CHIPS), operated by the New York Clearing House—account for less than 0.1 percent of the number of all payments in the United

States; however, they account for more than 80 percent of the value of payments. When a Fedwire payment is processed, the Federal Reserve debits the account of the sending bank and credits the account of the receiving bank. Payment instructions are for the immediate delivery of "central bank money," and Fedwire payments are settled when the amount of the payment is credited to the receiving bank's account with the Federal Reserve or when the receiving bank is notified of the payment. The Federal Reserve "guarantees" the payment to the bank receiving the Fedwire and assumes any credit risk if there are insufficient funds in the Federal Reserve account of the bank sending the payment.

Payments processed over CHIPS, however, are settled only when CHIPS participants fund their net obligations resulting from the day's payment instructions over CHIPS at the close of the business day. Settlement of CHIPS obligations occurs by Fedwire transfers initiated by those in a net debit position for the day's CHIPS activity. If the bank receiving a CHIPS payment makes funds available to its customers before settlement occurs at the end of the day, it is exposed to some risk of loss if CHIPS settlement cannot occur. To ensure that settlement occurs, the New York Clearing House has put in place risk control mechanisms (see description below).

. . .

As indicated, the Federal Reserve Banks extend intraday credit to banks in conjunction with the payment services they provide. Similarly, banks often extend intraday credit when they make payments on behalf of their customers. Thus, both the Federal Reserve and private banks are exposed to credit risk in processing payment transactions. Private banks are also exposed to liquidity risk.

Banks typically control their risk by establishing intraday credit limits for their customers and by monitoring their customers' use of such credit. In some cases, banks require their customers to pledge collateral to cover daylight credit exposures. The Federal Reserve Banks have also adopted risk control procedures: they use "net debit caps" (or ceilings for net debits) to limit the amount of credit extended to individual banks that use Federal Reserve payment services. The Reserve Banks monitor the use of intraday Federal Reserve credit for healthy banks, in most cases, by examining historical data through an ex post monitoring system. On-line, real-time account monitoring is used for the continuous control of intraday credit for certain institutions, especially those under financial stress. Real-time monitoring enables the Federal Reserve to reject or hold funds transfer requests pending the availability of funds to cover them. In some cases, the Reserve Banks may also require banks to pledge collateral to secure the intraday credit they use.

GROSS VERSUS NET SETTLEMENT

The settlement of payments occurs on either a gross or a net basis. When payments are settled on a gross basis, each transaction is settled individually. For example, Fedwire is a gross settlement system. When payments are settled on a net basis, the parties to the payments offset the amounts they are due to pay and receive with each other (or with a central party, or clearing-house) and maintain a running balance of the netted amounts. The offsetting of payable and receivable amounts can occur between two parties (bilateral netting) or among many parties (multilateral netting).

In markets characterized by a high volume or high value of transactions among a fixed group of participants, net settlement typically improves the efficiency of payment processing; reduces liquidity needs; and, depending on the type of legal foundation and risk controls used, can help control credit exposures. Netting may be applied in many real and financial markets. For example, petroleum companies active in trading crude oil have bilaterally netted their oil trades for many years and have also participated in a multilateral netting arrangement. Many organized exchanges for commodities and securities also employ forms of netting, usually through formal clearinghouses. Banks themselves actively participate in clearing-houses through which they exchange and net payment transactions.

Bilateral Netting

Interbank payments are often cleared and settled in bilateral arrangements. For example, two banks that exchange large volumes of payments may agree to exchange certain types of payments, such as checks ..., and settle the net value of the payments between themselves at a specific time. This type of agreement reduces the value of settlement between the two banks participating in the exchange because they can total the net value of customer transactions payable to and receivable from each other and substitute a single, smaller, net settlement (see box 1). Two banks may also enter into an agreement to net financial contracts, such as those involving foreign exchange, and settle the net amount resulting from the trading.

Multilateral Netting

.   .   .

Box 2 [below] shows a simple numerical example of a funds transfer netting arrangement involving four participants; it illustrates settlement from the perspective of the clearinghouse. In this example, if the four banks did not participate in the clearinghouse, they would collectively need to make a total of ten interbank· settlement payments with an aggregate value of $800 in connection with the underlying customer payments. As a result of multilateral netting, only one participant (Bank D) has an obligation to transfer money to the clearinghouse, and the clearinghouse must transfer money to three participants. Multilateral netting and the use of a clearinghouse have allowed these efficiencies to occur.

. . .

1. Effects of the Netting of Payments

The following example illustrates the differences between the exchange of a series of gross payments and the bilateral and multilateral netting of the series of payments from the standpoint of one organization. The assumptions in the example are that Bank A makes payments to and receives payments from nine other banks on a given day. It makes ten $100 payments to and receives ten $95 payments from each of five banks. It also makes ten $95 payments to and receives ten $100 payments from each of four banks. The settlement activity in each of the three cases is as follows:

Gross Settlement

Bank A makes ninety payments worth $8,800 and receives ninety payments worth $8,750.

Total number of payments made or received by Bank A	180
Total value of payments made or received by Bank A that must be settled	$17,550
Day's settlement effect on Bank A	—$50

Bilateral Netting

Bank A nets payments with each of the nine counterparties throughout the day and settles at the end of the day with each. Bank A pays each of five banks $50 for a total of $250 and receives $50 from each of four banks for a total of $200.

Total Number of settlement payments made or received by Bank A	9
Total value of settlement payments made or received by Bank A	$50
Day's settlement effect on Bank A	— $50

Multilateral Netting

Bank A nets payments with all nine counterparties as a group throughout the day and settles at the end of the day through a common agent for the multilateral netting arrangement. It makes a single payment of $50 for its obligation to this agent.

Total Number of settlement payments made by Bank A	1
Total value of settlement payments made by Bank A	$50
Day's settlement effect on Bank A	— $50

In each case, the settlement result at the end of the day for Bank A is the same (as long as net settlement occurs normally); however, the number and the value of settlement payments drop dramatically with netting. In bilateral netting, the number of payments to Bank A's counterparties is reduced to just 9 from 180 in gross settlement. In multilateral netting, Bank A need make only a single payment to satisfy its obligation to the group. Because a much smaller amount of money actually changes hands, liquidity needs are also dramatically reduced.

2. Transactions among Four Participants in a Funds Transfer Clearinghouse

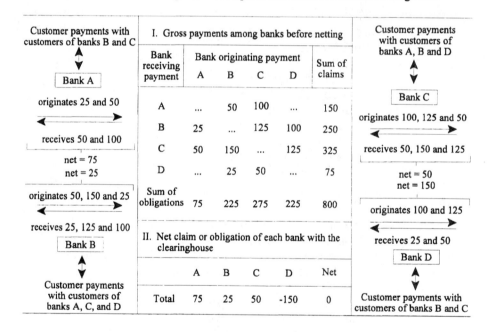

Risks in Netting Arrangements

Two types of risk arise in bilateral and multilateral netting arrangements: namely, credit and liquidity risk. A third type of risk, systemic risk, may also be present in multilateral netting arrangements.

. . .

In the case of bilateral netting arrangements, banks must evaluate the credit and liquidity risk assumed with the bank on the other side of the bilateral netting arrangement—the "counter-party." If there is doubt about a counterparty, a bank receiving payments from the counterparty on behalf of a customer may choose not to allow the customer access to the funds until settlement has occurred.

A mutualization of the credit risk occurs when more than two banks participate in a netting arrangement. In particular, the timely completion of all the underlying gross transactions that are included in a multilateral netting depends on the ability of each party to meet its single net settlement obligation arising from the netting. If even one participant fails to meet its net settlement obligation, then settlement for all the underlying transactions could be delayed or otherwise disrupted, creating credit and liquidity risks for the participants. Indeed, even a bank that has no dealings with the participant in a multilateral netting that does not settle may be exposed to risk. For example, in the situation described in the table above, participant A has no direct dealings whatsoever with participant D: A does not make payments to D, nor does it receive payments from D. Nonetheless, participant D has a net obligation to the clearinghouse of $150, and participant A's net credit of $75 would be funded from participant D's settlement. Accordingly, participant A depends on participant D to meet its settlement obligation, even though the two have exchanged no payments.

The risks created by privately operated netting arrangements cannot be eliminated, but they can be effectively controlled and limited. The risks cannot be eliminated because extensions of credit between privately owned institutions are an inherent part of such arrangements, and these extensions of credit are subject to some degree of default risk. Two types of risk control systems are used—decentralized and centralized. In netting arrangements based on a system of decentralized controls, the individual participants are responsible for controlling their risk vis-à-vis the other participants with whom they deal as counterparties in the individual transactions (CHIPS is an example of a decentralized risk control arrangement).[4] In contrast, systems with centralized controls typically rely on a central body that becomes the counterparty—usually a clearinghouse—to every transaction cleared through the system: The central counterparty becomes a "buyer" to every seller and a "seller" to every buyer (clearing bodies in the futures and options markets are examples of centralized risk control arrangements).

---

[4] Controls, typically credit limits, are set on a decentralized basis, but they may be enforced through a central computer facility.

3. Risks in Netting Arrangements

Liquidity risk involves the possibility that a participant in a clearing arrangement will have insufficient funds at settlement to cover its obligation. If this situation occurs, other participants may be negatively affected if they have planned to use the proceeds from the settlement to cover other obligations or, in anticipation of settlement, have already permitted their customers to use such funds. Thus, other participants may have to find alternative sources of funding to cover their obligations while they wait for the "defaulting" participant's ultimate payment to meet its obligation.

Credit risk involves the possibility that a participant in a clearing arrangement will be unable to meet its settlement obligation, either in whole or in part, because of its insolvency. In this case, other participants not only face a liquidity problem but also may incur actual losses.

Systemic risk involves the possibility that one participant's inability to settle in a clearing arrangement will cause other participants in that clearing group to be unable to meet their obligations either to their customers or to other banks. The value of the transactions exchanged among participants in a clearing arrangement directly affects the degree of systemic risk associated with the arrangement. When high-value payments are exchanged and the turnover of funds within the arrangement is also high, the degree of systemic risk is generally high as well. Consequently, high systemic risk is usually associated with private large-value funds and securities transfer systems.

Clearing arrangements that use either decentralized or centralized risk controls use combinations of the following techniques. To protect participants against credit risk, many clearing organizations establish membership standards, which are used to screen participants when they apply to participate in the arrangement and which are monitored on an ongoing basis. Some clearing organizations require each participant to establish bilateral credit limits with every other participant whereby the volume of payments received from each other participant can exceed the volume sent to each other participant only by a predetermined amount. Bilateral credit limits thus provide a mechanism for controlling the risk that the participants face in exchanging payments with each other participant in the arrangement. To the extent that participants agree to share losses arising from the default of one or more other participants and that these loss-sharing arrangements are tied to the bilateral credit limits, incentives are created for each participant to manage its bilateral credit positions prudently.

Credit and liquidity risks may also be controlled by imposing limits on the net debit position of each participant. Such limits reduce the risk that any one participant may impose on the group and may be related in principle to each participant's ability to fund its daily settlement obligation. Assuming that such limits, or net debit caps, are set realistically, their use reduces the potential that an individual participant will be unable to settle its position at the close of business.

To handle settlement defaults, some clearing groups rely on settlement recasts and unwinds. In a recast, all of the defaulting participant's payments are deleted from the settlement, and the net settlement positions of the remaining participants are recalculated. As a last resort, if a clearing group is unable to achieve settlement after more than one recast, then it may decide to unwind *all* transactions. This procedure essentially requires all the participants to settle independently with each other.

For small-value arrangements, settlement recasts may be able to address both liquidity and credit risk without serious systemic implications. If a participant defaults, the clearing group relies on the resources of each remaining participant to fund its adjusted settlement position on the settlement day. Further, by removing all of the transactions of the defaulting participant, a settlement recast automatically allocates the losses associated with the default to the participants that dealt with the defaulting participant. Such an approach to resolving a settlement default is viable only when the value of payments exchanged is relatively low and the potential change in participants' settlement obligations is relatively small and can be funded easily by the remaining participants.

In a large-value netting arrangement, the recast of the settlement could remove significant credits that other participants were relying on to meet their own obligations and thus cause them to be unable to settle. Therefore, recasts or unwinds can be a significant source of systemic risk.

To avoid the undesirable effects of a recast, large-value multilateral netting arrangements—such as CHIPS—may provide special "assurances" of settlement akin to "guarantees." The nondefaulting participants may, for example, agree in advance to share the burden of meeting the defaulting participant's obligation to allow settlement to occur on schedule. Lines of credit or pools of collateral may be maintained, either of which can be used for overnight borrowing to provide the funds to achieve settlement on the day of the occurrence. In such arrangements, the nondefaulting participants would share losses after the settlement had occurred, based on some method of loss allocation agreed upon in advance. Such arrangements would help prevent the sudden market disruptions that might otherwise occur with recasts or unwinds.

Legal Basis for Netting

Netting must have a sound legal basis for the settlement to be certain. In particular, in the event that a participant in the netting becomes insolvent, it is important that the net obligations of the participants be legally recognized so that a receiver of the insolvent participant is not able to "cherry pick," that is, accept incoming payments while voiding outgoing payments.

A variety of legal approaches may be used to net obligations. For example, netting by novation would substitute a new legal obligation each time an additional payment instruction is sent or received. Netting among several participants in an arrangement may be accomplished by placing an intermediary between the counterparties so that all obligations are due to or from this new intermediary. These approaches are applicable to the netting of financial contracts, such as foreign exchange deals, as well as to payments. Recent work by the Group of Ten central banks has emphasized the need for significant netting arrangements to have sound legal foundations.

.   .   .

Payment Netting Arrangements

At present, CHIPS is the only "pure" payment netting arrangement for large-value transfers operating in the United States. It is the largest payment netting system in the world and processes nearly $1 trillion in payments daily. It has about 130 participants, the majority of which are branches or agencies of non-U.S. banks. Only twenty U.S. participants, however, are settling participants that actually send or receive net payments to settle on behalf of themselves and other, nonsettling participants.

Since its inception in 1970, CHIPS has adopted a variety of measures to control and reduce credit and liquidity risk. Currently, it employs admission standards; bilateral credit limits, which are used by each participant to establish its maximum exposure to each other participant in the event of a default; net debit caps, which are based on all bilateral credit limits established for each participant; explicit loss-sharing rules, which are based on the bilateral limits; and collateral requirements to ensure timely settlement.

Since moving to same-day settlement in 1981, CHIPS has used a special settlement account with the Federal Reserve Bank of New York to settle each day. Immediately after the system closes for the day at 4:30 p.m. eastern time, participants are notified of their final net settlement obligations. The settlement payments for the twenty U.S. banks that settle directly for themselves and the other participants are made over Fedwire into the special settlement account at the Federal Reserve Bank of New York.

If any participant fails to settle, the loss-sharing rules are invoked. In essence, an additional settlement obligation (ASO) is calculated for each participant that dealt that day with the defaulting member to make up that member's unpaid obligation, and the participants are given a reasonable period of time to cover this ASO. If any participant failed to meet its ASO, U.S. government securities held in a special CHIPS collateral account at the Federal Reserve Bank of New York would be tapped to collateralize a loan in the market to use for ensuring timely settlement. Sufficient collateral is kept in the special CHIPS account to cover any one participant's largest potential uncovered net debit. In certain cases, there would be sufficient collateral to cover several simultaneous defaults by participants with smaller uncovered net debits. Thus, the CHIPS collateral account ensures timely settlement for all but cataclysmic default situations.

.   .   .

CHIPS Changes in 2001

In 2001, there was a fundamental change in the operation of the CHIPS system. The following description of these changes relies heavily on Payments Risk Committee (of the Federal Reserve Bank of New York), *Intraday Liquidity Management in the Evolving Payment System: A Study of the Impact of the euro, CLS Bank and CHIPS Finality,* Report by the Intraday Liquidity Management Task Force (April 2000) (PRC Report). CHIPS changed from an end-of-day multilateral net payment system to one that supplies intraday finality, and arguably will eliminate most risk from a settlement failure. Two essential changes have been made. First, CHIPS replaced the current Treasury securities collateral, under the ASO system, with a prefunded balance maintained in a "prefunded balance account" on the books of the Federal Reserve Bank of New York (FRBNY). Prefunded balances should be roughly equivalent to the $3 billion of Treasury collateral under the existing ASO system. Second, CHIPS uses a computer program, "the balance release algorithm," to control the release of the payments to and from participants. Payments are only released against actual balances and are settled when made.

Each participant is required to deposit its initial prefunded balance requirement to the prefunded balance account at FRBNY no later than 9:00 a.m. Normally this would be done by Fedwire. The amount of the balance will be determined by the Clearing House based on a participant's past activity. Participants are not permitted to make any additional deposits to or withdrawals from the prefunded balance account between the time they have paid their initial prefunded balance and the final end of day clearing.

The balance in a participant's account during the day will vary based upon the release and receipt of payment messages to other participants. In no case, however, can a balance go below zero or rise to more than two times the initial prefunded balance. This latter limit prevents any one participant from absorbing system liquidity by building an excessive balance. Payment messages will ordinarily be released in batches, involving two or several participants (bilateral or multilateral netting). The balance release algorithm is designed to ensure that these debits and credits do not cause any participant's balance to fall below zero or exceed the maximum. This system should introduce more flexibility than the old system where transfers had to stay within bilateral and net debit cap limits. The netting and the posting of the debits and credits constitute final settlement of all payment messages in each batch. CHIPS payment messages are no longer subject to final settlement at the end of the day. They will be finally settled upon receipt.

CHIPS closes at 5:00 p.m. At that time, CHIPS runs an "initial closing netting and release." In this procedure, CHIPS removes the maximum available balance restraint and runs the balance release algorithm one more time. This should cause the release of additional payments. It is estimated that after this procedure 99.6% of all CHIPS messages comprising 97.5% of all value will have been released and settled. Only about $30 billion in payments will remain.

CHIPS then calculates a net balance for each participant without releasing any of the remaining payments. This net balance is then reduced by any remaining balance available to the participant, to establish a "final prefunded balance requirement." Participants then have 30 minutes to fund this amount. There is no longer a special class of settling participants. In the event that one or more participants do not send in final prefunded balances, CHIPS will run the balance release algorithm one final time, and release all payments that can be netted with the balances available. Any payment messages still unreleased will expire and CHIPS will so notify the senders. What would be the effect?

> In sum, in the event of a participant's failure to pay its final prefunded balance requirement, the effect is likely to fall predominantly on the participant that did not fund, few small participants will be significantly affected, and it is unlikely that participants will have to reroute payments with a gross value in excess of their present debit caps. These effects are in contrast to what would occur today if a participant were not to pay its net debit balance. Each of the remaining participants would have to take a piece of the participant's net debit balance (the remaining participant's additional settlement obligation, or ASO). If a remaining participant defaulted on its ASO, its collateral would be sold to its settling participant to meet its obligation. If more than two major participants failed to settle, the loss-sharing arrangement might not apportion all of the failed participants' settlement obligations among the remaining participants and there could be a settlement failure and all of the day's payment messages might have to be unwound. Id., at 51.

The simulations show that if the two participants with the largest final prefunded balance requirements did not pay these amounts, unreleased dollars would be around $2-2.8 billion. Would banks be at risk for not receiving these payments?

Notes and Questions

1. Fedwire is a real time gross payment system. There is no netting; each transaction settles separately on the Fed's books. It is owned and operated by the 12 Federal Reserve Banks and in 2000 transferred about $1.51 trillion per day (U.S. GNP was about $9.2 trillion in 1999), in about 430,000 transactions per day, with the average size of a transaction about $3.5 million. All depository institutions (not securities firms) may have access, including branches of foreign banks. Over 4000 do have direct access to Fedwire; others have indirect access through correspondents.

CHIPS is owned by CHIPCo, the shareholders of which are Citibank, ABN AMRO Bank, Bank of America, Bank of New York, Bank of Tokyo-Mitsubishi, JP Morgan Chase & Company, Deutsche Bank, HSBC Bank USA, and UBS AG. In 2000, transfers amounted to about $1.3 trillion per day (less than Fedwire) in about 238,000 transfers per day. The average transaction was about $6 million (more than Fedwire). There are presently about 60 total participants (down from 142 in 1989), the majority of which are foreign (from about 30 countries). The decrease in membership reflects a number of bank mergers plus the decision of a number of banks to access CHIPS indirectly, through correspondents, rather than maintain the systems required for direct access. CHIPS reportedly has a 95% share of international large-value payments but only about 5% of domestic large-value ones. The latter go over Fedwire. A significant portion of CHIPS volume is the dollar settlement of foreign exchange transactions.

2. Banks sending Fedwires commonly overdraft their accounts (daylight overdrafts). The total of all banks' peak daylight overdrafts per day was about $130 billion in 1993, while average overdrafts were $70 billion.[*] In 1999, peak overdrafts ranged between $76 to $82 billion, while average overdrafts ranged between $25 to $31 billion. If a bank fails with an overdraft outstanding, the Fed has a loss. The Fed does not take money back from the banks that received payments from the failed bank.

---

[*] The peak daylight overdraft for a given day is the greatest value reached by the sum of daylight overdrafts in Federal Reserve accounts for all depository institutions at the end of each minute during the day. Another measure of overdrafts is average overdrafts. This is the sum of average per-minute daylight overdrafts for all institutions. H. Richards, *Daylight Overdraft Fees and the Federal Reserve's Payment System Risk Policy*, 81 Federal Reserve Bulletin 1065, 1069 n.7 (1995); D. Hancock and J. Wilcox, *Intraday Management of Bank Reserves: The Effect of Caps and Fees on Daylight Overdrafts*, 28 J. Money, Credit and Banking 870, 873 (Figure 2) (1996).

The principal reason is that Fedwires are final when sent; they are "good funds." Receiving banks need to know that the funds are good so they can allow the receivers to use them. Finality supports the high velocity of money in the economy, particularly in the financial system. Could the Fed just prohibit overdrafts? This would risk a slowdown in the economy and possible gridlock. For example, Citibank wouldn't be able to send funds to Morgan until Chase sent them to Citibank, but Chase can't send to Citibank until it get funds from Morgan, but Morgan can't send funds to Chase until it gets them from Citibank. Do overdrafts on Fedwire cause systemic risk problems, i.e. a possible chain reaction of bank bankruptcies?

Overdrafts of Fed accounts can occur as a result of a variety of different transactions, including transfers of book-entry securities. When book-entry securities are bought by a dealer, such as Salomon Brothers, they are delivered electronically to its clearing bank's (CB) account with the Fed. CB's securities account is credited and its funds account is debited. CB then makes corresponding entries on its own books to the funds and securities accounts of Salomon. Deliveries of book-entry securities during the day are substantial, and cause very substantial overdrafts on the accounts of the clearing banks (there are only a handful with any volume). In 1993, of the total peak daylight overdrafts of about $130 billion, securities were close to $100 billion. The overdrafts are extinguished at the end of the day when the dealer sells out or finances (for example, by repo transactions in which securities are exchanged for cash for a defined period) its position. Is there the same risk to the Fed from an overdraft caused by funds transfer as compared to book-entry securities deliveries?

3. Let's look at how a net settlement works by examining the hypothetical example (Table 2) in the Juncker piece. What is A's situation? Bank A sent 25 to B and 50 to C: its obligations (funds owed) are 75. Bank A received 50 from B and 100 from C: its claims (funds owed to it) are 150. Thus, its net position, the net of its obligations of 75 and claims of 150, is a net claim of 75. Under a delete and unwind rule (CHIPS Rule 13) if D fails to settle, all transactions involving D would be deleted. The new settlement positions of the banks would be as follows:

	A	B	C	D	Net
Pre	75	25	50	-150	0
Post	75	-50	-25	xx	0

How would A, B and C be affected? What would the Fed do in this situation?

It would not be a matter of indifference if the Fed were to lose money as a result of dishonored Fedwire daylight overdrafts or a CHIPS settlement failure. This would reduce the yearly dividend the Fed sends the Treasury, which in 1998 totaled $27.6 billion.

4. The Federal Reserve System has authored a report evaluating various options for its role in the payment system, including the possibility of withdrawing from a processing role in retail payment systems, particularly in offering check collection or automated clearinghouse (ACH) services. Committee on the Federal Reserve in the Payments Mechanism, *The Federal Reserve in the Payments Mechanism* (January 1998). The Committee concluded that the Fed should not withdraw since it might increase the costs to smaller depository institutions and divert resources away from other priorities. In the case of ACH services, it was concerned that one or at most two providers would come to dominate the market. This report was limited to retail systems (although, in fact, ACHs process sizeable corporate as well as individual payments). Should consideration be given to turning over Fedwire operations over to the private sector?

5. For an excellent overview of payment systems issues, see D. Folkerts-Landau, P. Garber and D. Schoenmaker, *The Reform of Wholesale Payment Systems and Its Impact on Financial Markets*, Occasional Paper No. 51, Group of Thirty (1996).

B.   FEDWIRE AND CHIPS: RISK REDUCTION MEASURES

1.   FEDWIRE

The Fed has adopted a two-pronged strategy to control daylight overdrafts on Fedwire, ceilings on and pricing of overdrafts. Pricing is effective as of April 14, 1994.

a.   CEILINGS

BOARD OF GOVERNORS OF THE FEDERAL RESERVE SYSTEM, FEDERAL RESERVE POLICY STATEMENT ON PAYMENT SYSTEM RISK
57 Federal Register 40455, 40457 (1992).

D.   Net Debit Caps

To limit the aggregate amount of daylight credit extended by Reserve Banks, each institution that incurs daylight overdrafts in its Federal Reserve account must adopt a net debit cap, i.e., a ceiling on the aggregate net debit position that it can incur during a given interval. Alternatively, if an institution's daylight overdrafts generally do not exceed the lesser of $10 million or 20 percent of capital, the institution may qualify for the exempt-from-filing status. Subject to the provisions for special situations described below, an institution must be financially healthy and eligible to borrow from the discount window in order to adopt a cap greater than zero or qualify for the filing exemption.

Cap categories and associated cap levels, set as multiples of capital, are listed below:

An institution is expected to avoid incurring net debits that, on average over a two-week period, exceed the two-week average cap, and, on any day, exceed the single-day cap. The two-week average cap provides flexibility, in recognition that fluctuations in payments can occur from day-to-day.

Net Debit Cap Multiples

Cap Category	Two-Week Avg.	Single Day
High	1.50	2.25
Above Avg.	1.125	1.875
Average	0.75	1.125
De Minimis	0.20	0.20
Exempt-from-filing	$10 million (0.20)	$10 million (0.20)
Zero	0.0	0.0

The purpose of the higher single-day cap is to limit excessive daylight overdrafts on any day and to assure that institutions develop internal controls that focus on the exposures each day, as well as over time.

The two-week average cap is measured against the average, over a two-week reserve maintenance period, of an institution's daily maximum net debit positions in its Federal Reserve account. In calculating the two-week average, individual days on which an institution is in an aggregate net credit position throughout the day are treated as if the institution was in a net position of zero. The number of days used in calculating the average is the number of business days the institution's Reserve Bank is open during the reserve maintenance period.

The Board's policy on net debit caps is based on a specific set of guidelines and some degree of examiner oversight. Under the Board's policy, a Reserve Bank may prohibit the use of Federal Reserve intraday credit if (1) an institution's use of daylight credit is deemed by the institution's supervisor to be unsafe or unsound, (2) an institution does not qualify for a cap exemption, does not perform a self-assessment, or does not file a board-of-directors-approved *de minimis* cap, and (3) an institution poses an excessive risk to a Reserve Bank.

The net debit cap provisions of this policy apply to foreign banks to the same extent as they apply to U.S. institutions. The Reserve Banks will advise home-country supervisors of banks with U.S. branches and agencies of the daylight overdraft capacity of banks under their jurisdiction, as well as of other pertinent conditions related to their caps. Home-country supervisors that request information on the overdrafts in the Federal Reserve accounts of their banks will be provided that information on a regular basis.

1. Cap Set Through Self-Assessment

An institution that wishes to establish a net debit cap category of high, above average, or average must perform a self-assessment of its own creditworthiness, credit policies, and operational controls, policies, and procedures. The assessment of credit worthiness should address the overall financial condition of the institution, placing emphasis on conformance of the institution's capital with supervisory standards for capital adequacy. The institution should also assess its procedures for evaluating the financial condition of its customers and should establish intraday credit limits that reflect these assessments. Finally, an institution should ensure that its operational controls permit it to contain its use of Federal Reserve intraday credit and restrict its customers' use of credit to the limits it has established. The *Users' Guide* to the Board's Payments System Risk Reduction Policy, available from any Reserve Bank, includes a detailed explanation of the steps that should be taken by a depository institution in performing a self-assessment to establish a net debit cap.

Each institution's board of directors is expected to review the self-assessment and determine the appropriate cap category. The process of self-assessment, with board-of-directors review, should be conducted at least once in each 12-month period. A cap determination may be reviewed and approved by the board of directors of a holding company parent of a depository institution, or the parent of an Edge or agreement corporation, provided that (1) the self-assessment is performed by each entity incurring daylight overdrafts, (2) the entity's cap is based on the entity's own capital (adjusted to avoid double-counting), and (3) each entity maintains for its primary supervisor's review its own file with supporting documents for its self-assessment and a record of the parent's board-of-directors review.

In applying these guidelines, each institution is expected to maintain a file for examiner review that includes (1) worksheets and supporting analysis developed in its self-assessment of its own risk category, (2) copies of senior management reports to the board of directors of the institution or its parent (as appropriate) regarding that self-assessment, and (3) copies of the minutes of the discussion at the appropriate board-of-directors meeting concerning the institution's adoption of a cap category.

As part of its normal examination, the depository institution's examiners will review the contents of the self-assessment file. The objective of this review is to assure that the institution has applied the guidelines seriously and diligently, that the underlying analysis and methodology were reasonable and that the resultant self-assessment was generally consistent with the examination findings. Examiner comments, if any, should be forwarded to the board of directors of the institution. The examiner, however, would generally not require a modification of the self-assessment cap category unless the level of daylight credit used by the institution constitutes an unsafe or unsound banking practice.

The contents of the self-assessment cap category file will be considered confidential by the institution's examiner. Similarly, the actual cap level selected by the institution will be held confidential by the Federal Reserve and the institution's examiner. (However, cap information will be shared with the home country supervisor of agencies and branches of foreign banks.)

.   .   .

On January 20, 1994, 59 Federal Register 3104, the Board adopted some important modifications to its methodology for determining daylight overdraft ceilings. Its proposal on self-assessment and capital for offices of foreign banks, which was adopted without significant change, follows.

BOARD OF GOVERNORS OF THE FEDERAL RESERVE SYSTEM, PROPOSALS TO MODIFY THE PAYMENTS SYSTEM RISK REDUCTION PROGRAM; SELF ASSESSMENT PROCEDURES, CAPS FOR U.S. BRANCHES AND AGENCIES OF FOREIGN BANKS
58 Federal Register 44677 (1993).

.   .   .

Self-Assessment Procedures

Under the Board's policy, an institution's net debit cap (for a single day and on average over a two-week period) is based on its cap category. The three cap categories that permit the highest use of intraday credit are the Average, Above Average, and High cap categories. An institution that wishes to establish a cap in one of these categories must complete a self-assessment of its creditworthiness, intraday funds management and control, and customer credit policies and controls.

The Board is proposing to add a fourth component, operating controls and contingency procedures, to the self-assessment procedures. This component is critical to a thorough self-assessment because institutions could incur significant financial losses as a result of fraud and because operational failures at payment system participants could disrupt financial markets.

. . .

The Board is also proposing a change in the procedures for completing the creditworthiness component of the self-assessment. These new procedures are described fully in the draft Guide to the Federal Reserve's Payments System Risk Policy, which is available from any Reserve Bank. Since the inception of the self-assessment process for establishing net debit caps, concerns have been raised regarding the administrative burden raised by the self-assessment procedures. In an attempt to reduce burden on institutions electing to complete a self-assessment, the Board has developed a matrix that combines an institution's supervisory rating and Prompt Corrective Action capital category into a creditworthiness rating. This "Creditworthiness Matrix" is shown below.

Creditworthiness Matrix

	Supervisory composite rating		
Capital level	Strong	Satisfactory	Fair
Well Capitalized----------	Excellent	Very Good	Adequate
Adequately Capitalized--	Very Good	Very Good	Adequate
Undercapitalized----------	Full Assessment	Full Assessment	Below Standard

Note: Institutions with a capital level or supervisory rating not shown in the matrix would receive a creditworthiness of "below standard."

. . .

2. U.S. Agencies and Branches of Foreign Banks

For U.S. agencies and branches of foreign banks, net debit caps on daylight overdrafts in Federal Reserve accounts are calculated by applying the cap multiples for each cap category to consolidated "U.S. capital equivalency."[4]

For a foreign bank whose home-country supervisor adheres to the Basel Capital Accord, U.S. capital equivalency is equal to the greater of 10 percent of worldwide capital or 5 percent of the total liabilities of each agency or branch, including acceptances, but excluding

---

[4] The term "U.S. capital equivalency" is used in this context to refer to the particular capital measure used to calculate daylight overdraft net debit caps, and does not necessarily represent an appropriate capital measure for supervisory or other purposes.

accrued expenses and amounts due and other liabilities to offices, branches, and subsidiaries of the foreign bank. In the absence of contrary information, the Reserve Banks presume that all banks chartered in G-10 countries meet the acceptable prudential capital and supervisory standards and will consider any bank chartered in any other nation that adopts the Basel Capital Accord (or requires capital at least as great and in the same form as called for by the Accord) eligible for the Reserve Banks' review for meeting acceptable prudential capital and supervisory standards.

For all other foreign banks, U.S. capital equivalency is measured as the greater of: (1) The sum of the amount of capital (but not surplus) that would be required of a national bank being organized at each agency or branch location, or (2) the sum of 5 percent of the total liabilities of each agency or branch, including acceptances, but excluding accrued expenses and amounts due and other liabilities to offices, branches, and subsidiaries of the foreign bank.

In addition, any foreign bank may incur daylight overdrafts above its net debit cap up to a maximum amount equal to its cap multiple times 10 percent of its worldwide capital, provided that any overdrafts above its net debit cap are collateralized. This policy offers all foreign banks, under terms that reasonably limit Reserve Bank risk, a level of overdrafts based on the same proportion of worldwide capital. Consequently, banks chartered in countries that follow the Basel Accord and whose net debit cap is based on 10 percent of worldwide capital are not permitted to incur overdrafts above their net debit cap. All other foreign banks may incur overdrafts to the same extent as banks from Basel Accord countries, that is, up to their cap multiple times 10 percent of their worldwide capital, provided that sufficient collateral is posted for any overdrafts in excess of their net debit cap. In addition, foreign banks may elect to collateralize all or a portion of their overdrafts related to book-entry securities activity.

. . .

The policy with respect to capital for foreign bank offices (FBOs) was changed effective February 2002, Board of Governors of the Federal Reserve System, Policy statement, 66 Federal Register 64419 (December 13, 2001). For U.S. branches and agencies of foreign banks, net debit caps on daylight overdrafts will be calculated by applying the cap multiples for each cap category to the FBO's U.S. capital equivalency measure, which is equal to the following: (1) 35 percent of capital for FBOs that are FHCs (financial service holding companies); (2) 25 percent of capital for FBOs that are not FHCs and have a strength of support assessment ranking (SOSA) of 1; (3) 10 percent of capital for FBOs that are not FHCs and are ranked a SOSA 2; and (4) 5 percent of the liability "net due to related depository institutions" for FBOs that are not FHCs and are ranked a SOSA 3.

The SOSA ranking is composed of four factors, including the FBO's financial condition, the supervisory system in the FBO's home country, the record of the home country's government in support of the banking system, and the ability of the FBO to access and transmit U.S. dollars.

The collateral provisions of the old policy became unnecessary due to the new authority for all banks to use collateral, as discussed below.

Notes and Questions

1.   Does it make sense to use capital as a base for the ceilings on daylight overdrafts? Why are ceilings generally enforced only by ex-post rather than real time monitoring?

2.   Why shouldn't the capital base for foreign banks be their entire worldwide capital? Although the 2002 revision in policy gives increased capacity to foreign banks for daylight overdrafts, they are still limited at best to 35 percent of worldwide capital.

b.   PRICING

In addition to ceilings, daylight overdrafts have been priced since April 1994.

BOARD OF GOVERNORS OF THE FEDERAL RESERVE SYSTEM, MODIFICATION OF THE PAYMENTS SYSTEM RISK REDUCTION PROGRAM; DAYLIGHT OVERDRAFT PRICING
57 Federal Register 47084 (1992).

The overdraft fee will be 60 basis points (annual rate), quoted on the basis of a 24-hour day. To obtain the daily overdraft fee (annual rate) for the standard Fedwire operating day, the quoted 60 basis point fee will be multiplied by the fraction of a 24-hour day during which Fedwire is scheduled to operate. Under the current 10-hour Fedwire operating day, the overdraft fee will equal 25 basis points (60 basis points multiplied by 10/24/92), the same price as originally proposed by the Board. Daylight overdraft pricing is effective April 14, 1994, six months after the October 14, 1993, effective date of the Board's new overdraft measurement procedures, published elsewhere in today's Federal Register (Docket No. R-0721).

The Board plans to phase in the 60 basis point fee (times an operating hour fraction) over a three-year period. On April 14, 1994, the fee will be 24 basis points, rising to 48 basis points on April 13, 1995, and 60 basis points on April 11, 1996. Under current Fedwire operating hours, these phase-in fees are equal to the proposed phase-in fees of 10, 20, and 25 basis points. A change in the length of the scheduled Fedwire operating day would not change the effective fee because the fee is applied to average overdrafts which, in turn, would be deflated by the change in the operating day. After evaluating the market's response to pricing, the Board may slow or accelerate the phase-in, cease the phase-in at a level below 60 basis points, or increase the fee above 60 basis points at the end of the phase-in or at a later date.

The fee will apply to combined funds and book-entry securities intraday overdrafts in accounts at the Federal Reserve. The average daily overdraft will be calculated by dividing the sum of the negative reserve or clearing account balances at the end of each minute of the scheduled Fedwire operating day (with credit balances set to zero) by the total number of minutes in the scheduled Fedwire operating day.

· · ·

c.   COLLATERAL

In December 2001, the Board took an important new step by allowing depositary institutions to obtain additional daylight credit by pledging collateral which was intended to address the liquidity needs of a the few institutions that might be actually constrained by their net debit caps. Board of Governors of the Federal Reserve System, Policy statement, 66 Federal Register 64419 (December 13, 2001). Banks were permitted to use existing collateral pledged to support discount window loans when that collateral was not being used for that purpose. The Board expected that very few banks would use the new facility since 97 percent of all Fedwire users use less than 50 percent of their net debit caps for their average peak overdrafts.

Notes and Questions

1.   Assume a U.S. bank has $10 billion in capital and $6 billion in daily average overdrafts over the current 10 hour Fedwire operating day (8:30 a.m. to 6:30 p.m.). How much will the bank pay in daylight overdraft fees to the Fed, assuming pricing has been fully phased-in, that is after April 11, 1996, and there are no further changes to the pricing methodology? Consider that the Fed allows a bank to deduct 10% of its capital from daily average overdrafts. Note that as of December 8, 1997, the Fed shifted to an 18 hour operating day (12:30 a.m. to 6:30 p.m.)

2.   Is the 60 basis point fee high or low? How could that be determined? The Fed decided in March 1995 to slow down the phase-in of daylight overdraft charges. The initial fee from April 1994 to April 1995 was 10 basis points (based on the 10 hour operating day). Fees increased in April 1995 to 15 basis points rather than 20 as originally proposed, and will stay at that level for at least two years. Since the inception of pricing, daylight overdrafts have dropped by 40%. Peak overdrafts fell from nearly $125 billion per day, on average, during the six months preceding April 14, 1994 (the inception of the 10 basis point fee)

to about $70 billion in the six months following April 14, and currently are around $100 billion. While the absolute amounts of daylight overdrafts have now risen substantially from 1994 post-pricing, the ratio of the average value of funds-related overdrafts has remained relatively constant at 1.5 percent. S. Coleman, *The Evolution of the Federal Reserve's Intraday Credit Policies,* Federal Reserve Bulletin 68, 77 (February 2002) (Coleman). Pricing also seems to have affected the concentration of overdrafts. In the six months preceding the implementation of fees, ten institutions with the largest overdrafts accounted for 80 percent of total average overdrafts; post-pricing they now account for only 70 percent. H. Richards, *Daylight Overdraft Fees and the Federal Reserve's Payment System Risk Policy*, 81 Federal Reserve Bulletin 1065, 1071-1072 (1995).

Since the Federal Reserve began pricing daylight overdrafts, an average of only about 350 depositary institutions have paid fees in a given year, and most of these institutions pay less than $1000 per year. In 2000, total fees paid were only $25.2 million. A few banks account for most of these fees. Coleman, supra at 81.

An important consideration in the slow down of price increases was the fear that volume would switch to netting systems (like CHIPS) thus increasing systemic risk in the Fed's view. 60 Federal Register 12559 (1995). The following Chart, Richards, *supra,* at 1076, indicates the change in dollar value on Fedwire and CHIPS from 1990 to early 1995. Does this Chart suggest Fedwire pricing has led to increased use of CHIPS? Why was there a spike in CHIPS volume immediately preceding pricing?

3. If a substantial amount of Fedwire volume has switched or will switch to CHIPS as a result of pricing, would this be of concern to the Fed? Doesn't an important part of the answer to that question depend on the effectiveness of risk reduction techniques on CHIPS?

4. Can banks simply pass on to customers the costs of their daylight overdrafts?

5. The most intense controversy over pricing of daylight overdrafts had to do with the measurement of daylight overdrafts. There are many transactions other than the sending or receiving of Fedwires that can affect the level of balances in Fed accounts, for example check debits and credits. The Fed has adopted a complicated measurement system, see Board of Governors of the Federal Reserve System, Modification of the Payments System Risk Reduction Program; Measurement of Daylight Overdrafts, 57 Federal Register 47093 (1992). The system was changed somewhat in 1996, 61 Federal Register 58691 (November 18, 1996).

6. Any real time gross settlement system like Fedwire requires users to have a certain amount of liquidity—Fed balances—to support payments during the day. While the allowance of daylight overdrafts reduces what

10. Change in dollar values of Fedwire and CHIPS funds transfers, 1990-95

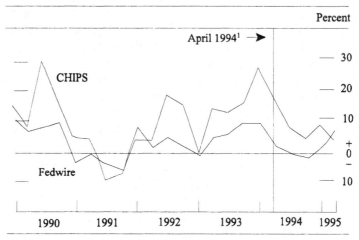

Note: Four-quarter change of quarterly averages of daily values.
1. 10 basis point daylight overdraft fee implemented.

would otherwise be the liquidity requirement, it does not eliminate it given ceilings, and they come at a cost given pricing. One way banks seek to reduce their liquidity costs on Fedwire is to concentrate payments at peak times, and then synchronize them with other banks to avoid gridlock. Outgoing payments during peak times can be funded by synchronized incoming payments thus reducing what would other be the Fed balance requirement, given that outgoing payments in non-peak times would have to be funded by the bank's own Fed balances. This peak time payment activity is concentrated around 4:30 p.m. in the afternoon. J. McAndrews and S. Rajan, *The Timing and Funding of Fedwire Transfers,* 6 Federal Reserve Board of New York Economic Review 17 (2000). See also, M. Bech and K. Soramäki, *Gridlock Resolution in Interbank Payment System,* Discussion Paper 9 (June 13, 2001).

7. Under the new 2002 policy, collateral is an option not a requirement. One can still incur daylight overdrafts under one's cap without any consequences, i.e. without fees or collateral. Should the next step be to make collateralization of all overdrafts mandatory and to abandon pricing? This is the approach taken in some foreign systems.

2. CHIPS

In the CHIPS system, three principal devices (apart from membership admission requirements) were employed to minimize the probability and impact of a settlement failure: (1) ceilings in the form of bilateral and net debit caps; (2) collateralized "Additional Settlement Obligations" (ASOs); and (3) ensuring the validity of netting in bankruptcy. With the change in 2001, ceilings and ASOs have been dropped. Netting validity remains important.

The whole CHIPS system is built on multilateral netting. Each participant has a net debit or credit position vis a vis the system. If a participant fails, the collateralized ASO obligations should insure the completion of the settlement. As we have seen, these ASOs represent allocated portions of the failed bank's net debit position.

The ASO providers would then have a claim against the failed bank for their ASOs—which might be partially secured by whatever collateral the failed participant had posted with the N.Y. Federal Reserve Bank. In the United States, bank bankruptcies are not dealt with under the Bankruptcy Code; instead, almost all bank bankruptcies are handled under banking law rules by the FDIC, as a receiver.

A major issue of concern would be whether the FDIC as receiver would respect the CHIPS netting. Suppose the failed bank (FP) had a net debit position of $5 billion, which resulted from having sent out transfers of $12 billion, and having received transfers of $7 billion.

The FDIC might ignore the CHIPS netting, and the ASO arrangements based on it, and take the position that FP has not been paid for the $7 billion in funds it received, and make claims against the CHIPS participants that sent these funds to FP. This would remit the CHIPS banks to making unsecured claims for $12 billion against the FDIC. Under the netting arrangements, the maximum loss (assuming FP's assets were worth zero) of the banks would be the net debit position, $5 billion. Under a FDIC gross approach, disaggregating transfers sent from those received, the maximum loss of the banks would be $19 billion. They would pay for the $7 billion in transfers sent to FP and get nothing for the $12 billion in transfers received.

The Payments System Risk Reduction provisions of the Federal Deposit Insurance Corporation Improvement Act of 1991, 12 U.S.C. § 4401 et seq. deal with this problem. The key provision affecting CHIPS, 12 U.S.C. § 4404, provides:

§ 4404. Clearing organization netting

(a) General netting rule

Notwithstanding any other provision of law, the covered contractual payment obligations and covered contractual payment entitlements of a member of a clearing organization to and from all other members of a clearing organization shall be netted in accordance with and subject to the conditions of any applicable netting contract.

(b) Limitation of obligation to make payment

The only obligation, if any, of a member of a clearing organization to make payment with respect to covered contractual payment obligations arising under a single netting contract to any other member of a clearing organization shall be equal to its net obligation arising under that netting contract, and no such obligation shall exist if there is no net obligation.

(c) Limitation on right to receive payment

The only right, if any, of a member of a clearing organization to receive payment with respect to a covered contractual payment entitlement arising under a single netting contract from other members of a clearing organization shall be equal to its net entitlement arising under that netting contract, and no such right shall exist if there is no net entitlement.

(d) Entitlement of failed member

The net entitlement, if any, of any failed member of a clearing organization shall be paid to the failed member in accordance with, and subject to the conditions of, the applicable netting contract.

(e) Obligations of failed members

The net obligation, if any, of any failed member of a clearing organization shall be determined in accordance with, and subject to the conditions of, the applicable netting contract.

(f) Limitation on claims for entitlement

A failed member of a clearing organization shall have no recognizable claim against any member of a clearing organization for any amount based on such covered contractual payment entitlements other than its net entitlement.

(g) Effectiveness notwithstanding status as member

This section shall be given effect notwithstanding that a member is a failed member.

This statute only goes so far. Suppose a failed participant is not a U.S. bank. CHIPS participants include substantial numbers of branches of foreign banks whose bankruptcy would be handled abroad, and foreign countries may not have clear rules establishing the validity of netting in bankruptcy.

The major industrialized countries' central banks have promulgated minimum standards for "Netting Schemes" which includes the requirement that "[n]etting schemes should have a well founded legal basis under all relevant jurisdictions," Bank for International Settlements, Report of the Committee on Interbank Netting Schemes of the Central Banks of the Group of Ten Countries 5 (1990) (Lamfalussy Report). The

New York Fed has received letters from counsel to CHIPS participants stating that their home countries would respect the netting. But these are only opinions; in many cases the law is unclear. Furthermore, it is clear that in some major countries netting would not be respected. In Italy and the Netherlands, bank liquidators employing the so-called "zero-hour" rule were able to revoke all payments of a failed bank on the day it becomes bankrupt so that the situation of the bank is restored to that prevailing at the end of the previous day (literally midnight or the "zero hour"). Working Group on EC Payments Systems, Report to The Committee of Governors of The Central Banks of The Member States of the European Economic Community on Minimum Common Features for Domestic Payment Systems 27 (1993).

The problem of the uncertainty of foreign laws may not be that serious, however, for U.S. banks. As the BCCI bankruptcy demonstrated, any foreign bank that fails will have substantial dollar balances held with U.S. banks, and U.S. authorities are likely to use these assets for the benefit of U.S. creditors, including U.S. banks. See H. Scott, *Multinational Bank Insolvencies: The United States and BCCI*, in Comparative Commercial Insolvency Law (J. Ziegel ed., 1994).

The Lamfalussy Minimum Standards for Netting, in addition to the requirement for a sound legal basis (standard #1), are:

2. Netting system participants should have a clear understanding of the impact of the particular system on each of the financial risks affected by the netting process.

3. Multilateral netting systems should have clearly-defined procedures for the management of credit risks and liquidity risks which specify the respective responsibilities of the netting provider and the participants. These procedures should also ensure that all parties have both the incentives and the capabilities to manage and contain each of the risks they bear and that limits are placed on the maximum level of credit exposure that can be produced by each participant.

4. Multilateral netting systems should, at a minimum, be capable of ensuring the timely completion of daily settlements in the event of an inability to settle by the participant with the largest single net debit position.

5. Multilateral netting systems should have objective and publicly-disclosed criteria for admission which permit fair and open access.

6. All netting systems should ensure the operational reliability of technical systems and the availability of backup facilities capable of completing daily processing requirements.

The Federal Reserve Board implemented these requirements in December 1994, 59 Federal Register 67534 (1994) (Fed Netting Policy).

3. GROSS VERSUS NET SETTLEMENT

The United Kingdom had a version of the pre-2001 CHIPS net settlement system called CHAPS but had no equivalent to Fedwire. Mr. Allsopp, former head of the Payments System Division of the Banking Department of the Bank of England, describes why CHAPS was converted into a Fedwire, real-time gross settlement system.

P. ALLSOPP, PAYMENTS SYSTEMS AND RISK
Banking World, May 1993, at 22, 23-24.

Reduction. In an end-of-day settlement system it is not possible for a bank to avoid acquiring an involuntary exposure to another bank, if it wishes to receive payments for credit to its customers. It is, however, possible to take steps to control those exposures.

One way is to place explicit limits on them: such limits have, for instance, been a feature of CHIPS, in New York, for some years, and they have successfully begun to be implemented in CHAPS from last year.

There is, however, a level below which these limits cannot be reduced, even by means of collateral, if the payment system is to continue to function efficiently, by which I mean that it will handle in a timely fashion the legitimate payment needs of the participating banks and their customers. Thus a regime of limits, however, constructed, is liable to leave some residual risk in the system.

The problem for any central banks is that, if it accepts that one of its domestic payment systems should retain a residual risk, in the event that the risk crystallizes, the central bank may find that it has inescapably picked up part, if not all, of the responsibility for covering it. It is not acceptable to have a private sector payment system relying on implicit central bank support against a risk inherent in the design of the system. Public funds cannot be used to, in effect, underwrite private sector risks. Hence the third stage, elimination of this interbank credit risk.

Risk elimination. One approach to this, which has been accepted by the members of CHAPS as an objective for 1995, and is being pursued in a number of other countries also, is to transform the end-of-day net settlement system into a real time gross settlement system, in which each payment instruction from the sending bank is settled across the accounts of the two banks in the books of the central bank before it is sent on to the beneficiary bank. Thus, the beneficiary bank receives final funds, by way of an irrevocable credit to its account with the central bank, and it can immediately pass good value to its customer, or use the funds to meet its own obligations elsewhere, without any exposure to the sending bank.

What that approach does, of course, imply is that if the payment is transferred between the accounts of the two banks before the sending bank has sufficient good funds to support the outpayment, the central bank—the Bank of England, for CHAPS—will itself acquire an exposure to the sending bank.

Padoa-Schioppa, who was appointed an Executive Director of the European Central Bank in 1998, compares the relative virtues of gross and net settlement systems.

T. PADOA-SCHIOPPA, CENTRAL BANKING AND PAYMENT SYSTEMS IN THE EUROPEAN COMMUNITY,

Symposium Proceedings, International Symposium on Banking and Payment Services,
Sponsored by Board of Governors of the Federal Reserve System
35-40 (Mar. 10-11, 1994).

The first issue is whether RTGS should supplement or substitute netting systems. And a related issue is whether substitution would be the natural outcome of market developments (i.e., the ascendancy of a superior technology) or the effect of central bank regulations imposing gross settlement for certain classes of payments.

. . .

Conceptually, if the two systems were designed so as to entail equal risks, payment operations would distribute themselves between the two systems in a way that minimized their cost. And it is reasonable to expect that, for certain classes of payment, netting systems would continue to be the cheapest mode. In general, this would be the case whenever intraday timeliness is not important. In practice, of course, it is almost impossible to design risk reduction measures that would equalize risks in the two systems. Moreover, it is not possible to leave the choice between the two modes completely free for every class of payment: there are, for instance, organized markets for which the decision has to be taken, as part of their organization, whether transactions are to be settled on a gross or on a net basis.

The second issue concerns how and on what conditions the amount of central bank money required to meet demand is to be supplied. A "pure" RTGS would require, for a given volume of gross transactions, a greater intraday supply of central bank money than a pure" netting system (i.e., with no specific risk management measures) because the increase in velocity is unlikely to be sufficient to finance the larger volume of reserves required to settle on a gross basis.

Today, most European—and non-European—central banks are facing what is called the problem of liquidity provision to RTGS. Queuing, compulsory reserves, overdrafts, limits, pricing and collateral for overdrafts are elements of the architecture of systems that exist or are in the process of being implemented. The trade-off between efficiency and stability and the complexity of the factors at work make it very difficult to design *the* optimal architecture of an RTGS or, more generally, of a large-value payment system. Central banks are following a pragmatic approach, and bearing part of the higher cost associated with the introduction of gross settlement.

I believe however that, even in the provision of intraday liquidity for RTGS, central banks should not depart from the classic principles regarding lending of last resort, such as those laid down by Bagehot and Thornton. First of all, commercial banks should not perceive the provision of intraday central bank money as an automatic guarantee supplied by central banks. Some elements of discretionality should be preserved by central banks, for instance by offering lines of credit that can be revoked even with short notice. Second, the cost of this advance of liquidity should not be negligible in order to preserve the incentives for commercial banks to reduce exposures through market mechanisms (for instance: better synchronization of receipts and payments, bilateral caps, etc.). Finally, if an RTGS requires the provision of intraday credit by the central bank, the exposures should always be covered by adequate collateral.

Another issue in the European debate about the evolution from net to gross settlement can be termed "reduction versus elimination" of systemic risk. To put it simply: can we say that with a complete transition to RTGS systemic risk will fall to zero?

Central banks may be tempted to answer positively because, almost by definition, a sequence of final payments cannot be unwound. In other words, the danger of a collapse of all the payments of one day seems to disappear in a gross settlement system. I am, however, of the opinion that the systemic risk inherent in payment systems does not disappear completely, and that it may be difficult to separate it from the risk of a domino effect in payment-credit relationships. After all, the payment system is an amplifier, not the cause, of contagion risk. Even in a gross settlement world, failure by one bank to meet a payment obligation at the time due may set off a chain reaction if the density of interbank payment flows becomes very high. The nature and effects of this chain reaction are very similar to those occurring in a netting system. In fact, a netting system can be looked at as the limit to which an RTGS tends when the density of payments per unit of time tends to infinity. This is why it is more appropriate, I think, to speak of risk reduction, or minimization, than of risk elimination.

· · ·

The following study has compared the total costs of net settlement under CHIPS and gross settlement under Fedwire.

D. SCHOENMAKER, A COMPARISON OF ALTERNATIVE INTERBANK SETTLEMENT SYSTEMS

London School of Economics Financial Markets Group Discussion Paper No. 204, 1995 at 26.

Table 3. Total costs of net and gross settlement (in $ mln).

NET SETTLEMENT	Repayment ratio m		
	m = 0	m = 0.4	m = 0.8
Cost of settlement failure	37.4	22.5	7.5
Cost of pledging collateral	6.1	6.1	6.1
Cost of settlement delay	26.8	26.8	26.8
Total costs	70.3	55.4	40.4
GROSS SETTLEMENT	Turnover ratio V = 27.8		
Cost of pledging collateral	65.1		
Cost of settlement delay	48.9		
Total costs	114.0		

The cost of settlement failure is the maximum level of intraday overdrafts multiplied by the probability of bank failure. Overdrafts on CHIPS are the sum of the net debit positions to be settled at the end of the day. The bank failure rate, .16%, is based on data from 1960-1990 on U.S. bank failures. The study considered repayment rates of the failed bank of 0, 40 and 80 percent. The turnover ratio is total payments divided by total overdrafts. The cost of pledging collateral in CHIPS is based on the amount of collateral pledged and an opportunity cost of 25 basis points on an annual basis. The cost of pledging collateral in Fedwire, where there is actually no such pledge, is the fees paid under pricing for overdrafts. The cost of settlement delay was derived from a complicated calculation as to the costs banks would incur in trying to reduce collateral costs in CHIPS or pricing costs in Fedwire.

The study concludes that gross settlement systems are more expensive. "The result is intuitive. To make the payment system failure proof, banks have to cover their payments with collateral or reserves [or pay pricing fees]. The cost of maintaining sufficient collateral or reserves is considerable under gross settlement. In contrast, the cost of improving the risk management of netting schemes is found to be moderate." *Id.* at 29.

Notes and Questions

1. The new version of CHAPS became operational in April 1996. Do you agree with the approach being taken in the United Kingdom? Would it be better to have both a gross and a net payment system?

2. Does the Schoenmaker study persuade you that the Bank of England's approach is wrong? What is its implication for Padua-Schioppa-'s point that both systems, side-by-side, are desirable? One author has characterized the trade-off between net settlement and RTGS systems as follows: "Net settlement increases probability of defaults or 'abnormal settlements' thereby raising the costs associated with potential defaults, and gross settlement [RTGS] increases the costs associated with holding reserves. The relative merits of the two types of settlement depend on the relative size of these two costs." C. Kahn and W. Roberds, *The Design of Wholesale Payments Networks: The Importance of Incentives,* Federal Reserve Bank of Atlanta, Economic Review 30, 31 (Third Quarter 1999). How will the new changes in CHIPS affect competition between CHIPS and Fedwire?

3. The Committee on Payment and Settlement Systems of the BIS has formulated *Core Principles for Systemically Important Payment Systems*, January 2001. Among the principles is the requirement that "[a] system in which multilateral netting takes place should at a minimum be capable of ensuring the timely completion of daily settlement in the event of an inability to settle by the participant with the largest single settlement obligation." Does the new CHIPS system satisfy this requirement?

C. HERSTATT RISK

An important risk in the payment system is the settlement risk on foreign exchange transactions. This is often called Herstatt risk after a German bank that failed in 1974. Reduction of this risk is a top priority for central bankers.

BANK FOR INTERNATIONAL SETTLEMENTS,
SETTLEMENT RISK IN FOREIGN EXCHANGE TRANSACTIONS
5-9, 15-17, 22-24, 36-38 (1996)

. . .

The market, and in particular the major correspondent banks in each country, now realize that every individual commercial bank and banking sector (however defined) is vulnerable to unexpected endogenous or exogenous events, which could occur on a sufficient scale to cause one or more banks to be unable to settle their foreign exchange trading obligations on any one day.

The scale of these potential settlement problems is demonstrated by the latest survey of FX market turnover. The BIS estimates the average daily turnover of global exchange markets spot, outright forward and foreign exchange swap contracts at US$ 1,230 billion in April 1995. Since each trade could involve two or more payments, daily settlement flows are likely to amount, in aggregate, to a multiple of this figure, although no comprehensive data are available.

Given the serious domestic and international repercussions that a significant FX settlement disruption could have in a market of this size, a bank might believe that public authorities in some countries would not close a major FX market participant during the day or permit it to default unexpectedly and cause significant losses during the settlement process. This belief might make a bank unwilling to reduce its present settlement exposures, or even increase its willingness to take on even greater settlement exposures with its counterparties. To the extent that this belief is widely held in the market. it has already produced an unacceptable level of risk in the financial system.

Moreover, the extent of this risk is in reality substantially greater than is suggested by estimates of market turnover and settlement flows. The definition of and methodology for measuring FX settlement exposure, as set out in this report, make it clear that it is not just an intraday phenomenon: in practice, FX settlement exposure typically represents overnight risk; it can last for several business days; and it will therefore be present over weekends and public holidays. Furthermore, at any point in time a bank's FX settlement exposure can greatly exceed its capital.

It is also the case that the market's belief that a major FX market participant will not be closed during the day is ill-founded. There is in fact no time, during a weekday, at which the large-value payments systems of every major currency are closed. To the extent that commercial banks maintain this belief, an unnecessary and avoidable element of risk remains in the market.

Set out below are brief summaries of five case studies that demonstrate the ways in which a settlement problem can arise. They also demonstrate that despite the steps that have been taken since 1974 to improve coordination between banking supervisors and to begin to introduce settlement risk control measures in the major financial centres, the possibility of a bank failing or being closed during the business day remains, and any collapse will almost inevitably occur during the business day of one financial centre or another. While the timing of the withdrawal of a banking authorisation may in some circumstances be controllable so as to minimize shocks to the markets, there will be other cases in which a banking supervisor may have little choice as to the timing of its actions. If, for example, a banking supervisor becomes aware that a bank has sustained major losses, sufficient to seriously impair its capital base, it may need to take immediate action of some sort to protect depositors. The timing of this action may also be influenced by the need to ensure that a bank does not continue to trade while insolvent, and by the need in such circumstances to act quickly lest the fact that the institution is in difficulty becomes publicly known, precipitating a "run" on the bank. In some countries it is not legally possible to put a bank into liquidation outside the business hours of the court that must appoint the liquidator.

2.2.1 *The failure of Bankhaus Herstatt (1974)*

On 26th June 1974 the Bundesaufsichtsamt für das Kreditwesen withdrew the banking licence of Bankhaus Herstatt, a small bank in Cologne active in the FX market, and ordered it into liquidation during the banking day but after the close of the interbank payments system in Germany. Prior to the announcement of Herstatt's closure, several of its counterparties had, through their branches or correspondents, irrevocably paid Deutsche Mark to Herstatt on that day through the German payments system against anticipated receipts of US dollars later the same day in New York in respect of maturing spot and forward transactions.

Upon the termination of Herstatt's business at 10.30 a.m. New York time on 26th June (3.30 p.m. in Frankfurt), Herstatt's New York correspondent bank suspended outgoing US dollar payments from Herstatt's account. This action left Herstatt's counterparty banks exposed for the full value of the Deutsche Mark deliveries made (credit risk and liquidity risk). Moreover, banks which had entered into forward trades with Herstatt not yet due for settlement lost money in replacing the contracts in the market (replacement risk), and others had deposits with Herstatt (traditional counterparty credit risk).

2.2.2 *Drexel Burnham Lambert (1990)* [omitted]

2.2.3 *BCCI (1991)*

The appointment of a liquidator to BCCI SA on 5th July 1991 caused a principal loss to UK and Japanese foreign exchange counterparties of the failed institution.

An institution in London was due to settle on 5th July 1991 a dollar/sterling foreign exchange transaction into which it had entered two days previously with BCCI SA, London. The sterling payment was duly made in London on 5th July. BCCI had sent a message to its New York correspondent on 4th July (a public holiday in the United States) to make the corresponding US dollar payment for value on 5th July. The payment message was delayed beyond the time of the correspondent bank's initial release of payments (at 7 a.m.) by the operation of a bilateral credit limit placed on BCCI's correspondent by the recipient CHIPS member. The payment remained in the queue until shortly before 4 p.m. (New York time), when it was canceled by BCCI's correspondent, shortly after the correspondent had received a message from BCCI's provisional liquidators in London on the subject of the action it should take with regard to payment instructions from BCCI London. In this way, BCCI's counterparty lost the principal amount of the contract.

A major Japanese bank also suffered a principal loss in respect of a dollar/yen deal due for settlement on 5th July, since yen had been paid to BCCI SA Tokyo that day, through the Foreign Exchange Yen Clearing System, and the assets of BCCI SA in New York State were frozen before settlement of the US dollar leg of the transaction took place.

The UK institution's loss illustrates a particular aspect of the difficulties which face the private sector under current circumstances in any attempt to coordinate the timing of payments; in this instance, the loss would almost certainly not have occurred but for the measures in place to reduce risk domestically within CHIPS. Moreover, the closure of BCCI by the banking supervisors illustrates that it is generally not possible to close a bank which is active in the foreign exchange market at a time when all the relevant payments systems have settled all its transactions due on a given day. In this case, the closure required the Luxembourg Court to appoint a liquidator, an action which under Luxembourg law can take place only within the normal business day of the Court.

2.2.4 The attempted Soviet coup d'état (1991) [omitted]

2.2.5 The Barings crisis (1995) [omitted]

2.3 Defining and measuring foreign exchange settlement exposure

To contain the systemic risk inherent in current arrangements for settling foreign exchange transactions, it is first necessary to develop a realistic understanding of the nature and scope of FX settlement exposures. On the basis of discussions with market participants, the CPSS has adopted the following definition of foreign exchange settlement exposure:

> *A bank's actual exposure - the amount at risk - when settling a foreign exchange trade equals the full amount of the currency purchased and lasts from the time a payment instruction for the currency sold can no longer be canceled unilaterally until the time the currency purchased is received with finality.*

It is important to note that this definition is designed to address the size and duration of the credit exposure that can arise during the FX settlement process. It says nothing about the probability of the occurrence of an actual loss.

The definition also does not specifically address the *ability* of a bank to measure and to control its FX settlement exposure at a particular moment. To develop a practical methodology for measuring current and future FX settlement exposures in a manner consistent with the above definition, a bank would need to recognise the changing status - and, hence, the changing potential settlement exposure - of each of its trades during the settlement process. Although settling a trade involves numerous steps, from a settlement risk perspective a trade's status can be classified according to five broad categories:

Status R: *Revocable.* The bank's payment instruction for the sold currency either has not been issued or may be unilaterally canceled without the consent of the bank's counterparty or any other intermediary. The bank faces no current settlement exposure for this trade.

Status I: *Irrevocable.* The bank's payment instruction for the sold currency can no longer be canceled unilaterally either because it has been finally processed by the relevant payments system or because some other factor (e.g. internal procedures, correspondent banking arrangements, local payments system rules, laws) makes cancellation dependent upon the consent of the counterparty or another intermediary; the final receipt of the bought currency is not yet due. In this case, the bought amount is clearly at risk.

Status U: *Uncertain.* The bank's payment instruction for the sold currency can no longer be canceled unilaterally; receipt of the bought currency is due, but the bank does not yet know whether it has received these funds with finality. In normal circumstances, the bank expects to have received the funds on time. However, since it is possible that the bought currency was not received when due (e.g. owing to an error or to a technical or financial failure of the counterparty or some other intermediary), the bought amount might, in fact. still be at risk.

Status F: *Fail.* The bank has established that it did not receive the bought currency from its counterparty. In this case the bought amount is overdue and remains clearly at risk.

Status S: *Settled.* The bank knows that it has received the bought currency with finality. From a settlement risk perspective the trade is considered settled and the bought amount is no longer at risk.

. . .

Bilateral netting services. FXNET, S.W.I.F.T. and VALUNET currently provide bilateral obligation netting services to many banks. As of December 1995, FXNET provided this service to 29 institutions operating out of 57 offices in 9 locations, including New York, London, Zurich, Tokyo and Singapore, and an additional 19 offices were in the process of joining the system. Three new locations (Geneva, Sydney and Toronto) would be introduced with the planned expansion. Accord, which is operated by S.W.I.F.T. (Society for Worldwide Interbank Financial Telecommunication), provides confirmation matching and bilateral obligation netting services. As of December 1995, 370 users employed the Accord matching services, including 27 subscribers to its netting services. VALUNET, the smallest of the service providers, is operated by International Clearing Systems (service provider for the proposed Multinet International Bank, which is discussed below). As of December 1995, VALUNET provided bilateral obligation netting services to 10 institutions operating out of 17 offices in 5 locations. In addition to these industry services, many pairs of banks have set up bilateral netting arrangements on their own, often using a standardised contract such as the *International Foreign Exchange Master Agreement (IFEMA).*

However, despite the potential risk-reducing benefits, the market survey indicated that not all banks use bilateral obligation netting agreements. When they do net, more often than not their netting is limited to close-out provisions (mainly to take advantage of favourable capital treatment of netted positions or to improve their leverage ratios)* while routine settlements continue to be conducted on a gross, trade-by-trade basis. Obligation netting is mostly confined to the largest banks and their largest counterparties.

Banks cite costs and operational capacity as barriers to the greater use of bilateral netting by novation or other methods of obligation netting. In several countries, banks also expressed concern about the lack of legal certainty of netting arrangements. Some of the discussions suggested a possible role for the European Commission or for some individual central banks in validating netting contracts. In contrast, some banks find it cost-effective to informally settle their foreign exchange trades by paying and receiving their obligations on a net basis. However, uncertainty regarding the legal soundness of such arrangements could potentially increase systemic risk.

Multilateral netting and settlement services. ECHO (Exchange Clearing House) began operations in August 1995 and the proposed Multinet International Bank hopes to start in 1996. Both systems are designed to transform bilaterally arranged individual FX trades into multilateral net settlement obligations and to provide risk controls that ensure the timely settlement of these obligations. In essence. these controls are designed to reduce credit and liquidity risks by assuring participants that the final settlement of each currency will

---

* "Close-out netting" only applies upon the occurrence of an event such as the appointment of a liquidator to one of the counterparties, eds.

take place even if a participant in the group is itself unable to settle its obligations on the due day.

ECHO began operations with 16 participant users in 8 countries netting trades in 11 currencies. ECHO hopes to expand its services to banks in more than 90 countries for trades in 25 currencies. Multinet plans initially to provide services to 8 banks in North America for their trades in US and Canadian dollars and other major currencies within the first year. Multinet also hopes to add further currencies and participants in other countries over time. It may be noted that central banks have successfully used the minimum standards and cooperative oversight principles set out in the Lamfalussv Report when reviewing these systems.

Other multi-currency settlement mechanisms. More recently, the newly formed "Group of 20"[13] has been actively exploring other possible multi-currency settlement mechanisms. Rather than directly netting the underlying FX trades, the models currently under study could be designed to support the settlement of individual trades or trades which have already been netted under other bilateral or multilateral obligation netting arrangements. Although these multi-currency settlement mechanisms would not, by themselves, provide the risk-reducing benefits of obligation netting, they could lower credit risks by assuring participants that the final transfer of one currency will occur if and only if the final transfer of the other relevant currency or currencies also occurs. Multi-currency settlement mechanisms could also, if designed accordingly, lower liquidity risks by assuring participants that if they settle their payment obligations then they will receive their expected funds on time.

Prospects for collective action. Although some of these industry-wide initiatives are well under way, many banks remain skeptical about the business case for committing resources to efforts to reduce FX settlement exposures. As a result, many individual banks have been slow to join these efforts. Without adequate motivation for a sufficient number of FX market participants to support and use one or more of these current or prospective industry-wide multi-currency services, their short-term (let alone long-term) viability is uncertain.

.   .   .

---

[13] The Group of 20 was formed in 1994 as a common interest group of international commercial banks from Asia Europe and North America. The purpose of the group is to identify and cause the implementation of private sector solutions that reduce the risk and increase the efficiency of the clearance and settlement of linked transactions primarily originating from foreign exchange activity.

Notes and Questions

1. Global FX market turnover has more than doubled between 1990-1996 to reach a daily average of $1.3 trillion generating more than $3 trillion dollars in daily payments in various currencies. In some payment systems, they account for more than 50% of daily payment traffic. P. Allsopp, *Settlement Risk in FX Transactions: The G-10 Central Banks' Report,* Payment System Worldwide (Summer 1996)

2. FX settlement risk is not taken into account under the current BIS capital requirement formula because foreign exchange forward transactions with less than 14 days maturity are considered to have no credit risk. Should this be changed?

3. In December 1997 Fedwire began operating 18 hours per day. How might this reduce FX settlement risk? As of March 30, 1998, only 1 percent of volume, $10 billion, was being transferred in the early morning, from 12:30 a.m. to 7. It has been reported that many banks will not use the service because their business volumes do not justify staffing during the middle of the night. J. Haliford, *Fed's Extended Hours for Fedwire Slow to Take Hold,* Security Industry News, March 30, 1998.

4. Prior to the BIS Report, many bankers and commentators thought FX settlement risk was largely an intraday problem principally caused by the fact that payment systems, located in different time zones, had different operating hours. A major reason advanced in the Report as to why FX settlement risk is also interday is that banks may originate settlements in advance of their value date (the date on which they are due) and not be able to cancel them upon discovery that their counterparty cannot settle. What might be done to make it easier to cancel payments in advance of their value date? Note that under Article 4A of the United States Uniform Commercial Code, §4A-211, governing wire transfers, payments can, in principle, be canceled up to the time they are credited to the beneficiary, if intervening banks cooperate. However, CHIPS Rule 2 prevents cancellation of any order received by CHIPS, whether or not the order has been passed on to the beneficiary. Should this Rule be changed?

5. Will multilateral netting systems like ECHO and Multinet eliminate foreign exchange settlement risk? If so, won't they create a new multilateral payment risk? Multinet will be a bank that will pay net creditors and receive payments from net debtors, much as the Federal Reserve Bank of New York does in the CHIPS system. To perform this role for dollar settlements it needs access to Fedwire. The grant of such access will depend on the Fed's confidence that Multinet has adequate liquidity in dollars. This depends on Multinet's ability to convert foreign exchange balances into dollars or to get dollar credit lines against foreign balances.

CLS Services, Ltd. is championing a new system called Continuous Linked Settlement ("CLS"). In 1997, Multinet and ECHO merged with CLS Services. In principle, CLS would permit simultaneous transfers of both legs of a foreign exchange transaction through existing national payment systems. IBM is developing the system and Swift will provide the network communications system.   J. Sandman, *CLS Settlement System Set for October Launch,* Security Industry News, March 26, 2001. The cost of the project once estimated at $60 million has climbed to $300 million, and will cost over $30 million per year to run, raising the issue of whether Herstatt risk justifies such expenditures. *The Long Dark Shadow of Herstatt,* The Economist, April 14, 2001. See also *16 CLS Members to Participate in March 2000 Trials,* Global Investment Technology, December 6, 1999; C. Davidson, *IBM to Build Settlement System,* Securities Industry News, May 4, 1998.

The CLS Bank, which will be chartered as a U.S. Edge Corporation (a limited purpose bank), will settle currency transactions whose underlying obligations are either netted or gross. The Bank will settle the payments for the transactions on a real-time not netted basis, transferring funds on both currency legs of the transaction at the same time by postings to the accounts of its members, a so-called payment v. payment system. The CLS Bank will be the counterparty to both sides of the payment. CLS members will pay the CLS Bank and receive payments from the CLS bank. Members will hold multicurrency accounts at the Bank. The first wave of operations will involve seven currencies: the Australian dollar, the Canadian dollar, euro, Japanese yen, pound sterling, Swiss franc and the United States dollar. The Bank will pool member balances in each currency, and providing members have a sufficient overall net balance, will settle transactions in any currency. Like in the new CHIPS system, an algorithm is employed to make maximum settlement use of a CLS member's balances. CLS Bank will hold its own accounts at the central banks of the currencies involved. Members will be able to pay in funds and receive settlement proceeds through the national payment systems.

Each member will be required to pay in balances at CLS Bank to cover currency short positions within certain limits. Prior to each day's settlement period, which will last for the few hours that the major payment systems in all time zones overlap, CLS will commence the settlement of queued instructions. During the settlement cycle, new funds will be taken in, transactions will be settled, and funds will be paid out. Banks can incur overdrafts up to a set ceiling in individual currencies but must have positive balances overall, taking account of fluctuations in exchange rates. CLS Bank holds lines of credit with "liquidity providers" (the actual members themselves) to cover individual currency overdrafts. See C. Khan and W. Roberds, *The CLS Bank: A Solution to the Risks of International Payments Settlement?*, Carnegie-Rochester Conference Series on Public Policy 54 (2001), pp. 191-226; W. Mundt, *The Case for Continuous Linked Settlement,* Payment Systems Worldwide (Winter 1997-98); PRC Report, at 63-64. For an earlier version of the same idea developed in connection with the euro, see H. Scott, *A Payment System Role for a European System of Central Banks,* in Committee for the Monetary Union of Europe, For a Common Currency, pp. 77-106 (1990) and *The Role of the European System of Central Banks in the Payment System,* in Committee for the Monetary Union of Europe, The Economic and Monetary Union: The Political Dimension, pp. 101-115 (1991).

CLS is scheduled to begin with a pilot project in March 2002. 70 of the world's largest banks, as well as all of the world's main central banks, will participate. A Skorecki, *Forex system that takes waiting out of wanting,* Financial Times, January 4, 2002.

D. SOME ASPECTS OF THE INTERNATIONAL PAYMENT SYSTEM

1. TYPES OF DOMESTIC PAYMENT SYSTEMS

CHIPS (net) and/or Fedwire (gross) type systems exist in the currencies of major countries, as indicated in the following Table adapted from Bank for International Settlements, Committee on Payment and Settlement Systems, Statistics on Payment Systems in the Group of Ten Countries, Tables 10a-10b (2001) (Redbook).

Table A
Features of Selected Interbank Funds Transfer System[1,6]
(figures relate to 1999)

	Type[2]	Owner/Manager[3]	No. of Participants	of which direct	Settlement[4]	Membership[5]	Number of transactions (thousands)	Value of Transactions (USD billions)[12]	Ratio of transactions value to GDP (at annual rate)
Belgium[6]									
Clearing House	L+R	B+CB	101	44	N	O	4,950	113	0.5
CEC	R	B+CB	104	46	N	O	937,160	477	2.0
Canada									
LVTS	L	AS	14	14	N	RM	3,040	15,035	23.1
France[6]									
CH Paris[7]	L+R	AS	357	29	N	RM	683,689	903	0.7
CH Provinces[8]	R	CB	267	219	N	O	2,700,494	1,163	0.9
SIT	R	CB+B/AS	311	22	N	RM	5,913,372	2,505	1.9
CREIC	R	CB	16	16	N	O	304,530	30	0.02
PNS[9]	L	CB+B/AS	25	25	N/BN/RTGS	RM	5,197	25,647	18.9
Germany[6]									
EMZ (former DTA)	R	CB	2,662	2,662	GS	O	2,176,200	2,388	1.1
EAF (former EAF 2)	L	CB	68	68	N/BN	RM	12,100	41,610	19.7
Italy[6]									
Local clearing	R	CB	n.a.	135	N	O	103,942	666	0.6
Retail	R	CB[11]	942	211	N	O	959,750	1,279	1.2
Japan									
FEYCS	L	B	259	47	N/RTGS	RM	9,995	62,389	14.4
BOJ-NET	L	CB	409	409	RTGS[13]	RM	4,810	302,792	69.7
Netherlands[14]									
Interpay	R	B	71	71	N	O	2,152,500	1,431	3.6
Sweden[14]									
K-RIX	L	CB	23	23	RTGS	RM	343	12,208	50.6
Bank Giro System	R	B	18	18	N	O	338,000	395	1.6
Switzerland									
SIC	L+R	CB+B	291	291	RTGS	RM	141,700	28,805	111.2
DTA/LSV	R	B	161	161	GS	RM	104,600	245	0.9
United Kingdom[14,18]									
CHAPS Sterling	L	B	404	14	RTGS	RM	19,786	72,336	50.1
BACS	R	B	50,000 [15]	15	N	RM	3,095,405	2,850	2.0
Cheque/credit	R	B	471	12	N	RM	2,103,569	2,322	1.6 [19]
United States									
Fedwire	L	CB	9,994 [16]	9,994 [16]	RTGS	O	102,800	343,382	36.9
CHIPS	L	B	77	77	N	RM	57,300	297,934	32.0
European Union									
TARGET	L	CB	5,144	4,261	RTGS	O	42,258	240,574	
Euro 1	L	B	72	72	n.a.[17]	RM	17,646	44,418	

1 For additional information see relevant country chapters.

2 L = Large-value system, R = Retail system.

3 Owner/Manager: B = Banks, CB = Central Banks, AS = Payment Association.

4 N = multilateral Netting, BN = Bilateral Netting, RTGS = Real-Time Gross Settlement, GS = other Gross Settlement.

5 O = Open membership (any bank can apply) or RM = Restricted Membership (subject to criteria).

6 For information on the national components of the EU-wide TARGET system (namely, ELLIPS in Belgium, TBF in France, ELS in Germany and BI-REL in Italy) see the relevant country tables. Data on TARGET as a whole are shown in Table 10b under the euro area.

7 Clearing House in Paris.

8 Clearing Houses in the provinces.

9 Previous SNP system changed to PNS (Paris Net Settlement) during 1999.

10 Transactions can also be submitted on floppy disk.

11 System managed by the Interbank Society for Automation in the name and on behalf of the Banca d'Italia.

12 Converted at yearly average exchange rates.

13 The system has been designed to allow participants to enter funds transfer instructions continuously, in which case settlement takes place on the central bank's books immediately. It is, however, also used to settle on a net basis.

14 For information on the national components of the EU-wide TARGET system (namely, TOP in the Netherlands, E-RIX in Sweden and CHAPS Euro in the United Kingdom) see the relevant country tables. Data on TARGET as a whole are shown below under the euro area.

15 Estimated.

16 Fedwire participants as of 30 June 2000.

17 The legal structure of Euro 1 is based on the Single Obligation Structure (SOS), whereby on each settlement day, at any given time, each participant will have only one single payment obligation or claim with respect to the community of the other participants as joint creditors/debtors, which will be settled at the end of the day. In accordance with the SOS, no bilateral payments, claims or obligations between participants will be created by the processing of payments in the system. Nor will there be any form of set-off, novation or netting resulting from the continuous adjustment of the participants' single claim or obligation.

18 Interbank figures only.

19 Excludes Northern Ireland.

Source: Bank for International Settlements, *Statistics payment systems in the Group of Ten countries*, March 2001, Tables 10a, 10b

The following chart shows the global time-zone relationships between various national payment systems as of 1993. It is the lack of overlap that is at the heart of the Herstatt risk.

BANK FOR INTERNATIONAL SETTLEMENTS, CENTRAL BANK PAYMENT AND SETTLEMENT SERVICES WITH RESPECT TO CROSS-BORDER AND MULTI-CURRENCY TRANSACTIONS 19 (1993).

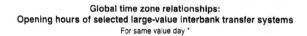

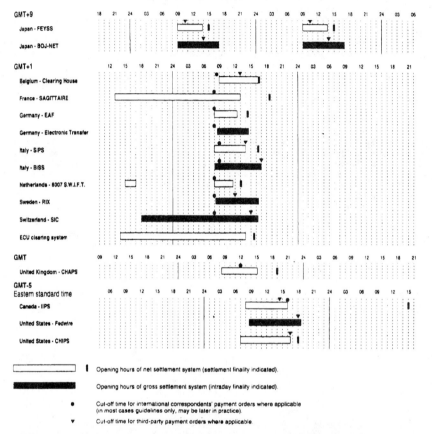

Note that the operating hours of the U.S. and Japanese systems have no overlap. Japan is 14 hours ahead of the U.S. so when CHIPS opens at 7:00 a.m. EST (12 noon GMT), it is 9:00 p.m. Tokyo time.

2. INTERNATIONAL PAYMENT SYSTEMS

In addition to domestic systems, there are payment systems that are set up to operate on a cross-border basis.

COMMITTEE OF GOVERNORS OF THE CENTRAL BANKS OF THE MEMBER STATES OF THE EUROPEAN ECONOMIC COMMUNITY, AD HOC WORKING GROUP ON EC PAYMENT SYSTEMS, PAYMENT SYSTEMS IN EC MEMBER STATES
294, 298-300 (1992).

3.2.1. Netting mechanisms

FX NET Limited is a limited partnership formed under English Law, owned by the UK subsidiaries of 12 major banks. It facilitates bilateral netting for spot and forward foreign exchange obligations between participating banks, using the concept of netting by novation. Banks are able to participate in FX NET by obtaining the necessary software package (prepared by Quotron) under license from FX NET for installation in their own in-house systems.

Through participation in FX NET, banks are able to reduce their credit and liquidity risks from gross to bilateral net positions for each of their branches which participate in the service, vis-à-vis branches of other banks.

Once a bank has installed the FX NET—Quotron software, it is then free to negotiate which other participants to net with and in which currencies. Within this process, FX NET provides well-documented model netting agreements which its participants may choose to use, though it is each participant's responsibility to obtain independent legal advice regarding the effectiveness of these agreements.

As of February 1992, 31 bank branches in London, New York, Los Angeles, Tokyo and Singapore were participating in FX NET, netting both within each centre and between different centres. In addition, a further 16 branches of existing, as well as new member banks, were preparing to join FX NET in these financial centres as well as in Hong Kong, whilst banks were also considering the establishment of FX NET in Paris and Zürich.

3.2.2. Central banks oversight

In early 1986, before FX NET was first implemented in pilot form, formal approval was sought from the Bank of England and the Federal Reserve Bank of New York (FRBNY). The Bank of England's approval was given in the following terms (similar to those of the FRBNY):

(i)   each participant bank would be expected to satisfy itself as to the legal validity of netting by novation in the UK, and in the country of origin of each of its participating counterparties;

(ii) a commensurate reduction would be expected in each participant's limits on such counterparties;

(iii) these aspects of participation would be subjects for discussion during the routine prudential interviews between each participant in the UK and the Bank of England in its role of banking supervisor.

Both the Bank of England's and the FRBNY's formal responses form part of the package for legal documentation that FX NET currently provides to its participants.

. . .

Another important part of the international payment system is S.W.I.F.T. The Society for Worldwide Interbank Financial Telecommunication (S.W.I.F.T.) is a private company, created in Belgium in 1973, which engages in the transmission of financial messages for the benefit of its shareholding member banks and of other approved categories of financial institutions.

S.W.I.F.T. transmits financial messages between the 7,000 financial institutions connected to the company's proprietary network which covers 192 countries. The core service offered by S.W.I.F.T. consists of handling the exchange of financial messages over its proprietary network (composed of computer facilities, switching equipment, leased lines and related software). The network functions comprise the acceptance, validation, storing and delivery of messages. The network, which is accessible 24 hours a day, seven days a week, handled a total message traffic of 1.2 billion in 2000. These messages are highly structured and cover a wide range of banking and other transactions such as payment orders, foreign exchange confirmations and securities deliveries.

To ensure confidentiality, each message is automatically encrypted by S.W.I.F.T. when it enters the network while users have the option to encrypt the message flow between their in-house terminals and their S.W.I.F.T. access point. Each message also contains an authenticator which permits the identification of the sender and receiver and which guarantees that the message text has not been modified during transmission. Authentication is based on a common algorithm provided by S.W.I.F.T. and on bilateral keys, known only to the sending and receiving pair of users. The network's operating system generates a broad range of automatic reports on individual users' message traffic, for instance relating to undelivered messages, but users may also request special reports, such as terminal error reports and delivery status reports.

With respect to message traffic, the S.W.I.F.T. network may be used for cross-border and internal domestic transactions involving member banks or participants. The proportion of domestic traffic in the total varies considerably from country to country, partly depending on the rules of the national telecommunications authority and partly on the types of alternative interbank telecommunication facilities available.

A S.W.I.F.T. message containing a payment order is different from the electronic messages that pass through domestic large-value funds transfer systems because the S.W.I.F.T. payment order does not, by itself or under S.W.I.F.T. rules, create an irrevocable obligation on the part of the sending bank. Financial institutions exchanging S.W.I.F.T. messages have to arrange the clearing and/or settlement of the incoming payment orders themselves, either by relying on bilateral correspondent relationships which they have with one another or by forwarding incoming orders to domestic interbank funds transfer systems.

Notes and Questions

1. RTGS systems differ in important respects. Some, like the Swiss SIC system, do not allow overdrafts and instead queue outgoing transfer instructions pending receipt of incoming funds. Where queues are used, pending messages may be centrally stored or kept at individual banks, and may be prioritized according to various criteria, or just treated on a first-in-first-out basis. Some RTGS systems are not owned by the central bank. CHAPS, for example, is owned by an association whose members are the direct participants and the central bank. See Bank for International Settlements, Committee on Payment and Settlement Systems of the Group of Ten Countries, *Real-Time Gross Settlement Systems* (March 1997).

3. OFF-SHORE DOLLAR PAYMENT SYSTEMS

Another aspect of the international payment system is offshore settlement. For example, there are various methods by which banks can clear dollar payments outside the United States through formal clearing systems. For example, there are the London Dollar Clearing Scheme (LDC) and the Tokyo Dollar Clearing system.

LDC clears United States dollar cheques and banker's drafts and payments (LDC items). Direct access to the clearing, administered by the Association for Payment Clearing Services (APACS) was limited in 1987 to seven major English banks (Settlement Banks), but other banks (Agency Banks) have indirect access to the clearing through correspondent accounts with the banks that have direct access.

LDC is a net settlement system. On the basis of a day's clearing activities in London each Settlement Bank has a net position. A Settlement Bank's net positions are settled through New York on the same business day that they arise in London. Positions are determined by 4:30 p.m. London time, or 11:30 a.m. New York time. Instructions to New York correspondents must be sent out by 12 noon New York time, leaving ample time during the same business day in New York to complete the settlement.

A net debtor Settlement Bank would instruct its New York correspondent to transfer funds to the New York correspondent account of the Settlement Agent (each Settlement Bank acts in this capacity on a rotating basis). This transfer could go through CHIPS or be a book transfer on the books of a New York bank which is the correspondent for both the Settlement Agent and the net debtor Settlement Bank. Conversely, the Settlement Agent transfers funds to the New York correspondent of a net creditor Settlement Bank.

In addition to the LDC net settlement among Settlement Banks, bilateral settlements must take place between LDC Settlement Banks, e.g. Lloyd's Bank, and their Agency Banks, e.g. Bankers Trust's London branch (BTL). Thus, for a day's LDC clearing, (BTL) may be in a net credit or net debit position with Lloyd's. If BTL is in a net credit position, Lloyd's would transfer funds, through its correspondent in New York, via CHIPS, to Banker Trust's New York head office (BTNY) for the account of BTL, and if BTL were in a net debit position, BTL would transfer funds, through BTNY, via CHIPS, to Lloyd's New York correspondent, the settlement could take place by book-entries on the books of BTNY to the accounts of BTL and Lloyd's.

The Tokyo Dollar Clearing (TDC), which has existed since the occupation of Japan after World War II, is presently a clearing of all types of electronic dollar transfers among more than 180 participant banks and branches in Tokyo, operated by Chase Manhattan's Tokyo branch (Chase-Tokyo).

Participating banks send electronic transfers to each other during the Tokyo day that may represent payments for any transactions between participants, e.g. the dollar payment on a foreign exchange transaction, or payments by a customer of one participant in favor of a customer of another participant. Customers receiving payments get credit on the books of their banks in Tokyo. All payments are routed through the computer system of Chase-Tokyo.

At the end of the day's clearing (3 p.m. Tokyo time), Chase calculates the net debit and net credit positions of participants, and communicates this information to the participants and to Chase New York. Chase New York then transfers credits to net creditors, on its books, through CHIPS, or by Fedwire, by 10 a.m. New York time (midnight same day in Tokyo). Net debtors must transfer credits to Chase in New York by the end of the CHIPS day. Net credit transfers by Chase are conditional on the net debtors settling with Chase by the end of the day.

As with LDC, TDC settlement takes place entirely in New York. But, also like LDC, the actual payments which underlie the TDC net calculation are made in Tokyo.

Notes and Questions

1. Could offshore dollar netting systems be used to avoid U.S. regulation of on-shore netting systems like CHIPS? Can this be controlled? The Fed Netting Policy applies to systems of a certain minimum size "that net payments or foreign exchange contracts involving the U.S. dollar...." Its policy would apply to offshore dollar clearings. How can the Fed enforce its policy against an offshore system? The Fed reserved the right to apply its rules to U.S. based non-dollar systems as well. Would there be difficulties in actually doing so?

2. Do these systems create risk to participants and to the U.S. payments system through which the net obligations are settled?

3. The Federal Reserve Board's September 1992 Payments System Policy Statement establishes guidance for offshore systems. They must be subject to central bank supervision, participants must identify significant risk, finality of settlement must be provided for, and settlement in the U.S. must be conducted through an identified settlement agent in a specified procedure.

4. EUROPEAN UNION

The European Union has taken three important initiatives with respect to large value payment systems within the EU: (a) formulation of minimum common standards; (b) improving the efficiency of cross-border retail transfers; and (c) preparation for EMU.

a. MINIMUM COMMON STANDARDS

In November 1993 the Committee of Governors of the EU central banks issued a report on "Minimum common features for domestic payment systems." This report established ten principles for EU Interbank Funds Transfer Services (EU IFTS) covering six areas: access conditions, risk management policies, legal issues, standards and infrastructures, pricing policies and operating hours. Three of the most important principles relate to access, the need for RTGS systems and the requirements for multilateral netting systems.

One of the access principles provides that "[n]o discrimination can be made between home-based credit institutions and credit institutions licensed in other EC countries which ask to participate in local interbank funds transfer systems, either through their local branches or directly from another member state. The applicants, however, may be required to establish that they can meet the relevant legal provisions of the host country. They also have to comply with the necessary technical requirements of the system; these requirements, however, should not be discriminatory."   This policy seems directly related to the goal of establishing a single market for banking services represented by the Second Banking Directive. In 1995, there were 162 branches of foreign banks participating in EU IFTS of which 104 were from other EU countries. Working Group on EU Payments Systems, Report to the Council of the European Monetary Institute, Developments in EU Payment Systems in 1994, at 4 (1995).

Remote access to payment systems (directly from the home country rather than through a local branch) has not yet been generally accepted due to various problems. For example, physical presence may be needed under back-up procedures requiring physical exchanges of data if electronic transmission is down. Having a settlement account with an overdraft facility at the local central bank is a condition for direct membership in most EU IFTS. Remote access raises the issue of whether and how the remote central bank can insure liquidity and perform the function of lender of last resort for the local system. *Id.* at 6-7.

Another important principle requires "[a]s soon as feasible, every Member State should have a real-time gross settlement system into which as many large-value payments as possible should be channeled. Such systems should settle across accounts at the central bank and have sound legal, technical and prudential features which are compatible across member states." By the end of 1996, RTGS systems are expected to be in operation in all EU countries with the exception of Austria and Luxembourg. *Id.* at 9. This principle, as elaborated below, is important for the implementation of EMU since EMU envisions using the linked RTGS systems of the participants to make Euro transfers.

A third principle states "[p]rovided that they settle at the central bank, large-value net settlement systems may continue to operate in parallel to real-time gross settlement systems but, in the near future, they should: (a) settle on the same-day as the exchange of the payment instruments; and (b) meet the Lamfalussy standards in full." The allowance of net settlement systems is significant given the general debate on the relative merits of RTGS and net settlement systems. However, the RTGS principle, requiring channeling into that system, seems to favor RTGS.

In May 1998, the European Parliament and Council adopted a Directive on Settlement Finality to insure the validity of payment netting. This is accomplished by providing for the legal enforceability of netting arrangements, the irrevocability of payment orders and the determination of which insolvency law is applicable in the event a payment system participant becomes insolvent. In addition, it recognizes the validity of collateral arrangements furnished in connection with payment systems. O.J. L 166, Directive 98/26/EC.

b.   EFFICIENT RETAIL CROSS-BORDER TRANSFERS

On December 4, 1995, the Council of Ministers adopted a Common Position with respect to certain retail (less than ECU 30,000) cross-border credit transfers, O.J. No. C353/52, 30.12.95. Each cross-border transfer of currency requires the cross-border processing of information and often requires a foreign exchange transaction, e.g. X with a French franc account in Paris wishes to pay sterling to a London account. Articles 3 and 4 of the new Directive requires that credit institutions explain clearly to clients (originators and beneficiaries) the terms and conditions under which a payment will be made.

Article 6 of the Directive sets an upper limit of five business days (absent agreement) that a credit institution can take to execute an originator's transfer instruction. If the originator's credit institution fails to meet its obligation, it must compensate the beneficiary's institution with interest from the end of five days (or any earlier agreed date) to the date the funds are credited; this interest is, in turn, passed on to the beneficiary. If the reason for delay is due to the action of an intermediary bank, the originating bank can look to it for indemnity.

Article 7 of the Directive obliges the originator's bank to execute a transfer for the full amount (without the deduction of fees) unless the originator has otherwise specified. It anticipates, however, that the beneficiary's bank can deduct fees from the beneficiary. The Commission hopes to avoid the situation where, due to the deduction of fees by the originating bank, the beneficiary would look back to the originator for additional compensation.

Finally, Article 8 provides that if a transfer is not complete within five business days, the originator has the option of asking for his money back, up to ECU 10,000, plus interest.   The originating bank, and each intermediary institution in turn, generally have the right to recover the recredited funds, plus related costs and interest, from its transferee.

In December 2001, the European Parliament and the Council issued Regulation No. 2560/2001 on cross-border payments in euro, O.J. L 344/13, 28.12.2001. It provides that charges for cross-border payments in euro of up to 50,000 will have to be aligned with domestic transaction charges within the home state of the executing bank. This prescription takes place for cash machines and bank cards of up to 12,500 euro in July 1, 2002, and for credit transfers of up to the same amount by July 1, 2003.   The rules will be extended to transactions of up to 50,000 by January 1, 2006. According to some studies, cross-border charges can be up to 20 times those for domestic transactions. Why would this be?

c.   EUROPEAN MONETARY UNION

EMU requires a large value transfer system for euro that needed to exist at the beginning of Stage Three of EMU—on January 1, 1999 (See

Chapter 7). The existence of such a system is especially important for the conduct of monetary policy which requires a reliable method for the European System of Central Banks (ESCB) to pay for and receive payment for euro-denominated bonds. EMI and its successor the European Central Bank (ECB) created a RTGS payment system called TARGET to fulfill this function. TARGET establishes a linkage, provided by SWIFT, between national RTGS systems. Only payments related to the implementation of the single monetary policy have to be processed through TARGET. Use of TARGET for other cross-border payments is optional. Banks access TARGET through a national RTGS system, which need not be their own. For example, Lloyds Bank in London can access TARGET through the Banque de France, if the Banque de France were to decide to allow such access.

TARGET is not itself a RTGS system because, unlike national RTGS systems, it provides no facility for the settlement of payments. TARGET transfers from Italian to German banks, for example, will be settled by correspondent accounts between Banca d'Italia and the Bundesbank.

There are two principal reasons the linkage approach was adopted, rather than the building of a new EU system. First, the countries participating in EMU were not known enough in advance to build a new system. Secondly, the EU principle of subsidiarity—not doing centrally what can be done locally—argues for keeping in existence, rather than replacing, national systems.

Unlimited but fully collateralized intraday credit is provided to RTGS participants fulfilling the general counterparty eligibility of the European Central Bank (ECB). In July 1998 the ECB decided to grant access to TARGET to national central banks (NCBs) and participants in RTGS systems operating in euro but located in non-euro area countries of the EU. The ECB will only provide intraday credit to a non-euro area NCB and its RTGS participants, if the non-euro ECB is in an overall credit position vis-a-vis the other NCBs participating in or connected to TARGET taken together. Non-euro area NCBs may provide collateralized intraday credit in euro to participants subject to certain conditions set by the ECB. European Central Bank, *Third Progress Report on the Target Project* ii-iii (November 1998).

In 2000, TARGET processed payments amounting to 263, 291 billion euro consisting of 47,980,023 billion transactions. Domestic traffic represented 58.2% in value and 78.8% in volume. European Central Bank, *TARGET Annual Report* (May 2001).

E. INTERNATIONAL STANDARDS

The Basel Committee on Payment and Settlement Systems has developed international standards for important payment systems. *Core*

Principles for Systematically Important Payment Systems, January 2001. The principles are as follows:

Core Principles for systemically important payment systems

I.   The system should have a well founded legal basis under all relevant jurisdictions.

II. The system's rules and procedures should enable participants to have a clear understanding of the system's impact on each of the financial risks they incur through participation in it.

III. The system should have clearly defined procedures for the management of credit risks and liquidity risks, which specify the respective responsibilities of the system operator and the participants and which provide appropriate incentives to manage and contain those risks.

IV.*   The system should provide prompt final settlement on the day of value, preferably during the day and at a minimum at the end of the day.

V.* A system in which multilateral netting takes place should, at a minimum, be capable of ensuring the timely completion of daily settlements in the event of an inability to settle by the participant with the largest single settlement obligation.

VI. Assets used for settlement should preferably be a claim on the central bank; where other assets are used, they should carry little or no credit risk and little or no liquidity risk.

VII.   The system should ensure a high degree of security and operational reliability and should have contingency arrangements for timely completion of daily processing.

VIII.   The system should provide a means of making payments which is practical for its users and efficient for the economy.

IX. The system should have objective and publicly disclosed criteria for participation, which permit fair and open access.

X. The system's governance arrangements should be effective, accountable and transparent.

* Systems should seek to exceed the minima included in these two Core Principles.

Responsibilities of the central bank in applying the Core Principles

A. The central bank should define clearly its payment system objectives and should disclose publicly its role and major policies with respect to systemically important payment systems.

B. The central bank should ensure that the systems it operates comply with the Core Principles.

C. The central bank should oversee compliance with the Core Principles by systems it does not operate and it should have the ability to carry out this oversight.

D. The central bank, in promoting payment system safety and efficiency through the Core Principles, should cooperate with other central banks and with any other relevant domestic or foreign authorities.

As we shall see in Chapter 22 on International Regulation, these core principles along with many others, are subject to IMF monitoring and probably will be subject to some kind of enforcement in the future. They apply, in principle, to all countries. Systemically important payment systems are those where, "if the system were insufficiently protected against risk, disruption within it could trigger or transmit further disruptions among participants or systemic disruptions in the financial area more widely." Id., at 7.

The first core principle requires a well founded legal basis under all relevant jurisdictions. This requires a clear law of contracts, rules to establish when the system achieves final settlement, and bankruptcy laws which insure the finality of payments made before a bank fails, including netting arrangements. It further requires clear laws regarding collateral since many systems depend on such collateral. Bank, *TARGET Annual Report* (May 2001).

Links to Other Chapters

The payment system is the core of the financial system, and concern about its potential collapse coupled with multiple bank bankruptcies around the world, is responsible for much of the banking regulation examined in this book. The payment system is also crucial to securities markets. Settlement of securities transactions requires payments, as well as the movement of securities. A major concern for regulators is whether the failure of securities firms to settle positions could trigger failures of other securities firms, and their banks. Thus, virtually all of the Chapters in this book require a basic understanding of the payment system.

CHAPTER ELEVEN

ASSET FREEZES

In this Chapter we use two cases to explore some political risks of holding eurodollar deposits. Libyan Arab Foreign Bank v. Bankers Trust Co. *(LAFB),* 1 Lloyd's Law Reports 259 (Q.B. 1988), involves the attempted freeze by the United States (the country of the currency) of eurodollar accounts held in the United Kingdom, while Wells Fargo Asia Limited v. Citibank, N.A., 936 F.2d 723 (2d Cir. 1991), *cert. denied* 505 U.S. 1204, 112 S. Ct. 2990, 120 L. Ed. 2d 868 (1992), *on remand from* 495 U.S. 660, 110 S. Ct. 2034, 109 L. Ed. 2d 677 (1990), involves a freeze on repatriation of dollars by the Philippines (the country where the deposits were placed).

A. FREEZES BY THE CURRENCY COUNTRY: *LAFB*

Mr. Justice STAUGHTON

The plaintiffs are a Libyan corporation, wholly owned by the Central Bank of Libya. They carry on what is described as an offshore banking business, in the sense that they do not engage in domestic banking within Libya. I shall call them "the Libyan Bank." The defendants are a New York corporation with their head office there. They no doubt have a number of branches in various parts of the world; but I am concerned with one in particular, their branch in London. I shall refer to them as "Bankers Trust," and when it is necessary to refer to particular offices as "Bankers Trust London" or "Bankers Trust New York."

In January 1986 the Libyan Bank had an account with Bankers Trust London, denominated in United States dollars. That was a call account, which meant that no cheque book was provided, interest was payable on the balance standing to the credit of the account at rates which varied from time to time, and some minimal period of notice might be required before instructions relating to the account had to be complied with. The suggestion in this case is that instructions would have to be given before noon if they were to be carried out that day. In English practice it would, I think be described as a species of deposit account. The amount standing to the credit of that account at the close of business on 8 January 1986 was U.S. $131,506,389.93. There may be a small element of subsequent adjustment in that figure. But the point is not material.

The Libyan Bank also had an account with Bankers Trust New York, again denominated in United States dollars. This was a demand account. No interest was paid on the balance, and no significant period of notice was required before instructions had to be complied with. But there was not, so far as I am aware, a cheque book. In England it would have been a current account. The amount standing to the credit of that account at the close of business on 8 January 1986 was U.S. $251,129,084.53.

Relations between Libya and the United States in January 1986 were not good. At 8.06 p.m. New York time on 7 January the President of the United States of America issued an executive order, which had the force of law with immediate effect. It provided, so far as material:

"Section 1. The following are prohibited, except to the extent provided in regulations which may hereafter be issued pursuant to this Order: ... (f) The grant or extension of credits or loans by any United States person to the Government of Libya, its instrumentalities and controlled entities."

That order did not in itself have any great effect on the events with which this case is concerned. But there followed it at 4.10 p.m. New York time on 8 January a second order, reading as follows:

"I, Ronald Reagan, President of the United States, hereby order blocked all property and interests in property of the Government of Libya, its agencies, instrumentalities and controlled entities and the Central Bank of Libya that are in the United States that hereafter come within the United States or that are or hereafter come within the possession or control of U.S. persons including overseas branches of U.S. persons. The Secretary of the Treasury, in consultation with the Secretary of State, is authorized to employ all powers granted to me by the International Emergency Economic Powers Act 50 U.S.C. 1701 et seq. to carry out the provisions of this Order. This Order is effective immediately and shall be transmitted to the Congress and published in the Federal Register.

Ronald Reagan

The White House

8 January 1986

It is not in dispute that Bankers Trust are a United States person; or that Bankers Trust London are an overseas branch of a United States person; or that the Libyan Bank are an agency, instrumentality or controlled entity of the Government of Libya. Consequently by the law of and prevailing in the State of New York (which I shall refer to as New York law for the sake of brevity) it was illegal at and after 4.10

p.m. on 8 January 1986 for Bankers Trust to make any payment or transfer of funds to or to the order of the Libyan Bank in New York, either by way of debit to the Libyan Bank's account or as the grant of credit or a loan. Similarly it was illegal, by the law of New York or of any other American state, for Bankers Trust to make any such payment or transfer of funds in London or anywhere else.

The United Kingdom Parliament did not enact any similar legislation. No doubt there were reasons of high policy for that forbearance; but with them I am not concerned. It is sufficient to say that nothing in English domestic law prohibited such a transaction. So the main issues in this case are concerned with the rules of conflict of laws, which determine when and to what extent the law of New York is given effect in our courts, and with the contractual obligations of banks. In a word, Bankers Trust say that they cannot, or at any rate are not obliged to, transfer a sum as large as U.S. $100m. or more without using the payment machinery that is available in New York; consequently they have a defence to the Libyan Bank's claim, because performance of this contract would have required them to commit an illegal act in New York. Alternatively they say that their contract with the Libyan Bank is governed by the law of New York, so that performance is for the time being illegal by the proper law of the contract.

The Libyan Bank's claims

These are as follows (using a slightly different system of numbering from that adopted in the pleadings and in argument):

(1) The first claim is for the balance of U.S. $131,506,389.93 standing to the credit of the London account at the close of business on 8 January 1986. It is said that this sum is due to the Libyan Bank, and can be claimed on a cause of action in debt. Alternatively it is said that Bankers Trust ought to have responded to demands for U.S. $131m. that were made by the Libyan Bank in various different ways after 8 January, and are liable in damages.

(2) If they are right on the first claim, the Libyan Bank further say that one or other of three sums ought to have been transferred from the New York account to the London account on 7 and 8 January, thus increasing the amount which they are entitled to recover. These are: (i) U.S. $165,200,000 on 7 January, *or* (ii) U.S. $6,700,000 on 8 January, *or* (iii) U.S. $161,400,000 on 8 January. Indeed it is said that the sum of U.S. $6,700,000 was in fact transferred to London on 8 January, with the consequence that the Libyan Bank are in any event entitled to recover that additional amount.

(3) Largely but not entirely as an alternative to the second claim, the Libyan Bank say that they gave a number of payment instructions to Bankers Trust New York for execution on 8 January, those instructions could and should have been executed before 4.10 p.m. on

that day, but were not. Consequently the Libyan Bank claim damages in the sum of U.S. $226,147,213.88.

. . .

(6) Lastly there is a claim which is quite independent of the events of 7 and 8 January 1986 and President Reagan's executive orders. It is said that during the period from April 1984 to November 1985 Bankers Trust operated a system of transfers between the New York account and the London account, which was not in accordance with their contract with the Libyan Bank. In consequence the Libyan Bank were deprived of interest for one day or three days on a succession of sums during that period. It is said that the loss suffered is of the order of $2m. Bankers Trust do not deny that, initially, the system of transfers which they operated during this period failed to accord with their contract. But they say that, by the doctrine of account stated or estoppel, the Libyan Bank are precluded from asserting this claim.

The issues thus raised, or at any rate those that arise under paragraph (1) above, are of great interest and some difficulty. Similar problems occurred a few years ago in connection with the freeze on Iranian assets by executive order of 14 November 1979, and litigation was commenced. But before any of those actions could come to trial the freeze was lifted. This time the problems have to be resolved.

History of the banking relationship

This can be considered in three stages. The first stage was from 1972 to 15 December 1980.

The Libyan Bank came into existence in June 1972.   A correspondent relationship was established between the Libyan Bank and Bankers Trust. Initially an account was opened for that purpose with the Paris branch of Bankers Trust. But in April 1973 that account was closed, and an account opened with the London branch. It was described as a 7-day notice account. However, any requirement that notice of that length should be given before debits were allowed on the London account was not enforced. In this period the Libyan Bank did not wish to have any account with Bankers Trust New York. Transfers for the credit of the Libyan Bank used regularly to arrive at Bankers Trust New York, in accordance with the system most often used for transferring large dollar amounts, which I shall describe later. But they were dealt with by an instruction from Bankers Trust New York to Bankers Trust London to credit the account of the Libyan Bank there. Indeed the Libyan Bank insisted on that from time to time. Thus on 14 July 1973 they said in a telex to New York: "We also request immediate transfer of any funds you may receive in future for our favour to your London office." And on 17 July 1973 to London:

> "When we have agreed to have the account of Libyan Arab Foreign Bank with Bankers Trust I have made it very clear that no balance

at all should be kept in New York and should be transferred immediately to our call account which started in Paris and now with you in London."

Certainly one motive for that attitude, and in 1973 possibly the only motive, was that dollar credit balances outside the United States earned a higher rate of interest than was obtainable in the United States. That is all that Eurodollars are—a credit in dollars outside the United States, whether in Europe or elsewhere. (It may be that one should add to this definition "at a bank" or "at an institution.") The interest rate is higher owing to the terms of the requirement imposed by the Federal Reserve Board that banks should maintain an amount equal to a proportion of the deposits they receive on deposit interest-free with the Federal Reserve system. That requirement is less demanding in connection with deposits received by overseas branches.

In fact Bankers Trust New York had operated an account in New York, for the handling of transactions by the Libyan Bank. But that account was closed on 17 December 1973 in consequence of the above and other protests by the Libyan Bank.

There followed a long period of discussion and negotiation. Bankers Trust were dissatisfied because the London, so-called 7-days' notice, account was used as a current account. Large numbers of transactions occurred on it, but interest was paid on the balance. This was not thought to be profitable for Bankers Trust. Furthermore, transfers to or from the account would commonly be made through New York, with a risk of delay and the possibility of error. On 23 November 1977 Mr. Ronai of Bankers Trust New York wrote to the Libyan Bank as follows:

" ... I am writing to outline our proposal for clearing up the operational difficulties encountered in your dollar-clearing activity through Bankers Trust in New York.

"I feel that the problems stem from the number of intermediate steps required to effect a large number of transfers to and from your London Call account via New York. In order to simplify this situation, my proposal is to set up a fully-managed account relationship with Libyan Arab Foreign Bank. This should provide you with several major benefits, among which are:

—more timely information for yourselves

—simplification of transactions

—greater ease in researching possible errors

—the ability to tailor the system to your requirements.

"The basic elements of a managed account consist of a current account in New York and a call account in London with Bankers Trust Co. The current account will be used for your daily dollar-clearing activity; the call account should be considered as an investment of liquid funds. An explanation of the operation of your managed account follows.

"On a daily basis, all transactions concerning the demand account are reviewed, and the balance is 'managed' so that it does not exceed or fall below a predetermined target or 'peg' balance. Excess funds will be credited to your call account, or your current account will be funded from your call account, as the case may be."

In 1980 that proposal was more actively pursued. At first it was suggested by Bankers Trust that the current account should be in London. But by the time of a meeting in New York on 7 July it was again proposed that there should be a demand account there. Following that meeting Bankers Trust wrote from London to the Libyan Bank with details of the proposed managed account system:

"We will establish a 'peg' (or target) balance for the demand account of U.S. $750,000. That amount is intended to compensate Bankers Trust Co. for the services which we expect to provide, and is subject to periodic renegotiation as appropriate, for example when our costs increase, when interest rates decline significantly or when our level of servicing is materially changed. Each morning our account management team will review the demand account's closing book balance from the previous business day. If that balance is in excess of the 'peg,' they will transfer in multiples of U.S. $100,000 the excess amount to your call account in London with value the previous business day.

"Similarly, if the demand account balance is below the U.S. $750,000 peg, they will transfer funds back from your call account with value the previous business day. ... As you can appreciate, our account management team must closely follow the balance in your call account. Given time zone differences with London, all entries to your call account must be passed by that team in New York, and all your instructions to effect payments or foreign exchange settlements must be directed to our money transfer department in New York."

The figure of U.S. $750,000 as the peg balance was later agreed at U.S. $500,000.

There was some discussion of political risk at the New York meeting. I am confident that political risk was at any rate in the minds of both parties, seeing that the freeze on Iranian assets had occurred only eight months previously. Mr. Abduljawad, then deputy chairman, is recorded as saying: "Placing at call is not an effort to avoid political risk, which he believes to be unavoidable." Whilst I accept that record as accurate, I also accept Mr. Abduljawad's oral evidence that "political risk is always being taken into consideration." Mr. Van Voorhees, who was among those attending the meeting on behalf of Bankers Trust, accepted that the Iranian crisis was at the back of everyone's mind in 1980.

A further meeting took place in Paris on 28 October 1980 between Mr. Abduljawad and Mr. Van Voorhees. At that meeting too no complete agreement was reached, so there was no new agreement or variation of the existing agreement. But important progress was made. Mr. Van Voorhees explained in plain terms that all the Libyan Bank's transactions would have to pass through New York. According to Mr. Van Voorhees, Mr. Abduljawad at first objected to that requirement, but later agreed to it. Mr. Abduljawad's evidence was that he did not reject it and equally did not agree to it. I do not need to resolve that conflict. It is plain to me that one of the terms which Bankers Trust were putting forward for the new arrangement was that all transactions should pass through New York; whether or not it was accepted at that stage is immaterial.

There followed a meeting in Tripoli and correspondence between the parties, and agreement was finally reached by 11 December 1980. Thus the managed account system was agreed on Bankers Trust New York would open a demand account for the Libyan Bank, with a peg balance of U.S. $500,000. Transfers between that account and the call account in London would be made, as the need arose, in multiples of U.S. $100,000. The need for a transfer would be determined each morning by examining the closing balance of the New York account for the previous business day; if appropriate a transfer to or from London would be made with value the previous business day—in other words, it would take effect from that date for interest purposes.

It was, as I find, a term of that arrangement that all the Libyan Bank's transactions should pass through New York. Although not mentioned in the correspondence by which agreement was ultimately reached, this had plainly been a requirement of Bankers Trust throughout the later stages of the negotiations, and I conclude that it was tacitly accepted by the Libyan Bank. It was virtually an essential feature of the system: Bankers Trust New York would know about and rely on the credit balance in London in deciding what payments could be made from New York; they might be exposed to risk if the balance in London could be reduced without their knowledge. It was argued that such a term is not to be found in the pleadings of Bankers Trust; but in my judgment it is, in paragraph 3(4)(v) of the re-re-amended points of defence. There remains an important question whether the managed account arrangement was irrevocable, or whether it could be determined. I shall consider that later.

The second stage ran from December 1980 to November 1985. Before very long Bankers Trust took the view that the remuneration which they received from the relationship, in the form of an interest-free balance of between U.S. $500,000 and U.S. $599,999 in New York, was insufficient reward for their services. On 15 March 1983 they proposed an increase in the peg balance to $1.5m.

Negotiations continued for a time but without success. By 15 March 1984 Bankers Trust had formed the view that the Libyan Bank would not agree to an increase in the peg balance; so, on 3 April 1984, they decided unilaterally on a different method of increasing the profitability of the relationship for Bankers Trust; and it was put into effect on 17 April.

The new method required a consideration of the balance on the New York account at 2 p.m. each day. If it exceeded the peg balance of U.S. $500,000 the excess was transferred in multiples of U.S. $100,000 to the London account with value that day. Consideration was also given on the following morning to the balance at the close of the previous day. If it was less than the peg balance, a transfer of the appropriate amount was made from London to New York on the next day, with value the previous business day; if it was more than the peg balance there was, it seems, a transfer to London with value the same day. The effect of the change was that the Libyan Bank lost one day's interest whenever (i) credits received after 2 p.m. exceeded payments made after 2 p.m., and (ii) the closing balance for the day would under the existing arrangements have required a transfer (or a further transfer if one had been made at 2 p.m.) to be made with value that day. If a weekend intervened, three days interest might be lost. I am not altogether sure that I have stated the effect of the change correctly; but precision as to the details is not essential.

Bankers Trust did not tell the Libyan Bank about this change. Indeed an internal memorandum of Bankers Trust dated 14 August 1984 wondered whether Libya (possibly referring to the Libyan Bank) would notice the drop in interest earnings. Although the effect was on any view substantial, I am satisfied that the Libyan Bank did not in fact appreciate what was happening until mid-1985; and they complained about it to Bankers Trust in October 1985. I am also satisfied that the Libyan Bank could have detected, if they had looked at their statements from Bankers Trust with a fair degree of diligence, that they were not receiving the full benefit by way of interest to which they were entitled. Indeed, they did, as I have said, eventually detect that. But I am not convinced—if it matters—that they could have divined precisely what system Bankers Trust were now operating.

The third stage began on 27 November 1985, with a telex from Bankers Trust which recorded the agreement of the Libyan Bank to a new arrangement. This telex is important, and I must set out part of it:

"As discussed with you during our last meeting in your office in Tripoli, we have changed the method of investment from same day by means of next day back valuation, to actual same day with investment cut off time of 2 p.m. New York time. ... In this regard, those credits which are received after our 2 p.m. New York time cut off which result in excess balances are invested with next day value. This you will see from observing your account. For your information, the way our same day investment system works, is as follows: each day, at 2 p.m. the balance position of your account is determined and any credits received up to that time, less payments and less the peg balance, are immediately invested. An example of this investment system can be seen for instance by comparing both statements of your demand and call accounts for 26 and 30 September 1985 which indicate same day investment on 26 September for U.S. $33.7 million which is reflected on your London call account statement on 27 September with value 26 September and on 30 September for U.S. $181.3 million which is reflected on your London call account statement on 1 October with value 30 September."

That was not in substance any different from the system which Bankers Trust had been operating since April 1984 without informing the Libyan Bank. It was now accepted by them.

7 and 8 January 1986

At 2 p.m. on 7 January the balance to the credit of the New York account was U.S. $165,728,000. (For present purposes I use figures rounded down to the nearest U.S. $1,000, save where greater accuracy is desirable.) Subject to two points which I shall consider later; a transfer of $165.2m. should then have been made to London. Mr. Fabien Arnell, an account manager of Bankers Trust New York says somewhat laconically in his statement.

"On 7 January 1986 I instructed the managed account clerk not to make a 2 p.m. investment. I cannot now recall the precise reason why I gave that instruction."

During the rest of that day there were substantial transfers out of the New York account, with the result that it would have been overdrawn to the extent of $157,925,000 if the 2 p.m. transfer had been made. There would then have had to be a recall of U.S. $158,500,000 from London on 8 January, with value the previous business day, to restore the peg balance. As no 2 p.m. transfer had been made, the closing balance was in fact U.S. $7,275,000 in credit.

On the morning of 8 January there was an amount of $6,700,000 available to transfer to London. The same amount would have been left as a net credit to the London account if $165.2m. had been transferred at 2 p.m. on 7 January and $158.5m. recalled on 8 January with value the previous day. An instruction for the transfer of U.S. $6,700,000 was prepared. But in the event the computer which kept the accounts in New York was not ordered to effect this transfer, nor was the London branch informed of it.

At 2 p.m. on 8 January the balance to the credit of the New York account was U.S. $161,997,000. After deducting the peg balance of U.S. $500,000 there was a sum of U.S. $161,400,000 available to transfer to London. No transfer was made. Those figures assume, as was the fact, that U.S. $6,700,000 had not been transferred to London in respect of the excess opening balance on that day.

Bankers Trust New York had received payment instructions totalling U.S. $347,147,213.03 for execution on 8 January. All of them had been received by 8.44 a.m. New York time. None of them were executed, for reasons which I shall later explain. (In case it is thought that not even the combined London and New York accounts could have sustained such payments, I should mention that substantial credits were received in New York during 8 January for the account of the Libyan Bank. If all the payment instructions had been implemented, there would still at the end of the day have been a net balance due to the Libyan Bank on the total of the two accounts).

In the hope of rendering those figures somewhat more intelligible, I set out a summary of the actual state of the New York account on 7 and 8 January 1986, with notes:

	U.S.	
Balance at 2 p.m. 7 January		(1)
Post 2 p.m. operations	$165,728,000	
Opening balance 8 January	(158,453,000)	(2)
Receipts before 2 p.m.	7,275,000	
Balance at 2 p.m. 8 January	154,722,000	(3)
Receipts after 2 p.m.	161,997,000	(4)
Closing balance 8 January	89,132,000	
	251,129,000	

Notes:

(1) $165.2m. available for transfer to London

(2) $6.7m. available for transfer

(3) $161.4m. available for transfer

(4) This figure contains some minor adjustments of no consequence.

Next I turn to the Civil Evidence Act statement of Mr. Brittain, the chairman of Bankers Trust. Late in the afternoon of 7 January he received a telephone call from Mr. Corrigan, the president of the Federal Reserve Bank of New York. Mr. Corrigan asked that Bankers Trust should pay particular attention on the next day to movement of funds on the various Libyan accounts held by Bankers Trust, and report anything unusual to him.

Late in the morning of the next day Mr. Brittain informed the New York Fed. (as it is sometimes called) that "it looked like the Libyans were taking their money out of the various accounts." (So far as the Libyan Bank were concerned, it will be remembered that they had already given instructions for payments totalling over U.S. $347m. on that day.) Later Mr. Brittain learnt that sufficient funds were coming in to cover the payment instructions; he telephoned Mr. Corrigan and told him that the earlier report had been a false alarm. Mr. Corrigan asked

Mr. Brittain not to make any payments out of the accounts for the time being, and said that he would revert later.

That assurance was repeated several times during the early afternoon. Mr. Brittain's statement continues:

> "Finally I telephoned Mr. Corrigan at about 3:30 p.m. and told him that we now had sufficient funds to cover the payments out of the various Libyan accounts and were going to make them. Mr. Corrigan's response to this was, 'You'd better call Baker' (by which he meant the Secretary of the United States Treasury, Mr. James A. Baker III). I said that I would release the payments and then speak to Mr. Baker. Mr. Corrigan's reply to this was. 'You'd better call Baker first'."

Mr. Brittain was delayed for some 20 minutes talking to Mr. Baker and to an assistant secretary of the Treasury on the telephone. Then at approximately 4.10 to 4.16 p.m. Mr. Baker said: "The President has signed the order, you can't make the transfers."

Mr. Brittain adds in his statement that this was the first occasion on which he became aware that an order freezing the assets was contemplated. In a note made a few weeks after 8 January he adds: "That is how naive I was." I am afraid that I can but agree with Mr. Brittain's description of himself. It seems to me that a reasonable banker on the afternoon of 8 January would have realised, in the light of the first executive order made on the previous day, the requests of Mr. Corrigan, and particularly his saying "You'd better call Baker first," that a ban on payments was a distinct possibility.

There is other evidence as to Mr. Brittain's telephone conversations. First, Mr. Blenk was in Mr. Brittain's office and heard what was said by him. There was not, it seems, any reference by name to Libyan Arab Foreign Bank, but merely to "the Libyans," which meant some six Libyan entities (including the Libyan Bank) which had accounts with Bankers Trust. Secondly, Mr. Sandberg, a senior vice-president of the Federal Reserve Bank of New York, heard Mr. Corrigan's end of the conversations. He accepted in evidence that the New York Fed. probably knew which Libyan banks held accounts with Bankers Trust.

(1) The U.S. $131 million claim

(a) Conflict of laws—the connecting factor

There is no dispute as to the general principles involved. Performance of a contract is excused if (i) it has become illegal by the proper law of the contract, or (ii) it necessarily involves doing an act which is unlawful by the law of the place where the act has to be done. I need cite no authority for that proposition (least of all my own decision in Euro-Diam Ltd. v. Bathurst [1987] 2 W.L.R. 1368, 1385) since it is well established and was not challenged. Equally it was not suggested that New York law is relevant because it is the national law of Bankers Trust, or because payment in London would expose Bankers Trust to sanctions under the United States legislation, save that Mr. Sumption for Bankers Trust desires to keep the point open in case this dispute reaches the House of Lords.

There may, however, be a difficulty in ascertaining when performance of the contract "necessarily involves" doing an illegal act in another country. In *Toprak Mahsullerr Ofisi v. Finagrain Compagnie Commerciale Agricole et Financière S.A.* [1979] 2 Lloyd's Rep. 98, Turkish buyers of wheat undertook to open a letter of credit "with and confirmed by a first class United States or West European bank." The buyers were unable to obtain exchange control permission from the Turkish Ministry of Finance to open a letter of credit, and maintained that it was impossible for them to open a letter of credit without exporting money from Turkey. It was held that this was no answer to a claim for damages for nonperformance of the contract. Lord Denning M.R. said, at p. 114:

> "In this particular case the place of performance was not Turkey. Illegality by the law of Turkey is no answer whatever to this claim. The letter of credit had to be a confirmed letter of credit, confirmed by a first-class West European or U.S. bank. The sellers were not concerned with the machinery by which the Turkish state enterprise provided that letter of credit at all. The place of performance was not Turkey.

> "This case is really governed by the later case of Kleinwort, Sons & Co. v. Ungarische Baumwolle Industrie Aktiengesellschaft [1939] 2 K.B. 678 where bills of exchange were to be given and cover was to be provided in London, but at the same time there was a letter saying, 'We have to get permission from Hungary.' It was said that because of the illegality by Hungarian law in obtaining it, that would be an answer to the case. But Branson J. and the Court of Appeal held that the proper law of the contract was English law; and, since the contract was to be performed in England, it was enforceable in the English courts even though its performance might involve a breach by the defendants of the law of Hungary.

> "That case has been quoted in all the authorities as now settling the law. ... The only way that Mr. Johnson (for the Turkish state enterprise) could seek to escape from that principle was by saying—' ... Although there was no term, express or implied, in the contract that anything had to be done in Turkey as a term of the contract, nevertheless it was contemplated by both parties. It was contemplated by both parties that the Turkish buyers would have to go through the whole sequence in Turkey of getting exchange control permission, and all other like things: and, if the contemplated method of performance became illegal, that would be an answer. Equally, if it became impossible, that would be a frustration.'

"I am afraid that those arguments do not carry the day. It seems to me in this contract, where the letter of credit had to be a confirmed letter of credit—confirmed by a West European or U.S. bank—the sellers are not in the least concerned as to the method by which the Turkish buyers are to provide that letter of credit. Any troubles or difficulties in Turkey are extraneous to the matter and do not afford any defence to an English contract ... "

From that case I conclude that it is immaterial whether one party has to equip himself for performance by an illegal act in another country. What matters is whether performance itself necessarily involves such an act. The Turkish buyers might have had money anywhere in the world which they could use to open a letter of credit with a United States or West European bank. In fact it would seem that they only had money in Turkey, or at any rate needed to comply with Turkish exchange control regulations if they were to use any money they may have had outside Turkey. But that was no defence, as money or a permit was only needed to equip themselves for performance, and not for performance itself.

.   .   .

Some difficulty may still be encountered in the application of that principle. For example, if payment in dollar bills in London was required by the contract, it would very probably have been necessary for Bankers Trust to obtain such a large quantity from the Federal Reserve Bank of New York, and ship it to England. That, Mr. Sumption accepts, would not have been an act which performance necessarily involved; it would merely have been an act by Bankers Trust to equip themselves for performance as in the Toprak case. By contrast, if the contract required Bankers Trust to hand over a banker's draft to the Libyan Bank in London, Mr. Sumption argues that an illegal act in New York would necessarily be involved, since it is very likely that the obligation represented by the draft would ultimately be honoured in New York. I must return to this problem later.

(b) The proper law of the contract

As a general rule the contract between a bank and its customer is governed by the law of the place where the account is kept, in the absence of agreement to the contrary. Again there was no challenge to that as a general rule; the fact that no appellate decision was cited to support it may mean that it is generally accepted. However, since the point is of some importance, I list those authorities that were cited. They are X A.G. v. A Bank [1983] 2 All E.R. 464; Mackinnon v. Donaldson, Lufkin & Jenrette Securities Corporation [1986] Ch. 482, 494; Dicey & Morris, The Conflict of Laws, 11th ed. (1987), p. 1292, n. 51; Rabel, The Conflict of Laws, 2nd ed., p. 17; American Law Institute, Restatement of the Law, Conflict of Laws 2d, vol. 4 (1979), para. 622, and the Memorandum of Law in the Wells Fargo case which I have referred to, and the Lexis report of judgment in that action.

That rule accords with the principle, to be found in the judgment of Atkin L.J. in N. Joachimson v. Swiss Bank Corporation [1921] 3 K.B. 110, 127, and other authorities, that a bank's promise to repay is to repay at the branch of the bank where the account is kept.

In the age of the computer it may not be strictly accurate to speak of the branch where the account is kept. Banks no longer have books in which they write entries; they have terminals by which they give instructions; and the computer itself with its magnetic tape, floppy disc or some other device may be physically located elsewhere. Nevertheless it should not be difficult to decide where an account is kept for this purpose, and it is not in the present case. The actual entries on the London account were, as I understand it, made in London, albeit on instructions from New York after December 1980. At all events I have no doubt that the London account was at all material times "kept" in London.

.   .   .

In my judgment, the true view is that after December 1980 there was one contract, governed in part by the law of England and in part by the law of New York.

.   .   .

I hold that the rights and obligations of the parties in respect of the London account were governed by English law.

.   .   .

(d) Means of transfer

The credit balance of the Libyan Bank with Bankers Trust constituted a personal right, a chose in action. At bottom there are only two means by which the fruits of that right could have been made available to the Libyan Bank. The first is by delivery of cash, whether dollar bills or any other currency, to or to the order of the Libyan Bank. The second is the procuring of an account transfer. (I leave out of account the delivery of chattels, such as gold, silver or works of art, since nobody has suggested that Bankers Trust were obliged to adopt that method. The same applies to other kinds of property, such as land.)

An account transfer means the process by which some other person or institution comes to owe money to the Libyan Bank or their nominee, and the obligation of Bankers Trust is extinguished or reduced pro tanto. "Transfer" may be a somewhat misleading word, since the original obligation is not assigned (notwithstanding dicta in one

American case which speak of assignment); a new obligation by a new debtor is created.

Any account transfer must ultimately be achieved by means of two accounts held by different beneficiaries with the same institution. In a simple case the beneficiaries can be the immediate parties to the transfer. If Bankers Trust held an account with the A bank which was in credit to the extent of at least $131m., and the Libyan Bank also held an account at the A bank, it would require only book entries to achieve an account transfer. But still no property is actually *transferred.* The obligation of Bankers Trust is extinguished, and the obligation of A bank to Bankers Trust extinguished or reduced; the obligation of A bank to the Libyan Bank is increased by the like amount.

On occasion a method of account transfer which is even simpler may be used. If X Ltd. also hold an account with Bankers Trust London, and the Libyan Bank desire to benefit X Ltd., they instruct Bankers Trust to transfer $131m. to the account of X Ltd. The obligation of Bankers Trust to the Libyan Bank is extinguished once they decide to comply with the instruction, and their obligation to X Ltd. is increased by the like amount. That method of account transfer featured in Momm v. Barclays Bank International Ltd. [1977] Q.B. 790.

In a complex transaction at the other end of the scale there may be more than one tier of intermediaries, ending with a Federal Reserve Bank in the United States. Thus the payer may have an account with B bank in London, which has an account with C bank in New York; the payee has an account with E bank in London, which has an account with D bank in New York. Both C bank and D bank have accounts with the Federal Reserve Bank in New York. When an account transfer is effected the obligations of the New York Fed. to C bank, of C bank to B bank, and of B bank to the payer are reduced; the obligations of the New York Fed. to D bank, of D bank to E bank, and of E bank to the payee are increased. That is, in essence, how the Clearing House Interbank Payments System (C.H.I.P.S.) works, by which a large proportion of transfers of substantial dollar amounts are made.

I shall call the three methods which I have described a correspondent bank transfer, an in-house transfer and a complex account transfer. There are variations which do not precisely fit any of the three, but the principle is the same in all cases. Sooner or later, if cash is not used, there must be an in-house transfer at an institution which holds accounts for two beneficiaries, so that the credit balance of one can be increased and that of the other reduced. In the example of a complex account transfer which I have given that institution is the New York Fed., which holds accounts for C bank and D bank.

Evidence was given by Professor Scott of a method which, at first sight, did not involve an in-house transfer at any institution. That was where different Federal Reserve Banks were used. However, the Professor assured me that an in-house transfer was involved, although it was too complicated to explain. That invitation to abstain from further inquiry was gratefully accepted.

Thus far I have been assuming that only one transaction affecting any of the parties takes place on a given day. But manifestly that is unlikely to be the case; there may be thousands, or tens of thousands. One purpose of a clearing system between banks must be to set off transfers against others, not only between the same parties but also between all other parties to the clearing system. Thus C bank and D bank, in my example of a complex account transfer, may have made many transactions between themselves on the same day. Only the net balance of them all will be credited to one by the New York Fed. and debited to the other at the end. So the identity of the sum which the payer wished to pay to the payee may be entirely lost in one sense. The net balance may be the other way, and a sum be credited to C bank and debited to D bank instead of vice versa. Or, by a somewhat improbable coincidence, the net balance may be nil.

There are two further complications. The first is that set-off occurs not only between C bank and D bank, but between all other participants to the clearing system. An amount which would otherwise fall to be debited to C bank and credited to D bank may be reduced (i) because F bank has made transfers on that day to C bank, or (ii) because D bank has made transfers on that day to G bank.

Secondly, an intermediate clearing system may be used, such as London dollar clearing. If the chain of transmission on each side reaches a bank that is a member of the London dollar clearing, and if the item in question is eligible for that clearing system, it may be put through it. Then it will go to make up the net credit or debit balances that are due between all the members at the end of the day—and they in turn are settled in New York.

(e) Particular forms of transfer

I set out below those which have been canvassed in this case, and discuss the extent to which they involve activity in the United States.

(i) In-house transfer at Bankers Trust London

This is quite simple, as has been explained. It involves no action in the United States. But it cannot take place unless the Libyan Bank are able to nominate some beneficiary who also has an account with Bankers Trust London.

(ii) Correspondent bank transfer

Again, this is relatively simple and involves no action in the United States. But for it to be effective in this case a bank must be found outside the United States where two conditions are satisfied: the first is that Bankers Trust have a credit balance there of U.S. $131m. or more; the second, that an account is also held there for the Libyan Bank or for some beneficiary whom they nominate.

(iii) C.H.I.P.S. or Fedwire

These are two methods of complex account transfer which are used for a high proportion of large dollar transactions. They can only be completed in the United States.

. . .

(vi) London dollar clearing

It may not be right to describe this as a means of transfer in itself, but rather as a method of settling liabilities which arise when other means of transfer are used, such as a banker's draft or banker's payment, or indeed a cheque. Bankers Trust are not themselves members of London dollar clearing, but use it through Lloyds Bank Plc.

Suppose H bank, also a member of the clearing, presented a banker's draft issued by Bankers Trust to or to the order of the Libyan Bank for U.S. $131m. At the end of the day net debits and credits of all the members of the clearing would be calculated—and settled by transfers in New York. As already explained, there would not necessarily be a transfer there of U.S. $131m. or any sum by Lloyds Bank or their New York correspondent to the New York correspondent of H bank. But somewhere in the calculation of the sum that would be transferred by some bank in New York to some other bank in New York the U.S. $131m. would be found.

That is the first aspect of the transaction which requires action in New York. But thus far only the liabilities of the clearing members between themselves have been settled. What of the liabilities of the banks that have used the clearing but are not members? Bankers Trust owe Lloyds Bank U.S. $131m. That sum will go into a calculation of all the credits and debits between Bankers Trust and Lloyds Bank on that day; the net balance will be settled by a transfer in New York between Bankers' Trust New York and Lloyds Bank or their New York correspondent.

Since I have assumed that H bank are a member of the London dollar clearing, no similar transfer is required in their case. They have already received credit for U.S. $131m. in the clearing process and the transfers which settled the balances which emerged from it.

There is another aspect of the London dollar clearing which featured a great deal in the evidence. This is that a rule, at the time unwritten, excluded from the clearing "cheques drawn for principal amounts of interbank Eurocurrency transactions." The system is described in the Child report, where it is said that "by mutual consent 'wholesale' interbank foreign exchange deals and Eurodollar settlements are excluded." That in turn raises a question as to the meaning of "wholesale." Bankers Trust argue that it includes transactions on interest-bearing call accounts between banks, at any rate if they are for large amounts. The Libyan Bank say that it refers only to transactions for time deposits traded between the dealing rooms of banks.

I prefer the evidence of Bankers Trust on this point. The reason for the exclusion appears to be that the introduction of a very large sum by one participant into the clearing system would impose an excessive credit risk. The average value of transactions passing through the system is U.S. $50,000, and the vast majority of items are of the order of U.S. $10,000. It is not normally used for transactions over U.S. $30m.; indeed, there were not many transactions in millions. I find that a transfer of U.S. $131m. by Bankers Trust to or to the order of the Libyan Bank would not, in the circumstances of this case, be eligible for London dollar clearing.

(vii) Other clearing systems outside the United States

Apart from the last point about eligibility, it seems to me that much the same considerations must apply to the other three systems discussed—Euroclear, Cedel and Tokyo dollar clearing. Although the identity of a particular transaction will be difficult or impossible to trace in the net credits or debits which emerge at the end of the clearing, these debits and credits must ultimately be settled in the United States. (The word "ultimately" constantly recurs and is of importance in this case, as was stressed in the course of the evidence.)

But whether that be so or not, there are other points relevant to the use of these systems. Euroclear in Brussels is a system run through Morgan Guaranty Trust Co. for clearing securities transactions and payments in respect of such transactions. If it so happened that Bankers Trust had a credit of U.S. $131m. in the system, it could arrange for that sum to be transferred to the Libyan Bank or any nominee of the Libyan Bank which had an account with Euroclear. That would be a species of correspondent transfer. Alternatively, it could order the transfer to be made anywhere else—but that would involve action in New York.

Cedel, in Luxembourg, is similar to Euroclear in all respects that are material.

The Tokyo dollar clearing system is run by Chase Manhattan Bank at its Tokyo branch. Bankers Trust did not have an account with the system. If they had done, and had used it to pay U.S. $131m. to the Libyan Bank, they would have had to reimburse Chase Manhattan via New York.

.   .   .

(ix) Cash—dollar bills

I am told that the largest notes in circulation are now for U.S. $100, those for U.S. $500 having been withdrawn. Hence there would be formidable counting and security operations involved in paying U.S. $131m. by dollar bills. Bankers Trust would not have anything like that amount in their vault in London. Nor, on balance, do I consider that they would be likely to be able to obtain such an amount in Europe. It could be obtained from a Federal Reserve Bank and sent to London by aeroplane, although several different shipments would be made to reduce the risk. The operation would take some time—up to seven days.

Banks would seek to charge for this service, as insurance and other costs would be involved, and they would suffer a loss of interest from the time when cash was withdrawn from the Federal Reserve Bank to the time when it was handed over the counter and the customer's account debited—assuming that the customer had an interest-bearing account. I cannot myself see any basis on which a bank would be entitled to charge, although there might be a right to suspend payment of interest. If a bank chooses, as all banks do for their own purposes, not to maintain a sum equal to all its liabilities in the form of cash in its vaults, it must bear the expense involved in obtaining cash when a demand is made which it is obliged to meet. If a customer demanded U.S. $1,000 or U.S. $10,000 in cash, I do not see how a charge could be made. When the sum is very much larger it is an important question—which I shall consider later—whether the bank is obliged to meet a demand for cash at all. If it is so obliged, there is not, in my opinion, any right to charge for fulfilling its obligation.

As I have already mentioned, it is accepted that there would be no breach of New York law by Bankers Trust in obtaining such an amount of cash in New York and despatching it to their London office.

(x) Cash—sterling

There would be no difficulty for Bankers Trust in obtaining sterling notes from the Bank of England equivalent in value to U.S. $131m., although, once again, there would be counting and security problems. Bankers Trust would have to reimburse the Bank of England, or the correspondent through whom it obtained the notes, and this would probably be done by a transfer of dollars in New York. But, again, it was not argued that such a transfer would infringe New York law.

(f) Termination of the managed account arrangement

Those means of transfer are all irrelevant so long as the managed account arrangement subsists; for I have found it to be a term of that arrangement that all the Libyan Bank's transactions should pass through New York. Apart from some minor teething problems at the start in 1980, that term was observed. The only entries on the London call account were credits from, or debits to, the New York demand account. It was the New York account that was used to make payments to, or receive credits from, others with whom the Libyan Bank had business relations. If the arrangement still exists, the London account can only be used to transfer a credit to New York, which would be of no benefit whatever to the Libyan Bank.

In my judgment, the Libyan Bank was entitled unilaterally to determine the managed account arrangement on reasonable notice, which did not need to be more than 24 hours (Saturdays, Sundays and non-banking days excepted).   The important feature of the arrangement from the point of view of Bankers Trust was that their operators could make payments in New York, on occasion giving rise to an overdraft in New York, safe in the knowledge that there was a credit balance in London which they could call upon and which would not disappear. If it were determined, Bankers Trust New York would be entitled to refuse to make payments which would put the account there into overdraft. For the Libyan Bank an important feature was that they obtained both the speed and efficiency with which current account payments could be made in New York, and the advantage of an account in London bearing interest at Eurodollar rates.   If the arrangement were determined and the Libyan Bank began once again to use the London account as if it were a current account, Bankers Trust would be entitled (again on notice) to reduce the rate of interest payable on that account, or to decline to pay interest altogether.

I find nothing surprising in the notion that one party to a banking contract should be able to alter some existing arrangement unilaterally. Some terms, such as those relating to a time deposit, cannot be altered. But the ordinary customer can alter the bank's mandate, for example by revoking the authority of signatories and substituting others, or by cancelling standing orders or direct debits; he can transfer sums between current and deposit account; and he can determine his relationship with the bank entirely. So too the bank can ask the customer to take his affairs elsewhere. In this case it does not seem to me at all plausible that each party was locked into the managed account arrangement for all time unless the other agreed to its determination, or the entire banking relationship were ended. I accept Mr. Cresswell's submission that the arrangement was in the nature of instructions or a mandate which the Libyan Bank could determine by notice. For that matter, I consider that Bankers Trust would also have been entitled to determine it on reasonable notice—which would have been somewhat longer than 24 hours in their case. I hold that the arrangement was determined, implicitly by the Libyan Bank's telex of 28 April 1986, and if that were wrong, then expressly by their solicitors' letter of 30 July 1986.

What, then, was the position after determination? The New York account remained, as it always had been, a demand account. Subject to New York law, Bankers Trust were obliged to make transfers in accordance with the Libyan Bank's instructions to the extent of the credit balance, but they were not obliged to allow an overdraft—even a daylight overdraft, as it is called when payments in the course of a day exceed the credit balance but the situation is restored by further credits before the day ends. The London account remained an interest-bearing account from which Bankers Trust were obliged to make transfers on the instructions of the Libyan Bank, provided that no infringement of United States law in the United States was involved. If Bankers Trust became dissatisfied with the frequency of such transfers, they were, as I have said, entitled on notice to reduce the rate of interest or bring the account to an end. And if I had not held that the rights and obligations of the parties in respect of the London account were governed by English law at all times, I would have been inclined to hold that they were once more governed by English law when the managed account arrangement was determined, although there is clearly some difficulty in recognising a unilateral right to change the system of law governing part of the relations between the parties.

(g) Implied term and usage

It is said in paragraph 4(2) of the re-re-amended points of defence that there was an implied term that transfer of funds from the London account, whether or not effected through the New York account

> "would be effected by instructing a transfer to be made by the defendants' New York Head Office through a United States clearing system to the credit of an account with a bank or a branch of a bank in the United States nominated or procured to be nominated by or on behalf of the plaintiffs for that purpose."

In other words, of the various forms of transfer which I have mentioned, only C.H.I.P.S. or Fedwire were permitted. That term is said to be implied (i) from the usage of the international market in Eurodollars, and (ii) from the course of dealing between the parties since 1980.

. . .

The high point of Bankers Trust's case on this issue lies in the expert report of Dr. Stigum from which I quote some brief extracts:

> "The usages and practices that apply to wholesale Eurodollar accounts are moreover, well understood by *all* wholesale participants in the Eurodollar market ... Cash transactions are a feature of only an insignificant portion of total Eurodollar deposits, namely those held by small retail accounts. At the wholesale level, the Eurodollar market is understood by *all* participants to be a *strictly non-cash* market. ... *All* wholesale Eurodollar transactions (these occurring not just in London, but in other centres around the world as well) must, unless they involve a movement of funds from one account at a given bank to another account at that same bank, be cleared in the United States. The reason for this custom and

usage is that the ultimate effect of the clearing of a wholesale, Eurodollar transaction is to remove dollars from the reserve account of one bank at the Fed. to the reserve account of another bank at the Fed."

Even as it stands, that passage does not support the implied term pleaded, that transfers would be made "through a United States clearing system." However, it is fair to say that in the particulars of usage there were added by amendment to the points of defence the words "save where book transfers fall to be made between accounts at the same branch"—which would allow, as Dr. Stigum apparently does, both an in-house transfer and a correspondent bank transfer.

Dr. Stigum is an economist and not a banker. I did not find her oral evidence impressive. On the other hand, Mr. Osbourne, who was until 1985 an assistant general manager of Barclays Bank, did seem to me an impressive witness, whose evidence was very sound on most points. His views were inconsistent with the usage alleged, at any risk in the case of an account such as that of the Libyan Bank with Bankers Trust London.

Furthermore, the supposed usage was inconsistent with the course of dealing between the parties, to which I now turn. It is, of course, true that from December 1980 to January 1986 all transactions by the Libyan Bank were carried out in New York. That is not in itself proof of a course of dealing, since, as I have found, there was an express term to that effect—until the managed account arrangement was brought to an end. What happened between 1973 and December 1980? Fortunately the parties agreed to treat one month as a suitable sample. That was December 1979, in which there were 497 transactions. They have been analysed as follows:

"Entries generated internally by Bankers Trust London,
that is to say, mostly intra-branch transfers   15
London clearable bank drafts, London dollar clearing
eligible bank drafts   8
London dollar clearing bankers payments   1
Intra-branch transfers between Bankers Trust London
and accounts at Bankers Trust New York   68
Intra branch transfers between Bankers Trust London
and accounts at Bankers Trust Paris   3
Payments through Fedwire   13
Payments through C.H.I.P.S.   389."

There was still a slight dispute as to how the London/Paris transfers were effected but that is not material.

The vast majority of those transactions (402) were, as the suggested implied term required, through a United States clearing system. If one adds the in-house transfers of one kind or another in Bankers Trust, as Dr. Stigum's custom permits, the total reaches 488. But there were 9 transactions in that month alone (London bank drafts and a London banker's payment) which were not permitted, either by the implied terms which Bankers Trust allege or by Dr. Stigum's custom and usage, although they may very well have been for relatively small amounts.

I find difficulty in seeing how course of dealing by itself could support a negative implied term of the kind alleged. The phrase is often used to elucidate a contract or to add a term to it. But if course of dealing is to eliminate some right which the contract would otherwise confer, I would require evidence to show, not merely that the right had never been exercised, but also that the parties recognised that as between themselves no such right existed. In other words, there must be evidence establishing as between the parties what would be a usage if it applied to the market as a whole. But whether that be so or not, I find no implied term such as Bankers Trust allege to be established either by usage, or by course of dealing, or by both.

There was a great deal of evidence as to which Eurodollar transactions could be described as "wholesale" and which as "retail." I am inclined to think that the answer depends on the purpose for which the description is used. I have found that a payment of U.S. $131m. by Bankers Trust to the Libyan Bank would be excluded from London dollar clearing. In that context it may, perhaps, be described as wholesale. But I have also found that no usage applies to the Libyan Bank's account. I do not exclude the possibility that some usage applies to time deposits traded between the dealing rooms of banks. If the word "wholesale" is applied to that class of business, the Libyan Bank's account is not within it.

(h) Obligations in respect of the London account

Having considered and rejected the two methods by which Bankers Trust seek to limit their obligations in respect of the London account—that is, an express term from the managed account arrangement still subsisting, or an implied term—I have to determine what those obligations were. What sort of demands were the Libyan Bank entitled to make and Bankers Trust bound to comply with? As I said, earlier, it is necessary to distinguish between services which a bank is obliged to provide if asked, and services which many bankers do provide but are not obliged to.

Dr. F.A. Mann in his book *The Legal Aspect of Money,* 4th ed. (1982), pp. 193-194, discusses this question in the context of the Eurodollar market. I have given careful attention to the whole passage. His conclusion is:

"The banks, institutions or multinational companies which hold such deposits, frequently of enormous size, and which deal in them are said to buy and sell money such as dollars. In law it is likely, however, that they deal in credits, so that a bank which has a large amount of dollars standing to the credit of its account with another (European) bank probably does not and cannot expect it to be 'paid' or discharged otherwise than through the medium of a credit to an account with another bank. In the case of dollars it seems to be the rule (and therefore possibly a term of the contract) that such credit should be effected through the Clearing House Interbank Payments System (C.H.I.P.S.) in New York. ... In short, as economists have said, the Eurodollar market is a mere account market rather than a money market."

Dr. Mann cites Marcia Stigum's book, *The Money Market* (1978) and finds some support for his view—which he describes as tentative—in an English case which has not been relied on before me. The passage in question appeared for the first time in the 1982 edition of Dr. Mann's book after the litigation about the Iranian bank freeze.

I am reluctant to disagree with such a great authority on money in English law, but feel bound to do so. There is one passage, at p. 194, which appears to me to be an indication of economic rather than legal reasoning:

"it could often be a national disaster if the creditor bank were entitled to payment, for in the last resort this might mean the sale of a vast amount of dollars and the purchase of an equally large sum of sterling so as to upset the exchange rates."

But if a person owes a large sum of money, it does not seem to me to be a sound defence in law for him to say that it will be a national disaster if he has to pay. Countries which feel that their exchange rates are at risk can resort to exchange control if they wish.

Furthermore, the term suggested by Dr. Mann—that all payments should be made through C.H.I.P.S.—is negatived by the evidence in this case. It may for all I know be the rule for time deposits traded between the dealing rooms of banks, but I am not concerned with such a case here.

R.M. Goode, in *Payment Obligations in Commercial and Financial Transactions* (1983), p. 120, writes:

"Would an English court have declared the Executive Order effective to prevent the Iranian Government from claiming repayment in London of a dollar deposit maintained with a London bank? At first blush no, as it is unlikely that an English court would accord extra-territorial effect to the United States Executive Order. However, the argument on the United States side (which initially appeared to have claimed extra-territorial effect for the Order) was that in the Eurocurrency market it is well understood that deposits cannot be withdrawn in cash but are settled by an inter-bank transfer through the clearing system and Central Bank of the country whose currency is involved. So in the case of Eurodollar deposits payment was due in, or at any rate through, New York, and the Executive Order thereby validly prevented payment abroad of blocked Iranian deposits, not because the order was extra-territorial in operation but because it prohibited the taking of steps within the United States (i.e. through C.H.I.P.S. in New York) to implement instructions for the transfer of a dollar deposit located outside the United States."

That was published in 1983. I have not accepted the argument which Professor Goode refers to, that it is well understood that deposits cannot be withdrawn in cash. I find that there was no implied term to that effect.

I now turn again to the forms of transfer discussed in subsection (e) of this judgment, in order to consider in relation to each whether it was a form of transfer which the Libyan Bank were entitled to demand, whether it has in fact been demanded, and whether it would necessarily involve any action in New York.

.   .   .

(ix) Cash—dollar bills

Of course it is highly unlikely that anyone would want to receive a sum as large as $131m in dollar bills, at all events unless they were engaged in laundering the proceeds of crime. Mr. Osbourne said in his report:

> As to the demand for payment in cash, I regard this simply as the assertion of a customer's inalienable right. In practice, of course, where such a large sum is demanded in this manner, fulfilment of the theoretical right is unlikely, in my experience, to be achieved. A sensible banker will seek to persuade his customer to accept payment in some more convenient form, and I have yet to encounter an incident of this nature where an acceptable compromise was not reached, even where the sum was demanded in sterling.

I would substitute "fundamental" for "inalienable"; but in all other respects that passage accords with what, in my judgment, is the law. One can compare operations in futures in the commodity markets; everybody knows that contracts will be settled by the payment of differences, and not by the delivery of copper, wheat or sugar as the case may be; but an obligation to deliver and accept the appropriate commodity, in the absence of settlement by some other means, remains the legal basis of these transactions. So in my view every obligation in monetary terms is to be fulfilled, either by the delivery of cash, or by some other operation which the creditor demands and which the debtor is either obliged to, or is content to, perform. There may be a term agreed that the customer is not entitled to demand cash; but I have rejected the argument that there was any subsisting express term, or any implied term, to that effect. Mr. Sumption argued that an obligation to pay on demand leaves very little time for performance, and that U.S. $131m. could not be expected to be obtainable in that interval. The answer is that either a somewhat longer period must be allowed to obtain so large a sum, or that Bankers Trust would be in breach because, like any other banker they choose, for their own purposes, not to have it readily available in London.

Demand was in fact made for cash in this case, and it was not complied with. It has not been argued that the delivery of such a sum in cash in London would involve any illegal action in New York. Accordingly I would hold Bankers Trust liable on that ground.

(x) Cash-sterling

Dicey & Morris, The Conflict of Laws, 11th ed. state in Rule 210, at p. 1453:

> "If a sum of money expressed in a foreign currency is payable in England, it may be paid either in units of the money of account or in sterling at the rate of exchange at which units of the foreign legal tender can, on the day when the money is paid, be bought in London ...."

See also *Chitty on Contracts,* 25th ed., para. 2105.

> "Where a debtor owes a creditor a debt expressed in foreign currency ... the general rule is that the debtor may choose whether to pay in the foreign currency in question or in sterling."

. . .

Given that a foreign currency debtor is entitled to choose between discharging his obligations in foreign currency or sterling, I consider that he should not be entitled to choose the route which is blocked and then claim that his obligation is discharged or suspended. I prefer the view that he must perform in one way or the other; so long as both routes are available he may choose; but if one is blocked, his obligation is to perform in the other.

. . .

(2) The claim that a further sum should have been transferred from New York

This arises in three different ways on the facts. First it is said that U.S. $165.2m. should have been transferred to London at 2 p.m. on 7 January 1986.

Bankers Trust have two answers to this claim. First they say that instructions had been received and were pending for further payments to be made on 7 January after 2 p.m., which exceeded the amount then standing to the credit of the New York account (and, for that matter, the London account as well). It was only because further receipts also occurred after 2 p.m. that the New York account ended the day with a credit balance of U.S. $7.275m., and the London account remained untouched.

Secondly, Bankers Trust say that, if they were obliged to make a transfer to London on 7 January, they could lawfully have postponed it until after 8:06 p.m. New York time, when the first Presidential order came into force. Thereafter, they say, the transfer would have been illegal because it would have left the New York account overdrawn and would have constituted the grant of credit or a loan to the Libyan Bank.

In my judgment both those arguments fail. The telex of 27 November 1986, from which I have already quoted, contained this passage:

> Each day, at 2 p.m., the balance position of your account is determined and any credits received up to that time, less payments and less the peg balance, are immediately invested.

It is said that "payments" there are not confined to payments actually made, and include payments for which instructions were pending. In view of the precision with which the time of 2 p.m. is stated, and the word "immediately," I do not consider that to be right. Mr. Sumption argued that "immediately" is coloured (one might say contradicted) by the illustration given in the telex; but I do not agree. The argument that Bankers Trust were entitled to delay the transfer until after 8:06 p.m. also fails, for the same reason, and it is unnecessary to decide whether it would have been a breach of the first Presidential order to allow an overdraft in New York which was less than the credit balance in London. They would certainly have been entitled in any event not to make payments which exceeded the net credit balance of the two accounts. But after credits which were received during the afternoon there was no need to do that.

Mr. Sumption also argued that the passage in the telex set out above was merely an illustration of how the arrangement would work, and not part of the revised terms of the managed account arrangement. That argument I also reject.

Some attention was paid to the course of dealing on these points. Mr. Blackburn's evidence showed that there was no consistency in the treatment of unprocessed payments, sometimes they were taken into account in deciding whether a 2 p.m. transfer should be made, and at other times they were ignored. As to the actual timing of the transfer, it was always booked in New York on the same day, and in London on the following day with one day's back value. The important feature to my mind is that, so long as there was no legislative interference, it did not make any difference to the parties whether the actual transfer was made at 2 p.m. or at any time up to midnight. Banking hours in London had already ended. Nor did it necessarily make a difference whether unprocessed payments were taken into account; if they were not, and a debit balance in New York resulted at the end of the day, Bankers Trust would recall an appropriate amount next morning from London, with one day's back value. It was only when the Presidential orders came to be made that timing became important. Bankers Trust were, as I hold, in breach of contract in failing to transfer U.S. $165.2m. to London at 2 p.m. on 7 January.

If they had done so, they would have been entitled to recall U.S. $158.5m. from London next morning, so that the net loss to the London account was only U.S. $6.7m. Mr. Cresswell argues that, in practice, Bankers Trust only recalled sums from the London account late in the day, and therefore after 4:10 p.m. when the second Presidential order came into effect; a transfer from London would thereafter have been illegal. In point of fact that may well be correct. But I have no doubt at all that, if there had been a large overdraft on the New York account on the morning of 8 January 1986, Bankers Trust would on that particular day have recalled the appropriate sum from London with the utmost despatch.

No transfer to London having in fact been made on 7 January, and no recall the next morning, U.S. $6.7m. should then have been transferred, as the amount by which the New York balance exceeded the peg of U.S. $500,000. The only issue of potential importance here is whether the transfer was actually made. Although preparations were made for effecting the transfer, I am satisfied that it was countermanded and did not take effect. There is no need for me to decide precisely when the transfer ought to have been made, since that is subsumed in the next point.

The Libyan Bank's third complaint under this head is that, no transfers between New York and London having in fact been made at 2 p.m. on 7 January or in the morning of 8 January, the balance in New York at 2 p.m. on 8 January was U.S. $161,997,000. It is said that a sum of U.S. $161.4m. should then have been transferred to London. In answer to that Bankers Trust rely on points that are the same as, or similar to, those raised in respect of 2 p.m. on 7 January: they say that they were entitled to take pending payment instructions into account; and that they were entitled to delay payment until after 4:10 p.m. when the second Presidential order had been made, which certainly prohibited such a transfer. I reject both arguments for the reasons already given, based on the telex of 27 November 1985. It is true that if the pending payment instructions were to be executed in the afternoon, there were grounds for apprehension that the New York account would become overdrawn, which might be a breach of the first Presidential order, and even that the total of both accounts would be overdrawn, which would plainly be a breach of that order. The solution for Bankers Trust was not to execute those pending instructions unless and until further credits were received in New York. Some were in fact received—the New York account ended the day in credit to the extent of U.S. $251,129,000. Payment instructions for that day totalled U.S. $347,147,213.03, and none of them were in fact executed. So on any view the New York account would have been overdrawn if all had been executed, and that much more overdrawn if in addition U.S. $161.4m. had been transferred to London at 2 p.m. But the net total of the two accounts would still have been a credit balance. If Bankers Trust took the view that an overdraft on the New York account would itself be a breach of the Presidential order, and if they were right, the solution as I have said was to execute the pending instructions only as and when credits received permitted them to do so.

Accordingly I hold that (i) Bankers Trust were in breach of contract in failing to transfer U.S. $165.2m. to London at 2 p.m. on 7 January; (ii) if they had done that, they could and would have recalled U.S. $158.5m. from London in the morning of 8 January; but, (iii) on the assumption that both those steps had been taken, there would have been a further breach in failing to transfer U.S. $154.7m. to London at 2 p.m. on 8 January. (I trust that the calculation of this last figure is not too obscure. The 2 p.m. transfer on 8 January should have been U.S. $161.4m. if *neither* of the previous transfers had been made—as in fact they were not. If they had both been made, the figure would have been reduced to U.S. $154.7m.)

The balance resulting from those three figures is a net loss to the London account of U.S. $161.4m. I hold that this must be added to the Libyan Bank's first claim, as an additional sum for which that claim would have succeeded but for breaches of contract by Bankers Trust. It is said that this loss is not recoverable, because it arose from a new intervening act and is too remote. In the circumstances as they were on 7 and 8 January I have no hesitation in rejecting that argument.

.   .   .

Conclusion

The Libyan Bank are entitled to recover U.S. $131m. on claim (1) and U.S. $161m. (the amount of their demand) on claim (2). Claims (3) and (4) fail. Claim (5) would have failed if it had been material. On claim (6) the Libyan Bank must have judgment for damages to be assessed.

Postscript

In August of this year there were 20 working days. Fourteen of them were entirely consumed in the preparation of this judgment. In those circumstances it is a shade disappointing to read in the press and elsewhere that High Court judges do no work at all in August or September and have excessively long holidays.

Judgment for plaintiffs.

Notes and Questions

1.   The basic features of the managed account relationship are set out below:

New York	London
Operational Accounts	Investment Account
(for payments)	(Call account at Libor+)

Peg Arrangement

1.   NY balances in excess of $500k peg transferred daily at 2:00 p.m. NY time to London account for same day value.

2.   If at 2:00 p.m. NY time, NY balance below $500k peg, transfer from London account to NY account, value previous day.

Transfer Mechanics (e.g. to London)

1.   BTNY credits BTL branch on its books, with notice to BTL of amount.

2.   BTL credits LAFB on its books.

What was the point of this arrangement for LAFB and for BT?

2.   Let's look at some freeze basics. Let's start with the first freeze order of January 7, 1986. At 8:06 p.m. NY time, President Reagan signed an Executive Order prohibiting "U.S. persons," which included foreign branches but not foreign subsidiaries of U.S. banks, from extending credit to certain Libyan entities. This prohibited BTNY or BTL from extending credit to LAFB.

At 2:00 p.m. that day, the NY account had a balance of $165.7 million. Under the peg arrangement $165.2 mm (165.7– .5) should have been transferred to London account but was not. Why wasn't this transfer made?

The second freeze order came at 4:10 p.m. on January 8, 1986. At 8:44 a.m., BTNY had on hand $347.1 million in payment instructions. Why were none of these payments ever made? At 2:00 p.m., the NY account had a balance of $161.997, but there was no transfer to the London account. Why not? How naive was Mr. Brittain?

When the freeze was imposed, there was $251.1mm in the NY account and $131.5mm in the London account.

3.   The second freeze order (1) prohibited transfers or cash withdrawals from Libyan accounts; (2) applied only to foreign branches of U.S. banks, not subsidiaries; (3) applied only to dollar accounts; and (4) prohibited any transaction whose purpose or effect was to evade the freeze.   Why didn't the U.S. impose the freeze order on foreign subsidiaries of U.S. bank holding companies or foreign currency accounts of foreign branches of U.S. banks?

4.   There were various actors affected by the freeze: (1) the United States; (2) the United Kingdom; (3) U.S. banks (including BT); and (4) foreign banks. How did they view the benefits and costs of the freeze? Did they want it to be effective?

5.   Let's turn to the issues in the lawsuit. The main claim by LAFB was for the $131mm in the U.K. account, brought as a cause of action for debt. LAFB asked that these funds be paid in cash or by any reasonable method of making a payment. It said it would accept payment in sterling, as well as dollars. In particular, it asked that the funds be transferred to its account with UBAF Bank Limited London, an arab owned consortium bank. You should focus on this claim.

LAFB also claimed funds in New York that it contended should have been in London. There were various theories about how to calculate this amount. One version was rather straightforward: BTNY should have transferred $161.4mm on January 8. This was the version the court accepted.

LAFB also claimed damages with respect to BTNY's failure to execute payment instructions to third parties on January 7. This claim was disallowed. Finally, there was a successful fraud claim for damages with respect to a unilateral change made by BT in the way interest was calculated under the peg arrangement.

6.   BT contended that there was an established usage that all dollar payments had to be made through the United States (New York). Why was this an important argument in the lawsuit? Was there such a usage? Are there ways to transfer dollars abroad without going through the United States?

7.   As a result of the court's decision, BT was required to pay LAFB approximately $300 million in dollar cash or sterling. How could BTL actually pay this judgment? Could the bank actually get the dollar cash? If it couldn't get dollars, why didn't BTL have a valid impossibility defense to its contractual obligation?

8.   Do you think a London bank should be required to pay off dollar accounts in sterling if it can't do so with dollars?

9.   Could BT pay this judgment in sterling without being subject to criminal penalties in the United States? Couldn't the United States (through a U.S. court) enjoin BT from making the sterling payment? If the United States did this, what legal remedies might LAFB pursue in the United Kingdom?

10. Judgment was given in dollars, but the statutory judgment interest rate was 15% (near the market interest rate on sterling but considerably in excess of the 7% dollar interest rate). What impact might this have had in persuading the Treasury to issue a license to BT—which

Treasury, in fact, did—to enable BT to pay the judgment? Ironically, BT made the payment under the license through a CHIPS transfer.

11. On the general issues raised by this case, see H. Scott, *Where are the Dollars?—Off Shore Fund Transfers,* 3 Banking and Finance Law Review 243 (1989) and J. Sommer, *Where is a Bank Account,* 57 Maryland Law Review 1 (1998).

12. What lessons can the United States learn from *LAFB* about how to impose more effective asset freezes in the future?

B.   FREEZES BY THE HOST COUNTRY

There follows the Supreme Court decision in *Wells Fargo* followed by the Second Circuit's decision on remand.

Justice KENNEDY delivered the opinion of the Court.

At issue here is whether the home office of a United States bank is obligated to use its general assets to repay a Eurodollar deposit made at one of its foreign branches, after the foreign country's government has prohibited the branch from making repayment out of its own assets.

I

The case arises from a transaction in what is known in the banking and financial communities as the Eurodollar market. As the District Court defined the term, Eurodollars are United States dollars that have been deposited with a banking institution located outside the United States, with a corresponding obligation on the part of the banking institution to repay the deposit in United States dollars. See App. to Pet. for Cert. 42a; P. Oppenheim, International Banking 243 (5th ed. 1987). The banking institution receiving the deposit can be either a foreign branch of a United States bank or a foreign bank.

A major component of the Eurodollar market is interbank trading. In a typical interbank transaction in the Eurodollar market, the depositing bank (Bank A) agrees by telephone or telex, or through a broker, to place a deposit denominated in United States dollars with a second bank (Bank X). For the deposit to be a Eurodollar deposit, Bank X must be either a foreign branch of a United States bank or a foreign bank; Bank A, however, can be any bank, including one located in the United States. To complete the transactions, most banks that participate in the interbank trading market utilize correspondent banks in New York City, with whom they maintain, directly or indirectly, accounts denominated in United States dollars. In this example, the depositor bank, Bank A, orders its correspondent bank in New York (Bank B) to transfer United States dollars from Bank A's account to Bank X's account with Bank X's New York correspondent bank (Bank

Y). The transfer of funds from Bank B to Bank Y is accomplished by means of a wire transfer through a clearing mechanism located in New York City and known as the Clearing House Interbank Payments System, or "CHIPS."   See Scanlon, Definitions and Mechanics of Eurodollar Transactions, in The Eurodollar 16, 24-25 (H. Prochnow ed. 1970); Brief for New York Clearing House Association et al. as *Amici Curiae* 4. Repayment of the funds at the end of the deposit term is accomplished by having Bank Y transfer funds from Bank X's account to Bank B, through the CHIPS system, for credit to Bank A's account.

The transaction at issue here follows this pattern. Respondent Wells Fargo Asia Limited (WFAL) is a Singapore-chartered bank wholly owned by Wells Fargo Bank, N.A., a bank chartered by the United States.   Petitioner Citibank, N.A., (Citibank), also a United States-chartered bank, operates a branch office in Manila, Philippines (Citibank-Manila). On June 10, 1983, WFAL agreed to make two $1 million time deposits with Citibank-Manila. The rate at which the deposits would earn interest was set at 10%, and the parties agreed that the deposits would be repaid on December 9 and 10, 1983. The deposits were arranged by oral agreement through the assistance of an Asian money broker, which made a written report to the parties that stated, *inter alia:*

" 'Pay: Citibank, N.A. New York Account Manila

" 'Repay: Wells Fargo International, New York Account Wells Fargo Asia Ltd., Singapore Account # 003-023645,' " 852 F.2d 657, 658-659 (CA2 1988).

The broker also sent WFAL a telex containing the following "'[i]nstructions' ":

" 'Settlement—Citibank NA NYC AC Manila

" 'Repayment—Wells Fargo Bk Intl NYC Ac Wells Fargo Asia Ltd Sgp No 003-023645,' " id., at 659.

That same day, the parties exchanged telexes confirming each of the two deposits. WFAL's telexes to Citibank/Manila read:

" 'We shall instruct Wells Fargo Bk Int'l New York our correspondent please pay to our a/c with Wells Fargo Bk Int'l New York to pay to Citibank NA customer's correspondent USD 1,000,000.' " Ibid.

The telexes from Citibank/Manila to WFAL read:

" 'Please remit US Dir 1,000,000 to our account with Citibank New York. At maturity we remit US Dir 1,049,444.44 to your account with Wells Fargo Bank Intl Corp NY through Citibank New York.' " Ibid.

A few months after the deposit was made, the Philippine government issued a Memorandum to Authorized Agent Banks (MAAB 47) which provided in relevant part:

" 'Any remittance of foreign exchange for repayment of principal on all foreign obligations due to foreign banks and/or financial institutions, irrespective of maturity, shall be submitted to the Central Bank [of the Philippines] thru the Management of External Debt and Investment Accounts Department (MEDIAD) for prior approval.' " Ibid.

According to the Court of Appeals, "[a]s interpreted by the Central Bank of the Philippines, this decree prevented Citibank/Manila, an 'authorized agent bank' under Philippine law, from repaying the WFAL deposits with its Philippine assets, i.e., those assets not either deposited in banks elsewhere or invested in non-Philippine enterprises." Ibid. As a result, Citibank/Manila refused to repay WFAL's deposits when they matured in December 1983.

WFAL commenced the present action against Citibank in the United States District Court for the Southern District of New York, claiming that Citibank in New York was liable for the funds that WFAL deposited with Citibank/Manila. While the lawsuit was pending, Citibank obtained permission from the Central Bank of the Philippines to repay its Manila depositors to the extent that it could do so with the non-Philippine assets of the Manila branch. It paid WFAL $934,000; the remainder of the deposits, $1,066,000, remains in dispute. During the course of this litigation, Citibank/Manila, with the apparent consent of the Philippine government, has continued to pay WFAL interest on the outstanding principal. See App. to Pet. for Cert. 48a.

After a bench trial on the merits, the District Court accepted Citibank's invitation to assume that Philippine law governs the action. The court saw the issue to be whether, under Philippine law, a depositor with Citibank/Manila may look to assets booked at Citibank's non-Philippine offices for repayment of the deposits. After considering affidavits from the parties, it concluded (1) that under Philippine law an obligation incurred by a branch is an obligation of the bank as a whole; (2) that repayment of WFAL's deposits with assets booked at Citibank offices other than Citibank/Manila would not contravene MAAB 47; and (3) that Citibank therefore was obligated to repay WFAL, even if it could do so only from assets not booked at Citibank/Manila. Id., at 31a-35a. It entered judgment for WFAL, and Citibank appealed.

A panel of the United States Court of Appeals for the Second Circuit remanded the case to the District Court to clarify the basis for its judgment. The Second Circuit ordered the District Court to make supplemental findings of fact and conclusions of law on the following matters:

"(a) Whether the parties agreed as to where the debt could be repaid, including whether they agreed that the deposits were collectible only in Manila.

"(b) If there was an agreement, what were its essential terms?

"(c) Whether Philippine law (other than MAAB 47) precludes or negates an agreement between the parties to have the deposits collectible outside of Manila.

"(d) If there is no controlling Philippine law referred to in (c) above, what law does control?" Id., at 26a.

In response to the first query, the District Court distinguished the concepts of repayment and collection, defining repayment as "refer[ring] to the location where the wire transfers effectuating repayment at maturity were to occur," and collection as "refer[ring] to the place or places where plaintiff was entitled to look for satisfaction of its deposits in the event that Citibank should fail to make the required wire transfers at the place of repayment." Id., at 14a. It concluded that the parties' confirmation slips established an agreement that repayment was to occur in New York, and that there was neither an express agreement nor one that could be implied from custom or usage in the Eurodollar market on the issue of where the deposits could be collected. In response to the second question, the court stated that "[t]he only agreement relating to collection or repayment was that repayment would occur in New York." Id., at 18a. As to the third query, the court stated that it knew of no provision of Philippine law that barred an agreement making WFAL's deposits collectible outside Manila. Finally, in response to the last query, the District Court restated the issue in the case as follows:

"Hence, the dispute in this case ... boils down to one question: is Citibank obligated to use its worldwide assets to satisfy plaintiff's deposits? In other words, the dispute is not so much about where repayment physically was to be made or where the deposits were collectible, but rather which assets Citibank is required to use in order to satisfy its obligation to plaintiff. As we have previously found that the contract was silent on this issue, we interpret query (d) as imposing upon us the task ... of deciding whether New York or Philippine law controls the answer to that question." Id. at 19a.

The District Court held that, under either New York or federal choice-of-law rules, New York law should be applied. After reviewing New York law, it held that Citibank was liable for WFAL's deposits with Citibank/Manila, and that WFAL could look to Citibank's worldwide assets for satisfaction of its deposits.

The Second Circuit affirmed, but on different grounds. Citing general banking law principles, the Court of Appeals reasoned that, in the ordinary course, a party who makes a deposit with a foreign branch of a bank can demand repayment of the deposit only at that branch. In the court's view, however, these same principles established that this "normal limitation" could be altered by an agreement between the bank and the depositor: "If the parties agree that repayment of a deposit in a foreign bank or branch may occur at another location, they authorize demand and collection at that other location." 852 F.2d, at 660. The court noted that the District Court had found that Citibank had agreed to repay WFAL's deposits in New York. It concluded that the District Court's finding was not clearly erroneous under Federal Rule of Civil Procedure 52(a), and held that, as a result, WFAL was entitled "to collect the deposits out of Citibank assets in New York." 852 F.2d, at 661.

We granted certiorari. 493 U.S. ___ (1989). We decide that the factual premise on which the Second Circuit relied in deciding the case contradicts the factual determinations made by the District Court, determinations that are not clearly erroneous. We vacate the judgment, and remand the case to the Court of Appeals for further consideration of the additional legal questions in the case.

II

Little need be said respecting the operation or effect of the Philippine decree at this stage of the case, for no party questions the conclusion reached by both the District Court and the Court of Appeals that Philippine law does not bar the collection of WFAL's deposits from the general assets of the Citibank in the State of New York. See 852 F.2d, at 660-661; App. to Pet. for Cert. 18a. The question, rather, is whether Citibank is obligated to allow collection in New York, and on this point two principal theories must be examined. The first is that there was an agreement between the parties to permit collection in New York, or indeed at any place where Citibank has assets, an agreement implied from all the facts in the case as being within the contemplation of the parties. A second, and alternative, theory for permitting collection is that, assuming no such agreement, there is a duty to pay in New York in any event, a duty that the law creates when the parties have not contracted otherwise. See 3 A. Corbin, Contracts § 561, pp. 276-277 (1960).

The Court of Appeals appears to have relied upon the first theory we have noted, adopting the premise that the parties did contract to permit recovery from the general assets of Citibank in New York. Yet the District Court had made it clear that there is a distinction between an agreement on "repayment," which refers to the physical location for transacting discharge of the debt, and an agreement respecting "collection," which refers to the location where assets may be taken to satisfy it, and in quite specific terms, it found that the only agreement the parties made referred to repayment.

The Court of Appeals, while it said that this finding was not clearly erroneous, appears to have viewed repayment and collection as interchangeable concepts, not divisible ones. It concluded that the agreement as to where repayment could occur constituted also an agreement as to which bank assets the depositor could look to for collection. The strongest indication that the Court of Appeals was interpreting the District Court's findings in this manner is its answer to the argument, made by the United States as *amicus curiae,* that the home office of a bank should not bear the risk of foreign restrictions on the payment of assets from the foreign branch where a deposit has been placed, unless it makes an express agreement to do so. The court announced that "[o]ur affirmance in the present case is based on *the district court's finding of just such an agreement.*" 852 F.2d, at 661 (emphasis added).

That the Court of Appeals based its ruling on the premise of an agreement between the parties is apparent as well from the authorities upon which it relied to support its holding. The court cited three cases for the proposition that an agreement to repay at a particular location authorizes the depositor to collect the deposits at that location, all of which involve applications of the act of state doctrine: Allied Bank International v. Banco Credito Agricola de Cartago, 757 F.2d 516 (CA2), cert. dismissed, 473 U.S. 934 (1985); Garcia v. Chase Manhattan Bank, N.A., 735 F.2d 645, 650-651 (CA2 1984); and Braka v. Bancomer, S.N.C., 762 F.2d 222, 225 (CA2 1985). Each of these three cases turns upon the existence, or nonexistence, of an agreement for collection. In *Garcia* and *Allied Bank,* the agreement of the parties to permit collection at a location outside of the foreign country made the legal action of the foreign country irrelevant. See *Garcia,* 735 F.2d, at 646 (agreement between the parties was that "Chase's main office in New York would guarantee the certificate [of deposit] and that [the depositors] could be repaid by presenting the certificate at any Chase branch worldwide"); id., at 650 (purpose of the agreement was "to ensure that, no matter what happened in Cuba, including seizure of the debt, Chase would still have a contractual obligation to pay the depositors upon presentation of their CDS"); *Allied Bank,* supra, at 520 (agreement between the parties was that Costa Rican banks obligation to repay various loans in New York "would not be excused in the event that the Central Bank [of Costa Rica] failed to provide the necessary United States dollars for repayment"). In *Braka,* the agreement between the parties was that repayment and collection would be permitted only in the foreign country, and so the foreign law controlled. See 762 F.2d, at 224-225 (specifically distinguishing *Garcia* on the ground that the bank had not guaranteed repayment of the deposits outside of Mexico). By its reliance upon these cases, the Court of Appeals, it seems to us, must have been relying upon the existence of an agreement between Citibank and WFAL to permit collection in New York. As noted above, however, this premise contradicts the express finding of the District Court.

Under Federal Rule of Civil Procedure 52(a), the Court of Appeals is permitted to reject the District Court's findings only if those findings are clearly erroneous. As the Court of Appeals itself acknowledged, the record contains ample support for the District Court's finding that the parties agreed that repayment, defined as the wire transfers effecting the transfer of funds to WFAL when its deposits matured, would take place in New York. The confirmation slips exchanged by the parties are explicit: the transfer of funds upon maturity was to occur through wire transfers made by the parties' correspondent banks in New York. See supra, at 3.

As to collection, the District Court found that neither the parties' confirmation slips nor the evidence offered at trial with regard to whether "an agreement concerning the place of collection could be implied from custom and usage in the international banking field" established an agreement respecting collection. See App. to Pet. for Cert. 16a-17a. Upon review of the record, we hold this finding, that no such implied agreement existed based on the intent of the parties, was not clearly erroneous. The confirmation slips do not indicate an agreement that WFAL could collect its deposits from Citibank assets in New York; indeed, Citibank/Manila's confirmation slip, stating that "[a]t maturity *we* remit US Dlr 1,049,444.44 to your account with Wells Fargo Bank Intl Corp NY *through Citibank New York,*" see supra, at 3 (emphasis added), tends to negate the existence of any such agreement. The telexes from the money broker who arranged the deposits speak in terms of repayment, and indicate no more than that repayment was to be made to WFAL's account with its correspondent bank in New York; they do not indicate any agreement about where WFAL could collect its deposits in the event that Citibank/Manila failed to remit payment upon maturity to this account.

Nor does the evidence contradict the District Court's conclusion that the parties, in this particular case, failed to establish a relevant custom or practice in the international banking community from which it could be inferred that the parties had a tacit understanding on the point. Citibank's experts testified that the common understanding in the banking community was that the higher interest rates offered for Eurodollar deposits, in contrast to dollar deposits with United States banks, reflected in part the fact that the deposits were not subject to reserve and insurance requirements imposed on domestic deposits by United States banking law. This could only be the case, argues Citibank, if the deposits were "payable only" outside of the United States, as required by 38 Stat. 270, as amended, 12 U.S.C. § 461(b)(6) and 64 Stat. 873, as amended, 12 U.S.C. § 1813(l)(5). It argues further that higher rates reflected the depositor's assumption of foreign "sovereign risk," defined as the risk that actions by the foreign government having legal control over the foreign branch and its assets would render the branch unable to repay the deposit. See, e.g., App. at 354-367 (testimony of Ian H. Giddy).

WFAL's experts, on the other hand, testified that the identical interest rates being offered for Eurodollar deposits in both Manila and London at the time the deposits were made, despite the conceded differences in sovereign risk between the two locations, reflected an understanding that the home office of a bank was liable for repayment in the event that its foreign branch was unable to repay for any reason, including restrictions imposed by a foreign government. See, e.g., App. at 270-272 (testimony of Gunter Dufey).

A fair reading of all of the testimony supports the conclusion that, at least in this trial, on the issue of the allocation of sovereign risk there was a wide variance of opinion in the international banking community. We cannot say that we are left with "the definite and firm conviction" that the District Court's findings are erroneous. United States v. United States Gypsum Co., 333 U.S. 364, 395 (1948). Because the Court of Appeals' holding relies upon contrary factual assumptions, the judgment for WFAL cannot be affirmed under the reasoning used by that court.

Given the finding of the District Court that there was no agreement between the parties respecting collection from Citibank's general assets in New York, the question becomes whether collection is permitted nonetheless by rights and duties implied by law. As is its right, see Dandridge v. Williams, 397 U.S. 471, 475-476 and n. 6 (1970), WFAL seeks to defend the judgment below on the ground that, under principles of either New York or Philippine law, Citibank was obligated to make its general assets available for collection of WFAL's deposits. See Brief for Respondent 18, 23, 30-49. It is unclear from the opinion of the Court of Appeals which law it found to be controlling; and we decide to remand the case for the Court of Appeals to determine which law applies, and the content of that law. See Thigpen v. Roberts, 468 U.S. 27, 32 (1984); *Dandridge,* supra, at 475-476, and n. 6.

One of WFAL's contentions is that the Court of Appeals' opinion can be supported on the theory that it is based upon New York law. We do not think this is a fair or necessary construction of the opinion. The Court of Appeals placed express reliance on its own opinion in Garcia v. Chase Manhattan Bank, N.A., 735 F.2d 645 (CA2 1984), without citing or discussing Perez v. Chase Manhattan Bank, N.A., 61 N.Y.2d 460, 463 N.E.2d 5 (1984). In that case, the New York Court of Appeals was explicit in pointing out that its decision was in conflict with that reached two days earlier by the Second Circuit in *Garcia,* supra, a case that the *Perez* court deemed "similar on its facts." See 61 N.Y.2d, at 464, n. 3, 463 N.E.2d, at 9, n. 3. Given this alignment of authorities, we are reluctant to interpret the Court of Appeals' decision as resting on principles of state law. The opinion of the Court of Appeals, moreover, refers to "general banking law principles" and "United States law," 852 F.2d, at 660; whether this is the semantic or legal equivalent of the law of New York is for the Court of Appeals to say in the first instance.

Alternatively, if the Court of Appeals, based upon its particular expertise in the law of New York and commercial matters generally, is of the view that the controlling rule is supplied by Philippine law or, as Citibank would have it, by a federal common law rule respecting bank deposits, it should make that determination, subject to any further review we deem appropriate. In view of our remand, we find it premature to consider the other contentions of the parties respecting the necessity for any rule of federal common law, or the preemptive effect of federal statutes and regulations on bank deposits and reserves. See 12 U.S.C. §§ 461(b)(6), 1813(l)(5)(a); 12 CFR § 204.128(c) (1990). All of these matters, of course, may be addressed by the Court of Appeals if necessary for a full and correct resolution of the case.

The judgment of the Court of Appeals is vacated, and the case remanded for further proceedings consistent with this opinion.

It is so ordered.

The Second Circuit decision follows.

Before TIMBERS, KEARSE and MAHONEY, Circuit Judges.

KEARSE, Circuit Judge:

This action, brought by plaintiff Wells Fargo Asia Limited ("WFAL") to recover funds deposited with the Philippine branch of defendant Citibank, N.A. ("Citibank"), returns to us on remand from the United States Supreme Court, see Citibank, N.A. v. Wells Fargo Asia Limited, ___ U.S. ___, 110 S.Ct. 2034, 109 L.Ed.2d 677 (1990), vacating and remanding 852 F.2d 657 (2d Cir.1988), aff'g 660 F.Supp. 946 (S.D.N.Y.1987) (Knapp, J.), for a determination of what law applies to the present controversy and the content of that law, and for resolution of the controversy in light of those determinations. For the reasons below, we affirm the district court's ruling that the law of New York is applicable and its award of judgment in favor of WFAL.

I. BACKGROUND

The background of this action has been recounted in several opinions, including Citibank, N.A. v. Wells Fargo Asia Limited, ___ U.S. ___, 110 S.Ct. 2034, 109 L.Ed.2d 677 ("WFAL IV"); Wells Fargo Asia Limited v. Citibank, N.A., 852 F.2d 657 (2d Cir.1988) ("WFAL III"), Wells Fargo Asia Limited v. Citibank, N.A., 695 F.Supp. 1450 (S.D.N.Y.1988) ("WFAL II"), and Wells Fargo Asia Limited v. Citibank, N.A., 660 F.Supp. 946 (S.D.N.Y.1987) ("WFAL I"), familiarity with which is assumed. Briefly, in 1983, WFAL, a Singapore-chartered bank wholly owned by the United States-chartered Wells Fargo Bank, N.A., placed two six-month-nonnegotiable U.S. $1,000,000 deposits with Citibank for its branch in Manila, Philippines ("Citibank/Manila"). The deposit agreement called for WFAL to pay this amount to Citibank in New York for deposit at Citibank/Manila; it called for Citibank to repay Wells Fargo International's New York account for WFAL.

The deposits were to mature in December 1983. In October 1983, however, the Philippine government issued a Memorandum to Authorized Agent Banks ("MAAB 47"). As described in our earlier opinion, MAAB 47 provided, in pertinent part, as follows:

Any remittance of foreign exchange for repayment of principal on all foreign obligations due to foreign banks and or financial institutions, irrespective of maturity, shall be submitted to the Central Bank [of the Philippines] thru the Management of External Debt and Investment Accounts Department (MEDIAD) for prior approval. As interpreted by the Central Bank of the Philippines, this decree prevented Citibank/Manila, an "authorized agent bank" under Philippine law, from repaying the WFAL deposits with its Philippine assets, i.e., those assets not either deposited in banks elsewhere or invested in non-Philippine enterprises. Citibank/Manila did not repay WFAL's deposits upon maturity.

WFAL III, 852 F.2d at 659. After WFAL commenced the present suit for repayment of the deposited amounts, Citibank/Manila sought and received permission from the Central Bank of the Philippines to repay its foreign depositors to the extent it could do so with non-Philippine assets. Citibank/Manila thereafter repaid WFAL $934,000, leaving $1,066,000 in dispute.

The district court, Honorable Whitman Knapp, *Judge,* entered judgment in favor of WFAL, rejecting Citibank's contention that MAAB 47 made it impossible to repay the WFAL deposits. Noting that MAAB 47 allows obligations to foreign banks to be repaid if the consent of the Central Bank is obtained, and further noting that Citibank had not satisfied its good faith obligation to seek that consent, the court concluded that Citibank's impossibility defense must fail. Though originally making this ruling on the hypothesis that the law of the Philippines applied, *see WFAL I,* 660 F.Supp. at 947, the district court concluded, upon request from this Court for clarification, that New York law, rather than Philippine law, governed the dispute, *WFAL II,* 695 F.Supp. at 1454. It ruled that under New York law, Citibank's worldwide assets were available for satisfaction of WFAL's claim. Id.

We affirmed. Though the district court had concluded (a) that repayment and collection are independent concepts, and (b) that the parties had not reached an agreement as to the situs of collection, and we did not disturb those rulings, we concluded that the

authorities suggest that a debt may be collected wherever it is repayable, *unless* the parties have agreed otherwise. Since the court found here that there was no separate agreement restricting where the deposits could be collected, and we are aware of nothing in the record that contradicts that finding, we conclude that WFAL was entitled to collect the deposits out of Citibank assets in New York.

WFAL III, 852 F.2d at 661 (emphasis added).

The Supreme Court vacated our decision, stating that we appeared to have treated the concepts of repayment and collection as interchangeable rather than independent and to have "rel[ied] upon the existence of an agreement between Citibank and WFAL to permit collection in New York." *WFAL IV,* 110 S.Ct. at 2040. The Supreme Court concluded that the district court's finding that there was no agreement as to the situs of collection was not clearly erroneous; it also endorsed "the District Court's conclusion that the parties, in this particular case, failed to establish a relevant custom or practice in the international banking community from which it could be inferred that the parties had a tacit understanding on the point." Id. at 2041. Concluding that our decision could not be upheld on the theory that there was an agreement as to the place of collection, the Supreme Court remanded for a determination of whether WFAL's claim is governed by New York law, Philippine law, or federal common law, and what the content of the governing law is, and directed us to decide the appeal in light of those determinations:

> Given the finding of the District Court that there was no agreement between the parties respecting collection from Citibank's general assets in New York, the question becomes whether collection is permitted nonetheless by rights and duties implied by law. As is its right, ... WFAL seeks to defend the judgment below on the ground that, under principles of either New York or Philippine law, Citibank was obligated to make its general assets available for collection of WFAL's deposits .... It is unclear from the opinion of the Court of Appeals which law it found to be controlling; and we decide to remand the case for the Court of Appeals to determine which law applies, and the content of that law.

Id. at 2042.

Accordingly, we proceed to those questions.

II. DISCUSSION

In response to this Court's earlier inquiry, the district court discussed the choice-of-law question as follows:

> The legal principles governing our determination are straightforward. Jurisdiction in this action is asserted both on the basis of diversity and federal question involving 12 U.S.C. § 632. In diversity cases, of course, we must apply the conflict of law doctrine of the forum state. Klaxon Co. v. Stentor Elec. Mfg. Co. (1941) 313 U.S. 487, 61 S.Ct. 1020, 85 L.Ed. 1477. In federal question cases, we are directed to apply a federal common law choice of law rule to determine which jurisdiction's substantive law should apply. Corporacion Venezolana de Fomento v. Vintero Sales Corp. (2d Cir.1980) 629 F.2d 786, 794-95, cert. denied (1981) 449 U.S. 1080, 101 S.Ct. 863, 66 L.Ed.2d 804. The rule in New York is that "the law of the jurisdiction having the greatest interest in the litigation will be applied and that the facts or contacts which obtain significance in defining State interests are those which relate to the purpose of the particular law in conflict." Intercontinental Planning, Ltd. v. Daystrom, Inc. (1969) 24 N.Y.2d

372, 382, 300 N.Y.S.2d 817, 825, 248 N.E.2d 576, 582. Federal law invokes similar considerations, see, Corporacion Venezolana, 629 F.2d at 795, and the place of performance is considered an important factor. *Citibank, N.A. v. Benkoczy* (S.D.Fla.1983) 561 F.Supp. 184, 186 and cases cited therein.

Regardless of whether the New York or federal test is used, application of these standards leads us to the conclusion that New York law should be used to evaluate Wells Fargo's contention that Citibank's worldwide assets are available for repayment of the deposits. As the New York Court of Appeals has recognized, "New York ... is a financial capital of the world, serving as an international clearing house and market place for a plethora of international transactions ... [.] In order to maintain its preeminent financial position, it is important that the justified expectations of the parties to the contract be protected." J. Zeevi and Sons, Ltd. v. Grindlays Bank (Uganda) Ltd. (1975) 37 N.Y.2d 220, 227, 371 N.Y.S.2d 892, 898, 333 N.E.2d 168, 172. In our view, these expectations will be best promoted by applying a uniform rule of New York law where, as here, the transactions were denominated in United States dollars and settled through the parties' New York correspondent banks, and where the defendant is a United States bank with headquarters in New York. Since Eurodollar transactions denominated in U.S. dollars customarily are cleared in New York ... the rationale for application of New York law becomes even stronger. If the goal is to promote certainty in international financial markets, it makes sense to apply New York law uniformly, rather than conditioning the deposit obligations on the vagaries of local law, and requiring each player in the Eurodollar market to investigate the law of numerous foreign countries in order to ascertain which would limit repayment of deposits to the foreign branch's own assets.

WFAL II, 695 F.Supp. at 1453-54.

As to the content of New York law on the matter, the district court noted that the most recent pronouncement of the New York Court of Appeals, see Perez v. Chase Manhattan National Bank, N.A., 61 N.Y.2d 460, 468, 474 N.Y.S.2d 689, 691, 463 N.E.2d 5, 7, cert. denied, 469 U.S. 966, 105 S.Ct. 366, 83 L.Ed.2d 302 (1984), indicated that the parent bank is ultimately liable for the obligations of the foreign branch. Though the district court reasoned that an actual expropriation by the foreign government would be treated differently, it concluded that in the present case, there having been no expropriation and no limitation of the depositor's rights but only action affecting the assets of the branch, New York law would allow collection of the debt in New York:

[I]f the Philippines had confiscated plaintiff's deposits, New York courts would interpret the expropriation as a compulsory assignment of the depositor's rights, so that payment to the Philippine assignee would discharge the debt. A New York court

> would further recognize such compulsory assignment as an act of a foreign sovereign unreviewable under the Act of State doctrine. *Perez,* supra, 61 N.Y.2d 460, 474 N.Y.S.2d 689, 463 N.E.2d 5. We believe New York would take a similar approach in the situation where a foreign government had effected a partial confiscation in the form of a tax on a deposit made at a foreign branch. See, Dunn v. Bank of Nova Scotia (5th Cir.1967) 374 F.2d 876. However, we are aware of no persuasive authority to tell us to what extent, if any, a New York court would defer to local law in the situation here presented, where the foreign sovereign did not extinguish the branch's debt either in whole or in part but merely conditioned repayment on the obtaining of approval from a government agency. Fortunately, we need not resolve that troublesome question.

WFAL II, 695 F.Supp. at 1454-55. The court found it unnecessary to determine whether New York law would hold that a foreign government's refusal to give the prerequisite consent constitutes an excuse for refusal to make repayment, in light of its earlier finding that Citibank "had not satisfied its good faith obligation to seek the [Philippine] government's consent to use the assets booked at Citibank's non-Philippine offices." Id. at 1455. The court reaffirmed that finding.

We agree with the district court's analysis, and we conclude, substantially for the reasons that court stated; that New York law governs the present claim and that under New York law, Citibank was not excused from making repayment. In urging that we reach the contrary conclusion. Citibank argues that there is a clear federal policy placing the risk of foreign-law impediments to repayment on the depositor. In so arguing, it relies on federal banking rules such as 12 U.S.C. § 461(b)(6) (1988), which provides that banking reserve requirements "shall not apply to deposits payable only outside the States of the United States and the District of Columbia," and 12 C.F.R. § 204.128(c) (1990) (issued at 52 Fed.Reg. 47696, Dec. 16, 1987), which provides that "[a] customer who makes a deposit that is payable solely at a foreign branch of the depository institution assumes whatever risk may exist that the foreign country in which a branch is located might impose restrictions on withdrawals." Citibank's reliance on these provisions is misplaced. Federal law defines a deposit that is "payable only at an office outside the United States" as "a deposit ... as to which the depositor is entitled, *under the agreement with the institution,* to demand payment *only* outside the United States." Id. § 204.2(t) (emphasis added). The provisions relied on thus do not reveal a policy allocating the risk to depositors as a matter of law where there is no such agreement. So long as state law does not restrict a bank's freedom to enter into an agreement that allocates the risk of foreign sovereign restrictions, state law does not conflict with the federal policy reflected in current statutes or regulations. We see no such restriction in the law of New York, and hence there is no " 'significant conflict'," Mires v. DeKalb County, Georgia, 433 U.S. 25, 31, 97 S.Ct.

2490, 2494-95, 53 L.Ed.2d 557 (1977) (quoting Wallis v. Pan American Petroleum Corp., 384 U.S. 63, 68, 86 S.Ct. 1301, 1304, 16 L.Ed.2d 369 (1966)), between New York law and federal law such as would be necessary to justify the creation of a federal common law.

We conclude that under New York law, unless the parties agree to the contrary, a creditor may collect a debt at a place where the parties have agreed that it is repayable. In applying this principle to the circumstances of the present case to affirm the judgment in favor of WFAL, we do not assume the existence of an agreement between Citibank/Manila and WFAL to permit collection in New York; rather, in light of the express finding of the district court that the parties had no agreement as to permissible situses of collection, we rely on the absence of any agreement forbidding the collection in New York.

Finally, we note that on the present remand, WFAL urged us to affirm on the basis of recently submitted evidence that in fact Citibank, while refusing to use non-Manila assets to pay Citibank/Manila's debts, has received profits of at least $25 million from Citibank/Manila during the period 1984-1989. WFAL contends that it is entitled to have its deposits repaid out of these profits. Citibank does not dispute that it received these profits (see Citibank reply brief on remand at 20, n. 18, stating that these transfers "represent a small yield on capital investment that the Central Bank permits Citibank/Manila to remit to its home office") but takes the position that it is not required to use these profits to pay persons whose deposits in Citibank/Manila remain unpaid. We need not resolve this question. Suffice it to say that Citibank's acknowledged ability to obtain Philippine Central Bank approval of transfers to it of moneys as profits appears to support the district court's finding, if further support were needed, that Citibank in fact did not satisfy its good faith obligation to seek that government's approval of repayment of WFAL's deposits to WFAL.

CONCLUSION

We have considered all of Citibank's arguments on this appeal and have found them to be without merit. The judgment of the district court is affirmed.

Notes and Questions

1. Make sure you understand how this freeze affected Citibank. Wells Fargo Asia Ltd. (WFAL), a bank chartered in Singapore (a subsidiary of Wells Fargo Corp., a U.S. bank holding company), placed two $1 million 6 month time deposits with the Manila branch of Citibank–NY (Citibank/Manila), on June 10, 1983, repayable on December 9-10, 1983. After the transaction, the account entries on Citibank's balance sheets were as follows:

Citibank Manila (C/Manila)		Citibank New York (C/NY)	
A	L	A	L
$2mm C/NY	$2mm WFAL	$2mm	$2mm C/Manila

After the deposits had been made, the Philippines issued the "Memorandum to Authorized Agent Banks" which prevented C/Manila from repaying the WFAL deposits with its "Philippine Assets." Philippine assets were local assets, assets denominated in pesos. They did not include deposits in banks outside the Philippines or invested in non-Philippine enterprises.

The purpose of the decree was to limit the outflow of Philippine foreign exchange reserves. This would happen if C/Manila were to use Philippine assets, denominated in pesos, to obtain dollars from the Philippines Central Bank, and remit these dollars to foreign creditors such as Wells Fargo.

If C/Manila had the full $2 million in a deposit at C/NY, it could have used these funds to pay WFAL. But it did not; it had invested this money in various assets, some Philippines, some not, along with funds from other C/Manila depositors. It was able to pay WFAL $934K from non-Philippine assets (WFAL's pro rata share), but still owed $1,066,000.

2.   Why did Wells Fargo place $2 million in time deposits with the Manila branch of Citibank rather than with Citibank's New York head office or London branch?

3.   The Federal Reserve Bank of New York sided with Citibank's position that the head office should not be responsible for foreign branch liabilities. Why?

4.   Under existing case law, it is clear that Head Office would be responsible if the parties had contracted to this effect—although courts have varied in how liberally contracts would be read to find such an agreement. The first decision by the Court of Appeals thought there was such a contract. Do you agree with the Supreme Court that there wasn't?

On remand, the Court of Appeals held that under applicable New York law, absent contract to the contrary, the Head Office was responsible for branch deposits, and the Supreme Court denied further review. How do you suppose this decision affected eurodollar interest rates? Was this the right result?

5.   In 1994, new section 25C was added to the Federal Reserve Act, 12 U.S.C. §633, which provides as follows:

(a) Exceptions from repayment requirement

A member bank shall not be required to repay any deposit made at a foreign branch of the bank if the branch cannot repay the deposit due to—

(1) an act of war, insurrection, or civil strife; or

(2) an action by a foreign government or instrumentality (whether de jure or de facto) in the country in which the branch is located;

unless the member bank has expressly agreed in writing to repay the deposit under those circumstances.

(b) Regulations

The Board and the Comptroller of the Currency may jointly prescribe such regulations as they deem necessary to implement this Section.

Do you prefer this result to the one reached by the Court?

Links to Other Chapters

Obviously asset freezes are directly linked to the payment system, the details of which were examined in the prior Chapter. Control of the domestic payment system is a major weapon at the disposal of national sovereigns that may permit them—if they are willing to use it—to exert control over offshore markets. For example, the Japanese could effectively stop Euroyen transactions by not allowing them to clear through the Japanese payment system. The desire of countries to control offshore markets, particularly in their own currency, is a recurring theme in this book.

CHAPTER TWELVE

EUROBONDS AND GLOBAL SECURITIES

This Chapter looks at eurobonds and global securities. With respect to eurobonds, we first look at the development and some important characteristics of the market. We will then examine two key issues, issuing procedures and withholding taxes. As to global securities, our focus is on what they are, how they relate to non-global securities, and what obstacles have to be overcome for their further expansion.

A. EUROBONDS

1. THE MARKET

THE INTERNATIONAL BOND MARKET
31 Bank of England Quarterly Bulletin 521-528 (1991).

Eurobonds are traditionally defined as bonds which are issued, and largely sold, outside the domestic market of the currency in which they are denominated. They are typically underwritten by an international syndicate of banks, are exempt from any withholding taxes (ie taxes on coupon payments deducted at source), and are bearer in nature (ie no register of ownership is maintained). Originally, investors were attracted in particular by (and thus prepared to pay a premium for) the bearer status of eurobonds and their freedom from liability to withholding tax, although it is an over-simplification to characterise all eurobonds as having such distinctive features—practices vary between currency sectors and have altered with time. Eurobonds are distinct from domestic and foreign bonds. For the purposes of this article domestic bonds can in general be taken to mean bonds issued by largely domestic borrowers through domestic syndicates of banks and securities houses to predominantly domestic investors. "Foreign" bond markets can be viewed as subsets of domestic bond markets, comprising domestic bonds issued by foreign borrowers.

Early development of the eurobond market

An international bond market can be traced back to the 19th century, when, for example, foreign governments launched bonds in London.   However, the eurobond market developed much more recently, in the early 1960s, as an offshore market in, primarily, dollar bonds. A contributory factor to its development was the prior growth of a London eurodollar deposit market in the post-war period reflecting, *inter alia,* the emergence of a substantial US current account deficit in the early 1960s and restrictions on the maximum rate of interest which US-based banks could pay on US-held dollar deposits under Regulation Q.

Over time, eurodollar depositors diversified into the first important foreign bond sector—"Yankee" bonds (US dollar bonds issued in New York by non-US borrowers).   Although Yankee bond issues were normally underwritten by US securities firms in New York, European intermediaries were often invited to help distribute the bonds abroad. As European investors and issuers became more important in the Yankee bond market, the necessary conditions were in place for European securities firms to avoid the listing and disclosure requirements of the US bond market by themselves lead managing and underwriting dollar bond issues in London.

The introduction in July 1963 of an Interest Equalisation Tax, in response to the deterioration in the US current account, gave the decisive impetus to the development of the eurobond market. The Interest Equalisation Tax was levied on US investors' purchases of foreign securities and in turn raised the cost of foreign borrowing in the US market by 1%. The effect was a sharp contraction of issuance in the Yankee bond market and, with access to a number of other foreign bond markets subject to restrictions, issuance was diverted to the emerging eurodollar bond market.   Reinforcing this, in 1965 the Voluntary Restraint Program established voluntary limits on foreign direct investment out of the United States (unless matching balance of payments earnings accrued) and in 1968 the guidelines were replaced by mandatory restrictions. As a result, US multinationals had little alternative but to fund their foreign subsidiaries through the euromarkets.

Eurobond market issuance expanded rapidly in the 1960s (reaching $3 billion in 1970) and the currency base of the market broadened (in particular, markets in deutschemarks.   Dutch guilders, yen and Canadian dollars became well established). In the 1970s, some of the factors which contributed to the early development of the eurobond market ceased to have effect: for instance, the Interest Equalisation Tax was abolished in 1974.   Nevertheless, the eurobond market consolidated its position as a channel of intermediation for international capital flows, largely because an infrastructure for economical primary distribution and secondary trading had become well established, and because many domestic bond markets were subject to strict issuing requirements.

During these early stages of the eurobond market, London became established as the main centre for issuance and trading. Apart from the advantages possessed in terms of time zone and language, London also benefited from the international, innovative and entrepreneurial traditions of many of its institutions, as well as the relatively restrictive regulatory and fiscal regimes in other centres.

Eurobond market: 1980-90

The past decade has seen the eurobond market evolve considerably in terms of growth of issuance, currency diversification, shifts in the patterns of instruments and borrowers, and innovation.

Total issuance

Eurobond issuance grew very rapidly, increasing from $26 billion in 1980 to $185 billion in 1986.

.   .   .

Currency diversification

Deregulation has contributed to a widening of the range of currencies in which eurobonds are issued from 11 in 1980 to 21 in 1990. New currency sectors have included, for instance, the French and Luxembourg francs, the lira and the Swedish krona. The increased spread of currencies in the eurobond market has presented a means through which investors may diversify their portfolios without incurring the complications of investing in domestic markets (eg tax). It has also contributed to a natural widening in the investor and issuer base of the eurobond market.

.   .   .

Instruments

Straight fixed-rate eurobonds have been the dominant instrument in the eurobond market, although their relative importance has diminished from 72% of eurobond issuance in 1980 to 61% in 1990 (Table A).

.   .   .

Table A
Eurobond issues by instrument type

$ billions

Year	Straight fixed-rate	Floating- rate note (FRNs)	Equity-related bonds			Total
			Equity warrant	Convert-ible	Bonds with non-equity warrants(a)	
1980	18.6	3.5	—	3.6	—	25.7
1981	18.7	7.6	—	2.6	0.3	29.2
1982	36.4	12.4	0.4	1.4	1.1	51.7
1983	29.1	14.1	1.6	3.3	1.3	49.4
1984	40.8	33.5	2.7	4.6	5.6	87.2
1985	73.1	55.0	2.7	4.8	1.6	137.2
1986	115.2	46.7	15.3	5.9	2.0	185.1
1987	91.7	11.4	23.0	13.0	2.5	141.6
1988	126.6	23.4	28.3	5.4	0.7	184.4
1989	125.1	26.8	67.0	4.6	0.2	223.7
1990	129.9	57.2	20.6	4.3	0.1	212.1

Source: Bank of England ICMS database.

(a) Currency, debt, gold.

. . .

Borrowers

Eurobond market investors have typically been "name-conscious", so most issuers have been highly-rated borrowers from OECD countries. (Between 1985 and 1990, issues by non-OECD countries averaged 3.7% of total eurobond issuance.) Over the last decade (Table B), issuance of eurobonds by the US private sector, the largest national group of issuers in the early 1980s, more than halved for a variety of reasons: for example, the use of shelf registration in the United States accelerated the process of domestic bond issuance and reduced one of the competitive advantages enjoyed by the eurobond market; the abolition of withholding tax in the US domestic market also contributed to a decline in the attractiveness of the eurobond market to US borrowers; and in recent years increased corporate indebtedness, often associated with large takeover bids, has led to heightened investor awareness of the credit risk of US corporations.

. . .

Investors

The bearer status of eurobonds precludes a comprehensive analysis of the investor profile, but a number of observations can be made.

UK residents' purchases of eurobonds were limited until the abolition of exchange controls in 1979, since then they have been free to purchase eurobonds without restriction. In the United States, domestic investors are inhibited from buying eurobonds through an

Table B
Gross flows in the eurobond market: borrowing by nationality
Percentages

	United States	Japan	United Kingdom	West Germany(a)	France	Canada	International Institutions	Other
1980	19.0	6.3	6.3	—	8.4	5.0	18.5	36.5
1981	22.2	9.9	4.2	0.2	7.2	16.8	13.5	26.0
1982	26.2	4.2	2.2	2.9	14.3	13.4	12.3	24.5
1983	13.2	9.6	3.4	4.8	11.5	7.8	19.9	29.8
1984	26.9	11.2	5.1	2.1	8.2	5.4	9.7	31.4
1985	27.4	10.2	10.3	2.0	7.9	5.3	8.9	28.0
1986	19.9	12.3	10.1	5.3	6.7	7.8	7.1	30.8
1987	14.1	23.3	6.9	5.9	5.0	4.2	10.4	30.2
1988	8.5	20.9	12.8	5.6	7.8	5.1	8.8	30.5
1989	6.9	36.7	10.2	4.1	5.0	4.3	7.6	25.2
1990	9.3	22.1	9.7	3.0	8.1	2.3	10.7	34.8

Source: Bank of England ICMS database.

(a) Includes borrowing by East German institutions following unification.

initial public offering which has not been registered with the SEC(although they may be sold freely after an official "seasoning period" of 40 days). US investors have, in any case, ready access to large and liquid domestic capital markets. Continental European investors—traditionally "name- conscious" and placing a premium on bearer instruments and freedom from withholding tax—have been a major source of demand for eurobonds. And in recent years Japan has become a major source of demand as its external surplus has grown; in addition, equity-warrant bond issues in the eurobond market have become a significant channel of intermediation between Japanese borrowers and investors.

A separate development has been a change in the character of certain segments of the eurobond market. Small private investors ("retail" investors) were a significant feature of the early days of the market, and remain important in high interest rate currency sectors characterized by comparatively small, illiquid issues (eg Australian and New Zealand dollars). However, other currency sectors (eg US dollar, Ecu, yen, sterling) have become increasingly institutionalized (ie the proportion of funds professionally managed, rather than being managed directly by the final investor, has increased); as a result, a demand for liquidity in the secondary market, and hence for large primary issues, has been created. Nevertheless, institutional investors are usually subject to restrictions on the diversification of their investments (eg German life insurance companies may only invest a maximum of 5% of their assets in overseas securities).

The global nature of the eurobond market—intermediating between borrowers and investors throughout the developed world—is matched by the wide nationality range of bookrunners (Table C). Banks and securities houses have traditionally maintained especially close links with issuers and investors from their home country. Consequently, the market shares of bookrunners have changed to reflect the pattern of

Table C
Distribution of eurobond bookrunners by nationality
Percentages

	United States	Japan	Continental Europe	United Kingdom
1980	19.5	4.9	52.4	12.0
1981	26.9	10.0	42.2	11.3
1982	28.6	5.5	51.3	8.1
1983	16.6	6.3	59.1	9.4
1984	34.4	8.9	40.4	9.3
1985	33.6	12.2	39.5	10.0
1986	27.2	24.3	37.5	7.5
1987	18.1	36.9	33.6	9.8
1988	19.6	44.8	25.8	6.6
1989	19.7	44.8	25.8	6.6
1990	18.8	29.1	40.8	8.1

intermediation through the eurobond market (eg Japanese firms have been bookrunners for virtually all equity warrant bond issues by Japanese companies), although there remain some banks and securities houses with a significant presence in a variety of countries and currency sectors.

. . .

Innovation

The eurobond market—just like the US domestic bond market—has traditionally been a leading channel of financial market innovation, allowing financial structures to be adapted to accommodate the requirements of issuers and investors more flexibly than has been possible in some domestic capital markets. For instance, the use of swaps in the eurobond market was a natural consequence of the increased internationalisation of bond markets, while the eurobond market also witnessed the development of the Japanese equity warrant. Other instruments, such as asset-backed securities, had earlier developed into a sizable market in the United States, and became an important part of the eurobond market (with issuance rising to $15 billion in 1990). . . .

Secondary market

Investors' desire for liquidity (eg the ability to buy or sell bonds in sizable amounts before they mature without much influencing the price) has led to the development of a sizable secondary market in eurobonds.

The secondary market is primarily an over-the-counter market, even though most eurobonds are listed on the London or Luxembourg Stock Exchanges. (Listings are normally obtained because some institutional investors are not allowed to purchase unquoted securities). Secondary market trading has expanded rapidly in recent years: Table E shows the growth in secondary market trading through the international clearing systems (Euroclear and Cedel).

The rapid growth of secondary trading is closely linked to structural changes in the market, in particular the increased institutionalisation of the investor base. During the early development of the market, issues were small (particularly in relation to government bond issues in domestic markets) and the market was oriented towards retail investors who were attracted by the anonymity and perceived tax advantages of eurobonds. Institutional investment was focused on domestic capital markets, partly reflecting exchange controls, while the lack of competitive market-making, inefficient settlement systems and unsophisticated communications technology represented further disincentives to sizable institutional investment in the eurobond market. As a result, there was little secondary market trading and bid/offer spreads were wide.

Table E
Secondary Market turnover[a]
$ billions

Year	$ billions
1980	240
1981	404
1982	864
1983	896
1984	1,512
1985	2,208
1986	3,570
1987	4,666
1988	4,627
1989	5,084
1990	6,262

Source: AIBD.

(a) Compromises secondary market turnover of fixed-income bonds, floating-rate notes, certificates of deposit and short and medium-term notes in euro and domestic sectors through Euroclear and Cedel.

. . .

Convergence of bond markets

In recent years there has been a growing integration—in terms of increased substitutability and interactions—between the euro, domestic and foreign bond markets. Moreover, the term "eurobond" as a synonym for an international bearer bond which is exempt from withholding tax has become something of a simplification in view of both the diverse arrangements in different currency sectors, and the expansion of the number of currencies in which eurobonds are issued.

The two major differences of form which distinguished eurobonds from domestic and foreign bonds have gradually been eroded. Fiscal reforms have led to the dismantling of withholding tax regimes in a number of major OECD countries (eg in the United States in 1984, Germany in 1989 and France—for foreign investors only—in 1989); and, in those countries which retain withholding taxes, procedures often exist for the reclaiming of tax under double taxation agreements for at least some categories of investor. The bearer status of eurobonds was not at the outset a unique feature of eurobonds: bearer bonds were, and are, issued in a number of domestic markets eg Germany, Switzerland and Luxembourg. Moreover, the increasing role of institutions as eurobond investors means that the anonymity associated with bearer status is less valued. The settlement of eurobond trades through the two clearing systems (Cedel and Euroclear) is also no longer a distinguishing feature; a significant amount of domestic bonds, notably government bonds, are now settled in the same way.

The integration of euro and national bond markets has been enhanced by the "global" bond which can be readily transferred between depositories in these sectors. To facilitate this transfer links have been created between Cedel and Euroclear in Europe and Fedwire in the United States. The enhanced worldwide marketability of "global" bonds increases their liquidity and thus the attractiveness of these issues to institutional investors, enabling the borrower to launch an issue at a lower spread than would have been attained had separate tranches been issued in more than one market. The first fully fungible global issue was a US $1.5 billion issue by the IBRD in September 1989 which was distributed and settled simultaneously in North America, Europe and the Far East.

The eurobond market is no longer the only bond market which is genuinely international in character. Over the years the traditional domestic bond markets have attracted increasing international investor interest as a result of factors such as improved communications technology and dismantlement of exchange controls. At the same time, portfolio diversification across markets has become an accepted component of investment strategy: for instance, the Employee Retirement Income Security Act (ERISA) in the United States promoted overseas investment as helping to reduce risk. The process of international portfolio diversification has been further stimulated by the development of markets in swaps, futures, options, etc, which have facilitated the elimination or transformation of currency and interest rate risks.

Furthermore, eurobonds are no longer characterised by the composition of the syndicate, or by their syndication procedures. Traditionally, eurobond issues were underwritten by an international syndicate, while domestic issues were underwritten by local firms. However, domestic bond markets have been increasingly opened up to foreign-owned financial institutions (eg from May 1985, foreign-owned banks were permitted to lead-manage deutschmark domestic bond issues), while primary market syndication procedures have become increasingly similar in many domestic and eurocurrency sectors: for example, the negotiated fixed-price re-offering, a method already adopted in the US domestic market, was re-introduced in the eurodollar bond market in June 1989.

Chart 3

Euro dollar/US domestic bond yield differential [(a)]

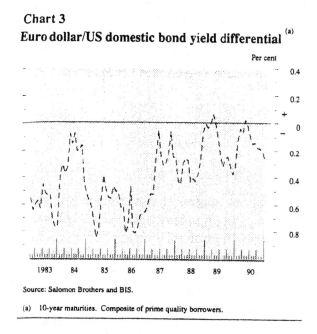

Source: Salomon Brothers and BIS.

(a)   10-year maturities. Composite of prime quality borrowers.

The effect of all these developments has been the evolution of an increasingly international bond market in which the previously rather distinct domestic, foreign and euro sectors have become more inter-linked. Instruments traded in different markets are becoming more homogeneous, as is the investor base in different markets. Nevertheless, the process is far from complete: although yield differentials between domestic and eurobond markets have been substantially arbitraged away in recent years, they still exist (Chart 3). The substitutability of euro and domestic sectors of the bond market is limited by a number of factors: for example, restrictions on domestic financial institutions' investment in overseas securities and differences in the registered/bearer status of certain domestic bonds and eurobonds.

If the eurodollar bond market is set in the context of US domestic bond markets (a comparison which gains validity as a truly international bond market becomes a more relevant paradigm), it is apparent that, although the rate of growth of issuance of the euro sector of the US dollar market has outstripped the rate of growth of issuance in the domestic sector during the last ten years, the euro sector remains quite small relative to the domestic sector (Table F). The greater size of the domestic sector partly reflects government borrowing, although the domestic market is also a much larger source of finance than the euromarkets for corporate borrowers: for instance, corporate borrowing in the eurosector of the US dollar bond market is only just over a quarter of the size of corporate borrowing in the domestic sector.

Table F
US dollar sector—bond issuance
$ billions

	Total			of which: corporate		
	Domestic(a)	Foreign	Euro	Domestic	Foreign	Euro
1980	267.8	1.8	14.5	42.2	0.5	4.4
1981	284.0	6.7	22.7	40.1	1.7	9.4
1982	392.9	5.9	40.9	53.0	0.3	13.8
1983	434.8	5.2	35.8	45.4	0.2	7.4
1984	557.8	1.8	67.3	66.8	0.1	16.3
1985	754.2	3.5	95.1	111.5	—	26.4
1986	819.8	6.1	115.3	189.7	0.5	35.0
1987	744.7	4.7	57.9	152.8	0.1	33.4
1988	736.2	9.8	73.4	169.5	1.7	39.8
1989	761.2	8.1	121.3	158.2	1.5	72.4
1990	831.7	12.8	74.0	151.0	3.8	29.0

Source: OECD *Financial Statistics Monthly* for domestic bond market data, and Bank of England for foreign and eurobond market data.

(a)   From 1987, data exclude issues by central government agencies. (Government agencies accounted for approximately 6% of total domestic issuance, and 9% of public sector bond issuance in 1986, the last year for which these data are available.)

.   .   .

a.   DEFINITION OF A EUROBOND

What exactly is a Eurobond?   The following piece expands on the Bank of England definition.

F. GRAAF, EUROMARKET FINANCE: ISSUES OF EUROMARKET SECURITIES AND SYNDICATED EUROCURRENCY LOANS
13-14 (1991) (Euromarket Finance).

Eurobonds, whether they be dollar instruments or denominated in another currency, can be defined as follows. They are:

(a) normally unsecured debt instruments, whereby the issuer promises to pay the amount specified on the bond at a stated future date (the *"maturity date"*) and to pay an annual rate of interest until such date to the holder of the bond; and

The trend towards asset-backed issues in the Euromarket will be discussed later (see Chapter 2 § (k)(5)); these, however, do not detract from the general rule that Eurobonds are mostly unsecured.

(b) issued by large, generally multinational corporations, sovereign states, public sector entities and supra-national institutions in order to raise large scale debt finance for a medium to long period of time; and

(c) issued simultaneously in a number of countries across the globe (other than the country in whose currency they are denominated) to a wide range of investors through a multinational syndicate of underwriting securities firms and banks and in a manner which does not subject the bonds, the issuer or the syndicate to national constraints in any of the countries; and

The crucial characteristic of Eurobonds is that they *are not issued on or into a single market* but are marketed internationally and that they are generally offered and placed in a non-public, semi-private fashion so as to avoid the securities legislation on public offerings in the various countries into which distribution takes place. These laws would otherwise impose prospectus, licence, registration or listing requirements incompatible with the nature and purpose of a Eurobond issue.   Broadly speaking, syndicate members will generally make use of either a 'private placement' exemption or a 'professional-investors-only' exemption under local securities laws.

As it would be extremely difficult for the managers or the issuer to provide comprehensive guidance on compliance with all local laws which could possibly be relevant in distributing Eurobonds, it will generally be stated in the relevant contracts that each syndicate member is responsible for making certain that its distribution efforts are legal in the various jurisdictions in which it approaches investors and the issuer will normally disclaim any responsibility with respect to the qualification of the securities in any specific jurisdictions.

Obviously, for certain currencies investor demand tends to be strongest in their home country so that such issues are for a substantial part placed with end-investors from that country.

In the Eurobond market the buyers of bonds in the first instance are exclusively financial institutions. Eurobonds are never offered directly to the public, but are offered mostly to banks and other financial institutions for placing with central banks, insurance companies, investment funds, pension funds or multinational corporations.

(d) denominated, therefore, in a currency that is not necessarily native to the borrower, the investors or the syndicate members through whom the securities are sold; and

Investors in Eurobonds, therefore, take both credit and foreign exchange risks. In addition, a number of foreign jurisdictions are involved whose rules could all impact on the value of the investment while the paying agents, to whom the investors must turn for their funds, are often located in foreign jurisdictions. This and the absence of credit ratings for Eurobonds helps to explain why the market is used almost exclusively by '*prime*' issuers, i.e. top-quality international corporations and banks, international organisations and sovereign states (see § (f) below), and why the investors require the securities to be easily traded, i.e. payable to bearer.

(e) generally bearer instruments to allow negotiability (high liquidity and, therefore, easy cash convertibility) and anonymity of the ultimate investors; and

(f) either issued with the benefit of a stock exchange listing, normally in London or Luxembourg, and therefore a 'public offering' according to the laws of the country of the exchange (although still placed with investors in the various countries on an essentially private basis) or placed with such investors without a listing.

The general method of distribution discussed under (c) above should be distinguished from those Eurobond issues that are taken up entirely by a small number of institutional investors (or even by a single investor) already identified before the managers sign the subscription agreement with the issuer, and which will buy the securities directly from the managers (no syndicate being required) and hold such securities generally until their maturity. These so-called '*private-private*' placements of Eurobonds are not publicly announced and are not normally listed on a stock exchange (at least initially). This book will not deal with such private placements of Eurobonds which are, in effect, syndicated (or single lender) loans that are, for one reason or another, documented as an issue of securities.

b.   EXPLANATIONS FOR GROWTH

As the Bank of England notes, in the early 1960s the U.S. imposed an interest equalization tax (initially 15%) on interest paid by foreign debt issuers to investors in the United States. The tax was intended to decrease U.S. investment in these securities because such transactions were putting downward pressure on the dollar. Since there were fixed exchange rates at this time, the U.S. had to offset market pressure by buying dollars with its reserves. Investments in foreign bonds denominated in dollars resulted in the issuer exchanging the dollar proceeds for local currency. The tax discouraged the investments because it increased the cost of borrowing in the U.S. market by 1%, since the issuer had to compensate investors for the tax.

So foreigners issued their dollar denominated bonds to U.S. and other investors outside the United States. Thus originally, the eurodollar bond replaced yankee bonds, bonds issued by foreigners to U.S. investors in the United States.

The Eurobond market prospered even after the tax was abolished in 1974. Total Eurobonds issued in 1993-1995 were:

Total Eurobonds Issued ($ billions)

1993	394.6
1994	368.4
1995	447.4

Sources: OECD/DAF.

The 1993 $400 billion in Eurobonds compares with $481 billion in international bonds, which counts foreign as well as Eurobonds. To recall, foreign bonds are issues in domestic markets by foreign issuers, for example a Japanese issuer sells dollar bonds in the United States. Given the difficulties in distinguishing between Eurobonds and international bonds, statistics after 1995 generally refer only to international bonds.

An important factor in the dramatic growth in 1993 was the continued expansion of Eurobond issues by emerging countries, as detailed below.

2. EMERGING MARKET ISSUES

FINANCIAL MARKET DEVELOPMENTS
33 Bank of England Quarterly Bulletin 469, 471 (1993).

Non-OECD borrowing in the international bond markets

Non-OECD borrowers regained access to the international bond markets in 1989. Since then they have made increasing use of these markets (see the chart)—in the third quarter of 1993, $10 billion was raised by non-OECD borrowers, more than double the amount raised in the same quarter of the previous year (see the table). This rise reflects the return of investor confidence in Latin America and the increasing attraction of investment in Asian economies. Eastern European borrowers have also begun to tap the international bond markets, although on a smaller scale (the Hungarian and Czech central banks have been the only issuers from the region so far).

An important factor behind the increase in non-OECD borrowing has been the low interest rate environment in the United States and Japan over the past few years. This has led investors to search for higher yields than are available on eurobonds from high-quality borrowers from the OECD area. Latin American borrowers, as well as those from other emerging regions, particularly Asia, have taken advantage of this.

Several factors have contributed to the steady increase in non-OECD borrowing in recent years, in particular the confidence induced in foreign investors by the adoption of stability- oriented policies and the completion of debt restructurings. Latin American issues have not been confined to bonds, and issuers have diversified their range of borrowing instruments and the markets from which they borrow. Mexican, Brazilian and Argentinian borrowers have, for instance, issued euromedium-term notes and eurocommercial paper. Mexico has also issued sovereign debt in the US foreign bond market, and some Mexican borrowers have issued US domestic commercial paper.

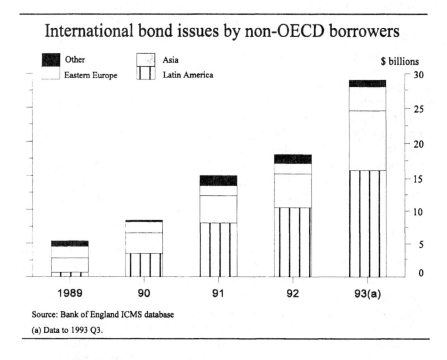

International bond issues by non-OECD borrowers

Other Asia $ billions

Eastern Europe Latin America

Source: Bank of England ICMS database

(a) Data to 1993 Q3.

Emerging market issues fell sharply after the Mexican peso crisis at the end of 1994. In the last quarter of 1994 they were $13.6 billion, but fell to $5.3 billion in the first quarter of 1995. By the fourth quarter of 1995 they had recovered, reaching $12.1 billion. Indeed, in November 1996, the Russian Federation issued $1 billion in Eurobonds, their first international bond issue since 1917.

3. EURO-DEUTSCHMARK ISSUES

Another factor in the growth of the market, was the importance of euro-deutschmark (euro-DM) issues. In 1993, these issues accounted for 13 percent of new issues, surpassing both yen and sterling.

K. MUEHRING, KING OF THE EUROPEAN BOND MARKETS
Institutional Investor, Feb. 1993, at 25.

The Euro-Dm market has always been considered a relative backwater in the Euromarket—a great irony considering the importance of the deutschmark as an international currency. For one thing, borrowers were never able to issue in size. The average bond issue was barely Dm262 million by the fourth quarter of 1991. Also, the market was illiquid and underwriting fees were high (as they still are in traditionally syndicated issues). The typical commission for a ten-year issue was an astounding 3 percent, versus 1.875 percent in the Eurodollar market for traditional syndications.

The reasons for these conditions lay mainly in the buy-and-hold habits of the retail investors who dominated the market. According to estimates by Moody's Investors Service, at the end of 1991, retail investors still held more than half the outstanding Dm245 billion of Euro-Dm paper. Accounting for another 13 percent of the investor base were German domestic banks, who also tend to buy and hold. That left foreign institutional investors with less than a third of the outstanding paper. "From a purely Anglo-Saxon point of view," notes Gordon Anderson, senior vice president for trading at Commerzbank in Frankfurt, the market does not work well because there is a natural tendency towards illiquidity."

Three developments helped make the market deeper and more liquid. The first was a set of legal changes that the Bundesbank announced last July, with the goal of making Euro-DM issuance more flexible. The new rules permitted listing on foreign exchanges, issuance under foreign rather than German law and clearance of bonds through Cedel or Euroclear in addition to (or instead of) the *Kassenverein,* the German bond-clearing system. The Bundesbank also removed the minimum two-year maturity for foreign issues, which should boost the Euro-Dm medium-term and commercial paper markets.

By themselves, the legal changes would probably have given the market only a minor lift. But their introduction last August came a month after the collapse of the primary market for European currency units in the aftermath of the Danish vote against the Maastricht treaty. Issuers, particularly sovereign issuers, raised some funds in Eurodollars, but had to look elsewhere for large-scale funding requirements, especially if they needed longer maturities. And the only

European market open to them, given the relatively small size of the other markets, was in deutschmarks.

Finally, the withdrawal of the lira and the pound from the ERM in September and the turmoil that followed brought institutional investors running to the deutschmark. The realignment pressures within the ERM overshadowed the economic difficulties Germany was having with reunification and any doubts over the Bundesbank's success in quelling domestic inflation. The first stop for foreign investors in Germany tends to be the Dm500 billion, ultraliquid market for German government paper, especially five-year *Bundesobligationen (Bobls)* and ten-year government Bunds. Foreign purchases in the German bond market, for instance, tripled from August to September to Dm34 billion-a level that was about six times higher than in September 1991.

But with the foreign inflows depressing government yields, the spread to Euro-Dm paper widened, causing institutional funds to overflow into the Euro-sector. By then larger Euro-Dm issues were coming to market, making the sector "an attractive alternative to the Bund market, with high credit quality, liquidity and a little yield pickup to boot," says Thierry Porté, Morgan Stanley's managing director for capital markets in London. Adding to the market's attractiveness to foreign institutional investors, says Porte, has been the growing use of the fixed-price reoffer as the syndication technique best suited to tailoring a new issue for institutional demand.

. . .

Look back at Table 3 in Chapter 1 which shows the international bond activity for 1994-2000. New issues rose from $385.7 billion in 1994 to about $1.8 trillion in 2000, and at year-end 2000 there were about $6 trillion in outstanding international bonds. Table A below, 37 Bank of England Quarterly Bulletin 33 (1997), gives the currency composition of international bond issues from 1994-1997.

The introduction of the euro in 1999 had a significant effect on the currency denomination mix. Euro denominated issues accounted for $603 billion or 44.6% of all new international bond issues, as compared with $574 billion in US dollar denominated bonds, 42.5% of new international bonds. V. Boland, *Euro bonds overtake issues in dollars,* Financial Times, January 10, 2000.

The international equity market (cross-border or cross-exchange issues) is growing significantly. Again looking at Table 3 in Chapter 1, we see that new equity issues increased from $82.6 billion in 1995 to $314 billion in 2000. New equity issues in 2000 were about 15% of combined bond and equity issues for the year, a slight increase from the 13% in 1996. Much of the new equity issue activity is due to privatization, see e.g. OECD, Financial Market Trends, Feb. 1999, at 49-77.

Table A
Currency composition of international bond issues
percent

Currency denomination	1994	1995	1996	1997
US dollar	34.9	39.2	46.2	45.2
Yen	18.4	18.4	13.4	11.4
Deutsche Mark	9.4	13.9	10.6	8.3
Sterling	7.0	4.3	6.8	10.2
French franc	6.8	2.7	5.4	4.5
Swiss franc	4.9	6.1	3.3	4.8
Italian lira	4.1	2.4	4.6	2.9
Ecu	1.8	1.8	0.6	2.2
Other	12.6	11.2	8.9	10.2
Total (U.S. billions)	**421.9**	**482.0**	**782.9**	**883.0**

Source: Bank of England Quarterly Bulletins

Notes and Questions

1. What accounts for the continued growth of the eurobond market in general? How can one explain the variations in the size of the DM sector? While international deutschmark issues slumped in 1994 to 9.4% of new international bond issues from 11.6% in 1993, they rose to about 14% in 1995, but by 1997 had fallen to 8.3%. How could Germany control the issuance of Euro-DM bonds? Why has it now liberalized its restrictions? How might this be connected to EMU?

New Yen-denominated issues grew from 12% in 1993 to about 18% in 1994 and 1995. One view about the source of Yen growth was the demand of Japanese retail investors for higher yields than are available in local currency investments where interest rates are quite low. Why might Euroyen rates be higher than domestic yen rates? In 1997 Euroyen issues had fallen to 11.4%. Why might this be? In 1995, there were major Euroyen bond issues by the governments of Italy and Brazil. Why would these governments issue yen denominated bonds?

The total size of the international bond market must be kept in perspective. As of September 1999 year-end stock of international debt securities of $45 billion was about 18.7% of total domestic securities. See Table 3, Chapter 1. The international segment has been growing. In 1995, international debt was only 12% of domestic debt. Bank for International Settlements, *International Banking and Financial Market Developments* (1996).

2. In the first Bank of England reading, Chart 3 above, eurodollar bond yields are lower than U.S. domestic bond yields, with the gap narrowing. Why is this? In December 1995, General Electric Capital

Corporation, the finance and securities subsidiary of General Electric Corporation, issued $250 million in international bonds at a yield of three basis points below the U.S. Treasury rate on a bond of the same maturity. Does this mean GE is a better credit risk than the United States? Do you think this would be affected by new Treasury or other eurodollar bond issues in December or the fact that there were more than $11 billion in planned redemptions of U.S. dollar denominated bonds in December, significantly more than the average $7 billion? See C. Middlemann, *Dollar Eurobonds Offer Cheaper Rates*, Financial Times, Dec. 1, 1995. Why have interest rates on Eurocurrency issues of European Union countries converged? See Chapter 7.

3.   As the Bank of England indicates, Eurobond market investors are very name conscious. As a general rule, only highly rated companies issue in the market. For example, one triple-A rated issuer with an excellent name, and that is close to our hearts, Harvard University, had a $100 million Eurobond issue in January 1996. Average seven year eurobond spreads over government bonds for triple-A rated borrowers are in the low 20s (basis points), rising to close to 50 basis points for single-A borrowers, and jumping to 450 basis points for borrowers with speculative grade ratings. *Investors Resume Search for Yield*, Financial Times, July 17, 1995. In 1998, given generally low interest rates in the world's most developed economies, investors have looked for higher yield in the euromarkets, with the result that some euro junk bonds (bonds with a sub-investment grade rating) have been issued. E. Luce and S. Davies, *World loan and bond market double act falls victim to crisis*, Financial Times, February 16, 1998.

4.   Trade associations, like the International Primary Market Association and the International Securities Market Association play an important role in the creation of standardized terms for Eurobond offerings. For example, they have proposed to change the method of calculating interest from assuming there are 360 days in a year, with 12 months of 30 days, to using 365 days and the actual days in any month to calculate interest. Financial Times, May 30, 1997.

5.   Will there be a Eurobond market for the currencies of countries taking part in EMU, e.g. will a euro Eurobond replace the Deutschmark and French Franc Eurobonds?

6.   The Asian financial crisis has led to some new developments in the pricing of Eurobonds. The problem was how to price the issuance of bonds in highly uncertain economic circumstances. One technique used in a $300 million bond offering in June 1997 by the state-owned Korean Development Bank is to offer early redemption rights if the issuer's credit is downgraded. It provides disaster insurance to investors and permits the Korean borrower to borrow at lower rates. E. Luce, *Goldman Sachs behind $300m S Korean bond*, Financial Times, June 17, 1997. Another

related technique was used by the government of Argentina in a $500 million offering in October 1997. Due to market uncertainty (the fear that the Asian crisis could spread to Argentina), Argentina was forced to pay 100 basis points more over the U.S. treasury rate than it would have paid absent the turmoil. However, the bond provided that the spread over the treasury rate would be adjusted at regular intervals during the life of the bond through an auction. E. Luce, *Argentina launches $500m 'adjusted spread' bond offering*, Financial Times, December 10, 1997.

4. ISSUING PROCEDURES

a. REGISTRATION

Eurobonds do not generally have to be registered when sold in European countries. Issuers can take advantage of exemptions in local law for bonds distributed to institutional buyers. As we have seen, banks are the initial buyers of eurobonds. But note, that if a euroyen bond were sold in the United States it would have to be registered unless it met the terms for a private placement exemption. The European markets generally have a more broadly defined exemption. Also, you may recall that "eurosecurities" are exempt from the EU's POP.

The fact that eurobonds are usually exempt from registration requirements does not mean that there are no disclosures made about the issuer. If the bonds are listed in London or Luxembourg, they are subject to the exchanges' disclosure requirements and the minimum standards of the Listings Directive. In addition, since many eurobonds are sold in London, their distribution will be subject to the disclosure requirements of the International Primary Market Association (IPMA), a London-based membership group for euro- issuers. Such disclosure requires a degree of due diligence—checking up on material facts—by the issuer and, to some extent, the lead manager. Issuers may be less concerned about due diligence in the euromarkets than in domestic markets because (a) they are generally better credits and (b) lead managers, in order to preserve their reputation with institutional investors, may be prepared to compensate investors. R. Foster, *Due Diligence: An Accident Waiting to Happen*, International Financial Law Review, Mar. 1996, at 23 (Due Diligence).

Eurobonds can be issued through so-called MTN (medium term note programs). These programs set up general documentation which permits multiple issues over time without new prospectuses. Despite the name, the actual maturities are the same as for Eurobonds. The original documentation costs of MTNs are greater than stand-alone Eurobonds, $131,500 compared to $100,000 (legal is $100,000 for MTNs). MTNs are growing in popularity. Outstanding MTN programs now represent 45% of outstanding Eurobond issues compared with 14% in 1991. *A Vision of the Future*, Euromoney, Mar. 1996, at 114. IPMA has been concerned with disclosure standards for MTNs. Although their documentation is minimal, liability might still attach in some jurisdictions for the failure to disclose material information. Due Diligence, *supra*.

What is the rationale for the general exemption from disclosure requirements? The idea is that this is an institutional market. There is, however, substantial argument as to whether the ultimate investors in these bonds are institutional or retail. Although securities are initially bought by banks, they may be quickly resold to retail investors. It is difficult to determine how much retail investment there is since the bonds are in bearer form. The Bank of England thinks this market has become largely institutional. On the other hand, some eurobond issues are apparently aimed directly at retail investors. On March 14, 1996 the Financial Times reported: "The eurobond market had an active session yesterday, but most of the new issues were short-dated, relatively small and targeted at European retail—currently the only investors willing to buy new bonds." C. Middelmann, *Issuers Tap Demand from European Retail Investors*, Financial Times, Mar. 14, 1996.

Why do issuers seek to avoid registration? Naturally, they seek to avoid the costs and potential liabilities. But perhaps most importantly bonds can be brought promptly to market based on market conditions. There is no need to wait for approval or clearance of a registration statement. Lack of registration may make it difficult for lower credit rated companies to sell eurobonds—institutional investors would want disclosure on no name companies. Eurodollar issuers have higher credit ratings than issuers in the U.S. domestic market, 47 percent of SP ratings in eurobonds are AAA, compared to 2 percent in U.S. bonds.

Can U.S. investors buy (or can issuers sell to them) eurobonds that have not been registered in the United States? This depends on the treatment of the issue under Regulation S. If there is high "substantial U.S. market interest," (SUSMI), which would certainly be the case if the bond issuer was a U.S. "reporting" company (had public issues in U.S. market), the issuer would have to comply with the Regulation S restrictions. Regulation S provides that in such case, U.S. investors cannot buy the bonds for 40 days after the initial distribution, the "seasoning" period. By this time the market has already incorporated relevant information about the issuer into the price of the bond. During this period, no bearer bonds can be issued because bearer bonds could be easily bought by U.S. investors. So, a temporary global note is used for the first 40 days, requiring investors to register—during this period investors can buy or sell interests in the note.

b.   UNDERWRITING

The following two pieces discuss the underwriting process for Eurobonds.

EUROMARKET FINANCE
at 53-89.

.   .   .

(B) Eurobond Issuing Procedures

Before discussing the legal aspects of Eurobond documentation it seems practical to describe the process of making a new issue of Eurobonds or FRNs. A new issue first moves through the primary market before being traded on the secondary market.

The IPMA Recommendations are presumed to be followed in the primary market (unless a departure is indicated in the invitation telex for a particular issue) and the AIBD's rules govern secondary market activities (including so-*called 'gray market' trading and primary settlement procedures both of which are discussed in detail below).*

The primary market starts with banks, securities houses and financial institutions competing for a new issue by a particular borrower, i.e. trying to obtain a lead management *'mandate'* or to become co-managers or underwriters. Building the contractual structure of participants together forming the *'syndicate',* which is responsible for finding investors for the issue is the second stage of the primary market and is known as the *'syndication process'* or simply *'syndication'.* The lead manager controls it. It ends when no further indications of interest in acting as an underwriter or selling group member can be made and the final *'allotments'* of securities to the syndicate members are determined and, where necessary, accepted, meaning that all securities have been subscribed for. The primary market ends with the *'primary settlement'* when the issue proceeds are made available by the syndicate to the issuer in exchange for the delivery of the bonds. The secondary market commences immediately thereafter.

Before moving to the main stages of the issuing process, the various structures of an issue syndicate, formed in the primary market, and the respective duties and responsibilities of its members will be reviewed. Thereafter, the stages of the issuing process will be highlighted for each type of issue syndicate.

Structure of the Issuing Syndicate

Until the early 1980s the conventional syndicate structure comprised three-tiers and the prevailing underwriting method used in this structure was *'negotiated'* or *'open priced'* underwriting.

To *'underwrite'* means to assume a contractual obligation to place a certain number of securities (this can be the entire issue or an agreed share of the issue) with investors, either as principal or as agent for the issuer, failing which one is bound to subscribe for any unsold bonds. An underwriter's success (or lack of it) in finding investors willing to purchase securities from it will thus determine its exposure vis-a-vis the issuer. The underwriting risk materialises at *'closing'* when *primary settlement* occurs and the issuer must receive the proceeds of the bonds (less certain agreed fees).   The issuer is assured by the management group's underwriting commitment that any lack of demand in the market will not result in a proportional reduction of the proceeds. In essence, the underwriting commitment shifts market risk from the issuer to the syndicate (save for force majeure situations).

In *'open priced'* underwriting the bond issue was launched on tentative terms (i.e. coupon and issue price) in order to test market demand and, based upon market response, final pricing terms were then agreed with the issuer.   Only then were legally binding underwriting commitments entered into.   In this method the issuer takes a risk that during the period in which the market is sounded out (the *'offering period'*), market rates move against the rate it would prefer to pay on its bonds.

During the early 1980s, the speed with which an issue was brought to the market had to increase due to rapid currency and interest rate fluctuations and, as a consequence, since that time a new method of underwriting known as the *'bought deal'* (or *'pre-priced deal'*) has been used in the overwhelming majority of new euromarket issues of bonds and FRNS. It involves a greatly simplified syndicate structure.

A further factor in the emergence of pre-priced deals is the fact that many issues are swap-driven, i.e. would not be brought to the market were it not for the opportunity, on the part of the issuer, to enter into a currency or an interest rate swap (or both).   As swaps require pre-established issue and coupon prices, the issuer must ensure that these are not modified. An open-priced issue would not accomplish this.

Under this technique one or more lead managers jointly and severally agree with the issuer before and regardless of syndication to firmly underwrite the entire issue at a fixed issue price and a specific coupon, so that the issuer has certainty as to its cost of funds. Only after the issuer has agreed these fundamental terms with the lead manager does the lead manager launch the issue and invite other managers to underwrite a portion of the issue at the terms already agreed. Pre-priced issues require realism on the part of the managers, as they and the borrower may be locked into a very bad deal if interest rates fall below the agreed rate after the announcement. If these rates rise above the agreed rate, there will not be sufficient demand and underwriters will be called upon to take the securities on their books (and suffer a loss if they are unable to sell the securities profitably later on in the secondary market). To mitigate these risks somewhat, the offering period is reduced to a few days and the timetable for pre-closing events is generally accelerated. In an extreme case the management group may terminate their commitments pursuant to the *'market out clause'* commonly contained in the subscription agreement with the issuer (see § (c)).

More recently the market has witnessed a gradual retreat from bought deals and a return to open priced underwriting as a result of several developments in relation to bought deals. Firstly, in an increasingly competitive primary market, lead managers have been bidding for mandates to issue Eurobonds and FRNS on unrealistic terms that investors were unable to accept, thereby forcing co-managers to mark down their re-sale prices to such an extent that Euromarket underwriting has become increasingly unprofitable. Secondly, a further erosion of managers' commissions occurred as a result of the fact that deliberately aggressive or mispriced new issues force the lead manager to influence the market price of the paper for the first few weeks through transactions that provide price support (a practice known as *'stabilisation'* which will be discussed in greater detail below). The lead manager's stabilisation losses are traditionally deductible from the co-managers' underwriting fee (and not against the management fee), so that in essence the lead managers shift the costs of bringing mispriced issues to the market onto their syndicate. In response to these developments a reform of new issue procedures and stricter rules on stabilisation have been called for. The latter has resulted in a change in IPMA's recommendations in April 1989. The former has led several of the principal lead managers in the market to introduce new underwriting procedures derived from the 'negotiated underwriting' technique. These new procedures, known as *'fixed price reoffering'*, allow the managers to test investors' appetite and obtain commitments before the final pricing of the issue is agreed with the issuer. Accordingly, using this technique, new issues should be priced more closely to the market so that stabilisation by the lead manager and price dumping by co-managers become rare. The syndicate structure used in a fixed price reofferings is a middle ground between classic 'negotiated underwriting' and the 'bought deal.'

Although the classic Euromarket syndicate is now mainly of historical interest, it is important for an understanding of both bought deals and fixed price reofferings. On the other hand, it is not certain at this stage whether the latter will displace bought deals. Consequently, the following discussion devotes attention to all three underwriting techniques in the order of their historical development.

. . .

Pre-priced underwriting

In a bought deal the syndicate structure is much simpler than in open priced issues. Normally, there will be no (sub-)underwriters or selling banks and the entire issue is syndicated among managers only, so that the only underwriters are the managers led by the lead manager. Consequently, the group of managers tends to be larger than in open priced underwriting. Bought deals have a short pre-launch period; immediately after the lead manager has agreed the major terms of the issue, the issue price and the fee structure with the issuer, it will announce the forthcoming issue on screen displays and commence syndication, i.e. approach co-managers informally to obtain indications as to their interest to join the syndicate. Obviously, this has priority for the lead manager: it needs to ensure that a large portion of its overall commitment to the issuer is taken over. This is then followed by invitation telexes which confirm the offering and its *fixed* terms and request the addressees whether and to what extent they would be willing to assume an underwriting commitment and to state their sales demand (i.e. the quantity of bonds or notes they actually require for sale to their customers) before a certain deadline. Within the same timeframe, underwriting acceptances are to be received from co-managers. The management group itself is responsible for placing the issue with investors although occasionally there might be a certain amount of bonds to be distributed by a selling group.

> At the same time, draft agreements (primarily the subscription agreement, the agreement among managers, the fiscal agency agreement (or trust deed)) are being prepared, discussed and distributed together with the preliminary offering circular in the event that the bonds are to be listed. Steps will be taken to agree the text of the preliminary offering circular with the stock exchange.

Simultaneously with or even prior to syndication, the lead manager will start *'pre-selling'* large portions of the issue itself on an *'if, as and when issued basis'* to institutional investors, banks and others in order to further reduce its overall exposure to the issuer. As the terms of the issue are fixed, there is no pricing or offering day in a bought deal. As soon as possible after receipt of underwriting acceptances and statements of selling interest the lead manager will therefore make the allotments to the managers and, where applicable, the selling group members by despatching allotment telexes.

> IPMA Recommendations require that in pre-priced issues that are syndicated among managers only, final allotments must be made within one business day from and including the day of the first invitation (i.e. the launch day) or as soon as practicable after the management group is formed, if earlier. Where a statutory, stock exchange or conduct of business rule prohibits allotments before a prospectus is issued, a deviation from this rule is generally agreed in advance. In these circumstances the

lead manager will only give 'indications of proposed allotments' while 'formal allotment' is delayed until the time allowed under the relevant provisions.

On the signing day the subscription agreement and the agreement among managers, which should previously have been sent to and approved by the co-managers, are executed and the final offering circular is bulk printed and distributed to the managers and, where applicable, the selling group members and the stock exchange.

The procedure for primary settlement on the closing day is identical to that for open-priced bond issues. The period from the launch date to the closing is generally fixed in advance in a bought deal (often to coincide with the timing of the related swap agreement(s)). It generally takes between one to four weeks. If there should be insufficient investor demand, the shortfall is taken by the management group in proportion to the respective underwriting commitments agreed upon in the agreement among managers.

The fee structure in pre-priced issues is the same as in open priced issues and, similar to open priced issues, there is no restriction on the managers as to the price at which they should offer the issue (or at least that part of it allotted to them) to the market. Each manager may quote a different price and each is free to give up all or part of its fees by quoting discounts below the issue price. If an issue has been priced unrealistically by the lead manager and the issuer, the likelihood of such *price dumping* by the syndicate is quite high. It is this practice which fixed price reofferings intend to eliminate.

Fixed price reofferings

So far, fixed price reofferings have used a small syndicate of co-managers assisted occasionally by a selling group. This inevitably means that their underwriting commitments are much larger than in a bought deal where the group of managers is larger. The essence of this new syndication method, however, is that all managers agree with each other and the issuer to offer the bonds or notes only at (or, alternatively, at or above) the agreed issue price during the primary market until such time as the lead manager decides to release the syndicate from this obligation (referred to as *'breaking the syndicate'*). In return the managers are allowed to take part in agreeing the issue price with the issuer which takes place only after they have tested demand and perhaps pre-sold parts of the issue to their customers on tentative terms. Furthermore, the lead manager undertakes to stabilize the issue only in unusual circumstances and not to start its own pre-sales until some time after sending out invitation telexes. As the bonds are priced at a level where they should sell and because of the managers' pre-marketing activities, very swift placement by the syndicate in the primary market is possible so that syndicate price-discipline can normally be lifted within 24 hours from the allotments.

Because the group of managers is small, it will be easier for the lead manager to enforce this price-discipline. Those managers that do not have genuine capacity to place correctly priced paper with investors and consequently must sell below the agreed issue price to professional traders rather than investors will be identifiable. Due to a different fee structure there is no incentive for managers to ask for an allotment of bonds that is larger than they can actually place with their customers. The management and underwriting fees will be a uniform percentage (in total anywhere between 0.25% and 0.4%), the lead manager does not take a praecipium before paying out the management fee and a selling concession of 0.125% is granted. Because the syndicate is not allowed to give up its fees in the form of a discount to the issue price when offering the issue to their customers and because the lead manager rarely conducts stabilisation, underwriting fees are not lost or uncertain.

A further interesting aspect of this new type of underwriting is that the period from launch to closing is shortened substantially compared to the other syndication methods; parties will normally aim for the closing day to occur approximately 7 days from launch. The reason for this is to limit the period in which *'grey market'* is active and to start secondary market trading as soon as possible. To facilitate this sharp timing standardized documentation is necessary.

The issuer's risks in this syndication technique are the same as in classic negotiated underwriting, i.e. it assumes a certain market risk and in most cases it will not be able to launch a bond issue for the sake of an attractive swap opportunity.

K. MUEHRING, THE EUROBOND MARKET AT 30
Institutional Investor, May 1993, at 57, 60-64.

Increasingly, underwriters won bought-deal mandates by overpricing new issues (which a bull market enabled them to do) and putting together largely meaningless syndicate groups whose members, ever keen for prestige and league-table position, would accept loss-making co-management positions in hopes of establishing client relationships—which rarely materialized.

"It was a way of transferring wealth from the weak to the strong," jokes Tikuma Shibata, now head of investment banking at Nomura International. Co-managers eventually tired of the losses, and learned to routinely sell their allotted bonds via brokers back to the lead manager. Lead managers, in turn, often withdrew the support bid during the offering period to allow the bonds to falter, or refused to allot the bonds to co-managers, forcing them to pay hefty premiums if bonds had been shorted. The resulting frenzy of syndicate shorting and squeezing and secondary ramping finally drove scores of fund managers out of the new-issue market altogether. "Investors simply got sick of it all," recalls Andrew Pisker, Lehman Brothers International's head of syndicate.

Sanity in syndicate

Things had to change, and they did. Tightly priced bought deals mandated through competitive bidding have given way to more negotiated mandates at prices that have attracted institutional investors back to the primary market. There is also a growing number of deals with joint-book numbers requiring a higher degree of cooperation among underwriters, albeit with the business going to a smaller bracket of firms. There is far more dialogue among syndicate members and investors on pricing, and the houses take down more realistic allotments and make firmer commitments to trading an issue in secondary. "The will to talk and to share the obligations is there much more than ever before," says UBS's Harwood. Even Goldman, Sachs & Co., considered the most aggressive of the underwriters, has now jointly run books with such rivals as Warburg, Lehman, CSFB and Banque Paribas. Among Goldman's joint-book deals: a landmark $500 million 30-year issue, done last March for the African Development Bank with Lehman.

.   .   .

The underlying trend here is a change in the nature of the market's liquidity. The Eurobond market's traditional liquidity—the result of multiple-market makers who quote both bids and offers—is giving way to the customer-driven, bid-side liquidity of the U.S. corporate bond market. This means that bond houses can better control their inventory and concentrate on relative-value and credit-arbitrage research for clients. "There has been a sea change in the nature of the liquidity," confirms William Watt, who heads international fixed income at Kidder Peabody. "What the investor needs to see is a reasonable, continuous bid in the paper, and the bid-side liquidity is as high as I have ever seen it."

This new cooperative spirit also has a certain balance-of-terror aspect to it. The sheer size of the deals and their attendant risks have made underwriters want to team up only with those they know well or can control reliably. Supporting an issue in the secondary market is crucial and difficult; best to put the paper in a few reliable hands, where it can be watched closely. "I screen you, and you screen me," is how Nomura's Shibata puts it. This kind of cooperation doesn't extend much beyond the narrowing universe of reciprocity-minded firms that comprise the emergent Euro-bulge bracket.

A semblance of order

Yet there is reason to believe that the cycle may be broken this time around. The introduction of the fixed-price reoffer—the standard Wall Street syndicate management method—by Morgan Stanley for a $500 million issue for New Zealand in mid-1989 is usually cited as the watershed. Since then almost all Eurobonds in any currency—save the most retail-driven currencies, such as the Australian dollar—are now launched as fixed-price reoffers. "There is no question that there is a semblance of order to which you have to credit the fixed-price reoffer," says Salomon's Tye.

The fixed-price reoffer—in which the bonds are reoffered, or sold, to any bank or institution outside the syndicate at a single, firm price—imposed a new discipline in several ways. It eliminated the advantage to the lead manager of pocketing the ⅛ praecipium, for instance, as well as the lead manager's nasty habit of forcing other syndicate members to pay whatever the lead decided were the stabilization costs in maintaining a support bid. Investors also took to the single price of the bonds reoffered because it removed doubt over the likely value of the bonds when they were seasoned. "Before, there was an element of uncertainty about it because you would never know how much they actually sold and how much was on their books," recalls Gordon Johns, managing director of Kemper Investment Management's $1.5 billion portfolio in London.

But the fixed-price reoffer is in fact less a cause than an effect. What lies behind its acceptance has been the preference—some would say obsession—on the part of institutional investors for valuing Eurobonds (in nearly every currency sector) in terms of the spread between them and the relevant benchmark government bonds. Retail investors were interested in the issuer's name and a bond's absolute coupon level. Institutions, by contrast, are concerned with relative performance. Institutions move in and out of currencies or sectors in search of the highest return, always with the domestic government bond markets as the investment touchstone. This style of portfolio management, together with the related growth of the swaps market and the widespread use of futures markets for hedging purposes, has produced a fundamental shift in the way Eurobonds are valued.

Eurobonds, for the most part, have evolved into a complementary asset in the institutional view. "It is governments [first, and then] everything else," remarks Kemper's Johns. "The major return is in getting the currency and market right first. Buying Eurobonds [for their relative value to governments] marginally adds to income, but it certainly comes with illiquidity and credit risk as well."

New benchmark

The signs are unmistakable. The Eurobond market is moving into closer alignment with domestic capital markets—especially the mammoth U.S. bond market. These days nearly all bonds are quoted in terms of their spread above governments, and one often has to check the *International Financing Review* for the coupon level. And J.P. Morgan's Gray is quite clear on who's responsible for this fundamental shift: "The really big changes in thinking have come from the investors and issuers; the latter in being much more attuned to the performance in secondary, and the former in simply being much more institutionalized, and all that goes with it."

For the bond houses it is a new mind-set. They must make realistic bids for mandates, and the lead manager must enforce syndicate discipline. "You have to support your deals ruthlessly, because otherwise the borrower will lose confidence in you," says Goldman Sachs' Sherwood. Deals are no longer judged in terms of the price on issue day but rather according to the bonds' ongoing performance—until their price rises so high that their yield crosses that of the underlying governments, indicating its passage into retail hands or asset swaps, and illiquidity.

Notes and Questions

1. In a "bought deal" the underwriter buys bonds (or equities) from the issuer at a fixed price, meaning with a fixed coupon and with an agreed amount of proceeds going to the issuer. Standard documentation is set by a dealers association (ISMA). Suppose the underwriter agrees to give the issuer $10 million in proceeds at a coupon rate of 8.25 percent. Further assume that each bond is $100 (there are 100,000 bonds). How does the underwriter make money? How might the underwriter lose money?

2. Will the underwriter seek to have a higher or lower coupon rate than the market demands? How can the issuer control the underwriter setting the premium too high? An example of an equity bought deal is the £500 million sale of the U.K. government's 1.8% stake in British Petroleum, which is a very widely held stock. A competitive auction was held on Monday, December 4, 1995 which was won by SBC Warburg. By Tuesday afternoon, the shares had been placed with investors. A. Sharpe *Speed of BP Sell-off Sparks Debate on Marketing Routes*, Financial Times, Dec. 11, 1995.

3. Negotiated or "bookbuilding" deals, which originated in the United States, have now become the standard practice in the Euromarket, at least for equities, id. In these deals, the issuer retains an underwriter, who structures the terms of offering. The price of the issue is set after the prospectus is circulated to an underwriting group without a price and preliminary indications of interest are obtained; then the issue is priced. During this period, the registration can become effective, i.e. cleared by the SEC—which might take up to three weeks.

The underwriter fixes a price, usually in terms of a discount from par, to make a spread on the transaction that compensates for the service, e.g. the issuer gets 99 with 8.25 bond that the underwriter knows it can sell at par. The service is structuring the deal, a corporate finance function, as well as delivering the agreed proceeds to the issuer.

An example of a bookbuilding equity deal is the sale by SBC Warburg of Unigate's 29% stake in Nutricia, the Dutch baby food company that was not widely known or held outside Holland. *Id.*

How would you compare the virtues of bought and negotiated deals? Is one method more appropriate for bonds as compared with equities? What kind of deals would underwriters prefer?

4. Shelf registration was introduced in the United States in 1982. You may want to review the idea, as set forth in Chapter 2. Why did shelf registration make bought deals possible for the first time in the U.S. market?

5. How does a fixed-price reoffer system of distribution work, as compared with the type of pricing that preceded its adoption? Which system would bond buyers prefer? Which system would syndicate members prefer?

Under the fixed-price reoffer system, once the lead manager is satisfied that most of the bonds have been placed with end investors the bond issue is allowed to find a free market price. Borrowers, however, expect the lead manager to support the bond price at the fixed-price reoffer level; however other participants in the deal do not feel obliged to do so. S. Webb, *Bond-dumping Rears it Head*, Financial Times, Apr. 11, 1994. Indeed, members of syndicates who cannot sell their bonds sometimes sell them back anonymously to the lead manager via a broker, contrary to the syndicate rules, and still pocket their underwriting fees. A. Sharpe, *Eurobond Market Shows Signs of Wear and Tear*, Financial Times, Apr. 26, 1995. One suggested solution to this problem is to allocate bonds from a new issue only to houses that have actual demand or having the lead manager set up a selling group of non-underwriters which only earn a fee on the bonds they sell. *Id.*

In 1994, there was some evidence that banks were not fully living up to their fixed-price reoffer obligations. In a number of issues banks were left with an inventory of bonds they could not sell at the fixed-price. As a result, some banks appeared to offer clients bonds at a discount during the fixed-price period. One way around this problem would be for the lead managers to set more realistic prices; however intense competition among prospective lead managers has made this difficult. All-in fees for raising funds through eurobonds have shrunk from 2.5% of the money raised twenty years ago to .25% today. *Warburg Exit Highlights Pressure on Margin*, Financial Times, Jan. 16, 1995.

6. The trading of bonds is very different than equities. Bonds are mostly sold over-the counter, not on exchanges. Traders quote their own prices; there is no equivalent of the transparent prices quoted by stock exchanges. There are various plans to make the trading process more efficient, e.g. replacing phone-based trading with electronic trading, but it may be difficult to have them traded on exchanges. There would be less investor interest since many bonds are held to maturity, and thus less liquid, and their prices are much less volatile than stock prices. *E-bonds, licensed to kill,* The Economist, January 15, 2000.

c. TAXATION

T. PRIME, INTERNATIONAL BONDS
AND CERTIFICATES OF DEPOSIT
45-54 (1991).

The nature of withholding taxes

The incidence of withholding taxes or, as they are more familiar to English eyes, taxes levied at source on the payer of interest, have a very significant impact upon the structure of international bond financing. The idea behind a withholding tax is quite simple, and dictates that the payer of interest should deduct from the interest payment the tax at the appropriate rate attributable to the payment, and forward this to the relevant revenue authorities. Such taxes are well accepted revenue devices facilitating the collection of tax, and, indeed, are commonly used even where borrower and lender are resident in the same jurisdiction. They become of even more crucial importance in international transactions, since, once the interest has departed from the jurisdiction of the borrower, the revenue authorities of that jurisdiction would be left with no effective means of collection in the absence of the use of the device. It is a feature of the Eurobond market that interest on the coupon should be paid free of tax, so that the set interest rate is actually received by the bondholder. Given this expectation of the bondholder, an issue will not be generally acceptable to the market unless the bondholder's position is secured in this respect.

Bond terms

The bonds themselves usually make explicit provision in their terms to cover the difficulties of the tax situation. The terms provide that payment of principal and interest will be made without deduction on account of any present, or future, taxes or duties, levied by the jurisdiction of the issuer. If, however, the matter was simply left there the issuer would be left in an unsatisfactory position, because he would be left to pay the commercial rate of interest and the tax upon it at a grossed up amount. His borrowing would, therefore, be crippling to him.

Arrangements on issue

Accordingly, as a matter of practice, international bonds are not issued by issuers subject to a withholding tax in their own jurisdiction at the time the issue is made. The sophistication of the techniques used in the international financial market is such that this problem can be overcome by companies incorporated in a jurisdiction which imposes a withholding tax. The means employed is the use of one of the many countries in the world, operating a tax system which looks kindly upon the tax implications of commercial transactions (and often the acquisition of wealth by individuals as well), commonly referred to as 'tax havens'. In particular, what is needed is a country which allows payment of interest to be made free of withholding tax, such as the Netherlands Antilles and the Cayman Islands.

The means employed is for the corporation wishing to undertake the loan to form a subsidiary in the tax haven, and for the issue to be made by the foreign subsidiary, which then receives the results of the issue, and lends them on to the parent company. The loan made by the subsidiary to the parent company is interest bearing, and the interest is at a rate which allows the subsidiary to finance the interest on the coupons of the bonds. In this way the parent corporation receives the required funds, and is able to undertake the issue on normal commercial terms.

Choice of tax haven

The choice of a satisfactory tax haven depends upon two separate sets of considerations. The first of these relate to the tax haven itself. To be satisfactory as a tax haven for the location of the subsidiary in an international bond issue, the laws of the jurisdiction must be such as to allow the subsidiary to make payments of interest to the bondholders without the deduction from the agreed sum of any withholding tax. Secondly, the tax haven must either charge no local stamp or documentary taxes, or, if any are levied, they must be at such an insignificant level as not to give rise to any major cost to the issuer. Thirdly, the jurisdiction chosen must not seek to impose any capital, or inheritance, taxes upon bondholders merely because the issue was made within that jurisdiction. Fourthly, the chosen jurisdiction must be free of any local exchange control regulations, which would either prohibit or make difficult the payment of interest to bondholders, or the ultimate repayment of their capital to them, or the repatriation of the proceeds of the issue to the jurisdiction of the parent company. Fifthly, since the subsidiary is incorporated merely to raise the loan, there must be no requirements of the local corporate law that a significant proportion of share capital be subscribed in relation to the borrowing being undertaken, for the parent would find this an unacceptable burden since its interest in the subsidiary is purely for the raising of capital and not for trading purposes. Sixthly, the cost of incorporation and administration of the subsidiary under local corporate law must be inexpensive. Finally, the political complexion of the local jurisdiction must be considered, for it is important that the benign fiscal and commercial environment should continue and not be brought to an abrupt end by political developments, causing a new administration with radically opposed policies to come into power.

The second set of considerations arise from the jurisdiction of the parent company, and the relations between that jurisdiction and the tax haven itself. In particular, not only is it important that the subsidiary be able to make payments of interest without deduction of tax, but the parent must be entitled to make payments free of tax to the subsidiary without the imposition of a withholding tax, and also, in due course, be able to repatriate the funds to the subsidiary to redeem the bonds without falling foul of tax or exchange control regulations. Secondly, the subsidiary having no significant assets of its own, the issue will be made palatable to the market by the parent company guaranteeing its subsidiary's issue, thereby substituting its own credit-worthiness for that of the subsidiary.[1] If, therefore, the parent is called upon to make payment under the guarantee, it is important that these too can be made free of any tax or exchange control regulations. Finally, since in the hands of the parent the interest paid on its bonds is an operational expense for its trading purposes, it is vital that the interest should be deductible in the computation of the parent's tax liability for its trading operations in its own jurisdiction.

In evaluating the position of the parent company with regard to both the allowance of interest in the calculation of its tax liability and the impact of exchange control regulations, the law of its own jurisdiction must be considered at the time that the issue is made. If the laws of that jurisdiction prove to have insurmountable obstacles, it will not be possible to undertake an issue by the parent corporation beneficially. With regard to the impact of withholding taxes, the matter to be investigated is whether the country in which the subsidiary is to be incorporated has a sufficiently favourable double taxation treaty with the jurisdiction of the parent.

Stamp duties and other documentary taxes levied in many jurisdictions are another area of taxation which may give rise to difficulty to an issuer by increasing the cost of the issue. In international finance they can take the form of taxes imposed upon the securities which are issued, and which may be calculated by reference to a small percentage of their face value. Equally, some jurisdictions levy a straight issue tax on the value of bonds issued, or, in the case

---

[1] He would pay in all the notional interest which would, less the tax at the appropriate rate, give the actual interest agreed—a significantly higher figure than the appropriate rate of tax on the net agreed figure.

CHAPTER 12   EUROBONDS AND GLOBAL SECURITIES

of convertible bonds, on the share capital into which the bonds may be converted. It is necessary to investigate the tax position in the jurisdiction of the issuer with regard to these matters, which can significantly increase the cost of the issue to the issuer.

. . .

U.S. CORPORATIONS IN THE EUROBOND MARKET

The U.S. also operates a withholding tax. This was introduced in 1936 at a rate of 10 per cent. Slight modifications were made in the following two years, and the modified version of the tax became part of the Internal Revenue Code of 1939 at general rates of 10 per cent for individuals and 15 per cent for corporations. Subsequently, by degrees, the rates were raised to 30 per cent where they remain to this day.

Inevitably therefore, when the international bond market developed and U.S. corporations wished to participate, this tax represented a problem to be overcome. The finance subsidiary was pressed into use, but the form depended on whether or not the parent corporation's activities were almost exclusively foreign or largely domestic. If the U.S. parent corporation's activities were almost exclusively foreign, and the money raised was to be invested in foreign affiliates, the parent corporation could use a domestic international finance subsidiary (IFS). The intermediary is usually referred to as an 'eight-twenty company.' The domestic IFS would be wholly owned by the U.S. parent, issuing securities guaranteed by the parent, and lent the proceeds to the foreign affiliates. The affiliates would necessarily pay interest on the money borrowed to the affiliate and this would represent the whole, or virtually the whole, of the income of the domestic I.F.S. Since the operations of the foreign affiliates were largely, or even exclusively, overseas, the interest payments paid to the I.F.S. would be largely non-U.S. source income in its hands. Under the terms of the Internal Revenue Code a U.S. company (which includes a domestic I.F.S.), which derives less than 20 per cent of its gross income from U.S. sources, is not required to withhold tax on interest paid to foreigners.

This was an effective means of dealing with the problem of withholding tax where the parent company's interests were largely overseas, and the bond issue was made to capitalise this. Where however this was not the case, or if it was likely that its operations would not continue to be so heavily based overseas, other means had to be considered. In such circumstances the natural solution was the overseas I.F.S. Naturally, such an I.F.S. would need to be situated within a jurisdiction offering the advantages already considered, and, while a number of satisfactory locations were available, it was the Netherlands Antilles which came to be the most used.

The use of the Netherlands Antilles for this purpose depended on the terms of the tax treaty between itself and the U.S., and the local law of the Netherlands Antilles. Under local law non–residents are free of withholding tax on their income receipts, and also free of any other taxes which would adversely affect the position. Under Article VIII of the treaty, interest receipt of the Netherlands Antilles subsidiary from the U.S. are in general not subject to U.S. withholding tax. Effectively, the only real cost in respect of the borrowing were comparatively minor administrative and legal costs.

However, since 1980 the U.S. has applied deeper thought to the position of the U.S. corporation in relation to the Eurobond market. On the one hand, to have a tax system which drives its own corporations to the necessity of complex overseas arrangements to raise the capital they need to develop and expand their overseas activities, was hardly beneficial to U.S. economic (and probably political) interests. On the other hand, there was a concern that holders of bearer securities could draw income entirely anonymously from their investments, and not declare it as part of their income on their tax returns. This latter consideration was of far wider implication than the Eurobond market, since so many different forms of investment can be held in bearer form with the consequent anonymity which this brings. Having thus analysed the real issues with which it wished to deal, the U.S. passed legislation accordingly. The effect of the legislation is that U.S. issuers may now issue direct into the market without the use of an I.F.S., and will not suffer fiscally as a result, provided strict conditions are met.

In order to issue bearer securities that will be free of withholding taxes U.S. issuers must now comply with three separate, but interrelated, sets of tax rules. These are contained in or based on three separate statutes, the Tax Equity and Fiscal Responsibility Act of 1982 (TEFRA), the Tax Reform Act 1984 (the TRA), and the Interest and Dividend Tax Compliance Act of 1983 (I.D.T.C.A.).

The fundamental purpose of TEFRA was to move issuers away from the use of bearer securities to those requiring registration by means of fiscal disincentives. It achieves this with the aid of temporary regulations introduced in August 1984 by worsening the tax position of parties on the issue of bearer securities, with a view to ensuring that they would not be sold to U.S. investors in the initial distribution of the securities. The particular fiscal disincentive applied is the imposition of an excise tax equal to 1 per cent of the face value of the securities issued multiplied by the number of years to maturity. However, since the U.S. authorities were primarily concerned with their foreign and domestic markets and not with the Eurobond market, in which they wished their corporations to be able to issue freely as desire and necessity arise, they were content to include an express 'Eurobond exception' applicable if three criteria are satisfied. First, interest must be payable on the bearer securities only outside the U.S. Secondly, the face of each security and detachable coupon must bear a legend setting out that any U.S. person holding such security or coupon will be subject to various limitations under the revenue laws of the U.S. Finally, the securities must be sold under 'arrangements reasonably designed' to ensure that the securities will not be sold or distributed to any U.S. person (other than qualified U.S. financial institutions such as banks, brokers and insurance companies).

IDTCA was introduced to build on the basis established by TEFRA. IDTCA imposed stronger information and reporting requirements than TEFRA to improve compliance with U.S. tax laws, particularly the taxation of interest and dividends. Issuers, paying agents, and brokers are all required to obtain and report the tax identification numbers of investors receiving payments of interest or dividends on, or the proceeds of sale of, securities. If this is not done a 20 per cent withholding tax must be withheld from the payments of interest, dividends, or sales proceeds.

The choice imposed by the form of the legislation is plainly unacceptable to the international bond market, which has always demanded payment of interest free of taxes, and also respect for and preservation of the traditional anonymity of the market. As a result of pressure from those who are involved in, or wish to use, the Euromarkets, temporary regulations have now been introduced to protect the needs of the market.* Issues made in compliance with the TEFRA Eurobond exception are free of the information and reporting requirements if all payments of interest and principal are made outside the U.S., and neither the issuer nor the paying agent has actual knowledge that the holder is a U.S. person. Further, information and reporting requirements do not apply to sales proceeds paid to investors by non-U.S. custodians and brokers that are not controlled by a U.S. person and derive most of their income from outside the U.S. Where, however, the custodian or broker is controlled by a U.S. person, or derives most of its income from the U.S., information must be reported, unless the institution has on its files evidence of the holder's non-U.S. status.

If the thrust of these reforms were to insist on less anonymity for investors and therefore greater fiscal rectitude, at some risk to the traditions of the international bond market until specific exemptions were made for it, the thrust of the Tax Reform Act was to try to assist the market by eliminating the need for a foreign I.F.S. This it achieved by repealing the 30 per cent withholding tax on 'portfolio interest' in the case of a debt-securities issued to non-resident alien individuals and foreign corporations after 18 July 1984. Three types of debt-securities produce income qualifying as portfolio interest, two of the exceptions relating to registered debt securities in particular circumstances and the third being 'obligations in bearer form issued in compliance with the

---

* These regulations are now found in §1.163-5 (1995), eds.

TEFRA Eurobond exception.' Coupled with the creation of this means for U.S. issuers to issue international bonds without the use of an IFS, the Inland Revenue Service took steps to clamp down on the use of the Netherlands Antilles finance subsidiary structure.

The overall effect of these provisions is, therefore, now to create a means whereby U.S. issuers can freely make use of the international bond market without the impositions of financial penalties. Indeed U.S. issues are now made direct without the use of an I.F.S.

Notes and Questions

1. Until 1984, the United States imposed a withholding tax on interest paid to foreigners. Assuming there was no way to avoid the tax, was this a good policy? How did U.S. companies, in fact, use the Eurobond market to issue debt to foreigners free of this tax? How could foreigners be sure that no tax would be imposed?

2. In June 1987, the Treasury announced that it would terminate the Netherlands Antilles tax treaty. Why was this a problem for bonds issued before 1984?

3. As the Prime article relates, U.S. withholding taxes are no longer a problem. What about the one percent excise tax on issuing bearer securities? Is this a problem?

4. Until late 1992, eurolira bonds issued by supranationals, like the World Bank, to Italian investors in the euromarket—outside Italy—were not subject to the normal Italian 38% withholding tax. Italian investors in these bonds were subject to an income tax on interest earned, but given massive tax cheating in Italy, these issues were effectively tax-exempt. Italy has now made new issues of these bonds sold to Italians subject to a reduced withholding tax of 12.5%.

Before imposition of the new withholding tax a high proportion of World Bank funds were raised through eurolira bond issues. Why? What did the World Bank do with all this lira?

5. The European Union agreed on June 20, 2000, after many acrimonious debates, to a framework for tax on the payment of income on savings in the long run. The idea was to tackle widespread tax evasion which is facilitated by the use of bearer bonds. At the time, 11 of the 15 member states of the EU did not tax interest on the savings of individuals based in other member states, some say to attract capital. The agreement adopted two tools to deal with this problem. A minimum tax on European savings could be imposed by paying agents (banks paying out interest for issuers) on most European bondholders at source in the form of a 20% withholding tax on cross-border payments to individuals within the EU. Alternatively, paying agents on bonds or other liabilities could provide information about the income to their own fiscal authorities, who would pass it on to the tax authorities of the state in which the beneficial owner

resided for tax purposes. The June 2000 agreement provided a timetable to resolve important issues, then decide whether to use both tools as a transition measure and by 2010 rely entirely on information exchange, the second tool. J. Kirwin, *EU States Agree to Long-Term Framework for Cross-Border Tax on Savings Income,* BNA Banking Report, June 26, 2000 at 1173 (Kirwin).

The problem for the EU was that the use of either tool could harm some member's financial market. A withholding tax might cause the center of activity for the Eurobond market to move from the U.K. to Switzerland or at least pose heavy administrative costs on issuers which may ultimately fall on investors. R. Baron, *Serious Damage: The Impact of the Withholding Tax on the City of London* (Centre for Policy Studies 1999). ISMA, *The May 1998 proposal for the taxation of cross-border interest payments,* Circular No. 3 (1999). An exchange of information might end the appeal of a country with strong bank secrecy laws like Luxembourg, where non-residents held 90% of all accounts. See Kirwin. Even if all EU members used these tools, other countries might not and so gain a competitive advantage in financial markets.

The June 2000 agreement addressed these problems. In 2001 and 2002, the European Commission would negotiate with Switzerland, the US, and other key countries to get them to accept measures equivalent to information exchange. EU members would negotiate with associated states, such as the Channel Islands, to the same end. If both sets of non-EU countries adopted equivalent measures, then EU members would decide by unanimous vote whether to adopt a regime allowing each country either to tax non-residents' savings income at 20% or exchange information about that income with the appropriate tax authorities. In 2010, information sharing would become mandatory and the tax would end. See Kirwin. Several countries, including Luxembourg, would have to modify their bank secrecy laws during this transition.

The EU gave some consideration to exempting eurobonds from the proposal. ISMA has noted, however, that Eurobonds are exceedingly difficult to define. They note that "no *universally accepted*, legal definition exists for the term 'Eurobond' itself. Even the markets most basic understanding that a Eurobond is a bond issued outside the home market of its currency has been thrown into question with the introduction of the euro...." Id., at 12. The U.K. got the EU to agree that tax evasion, not tax harmonization, was the problem being addressed, and then proposed that tax evasion can be solved by a "system of information exchange." Such a system would make withholding taxes unnecessary, according to the UK. E. Crooks, *G7 Accord Backs Chancellor on Withholding Tax,* Financial Times, April 17, 2000.

In November 2000, the EU grandfathered all euro-bonds in circulation before March 1, 2001, exempting them from the 20% tax that could be imposed in 2003. It was not clear, however, if the exemption applied to bonds circulating before the cut-off date but later increased by the issuer. Sovereign borrowers often increase outstanding bonds rather than issue new ones in order to take advantage of the liquidity of the existing security. P. Norman and V. Boland, *EU Finance Ministers Reach Deal on Savings Tax*, Financial Times, Nov. 28, 2000, and A. Ostrovsky, *Sovereigns Wrong-Footed by Withholding Tax Change*, Financial Times, Mar. 2, 2001.

Swiss officials and bankers made it clear that they favored a withholding tax, opposed general information sharing, and would respond to requests about tax fraud (but not tax evasion) from other governments. This is their system now. They also insisted that all financial centers, including Hong Kong and Singapore, participate in any agreement the Swiss reached with the EU. J. Kirwin, *Swiss Banks Demand Global Agreement on Deal for Cross-Border Tax on Savings,* 75 BNA Banking Report 834, Dec. 26, 2000. In April 2001, the Swiss delegate to negotiations with the EU said that the proposal to share information conflicts with Swiss bank privacy laws. *Swiss Official Says Information-Sharing Sought by EU Conflicts With Country's Law*, BNA Banking Report, Apr. 23, 2001, at 725.

How will investors react to the agreement, given that bond yields on most eurobond issues have fallen significantly since issue?

B.   GLOBAL SECURITIES

The eurobond market has been the heart of the international bond market. Issuers used off-shore markets to tap investors from a variety of domestic markets, including their own. Thus, a U.S. issuer might issue eurodollar bonds through London rather than U.S. or Japanese domestic bonds (subject to the market regulations of those two countries). Similarly, a Japanese issuer would issue euroyen through London rather than use the domestic markets of the U.S. or Japan. The advent of global offerings is changing this pattern. A global offering is a simultaneous offering in all major markets, including the issuer's home country. New issues of international bonds in 1993 were $481 billion, of which $35 billion, or about 7.2%, represented globals. As of the third quarter 1996, new international bond issues were $522.4 billion, of which $79.6 billion, or about 15.2% were global.

K. MUEHRING, THE GLOBAL COMES OF AGE
Institutional Investor, Dec. 1993, at 82.

Four years old

In the four years since the World Bank launched the concept with a $1 billion issue in September 1989, there have been 61 globals, worth a total of $88.4 billion, according to IFR Securities Data. Although the World Bank still accounts for about a quarter of the outstanding volume, issuers now include several European sovereigns (Sweden, Italy, Finland and Portugal), a handful of Canadian provinces, two corporates and a string of U.S.-bank-issued credit-card-backed receivables. And though most globals have been denominated in U.S. dollars, issues have also been launched in Canadian dollars, yen, New Zealand dollars, Australian dollars and, most recently, deutsche marks.

An instrument that offers to integrate the world's bond markets by offering investors and issuers the bonds at a single price worldwide has such broad appeal that it is surprising the global took so long to come about. The structure is seemingly simple: Globals differ from Eurobonds and international bonds in being launched simultaneously in the U.S., Europe and Asia, with trading within and among all three markets.

Globals are inherently large and liquid. The issues are usually $1 billion or larger in size, which enables market makers to quote prices in secondary worldwide with a 5-to-10-cent dealing spread on lots of up to $25 million. Compared with 3 cents on on-the-run U.S. Treasuries and 15-to-50-cent dealing spreads on most Eurobonds, globals are the most liquid alternative to on-the-run government bonds. The World Bank's four yen-denominated globals, for instance, are the most actively traded paper in the yen market after the benchmark ten-year Japanese government bond, notes the World Bank's Lay.

. . .

Ensuring liquidity

But the biggest factor in the global's success has been the assurance of liquidity. "We take positions as an active investor," says Ian Kelson, head of fixed income at Morgan Grenfell Asset Management in London, "which means, of course, that we are looking to get out of the position as well." To Kelson, liquidity means the ability to trade in tickets of $25 million "without having a material effect on the price." Indeed, institutional investors—who are likely to be taking not long-term positions on yield but shorter-term ones on currency, spread or interest rates—are willing to pay a premium for liquidity. "The global has proved the issuer can get size without any concession on price," says John McNiven, a managing director at Merrill Lynch International in London.

. . .

In theory, the primary distribution is spread evenly throughout all three main investor markets. But in reality, the bulk of the paper is sold into the market where the bid is strongest. For instance, more than half of the 30-year tranche of Italy's $3.5 billion global in October sold into the U.S., though barely a fifth of Sweden's $1 billion three-year floater went into U.S. accounts.

The result is a uniformly lower price for issuers. Five years ago, says the World Bank's Lay, the Bank's paper was trading at 15 basis points above federal agency paper, whereas it is now trading in the U.S. at more than 10 basis points below the federal agency paper. Lay strongly believes that the global program has been instrumental in achieving this lower cost of funding.

. . .

The following reading discusses some issues with the use of globals.

E. GREENE, A. BELLER, G. COHEN,
M. HUDSON, JR., AND E. ROSEN, U.S. REGULATION OF THE
INTERNATIONAL SECURITIES MARKETS
§§ 6.01, 6.02 (1999).

§ 6.01 GLOBAL EQUITY OFFERINGS

Large companies in need of significant amounts of capital and shareholders seeking to sell very sizeable equity stakes frequently engage in "global offerings"—that is, offerings in the issuer's home country combined with offerings in other markets (*e.g.*, the United States, Japan or Europe).

. . .

[1] The U.S. Pattern

U.S. rules and regulations have imposed a standard pattern on public offerings in the United States, and much of the complexity of global offerings is generated by the way in which foreign regulatory regimes impose conflicting patterns.

The standard pattern for a U.S. public offering is as follows:

— No offer can be made in the United States until a registration statement is filed with the SEC. The registration statement includes a preliminary prospectus, which is generally printed and distributed to potential purchasers after filing. The preliminary prospectus is the only document that can be used to make offers in writing.

— After the filing is made, the SEC can be expected to comment on the registration statement, especially if it is the first offering by the company in the United States. Although it typically takes about one month to receive comments, the SEC may be willing to provide comments in a shorter period of time to accommodate the timing of global offerings by non-U.S. companies. It should generally be possible to respond to those comments within a week or two, and then to file an amended registration statement, including the form of amended preliminary prospectus used in roadshows or other marketing efforts, or if the offering timetable calls for it, the form of final prospectus (the final prospectus would not include pricing information if such information is to be added to the final prospectus pursuant to Rule 430A). After the amended registration statement containing the form of final prospectus is filed, the SEC will declare the registration statement effective on request.

— At about the time the amended registration statement is declared effective, the underwriting agreement is signed and the share price is set. During the period between filing and effectiveness, executive officers of the issuer will have participated in roadshows, and the underwriters will have obtained indications of interest at various prices from their customers. The lead underwriter will then negotiate the price and the ultimate size of the U.S. tranche with these indications of interest in mind. In a public offering of shares that are already listed on an exchange, pricing is usually based on the quoted share price, or a formula related to such price.

— After effectiveness, and as soon as possible after pricing, the final prospectus (including the pricing information) is printed and the underwriters confirm sales to their customers. In purely domestic U.S. transactions, the closing typically occurs three or four business days later while in U.S.-registered offerings by non-U.S. issuers, the closing sometimes does not occur until five days after sales are confirmed. Regardless of the length of time of the settlement period, the closing is subject to certain conditions being met, including the delivery of legal opinions and accountants' comfort letters and the absence of material adverse changes in the issuer's business or serious disruptions in the financial markets.

There is more flexibility in a U.S. private placement, since the registration requirements of the Securities Act do not apply and the SEC is not involved.

[2] Selected Foreign Regulatory Regimes

The pattern for a global equity offering must be determined in the context of both the U.S. rules and regulations and the regulatory regimes abroad. In many cases, the foreign component of a global offering is made in a way that is exempt from the application of most foreign regulations. The exemption typically relied on in many countries, such as the United Kingdom, is the so-called "professionals" exemption, which in certain circumstances permits offers and sales of securities to be made to institutions and other market professionals with few regulatory requirements. If the international offering includes a public offering in a national market, however, various registration and regulatory requirements of that country may apply, and these requirements will have to be integrated with the U.S. rules. In such a situation, complex issues are likely to arise that could expose the issuer or the underwriters to risks not otherwise encountered.

[a] United Kingdom

The standard U.S. pattern was modified for the privatizations in the United Kingdom in the 1980s that were combined with U.S. public offerings. In those offerings, marketing in both countries prior to pricing was done on the basis of a "pathfinder" prospectus, which took the form in the United States of a preliminary prospectus included in a registration statement filed with the SEC. Pricing took place on "impact day," which occurred about three weeks following release of the pathfinder prospectus and also marked the beginning of a one- to four-week subscription period in the United Kingdom. Although the SEC could have been asked to declare the registration statement effective on impact day, thus allowing the U.S. underwriters to confirm sales and eliminate much of their underwriting exposure, this result was unacceptable to the participants in the offering in the United Kingdom. An effective registration statement would result in "grey-market" trading of the shares on a "when-issued" basis in the United States, and potentially the United Kingdom, during the U.K. subscription period; and the possibility of such trading was considered potentially disruptive. As a result, the U.S. underwriters were required to sign the underwriting agreement and commit themselves to purchase the shares on impact day but were not permitted to request the SEC to declare the registration statement effective or to confirm sales to their customers until "allotment day" when the U.K. subscription period ended. This extended period between pricing and confirmations of sales subjected the U.S. underwriters to risks that were not borne by their U.K. counterparts, who typically "laid off" their underwriting commitments on large U.K. institutions acting as sub-underwriters prior to impact day.[5]   When this extended underwriting period was combined with the absence of a *force majeure* clause in the underwriting agreement, the underwriting disaster in the 1987 British Petroleum offering became possible.

More recent U.K. privatizations have adopted procedures that minimize the risk to underwriters and the inconsistency between U.S. and U.K. underwriting practice. In the 1991 secondary offering by the British Government of shares in British Telecommunications public limited company ("BT"), which involved a registered public offering in the United States, marketing took place on the basis of a "pathfinder" prospectus abroad and a preliminary prospectus in the United States, but pricing did not occur on impact day. Institutional U.K. offerees and offerees elsewhere around the world tendered bids for shares beginning on impact day and the British Government and the global coordinator set the final offer price for both the tender offer and retail tranches at the end of the subscription period based on those bids. The U.S. registration statement was declared effective at the end of the subscription period before the final offer price was set. This process more closely resembles pricing practices in U.S. public offerings, where the formal "tender offer" process of the BT offering is analogous to the somewhat less transparent U.S. "book-building" process.

.   .   .

[v] Comparison of U.S. and U.K. Rules

It is useful to contrast the U.S. and U.K. rules on publicity and distribution of research reports in order to highlight some of the difficulties that arise in global offerings. The United Kingdom, like many other jurisdictions, permits much more publicity about an offering outside the offering document than does the United States. Large global equity offerings in the United Kingdom and elsewhere in Europe are sometimes preceded by full-scale television and press advertising campaigns and distributions of brochures describing the issuer and the offering process. Such advertising is permitted if certain procedural requirements are followed. U.K. law also would permit unlimited distribution of advertisements that do not comply with such procedural requirements so long as distribution is limited to certain professionals. Notwithstanding such permitted advertising, offers by U.K. companies technically can be made to the public in the United Kingdom, as in the United States, only on the basis of prospectuses that contain mandated disclosure.

---

[5] The U.S. underwriters could not arrange for sub-underwriting in this manner, since sub-underwriting commitments from institutional investors, like other binding commitments to purchase securities, can only be obtained after the registration statement is declared effective.

Conflicts between the U.K. and U.S. systems arise in global offerings involving both jurisdictions because the U.K. publicity efforts must be restricted as described above to jurisdictions outside the United States.   Difficulties arise, for example, when placing advertisements in publications such as *The Financial Times* and *The Economist.* Such publications are distributed in the United States, and steps must be taken to prevent the publication of advertising materials in their U.S. editions.   In some recent transactions, offering participants have sought to document their efforts to avoid U.S. publicity by getting certain publications to agree in writing not to publish advertisements in specified jurisdictions.[57]   The need to coordinate conflicting legal systems has led to the practice of distributing written publicity guidelines to all participants in a global offering that synthesize the legal requirements in all relevant jurisdictions. Since compromises often need to be made to place all syndicates on an equal footing, these guidelines typically reflect the most restrictive elements of the participating jurisdictions' legal systems.

This is an area that the SEC is particularly sensitive about. In a global equity offering involving a U.K. issuer, where advertisements prepared for publication outside the United States inadvertently appeared in the U.S. edition of *The Financial Times*, the SEC expressed concern and requested an explanation from the offering participants.

While the U.S. prohibition against pre-offering publicity will continue to prevent offering participants from placing paid

---

[57] While it may be possible to get such publications to agree not to publish advertisements in specified jurisdictions, they generally will not agree to restrict ordinary articles to certain editions. As discussed in Chapter 5, Regulation S provides a safe harbor from the registration requirements of the Securities Act for certain non-U.S. offering activities (including offshore press activities) that may be conducted contemporaneously with a registered U.S. public offering. However, as a result of uncertainty regarding the impact of press activities that involve such publications, securities lawyers have generally advised that one-on-one interviews and similar meetings with such publications are not possible prior to filing a registration statement that contains a preliminary prospectus and that, following the filing of the registration statement, such interviews are possible only as long as they are limited to information contained in the preliminary prospectus. *See, e.g.,* Letter from John Makinson, Managing Director, *The Financial Times*, to Elise B. Walter, Deputy Director, SEC (June 30, 1994), and letter from Elise B. Walter, Deputy Director, SEC, to John Makinson, Managing Director, *The Financial Times* (July 12, 1994)(available from Cleary, Gottlieb, Steen & Hamilton, New York). To combat this uncertainty, the SEC has recently adopted a safe harbor which, subject to certain restrictions, permits members of the U.S. press to participate in offshore press activities conducted by or on behalf of a non-U.S. issuer in connection with a concurrent U.S. and offshore offering, including attending one-on-one meetings with the issuer, so long as access also is provided to members of the non-U.S. press and any offering-related materials provided to the press which may be of significant interest to U.S. investors contain a prescribed cautionary legend. *See* SEC Release No. 33-7470 (Oct. 10, 1997); §5.02[1][b].

advertisements in U.S. publications or U.S. editions of non-U.S. publications, a recently adopted safe harbor Rule 135e under the Securities Act, should have the effect of permitting a broader range of offshore publicity activities by non-U.S. issuers in global public offerings without running a risk that coverage of such activities by the U.S. press will result in "gun-jumping."   However, the proposed changes will not shield offshore activities during an offering by a U.S. issuer or an offering by a non-U.S. issuer being conducted exclusively in the United States. This results in the slight anomaly that offshore activities leading to U.S. press coverage may be permissible where sales to U.S. persons are supposed to be prohibited (*i.e.*, in a pure Regulation S non-U.S. offering), while a more restrictive view is taken with respect to an exclusively U.S. offering, in which investors enjoy the protections of a detailed statutory framework.

The requirement that no U.S. publicity efforts begin before circulation of the preliminary prospectus led to certain difficulties in a number of global public offerings. For instance, in the 1992 Wellcome offering, the offering participants felt that lengthy pre-marketing was necessary in all jurisdictions, and in the United States especially, to educate investors about a company that was not widely known outside the United Kingdom.   Since this pre-marketing could begin in the United Kingdom and elsewhere before a prospectus was prepared, the original intention was to distribute the preliminary prospectus about a month before pricing, but to begin other marketing efforts (including an advertising campaign) about two months before pricing. Marketing efforts could not begin in the United States before the filing of the preliminary prospectus, so the U.S. underwriters convinced the other underwriters that it was important to file a preliminary U.S. prospectus one month early for distribution to a limited audience of key U.S. investor groups. The early filing contained the full substance of the preliminary prospectus that would be widely distributed one month before pricing, but omitted certain details about the offer structure. Since the U.S. syndicate would be circulating a preliminary prospectus, the U.K. and other syndicates decided to do the same in order to maintain a consistency of marketing efforts, so they simultaneously issued a pathfinder prospectus outside the U.S.   The preliminary prospectus that was distributed on a limited basis was referred to by the non-U.S. offering participants as a "pink herring,"[58] since it came

---

[58] The "pink herring" has since become a common feature of global offerings, especially in the privatization context, and the SEC has accepted their use subject to a requirement that each recipient of the pink herring also be sent a copy of the "red herring" (the standard preliminary prospectus).   See Note 39.   Typically the pink herring omits pricing information but includes an indication of the total number of shares to be offered globally (although no indication of the size of U.S. portion of the offering is given). However, the pink herring filed with the SEC in connection with the proposed privatization of France Telecom—which was delayed following French parliamentary elections in May 1977—in 1997 omitted both pricing information and any indication of the number of shares that would be offered. *See* France Telecom,

one month earlier than the intended date of distribution of the "red herring" prospectus, and contained slightly less information than the red herring.

Certain conflicts between the U.S. and U.K. rules on distribution of research reports also became apparent in the BT and Wellcome offerings. Notwithstanding that Rule 139 would have permitted research reports to be distributed by certain underwriters during the offerings, the U.K. liability concerns associated with distributing a research report during an offering caused the U.K. offering participants to impose a black-out on the distribution of research reports anywhere in the world for at least one month (two months in the case of the 1991 BT offering) prior to commencement of the offering.[59] Although similar liability concerns exist in the United States, as a technical matter, U.S. offering participants are permitted to publish Rule 139 reports during a distribution.[60]

U.S. and U.K. rules were also inconsistent during the period prior to the black-out period. Rule 139 would have permitted certain underwriters to publish research reports with profit and other forecasts different from the ones previously published by the underwriter. However, concerns about liability for the issuer in the United Kingdom for such forecasts caused the U.K. advisers to prohibit the publication of new forecasts in reports that otherwise could be distributed under U.S. and U.K. law. U.K. rules also required share recommendations to be omitted from the research reports published in the period before the black-out period. Not only would Rule 139 have permitted such recommendations to be included (although not improved because of then-applicable market manipulation rules), but their inclusion is entirely customary in U.S. research reports.

Preliminary Prospectus (Apr. 21, 1997) included in Registration Statement on Form F-1 (no. 333-06814).

[59] This black-out was interpreted by the U.K. offering participants to apply even to research reports previously published by underwriters and included on electronic systems operated by third parties. The global coordinators for such offerings asked the underwriters to have such previously published research reports deleted from these electronic systems during the black-out period, although the U.S. underwriters explained that their agreements with such third parties did not all permit them to have such reports deleted upon request. Consequently, certain U.S. underwriters committed that research not capable of being deleted would not be updated during the black-out period.

Some recent offerings have omitted a black-out period or imposed one shorter than one month on the theory that a black-out period may not in fact be very useful under U.K. law in protecting against liability for research reports.

[60] Notwithstanding the technical availability of Rule 139, many U.S. investment banks restrict distribution of research in the United States during an offering. Even those which permit some distribution of research will stop all such distribution for a period of time, generally several weeks, immediately preceding the distribution of the preliminary prospectus.

As in the case of the rules regarding publicity, the practice in global offerings is to distribute research report guidelines to all offering participants that synthesize the rules applicable to the various syndicates.

. . .

§ 6.02 GLOBAL DEBT OFFERINGS

. . .

[1] TEFRA Considerations

The anti-bearer bond rules ("TEFRA") of the U.S. Internal Revenue Code of 1986 (the "Internal Revenue Code") add a further dimension to global offerings of debt securities. In many foreign markets bonds are typically offered and sold in bearer form to comply with local custom and, in some cases, to comply with local law. TEFRA, however, prohibits bearer bonds from being offered or sold in the United States, whether in a public offering or a private placement, as part of their original issuance. As a result, bonds offered and sold in the United States must be in registered form and, moreover, cannot be convertible into bearer form. Thus the issuer and underwriters in a global debt offering must decide either (i) to offer and sell bearer bonds outside the United States and registered bonds in the United States, with the consequent impairment of trading between markets, since investors outside the United States may be unwilling to purchase bonds in registered form in the secondary market, or (ii) to offer and sell bonds in registered form both in the United States and outside, with the consequent shrinking of the market for the bonds outside the United States, since many investors in foreign jurisdictions may only wish to purchase bonds in bearer form. What is more, if the issuer of bonds in registered form is a U.S. company, U.S. tax rules will require each foreign investor to provide an Internal Revenue Service form W-8, identifying itself, in order to receive interest payments free of U.S. withholding tax. This requirement is inconsistent with the desire of many foreign investors to remain anonymous and is likely to further reduce the attractiveness of bonds in registered form.

In some cases it is possible for non-U.S. issuers to reconcile the foreign preference for obligations in bearer form with TEFRA by creating instruments that are considered to be in registered form for TEFRA purposes but are denominated as bearer obligations and are generally treated as such under local law.

It is also possible, through the use of global bonds registered in the name of clearing systems or their nominees, to reconcile the requirements of TEFRA with the desire of European investors to remain anonymous, at least in the case of offerings by foreign issuers to which the W-8 requirement does not apply, and at the same time to offer and sell identical securities in the United States and abroad. Because a global bond registered in the name of a clearing system or its nominee is a registered bond for purposes of TEFRA, interests in the global bond may be offered and sold in the United States, and so long as the bond remains in global form the beneficial owner can remain undisclosed. In the case of a U.S. issuer, the requirement to deliver a form W-8, which applies to the beneficial owner, in order to receive interest payments free of U.S. withholding tax, makes this a less than a complete solution.

Offerings of bonds in registered form both in the United States and outside have been made by the World Bank and a few other issuers. Certain other issuers and underwriters have explored the possibility of conducting global bond offerings in such a manner to ensure the fungibility of the entire issue. In cases where the bonds are publicly sold in the United States, either pursuant to registration under the Securities Act or, as in the case of the World Bank, an exemption from registration, the securities sold in the United States and outside will be fungible. Complete fungibility is more difficult to achieve where bonds are sold in the United States pursuant to the private placement exemption from registration under the Securities Act, including under Rule 144A thereunder.

. . .

Notes and Questions

1. The World Bank in *Global Bonds* (1994) has singled out four key characteristics of global bonds.

- The bonds are legally eligible for primary market sale into each of the world's major bond markets, without the imposition of lock-up provisions.
- The bonds can be settled and cleared on any one of several systems and they can flow back and forth between systems with minimal transactions costs.
- The offering price at launch is validated through an extended period of price discovery through bookbuilding.
- The bonds are distributed by carefully selected international syndicates of bond dealers.

2. Why are global offerings becoming more attractive than eurobonds given that issuers must comply with different national market regulations?

3. The reading excerpt gives an illustration of the coordination problem. What differences in market rules between the U.S. and the U.K. accounted for the fact that the underwriters did not want the registration

statement to be effective on "impact day?" Why did the solution, delaying the U.S. effective date to the end of the U.K. subscription period, increase the risks for the U.S. underwriters? How did the 1991 BT offering reduce this risk?

4. Global offerings have generally used a negotiated or open priced style of underwriting, as opposed to a bought deal. The BT3 offer in July 1993 used "a formal bookbuilding process, in which managers are involved in the solicitation of 'non-binding indications of interest in purchasing shares' which are communicated through a formal process to the Global Co-ordinator (S.G. Warburg Securities for BT3), and which leads to a final pricing and allocation decision, following which the managers become legally bound to underwrite the offer." E. Greene and W. Underhill, *Structuring A Successful Global Offering—The BT3 Offer, in* Recent Developments in International Securities Law (American Conference Institute), Oct. 25-26, 1993, at 6. Allocation decisions among bidders were based on four "quality" considerations, in addition to price: (1) price leadership (high bids early in the process); (2) after market support (bids from investors likely to hold in the immediate after market); (3) pre-sale support (bids from investors who increased their bids during the bidding period); and (4) no adverse activity (bids from investors believed not to have engaged in adverse market activity, for example, short sales). The shares are actually allocated to the underwriters who then sell the shares to the underlying bidders.

Why have globals used open priced underwriting? Why allocate shares on any basis other than price?

5. One advantage of globals over eurobonds is that globals immediately reach retail investors in domestic markets. Many eurobonds will be subject to a 40 day lock-up under Regulation S--those with substantial U.S. market interest. Consider a foreign issuer who is deciding whether to issue eurodollar bonds in the U.K. or global bonds in the U.S., Japan and Germany. Institutional investors can all easily buy in the U.K., but retail investors may have a harder time in doing so. The ability to reach retail investors may make the bond issue more liquid, thus reducing the price (yield).

6. There is a lot of hype in connection with going "global." Issuers and underwriters may describe an issue as global because, in principle, it is supposed to be marketed simultaneously in the major markets whereas in reality it isn't. One syndicate manager described a $1 billion global bond issue by Argentina as a "dressed-up Yankee" since 75 percent of the issue was sold in the United States.

7. Economists are very interested in the degree to which financial markets between countries are integrated. One useful concept to describe the extent of such integration is the law of one price, or as one study has termed it, the "global financial law of one price." McKinsey Global

Institute, The Global Capital Market: Supply, Demand, Pricing and Allocation 12 (1994). This "law" requires:

*In the absence of impediments to exchange, all tradable financial instruments and currencies with equivalent risk must sell at the same price everywhere, allowing for transaction costs.

*The relationship between the prices of tradable instruments with equivalent risk is brought about through financial arbitrage.

*In the short and long run, the financial arbitrage of tradable instruments causes all financial instruments and currencies to trade at their relative financial risk/return parity to each other.

The McKinsey study found that the law of one price basically obtains in foreign exchange markets given the existence of covered rate parity, the condition that interest rates across countries be equal when they are contracted in the same currency. This means that investors can obtain the same return from a 3-month, U.S. dollar-denominated instrument or a 3-month, deutschmark-denominated instrument with a forward exchange rate contract to purchase dollars at the maturity date.

The McKinsey study also found evidence for the law of one price in Japanese, German and U.S. government bond markets. As of October 11, 1994, the real long-term government bond yields for these three countries were 4.73 for Japan, 4.72 for the U.S., and 4.51 for Germany, ironically much more yield convergence than exhibited within the EC (U.K. yields were 6.47, Italian yields were 7.9). The range was less than 25 basis points. On October 11, the holding period premium range (the spread between the long-term government bond yield and the 3-month rate) was within 35 basis points (Japan-2.42, Germany-2.26, and the U.S. 2.07). This compared with a 2.97 percent spread on August 12, 1992.

A study of the markets for government bonds in Germany, the U.K., and the U.S. found that when global finance is in turmoil (e.g., the 1992 crisis for sterling or the financial crisis in Asia) the factors affecting yield curves are primarily international. Otherwise, domestic factors primarily affect yield curves. The authors speculated that global investors were reallocating their bond portfolios and domestic investors were adjusting their expectations because of the crises. So contagion is important in bond markets. A. Clare and I. Lekkos, *An Analysis of the Relationship Between International Bond Markets*, Bank of England, 2000.

Some key factors causing increased integration of financial markets are increased international capital flows, the disappearance of capital controls, better technology and less onerous regulation of domestic markets. Is financial market integration good? How did the development of the euromarkets promote integration? Will the development of global markets promote integration even more?

Links to Other Chapters

To a large extent, the success of the eurobond market has depended on onerous regulation of domestic bond markets, examined to some degree for the U.S. (Chapter 2) and Japan (Chapter 8). The development of the global bond market represents a major challenge to eurobonds, and depends on further deregulation of domestic markets. Clearance and settlement arrangements, on a coordinated global basis, may be crucial to further expansion of global markets, a matter taken up in Chapter 15. Finally, the issue of both global and eurobonds may be driven by swap possibilities (Chapter 17). Chapter 21 deals with issues relating to the issuance of and default on eurobonds issued by emerging market countries.

CHAPTER THIRTEEN

INTERNATIONAL ASSET SECURITIZATION

A. INTRODUCTION

Securitization refers to many activities, each reducing to a search for liquidity. Firms securitize to become more liquid, lowering risk and cost. Their activity shifts liabilities or assets from intermediated financial markets, normally the province of commercial banks, to securities markets. The broader, more transparent, and standardized securities markets can provide funds at a lower cost than commercial banks, which tailor credit for borrowers that cannot tap the securities markets because of their peculiar needs or lower credit standing.

Pooling smaller loans to reach a scale that can tap securities markets is the form of securitization that this Chapter examines. Loans or other receivables are converted into tradable investments. A bank, for example, cannot sell just one of its mortgage loans in public securities markets. Too little is known about the borrower for investors to assess risk and the amount of the loan is too small to justify the cost of going to the market. Pooling many mortgages with similar characteristics surmounts these shortcomings. This activity differs from other forms of securitization, such as substituting securities for loans, as when a borrower shifts from bank credit to commercial paper, or decomposing a large standard bank loan into loan participations. See T. Frankel, *Securitization* 6 (1991) and H. Morrissey, ed., *International Securitisation* 5 (1992) (Morrissey).

The purchase of these pooled assets is funded, according to Morrison, *Securitization International Guide*, International Financial Law Review 3 (Supp. Aug. 1993), by issuing investment grade securities that are:

> primarily serviced by the cash flows of a discrete pool of receivables or other financial assets, either fixed or revolving, that by their terms convert into cash within a finite time period plus any rights or other assets designed to assure the servicing or timely distribution of proceeds to the security holders.

Although one might assume that a riskier company would be most likely to tap the capital markets using higher rated securities with strong receivables, in fact even investment grade originators can benefit from securitization. See S. Schwartz, *The Alchemy of Asset Securitization*, 1 Stanford Journal of Law, Business & Finance (Fall 1994).

The industry distinguishes between mortgage-backed securities (MBS) and asset-backed securities (ABS). MBS markets are big in the U.S., with amounts outstanding above $1 trillion by the mid-1990s. The receivables in the US were mainly single family mortgages, with the remainder split between retail and office mortgages. Multifamily mortgages (over 4 units) declined in share, while securitized commercial mortgages grew fast but remained a small fraction of all commercial mortgage credit.

ABS receivables, the subject of this Chapter, include automobile loans, credit card receivables, trade receivables, home equity loans, leases of real property or equipment like airplanes, education loans, junk bonds, boat loans, and even oil or gas reserves. These ABS appear routinely in the US, which dominates the market. In the US, publicly placed ABS issues amounting to $60 billion in 1993 made up about 80% of all ABS and grew to $200 billion in 2000 Auto and credit card assets backed about 65% of all ABS. Very few small business loans were securitized. ABS now appear increasingly in Europe and Japan. The assets are often less standardized than mortgages and may introduce additional complexity, such as receipts in various currencies.

This Chapter describes cross-border asset securitization in general, including the reasons a firm securitizes and the elements of a securitized transaction. It presents for comparison the development of the ABS markets in the US, Germany, Japan, and India. The Chapter raises legal problems common to cross-border ABS. Finally, it summarizes the proposal by the Basel Committee to expand capital adequacy rules governing ABS.

B.   ELEMENTS OF A SECURITIZED TRANSACTION AND THE REASONS TO SECURITIZE

Some years ago, the Australian firm Broken Hill Proprietary Ltd. (BHP) securitized loan receivables it held in a cross-border transaction arranged by Deutsche Bank—Germany's largest bank. Based in Melbourne, BHP was Australia's largest publicly-owned company and one of the biggest natural resources companies in the world. While almost 70% of its assets were in Australia, BHP had sizable overseas operations in North America, the United Kingdom, South America, and in the Pacific/Oceania region. Worldwide it had about 48,000 employees. Its 218,000 shareholders were distributed over 77 countries, and BHP shares were listed on stock exchanges in Australia, Germany, Japan, New

Zealand, Switzerland, the US and the United Kingdom. The company controlled about 450 subsidiaries worldwide.

BHP had made interest-free loans to its employees to buy BHP stock, but it wanted to remove the loans from its balance sheet, replace them with profitable assets, and reduce its large US dollar debt. BHP decided to sell a portion of the loans and use the proceeds from the sale for other purposes. Of course, although the assets left BHP's books, the employee-borrowers continued to pay BHP the interest and principal due. BHP passed their payments on to the new owner of the loans. This securitization was cross-border. The receivables, in Australian dollars, were sold to the Australian unit of a trust in Jersey. Another unit, based in Jersey, issued euro-CP to fund the purchase, mainly in DM and dollars, to investors in Europe and Asia. The German bank supplied many supporting services.

Firms may securitize for a variety of reasons including a desire for liquidity, to reduce financing costs or mismatches between assets and liabilities, and to manage balance sheets better. The simple schematic illustration in Exhibit 1 below shows the elements of an ABS transaction.

The Corporation, in Exhibit 1, originates the assets for the ABS using receivables from loans, credit cards, or other assets. BHP had loan receivables due from its employees, the Debtors in Exhibit 1. The originator, a company or a bank, sells the assets to a Special Purpose Vehicle (SPV), which is a trust or corporation created for the transaction by the originator or a third party, such as a bank. BHP sold the loan receivables to an SPV called Rhein-Main Securitisation No. 4 Ltd (RMS No. 4), based in Australia and part of a group set up by Deutsche Bank in the financial center of Jersey.

The role of the SPV is described in detail in Part B2. It pays the originator with funds it receives by issuing securities backed by the cash flow from the assets. Rhein-Main Securitisation Ltd, a sister unit of RMS No. 4, issued euro-commercial paper to investors mainly from the Mid-East and Europe. The originator usually services the receivables, for a fee, collecting principal and interest payments from the debtors and transferring them to the SPV for the investors. BHP did this. Third parties, usually banks, guarantee the credit and liquidity of the SPV so the note or bond issue can win a top rating from rating agencies like Standard and Poor's. Deutsche Bank, with the highest possible rating, guaranteed the BHP SPV. Third parties may also provide other services, arranging the transaction, underwriting and dealing in the securities where appropriate, acting as trustee, issuing and paying agent, and administering the SPV's activities. For BHP, Deutsche Bank provided these services.

EXHIBIT 1

Simplified Structure of an ABS Transaction

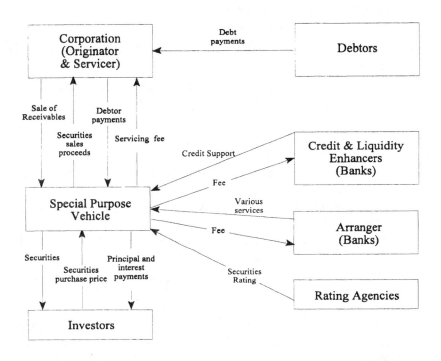

The following sections present the types of assets, or receivables, that are securitized, the characteristics of SPVs, their forms, and the ways in which they and their assets are protected from various claimants, such as creditors in bankruptcy and tax collectors. The types of investors and securities are described, along with the process for rating the instruments. The BHP securitization illustrates each factor. It is, of course, one of many types of securitization.

1. SECURITIZABLE ASSETS

Investors in securitized paper often seek the following features in receivables to reduce their risk:

- Large pool: Scale makes an ABS issue feasible, since it is too expensive to market an issue of a few hundred thousand dollars and since it permits reliable performance forecasts.

- Low default rate: High asset quality and small credit risk reduce the financing cost for the ABS.

- Insensitivity to interest rate changes: The debtors' payments should not be altered by changes in interest rates.

- Limited prepayment risk: The debtor should not be able to repay the loan prematurely. Prepayment can reduce the interest earned on the receivable for the originator and the SPV, and exposes them to the reinvestment risk of the liquidated receivables which can be particularly damaging if interest rates are falling.

- Short maturity: Shorter maturities of the receivables ease management of the interest rate risk.

- "Relatively homogeneous pools": Similar "credit quality, maturity and interest rate profile" help one forecast uncertain financial flows. See Morrissey 151.

Not all assets have these features, so not all are equally amenable to securitization. Mortgages most readily fit the criteria. Indeed, securitization began with mortgages and now over one-third of all mortgages in the US are securitized. Consumer loan receivables, in particular automobile loans and credit card balances, were the first types of assets used for ABS because they meet a number of the requirements. Increasingly, non-consumer receivables are being securitized, particularly trade receivables, leases, and commercial mortgages.

The assets BHP securitized were interest-free loans it had made to its employees to help them buy BHP stock or options when the company was threatened with an external take-over. About 70% of its employees participated and their purchases were substantial. While the employees had to have fully paid back the loans they received to buy options by the time they exercised the option (usually 3 to 5 years after purchase), loans to buy shares had a maximum maturity of 20 years.

The sale of employee loans was not a common practice. While there had been a number of such sales in the United States, BHP was the first Australian company to undertake such a transaction. The BHP deal was apparently also the first of its kind worldwide to securitize loans made to help employees buy company shares.

2. THE SPECIAL PURPOSE VEHICLE

The SPV must have a legal form, own the receivables, and manage the cash flows in a way that maintains the value of the funds flows and does not subject them to claims by people other than the investors. Others who might claim could be creditors of a bankrupt originator of the receivables or founder of the SPV, other creditors of the SPV, or tax authorities. Often imaginative legal design is required.

This section describes the SPV for BHP and the major problems that an SPV must avoid in its own design and the structure of the transaction. Later sections examine each of the problems and solutions.

The SPV for BHP's loans was designed by Deutsche Bank for European corporations wishing to securitize assets and for European investors in ABS. The bank set up the Rhein Main Securitization Group (RMS Group) in Jersey, giving it three characteristics: it was a multi-seller vehicle using euro-commercial paper in multiple currencies. The multi-currency aspect was the SPV's capability to issue asset backed CP in a variety of currencies. Euro-CP allowed the SPV flexibility to add receivables of different originators to the asset pool and fund them with new CP issues. The SPV was a multi-seller because it could simultaneously hold different kinds of assets (receivables) from a variety of corporate originators. These receivables backed the securities issued by the SPV.

Care is taken setting up an SPV to make it remote from claims in bankruptcy. The SPV's only assets are the receivables. These service the asset-backed security. If the SPV is not a legal entity separate from all others, such as the originator or the bank that set it up, claimants on the others might have a claim on the assets of the SPV. If ownership of assets held by the SPV was not transferred to the SPV, then claimants on a bankrupt seller-originator could have a claim on the assets that were supposed to be off the originator's balance sheet and solely securing the investors' funds. This requires a true sale, discussed below. Failure to achieve separate legal status or true sale would increase the risk for ABS investors, because the assets would be subject to the claims of others. This would either raise the cost of the securitization or scuttle it. Investors will not accept such a risk given the narrow margins they receive (the low margins make securitization attractive to the originator).

The SPV must also be free of tax. Costs of securitization rise if the flow of funds is taxed as it passes through the originator and SPV before reaching the investor. The tax would reduce the value of the cash flow.

So the SPV must be both separate from the originator and not taxed. This generally requires special legal treatment. The SPV must also meet investors' requirements about accounting rules and rating if securitization is to be feasible. The following sections examine these factors.

3. THE FORM OF THE SPV AND THE INVESTOR'S INTEREST IN IT

The SPV can take the legal form of a trust or corporation. The trust is common in Anglo-American jurisdictions. In most civil law countries,

which lack the trust concept, a separate corporation must be established.*
The legal form can have important tax implications and affects the
securities the SPV can issue, as in the United States.

Rhein-Main Securitisation Holding Ltd. and Rhein-Main Charitable
Trust, a corporate shell, satisfied legal requirements for the SPV. The
holding company was a Jersey limited liability company. Net income
generated by its subsidiaries would be distributed to the charitable trust.
This dividend was usually nominal, not by law but by practice. Jersey
law prohibited RMS Trust from accumulating or capitalizing income it
received. It had to apply the income for its stated charitable purposes.
The trust was set up by an unrelated third party through a donation.

Deutsche Bank held no ownership interest in any affiliate of the
Rhein-Main Group. No personnel interlock existed between Deutsche
Bank staff and directors and officers of the Rhein-Main Group. A
violation of the strict separateness of the SPV could force Deutsche Bank
to consolidate the SPV. Deutsche Bank and its affiliate, the British
merchant bank Morgan Grenfell, did provide administrative and
consulting services to the RMS SPV. They acted as cash administrator,
issuing and paying agent, arranger, and manager.

A separate limited liability company was used for each originator; the
one for BHP was called Rhein-Main No. 4 Ltd (RMS No. 4). Marketing
and tax considerations rather than law, accounting rules, or rating
agencies prompted this. Originators in Europe preferred to separate their
asset pool in this way to avoid commingling with other asset pools.
Potential originators in Germany, newcomers to the market, might be
more willing to securitize through this structure than if one company held
several pools. In addition, Deutsche Bank found that it could manage
each pool better in a separate company. Administrative procedures and
accounting were easier than if multiple pools were held by one company,
particularly with pools in different currencies. By contract, the operations
of RMS No. 4 were carried out by the staff of Deutsche Bank's Asset
Backed Securities Group in Frankfurt

Deutsche Bank decided not to have each securitization company issue
securities itself. One reason was that multiple issuers with very similar
names would confuse investors. The single issuer, Rhein-Main Securitisation Ltd. (RMS Ltd), was a limited liability company set up under Jersey
law. It was managed by a board of directors appointed by its sole
shareholder, Rhein-Main Securitisation Holding Ltd.

The investor may hold either debt or equity issued by the SPV, or
some combination of the two. Three basic structures exist:

---

* An exception is the French system of fond communs de creances. They amalgamate
the trust and investment fund concepts created for French securitization. See P. Billot,
Securitisation à la Française, International Financial Law Review 12 (Mar. 1989).

- <u>Pass through</u>: The SPV sells the investor a share or participation representing an undivided pro-rata interest in the pooled assets and a right to a pro-rata share of cash flows. In the U.S., to comply with tax law, the SPV must take the form of a passive self-liquidating trust which passes the payments directly to the investor without reconfiguring them, if the trust is to escape tax. This means the trust provides no protection against prepayment of receivables by the debtors. The investor's interest is equity-like in several ways. It has a property interest in the assets of the SPV. Its receipts vary with the performance of the SPV.

- <u>Pay through</u>: The SPV sells investors securities that reconfigure the cash flows from the assets, often creating two or more classes of security. Each class is entitled to payments from the single pool's cash flow, but one class is senior (for example, with rights to the immediate maturities or fixed payments) and the others junior (eg., with rights to the longer maturities or a residual). The junior security is a buffer for the senior security against prepayment and other fluctuations or losses in the cash flow. The senior security is debt, the junior more like equity. Risk is allocated this way in order to tap investors with different preferences for risk. Sophisticated investors, often institutions, are more able to evaluate the risk of the junior securities. Less sophisticated investors are more likely to take the senior securities. Pay throughs are a common flexible form of ABS. They may offer floating rates or divide interest and principal revenue streams into IOs ("interest only") and POs ("principal only"). When the SPV takes the form of a corporation, it is subject to corporate income tax but the interest it pays on the debt is deductible. The investor's interest is only in the securities issued by the SPV, not the underlying assets, although the investors may take a security interest in those assets as further protection.

- <u>Collateralized debt</u>: An originator/issuer sells investors debt giving the right to receive a stated interest and principal, independent of the assets' cash flow but generated by it and secured by the assets as collateral. Since the assets remain on the originator's books, they are not issued by commercial banks which securitize to remove assets from their books.

The RMS/BHP SPVs combine elements of both pass-through and pay-through.

4. BANKRUPTCY REMOTENESS

The SPV must be protected further from its own bankruptcy and from the bankruptcy of the originator or the obligors on the underlying assets. Protection includes contractual arrangements, limitations in the SPV's charter, assuming a true sale, support by the originator, and credit and liquidity enhancement by third parties.

Contractual and charter protection. An SPV's corporate charter and its contractual arrangements severely limit the activities in which it may engage. Typically, the SPV may incur no debt other then issuing the ABS. RMS No. 4 was a separate special purpose company which could not incur any material debt other than that relating to the purchase of receivables from the originator. RMS Ltd, the issuer, was a special purpose company that could only incur the debt of the CP it issued (backed by the flow from the receivables). Every party to a contract with the issuer or securitisation company had to sign a "no petition" agreement not to file for the issuer's or securitisation companies' bankruptcy until one year and a day after all sums outstanding and owing under the latest maturing commercial paper had been paid. These agreements were valid under Jersey law. RMS Ltd's commissioning agreements with RMS No. 4 and the other securitisation companies and the credit facilities agreement between those companies and the liquidity and credit enhancers restricted the issuer's business activities to issuing CP and incidental operations. RMS No. 4's assets must consist almost exclusively of the transferred receivables that backed the CP. The contract with BHP incorporated minimum standard terms that met the rating agencies' requirements.

A true sale. The SPV relies on the quality of the transferred assets, not the creditworthiness of the originator. A true sale from the originator to the SPV (and the "corporate separateness" of the SPV) should preclude a court dealing with an originator's bankruptcy from piercing the corporate veil and reclaiming assets transferred to the SPV as a fraudulent conveyance. A true sale requires the transfer of all risks and benefits to the purchaser. It must be irrevocable and without recourse. US courts will generally examine the transfer, its documentation, accounting, timing and price. Most European countries have similar anti-fraud standards to protect other creditors of a bankrupt originator. In Germany, France, Belgium, the UK, the Netherlands and Spain bankruptcy law requires the sale to have taken place before the originator became legally insolvent or initiated bankruptcy proceedings. If the sale prejudices other creditors, and the purchasing SPV is aware of this, the sale is not effective. Asset sales contracts may prohibit the transfer of assets when a covenant of the sales contract (e.g. debtor in default, insolvency etc.) is broken. In order to avoid a recharacterization or annulment of the intended sale, the parties must consider whether such a clause would violate the true sale criterion in the originator's jurisdiction. See R. Palache and I. Bell, *Legal and Tax Issues*, *in* Morrissey at 91.

The contract between RMS No. 4 and BHP provided that BHP would sell the loans to RMS No. 4 at face value. For servicing the loan receivables, BHP would receive a service fee. RMS No. 4 would own a portion of all BHP's employee loan receivables and receive a share of all loan payments made to BHP.

BHP paid two monthly fees to RMS No. 4. A fixed amount was for administrative and management costs, including fees for credit and other enhancements. A variable amount incorporated the cost of issuing and servicing the securities, including the cost of building reserves to pay interest on the commercial paper (CP). The assets were not overcollateralized.

BHP would absorb costs due to changes in the environment of RMS No. 4, such as tax or regulatory changes.

BHP guaranteed that none of the transferred loan receivables was in default and that no legal risks existed in the validity and enforceability of the loan agreement between BHP and the loan debtors and in the assignment to RMS No. 4. The nominal amount of the transferred receivables must equal or exceed the money raised by the issuer's sale of the asset-backed CP. Through the assignment of the loans, Deutsche Bank received the right of recourse to the debtor's BHP stock if the loan debtor defaulted on the repayments. BHP accepted a number of covenants specifying performance indicators for the loans. Historically, the employee loans had very high quality, as BHP staff had almost never defaulted. The continuous increase in the value of BHP's stock in the past five years meant that it had outperformed the benchmark Australian All Ordinaries Index by more than 50%. BHP retained the dividends on the employees' shares and credited them to the employees' outstanding loan balance. BHP had a record of over 50 consecutive years of stable or increasing dividend payments.

RMS No. 4 would monitor the quality of the assets. BHP would regularly report the loan repayment performance of the debtors, the remaining outstanding volume, and other characteristics. Three times each year, BHP's independent auditing firm Arthur Andersen had to certify to RMS No. 4 the existence and volume outstanding of the transferred loans.

If BHP broke any covenant, a two-step process would start. During a grace period of three days to one week, BHP could have to provide updated information to Rhein-Main No. 4 and clarify the situation. If the problem was not corrected, RMS No. 4 could take a number of steps, the most drastic of which would be to stop buying BHP loans, as required by the liquidity and credit enhancement contracts. The portion of the BHP loan portfolio owned by RMS No. 4 would be liquidated. Issuance of CP backed by BHP receivables would stop.

The true sale and corporate separateness criteria also have important accounting, tax, and regulatory implications. The overall effect is to encourage parties to choose the most friendly jurisdiction for each part of the transaction.

5. ACCOUNTING TREATMENT

Accounting treatment may guide the tests for true sale and consolidation. US rules set three requirements for a sale: the originator transferred control of the economic benefits of the receivables to the SPV; the originator's obligations under the recourse provisions are reasonable; and the originator is not obliged to repurchase the assets except under the limited recourse provisions. See S. Almond and C. Henderson, *Accounting for International Securitisation*, in Morrissey at 151.

Consolidation of the underlying assets with the originator's could gut the securitization. In addition to its impact on the investors, who would bear the risks of the originator, consolidation would change the balance sheet of the originator. Consolidation would increase the originator's assets and require increased debt or equity, which must be serviced and for which the costs rise as leveraging increases due to the consolidation.

Consolidation is generally required if the originator controls the SPV. The SPV can avoid consolidation by ensuring that no originator holds equity in the SPV, as was true for RMS. Where the trust structure is not available, banks frequently rely on unrelated parties to raise the necessary minimum equity to set up an SPV and become the pro-forma shareholders.

6. TAXATION

International asset securitizations allow tax forum shopping. The parties that meet the choice of law rules can shape the tax treatment of the transaction in their choice of jurisdiction and design of the SPV. Three important areas are tax on:

> The receivables transfer;
>
> The cash-flows between debtor, SPV, and investors; and
>
> The SPV.

The tax for each party depends on the jurisdiction in which each is located for tax purposes.[*]

The receivables transfer may generate a sales tax or force the originator or SPV to recognize a gain or loss. Some countries levy a registration or stamp duty on the originator's sale. When the purchase price exceeds the face value of the asset, gain may be taxed as income to the originator. A loss would also be recognizable. Some countries like the

---

[*] Much of this discussion draws on R. Palache and I. Bell, *Legal and Tax Issues, in* Morrissey at 91.

UK use the fair market value of the receivables rather than their face values to determine gains and losses.

Australia taxes the transfer of interest-bearing securities whenever the sale is to a non-resident. This is a form of sales tax. To avoid this unfavorable Australian tax treatment, the Jersey-based RMS Group incorporated its subsidiary RMS No. 4 in Australia. This entity was established solely to buy the BHP employee loans. Australian law governed the contract between RMS No. 4 and BHP, including the assignment of the loan receivables. Selling to an Australian entity and issuing through a Jersey-based conduit reduced the tax burden both for the originator BHP and the potential CP investors.

Some countries withhold tax on interest payments in general or if the payments leave the country. Many countries do not. The ABS transaction would be structured to avoid withholding tax on interest paid either by the debtors to the SPV or by the SPV to the investors. Cross-border payments often find relief in double tax treaties between the affected countries.

To avoid double taxation, the SPV must be designed to avoid treatment as a corporate entity for tax purposes. The US, UK, and France permit tax-exempt trusts or trust-like SPVs. Otherwise, a tax haven like the Cayman Islands serves the purpose, though some havens lack double taxation treaties. Competition among tax havens leads them to strengthen their infrastructure. The Cayman Islands, for example, launched a stock exchange in January 1998 that lists many structured debt securities, such as collateralized bond or loan obligations. See A. Nealon, *New Focus for Cayman's Stock Exchange*, International Financial Law Review 52 (December 1998). Concern about possible abuse led the U.S. Internal Revenue Service to propose rules that would restrict activities and arrangements of Financial Asset Securitization Investment Trusts. C. Adelman, *New FASIT Regulations Pose Hurdles for Securitization Industry*, International Financial law Review, May 2000 at 13.

Deutsche Bank chose the tiny channel island of Jersey, off the English and French coasts, as the jurisdiction for RMS. The many foreign financial institutions with offices on the island generated 40% of its gross domestic product. The U.K. managed Jersey's external relations, Jersey set domestic policy, and was excluded from almost all aspects of the EU. Jersey maintained its fiscal independence. Capital movements were unrestricted. Jersey levied no capital gains tax, capital transfer tax, withholding tax, gift tax, wealth tax, estate duty or sales taxes of any sort; the only significant tax was income tax. Its moderate flat income tax rate of 20% had remained unchanged since 1940 and, as many exemptions from this tax were available, more than two-thirds of all Jersey-registered companies paid no income tax at all. Every wholly owned subsidiary of the Jersey company RMS Holding based abroad could benefit from Jersey tax and corporate laws.

Jersey's corporate law imposed few hurdles for incorporation and operations of a company on the Island. A minimum of three shareholders was needed to incorporate a limited liability company. Nominees could keep the identity of the beneficial owner anonymous. The company had to have its registered office on the island. Auditors need not be appointed and an income-tax exempt company did not have to file any returns or accounts. Minimum capital and paid-in capital requirements were low. Incorporation could occur in a week at a cost of less than US$2,000.

7. CREDIT, LIQUIDITY, AND OTHER ENHANCEMENTS

Investors usually demand very high investment grade securities in an ABS. The assets themselves do not earn this grade without enhancements that reduce risks of credit, liquidity, currency, and prepayment.

Credit enhancement reduces the effect of default by the debtors on the underlying assets. It is based on the historical performance of the receivables, and usually covers between 5% and 20% of the outstanding receivables.[*] It may be provided internally, by extra collateral or by the sponsor taking the equity, or it may be provided by third party guarantors. Over-collateralization sets the nominal amount of the receivables above the nominal value of the ABS issued, to provide a buffer against debtor default. A spread account accumulates differences in the interest rates on the receivables and the lower rate on the ABS in a reserve to offset debtor defaults. A senior/subordinated debt structure protects the senior securities. In many, the underwriters or dealers of the security agree to buy the complete subordinated tranche. Other forms of collateral (other than the receivables themselves) may secure the debtors' payments to the originator. The SPV may receive a claim against this collateral. Third parties, usually banks or insurers, provide unconditional guarantees, such as irrevocable standby letters of credit, on which the SPV can draw if debtors default.

The RMS credit enhancement applied to non-performing receivables. It consisted of a standby letter of credit and sometimes a subordinated loan. The maximum amount covered by the letter of credit was based on the historical performance of the receivables, potential debtor concentrations, and performance triggers related to the originator. This limited the credit facility to a percentage of the receivables RMS No. 4 held. For it, as well as the other RMS securitization companies and therefore for each originator, this percentage was calculated individually

---

[*] A. Carron *in* Fabozzi at 654. For automobile ABS in the US, historically the range has between 8% and 15%, whereas for credit cards it was between 8% and 20%.

and specified in the receivables transfer contract between the originator and the securitisation company. Each securitization company's credit enhancement could be called to support non-performing assets in another company once the credit enhancement for the first was exhausted. The credit enhancer, which the rating agencies required to be A-1+/P-1 rated, was Deutsche Bank. Deutsche Bank enhanced credit with a standby letter of credit for 5% of the pool of outstanding receivables in the BHP securitization. If debtors defaulted, the credit enhancement facility made up the shortfall up to 5%.

Liquidity enhancement reduces the risk that a failure by the servicer to transfer the debtors' payment to the SPV on time might prevent ABS investors from being paid. Liquidity may be enhanced by the same internal techniques as credit enhancement (over-collateralization, spread account, etc.) or by third party guarantees. These bridge the timing differences between the due dates of the ABS and the receipt of payments from the debtors.

RMS No. 4 had a liquidity facility to ensure that payments were made in full to the investors when they fell due as long as the assets met the quality standards. A syndicate of banks led by Deutsche Bank, all rated A-1+/P-1, covered fully any shortfalls in the payment stream through RMS No. 4, due to timing differences. If new CP could not be issued in sufficient value to meet the issuers's obligations in outstanding CP, the reserve for interest, the liquidity facility, and the credit enhancement would be used to repay maturing CP.

The liquidity facility for RMS No. 4 supported only performing receivables; they could not be in default or more than a certain number of days past due. The liquidity banks would pay, in the same currency as the receivables, advances due to RMS No. 4, which would transfer the funds to the issuer. The liquidity facility addressed three other risks:

1. Commingling: As it serviced the receivables, the originator received the payments by the debtors and usually deposited these payments in the same bank accounts used for receipts from non-securitized receivables. In the originator's bankruptcy, it could be extremely difficult to separate these funds. The liquidity banks would fund the amounts due until the payments on receivables were credited to the securitization company's bank account.

2. Dilution: even if the originator's debtors claimed set-off, trade discount, or other reductions in their payments due, the originator was obliged to pay the securitisation company the full amount owed, but the liquidity banks would pay if the originator failed to do so.

3. Invalid assignment: if the assignment of the receivables to the securitisation company was invalid or contested, the liquidity banks would provide the funds.

RMS Ltd was required to ensure that the liquidity facility always fully covered the total amount of CP outstanding. Both facilities were in the same currencies as the receivables. This preserved the total amount and denomination of the asset pool. Since RMS group was a multi-currency vehicle, however, the currency of the receivables was not necessarily identical to that of the CP whose issue was backed by those receivables.

Enforcing the credit and liquidity enhancement. Where third parties enhance credit or liquidity for the SPV, they must be rated at least as high as the SPV. To protect the investors in the outstanding ABS, contracts between the third party enhancers and the SPV usually provide payout event triggers. These start to wind down the ABS transaction, liquidating the receivables portfolio and prohibiting further debt issuance by the SPV. Typical trigger events are a deterioration of the receivables quality, the rating agencies' downgrading of the SPV, originator or servicer, bankruptcy, invalidity of the receivables transfer, or the breach of the originator's warranties relating to the receivables.

RMS No. 4 entered a commissioning agreement with the issuer (RMS Ltd) that allowed the former to instruct the issuer to issue CP periodically and remit the proceeds to it. RMS No. 4 had to satisfy all the issuer's payment obligations in issuing the CP. The commissioning agreement specified the events that trigger the stop issuance mechanism for RMS No. 4. Termination events defined in the asset transfer contract between RMS No. 4 and BHP prevented the securitisation company from buying more receivables from the originator. If one occurred—say, the liquidity enhancement contract expired—RMS Ltd. could issue no further CP. Indeed, whenever all expenses relating to outstanding CP for BHP could not be met because the bundle of resources was inadequate, a stop-issuance mechanism prevented further issuance of CP. The liquidity reserve would be drawn.

Currency risk hedging in international asset securitizations shield the investors from exchange rate movements against the currency of the receivables and the ABS. Third parties, usually banks, provide foreign exchange or currency swap agreements.

RMS No. 4 had to hedge fully the currency risk in a cross-currency securitisaton by short-term foreign exchange agreements or long-term currency swaps with A-1+/P-1 rated counterparties such as Deutsche Bank. This hedged the effect of a mismatch between currencies of the outstanding commercial paper and those of the receivables in the securitized pool. The CP stop-issuance mechanism ensured that currency movements which increased the funding cost for a pool of receivables would not negatively affect the timely and full payments due the investors of the CPs already issued and still outstanding.

An adverse change in interest rates had the same consequences as the exchange rate movement by increasing the effective interest rate on future CP issues, and therefore the cost of their funding, over RMS No. 4's projection at the time of purchase. Unless there was a sufficient reserve to cover all interest due on outstanding CP, the stop-issuance mechanism prevented the issuance of a new tranche of securities.

Other enhancements. Receivables with a longer maturity, like mortgages or automobile loans, usually carry a prepayment risk. Many investors look for a predictable cash flow. They seek payment at a known date because they need funds then and not before or after. Institutional investors like pension funds or insurers forecast their funding requirements and gear the maturity of their assets to these needs. For them, a risk is that the debtors may fully repay their debt before the end of the contracted period. In a falling interest environment, the earlier liquidation of the receivables exposes the SPV to a reinvestment risk, i.e. the repaid funds can only be reinvested at lower rates of return. Guaranteed investment contracts (GIC), provided by banks or insurers, can reduce the reinvestment risk. Pay-throughs manage prepayment by permitting an agreed flow of funds to the investor.

8. INVESTORS AND THE TYPES OF ASSET BACKED SECURITIES

The size and characteristics of the targeted investor group largely determine the form of the asset backed security. Investors in asset backed securities tend to be institutions, particularly in the euromarkets. They are primarily interested in the price, yield, and maturity of the ABS. Rates can be fixed or variable and maturities do not have to correlate with that of the underlying receivables because the asset backed securities are in different classes designed to have various maturities and interest rates.

Market liquidity is important to ABS investors. Rather than hold longer-term bonds to maturity, they usually require an active and liquid secondary market. Commercial paper is attractive to investors because its maturities of less than one year reduce funding and credit risk. This allows the investor to accept a lower return, which makes commercial paper attractive to issuers. Investors usually hold commercial paper to term. Since CP are privately placed and do not require a secondary market, the minimum needed for an issue is considerably less, so issues of $20 million or even less are feasible.

The commercial paper. The RMS CP were privately placed at a discount and redeemed at par mainly with institutional investors in Germany (40%), elsewhere in Europe (25%), and in the Middle and Far East. The CP were not marketed in Japan. Most of the CP had been in Deutschmark and eurodollars, but also included the European currency unit (ECU), Swiss Francs, Canadian Dollars, and Dutch Guilders. The maturity of the CP ranged between seven days and one year, but the bulk of the paper matured in one to three months, with a small percentage going up to six months. While there was no legal requirement to receive a rating in the Euromarket, the CP had a top rating, A-1+/P-1. Deutsche Bank and Lehman Brothers, the dealers, handled all investor relations, including marketing, and periodically reported to RMS Ltd. Pricing reflected investor demand. Deutsche Bank decided that the CP required active marketing, particularly to German investors to familiarize them with the concept and structure of the SPV. The effort to educate German investors was hampered by the unwillingness of the German corporations that securitize their receivables through RMS to shed anonymity.

RMS Ltd continuously issued CP backed by the securitisation companies' receivables and enhancements. Investors were informed that receivables funded the CP. They did not know all the originators or which pool of receivables backed their CP, though RMS kept track through internal accounting. Overcollateralization of one pool could be used to pay investors in CP issued for another pool. If one pool encountered problems, the credit enhancement contracts with Deutsche Bank allowed the investors the protection of all the bank's letters of credit. CP gave the SPV more flexibility to pool receivables from different originators. Most eurobond issues created a new issuing company for each pool of receivables.

Regulatory issues affect the form of security. Many jurisdictions require registration and reporting for publicly offered and traded securities. Some securities, like commercial paper or eurobonds, may be exempt from registration requirements. Institutional investors like insurance companies or pension funds may be limited by law or their corporate statutes in the amount or type of a particular class of securities they may buy.

German law was important to RMS, which placed much of its CP with German investors. The Bundesbank regulated German's money market. It prohibited banks from issuing debt securities with a maturity of less than two years; this included euro-DM CP. The rule did not extend to non-banks. RMS Ltd. was not considered a bank.[*] A potential CP issuer would be unwise not to consult with the Bundesbank when selling euro-DM CP to buyers in the German market. Deutsche Bank presented its RMS structure to the Capital Market Division of the Bundesbank which voiced no objection and approved the transaction informally. Had the Bundesbank given a negative opinion, Deutsche Bank would not had pursued the venture as planned. It prized its good relationship with the German central bank and its position as a primary dealer for Federal Treasury paper.

---

[*] This conclusion was reached by analogy to factoring companies whose operations did not fall within the scope of the definition of "banking business" of the German Banking Law (Kreditwesengesetz).

The commercial paper designated the provisions about debentures in the German Civil Code (BGB) as applicable law. Debentures in bearer form, such as the CP issued by RMS Ltd., could easily be assigned by the creditor to another party which then assumed the rights under the debenture. The issuer need not be notified. The law was silent about accelerating debentures, but the Rhein-Main CP could not be accelerated. If the issuer defaulted, the creditors could not require that the outstanding balance be paid before maturity. A major default by debtors could, however, stop issuance of new CP.

German securities law generally required disclosure of detailed information in a prospectus. The obligation did not apply to CP with a maturity of less than one year or to securities offered only to institutional investors. Germany had adopted the EU rules and exemptions. For euro-securities, no prospectus was required if the minimum tranche sold to an individual investor was more than DM 80,000. See §2 Law Regarding Securities Prospectuses (Gesetz ueber Wertpapier-Verkaufspros-pekte vom 13.12.1990). See the definition of a euro-security below. Since the Rhein-Main CP would qualify under all three exemptions, it had no obligation to publish a prospectus.

Deutsche Bank got the informal approval of other central banks in whose currencies it planned to issue CP. Several selling restrictions applied. In the UK and Australia, the CP could be advertised and sold only to institutional investors. For Switzerland, the dealers agreed to comply with any laws, regulations, and guidelines of the Swiss National Bank about the offer and sale of the CP. The CP could not be offered or sold to persons residing in Jersey, as this might affect the income-tax exempt status of the issuer, RMS Ltd.

RMS No. 4 had to pay RMS Ltd, the issuer, the amount due on the CP ahead of any fees due the servicer and interest due on the credit enhancement. Liquidity enhancers ranked equally with the investors. Payment on the notes may be preceded by tax claims or other fees and payments due to other debtors of RMS No. 4.

The Euro-CP Market. The boundaries of the euro-CP market were unclear. Deutsche Bank considered CP denominated in DM and issued by a Jersey corporation to be Euro-CP even if the buyers were in Germany. The definition used in this Textbook specifies an international selling syndicate and a currency other than that of the country of issue. Other definitions identify when a security becomes a euro-security for a specific purpose. For example, when setting prospectus requirements, Germany defined a "euro-security" as a transferable instrument distributed by a group with members registered in two different states, offered in one or more states than that of the issuer, and acquired first through a financial institution.

Commercial paper programs could profit from the steepness in the yield curve, i.e. the difference between higher long-term and lower short-term interest rates. This made the repackaging of higher-interest longer-term loans attractive, as they could be replaced by revolving, lower-priced CP.

9. RATING

Rating agencies play pivotal roles in the ABS market. Investors force the SPV to get independent ratings of its securities. As a separate legal entity without deep pockets, the SPV lacks the reputation of a large corporation and cannot rely on its name. The complex technical detail in an asset securitization means rating agencies offer a quick professional estimate about the quality of the issuer at great savings to the potential investor.

A rating is an opinion about the ability and obligation of the SPV to make full and timely payments on the security. Standards vary for short-term (less than one year) and long-term securities.[*] Rating agencies, which are paid by the SPV, generally examine five types of risk: debtors' credit risk, operational risks of payments among all parties, legal and tax risks for the receivables and securities, risk that any party will not perform, and sovereign risk. The criteria to judge these risks depend on the assets and jurisdictions. Although the rating agencies prescribe no specific structures to achieve certain ratings, generic structures have evolved that are modified to fit the transaction. Examples of long-term ratings by S&P's, Moody's, and Fitch's are in Exhibit 2.

Exhibit 2

Comparative Ratings for Long-Term Securities

LEADING BOND RATING SERVICES Explanation of corporate/municipal bond ratings	RATING SERVICE		
	Fitch	*Moody's*	*Standard & Poor's*
Highest quality, "guilt-edged"	AAA	Aaa	AAA
High quality	AA	Aa	AA
Upper medium grade	A	A	A
Medium grade	BBB	Baa	BBB
Predominantly speculative	BB	Ba	BB
Speculative, low-grade	B	B	B

[*] This is required by law in France, where Article 40 of the 1988 Securitisation Law (Loi No. 88-1201) requires that the SPV receive a rating from an officially accredited independent rating agency.

LEADING BOND RATING SERVICES Explanation of corporate/municipal bond ratings	RATING SERVICE		
	Fitch	*Moody's*	*Standard & Poor's*
Poor to default Highest speculation Lowest quality, no interest	CCC CC C	Caa Ca C	CCC CC C
In default, in arrears, questionable value	DDD DD D		DDD DD D

Ratings have a long tradition in the United States but are relatively new in the European markets. The need for a rating is particularly new to the German market. Large German corporations usually issue unsecured CP without any rating and German investors rely on the name and recognition of the issuer. Rating agencies have been less important in Germany because, compared to the U.S., Germany's economy and financial system are smaller so that the major players know each other better, the major banks' dominance and corporate role means they have much better information about issuers than would investors in the U.S., and the banks and issuers are so closely linked that the borrowers' mobility is limited.

BHP had an A rating from Standard & Poor's and A2 by Moody's for its long-term US dollar debt, which accounted for about 63% of its total outstanding debt. Its short-term ratings were A-1 (one step below A-1+) and P.

Deutsche Bank's strong capital position was reflected in its outstanding credit ratings: S&P's AAA and A-1+, and equally high ratings from Moody's and Fitch's. It was one of only a handful of European banks in this category. Deutsche Bank was the largest bank in Germany and among the top ten world-wide, with operations in more than 50 countries.

The commercial paper issued by RMS received the top rating that Standard & Poor's and Moody's Investor Service assigned for short-term securities (A-1+, P-1). The sponsor had to make sure the structure conformed with the key requirements of the rating agencies in order to obtain the desired rating.

Notes and Questions

1. Why securitize? What are the costs and benefits of securitization to the originator?

2. Consider the features sought in securitizable assets listed in Section 1 above. What is the idea behind them? When banks originate their own assets, they seek assets with the listed features. But they have

many other assets, often in the form of commercial loans, that lack many of these features. What would be the impact of being able to securitize these assets?

   3.   Concerning bankruptcy remoteness:

   a   Why is it important to rely on asset quality rather than the originator's creditworthiness?

   b.   How would relying on asset quality facilitate international transactions in ABS?

   c.   How important would the originator's home country be in asset securitization? Would it matter if the country was Australia or Zambia?

   d.   When a bank originates assets, it is important to the investors that the SPV be remote from the bank. What reasons would the bank have to be sure the SPV was remote?

   e.   How does the need for bankruptcy remoteness affect the structuring of funds flows?

   f.   Under what circumstances should a court recharacterize a sale of assets for the ABS? Suppose the seller guarantees the collection of all the receivables. Canadian courts take the view "that the retention of significant risk by the seller . . . should not compromise a lawyer's ability to provide a clean true sale opinion. . . . Where the parties' intention to sell assets is clearly evidenced . . . , the courts will not recharacterize the transaction . . . ." M. Fingerhut, *Securitization Takes Off in Canada*, International Financial Law Review, Nov. 2000 at 39.

   4.   Why are credit, liquidity, and other enhancements necessary if the quality of the assets is kept so high? Who benefits from the use of enhancements?

   5.   How important are rating agencies for securitization? Why? Could securitisation take place in countries that lack rating agencies? What are the alternatives to rating?

C. THE DEVELOPMENT OF NATIONAL ABS MARKETS

This section presents the law governing securitization in four countries, representing a range of approaches. The U.S. led the way. Germany and Japan lagged, then pushed reforms in the late 1990s, addressing problems posed by, among other things, their code law systems. India, although it has a common law system that is supposed to be conducive to ABS, has identified many hurdles in the law that should be removed if securitization is to play an important role in the country, as the central bank seems to want. As you read this part, please consider why a country would want to promote securitization and what is required to develop ABS markets within a country.

1. THE US ABS MARKET

The US ABS market evolved from the mortgage backed securities market In 1985, Sperry Computer made the first ABS offer, backed by computer leases. Since then, public ABS issues grew steadily, from about $25 billion a year in the late 1980s to $50 billion in 1990, just over $100 billion in 1995, and over $200 billion in 2000. Compared to corporate bond issues, they rose from 20% in the late 1980s to 67% in 2000. ABS consistently won more stable ratings and had a much lower default rate. Private ABS issues were much smaller. See A. Sharma and H. Paris, *Securitization in Emerging Markets: A Development Opportunity, International Finance Corporation Development Paper*, Feb. 2001, at 5, citing data from Moody's Investors Service and Standard & Poor's (Sharma and Paris).

Most US ABS assets are credit card receivables and automobile loans. They account for about two-thirds, with much of the remainder in trade receivables, equipment leases, and student loans. Most take the form of bonds or trust certificates, but CP are growing. Total outstanding ABCP (stock, not flows) rose from $50 billion at the end of 1993 to $600 billion at the end of June 2000. Many see the instruments as so standard as to be a commodity. By 2001, a concern was that consumers would not be able to service their debt as the U.S. economy grew more slowly. Indeed, in the first quarter of the year, delinquencies and charge-offs on credit cards rose for the third consecutive quarter. If investors reduced their demand for ABS, consumer lending would slow, creating a vicious cycle. Fitch IBCA, Duff & Phelps, *Asset Backed Special Report*, August 3, 2000 at 3; M. Walker, *New Frontiers in Securitization*, Euromoney, Feb. 2000, at 55; G. Silverman, *$92bn Credit Where Credit's Due*, Financial Times, May 11, 2001.

Paving the way for the ABS markets in the United States were the existing MBS markets. The following describes the development of US MBS.

S. ALMOND AND C. HENDERSON, ACCOUNTING FOR SECURITIZATION
Morrissey at 151.

The US mortgage-backed securities (MBS) market has undergone dramatic expansion since the first deals were made in the 1970s, and now boasts the stature of one of the most significant capital markets in the world. ....

Home ownership has long been an integral part of the "American dream," and has received official encouragement in the form of various initiatives dating back as far as the early 1930s and designed in the first instance to help the economy recover from the Depression. These include the tax deductibility of mortgage interest payments; government programmes and agencies created to promote housing finance; and the structure of the "Savings and Loan" industry, traditionally the main provider of residential mortgages. ... These factors and rapid economic expansion led to a flourishing primary mortgage market, with the volume of outstanding mortgage debt growing from US$73.1 billion in 1950 to US$3,852.0 billion in 1990.

. . .

The US government established the Federal Housing Administration (FHA) in the 1930s to insure residential mortgage loans made to lower income Americans against default. This helped to improve the level of finance available for home purchase at a time when confidence was low as a result of the Depression. Later, the Veterans Administration (VA) established a similar programme to the FHA insurance scheme, whereby it guaranteed the mortgage loans of home purchasers who had served in the US military forces.

The government also established three agencies to promote housing finance through the development of secondary debt markets. The first of these, the Federal National Mortgage Association, known as FNMA or "Fannie Mae", was founded in 1938, to buy and sell mortgage loans insured by the FHA. Fannie Mae bought these loans from their originators, boosting the lenders' capacity to make new loans. The purchases were initially funded through Fannie Mae's issuance of straight corporate debt paper, creating the first link between the US housing finance and wholesale capital markets. The second housing agency, the Government National Mortgage Association, known as GNMA or "Ginnie Mae", was established within the US Department of Housing and Urban Development ("HUD") in 1968. Its mandate was to encourage the development of the secondary market for FHA-insured or VA-guaranteed mortgages. GNMA issued the first US mortgage-backed securities in 1970. Finally, the Federal Home Loan Mortgage Corporation, FHLMC or "Freddie Mac" was established in 1970 to provide the same function for non-government, or "conventional", mortgages as Ginnie Mae provides for FHA and VA loans. Freddie Mac made its debut issues in 1971.

The early GNMA and FHLMC issues were "pass-throughs."

. . .

Much of the innovation within the US MBS market over the past decade has indeed been driven by the recognised need to deal with prepayment risk. Collateralised Mortgage Obligations (CMOs), for example, consist of several tranches with differing priorities over the cash flows on the underlying collateral.... The CMO structure was created by First Boston in 1983, and has become one of the most important types of US mortgage security. During the 1970s, however, the agencies continued issuing pass- throughs and the secondary mortgage market grew slowly, lacking an impetus such as strong investor demand or support from Wall Street.

The thrifts' early mortgage-related securities were mortgage-backed bonds... [that] do not achieve the comprehensive transference of risks off balance sheet that is accomplished via the pass-through structure. The first US mortgage-backed bond issue was brought by California Federal ("Cal Fed") Savings and Loan in 1975. The mortgages collateralising this deal were FHA-insured or VA-guaranteed, with an initial collateralisation of 175% of the issue.... Other mortgage-backed bonds were subsequently issued in the mid-1970s by thrifts, on the basis of FHA, VA and conventional mortgage loans.

US savings and loan institutions, hit by soaring deposit interest rates in the late 1970s and early 1980s and low interest on long-term mortgages, were helped by Congress in September 1981. But the continuing mismatch and even riskier lending forced a massive bailout of saving and loan institutions in 1989. Despite the insolvent thrifts' huge MBS holdings, the favorable risk-weightings applied to agency MBS for the purposes of the BIS capital adequacy requirements for banks, and growth in overseas investor interest, contributed to healthy demand for US mortgage product. Almond and Henderson continue:

> Today's investor in the US secondary mortgage market has a choice of instruments offering fixed or floating rates, the whole spectrum of maturity structures, agency or "private label" credit status and bearing very different levels of prepayment risk.

US government policy affected the MBS market in other ways. The Tax Reform Act of 1986 created real estate mortgage investment conduits (REMICs) through which MBS could be safely issued without tax at the SPV level. Issuers of MBS are exempt from the requirements of the Investment Company Act of 1940. Registration of MBS pursuant to the Securities Act of 1933 is by a special form. The Comptroller of the Currency regularly supports the authority of national banks to issue MBS. Glass-Steagall rules do not prevent banks from selling MBS without recourse.

US laws provide ABS much less special treatment. In 1996, Congress authorized a vehicle for securitizing debt called the Financial Asset Securitization Investment Trust. See C. Adelman, *New FASIT Regulations Pose Hurdles for Securitization Industry*, International

Financial Law Review, May 2000 at 13. Other laws affecting ABS include the following:

Federal Securities Law:[*] The Investment Company Act of 1940 does not apply to issuers of nonmortgage assets who are

> primarily engaged in purchasing 'notes, drafts, acceptances, open accounts receivable, and other obligations representing part or all of the sales price of merchandise, insurance and services' or 'making loans to manufacturers, wholesalers, and retailers of, and to prospective purchasers of, specified merchandise, insurance, and services.'

The Securities Act of 1933 expedites SEC review of the registration statements

> for the issuance of both mortgage and nonmortgage asset-backed debt securities if the issuer is a majority-owned subsidiary of an established company that is obligated to file periodic reports under the Securities Exchange Act of 1934 (1934 Act).

Bank Regulation: National Banks, according to the Comptroller of the Currency,

> are authorized to issue securities backed by or representing interests in mortgages and other assets. Depending on the accounting, tax, and other structural aspects, securitization activities of national banks have been justified as a means of either borrowing funds or selling assets. In both cases, securitization of bank assets is perceived as a way to enhance liquidity; manage capital and other balance sheet ratios, as well as interest rate exposure; reduce asset concentrations; and diversify income sources.

Sale of Assets Using Participation Certificates: "Under both GAAP and RAP, the transfer of mortgage or other assets entirely without recourse to the transferor is normally treated as a sale."

Small Business Loan Securitization: In 1994, the US Congress reduced accounting problems created by regulations that hindered banks from securitizing small business loans when the transactions involved some recourse. A goal was to enhance the liquidity and marketability of these loans.

Capital Adequacy: In 1997, the Federal Reserve Board proposed to change the risk weight for asset backed securities from 100% to 20% (see Chapter 4). This would allow banks to hold capital equivalent only to 1.6% of the value of the ABS, rather than 8%. The Basel Committee on Bank Supervision proposed changes to its guidelines in 2001, as described later in this Chapter.

---

[*] Summarized from R. Dayan, et al., *Legal Overview of Asset-Backed Securities*, *in* The Handbook of Asset-Backed Securities 41 (J. Lederman ed., 1990).

The ABS market was a smaller offshoot of the MBS market. One difficult issue for regulators was how to treat participations in short-term loans sold in their entirety by the securitizing bank, which kept no interest. Bank regulators advised that the bank's policy should make clear that "loan participants are not investing in a business enterprise. Second, banks should sell these participations only to investors with experience...." Third, banks should only sell to borrowers meeting their credit standards. Fourth, potential buyers should be able to examine information about the originator's credit standing, to make informed investments. See O. Domis, *Banks Advised How to Avoid Classifying 100% Loan Participations as Securities*, American Banker, Apr. 24, 1997.

The MBS market confounded US monetary policy in 1993-94. The Fed was trying to tighten monetary policy. One of the Fed's goals was to flatten the yield curve by reducing inflationary expectations that would raise long-term interest rates. The opposite happened in 1993-4. A partial explanation lay in the MBS market. MBS dealers hedge against the risk that the duration of their MBS portfolios will lengthen if interest rates rise. As rates rise, fewer mortgages are prepaid and refinanced, so the expected maturity of the MBS grows. Dealers hedge against this "extension risk" by short selling Treasury bonds with maturities that match the maturities of the dealers' long positions in MBS. As MBS maturities lengthen, dealers shift to T-bonds with longer maturities. This raises the yields on the longer T-bonds relative to shorter ones: buyers must pay more since demand has grown. The markets are big; perhaps $300 billion in 10-year equivalents were sold from October 1993 to April 1994. One study concluded the effect on Treasury yields was significant. Long-term rates rose more than short-term. See J. Fernald, F. Keane, and P. Mosser, Federal Reserve Bank of New York, *Mortgage Security Hedging and the Yield Curve* (1994).

During the 1990s, prepayment became a problem in various ways. In 1994, it became a problem in reverse as interest rates rose. Mortgage holders stopped prepaying at earlier rates, which stretched out payments on pass- and pay-through MBS far beyond the forecast period. Volatility made pricing of new MBS difficult. Homeowners also took many fewer new mortgages, which reduced new MBS issues dramatically (by 75% in the second quarter of 1994). One fund achieved notoriety by losing much of its investors' $600 million and going bankrupt in April 1994: Askin Capital Management was a leveraged CMO fund that took many exotic interests, such as reverse interest only strips, and bet wrong. Investors in the junior paper sought the risk and some were wiped out. But by 1998, one analysis concluded that homeowners' propensity to refinance had increased due to structural changes in information technology that make the U.S. mortgage market more competitive. See P. Bennett, R. Peach, S. Peristiani, *Structural Change in the Mortgage Market and the*

Propensity to Refinance, Federal Reserve Bank of New York Staff Reports (September 1998).

Notes and Questions

1.   How important to the evolution of markets for MBS in the US was the existence of Ginnie Mae, Fanny Mae, and Freddy Mac and these other policies? What explains these policies?

2.   Compare the various forms of US government support for the MBS and ABS markets. How important was this support for the relative development of each in the US?

2. ABS MARKETS IN EUROPE AND GERMANY

ABS markets in Europe are smaller than those in the US and grew more slowly until the mid-1990s, then surged. From less than 10% the size of the US market in 1995, the European ABS markets grew to 40% by 1999. Sharma and Paris at 6. Asset backed bond issues were forecast to grow 20% in 2001 to $100 billion. A. van Duyn and J. Chaffin, *Asset-Backed Bonds Set for Year of Growth*, Financial Times, Jan. 26, 2001.

National ABS markets in Europe grew at various speeds. From the late 1980s, the U.K. dominated in Europe though its share fell to about 50% of all structured issues in 2000. In the mid-1990s, France ranked second and Italy third, but Germany rose from a trivial 0.1% of all ABS issues to second place by the end of the decade, accounting for 13% in mid-2000. Anticipating the euro, several countries streamlined their markets, including France, Italy, and Spain. Germany followed a bit later and its markets seem to have responded to the new policy. The ABS funded mergers and acquisitions, synthetics described below, and non-performing loans. The following material describes securitization in Germany. See E. Hagger, *The Quest for Securitization*, Euromoney, Sep. 1998, at 170, citing Fitch Investors Service; M. Peterson, *Securitization: Any Flavour But Vanilla*, Euromoney, Sep. 2000, at 334.

Receivables originated by German companies can be securitized, since a creditor may assign receivables to a third party. The assignee is subject to the debtor's defenses against the assignor at all times. Assignment is permitted unless excluded by the contract, but German companies tend to exclude it because they want to know to whom they are indebted. Notification of the debtor is not required, but payment by an unnotified debtor to the original lender is a defense against an assignee.

In Germany, a debt security called the Pfandbriefe, in existence since 1769, has been a major financing tool for mortgage banks which were governed by a special mortgage banking law. Many of the mortgage banks were owned by the big German universal banks. The Pfandbriefe allowed the mortgage bank to refinance long-term mortgage loans by selling interests in a pool of such loans on the bank's books to investors.

Pfandbriefe were collateralized by the bank's pool of residential mortgages, but no specific mortgages backed particular Pfandbriefe. Strict loan-to-value limits and tight regulatory supervision minimized the risk of these securities, and they bore no prepayment risk. The law required the volume and interest rate of the mortgage loans on the bank's books to be at least as high as those of the Pfandbriefe, to protect the investors. If the mortgage bank defaulted, the Pfandbriefe investors might have recourse to the bank's other assets. Institutional investors like insurance companies were subject to no ceiling on their holdings of Pfandbriefe, which counted toward the insurers' mandated coverage ratios. Big German universal banks were major investors in Pfandbriefe. Thus they could be on both sides of the transaction. They benefit from increased liquidity even though as the originator they would remain liable.

Mortgage bonds and communal bonds, like the Pfandbriefe, are found in many countries in Europe. One estimate at the end of 1993 set their total volume in 15 countries at $900 billion, just short of the MBS market in the U.S. Germany accounted for over half of the total volume in Europe. See J. Thompson, *Securitization: An International Perspective* 16 (1995). German Pfandbriefe became increasingly popular among foreign investors in the mid-1990s. They were issued in various currencies, including french franc, dollars, and euro. A growing number of jumbo issues were mortgage-backed, but most were backed by government debt. By early 1999, when jumbos were redenominated in euro, outstanding Pfandbriefe equaled $1.1 trillion. The ECB allowed Pfandbriefe to serve as Tier 1 capital. See L. Covill, *What's Behind the Flight of the Jumbo*, Euromoney, April 1998, at 138; U. Harnischfeger, *Pfandbrief Success Encourages Imitators*, Financial Times, April 15, 1999.

Candidates for securitization in Germany include auto loans, credit card and other consumer loans, and even public sector receivables. None was securitized in Germany until mid-1998. The following paragraphs explain why.

Captive financing companies of the car manufacturers supply much of the auto loans in Germany. The spreads on the loans are very narrow, since financing is an important marketing tool. Some domestic car manufacturers securitized their North American receivables through ABS-programs in the US. Daimler Benz of North America issued two public ABS totalling US$1.2 billion. Volkswagen and BMW securitized through US vehicles.

Credit cards were introduced in Germany in the mid-1980s, but were only modestly used. An alternative was the Arecaceae, a standardized check accepted across Germany and Europe to pay for goods and withdraw funds from a bank account. The ECB Card, a combination ATM and debit card, supplements the Arecaceae. The ECB card issuing bank guaranteed every Arecaceae to a certain level. ECB Card and

Arecaceae fees to consumers and merchants were a fraction of a percentage point, much lower than those for credit cards. Balances were either immediately deducted from the user's account or cleared at the end of the month.

Consumer loans were plentiful. Most purchases they funded were subject to guaranty and warranty periods of at least 6 months for the goods purchased. If the goods were inadequate, the consumer could refuse to pay the loan, exchange the goods, or lower the purchase price. This made it difficult to securitize the loan.

The large infrastructure projects in East Germany after reunification in 1990 and the ensuing budget crisis prompted debate about public finance. One suggestion was to securitize public sector receivables from infrastructure projects like interstate highways and sewage treatment. Most Germans were skeptical about this proposal.

In Germany, the major source of revenue for municipalities is a tax on business. Local governments tax the income and net assets of companies, including 50% of each company's long-term debt and the interest payments on that debt. A special purpose vehicle with no significant income would be liable for tax on the ABS it issued. Since January 1, 1993, a withholding tax applied to interest payments on German-issued ABS.

German receivables could instead be securitized through SPVs abroad. A few German corporations securitized their assets anonymously through off-shore vehicles, but through 1995 only Continental Tire AG had publicly even announced its intention to securitize its domestically originated trade receivables. Other larger German corporations like Daimler-Benz and Volkswagen were rumored to be actively securitizing German assets, but had not publicly admitted it. German corporations were reluctant to sell their receivables. This still carries the stigma of a last resort financing effort by companies in financial distress.

Banks comfortably exceeded the minimum ratios prescribed by the capital adequacy rules. Until 1997, the Federal Banking Supervisory Office, which regulates banks, opposed the securitization of bank loans, citing residual legal or moral recourse risk which would not be reflected in the bank's balance sheets. The only publicly known transaction in Germany, a securitization of consumer loans by Citibank's German subsidiary KKB Bank via an SPV in the Cayman Islands in 1990, was apparently not prohibited because the regulators learned about it too late to stop it. While no formal opinion, law, or regulation prohibited banks from securitizing their loans, the bank regulators repeatedly stated their serious concerns.

In February 1996, Deutsche Bank managed the securitization by Volkswagen of German receivables at a time when VW was performing exceptionally well. The securities were issued in the euro-markets. Some saw this as a watershed.

A basic shift in government policy preceded the take-off of Germany's ABS market in the late 1990s. Several government actions made ABS easier. In May 1997, Germany's Banking Supervisory Office issued the "Circular Regarding the Sale of Customer Receivables of Credit Institutions in Connection with ABS Transactions." Advisory rather than with the binding force of law, the circular explained how lenders could remove receivables from their balance sheet (for purposes of determining required capital) and how bank secrecy rules could be respected when receivables were transferred as part of an ABS. The circular required a true sale, no recourse, no substitution of receivables, and limited repurchase of receivables. It limited the originator's ability to finance the SPV and the originator's moral obligation for the receivables. In September 1997, the Supervisory Office issued a circular permitting banks to repackage sovereign and quasi-sovereign loans for OECD countries and, carefully limited, other countries. A German Insolvency Code, which took effect at the start of 1999, clarified the rights in bankruptcy of the liquidator against assigned assets, but excluded true sales used to create ABS. E. Reudelhuber, *The Issuance of Asset-Backed Securities by Credit Institutions in Germany*, Part 2, Butterworths Journal of International Banking and Financial Law, Mar. 1998 at 98 (Reudelhuber). See A. Vogt and K. Dittrich, *Germany Issues Guidance on Asset-Backed Securities,* International Financial Law Review, August 1997, at 15; and M. Weller, K. Vasu, and J. Rinze, *Securitization*, International Financial law Review, Special Supplement, April 1998, at 39; E. Reudelhuber and A. Vopgt, The Issuance of Asset Backed Securities by Credit Institutions in Germany (Part II).

The law remained unclear in several ways. One was a requirement in the Legal Services Act that the local court approve "the commercial collection of another party's receivables and of receivables assigned for collection purposes." The exception for credit institutions that collect from their customers did not appear to apply even to banks collecting for the SPV, which was not a customer of the bank. Another unresolved issue was the status of a cross-border ABS using a trust. The German Federal Supreme Court said that when German law governed the receivables, no trust can be created. German law was not consistent with the trust concept. When the law of a common law jurisdiction governed the receivables, a trust for them would be valid. Germans could transfer assets governed by German law to a trust subject to common law. Uncertainty created by these rules led Germans instead to use a "collateral agent" to hold the assets as a fiduciary for the investors. The practice, based on case law rather than legislation, is known as *Treuhand*, and translated as fiduciary administration or fiduciary transfer.

Insolvency of the collateral agent is not a problem for investors. Reudelhuber.

Insolvency of the originator continues to raise minor issues. Future assets, which come into existence or the originator's possession after the ABS agreement is executed, may not be subject to the prior assignment of assets to the SPV. In German law, a global assignment transfers receivables. Upon the originator's bankruptcy, the SPV can have all the assets it then owns separated from the originator's assets. But suppose that at the time of bankruptcy, under a partly performed contract between the originator and the source of the receivables, further receivables would come into existence if the contract were fully performed. Suppose that these receivables were anticipated as part of the funding to service the ABS. Under German law, these future receivables are not assigned to the SPV (the rationale seems to be that the bankruptcy allows the administrator not to perform the contract). If the originator does receive them, the SPV would not be able to separate them from the bankrupt's assets. Reudelhuber at 100.

A year after the governmental initiative started, German banks began to issue MBS and, using their own corporate loans as receivables, ABS. In April 1998, Dresdner Bank issued a DM 2 billion ABS using commercial paper and medium-term notes. Dresdner was allowed to provide liquidity to the SPV. Deutsche Bank issued a DM 1.4 billion ($800 million) MBS one month later and an ABS three months later. The MBS broke new ground in Europe with an unrated tranche and interest-only tranches. The ABS attracted investors by offering a way for them to take positions in German corporations, since Germany's bond market is undeveloped. One estimate put the potential German MBS market at over $10 billion annually if banks merely securitized each year 5% of outstanding mortgages, DM 1.9 trillion at the end of 1997. Even the mortgage banks that offer pfandbriefe securitize as well. Their governing law limits their use of mortgages to back their *pfandbriefe* to 60% of their total mortgages. Commerzbank solved one traditional problem by successfully offering an ABS without disclosing the identify of some of the corporate borrowers, thus preserving the bank's relationship with these customers. E. Hagger, *The Quest for Securitization*, Euromoney, Sep. 1998, at 170; J. Walsh, J. Fried, *Securitisation of German Mortgages*, Butterworths Journal of International Banking and Financial Law, Oct. 1998, at 425; C. Harris, *Commerzbank Breaks Ground in Loan Risk*, Financial Times, Nov. 10, 1998.

Synthetic securitization blossomed in Germany in 1999, possibly substituting for ABS. In a synthetic transaction, a bank swaps the credit risk on 80%-90% of a portfolio of its loans, retaining the rest or restructuring it as a junior ABS bond. The credit default swap, which is the senior tranche, is with another bank, which often swaps again with insurance companies. The swap leaves the assets on the originating bank's books and raises no new funds for the bank, but requires only 20% capital because the swap is with an OECD bank, rather than the 100% capital needed for loans to private borrowers. Deutsche Bank introduced this to Germany in 1999, drawing on U.S. innovations. In 2000, almost $40 billion in synthetic transactions took place. It was not clear, however, if the synthetics and traditional ABS were substitutes or met different needs. J. Burke, *The Synthetic Solution*, Institutional Investor, Jan. 2001, at 33.

Notes and Questions

1. What explains the late development of the German markets for MBS and ABS?

2. How close a substitute for an MBS is the Pfandbriefe? Are they identical? If not, are the differences important?

3. How important is German government policy and law in the development of Germany's MBS/ABS markets? Why would the bank regulators be seriously concerned about securitization by banks?

4. German banks are universal banks supplying most corporate finance in the form of commercial loans. German capital markets have been traditionally weak compared to those of the US or UK. How would this affect the development of the German ABS market?

5. No German rating agencies exist to rate the securities. What would account for this? How important would it be for the development of the ABS market in Germany?

6. What potential do you foresee for the development of a domestic German securitization market? What further changes would be needed in policy or the financial context?

3. ABS MARKETS IN JAPAN

After reluctantly letting securitization markets grow for many years, in 1996 with the Big Bang the government began to promote securitization and by 2000 Japan's markets ranked second to those in the US, albeit a distant second.

During much of the 1990s, Japanese law made securitization expensive and cumbersome. The transfer of each individual loan or receivable required the certificate of a notary, except that from 1993 leasing and credit companies did not need notarization to register their transfers. Establishing an SPV was costly: a corporate SPV needed ¥10 million capital (about $100,000) and 3 directors. Regulation was "complex and inflexible, . . . [and] divided ministries . . . had jurisdiction over divided industries." H. Kanda, *Securitization in Japan*, 8 Duke Journal of Comparative & International Law 359, 360 (1998) (Kanda). MBS started a bit earlier than ABS in the mid-1980s. The MBS quickly acquired a reputation for fraud, which did not reassure regulators about the wisdom of promoting securitization.

ABS in Japan include bank loans (since 1989), equipment leases, car loans, installment sales, and credit cards. In the early 1990s, few of the instruments were defined as a security, which limited demand for them, though amendments to the Securities Law in 1992 expanded the definition a little. The Law for Regulating Business of Specified Claims, No. 77 of 1992 (MITI Law) took effect June 1993. The Ministry of Trade and Industry implemented it, and imposed "additional layers of regulatory control," according to Kanda at 371, MITI added a review of each plan by the Structured Finance Institute of Japan and requiring a license from MITI and the Ministry of Finance (MOF) if the SPV was not incorporated. This law did not permit entities other than leasing and credit companies to originate ABS. This would exclude banks and industrial companies from direct business in the markets.

In the late 1990s, the government began to make securitization easier. The Special Purpose Companies Law of September 1998 made SPCs remote from bankruptcy, gave them tax benefits, reduced their minimum capital to ¥3 million, allowed them to have only one director, and limited their additional debt. Mondellini at 98.

The obligation to notify each debtor repeatedly was addressed by the Law Prescribing Exceptions to the Requirements for the Perfection of Assignment of Receivables under the Civil Code (Law No. 104 of 1998) (the "Perfection Law"). Registration by public filing would perfect an assignment against third parties without notification. Almost any financial asset, including receivables, is covered. "Many participants think it could boost the creation of new asset types in the securitization market." L. Mondellini, *A Rapid Take-Off, But Can the Sector Keep Flying?* Euromoney, November 1999 at 98 (Mondellini). Unfortunately, this new rule had defects. It did not perfect assignment against a party to the ABS, including the underlying obligor. The danger is that the obligor may claim a set off against the originator. The only solution is get the obligor's consent without reservation or to give notice with a certified copy of the registration. This is therefore called the "Imperfection Law." C. Lewis, Securitization of Consumer Loan Receivables in Japan, *The Asian Securitisation and Structured Finance Guide 2000* (1999) at 44 (Lewis). Moreover, it was not clear that the goal of the law was entirely accomplished. Notice to the borrower of the assignment is still required by the Moneylenders Law, independently of the rules for perfection. For revolving credits, such as consumer loans, detailed notice is required with each draw down. Lewis at 47.

To promote ABS issues by non-banks, the government passed the Law Concerning Bond Issuance by Commercial Lenders for Lending Activities (Law No. 32 of 1999, called the Non-Bank Bond Law). This law made it easier for lenders that were not banks to issue ABS. The law provided that the originators were not operating illegally as banks, which prior law implied. The new law required the non-banks to register with the Financial Reconstruction Commission, have a minimum capital, and disclose substantial information about such things as bad debts and interest rates. This is particularly important for consumer finance receivables. Lewis at 47.

The ability to securitize future assets is a problem in many code law countries, of which Japan is one. In 1999, the Supreme Court broadened the range of future assets that could be securitized to include any that were sufficiently specified, a standard test in many countries. The court said that the assets could come into existence at any time in the future, no longer within the 1 year limit set by courts earlier. Lewis at 47.

The ability of non-lawyers to manage and collect debt is limited. Japan's Lawyers Law (Law No. 205 of 1949, as amended) "prohibits third party non-lawyers from settling or taking legal action with respect to debts." Lewis at 48. To reduce the problems this creates for securitization, Japan passed The Law for Special Measures Concerning the Debt Management and Collection Business (the Service Law) in 1998. Companies that qualify can get a license to manage and collect a limited set of assets. Thus a licensed moneylender, if it is a bank subsidiary, can manage and collect only receivables secured by real property and owed by certain commercial firms. The 1998 law did not promote securitization across the board, however. Consumer loan receivables remain subject to the Lawyers Law. Any third party can manage them until "a case or controversy arises," at which point "only the new owner, a lawyer or possibly the originator may service the loan." Lewis at 48. So Japan does not seem to have solved this problem and Germany seems not to have addressed it.

Japan's financial markets rose to the opportunity. From 1996 to 1998, loans to corporations were the main securitized asset, as banks sought to get the loans off their balance sheets. The banks slowed this process in 1999 after receiving capital injections from the government. In 1999, the major asset became consumer finance (e.g., car loans, consumer loans, promissory notes). Consumers were seen as very low risk because of their almost unblemished record servicing their debt. Large portions of the ABS (and MBS) were sold to foreign investors. While foreign securities firms arrange most cross-border securitizations, the big domestic banks dominate those sold within Japan. Mondellini at 100-1.

In the sister market securitizing real property loans, residential and commercial mortgage backed securities also grew quickly from 1999, when banks did start to remove them from their balance sheets. The potential for the market was large. One estimate, including the bank's bad loans and the need of companies for liquidity, predicted almost $50 billion in MBS by 2005. Morgan Stanley Dean Witter was the only investment bank prepared to securitize non-performing real estate loans in 2000. It assembled loans for 441 property in the major commercial cities of Tokyo and Osaka and had an SPV in the Cayman Islands issue yen bonds in four tranches worth $46 million. The total maturity was 5 years, but people expected most loans to be repaid within one year. Investors were based in Japan, Europe, and the US, and the issue was oversubscribed by 100%. A. Harney, *MSDW Prices Property Loan Securitisation*, Financial Times, Aug. 9, 2000.

4. ABS MARKETS IN INDIA

India recently investigated what would be needed to permit markets for securitization to grow.   Over more than five decades since independence, the country reshaped the common law system that the English left. By the late 1990s, people in government and the financial sector expressed the need to have laws that would support the development of securitization. The market was negligible.

In 1999, one Indian lawyer said, "The Indian legal framework is not generally geared to providing a suitable legal structure to promote and regulate the issuance, transfer, trading, and enforcement of securitized instruments (whether in the nature of pass-through certificates or pay-through certificates)." A. Ghoshal, *Securitisation: Legal Framework in India,* The Asian Securitisation and Structured Finance Guide 2000 19 (Dec. 1999) (Ghoshal).

Answering the question of what changes were needed to make the law suitable, the Reserve Bank of India published the *Report of the In-house Working Group on Asset Securitisation*, Dec. 29, 1999 (RBI Report). In a wide ranging review, the report identified the following ways that the legal system created impediments to ABS. The analysis of impediments to MBS is not reported here. The discussion incorporates observations by Ghoshal.

    a.   Laws Affecting the Investor Base.

Pass-through certificates do not clearly qualify as securities for purposes of the securities law. Many financial institutions lack the unambiguous power to invest in ABS. Capital adequacy rules fail to define the risk weights for ABS held by banks. Disclosure of information about the assets is inadequate for informed investor choice.

    b.   The Regulatory Environment.

True sale lacks clear definition. Regulators have not given insurance companies clear guidelines about their investment in ABS. Existing regulations for non-bank financial institutions are applied to SPVs but are inappropriate.

c. Legal Provisions, including Tax Law.

Securitization is not defined in any law. This creates problems as legislators and regulators try to strengthen the many laws and rules that need attention.

Fees and taxes raise the cost of securitization. High fees must be paid to register asset transfers. Stamp duties on the assignment of receivables vary by each state and are so high in many states that they make securitization too expensive. While some stamp duties are very low flat fees, many others are imposed ad valorem and substantial rates. States impose stamp duties at every stage of the transaction, with a devastating cumulative effect. The RBI Report proposes a low national stamp duty. Income tax is deducted at source at every point funds are transferred, for example on the transfer from the originator to the SPV, and when the SPV pays the investors (Income Tax Act 1961). This is because a person who transfers income without also transferring the underlying asset must pay income tax (Income Tax Act, 1961, §60), making it difficult to establish an SPV as a tax free conduit.

Certain types of assignment are inadequately defined, and therefore not permitted, by the law. Transfer of future receivables is not possible for ABS. By law, the property being transferred must exist to be transferred (Transfer of Property Act, 1882). If the property does not exist, the contract is executory and the liquidator can terminate it. So claims that are contingent or conditional cannot be transferred. Partial assignment of a claim has been prohibited by the courts as possibly forcing the debtor to take part in multiple cases involving a single debt (Code of Civil Procedure, 1908, Order II Rule 2).

Some limitations arise from the form of the SPV. Corporate SPVs cannot be bankruptcy remote because the Company Act allows a court to wind up any company with a debt as low as Rs. 500 (about $10) unpaid for three weeks. The corporate SPV may find that the funds it receives are treated as corporate deposits, according to the Company Act 1956 §§58A and 58B, in which case the law substantially restricts the use of the funds (Ghoshal at 21). SPVs that are trusts may not be able to list the securities they issue on an Indian stock exchange, since no regulations govern them. If the SPV is a pay-through trust, it may be subject to complex and inappropriate regulations issued by the RBI for non-banking finance companies (Ghoshal at 21).

Secrecy laws prevent a publicly owned financial institution from divulging any information about its debtors to anyone other than other banks and financial institutions. This would make it difficult for the firm to originate receivables as assets.

The RBI Report proposed a schedule that would resolve these problems over the following two years.

While the report identified many problems that the law creates for ABS, it did not address all legal problems that ABS could face. Three examples follow.

Notice to the debtor and third parties about the assignment is difficult with ABS backed by intangible financial assets. Indeed, how do third parties in India know that an SPV owns some or all of the receivable? The RBI Report briefly alludes to the Registration Act, 17(1)(b), which is optional for interests in personal property.

Security interests are common in pay-through ABS. The investor acquires no proprietary interest in the underlying asset but often receives a security interest in it. The laws governing secured transactions in India are complex and often unclear. Effective notice by registration is only possible for companies, which must use the company registry. Company registries, moreover, are at the state level, not centralized. This makes it very difficult to notify other possible prior or future claimants to the asset assigned by a non-corporate originator. Priority is difficult to establish because the timing, and therefore the rank, of claims cannot be certain in advance of bankruptcy. In India, a registered secured creditor may not have priority even over later registered secured creditors, let alone over other unregistered secured creditors or assignees of the receivable. W. Fleisig, N. de la Pena, and P. Wellons, *Secured Transactions Law Reform in Asia: Unlocking the Potential of Collateral*, Asian Development Bank (2000). The RBI Report does not address the problems this may cause or suggest solutions to the problems.

Enforcement is very slow. It often takes over eight years in contested cases to resolve disputes in Indian courts, an exceedingly long time even by emerging market standards.

Questions

1. On which legal reforms should India concentrate? What can India learn from the experience of Germany and Japan to promote its own ABS markets?

D. LEGAL ISSUES FOR CROSS-BORDER ABS

Cross-border ABS raise a set of legal problems not found in purely domestic securitization. An ABS can achieve cross-border status in various ways. The originator may be in one country and those receiving the proceeds may be in another. The SPV company or trust may be in a country other than the assets. The assets may be in one currency, while the payments to the investors are made in another. If, for example, the originator were a Thai company, the receivables were dollar earnings from computers it exported, and the SPV were based in Jersey, the trust would receive payments and distribute them to investors without the funds ever being in Thailand, the originator's country. Cross-border assets that are securitized also include long distance phone charges and airline ticket receivables.   But cross-border ABS often securitize assets in the originator's home country, such as consumer credit and credit card receivables.

Cross-border securitization brings several benefits to the parties to the transaction and to their economies, according to Tamar Frankel, *Cross-Border Securitization: Without Law, But Not Lawless*, 8 Duke Journal of Comparative & International Law 255, 265 (1998) (Frankel 1998). By disaggregating functions across countries, she says, the parties can structure the transaction so that each stage can be performed in the country where it can be done most efficiently or most cheaply. Of course, she adds, a country must manage the downside, which is that this also permits avoidance of regulation, taxes, and exchange restrictions. The cost of regulation should fall if powerful external investors replace the national regulators as disciplinarians of the issuer and intermediaries. Generally, the cross-border ABS market offers an alternative to inefficient local financial institutions.

An ABS tries to "separate the inherent value of an issuer's asset pool from one aspect of its environment (the bankruptcy laws), [and] cross-border securitization seeks to partially separate the inherent value . . . from another aspect . . . (the country in which it is located)." E. Arca, *Cross-Border Securitization*, 12 The Review of Banking & Financial Services 21, 26 (Feb. 14, 1996) (Arca). But the separation is not complete. For example, to the extent that the underlying assets are in a country other than that of the investor, country risk exists. The security itself is usually issued offshore, raising special problems. A collateralized bond obligation (CBO) issued offshore will require a global custodian and local sub-custodians, introducing additional risks for the investor. Foreign exchange issues arise, which parties reduce by using swaps and forwards. See S. Schwarcz, *The Universal Language of Cross-Border Finance*, 8 Duke Journal of Comparative & International Law 235, 247-8 (1998) (Schwarcz 1998).   According to Arca at 26-7, the "complex matrix of factors" at work in cross-border markets creates additional volatility in the flow of funds, forcing investors to rely more on-going rating. So cross-border ABS markets introduce risks not found in domestic securitization.

Complex issues involving applicable law and its substance arise from cross-border ABS. The issues are relatively straight-forward for matters involving the contractual relations between the investors and the SPV that issues the securities to them: the security can designate the applicable law. The problems arise for proprietary matters involving the investors' and the SPV's ownership rights in the assets. For example, a major potential trap for the SPV, the investors, and trustee is that the originator continues to manage most assets. The receivables' obligors continue to pay the originator, not the SPV directly. The originator could convey multiple interests in the same asset, some preceding and some following when the interest was conveyed to the SPV. The debtor and others acquiring an interest in the asset could conclude that it was still the property of the originator or unencumbered by any security interest. This is, of course, the problem for any interest in an intangible. It is not possible to transfer physical possession of the asset—a right to payment—to the new owner or secured party, and transferring the documents is often not feasible either. Resolving this problem is at the heart of any system of secured transactions.

The problems for proprietary interests arise at two levels in the ABS transaction:

- At the Originator/SPV level, the SPV's interests in the assets provided by the originator must be fully protected from claims by others with a possible interest in them. The others may be other assignees, holders claiming a security interest in the assets, and the company's general creditors in bankruptcy. It may be necessary to give notice of the SPV's ownership, which in many countries is difficult since the receivables are intangible and lack a physical location.

- At the SPV/investor level, the investors' interests in the assets taken by the SPV must be protected as well. (a) In a pay-through SPV, the investors' interest is in the flow of funds. The investors do not own the underlying assets (as they do in a pass-through), but they sometimes take a security interest in the SPV's assets. (b) In some circumstances—such as when bonds are issued—a trustee is appointed to represent the interests of the investors. The SPV may give the trustee a security interest in the assets it owns. In other circumstances—like the BHP ABS described earlier in this chapter—several Tier 1 SPVs each will contract with its originator to take an asset pool and the Tier 2 SPV will issue the securities to the investors funded by the flow from all asset pools. The Tier 2 SPV will take a security interest in the asset pools of each Tier 1 SPV. The security interests must usually be registered or notice of them given in some other way to make them effective against third parties.

It can be difficult to identify which jurisdiction's law applies at either level. At the Originator/SPV level, covenants in the originator's other financial contracts may limit its ability to assign or transfer the assets: e.g., a prior negative pledge in another loan. Determining what law governs can be very difficult. Suppose, for example, that the covenant against liens is in a loan agreement governed by English law but the originator is located in Mexico, whose law may govern the lien. More generally, what law should govern? Should it be the law where the receivable is located, the law of the contract creating the receivable, the law where the assignor is located, or where the obligor is located? The challenge is severe when receivables or obligors are located in many jurisdictions. Schwarcz 98 at 240-3, and see S. Bazinas, *An International*

Legal Regime for Receivables Financing: UNCITRAL's Contribution, 8 Duke Journal of Comparative & International Law 315 (1998) (Bazinas).

At the SPV/Investor level, to protect the security interests in assets owned by the SPV one must consider different sets of laws depending on where rights are enforced, the type of asset, and the nature of the interest in it. The following example is given for the U.K. by Xin Zhang, *Trends and Developments in Cross-Border Securitisation, Part 1: Legal Structures and Analysis*, Butterworths Journal of International Banking and Financial Law, July/August 2000, at 269 (Xin Zhang 1). He describes the problem of determining applicable law when the securitized assets are securities themselves. The applicable law depends on whether the legal issue is contractual or proprietary. The contractual aspects (relations between the parties) are governed by the law governing their contract (called the proper law in the UK). The proprietary aspects – the nature of their interest in the assets – are governed by the country in which the asset is located (*lex situs*). Rules for *lex situs* vary with the type of asset and the interest in it. Various asset types, and their *lex situs* are:

– bearer securities: where the certificates are situated;

– registered securities: where they are registered;

– shares: the place of the issuer's incorporation, either at the particular registry or, if transferred by delivery, "where the relevant document is situated." Xin Zhang 1 at 276.

This rule "is disastrous," according to Xin. When "there are a number of underlying bonds in the portfolio of a CBO and the portfolio itself is managed on an ongoing basis, it would be impracticable for the SPV and the trustee to identify the situs of the varied bondholdings and to observe the formalities in each relevant country, especially where there are intermediate holdings and securities are transferred electronically." Xin Zhang 1 at 276.

Xin argues that when the securitized assets are securities the rule, which is from *Macmillan Inc. v. Bishopsgate Investment Trust plc (No. 3)* [1996] 1 WLR 387, should exclude securities held by intermediaries, such as a global custodian. The custodian's interest in the asset is as a trustee. While U.K. law offers no direct rule about the *lex situs* of trust interests in securities held by an intermediary, the general rule looks to the location of the trustee, which would be the place of the global custodian. "If the global custodian is located in London, English law will govern the attachment, perfection, and priority of the security interest created upon the bond portfolio." If the shares are held through a clearing system, perfection must accord with the clearing system's local law. "A two-tiered legal compliance strategy . . . [is needed] for proprietary issues of cross-border collateralization in a CBO. . . the law of the place of the global custodian and the law of the clearing system." Xin Zhang 1 at 277.

The applicable substantive law to protect the SPV's or investors' interests may be complex, confusing, or inadequate. For example, in a structure with two SPVs, in which Tier 1 holds assets in different countries and Tier 2 issues the security, the Tier 2 SPV may need a security interest in the entire business of Tier 1 SPV. Because Tier 2 needs the assets to continue to generate income (e.g., projects in various countries), it wants to be able to take over the entire business of the Tier 1 SPV. In UK law, which is an example of the complexity, this requires a fixed charge, a future charge, an assignment of rights and benefits of contracts, and a mortgage of the shares of the project. Xin Zhang 1 at 275-6. Many countries do not, however, have such a broad security interest. Instead, they permit only interests in certain types of property, often not clearly providing for security interests in receivables. These laws are inadequate to the needs of the ABS.

It is necessary, however, to perfect the interest and establish priority against third parties, whatever the level of the interest. Cross-border ABS encounter problems perfecting the interest under the applicable law. Local law in many countries is not certain (e.g., the role of filing to perfect a claim may be ambiguous). Actions required by law may be expensive, requiring notice to each obligor even where there are many (e.g. trade receivables). Actions required by law may not be culturally acceptable, as for example when giving notice to obligors sends a bad business signal (Germany has been a case in point). Schwarcz 98 at 240.

Cross-border ABS encounter problems establishing priority under applicable law due to difficulties filing or the limited scope for security interests in, for example, future property. Most systems require notice against third parties, and filing or registration is the most efficient way to give notice. But many countries have an ineffective or non-existent filing system. Many countries using code law systems have registries limited to interests in certain assets, such as vessels or heavy equipment. It is not possible to identify all persons that may have an interest in an asset that is serving as collateral. Many countries, particularly in emerging markets but not limited to them, have registries that are not centralized, are costly, or take a very long time to register.

Filing may be necessary for a sale as well as a security interest. In the U.S., filing by the U.C.C.-1 filing form puts third parties on notice of the transfer. For ABS, one danger is that filing might be considered evidence that the transfer was a secured loan rather than a true sale. In the U.S., "Any [such argument . . . can be obviated by stating on the financing statement that the intention is to create a sale and that the filing is being made because the U.C.C. requires it." Schwarcz 98 at 240. This is not always the case in other countries.

For receivables, a major potential problem is that the assets may not exist when the ABS is concluded and filing takes place. ABS may securitize, for example, receivables for credit card debt or auto loans that

CHAPTER 13   INTERNATIONAL ASSET SECURITIZATION   **813**

will be incurred in the future. In addition, ABS practice often allows the originator to substitute like assets for those originally identified. Xin Zhang 1 at 277. Establishing priority in these future financial assets can be difficult if not impossible. In many countries with code law systems, the property must be identifiable to establish priority against other possible interests. Thailand is one example. ADB Report at 28. Even common law countries may have problems. The longstanding English case law for assignment of receivables only resolved the issues for present receivables, not future ones. Xin Zhang 2 at 320. India and Pakistan, both common law countries, permit security interests in future property (after-created and after-acquired), for example, but in some circumstances priority is uncertain against other security interests that intervene between the filing of the first interest and the creation or acquisition of the asset. ADB Report at 28-29. Credit enhancement is a partial solution. Arca at 24.

Cross-border ABS with below-investment grade assets offer one way for originators with substantial bad debts to remove the debts from their balance sheets and at the same time tap sources of foreign currency. An example is the initiative by Morgan Stanley Dean Witter in Japan described above in the section on that country. These stand in vivid contrast to typical ABS, which take the best assets from an issuer with a rating lower than the best and, helped by credit enhancement, must win the highest rating to reduce the financing cost for those assets that the originator must pay. Emerging market structured bonds (CB0) did so using overcollateralization and subordination of junior tranches, particularly before the financial crises of 1997. Xin Zhang 1 at 274. A review by the International Finance Corporation since then revealed that ABS of originators from countries that later came under stress, such as Japan, Indonesia, Pakistan, Thailand, Argentina, and Mexico were serviced and continued to perform. Sharma and Paris at 17.

Questions

1.   When the originator sells the receivables to the SPV, how is that transfer made effective against third parties?

2.   What can be done to protect the SPV's interests in future assets, acquired or created after the transfer, in Germany and Japan?

E.   PROPOSED CAPITAL ADEQUACY RULES FOR ABS

The Basel Committee on Banking Supervision issued a consultative document on capital adequacy for asset supervision in January 2001 and asked for comments by May 31, 2001. The document offered a framework to provide adequate capital for what it called the explicit risks of traditional securitization and synthetic securitization. It briefly discussed the implicit and residual risks, such as the possibility that an originator may feel the need to protect its reputation if the value of underlying assets falls. The document listed the types of quantitative and qualitative disclosure banks should make when they act as originators or sponsors, or set up SPVs. This section presents the proposals for capital for explicit risk associated with traditional securitization.

Building on its general proposal for capital adequacy regulation, the Committee offered different rules depending on whether a bank used the standardized approach or the internal ratings-based (IRB) approach (see Chapter 4). For each approach, it distinguished among originating banks, investing banks, and sponsoring banks.

The standardized approach for originating banks set minimum operating criteria to achieve a clean break when removing the assets from the bank's books. A legal opinion must confirm that the assets were beyond the reach of the transferor and its creditors at any point. The SPV and those who hold beneficial interests in the SPV must "have the right to pledge or exchange those interests," and the transferor may have no "effective or indirect control over the . . . assets." A bank that fails any of these tests must treat the assets as its own and hold capital even if the transfer meets local true sale tests.

Originating banks may provide services, credit enhancement, and liquidity, but only in limited ways. They can enhance credit, but only at the start of the scheme; this includes the payment of servicing fees. They may provide short term liquidity only according to the terms of the contract, to avoid the possibility that circumstances might push the bank into providing liquidity in a way that negates the true sale. A liquidity facility advances "cash to ensure an uninterrupted flow of payments to investors." The advances may only have "very low credit risk" and must be reimbursable. Reimbursement must have priority over payments due to the investors from the assets' cash flow or credit enhancements. Capital would be required as follows. For credit enhancement, the originating bank "must deduct the full amount of the enhancement from capital." For liquidity facilities, the originating bank must treat these advances "as commitments," converting them to their on-balance-sheet equivalent at 20% of the fixed notional amount of the facility (or, if none is set, the full asset pool), and risk-weighting them at 100%.

Banks originating revolving credit securitizations are usually subject to early amortization clauses requiring the early termination of the program if the credit quality of the assets falls substantially. A downturn in the economy, for example, may raise the risk of default on consumer loans, for example. Early termination means that the bank, instead of selling the new receivables to the SPV, would have to keep them on its own books, fund those assets, and hold capital against them. To avoid these costs, a bank might try to provide implicit recourse, enhancing credit beyond the terms of the contract. Now supervisors impose operational requirements to assure a true sale, but the Basel Committee believes capital should be required. It proposes that the originating bank convert the tranche to its credit equivalent using a 10% to 20% conversion factor on the notional amount of the pool off the balance sheet. The factor rises from 10% to 20% depending on operational factors, such as the speed with which the amortization is due.

Banks investing in ABS must hold capital using risk weights based on external credit ratings when ratings exist. The weights are 20% (AAA to AA-), 50% (A+ to A-), 100% (BBB+ to BBB-), and 150% (BB+ to BB-). Tranches rated B+ and below, or unrated, are seen as credit enhancement and deducted from capital. An exception is made for unrated tranches that meet certain criteria. For them, the regulator looks through the securitization to the risk category of the underlying asset. The criteria identify a senior tranche, in which "the investors are exposed to the risk of the underlying asset and not to the issuer." Junior tranches bear 100% risk or, if held by the originating bank, are deducted from capital. National supervisors must decide when to look through.

Sponsoring banks in conduit programs, such as asset-backed commercial paper (ABCP), may offer a facility that ostensibly provides liquidity but really enhances credit. Current rules give liquidity facilities a zero conversion rate, so the incentive to cheat is great. The Committee proposes to raise the conversion rate to 20% and have a 100% risk weight if the facility passes certain tests, such as being an obligation to the SPV rather than the investors, allowing the SPV to have a third party provide the facility instead, and not being subordinate to the investors' interests. A facility that does not meet these tests is considered to be a credit enhancement. It takes the risk weights based on external ratings described above, like other second loss enhancements. In general, a "first-loss" credit enhancement–which like a junior tranche would absorb losses before the "second loss" senior tranche–should be deducted from capital."

The IRB approach to traditional securitization is outlined in the Consultative Document. Issuing banks would have to deduct "the full amount of retained first-loss provisions . . . from capital." But the Committee was considering a proposal to let issuing banks use an internal ratings-based approach (like that for credit risk) if the tranche was rated. Investing banks could calculate the probability of default using external ratings or their own internal system, then calculate the likely effect of that default using parameters set by the Basel Committee. The Committee recognized that substantial additional work was required.

Questions

1.   How well would the Basel capital adequacy proposals for ABS deal with risks to banks of giving credit enhancement and liquidity facilities?

eneral knowledge of financial markets for banking and securities and their regulation, both in the U.S. (Chapters 2 and 3) and Europe (Chapters 5 and 7). Bank regulatory issues arise concerning capital adequacy for Deutsche Bank (Chapter 4). Basic decisions about structuring the BHP transaction involved Jersey's special status as a tax haven, which is permitted by the European Union (Chapters 5 and 7), and the hedging of currency risk (Chapter 6). Telmex issued $1.5 billion in telephone purchase receivables a few years after the securities issue described in Chapter 20.

CHAPTER FOURTEEN

STOCK MARKET COMPETITION

One important feature of the world's financial system is increased competition between stock markets (including electronic networks) both within and among countries. Within countries such competition is usually zero-sum in that issuers are unlikely to list on more than one exchange. On an international level the issue is more complicated. If an issuer lists on only one exchange, for most companies in the U.S. and Japan that exchange is likely to be in the home country. For European issuers, however, given the variety of exchange choices in a single time zone and the adoption of the euro, there is active competition for single listings among countries. Increasingly, major issuers cross-list securities, that is they list securities on foreign as well as their domestic exchanges. Multiple listings may change the risk characteristics of the securities, e.g. market covariance or beta, making such securities more generally attractive. K. Smith and G. Sofianos, *The Impact of an NYSE Listing on the Global Trading of Non-U.S. Stocks,* NYSE Working Paper 97-02 (June 1997). Cross-listings on either the NYSE or the London Stock Exchange seem to be associated with a considerable increase in firm visibility. In effect, cross-listing is a form of advertising. H. Baker, J. Nofsinger, and D. Weaver, *International Cross-Listing and Visibility*, NYSE Working Paper 99-01 (January 1999).

Cross-listings may also provide increased access to capital when local markets cannot provide enough capital, provide access to a currency (foreign stock) for stock-based takeovers, serve as a means of compensating and motivating executives, e.g. U.S. executives of a foreign firm may find U.S. market stock options attractive. Several studies have found that non-U.S. firms benefit from a U.S. listing by decreasing the cost of capital. K. Lins and D. Strickland, *Do non-U.S. firms issue stock on U.S. equity markets to relax capital constraints,* Working Paper (November 1999). Cross-listings may also reflect the desire of issuers to "bond" themselves to more strict disclosure rules and enforcement so as to win the trust of investors. See J. Coffee, Jr., *The Coming Competition Among Securities Markets: What Strategies Will Dominate,* Paper prepared for the 9th Annual Singapore Conference on International Business Law (September 14, 2001).

In some cases cross-listing results in losses of trading volume in the home country, in others it increases home country volume as the cross-listing expands the total volume of trading. Cross-listing has triggered competition among exchanges for cross-listings, e.g. the NYSE and the London Stock Exchange may compete for the foreign listing of a German company, and for the share of volume in cross-listed stocks.

Competition among exchanges may force needed changes in the home country rules and systems. As will be shown later in this Chapter, this has been the story in Europe, where competition between London and the continent has caused dramatic changes in the way the exchanges are operated. Stock market liquidity, which often accompanies growth, is positively correlated with economic growth, capital accumulation and productivity improvements. R. Levine and S. Zervos, *Stock Markets, Banks and Economic Growth,* 88 The American Economic Review 537 (1998). Thus, countries may have a great interest in the results of stock market competition.

This Chapter examines the terms and consequences of this competition. It begins by looking at competition in the U.S. market, and then turns to a comparison of other major markets.

A. U.S. MARKET

We begin with the 1994 study of the Securities and Exchange Commission on U.S. securities markets. We then turn to competition between the NYSE and NASDAQ, and the effect of regulation on competition, using circuit breakers as an example.

1. OVERVIEW OF U.S. MARKET

SECURITIES AND EXCHANGE COMMISSION, MARKET 2000, AN EXAMINATION OF CURRENT EQUITY MARKET DEVELOPMENTS
Study II, Jan. 1994.

A. The Users of the Markets

The predominant trend of the past 20 years has been the growth in size and diversity of users of the equity markets. Current market participants include numerous large entities, representing both retail customers and professionals. In the Securities and Exchange Commission's ("Commission") 1971 Institutional Investor Study, this trend was described as the "institutionalization" of the market. The institutional presence in the markets has continued to grow. For example, in 1975, institutions owned 30% of U.S. equities, but by 1992 they owned slightly more than 50% (Exhibit 1).[*]

...The absolute amount of retail investor activity is greater than in years past, but the *percentage* of market activity attributable to direct individual investor participation in the market has declined. In 1992, block trades, which are effected almost exclusively by institutions, accounted for 50% of NYSE volume, an increase from 16% in 1975. Program trades, negligible in 1975, accounted for another 11% of NYSE volume in 1992. Activity by market professionals, such as options market makers and equity trading desks, accounted for an additional significant portion of NYSE volume. Thus, of the total volume on the NYSE, a minority results from the direct activity of individual investors. This trend is not as pronounced for the OTC market, but there is increasing institutional activity in that market as well, especially for OTC stocks included in the major market indexes.

Although there has been a decline in the percentage of *direct* individual participation, there actually has been an increase in *indirect* participation in the equity securities market. Individual investors are more likely to participate through institutions, such as mutual funds, public pension plans, private pension plans, or insurance companies. Together with the endowment funds of colleges and religious organizations, these entities now own over $2.3 trillion of U.S. equities.

. . .

B. Structure of the Equity Markets

. . .

1. Primary Exchanges (NYSE and Amex)

There are seven registered stock exchanges in the United States. The two primary exchanges—the NYSE and the Amex—list most of the stocks traded on an exchange. The five U.S. regional stock exchanges include: the Boston Stock Exchange ("BSE"), the Philadelphia Stock Exchange ("Phlx"), the Cincinnati Stock Exchange ("CSE"), the Chicago Stock Exchange ("CHX"), and the Pacific Stock Exchange ("PSE"). These exchanges primarily trade securities that also are listed on the primary markets.

The primary exchanges operate as modified auction markets. In the exchange auction all order flow for a stock is directed to a central location, the trading post for the specialist in the stock, and orders interact to the maximum extent possible. A specialist acts as a market maker by trading for its own account to ameliorate temporary disparities in supply and demand for the stock and also acts as the

---

[*] Exhibits are omitted.

agent for orders left on the limit order book. This structure proved inadequate to accommodate large block orders in the late 1960s and early 1970s. The NYSE and the Amex responded by modifying their auction rules to enable block orders to be negotiated by the trading desks of member firms off the floor of the exchange. The trading desk would find a customer to take the other side of the block, acting as an agent for both sides in the transaction, or would commit its capital by taking the other side of the block itself. In either event, a negotiated price for the block would be established off the exchange (i.e., upstairs), and the transaction would then be brought down to the trading post and exposed to the trading crowd and to any limit order book interest.

The modified auction structure served the NYSE well when it was practically the sole price discovery mechanism for stock. In 1975, the NYSE captured approximately 86% of the volume in NYSE-listed stocks. This concentration of volume allowed the NYSE to operate as a self-contained auction, albeit modified for block trading, which at the time accounted for only 16.6% of NYSE volume. Third market makers (discussed shortly) garnered a modest share of small customer orders.

In contrast, in the first six months of 1993, the NYSE accounted for only 70% of the total orders and 79% of the volume in NYSE-listed stocks. Moreover, block transactions, which often are negotiated off the floor of an exchange, accounted for half of the NYSE volume. Some blocks are sent to regional exchanges for execution, whereas blocks accounting for over 2 million shares per day are executed off the exchange after the close of regular trading hours. A substantial portion of small orders for public customers (i.e., orders for 3,000 shares or less) is sent to the regional exchanges or third market dealers for execution (Exhibit 11). Proprietary trading systems handle 1.4% of the volume in NYSE stocks, usually in the form of portfolio trades or block trades. Several large institutions or money managers cross portfolio orders internally between accounts. These crosses account for up to 1 million shares on any given day.

Almost 200 NYSE stocks are traded on foreign exchanges. Foreign trading accounts for several million shares per day in these stocks. Ten million shares per day are executed as program trades after the NYSE closes, either on the NYSE's after-hours crossing session or through the foreign desks of U.S. broker-dealers. Perhaps most importantly, active options and index futures markets provide an alternative means of trading NYSE stocks. The aggregate dollar value of trading in these markets far surpasses the dollar value of trading on the NYSE.

Although order flow is dispersed, the NYSE still receives the majority of small orders. Its market share in these orders, however, has eroded steadily over the past decade. The NYSE generally has retained the 3,000 to 25,000 share trades, which are too large for the small order systems of the regional exchanges and third market and too small to be handled by block positioners. These orders benefit from the liquidity provided by the NYSE floor, but they are also often difficult for the NYSE specialists to handle because the orders require capital commitment and trading acumen. In addition, the NYSE attracts orders that need special handling as well as trades for which the institutional customer wants to "see a NYSE print."

Despite the fact that it has lost some volume, the NYSE still plays an important price discovery function as does the Amex. Most securities markets set prices equal to or based on the primary market prices. For example, the regional exchanges and third market makers usually base their quotations on the primary market quote, and many of them simply autoquote the primary markets. Block positioners use the NYSE price as the reference point for negotiating block prices. Much after-hours trading is executed at NYSE closing prices. Similarly, proprietary trading systems often use the NYSE quotes as a pricing reference. The derivatives markets obviously rely on NYSE (as well as Amex and NASDAQ) prices to price options and futures. There are also numerous transactions involving equities that use NYSE prices.

The NYSE also serves as the market of last resort during times of market stress. During volatile market conditions, when normal liquidity is unavailable in the index-derivatives markets, market participants channel their stock orders to the NYSE. Moreover, supplemental sources of liquidity to the floor, such as block positioners, are less active during such periods. The NYSE has attempted to accommodate periodic surges of demand by upgrading the capacity of its automated floor systems and by increasing the amount of capital that specialists are required to have available. At the same time, the NYSE has adopted certain circuit breaker provisions, such as NYSE Rules 80A and 80B, which are designed to dampen these surges. Users of the market must understand that, if the NYSE is to perform the role of market of last resort, they will have to pay for this service in some manner.

2. Regional Exchanges

At an earlier point in their history, the regional exchanges served as "incubator" markets for small, local companies. For the past 20 years, however, the overwhelming percentage of regional stock exchange business has been in the stocks of NYSE-and Amex-listed companies that the regional exchanges trade pursuant to grants of unlisted trading privileges ("UTP"). In 1992, over 97% of the regional stock exchanges' volume derived from issues traded pursuant to UTP.

...The regional exchanges captured 20% of the orders in NYSE issues in the first six months of 1993. Most of this market share derives from small orders from individual customers. During the 1970s and 1980s, the regional exchanges built automated systems that enabled member firms to route small customer orders to their specialist posts....Because of the speed and efficiency of these systems, lower transaction fees, and the guarantee of the ITS* best bid or offer, many retail broker-dealers send some of their small order flow to the regional exchanges.

3. Third Market

OTC trading of exchange-listed securities is commonly known as "third market" trading. Third market dealers handle order flow sent to them by other broker-dealers. At the time of the Institutional Investor Study, third market volume derived principally from two sources. First, institutional investors desiring to avoid the NYSE fixed commission schedule entered into various order flow arrangements with third market dealers and regional exchange members. The unfixing of commission rates in 1975 caused this business to decline. Second, a few third market dealers acted as block positioners; the services of these firms were especially in demand when the NYSE was closed. Some third market firms continue to act as block positioners, but their role has been partially undercut as NYSE member firms have developed the ability to effect transactions in blocks at their foreign desks.

The past few years have seen third market trading increase, principally from operations established by a few third market makers to handle small customer order flow. The third market makers act much like NASDAQ market makers in that they accept orders of up to a few thousand shares in the most active listed stocks from retail firms or discount brokers. Market orders are executed against the best bid or offer on ITS, and limit orders are handled according to preestablished execution parameters.

Third market makers offer three advantages to firms with large retail order flow. First, third market makers have automated their operations so that they provide virtually instantaneous executions and reports. Second, they do not charge transaction fees, membership fees, or limit order commissions. Third, they usually pay $0.01 to $0.02 per share for order flow.

Third market activity is concentrated in the 400 most active NYSE stocks and a much smaller number of Amex stocks. The remaining NYSE- and Amex-listed stocks are not sufficiently active for third market operations. In 1989, the third market garnered 3.2% of reported NYSE volume and 5% of the reported trades; in 1993, this percentage had increased to 7.4% of reported NYSE volume and 9.3% of the reported trades.

---

* The Intermarket Trading System (ITS) is a communications system allowing specialists and floor brokers on one exchange floor to transmit buy or sell orders to market makers on another exchange floor, eds.

4. NASDAQ

NASDAQ is an interdealer quotation system operated by the National Association of Securities Dealers ("NASD"), which is registered as a national securities association under Section 15A of the Securities Exchange Act of 1934 ("Exchange Act"). NASDAQ consists of competing market makers for each security. Customer orders are not normally reflected in the market makers' quotes. Unlike the exchange market, limit orders are handled individually by each market maker.

At the time of the Securities Acts Amendments of 1975, Congress and the Commission found it unnecessary to regulate NASDAQ as an exchange. Although certain trading characteristics of NASDAQ are functionally similar to those of the traditional exchanges, the Commission believed that these similarities did not transform NASDAQ into an exchange. Nevertheless, the NASD is subject to regulation under Section 15A of the Exchange Act that is substantively similar to the regulation for national securities exchanges under Section 6 of the Exchange Act.

At its inception in 1971, NASDAQ publicly displayed only representative bids or offers; nevertheless, it revolutionized OTC trading by increasing the availability of quotes for OTC securities. As a result, spreads for these stocks narrowed, volume increased, and liquidity improved. In addition, NASDAQ led to greater visibility for its issues and expanded coverage in the media. NASDAQ also reduced dealers' reliance on the telephone and enabled integrated firms to compete as market makers with wholesale firms.

NASDAQ has made tremendous strides in automating OTC market making and increasing the efficiency and transparency of the OTC market, including: (1) the display of all market makers' quotes; (2) the implementation of real-time trade reporting for NASDAQ/NMS securities in 1982 and NASDAQ Small-Cap stocks in 1992; (3) the display of market maker quote size; (4) the introduction of its Automated Confirmation Transaction Service; and (5) the development of SelectNet. In addition, all NASDAQ/NMS securities have been marginable pursuant to Federal Reserve Board guidelines since 1984. They also are exempt from state blue-sky registration provisions in most states.

Initially, NASDAQ was considered primarily an "incubator" market. When its companies matured financially, they usually became listed on exchange markets. NASDAQ now is a major market in its own right. Based on volume, it is the second largest securities market in the world after the NYSE. Its dollar volume of trading is 43% of the NYSE's dollar volume. Its NMS market trades 3,104 companies, many of which qualify for listing on the primary exchanges but choose to remain on NASDAQ. Although most of the most highly capitalized companies are listed on the NYSE, a significant portion of the younger, widely held companies are quoted on NASDAQ. The three primary markets compete aggressively for listings.

NASDAQ is not a completely automated market. With the exception of its Small Order Execution System ("SOES") and SelectNet features, order entry and execution for NASDAQ stocks still occur by telephone. Moreover, it is difficult for a customer to have a limit order exposed on NASDAQ. As a result, proprietary trading systems, which offer both automation and limit order exposure, have been able to capture 13% of the volume in NASDAQ/NMS stocks.

NASDAQ now is linked with the exchanges through the interface between ITS and the NASDAQ's Computer Assisted Execution System ("CAES"). Through this linkage, NASDAQ market makers are linked to ITS for listed stocks that are not subject to off-board trading restrictions. The NASD has proposed to expand the linkage to all NYSE and Amex stocks.

5. Automated Trading Systems

Several types of automated trading systems offer institutions and broker-dealers the opportunity to trade off the exchanges and NASDAQ. The first are proprietary trading Systems ("PTSs"), screen-based automated trading systems typically sponsored by broker-dealers. PTSs are not operated as or affiliated with self-regulatory organizations ("SROs") but instead are operated as independent businesses. PTSs currently permit trading in equities, government securities, corporate debt, and options. As a practical matter, participation in these systems is limited to institutional investors, broker-dealers, specialists, and other market professionals.

Advancements in telecommunications and trading technology over the past decade have fostered the growth of PTSs. They have been used by institutional investors to reduce execution costs, avoid the market maker spread, and trade in size without incurring the market impact costs that could result if orders were handled on the organized markets. The popularity of PTSs has been fueled by two phenomena. For listed securities, they are attractive to passive managers or other patient investors who are sensitive to transaction costs, but do not need the instant liquidity that the exchanges provide and do not want to pay the market spread. For NASDAQ securities, they are used by institutional investors who do not want to go through NASDAQ market makers to enter an order or who want to avoid paying the bid-ask spread, but instead prefer to seek liquidity through interaction with other institutional investors.

PTSs have combined technology with features attractive to institutional investors to gain an increasing share of volume in the past few years. For the first half of 1993, the total share volume on PTSs was 4.7 billion shares, which was almost equal to their entire volume in 1992. The total share volume for 1992 was nearly 4.9 billion, an increase of more than 60% from the 1991 volume of 2.9 billion.

Trading in NASDAQ stocks represented 87% of PTS volume in the first half of 1993. During this same period, listed stocks were only 13% of PTS volume.

Even though PTS volume is growing rapidly, it is important to keep these numbers in perspective. First, the rising trend in PTS volume is consistent with the increasing volume occurring in the equity markets as a whole. Second, these systems represent only a small segment of primary market activity....Third, many institutional investors still consider these systems to be experimental and have not sought access to PTSs.

The second type of automated trading systems are, as described above, internal crossing systems operated by several large broker-dealers. These systems cross orders submitted by the broker-dealer's customers and, in some cases, orders from other broker-dealers. The systems route crosses in listed stocks to exchanges for execution. Crosses in NASDAQ stocks are submitted to NASDAQ for trade reporting.

6. Fourth Market

The fourth market refers to the trading of shares directly between institutional investors without the intermediation of a broker-dealer. This type of trading differs from the trading done through PTSs because the latter must either register as broker-dealers or secure the services of a registered broker-dealer in order to process and guarantee the trades. The distinction is important because trades effected through PTSs are, for the most part, subject to transparency rules, and they are subject to oversight by the NASD.

The Division requested data on the extent of fourth market trading, but commentators did not submit any information on this market. The Division understands, however, that the fourth market consists of internal crosses of orders between different accounts of the same institution or money manager. A few large institutions or money managers use this technique to avoid brokerage commissions and to limit the search for alternative sources of liquidity. Internal crossing of orders is used primarily for passively managed accounts that are cost-sensitive but do not need immediate liquidity. Although it is impossible to quantify the amount of fourth market trading, the Division estimates that such trading averages several million shares per day. In addition, some trading may be conducted in a "rolodex market" of institutions that call one another to solicit contra-side interest to an order, but this activity does not appear to involve significant volume.

7. Foreign Markets

Over the past 20 years it has become easy to trade securities around the world because of advances in telecommunications. Hundreds of U.S. equities are traded on foreign stock exchanges by the larger U.S., Japanese, and European broker-dealers, which have established trading desks at the major securities markets around the world.

The trading of U.S. equities by U.S. broker-dealers on foreign exchanges amounts to several million shares per day. Most of this trading is done abroad because of time zone differences between the major markets in New York, Tokyo, and London. Institutional investors that wish to trade when U.S. markets are closed seek the markets open at the time. By and large, this trading is concentrated on the London Stock Exchange ("LSE") and occurs shortly before the opening of the NYSE. Most additional trading abroad is not done on foreign markets but results from orders faxed by U.S. broker-dealers to their foreign desks. These orders usually involve a large block in a single stock or a large basket of multiple stocks. Currently, this "fax" trading amounts to approximately 7 million shares per day in NYSE stocks.

8. Block Positioning

Most transactions involving block trades over 50,000 shares (and many from 25,000 to 50,000 shares) are effected with block positioning firms. Block prices are negotiated based on current prices disseminated from the exchange floor or NASDAQ, with a block premium added or subtracted. Block positioners supplement the liquidity of the NYSE and NASDAQ by "shopping" their customer's block order upstairs to find a contra-side. They also take the other side of the transaction, keeping the block as a proprietary position.

Once price is negotiated for a block of NYSE stock, the transaction is executed on the exchange floor. Block positioners who are not members of the NYSE are not required to execute the block transaction on the exchange. When a block transaction is executed on the NYSE floor, it is subject to special auction market procedures designed to allow the limit order book or the trading crowd to participate. Block positioners prefer not to have the block broken up by the trading crowd or the limit order book. In some cases they use a regional exchange to execute the transaction (i.e., "print the block"). ...Until the October 1987 market break, upstairs firms often would commit capital to position a block. The market break and volatility that followed dampened the enthusiasm to commit capital. In addition, some commentators have suggested that the shrinking level of commission dollars and the rise in soft dollar practices have further reduced block positioning liquidity. Block positioners today are more likely to attempt to find contra-side interest for the block order, execute the cross, and collect agency commissions than to position the block.

Most blocks in NYSE stocks are negotiated off the exchange (i.e., "upstairs") but are executed on the exchange. A small percentage is executed on the regional exchanges. Indeed, the NYSE captures over 90% of the blocks in its stocks during regular trading hours. Some blocks, comprising approximately 2 million shares per day, are faxed by NYSE member firms to their foreign desks, where they are executed nominally in a foreign OTC market in order to comply with the NYSE's off-board trading restrictions. Because these trades are not reported to the consolidated tape, they avoid U.S. transparency requirements.

. . .

C. Off-Shore Trading

Overseas markets generally compete for volume in U.S. stocks after regular U.S. business hours. This competition has arisen partly from the practice of U.S. broker-dealers "booking" trades through their foreign desks or foreign affiliates to avoid U.S. transparency requirements, off-board trading restrictions, transaction fees, or limits on short sales. In what is commonly referred to as the "fax market," for instance, a U.S. broker-dealer acting as principal for its customer negotiates and agrees to the terms of a trade in the United States, but transmits or faxes the terms overseas to be "printed" on the books of a foreign office without reporting the trade in compliance with U.S. requirements. The Division estimates that approximately 7 million shares a day in New York Stock Exchange ("NYSE") stocks are faxed overseas. Many of these trades are nominally "executed" in the London over-the-counter market. Transparency standards in overseas markets are often much weaker than in the United States, thus, off-shore trades generally are not reported publicly. Rather, they are reported weekly for regulatory purposes only to the NYSE pursuant to NYSE Rule 410B or to the National Association of Securities Dealers ("NASD") on Form T.

Fairness and efficiency in U.S. secondary markets is directly related to the public availability of current transaction and quotation information. Transparency is weakened when trades in U.S. securities are negotiated and arranged in the United States, but sent off-shore for nominal execution. Due to the absence of an international consensus on adequate transparency standards, the Division believes it is necessary to examine which off-shore trades should be included in U.S. transaction reporting mechanisms.

The Division notes that the United Kingdom's Securities Investments Board ("SIB") takes a different approach toward off-shore transactions. In SIB's view, the issue with respect to off-shore transactions is not whether there is public reporting, but whether there is regulatory reporting. The Division disagrees with this viewpoint: regulatory reporting cannot substitute for transparency and its benefits of fair and accurate price discovery.

Thus, the Division is of the view that the U.S. transaction reporting system should capture trades in reported securities when the price discovery occurs in the United States, but the trades are nominally booked overseas for execution. For example, a U.S. money manager decides to sell a block of 500,000 shares in an NYSE security. The money manager negotiates a price with a U.S. broker-dealer, who sends the order ticket to its foreign trading desk for execution. The price discovery for this trade occurred in the United States as much as if the trade had been executed by the broker-dealer's U.S. trading desk.

. . .

D. U.S. Activity by Foreign Exchanges

As interest in trading foreign equities grows, U.S. investors are seeking more direct, efficient, and economical means of executing cross-border trades in foreign markets. Assisted by rapid technological advances in data processing and telecommunications, foreign exchanges now are able to provide U.S. investors with direct access to their quotation and execution capabilities. It is technologically possible for a foreign, non-U.S. registered exchange and its facilities (including specialists and market makers) to reach U.S. investors without intercession by a U.S. exchange or a foreign entity ("cross-border exchange access"). When a foreign exchange provides this kind of direct access to U.S. investors and broker-dealers, whether through exchange-owned terminals located in the United States, software that permits a U.S. investor's own computer system to gain access to the foreign exchange, or any other mechanism using U.S. jurisdictional means, the foreign exchange conducts activity and establishes a presence in the United States that is subject to the Commission's jurisdiction.

In this context, the Division has two concerns: (1) that U.S. investors executing a trade through a foreign exchange facility located in the United States should be afforded the same or similar protection that U.S. investors who execute trades on domestic exchanges in the United States receive; and (2) that the proper level of U.S. regulation for foreign exchanges with a limited presence in the United States be determined.

. . .

E. After-Hours Trading

1. Introduction

Over the past few years, after-hours trading has been the subject of much discussion. Some market participants are of the view that after-hours trading will increase as a result of four factors: (1) advances in telecommunications and computer technology; (2) the development of a global economy with multinational corporations demanding both international communication and international sources of capital; (3) the emergency of huge institutional investment funds that require cross-border diversification; (4) and regulatory changes such as those that open stock exchanges to foreign membership. These factors are also contributing to an increase in international trading.

To date, volume of after-hours trading in U.S. equities is modest. Most customers and broker-dealers prefer to trade during primary market hours, when liquidity is greater, spreads are narrower, and information is more current. As a consequence, an active 24-hour market in U.S. equities has not developed. For instance, during the first six months of 1993, NYSE members executed after-hours trades involving only several million shares per day in NYSE stocks, with most of this nominally executed overseas; proprietary trading systems ("PTSs") that operate after-hours captured only one million shares per day in NYSE stocks; and broker-dealers averaged slightly over one million shares of after-hours trading in stocks quoted on the National Association of Securities Dealers Automated Quotation ("NASDAQ") system.

Given existing capabilities to trade on a 24-hour basis and the expansion of global securities trading, however, after-hours trading may develop further in the future. To attract order flow associated with certain trading strategies, several U.S. markets have already taken steps toward 24-hour trading. The NYSE, for example, has developed a multi-phase plan to respond to the evolving demand among NYSE members and customers to trade outside the 9:30 a.m. to 4:00 p.m. trading session. Phase one consists of revisions to its market-on-close procedures...that permit firms to enter orders for guaranteed execution at the closing price, including matched buy and sell orders. Phase two...is an "Off-Hours Trading" ("OHT") facility that operates after the close of the regular NYSE trading day. (The OHT permits NYSE members to enter orders on closing-price, single-sided, and coupled orders from 4:00 p.m. until 5:00 p.m., and to enter orders for program trades from 4:00 p.m. until 5:15 p.m.)

.   .   .

EXHIBIT 42

NEW YORK STOCK EXCHANGE
DISTRIBUTION OF REVENUE BY SOURCE

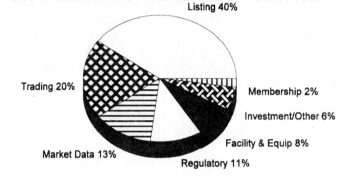

Listing 40%

Trading 20%

Membership 2%

Investment/Other 6%

Facility & Equip 8%

Market Data 13%

Regulatory 11%

CALENDAR YEAR 1992

In 1998, the NYSE earned $101.3 million on revenue of $728.8 million. Listings accounted for 41% of revenue. Trading revenue had fallen to 17% and market data fees had risen to 15%. All in all the share of revenue sources remained fairly constant.

The preceding material discussed the rise of Alternative Trading Systems as an expanding area of off-exchange trading. In 1999, a new SEC rule, Release No. 34-41297 (April 16, 1999) went into effect changing the way Alternative Trading Systems are regulated.

S. MILLER AND L. MULLEN, ALTERNATIVE TRADING SYSTEMS
Traders Magazine (March 1, 1999).

On Dec. 8, 1998, the Securities and Exchange Commission adopted a new regulatory scheme for alternative trading systems (ATS). The new scheme requires an ATS either to register as a national securities exchange or as a broker dealer and comply with new requirements under Regulation ATS.

The agency has revised its interpretation of the term exchange to apply to ATSs through new rule 3b-16. Previously, the agency relied on the definition in the Securities Exchange Act of 1934 to identify those entities subject to exchange regulation.

Over the past 30 years, the SEC has examined how to apply the term "exchange" to systems that have been variously called proprietary trading systems (PTSs), broker-dealer trading systems, and most recently, ATSs. In 1990, the SEC excluded PTSs from exchange treatment in its Delta release. In 1995, the SEC adopted rule 17a-23, which treated these systems as broker dealers and imposed certain record keeping and notice obligations on PTSs.

Many market participants thought rule 17a-23 ended the debate on regulating these systems. In 1997, however, the SEC questioned its historic treatment of PTSs as broker dealers, ultimately adopting the new regulatory scheme.

New Interpretation

New Securities Exchange Act rule 3b-16 expands the concept of an exchange to mean any "organization, association, or group of persons that:

(1) Brings together the orders for securities of multiple buyers and sellers; and

(2) Uses established, non-discretionary methods (whether by providing a trading facility or by setting rules) under which such orders interact with each other, and the buyers and sellers entering such orders agree to the terms of a trade."

The new interpretation is intended to capture systems that centralize orders, either by the display or the processing and execution of orders. Orders include "any firm indication of a willingness to buy or sell a security, as either principal or agent, including any bid or offer quotation, market order, limit order, or other priced order," and are executable without further meaningful negotiation.

An exchange-run system must deal with multiple buyers and sellers in contrast to systems operated by a single dealer who acts as a counterparty to all trades. Similarly, systems that do not provide for order interaction, such as those that route orders to order-execution facilities, will not qualify as exchanges. In addition, exchanges must use "established, non-discretionary methods" for order interaction.

These methods include rules governing trading conduct and trading facilities that standardize the manner of order interaction, such as computer algorithms. Most importantly, the system operator cannot exercise discretion in working orders.

Regulation ATS

An ATS includes any system that qualifies as an exchange and does not exercise self-regulatory functions. Regulation ATS applies to any ATS that chooses broker-dealer registration over exchange registration, although certain systems are not required to comply with Regulation ATS. These include, among others, those registered, or exempt from registration, as national securities exchanges, and systems operated by national securities associations.

The requirements of Regulation ATS are designed to ensure that adequate information about ATSs is available. They are also designed to protect confidential subscriber trading information, and to ensure cooperation in investigations of ATSs and their subscribers.

An ATS with five percent or more of the trading volume in any listed or NASDAQ National Market or Small-Cap security, that displays orders for those securities to more than one subscriber or other user, must link with a self-regulatory organization (SRO) to display the ATS's best bids and offers for those securities on the SRO. The ATS must also provide the SRO's members with access to those bids and offers on equal terms as other bids and offers on the SRO.

An ATS with 20 percent or more of the trading volume for most equity securities and certain categories of debt securities must also provide fair access to membership in the ATS. The ATS must also maintain adequate systems capacity, integrity and security standards.

The Impact

Broker dealers operating ATSs must weigh exchange registration against broker-dealer registration that comes with additional requirements. Some market participants have expressed an interest in becoming stock exchanges. What's their motivation?

For one thing, these market participants may want to capture tape revenue. For another, they may want to avoid being governed by an unrelated SRO, which may, incidentally, operate a competing system.

Whatever the motivation, exchange registration brings with it substantial obligations to fulfill self-regulatory functions. Moreover, membership must be limited to broker dealers, which means institutional and retail customers would no longer be able to directly subscribe to a system that chooses to register as an exchange.

Trading systems created in the future will need to determine if they qualify as exchanges, and if so, these must comply with the new regulations, and must determine which regulatory status best suits their operations.

The ATS rules will greatly expand the transparency of orders in the marketplace, and will, for the first time, require the public display of institutional orders that are displayed in the largest ATSs. Thus, the SEC's dedication to transparency, that drove the order handling rules, has taken a significant step further.

Both sets of rules were launched during highly-favorable market conditions. A more trying environment will provide a more meaningful test.

Notes and Questions

1. Stock markets compete over trading volume in securities. Trading increases the commissions for firms that are members of the market. An important element of trading volume is listings. Listings also produce revenue in their own right; listings can cost as high as $500 and $50 thousand per year, respectively on the NYSE and NASDAQ. The amount of listing revenue reduces transaction fees charged to firms and thus increases their net profit per trade.

2. As indicated in the introduction to this Chapter, a foreign company that cross-lists in the U.S. may reduce its cost of capital. As discussed in Chapter 2, this may result from the fact that investors have more protection when companies are subject to U.S. rules, for example minority shareholders in takeovers. This assumes that the cross-listing company's home country offers less protection for shareholders than the U.S. This same reasoning underlies the paper of A. Ahearne, W. Griever and F. Warnock, Information Costs and Home Bias: An Analysis of U.S. Holdings of Foreign Equities, Board of Governors of the Federal Reserve System, International Finance Papers No. 691 (December 2000). They find that the home country bias of U.S. investors to underweight foreign equities in their portfolios—they hold 12% whereas foreign equities account for about 50% of the value of equities worldwide—is significantly due to inadequate disclosure rules in many foreign countries. They show that countries with a greater share of firms that have public U.S. listings, either debt or equity, tend to be less severely underweighted in U.S. equity portfolios.

A. Licht, *Managerial Opportunism and Foreign Listing: Some Direct Evidence* Draft, January 10, 2001, looks at the case of Israeli companies which list only in the United States and not in Israel. He argues that this may result from managerial opportunism since some disclosure requirements, in particular conflict of interest disclosures, are higher in Israel than for foreign companies listing in the U.S. This is due to the less demanding disclosure standards under 20-F for foreign issuers than for domestic issuers with respect to matters of aggregate remuneration and options. As discussed in Chapter 2, these lower standards for foreign issuers were probably adopted on the assumption that such disclosures were not required in the home country, and that requiring them in the U.S. would unduly deter foreign issuers from entering into the U.S. public capital markets. This assumption may not always be the case. Licht does not explain why the market would not penalize Israeli companies through lower stock prices for trying to avoid disclosure of potentially negative information.

3. Some commentators have criticized the SEC's new rules regarding ATSs. ATSs now handle 4% of orders in NYSE listed securities and 20-30% of all order-flow in the over-the-counter market. The criticism stems from the fact that the new regulation does not allow the ATS to be

grouped and regulated along "functional" lines. Rather, the new rules call for the ATSs to fit into two different regulatory molds little different from those employed by the original Securities Exchange Act: national securities exchanges or broker dealers. The critics contend that only by creating flexible regulatory regimes that adapt as the technology changes will the US be able to ensure its competitiveness. Do you agree? How would you consider crafting regulation to handle the ATSs? See J. Macey and M. O'Hara, *Regulating Exchanges and Alternative Trading Systems: A Law and Economics Perspective*, 28 J. Legal Stud. 17 (1999).

4. As a result of 1975 amendments to the Securities Acts and implementing rules of the SEC, the NYSE participates with the seven regional exchanges and the National Association of Securities Dealers (NASD) in three plans to distribute market data: (1) the Consolidated Tape Association Plan (CTA Plan) which consolidates and reports trade data from all participating markets; (2) the Consolidated Quotation Plan (CQ Plan) which consolidates and reports quotation data from all participating markets; and (3) the Intermarket Trading System (ITS) Plan which permits participants to route orders among the participating markets to execute trades with the best-priced quotes. Subscribers pay for the CTA Plan and CQ Plan data. The revenue from the NYSE data, provided to the Plans through so-called Network A, after expenses, was about $125.2 million in 1998, of which the NYSE only captured $93.2 million or 74%; the balance is distributed to NASD and the regional exchanges. The SEC issued a Concept Release on the Regulation of Market Information Fees and Revenues Agency on December 9, 1999, Release No. 34-42208, in order to review the arrangements currently in place for the dissemination of market data and subsequently formed an Advisory Committee to look into the issue.

The NYSE has been concerned that some broker-dealers and ECNs are using the current arrangements to free-ride on NYSE market information in order to internalize trades and to use the NYSE liquidity to lay-off their proprietary positions, and are vastly underpaying for the services. As a result, the NYSE has authorized its withdrawal from the CTA and CQ Plans, subject to SEC approval. NYSE Letter to the SEC commenting on the Concept Release (April 10, 2000). Additionally, the NYSE has stated that it sees no need for a mandated ITS since broker-dealers have developed their own technology to perform the same function more efficiently. NYSE, Press Release, April 6, 2000. On the other hand some brokers, like Charles Schwab, are complaining that existing fees are discriminating against on-line brokers, M. Hendrickson, *Data Panel Unlikely to Reach Consensus,* Securities Industry News, April 23, 2001.

An SEC Advisory Committee issued its report on *Market Information: A Blueprint for Responsible Change* (September 14, 2001). The Report recommended no changes in how the SEC reviews existing fees for market data. Instead, it focused on how consolidated market data is distributed.

It recommended that the SEC should permit a new system of competing consolidators rather than having the CTA as the sole consolidator.

5. The SEC has adopted Rules 11Ac1-5 and 11Ac1-6 to require markets and broker-dealers to make available to the public reports that include uniform statistical measures of execution quality on a stock-by-stock basis. The measurements include price improvement and disimprovement, speed of execution, limit order fill rates and the "realized spread"—the spreads actually paid by investors (not just quoted spreads). The rules are preceded by a preliminary note saying the rules do "not create a reliable basis to address whether any particular broker failed to obtain the most favorable terms reasonably available under the circumstances for customer orders." Broker-dealers will have to disclose the existence of any payment-for-order flow or internalization arrangement they engage in. These rules were the result of the Commission's more general consideration of market structure issues discussed later in this Chapter. How will the adoption of these rules affect competition between NASDAQ and the NYSE?

6. Why would a broker-dealer care whether an order for a stock traded on both NASDAQ and SEAQ (the London Stock Exchange) was executed on one or the other market?

7. A 1999 study by M. Pulatkonak and G. Sofianos, *The Distribution of Global Trading in NYSE-Listed and Non-U.S. Stocks,* NYSE Working Paper 99-03 (March 1999), identifies various factors that explain the share of trading of the NYSE and home exchanges in cross-listed stocks. The most important factor is the time zone effect which explains 40% of the variation in U.S. market share. The closer the home exchange to New York, the greater the NYSE share. Another important factor is whether the stock is from a developed or emerging market. Competing with a developed home market lowers the U.S. market share by 30 percentage points. R. Portes and H. Rey, *The Determinants of Cross-Border Equity Flows: The Geography of Information,* Working Paper (January 2000), find that market size, efficiency, and geographic proximity are the most important determinants of cross-border purchases and sales of equity. Regulation may also place an important role. In an interesting study, U. Bhatttacharya and H. Daouk, *The World Price of Insider Trading,* Working Paper (2000) found that of the 103 countries that have stock markets, 87 had insider trading laws, but only 38 had ever enforced them through a prosecution. While the cost of equity in a country did not change after the introduction of insider trading laws, it decreased significantly after the first prosecution.

8. NASDAQ International has for some time traded NASDAQ listed stocks in London during SEAQ operating hours in order to prevent SEAQ from capturing trading in NASDAQ stocks after NASDAQ closes; this has had very little success.

2. NYSE versus NASDAQ

The NYSE is principally an order market in which brokers bring customer orders to a central point to be matched. On the NYSE this matching is not automatic, it is done through the specialist. The following excerpt discusses the system.

OFFICE OF TECHNOLOGY ASSESSMENT, ELECTRONIC BULLS AND BEARS
at 42 (1990).

Stock exchange specialists act as both brokers and dealers. As brokers, specialists buy and sell for the public, by executing limit orders that are brought to them on behalf of customers by floor brokers; they also execute market orders that reach them through the automated order routing system, SuperDOT. (A limit order specifies the price at which an investor is willing to buy or sell. Limit orders are put in the specialist's "book" until they can be executed at the designated price or a better price. A market order is an order to buy or sell immediately, at the prevailing price.) Specialists are prohibited by law from handling customer orders other than limit orders. The specialist's book was once a looseleaf notebook but now it is, for most NYSE stocks, a computer screen. The specialist is not, with some exceptions, required to show this screen to other traders, exchange members, or the public, although he must disclose aggregate price information.

As dealers, specialists buy and sell for their own account. They have an "affirmative obligation" to do so when it is necessary to provide liquidity. Specialists provide liquidity by buying or selling when there are no other bidders or offerers at or near the market price. The specialist tries to keep prices from making big jumps, by making a bid or offer that acts as a bridge when there is a wide gap between bids and offers. The specialist also has a "negative obligation," *not* to trade for his own account when there are already customers wanting to trade at or near the market price.

NYSE figures in 1990 show that specialists' purchases and sales as dealers accounted for 19 percent of all sales on the exchange. Id.

In a quote market, like NASDAQ, dealers quote bid and offer prices to other dealers. On NASDAQ, many dealers make markets in the same stock. Their inventory consists of their own positions and those of their customers. For example, a dealer may quote a bid of 95 (the price at which she will buy) and an offer of 98 (the price at which she will sell). The bid-offer spread compensates the dealer for the risk of taking positions in a stock (which decreases as the trading depth and volume increases).

In share of U.S. equity trading volume, NASDAQ has caught up and gone ahead of the NYSE. In 1992, NASDAQ average dollar daily trading volume was approximately $3.5 billion as compared with approximately $7 billion on the NYSE Market 2000, Exhibit 13. This can be compared to 1982, when NASDAQ was at approximately $.3 billion compared with the NYSE at approximately $2 billion. By year-end 1999, NASDAQ had surpassed the NYSE, having $41.5 billion compared with $35.4 billion for the NYSE, although the NYSE's market capitalization of $11.4 trillion was more than double NASDAQ's of $5.2 trillion. NASDAQ gained trading market share over this period despite the fact that from May 1989 to May 1993 the trade-weighted average spread on NASDAQ's National Market increased from 43 cents to 59 cents while the spread on NYSE held steady at 21. Does this mean customers are getting a raw deal on NASDAQ trades? Or is this gain in NASDAQ market share merely explained by the interest in "tech" stocks like Microsoft which have NASDAQ listings? Also, note that comparison of trading volume on NASDAQ and NYSE is fraught with difficulty because trading is measured differently. Trends are, however, more reliable. Consider this recent assessment of the state of the New York Stock Exchange.

J. WILLOUGHBY, EXCHANGE OR DIE

Institutional Investor, November 1998, at 42, 43.

Throughout its 206-year history, the [NYSE] has defined itself as an auction, as opposed to a dealer, market. All NYSE trades pass through the exchange floor, where specialists maintain the open, continuous auction. Today the NYSE's system is rare–nearly every other exchange in the world has moved, or is moving, to dealer markets, in which brokers trade directly with each other over computer screens or telephones. Although the Big Board's preeminence provides evidence that the auction system has its merits, its linchpin, the specialist, has become undercapitalized and spread increasingly thin. [The Chairman of the Exchange, Dick Grasso,] must make changes to ease pressure on the floor and restore stability, despite a fractious NYSE membership resistant to change.

In fact, Grasso rides herd over an institution long split by multiple constituencies. Above all, he must serve its members, from floor traders and specialists to brokerage firms and banks "upstairs" to absentee landlords who lease seats. But he must also cater to institutional investors whose activity generates the bulk of the trading while keeping individual investors firmly in mind. As the central marketplace for equities, the NYSE is, its private, not-for-profit status notwithstanding, a public trust. And so he must bow to the U.S. Congress and securities regulators, who uneasily watch the NYSE's continued dominance.

Each of these groups has its own unique self-interest. Independent floor traders -- the "crowd" that buys and sells, setting stock prices -- are near rebellion, squeezed by costs and new technology that routes trades away from them. They worry that growing volumes and the institutions' increasing influence over exchange policy will stifle the auction system. Meanwhile, heavy volume and the growing number of new listings—one of Grasso's priorities—threaten to overwhelm specialists. "There's an inherent conflict between the administration, which is in the business of listing stocks, and the specialist, which is in the business of trading stocks," says Wagner Stott's Sullivan, who was an NYSE vice chairman between 1993 and 1995.

. . .

NASDAQ and the NYSE are also tough competitors for foreign listings which both markets see as crucial to their future growth. As of year-end 1999, NASDAQ had listings for 429 foreign companies, up from 256 at the end of 1990, while the NYSE had 406 foreign listings, up from just 96 in 1990.

Why aren't competitive market makers operating over a screen in a certain stock (NASDAQ), better than a live auction market in which a specialist is given a monopoly in making a market in a stock (NYSE)? Consider the following justification.

L. BENVENISTE, A. MARCUS AND W. WILHELM, WHAT'S SPECIAL ABOUT THE SPECIALIST
32 Journal of Financial Economics 61 (1992).

The former chairman of the New York Stock Exchange, William Donaldson, has asserted:

When you have a human being in the middle of a trade working for you and a crowd of other buyers and sellers you can get the benefits of better bids and offers. (*Business Week*, Nov. 5, 1990, at 121)

This claim is representative of the widely-held belief among exchange members that the professional relationships that evolve on exchange floors yield benefits not easily duplicated by an anonymous exchange mechanism.

. . .

Floor brokers are easily identified and trade repeatedly with the specialist. We contend that this previously ignored layer of intermediation on exchange floors offers an opportunity for the specialist to reduce the costs of asymmetric information.

. . .

Although it may be relatively difficult for specialists to identify in advance floor brokers exploiting information on behalf of their principals, the stability and relatively small size of the trading community limit brokers' ability to systematically exploit private information by increasing the probability that those doing so will be identified after the fact.

. . .

An anonymous trading environment necessarily implies pooling of liquidity traders and information traders. As does earlier work, we find that in a pooling equilibrium, the specialist's inability to distinguish between members of the two classes of traders leads to a positive bid-ask spread (reflecting a transfer from uninformed to informed traders) that increases with the expected value of such information.

L. Chan and J. Lakonishok, *A Cross-Market Comparison of Institutional Equity Trading Costs*, National Bureau of Economic Research Working Paper No. 5374 (1995) ("Trading Costs") investigated the comparative execution costs of trading on NASDAQ and the NYSE, as measured by commissions and market impact, for institutional investors, the investors most sensitive to cost differences. The authors found that NASDAQ had a comparative advantage for stocks with a 1991 market capitalization below $1.2 billion, which accounted for 88% of the NASDAQ trading programs (where a manager carries out a program to buy or sell a stock over a period) or 69% of the value traded. The NYSE, on the other hand, has a distinct advantage in trading the largest stocks, with market capitalization over $4.5 billion, which constituted 32% of the NYSE trading programs or 51% of the value. What might explain these findings? The authors suggest the following:

TRADING COSTS
at 77

On the NYSE, large or difficult transactions are generally accomplished through a block broker on the upstairs market who 'shops the block' and solicits interest from other investors who may be more natural suppliers of liquidity. Typically, the block broker serves only as agent for the investor and does not take a position in the stock, receiving instead only commission income. There is, however, on the NASDAQ market no corresponding central message post where prices and order flows can be concentrated. For a NASDAQ issue, therefore, a dealer is more likely to be involved as a self-interested principal, either as a market-maker or a contraparty in a block trade. The relation between an investor and a dealer on the over-the-counter market is thus more likely to be adversarial in nature. Given the difficulty of assessing the quality of execution for large or complicated trades, the dealer has greater leeway in increasing its profit margin at the expense of the investor.

Most studies have found that the costs of trading on exchanges like the NYSE are lower than NASDAQ, as measured by the impact of the trading on prices and the total bid-ask spread. See J. Affleck-Graves, S. Hedge and R. Miller, *Trading Mechanisms and the Components of the Bid-Ask Spread*, 49 Journal of Finance 1471, 1472 (1994). A 1996 study found lower costs for large, medium and small capitalization stocks. H. Bessembinder and H. Kaufman, *A Comparison of Trade Execution Costs for NYSE and NASDAQ-Listed Stocks*, Working Paper (November 1996). See also, R. Huang and H. Stoll, *Dealer versus Auction Markets: A Paired Comparison of Execution Costs on NASDAQ and the NYSE*, Journal of Financial Economics 41 (1996) (NYSE costs lower in study of high capitalization stocks). A 2001 SEC Study reaches the same result. *Report on the Comparison of Order Executions Across Equity Market Structures* (January 8, 2001). On small market orders of 100-499 shares, NASDAQ is faster but NYSE spreads are narrower. On medium orders of 500-1999 shares, the NYSE has a small advantage on both speed and spreads, and on very large orders, 2000-4999, the NYSE has a pronounced advantage on both speed and spreads.

It is curious that the competitive market-making structure of NASDAQ, under which there are several market makers for one stock, produces higher spreads than the NYSE where there is only one specialist per stock. P. Schultz, *The Market for Market-Making*, Working Paper (February 2000) offers the explanation that the market-makers do not actively compete: trading in individual stocks is highly concentrated. This concentration seems attributable to advantages in obtaining order flow, e.g. from brokerage affiliates.

The NYSE is in the process of introducing more automatic trading for small orders through a new system called NYSE Direct+[TM]. This system will allow member firms (and will permit member firms to allow their customers) to specify limit orders of 1,099 shares or less as "Auto ex" orders. These orders will receive automatic electronic execution against the NYSE quotation to the extent a matching bid or offer is available at the time the Auto ex order is received. Were all less-than-1,100 share system limit orders to flow to NYSE Direct+[TM], 71% of the NYSE's system limit orders (representing 8% of overall volume) could receive automatic executions. NYSE Special Committee on Market Structure, Governance and Ownership, *Market Structure Report*, March 23, 2000, at pp. 35-36 (NYSE Market Structure Report). This initiative is part of a more general plan of the NYSE to give customers the choice as to how they want to trade, whether though the floor auction process or through automatic matching; they call this Network NYSE.

In the past, the NYSE has attempted to enhance its competitive position by limiting the ability of member firms to trade off its exchange. The Rule has been extensively debated over the years.

J. HASBROUCK, G. SOFIANOS, AND D. SOSEBEE, NEW YORK STOCK EXCHANGE SYSTEMS AND TRADING PROCEDURES 19-20 ("SYSTEMS AND TRADING PROCEDURES")

NYSE Working Paper No. 93-01(1993).

The purpose of NYSE Rule 390 is to encourage order flow concentration and to discourage member firms from matching orders internally without exposing them to the auction process. Rule 390 prohibits, with certain exemptions, member firms from effecting proprietary trades and in-house agency crosses in NYSE-listed securities off an organized exchange. In 1976, the SEC limited the scope of Rule 390 by exempting agency transactions, provided the same member firm does not represent both sides of the trade (in-house agency crosses): *member firms may effect one-sided agency trades anywhere, anytime.*[56] In addition, SEC Rule 19c-3 exempts from Rule 390 securities *initially* listed on a U.S. exchange after April 26, 1979.[57] Member firms may trade, at any time, NYSE-listed securities on any organized domestic exchange where the securities are cross-listed or have unlisted trading privileges (see page 20) as well as on organized foreign exchanges.[58] Outside of Exchange business hours, member firms may also trade NYSE-listed securities in *foreign* over-the-counter markets. Broker-dealers that are not members of the NYSE are not subject to Rule 390.

Examples

> Broker-dealer John is a NYSE member and stock XYZ is listed on the NYSE since 1968 (XYZ is a "Rule 390 stock"). John cannot buy or sell XYZ for his own account in the U.S. over-the-counter market even outside NYSE trading hours.
>
> John has a 1,000-share customer buy order in XYZ and a 1,000-share customer sell order also in XYZ. During NYSE trading hours, John must cross the two orders (agency cross)

---

[56] In-house (two-sided) agency crosses remain subject to Rule 390.

[57] A security initially listed on another exchange that subsequently transferred to the NYSE is subject to Rule 390 if the initial listing day (on the other exchange) was before April 26, 1979. Such a security is subject to Rule 390 even if the transfer to the NYSE occurred after April 26, 1979 (see example 6).

[58] Trading of U.S. securities on foreign exchanges is subject to the registration and listing requirements of those exchanges.

on an organized (domestic or foreign) exchange. Outside NYSE trading hours, John may cross them in a foreign over-the-counter market.

John, however, can buy or sell XYZ for a customer (a one-sided agency trade) in the U.S. (or in a foreign) over-the-counter market during NYSE trading hours.

John can buy XYZ for his own account in a foreign over-the-counter market outside NYSE trading hours.

Stock ABC was initially listed on the NYSE in 1992; it is therefore a "19c-3 stock" and is not subject to Rule 390. John can buy or sell ABC for his own account in the U.S. over-the-counter market even during NYSE trading hours.

Stock CBA was initially listed on the Amex in 1983. In 1992 the stock moved to the NYSE. Stock CBA is subject to Rule 390 [We think not, eds.].

Broker-dealer Mary is not a member of the NYSE and therefore is not subject to Rule 390. Provided Mary is not restricted by the rules of other U.S. exchanges she is a member of, she may buy and sell XYZ in the U.S. over-the-counter market even during NYSE trading hours.

At the end of 1992, 54 percent of NYSE-listed stocks were classified as 19c-3 stocks and were not subject to Rule 390. In December 1992, 19c-3 stocks accounted for 40 percent of NYSE share volume and 31 percent of NYSE dollar volume. The Exchange accounts for 82 percent of the share volume in 19c-3 stocks and 83.2 percent of the share volume in Rule 390 stocks.

On December 10, 1999, the NYSE filed with the SEC a proposed rule change to rescind Rule 390 which the Commission approved on May 5, 2000, Release No. 34-42758. The rescission will allow NYSE members to act as over-the-counter market makers or dealers in all NYSE-listed securities. The SEC had previously approved a change to the ITS Plan, favored by NASD, that allows NASD members unrestricted access to ITS, so as to allow it to trade all of the NYSE securities. Release No. 34-42212 (December 9, 1999).

When the SEC published the proposed Rule 390 change for comment, Release No. 34-42450 (February 23, 2000), it expressed concern that as a consequence of the change, a significant amount of order flow that currently is routed to the NYSE may be divided among a number of different dealers in the over-the-counter market, where there may be a reduced opportunity for order interaction, thus reducing quote competition and the opportunity of transactors to obtain the best price. The Commission is really concerned with two sources of fragmentation, internalization, which occurs when a broker-dealer matches buy and sell orders internally without exposing them to competing orders in other trading locations, and payment for order flow, which occurs when a broker or dealer receives compensation to route an order to a particular market, whether or not that market will produce the best price for the customer. The SEC asked whether fragmentation of securities trading is a problem and, if so, what to do about it. The issue of market fragmentation appears to be a major issue for the future. Some of the problems of fragmentation are illustrated by the Chart below.

How Market Structure Affects Orders

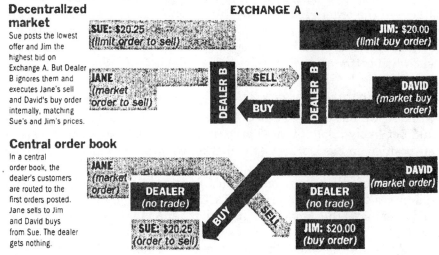

Source: M. Schroeder and R. Smith, *Sweeping Change in Market Structure Sought*, The Wall Street Journal, February 29, 2000

Fragmentation is much more of a problem for NASDAQ than for the NYSE. The NYSE executes about 82.5% of the trading volume in NYSE-listed securities, NYSE, *Fact Book for the Year 1999* (May 2000), while nine ATS's collectively accounted for 28% of trades in NASDAQ equities.

The SEC has outlined six options for dealing with fragmentation: (1) markets and brokers improve on the disclosure of the details of trade execution and order routing so that investors have more complete information to base their decisions on; (2) brokers and dealers make internally crossed trades only at a price better than the National Best Bid or Offer (NBBO) then outstanding (this is the NYSE's proposal); (3) all market centers would be required to expose their market and marketable limit orders in an acceptable way to price competition, for example, a market maker would be required to expose certain orders to the market before executing trades as principal; (4) markets would be required to satisfy the first order or quote that improved on NBBO before executing other trades at that price; (5) intermarket trading priorities would grant time priority to the first limit order or dealer quotation that improved the NBBO for a security; and (6) a national market linkage system would be established which would provide price/time priority, a centralized limit order book (CLOB).

The CLOB alternative has been advocated by some of Wall Street's largest firms, self-styled the "Working Group." They agree with the NYSE that the ITS system should be eliminated, but propose to replace it with a "Super National Market System." The new market would be built around a central order book with price-time priority, so that orders to buy a stock at a particular price would be executed across different markets in the order received, no matter which trading system they are placed on. This would prevent firms such as Schwab from matching customer orders internally or through selected brokers on a pay for order basis, when better or earlier orders are available from other markets. M. Schroeder and R. Smith, *Sweeping Change in Market Structure Sought*, Wall Street Journal, February 29, 2000.

The NYSE has opposed CLOB for several reasons. First, since CLOB would not likely apply to large orders—firms would not want to expose their position on block orders—the market would be fragmented between large and small orders. Second, the proposal would favor some players at the expense of others, e.g. large-firm CLOB proponents will use CLOB retail prices to price large orders off CLOB. Third, most CLOB models would eliminate the liquidity supplied by specialists, which would be particularly troublesome in a steeply declining market, and would generally result in wider bid-ask spreads. Fourth, CLOB will be a marketplace mandated by regulation, and will eliminate competition between markets. NYSE Market Structure Report, at pp. 27-33. This last point has also been made Federal Reserve Board Chairman Greenspan in testimony before the U.S. Senate Committee on Banking, Housing, and Urban Affairs, April 13, 2000.

Notes and Questions

1. What is the argument for the value of a specialist? Do you agree with it? Note that the number of specialists has shrunk rapidly in recent years. There are now only 7 specialist firms, and all but one are affiliated with large financial service firms like Goldman, Sachs who acquired Speer Leeds in 2000. Indeed, the top 5 firms do 80% of the business. Specialists acquire the right to make the market in a stock by applying to an Allocation Committee, which is formally not part of the NYSE; absent misbehavior, there is rarely a switch from one specialist to another, so most of the competition relates to new listings. Should this specialist concentration be of concern to the NYSE?

2. Is it a good idea to repeal Rule 390 entirely? After repeal, quoted spreads decreased by 16 percent on average, while effective spreads decreased 6 percent. Moreover, quoted depth at the NYSE increased by

5 percent. This suggests that specialists improved liquidity to remain competitive with possible off-exchange trading. T. Kam, V. Panchapagesan, D. Weaver, *The Revocation of Rule 390 - A First Look,* Working Paper (December 7, 2000). What do you think of the "Working Group" proposal? Is there a need for an international version of such a proposal?

3. Another NYSE rule that some claim restricts competition is Rule 500 which requires that companies can only delist after obtaining a two-thirds majority shareholder vote, with no more than 10% objecting. How would such a rule effect competition between the NYSE and other exchanges? G. Ip, *Big Board May End Rule That Prevents Defections,* Wall Street Journal, July 3, 1997.

4. In another attempt to compete with NASDAQ, the NYSE has changed its listing standards for the first time in 30 years to attract fast growing foreign firms. Before the change foreign firms needed to have overall earnings of $100 million for the three previous years and at least $25 million in each of those years. The overall three year $100 million requirement was retained but now a firm can have lost money in the first year. The changes are designed to lure precisely those companies that have been attracted to the NASDAQ market.

5. Both the NYSE and NASDAQ are considering demutualization. Both would form companies and sell stock in their companies to the public. This would require the NYSE to buy up members' seats—one sold for $2.6 million in 1999—which might have adverse tax consequences to the sellers. It would also require NASDAQ to become a formal "exchange." The market hasn't needed that designation because of its ownership by NASD, which would of course be changed if NASDAQ went public. The asserted benefits from going public are that it would remove the conflict of having member firms deciding the affairs of the exchanges while also competing with them. It would also facilitate mergers and acquisitions, both nationally and internationally. Major exchanges in Europe, e.g. Deutsche Börse, the London Stock Exchange and Euronext, have already demutualized.

6. Competition among exchanges has also led to after-hour trading, on ATS systems. In March 2000, volume was at 58 million shares in contrast to billion share volume during regular hours. Volatility in traded stocks is quite substantial. For example, on February 24, 2000, Wal-Mart's price rose 8% on volume of just 400 shares, and its next day price came down to approximately that of the regular closing on the previous day. The NYSE has criticized such trading, but has a self-interest in doing so since less after-hour off-exchange trading might mean more regular hour on-exchange trading. See S. Pulliam, *Grasso's Blunt Letter Hits After-Hour Trades,* Wall Street Journal, June 2, 2000.

3. NASDAQ REFORMS

The NASDAQ market came under attack in 1994 for colluding to maintain wide spreads on its quotes. W. Christie and P. Schultz, two economists, found that NASDAQ's dealers' quotes rarely ended in odd-eighth amounts, i.e. 5 1/8, 5 3/8, instead moving in even-eighths, i.e. 5 2/8, 5 4/8 (quarter-dollars). *Why do NASDAQ Market Makers Avoid Odd-Eighth Quotes?*, 49 Journal of Finance 1813 (1994). The study suggested that this resulted from collusion and that collusion might also explain NASDAQ's relatively high bid-offer spreads. This study triggered a wide scale investigation in October by the U.S. Department of Justice. Do wide quote spreads necessarily indicate inefficiency?

Some studies have determined that only 35% of NYSE trades as compared with 45% of trades on the London Stock Exchange (with a similar system to NASDAQ) actually take place within posted prices. *Spread-em*, Economist, Nov. 5, 1994, at 81. See also, A. Kleidon and R. Willig, *Why Do Christie and Schultz Infer Collusion From Their Data* (1995). This would strongly imply that one cannot rely on posted prices to judge spreads. Moreover, this does not take the cost of commissions into account.

In August 1996, the SEC promulgated rules that took effect in 1997 designed to protect investors trading on NASDAQ. The rules force NASDAQ dealers to publicly display all investor limit orders that are between 100-10,000 shares, to notify the public of the absolute best prices at which they are willing to trade any stock (this includes quotes supplied in "private" markets such as Instinet), and to expand the size of any offered block of stock at the best market-wide price to include a customer's limit order at the same price (a dealer's offer to sell 500 shares of stock would have to be expanded to 700 if a customer delivered a 200 share offer at the same price). J. Taylor, *A Fairer NASDAQ? SEC Approves its New Rules*, Wall Street Journal, August 29, 1996. Two recent studies suggest that trading costs of NASDAQ securities have fallen in the presence of the new rules. See M. Barclay, et al, *The Costs of Trading NASDAQ Issues: The Impact of Limit Orders and ECN Quotes*, Charles Dice Center for Research in Financial Economics Working Paper 97-8 July, 1997; P. Schultz, *Regulatory and Legal Pressures and the Costs of NASDAQ Trading*, December 1998.

H. Bessembinder, *Trade Execution Costs on NASDAQ and the NYSE: A Post-Reform Comparison*, NYSE Working Paper 98-03 (August 1998) found that after the implementation of these reforms, NASDAQ's trade execution costs were still larger than those of the NYSE, though the differential was smaller than that documented in earlier years. The average of quoted spreads was 0.78% of the share price on the NYSE as compared to 1.03% on NASDAQ. Differences in commissions between the two exchanges, at least for retail customers, did not appear to account for the difference.

NASDAQ also agreed to settle its dispute with the SEC over collusion by spending $100 million to improve its surveillance of the market. J. Taylor, *NASD's SEC Pact Calls for $100 Million Outlay,* Wall Street Journal, August 7, 1996. And in November 1996, NASDAQ significantly raised its listing standards.

NASDAQ recently considered a major overhaul of its system which it has called Next NASDAQ. Plans for the new system originally called for a greater scope for automatic order matching, currently only available for small orders through SOES, and the creation of a central limit-order book. However, in the face of intense opposition from market-makers, the NASD has canceled plans for Next NASDAQ, specifically, scrapping the central limit order book concept.

NASDAQ has formally separated itself from its parent association, NASD, the National Association of Securities Dealers. At the same time, NASDAQ has applied to the SEC to become an exchange, which would permit it to become an SRO. This is important if NASDAQ is to retain control of hundreds of millions of dollars in annual market data fees. Apparently, it would be unable to charge for such data about trading in NASDAQ stocks unless it were an exchange. J. Labate, *Nasdaq in New Bid to Become Exchange,* Financial Times, December 11, 2000.

In January 2001, the SEC approved a new quotation system for NASDAQ called SuperMontage. The system will make NASDAQ more of a conventional stock exchange and less a network of market makers by centralizing and displaying more of the market's stock quotes. New trading screens will display the three best bids and offers for every stock, as well as each market maker or ATS's single best bid and offer. At present, NASDAQ only shows each market maker or ATS's best price. Large institutions can post bids or offers anonymously, an important right to facilitate the trading of large blocks. The system offers investors to direct orders to the ATS or market maker of their choice. NASDAQ dealers profit from the spread while ATS' charge an access fee as much as 1.5 cents per share. The prices quoted will take account of the access fees. Orders can only be preferenced on the basis of best bids or offers; the SEC rejected preferencing options based on size and price which would have allowed big blocks to trade ahead of smaller ones. M. Schroeder and G. Ip, *Plans to Upgrade Nasdaq Trading Passes the SEC,* Wall Street Journal (January 11, 2001); M. Hendrickson, *Concessions Lead to SuperMontage OK,* Securities Industry News (January 15, 2001). Island, one of the largest ECN's, which accounts for 11 percent of the trading in NASDAQ stocks, announced its intention to join SuperMontages in the sense of continuing to channel its trade quotes through NASDAQ, and to report those trades through NASDAQ as well.

I. Clary, *SEC: Who Can Trade OTC Stocks* and I. Clary, *Island May cut fees on Montage*, Securities Industry News, April 22, 2002.

Many believe that price competition between NASDAQ and the NYSE will be further improved, and spreads narrowed, by decimalization, quoting stocks in cents rather than 16ths (6.25 cents). The SEC pressed this changeover. SEC, Press Release, Release 34-42685 (April 13, 2000). The NYSE converted to decimalization in February 2001, and NASDAQ fully converted by April 2001. A preliminary analysis of conversion indicates a tightening of bid-ask spreads by 37% on NYSE-listed stocks and 50% on NASDAQ traded stocks. Both quoted and effective spreads of NASDAQ stocks remained wider than comparable stocks traded on the NYSE. K. Chung, B. Van Ness, and R. Van Ness, *Are Nasdaq stocks more costly to trade than NYSE stocks? Evidence after decimalization,* Working Paper (July 2001).

4. CIRCUIT BREAKERS

Following the market break of 1987, the NYSE adopted certain circuit breakers to halt trading when there was a steep fall in the market. Starting on October 19, 1988, if the Dow Jones Industrial Average were to decline by 250 points from the previous day's close, then trading in all stocks would be halted for one hour. Additionally it was decided that if the Dow were to plummet by 400 points from the previous day's close, then trading in all stocks would be halted for two hours. *Systems and Trading Procedures*, NYSE Circuit Breakers, March 31, 1993.

When the rule went into effect in 1988, a 250 point move was 12% of the average and a 400 point move was 19% of the Dow Jones Industrial Average (DJIA or Dow). Given the rise of the Dow, by March 13, 1996, a 250 point move represented only 4.5% of the average. It was widely perceived that the "devaluation" was a problem, but there was debate about how it should be fixed. Some argued that the circuit breakers should be expressed in terms of percentages of market averages; but others contended that a well known and certain circuit breaker, i.e. 250 points, would have a stronger ex-ante effect in restraining breaks since the amount of a triggering price break, expressed as a percentage of the DJIA, would constantly change with changes in the average. Some suggested doing a split of the Dow much as highflying stocks are split.

In February 1997, the SEC approved changing the 250 point - 1 hour circuit breaker to a 350 point - 30 minute rule, and also changing the 400 point - 2 hour breaker to a 550 point - 1 hour rule. The 350 point rule required a drop of about 5% when adopted. The Commodity Futures Trading Commission also approved changes in the futures rules. Trading of futures on the S&P 500 stock index will stop when the index is down 45 points, and again when down 75 points; the previous limits were 30 and 50 index points. Wall Street Journal, February 3, 1997.

The 350/550 circuit breakers were triggered for the first time on October 27, 1997. The 350 point level, which represented a 4.5% decline in the Dow, was reached at 2:36 p.m. When trading resumed at 3:06 p.m., the Dow declined an additional 200 points, and the second circuit breaker was triggered at 3:30 p.m. which had the effect of closing the market (the normal closing time is 4:00 p.m.). The market had declined 554 points for the day, the largest single-day point drop in Dow history, but this only represented a total decline of 7.2%, making it the 12th highest percentage fall, only one-third of the Dow's 22.7% decline on October 19, 1987. J. Cochrane, Senior Vice President and Chief Economist, New York Stock Exchange, *Trading Halts and Program Trading Restrictions,* Testimony before the Subcommittee on Securities of the U.S. Senate Committee on Banking, Housing and Urban Affairs (January 29, 1998).

This experience set off another round of debate on circuit breakers. Apart from the renewal of the argument over absolute numbers versus percentages, there was additional concern over whether the market should be closed as a result of the triggering of a circuit breaker. This made it impossible for investors to effectively place "market on close" orders, orders instructing brokers to buy/sell at the closing price. Normally, closing sell order imbalances are published at 3:50 p.m. to attract buyer interest. Such buy orders may play a key role in bringing the market into balance without large price movements. Some believed that selling pressure was accelerated on October 27 by investors who believed that the circuit breakers would preclude this procedure.

M. Goldstein and K. Kavajecz, *Liquidity Provision during Circuit Breakers and Extreme Market Movements,* NYSE Working Paper 2000-02 (January 2000) conducted a study of the 1997 market break. They found that upon the first execution of the circuit breaker (2:36 p.m.), little liquidity was provided to the market, i.e. there was a lack of order submission, cancellation or change in the limit order book (orders at specific prices). But more dramatically, on Tuesday, October 28, 1997, there was a liquidity drain, as the limit order book was uncharacteristically thin and empty; it was left to floor members and specialists to supply liquidity.

A new revision of the circuit breakers went into effect in April 1998. It operates as follows: (1) a 10% drop halts trading for one hour if it occurs before 2:00 p.m., and for 30 minutes if it occurs between 2 and 2:30, but does not halt trading at all after 2:30; (2) a 20% drop occurring before 1:00 p.m. halts trading for two hours, and between 1:00 p.m. and 2:00 p.m. for one hour, and closes the market for the day after 2:00 p.m.; and (3) a 30% drop closes the market for the day no matter when it occurs. These percentages are actually expressed as absolute numbers, calculated on a quarterly basis.

Notes and Questions

1. Are circuit breakers, in general, a good idea? If so, what do you think of the latest round of revisions? Will the adoption of circuit breakers in the U.S. market influence the competition between U.S. and foreign markets for listings?

2. Assuming a foreign company trades on both a U.S. and foreign exchange in the same or an overlapping time zone, what will be the effect of a U.S. circuit breaker on trading in the foreign market, assuming trading in the company is not suspended in the foreign market in coordination with the U.S. suspension?

B. FOREIGN MARKETS

We turn now to the characteristics of two important foreign exchanges, London's SEAQ International and the Tokyo Stock Exchange (TSE).

R. HUANG AND H. STOLL, MAJOR WORLD EQUITY MARKETS: CURRENT STRUCTURE AND PROSPECTS FOR CHANGE

Monograph Series in Finance and Economics 2-20, 43-47
(New York University ed., 1991).

II. London: Back to the Future

In the early 1970s, predictions in the United States of the demise of stock exchanges as then organized were commonplace. The Securities Acts Amendments of 1975 called for a National Market System in which the computer would make possible efficient trading of securities without the need for face-to-face contact on an exchange floor. Trading on the New York Stock Exchange (NYSE) has continued to flourish, albeit its market share has declined. But in the United Kingdom, the predicted future has arrived. Along with a variety of other significant changes, the "big bang" of October 1986 shifted trading to upstairs computer screens. In the wake of the "big bang" have come a variety of dislocations and problems, leading some observers to suggest that London's dramatic step into the future has been a backward step; but others argue that the changes in London are a vast improvement over the preceding antiquated system.

. . .

B. The Functioning of the London Securities Market

1. The Trading System

The trading system of the London Stock Exchange is a competing dealer market in which dealers display quotes over computer terminals. The system is essentially the same as the NASDAQ system. The heart of the London market is the SEAQ system, which allows registered market-makers to change quotes and report transactions, but several different systems constitute the London market. The "big bang" brought major improvements in the *information system.* Data on transaction volumes, prices and bid-ask quotations received by SEAQ computers from dealers is disseminated over TOPIC, the London Stock Exchange's viewdata system. As in NASDAQ, a level one display gives the inside quote for any stock on the system, and a level two display gives the quotes of all dealers making a market in the stock. Prior to the "big bang" neither the inside quote nor the individual quotes of dealers were available to the public. Computer readable information on transactions and quotes is provided over the CRS-Lynx system to interested firms who wish to use the data to support internal trading systems.

. . .

3. Cost of Trading

The London Stock Exchange's Quality of Markets Unit carries out surveys of commission cost and tracks bid-ask quotes of dealers.

. . .

(b) Bid-Ask Spread

Much attention has focused on the problems of competing market-makers in the London market, the presence of aggressive quote setting and the resultant lack of profitability. Table 4 provides information on average inside quoted bid-ask spreads for standard transaction sizes...by stock category. These spreads are not low by NYSE standards. According to data from McInish and Wood (1989) shown in Table 5, the average spread for the most active twenty percent of NYSE stocks (about 280 stocks) was 0.62 percent in 1987.

Table 4. Inside Quotes by Stock Category and Time Period, International Stock Exchange, In percent

Time Period	[Most Active]		[Least Active]
Pre-crash	0.83	1.76	3.00
December, 1987	1.52	3.82	6.12
December, 1988	0.85	3.20	5.30
December, 1989	1.20	3.40	6.30

Source: ISE, *Quality of Markets Quarterly Review,* October/December, 1989.

**Table 5. Bid-Ask Spreads for NYSE Stocks Classified into
Quintiles According to Trading Frequency,
Calendar Year 1987**

	Percentage spread
Most active	0.62
2	0.99
3	1.38
4	1.59
Least Active	2.06

Source: McInish and Wood (1989), Table 1. The spreads are those prevailing at the end of the day.

The spread on the London Stock Exchange is comparable to the spread on NASDAQ, perhaps somewhat lower. Stoll (1989, p. 128) reports spreads for 820 NASDAQ/NMS stocks in December 1984. Spreads range from 1.16 percent for the 10 percent of most actively traded stocks to 6.87 percent for the 10 percent of least actively traded stocks. While these spreads in 1984 are somewhat higher than London Stock Exchange spreads in 1989, they are not markedly different. Furthermore, no attempt has been made to control for differences in volume, risk and other factors. It is difficult to say that London Stock Exchange spreads are too high or too low.

Differences in reported spreads are to be expected between the NYSE and either the NASDAQ market or the London Stock Exchange even when comparable stocks are examined. First, the limit order book on the NYSE tends to narrow spreads, as Stoll (1985) notes. Limit orders act like a competing dealer and thereby reduce spreads just as competing dealers reduce spreads. Probably more important is the fact that public limit orders offer free trading options to the rest of the market. When market prices changes slightly and limit orders are not adjusted, spreads will be smaller than the inside spread of competing dealers who adjust quotes quickly to reflect current market conditions

Second, spreads also tend to be larger in a competing dealer market because it is more difficult to guard against informational trading. A trader with information can "hit" each of fifteen dealers in a stock with 1000 shares, thereby disposing of 15,000 shares at the current quote. Each of the 15 dealers must set a quote that provides protection against this possibility and against the greater difficulty of liquidating his position when all other dealers acquire similar positions. If there is only one dealer, he can trade the first 1000 shares (or even a larger amount) at a narrow spread and then adjust the price as additional orders arrive. The final effect is the same, but the spread is greater in the multiple dealer market.

. . .

(c) Disclosure of Transaction Prices

One of the most controversial accommodations to market-makers was the London Stock Exchange ruling in February 1989 permitting the delayed publication of the transaction size and price until the following day for transactions exceeding 100,000 pounds. The argument for such delay was that market-makers disclosing such a large trade would cause prices to move against them and make it difficult to unwind their position. The Elwes committee brought this argument and recommended a smaller delay of up to 90 minutes (now implemented) in the publication of price information for transactions more than three times NMS (£750,000).[1]

The failure to disclose block trades disadvantages public investors who trade at unfair prices. Indeed, the argument that disclosure must be postponed to give the market-maker time to dispose of the block is based on the proposition that market-makers have a right to trade on inside market information, something that would not be permitted in the United States. The predicament of the market-maker who must dispose of a block is understandable, but if the block is fairly priced, disclosure of that price might encourage traders to buy. In U.S. markets, prices tend to rebound from the block price, thereby giving buyers of blocks a positive return and an incentive to participate.

Immediate disclosure of block prices might alter the procedures by which blocks are traded in the U.K. For example, a market-maker might try to find the other side of a block before executing the trade (as is often the case in the U.S.). Under current and proposed arrangements, the block is traded by the dealer at the wrong price and then sold to the unsuspecting public at the wrong price. It would be preferable to negotiate before the block and determine a fair price that could immediately be disclosed to the public. If the risk is great, the price of the block can incorporate a discount for that risk.

.   .   .

The London Stock Exchange (LSE) made a fundamental change in the way its stocks were traded by adopting a new trading system, SETS, in October 1997. SETS has a two-tiered system where smaller orders may be crossed on brokers' own books, or can be pooled into bigger orders that qualify for matching. Very large "block trades" may be matched or done through a registered principal trader. Unlike the old market makers, registered principal traders will only be obliged to deal in particular shares when there are no offers to buy or sell from other traders on the electronic book. This is quite close to the NYSE specialist system.

Proponents of the change pointed to the comparative efficiency of competitor home-country order-driven systems like the Paris Bourse, the

---

[1] NMS means normal market size.

implementation of the Investment Services Directive which now allow stocks on Paris and other European exchanges to be traded on screens in London, and the launch in September 1995 of the Tradepoint Investment Exchange an order-driven London exchange, offering trading in 400 big British companies. Tradepoint has as yet not posed a threat to LSE; its volume is less than 1% of LSE. However, in May 1999, a group of leading global brokerages and a U.S. management firm formed a consortium to invest $22 million in Tradepoint and take control. S. Stirland, *Big Players Join to Remake Tradepoint*, May 10, 1999. In March 1999, Tradepoint was permitted to operate in the United States without registering as an exchange (before the SEC adopted its new alternative trading system rules). Release No. 34-41199 (March 22, 1999). We will have more to say on this at the end of the Chapter.

By mid-1998, SETS had roughly 125 companies, yet had been beset by problems of low usage and volatile prices. Complaints from company executives about the dramatic swings of their stock prices on SETS, especially during the beginning and end of the trade day, prompted the LSE to institute a number of reforms designed to increase liquidity. The LSE delayed its opening time to make it more difficult for traders to manipulate the market in the early-opening hours. Additionally, the LSE introduced a system to correct the erratic swings in its prices. See C. Kentouris, *With Usage Low, LSE Modifies SETS Order Book*, Securities Industry News, June 1, 1998; G. Graham, *London Stock Exchange Opens Later For Trading,* Financial Times, July 20, 1998; P. John, *London Stock Exchange Sets Out Its Revamped Trading Stall*, Financial Times, December 14, 1998.

The primary purpose of SETS was to reduce the trading costs for small investors. In a study after the implementation of SETS, N. Naik and P. Yadav, *Evidence from the London Stock Exchange,* Working Paper (June 1999), found that public investors trading through limit orders (liquidity suppliers) benefitted from the change because they earned the spread. For example, an investor could place a limit buy order at 2 and a limit sell order at 2.5, and if both orders were fulfilled earn the .5 spread. When investors trade with dealers, who have superior information and no longer have to make two way quotes, they lose part of their spread. This is reflected in increased dealer positioning revenue after the change. The researchers were unable to determine whether public investors were better off as a result of the change because they had no date as to how investors would fare without limit orders, but it seems reasonable to assume the possibility of capturing spread does make public investors better off. Dealers may be worse off. Although they capture some of the spread on limit orders, they also face more competition from public investors placing limit orders.

Under the LSE market-making system, counterparties are not anonymous and, as we shall see in Chapter 15, the exchange does not guarantee performance, i.e. payment or delivery of securities. In 1999, LSE announced plans to change this system to one of a central (the exchange) and anonymous counterparty.

LSE demutualized in 2000 and raised over an additional $2 billion by a share offering in 2001.

We now turn to the Tokyo Stock Exchange.

M. SATO, THE TOKYO EQUITY MARKET: ITS STRUCTURE AND POLICIES

Capital Markets and Financial Services in Japan 40-55
(Japan Securities Research Institute ed., 1992).

2. Mechanism/Structure

Structurally, or in terms of trading mechanism, the Tokyo market is characterized by three major elements: a continuous auction market based on order-book system; a high degree of automation; and integration of cash and derivative markets.

(1) Continuous Auction Market

First of all, the Tokyo market is a continuous public auction market based on an order-book system. All orders, either limited or at market, are placed by member broker/dealer firms with what we call "Saitori" members who are solely in charge of matching these orders in their order-books in accordance with the auction principles, i.e., price priority and time precedence. The Saitori members are not allowed to trade any listed stocks for their own accounts. Thus, the Tokyo market is a pure "order-driven" market without any responsible market-makers.

From the international perspective, the market differs from some European markets in that it adopts a "continuous", as against "call" method of trading, meaning that any listed stocks are available for trading during the entire trading hours. It is also different from a "dealer" market in that it is "order-driven" rather than "quote-driven". A typical dealer market exists in London and over-the-counter market in the United States, known as NASDAQ, where market-makers competitively indicate their asks and bids on screen to which brokers and public investors react. Further, within the family of order-driven market, it is unlike some Asian exchanges or derivative markets in the United States in that it uses an order-book system rather than "board" or "open-outcry" system to match buy and sell orders continuously. Finally, even within the group of order-driven market based on order-book system, the market is not perfectly the same as others in that it is without any help of responsible market-makers such as "specialists" on the New York Stock Exchange and elsewhere.

Rationales behind the features are several. First, need for providing immediacy of trading has commanded the adoption of a continuous rather than call method of trading, although a batch trading is used at the opening of trading session since the market does not trade for 24 hours. The method also permits to provide market information on a continuous basis, of course. Indeed, the immediacy requirement has caused many markets in the world to shift from a call to continuous method of trading, most notably in France in 1986.

Second, an order-book system is preferred to a board or open-outcry system chiefly because of fairness consideration. An open order-book permits the fairest treatment of all orders, large and small, by matching them in strict compliance with the auction principle and making the matching process visible to all concerned. A board system seems to favor floor traders and investors represented by them as against those not represented because of the absence of an order-book widely publicized. An open-outcry system may not achieve time precedence, since all orders must be handled as "discretionary" orders. In addition, the Tokyo market trades too many shares to be handled by bilateral bargains in a crowd, and too heavily to permit brokers/dealers themselves to write offers on the trading board; hence a middleman specialized in matching operation is needed and can be afforded by the market.

Third and more importantly perhaps, there are several reasons why the Tokyo market adopts an order-driven rather than quote-driven system. Historically, Japan has no tradition of dealers' quoting asks and bids to make markets for brokers and public investors. More essentially, Japan, as a matter of capital market policy, emphasizes the importance of concentrating all orders into a single market in order to provide best prices to investors. Given this policy, public limit orders, which are not allowed to compete with market maker asks and bids under a quote-driven system, must be fully provided for. If not, there will be an incentive for brokerage firms handling public orders to create in-house limit-order books and order matching systems or to act as dealers, resulting in fragmentation of market to the detriment of investors' interests. Further, admitting that a quote-driven system can maximize market liquidity by providing immediacy of trading, an order-driven system may achieve the same goal by strengthening investor confidence in fairness of the market and providing maximum opportunity for orders to meet with counter-orders. While actual quote-driven markets are said to be less transparent in actual trade consummation than they first appear, an order-driven market with open order-book permits maximum transparency to ensure the fairest price formation. Finally, advantages of quote-driven market would not be too great and disadvantages rather pronounced in the particular circumstances of Japan. Generally, a quote-driven system can take care of "block" orders better than an order-driven one, given sufficient capital base of market makers, but competition among market makers is crucial to successful working of the entire system. In Japan, while block orders are being taken care of by so-called "crossing" technique, proper competition among market makers would not be too easy to achieve, given the industrial structure of securities business in Japan.

Thus, the Tokyo market is purely of public auction type. Then, the question may be, "How can the market be stable without any market makers responsible for the stabilization?"

Both phenomenal and institutional factors may answer the question. Phenomenally, there is active private, or individual, participation in the market, tending to stabilize stock prices with diverse investment judgements. Of a total turnover of 190 trillion yen (or US $1.3 trillion) and total 29 million trades in 1990, roughly one third is accounted for by individual investors. Numbering approximately 10 million, they act as stabilizer, as shown by the fact that they bought massively immediately after stock falls like 1987 October crash and recent plunges. Institutional traders appear to behave more on a "herd instinct" due perhaps to their concern about self-protection. Also, phenomenon of cross-holding of shares within the corporate sector, unique to Japan, may provide a sort of "downward rigidity" in critical times.

Institutionally, member broker/dealer firms, especially the big-sized, can and do act as de facto market makers since they are allowed to trade on their own accounts, though on certain conditions. Also, "crossing" of orders substantially mitigates the impact of block trading upon stock prices, under which a broker finds counterparty to large orders beforehand or he himself becomes counterparty if he finds no one to counter, with actual crossing being effected in the order book in accordance with the auction principle. Further, a so-called "circuit-breaker", i.e., price limit and trading halt, does work to stabilize the market especially when investors behave rather irrationally.

(2) Highly Computerized Market

The Tokyo equity market is also characterized by a high degree of automation of exchange operations.

In the Exchange, there are two different kinds of trading facilities. One is a trading floor where people meet to trade stocks in a traditional manner, the other a totally computerized trading system called "Computer-assisted Order Routing and Execution System" ("CORES"), introduced in 1982. More than 1,400 of all domestic stocks and all foreign stocks are at present traded by CORES, leaving the most active 150 stocks to the floor trading.

CORES is believed to have performed quite well. Operational efficiency has been enhanced mainly through elimination of data reentries which had been necessary before in the sequential process of order collection, routing, matching, trade confirmation and clearing and settlements. Accuracy of trading has been achieved because of the avoidance of errors in such processes that are inherent in manual works. Also, cost-savings have taken place on the members' side in the form of elimination of traders on the floor, and the market as a whole has enjoyed an increased capacity to handle trades thanks to greatly reduced burdens of trade comparison.

Regarding the quality of market, visibility has been enhanced by duplicating the order-book on screens at members' headquarters and information dissemination quickened and improved, both of which, together with speedier order routing and matching, are believed to have contributed to more liquidity of the market.

Then, the question may be, "Why not go to entire automation to cover all the trades on the Exchange?" The issue has been considered in light of the advantages of modern technology on one hand and those of traditional physical floor on the other. True, CORES has proved efficiency, accuracy and speediness of trading. However, liquidity of the market might suffer from entire automation, since order flows are generated, to some extent at least, by subtle interactions of human activities on the floor, including general atmosphere at the floor, facial expression of rivals, so-called "floor gossips", and so on, all of which can hardly be computerized. Also, volatility of the market might be enhanced, were it not for the physical floor where information behind price moves can be quickly exchanged among traders. In other words, prices might be "over-shooting" or "under-shooting" if traders are just reacting to price moves on screen without well understanding the reasons for the moves. Difficulty might be compounded by less easy crossing of orders on the screen than on the floor due to the "mechanical" nature of screen trading. All these, together with costs involved in an entire automation, not to speak of nostalgia of older generations and tourist consideration, have led the Exchange to a new system which maintains but restructures the floor by using the modern technology.

The system is essentially to combine the advantages of the technology, efficiency and accuracy, with those of trading floor, intimacy and visibility. While small orders, up to 3,000 shares, are routed, matched and reported back all electronically, larger orders are routed through members' booths located on the floor down to the trading posts where the orders are merged with the small orders by key operation of Saitori members. The new system, fully operative since this March, enables us to smoothly handle a trading volume of 5 billion shares a day, instead of 2 billion shares under the old system.

Besides, all the derivative markets on the Exchange have been computerized in the same fashion as CORES, futures on Japanese government bonds, options on the futures, futures and options on

"TOPIX" ("Tokyo Stock Price Index") and futures on U.S. Treasury bonds.

———————

This description of the Tokyo Stock Exchange in the article above is not altogether clear on how market orders are handled. As the article indicates, TSE does have market as well as limit orders. After the opening (which uses a special procedure called itayose), market orders are "matched" under the zaraba (continuous trading) method as follows.

1.   Assume the last trade was at 100¥ and assume there is a limit buy order at 100¥. A market sell order is fulfilled at the price of the last trade and matched against the limit buy order.

2.   Assume the last trade was at 100¥ and assume the best limit buy order is 99¥. A market sell order is fulfilled at 99¥ and matched with the best limit buy order.

3.   Assume the last trade was at 100¥ and there is no limit order. A market sell order is matched against a market buy order at 100¥.

4.   Assume the last trade was at 100¥ and there is a limit buy order at 101¥. A market sell order is matched against the limit buy order at 100¥. This gives price improvement to the buy order.

5.   Assume the last trade was at 100¥ and there is a limit buy order at 101¥ but there is no market order. After a warning, the next market sell order is matched at 101¥ with the limit buy order.

The article is outdated in two respects, there are no longer saitori and all trading is automatic (there is no trading floor). In addition, there are two procedures to limit volatility. First, when there is a major order imbalance, special quotes are publicly disseminated. If counter orders come in the orders will be matched at the special quote and the quote will be withdrawn. If no orders come in at the quote, the quotes are adjusted up or down within certain parameter. Second, TSE sets daily price limits (including special quotes), in absolute yen amounts, for individual stocks.

Notes and Questions

1.   The terminology used to describe the structure of equity markets can often appear confusing. Markets are sometimes said to be either order-driven or dealer-driven. Additionally, markets are known as floor or as screen exchanges. However, these terms are not mutually exclusive and it is important to note that in many cases markets are a hybrid of these varied features. For example, the NYSE is floor exchange that is characterized as an order-driven market, yet uses a specialist (dealer) to help clear the market in a particular stock. The Tokyo Stock Exchange, on the other hand, is also a floor exchange that is an order-driven market. It differs from the NYSE in that it relies on a screen-based order-book

system to match buy and sell orders in the market place, without the help of a specialist. As you begin to think about the differences among the exchanges, pay close attention to how the terminology is used to describe hybrid features of the different world exchanges.

2. How would you compare the trading and price reporting systems of SEAQ and TSE, as described above, to the NYSE and NASDAQ?

3. The Market 2000 study indicates that most blocks in NYSE stocks are negotiated off the exchange ("upstairs"), but are executed on the exchange ("downstairs"). However, a later study of Dow Jones stocks found that 83 percent of trading value in orders of 10,000 shares or more are directly executed downstairs without upstairs intervention. However, the mean size of the downstairs sample was smaller, 19,520 shares, compared with the mean of 38,600 shares for the upstairs sample. The study found that the downstairs market accommodated large-block trades with minimal price movements and observed that the downstairs market offers immediacy and less potential for information leakage. The study suggests that these benefits may be less important when traders in upstairs markets can credibly signal that their trades are not motivated by superior information. It concludes that the primary benefit of the upstairs market may not be to the initiator but to the counterparties who are reluctant to submit large limit orders and thus offer free options to the market. Upstairs markets "allow these traders to selectively participate in trades screened by block brokers who avoid trades that may originate from traders with private information. Thus the upstairs market's major role may be to enable transactions that would not otherwise occur in the downstairs market." A. Madhavan and M. Cheng, *In Search of Liquidity: Block Trades in the Upstairs and Downstairs Markets* 10 Review of Financial Studies 175, 201 (1997).

Consider this example of off-exchange trading of blocks. In May 1997, Carl Icahn sold his 19.9 million-share stake in RJR Nabisco Holdings Corp. to Goldman, Sachs & Co. for more than $730 million. Goldman bought the stock outside the U.S. after markets there closed and resold it before the markets opened up the next day. Neither the purchase or resale hit the NYSE tape although it was reported to the Exchange. Icahn knew he might have taken a discount, since he did not get a "market" price for his stock, but was concerned that a sale on the exchange would prompt short selling, and wanted to get the deal done quickly. G. Ip, *More Big Stock Sales are Handled 'Off Board'*, Wall St. Journal, April 9, 1997.

Given that downstairs trades on the NYSE are immediately reported, would you conclude from this study that SEAQ gets an insignificant competitive advantage from delaying reporting of large block trades?

One study found that on SEAQ only about 15% of the volume of large trades is unwound in the 90 minute delay period, and that most of this post-trade positioning was accomplished within 45 minutes. It further found that reducing the level of information could only be justified in 50% of the cases in which it is now allowed. J. Board and C. Sutcliffe, *The Effects of Trade Transparency in the London Stock Exchange: A Summary* (London Stock Exchange Financial Markets Group Special Paper No. 67, 1995). G. Gemmill, *Transparency and Liquidity: A Study of Block Trades on the London Stock Exchange under Different Publication Rules*, LI Journal of Finance 1765 (December 1996) found that spreads and liquidity on blocks were unaffected by the different publication regimes employed on the London Stock Exchange at various points in time, immediate (1987/88), 90 minutes (1991/92) and 24 hours (1989/90). One explanation is that prices leak out immediately despite delayed publication rules.

4. Listing costs, which include but are not restricted to fees, vary significantly among exchanges. A Tokyo listing is reported to cost three to four times as much as other leading markets, $170,000 - $225,000 per year, mainly for translating reports for Japanese permits and observing regulations. The poor performance of the TSE, and the low trading volume, has caused foreign a significant number of foreign companies to delist. As of September 1997, 64 foreign companies were listed, as compared to 127 in 1991. There has been a steady fall in listings over the 1991-1997 period despite the fact that listing fees were lowered in December 1994. They are currently at a maximum of about $235,000 (the actual fees depend on total number of shares issued and the number of Japanese shareholders). In 1997, TSE lowered other listing requirements. Minimum shareholder equity is now reduced to $8.4 million from the old level of $84 million and minimum profits required for the three years before listing have been reduced to about $1.68 million from $16.8 million. G. Robinson, *Tokyo Exchange to Relax Rules*, Financial Times, September 18, 1997; *Relaxation of Listing Requirements for Foreign Companies*, Securities & Capital Markets Law Report, Feb. 1995.

5. A new market, NASDAQ Japan, which operates as a section of the Osaka Securities Exchange, was launched in June 2000, to trade growth companies. This is a joint venture between NASDAQ and Softbank, a leading Japanese company. One commentator stated that this initiative did not address one of the main obstacles to new listings, a Japanese Commercial Code requirement that the par value of shares be at least ¥50,000 ($473) which limits the number of shares issued and encourages volatility. B. Rahman, *Nasdaq Japan passes early test,* Financial Times, June 27, 2000. The Tokyo Stock Exchange launched its own market for venture companies, Mothers, in December 1999. As of June 2001, NASDAQ Japan had only 56 listings with no high profile names. Mothers only lists 29 stocks. Of course, given the general doldrums of the Japanese market and the U.S. bubble burst on technology stocks, this may not be the most propitious time to build up listings.

C. WORLDWIDE COMPETITION BETWEEN STOCK MARKETS

The following pieces examine some important aspects of the competition between stock markets worldwide.

1. TRADING SYSTEMS

A. RÖELL, COMPARING THE PERFORMANCE OF STOCK EXCHANGE TRADING SYSTEMS

The Internationalization of Capital Markets and The Regulatory Response 167-177
(J. Fingleton ed., 1992).

.   .   .

8.2 THE MARKETS IN CROSS-LISTED FRENCH EQUITIES

It is not easy to compare the liquidity of the Paris Bourse and London's SEAQ International. The reason is that the trading systems are so different that one invariably finds oneself comparing apples with pears.

Measuring liquidity in Paris is relatively easy. The CAC (Cotation Assistée en Continu) electronic auction system provides a continuous picture of the reigning limit order book. Any trader who requires *immediacy* (trading without any delay to search for, or simply hope for, better terms of trade) need only hit these limit-orders to obtain a deal. Thus, with a picture of the limit order book in hand, it is simple to compute the cost of trading for any given deal size.

Figures 1 and 2 show typical examples of the Paris limit order book. Figure 1 plots the average price a broker looking at the limit order book knows that he can obtain (pay) for sell (buy) orders of different size, for shares in a major French company (BSN). Note that the market is very *tight:* the 'fourchette', or bid-ask spread for minimal size deals, is very small indeed (less than 0.5%). On the other hand the market is not very *deep.* For larger deals, say of size 20,000 shares or more (about FF 20 million or more in value), the effective spread is quite wide: the average price obtained when selling a block this size would be more than 5% below the price paid when buying it. And beyond this size the limit order book soon runs out altogether. Figure 2 rounds out the picture by giving an impression of the extra liquidity supplied to the market by 'hidden orders': that is, portions of limit orders that are there

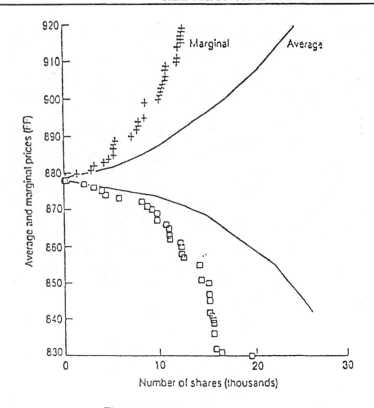

Fig. 1. Paris Limit orders, BSN, 24 June 1991.

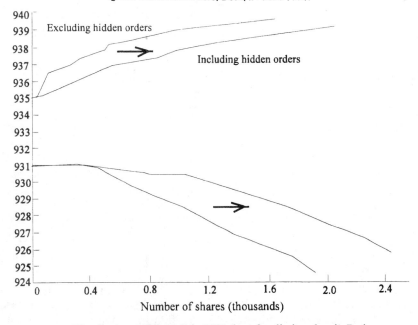

Fig. 2. Axa-Midi, 22 July 1991, best few limit orders in Paris.

to be executed against but invisible to the users of the system. Agents like to hide part of their larger orders in this way so as not to alarm market participants. In any case these 'hidden orders' do not seem to be over-whelming in relative size: in Figure 2, a typical case, they enhance the depth of the market by increasing the size one can trade at any given bid-ask spread by roughly 1/3 to ½.

If you are contemplating a trade in Paris, what you see is what you get (apart from the hidden orders). Measuring the liquidity of the London market is more difficult, because prices are often negotiated to yield a better deal than is quoted on screen. Market makers display bid and ask prices on screen, together with the quantity for which they undertake to guarantee these prices to all customers (i.e. the trade size for which their price is 'firm'. This quantity must equal at least the NMSW—Normal Market Size—for the security in question, set by the Stock Exchange at roughly the median trade size). But in practice customers who telephone a market maker to execute a deal can generally negotiate a better price or a larger quantity than quoted, especially if the deal is of substantial size.

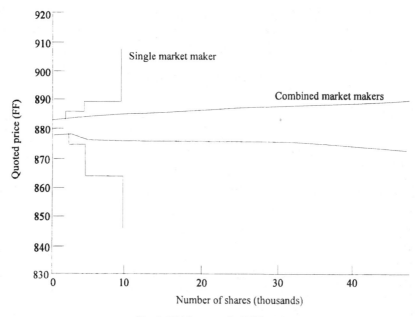

Fig. 3. SEAQ quotes for BSN, 24 June 1991.

As shown by the 'single market maker' prices in Figure 3, the London market in French equities is not very tight. The market touch (the difference between the best bid and ask quotes) at minimum trade sizes generally exceeds that in Paris by a factor of about 2. If it were the case that traders could only rely on the firm quotes of single market makers, the market would not be very deep either. Figures 1 and 3 concern the same security (BSN) at the same moment of time, and are drawn to the same scale. Based on these figures one would conclude that the cost of immediacy in French equities is lower in Paris over the entire range of trade sizes.

Realised transaction prices present a rather different picture from market makers' quotes. Table 1 displays the average deviation between the transaction price and the quoted market mid-price for a selection of French equities on SEAQ International. This measure roughly represents half the realised bid-ask spread (but note that inaccurate reporting of deal times leads the transaction price to stray away from the presumed contemporaneous mid-price, so that this measure may be an overestimate). In Table 1, average realised spreads *decrease* with transaction size. Moreover, trade sizes far exceeding NMS and market makers' quoted sizes are commonplace. Thus the market is rather deeper than one would infer by looking at market makers' quotes.

Table 1 Average percentage deviation of transaction price from market mid-price on SEAQ International, May-July 1991, for selected French equities

Stock	Normal market size (NMS)	Median trade size	Price deviation for trade size ranges			
			All	1/10 NMS and below	1/10 NMS to NMS	Above NMS
Axa-Midi	1000	1000	0.823	1.522 (30)	0.736 (183)	0.794 (177)
B.S.N.	2500	1000	0.565	0.693 (202)	0.498 (659)	0.652 (214)
Carrefour	500	500	0.690	0.939 (73)	0.704 (428)	0.611 (456)
Elf Aquitaine	5000	4800	0.670	0.860 (138)	0.659 (703)	0.639 (588)
Gen. Des Eaux	500	500	0.572	0.726 (102)	0.549 (497)	0.563 (505)
L'Oreal	2500	1500	0.687	1.031 (52)	0.638 (353)	0.686 (198)
Pernod-Ricard	1000	615	0.673	1.084 (37)	0.597 (152)	0.685 (106)
Schneider	2000	1500	0.852	1.291 (37)	0.872 (157)	0.640 (91)
Un Ass Paris	2000	3000	0.659	0.824 (19)	0.600 (264)	0.693 (369)

Number of transactions in parentheses.

It is not clear, however, whether Table 1 really represents the price immediacy. Did the larger deals require extensive negotiation or delay before the price could be agreed? The data do not provide this information.

To summarise the facts: there has been considerable migration of trading volume, and in particular of larger deals, towards SEAQ International. Indeed, on occasion the day's trading volume in a blue-chip continental European equity on SEAQ international can exceed that on the domestic market, though on average the domestic market trading volume remains considerably higher (by a factor of about 3 in the case of France). The data on trading costs and liquidity suggest that Paris's electronic auction market provides tighter spreads for small deals but that the limit order book is not deep enough to accommodate large deals at prices that are competitive with those obtained from London's market makers. The London market makers' firm quotes are not particularly tight or deep; but the transaction data suggest that when asked to improve upon their firm quotes, they routinely do so; especially for large deals.

8.3 DISCUSSION OF TRADING STRUCTURE AND POLICY ISSUES

It is not just for French equities that large deals have migrated to London following their introduction onto the SEAQ International system. There is the same pattern in the trading of blue-chip equities from many other European countries such as Spain, Italy and Sweden. One can think of a number of different reasons why this might be so. Some are inherent in the trading systems used. Some concern additional specifications not inextricably tied to the trading system used. And some have nothing to do with the methods and regulation of trading at all.

In Paris, Madrid, Stockholm and now Milan also, shares are traded on a continuous electronic auction, using variants of a system developed by the Toronto stock exchange. This system differs from London's SEAQ system along a number of different dimensions.

Public Limit Order Exposure

One important difference lies in the way entry into market making is regulated. In Paris, any member of the general public is free to 'make' the market by instructing a broker to input limit orders into the system on his behalf. Thus in theory everyone can come in and provide liquidity on the spur of the moment. In London, only registered market makers can display their limit orders on the screen: there is no 'public limit order exposure' (PLOE). While there is no great barrier to entry into market making (any stock exchange member who passes minimum competence and capital adequacy standards qualifies), day-to-day liquidity provision by members of the public is ruled out. Thus ordinary members of the public cannot trade directly with each other as in Paris; all trading must go via the market makers (unless one has access to a network of potential counterparties to trade with, and that is not worth building up except for large institutional investors who trade regularly and in size).

It is a common perception that this lack of PLOE alone increases transaction costs in London because ordinary traders cannot avoid giving a cut to the intermediary, namely the market maker's spread ('jobber's turn'), even when willing counterparties are available. But would not competition among market makers eliminate such an opportunity for excessive profit? Figure 4 shows the number of market makers per share for the French equities traded on SEAQ International. Securities with less than 10 registered market makers are rare. It seems unlikely that there are substantial opportunities for oligopoly profit.

More prosaically, the high spread in London for smaller deals may simply reflect the order processing costs involved. The process of trading by telephoning a market maker and the paperwork involved are costly in terms of time and trouble. Paris's automatic system, where trades are executed directly and electronically at the touch of a button, is simply less costly. And even with automatic execution of small orders in London, a trade between two final customers would still tend to be more costly as it necessarily involves intervention of a market maker, i.e. two separate transactions. Such order processing cost differentials clearly loom larger for smaller deals, explaining why London is less competitive in that category of trades.

Fig. 4. SEAQ market makers per security.

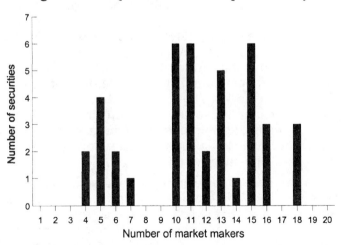

Transparency and Last Trade Publication

A second important difference, and the focus of the current debate about EC regulatory policy, is the *transparency* of the two types of market. Can all participants see the order flow promptly and simultaneously? On the electronic auction markets, all trades are necessarily inputted into the system at the moment they are executed. It is thus relatively simple for the exchange authorities to publish a wide range of information about recent deals: their size and price, and even the identities of the brokers involved. On a telephone dealing market accurate and prompt publication of trading information is harder to achieve. Traders have to be explicitly required to report their trades promptly and accurately. And traders who do not wish to reveal information about their current deals can easily evade such requirements and delay their trade reports, for instance by entering into provisional agreements to trade that are not officially finalised until some time later. In short, the London system is inherently less transparent.

In addition, the exchange authorities in London have deliberately chosen not to try to enforce immediate trade reporting and publication. In the international equity section of the market exchange the authorities have not imposed any trade publication requirements at all, while for domestic equities (in response to pressure from market makers) publication of large deals is quite slow. The justification for this is that market makers can quote a better price if they are able to lay off a position they take on before it becomes publicly known that the deal is overhanging the market, moving the market price adversely.

It should be emphasized that there is a pure redistribution of trading costs from large and informed traders to small traders at work here. Why would a market maker offer a better price for large deals that are not published? Precisely because large deals in particular convey information; the market maker can take advantage of the fact that others do not have this information by trading at a price that does not reflect it yet, after completing the initial deal. So the initial trader's gain is the rest of the market's loss. In equilibrium, market spreads for all deals (in particular those that are too small to convey much information) will widen, as market makers need to protect themselves against competitors who have superior order flow information, as well as against traders with superior information.

Clearly, a market maker who is not subject to immediate trade publication can out compete those who are, who have no window of time before everyone else knows about a trade. Thus it is not surprising that large trades gravitate towards the market with the slowest publication of trades: large institutional traders, and the market makers who vie for their business, prefer a market with slower trade publication. This point has been recognised by policy-makers. Thus in the debate about EC regulations, continental exchange authorities have tended to push for the imposition of greater transparency across the board, and in particular, for faster trade publication in London. Meanwhile London authorities argue that the current system is very successful and that prompt trade publication would drive away business (not just back to continental Europe, but also back to the USA and other countries whose shares are traded on SEAQ International). If it ain't broke, why fix it?

In this context it is interesting to note the new Paris proposals for reporting of block trades. Up to now, stock exchange member firms who arrange negotiated block deals have been required to report them promptly as a 'cross transaction' on the CAC system, where the information is displayed to all participants. The new proposals delay the publication of this information. It is hoped that this will increase the volume of block deals done in Paris and within exchange trading hours.

This tendency towards reduced market transparency as a result of competition among exchanges has a beggar-thy-neighbour ring to it. Why not have the EC impose greater transparency, a principle that has long guided US policy-making. Or would the damage to London's position as an international marketplace for large transactions be too great?

Negotiating Deals

Both the limit order book in Paris and the firm quotes of the market makers in London are generally not deep enough to accommodate most of the transactions exceeding the median trade size in London. This is not surprising. Any agent who places a limit order (or displays a firm quote) is in effect giving an option to trade at a fixed price to counterparties. If a counterparty trades just as the market price moves through the limit order, or if he trades on superior information, the placer of the limit order loses out.

Thus it is not surprising to see a reluctance to provide continuous liquidity. Telephone negotiation of large deals (for smaller deals, negotiation is not worth the time and trouble) allows the market maker to check whether there is anything untoward going on at the instant of trading, and also to form an opinion about the possible trading motives of the counterparty: (Can he give a convincing reason for needing to trade that is not based on superior information? Is he a trusted repeat customer with a good reputation? etc.) This means that the transaction prices that can be obtained through negotiation are typically better than the electronically displayed quotes or limit orders. And in equilibrium, the latter are likely to be wider apart than they would be in a market where there is no scope for negotiation.

This explains why even in Paris, very large deals must be arranged outside the electronic limit order book. It does not explain why large deals gravitate to London. There is no fundamental reason for there not to be well-known large institutions in the home markets, who are prepared to trade blocks upon inquiry, effectively acting as market makers for large deals.

· · ·

8.4   CONCLUDING COMMENTS

How and why has London's SEAQ International been able to capture such a large share of trading volume in European equities? The data on dealing spreads in this paper agree with the actual patterns of trading volume: London's advantage is confined to larger sized deals. Why is this so? Apart from London's pre-eminent position as an international centre, there are a number of innate features of the market maker based dealing system which makes it suitable for large scale deals. Amongst these, slower trade reporting seems to be a significant factor in its attractiveness to large-scale dealers. One would expect harmonisation of trade publication speeds—either through stricter EC rules or through laxer rules on the Continent—to lead to some repatriation of trading activity to the domestic stock exchanges.

2. COMPETITION IN EUROPE

Competition among Europe's complex web of markets began historically with different national exchanges separated by different market structures and nationalist sympathies. It evolved by showing a steady trend toward convergence of the different structures. Now we are witnessing substantial mergers of markets, most notably of the London and Frankfurt exchanges. The material in this section attempts to sketch a picture of this evolving and still quite dynamic European market environment.

a. BACKGROUND ON EUROPEAN STOCK MARKETS

EUROPEAN STOCK MARKETS, TOO MANY TRADING PLACES
The Economist, June 19, 1993, at 21.

How many stock exchanges does Europe with a single capital market need? Nobody knows. But a part-answer is clear: fewer than it has today. America has eight stock exchanges, and seven futures and options exchanges. Of these only the New York Stock Exchange, the American Stock Exchange, NASDAQ (the over-the-counter market), and the two Chicago futures exchanges have substantial turnover and nationwide pretensions.

The 12 member countries of the European Community (EC), in contrast, boast 32 stock exchanges and 23 futures and options exchanges. Of these, the markets in London, Frankfurt, Paris, Amsterdam, Milan and Madrid—at least—aspire to significant roles on the European and world stages. And the number of exchanges is growing. Recent arrivals include futures exchanges in Italy and Spain.

In eastern Germany, Leipzig wants to reopen the stock exchange that the Russians closed in 1945.

.   .   .

Co-operate or die

[C]ompetition-through-diversity has encouraged European exchanges to cut out the red tape that protected their members from outside competition, to embrace electronics, and to adapt themselves to the wishes of investors and issuers. Yet the diversity may also have had a cost in lower liquidity. Investors, especially from outside Europe, are deterred if liquidity remains divided among different exchanges. Companies suffer too: they grumble about the costs of listing on several different markets.

So the third response* of Europe's bourses to their battle has been pan-European co-operative ventures that could anticipate a bigger European market. There are more wishful words here than deeds. Work on two joint EC projects to pool market information, Pipe and Euroquote, was abandoned, thanks mainly to hostility from Frankfurt and London. Eurolist, under which a company meeting the listing requirements for one stock exchange will be entitled to a listing on all, is going forward— but this is hardly a single market. As Paris's Mr. Théodore puts it, "there is a compelling business case for the big European exchanges building the European-regulated market of tomorrow". Sir Andrew Hugh-Smith, chairman of the London exchange, has also long advocated one European market for professional investors.

One reason little has been done is that bourses have been coping with so many reforms at home. Many wanted to push these through before thinking about Europe. But there is also atavistic nationalism. London, for example, is unwilling to give up the leading role it has acquired in cross-border trading between institutions; and other exchanges are unwilling to accept that it keeps it. Mr. Théodore says there is no future for the European bourses if they are forced to row in a boat with one helmsman. Amsterdam's Baron van Ittersum also emphasises that a joint European market must not be one under London's control.

Hence the latest, lesser notion gripping Europe's exchanges: bilateral or multilateral links. The futures exchanges have shown the way. Last year four smaller exchanges led by Amsterdam's EOE and OM, an options exchange based in Sweden and London, joined together in a federation called FEX. In January of this year the continent's two biggest exchanges, MATIF and the DTB, announced a link-up that was clearly aimed at toppling London's LIFFE from its

---

* The two others were protectionism, e.g., Club Med, and cost cutting, eds.

dominant position. Gérard Pfauwadel, MATIF's chairman, trumpets the deal as a precedent for other European exchanges. Mr. Breuer, the Deutsche Börse's chairman, reckons that a network of European exchanges is the way forward, though he concedes that London will not warm to the idea. The bourses of France and Germany can be expected to follow the MATIF/DTB lead.

It remains unclear how such link-ups will work, however. The notion is that members of one exchange should be able to trade products listed on another. So a Frenchman wanting to buy German government-bond futures could do so through a dealer on MATIF, even though the contract is actually traded in Frankfurt. That is easy to arrange via screen-based trading: all that are needed are local terminals. But linking an electronic market such as the DTB to a floor-based market with open-outcry trading such as MATIF is harder. Nor have any exchanges thought through an efficient way of pooling their settlement systems.

. . .

c. LONDON VERSUS THE CONTINENTAL EXCHANGES

The 1990s have seen the continental exchanges improve their competitive position vis-à-vis London.

In Chapter 5, when we looked at the Club Med countries' position on the Investment Services Directive, it appeared that their competitive strategy was protectionism, i.e. keep other exchanges like SEAQ from trading Club Med country securities. We also saw that strategy failed. France, one of the leaders of Club Med, has now shifted its strategy to one of forceful competition with SEAQ. And the Paris Bourse is promoting the virtues of its order-driven system over SEAQ's market-maker system (which SEAQ, in turn, has changed). It also has adopted new rules for trading large blocks.

All CAC trades were traditionally required to be made at a single price whatever the size of the order; all supply and demand was matched centrally at a single price. Under the new rules, block trades can be separately negotiated at a price within a weighted average price spread for standard block sizes determined by the Council dès Bourses de Valeur (CBV, the governing board of the exchange). The weighted average price spread for a particular share offering is calculated from the outstanding sale and purchase order for a standard block size registered in the market. The standard block size is set for each quarter based on the volumes of transactions and quantities of shares normally marketed in the previous quarter, with a minimum size of FF one million ($195,000) or 2.5% of the value of trades transacted daily whichever is higher. So called "structuring" blocks, an amount either in excess of FF550 million ($97.7 million) or 10% of a company's capital have greater leeway. There has been no compromise, however, with prompt reporting. Once these off-market block trades have been completed, they must be promptly reported.

Another competitive move by CAC in 1996 was to deploy a communications system in London that allows traders in London to trade CAC stocks from screens in their London offices in real time. This takes advantage of the Investment Services Directive to offer cross-border services. CAC has also set up its Eurocac system for dealers to trade in the stocks of European blue chips regardless of where they are listed. As of 1997, it had 60 stocks, 30 of which were Italian and 10 German. M. Anslow, *Selling SuperCAC*, Security Industry News, May 19, 1997. Finally, it is important to note that the French stock trade transaction tax was eliminated in 1993.

It appears that CAC and other continental exchanges have made inroads into SEAQ's market share in the trading of their securities. While SEAQ initially may have traded 25% of the volume in French equities, and perhaps even 50% in French blue chips, according to Paris Bourse officials in 1995, trading in blue chips on SEAQ was only 25% of total volume. A. Benos and M. Crouhy, Changes in the Structure and Dynamics of European Securities Markets 4 (HEC School of Management Discussion Paper, July 1995). M. Pagano, *The Changing Microstructure of European Equity Markets*, paper presented at the University of Genoa Conference on European Investment Markets, September 1996, finds that the Italian, German and French markets repatriated a substantial portion of trading from SEAQ. He offers three reasons: (1) the increase in liquidity, immediacy and transparency of Continental markets; (2) the declining willingness of London dealers to commit substantial capital to market making in Continental stocks following significant losses on such stocks in the early 1990s; and (3) a preference of institutional investors for the Continental trading systems.

Paris has also been a pioneer in selling its trading technology to other exchanges. In 1997 it made major sales of its technology to the Sao Paulo stock exchange and the Chicago Mercantile Exchange. Technology sales could be an increasingly important revenue source, and basis for competition, among exchanges.

Germany has also made some strides in becoming more competitive. Germany's equity market has not been traditionally important due to the predominance of bank financing. Equity investment in Germany is estimated at between 5.5 and 11 percent of total investment, as compared with 18 percent in the U.K. and 21 percent in the U.S. R. Butler, *Last Call for Germany's Equity Market*, Institutional Investor, November 1996. However, the privatization of East German companies, the general advantages of capital market financing, together with the desire of the country to become a major player in international capital markets, is producing change. About 12.33 million people, or about 19.3 percent of the population, owned shares at the end of 2000, about double the level of 1997, and investors in mutual funds increased by 10 percent aver the same period. R. Benoit, *Big rise in number of Germans owning shares,* Financial Times, January 10, 2001.

Germany's regulatory system has been greatly strengthened through the creation of the Federal Supervisory Office for Securities Trading and the adoption of prohibitions on insider trading. Germany, like the United States, has regional exchanges, eight in number. These exchanges use an open-outcry trading method under which public orders and market-makers compete for exposed individual orders in a system somewhat like that of the NYSE. Frankfurt's exchange has 75% of German exchange trading. For a comprehensive review of changes in Germany, see J. Fries, Jr., *An Outsider's Look into the Regulation of Insider Trading in Germany: A Guide to Securities, Banking, and Market Reform in Finantzplatz Deutschland*, 19 Boston College International and Comparative Law Review 1 (1996).

Stock market competition in Europe occurs in the context of competition between London and Frankfurt for supremacy as a financial center. London outstrips Frankfurt by most measures, e.g assets under management, $4.132 billion versus $1.456 billion, number of foreign banking institutions, 478 versus 320, cross-border bank lending share, 31% versus 5.4%, foreign equity turnover share, 52% versus 5.8%, and OTC derivatives trading share, 36% versus 12.7%. However, Frankfurt is well positioned with respect to the increasing importance of the euro and as the home of the European Central Bank. C. Batchelor, E. Crooks and T. Major, *More big money flows into London as Deutsche Bank plans a 'leaning tower,'* Financial Times, February 8, 2002.

d. ALLIANCES AND MERGERS

In July of 1998 the London and Frankfurt Stock Exchanges announced the formation of a strategic alliance apparently ending an acrimonious struggle between the two exchanges over supremacy in the quickly converging European market. The merged exchange, which was to open in January 1999, was to feature the top 300 companies in the European Union. Members of the two exchanges were to have reciprocal membership with each other. As such, the London Stock Exchange would no longer deal in German stocks and vice-versa. Instead, members of the London exchange that wanted to deal in German equities would do so as regular remote members of the German exchange and the same would be the case for German traders wishing to deal in London equities. Further, the two exchanges were to have a common index, the listing criteria were be the same, and the hours between the two markets were to be harmonized. G. Graham, *London and Frankfurt Launch Offers,* Financial Times, Nov. 5, 1998; V. Boland, *Europe's Exchanges Meet to Bolster Alliance*, Financial Times, Dec. 18, 1998; P. John, N. George, and V.

Boland, *Move to Synchronise European Dealing Hours*, Financial Times, March 1, 1999.

This was to be the first step in the creation of a pan-European exchange. After London and Frankfurt took the lead, the Paris, Madrid, Milan, Amsterdam, Brussels and Zurich exchanges joined the alliance. However, the exchanges were unable to solve some basic problems, most importantly the adoption of common trading systems, which would have required significant technology changes with high attendant costs, and common clearing and settlement systems (Chapter 15 elaborates on these problems). As a result, the participating bourses adopted a "virtual" solution that would allow users of each exchange access to stocks listed on the other using existing technology. V. Boland, *Plan for single Europe bourse shelved,* Financial Times, September 24, 1999.

The idea of one pan-European exchange came to a halt, at least temporarily, when the Paris Bourse merged in March 2000 with the Brussels and Amsterdam exchanges under the name of Euronext, with a combined market capitalization of $1.7 trillion. It appears that this was a preemptive move by Paris after its discussions for a merger with the London Stock Exchange broke down. V. Boland, *Paris exchange seeks to woo new partners*, Financial Times, April 26, 2000. Each exchange remains intact as a subsidiary of a Euronext, N.V. a Dutch-based holding company, and each continues to have its own listings and trading systems, and separate regulator. Euronext claims to have a "single trading platform," but this only means that members on one exchange can trade in the same capacity on all three exchanges. S. Hirsch and V. Marquette, *EURONEXT: The First Pan-European Exchange, An Overview from Creation to Completion,* Journal of International Financial Markets 105 (2001). In 2001, Euronext became a more formidable competitor when it acquired Liffe. the London International Financial Futures and Options Exchange, when it outbid LSE.

The Paris led merger was followed by the announcement of a merger of the London and Frankfurt stock exchanges on May 3, 2000, under the new name of iX for International Exchange. This plan was abandoned on September 13th of the same year but it is interesting to review the proposed structure and why the merger failed.

Each exchange was to own 50 percent of iX. Since the big German banks were the major owners of the Frankfurt exchange, while LSE ownership was diffused among 290 members, the German banks would have been the biggest shareholders of the new combined entity. Deutsche Bank, for example, would have owned 8.5 percent of the new exchange.

As of March 2000, the LSE had a market capitalization of about $2.8 trillion with the Deutsche Börse at $1.5 trillion, and LSE had average daily dollar volume of $468 billion as compared with $365 billion for Deutsche Börse. The combined market capitalization of $4.3 trillion made it the 4th largest stock market in the world, after the NYSE ($11.2 trillion), NASDAQ ($6.2 trillion) and Tokyo ($4.5 trillion). While London was bigger at the time of the proposed merger, the growth rate and profitability of Frankfurt was higher.

iX was to have been headquartered in London under the leadership of the former CEO of the Frankfurt exchange, Werner Siefert. Blue-chip stocks were to be traded in London under U.K. regulation and technology stocks were to be traded in Frankfurt under German regulation. iX had agreed to have a central counterparty to trades but it was unclear exactly how that would have been arranged. Several other issues, such as the currency in which stocks would trade in London (euro, sterling or both) and the integration of trading and clearing and settlement systems remained to be resolved. Deutsche Börse's 50 percent ownership of Clearstream (formerly Cedel) was left outside of the deal (see Chapter 15 for more information on Clearstream). This was apparently done because Deutsche Börse would have been the dominant partner in a merger including its Clearstream ownership.

iX was to have a link with NASDAQ. NASDAQ planned to trade the technology stocks centered in Frankfurt when Frankfurt was closed. This fit into NASDAQ's general strategy to be the centerpiece of 24 hour global trading.

It is not clear exactly why the merger failed, but four factors seemed to play important roles. First, the division between the blue chip trading in London and the technology trading in Frankfurt was not altogether clear. Second, there was criticism of the brokerage community of the failure to create a common clearing and settlement system for stocks traded on the two exchanges. Third, there were significant regulatory issues arising out of the differences in regulation in the two countries. Foremost of these was transparency, or price reporting. In London, a five day delay was permitted for the reporting of block trades, unless the block trade has been 90% unwound in which case the trade must be reported immediately, while in Frankfurt it appears that traders must report trades by the end of the day unless they are executed off the exchange (amounting to 30 percent of all trades) in which case they are not reported at all. NYSE Research, April 24, 2001 (communication to authors). Deutsche Börse announced, however, that it was in favor of using the London rules for the price reporting of all issues. The German and British regulatory authorities, the Federal Securities Trading Supervisory Office (BAWe) and the Financial Services Authority, issued a joint statement on August 21, 2000 describing six task forces that had been set up to review regulatory issues. The work of these task forces is elaborated on in S. Bergstrasser (Head of International Affairs of the BAWe), *Regulatory Implications of an Exchange Merger,* Working Paper delivered at Capital Markets in the Age of the euro, Genoa, Italy, November 10-11, 2000 [Bergstrasser].

Apart from the transparency issue, there were problems of corporate structure and governance that would have made a complete merger impossible. Under German law, at least, the exchange would have had to remain a separate body, as it was a quasi-public corporation. There were also problems as to how the disclosure regimes in the two countries were to work together. While there were differences in how listing standards, and periodic and ad hoc disclosure, were dealt with by the two exchanges, it is unclear why these differences would have prevented the merger, as the shares in Frankfurt could have traded under Frankfurt rules, and the shares in London under London rules. There were also issues about how the two different regimes for insider trading and market manipulation would have been handled. Again, it is not clear why these differences could not have been preserved, particularly if the there were no dual listings, all trading in a given stock would have been in one country.

The final factor that may have accounted for the merger failure was the hostile bid for the LSE launched in September 2000 by the OM Group, a technology group that runs the Stockholm stock exchange. Although, the hostile bid was eventually rejected on November 11 (after the friendly merger fell through), the OM bid may have raised issues about the pricing of the friendly merger, particularly whether the 50-50 approach undervalued London. *Shocking times in Throgmorton Street,* The Economist, September 2, 2000.

Notes and Questions

1. Röell finds that bid-offer spreads on CAC (Paris order market) are narrower on small trades but larger on big trades than SEAQ (quote market). Why might narrow spreads be an indication of market efficiency? Should brokers execute all small trades on CAC rather than SEAQ? Why might a quote market be more efficient for large trades?

2. Some studies have found that one advantage of trading on SEAQ, a dealer market, over CAC, an order market, is that trading on SEAQ need not be anonymous. This permits the disciplining of traders exploiting informational advantages, which, as we have seen, is a major justification of the NYSE's specialist system, *see supra* at 770. L. Glosten, *Is the Electronic Open Limit Order Book Inevitable?*, 49 Journal of Finance 1127, 1152-1153 (1994). See also G. Franke and D. Hess, Anonymous Electronic Trading Versus Floor Trading 32-33 (Internationalisierung der Wirtschaft, Sonderforschungsbereich 178, Serie II, No. 285, 1985).

3. NASDAQ has formed an alliance with the Quebec Stock Exchange and has a joint venture with Softbank to trade high technology stocks on the Osaka Stock Exchange as of June 2000. Following the demise of the LSE-Deutsche Börse merger, NASDAQ attempted to make an alliance

with the LSE, but that apparently has proved unsuccessful. NASDAQ believes that one of the key obstacles preventing its global expansion is the difficulty of trading foreign shares in the U.S. While investors can trade shares by doing so abroad, the SEC prevents them from doing so through screens of foreign exchanges in the U.S., as this would allow a foreign exchange to operate in the U.S. without fulling complying with U.S. rules.

Announcement of the planned NASDAQ linkage with iX, was followed by talks between the NYSE and Euronext about a linkage of their own, and the NYSE is also exploring linkages with the Toronto, Mexico City and Tokyo exchanges. *NYSE Talks to Markets in Latin America, Europe, Canada About Possible Alliances,* Wall Street Journal, May 10, 2000.

4. There are significant efforts to establish Pan-European stock-markets for second-tier firms. The EU Commission has promoted this idea. EASDAQ (European Association of Securities Dealers Automated Quotation) began operations in September 1996, using the NASDAQ market-maker quote based system to establish a market for fast growing companies. It has had somewhat of a slow start. By January 31, 2001, it only had 60 companies and a small market capitalization. In April 2001, NASDAQ announced its acquisition of a 58 percent stake in EASDAQ, which will now be called NASDAQ Europe. NSCC the clearing arm of the U.S.'s DTCC will help manage clearing and settlement services. J. Labate and A. van Duyn, *Nasdaq dispels any doubts over its European ambitions*, Financial Times, March 31/April 1, 2001. EASDAQ has competition from another venture to trade smaller capitalized companies, Euro NM, which has linked four new national systems trading small companies, the French Nouveau Marché, the German Neuer Markt (part of the Frankfurt Stock Exchange), the Belgian Nouveau Marché, and the Dutch NMAX. The link between the Belgian and French markets was operational in February 1998 and the links with the other two markets began at the end of 1998. By June of 1998 Euro NM had 101 listings and a market capitalization of over $20 billion. In December of 1998, Euro NM announced plans to have Sweden, Denmark, and Switzerland join, giving it a clear edge in its battle with EASDAQ.

The German Neuer market has grown to be by far the biggest member of Euro NM. As of May 2000, it had 60 percent of the listings and more than 80 percent of the market capitalization. 20 percent of its listings are foreign issuers. Due to the dot.com crash, it had a 90 percent downturn between January 2000 and July 2001, resulting in some calling for stricter regulation and listing standards. Some now refer to this as the Suckermarkt.

EASDAQ requires companies applying for admission to trading to publish a prospectus, and public offerings of EASDAQ listed securities would be subject to the European Union POP Directive examined in Chapter 5. EASDAQ securities can be traded through screens placed in a number of EU countries. As was also seen in Chapter 5, this method of cross-border trading was facilitated by the Investment Services Directive. EASDAQ has a close connection with NASDAQ reflected in the choice of name and the fact that EASDAQ rules and systems have been modeled after NASDAQ. Further, companies already listed on either of the two markets are normally granted easy access to the other. V. Boland, *EASDAQ and Euro NM Are Fighting to Obtain Company Listings But Nationality Still Seems to Play a Role*, Financial Times, June 22, 1998; V. Boland, *Three More Countries to Join Euro NM*, Financial Times, Dec. 18, 1998.

Finally, one should not ignore the competition from ATS's, like the U.K's Tradepoint, to the traditional European exchanges. In October 2000, Tradepoint announced a merger with the Swiss Stock Exchange (SWX) which formed a combined trading system, Virt-X that opened for trading in June 2001. Trading in all Swiss blue chip shares and Tradepoint's pan-European trading will be based in London and governed by U.K. regulatory standards. V. Boland, *Tradepoint and SWX seal virt-x merger,* Financial Times, October 24, 2000.

5. With respect to merger possibilities, note that in November 1993, the Chicago Board of Options Exchange made an offer to buy the Philadelphia Stock Exchange through making an offer for each of the Philadelphia's 505 memberships. The Board of the Philadelphia Exchange rejected the offer, however. Chapter 16 deals more generally with the issue of competition between derivatives exchanges. In April 1994, the members of New York's two major futures exchanges, the New York Commodity Exchange and the New York Mercantile Exchange, approved a merger, and the two Chicago exchanges, the Chicago Board of Trade and the Chicago Mercantile Exchange entered into merger discussions in January 1996, R. Lapper, *Chicago Exchanges to Discuss Merger*, Financial Times, Jan. 25, 1996. Most recently, AMEX, NASDAQ and the Philadelphia stock exchange announced their combination, G. Ip., *Philadelphia Exchange to join NASDAQ, Amex*, Wall St. Journal, June 10, 1998. Presently, however, NASD, the joint owner of the three exchanges has separated itself from NASDAQ and is seeking to sell its interest in AMEX. Do you think there is a relationship between competition for trading in derivatives and stocks, given modern trading strategies?

6. A key question is how the euro will affect the development of stock markets in Europe. It is likely that a common currency has already contributed to the attractiveness of the London-Frankfurt merger and will continue to promote further integration of national markets.

7. Note that the problems of competition between some derivative markets may be different in one important respect from trading in stocks. The market that first designs some derivative products may have a proprietary right that requires its consent before the product is traded elsewhere. Thus, the Chicago Mercantile Exchange and the Chicago

Board of Trade have competed for the right to make a market in the Major Market Index (a stock index future). The rights to trade in the index are licensed by the American Stock Exchange.

3. COMPETITION BETWEEN EUROPE AND THE UNITED STATES

M. Pagnano, A. Röell and J. Zechner, *The Geography of Equity Listing: Why do European Companies List Abroad,* Working Paper (December 11, 1999), show that between 1986-97, the number of European companies cross-listing their shares increased considerably, but most of the increase went to U.S. exchanges (half to NYSE). At the same time the number of U.S. firms cross-listing in Europe fell by one-third. The authors found that this was part of a bigger picture, the inability of European exchanges to attract any new listings, with the exception of Frankfurt and to some extent London. The companies most likely to cross-list in the United States are high tech companies and/or companies that have rapidly expanded through leverage and are in need of capital. The European exchanges have lost out to the U.S. according to the authors, because they have the higher trading costs—with the exception of the U.K., and lower accounting standards and shareholder protection. The U.S., on the other hand, has relatively lower trading costs and higher accounting standards and shareholder protection. In addition, U.S. markets have a better analyst following for high tech companies, are more liquid and larger. These advantages may decrease as European capital markets integrate in the post-euro period.

The authors' analysis does not account entirely for the possibility of European stock exchanges or ECNs expanding into the U.S. and U.S. exchanges expanding into Europe. Competition may really be between types of trading systems rather than between exchanges located in a particular geographic area.

Worldwide cross-listings should generally increase as regulatory differences among countries decrease. As we saw in Chapter 2, high U.S. disclosure standards, and the present requirement for U.S. GAAP reconciliation, have deterred many foreign companies from listing in the U.S. If foreign countries were to move closer to U.S. disclosure standards and if the U.S. were to accept IASC accounting standards cross-listings in the U.S. should increase. This was suggested in a recent study of N. Yamori and T. Baba, *Japanese Management Views on Overseas Exchange Listings: Survey Results,* Pacific Basin Working Paper Series, Working Paper No. PB99-05 (December 1, 1999) where the authors predicted that cross-listing of Japanese companies should increase as a result of Big Bang since Japanese companies will be required to adopt international disclosure and accounting standards.

In this light, recall the earlier discussion of NASDAQ Europe, the attempt of NASDAQ to take trading away from the European exchanges.

European based systems may also try to come to the U.S. to compete with U.S. exchanges. Again, consider the earlier discussion of Tradepoint's approval to operate in the United States without being required to register as an exchange. Such approval permits investment fund managers to trade LSE stocks in the U.S. without using a broker as an intermediary—all traders on registered exchanges must be registered broker-dealers. This move by Tradepoint is part of the growing picture of cross-continental competition by which exchanges on one continent expand into others through the use of computer technology. Tradepoint will be trading LSE listed stocks in the U.S. during U.S. operating hours which include times at which the LSE will be closed, thereby hoping to capture LSE listed stock trading volume both in London and the United States.

The SEC's grant of an exemption to Tradepoint from stock exchange registration, with the cost and regulation that would attend, is conditional on low volume. Its average daily volume involving a U.S. member cannot exceed $40 million and its worldwide average daily volume cannot exceed 10 percent of the average daily volume of the LSE. This indicates that the SEC could well have a different approach for exchanges with more appeal.

Tradepoint will have two different levels of service—one for all U.S. Members ("Public Market") and one limited to U.S. members who are QIBs as defined in Rule 144A, see Chapter 2. The Public Market will trade U.K. securities registered in the U.S., while the other service will trade the unregistered shares. Members must be institutions such as broker-dealers, institutional investors and market-makers. Note that the ability of Tradepoint to trade unregistered U.K. securities is not limited to Rule 144A securities and thus is an alternative to the Pink Sheets for those securities. Tradepoint was approved by the SEC in December 1998 just months before the SEC's new ATS regulation, discussed earlier in this Chapter, became effective. It is unclear how future exemption applications from foreign exchanges will be affected by the adoption of this regulation. There are increasing calls from foreign exchanges to reform the U.S. registration process. Foreign exchanges would, indeed, like the same automatic access to the U.S. that EU exchanges have for EU countries under the Investment Services Directive, J. Clarke, *European Invasion*, Securities Industry News, June 18, 2001.

In May 1999, the NYSE announced plans to extend its operating hours to 10 p.m. This move would help counter the plans of alternative trading systems to trade NYSE stocks in the NYSE after-hours which are in turn catering to the demand of internet investors to trade in the evenings. While it is believed that NYSE will operate in usual fashion during the extended hours, it is possible that in the longer run it will itself operate an electronic non-floor or specialist based market during these after-hours. Note that this move is not aimed at competing with the European exchanges; this would require the NYSE to open earlier since Europe is six hours ahead of the U.S. The NYSE has considered such a move but appears to have shelved it for the time being.

Ultimately, the major determinant of the outcome of stock market competition will be trading costs. We have already looked at this issue in the context of NYSE versus NASDAQ. Two recent studies have compared trading costs over a wide variety of markets. I. Domowitz, J. Glen and A Madhavan, *Liquidity, Volatility and Equity Trading Costs Across Countries and Over Time,* 4 International Finance 221 (2001) compared implied costs, defined as the price impact of a trade, and explicit costs such as brokerage fees and taxes. Here is the data (in basis points) for selected countries:

	Total Costs	Explicit Costs	Implicit Costs
France	29.5	22.8	6.7
Germany	37.7	24.3	13.4
Japan	41.3	31.7	9.5
Korea	197.5	63.1	134.4
UK	54.5	39.3	15.2
USA	38.1	8.3	29.8

A second study by GSCS's Best Execution Comparison Service, a transaction cost tracker, found the following (French data was not given in the report), comparing the sum of commission costs and cost of execution (in basis points), as measured by the difference between the price at which an investment makes a trade and an average of all prices the stock trades on that day, A. Beard, *Stock transaction costs vary across the globe,* Financial Times, July 26, 2001:

	Total Costs	Commission Costs	Execution Costs
Germany	35.4	17.7	17.7
Japan	19.0	11.7	7.4
Korea	46.0	34.7	11.3
UK	22.6	15.5	7.0
USA	27.5	12.9	14.9

What conclusions could you draw from this data?

Links to Other Chapters

Competition among stock markets depends on some understanding of domestic securities markets. We have already looked at the U.S. (Chapter 2), Europe (Chapters 5 and 7), and Japan (Chapter 8). Domestic considerations and regulation have a significant impact on the ability of domestic markets to compete for international business. The next Chapter, 15, focuses on a very important term of competition, clearance and settlement, and Chapter 16 on Futures and Options looks at some issues affecting competition between derivatives exchanges. Finally, Chapter 21 on emerging markets, looks at competition for listings of emerging market companies between emerging markets and developed exchanges.

CHAPTER FIFTEEN

INFRASTRUCTURE: CLEARANCE AND SETTLEMENT

This Chapter examines the clearance and settlement of securities. Efficient and reliable systems are a necessity for domestic and cross-border portfolio investment. First, we look at the basic elements and mechanics of the clearing and settlement process, with emphasis on the clearing and settlement of U.S. equities through the National Securities Clearing Corporation (NSCC).

Second, we explore the risks, systemic and nonsystemic, of clearing and settlement, and the Group of 30 recommendations to reduce them.

Third, we explore the mechanisms through which securities traded in one market can be cleared and settled in another market. The focus will be on inter-market linkages and international systems such as Euroclear.

Finally, we look at how clearing and settlement systems may evolve in the future.

A. THE BASIC ELEMENTS

1. OVERVIEW

This section begins with an overview of how clearance and settlement works, and then turns to the risks its involves.

OFFICE OF TECHNOLOGY ASSESSMENT, U.S. CONGRESS,
TRADING AROUND THE CLOCK*
ch. 5 (1990)("Trading Around the Clock").

"Clearing and settlement" is the processing of transactions on stock, futures, and options markets. It is what happens after the trade. "Clearing" confirms the identity and quantity of the financial instrument or contract being bought and sold, the transaction price and date, and the identity of the buyer and seller. It also sometimes includes the netting of trades, or the offsetting of buy orders and sell orders. "Settlement" is the fulfillment, by the parties to the transaction, of the obligations of the trade; in equities and bond trades, "settlement" means payment to the seller and delivery of the stock certificate or transferring its ownership to the buyer. Settlement in futures and options takes on different meanings according to the type of contract.

Trades are processed differently depending on the type of financial instrument being traded, the market or exchange on which it is traded, and the institutions involved in the processing of the trade (i.e., an exchange, a clearinghouse, a depository, or some combination).

. . .

The differences in countries' clearing and settlement are important because clearing and settlement systems used for domestic trading are now being called on to accommodate international participants. The integrity and efficiency of a nation's clearing and settlement systems are important to both its internal financial and economic stability and its ability to compete with other nations.

Many markets have "clearinghouses" that handle both the clearing process and some of the settlement process. This is the most common system in the United States for exchange-traded financial products. Many markets, including the U.S. markets, have "depositories," that hold stocks and bonds for safekeeping on behalf of their owners.

Where clearinghouses do not exist (e.g., in some European markets), depositories may take on functions of clearinghouses. Depositories may transfer ownership of stocks and bonds by "book entry" (a computer entry in the depository's record books) instead of physical delivery of certificates to the buyer, which saves time and money. There are also markets in which exchanges perform some of the clearing and settlement functions (e.g., London's International Stock Exchange), and markets in which neither clearinghouses nor depositories exist (e.g., until very recently, foreign exchange, or "forex," markets).

---

* Significant changes since publication of this piece have been inserted in brackets.

THE GOALS OF CLEARING AND SETTLEMENT

Differences in the clearing and settlement process among countries are often linked to historical, economic, and cultural factors in their laws and customs. These differences can expose international investors to extra risk in some instances. Perceptions of the purposes of the clearing and settlement process vary widely among countries. In the United States and Canada, where public policy supports broad public access to the markets, the reduction of risk, through the clearinghouse as an intermediary, is a major goal of clearing and settlement. These policies are reflected in a hierarchy of protections for the clearinghouse, including minimum capital requirements for clearinghouse members.

In many other countries, risk reduction is imposed before trading takes place, by controls on who is allowed to participate, or by the participants "knowing their trading partners," and, in equities, by reducing the time allowed to settle a transition. In these markets, clearinghouse guarantee funds are generally small or nonexistent, and settlement is seen merely as a delivery function, rather than as a mechanism for risk reduction.

These different views of the purpose of clearing and settlement have become significant as more investors begin trading in markets other than their domestic markets. U.S. investors, accustomed to domestic markets where safeguards are in place, may assume that the clearing and settlement of their trades in a foreign market has risks comparable to those in the United States, where there are guarantees provided by clearing and settlement organizations.

The chief aims of clearing and settlement in the United States and some other countries are efficiency and safety. The faster and more accurately a trade can be processed, the sooner the same capital can be reinvested, and at less cost and risk to investors. Therefore, as markets become global, one could expect that investment capital will flow toward markets that are most attractive on a risk-return basis, and that also have efficient and reliable clearing and settlement systems.

The soundness of clearing and settlement systems in one nation can also impact other nations. The failure of a clearing member at a foreign clearinghouse could affect a U.S. clearinghouse through the impact on a common clearing member. To reduce the risk of such an occurrence, different countries' clearing and settlement systems must be coordinated with each other, for example, by sharing risk information and harmonizing trade settlement dates. Both the private sector and Federal regulators have begun to take steps in this direction. It is doubtful that the private sector can achieve the needed changes without national governments taking a prominent and concerted role.

HOW CLEARING AND SETTLEMENT WORKS

Many kinds of organizations are involved in clearing and settlement. Their functions vary from market to market, and not all of these organizations exist in every country. For instance, clearinghouses play a key role in the United States and some Asian markets; but in many European markets, depositories are more important.

A key role of a clearinghouse is to assist in the comparison of trades and sometimes, as in the United States, also to remove counterparty risk from the settlement process. Clearinghouses can provide the buyer with a guarantee that he will receive the securities—or other interest—he purchased, and provide the seller with a guarantee that the payment will be received.

In the United States, the clearinghouse has a number of working relationships, or interfaces, with other institutions (figure 5-1). A trade in the United States (as well as in Japan, Canada, and some other countries) cannot settle through the central systems until it has been matched, i.e., buyers' and sellers' records of the trade are compared and reconciled. A clearinghouse has an interface with a market in which trades are executed and from which the clearinghouse receives information on the trades. The clearinghouse may receive previously "locked-in" trades (trades which have already been matched), or it may match the trades itself.

A second interface is with its clearing members, i.e., the member firms of an exchange or market. A clearing member delivers trade information to the clearinghouse and may hold positions both for itself (proprietary positions) and on behalf of its customers. Other traders in a market, who are not clearing members, must clear their trades through a member of a clearinghouse for that market. A clearinghouse controls the risks of the clearing and settlement process through its relationships with its clearing members. For example, it may have minimum capital requirements for clearing members, use margins or mark-to-market procedures, and require that its clearing members place collateral in a guarantee fund as protection against default by other clearing members. In the event of the failure of a clearing member, the clearinghouse may also have the ability to assess all other clearing members. It may also provide its clearing members with a trade-matching service and notify members about the way a trade is to be settled (the settlement date, and the way payment and delivery or transfer of ownership will be accomplished).

A third interface is with clearing and credit banks. The clearinghouse and the banks work together in the payment and collection process, since clearinghouses today do not have direct access to the payment system, e.g., Fedwire in the United States. The banks also provide credit to clearing members.

In the securities markets—but not typically in futures and options markets—there is often a fourth interface with the depository. The depository records and arranges the legal transfer of ownership of securities, and holds securities for safekeeping. The clearinghouse instructs the depository on how the transaction is to be settled. The depository may act as an agent, on behalf of the clearinghouse, to receive funds to settle the transaction.

Figure 5-1—Interfaces Among Clearing Participants

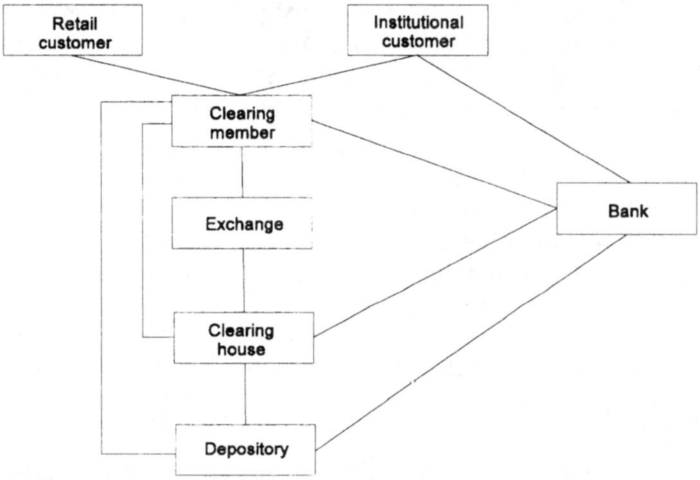

SOURCE: Office of Technology Assessment, 1990.

In addition to the relationships between clearinghouses, markets, depositories, and banks, these organizations also have relationships with each other. Clearing members of a designated market deal with the banks to settle with the clearinghouse and to obtain credit. There is an important relationship between the banks and the depository. When a bank acts in a custodial role, e.g., delivering securities and receiving payments in behalf of its customers, instructions on payment and title transfer are sent to the bank by the customer. The depository, in turn, as an accounting system for immobilized or dematerialized instruments, and/or as a central vault for the physical instruments themselves, interfaces with the banks as custodian. It may also, as custodian, have an interface with the banks for payment.

RISKS FROM DIFFERENCES IN CLEARING AND SETTLEMENT MECHANISMS

These differences—the use of guarantee funds, the time allowed to settle a trade, etc.—in countries' clearing and settlement systems are a major constraint on global trading and may impose risks on traders and investors. Defaults in a national clearing and settlement process can propagate through other national systems, since multinational financial institutions may be active in several national markets. Collapse of a major settlement system could endanger financial systems in both its own and other countries.

Even in day-to-day operations, differences in clearing and settlement systems and in their performances constrain some kinds of trading. For example, in Japan, settlement in equities and bonds is normally on the third day after a trade (T+3) and in the United States it is normally on the fifth day (T+5). [In 1995 the United States moved to T+3 but the following example could apply to other countries, eds.]. An investor trading General Motors (GM) stock on both the New York Stock Exchange (NYSE) and the Tokyo Stock Exchange (TSE) would have trouble perfectly arbitraging his holdings. If the investor were to buy GM shares on the NYSE and simultaneously sell them on the TSE, because the U.S. settlement period is 2 days longer, the GM shares would be delayed by 2 business days for the Japanese settlement. If the investor were to buy GM stock on the TSE and sell GM stock that same day on the NYSE, the shares could be available for the NYSE settlement because that is 2 days later than Tokyo's. The Japan Securities Clearing Corp. (JSCC)—through its link with International Securities Clearing Corp. (ISCC) in the United States—holds the U.S. shares at The Depository Trust Co. (DTC); therefore instead of physical movement of certificates there simply would be a book entry delivery at DTC.

. . .

Trading in European markets, unlike in the United States, mostly does not rely only on stock exchanges. In Japan, there is as yet no central depository, but there is a clearing and custody system at TSE. Many European countries have depositories, but their functions vary from country to country, and are often different from U.S. depositories.

There are three principal models for clearing and settlement in the world's major stock markets. The first model has no centralized depository or independent clearinghouse beyond the stock exchange. The exchanges usually perform as many of the clearing and settlement functions as are feasible. These include trade matching, confirmation, and some type of settlement facility—usually a central location where market participants can deliver and receive securities and payments. The equities market in the United Kingdom is an example.

The second model of clearing and settlement is one in which there is a central depository structure, with trade matching and confirmation services provided by the exchanges. Once trades have been matched and confirmed, the trade data are sent to the depository for settlement.

There are variations on this model with differing degrees of settlement services provided by the depository. The depository may offer book-entry transfer of ownership of immobilized securities, with limited provisions for varying payment methods. Or the depository may provide book-entry transfer of dematerialized securities and the ability, through direct links to local payment systems, to simultaneously and irrevocably transfer funds for each settlement. An example is West Germany and its Deutscher Kassenverein (KV) depository system.

The third model has not only a stock market and a central depository, but also a clearinghouse that stands between the stock market and depository to reduce risk. The stock market, along with the clearinghouse, provides trade matching and confirmation services. A trade is confirmed by the market participants and is then passed to the clearinghouses which substitutes itself as the counterparty to each trade. This gives a degree of financial assurance to the markets since the clearinghouse will honor the obligations of a clearing member if necessary. The clearinghouse then passes the trade information to the depository for delivery versus payment on the settlement date. An example is the United States equities market.

In most European equities markets, there are no central clearing organizations that assume the role of counterparty to every trade or provide other kinds of mechanisms to ensure the financial integrity of all market participants in the clearing and settlement phase. Where there is no third-party guarantee mechanism for trade settlement, market participants are forced to choose their counterparties based on their own credit assessment.

. . .

Appendix

Clearing and Settlement in Major Market Countries

Clearing and Settlement in the United States

Three [two] clearinghouses and three [two] depositories serve the Nation's 7 stock exchanges, NASDAQ, and other over-the-counter dealers; 9 clearinghouses serve the 14 futures exchanges; and 1 clearinghouse serves all the equities options markets. The major clearing members, who also clear for non-clearing members of a clearinghouse, tend to be highly automated for lower costs and greater operating efficiency. For safety purposes, U.S. clearinghouses also tend to be financially structured such that a failing clearing member can be isolated quickly and its problems resolved without a ripple effect.

While arrangements between clearinghouses and their clearing firms vary, the general goal is that the clearinghouse maintain adequate resources and commitments to assure settlement if a clearing firm or its non-clearing firm customer defaults. These include capital requirements for members, claims on items in process, if any, as well as claims on the defaulting member's remaining assets on deposit with the clearinghouse (e.g., cash, letters of credit, Treasuries, or securities posted as collateral for margin). The clearinghouse also has claims on other assets of the failed clearing member. The clearinghouse's guarantee fund is another resource. Finally, the clearinghouse can make assessments against other clearing member firms. This succession of fallbacks is a buffer against shocks ranging from sudden large drops in the prices of securities and futures to defaults by members. As a result, there have been few cases of a failure of a clearing member in the United States, and no instances of a failure of a clearinghouse [Adler, Coleman Clearing Corp., a clearinghouse for penny stocks, failed in 1995].

Equities Clearing Organizations

The National Securities Clearing Corp.—NSCC processes 95 [99] percent of all equities trades in the United States. It is jointly owned by the principal equities markets: the New York Stock Exchange (NYSE), American Stock Exchange (AMEX), and National Association of Securities Dealers (NASD). It serves 1,800 [2,000] brokers, dealers, banks, [mutual funds] and other financial institutions, through about 400 [450] direct participants.

NSCC's clearance and settlement process normally requires five [three] business days. Trade information is received either in the form of locked-in trades already matched by the computer systems of the exchange or market; or, as buy and sell data reported by market participants. The latter still must be compared and buy and sell orders matched. Locked-in trades are entered directly in the NSCC computer system on the same day as the trade. This sharply reduces the need for the matching of buy and sell orders at the clearinghouse level. On a typical day, about 75 [96] percent of the trades on the NYSE are locked-in (a smaller proportion by dollar value).

UNITED STATES GENERAL ACCOUNTING OFFICE,
PAYMENTS, CLEARANCE AND SETTLEMENT,
A GUIDE TO THE SYSTEMS, RISKS, AND ISSUES
51-55 (1997).

The Clearance and Settlement Process

Equities are cleared and settled through NSCC and DTC. Clearance begins after the trade occurs and involves NSCC guaranteeing the trade and then netting the delivery and receipt of settlement obligations. Settlement usually occurs on T+3, with the equity shares settlement usually performed through book-entry moves at DTC and the money settlement through NSCC and settlement banks. Equities that are eligible for depository processing through DTC enter the Continuous Net Settlement (CNS) System, which, according to NSCC officials, is where the vast majority of equity trades settle. NSCC has three different settlement systems: one for depository-eligible issues, one for settlement of nondepository-eligible issues, and one for trades that bypass the netting process and are settled separately.

Table 2.2: NSCC Clearance and Settlement Process for Depository Equity Shares

T+3 day	Clearance and Settlement
T (trade date)	Trade occurs and trade information is sent to NSCC, mostly on a "locked-in" basis.
T+1	Results of trade comparison and matching are sent to direct participants.
T+2	NSCC determines participants' net settlement positions.
T+3	Settlement date—securities are delivered and payment is made.

NSCC officials said that the completion of transactions may not always occur on T+3.

Source: NSCC.

Figure 2.1: T+3 Clearance and
Settlement of Depository-Eligible
Equity Shares

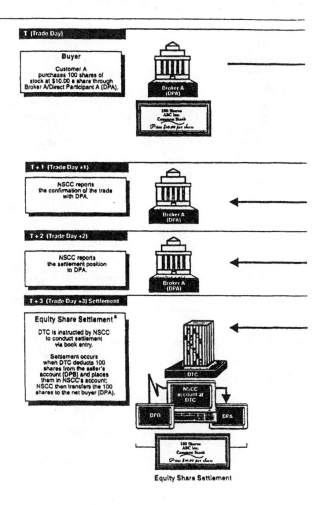

T (Trade Day)

Buyer

Customer A
purchases 100 shares of
stock at $10.00 a share through
Broker A/Direct Participant A (DPA).

Broker A
(DPA)

100 Shares
ABC Inc.
Common Stock
Price $10.00 per share

T + 1 (Trade Day +1)

NSCC reports
the confirmation of the trade
with DPA.

Broker A
(DPA)

T + 2 (Trade Day +2)

NSCC reports
the settlement position
to DPA.

Broker A
(DPA)

T + 3 (Trade Day +3) Settlement

Equity Share Settlement[a]

DTC is instructed by NSCC
to conduct settlement
via book entry.

Settlement occurs
when DTC deducts 100
shares from the seller's
account (DPB) and places
them in NSCC's account;
NSCC then transfers the 100
shares to the net buyer (DPA).

DTC

NSCC
account at
DTC

DPB   DPA

100 Shares
ABC Inc.
Common Stock
Price $10.00 per share

Equity Share Settlement

(continued from previous page)

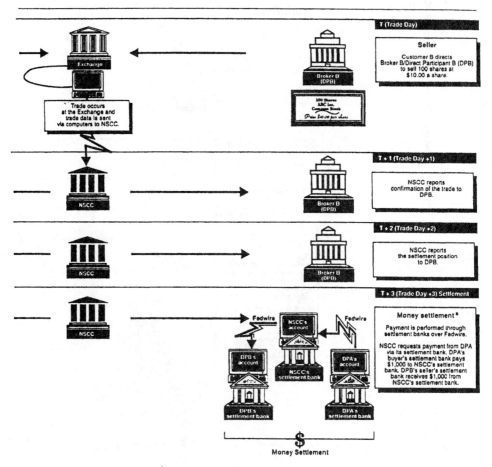

Figure 2.1 describes in a simplified manner the T+3 trading, clearance, and settlement of a single depository-eligible equity trade that is not netted with other trades.

The 3-Day Clearance and Settlement Cycle

Trade Day (T)

The 3-day cycle of clearance and settlement for NSCC begins on the day of the trade (T). Trade information is recorded at the exchanges and then is transmitted to NSCC (via computers) through a variety of automated marketplace trading systems.

Most of the trades are transmitted as "locked-in" transactions—the details of the trades from the buyer and seller have already been matched by the computer systems of the exchanges or OTC market, which means that NSCC does not perform a trade comparison. However, if trades are not locked-in, the buy and sell data have to be reported by direct participants to NSCC, and NSCC then compares and matches the data. NSCC officials said that trades mostly occur on a locked-in basis.

Once the trade data have been compared, NSCC guarantees the transaction. This is referred to as "novation" or the substitution of one party for another (NSCC becomes the buyer to every seller and the seller to every buyer.) The guarantee begins on midnight of the day that the trade is reported back to direct participants as having been compared.

T+1

On T+1, results of the comparison and matching process are reported to direct participants. NSCC transmits to direct participants computerized reports (known as contracts) that show every buy and sell order reported by the participant and the marketplace on T, and also confirm that each transaction has been compared and is ready for settlement.

T+2

Participants are informed of their net settlement positions for trades that occurred on T and are due to settle on T+3. NSCC issues a report to direct participants that tells them what their net settlement is that day and projects what their net settlement will be on T+3. To do this, NSCC uses its CNS system, which "reduces or nets the total number of financial obligations requiring settlement." Participants then are advised whether they are net buyers or net sellers for each issue of stock.

T+3

T+3 is settlement day for trades that began on T—to the extent that securities are available for delivery, delivery will be made, and participants with payment obligations will be required to pay. The participants' net settlement positions are determined by the CNS system netting all their trades due to settle that day against the prior days' unsettled long (buy) and short (sell) positions (referred to as fail positions or unsettled positions) for each issue of equity.

Equity Settlement Has Two Parts

Equity share settlement. The settlement of equities has two parts—equity share settlement and money settlement. The first phase is equity share settlement. The movement of the shares takes place through DTC accounts. NSCC instructs DTC to move shares from the accounts of net sellers to NSCC's account and then from NSCC's account to the accounts of net buyers. If the amount of shares is insufficient to satisfy all delivery obligations, NSCC uses a random allocation algorithm to determine to whom securities should be delivered. The CNS automatic delivery process occurs in two cycles: (1) the night cycle at about 1:30 a.m. on (T+3) and (2) the continuous "day cycle" later that day.

Money settlement. The final phase of settlement is the money settlement. The CNS net money settlement is determined on T+3 and can be settled with a single payment between NSCC and participants through settlement banks.[5] Every trading day, NSCC is to generate a settlement statement. This statement is to include a line item that tells each participants what its net CNS money obligation is, based upon the dollar value of the participant's equity shares delivered and the dollar value of its payment obligation. Each participant has a settlement bank that has guaranteed that it will pay or receive the money settlement on the participant's behalf.[6] Settlement banks are required to make payment before Fedwire's funds transfer system closes.

TRADING AROUND THE CLOCK

In 1989, the fail rate—the percentage of trades which do not settle on the settlement date—in trades cleared through CNS was 8.13 percent of the total net dollar value of cash and securities due on the settlement date. Since the NSCC takes the counterparty position and guarantees the settlement of all CNS-matched trades, NSCC is exposed to various credit, market, and non-market risks. The ways in which clearinghouses protect themselves against such risks are critically important.

NSCC protects against credit risk, first of all, by retaining a lien over securities which the receiving participant has not paid for. For trades not settled by T+5 [T+3], NSCC uses a mark-to-market procedure to limit its market risk until settlement does occur. Market risk is kept to 1-day's market movement by adjusting members' settlement obligations to current market prices. Members pay or are paid at settlement based on the current value of their open positions on and after T+5 [T+3], rather than their value when they made the trade.

---

[5] NSCC has operated a same-day funds settlement system since Feb. 22, 1996.

[6] In order to qualify as a settlement bank, each bank has to meet specific criteria established by NSCC.

In the interim, until the position settles, members pay or receive the net difference in market price movement. NSCC's guarantee fund for CNS takes account of potentially adverse movements on trades which have not settled before T+5 [T+3]. It is based on the total size of all positions open. These include those pending (before settlement); trades settling on T+5 [T+3]; and trades for which T+5 [T+3] has passed and settlement has not occurred. In addition, a percentage of the market value of securities for next-day (T+1) delivery must be deposited in order to protect the NSCC in the event the member defaults. This calculation is done daily for all members and can be collected more frequently than the monthly norm. All NSCC clearing members are required to contribute to the guarantee fund. NSCC's total funds on deposit, not including lines of credit, totaled over $400 million in 1989 and 1990 [$262 million in 1995].

The NSCC also maintains a full compliance-monitoring system to ensure its continuing ability to judge the creditworthiness of its participants. It shares risk information with other SEC-registered clearinghouses, both through the SEC's Monitoring Coordination Group and the Securities Clearing Group. NSCC and a number of futures clearinghouses are now discussing proposals for increasing the sharing of risk information; e.g., data on market participants' holdings on various exchanges.

The NSCC is linked to its clearing members by means of the Securities Industry Automation Corp. (SIAC), which operates NSCC's technology base. Most participants now have direct computer links; only about 1 percent of the full-service members continue to report trades via computer tape [tapes have now been eliminated].

. . .

The International Securities Clearing Corp.—ISCC is a subsidiary of the NSCC and is an SEC-registered clearinghouse. It was founded in 1985 to assist in clearing and settlement and to provide custody services for securities traded among American brokers and banks and their counterparties across national borders. It has links with clearinghouses and depositories in foreign markets, including:

- the International Stock Exchange (ISE), in London;
- the Centrale de Livraison de Valeurs Mobilieres (CEDEL), in Luxembourg;
- 20 depositories and custodians in Europe and Asia, indirectly linked by means of a conduit provided by CEDEL;
- the Japan Securities Clearing Corp. (JSCC), the Tokyo Stock Exchange's clearing and custody organization;

- the Central Depository subsidiary of the Stock Exchange of Singapore; and

- the Canadian Depository for Securities (CDS), in Toronto, linked through NSCC.

ISCC also serves as the clearing system for the NASD's PORTAL market for foreign private placements exempt from SEC registration by virtue of Rule 144A.

2. RISKS OF CLEARANCE AND SETTLEMENT

We begin by looking at the basic risks presented by the failure to settle trades and then turn to mechanisms to deal with them.

a.   THE NSCC FAIL PROCESS

When trades are matched, NSCC becomes the counterparty to the trades. This now occurs at midnight of T+1. Suppose A sells B 100 IBM at $100 per share, and the trade is locked-in at T+1. What is the risk for NSCC? First, there is the risk that B may fail to pay NSCC. If this occurs, NSCC must still pay A $10K on the settlement date, T+3. If the price of IBM has gone down, the IBM shares NSCC gets from A may be worth less than $10K. If they were worth only $5K, because they are now selling at $50 per share, NSCC has a $5K loss.

It is also possible that A may not deliver the shares to NSCC on T+3, even though NSCC must deliver the shares to B. If the price of IBM shares has gone up, NSCC must buy the shares at a higher price than $10K, the funds it gets from B. If the shares were worth $15K, because they are now selling at $150 per share, NSCC has a $5K loss.

How does NSCC protect itself against these risks? There are two periods of concern, the interim period (between the trade and settlement), T to T+3, and the period after settlement, T+3 and after. Securities' settlement is actually supposed to take place before 3:00 p.m. on T+3. Money settlement occurs between 4:00 - 5:00 p.m.

In the interim period, the clearing fund for each member is supposed to cover potential losses, based on a 20 day rolling average of a participants' portfolio value away from the stock price. Participants pay in on sells where the stock rises, and on buys where the stock falls. But the 20 day average measures positions and market risk in the past; this could have already changed as of today, and could further change in the future. Normally, the money due is only actually collected once a month, but it can be collected as often and as quickly as needed.

After the interim period, if the party does not settle a trade on T+3, NSCC must perform as counterparty. Failures to pay can result in NSCC closing out the position of the failing party. Failures to deliver usually result in a mark-to-market procedure. These procedures are further elaborated below.

Failure to Pay

Failure to pay usually means insolvency. However, there can be unusual situations, floods, riots etc. Payment settlements are now all by Fedwire. Late payments must include interest.

In case of insolvency, NSCC closes out the failing broker's (FB) positions on T+3. It will pay for/deliver securities according to FB's contracts. NSCC has a 3 day market risk on FB's positions. It loses on price decreases on long positions (NSCC must pay the delivering broker the contract price in exchange for securities worth less than the contract price) and price increases on short positions (NSCC must pay for securities at the T+3 price and only gets back the lower contract price).

Failure to Deliver

(a) The routine case

A failure to deliver occurs routinely when the delivering broker (DB) does not have the required securities. DB may not, for example, have received them from the customer and is unwilling to borrow them.

If DB fails to deliver on T+3, it must pay NSCC any positive difference between the T+2 price (the last closing market price) and contract price. Thus, if the trade was at $100 and the price at T+2 was $150, DB must pay NSCC $50 on T+3. The $50 is passed on to the receiving broker (RB) on the same date. NSCC has no loss, because it has taken no position in the stock. DB has paid over its $50 loss, as of T+2, to RB which had a corresponding $50 gain.

If DB delivers on T+4, RB would pay the T+2 closing price, $150 to NSCC (the mark-to-market price), and NSCC would pay DB $150. In effect, the deal is still done at the $100 contract price. RB has paid $150 on T+4, but had previously received the $50 mark payment on T+3; net payments are $100. DB gets $100 net, $150 from NSCC minus its previous mark payment of $50.

(b) Insolvency

We set out below what happens when DB declares insolvency on either T+3 or T+4. Chart I below shows how the mark-to-market system works, assuming the market prices in the left column.

CHART I: NSCC's Mark-to-Market System

Day	Closing price of stock	Mark-to-market price	Mark
T (day of trade)	100 (trade price)	N.A.	N.A.
T + 2	150	N.A.	N.A.
T + 3	190	150	50
T + 4	220	190	40
T + 5	250	220	30

Note: T = day of trade. NSCC becomes counterparty at midnight on T+1.

The mark-to-market price is the price RB pays for the delivery of stock and the mark is the amount the DB must pay if delivery is not made on the indicated date.

Chart II below shows NSCC's exposure on T+3 and T+4 depending on whether or not NSCC can purchase the stock on the date of insolvency before the market closes, and whether or not DB has paid the mark due on the date of insolvency.

CHART II: NSCC's Exposure when Broker Fails to Deliver and Becomes Insolvent

Day insolvency occurs	Timing of insolvency on the day insolvency occurs:			
	after market close		before market close	
	before mark payment	after mark payment	before mark payment	after mark payment
T + 3	$P_{T+4} - K$ (1)	$P_{T+4} - C_{T+2}$ (2)	$P_{T+3} - K$ (3)	$P_{T+3} - C_{T+2}$ (4)
T + 4	$P_{T+5} - C_{T+2}$ (5)	$P_{T+5} - C_{T+3}$ (6)	$P_{T+4} - C_{T+2}$ (7)	$P_{T+4} - C_{T+3}$ (8)

Note: K = contract price (established on day T)
      P_x = market price of stock on day X
      C_x = closing price of stock on day X
      Numbers in parentheses correspond to the various cases described below.

Let's go through each of the cases represented in Chart II (case number in parentheses). For purposes of this discussion, we shall use the prices given in Chart I, and we shall assume for simplicity that the market price at which NSCC can acquire the stock on a given day is equal to that day's closing price.

Case 1

NSCC must purchase the stock at the T+4 price, P_{T+4}, because DB became insolvent after the market closed on T+3. NSCC receives the contract price, K, from RB. NSCC thus loses up to P_{T+4} - K (there would be no loss if P_{T+4} turned out to be less than K). Assuming the prices given in Chart I, NSCC loses 220 - 100 = 120.

Case 2

NSCC must again purchase the stock for P_{T+4}. Since the position has been marked to market, and RB has already received a mark payment of 50, RB pays NSCC the T+3 mark-to-market price, C_{T+2}, that is 150. NSCC thus loses 220 - 150 = 70.

Case 3

NSCC can purchase the stock at T+3 since the insolvency occurs before the market closes and will pay RB the contract price, K. NSCC thus loses 190 - 100 = 90.

Case 4

NSCC can purchase the stock at T+3, but here RB has received the 50 mark, and the position is marked to market on T+3 to the T+2 closing price, 150. NSCC loses 190 - 150 = 40.

Case 5

NSCC purchases the stock for P_{T+5}. We assume no T+4 mark has been paid, so that the position has not been marked-to-market on T+4. RB pays the T+2 closing price, i.e., the T+3 mark-to-market price. Note that RB's payment is equal to the contract price of 100 plus the T+3 mark of 50. NSCC loses 250 - 150 = 100.

Case 6

NSCC again purchases the stock for P_{T+5}. RB has received two marks, 50 on T+3 and 40 on T+4, and pays 190, the T+4 mark-to-market price (which is the T+3 closing price). DB has paid the contract price plus the two marks. NSCC loses 250 - 190 = 60.

Case 7

NSCC purchases the stock before the market closes for P_{T+4}. Since no T+4 mark has been paid, and the position has not yet been marked-to-market, at T+4 DB pays 150, the T+3 mark-to-market price (which is the same as the T+2 closing price). NSCC loses 220 - 150 = 70.

Case 8

NSCC again purchases the stock for P_{T+4}. As in Case 6, RB pays 190, the T+3 closing price (i.e., the T+4 mark-to-market price). NSCC loses 220 - 190 = 30.

b.   CONTROL OF RISK

STAFFS OF BOARD OF GOVERNORS OF THE FEDERAL RESERVE SYSTEM AND THE FEDERAL RESERVE BANK OF NEW YORK, CLEARANCE AND SETTLEMENT IN U.S. SECURITIES MARKETS 1-20 (1992).

.   .   .

3. Credit, Liquidity, and Operational Risks in Clearance and Settlement

Definitions

At the outset, the terms *credit risk, liquidity risk,* and *operational risk* must be defined precisely. The definitions of credit risk and liquidity risk used in this paper are those used by the Committee on Payment and Settlement Systems (formerly the Group of Experts on Payment Systems) and the Committee on Interbank Netting Schemes in analyzing interbank systems for clearance and settlement of payment orders and foreign exchange obligations. *Credit risk* is the risk that a trade will not settle for full value, either when due or at any time thereafter. *Liquidity risk* is the risk that settlement will be made not at the appointed time, but at some unspecified time thereafter. Although the distinction between credit and liquidity risks is important, it is worth noting that at the time a settlement failure is detected, the counterparties of the participant that failed to settle may not know whether a credit problem or a liquidity problem is involved.

Operational risk is the risk of a breakdown of some component of the hardware, software, or communications systems that are critical to settlement of financial transactions. Such breakdowns clearly could create serious liquidity problems by delaying settlement of transactions. Breakdown of a key operational component also could heighten credit risks in at least two ways. First, it could hamper the ability of participants in the settlement process to monitor and control their credit exposures. Second, as is discussed below, any development that increases the time between a trade and its settlement increases credit risk.

As noted in section 1, policymakers have been especially concerned about the potential for clearance and settlement arrangements to create systemic risks. Here again, a precise definition of systemic risk is needed. In previous work by various Group of Ten groups, systemic risk was defined as the risk that the inability of one counterparty to meet its obligations when due (for either financial or operational reasons) will cause other counterparties also to be unable to meet their obligations when due. If the obligation were met at a later time, the systemic risk in question would be a liquidity risk; if not, it would be a credit risk. Defined this way, systemic liquidity risks are commonplace; for example, failure of one counterparty to make timely delivery of a security frequently causes the receiver to fail to make timely redelivery. Private market participants have developed banking and other contractual arrangements that allow them to manage such routine liquidity pressures.

Thus, although this definition of systemic risk is precise, it covers events that most central bankers probably would not include in their definition of systemic risk. From a central banker's perspective, *systemic risk* is the risk that credit losses and liquidity pressures arising from financial or operational problems (of a clearing organization, a participant, or a settlement bank) could be sufficiently large that they cannot be managed and contained using the established banking and contractual arrangements and that, as a result, the stability of financial markets could be jeopardized.

Credit Risk

The counterparties to a financial transaction are exposed to credit losses in the course of clearing and settling the transaction because (1) the price of the security involved can change between the time the trade is initiated and the time it is settled and (2) delivery of the security and payment in many cases are not synchronized. Credit risk that stems from changes in security prices is often called market risk. However, to avoid confusion with the risk of capital loss (absent a default by a trading counterparty), it seems appropriate to adopt the terminology used by the Committee on Interbank Netting Schemes and refer to such credit risk as *replacement-cost risk.* (This terminology reflects an assumption that if a counterparty defaults prior to settlement, the nondefaulting counterparty would not complete its settlement obligation, but instead would promptly replace its obligation to deliver or receive the security with a new contract with a third party.) Credit risk that stems from gaps in the timing of payments and receipts on the settlement date is termed *principal risk.*

At the time a transaction is initiated, it generally can be replaced at virtually no cost, because the market price of the security—the price at which the replacement transaction would be consummated—presumably would be quite close to the original contract price. As time passes, however, the market price may move away from the contract price. Depending on the direction of the price change, one of the counterparties would suffer a loss in replacing the transaction—the buyer if the price had increased, the seller if the price had decreased. Because the direction of change in market price is uncertain, both parties to the transaction are exposed to replacement-cost risk. The magnitude of the risk depends on the volatility of the security price and the length of time between the transaction and its settlement.

Even so-called cash or spot market transactions can involve significant replacement-cost risk. Relatively few transactions are settled on a same-day, much less a real-time, basis. In U.S. securities markets, the lag between trade and settlement typically is one day for U.S. government securities, five days for equities and most corporate and municipal bonds, and as much as thirty days for certain mortgage-backed securities. To cite an extreme example of replacement-cost risk, the prices of ten of the thirty stocks making up the Dow Jones Industrial Average declined 35 percent or more over five-day intervals in October 1987. A default by a buyer of one of the stocks during that period would have exposed the seller to losses of that magnitude. Forward contracts can entail quite substantial replacement-cost risk. In fact, if the seller defaults and the market price of the security has more than doubled since the transaction, the added cost to the buyer would exceed the value of the security at the time of the original trade. However, such extreme movements in security prices are the exception rather than the rule.

The largest credit exposures in clearance and settlement typically occur on settlement day, when the full principal value of the security can be at risk. In some markets, delivery of the security and delivery of the payment often are not synchronized. If the security is delivered prior to receipt of payment, the deliverer risks losing the full value of the security. If payment is made prior to delivery, the payor risks losing the full value of the payment. In some cases, the sequence in which deliveries and payments will occur is known in advance and principal risk is clearly asymmetric. In other cases, the sequence is not known in advance; indeed, even on settlement day the counterparties may lack real-time information on the status of deliveries and payments.

Liquidity Risk

Both counterparties to a financial transaction are exposed to liquidity risk on settlement day. The seller has an incentive to minimize its holdings of relatively low yield transactions balances. Consequently, if its counterparty does not pay on settlement day, the seller generally must borrow funds or liquidate assets to offset the resulting shortfall in its transactions account. The cost to the seller of covering the shortfall depends on the time of day the payment is due; because access to sources of liquidity often becomes limited as the end of the business day approaches, payment failure late in the day can be especially costly.

On the other side of a transaction, the buyer may have engaged in subsequent transactions that require it to deliver the security in question. If the seller defaults, the buyer must either borrow the security from a third party or fail to complete its delivery obligation. The liquidity of markets for borrowing and lending securities varies widely. Moreover, borrowing and lending securities in turn involve credit, liquidity, and operational risks.

4.   Potential Benefits of Clearing Organizations

Types and Functions of Clearing Organizations

Two types of specialized financial intermediaries (or *clearing organizations*) have been developed to reduce credit and liquidity risks (as well as transactions costs) to participants in securities clearance and settlement. *Clearinghouses* perform multilateral netting of securities transactions among their participants; many also provide trade comparison (confirmation and matching) services. *Depositories* immobilize or dematerialize securities and typically integrate a book-entry securities transfer system with a money transfer system to achieve delivery against payment.

Trade Comparison

Trade comparison is the process of confirming and matching the terms of a securities transaction (the issue, price, quantity, and counterparties). This function may be performed by the clearinghouse or, in the case of securities traded on an exchange, by the exchange itself. By speeding up the matching of trades, a trade comparison system reduces credit risk in several important ways. First, it provides a clearing organization and its participants with more timely information on the magnitude of unsettled positions and associated risks. Some clearinghouses have moved to replace batch, end-of-day comparison systems with on-line systems, thereby making it possible to monitor and control intraday exposures. Second, by decreasing the time between trade and settlement, a trade comparison system generally reduces replacement-cost risk, both because potential changes in securities prices between trade and settlement are smaller and because the number of unsettled trades tends to decrease. Finally, a trade comparison system, with its quicker matching of trades, allows trades to be netted more promptly.

Multilateral Netting

Both the legal foundations and the economics of multilateral netting of securities transactions closely parallel those for the netting of payment orders and foreign exchange transactions, which have been studied in detail by the Committee on Interbank Netting Schemes. In securities markets, *multilateral netting* is achieved in several ways. In some cases, the clearinghouse acts as a central counterparty. Participants enter into a transaction bilaterally. If certain conditions are met, the clearinghouse subsequently is substituted as the buyer to the seller and the seller to the buyer, and any obligations between the participants pursuant to the original transaction are discharged. The clearinghouse keeps a running record of its net position vis-á-vis each participant for each security and each settlement date. For a given set of transactions, this process leaves each participant with net obligations to deliver to, or receive from, the clearinghouse amounts of securities equal to its multilateral net position vis-á-vis other participants in the clearinghouse. For each settlement date, each participant's payment obligations are settled by a single payment to, or from, the clearinghouse.

In other multilateral netting schemes, the clearinghouse guarantees completion of all matched, unsettled transactions among its participants. In still other arrangements, the clearinghouse calculates a multilateral net position for each participant vis-á-vis other participants but neither substitutes itself as central counterparty nor guarantees completion of transactions. The latter arrangements are what the Committee on Interbank Netting Schemes called "position netting"; obligations are routinely settled by delivery and payment of the net amounts, but in the event of a default, the multilateral net positions are not legally binding on participants.

Legally binding multilateral netting has the potential to reduce both principal risk and replacement-cost risk. Principal risk can be reduced because the value of the securities that must be delivered to settle a given value of trades typically is far smaller than the gross value of the securities traded. Replacement-cost risk can be reduced because potential losses from replacing some trades are offset by gains from replacing other trades. The magnitude of potential risk reductions depends on trading patterns. Principal risks can be reduced dramatically when participants both buy and sell substantial amounts of the same securities. Assuming that securities prices are positively correlated, smaller but still significant reductions in replacement-cost risk can be achieved if participants are buyers of some securities and sellers of others.

Regardless of the pattern of trading, multilateral netting by a clearinghouse can reduce replacement-cost risk by facilitating prompt closeout and replacement of unsettled transactions. Because a single counterparty or guarantor replaces multiple counterparties, there is no need for multiple negotiations to close out unsettled transactions. Also, multilateral netting arrangements generally specify procedures for determining the value of unsettled positions and for allocating losses to surviving participants.

Netting arrangements also are designed to reduce liquidity risk. In a multilateral netting system, all of a participant's obligations to deliver or receive a *particular* security on a specific settlement day are discharged through making or receiving a single delivery. In addition, *all* of a participant's obligations to make or receive payment on settlement day are discharged through making or receiving a single payment. If a security is to be received, the amount to be received is no larger, and generally is considerably smaller, than the sum of the amounts that would be delivered in the absence of netting. Likewise, if a cash payment is to be received, the amount to be received is reduced by netting. Consequently, the liquidity pressures arising from unanticipated failures to receive securities or payments can be greatly diminished by legally binding multilateral netting. Clearinghouses in the United States typically report that multilateral netting reduces the value of deliveries by 70 percent to 90 percent, implying potential reductions of that magnitude in both principal and liquidity risks.

Delivery Against Payment

Credit and liquidity risks can also be reduced through creation of a depository. A depository immobilizes or dematerializes securities and uses a computerized accounting system to record and transfer ownership of securities. By integrating a book-entry system with a money transfer system, a depository can substantially reduce or even eliminate principal risk. Elimination of principal risk requires a *delivery-against-payment* system, which provides assurances to participants that final securities transfers (deliveries) will occur if, and only if, final money transfers (payments) occur. In such a system, when instructed to transfer ownership of a security from one participant to another, the depository debits the security account and credits the money account of the first participant, and simultaneously credits the security account and debits the money account of the second participant for the same amounts.

In the United States, debits and credits to securities and money accounts in the Federal Reserve's book-entry system for U.S. government securities are final (irrevocable and unconditional) as soon as they are posted; both the securities and funds transfer systems are gross, real-time systems. In contrast, at private depositories, both the money and securities transfers in these systems initially are provisional. Participants receive final payment in the form of a claim on the Federal Reserve or on a settlement bank. Payment typically must be made by the end of the day. Throughout the day, debits and credits to money accounts are netted. At the end of the day, participants in a net debit position make final payment to the depository, and participants in a net credit position receive final payment from the depository. Securities transfers in the system become final only when all participants in a net debit position have completed final payment. Private depositories typically employ a variety of safeguards (discussed in section 6) designed to assure participants that the net settlements will be completed on schedule.

. . .

6. Risk Management by Individual Clearing Organizations

Key Issues

To ensure that they realize their potential benefits, U.S. securities clearing organizations have established risk-management systems designed to limit potential credit losses and liquidity pressures from participant defaults and to ensure that even if defaults occur, settlement can be completed on schedule and losses recovered from surviving participants. They also have sought to ensure the operational reliability of all the hardware, software, and communications systems that are critical to the completion of settlements. Although the approaches to achieving these objectives vary from clearing organization to clearing organization, all well-designed systems have addressed several key issues: responsibilities and incentives for risk management; standards for membership; safeguards against credit and liquidity risks; and operational safeguards. Table 3 summarizes safeguards at selected U.S. clearing organizations.

Responsibility for Risk Management

The most basic issue in risk management is the division of responsibility for risk management between the clearing organization and its participants. A clearing organization may seek to preserve incentives to manage risks bilaterally (a decentralized approach to risk management), or it may itself assume primary responsibility for risk management (a centralized approach). Either approach can prove effective in limiting risks; what is critical is that participants understand clearly where the responsibility rests.

Many U.S. clearing organizations assume total responsibility for risk management. They typically employ a full-time staff that reviews membership applications and continually monitors member compliance with financial and operational requirements. Participants are not expected to manage their counterparty exposures and have little or no incentive to do so. Participants in a clearinghouse, for example, might be expected to be responsible for losses from their bilateral dealings with a defaulting counterparty if the default occurred before the substitution of the clearinghouse as counterparty (or prior to the time when its guarantee became effective). However, when defaults have occurred, clearinghouses sometimes have accepted responsibility for all matched trades, even if the substitution (or guarantee) had not taken effect prior to the default. In such instances, the extent of participants' bilateral dealings have had no effect on their losses from a default. Consequently, participants in such systems may perceive the clearing organization to have assumed complete responsibility for risk management and may differentiate among trade counterparties only on the basis of their reliability in reporting terms of transactions promptly and accurately, if at all.

Although assumption of complete responsibility for risk management by the clearing organization is common in U.S. markets, several recently established organizations for clearing and settling over-the-counter transactions have been structured to encourage participants to manage credit risks bilaterally. These organizations (Participants Trust Company (PTC), the Government Securities Clearing Corporation (GSCC), the Depository Trust Company's (DTC) same-day funds settlement (SDFS) system, and the MBS Clearing Corporation (MBSCC)) have, for example, instituted loss-sharing rules that allocate credit losses to surviving participants on the basis of their bilateral dealings with the defaulting participant.

Even though they require loss sharing, however, most of these clearing organizations have retained substantial responsibility for risk management.

None has adopted an approach as highly decentralized as that of the Clearing House Interbank Payment System (CHIPS), in which limits on a participant's activity are based solely on bilateral credit decisions by other participants.

. . .

Notes and Questions

1. The clearing of securities involves two basic functions, matching of trades and the net position calculation. Trade matching requires confirming the identity and quantity of the security being traded, the transaction price and date, and the identity of the buyer and seller. This is often referred to as the trade comparison process. The net position calculation involves calculating the net position of the participants in terms of securities that must be delivered and funds that must be paid. How does trade matching occur when securities are traded on an exchange. How are the trade facts captured?

2. Net position calculation can be on a bilateral or multilateral basis. If A buys from B 100 shares of IBM at $1 per share and sells to B 50 shares of IBM at $3 per share, what are their net securities and cash positions? If A buys 100 IBM from B at $1, B buys 50 IBM from C at $3, and C buys 40 IBM from A at $2, what are the net securities and cash positions of the three parties if there is a multilateral netting?

3. The settlement of the securities and cash positions may take place through a variety of mechanisms. The actual transfer of the securities may occur by physical delivery of certificates or by book entries denoting

a change of ownership. Where transfer is by book entries, the securities may be held by a central depository which will make the appropriate debit or credit entries to the appropriate parties. Cash payments are usually by cashiers checks or wire transfers. For exchange trades, who has the obligation to deliver the securities and pay the funds? How does this affect the risk of trading?

4. It is quite important whether or not the delivery of securities and the payments occur relatively simultaneously. If securities are delivered before funds, the party that has delivered the securities is out the cash, and is at risk for a failure to pay. Conversely if funds are paid out before securities are received, the party that has paid the funds is at risk for the failure to deliver the securities. This is why some systems have a delivery versus payment (DVP) requirement.

5. Note that settlement occurs at two levels: between the parties to the trade, e.g. two broker-dealers (b/d), and between the b/ds and their customers. The timing between these two levels may be important. If a b/d must settle with another b/d before settlement occurs between the b/d and the customer, the b/d may have risk, e.g. b/d purchases the security, it goes down in value and the customer does not pay.

6. Let's now look specifically at the NSCC process. Until it was acquired by DTC in 1999, NSCC was owned by the NYSE, Amex and NASD. It has over 400 direct participants, and a total of direct and indirect participants of 1800 (indirect participants trade through direct participants). NSCC effects clearing and settlement of 95% of all equity trades in the United States, and also clears corporate bonds, as well as some other securities, e.g. municipal bonds. NSCC does not clear all securities or derivatives. U.S. treasuries are cleared by the Federal Reserve and other clearing corporations clear commercial paper, options, and futures. In 1998, NSCC processed about 950 million securities transactions valued at almost $45 trillion.

DTC is a New York limited purpose trust company, a quasi-bank, which is the world's largest securities depository. It is owned by 600 bank and securities firm participants. DTC holds securities (individual or global certificates) and accounts for the ownership interests of its participants in the form of book-entries, e.g. A + 100 IBM. It also has funds accounts in connection with institutional settlement. It holds some securities that are not cleared by NSCC, e.g. commercial paper. In 1999, it had $23 trillion worth of securities in custody.

Ownership of shares is handled through a tiered system of book-entries more specifically dealt with later in this Chapter. Corporate registrars have a limited role in accounting for changes in ownership since most shares on registers are held in the name of Cede & Co., the nominee name of DTC. So when investor A sells to investor B, no change is made on the books of the registrar when the issue is held at DTC. DTC accounts on its books for the ownership interests of its members, broker-dealers and custodian banks, and the broker-dealers and custodians then account for the ultimate ownership of customers on their books.

DTC apart from accounting for the ownership of securities and funds, also performs other functions, e.g. it collects and distributes dividends and interest.

7. The NSCC system to deal with fails does not eliminate all of NSCC's risk. How would you summarize its maximum risk in the interim and later periods? What can NSCC do to protect itself against these remaining risks?

8. Does NSCC have a DVP system? As of February 1996, payments for securities settlements were made in same day funds over Fedwire. Does this make the system DVP?

9. The Group of Thirty, an industry supported think tank played a key role in formulating industry standards for clearance and settlement, although in the U.S. implementation of the T+3 standard required active intervention by the SEC. While the Group of Thirty's work in this area has receded into the background, other industry groups like the International Securities Services Association (ISSA) continue its work, see Recommendations 2000 (2000). In addition, the Bank for International Settlements has hosted a joint effort between its Committee on Payment and Settlement Systems and IOSCO to formulate recommendations for clearance and settlement systems worldwide. *Report of the CPSS-IOSCO Joint Task Force on Securities Settlement Systems, Consultative Report* (January 2001).

B.   GROUP OF THIRTY PROPOSALS

Many of the changes in clearance and settlement in the 1990's have been spurred on by the Group of Thirty's proposals which called for:

1. By 1990, all comparisons of trades between direct market participants (i.e., brokers, dealers, and other exchange members) should be compared within 1 day after a trade is executed, or "T+1."

2. Indirect market participants–institutional investors, or any trading counterparties which are not broker/dealers–should be members of a trade comparison system which achieves positive affirmation of trade details.

3. Each country should have an effective and fully developed central securities depository, organized and managed to encourage the broadest possible industry participation.

4. Each country should study its market volumes and participation to determine whether a trade netting system would be beneficial in terms of reducing risk and promoting efficiency.

5. Delivery versus payment should be the method for settling all securities transactions.

6. Payments associated with the settlement of securities transactions and the servicing of securities portfolios should be made consistent across all instruments and markets by adopting the "same day" convention. (No date has been set for achieving this objective.)

7. A "rolling settlement" system should be adopted by all markets. Final settlement should occur on T+3 by 1992. As an interim target, final settlement should occur on T+5 by 1990 at the latest, except where it hinders the achievement of T+3 by 1992.

8. Securities lending and borrowing should be encouraged as a method of expediting the settlement of securities transactions. Existing regulatory and taxation barriers that inhibit the practice of lending securities should be removed by 1990.

9. Each country should adopt the technical standard for securities messages developed by the International Organization for Standardization (ISO Standards 7775 and 6166).

The following Table gives the status at year-end 1999 of implementation of those proposals in major countries. There are three categories for DVP (delivery versus payment): (1) complete, where there is a simultaneous and irrevocable exchange of securities (on the delivery side) and cash value (on the payment side); (2) qualified, where there is no simultaneous exchange of cash and securities but where there are "conditions or safeguards providing conditions close to those" found in a "complete" system; or (3) non-DVP. Note that France (the Paris Bourse) had a monthly settlement cycle. This will be changed to T+3 in September 2000. S. Iskandar and V. Boland, *French move to harmonize settlements,* Financial Times, February 28, 2000.

Group of Thirty: Current Status of International Settlement Recommendations-Equities

Recommendation No.	1	2	3	4	5	6	7	8	9
Country:	Institutional Comparison	T+2 Affirmation	Securities Depository	Securities Netting	DVP	Same-Day Funds	Rolling Settlement on T+3	Securities Lending	ISO/ISIN
Australia.............	Yes	Yes	Yes	Yes	Complete	Yes	T+3	Yes	Yes
Austria................	Yes	No	Yes	Yes	Complete	Yes	T+3	Yes	Yes
Belgium...............	Yes	Partial	Yes	Yes	Qualified	Yes	Bi-weekly	No	Yes
Canada................	Yes	Yes	Yes	Partial	Qualified	Yes	T+3	Yes	No
France.................	Yes	Yes	Yes	Yes	Qualified	Yes	Monthly	Yes	Yes
Germany.............	Yes	Yes	Yes	Yes	Qualified	Yes	T+2	Yes	Yes
Hong Kong..........	Yes	Yes	Yes	Yes	Qualified	Yes	T+2	Yes	Yes
Italy.....................	Yes	Yes	Yes	Yes	Qualified	Yes	T+3	Yes	Yes
Japan...................	Yes	No	Yes	Yes	Qualified	Partial	T+3	Yes	Yes
Singapore............	Yes	Yes	Yes	Yes	Qualified	Partial	T+5	No	Yes
Spain...................	Yes	Yes	Yes	Yes	Qualified	Yes	T+3	Yes	Yes
Switzerland........	Yes	No	Yes	No	Complete	Yes	T+3	Yes	Yes
United Kingdom	Yes	Partial	Yes	No	Qualified	Yes	T+5	Yes	Yes
United States...	Yes	Partial	Yes	Yes	Qualified	Yes	T+3	Yes	CUSIP

Source: State Street Bank and Trust Co., The Guide to Custody in World Markets (1997, 2000).

1. THE UNITED STATES

The most contentious part of the Group of Thirty's recommendations for the United States was the T+3 proposal. The following piece discusses some of the difficulties.

GROUP OF THIRTY, CLEARANCE AND SETTLEMENT STATUS REPORTS

(Autumn 1992) (United States).

. . .

F. T+3 Settlement

In its discussions of shortening the settlement cycle, the Working Committee initially identified several issues that needed to be addressed to move T+3. These included the receipt of a written confirmation by the retail customer as a trigger for payment, the lack of an electronic payment system for retail transactions, and the current affirmation process for institutional trades. Of equal importance was the issue of changing customer behavior regarding long-standing business practices. Each of these issues was discussed at length by the Working Committee and later by the Bachmann Task Force.

Receipt of Confirmations

• The Legal and Regulatory Subgroup quickly dismissed the significance of the confirmation issue by determining that the receipt of the confirmation is not legally required for the settlement of an equities transaction, although there is a legal requirement to send a confirmation.   However, since many customers are accustomed to receiving a confirmation before paying for their transactions, the confirmation issue becomes one of modifying customer behavior.   The Working Committee concluded that modifying customer behavior can be achieved through industry-wide information and education efforts.

Electronic Retail Payment System

• Many firms rely on checks to send and receive customer funds. The current mail delivery time frames in many cases would not accommodate payment by check in a T+3 settlement period. Recognizing that collection of funds from customers was a major issue in moving to T+3, the Working Committee determined that some type of electronic retail payment system was necessary.

.   .   .

Notes and Questions

1.   The G–30 has made a number of recommendations to standardize clearing and settlement in different countries.   Is standardization a desirable objective?   If so, why?

2.   What changes did NSCC have to make to comply with the G–30 recommendations? And what were the costs and benefits of making those changes?   It is important to note that the SEC adopted a new Rule 15c6–1 on October 6, 1993, which required T+3 settlement by June 1, 1995, 58 Federal Register 52891 (1993); the industry did not do so voluntarily.   In line with the SEC change, the Federal Reserve Board amended Regulation T (Credit by Brokers and Dealers) by shortening by two days the time for customers to meet initial margin calls or make full cash payment to broker-dealers.   Under the new rule, customers have two business days after the completion of the standard settlement cycle.   That cycle is T+3 as of June 1995, 59 Federal Register 53565 (1994).

The SEC has permitted another important change, allowing customers to have certificateless direct registration of certificates; the customer's name can appear directly on the books of the issuer and the customer receives a statement of ownership from the issuer rather than a certificate.   Before customers could only avoid holding certificates by holding them in street name through their brokers. Or put another way, customers seeking to hold securities directly had to do so by keeping the paper themselves. 62 Federal Register 64034 (1997).

3. There is no stopping with T+3. Already some countries, like Germany and Hong Kong, have T+2, and Hong Kong is debating going to T+0. C. Kentouris, *Hong Kong Custodians Balk at T+0,* Security Industry News, July 19, 1999. Both the Fed and the SEC have urged that the U.S. go to T+1. It now appears that this cannot be done before 2004. The cost of moving to T+1 in the United States is estimated to be $8 billion but this will be recouped by lower costs. Importantly, movement to T+1 would reduce daily settlement exposure by $750 billion daily and as a consequence reduce by one-third the size of the required clearing fund to guarantee trades. C. Kentouris, *SIA Report: Shorter Settlement Feasible No Earlier than 2004,* Security Industry News, July 31, 2000. A T+1 settlement date for cross-border trades would create significant difficulty because under current arrangements the foreign exchange trade needed to provide the settlement currency would not be completed until T+2.

2. THE UNITED KINGDOM

Until 1994 the United Kingdom had a fortnightly settlement (once every two weeks). They also had a paper based settlement system with no central depository. The following pieces describe some of their difficulties in changing to the present system. What did the sorry state of the LSE settlement system say about the importance of such systems in competition between stock exchanges?

R. WATERS, THE PLAN THAT FELL TO EARTH
Financial Times, Mar. 12, 1993.

The City yesterday turned its back on a complicated and expensive stock market settlement system in favour of a "quick fix". Hundreds of millions of pounds of development costs, incurred by more than 150 financial institutions in the City and many more listed companies, were formally abandoned at 3 pm, when news of the decision was announced.

The London Stock Exchange board's decision to drop its blighted Taurus project has shaken the confidence of the City establishment. It was planned by a wide range of institutions with interests in the securities industry to be an electronic system of ownership and transfer of shareholdings.

City leaders had always stressed that it was an essential part of the infrastructure needed to underpin London's stock market and reinforce its claim to being Europe's leading financial centre. In the event, it proved only that the City establishment is incapable of overcoming the conflicting self-interests of its members to put London as a financial centre first.

Mr. Peter Rawlins, chief executive of the Stock Exchange, yesterday resigned, to take responsibility for the failure of the project. But Sir Andrew Hugh Smith, exchange chairman and chief executive for the moment, pinned the blame largely on the fact that the early design for Taurus, developed by the exchange, was rejected in 1989. Service registrars, who maintain share registers for listed companies, voted down the idea because it could have put them out of business. "It wasn't surprising—after all, turkeys don't vote for Christmas."

Yesterday's move also raises serious questions about the future of the Stock Exchange, which has been traumatised by its failure to complete Taurus. Settlement is one of the exchange's core services, providing £47.5m of its £194m of income last year.

Yesterday, it was effectively shunted aside by the Bank of England, which stepped forward to take over responsibility for over-hauling stock market settlement in London. ...

R. SMYTH, BANK OF ENGLAND BLUEPRINT FOR LSE SETTLEMENT SYSTEM

International Financial Law Review, Oct. 1993, at 21–23.

The Bank of England's task force on securities settlement, set up in March this year when the London Stock Exchange (LSE) abandoned Taurus, has pronounced. Its report, dated June 30, recommends a new LSE UK equity settlement system code-named (not acronymed) CREST to replace Talisman.

CREST will:

- save time and money by eliminating stock transfer forms and share certificates ie, paper; it will substitute electronic transfers and evidence legal title by register (book) entries alone, and not also certificates;

- limit counterparty risk through closer delivery-against-payment (DVP);

- remove post-settlement market risk through irreversible DVP; and

- accelerate registration and settlement through registration on the same day as settlement ie, closer DVP, and, in time, settlement in under T+5.

This will make the LSE a more attractive market, although only for UK equities at first because, initially, CREST will not cover other securities. The LSE is already the principal market for UK equities and there seems to be no sign of this changing. CREST should therefore increase LSE UK equity trade volume rather than stop the trades going elsewhere.

The UK equity limit should be noted. CREST may eventually include, albeit with difficulty, non-UK ('international') equities. Without them, roughly half LSE equity trading value on recent figures will be outside it—and at a time when international is growing faster.

. . .

Only LSE Trades

CREST will exclude off-market ie, off-LSE transfers, and therefore will apply only to LSE trades. Taurus, on the other hand, would have covered all transfers, both on- and off-market. This savagely complicated it because many transfers of shares in UK companies with large registers are off-market. They include, for instance, transfers between relatives and on death, and all gifts.

CREST will not cover securities not traded on the LSE. Initially, it will include only LSE-traded UK equities ie, shares, not debt securities, issued by UK-incorporated companies. Therefore, at first, it will exclude all non-UK company securities and all UK company debt securities, even if LSE-traded. LSE-traded UK company debt securities will probably join later (it is not clear why not initially). Unlike Taurus, even LSE-traded non-UK company securities may do. The difficulty here is linking settlement with legal ownership, since what constitutes legal ownership will depend on local, not UK, law. A solution may be to include UK depositary receipts for these securities. UK government securities, or gilts, will continue to have a separate settlement system outside CREST.

CREST—key points
• Simpler and cheaper than Taurus

• London Stock Exchange (LSE) players only	• LSE trades only
• Company securities only (initially, just UK equities)	• No paper—electronic stock and money transfers
• Closer delivery-against payment (DVP)	• Irreversible DVP
• Same day settlement and registration	• No netting
• Payment through settlement banks	• No central nominee shareholder
• Registration intact	• No central register
• Continuous register updates	• Bank of England-operated
• Less new law than Taurus	• Rolling short settlement (T+5) pre-CREST

Timetable (provisional)

T+10—July 1994
T+5—January 1995
CREST—March 1997 or earlier
Under T+5—post-CREST

Paperless back office

There will be no paper to transfer or evidence legal title. Electronic messages effecting register entries will replace stock transfer forms (paper) for UK equity trades between CREST participants. The only written part of this transfer process will be the register entries—book-entry transfers or BETs—which will remain *prima facie* evidence of legal title to the corresponding shares. Share certificates will go and nothing will replace them. It should be noted that even investors outside CREST may be able to choose not to have them for CREST shares. Even now there is no paper to transfer title to UK equities between LSE market makers or certificates to evidence their title. SEPON is the legal owner of all their UK shares and therefore UK share transfers between them do not affect legal title. The UK Companies Act 1985 does not require companies to issue share certificates to SEPON, and as a result they do not.

CREST will involve closer, and irreversible, DVP, and, potentially, real, irreversible, DVP. Real DVP is simultaneous delivery and payment ie, you get the shares (delivery) when you pay for them, like goods you buy for cash in a shop. You still do not necessarily get them when you order them ie, when you deal (trade). Closer DVP will be same day delivery and payment. If delivery and payment are irreversible, so that, unlike now, completed LSE UK equity deals cannot be unwound, DVP removes:

- counterparty risk, since delivery and payment are simultaneous, the risk your counterparty fails to pay or fails to deliver and leaves you without the stock and without the money because you have already delivered or paid, respectively; and

- post-settlement market risk, since delivery and payment (together, settlement) are irreversible, the risk that if your trade is unwound, you can replace it only at a worse price.

Closer DVP and, potentially, real DVP will come through (i) treating delivery of UK equities as the transfer of their legal ownership ie, as registration in the buyer's name, and (ii) electronically linking this, with the transfer of money the other way, therefore from the buyer's bank to the seller's. Closer DVP will mean same day settlement and registration, and real DVP, simultaneous settlement and registration.

Irreversible DVP will come by legal means alone, by a stipulation in CREST's rules, which will bind participants contractually or as the law of the land. As stated, UK share transfers between LSE market makers do not affect legal as distinct from beneficial title. If closer and irreversible DVP will apply here (which is unclear), it will probably come through electronic links between SEPON account entries, which transfer the beneficial title, and payment.

No netting

Curiously, it seems impractical to combine irreversible share DVP with the netting of settlement payments with the market as a whole, with a system where each participant makes or receives a single payment for each settlement period. Instead, CREST settlement will be trade-by-trade. In contrast, under the Talisman system, the LSE nets payments due between market makers, brokers and Institutional Net Settlement Participants (INSPs), a blessing given the number of trades in each two- or three-week settlement period.

Why no netting? It would require either (1) a guarantee by the CREST operator, the entity effecting the netting (the 'central counterparty'), against the default of any of the original parties to the various deals being netted or (2) a facility, as is the case now, to unwind completed deals. They are alternatives because a guarantee preserves the market chain whereas unwinding breaks it.

The difficulties with the alternatives are: (1) the operator would require security for its guarantee from the potential beneficiaries, all the CREST participants, and only their shares passing though the CREST system could provide it in practice. The operator would dislike this because share prices are volatile. Margining to preserve its value would be impractical because a rapid fall would require repeated margin calls; and (2) unwinding completed deals defeats irreversibility, and so the point of DVP.

Closer DVP will involve electronic cash transfers between banks admitted to the CREST system ie, settlement banks because only electronics will be able eventually to make the cash and share transfers simultaneously, and so achieve real DVP. The only other route is the impractical goods-in-shop approach ie, manual amendment of the share register at the same time as manual delivery of cash (not even of a cheque, because it is a mere promise of cash!).

A settlement bank will have to be a direct member of the CHAPS network. Payment will operate through two tiers of accounts. Both the purchaser and seller of shares will have an account with a settlement bank (tier one) and each settlement bank will in turn have one with the CREST system's bank, the Bank of England (tier two). To enable even trade-by-trade as distinct from netted settlement without the CREST operator's guarantee, the purchaser's settlement bank will have to have sufficient funds in its account with the Bank for the Bank to be able to transfer the purchase price to the seller's settlement bank's account with the Bank at the settlement time ('pre-funding'). It will, of course, be up to the purchaser's settlement bank whether it requires funds from the purchaser or gives him credit.

There will be no central nominee shareholder. A central nominee shareholder would be the nominee on registers for all CREST participants' CREST shares, and, as such, the sole legal owner of them, as SEPON is now for all LSE market makers' UK shares. The participants or their clients would be the beneficial owners. The advantage would be that a deal in CREST shares between CREST participants would not result in alteration of a register because the central nominee would be the registered holder both before and after the deal. Only amendment of the central nominee's own stock accounts would be necessary. The disadvantages the report identifies are (1) the legal uncertainty of an interest in a pool of shares—here, a pool of all the shares of a particular type held (through the nominee) by CREST participants; (2) the nominee's custody functions; and (3) the reduction in shareholder visibility to the companies in which the nominee held shares—which would, of course, be, at a minimum, all UK companies with LSE-traded shares.

Legal uncertainty and visibility are unconvincing. Admittedly, pooling in practice means pool members are tenants in common. So, if there are 1,000,000 shares in a pool and you have ten of them, you have a 100,000th interest in each, not ten particular ones. This is hard to explain to private investors, but not legally uncertain. For instance, the LSE has operated its Talisman pools in this way since 1979 without no apparent hitch. As for general visibility, a central CREST nominee would only add a further nominee layer to an existing registration in the name of a nominee—for an INSP, brokers' clients or LSE market makers. Custody is a fair objection. There would have to be electronic facilities for participants to instruct the central nominee on stock situations, and at the right time, as well as for the nominee to relay them to the intended recipient, again at the right time. This is fiendish to devise, as Taurus proved.

The UK share registration system will remain intact. The task force rejects as unnecessary a central share register ie, a single registrar for all UK companies with LSE-traded shares. Each UK company now has one register for each class of its shares, and this would continue. The centralisation would therefore reduce, pace, its name, the number of registrars (to one), not registers. The fragmented UK registration industry might find this unattractive.

CREST will require continuous register updates, as is the case now, for LSE UK equity trades ie, an update for every settlement day. Rolling settlement, with each working day a settlement day, will therefore mean daily updates, although it is not yet clear how up to date ie, how long after settlement they will be. For instance, a daily update to a date six weeks previously is less informative than one to yesterday. Continuous is in contrast to periodic. A periodic update is only once in a period covering more than one settlement day, and is confusing. For instance, Taurus could have combined rolling settlement with five-weekly updates! Currently, for LSE UK equity trades, there are continuous updates, once an account, and so every two or three weeks, depending on whether it is a two-or three-week account. The importance of continuous updates is to open the way to real DVP, since real DVP means updating at the same time as settlement.

The Bank of England will probably operate CREST. Probably, because it will consider it only if no private sector interests want to. They are unlikely to, because, apart from anything else, few will now be credible for the task post-Taurus. If the Bank does, it will be on a fully commercial basis and so it will aim to make a profit out of it.

Less New Law

CREST will mean less new law than Taurus because it will be simpler. Obvious changes will be removing stock transfer forms and share certificates for CREST trades and holdings. The legal delivery mechanism will probably be the same as for Taurus, a statutory instrument under section 207 of the Companies Act 1989, supported by rules made by the CREST operator. Again as for Taurus, the rules will probably have the force of law, like the statutory instrument, rather than being just a private contract between CREST participants. Assuming it is made under section 207, the instrument will have to 'secure that the rights and obligations in relation to securities dealt with under the new procedures correspond, so far as practicable, with those which would arise apart from any regulations under this section' ie, make as few changes as possible to the existing law. Be warned—despite this injunction, Taurus managed to produce over 1,000 pages of regulations and draft rules and procedures.

Rolling on

You may be wondering what has become of rolling short LSE UK equity settlement, one of Taurus' principal, and simpler, benefits. Rolling means settling a fixed number of days after a trade so that every working day is a settlement day. This is unlike the current LSE system of account settlement for UK equities, where all deals within the two- or three-weekly account settle on the same day, six working days, the second Monday, after the end of it. Whilst an interesting City relic of pre-railway communications, this is slow, creates spasmodic two or three weekly workloads, and puzzles the private investor—at least if he is selling, and so waiting for money.

Short means shorter than now, which is therefore a minimum of six, and a maximum of 15 or 20, working days after a trade. The task force has decided, as many thought, that rolling short LSE UK equity settlement is practical without dematerialisation, and so with paper and without Taurus or CREST. So, the LSE should introduce settlement 10 working days after a UK equity trade (T + 10) in July 1994, and T + 5 in January 1995. Further reductions will be post-CREST, which should itself arrive by March 1997. They will probably apply only to CREST trades, unlike T + 10 and T + 5, because of the difficulty of achieving paper (non-CREST) settlement (stock transfer forms one way, cheques the other) in under five working days.

Notes and Questions

1. How much of an improvement is CREST over Talisman?

2. The LSE did, in fact, move to a rolling T+10 settlement in 1994, and then to T+5 in June 1995. It went to T+3 in February 2001. CREST imposes fines for late settlement but waives them where there is unusually heavy trading. V. Boland, *CrestCo cuts fines for late settlement,* Financial Times, February 22, 2000. CREST began operations in July 1996 and was fully operational by the end of 1997. The ownership structure has now been established with 69 shareholders subscribing to £12 million in capital of CRESTCo. the operating company. The Bank of England led the effort to develop the service. *The CREST Project,* 35 Bank of England Quarterly Bulletin 60 (1995).

3. Until February 2001, CREST had no netting and settled trades on a trade-by-trade basis on both the securities and cash side. On the cash side, customers authorized their banks to settle the cash side of trades, and CREST originated debit orders to these accounts to settle the trade. The payments were then made through CHAPS which has become a RTGS system, see Chapter 10. The system was close to a DVP system.

Given the lack of netting, was there any reason for CREST to follow the G-30 standards?

In February 2001, LSE, CREST and the London clearing House (LCH) commenced operations for a central counterparty (CCP) facility for trades on the LSE's Sets electronic order book system. As of yet, however, there is no multilateral netting. J. Clarke, *U.K. CCP Service Launched, But Concerns Linger,* Security Industry News, March 5, 2001. Does a CCP arrangement make sense without multilateral netting? Which system is better, CREST or the NSCC-DTC system used in the United States?

4.   In the past, there have been problems with stock lending in the United Kingdom. The availability of stock lending is important in avoiding failures to deliver. If a party does not have the security, and has sold it (has shorted the stock), it can borrow it from another party. This has raised tax problems for the Inland Revenue. Prior to July 1, 1991, a 15% withholding tax was imposed on the lender on dividends paid on shares which were part of a borrowing arrangement. The concern was that "stock lending" might be used as a device by which domestic "borrowers" that really bought the stock would escape the withholding tax. The lender recovered the tax from a charge to the borrower, thus raising the cost of stock borrowing. Many of these lenders were foreign institutions, who would normally not have a withholding tax imposed on dividends under various U.K. tax treaties. After July 1, no withholding tax was to be imposed on qualified "pool" foreign lenders.

5.   In recent years, GSCS (Global Securities Consulting Services) has published benchmark measures—relative to 100—on settlement efficiency, safekeeping efficiency and operational risk across 20 equity markets, GSCS, *The 1995 Review of Major Markets*, The 1995 Review (1995) (GSCS 1995). The settlement benchmark reflects the overall cost to market participants of failed trades, based on average trade size, local market interest rates, the proportion of the trades that fail, and the length of time for which they fail. The safekeeping benchmark compares the efficiency of different markets in terms of the collection of dividends and interest, reclamation of withheld taxes, and protection of rights in the event of corporate action. The operational risk benchmark takes into account both the settlement and safekeeping benchmarks, as well as other operational factors such as compliance with the G30 recommendations, constraints on capital flows, counterparty risk and force majeure risk. GSCS assigned the following ratings for 1994:

Country	Settlement	Safekeeping	Operational
Australia	94.8	93.6	82.2
Austria	87.4	92.0	77.9
Belgium	88.0	89.5	78.2
Canada	92.6	93.8	82.2
France	92.8	90.1	82.3
Germany	91.1	91.4	83.2
Hong Kong	91.7	94.8	77.6
Italy	92.9	77.8	72.6
Japan	93.8	94.5	81.3
Singapore	88.5	91.9	72.5
Spain	77.8	88.9	65.9
Switzerland	85.9	91.1	76.9
United Kingdom	86.4	95.1	79.3
United States	96.7	95.5	86.5

The correlation coefficient between changes in cross-border equity volume and the settlement benchmark is -0.041, that is there is no evidence of a statistically positive link between improvements in the efficiency of clearance and settlement and cross-border trading. I. Giddy, A. Saunders and I. Walter, European Financial Market Integration: Clearance and Settlement Issues 38 (New York University Salomon Center, Working Paper No. S-95-19, 1995) (Giddy, et. al.). What does this tell us about the importance of clearance and settlement? Does it suggest that the types of reforms advocated by G30 are relatively unimportant?

The U.K. settlement rating only increased to 86.4 in 1994 from 85.4 in 1993 despite the implementation of ten-day rolling settlement in 1994. It appears that this was due to an increase in the fail rate, to 10.4% from 8.7%. Does this suggest that increasing the speed of settlement may not always be efficient?

C.   INTERNATIONAL DIMENSIONS

We now turn to some international aspects of clearing and settlement. As the Chart below indicates, Bank for International Settlements, Report of the Committee on Payment and Settlement Systems, *Cross-Border Securities Settlements*, 13 (1995), there are various alternative channels through which a non-resident of the country of issue of a security could effect settlement of a cross-border trade: (1) through direct access to (membership in) the Central Securities Depository (CSD) in the country of issue, e.g. DTC in the United States; (2) through a local agent (a local bank that is a member of the CSD in the country of issue); (3) through a global custodian that employs a local agent as sub-custodian; (4) through a CSD in the non-resident's own country that has established a link (usually direct) to the CSD in the country of issue; or (5) through an International Central Securities Depository (ICSD), e.g. Euroclear or Clearstream, that has established a direct or indirect (though a local agent) link to the CSD in the country of issue.

Direct access is often not a real alternative since CSDs typically prohibit foreign residents from becoming participants, with the exception of foreign CSDs and ICSDs. Moreover, certain functions would be difficult to perform without a local presence, e.g. matching of settlement instructions. Use of a local agent in the country of issue is probably the most common method for settling cross-border trades. Foreign residents may contract with local agents directly or use global custodians to do so. "A global custodian provides its customers with access to settlement and custody services in multiple markets through a single gateway by integrating services performed by a network of sub-custodians, including the global custodian's own local branches and other local agents." *Id.* at 15.

Numerous CSD-CSD links have been established which are used primarily to settle trades of stocks listed in two countries. Suppose investor A buys IBM shares on the Tokyo Stock Exchange (TSE) from seller B. How would the transaction be cleared and settled. The Japanese Securities Clearing Corporation (JSCC), which is the Japanese version of NSCC, holds an account at DTC that contains securities deposited into JSCC by traders in Japan. If the selling party had securities held by JSCC, JSCC accounts for securities transferred on its books, e.g. debit B. DTC, in turn, would debit the JSCC account and credit A's account (if A had a DTC account) or A's agent. If the selling party did not have securities deposited with JSCC, it would have to deliver these securities to DTC for the account of JSCC, before JSCC could account for the trade. It would typically do so through its custodian bank. Payment for the shares would be in Yen transferred through the Japanese payment system.

What is the purpose of such links? Investors typically hold securities in custody in the home country of the traded security. This is because this is where most of the trades with respect to that security occur. Without the linkage, the selling party's custodian would physically have to move the security to Japan where it would be received by the buyer. The buyer, in turn, even if Japanese might want to move the security back to the U.S. Securities would constantly be moved in and out of the trading country with the attendant expense.

Alternative channels for settling cross-border securities trades

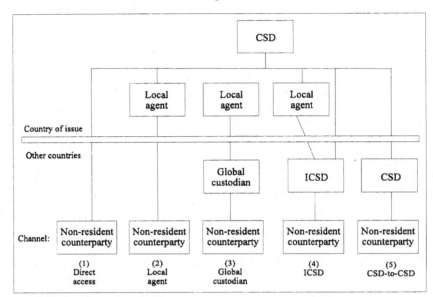

Source: Bank for International Settlements.

The advent of the euro in 1999 could have a significant impact on clearing arrangements. Since securities in different countries will be trading in a common currency, linkage could combine funds and securities settlement, and make local depositories more competitive with the ICSDs described below. C. Kentouris, *Advance of euro Spurs National Depositories to Unite*, Security Industry News (March 24, 1997).

1. ICSDs

The ICSDs, Euroclear and Cedel (now Clearstream), were originally set up to provide settlement and custody services for Eurobonds. Euroclear was founded in 1968 by the Brussels office of Morgan Guaranty Trust Company of New York (MGT). The Euroclear System is run by a Belgium cooperative, the Euroclear Clearance System Société Coopérative which is ultimately owned by 1,400 of the 2000 worldwide participants. MGT continues to run the system through its European Operations Centre in Brussels. ICSDs are major players. In 1999, turnover was $46 trillion and the value of securities in custody was $3 trillion. This compares with 1999 turnover of DTC-NSCC of $45 trillion and 1999 custody of $23 trillion. The following piece gives some detail on Euroclear.

EUROCLEAR, THE EUROCLEAR SYSTEM
4-8, 11-16 (June 1996).

.   .   .

Description of Euroclear Services

Participants in the Euroclear System are able to make use of four basic services through a single point of entry at EOC in Brussels: multi-currency securities clearance and settlement, securities lending and borrowing, custody and money transfer.

Securities Clearance and Settlement

Before describing the settlement process, it is important to understand the daily instruction processing cycle and the matching of trade information.

Participants provide EOC with instructions to receive securities if they are purchasers, or to deliver securities if they are sellers. Such instructions are validated in real-time for processing. Invalid instructions are rejected immediately. EOC attempts to match a Participant's valid receipt instruction with a counterparty Participant's delivery instruction to ensure that the terms of the trade are identical. The matching process takes place continuously throughout the day; valid instructions are submitted for matching as they are received. Information required for matching includes (1) account numbers, (2) settlement date, (3) quantity of securities, (4) the security code number of the issue traded, and (5) currency and cash countervalue.

Unmatched instructions remain in an inventory of valid instructions and continue to be put through the matching process until they either match or are cancelled. Participants can obtain reports of matched and unmatched instructions via ACE, which is a trade confirmation and matching procedure developed in 1987 in cooperation with Cedel and with the support of the International Securities Market Association ("ISMA"). ACE was designed to meet the market's need for a simple, secure and fast confirmation and matching system for international securities transactions.

EOC takes matched instructions for a given settlement date along with any unsettled transactions from previous days and proceeds to the next step in settlement processing.

Euroclear securities settlement processing takes place in the pattern recommended by the Group of Thirty. Overnight processing takes place during the night prior to the relevant value date for settlement, and daylight processing takes place on settlement date. Transactions may be settled against payment in more than 30 settlement currencies. Delivery versus payment is ensured because settlement cannot occur unless the seller has securities and the buyer has cash available to exchange.

In the Euroclear System, there is no separate cash payment cycle and, in part because of the risks that a separate payment cycle would represent are absent, no netting of transactions. The System operates through simultaneous book-entry movement of cash and securities through a transaction-by-transaction program that recycles cash and securities received during the securities settlement processing in order to enable Participants to settle as many matched transactions as possible with all available resources. Participants may link instructions and/or specify the priority which controls the sequence in which their instructions are processed.

Interest payments and redemption proceeds are available during the overnight processing for the value date. Generally, where the issuer is creditworthy, such payments are credited conditionally on the scheduled payment date in anticipation of the receipt of funds from the issuer.

The value dates of cash and securities debits and credits are directly related to the type of security and whether or not it must be delivered outside the Euroclear System. The most notable cases - where the value date is not the same as the processing date - are certain transactions involving transfers to and from domestic markets, and distributions and primary market trades of new issues.

Cash and securities positions resulting from the overnight settlement process are reported to participants in the early morning (Brussels time). At the end of each securities processing cycle, EOC provides Participants with reports listing which securities transactions settled and which did not. An important advantage of overnight processing is that, at the beginning of each business day, Participants know their resulting cash and securities positions, can manage cash balances in same-day value currencies, and can further manage the use of their securities management capabilities through the daylight securities settlement processing.

. . .

Securities Lending and Borrowing

The Euroclear securities lending and borrowing program is designed to improve the efficiency of securities settlement and increase market liquidity. The service allows Participants with buy and hold portfolios of securities to earn lending fees thereby increasing overall portfolio yield (without loss of ownership benefits) by lending securities to other Participants who seek to avoid fails because of lack of securities.

Borrowers in the program are usually active traders such as market-makers or broker-dealers. Participants may be either automatic borrowers, which provide standing instructions to EOC both to identify and, if possible, meet their borrowing needs, or opportunity borrowers, which retain the responsibility for submitting their borrowing requests on an ad hoc basis. Borrowers also benefit from the automatic reimbursement program, in which borrowings are automatically reimbursed as soon as sufficient securities are credited to the account of the borrower. All borrowers may choose the classes of securities, currencies and specific issues for which they wish to borrow.

Lenders in the program are mainly portfolio managers and custodians who are not active traders. These Participants may become either automatic lenders or opportunity lenders. Automatic lenders provide standing instructions to EOC to lend certain portions of their portfolios when opportunities arise and authorize EOC to determine the securities available for lending under program rules. Lenders may also exclude certain securities, types of instruments or currencies. Opportunity lenders may be requested by EOC to lend securities whenever the supply of securities from automatic lenders is expected to be inadequate to meet all borrowing needs.

The benefit of integrating securities lending and borrowing into the securities settlement processing is that borrowings correspond exactly to Participants' needs, thereby eliminating the risk of over- and under-borrowing. Settlement efficiency has been further enhanced by the inclusion of equities in the borrowing program.

In fact, borrowers may reserve securities for borrowing at a future date. This enables borrowers to control their borrowing needs better and reduces the risk of fails because of an inability to borrow. Lenders that agree to reservation of lendable securities are assured of certain level of returns. New categories of loans permit fixed-term lending.

To protect against concentrated borrowings, aggregate borrowings in an issue and borrowing by a single Participant are each limited to specified percentages of the outstanding issue.

Lenders may recall any loan within a recall period of 3 to 6 days depending on the type of security. Morgan Guaranty guarantees the return of securities lent (or the cash equivalent) if a borrower fails to return the securities. Lenders are automatically credited with interest proceeds and any other distributions as if they still held the lent securities. Lenders retain the collateral value of securities lent out in order to secure their own borrowings through the System.

EOC provides Participants with comprehensive reports of their lending and borrowing activity.

Custody

Euroclear Participants have access to extensive custody-related services, including safekeeping, administration of interest, dividend and redemption payments, assistance with recovery of tax withheld, exercise of warrants, conversions and other options and assistance with corporate actions.

The entire custody operation of the Euroclear System is designed to minimize the need to move physical securities. Securities are immobilized in the Euroclear depositary network, which includes major depositary banks, national clearing systems and central banks in more than 25 countries around the world.

Central management of the network, including effecting and monitoring of external receipts and deliveries of securities, is carried out by EOC.

Each issue of securities accepted into the Euroclear System is assigned to and held by one depositary, usually the most conveniently located of the Euroclear depositaries (specialized depositary). Once deposited into the System, all securities are held on a fungible basis.

If a depositary accepts the deposit of a physical security for which it is not the specialized depositary, its ability to authenticate that security may be limited. For that reason, the particular security is "frozen" until it is authenticated by the specialized depositary. In addition, the number of entry points where particular types of securities can be accepted is limited. This helps determine clear responsibility for deposited securities and, by enhancing controls, both the System and its Participants are protected.

.   .   .

Money Transfer

In order to facilitate the transaction settlement processing, Participants open a cash account with Morgan Guaranty Brussels. This cash account is divided into sub-accounts, one for each currency accepted in the Euroclear System.

The cash accounts are used primarily for settlement of securities transactions. In addition, money transfer transactions can be executed through the Participants' cash accounts: book transfers of funds between Participants, wire transfers by debit of a cash account for payment outside the System, preadvices of funds to be received, foreign exchange conversions, and crediting of funds by a correspondent.

Participants can manage their cash accounts on the basis of daily cash reports, which give details of pending and processed cash movements and balances.

Participants are able to use EUCLID, S.W.I.F.T., telex or mail to send money transfer instructions.

New Issues

Virtually all new issues of internationally-traded securities and euro-commercial paper, and many important international equity distributions, are closed and distributed on a same-day against payment basis through the two international clearance and settlement systems. Approximately 70% of all primary distributions of securities issued in the euromarkets are through the Euroclear System. Distribution of securities either against payment or free of payment facilities centralized control of allotment payments from Participants to the lead manager. Assistance in connection with the administration of the exchange of global certificates for definitive certificates is also provided.

· · ·

Notes and Questions

1.   Could Euroclear clear and settle a trade in IBM on the NYSE? How would this work? Would parties want to use Euroclear rather than NSCC?   Section 17A of the 1934 Securities Act requires "clearing agencies" clearing U.S. securities to be registered with the SEC. Neither Euroclear or Clearstream have registered, so as to avoid U.S. regulation. However, Clearstream and Euroclear have obtained SEC exemptions from the requirement to clear and settle U.S. Treasury securities and equities with foreign counterparties.

Cedel's (the predecessor of Clearstream) argument for the exemption for the clearance of government securities was based on its development of the Global Credit Support Service, a real-time system for posting and receiving collateral among swaps counterparties which could substantially reduce swaps credit risk (more on this in Chapter 17). Euroclear sought approval to bolster its securities lending and repo capabilities.   The permissions were conditioned upon a volume limit of five percent of the total average daily dollar value of the aggregate volume of U.S. entities in treasuries, and agreement to notify the SEC of any changes in the organizations' operational rules. In principle, why should Cedel or Euroclear be required to register with the SEC in order to clear U.S. securities?

In granting the exemption to Cedel, the SEC detailed the various standards for clearing agency registration and the means by which Cedel addressed the standard. These standards relate to the organization and processing capacity and financial strength of the applicant, as well as principles of corporate governance, and access. The SEC side-stepped an access issue of some import. Cedel Bank limits participation to commercial, investment banks and broker-dealers, excluding investment companies from direct participation. Investment companies hold securities at Cedel through bank custody accounts. Section 17A(b)(3) says investment companies must have access to clearers, but the SEC concluded that Cedel's practice was acceptable. The SEC also ignored the 17A requirement that the clearing agency be able to enforce compliance with its rules. See K. Tyson-Quah and S. Weinberger, *Cedel Wins SEC Exemption to clear T-bills*, International Financial Law Review (May 1997); E. Luce, *Euroclear to settle U.S. Treasuries*, Financial Times, June 19, 1997. In February 1998, the SEC also granted an exemption to Euroclear for government securities. Release No. 34-39643.

Both Cedel and Euroclear were given approval later in 1998 to clear U.S. equity trades involving foreign counterparties. This enabled Euroclear to settle trades of the handful of U.S. securities listed on Easdaq for which Euroclear generally acts as settlement agent. Euroclear's role in settling U.S. equities was further extended in April 1999 when it began generally settling U.S. equities for non-U.S. Euroclear participants.

2. Euroclear and other international clearing mechanisms may rightly be seen as competing with domestic arrangements. These international mechanisms may eventually make domestic systems obsolete. They offer greater market liquidity, more efficient use of member collateral to back borrowings and potential economies of scale. Giddy et. al, at 15-17. One might question the need to improve these systems, with the attendant expense, when an international alternative exists. This also calls into question the entire effort of the G–30.

The share of international clearance and settlement services (ICSDs), like Euroclear and Clearstream, is quite high with respect to cross-border debt such as eurobonds, and they have some significant share of national debt instruments, but their share of equities is less than one percent. This has been attributed to lack of harmonization among national markets with respect to certain practices. Giddy et. al. argue that differences in settlement cycles impede ICSD settlement. For example, they point out that an investor selling U.K. stocks (T+5 settlement) and buying German stocks (T+2) would have to borrow money for 3 days to bridge the settlement date differences. Other examples cited by the authors are differences in paper versus book-entry securities, bearer versus registered shares, taxation of cross-border transactions, and multiple currencies. *Id.* at 20-30. One might add potential choice and conflict of law problems—at least two countries' laws are potentially applicable. Why should these kinds of differences between markets provide an obstacle to ICSD settlement. The authors appear to assume that ICSD settlement is only advantageous for cross-border trades. Is that correct?

3. DVP is an important requirement for a settlement system. How does Euroclear achieve this? When a trade is between two Euroclear participants, each trade is final during the overnight cycle so that in the morning sellers get final credits. However, since most of the markets are closed when the processing cycle is finished, Morgan Guaranty cannot be sure that its cash correspondents have received funds from buyers. Thus, Morgan assumes a credit risk. Similarly, it may have to assume risk for settling a trade between a Euroclear participant and a party who has elected to settle in a local CSD. For example, it may give out the cash proceeds to a participant seller before receiving cash through the local CSD. M. Dine, *Delivery Versus Payment In A Cross-Border Environment*, 7 Payment Systems Worldwide 29 (1996). Does Morgan's assumption of risk raise any problems?

Euroclear switched to a new "real time" settlement system in a phase-in process that began in April 1998. Under the new procedures, instructions to settle with another Participant, for most instruments, may be sent until around 18:00 on the Settlement Date (S) rather than the old deadline of 19:45 on S-1. "Participants receiving French BTANS [bonds], for example, will have full use of these securities early in the day on S for same-day turnaround, financing or lending opportunities since the securities will be credited in real time to their Euroclear accounts as soon as confirmation is received from RGV, SICOVAM's [the clearance system for French securities] new real-time settlement system. Today, finality in the French market is achieved at the end of the day and securities received are credited to Participant accounts on S+1." Euroclear, Real-time Settlement (1998). The system became fully operational in 1999.

In May 1999, Clearstream announced that it would move to continuous settlement, without any batch processing. This was after it had announced a merger with Germany's Deutsche Börse Clearing (DBC).

4. In September 1999, J.P. Morgan announced it was bowing out of Euroclear. Euroclear's European users were uncomfortable that a principal U.S. banking organization was the operator of their clearing system, reportedly earning $235 million in 1998. In contrast, Clearstream was more European. A new bank called Euroclear will take over Morgan's operations in 2001. At the same time, Euroclear extended its reach by becoming the clearer for EURONEXT, the new stock exchange formed out of the Paris, Belgian and Amsterdam exchanges. Related to this development, in March 2000 Sicovam, the French clearing organization, merged with Euroclear, becoming a subsidiary of the Euroclear bank, named Euroclear France.

5. Users of Euroclear and Clearstream (formerly Cedel) would like to see one European clearing and settlement system. Currently there are over 20 clearing organizations and existing networks are expensive. There

is much debate about how expensive. Some have estimated that clearing and settlement costs in Europe are 7-10 times those of the United States but this is disputed. See K. Lannoo and M. Levin, *The Securities Settlement Industry in the EU: Structure, Costs and the Way forward,* CEPS Research Report (December 2001); C. Kentouris, *DTCC Disputes European Study Results,* Securities Industry News, April 8, 2002. Users would also like to see one CCP, whereas tody various organizations such as the LCH (London Stock Exchange), Clearnet (Paris Bourse) and Eurex Clearing (Deutsche Börse) now compete. P. Kent and D. Fox, *Why Providers should merge,* Financial Times, March 28, 2001. Some estimate that one CCP would reduce costs by $950 million per year. *European share trading, Nothing Settled,* The Economist, January 20, 2001.

The Wise Men Report in 2001, on needed improvements in securities regulation in the EU, see Chapter 5, urged the consolidation of clearing and settlement systems. Since then, the Commission has launched an investigation into whether anti-competitive practices are responsible for the lack of consolidation. The focus is on so-called "vertical silos" which refers to the arrangements under which trades on certain exchanges must be cleared through particular agents. Thus, trades on Deutsche Börse must be cleared through Clearstream, which is owned by Deutsche Börse, and trades on Euronext, the combined Paris-Amsterdam-Brussels exchange, must be cleared through Euroclear. J. Clarke, *Commission Tackles European Processing,* Securities Industry News, April 9, 2001; A. Skorecki, *Deutsche Börse wraps up deal for Clearstream,* Financial Times, April 17, 2002. The Commission is reportedly interested in whether these arrangements are illegal tie-ins and whether all operators can use the clearing systems on the same terms, D. Hargreaves, *Brussels looks into clearing and settlement,* Financial Times, April 6, 2001. Vertical silos contrast with the situation in the United States where one user-owned organization, DTCC, clears and settles trades for all exchanges. The vertical approach permits the integration of clearance and settlement with trading but inhibits the integration of clearance and settlement across different exchanges. Japan had adopted the U.S. approach, C. Kentouris, *Japan's Jasdec Picks Horizontal Structure,* Securities Industry News, April 15, 2002.

Another part of the problem is that some countries, e.g. Italy and Spain, provide that only one organization can hold electronic shares in their country. This makes it difficult for international clearers to compete with the locally authorized depository.

6. DTCC has begun an initiative to become a global CCP. In discussing the possibilities of consolidation, DTCC states: "[d]ifferences in law, which impact the perfection of legal rights that a CCP may have to exercise in the event of a participant's failure, may be difficult to reconcile.

And regulators may legitimately oppose cross-jurisdictional mergers since it is they who must protect information; ensure fair access to services, and safe and sound operations; and intervene if the CCP itself fails." DTCC, *Central Counterparties: Development, Cooperation and Consolidation* (October 2000). Does this suggest that regulatory integration must precede securities market integration?

2. SETTLEMENT FOR GLOBAL BONDS

Clearing and settlement arrangements are an important feature of global bonds. Consider the following excerpts from the World Bank Prospectus for the issuance of DM 3 billion in global bonds.

WORLD BANK, PROSPECTUS DM 3 BILLION
Oct. 20, 1993.

CLEARANCE AND SETTLEMENT

Summary

Clearing and settlement arrangements, including links between DKV, Euroclear, Cedel and DTC, will provide investors access to four major clearing systems. At initial settlement, the Bonds will be represented by two permanent global certificates which will not be exchangeable for definitive bonds. One permanent global certificate, to be held in DKV, will be issued in bearer form (the "DKV Certificate") and will represent the Bonds held by investors electing to hold Bonds through financial institutions that are participants in DKV ("DKV participants"). Euroclear and Cedel participate in DKV by virtue of being participants in the Deutscher Auslandskassenverein AG, Frankfurt am Main ("AKV"), which provides access to DKV for certain foreign institutions; Bonds held by investors electing to hold Bonds through financial institutions that are participants in Euroclear and Cedel ("Euroclear and Cedel participants") are thus included in the DKV Certificate. The other permanent global certificate, to be held by Citibank N.A. acting through its Frankfurt branch ("Citibank Frankfurt") as custodian for DTC, will be issued in registered form (the "DTC Certificate") and will represent the Bonds held by investors electing to hold Bonds through financial institutions that are participants in DTC ("DTC participants").

Together, the Bonds represented by the DKV and DTC Certificates will equal the total aggregate principal amount of the Bonds outstanding at any time. When subsequent secondary market sales settle between the DKV and DTC clearing systems, such sales shall be recorded on the Register and shall be reflected by respective increases and decreases in the DKV and DTC Certificates.

The Bank will appoint Citibank Frankfurt as the registrar and transfer agent for the Bonds (the "Registrar and Transfer Agent"). Citibank Frankfurt provides the link between DKV and DTC as an indirect DTC participant through Citibank Issuer Services N.Y. ("Citibank IS-NY") and, as a German credit institution, it is also a DKV participant.

.   .   .

Primary Market

Customary settlement procedures will be followed for participants of each system at initial settlement. The DKV and DTC Certificates will be delivered at initial settlement to DKV and Citibank Frankfurt (as custodian for DTC), respectively. Through the Same-Day Funds Settlement ("SDFS") system, DTC participants will have their securities accounts credited with Bonds against payment in same-day funds on the settlement date. Settlement procedures applicable to the domestic DM bond market will be followed for DKV participants; Bonds will be credited to their securities accounts on the settlement date, against payment in Deutsche mark in same-day funds. Settlement procedures applicable to DM Eurobonds will be followed for Euroclear and Cedel participants. Bonds will be credited to their securities accounts on the settlement date against payment in same-day funds.

Secondary Market

Secondary market sales of Bonds within each clearing system will be settled in accordance with the rules and procedures established by that system. This means that regular sales at the Frankfurt Stock Exchange will settle within DKV on a two business-day basis. Sales within Euroclear or Cedel and between Euroclear and Cedel will normally settle on a seven-day basis unless parties specify a different period (which may be as short as two days). DTC is a U.S. dollar based system but sales may be settled in other currencies on a free-delivery basis. Sales within DTC denominated in U.S. dollars can settle on a same-day basis; in the case of non-U.S. dollar denominated sales within DTC, the bonds can be delivered same-day, but payment will be made outside DTC.

Secondary market sales between DKV participants and Euroclear or Cedel participants. These trades normally settle on a seven-day basis (unless parties specify a different period, which may be as short as two days).

Secondary market sales from a DTC participant to a DKV, Euroclear or Cedel participant. Two days prior to settlement, a DTC participant selling Bonds to a DKV, Euroclear, or Cedel participant will notify Citibank IS-NY of the settlement instructions and will deliver the Bonds to Citibank by means of DTC's Deliver Order procedures.

Citibank IS-NY sends the settlement instructions to Citibank Frankfurt. One day prior to settlement, Citibank Frankfurt enters delivery-versus-payment instructions into DKV for settlement through its DKV transfer account; the Euroclear or Cedel participant will instruct its clearing system to transmit receipt-versus-payment instructions (via the AKV link) to DKV, and the DKV participant will transmit such instructions directly to DKV, with Citibank Frankfurt as counterparty. On the settlement date, Citibank inputs a Deposit/Withdrawal at Custodian (DWAC) transaction to remove the Bonds to be sold from its DTC securities account; matched and pre-checked trades are settled versus payment--the DKV or Cedel participant's securities account is credited same day value, the Euroclear participant's securities account is credited not later than the next day for value the settlement date, and Citibank Frankfurt causes the DTC participant's pre-specified DM account, at Citibank AG, Frankfurt to be credited for same day value, or any other DM account pre-specified by such DTC participant for value the next day.

Secondary market sales from a DKV, Euroclear, or Cedel participant to a DTC participant. Two days prior to settlement, a DTC participant sends Citibank IS-NY the details of the transaction for transmittal to Citibank Frankfurt and instructs its bank to fund Citibank Frankfurt's DM account one day prior to settlement.

A Euroclear or Cedel participant will instruct its clearing system no later than one day prior to settlement to transmit delivery-versus-payment instructions (via the AKV link) to DKV, and a DKV participant will transmit one day prior to settlement such instructions directly to DKV, naming Citibank Frankfurt as counterparty with further credit to DTC. At the same time (i.e., one day prior to settlement), Citibank Frankfurt transmits receipt-versus-payment instructions to DKV.

On the settlement day, upon settlement of the trade in DKV, Citibank Frankfurt so informs Citibank IS-NY; the DTC participant initiates a DWAC deposit transaction for Citibank IS-NY to approve, resulting in a deposit of Bonds in the DTC participant's securities account same day value. The DKV, Euroclear or Cedel participant's accounts are credited with the sales proceeds same day value.

Settlement in other currencies between the DTC and DKV systems is possible using free-of-payment transfers to move the Bonds, but funds movement will take place separately.

Notes and Questions

1. Notice that settlement times for bond trades across clearing systems may be longer than trades within systems. Also, settlement arrangements for bonds are distinct from those of equities. Thus, U.S.

bond trades can settle on DTC on a same-day basis, whereas equity trades currently settle at T+3, and bond trades across systems, according to the 1993 prospectus, normally settle at T+7.

2. Do differences between settlement times within and across markets affect the development of global bonds? A trade organization of major securities firms, the International Securities Market Association (ISMA), promulgated a rule in 1994 that certain international bond trades would settle on T+3 as of June 1, 1995, T. Corrigan, *ISMA Moves on Settlement Period*, Financial Times (June 3, 1994), and that rule has been implemented. This has been facilitated by the use of ISMA's electronic trade confirmation system TRAX which has replaced previous paper-based procedures. An excellent survey of current arrangements for the clearance and settlement of cross-border trades is Bank for International Settlement's, *Cross-Border Securities Settlements* (1995).

3. RIGHTS IN DEMATERIALIZED SECURITIES

ICSD arrangements involve the indirect holding of investments. The investor holds his securities through a facility such as Euroclear which delegates the holding to a national depositary. This raises some important legal issues as to the investors' rights in the securities that are explored in the following piece.

R. GOODE, THE NATURE AND TRANSFER OF RIGHTS IN DEMATERIALIZED AND IMMOBILIZED SECURITIES

The Future For The Global Securities Market: Legal and Regulatory Aspects 114-124 (F. Oditah ed., 1996),

Chain of entitlements and the multi-tiering of intermediaries and security entitlements

The relationships between the various parties engaged in trade in an international issue can be viewed from opposite ends of the chain: from the issuer through the various tiers of intermediary to the ultimate investor and from the ultimate investor back through the different intermediaries to the issuer. This can best be illustrated by two examples, a new international issue in which the issuer deposits a permanent global note with the two ICSDs to be held in agreed proportions with a common depository, and a receipt into an ICSD or other depository of securities already in issue.

In the case of the new issue, participants pay for their participation through their account with their ICSD, which transfers funds to the lead manager for payment through the common depository against delivery of the global note. The ICSDs are the sole holders of record in the books of the issuer and in the ordinary way no investor will ever come into a direct relationship with the issuer or have a direct claim on the issuer. Since the global note which represents the underlying security is permanently immobilized, customers of the ICSD cannot normally acquire definitive notes or procure physical delivery; their interest takes the form of a securities entitlement against their ICSD, with associated rights to dividends, interest, redemption payments, etc. It is not an entitlement to a specific security from the issuer but a right to share *pro rata* in the pool of fungible rights in the issue held by the ICSD. But a customer, in addition to taking an allotment for itself, may also hold for clients of its own, typically in a fungible or omnibus account for clients collectively, without segregation as between one client and another. Alternatively the customer, having initially bought on its own account, may sell the whole or part of its interest to a client. In either event the customer of the ICSD holds for its clients, and each client's relationship will be only with that intermediary (i.e. with the customer of the ICSD), not with the first-tier intermediary (the ICSD) or with the issuer. Not uncommonly there are lower tiers of intermediary and client.

Looked at from the other end of the chain, an investor holds securities through an omnibus account with his bank, a global custodian, and his rights are against that bank, not against the issuer. The global custodian will in turn hold accounts with its sub-custodians in different countries, and they will be account-holders with their local CSDs. Some CSDs have a direct relationship with an ICSD. In other cases the ICSD's relationship with a local CSD will be indirect, i.e. through a local bank which is a member of the CSD. Each account-holder's relationship is solely with the intermediary with whom his account is maintained.

Let us suppose that an ICSD is holding a permanent global note issued by I and that A Bank is a customer of the ICSD and has acquired a five per cent participation in the issue represented by the global note, of which one per cent is acquired for itself and the rest for its customers, including B Broker who has in turn placed an order on behalf of its client, C. The ICSD is the first-tier intermediary, standing between the issuer and the primary investor, and A Bank's rights in relation to the ICSD can conveniently be described as a first-tier entitlement. A Bank is the second-tier intermediary and B Broker's rights in relation to A Bank constitute a second-tier entitlement. B Broker is the third-tier intermediary and C holds a third-tier entitlement.

LEGAL ISSUES

A critical question, which we shall address shortly, is the nature of each entitlement, and whether either of the lower-tier entitlements is to be considered original or to be considered derived from, or carved out of, the entitlement immediately above it. But first it is necessary to devote a few words to the concept of fungibility.

Fungibility

A securities account in the name of an investor may be fungible or non-fungible. Property is fungible when any unit of it is considered interchangeable with any other unit for the purpose of delivery or transfer obligations. Whether property is fungible depends not on its physical characteristics but on the nature of the obligation owed with respect to it. If the depositee is not obliged to return the deposited property *in specie* but has the right to deliver its equivalent in type and number or amount the asset is fungible. Such a right is typically conferred by contract but may also be given by national legislation, as in the case of the Decrees governing Cedel Bank and Euroclear. If the depositee has to return the very same item deposited with him it is non-fungible. Securities are usually fungible if forming part of the same issue or of another issue made on identical terms.

The division between fungible and non-fungible entitlements is not the same as that between purely contractual and proprietary rights. There are fungibles and fungibles. In terms of pure exchangeability the deposit of securities in a fungible securities account is conceptually indistinguishable from the deposit of money with a bank. In either case the depositee is free to use the specific items deposited (securities, notes and coin) as its own, its obligation being merely to redeliver an equivalent type (securities) or amount (money). But whereas the depositor of money has a purely contractual claim, there being no obligation on a bank to segregate deposited funds for customers either individually or collectively, the custodian of securities in a fungible account will typically be required by the deposit agreement or by law to hold the pool of securities of that type for all interested depositors collectively, whether by way of trust (as in England) or under some other legal regime which confers on depositors co-ownership rights (as in Belgium and Luxembourg). The distinction is of great importance in the event of insolvency of the custodian, for the depositor of money will be a mere unsecured creditor (though in some legal systems having priority rights), whereas the depositor of securities will have co-ownership rights and the securities will not form part of the custodian's assets available for distribution among its creditors.

Tangible securities may be fungible or non-fungible. The position of intangible securities is less straightforward. Where they are unnumbered they are clearly fungible, there being nothing to distinguish one unit from another. The same applies where, though numbered, they have been made fungible by contract (e.g. by agreement to credit them to a fungible account) or statute. The situation regarding numbered intangible securities which have not been made fungible by contract or statute is not so clear. Being intangible they are not capable of physical segregation, so that in principle one unit is the equivalent of any other unit, and a person who agrees to transfer securities bearing numbers different from those he actually holds is considered to have agreed to make the transfer from units of the numbers he does hold. But though intangible securities cannot be physically identified, their numbering could facilitate a tracing claim. For example, if a custodian, D, holds shares numbered 1-50 for A and shares 51-100 for B and without authority purports to transfer shares 51-100, then though these have no physical manifestation we can say that the transfer shows an intention to dispose of B's holding rather than A's. In other words, as has been aptly pointed out, though intangibles may not be capable of identification in the physical sense they *are* capable of allocation. Securities traded internationally are usually fungible; indeed, Euroclear, unlike Cedel Bank, does not open non-fungible accounts. Cedel Bank treats all securities as fungible unless otherwise instructed by the customer.

The position of the indirect holder

Even a direct holder of securities carries the risk of insolvency of the issuer but at least he possesses or controls the securities and associated rights. An indirect holder carries a triple risk: the inability to enforce rights directly against the issuer where the custodian is the holder of record and is unable or unwilling to do so on his behalf; the insolvency of the custodian, to the extent of any deficiency in the pool of securities available to account holders; and the loss of securities held by the custodian in circumstances where it is able to disclaim responsibility for the loss.

As regards permanent global notes, the right of direct enforcement, so far as not given by the applicable law, can be taken care of in various ways: by provisions in the trust deed (where there is one) executed by the issuer; by an irrevocable deed of covenant executed by the issuer at the time of issue of the global note by which, in the event of the permanent global note becoming void, account-holders acquire direct rights against the issuer; and by provisions in the global note itself entitling the custodian to exchange it for definitive certificates in stated events, such as an event of default. In the absence of such an event the account-holder relies on the contractual duties assumed by the custodian to perform services on his behalf, such as collecting and crediting dividends, interest and redemption moneys, exercising voting rights, and the like.

For protection against insolvency of the custodian the account-holder (investor or secured creditor) needs assurance that the law will recognize the priority of his entitlement over the claims of the custodian's general creditors. Specifically the investor or secured creditor needs to know that securities in the hands of the custodian for his account will not be available to the custodian's own creditors but will be held for him to the extent of his interest or, if securities or moneys have been lost, proportionate to his interest.

This raises a number of potentially difficult questions. First, what is the subject-matter of the account-holder's entitlement? In particular, is it a proprietary right which can be asserted against the custodian's trustee or liquidator or the purely personal right of an unsecured creditor? Secondly, where the account holder seeks to rely on the right as proprietary, and in particular where he claims the status of a pledgee or other secured creditor, has he taken all necessary steps to perfect his interest under the applicable law and preserve its priority against other claimants, including a trustee in bankruptcy or liquidator? Thirdly, what law is to be applied to determine the first two questions? Fourthly, what is the effect of mandatory perfection requirements under the law of another State having a claim to regulate perfection, for example, the State in which the grantor of a security interest is incorporated? Finally, where the custodian has itself deposited the securities with a sub-custodian who becomes insolvent or causes loss of the securities through negligence or fraud, does the loss fall on the custodian or the account-holder, and what law governs this question?

In analyzing these questions it is helpful to take separately the first-tier entitlements and lower-tier entitlements.

Possible characterisations of the first tier entitlements

Where securities are deposited in an account with a first-tier securities intermediary there are at least three different ways in which the applicable law might characterize the account-holder's entitlement:

(1) As a mere personal right to the transfer or (in the case of tangible securities delivery) of securities of the same type and value

This, of course, would be disastrous for the account-holder. Yet it is a risk in jurisdictions (particularly civil law jurisdictions) which have not modernized their law. For example, many civil law jurisdictions do not possess the trust institution, insist on specificity or segregation of assets as a condition of ownership or security and do not recognize co-ownership of, or security interest in, pools of fungible assets. In these countries account-holders and pledgees may be at risk in the absence of appropriate legislation. Several civil law jurisdictions have in fact provided co-ownership rights by statute.

(2) As continuing ownership of the deposited securities

Under English law this is the case where the securities are deposited in a non-fungible account, so that the intermediary is under a duty to return them *in specie* and is thus a mere bailee of the deposited notes or certificates. However, if the securities are intangible securities registered in the name of the intermediary legal title will be in the intermediary and the indirect holder having merely equitable ownership, whilst if the securities are bearer securities the location of the legal title intention of the parties. In practice most accounts in relation to internationally-traded securities are fungible accounts, and this will be assumed in what follows.

(3) As a combination of personal rights and co-ownership of a pool of fungible securities

The theory here is that all deposited securities of a given issue are fungible, so that the depositor transfers ownership of the particular securities to the intermediary and acquires in their place a personal right to the delivery or transfer of their equivalent in class and value and co-ownership of the pool of fungible securities held at any given time by the intermediary as custodian. How that co-ownership is characterized in different legal systems (beneficial ownership under a trust, legal ownership, etc.) is generally of no great significance in itself; what matters is that the rights are proprietary in character and that the securities pool is not available to general creditors of the custodian. This is the position under Belgian law in relation to Euroclear and under Luxembourg law in relation to Cedel Bank and is the principle established in the newly revised Article 8 of the Uniform Commercial Code.

English law has no difficulty with the co-ownership concept so long as it forms an express or implied term of the contract with the custodian or alternatively is established by a trust in favour of the account-holder. There is no problem of lack of ascertainment of the subject-matter, and no need for physical segregation, since what the account-holder acquires by the agreement is not an interest in unidentified securities forming an unsegregated part of a bulk of securities but co-ownership of, or (in the case of security) a security interest in, the entire bulk. The position is otherwise where the depositor makes an unconditional transfer of ownership to the custodian and stipulates merely for a right to delivery or transfer to him of their equivalent in type and amount at a later date without any express or implied agreement for, or trust, of a share in the pool of deposited securities. In such a case he is a mere unsecured creditor, in just the same way as the depositor of money with a bank. The right to call for delivery or transfer is a mere personal contractual right, not a proprietary right, for that is the bargain. In the case of bearer securities an undertaking by the depositary to hold for the account-holder a given number and value forming part of the total holding would fail for lack of ascertainment of the subject matter in much the same way as in the case of an agreement for sale of an undivided part of a bulk of goods. This is not so in the case of registered securities, since these are incapable of physical segregation.

Similar considerations apply to a security interest. Under English law this can be created by agreement or trust relating to a fund of intangibles and is effective against the trustee or liquidator of the party granting the security interest so long as any applicable perfection requirements have been.

The nature of lower-tier entitlements

Let us go back to our chain of I (issuer) ICSD-A Bank-B Broker. The first question to consider is whether the first-tier entitlement, namely that held by A Bank in relation to the ICSD, is proprietary or purely contractual in character; the second, whether the lower-tier entitlement is original or derivative, that is to say, whether its content is determined independently of the nature and quantum of the interest held by the securities intermediary with which the account is held or is derived from and a sub-set of the intermediary's own rights against the higher-tier intermediary with which its account is held. There are several different possibilities, depending on the legal regime applicable.

Let us assume in the first place that A Bank's rights against the ICSD are purely personal (contractual). We know that this is not the case as regards Cedel Bank under Luxembourg law or Euroclear under Belgian law, but we might hypothesize another ICSD governed by a different law under which the rights might be purely contractual. In that case it is obvious that B Broker cannot have proprietary rights in any part of the pool of securities held by the ICSD. At best it is the beneficial owner (e.g. under a trust or similar device) of A Bank's contractual rights against the ICSD, which would protect it against the creditors of A Bank on A Bank's insolvency but not against creditors of the ICSD if it were to become insolvent. But in jurisdictions which do not possess the trust concept B Broker might be no more than an unsecured creditor of A Bank.

Our alternative assumption is that A Bank is co-owner of the pool of securities held by the ICSD. It does not follow that B Broker's rights against A Bank (on the assumption that A Bank purchased part of its participation for B Broker) are themselves proprietary in character. That depends on the terms of the agreement between B Broker and A Bank and on the law governing the proprietary effects (if any) of that agreement. It is perfectly possible to envisage a legal scenario in which B Broker has a purely contractual right to the portion of the issue acquired by A Bank in accordance with B Broker's instructions. In market terms such a result would be highly undesirable, since it leaves B Broker to bear the risk of A Bank's insolvency. The needs of the market require that B Broker's entitlement should be treated as proprietary in character. That could be done by giving him direct proprietary rights against the ICSD. But that solution would breach another market requirement, namely that each account holder's relationship should be confined to the intermediary with which the account is held. The only way in which both market needs can be met is by characterising B Broker's interest as a derivative interest of the same character as the interest from which it is derived. In other words, B Broker would be co-owner with other account-holders of A Bank of such part of A Bank's participation as can be shown to have been acquired on their behalf. So A Bank would have a five per cent co-ownership interest in the pool of securities held by the ICSD, and B Broker and other account holders of A Bank would be co-owners of the 80 per cent of A Bank's participation acquired by A Bank on their behalf.52 Moreover, if lower-tier interests are characterized as derivative then it follows that (a) their value cannot exceed a due proportion of the recoverable value of the issued securities; (b) transfers of or security rights over higher-tier interests which are effective under the law applicable to them are binding on the holders of lower-tier interests; and (c) no holder of an interest can have rights to securities greater than those possessed by the holder of the higher-tier interest from which the former interest is derived.

So far we have assumed that the custodian itself holds a security entitlement sufficient to cover the security entitlements it has agreed to give its own customers. To the extent of any shortfall the security entitlements of those customers abate proportionately, though their personal rights remain unaffected. If the custodian has purported to credit its customers with an entitlement from an interest it has not itself yet acquired, their rights will necessarily be purely personal until such acquisition.

The applicable law

In order for the account-holder or secured creditor to form a view as to whether he is adequately protected by the legal regime governing his entitlements it is first necessary to determine what law applies. This is controlled by the conflict of laws rules of the forum. For dealings in movable property English courts, in common with those of many other jurisdictions, apply the *lex situs*. However, in an extremely interesting and well-reasoned judgment Mr. Justice Millett (as he then was) held that whether the securities are tangible (i.e. bearer securities) or intangible, the applicable law is the *lex loci actus,* the place where the transfer is effected.

In the case of tangible securities it is important to bear in mind that what is relevant is not their tangible character as such but the manner in which a transfer of them is effected. While they are immobilized in the vaults of a custodian and transfers are effected by book entry, the location of the certificates is irrelevant, for the transfer has not been effected by physical delivery but by book entry, and whether one applies the *lex situs* or the *lex loci actus* the applicable law is that of the place where the entry is made. This approach corresponds closely with the terms of the recently revised Belgian decree governing the Euroclear operations, which make it clear that the decree applies, and the interest in securities (as defined by Belgian law) held by Euroclear, is to be considered located in Belgium, even if the certificates representing the securities are physically held by sub-custodians outside Belgium. But if the custodian or sub-custodian of securities that are tangible under the law of the issuer's incorporation were to transfer them by physical delivery outside the ICSD system, the effect of the transfer would be governed by the place of delivery, which is the same as the location of the certificates at the time of delivery. The legal regime for Cedel Bank contains corresponding legislation stating that the lex situs of securities deposited with Cedel Bank is Luxembourg law, irrespective whether such securities have been deposited in a location outside Luxembourg.

It is also necessary to treat each level of interest separately. Each tier of intermediary holds a bundle of intangible rights for its own customer and each bundle of rights represents a distinct interest. This follows from the fact that the book-entry entitlement of any customer features only in the records of its own intermediary, not in the records of higher-tier or lower-tier intermediaries. So first-tier interests would be governed (according to the theory adopted) by the *lex situs* of that interest or the law of the place of its transfer.

We have noted that in the *Macmillan* case the applicable law for book entry transfers was held, at first instance to be the *lex loci actus* and, on appeal, the *lex situs*. The *lex loci actus* does, indeed, appear to have much to commend it, since it looks at the way in which the transfer is effected rather than the nature of the security transferred and can thus be applied whether the securities are tangible or intangible and, in the case of tangible securities, whether the transfer is effected by physical delivery or by book entry. It also avoids the need to ascribe an artificial *situs* to the intangible securities. However, it suffers the serious disadvantage that in the case of an intermediary with an international network of branches or offices connected by a computer network the place of record of an entitlement or transfer may be quite arbitrary so far as the account-holder is concerned, and, indeed, may change from time to time, with consequent uncertainty as to the applicable law governing any particular transaction. Further, the rights of different account-holders might be governed by different laws. There is therefore much to be said for discarding both the *lex situs* and the *lex loci actus* as the law applicable to book-entry transfers and substituting the law of the intermediary's place of incorporation, or alternatively the law of the place where it has its seat.

It is a generally accepted principle of the conflict of laws that the nature of a security issued by a company, including the question whether it is to be characterized as tangible (and thus transferable by mere delivery) or intangible, is governed by the *lex societatis*. So if share certificates relating to registered shares issued by a New York company are deposited with a bank in London by way of pledge, an English court, applying New York law to characterize the transferability of the shares, will recognize the effectiveness of the pledge even though under English law registered shares are incapable of pledge. Conversely, if certificates to registered shares or bonds issued in England are pledged with a bank in New York, one might expect New York courts to apply English law to determine the character of the shares or bonds and thus to conclude that they are incapable of pledge.

Notes and Questions

1. The problems raised by Professor Goode are not unique to ICSDs. Within national jurisdictions many investors, particularly large institutional ones, hold securities through custodians. In the ICSD, however, the laws of more than one jurisdiction are necessarily involved.

2. Consider the following hypothetical devised by Professor Goode. Assume that a German corporation issues debt securities represented by a single global certificate immobilized at the Depository Trust Company (DTC) and registered in the books of the issuer in the name of Cede & Co., DTC's nominee, with part of the initial distribution being made to U.S. investors and part of it being made to non-U.S. investors. An English broker purchases an interest in the securities and takes delivery of the interest by book-entry to its account with Morgan Guaranty Trust Company, Brussels office, as operator of Euroclear. The Euroclear operator holds a position in the securities for the benefit of Euroclear participants through an account with a New York bank participant of DTC. Under new Article 8 of the Uniform Commercial Code interests in securities held through accounts with the New York bank and DTC would be defined as "security entitlements." Interests in securities held through the Euroclear operator are defined by Belgian Royal Decree No. 62 as non-traceable co-proprietary rights or a "universalité" represented solely by an account in Belgium (i.e. a package of rights very similar to a security entitlement). Suppose that the English broker sells the securities to a French broker by book-entries on the records of the Euroclear operator. Which jurisdiction's law would or should govern the validity of the transfer from the English broker to the French broker?

a. New York law because the global certificate is located in New York?

b. German law because the issuer is organized under the laws of Germany?

c. English law because the English broker/transferor is an English company?

d. French law because the French broker/transferee is organized under the laws of France?

e. Belgian law because the Euroclear accounts are located in Belgium? (This would be the result under Section 8-110 of new Article 8 of the UCC and under Belgian law).

3. In *Fidelity Partners, Inc. v. First Trust Company of New York*, 1997 U.S. Dist. LEXIS 19287 (SDNY), Fidelity Partners, a judgment creditor by assignment of the Philippine Export and Foreign Loan Guarantee Corporation ("PG") brought an action to recover PG's $1.75 million interest in certain bonds issued by the Philippine government. Under the Foreign Sovereign Immunities Act ("FSIA"), 28 U.S.C. §1610, it could only levy on property in the United States because PG is a Philippine government agency. PG's interest in the bonds was held through ING Bank of Manila ("ING") located in the Philippines. ING held its interest in the bonds on the books of Euroclear, through Morgan Guaranty's Brussels branch. Morgan Guaranty's London office was the sub-custodian of the bonds since it is the only recorded owner of the global bond of which PG's interest comprises a part. First Trust Company of New York was the fiscal and paying agent, registrar, transfer agent and authenticating agent for the bonds. The court denied Fidelity's attempt to levy on the various accounts, holding that Fidelity could only garnish the ING account, since this was the only the account on which PG's interest was recorded, and a levy on that account, located in the Philippines, was barred by the FSIA.

Assuming the global bond was held in custody in New York by Morgan, New York, should Fidelity have been able to garnish the New York account and recover its share by forcing Morgan to issue a definitive bond for $1.75 million?

4. One of the terms of competition between Clearstream and Euroclear is the legal framework protecting investors holding securities in the two systems. The rights in Clearstream are governed by Luxembourg law and the rights in Euroclear by Belgian law. In 1998, E. Bettelheim wrote an article concluding that Luxembourg law was preferable since (1) Belgian law does not "deem" all securities credited to accounts with the Euroclear Operator as being located in Belgium (and, therefore, might not be governed by Belgian law under conflicts of law analysis); (2) Belgian law does not provide for the transfer of title by book entry or for the enforceability of transfer of title clauses in collateral transactions; (3) there is no broad statutory provision in Belgian law for netting on insolvency; and (4) Belgian law does not provide a firewall against the insolvency of a clearing agency like the Euroclear Operator. *Collateral Held in Euroclear and Cedel: A Legal Comparison* 8 Journal of International Banking and Financial Law 363 (1998). This was the subject of a rebuttal in an article by Euroclear lawyers, L. De Ghenghi and B. Servaes, *Collateral Held in the Euroclear System: A Legal Overview,* 9 Journal of International Banking and Financial Law 83 (1999).

4. FUTURE ARRANGEMENTS

Where will we go in the future? The following report sets out some basic criteria for evaluating future changes and then sets forth some possible infrastructure models for the future. The excerpt describes three models: (1) Worldclear; (2) Global Hub; and (3) Bilateral Links. As you read the report, consider whether you prefer any of these models to our existing system and whether any one model is clearly the best.

MORGAN GUARANTY TRUST COMPANY OF NEW YORK, BRUSSELS OFFICE AS OPERATOR OF EUROCLEAR, CROSS-BORDER CLEARANCE, SETTLEMENT AND CUSTODY: BEYOND THE G30 RECOMMENDATIONS
(1993).

The G30 Report concluded that "the development of a single global clearing facility was not practicable," but determined that "agreement on a set of practices and standards that could be embraced by each of the many markets that make up the world's securities system was highly desirable." It therefore made nine recommendations designed to improve the quality and standardize the practices of *national* clearance and settlement systems. These recommendations were centered around the establishment of one or more central securities depositories ("CSDs") in each market.

The Group of Thirty focused on the efficiency of individual national systems; it did not conduct an analysis of the specific costs and risks that impede the efficiency of *cross-border* settlement when these systems operate together. It therefore did not analyze the complexities of settling transactions in a *multi-currency, multi-time-zone* environment, or identify the conditions that must be satisfied to maximize cross-border efficiency.

. . .

Friction Costs

The unrealized benefits of international portfolio diversification give a sense of urgency to minimizing an important category of *friction costs* in international financial markets—those associated with cross-border securities clearance, settlement, and custody. These can be explicit (e.g., fees) or implicit (e.g., risks). They can arise in connection with a securities transaction or over the life of a security (e.g., settlement or custody fees). They can be borne by market participants or absorbed by CSDs, the banking sector, central banks, or other financial intermediaries (e.g., credit exposure of a seller to its buyer between trade execution and settlement or the credit exposure of a bank to a seller who is allowed to send a wire transfer in anticipation of confirmation of the final settlement of a buyer's payment).

The friction costs associated with cross-border clearance, settlement, and custody are readily identifiable when examined in the context of the *life cycle of a securities transaction.* Such a life cycle begins when market participants make decisions about whether to hold, buy, or sell a particular security and ends with investment management decisions about maximizing the risk-adjusted returns on the resulting portfolio of securities or cash. A decision to buy or sell a security requires the use of a settlement system to process the resulting transaction.

Settlement Pipeline

Settlement systems can be compared to factories. They take an array of inputs and transform them into an array of outputs. The clearance and settlement process itself, like a high-velocity manufacturing process, can be pictured as a *pipeline.* Work enters the pipeline at one end, and finished products flow out the other. Efficient processing reduces the time between when inputs are acquired from suppliers and finished products are delivered to consumers.

Similarly, an efficient clearance and settlement process reduces the time between when market participants must position their securities or cash for settlement and when their new securities or cash positions are available for redeployment. In other words, market participants wish to retain injecting them into the settlement pipeline, and to assert control over their proceeds (new securities or cash) as soon as possible after they emerge from the pipeline.

Pipeline Liquidity Risk

The G30 Report and other studies identified some of the major costs and risks associated with clearance and settlement. These studies did not focus, however, on what this paper calls *pipeline liquidity risk* —risk associated with delays in a settlement pipeline arising primarily from gaps in time between the processing cycles of various CSDs and between the processing cycles of CSDs and national payment systems. There was no need to focus on this risk because previous studies concentrated on domestic rather than cross-border transactions. Pipeline liquidity risk is less pronounced in domestic markets. Moreover, it has typically been absorbed on both the payment and delivery sides of purely domestic transactions by domestic banks, the relevant central bank, or other financial intermediaries.

These institutions absorb pipeline liquidity risk in the domestic context by providing intra-day or other *uncompensated* credit. For example, in domestic markets where a CSD achieves DVP at the end of the business day and the deadline for same-day payments through the national payment system occurs earlier in the day, pipeline liquidity risk arises on the payment side of a transaction. The banking sector typically provides intra-day cash advances to permit sellers to execute wire transfers so the anticipated proceeds from the buyer can be redeployed on the *same* day, before the payment system closes. If banks were not willing to make intra-day cash advances for this purpose, sellers could not use the proceeds until at least the *next* business day, resulting in at least one day's interest cost at market rates. Credit is also extended in real-time systems where DVP is achieved throughout the day. For example, the Federal Reserve currently absorbs the pipeline liquidity risk on the cash side of transactions in U.S. government securities that settle through the Fedwire system by extending intra-day overdrafts to buyers' banks that are short of cash at the time settlement occurs.

Pipeline liquidity risk also arises on the securities side of *back-to-back transactions* undertaken by customers of local custodians, and is typically bridged in domestic markets by extensions of intra-day credit by bank custodians. A simple back-to-back transaction consists of a pair of purchase and sale transactions in which a party agrees to purchase securities from one counterparty and sell them to another. Such a transaction creates a classic chicken-and-egg problem. The customer wants to use the securities from the purchase transaction to settle the sale transaction, and it also wants to use the proceeds from the sale transaction to settle the purchase transaction. However, because CSDs typically have only one processing cycle, the sale transaction cannot be settled on the same day as the purchase transaction, unless the customer prepositions the securities to be sold or the custodian arranges an intra-day securities loan to the underlying customer. If custodians cannot arrange intra-day securities loans, customers will incur the cost of borrowing securities for at least one day.

Pipeline liquidity risk can no longer be ignored in the cross-border environment. As recognized by the Committee on Payment and Settlement Systems of the central banks of the Group of Ten countries (the "G10 Committee"), credit and liquidity risks tend to be more complex and last longer in a cross-border environment. The number and size of *gaps in time* between the processing cycles of the various CSDs and between those of CSDs and national payment systems are greater. These gaps are the result of multiple currencies, localization of national payment systems, localization of CSDs, time-zone differences, and certain customs and traditions that complicate cross-border settlement.

It is difficult for domestic CSDs to shift this risk to the international banking sector because of the number of jurisdictions involved and the lack of financial incentive. If domestic CSDs or the international banking sector were not willing to supply the necessary credit, a participant could be forced to incur or forego one (or more) day's interest or securities borrowing fees on its daily purchase and sale transactions in different securities. For a trader with an average net daily volume of, for example, USD 500 million, this can generate annual interest expenses or foregone interest income of USD 25 million or more at current interest rates—a substantial friction cost.

If a CSD of one country establishes a bilateral link with that of another, pipeline liquidity risk can arise with respect to cross-market buyers, cross-market sellers, back-to-back traders, and the other CSD. Because CSDs have generally been unable or unwilling to assume the pipeline liquidity *risks* associated with settling transactions, their participants have faced the risk of incurring significant *costs* if they used the link to settle cross-border transactions. The existence of pipeline liquidity risks—and the failure of any intermediary to absorb them—results in friction costs that may explain why many of the existing bilateral links between domestic CSDs have yet to attract much traffic.

Although pipeline liquidity risks cannot be eliminated altogether, this paper recommends that steps be taken to reduce their duration and the probability that they will result in credit losses. This should help CSDs absorb risk, or assemble international banks to do so, to eliminate the pipeline liquidity friction costs otherwise associated with bilateral links or other cross-border settlement structures.

Legal Risk

National securities ownership, transfer, and pledging laws generally reflect a different era—when individual securities were held directly by owners in physical form. Instead, securities today are generally held indirectly through multiple tiers of intermediaries. Cross-border investment requires not only tiering of intermediaries, but also involvement by intermediaries in different countries, with each tier being subject to a different country's laws. Existing national laws contain unnecessary ambiguities when applied to such multi-tiered securities holding systems.

Basic Custody Services

Previous studies also have not concentrated on the friction costs associated with holding and maximizing the value of a security over its life. The life of a security begins with its issuance and, in the case of debt, ends with its maturity or redemption. The life of an equity security theoretically continues into perpetuity, although it can end with the repurchase of the security by, or the bankruptcy or merger of, the issuer. Along the way, market participants must engage in *income collection* and *withholding tax reclamation,* and react to any number of *corporate events.*

Most market participants today hold their securities positions through multiple tiers of local or global custodians, CSDs or other intermediaries, in what can be called a *multi-tiered securities holding system.* This reduces the cost and risk of holding securities and makes it easier for market participants to transfer them, thus increasing the liquidity of securities positions. ... Market participants rely on such intermediaries to collect dividends and interest, process withholding tax reclamations, transmit notices from issuers about corporate events, carry out instructions from customers, and perform other *basic custody services.*

The costs and risks associated with basic custody services vary greatly depending on the nature of the service. Income collection and withholding tax reclamation services are relatively low-risk activities. Other services, such as transmitting notices and instructions with respect to corporate events, can create more substantial costs and risks, if they involve delays or if inaccurate information is transmitted.

The business of supplying basic custody services to the market is becoming more standardized and, as a result, commoditized. Local and global custodians increasingly try to differentiate their services either by subsidizing basic custody services with revenues from more profitable *value-added services* or by assuming greater risks in their provision. For example, some global custodians now offer "contractual" settlement and "guaranteed" income and tax reclamation services. They may also offer sophisticated analytical and portfolio management services.

This paper recommends that CSDs be encouraged to develop the capacity to provide basic custody services so that the market can benefit from their economies of scale and scope. Measures should also be taken to reduce the costs of collecting corporate events information from different jurisdictions; acting on client instructions as to elected options, proxy voting, and the like; and of processing tax reclamation entitlements.

Progressive Displacement

The current status of basic custody services is reminiscent of the situation of safekeeping and settlement services a number of years ago. Local custodians historically maintained physical possession of securities in almost all domestic markets. They settled customer transactions through physical delivery of securities against cash. Over time, competition to supply these services became intense, and the services became standardized and commoditized. With settlement delays, the rate of failed transactions grew.

In many markets, the growing trading volumes, cumbersome nature of physical settlement, and lack of clear financial incentives to develop a commoditized service led to the back-office paperwork crisis of the

1960s. The response was to establish CSDs to perform the safekeeping and settlement functions on behalf of custodians or other market participants. CSDs achieved immobilization of securities and exploited economies of scale and scope in supplying safekeeping and settlement services. CSDs thus allow custodians to subcontract an otherwise low-margin service and focus on supplying more profitable custody services, sparing the industry the deficiencies of physical settlement.

The process by which CSDs displaced local custodians as the primary suppliers of safekeeping and settlement services occurred over a period of years. A similar process of *progressive displacement* seems now to be occurring with respect to basic custody services because of the economies of scale and scope that CSDs have in supplying these services. This paper recommends that CSDs develop the capacity to supply basic custody so that custodians will be able to subcontract aspects of their businesses with rapidly-deteriorating margins and focus on supplying more profitable, value-added custody services to their customers.

Regulatory Costs

Previous studies have also tended not to address the friction costs associated with regulating CSDs. CSDs generally provide clearance, settlement, and custody services only to wholesale market participants. This is particularly true with respect to cross-border transactions because retail investors hold and transfer securities through professional brokers and fund managers.

Regulatory burdens on innovation or intersystem linkages can substantially increase the costs and risks of clearance, settlement, and custody. It is essential that national regulators resist the temptation to assert extraterritorial jurisdiction over CSDs based in other countries, as they establish links with domestic CSDs. Otherwise, such other CSDs, which already have primary regulators, could become subject to overlapping and even conflicting regulation, which could substantially increase the costs and risks of cross-border settlement and the time required to implement improvements. To the extent local regulators have concerns about the local effects of cross-border links, their attention should be focused on the home-country CSD that is linked to the foreign CSD, and encourage international convergence of regulatory standards.

. . .

Multiple-Access Model
Description

The multiple-access model consists of one or more CSDs in each country, local custodians, ICSDs, global custodians, and market participants. The multiple-access model enables market participants to settle transactions in domestic, foreign, or international securities through a variety of channels.

Figure 3 below shows *some* of the possibilities; many more channels exist.

Figure 3. Multiple-Access Model

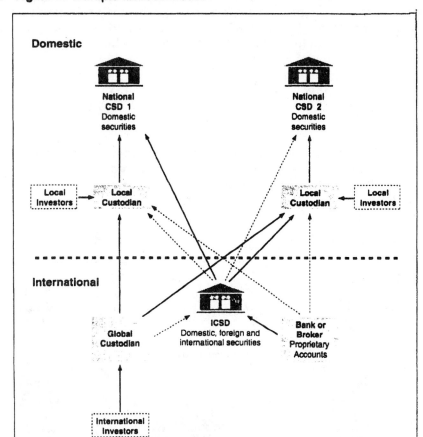

→ Signifies the access option selected for cost or efficiency reasons by each player (bank, broker, custodian or ICSD).

┄┄┄► Signifies an alternative option that might be selected on the basis of competitive analysis.

For example, the solid arrows from "international investors" show how investors can settle cross-border transactions in domestic securities in any market in the world through a global custodian that gains access to local CSDs through a network of local custodians. The global custodian could also obtain access to certain local CSDs through membership in an ICSD. ICSDs can obtain access to local CSDs either through their own networks of local custodians or by establishing direct links with local CSDs. Similarly, the solid arrows from banks or brokers trading for their own accounts show how traders can settle cross-border transactions through an ICSD, and the dotted arrows show the alternative of establishing a network of direct relationships with local custodians.

Alternative Models

Worldclear

Description

The Worldclear model is the most radical model for restructuring the cross-border settlement infrastructure. It assumes the establishment of a single, global CSD to perform the safekeeping, clearance, and settlement functions for all securities—domestic, foreign, and international. (See Figure 4).

Figure 4. Worldclear Model

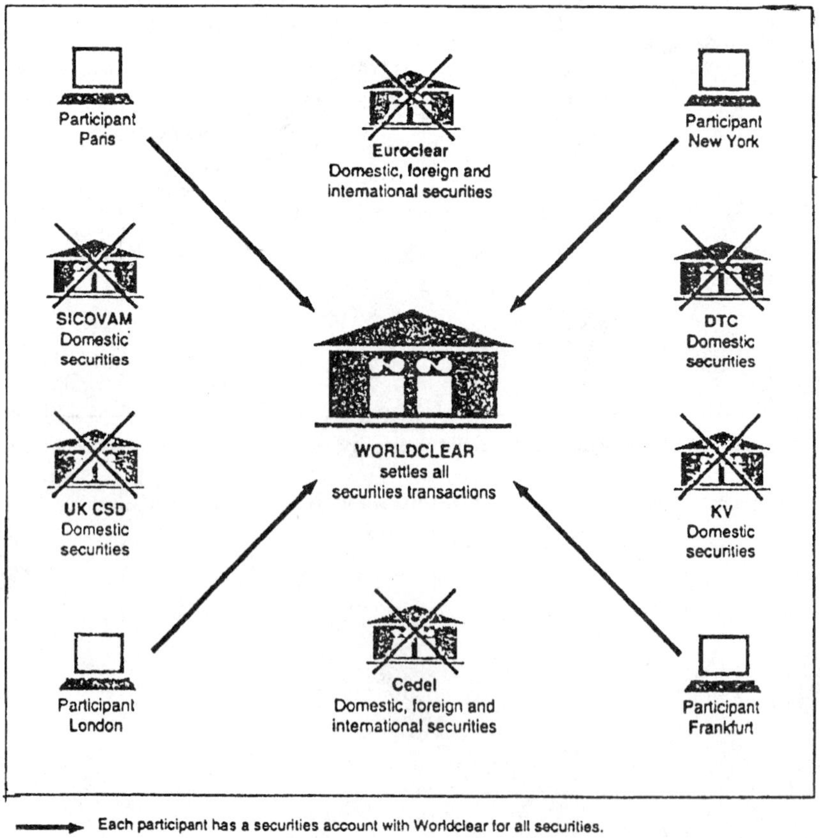

━━━━▶   Each participant has a securities account with Worldclear for all securities.

Worldclear would replace national and international CSDs with a single, centralized, global CSD.   All participants of existing CSDs would become participants of Worldclear.   It would maintain the cash and securities accounts for all wholesale market participants, and effect all transfers in its own electronic files.   Worldclear nevertheless assumes that multiple national currencies and payment systems continue to exist.

Global Hub

Description

The global hub model assumes the establishment of a single, global CSD with both "home-market securities" and "other-market securities" links with each national and international CSD for settling cross-market transactions in all securities.   A "home-market securities link" is a bilateral link in which the global hub essentially acts as a participant of a national or international CSD.   It would permit transactions to be settled between the global hub and any of the participants of the CSD with respect to securities held by such CSD ("home-market securities"). An "other-market securities link" is a bilateral link in which a CSD acts as a participant of the global hub.   It would permit transactions to be settled between any pair of CSDs with respect to securities that are not held by either CSD ("other-market securities").   (See Figure 5).

Each CSD would continue to perform the safekeeping function for all home-market securities.   Its securities accounts would reflect the positions both of its participants and of the global hub in its home-market securities.   Its securities accounts would also reflect the positions of its participants in all other securities.   It would perform the clearance and settlement function for all transactions in its home-market securities when at least one of the counterparties is a participant in its system.   It would perform the same function for transactions between two of its participants in all other securities.

The global hub would perform all clearance and settlement functions for all transactions between the various CSDs and ICSDs.   It would maintain cash and securities accounts for each CSD (but not their participants), and effect transfers in all securities through its own electronic records.

In contrast to an ICSD, the global hub would not have any participants except for other CSDs.

.   .   .

Figure 5. Global Hub Model

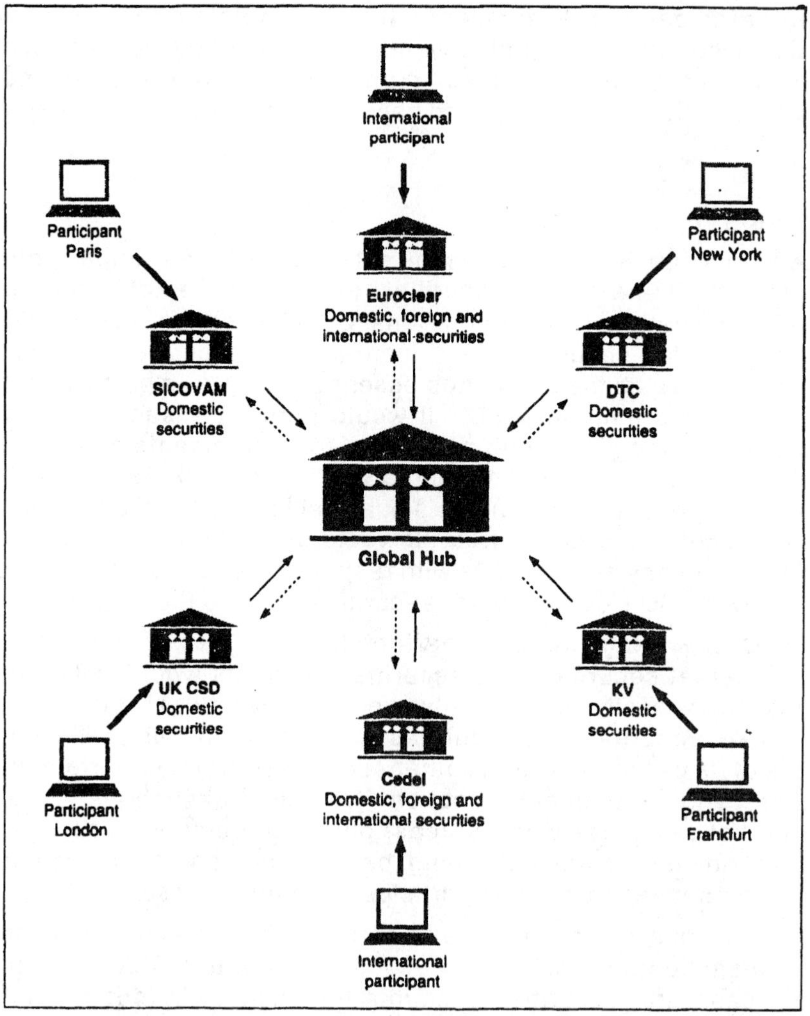

Each participant has a securities account with its home CSD for all home-market securities and all other-market securities accessible through the Global Hub.

Home-market Link: Global Hub has securities accounts with the home CSD reflecting its positions in home-market securities held for other CSDs. This allows the Global Hub to settle transactions between participants of the home CSD and other CSDs.

Other-market Link: home CSD has securities accounts with the Global Hub reflecting its positions in other-market securities. This allows its participants to settle transactions with participants of all other CSDs.

Bilateral Links

Description

The bilateral links model assumes the establishment of both "home-market" and "other-market" links between each pair of existing national or international CSDs. (See Figure 7). Each CSD would continue to perform the safekeeping functions for all home securities, maintain cash and securities accounts for each of its participants (including each other), and perform the clearance and settlement functions for all transactions in its home securities, as well as in all other securities.

Figure 7. Bilateral Links Model

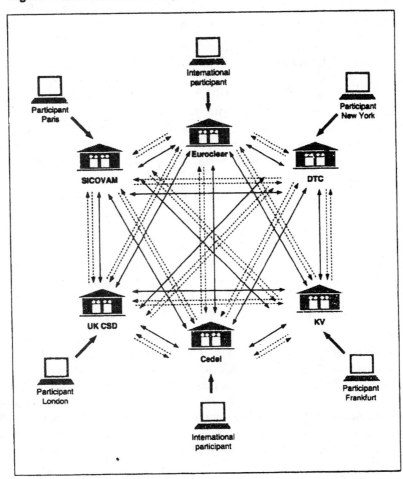

Each participant has a securities account with its home CSD for both home-market securities and all other securities accessible through its bilateral links.

Home-market Links: each CSD has securities accounts with each other CSD reflecting its positions in the other's home-market securities. These links allow each CSD to settle transactions between participants and those of the other CSD in the home-market securities of each CSD.

Other-market Link: each CSD has securities accounts with each other CSD reflecting its positions in third-market securities. This allows each CSD's participants to settle transactions with those of the other CSD in third-market securities.

. . .

Notes and Questions

1.   How would you appraise the costs and benefits of the existing Multiple-Access Model as compared with the various alternatives? For a study of the alternatives within the European context, see I. Giddy, A. Saunders, and I. Walter, *Alternative Models for Clearance and Settlement: The Case of the Single European Capital Market*, 28 Journal of Money, Credit, and Banking 986 (1996). How might the advent of the Euro affect clearing and settlement within Europe?

2.   In May 1999, Euroclear made a new proposal, *The Hub and spokes clearance and settlement model*, to establish a pan-European settlement system.   Under this proposal, Euroclear, the Hub, would continue to directly serve its global clients. National depositories, the Spokes, would no longer need to establish bilateral links, under the bilateral model proposed by the European Central Depositories Association, but would link to Euroclear, as under the Global Hub model discussed above, for cross-border trades. Euroclear as Hub to the Spokes, given its holding of cash accounts, would be able to provide DVP settlement which many securities depositories cannot do given that securities and cash transfers occur in two separate systems. What do you think of this proposal?

3.   Could clearinghouses in different countries coordinate their activities to reduce risk?   Could they share information?   Could they establish a common collateral pool? Is there any way they could work together to net off transactions in one clearinghouse against those in another? This would probably be difficult given different time zones. We will revisit this question when we come to the Barings case in the next Chapter.

Within the same time zone, there are moves one can make, as illustrated by current DTC–NSCC arrangements. DTC settles institutional trades and NSCC settles retail trades from the same exchange. There are two parts to the process: (1) 2:45 p.m. NSCC pays DTC on behalf of common clearing members that are owed a payment by NSCC and owe a payment to DTC, and (2) 4:00 p.m. DTC pays NSCC on behalf of common clearing members that are owed a payment by DTC and owe a payment to NSCC.

An Example: Participants' Net Positions

	DTC	**NSCC**	**Net**
Salomon	−100	+400	+300
Goldman	−200	+100	−100
Morgan	+100	−300	−200
Merrill	+600	−200	+400

(1) NSCC pays off DTC positions of Solly and Goldman: (−300); pays Solly 300, gets 100 from Goldman.

(2) DTC pays off NSCC positions of Morgan and Merrill: (−500); gets 200 from Morgan and pays Merrill 400.

(3) The NSCC and DTC positions do not net to zero because there are additional transactors.

Along the same lines, clearinghouses within the United States for mortgage, government and equity securities, have asked the SEC for approval to arrange cross-guarantee agreements. The agreements would allow one clearing corporation, after its claims against a defaulting broker have been satisfied, to release remaining funds in that broker's account for transfer to another clearinghouse facing a shortfall. Of course, this would prevent the collateral from going to the estate of the bankrupt firm for the benefit of other creditors. G. Wisz, *Clearing Corporations Seek Cross-Guarantee Approvals,* 7 Securities Industry News (August 12, 1996). It has taken some time for the clearinghouses to reach agreement on exactly how to share collateral, particularly where there is excess, but agreement was reported in April 1997. G. Wisz, *Agreement to Share Excess Unblocks Cross-Collateral Plan*, Security Industry News (April 7, 1997).

Links to Other Chapters

Clearance and settlement is an important aspect of all domestic securities markets (see Chapters 2 and 8), and is a key term of competition among those markets, as we saw in Chapter 14 on Stock Market Competition, and as we shall see again in Chapter 20 on Emerging Markets. A clearance and settlement system (for example, Euroclear) is also necessary for Eurosecurities like Eurobonds (Chapter 12). It must work hand in hand with national payments systems (Chapter 10). We will also see that the clearance and settlement systems for exchange traded derivatives (Chapter 16) are different in important respects from those for the underlying securities.

CHAPTER SIXTEEN

DERIVATIVES: FUTURES AND OPTIONS

A. INTRODUCTION

Derivatives are financial instruments whose value is based on or derived from other assets or variables. Futures and options are among the best known. A futures contract is an agreement to buy or sell an asset at a set time in the future for a set price. Two types of options exist. A call option gives the holder the right to buy an asset by a set date for a set price. A put option gives the holder the right to sell an asset by a set date for a set price.

Today financial futures and options markets span the globe. The underlying asset may be a deposit in a major currency, a bond issued by a major government, equity in a firm, or an index of a leading stock market. The exchanges that create and trade the contracts are scattered about the world. The players hale from many countries.

The markets have a long pedigree. Futures markets began hundreds of years ago, giving farmers and traders firm prices for crops well before harvest. U.S. futures exchanges opened during the mid–1800s. Options markets appeared in Europe and America in the 1700s, but not until the early 1900s was an exchange-like association set up. The Chicago Board of Exchange opened the first options exchange in 1973.

This Chapter examines the international financial futures and options markets. It proceeds with an introduction to futures and options, concentrating on their underlying theory, the mechanics of their trading, and the reasons behind their use. The second part of the Chapter links this descriptive foundation to a case study involving the collapse of Barings Bank. Overall, the chapter helps to sketch the risks users of derivative products encounter and the tools available to governments and exchanges to manage these risks. Thus, it is important that as you read this Chapter you pay particular attention to the risks presented by futures and options and ask which of these regulators can curtail.

B. FUTURES, OPTIONS, THEIR MARKETS: AN INTRODUCTION

1. FUTURES

Futures exist for many different types of assets. For example, there are futures contracts on wheat, on Treasury Bills, stock indices, like the FTSE 100, and even shares in individual companies. Hedgers and speculators are the two basic types of investors in futures. Hedgers are people who use futures contracts to offset their risks in regard to a particular asset. Speculators, on the other hand, buy and sell futures contracts with the sole goal of earning a profit. They usually base their decisions on their perceived sense of the price movement of the underlying asset in the contract.

This chapter mainly concentrates on a subset of futures contracts known as financial futures and, even more specifically, on interest rate futures. The following description of financial and interest rate futures is from A. Buckley, Multinational Finance 257 (1996):

> A financial futures contract is an agreement to buy or sell a standard quantity of a specific financial instrument at a future date and at a price agreed between the parties through...an organized financial futures exchange...

> Someone who buys an interest rate future has the right and obligation to deposit money to the nominal amount contracted for at a specified interest rate for a specified period with the seller. Someone who sells an interest rate future becomes available to take a deposit amounting to the nominal amount contracted at a specific rate of interest for a specific period of time.

The Chicago Mercantile Exchange has produced an account of some of the different kinds of interest rate futures available to investor. Chicago Mercantile Exchange, Using Interest Rate Futures and Options (1993):

> The 13–week U.S. Treasury bill futures contract is an agreement to buy or sell, at a given time in the future, a U.S. Treasury bill with 13 weeks to maturity and a face value of $1,000,000. The 3–month Eurodollar Time Deposit futures contract implies an agreement to place a deposit (lend) or to take a deposit (borrow), at a given time in the future, of $1,000,000 in Eurodollars for 3 months in the London Interbank Market. The One–Month LIBOR futures contract implies an agreement to place a deposit or to take a deposit of $3,000,000 in Eurodollars for one month in the London Interbank Market.

> The CME's three-month euro Deutsche mark (also known as Euromark) futures and options are the Exchange's first non-dollar denominated short-term interest rate contracts. The Euromark futures contract calls for a 3–month deposit of Deutsche marks. The

contract size is DM 1,000,000. With the addition of Euromark contracts, the CME's interest rate complex offers investors a way to utilize short-term interest rate markets on both sides of the Atlantic.

All of these contracts are traded using a price index, which is derived by subtracting the interest rate from 100.00. For instance, an interest rate of 10.00 percent translates to an index price of 90.00. If interest rates move higher, the price of the contract falls; if rates move lower, the contract price rises.

2. OPTIONS

An option gives the buyer the right to take a futures position from the seller. A call option confers the right to buy the futures at an agreed exercise or strike price. A put option confers the right to sell at the strike price. Option positions and investment strategies can become quite complex. For simplicity, we draw on examples of stock options (not complicated by interest payments). American options can be exercised at any point. European options cannot be exercised before the expiration date. The following material is from J. Hull, Introduction to Futures and Options Markets 213-20 (1991) (Hull). As you read it, consider its implications for determining the riskiness of individual options and managing that risk.

Hull describes profit and loss opportunities available to parties to option contracts. "On one side is the investor who has taken the long position (i.e., has bought the option). On the other side is the investor who has taken a short position (i.e., has sold or written the option). The writer of an option receives cash up front but has potential liabilities later. His or her profit/loss is the reverse of that for the purchaser of the option." The following figures show the profit and loss to buyers (Figures 7.1 and 7.2) and writers (Figures 7.3 and 7.4) of a call and put option.

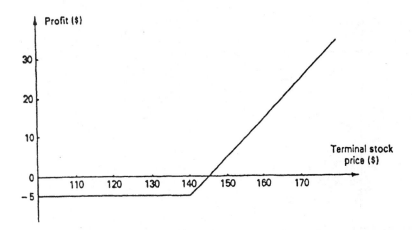

FIGURE 7.1   Profit from buying a European call option on one IBM share. Option price = $5, strike price = $140.

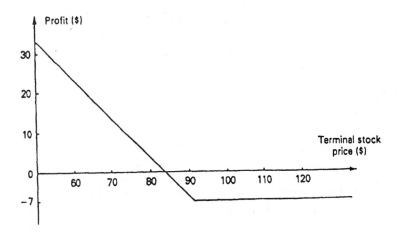

FIGURE 7.2   Profit from buying a European put option on one Exxon share. Option price = $7, strike price = $90.

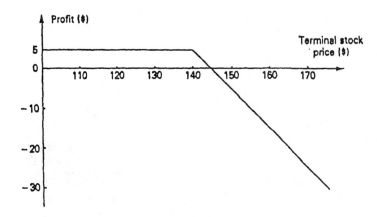

FIGURE 7.3   Profit from writing a European call option on one IBM share. Option price = $5, strike price = $140.

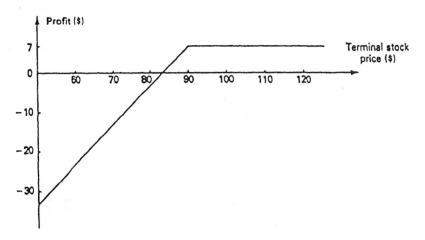

FIGURE 7.4   Profit from writing a European put option on one Exxon share. Option price = $7, strike price = $90.

Hull then describes four strategies involving a single option and the underlying stock. Focus on the protective put strategy (chart c and the elaborated version following this note). What is it? How do you interpret its profit curve? How does it compare to the normal long put curve? What happens with the protected put if at strike time the stock price is below the put strike price? Above the strike price? What does this profit curve resemble? Hull says:

> There are a number of different trading strategies involving a single option on a stock and the stock itself. The profits from these are illustrated in Figure 9.1. In this figure, and in other figures throughout this Chapter, the dashed line shows the relationship between profit and stock price for the individual securities constituting the portfolio, while the solid line shows the relationship between profit and stock price for the whole portfolio.
>
> In Figure 9.1a the portfolio consists of a long position in a stock plus a short position in a call option. The investment strategy represented by this portfolio is known as *writing a covered call*. This is because the long stock position "covers" or protects the investor from the possibility of a sharp rise in the stock price. In Figure 9.1b a short position in a stock is combined with a long position in a call option. This is the reverse of writing a covered call. In Figure 9.1c the investment strategy involves buying a put option on a stock and the stock itself. This is sometimes referred to as a *protective put strategy*. In Figure 9.1d a short position in a put option is combined with a short position in the stock. This is the reverse of a protective put.
>
> The alert reader will notice that the profit patterns in Figure 9.1a, b, c, and d have the same general shape as the profit patterns discussed [above] for short put, long put, long call, and short call, respectively. Put-call parity provides a way of understanding why this is so.

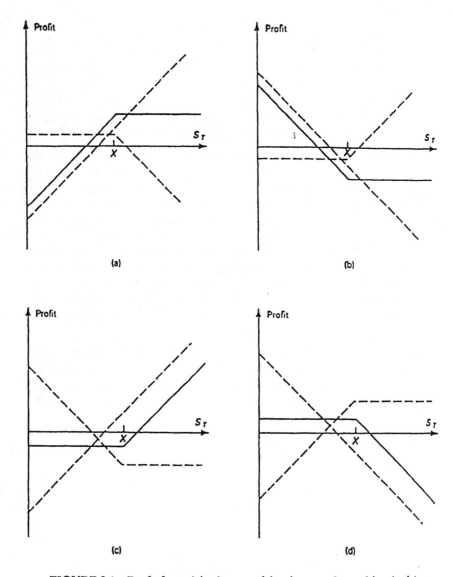

FIGURE 9.1   Profit from (a) a long position in a stock combined with a short position in a call, (b) a short position in a stock combined with a long position in a call, (c) a long position in a put combined with a long position in a stock, (d) a short position in a put combined with a short position in a stock.

The following chart elaborates the protective put in chart (c) above. The vertical axis is the profit on a position. Above point (b) the position runs a profit, below is a loss. The horizontal axis is the stock price, which increases to the right. The (x) represents the strike price. The (w) is basically the price at which the long stock was bought. The (z) is the cost of the put.

The dotted lines represent the profit and loss on two long positions. The straight diagonal sloping up to the right is the long stock, which becomes profitable when its market price exceeds the price at which it was bought, point (w). Two other items affect (w) (neither is separately calculated on the chart): any cost of funding the purchase of the stock reduces profit and any dividend received on the stock while it is held increases profit.

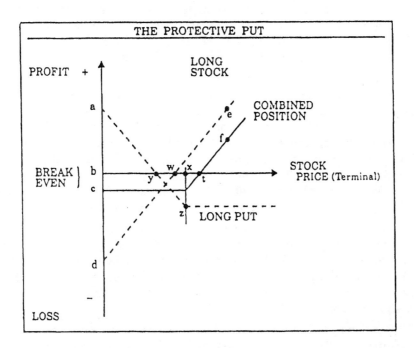

HOLD LONG STOCK AND LONG PUT IN THE STOCK

X = STRIKE PRICE

W = LONG STOCK PURCHASE PRICE

(X -> Y) = (X -> Z) = LONG PUT COST = (E -> F)

(B -> C) = (W -> Y) = LOSS ON LONG STOCK (B -> D) <u>LESS</u>

PROFIT ON PUT   (B -> A)

Put-call parity says that the current value of a call on a stock equals the current value of an associated put plus the current market price of the stock less the present value of the strike price. The relationship is most easily demonstrated with a European put and call on a stock that does not pay dividends, ignoring transactions costs, margins, and taxes. The idea is that if put and call prices are not in this parity, arbitrage is possible. One "could make a certain profit on zero investment by selling the relatively overpriced option and using the proceeds to buy the relatively underpriced option, together with an appropriate position in the stock and borrowing or lending .... The portfolio would require no cash outflow (or inflow) on the expiration date of the options." J.C. Cox and M. Rubenstein, Options Markets 39–44 (1985).

An example may help to illustrate this. Suppose you create two investment portfolios. For the first, you purchase a share of IBM for $50, and a put on IBM stock, with a strike price of $50 (the protective put strategy discussed, *supra*). At the same time, you make a second portfolio by buying a call option on a share of IBM, with an exercise price of $50. Additionally, you invest the present value of $50 in a savings account (so that on the exercise date you will have exactly $50).

Two outcomes on the exercise date are possible. IBM might be selling for more than $50. In the case of the first portfolio, you could sell your share for profit and discard the put. Likewise, in the second portfolio, you could take the $50 out of the bank account, exercise the call, and simultaneously sell the share back on the open market. In both cases, you will reap the exact same profit. On the other hand, IBM might be selling for less than $50. In the situation of the first portfolio, you will exercise your put and retain the $50. In the second portfolio, you will throw away the call, and hold onto the $50 from the savings account.

Under both outcomes, these portfolios have the same payoffs. Consequently, they should, theoretically, have the same price. Investors who engage in arbitrage look for differences among baskets of assets that should be priced equally. Thus, arbitrage is merely a way to make a profit by exploiting differences in the price of two portfolios that should have equivalent prices.

The options you mainly run into in this chapter are those on interest rate futures. The Chicago Mercantile Exchange has provided a description of the types of interest rate futures options available to the trader. See Chicago Mercantile Exchange, Using Interest Rate Futures and Options (1993):

A futures option contract confers the right from seller to buyer to take a futures position at a stated price. Two types of options are traded on the CME's Index and Option Market: calls and puts. Calls are the right to buy the futures at a predetermined "exercise" price. If the futures price rises above the exercise price, the calls will represent a bargain to the holder. Puts are the right to sell at that fixed price. If the futures price falls below the fixed exercise price, the puts give the holder the opportunity to sell the futures at an above-market price.

3. THE MARKETS

The Chicago Mercantile Exchange (CME) is one of over 75 futures and options exchanges around the world. Less than one-third are in the U.S. Many are in other industrial countries: the U.K. (8, including the London International Financial Futures Exchange—LIFFE), Japan (5, including the Tokyo International Financial Futures Exchange—TIFFE), Canada (5), Germany (originally, the Deutsche Terminborse—DTB, and then, in a joint venture with the Swiss exchange, Eurex), France (the Marche a Terme International de France—MATIF), and many other European countries. Exchanges exist in a few financial centers: the Hong Kong Futures Exchange Ltd and Singapore International Futures Exchange Ltd (SIMEX). A growing number of developing and transition countries have exchanges. For a discussion about whether emerging markets should develop futures and options exchanges, see G. Tsetsekos and P. Varangis, *Lessons in Structuring Derivatives Exchanges*, 15 World Bank Research Observer 85, 91, Feb. 2000 (Tsetsekos); and generally see K. Park and S. Schoenfeld, The Pacific Rim Futures and Options Markets (1992).

Most exchanges are owned by their members, but this is changing. In 2000, LIFFE opened to non-members and was later taken over. SIMEX merged with Singapore's Stock Exchange as the first step to selling shares to the public. CME plans to become a for-profit corporation. The Chicago Board of Trade (CBOT) planned to become a joint stock company with a subsidiary for electronic trading that would eventually be member-owned. The Sydney Futures Exchange, in Australia, planned to demutualize. C. Bowe, *CME Lays Out Demutualization Plan to Members*, Financial Times, Nov. 3, 1999; N. Tait, *CBOT Set to Vote on Move to Delaware*, Financial Times, June 28, 2000; W. el-Gabry, CBOT Revises Its Plans to Demutualise, Financial Times, Sep. 1, 2000; P. Montagnon and V. Marsh, *SFE in Modernisation Bid*, Financial Times, June 26, 2000.

As one of the largest exchanges ranked by trading volume, CME with the Chicago Board of Trade, accounted for 23% of worldwide futures and options trading in 1997, down from 38% in 1992. By 2000, in order of contracts traded during the year, Eurex was first, followed by CBOE and CBOT, MATIF, CME, Amex, Liffe, and KSE, the exchange in Korea. N. Tait, *Fierce Battle to Take Lead*, Financial Times, June 28, 2000.

CME formed in 1919 to trade futures, emerging from an exchange for agricultural commodities founded in 1874. It set up the International Monetary Market (IMM) in 1972 to trade foreign currency futures. Now it has over 600 general members and over 1000 IMM division members. Today, chicken and live hog futures and options trade alongside those in Yen and Swiss Franc, London's FT–SE 100 share index, Japan's Nikkei Stock average, and the S & P 500 index, among others.

The large U.S. exchanges still use open-outcry pits for trading, but are moving to electronic trading despite their statements that screens cannot beat the six seconds it takes human traders to close a trade. Getting to the floor, however, can take time. So even the big exchanges increasingly use screen trading at least for futures and options trading with low volumes or after hours. In this respect, the European exchanges lead those in the U.S. and the U.K. Eurex introduced an electronic governmental bond trading platform in 2000. The newer exchanges generally use electronic trading. See L. Morse, *CBOT Warming to the Computer*, Financial Times, Mar. 6, 1997; Tetsekos at 93.

Clearing mechanisms raise important issues for the markets. Should the clearing house be part of or separate from the exchange? Does it have the authority to impose and monitor margin and collection rules on all participants? We address this in the discussion of Barings. Should futures and securities exchanges each have their own clearing house or share one? In favor of sharing are scale economies that reduce cost, better information about the entire market, and easier monitoring by the regulators. Keeping them separate limits the bad effect of inadequate control by one clearing house. As discussed below, margin rules vary for the two types of markets. See Emerging Market Committee of the International Organization of Securities Commissions, Legal and Regulatory Framework for Exchange Traded Derivatives, June 1996.

Clearing mechanisms vary across countries. In Japan and France, for example, clearing is within the exchange. Most British exchanges use a separate entity, such as the London Clearing House Limited. In the U.S., futures clearing is closely associated with the exchange, either as a separate clearing house or, as for the CME, a department of the exchange. The clearing house monitors all transactions during a day to determine the net position of each member broker. Non-member brokers do business through members. In the U.S., the Options Clearing Corporation (OCC) issues and clears publicly offered options traded on the exchanges. The OCC is owned by five exchanges, including the New York Stock Exchange and the Chicago Board Options Exchange. Clearing houses are competing directly with the over-the-counter markets now. The London Clearing House (LCH) is expanding its clearance of swaps (see Chapter 17). N. Churikova, *LCH to Expand Swap Clearing*, Financial Times, Oct. 20, 2000.

Notional principal amounts outstanding are huge. The following table is from the Bank for International Settlements, 64th Annual Report 112 (1994) (BIS Annual Report); Bank for International Settlements, International Banking and Financial Market Developments (Feb. 1997 and Feb. 2000).

Markets for selected derivative instruments

Instruments	Notional principal outstanding							
	1988	1993	1996	1997	1998	1999	2000	2001
	in billions of US dollars							
Exchange-traded instruments	1,306.0	7,839.3	9,884.5	12,202.2	13,549.3	13,521.7	14,156.0	23,539.7
Interest rate:								
Futures	895.4	4,960.4	5,931.1	7,489.2	7,702.2	7,913.9	7,827.3	9,136.8
Options[1]	279.2	2,362.4	3,277.8	3,639.9	4,602.8	3,755.5	4,719.2	12,477.1
Currency:								
Futures	11.6	29.8	50.3	51.9	38.1	36.7	40.0	65.6
Options[1]	48.0	81.1	46.5	33.2	18.7	22.4	20.4	22.7
Stock market index								
Futures	27.8	119.2	198.6	211.5	321.0	334.3	366.5	294.6
Options[1]	44.0	286.4	380.2	776.5	866.5	1,458.9	1,182.5	1,542.9
Over-the-counter instruments[2]	--	7,076.9	24,292.0	--	--	--	--	--
Interest rate swaps	1,010.2	6,177.3	--	--	--	--	--	--
Currency swaps[3]	319.6	899.6	--	--	--	--	--	--
Other swap-related derivatives[4]	–	--	--	--	--	--	--	--

[1] Calls and puts. [2] Data collected by the International Swaps and Derivatives Association (ISDA) only; the two sides of contracts between ISDA members are reported once only; excluding instruments such as forward rate agreements, currency options, forward foreign exchange contracts and equity and commodity-related derivatives. [3] Adjusted for reporting of both currencies; including cross-currency interest rate swaps. [4] Caps, collars, floors and swaptions.

Sources: Futures Industry Association, various futures and options exchanges, ISDA and BIS calculations.

OTC data exclude forward rate agreements, OTC currency options, forward foreign exchange positions, equity swaps and warrants on equity. A detailed survey by the BIS of OTC foreign exchange, interest rate, equity and commodity derivative contracts outstanding on March 31, 1995 revealed a nominal value of $40.7 trillion after adjusting for double counting. Single currency interest rate contracts, mainly swaps, accounted for 65% (of which 35% was US dollar, 21% Yen, and 13% DM), FX products 32% (most involving the US dollar), and equity and commodity instruments 1% each. See Bank for International Settlements, International Banking and Financial Market Developments 53 (Feb. 1996).

Actual exposures are far less than the notional amounts. "The amount at risk through counterparty default, for example, represented on average on conventional assumptions between 2% and 4% of the contracts notional value." 32 Bank of England Quarterly Bulletin 402 (1992). For example, the 50 largest U.S. Bank Holding Companies reported a total notional value of $6.3 trillion at the end of December 1992. The replacement cost was merely 2.30% gross and 1.46% net, according to a report by the House Banking Committee minority staff on Financial Derivatives (Nov. 1993).

In the U.S., futures and options trading grew exponentially in the 1980s. From 10 million contracts in 1968 to 100 million in 1981, trading reached 360 million in 1992. Options only started to trade in 1982; since 1987, they accounted for about one-seventh of all trading. Non–U.S. trading rose from less than half the U.S. volume in 1986 to almost equal the U.S. in

1993, most as interest rate contracts. See Johnson and CFTC, October 1993. The CME's 3–month eurodollar future contract won the largest volume gains and was among the most traded contracts in the world during 1992. Then in 1995 growth fell in the U.S. and Europe. Contract volume dropped on the CME (down 11.4%), MATIF (23.92%), LIFFE (13.5%), CBOE (11.7%) and CBOT (4%). Enormous volume growth in Brazil (almost 50%) offset these declines in global counts, but the value of Brazilian contracts was small relative to much of Europe and the U.S. Explanations for the slowdown included a maturing industry worldwide, less interest rate volatility, and even the scandals. See Futures Industry 13 (February 1996). Growth recovered slightly in 1996 in the U.S. but not in Europe. Currency futures were reported to be too small and inefficient to compete with the OTC market run by banks. See S. McGee, *Why Are Currency Futures Languishing?*, Wall Street Journal, Apr. 10, 1995.

In 2001, the second leading exchange for futures and options, measured by volume of contracts, was Eurex. Following it were CME, CBOT, LIFFE, and Euronext. The leading exchange, however, was the Korea Stock Exchange, which had a small stock index contract that was very active. Futures Industry Association, *World Futures and Options Volume Up More Than 50 Percent in 2001*, News Release, Feb. 12, 2002.

Banks played a major role as buyers and sellers of futures and options. An analysis in 1992 revealed that banks took about one-third of short-term interest rate futures, and a quarter or less of futures for long-term interest, currency, and stock market indexes. They took from 45% to 55% of most types of call options and 30% to 50% of most types of put options. However, they had barely 1% to 12% of puts and calls on stock market indexes then. See International Monetary Fund, International Capital Markets, Part II, Table 9 (Aug., 1993). The big banks were the major players. In the U.S., the 10 largest BHCs held 95% of all BHC futures (and forwards), which had a notional value of $5.8 trillion on June 30, 1993, according to the Federal Reserve Board. They held 94% of the $2.2 trillion in options.

4. PROTECTING THE EXCHANGE: MARGIN RULES

The major tool used by exchanges to protect themselves are margin rules. This following describes the general approach to margining based on U.S. practice.

Margin rules generally. A key tool to affect trading and reduce risk is the margin rules and marking-to-market. Futures and options exchanges, supervised by their regulators, usually set margin rules for their brokers' transactions with them or with their clearinghouse and for the brokers' customers. The rules vary by country. A quantitative theoretical analysis concluded that margin rules will require the "right" amount of protection if the credit risk of the traders is transparent, but that when it is not transparent the rules will set higher standards if the cost of default is great and lower standards if it is small. T. Santos and

J. Scheinkman, *Competition Among Exchanges,* Center for Research in Security Prices Working Paper No. 514, Apr. 2000.

Margin rules for positions in stock. Suppose someone buys equity on the New York Stock Exchange. The Federal Reserve Board sets initial margin requirements. The Fed has such rules to protect the expansion of credit and the money supply. The buyer pays for part of the stock and gets a loan from the broker for the remainder of the cost until full payment is made. The broker holds the stock as security for the loan. The initial margin rules determine the amount of the loan by requiring a down payment as a percent of the stock's current market value. The Fed limits margin lending outside the U.S. For example, pursuant to Regulation T, the Fed lists foreign stocks that are eligible for margin lending by U.S. brokers and dealers in the same way as domestic stocks. See 12 CFR 224.1 and .2 (Jan. 1, 2000).

Some stock exchanges require adjustments after the initial margin; this is called a variation or maintenance margin. The Fed does not require it. The NYSE sets a minimum maintenance margin of 25% of the stock's current market value. If the customer's margin falls below that level as the stock price drops, the broker gives the customer a margin call to bring the margin up to the minimum. The purchased securities secure the loan, but since their value is volatile, they are marked to market daily.

The NYSE imposes maintenance margin requirements to protect its brokers. The securities secure the broker's loan to the customer, but their value is volatile. Daily marking to market and the minimum maintenance margin protect the brokers' loans. Brokers are not required to have margin accounts with their clearinghouses for stock operations.

If the initial margin were 50% and the stock's current market value were $5000, the customer must pay $2500 at purchase and the broker can only lend $2500. If the stock then fell in value to $2800, since the broker's loan was still $2500, the customer margin account would be only $300. But the maintenance margin is 25% of $2800 or $700. The customer pays the broker $400 on margin call to raise the margin account to $700.

Effective July 1, 1996, the Fed relaxed many restrictions on loans broker-dealers could make and security they can accept for margining. It acted to allow U.S. brokers to compete better in overseas markets and with those not subject to the rules. J. Wilke, *Fed Acts to Ease Many Regulations Affecting Margin,* Wall Street Journal, Apr. 25, 1996. But in early 2000, people testifying in Congress urged the Fed to raise margin requirements in order to counter what they saw as a bubble in asset prices on the U.S. exchanges.

Margin rules for customers' futures contracts. For customers' futures contracts, long and short positions are subject to margin rules. In the U.S., at the time of purchase, a customer buying a position pays an initial margin that is a share of today's cash future price. The amount is usually a small percentage and it varies depending on whether the position is a hedge or speculative and on the contract's variability. The customer may give cash or securities. No loan is made, since futures contracts take no initial payment. The maintenance margin is set daily against the current market value of the contract, which is marked to market daily. Any loss in value is deducted entirely from the margin account and any gain is added. This is called the variation. The broker passes the variation to the exchange, which in turn passes it to the broker on the other side of such a transaction, for the customer. The customer, who also has a margin account, can withdraw any amount above the initial margin. So any shift raises one margin account and lowers the other. Whenever a customer's margin account falls below the minimum maintenance level, the broker makes a margin call and the customer must return the margin deposit to its initial level. If the customer cannot meet a margin call and its margin account is insufficient to offset the decline in the contract's market value, the broker is obliged to pay the exchange any shortfall, on most exchanges in the US and Europe.

Margin rules for brokers' futures contracts. A member broker (or clearing member) has many customer accounts as well as its own proprietary accounts. Futures exchange clearing houses set margins for member brokers' futures contracts. The clearing house usually calculates gains or losses on each broker's total long positions and on its total short positions in each contract at the end of the trading day. Some net the sums, offsetting gains in short (or long) against losses in long (or short). Some rules gross them, adding both. The clearing house then adjusts the broker's clearing margin account for each contract by the gain or loss and the broker tops up or withdraws funds as appropriate.

Clearing houses protect themselves with more elaborate use of margin rules. U.S. futures clearing houses use "simulation analysis and ... pricing theory to measure the potential risk of one-day price moves to a specified level of probability." They adjust the methodologies "periodically to reflect changes in implied volatility." This form of risk simulation extends to surveillance. See CFTC October 1993. Clearing houses make "super" margin calls if a customer or proprietary position could endanger a member's capital and the member must post it within one hour. They require members to use settlement banks to make margin payments; if the settlement banks cannot advance the payment needed, the member will fall back on prearranged credit from other banks. So banks do their own credit check on members.

Margin rules for options. Margining for calls is described in the following excerpt from Hull, 179–81.

> When call and put options are purchased, the option price must be paid in full. Investors are not allowed to buy options on margin. This is because options already contain substantial leverage. Buying on margin would raise this leverage to an unacceptable level.

When an investor writes options, he or she is required to maintain funds in a margin account. This is because the investor's broker and the exchange want to be satisfied that the investor will not default if the option is exercised. The size of the margin required depends on the circumstances.

Writing Naked Options

Consider first the situation where the option is naked. This means that the option position is not combined with an offsetting position in the underlying stock. If the option is in the money, the initial margin is 30% of the value of the stocks underlying the option plus the amount by which the option is in the money. If the option is out of the money, the initial margin is 30% of the value of the stocks underlying the option minus the amount by which the option is out of the money. The option price received by the writer can be used to partially fulfill this margin requirement.

Example

An investor writes four naked call option contracts [with 100 shares per contract]. The option price is $5, the strike price is $40 and the stock price is $42. The first part of the margin requirement is 30% of $42 × 400 or $5,040. The option is $2 in the money. The second part of the margin requirement is therefore $2 × 400 or $800. The price received for the option contracts is $5 × 400 or $2,000. The additional margin required is therefore

$$\$5,040 + \$800 - \$2,000 = \$3,840$$

Note that if the option had been a put, it would be $2 out of the money and the additional margin requirement would be

$$\$5,040 - \$800 - \$2,000 = \$2,240$$

A calculation similar to the initial margin calculation is repeated every day. Funds can be withdrawn from the margin account when the calculation indicates that the margin required is less than the current balance in the margin account. When the calculation indicates that a significantly greater margin is required, a margin call will be made.

Writing Covered Calls

Writing covered calls involves writing call options when the shares that might have to be delivered are already owned. Covered calls are far less risky than naked calls since the worst that can happen is that the investor is required to sell shares already owned at below their market value. If covered call options are out of the money, no margin is required. The shares owned can be purchased using a margin account as described above, and the price received for the option can be used to partially fulfill this margin requirement. If the options are in the money, no margin is required for the options. However, the extent to which the shares can be margined is reduced by the extent to which the option is in the money.

Example

An investor decides to buy 200 shares of a certain stock on margin and to write 2 call option contracts on the stock. The stock price is $63, the strike price is $60 and the price of the option is $7. The margin account allows the investor to borrow 50% of the price of the stock less the amount by which the option is in the money. In this case, the option is $3 in the money so that the investor is able to borrow

$$0.5 \times \$63 \times 200 - \$3 \times 200 = \$5,700$$

The investor is also able to use the price received for the option, $7 × 200 or $1,400, to finance the purchase of the shares. The shares cost $63 × 200 = $12,600. The minimum cash initially required from the investor for his or her trades is therefore

$$\$12,600 - \$5,700 - \$1,400 = \$5,500$$

The Options Clearing Corporation (OCC) performs much the same sort of function for options markets as the Clearinghouse does for futures markets.

It guarantees that the option writer will fulfill his or her obligations under the terms of the option contract and keeps a record of all long and short positions. The OCC has a number of members, and all option trades must be cleared through a member. If a brokerage house is not itself a member of an exchange's OCC, it must arrange to clear its trades with a member. Members are required to have a certain minimum amount of capital and to contribute to a special fund that can be used if any member defaults on an option obligation.

When purchasing an option, the buyer must pay for it in full by the morning of the next business day. These funds are deposited with the OCC. The writer of the option maintains a margin account with his or her broker as described earlier. The broker maintains a margin account with the OCC member that clears its trades. The OCC member, in turn, maintains a margin account with the OCC. The margin requirements described in the previous section are the margin requirements imposed by the OCC on its members. A brokerage house may require higher margins from its clients. However, it cannot require lower margins.

Exercising an Option

When an investor wishes to exercise an option, the investor notifies his or her broker. The broker in turn notifies the OCC member that clears its trades. This member then places an exercise order with the OCC. The OCC randomly selects a member with an outstanding short position in the same option. The member using a procedure established in advance selects a particular investor who has written the option. If the option is a call, this investor is required to sell stock at the strike price. If it is a put, the investor is required to buy stock at the strike price. The investor is said to be *assigned*. When an option is exercised, the open interest goes down by one.

At the expiration of the option, all in-the-money options should be exercised unless the transactions costs are so high as to wipe out the payoff from the option. Some brokerage firms will automatically exercise options for their clients at expiration when it is in their clients' interest to do so. The OCC automatically exercises stock options owned by individuals that are in the money by more than $0.75 and stock options owned by institutions that are in the money by more than $0.25.

Cross margining. Cross margining programs permit the Options Clearing Corporation and a clearer of futures to "calculate and collect a single clearing system margin requirement ... based upon each participating member's total portfolio of offsetting options, futures, and options on futures." Some of a member's customers would have accounts that were not part of the cross-margining system. In a member's bankruptcy, it was necessary to ensure that those customers' margins would not be used for losses on positions subject to cross-margining. The CFTC wrote special rules to protect these customers. See Regulatory Activities Report 23. In 2000, CBOT and Eurex considered cross-margining.

Margin rules based on forecast price movements. A more sophisticated approach to margining uses portfolio analysis to estimate the risk of the investor's full range of securities. A system common to many of the larger exchanges is called SPAN. LIFFE used SPAN, and when LIFFE and the London Traded Options Market merged in March 1992, the LIFFE margining rules extended to options as described below. SIMEX also uses SPAN. SPAN assesses risk more precisely by taking an overall view of the trader's portfolio. See R. Waters, *Options Market Adopts Revised Margining Regime*, Financial Times, Mar. 24, 1992.

Notes and Questions

1. For margin rules for customers' futures contracts:

(a) Why use the futures' current market value? Why not use the current market value of the underlying asset?

(b) Work through the following example. Long Customer buys a long futures contract for $5000. The exchange sets the initial margin at 5% or $250. The maintenance level is 75% of the initial margin. If on the following day the current market value of the contract is $4900, the margin account of the Long Customer is only $150, below the maintenance level of $188. The broker gives a margin call for $100 to return the margin to its initial $250 level. The margin account of a Short Customer is increased by $100. If the current market value had fallen only $50, the margin account of the Long Customer would be reduced by that $50 but there would be no margin call. The Short Customer would receive $50 more in its margin account as a variation payment, which it could withdraw. The exchange is not exposed; the debit to the Long Customer's account funds the credit to the Short Customer's account.

(1) What is the role of the brokers for each customer?

(2) What is the role of the exchange?

(c) How do margin rules for futures differ from the margin rules for someone who buys stock long? Does the initial margin have the same function? What would explain why the maintenance margins are treated differently?

2.   For margin rules for brokers' futures contracts:

(a) Which is more important to mitigate systemic risk, individual customer margins with the broker or member margins with the exchange? As long as a member can meet its margin calls, is the exchange protected?

(b) Is it good policy to calculate positions and margin requirements at the end of the day? LIFFE, through the London Clearing House, CBOT, and CME make at least one intra-day assessment. SIMEX had the authority but rarely used it with Baring Futures (Singapore), the entity managed by Nicholas Leeson.

(c) Rules governing the treatment of a broker's proprietary accounts and its customers' accounts vary. Most exchanges require the broker to differentiate between them. SIMEX required separation, while OSE combined the accounts. LIFFE requires differentiation if the broker itself segregates the customers. Germany's DTB requires differentiation. If the broker defaults, LIFFE prohibits set-off between proprietary and customer accounts, while DTB merges all accounts. Why would LIFFE and DTB differ as to set-off between customer and proprietary accounts?

(d) In addition are other ways to defend the exchange/clearing house and the system. The Clearing House can:

— set net capital rules for each member;

— if a member defaults, transfer the customer accounts to other members.

— if a member defaults, "liquidate the member's positions and original margins, sell his exchange membership, use his contributions to the clearinghouse guarantee fund and its committed lines of credit, assess all clearing members, where permissible, and finally, use the clearinghouse's capital." See Office of Technology Assessment, Electronic Bulls and Bears (1990).

(e) How are the many different types of margin rules that one finds on exchanges likely to affect competition and cooperative ventures among exchanges?

(f) Overall, what is the purpose of the margin rules for futures contracts?

(g) Congress authorized the Federal Reserve Board to set margins for stock index futures in the Futures Trading Practices Act of 1992 and the Fed delegated that authority to the CFTC in March 1993. The SEC regulates margins for options on stock indexes. See Regulatory Activities Report.

3. For margin rules for options:

(a) What is the rule for buyers of calls? What protects against the risk that the buyer cannot come up with the strike price when it exercises the call? Note that not all exchanges follow this practice. LIFFE options buyers do not have to pay up front, but must hold margin accounts. Why would LIFFE have such a rule?

(b) For a seller of a naked call that is out of the money, assume a stock price of $5000, a strike price of $5500, an option price of $600, and a 30% initial margin requirement. The margin would be $400. What is the rationale?

(c) For a seller of a naked call that is in the money, assume a stock price of $6000, a strike price of $5500, an option price of $600, and a 30% initial margin requirement. The margin owed is $1700. What is the rationale for treating this transaction differently from the out of the money option?

(d) hat is the rationale for the margin rules governing sellers of covered calls?

(e) Why do margin rules for options differ from those for futures?

C. THE MECHANICS AND USE OF INTEREST-RATE FUTURES AND OPTIONS BASED ON THEM

Exchanges attract potential investors by describing their contracts. Selections from the CME brochure "Using Interest Rate Futures and Options," cited *supra*, follows. As you read it, remember it is a marketing tool. Identify the risks in these markets.

CHICAGO MERCANTILE EXCHANGE, USING INTEREST RATE
FUTURES AND OPTIONS
(1993).

INTRODUCTION

The Chicago Mercantile Exchange (CME) introduced the trading of financial futures in 1972. Since then the value of futures in transferring financial risk has been widely recognized and financial futures trading has experienced explosive growth.

The first financial futures were currency contracts. In 1976 the CME introduced the 13–week Treasury bill futures contract, the first interest rate futures contract based on a money-market instrument. Its success indicated the need to transfer short-term interest rate risk. In 1981 the CME initiated trading in another futures contract, based on three-month Eurodollar time deposits. In 1990, a contract based on one-month Eurodollar time deposits was introduced, the One–Month LIBOR futures contract.

In 1984, Eurodollar futures contracts, identical to those traded on the CME, began trading at the Singapore International Monetary Exchange (SIMEX). Under a linked clearing program, the Mutual Offset System, Eurodollar futures can be traded on one exchange and held or liquidated at the other. Since SIMEX is open when the CME is closed, this allows traders to have access to an extended trading day.

Options on Eurodollar futures were introduced in 1985, and options on Treasury bill futures were opened in 1986. Options, used separately or in combination with the futures, offer additional trading flexibilities and positioning choices.

. . .

Who Should Consider Interest Rate Contracts?

Banks, security dealers and other financial firms were the early users of financial futures and options for managing their interest rate exposures. Interest rate contracts are an obvious and effective risk management tool where uncertain interest income and expense are integral parts of a business.

Interest expense is, in fact, an important expense component in nearly any type of business. Interest rate volatility can have a major impact on any company's earnings and cash flows. Any firm with a substantial interest rate exposure—temporary or permanent—should investigate the risk-minimizing benefits financial futures and options can provide.

. . .

THE MONEY MARKET

. . .

Since the Eurodollar futures contract was introduced by the Chicago Mercantile Exchange in 1981, joining the Treasury bill futures contract, spreading between these two (the simultaneous purchase of one contract and sale of the other) has become increasingly popular.

The basic reason for trading the "TED" spread is to take action based upon an opinion of what will happen to the rate differential between the two instruments.

The TED spread represents a "quality play." One takes action on an opinion that, all else being equal, the gap between rates required for U.S. Treasury bills and rates required for Eurodollar time deposits will widen or narrow. As the gap in rates moves, so will the gap in the prices of the respective futures instruments. If the gap in rates widens, then the gap in prices will widen, and vice versa.

The LIBOR futures contract is identical to the Eurodollar contract except that it represents a one-month (versus three-month) London Interbank Offer Rate (LIBOR) on a $3,000,000 (versus $1,000,000) Eurodollar time deposit and settles monthly (versus quarterly).

In addition to providing more flexibility for financial managers, the LIBOR futures contract allows spreading against the Eurodollar futures (the "LED" spread) for a yield curve play and spreading against the T-bill futures (the "TEL" spread) for a combination quality and yield curve play.

Euromark futures and options offer the hedging, trading and arbitrage opportunities in Deutsche mark-denominated deposits (such as swaps, FRAs, caps, floors, etc.) that have been enjoyed for so long in dollar-based deposits by users of the CME's Eurodollar contracts. Among the many uses of the Euromark contracts are: hedging Euromark loans and deposits; hedging Euromark forward foreign exchange exposures and FRAs during U.S. trading hours; creating synthetic term rates for mark-denominated investments and borrowings; arbitraging with interbank deposits; and spreading with other CME futures contracts, such as Eurodollars and Deutsche marks.

THE MECHANICS OF FUTURES TRADING

Whereas trading in the money markets takes place over the telephone between dealers, interest rate futures trading occurs in an open outcry auction market, where all traders have equal access to the best price at the time of the trade. If interest rates move higher, the price of the contract falls; if rates move lower, the contract price rises. To protect against a rising interest rate, sell the futures contract (go short). If rates rise and the futures price falls, you can buy back the contract at a lower price, producing a profit on the transaction. Likewise, to protect against falling rates, buy the futures contract (go long). If rates fall and the futures price rises, you will be able to sell the contract at a higher price, producing a profit on the transaction.

. . .

Longs and Shorts

Before buying or selling a futures contract, you must open a trading account, depositing "initial margin" with a broker—either a cash deposit or another form of collateral. This margin serves as a good-faith deposit, guaranteeing performance. The price at which a buy or sell order is executed becomes the "entry" price, and at the end of trading on that day, the contract value is "marked-to-market." Your account balance is adjusted, reflecting the profit or loss based on the difference between the entry price and the "settlement" (or closing) price. This process continues for each day your position is open.

Because each futures contract covers $1 million face amount of three-month securities, each "basis point" (0.01) of price change is worth $25 (.01% $1,000,000 1/4 year = $25). Thus, if you took a long position, buying the contract at 91.05, and it settles at 91.20, you would be credited with a profit of 15 basis points $25 per point, or $375. If the price falls on the next day by 10 basis points, from 91.20 to 91.10, your account would then be debited with a loss of $250 for that day's trading. In other words, each day your contract position is marked to the new settlement price until you sell the same contract to close the position. At that time your position will be marked to the sale price.

If you sell a contract to open a short position, it works the same way, in reverse. If you short the contract at 91.05, and it settles at 91.20, your position would be debited with a loss of 15 basis points, or $375. The position would be "marked to market" daily until it is closed by buying an identical contract.

Profits that bring the brokerage account above the initial margin requirement can be withdrawn while a contract position is still open; but if daily losses cause the trading account to fall below a certain level (the "maintenance margin" level), further funds will be required to bring this account back to the initial margin level.

Futures Pricing

Although the cash and futures prices of a three-month security generally move in tandem, the price relationship between them, called the "basis," is affected by changes in the shape of the yield curve.

The futures price is directly related to the cash price of the *deliverable* security (for example, an already-issued one-year or six-month T-bill that will mature 91 days after the T-bill futures' first delivery day).[1] On the futures' delivery date, the futures contract becomes a cash position, so that the two prices are the same at that point. Prior to contract delivery, the futures price (yield) reflects the market price (yield) of the deliverable security, as well as the financing rate associated with holding the deliverable security until the contract delivery date.

If the short date financing rate is higher than the yield on the deliverable security, there is a cost of carrying the deliverable; and the

---

[1] Although Eurodollar Time Deposits are not transferable, market participants can generally place or take deposits for any date, so that the same pricing mechanism is in place.

yield implied by the futures price would tend to be lower than the deliverable's yield. Conversely, if the financing rate is lower than the deliverable's yield, there is a profit from carrying the deliverable, and the futures yield will have to be higher.

As the futures' delivery date approaches, the effects of yield curve changes on the futures price become smaller, until the futures, the deliverable and the current three-month security all become identical and thus assume the same price on the futures' expiration day.

Delivery

Although relatively few contract position holders ever take or make actual delivery of securities, the integrity of the contracts rests heavily on the Exchange's ability to provide an accurate, timely transfer when called upon to do so.

Eurodollar time deposits--since time deposits are not transferable, "delivery" is actually a cash settlement. The full contract value is not exchanged; rather, the long and short positions are simply marked to a price dictated by the cash market. More precisely, the settlement price of the futures is determined by an authoritative Exchange poll on the final contract trading day. The cash market offered rate for 3-month Eurodollar Time Deposits (the London Interbank Offered Rate, or LIBOR) is deducted from 100 to determine the final contract settlement price.

. . .

THE MECHANICS OF OPTIONS TRADING

Taking a position on a T-Bill or Eurodollar rate by buying a call or a put option requires no margin. The price paid for the option is the absolute limit of the buyer's risk; margin security is therefore unnecessary.

As an option buyer, you have the right, but not the obligation, to take a position in the underlying futures contract.[1] The decision whether to enter the futures market is entirely up to you, the option holder. Rather than "exercising" the option, you may re-sell it in the market, or simply let the option expire if it has no value.

Buying a call option gives you the right to take a long position in the underlying (same contract month as the option) futures at a specific price—the strike or exercise price. If the futures price rises (interest rate falls), the price of the call will tend to rise. The call's *likelihood* of profit increases, and therefore its price rises.

---

[1] Upon taking a futures position, a margin deposit will be required.

Buying a put option gives you the right to take a short futures position at a specific strike price. If the futures price falls (the interest rate rises), the price of the put will tend to rise. As the futures price falls, the probability increases that the put will bring a short futures position at a profit.

The option "writer," who sells the option to *open* a position, assumes the obligation of taking a futures position opposite to the option holder, if the option is exercised. The call writer stands ready to take a short futures position. The put writer stands ready to take a long futures position.[2]

The option writer sells the right to exercise in order to earn the option price with the passage of time and no movement or adverse movement in the futures price. Such a position carries unlimited risk, but can be liquidated at any time before expiration by buying the same option. Many option writers limit their risks by writing the option against an opposite futures, cash or option position. This enables any loss on the written option to be offset by profit from the other position.

Strike Prices

The strike price of an interest rate option is the price at which you would take a futures position upon exercise. The strike prices that currently are listed for trading are at every 25 basis points for the options on T-bills and Eurodollars.

As is the case with the futures contracts, trading for option contracts is on the March–June–September–December cycle. On the first day of trading for options in a new contract month, exercise prices for puts and calls will be listed above and below the settlement price of the underlying futures contract.

Each strike price and month represents a distinct option contract, just as puts and calls are distinct. For example, to offset a long March T-bill 93.00 call position, only the *sale* of that same call will do.

After the first day of trading, new exercise prices for puts and calls will be created based on the upward and downward movement of the underlying futures contract.

Option Prices

To simplify trading, option prices (or premiums) are quoted in terms of index points rather than a dollar value. Since the futures price, the option price and the strike price are quoted in the same terms, the price relationships are very evident. The dollar value of a T-bill or Eurodollar option price is equal to the quoted index price times $2,500. For

---

[2] The writer of an option is required to post a margin deposit when the position is opened. The amount of margin required is recalculated daily until the option position is closed. The writer of an option must post margin because it is the writer who must stand ready to take a futures position at an unfavorable price at any time before the position is closed.

example, an option quoted at 1.23 would cost $3,075 (1.23 $2500). One option covers one futures contract and, like the futures contract, has a minimum price change of .01 index points, equal to $25.

The price of an interest rate option is directly related to the underlying futures price, rather than to the current cash market interest rate. The option price is shaped by the following three factors.

1. Relationship of the Strike Price of the Option to the Current Underlying Futures Price

If the current futures price is higher than a call's strike price, the call is said to be "in-the-money." If the call holder exercises it today, he takes a long futures position at the strike price. The difference between the futures price and the strike price is the amount he will be credited, and is termed the option's "intrinsic value."

Similarly, if the futures price is lower than the strike price of a put, that put is "in-the-money." The exercise of an in-the-money put results in a sale of the futures at an above-market price.

In general, the greater an option's intrinsic value, the higher that option's price. If the option is "out-of-the-money" (currently has no intrinsic value because the futures price is lower than the call's strike or higher than the put's strike), the more out-of-the-money it is, the lower the option price.

2. Time

The more time that remains until an option's expiration, the higher the premium tends to be. The longer time period provides more opportunity for the underlying futures price to move to a point where the purchase or sale of the futures at the strike price becomes profitable. Therefore, an option with six months remaining until expiration will have a higher price than an option with the same strike price/futures price relationship and with only three months until expiration. The time component of an option's value tends to be largest when the underlying futures contract is trading near the exercise price of the option—that is, when an option is "at-the-money."

An option is a wasting asset. As the option approaches its maturity, the time value declines to zero. At expiration, the option's value is only its in-the-money amount.

3. Volatility

The more the futures price tends to fluctuate, the higher the potential profit on the option. *Volatility* is a measure of the degree of fluctuation in the futures price. More specifically in the case of options on the T-bill and Eurodollar futures, volatility is a measure of the degree of fluctuation in the *rate implied* by the futures contract price. If volatility increases, with all else remaining the same, the option price will rise; and if it declines, the option price will fall.

There are a number of different measures of volatility. The following exhibit, for instance, illustrates the two most common measures: historical volatility is based on the *futures* contracts' price movements over a specific time period in the past. In contrast, the implied volatility is a measure of variability "implied" by a given option's price. It is the volatility underlying each of the options prices determined by the marketplace.

The "Delta Factor"

How will the changing price of an option relate to changes in the price of the underlying futures contract? The relationship is usually not one-for-one. A price change in the futures will usually result in a smaller change in the option's price.

The option's potential is related to the time remaining and to the futures' volatility, as well as to the futures price. The option's price consists of intrinsic value, if any, and time value. The greater the intrinsic value portion of the option price, the more responsive it will be to a changing futures price. On the other hand, the more time value makes up the option price, the less responsive it will be to a changing futures price. The price-change relationship between the option and the underlying futures is summarized in what option theorists call the "delta factor."

The delta factor is a measurement drawn from the mathematical option pricing formula, and serves several purposes. Basically, it can be used to gauge the change in the option price for a given change in the futures price. For instance, if a call's delta is 50 percent, and the futures price rises quickly by 25 basis points, the call's price should rise by 12 or 13 basis points. If the futures fall, the delta will predict the loss in option value of similar magnitude.

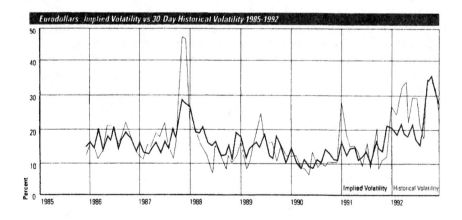

The table below lists hypothetical details for some calls with the futures price at 91.50, and with various lengths of time remaining until expiration. Notice the symmetry represented. Put deltas would have a very similar distribution if the strike prices across the top were reversed in order.

Hypothetical Call Deltas (with the futures price at 91.50)

call strikes:	90.50	91.25	91.50	91.75	92.50
time remaining:					
1 day	100%	96%	50%	4%	—
1 week 100%	75%	50%	25%	—	
1 month	90%	62%	50%	38%	10%
3 months	77%	57%	50%	43%	23%
6 months	70%	55%	50%	45%	30%
1 year	64%	54%	51%	47%	36%

The deltas can also be considered ratings of the probability that the option will expire in-the-money. If the 92.50–strike call is far out-of-the-money with the futures price at 91.50, it makes sense that as time to expiration diminishes, so does the delta. With only a week to expiration, a small futures price move would not attract many buyers to the call, so that call's price will not react. On the other hand, the 90.50–strike call is very likely to finish in-the-money with only a week to expiration. Even a small futures price change would reflect a change in the potential in-the-money amount at expiration, and, thus, the call's price varies nearly one-to-one with the futures.

The preceding table illustrates that deltas will vary with both changing futures prices and the passage of time. Deltas are also affected by changes in volatility. An increase in the futures' volatility would drive up the time value of the options, and consequently their prices. Higher time value would tend to drive up the out-of-the-money option deltas, and diminish the in-the-money deltas, leaving the at-the-money deltas nearly unaffected. A decrease in volatility would decrease the out-of-the-money deltas and increase the in-the-money deltas. The longer the time until expiration, the more effect a volatility change would have on the option prices and deltas.

Exercising Your Options

You may exercise an option on any business day the option is open for trading, including the day on which it is purchased. Exercise of a call results in a long futures contract at the call's exercise price, effective on the next trading day. Exercise of a put option results in a short futures contract at the put's exercise price. Your account would be credited the difference between the exercise price and the closing futures price, and you would be required to post futures margin. You could hold the futures position, or liquidate it immediately with an offsetting transaction.

You would want to exercise the call only if the current futures price is higher than the call's exercise price, and exercise the put only if the current futures price is lower than the put's exercise price. Further, you would normally exercise an option prior to the expiration day only if it is very deep in-the-money. If the option carries any time value in addition to its intrinsic value, you could profit more by selling the option and directly entering a futures position.

At expiration, an option has no remaining time value, so you probably would exercise any open in-the-money option contracts. Exercise of a T-bill option on expiration day results in a futures position that will have two to four weeks of trading life remaining. On the other hand, Eurodollar option exercise on expiration day results in a cash settlement instead of a futures position. Since the Eurodollar options and futures expire on the same day and the futures are settled in cash, exercise of expiring in-the-money options results in a cash payment to the option holder of the final in-the-money amount. The CME Clearing House automatically exercises expiring in-the-money Eurodollar options. However, the T-bill option is not automatically exercised, since it involves depositing margin and taking a futures position.

. . .

HEDGING WITH INTEREST RATE FUTURES

The idea behind hedging with interest rate futures is to offset an existing interest rate risk. This offset is accomplished by maintaining an appropriate futures position that will generate profits to cover the losses associated with an adverse interest rate move. You should note that a properly constructed futures hedge will also generate losses that will offset the effects of a beneficial interest rate move. Consider these hedge examples:

Hedging a Forward Borrowing Rate

In late September, a corporate treasurer projects that cash flows will require a $1 million bank loan on December 15. The contractual loan rate will be 1 percent over the three-month Eurodollar rate (LIBOR) on that date. LIBOR is currently 9.25 percent. The December Eurodollar futures, which can be used to lock in the forward borrowing rate, are trading at 90.45, implying a forward Eurodollar rate of 9.55 percent (100.00–90.45). By selling one December Eurodollar futures contract, the corporate treasurer hopes to ensure a borrowing rate of 10.55 percent for the three-month period beginning December 15. This rate reflects the bank's 1 percent spread above the rate implied by the futures contract.

By December 15, the existing Eurodollar rate rises to 11.10 percent, and the December futures price declines to 89.00 (reflecting an 11 percent rate). As a result, the treasurer's interest payment to the bank is $30,250 for the quarter ($1,000,000 x 12.10 percent x 1/4 year). However, the decline in the futures price produces a profit on the short futures of $3,625 (that is, 90.45–89.00 x $2,500 or, more simply, 145 $25). Thus, the net interest expense for this quarter is $26,625 for an effective annual rate of 10.65 percent.

This example illustrates that the realized cost of funds may differ somewhat from the cost of funds anticipated at the time the hedge is initiated. The difference can be accounted for by the difference between the spot market LIBOR rate and the rate implied by the futures contract at the time the hedge is liquidated. The LIBOR rate was 10 basis points higher than the rate implied by the December futures contract on December 15, accounting for the 10 basis point differential between the anticipated and realized cost of funds. In this case, the difference worked against the hedger; but in other situations the difference may prove beneficial. In general, this hedging inaccuracy, called "basis risk," is minimized the closer the loan-pricing date is to the delivery date of the futures contract.

Modifying Maturities

Asset managers can lengthen the effective maturity of short-term investment assets by buying futures contracts, and shorten the effective maturity of those assets by selling futures contracts. Liability managers can achieve the same effects by doing the opposite, i.e., selling futures to lengthen their liabilities and buying futures to shorten them.

For either assets or liabilities, hedging serves as an alternative to restructuring the portfolio in the cash markets. The use of futures may be attractive when physical restructuring is not possible (e.g., term deposits cannot be bought back prior to their maturity dates). It may also be cheaper to use futures because (a) transaction costs in the futures market may be lower than those in cash markets, or (b) liquidity conditions in the cash market would result in substantial market penalties.

. . .

Cross Hedging to Establish Yields or Costs

The asset manager who knows that funds will be available for investment beginning on some forward date may buy futures to establish a rate of return for this investment. Also, the liability manager who plans for a forthcoming debt issuance can prearrange funding costs by selling interest rate futures. In either case, the manager may hedge even if his risk does not involve precisely the same instrument that underlies a futures contract.

. . .

Locking in a Funding Rate

Consider the case of a bank that funds itself with three-month Eurodollar Time Deposits at the London Interbank Offered Rate (LIBOR). This bank has a customer who wants a one-year fixed-rate loan of $10 million, with interest to be paid quarterly. At the time of the loan disbursement, the banker raises three-month funds at 12.55 percent; but he has to roll over this funding in three successive quarters. If he does not lock in a funding rate and interest rates rise, the loan could prove to be unprofitable.

The three quarterly refunding dates fall shortly before the next three Eurodollar futures contract expirations in March, June, and September. At the time the loan is taken down, the prices of these contracts are 86.81, 86.45, and 86.20, respectively. These prices correspond to yields of 13.19 percent, 13.55 percent and 13.80 percent. Coupled with the initial funding rate of 12.55 percent, the banker could lock in a cost of funds for the year equal to the average of these four rates (13.27 percent). He would sell 10 contracts for each expiration, reflecting the funding need of $10 million per quarter. Then, on the refinancing dates, the banker would take in three-month Eurodeposits and simultaneously liquidate the appropriate hedging contracts by buying them back. With the March refunding, the March contracts would be liquidated; June contracts would be liquidated in June; and September contracts would be liquidated in September.

As it turns out, the banker is able to re-fund at 14.55 percent, 14.30 percent and 11.30 percent for the respective quarters. The corresponding futures are liquidated at 85.42 (14.58 percent), 85.73 (14.27 percent), and 88.92 (11.08 percent). The overall results are presented in Exhibit 3.

Exhibit 3
Quarterly Eurodeposit costs
Qtr 1: $10 million .1255 1/4 = $313,750
Qtr 2: $10 million .1455 1/4 = $363,750
Qtr 3: $10 million .1430 1/4 = $357,500
Qtr 4: $10 million .1130 1/4 = $282,500
$1,317,500
Less the futures profits
Mar: 10 contracts (8681- 8542) $25 = $34,750
June: 10 contracts (8645- 8573) $25 = $18,000
Sep: 10 contracts (8620- 8892) $25 = -$68,000
$15,250
Net Interest Expense
$1,332,750
Effective Rate
13.33%

(Note that the September futures contracts resulted in a loss of $68,000. This caused the overall hedge to produce a net loss of $15,250, which must be added to the Euro-deposit costs to result in the net interest expense.)

The unhedged interest expense over the four quarters would have been 13.18 percent, lower, in fact, than the hedged expense.

However, the funding rate was quite volatile over the period and could have easily resulted in a loss on the loan program. It should be recognized that effective futures hedges materially lock in an interest rate, precluding both advantage and loss from rate movement.

Recall that the banker had expected to lock up funding at 13.27 percent. In fact, funds actually were acquired at 13.33 percent, or 6 basis points higher. This discrepancy occurred because of less-than-perfect convergence between the cash refunding rates and the futures liquidation rates. If the bank had funded at exactly the same rate as the futures liquidation rate, the target would have been achieved. In this case, however, the actual funding over the term of the loan was, on average, six basis points higher than the futures liquidation rates. Put another way, these basis adjustments adversely affected the performance.

The minimal difference between the target rate and the effective funding rate can be attributed to the fact that the refunding dates were quite close to the futures expiration dates. If the respective dates were further apart, the funding rates and the futures rates would not necessarily converge so closely.

This example of a one-year loan funded with three-month deposits is an example of a negative interest rate "gap"—that is, where shorter-term liabilities are funding a longer-term asset and rising interest rates will have an adverse impact. The same basic hedging approach can be followed to remedy an overall balance sheet maturity mismatch.

HEDGING WITH OPTIONS ON INTEREST RATE FUTURES

Whenever T-bill or Eurodollar futures can be used to lock-in a rate, options on futures can be substituted to guarantee a rate floor or ceiling. As an alternative to a long futures position, which predetermines a forward investment return for an asset, a call can be substituted. The call gives the right to buy the futures contract at a stated price. This provides a floor for the asset return while preserving the opportunity for better performance. On the other hand, instead of taking a short futures position to predetermine a liability rate, a put option can provide protection. The put gives the right to sell the futures at a stated price, providing a ceiling for the liability rate, while preserving the opportunity for a lower cost of funds.

The floor or ceiling rate provided by the option is determined by its strike price and the premium paid. The "strike yield" (simply 100 minus the option strike price) is adjusted to reflect the cost of the option. For example, suppose the following prices were observed:

Sep Eurodollar futures	91.74
Sep 91.50-strike call	.43
Sep 92.00-strike call	.18
Sep 91.50-strike put	.18
Sep 92.00-strike put	.42

Under these conditions, the user of the futures contract could lock-in a target rate of 8.26 percent (100.00–91.74)—an asset return if long or a liability cost if short. Subject to basis risk, this yield would be locked up regardless of whether market rates rise or fall over the hedge period.

Using the 91.50–strike call to hedge a floating-rate investment, a hedger could guarantee a minimum return of 8.50 percent for a cost of 43 basis points. In other words, the realized minimum return would be 8.07 percent as a worst case (8.50–.43).

If the rate falls below 8.50 percent, futures prices would rise and the call option would increase in value. The fallen investment rate on the asset would be supplemented by the profit on the call to ensure a minimum net return of 8.07 percent. On the other hand, if the rate rises above 8.50 percent, the option would be worthless at expiration, and the investor would simply lose the cost of the option and receive the higher market rate on the asset.

Using the 92.00–strike call, the investment hedger would establish a minimum return of 7.82 percent (100.00–92.00–.18). Why would someone use the 92.00–strike call rather than the 91.50 strike call, when the 91.50–strike call offers a higher minimum return? The question goes to an important tradeoff consideration.

While it is true that the 91.50–strike call provides a more attractive worst-case scenario, it does so for a larger up-front cost. The purchaser of the 91.50–strike call pays $1,075 for this protection ($25 x 43 basis points), while the cost of the 92.00–strike call is only $450 ($25 x 18 basis points).

Options offer a special advantage for hedging contingent liabilities or investments. If it is not certain whether funds will be needed or available, interest rate options can secure a rate at the least risk. If the contingency is eventually not realized, forward or futures hedging commitments could present sizable losses. The potential loss on long puts or calls, on the other hand, is limited to their purchase price, known in advance.

Creating a Cap–Rate Loan

Suppose a financial manager has access to funding at three-month LIBOR plus ¼ percent, and he wants to put a limit on how high this rate could rise by the time he will borrow in September. In effect, he wants insurance that will pay off if rates increase, but will not generate losses if rates fall. A Eurodollar put will serve this purpose.

At the time of the decision (July 1), three-month LIBOR is 8¾ percent, the September Eurodollar futures are trading at 90.60 (9.40 percent), and the 91.00–strike put is trading at .72. At these prices, this put provides a maximum cost of funds equal to 9.97 percent (100.00 - 91.00 + .72 + .25—where .25 reflects the ¼ percent spread above LIBOR).

When the put is purchased in July, the manager knows what he can expect in September. If LIBOR at that time were less than 9 percent, the put would expire worthless, and the manager would simply borrow at LIBOR plus ¼ percent. Of course, he would have to add the initial .72 cost of the put option to his total cost, but even with that expense it would never be higher than 9.97 percent (9.00 + .25 + .72).

In the event that LIBOR were to rise above 9 percent, the price of the futures contract would decline, and the put would have intrinsic value at its expiration equal to LIBOR minus 9.00 percent. Suppose for example, LIBOR were to rise to 11.50 percent at the expiration of this option contract. In this case, the cost of funds from the bank would be 11.75 percent (reflecting the ¼ percent spread) for an interest cost of $29,375 per million for the quarter ($1,000,000 .1175 ¼ year). The final value of the 91.00–strike put would be $6,250 ((91.00 - 88.50) $25). The profit on the put, $6,250 less its initial cost (72 bps. $25 = $1,800), would be deducted from the interest expense. Net interest expense would thus be $24,925 per million for the quarter (29,375 - 6,250 + 1,800). On an annualized basis, the effective rate is calculated:

$$\frac{24,925}{1,000,000} x \frac{360}{90} = 9.97\%$$

Importantly, this same rate would result, regardless of how high market rates rise.

.   .   .

The combination of calls and puts can take any form to suit any set of expectations and hedging goals. The choice of strike prices for calls and puts allows the manager to tighten or expand the re-investment range, or to tilt it in one direction or the other.

The preceding examples are based on the simplest buy-and-hold strategy in order to keep the exposition simple. Delta and other option-pricing parameters can be used to weight option positions and manage them. Further study also will yield several other option combinations that can be useful to the sophisticated trader.

CONCLUSION

Determining which hedging strategy is best—using futures or options—depends on the goals of the hedger. A futures contract essentially locks in a rate, making the holder indifferent to the way interest rates move. On the other hand, the hedger who buys an option is purchasing one-way protection with upside potential. In return for the price of the option, he receives compensation if adverse conditions evolve; but if good news develops, he is able to reap the benefits.

The choice of which instrument to use is really a judgement call, reflecting the probability of an adverse interest rate change, the potential damage of such a rate adjustment, and the cost of protection. In all likelihood, different choices will be made at different times, as conditions change. For that reason an understanding of both futures and options will provide managers with the greatest opportunity for effective risk management.

Questions

1. Be sure you understand the basic terms.

a. What is a future? What is a long position? A short position? What is a three-month Eurodollar time deposit futures contract? Who benefits if the contract price rises in the future? What is the effect of this contract if LIBOR rises or falls in the future?

b. What is an option? What is the difference between a call and a put? What is a writer of a put or call? What is the holder? Buyers take long positions. Sellers take short positions.

c. How is an option different from a future on the same instrument?

2. Who designs future and option contracts? What factors would shape the design?

3. What factors shape the pricing of a 3 month eurodollar future contract and an option on this contract? How is a $1 million futures contract priced?

a. If LIBOR was 7% on the expiration date, what would be the price of the contract then?

b. Assume that at the time a contract was purchased, the market expected LIBOR to be 5% two months later when the contract expired. What would the price of the contract have been at purchase?

c. On the facts in (a) and (b), what would be the dollar value of the change from purchase to expiration? Which party pays, buyer or seller? If a player expects interest rates to rise, does it want a long or short position?

d. How much is at risk with a $1 million eurodollar contract? How would operations in the eurodollar futures market affect the underlying cash market?

4. Who would buy or sell futures generally and the 3 month eurodollar contract specifically? Give examples of hedgers, arbitrageurs, and speculators using the eurodollar contracts.

5. Who would buy or write options on futures generally and on the 3 month eurodollar contract specifically? Give examples of hedgers, arbitrageurs, and speculators using the eurodollar contracts. How would a call buyer and a call writer react to the following

    a. Whether the strike price should be set high or low?

    b. Whether the exercise date is set sooner or later in the future?

    c. Whether the underlying value of the future rises or falls? Whether it is volatile?

    d. Whether interest rates rise or fall?

6. In 2001, eurodollar futures were the most actively traded contracts in the world. To support trading, the CME introduced block trading off the floor for institutional investors and rich individuals and six months later relaxed its rules, lowering the fee, increasing the number of contracts, increasing the contract minimum, and lengthening the reporting time to 15 minutes. *CME Amends Trading Rules for Eurodollar Futures, Options,* World Securities Law Report, June 2001, at 27.

D. FUTURES AND OPTIONS EXCHANGES: COMPETITION AND REGULATION

Futures and options exchanges compete to be the first to design popular new contracts, which tend to be more successful than "me too" contracts. To succeed, the contract requires "a large cash market, volatility, an active dealer community, the absence of a good cross-hedging vehicle, multiple applications for its use and a careful specification ...." J. Raybould, *London's Futures Exchanges,* City Research Project of London Business School, Sept. 1994, at 5-6 (Raybould).

Exchanges usually compete over different contracts. LIFFE, for example, offers many futures and options contracts; MATIF (France), Eurex (the German and Swiss futures exchanges), CME, and CBOT each offer competing contracts on at least one of five underlying securities. LIFFE, which introduced futures and options on the German government security (the bund), continued to dominate trading in them until 1997, when Eurex won out. Most exchanges depend on a major contract (Raybould 16). In 1999, more than 33% of the Eurex trading volume was futures on the German bund, for example. But Eurex is changing this by increasing its products based on equities. Finally, exchanges use their fees to compete. Despite a reluctance to raise fees, for example, both CBOT and CME have had to do so as the exchanges expand. V. Boland and N. Tait, *Eurex Tops CBOT on Futures,* Financial Times, Jan. 4, 2000; V. Boland, *Eurex Expands in Equity and Index Products,* Financial Times,

Apr. 5, 2001; C. Bowe, *Futures Exchange Members Pay the Price for Change*, Financial Times, Nov. 20, 2000.

Exchanges have different strategies. LIFFE is an example. When it found it very difficult to introduce new contracts, its growth strategy was to win new users (pension funds and retail buyers), to trade two more hours in order to overlap with the Chicago market, and link with other exchanges. Most of LIFFE's customers are European. Other European exchanges offer electronic trading; LIFFE had only floor trading until late 1998 (see section 2). Even this transition presented a business opportunity, as LIFFE decided to sell the technology it used in the switch to other exchanges. In 2000, LIFFE introduced futures on individual stocks, leading its competitors and pushing the U.S. exchanges to press for legislative changes that would allow them to do the same. V. Boland, LIFFE *Gets New Capital for Connect*, Financial Times, Nov. 21, 2000.

Links among exchanges in other time zones have been tried repeatedly but with limited success. CBOT considered an alliance with Eurex in mid-2000. CME and the Tokyo Stock Exchange discussed a link in the markets for fixed-income and equity derivatives. CME and the Spanish futures exchange (Meff) decided to launch a contract on the S&P 350 index of European countries. A. van Duyn, N. Tait, and D. Grass, *CBOT Cool on Eurex Merger Hint*, Financial times, Aug. 16, 2000; B. Rahman and N. Tait, *Tokyo SE and CME in Alliance Talks*, Financial Times, Oct. 18, 2000; N. Tait, *CME and Meff Plan European Stock Index Contracts*, May 16, 2001.

Options trading is generally much less than futures trading on European exchanges. Options volumes were less than 25% of futures volumes on the four UK exchanges, 37% on MATIF. Only on DTB did options volumes exceed futures, for a share of 135%. See Raybould 69.

The U.S. exchanges' share of the volume on world exchanges has declined, despite their many efforts to innovate. London's futures exchanges grew much faster from 1987 to 1993 than the five largest U.S. exchanges. Noting this trend, a U.S. government study concluded that this was not due to lack of competitiveness. New volume elsewhere met foreign needs for local risk management. But in 1999 Eurex, the German/Swiss futures exchange, claimed the largest trading volume of all exchanges, including the CBOT. See Secretary of the Treasury, Financial Market Coordination and Regulatory Activities to Reduce Risks in the Financial System in 1993 and 1994, at 32 (1994) (Regulatory Activities Report), V. Boland and N. Tait, *Eurex Tops CBOT on Futures*, Financial Times, Jan. 4, 2000.

The U.S. exchanges pressed their regulators to reduce the impact of regulation on them in order to increase their competitiveness. In the US., the Commodity Futures Trading Commission (CFTC), an independent federal agency founded in 1974, regulates exchanges for futures on all commodities. The Commodity Futures Modernization Act (H.R. 5660)

(CFMA) was passed December 15, 2000 to streamline the role of the CFTC. To allow the exchanges to compete more effectively, particularly against OTC markets, the act reduced the CFTC's regulation of certain types of exchanges. The CFMA established three categories of markets, called designated contract markets, derivative transaction execution facilities (DTF), and markets exempt from CFTC regulation. "The three categories match the degree of regulation to the varying nature of the products and the nature of the participant having access to the market," according to the CFTC. Designated contract markets allow trading of derivatives on any commodity with any type of market participant. They are most thoroughly regulated. The intermediate category, DTF, is subject to minimal CFTC regulation. A DTF is open only to sophisticated traders in futures and options that are unlikely to be manipulable because their market is very big, their underlying cash market is very liquid, or there is no cash market. The exempt markets are electronic trading facilities only for sophisticated commercial entities and DTFs that trade financial futures other than securities or indexes on them. This was a major change from the governing regulatory regime, which did not discriminate among types of commodities or traders. See CFTC Staff Task Force, *A New Regulatory Framework* (Feb. 22, 2000) and M. Sackheim, *Foreign Brokers Win Access to US Futures Customers*, International Financial Law Review 16 (Feb. 2000); N. Tait, *CFTC Approves Regulatory Plan*, Financial Times, Nov. 23, 2000; Commodity Futures Trading Commission, *A New Regulatory Framework for Trading Facilities, Intermediaries and Clearing Organizations*, 66 Federal Register 14262, Mar. 9, 2001; *Broad New Futures Law Approved in Wake of OTC Derivatives Accord*, Bureau of National Affairs, Inc, Jan. 1, 2001, at 3.

The same Act repealed the ban on futures on single stocks, clarified that swaps are excluded from CFTC and SEC regulation, and gave foreign brokers easier access to U.S. investors. The end of the ban on futures for single stocks opened up a new market segment. LIFFE's first contract in January 2001 had prompted Congress to lift the ban. By March 2002, LIFFE listed 118 contracts from many countries and entered a joint venture with NASDAQ to trade in the U.S. Spain had the most active market, however. The CFTC had recognized two new exchanges for single stock futures, one—an electronic exchange set up by CME, CBOE, and CBOT—listing 30 contracts. The SEC and CFTC, sharing regulatory responsibility for single stock futures, issued rules. The most contentious involved margin rules since the rules differed for securities and futures markets (see below). N. Tait, *Three Chicago Exchanges in Options Link*, Financial Times, May 15, 2001; A. Ostrovsky, *Liffe Adds Stock Futures*, Financial Times, March 7, 2002; J. Levitt and J. Politi, *US Catches Up with Single Stock Futures*, Financial Times, Feb. 20, 2002; M. Young, *The Commodity Futures Modernization Act of 2000*, 34 Review of Securities & Commodities Regulation 89, 98 May 16, 2001; and Joint Letter by the Securities Industry Association and Futures Industry Association to the

Commissioners of the SEC and the CFTC, *Proposed Customer Margin Rules Relating to Security Futures,* Dec. 5, 2001.

The following section describes the CFTC's role approving new contracts.

1. CONTRACT DESIGN

When U.S. exchanges design a new future or option contract, they apply for approval to the CFTC, which regulates futures contracts on all commodities. The contracts may only be traded on an exchange regulated by the CFTC. The regulator must find that they are not contrary to the public interest. The CFTC does not regulate forward contracts (which are analogous to OTC futures) or OTC options. It would like this power, but legislation in 1997 continued to withhold it despite the problems even supposedly sophisticated large corporate investors have encountered with options. See R. Romano, *A Thumbnail Sketch of Derivative Securities and Their Regulation,* 55 Maryland Law Review 1 (1996).

The U.S. Senate considered, in 1996-7, whether to reduce the role of the CFTC in approving new contracts. An early proposal was to allow futures exchanges to introduce new contracts without CFTC approval. CFTC would have a veto if the contract would harm the public interest. This was modified in early 1997 to allow the CFTC 10 days prior review, down from 90 days, and then another 15 days to start proceedings, with a total of 120 days to complete them. See L. Morse, *US Proposes Overhaul of Derivatives,* Financial Times, Aug. 6, 1996; A. Lucchetti and J. Taylor, *Bid to Overhaul Futures Trading Sparks Debate,* Wall Street Journal, Feb. 19, 1997; Statements on Introduced Bills and Joint Resolutions, The Commodity Exchange Act Amendment of 1996 (Senate - September 16, 1996); and *Legislative Battle Over Commodity Exchange Act Intensifies in Washington,* 10 Swaps Monitor no. 8, Feb. 17, 1997, at 1.

An example of the CFTC's review of proposals for new futures and options contracts is in a memorandum dated November 20, 1992. The CFTC staff explained why it recommended that the Commission accept the CME's proposed Three-month Euroyen Time Deposit futures contract and options on the future. The memorandum reveals how the U.S. government and the exchange regulate futures and options markets.

The staff first reviewed the cash market, which was the Tokyo interbank market, and found it "extremely large," liquid, broad, and "characterized by a tight bid-ask spread and extensive arbitrage." It was technically sophisticated: "Real-time TIBOR quotes are publicly available on electronic quote screens." Indeed, a Euroyen futures contract already traded on the Tokyo International Financial Futures Exchange (TIFFE) was "one of the ten leading futures contracts in the world." The staff found "arbitrage between the TIFFE Euroyen futures contract and TIBOR cash markets."

The staff then summarized the terms and conditions of the proposed futures contract. "The unit of trading for the proposed futures contract is the interest on a three-month time deposit in the Tokyo interbank market with a principal value of 100,000,000 Japanese yen (¥100,000,000, i.e., approximately $833,000)." The pricing mechanism resembled that described above for eurodollar interest rate contracts: "Future prices for the proposed contract will be quoted on an index basis; that is, 100.00 minus the annual yield in percentage points on a three-month Euroyen time deposit. The minimum price fluctuation will be 0.01 index point (equal to ¥2,500, i.e., approximately $20.85 per contract)." The CME would rely on TIFFE's determination of the final "settlement price for its Euroyen futures contract." This was possible because the CME contract would expire at the same time TIFFE's contract expired.

CME's proposals to limit speculative positions to 5,000 contracts in all months and require reports of 25 or more contracts were acceptable to the staff.

The exchange thus satisfied the CFTC's guidelines. "(1) The cash settlement of the contract is at a price reflecting the underlying cash market" because the "price. . . [is] reliable, acceptable, publicly available, and timely." "(2) The cash settlement of the contract will not be subject to manipulation or distortion" because of the market's size and liquidity. The third requirement was "(3) the price series upon which the settlement price is based is reliable, acceptable, publicly available, and timely." This raised a problem. TIFFE would "not reveal the identities of the banks it surveys nor the actual data received from survey participants to either the CME or the Commission." The CME would have to monitor prices in Tokyo during the time when TIFFE made its survey.

The staff reviewed the trading months and hours, found the contract size and minimum price fluctuations acceptable, given similar practice for other contracts. It found the public interest would be served because "the proposed contract potentially could, or would, be used for hedging or price basing."

Buyers and sellers pay in yen. Variation payments on margin accounts must be in yen (although performance bonds can be in any of several currencies or government securities). CME took advantage of a change in the law in January 1990 allowing banks in the U.S. to hold foreign currency deposits. CME has yen accounts in its settlement banks and next day payment through them is possible in yen. Finality is through the Japanese banking system. According to CFTC rules governing the treatment of customer funds, the foreign currency accounts would be subordinate to U.S. dollar claims in bankruptcy. More generally, Chase Bank lets CME clearing firms buy or sell foreign exchange through it, making funds available the next day rather than on the second day, which is the normal settlement day in foreign exchange transactions.

A similar review of the proposed options on the futures contract reached the same conclusion.

Competition among exchanges is often intense enough to draw in home governments. SIMEX locked horns with several of its neighbors over instruments it introduced on their securities. In mid-1996, SIMEX announced that starting January 1997 it would offer a futures contract on the Taiwan stock index compiled by Morgan Stanley Capital International. CME proposed a similar contract. Taiwan securities regulators opposed this, at first, since they wanted such a contract introduced in Taiwan. They threatened to stop sharing data with Morgan, then backed down. In May 1996, days after CME announced its contract, CBOT announced that it was working with Taiwan to set up a futures and options exchange there. In June 1997, Taiwan adopted legislation that would permit a futures and options market and one was expected to open in early 1999. See *SIMEX Kicks Off New Year By Launching Taiwan Index Futures*, International Securities Regulation Report, Jan. 16, 1997, at 5; *The Big Fight*, The Economist, May 25, 1996, at 82, and P. Montagnon, *Taiwan Prepares to Launch Futures Trade By Year-End*, Financial Times, June 10, 1997. SIMEX also battled TIFFE over SIMEX contracts on Japanese instruments. What would account for this? Trading in TIFFE's Euroyen futures contract was about 15 million a year in 1990-2 (SIMEX's contract grew from 1 million to 3 million), 23 million in 1993 (4 million at SIMEX), 38 million in 1994 (vs. 8 million) and 36 million in 1995 (vs. 8 million). See Bank for International Settlements, International Banking and Financial Market Developments (Feb. 1996).

2. COMPETITION AND COOPERATION IN EUROPE

The advent of the European Monetary Union prompted exchanges to cooperate as well as compete. Futures exchanges in Europe competed to offer the first contracts in euro. MATIF and LIFFE designed interest rate futures based on euribor, the euro interbank rate. Many shorter-term interest rate contracts were displaced by the euro: LIFFE offered contracts for DM (so did DTB), FF (so did MATIF), Eurolira, and Ecu. MATIF depended on the FF contract for 50% of trading volume, LIFFE depended on two DM interest contracts, plus a UK interest contract for over 50%.

Key exchanges in continental Europe in 1998 joined to create two alliances that would have the scale to compete effectively with LIFFE. MATIF (and MONEP) in France allied with exchanges in Spain and Italy. DTB and SOFFEX of Switzerland created Eurex, aiming for a common electronic trading system by January 2002. They would first permit members of one to trade on the other. Then fixed income products would be listed and traded on one screen. Trades would cross-clear later, which would permit margins on one contract to offset another contract. Cash equity products would be linked by 2002. While DTB already used electronic trading, the French used pits. Eurex failed to convince CBOT to join the alliance, sharing Eurex's technology for a common electronic trading system. In early 1999, Matif, CME, and SIMEX announced the Globex Alliance, to trade electronically around the clock.

LIFFE counterattacked for years along various lines. In November 1998, LIFFE shifted to an electronic trading system to compete with Eurex. It offered MATIF traders special employment terms to strengthen its capacity to trade when the euro was introduced. LIFFE changed its trading hours to start 45 minutes before DTB. This seemed essential because DTB traded a larger share of bund futures than LIFFE starting in 1997. To raise capital, LIFFE offered its shares to non-members in December 1998. LIFFE received permission from the CFTC to open screens in the U.S. (see section 3 below) and arranged with CME to link electronic trading systems in 1999. See S. Iskandar, *LIFFE Seeks French Traders to Lift Share of Market*, Financial Times, November 18, 1997, S. Iskandar, *Frankfurt Outstrips London's LIFFE on Long Bonds*, Financial Times, October 23, 1997; D. Shirreff, *Battle for the euro*, Euromoney, Jan 1997, at 50; S. Iskandar, *Exchanges Square Up for a Fight*, Financial Times, Dec. 17, 1996; R. Lapper, *LIFFE Takes Pole Position in euro Contracts Race*, Financial Times, Nov. 9, 1996; and *The Big Squeeze*, The Economist, Nov. 7, 1996, at 69; E. Luce and N. Tait, *LIFFE Gets Green Light for US Screens*, Financial Times, July 27, 1999; N. Tait and V. Boland, *CME to Forge Alliance with UK Exchange*, Financial Times, Aug. 6, 1999.

The uneven history of attempts by exchanges to cooperate may have reassured LIFFE. In 1994, MATIF and DTB arranged "reciprocal trading of certain interest contracts." CME and Singapore Mercantile Exchange offered a reciprocal contract of "rolling spot options on DM futures." See J. McGrath, Derivatives under Global Scrutiny, International Financial Law Review, Oct. 1994, at 20. (McGrath). In November 1995, LIFFE and TIFFE agreed to a formal link, starting April 1996, that would allow participants to trade three month Euroyen futures contracts. Investors could trade the contracts in European time zones, after TIFFE hours. The two exchanges have at least fifty common members. CME and DTB agreed in 1997 that DAX stock index futures contracts will be traded on the CME. See Bank for International Settlements, International Banking and Financial Market Developments, Feb. 1996, at 24; and R. Lapper, *LIFFE to Trade in TIFFE Euroyen Futures Contracts*, Financial Times, Nov. 14, 1995; and *CME to Trade German-Based Stock Index Futures*, International Securities Regulation Report, Jan. 30, 1997, at 15.

These cooperative arrangements founder unexpectedly. For example, CBOT and LIFFE agreed in 1994 to cooperate starting in May 1997. LIFFE would exclusively trade CBOT's US T-bond futures contract after CBOT hours and CBOT would trade LIFFE's bund contract after LIFFE hours. After 1994, CBOT developed an electronic trading system called

Project A that could trade T-Bonds after hours. It performed very well, trading 17,000 contract a night, and would compete with LIFFE's floor trading of the T-Bond contract. But CBOT members preferred Project A, whose profits pass through to members as dividends, rather than floor trading fees, which go to the Exchange. Members wanted to change the 1994 agreement with LIFFE. See L. Morse, *Chicago Exchange Rethinks Liffe Link*, Financial Times, Mar. 3, 1997. In early 1999, similar thinking prompted CBOT to reject the link with Eurex.

Despite some progress, competition among the exchanges has made cooperation extremely difficult. In the early 1990s there was a sense of optimism among the exchanges that some level of cooperation could be achieved. However, in 1998, Reuters and MATIF closed Globex, the international after-hours screen trading system developed jointly by Reuters, the Chicago Mercantile Exchange, and the Chicago Board of Trade. See T. Corrigan, *Quirky Offshoots Gain Respect*, Financial Times, Oct. 20, 1993. Additionally, the MATIF/DTB arrangements foundered in 1997, and by 1997 electronic trading accounted for about one third of all trading.

In 2001, Euronext addressed the cooperation/competition dilemma by acquiring LIFFE, beating the London Stock Exchange and other bidders. Euronext, an amalgam of the Paris, Brussels, and Amsterdam stock exchanges, paid $805 million, a 112% premium over its market value at the time. Euronext planned to let LIFFE operate independently and to move its own derivatives operations to London. The enlarged LIFFE would rank first in Europe by number of contracts. C. Pretzlik, *High Price Paid to Secure Future*, Financial Times, Oct. 30, 2000.

Distinctions between exchange and OTC trading have begun to blur. There are many examples. Exchanges create instruments that replicate those offered OTC. CME and the Singapore Mercantile Exchange created "a series of rolling spot currency contracts ... to replicate foreign exchange cash transactions." See McGrath. CBOE designed Flex options in early 1993. The buyer–an institutional investor because the minimum price is $10 million–specifies the strike price and expiration of the options, which are initially on the S&P 100 and 500 indexes. CBOT extended this to other underlying securities, including in 1994 options on the value of Mexican, Tokyo, and Israel stock exchange indexes. Other exchanges copied this. See Raybould 10 and McGrath. "OTC derivatives dealers are among the largest users of US listed futures and options contracts" to lay off risk. L. Morse, *Traders Condemn Plan to Tax Futures*, Financial Times, Feb. 8, 1995.

3. CROSS-BORDER ELECTRONIC ACCESS TO FUTURES EXCHANGES

A growing problem for regulators of futures exchanges was how to treat foreign exchanges that wanted to provide screens in the regulators' country. Suppose Eurex wanted to let its members operating in the U.S. have Eurex computer terminals in the U.S. If the members wanted to trade as principals from the U.S., did Eurex have to be designated a U.S. contract market by the CFTC? What if U.S. customers wanted to trade?

In March 1999, the CFTC proposed a new Rule 30.11 to allow exchanges operating primarily outside the U.S. electronic access to exchanges in the U.S. without requiring the foreign exchanges to be designated as U.S. contract markets. Foreign electronic exchanges that automatically matched or executed orders could petition CFTC for an exemption. The new Rule described how to do so. See CFTC, *CFTC Issues Proposed Rules Concerning Order Routing and Electronic Access to Futures Exchanges Operating Primarily Outside the U.S.*, Release #4243-99, Mar.16, 1999. The CFTC set the following standards:

- the petitioner is an established board of trade that wishes to place within the United States an automated trading system permitting access to its products but whose activities are otherwise primarily located in a particular foreign country that has taken responsibility for regulation of the petitioner;

- the petitioner's home country has established a regulatory scheme that is generally comparable to that in the U.S. and provides basic protections for customers trading on markets and for the integrity of the markets themselves;

- except for certain incidental contacts within the U.S., the petitioner is present in the U.S. only by virtue of being accessible from within the U.S. via its automated trading system;

- the petitioner is willing to submit itself to the jurisdiction of the Commission and the U.S. courts in connection with its activities conducted under an exemptive order;

- the petitioner's automated trading system has been approved by the petitioner's home country regulator following a review of the system that applied the standards set forth in the 1990 International Organization of Securities Commissions ("IOSCO") report on screen-based trading systems (as . . . revised) or substantially similar standards; and

- satisfactory information sharing arrangements are in effect between the Commission and the petitioner and petitioner's regulatory authority.

The CFTC decided that it would consider the volume of U.S. trades to decide if a petitioner's U.S. contacts were so extensive that it required designation as a contract market in the U.S. But the CFTC did not fix a volume amount (or a ceiling for the U.S. share of total trading by the petitioning exchange) that would serve as a ceiling for an exemption. However, the petitioner could offer only products that could lawfully be offered in the U.S.

To determine if a home country regulatory system was "generally comparable to that in the U.S.," the CFTC would consider:

- prohibition of fraud, abuse and market manipulation relating to trading on the petitioner's markets;

- recordkeeping and reporting by the petitioner and its members;

- fitness standards for intermediaries operating on petitioner's markets, members or others;

- financial standards for the petitioner's members;

- protection of customer funds, including procedures in the event of a clearing member's default or insolvency;

- trade practice standards;

- rule review or general review of board of trade [exchange] operations by its regulatory authority;

- surveillance, compliance, and enforcement mechanisms employed by the board of trade and its regulatory authority to ensure compliance with their rules and regulations; and

- regulatory oversight of clearing facilities.

The CFTC adopted Rule 30.12 in August 2000, allowing foreign brokers, either affiliated with a U.S. futures commission merchant (FCM) or regulated in the jurisdiction of the U.S. FCM, to "accept orders from certain sophisticated U.S. customers, known as 'authorized customers,' provided the U.S. FCM carrying the authorized customer's account satisfies certain procedural safeguards and remains well-capitalized." *CFTC Eases Rules for U.S. Persons to Trade in Foreign Futures, Options,* Bureau of National Affairs, Inc. Aug. 2000, at 4.

In one view, the regulatory structure in place today is not equipped for electronic exchanges. The existing system assumes that members of the exchanges play a central role in all aspects of the exchange's activities and that the exchanges have the capacity to enforce their regulations against members. But in the new electronic market, the firms that used to be exchange members will recede to mere subscribers, for whom any single exchange will be much less important than in the past. The exchange will cease to be an SRO because it will have no "self" to regulate and its only power over subscribers will be to deny them access to the exchange. The appropriate regulator in the U.S. would be the National Futures Association (NFA), either directly or delegated by the CFTC. A new structure is needed for compliance, market surveillance, and investigation. Clearing, however, could possibly be left to corporate market participants to design, through the use of market power. P. McBride, *Getting to Grips with Self-Regulation in the New e-Markets,* International Financial Law Review, June 2000 at 41.

Notes and Questions

1. Compare this proposed euroyen future to the CME's 3 month eurodollar contract. What are the similarities? What accounts for the differences? Is this really a euroyen contract? What might explain its name?

2. A contract such as that described in Section 1 above can be coordinated more or less closely with almost identical contracts on other exchanges, such as TIFFE or SIMEX. How willing would TIFFE be to help CME develop this contract?

   a. Exchanges do not have identical rules. TIFFE's margin rules differ from those in the U.S.. TIFFE requires customers to close their position if they want to withdraw any equity (or surplus over the maintenance level) from their margin account. Until 1999, TIFFE's brokers charged fixed commissions at least twice as high as commissions for trading on SIMEX or CME. How would these rules affect the willingness of TIFFE to cooperate with CME on this contract?

3. Would the Japanese finance ministry support or oppose this proposed contract? How much leverage would the Japanese government have to affect the CME's decision about whether to list this contract? Suppose the government believed that options trading in Japan contributed to the stock market collapse over the last decade and the government had instituted policies to limit price movements on Japanese futures and options markets.

4. The impact of trading in derivatives markets on volatility in the underlying market is a major issue of academic research. A review of the largely Western literature in 1995 reported that most studies found interest rate futures or options markets either improve stability or have no effect on the cash market. Exchange rate futures, however, increase the volatility of the underlying market. See A. Chatrath, S. Ramchander, and F. Song, *The Role of Futures Trading Activity in Exchange Rate Volatility*, Journal of Futures Markets (1996). However, another study found that when options were not well regulated in the U.S., from 1973-80, they temporarily increased underlying stock prices (possibly due to market manipulation). After federal regulations took effect in 1980, options had a negative effect, dampening the price of the underlying stock for at least four years. See S. Sorescu, The Effect of Options on Stock Prices, Mar. 5, 1997. Two later studies found that European options reduced fundamental volatility and that in Japan, while Nikkei stock options traded on the Osaka exchange increased Nikkei volatility, similar options traded on SIMEX did not. For Korea during the 1997 crisis, the futures market destabilized the stock market. Index futures volumes rose dramatically starting 3 months before the crisis began, then reverted to normal. Foreign investors in the futures markets played a significant role. During the crisis, sales in the futures market undercut prices in the

cash market, an unknown phenomenon in Korea before then. S. Hwang and S. Satchell, *Market Risk and the Concept of Fundamental Volatility*, 24 Journal of Banking & Finance 759 (2000) and E. Chang, J. Cheng, J. Pinegar, *Does Futures Trading Increase Stock Market Volatility? The Case for the Nikkei Stock Index Futures Market*, 24 Journal of Banking & Finance 727 (2000); E. Ghysels and J. Seon, *The Asian Financial Crisis: The Role of Derivative Securities Trading and Foreign Investors*, Mar. 5, 2000.

Speculators attacking a country's currency sometimes also attack the country's equity market, in what is called a double play. Hong Kong faced this double play in August 1998. First, speculators sell stock short, either in the cash or futures market. Since they profit if the stock prices fall, the next step is to help that happen. They drive up interest rates by squeezing liquidity in the economy. Rising interest rates may weaken stock prices. One way is to make big spot sales of the currency, increasing its supply and forcing the central bank or monetary authority to tighten liquidity and drive up interest rates. A second way is to borrow big in the interbank market or other money markets (perhaps to finance the short sales of equity). The government is forced to intervene whether the economy is weak or strong. One analysis concluded that the government can "never simultaneously reduce speculation in the equity and the money markets." S. Chakravorti and S. Lall, *The Double Play: Simultaneous Speculative Attacks on Currency and Equity Markets*, Federal Reserve Bank of Chicago, Dec. 2000.

5. How would the CME euroyen futures contract look to potential investors in it? Who would be likely to use it?

6. Futures exchanges also competed by combining with the stock exchange that traded many of the underlying securities for the futures and options. In 1999, Singapore's SIMEX announced plans to merge with the Singapore Stock Exchange and Hong Kong's futures exchange and stock exchanges did the same. E. Luce, *SIMEX Leads Singapore's Bid for Asian Dominance*, Financial Times, Mar. 11, 1999.

7. In March 1999, Alan Greenspan, chairman of the Federal Reserve Board, said that "the success of derivatives traded outside of exchanges suggested that United States futures markets could operate with less Government oversight." *Less Oversight of Derivatives Is Supported By Greenspan*, New York Times Mar. 20, 1999. How well does the CFTC proposal for electronic access of foreign exchanges to U.S. markets reflect Greenspan's view?

E. A CASE STUDY IN THE REGULATION OF FUTURES AND OPTIONS MARKETS: THE BARINGS CASE

The oldest British merchant bank, Baring Brothers, collapsed over the weekend of February 25-26, 1995. A 28 year old employee based in

Singapore, trading futures and options contracts, had amassed losses exceeding £860 million.* Barings' capital was £540 million. A rescue effort by the Bank of England that weekend failed; other banks would not lend to Barings because, with the derivatives contracts still open, the full extent of Barings' losses could not be fixed.

On March 5, the Dutch bank Internationals Nederlanden Groep NV (ING Bank) won the bid to acquire Barings' securities, asset management, and investment banking operations for £1 (one pound). It then invested £660 million and assumed most debts. On March 8, the acquisition was approved by the U.K. High Court and by the court in the Cayman Islands, where Barings was incorporated.

This crisis raises important issues concerning the regulation of futures and options markets. To what extent is the reliance on margin rules sufficient to protect exchanges and the financial system? Are other safeguards needed? How significant is it that the exchanges and regulators missed what seem to have been major flaws in Barings' management of its futures and options operations? Is greater coordination among exchanges and their regulators needed? What are the implications of Barings' activities for deposit-taking institutions? What are the implications of the Bank of England's resolution of the crisis?

In this section we begin with a brief introduction to the Barings Group and then proceed to chronicle the activities that ultimately led to its collapse. Following this, we begin to analyze the performance of the key regulatory bodies which supervised Barings from 1992 until the time of the disaster. Of particular import are their techniques (notably margin rules), their handling of the crisis, and their subsequent efforts to join with other regulators and exchanges from around the world to avoid a re-run of the catastrophe. When reading this section, use the discussion of theory and market microstructure, presented in the first part of the chapter, to help you respond to the issues raised. Also, try to see how a sound understanding of the mechanics of futures and options is necessary to be able to design appropriate regulatory responses to the problems described.

The sources for most of this account are two official accounts: Bank of England, Report of the Board of Banking Supervision Inquiry into the Circumstances of the Collapse of Barings (1995) (BoE Report); and Inspectors appointed by the Minister for Finance, Baring Futures (Singapore) Pte Ltd (1995) (Singapore Report).

* At year-end, the exchange rate of a U.S. dollar for yen was ¥111.8 (1993) and ¥99.7 (1994), Singapore dollars was S$1.61 (1993) and S$1.46 (1994), and pound Sterling was £ 0.675 (1993) and £0.64 (1994)

1. THE BARINGS GROUP

Over 230 years old, Barings was a financial group based in London. Barings PLC, the holding company, had over 100 subsidiaries in scores of countries and five divisions: banking, equity brokering and trading, corporate finance, international finance, and operations. Its activities included merchant banking (wholesale deposit-taking, trading, corporate finance, mergers and acquisitions, venture capital), investment advice, fund and asset management and advice, unit and investment trust (like mutual funds) creation and management, stock registry, real estate investment, financing vehicles, and securities dealing and brokering. Supervision of the key Barings units was scattered among several countries' regulators.

For this story, the important units of Barings Group, and their supervisors, included:

1) Baring Brothers & Co., Ltd (BB&Co), the deposit-taking merchant bank incorporated in the U.K., had specialized in corporate finance and debt trading. The Bank of England was the lead supervisor of BB&Co in the U.K., but the U.K. Securities and Finance Authority (SFA) supervised its U.K. securities operations.

2) Baring Securities Ltd (BSL) was formed from a stock brokering firm acquired by BB&Co in 1984 that had a strong Asian network. It was BB&Co's first important venture into equity securities. Incorporated in the Cayman Islands and headquartered in London, BSL's U.K. operations were supervised by the Securities and Futures Authority there. From 1993, BSL handled clients' securities as a broker and a subsidiary, Barings Securities (London) Ltd (BSLL) made the proprietary investments. BSL owned the following three firms, among many others;

3) Baring Securities (Japan) Ltd (BSJ), incorporated in the Cayman Islands, was a broker-dealer in Japan and supervised by the Ministry of Finance there.

4) Baring Securities (Singapore) Pte Ltd (BSS) incorporated in Singapore to carry out Baring's securities business there. It was a member of the Singapore Stock Exchange and regulated by the Monetary Authority of Singapore.

5) Baring Futures (Singapore) Ltd (BFS), carrying out Barings' derivatives business in Singapore, incorporated there and became a non-clearing member of SIMEX in September 1986 and a clearing member on July 1, 1992. With one-third the staff of BSS and much less senior management attention than BSS, BFS was the unit Nicholas Leeson managed when the entire Group collapsed. SIMEX supervised BFS.

The Group managed its banking business (through BB&Co) and its securities business (through BSL) separately until 1992, when it started a long process of combining them into what was to become the Barings Investment Bank in late 1994. This slow amalgamation of two very different businesses and cultures contributed to serious confusion in the Group's management. Functions and lines for reporting were vague, overlapping, and often changed. Leeson, for example, nominally reported to senior Barings personnel in Singapore, London, and Tokyo.

2. THE SCAM

a. THE LEGITIMATE POSITIONS

Nicholas Leeson assumed responsibility for trading and for settlement in BFS. After he was denied a broker's license in the U.K. because of fraud in his application, in March 1992 Barings sent him to Singapore without revealing the U.K. denial when he applied for his license in Singapore. Originally he was responsible only for settlement and he continued to manage BFS's back office throughout his tenure. He had no experience trading futures, but began executing trades soon after BFS became a clearing member in July 1992.

BFS had four clients, three of them other Barings companies and the fourth the Tokyo office of Banque Nationale de Paris (BNP). BFS was mainly to execute trades for them, since it had no authority to take proprietary positions on its own behalf in 1993 and its authority in 1994 to take intra-day proprietary positions was quite limited. BSL, the largest client, acted as agent for its customers and BSLL took proprietary positions. BSJ used BFS to execute proprietary trades. In late 1992, BSJ's traders had begun to arbitrage baskets of stocks on the Tokyo Stock Exchange (TSE) cash market against Nikkei Index futures on the Osaka Stock Exchange (OSE), simultaneously buying/selling the basket and selling/buying the Index. They called this cash futures arbitrage.

The Nikkei 225 Stock Price Average is an index calculated by Nihon Keizai Shinbun, the leading financial news service in Japan. Modeled on the Dow Jones Index, it existed since 1950. The index is based on a portfolio of 225 stocks listed on the First Section of the TSE. These 225 shares represented about 20% of all shares listed on the First Section. Each of the 225 shares had equal weight. Their value was averaged regularly and divided by a constant to adjust for rights issues and other non-market factors. As the total price of the 225 stocks changed, the index changed proportionately. On January 17, 1995, the Nikkei 225 was at ¥19,421. The index itself is not traded on an exchange, though an investor can easily create it by buying individual stocks, as the BSJ traders did.

The BSJ traders discovered that they could reduce their costs by shifting the futures trading to the Singapore International Monetary Exchange (SIMEX) from the OSE, whose margin requirements (discussed below) were significantly higher. Contracts offering futures and options on the Nikkei 225 were traded on SIMEX (which first developed and traded them), OSE, and the Chicago Mercantile Exchange (CME). A SIMEX contract was 500 times the index, an OSE contract 1,000 times. If the index was at ¥19,000 the value of a single OSE contract was ¥19 million and SIMEX contract was half that. One study has found that OSE, SIMEX, and CME prices were cointegrated but that one particular market did not drive the others. Instead, "causality runs from the last trading market(s)...." See G. Booth, T-H Lee, Y. Tse, International Linkages in Nikkei Stock Index Futures Markets, 4 Pacific Basin Finance Journal (1996) at 59. SIMEX saw itself as a leader. It was the first exchange in East Asia to trade financial futures, starting in the mid-1980s. About 80% of SIMEX's business was from outside Singapore. Its trading volume more than trebled from 1991 to 1994 and increased 27% in the first quarter of 1995. See P. Montagnon and K. Cooke, *Prompt Treatment for Futures Shock,* Financial Times, Mar. 3, 1995.

The "SIMEX/OSE switching business" arose when BSJ discovered it could make money arbitraging price differences between the Nikkei futures indexes on SIMEX and OSE. It would buy a contract on one exchange and sell an offsetting contract on the other, making money on small spreads by investing large amounts. From early 1994, Barings allowed Leeson to make proprietary trades up to an intra-day limit of 200 Nikkei futures contracts. It also gave him a low intra-day limit to arbitrage Japanese government bond (JGB) futures on SIMEX against TSE prices. He was not allowed to hold positions overnight or in options. He was not subject to limits on agency trading. In fact, Barings' senior managers consistently described Leeson's activities as trading on behalf of Barings' customers.

Barings could arbitrage futures in two ways through Leeson. As discussed at the end of B(2), *supra*, arbitrage occurs when the same good can be simultaneously bought at a low price in one location and sold at a higher price in another. Switching was one way. Barings could arbitrage financial futures contracts traded in two futures markets, called "inter-exchange arbitrage profits," or switching. These were the contracts and exchanges:

1) Nikkei 225 contract: traded on SIMEX and OSE[**]

2) JGB futures contract: traded on SIMEX and TSE.

These contracts are identical in their specifications, except that the SIMEX contract is half the notional size of the corresponding Japanese contract. Leeson could only trade futures; he had no authority to trade options for a Barings account (although he ultimately did trade without authority).

[**] SIMEX offered an option on the N225 futures contract. OSE did not.

Barings would profit "from temporary price differences between the SIMEX and OSE Nikkei 225 contracts, buying the cheaper contract and selling the more expensive one and then reversing the trade when the price difference had narrowed, or even been eliminated, in calmer markets." (BoE Report p. 42). Price differences occurred because demand and supply differed: OSE had most Japanese demand, while SIMEX had offshore and local traders. OSE, with an electronic exchange, was slower than SIMEX, with floor trading. OSE would stop temporarily when bids or offers were not sufficient to make trades, which happened in volatile markets. Barings/BSJ did the same with futures on JGBs.

For example, assume the N225 futures contract is trading at 98 on SIMEX and 96 on OSE. Barings buys the cheaper (96) on OSE and sells the dearer (98) on SIMEX. It has locked in a 2 point spread which it realizes when it reverses the positions, whatever happens to the price.

a. Suppose the prices converge on the two exchanges to 97. Barings will: sell at 97 on the OSE, giving a one point profit because it bought at 96, and buy at 97 on SIMEX, giving one point of profit because it originally sold at 98.

b. Suppose the prices converge at 100. Barings will sell at 100 on the OSE, giving it a 4 point profit because it bought at 96, and buy at 100 on SIMEX, giving a 2 point loss because it originally sold at 98. This offsets the OSE profit, giving it, net, 2 points.

Of course, the actual price differences are measured in one or two basis points and they last only a short part of the day. Barings could do this because it had people at both exchanges who could detect these small price differences.

When Leeson traded for Barings, he took the positions on SIMEX and instructed BSJ, Baring's unit in Japan, to take the offsetting positions on the OSE or TSE. BSJ could initiate by taking a position in Japan and instructing Leeson to take the offsetting position on SIMEX.

Cash/Futures arbitrage was the second technique available to Barings and Leeson. Barings could also compare the price of the N225 index futures contract (on OSE or SIMEX) to the prices of the 225 shares traded on the TSE that made up the index (weighting those shares the same as they were weighted in the N225 index). If the prices of the index and underlying shares differed, Barings could buy the cheaper and sell the dearer. It would construct its own portfolio of the underlying shares that would mimic the index.

For example, assume the index was cheaper than the underlying share portfolio. Barings would buy the index (take a long position in the futures contract) and sell the underlying portfolio (short the stocks). Barings would realize the profit by reversing the positions simultaneously when the prices changed (presumably by converging). That is, it would sell the index and buy the stocks.

Or assume the index was more expensive than the underlying portfolio. Barings would short the index (take a short position in the futures contract) and buy the underlying portfolio (ie., become long in the stocks). Again, it would profit by reversing the positions simultaneously.

Here too the price differences would be very small and last only briefly. This would be a type of investment that would be best done intra-day.

Gradually Leeson became known as a successful trader of Nikkei 225 index futures and options. Barings was in a unique position to arbitrage because it was one of just a few brokers that had seats on both the OSE and SIMEX. As a member, it would see the order flow on both and know ahead of non-members how prices would move. Acting quickly, it could use this knowledge to invest in the stock index futures and options with little risk. Lesson managed this SIMEX/OSE "switching business," generating profits and losses that were booked to BSL, BSLL, and BSJ. His activities became the major profit center for BSL and BSL the major profit center for the Barings Group. Barings awarded Leeson a bonus of £115,000 for 1993 and planned, before his actions destroyed the Bank, to give him £450,000 for 1994. More senior Barings managers based in Singapore "viewed BFS as Mr Leeson's own responsibility and thus did not check Mr Leeson's activities. On the other hand, the Baring Group management in London maintained that BF was a Singapore company accountable in the first instance to its local managers," said the Singapore Report.

b. THE SECRET POSITIONS

On July 3, 1992, two days after BFS started trading on SIMEX, Leeson opened Account 88888, telling SIMEX that it was a house or BFS account for BSL. He then instructed a member of his staff to remove the computer-based link between the account and BSL (in London). Indeed, most people in other Barings companies asserted they had never heard of the account. Over the next 2.5 years, his consistent practice was to book trades initially in a BSJ or BSL account, since they were his "clients," then transfer trading losses to Account 88888 in a way that allowed him to show large profits for the BSJ and BSL accounts.

BFS's actual trading included many activities beyond Leeson's authority: unhedged Nikkei futures (rising from 189 long futures in August 1992 to 26,032 by January 31, 1995 and 61,039 by February 24, 1995); unhedged JGB futures (from 2,120 contracts traded in October 1993 to 54,325 in November 1994); and an unhedged combination of options called a short or top straddle, on which he earned S\$723 million by the end of 1994 and could have profited S\$274 million had he closed them then.

The top straddle became a major source of loss. Leeson created it by writing a put and a call on the Nikkei 225 future at the same strike price. He would profit only when the market price stayed close to the strike price. The call writer profits until the market price rises slightly above the strike price. The put writer profits until the market price falls slightly below the strike price. When put and call are combined, the writer loses money when the index moves beyond either point -- slightly above or below the strike price -- because it promised to deliver the cash value of the contract (call writer) or pay it (put writer). Leeson bought many in early 1995 at a strike price of about ¥19,000/contract and was in the money between ¥18,500 and ¥19,500. From February 8, the price moved down from ¥18,350 to ¥16,890 on February 27 and then hovered around ¥17,000 in early March.

Leeson used Account 88888 to hide unauthorized trading and enhance prices for BSL, BSLL and BSJ as follows. All trades must be executed on the SIMEX floor so that others could bid on them. To avoid this danger, he would tell two BFS floor traders to execute large trades in the 30 seconds before trading closed, transferring all unauthorized trades from the BSL, BSLL or BSJ accounts to 88888 so his reports to BSL, BSLL or BSJ would comply with his authority. Later he would adjust the prices and volumes so he could report small, apparently hedged trades throughout the day that would sum to the earlier large trade but, because the prices were false, show a profit to BSJ, BSLL or BSL in trades with 88888, which would take the loss. When BSJ, BSLL or BSL requested copies of the daily transaction list, the BFS traders would fax the falsified list then later rewrite the daily list to conform to SIMEX's own records and put it into the SIMEX's computer. BFS's settlement staff would put the adjusted prices and volumes in BFS's system for processing. The Singapore Report calculated that Leeson reported, in January and February 1995, trading profits of S$46 million for BSJ when the actual loss was S$9.2 million.

Leeson also booked fictitious trades, not executed on the SIMEX floor, to swell the BSJ, BSLL and BSL profits even more while 88888 would take the fictitious loss. The Singapore Report calculated that in January and February 1995, without these fictitious trades, BSJ's actual losses would have been S$37 million. These fictitious trades resulted in BFS under-reporting its actual positions to SIMEX. Leeson could do so because SIMEX relied on members' accounting systems to process transactions and report accurately. SIMEX would only uncover fraud in an audit. It lacked a way to track each members' clients' open positions. Although BFS's "settlements operations ... were linked by computer to BSL Settlements, Mr Leeson had suppressed information pertaining to trades that were booked in Account 88888 from the general trading information ('the trade feed') transmitted to BSL Settlements ..." according to the Singapore Report. The following table reports cumulative losses in Account 88888.

<u>Cumulative Losses on Account 88888</u>

End of period	Amount	
30 September 1992	¥658 million	(S$ 8.8 million)
31 October 1993	¥879 million	(S$ 12.9 million)
30 November 1993	¥4.4 billion	(S$ 65.7 million)
31 December 1994	¥25.5 billion	(S$373.9 million)
After collapse	¥135.5 billion	(S$ 2.2 billion)

The losses grew because Leeson regularly bet wrong in the unauthorized and unhedged proprietary positions he took. As the losses grew, so did his bets. In early January 1995, the Japanese markets moved in his favor, erasing some of the losses. Then the January 17 earthquake in Kobe undermined Japan's financial markets, which increased in volatility. Leeson took very large long positions in Nikkei futures and prices fell. He took massive net short positions in JGB futures and the price rose 2%. The top straddle options lost substantial amounts. Realized and unrealized losses on futures were ¥2.6 billion in January and ¥48.0 billion in February. Losses on options were ¥12.2 billion in January and ¥5.5 billion in February. In S$, he lost S$227.7 million in January and S$823.3 million in February.

c.   FUNDING THE LOSSES IN 88888

Funding for BFS's operations came almost entirely from its clients in the Barings group. BFS would instruct them to send it funds to meet the cost of trades and margins incurred for them. According to the Singapore Report, as BFS called for ever-increasing funds

> BSL found it more and more difficult to reconcile these amounts with the trades for which the fund were being requested. During 1993, BSL knew that between £15 million (S$35 million) and £20 million (S$46 million) remitted to the Barings Group's brokering companies in the Far East could not be reconciled with the trades in respect of which the funds had been requested.

The unreconciled amount rose to about £100 million (S$230 million) in 1994 and £320 million (S$736 million) in January and February 1995. Baring's headquarters referred to its payments to meet these unreconciled balances as "topping up."

Leeson told Barings' Group Treasury that he needed short-term funds "to meet intra-day advance margin calls by SIMEX" and to fund the positions of BSJ which, he said, took longer to raise funds than BSL. No one in the Group Treasury questioned this. According to the Singapore Report:

> The Barings Group's risk positions, trading limits and trading performance and the allocation of funding were monitored each day by a high-level Asset & Liability Committee (ALCO). ... ALCO discussed the issue of funding BFS on at least six occasions in January and February 1995. By this time Mr Leeson's reported

trading activities had assumed very large proportions, causing the Baring Group to almost miss a SIMEX margin call on 24 January 1995. However the preoccupation of these meeting was to arrange adequate funding lines to meet Mr Leeson's large requirements, rather than to investigate the causes underlying these requirements. At some stage, ALCO did decide that Mr Leeson should be asked to reduce his positions, but this decision was never effectively implemented.

On 20 February 1995, just days before the collapse of the Baring Group, the need to reduce Mr Leeson's position was again raised at ALCO. Mr Norris, the Chief Executive Officer of the Baring Group, informed ALCO that he had discussed this issue with Mr Leeson when they met in Singapore the previous week. Mr Norris informed ALCO that Mr Leeson had suggested that his positions should not be reduced and Mr Norris concurred with this. Mr Norris denied having had such a discussion with Mr Leeson or having briefed ALCO in this way, but both facts were corroborated by independent witnesses.

Funding for the S$2.2 billion in ultimate losses on 88888 was from creditor banks (S$100 million) and other Baring Group companies (S$2.1 billion). The Barings firms had remitted S$1.7 billion to BFS. Of this, S$770 million was from BSL, another S$270 million from BSLL, and the remaining S$690 million was from BSJ. In addition, BFS had held S$400 in margin payments SIMEX returned to it for trades for the other firms.

The Barings funders themselves raised much of their money from banks. BSL used its customers' funds or loaned its clients the money to meet margin calls, borrowing from BB&Co. BSLL borrowed from BB&Co and the interbank market. BSJ drew from its customers and Japanese banks, from which it borrowed yen and JGBs. BSJ used these sources to fund its payments to BFS and its own margin calls on Japanese exchanges. These calls grew as Barings' exposure on the Japanese exchanges grew dramatically in January and February 1995 because BSJ took the Barings positions in Japan believing BFS was hedging them in Singapore. At the collapse, BSJ owed Japanese banks over £375 million, of which £50 million was borrowed securities.

Auditors obviously failed to uncover Leeson's fraud, but they had at least identified the potential. According to the Singapore Report, an internal audit in the third quarter of 1994

> identified as one key issue to be examined further in Singapore, the fact that Mr Leeson occupied a very powerful position controlling both the front and the back offices of BFS. He was both chief trader and head of settlements and was thus in a position to record the trades that he himself had executed in any way he wished. The internal audit report, issued in the last quarter of 1994, specifically highlighted this fact as creating a significant risk that internal controls could be overridden. Nothing was done to remedy this. The

internal audit report noted that insofar as Mr Leeson's trade were almost all executed for other Baring Group entities, these trades would be subject to reconciliation controls, which would mitigate the extent of any irregularities that might arise from this situation. In fact no such reconciliation controls existed.

As early as 1993, auditors had warned about the need to separate management of front and back offices in BFS. They repeated the warning periodically and were ignored by senior managers until late January 1995.

The external auditor's work was also inadequate. They relied on Leeson and failed to check his explanations or purported transactions with the other parties he named. They accepted photocopies rather than originals. This was important because after Leeson left Singapore falsified documents were found in his desk, along with paste, scissors, and sources with holes cut in them. He had used them to prove the existence and support of "clients" to explain large trades. The auditors even failed to notice that a confirmation supposedly sent direct to them from a "client" actually had "From Nick & Lisa" at the top of both pages, indicating its source was Leeson's home fax machine. The Bank of England Report noted that Coopers & Lybrand (Singapore) concluded that BFS's internal controls were adequate in November 1994 even though back and front office responsibilities were combined in Leeson. The Report observed that C&L London should have made "more thorough" tests of the controls, given the high funding requests from BFS in early 1995. The C&L audit of Barings was not, however, complete by February 25, 1995.

Notes and Questions

1. Review the tasks Barings senior managers thought BFS was carrying out. What types of authorized positions on SIMEX did Leeson take? How risky were they? Why would they interest Barings? How profitable would you expect it to be? Why would Barings allow a person with Leeson's experience to carry out these tasks?

2. What would Leeson gain from the fraud?

3. Consider how a graph of the straddle would look. Why is it called a top straddle? Why would Leeson take on top straddles from late 1994 on?

4. The Singapore Report did not accept the Baring Group management's assertion that 88888 was an unauthorized account of which they were ignorant. Instead, the Report suggests, senior management was "grossly negligent, or wilfully blind and reckless to the truth." Do you agree? What other factors might also explain their failure to detect Leeson's activities until too late?

3. THE REGULATORY ROLE OF SIMEX

Countries regulate their futures and options markets in many ways. Regulators, such as the CFTC, generally must recognize contracts and clearing houses, setting minimum standards that include the public interest; foreign contracts and clearing houses may come under special scrutiny. To promote financial safety, regulators require adequate capital for intermediaries like clearing members and brokers, though many major countries do not set specific capital rules for exchanges or clearing houses. Clearing houses may set capital requirements for their members. Regulators expect exchanges like SIMEX, a corporation, to set margin rules, keep the markets under surveillance, and require customer funds to be segregated from the broker's own accounts. Supervision of records varies across countries. Regulators protect customers through rules about brokers' fitness, order execution, sales practices, and records. Market efficiency is the goal of rules about product design and market disruption. Manipulation is forbidden, though its definition varies. See CFTC, International Regulation of Derivative Markets, Products, and Financial Intermediaries (1993). Regulation of futures and options differs from that of securities. The CFTC explained in its October 1993 study:

> The futures exchange markets do not exist to facilitate the transfer of ownership of a cash commodity. Futures markets developed to reallocate the risk in commercial transactions and facilitate discovery of the efficient price for commodities in general commerce. Unlike the federal securities regulatory framework, the main focus of futures transaction regulation was on transactions in the "secondary" exchange market reflecting that all futures transactions were required to be effected on a centralized exchange and that there is considered to be no "issuer" of futures contracts and thus no offering process comparable to that for securities. All futures transactions were required to be conducted in the public marketplace and thus included in the auction price. This centralization was considered important for the effective functioning of the markets as a price discovery mechanism, and much of the regulatory scheme was directed at the proper reflection of price. In general, subject to certain financial protections, futures markets were not required to be "continuous" and until recently, affirmative market-making obligations to maintain liquidity were foreign to such markets. Although all large market participants were required to report their positions, regulatory financial requirements were directed solely to agents (brokers) transacting on behalf of customers.

> Exchange-traded stock and stock index options did not exist until the 1970s. At that time, options on individual equities were listed and in subsequent years significant regulatory and legislative attention was directed to the appropriate regulation of such products. Unlike futures regulators, domestic securities regulators deem the clearing entity to be the issuer of exchange traded options.

Exchange markets, both securities and futures, characteristically have had regulatory or self-regulatory criteria relating to the financial capacity and accountability of members entering into transactions for themselves or for others. These were necessary because transactions in such markets are concluded anonymously, without the benefit of individual credit judgments concerning counterparties. In exchange markets for securities, the clearing agency assures delivery of an asset against payment; in most derivative markets, the clearing system guarantees the obligation to make daily payments of losses.

Regulatory overlap exists in the options market in the U.S. Registered broker-dealers may engage in OTC option transactions, subject to NASD rules, position limits, SEC capital and fraud rules. If they are also members of options exchanges, some margin rules extend to their OTC transactions.

Futures and commodity options, including options on government securities and futures are within the jurisdiction of the CFTC. Options on securities, including on common stock and government debt, options on foreign currency when traded on exchanges, and options on stock indices, are within the SEC's jurisdiction.

SIMEX supervises compliance with exchange rules by its members, of which BFS was one. It is the self-regulatory organization for financial futures in Singapore and subject to the Monetary Authority of Singapore. SIMEX carries out general surveillance of BFS activities on the exchange and inspects on site. BFS had to submit quarterly and annual financial statements certified by an external auditor and daily position reports. SIMEX inspected BFS April 1993, fining it S$23,000 for several violations. It inspected BFS again in September 1994, looking only at segregation of client funds and client margins. SIMEX considered disciplinary action on five counts, telling BFS on January 16. BFS replied on January 30 and February 13 that the problems were clerical errors. SIMEX'S Audit and Review Department assessed BFS' liquidity in December 1994 and wrote to BFS on January 27, 1995 that its liquidity was low given the large positions on December 30. BFS replied on February 10, assuring SIMEX that there was no problem.

As BFS's positions grew in late 1994, SIMEX required BFS to give it daily reports of customer positions. Errors in these reports prompted SIMEX to call for a written explanation. Leeson drafted the reply. The financial surveillance led SIMEX to write to BFS twice in January. It appeared that BFS was financing customers' positions (because 88888 was presented as a customer account to SIMEX), which SIMEX rules forbade. BSL sent senior officials to Singapore, including the Barings Group Treasurer in early February, to assure SIMEX that BFS could meet all margin calls. BFS also stated that it did not deal directly with Barings' customers.

SIMEX's Market Surveillance Department noticed that BFS would periodically exceed its maximum allowed contracts per customer. According to the Singapore Report:

> Under SIMEX Rules, no client may hold a position in excess of 1,000 outstanding Nikkei futures except with SIMEX's approval. BFS had apparently been granted an extended limit of 10,000 ... for BSL's trading. This limit was to cover trading in both futures and options.

> Based on the positions reported to SIMEX, ... BFS had exceeded its approved limit on a few occasions. However, SIMEX relied on the fact that the margins were being met in full, and did not raise the matter with BFS.

a. SIMEX'S MARGIN RULES

The primary method SIMEX employed to protect itself was margin rules. The regulations they adopted tended to reflect that of most futures exchanges, as discussed, *supra*. The Singapore Report described SIMEX's margin rules as follows:

> The SIMEX Clearing House [which is a counterparty to all trades] maintains a strict "no debt" policy. In the "mark-to-market" process, the daily closing price is used to value all open positions at the end of each day. Clearing members with profitable positions have the profits credited to their accounts, while those with losses have their accounts debited. Each morning, SIMEX is notified by way of confirmation from settlement banks that all amounts due on losses incurred the previous trading day, known as settlement variations, have been collected from the accounts of all corporate clearing members.

> Clearing members place margin deposits to cover the potential losses on outstanding contracts with the SIMEX Clearing House. The clearing members, in turn, obtain margin deposits from their clients. The margin deposits required for particular types of contracts are fixed by SIMEX and revised periodically based on market volatility studies in accordance with international norms. SIMEX uses the Standard Portfolio Analysis of Risk ("SPAN") margin system to calculate margins. SPAN evaluates the overall risk of a portfolio of futures and options contracts and matches margins to risk. The system is able to consolidate the risks of a futures instrument with the risks of an option on the same futures instrument. SPAN simulates the reaction of a portfolio to a range of possible market changes and then covers the largest reasonable overnight loss.

> SIMEX margin requirements for open positions are computed on a gross basis. For this reason, one client's long positions may not be used to offset another client's short position in determining the amount of margins to be placed with the Clearing House. Also, SIMEX clearing members must separately maintain margins with the Clearing House for client positions and for their own house positions.

House and client positions cannot be used to offset one another for margining purposes.

SIMEX settlement prices are the official daily closing prices of individual contracts determined according to SIMEX Rules. The amounts to be received by or paid to SIMEX by clearing members as a result of marking the position to market are known as settlement variations.

All corporate clearing members are jointly and severally liable for the obligations of the Clearing House. As a result, corporate clearing members are required to maintain higher prescribed minimum levels of paid up share capital, net tangible assets, security deposits and adjusted net capital relative to other categories of members.

Although margin payments to and from SIMEX took place on T+1 for U.S. dollar transactions, SIMEX allowed payment on T+2 for Yen denominated transactions and it allowed initial margins for the Yen transactions to be posted in U.S. dollars. It also allowed an exception for margins "forthcoming in a reasonable time," which it defined as 3 days.

SIMEX's margins overall were less onerous than OSE's. SIMEX's effective rate could be as much as one-third below those of OSE, depending on the portfolio. For stock index futures, OSE set the initial margin for members at 10% of the contract value and for their clients at 15%. For stock index options, OSE set the members' initial margin at the premium plus 15% of the cash market index value and for customers at the premium plus 20%. SIMEX simply kept the option seller's premium. In other ways, OSE's margin rules were slightly less onerous. OSE permitted each member to keep only one account, in which it could net house accounts but not client positions. OSE margins were due from clients to members on T+2 and from members to the exchange (and vice versa) on T+3.

b. LEESON'S COMPLIANCE WITH SIMEX MARGIN RULES

Leeson was responsible for complying only with the margin rules of SIMEX; BSJ met the margin requirements of the Japanese exchanges. Leeson met the SIMEX margin rules mainly by raising funds from his three clients within the Barings group (BSL, BSLL, and BSJ), as described above. The non-Barings client, BNP Tokyo, was not a major source. Leeson also drew intra-day credit from Citibank, Singapore.

Barings' derivatives trading grew to a large share of total trading on both SIMEX and the Japanese exchanges. Barings' share of total volume on SIMEX was 2.5% in December 1992, 7.7% in December 1993, reached 12.1% in September 1994 and, after declining slightly, 12.7% in January 1995. Barings' share of Nikkei 225 options contracts on SIMEX was 10% in April 1993 and 40% by January 1995. In Japan, Barings' share of open futures contracts on the OSE was 5.2% on December 30, 1994 and rose to 15.6% by February 1995.

Near the end of 1994 as the volumes grew, Leeson needed much more to fund margins than in the past. He convinced BSJ to leave substantial funds with BFS to use to meet intra-day assessments even though SIMEX rarely assessed them. He sold options to raise funds in a round-about way. SIMEX would credit him with the purchase price but immediately debit his account for the full amount, which it held as margin. Leeson did not receive the purchase price. He asked BSL to advance the money for the option margin as if it had not been paid by the option purchase price. BSL did as requested. And Leeson lied to SIMEX about the size of BFS's positions, understating the amount to be margined. He did so by netting the BSJ positions with the 88888 offsetting positions even though SIMEX did not permit netting of this sort.

SIMEX eventually uncovered problems with Account 88888. According to the Singapore Report, Lesson had BFS's settlement clerks regularly reduce the monthly closing balances on 88888 to almost zero at the end of each month by an overnight transfer, on BFS's books, to BFS's Citibank account, which was reversed the next morning. This was done by false accounting entries. Since SIMEX was checking BFS's quarterly reports to it against BFS's accounts, rather than verifying the books' "completeness and accuracy," SIMEX inspectors did not notice the practice. But as trading picked up in late 1994, SIMEX noticed a S$100 million discrepancy. According to the Singapore Report,

> On 28 December 1994, in the course of monitoring BFS's compliance with SIMEX Rules on customer margin requirements, SIMEX requested BFS to submit a report showing the computation of the SPAN margin on account 88888, which had been reported to SIMEX as a sub-account of ... a BSL account. This led to the discovery of a discrepancy of US$100 million ... between BFS's stated margin requirement for [the overall] account ... of US$242.1 million, and SIMEX's computation, based on BFS's SPAN margin computation report, of US$342.1 million for account 88888.

The same day, SIMEX demanded an explanation. BFS told SIMEX it must wait for Leeson to return from a trip. On January 11, having no reply, SIMEX wrote to the senior Barings officer in Singapore. He had Leeson draft a reply that was sent on January 25.

After Barings collapsed and SIMEX closed out its business, SIMEX was able to return US$86 million to BFS. As it turned out, the margins it held more than protected it and its other members.

Notes and Questions

1. What danger did Leeson's fraud pose to SIMEX? Were SIMEX's rules to protect itself adequate? One could conclude that existing safeguards on SIMEX, and the Japanese exchanges, are adequate since neither exchange had to draw on more than the margins from Barings. Do you agree with this? Consider the implications of the timing of margin

payments on both SIMEX and OSE. Consider how important it should be to an exchange that a position is hedged or not. How easily could the exchange distinguish between the two in practice? What does each consideration suggest about the risk to the exchange? Should SIMEX have required same day payment of margins? Why might it not?

2. Did SIMEX react quickly enough after discovering BFS's failure to comply with various rules? If you think not, what could account for its delay?

3. How could Leeson's exposure have gone undiscovered by the exchange for so long?

a. SIMEX did not compare Leeson's reports against the books of other Barings units or Barings positions on OSE. Could SIMEX expect to get accurate information without doing so? Would closer cooperation with OSE have protected SIMEX much more?

b. Is this simply a matter of fraud, which no regulations can completely eliminate? Or did the regulations themselves, as written or implemented, contribute to the crisis? For example, OSE set higher margin requirements for customers than members while SIMEX set the same for both. Would one of these two approaches be more likely to have revealed Leeson's camouflaged positions sooner than the other? How significant is it that the exchanges missed what seem to have been major flaws in Barings' management of its futures and options operations?

4. THE REGULATORY ROLE OF SECURITIES AND FUTURES AUTHORITY (SFA)

According to the BoE Report:

The SFA, as a self-regulating organization under the Financial Services Act 1986 (FSA), authorized BB&CO, BSL, and BSLL to carry out certain types of investment business in the UK. The SFA has a duty to regulate the investment businesses of its member firms conducted in the UK in order to afford an adequate level of protection for investors. Accordingly, the SFA regulates its members in relation to: their financial resources; the security of investors' money and assets held by members; and the fair and proper conduct of investment business undertaken. The regulation of the financial resources of BB&Co was delegated by the SFA to the Bank under a Memorandum of Understanding (MoU) in April 1991.

As a matter of policy, the SFA accepts no responsibility for the subsidiaries of firms it regulates other than as counterparties to transactions with those firms. The FSA gives it no power to regulate the business of non-member firms. Thus the SFA would not have expected to know about, for example, large proprietary positions taken by BFS. By letter on October 6, 1994, the SFA specifically waived any requirement that BSL provide accounts of its overseas subsidiaries.

The SFA is interested in the operations of subsidiaries that could affect the financial integrity of its members. Only after the collapse, however, the SFA learned that BSL had not reported as counterparty risk balances for margined futures and options transactions it provided to BFS. One reason the SFA did not know this is that it did not receive internal audit reports from its members. The SFA did know that BSL had significant credits (from £100 to £500 million) from January 1994 to "trade debtors" identified as affiliates on behalf of the affiliates' customers. But the SFA did not learn that BFS was the major affiliate. The SFA said it would expect to see large amounts due from affiliates given the nature of BSL's international business.

During 1996, the SFA banned several former Barings managers who had supervised Leeson from holding similar positions for three years. See J. Gapper, *Former Barings Director Banned*, Financial Times, May 29, 1996.

Notes and Questions

1. The BoE report criticizes the policy that allowed the SFA not to examine key subsidiaries. This, it said, allowed key SFA officials to ignore market discussion of Barings' large exposures in the Far East. Do you agree? What would justify the SFA policy?

2. The BoE report also criticized the SFA for not requiring more information about the trade debt due from affiliates, but recognized that the SFA would not have known of a potential problem from the data submitted. Was this a dereliction of SFA's duty to protect the security of investors' money and assets held by members? What might account for SFA's approach?

5. THE ROLE OF THE BANK OF ENGLAND AS LEAD REGULATOR

Among financial regulators of U.K. institutions, BoE was the "lead regulator" of the Barings Group. It held this status by agreements -- memoranda of understanding -- with the other U.K. regulators, such as the SFA, rather than by statute. As lead regulator, BoE received and analyzed data for consolidated (Group-wide) capital ratios and consolidated large exposures and BoE assessed the risks to BB&Co from the non-bank units of the Barings Group. BoE did not supervise the non-bank units. The College of Regulators for the Barings Group included BoE, SFA, and two other agencies not germane here. The College regulated by exception, which meant that members only focused on institutions that a member specifically identified as a concern to it. At no meeting of the College was Barings identified.

As regulator of deposit-taking institutions, BoE supervised BB&Co itself. In this capacity, BoE worked with Barings as it tried to merge the business of BB&Co and BSL in the early 1990s, which included possible "solo consolidation" of their accounts, described below.

BoE was also the "lead regulator" for purposes of the Basel Concordat. The Basel Committee, which includes Japan and the U.K., meets quarterly. At no meeting was Barings identified as a concern. Singapore participates in the Offshore Group of Banking Supervision, represented by its Monetary Authority. The Committee and the Offshore Group agreed to principles that would help banking supervisors in member countries collaborate. One principle said that host authorities suspecting or discovering a material problem should communicate immediately with the parent authority. Another specified that host authorities should give parent authority adequate data, particularly about large exposures. Neither regulators in Singapore or Japan informed BoE of concerns or large exposures for Barings.

a. THE KEY INDICATORS

The BoE Report listed key indicators or warning signs that could have alerted observers to Barings' potential problems early enough to prevent collapse. The Report concluded that most indicators were not known to BoE. In the following list, only the last three were available to BoE. Consider why BoE would not receive information about the others.

a. The identification of the lack of segregation of duties in BFS between front and back offices, which was subsequently reflected in the internal audit report following the review of BFS's operations which was conducted in July and August 1994;

b. The unreconciled balance of funds ... transferred from Barings in London to BFS for margins;

c. The discovery of the purported transaction relating to an apparent receivable of ¥7.778 billion (approximately £50 million) ...;

d. The letter sent by SIMEX to BFS on 11 January 1995 ... which included specific reference account '88888' and its large funding requirements; and the letter set by SIMEX to BFS on 27 January 1995 (which was communicated to London) in which SIMEX sought assurance regarding BFS's ability to fund its margin calls should there be adverse market movements;

e. The high level of inter-exchange arbitrage (or 'switching') positions without any application of gross limits;

f. Market concerns circulating in January and February 1995;

g. Issues and questions arising out of Barings' reporting of large exposures and client money to supervisors and regulators;

h. The apparent high profitability of BFS's trading activities relative to the low level of risk as perceived and authorized by Barings' management in London; and

i. The high level of funding required to finance BFS's trading activities.

The following sections discuss the large exposures and the effect of solo consolidation for BSL with BB&Co.

b. LARGE EXPOSURES

The U.K. Banking Act requires banks to notify the BoE before incurring an exposure of more than 25% of its capital base to a person or closely related persons. A BoE notice in 1993 removed from BoE supervisors the authority to allow higher exposures in exceptional circumstances. UK banks must also file quarterly reports with BoE identifying all exposures over 10% of their capital base and their highest exposure in the period.

From January 1993 to December 1994, Barings did not report, before or after incurring them, its entire exposures to OSE: it excluded margins on segregated customer positions. Even so, its reported exposures exceeded the ceiling of 25% of its consolidated capital base (CCB) every quarter but one. The reported ratios were, by quarter: 31.6%, 44.6%, 37.1% 24.7%, 41.5%, and 27.9%. Barings told BoE in January 1993 that margins on Barings' proprietary positions should be seen as a Barings' exposure and margins on clients' positions should not. Barings added that margins on its proprietary positions should not be treated as a single large exposure. Instead, one should "look through" the exchange to its members, who were the first line of defense should the exchange be unable to meet its obligations and default on the margins.

BoE told Barings at a meeting in May 1994 that it would regard the entire margin amount, including that from segregated customer accounts, as Barings' exposure unless Barings got a legal opinion that Barings would not be exposed by a failure of the OSE to repay margin on segregated customer accounts. Barings replied that it could not do so because Japan lacked a clear agency law. BoE agreed to write its views in a letter to Barings, but failed to do so.

From then until the issue of "looking through" OSE was resolved, the BoE's supervisor for Barings acted as though he had given Barings an "informal" or unwritten concession allowing its margins with OSE to exceed 25%. The supervisor did not have the written approval of more senior BoE officials, although BoE's internal regulations seemed to call for that. He understood that Barings could not pre-notify the BoE of clients' margins because it was up to the client to decide when to take the position. The supervisor did not regard the exposure as endangering the financial health of Barings. He said that said he would have been concerned if the exposure/capital ratio exceeded 50% and it did not until February 1995, when it was 73% at the collapse. And he did not notify the SFA.

Barings treated its margin exposure to SIMEX the same way, although this was never discussed with BoE.

BoE gave its final decision in January 1995, two years later, only after Barings wrote on January 18, 1995 asking for BoE's decision. The BoE said it lacked discretion and that Barings must reduce the total exposure to 25%. BoE understood that Barings would need time to do so.

c.   SOLO CONSOLIDATION AND LENDING BY BB&Co to BSL for BFS

When Barings collapsed, BFS owed BSL £337 million and BSLL £105 millions. BSLL had funded most of this by borrowing from BB&Co, the treasurer for the Group. The rest BSLL borrowed from other banks. BSL had funded much of its clients' margin calls and drew on BB&Co to finance the credit. The total borrowed from BB&Co far exceeded 25% of the merchant bank's capital. This very large exposure was possible in part because BSL was "solo consolidated" with BB&Co.

BoE permits solo consolidation when the links between the bank and another company are strong, so that the parent bank manages the other and no obstacle would prevent the other from paying surplus capital to the bank, particularly if the other were to be wound up. The effect of solo consolidation is to treat the other company as a department of the bank.

When Barings began in 1992 to amalgamate the business of its merchant bank and its securities company, it started discussions with BoE to solo consolidate BSL with BB&Co. This would be a first: BoE had never before allowed a large securities firm to solo consolidate with a bank. A major problem for BoE was the different capital adequacy rules for the two. BoE wanted to avoid regulatory arbitrage. In November 1993, Barings received a letter from its BoE supervisor that seemed to allow provisional solo consolidation pending a resolution of the debate within BoE about capital adequacy. Barings proceeded with solo consolidation on the basis of this letter.

Although the 25% limit continued to govern lending by the solo consolidated group (BB&Co and BSL) to others in the Barings Group, the limit was not effective. As described above, BSL loaned substantially more to BFS. The BoE Report explained:

> The failure of controls in Barings meant that, following the solo consolidation of BSL with BB&Co, the connected lending limit did not provide an effective barrier between the solo consolidated group and BFS; funds which as a matter of law constituted loans by BB&Co to BSL were passed to BFS without limit. ...

By late 1994, BB&Co had loaned about £200 million to BSL, almost 40% of capital, and £150 million more than BB&Co had been allowed to lend BSL before the provisional solo consolidation.

BoE also gives "treasury concessions" for bank loans to certain other members of a group of companies related to the bank that allow the bank to lend much more than the normal 25% lending limit. The specific amount, called the treasury concession, may be 100% of the bank's unconsolidated or solo consolidated capital and often exceeds that amount "for historical reasons." For BB&Co, the concessions had been 257% in 1991 and fell to 117.5% by its collapse. No concessions existed for overseas securities subsidiaries, which were subject to the 25% connected lending limit. A concession of £85 million existed for loans to BSLL. From January 1993 to December 1994, however, errors reporting BB&Co's solo consolidated exposure to BSLL prevented BoE from learning the full amount. BoE staff recognized but did not discuss these errors with Barings. BoE waited instead, for example, for Barings to develop a group-wide audit system. BSLL had on-loaned some of this to BSJ. And the funds helped BSLL fund its margin requirements for Barings' proprietary positions executed by BFS.

BoE staff learned only in November 1994 that Barings' arbitrage business in the Far East was about £250-300 million. It learned because Barings asked to solo consolidate BSJ with BB&Co so that the merchant bank could fund BSJ's arbitrage. Barings' idea was to replace current funding from external banks with cheaper funding from BB&Co. The proposal failed because BSJ could not eliminate all its external funding, as required for solo consolidation.

Notes and Questions

1. Could the BoE have done a better job as lead regulator that could have prevented the Barings crisis? Please review the key indicators or warning signs in Section 5(a) above. Are there practical solutions to these problems?

2. Is the failure of both the U.K. College of Regulators and the Basel Committee/Offshore Group to identify Barings as a problem somehow inherent in their collaboration? After all, if the key regulatory agencies -- SIMEX and BoE – failed to identify the problem, is it likely that a committee could do more?

3. How concerned should bank regulators be about the role of Barings merchant bank (BB&Co) in the events leading to the crisis? Is this just a matter of requiring better prudential regulation or does it suggest that deposit-taking institutions should be completely separated from securities firms (recall the discussion of approaches to capital adequacy for securities operations in Chapter 4)?

4. The BoE Report concluded that the "informal concession" permitting BB&Co to exceed its large exposure limits to OSE and SIMEX without any limits on the size of the concession was "an error of judgment." Had Barings been held to the 25% limit for OSE, Leeson might not have been able to raise funds so readily in late January and February 1995, said the Report. The BoE Report also found that the informal way BoE granted solo consolidation for BSL meant BoE failed to "fully assess the impact of BSL being solo consolidated with BB&Co."

The Report did not pin the failures only on the individuals in BoE responsible for Barings. It does not, however, reveal compelling reasons for the informal approach, although BoE historically has been very informal in its supervision of banks. Certainly its senior managers did not push for a more formal approach. What does this story suggest about the ability of lead regulators to do their job?

5. BoE staff acted slowly, even had to be prodded, at several times and on several topics that turn out, with hindsight, to have been critical. How fast a reaction is fast enough, particularly in the derivatives markets? Could any reasons of policy explain the apparently slow reaction? How does BoE compare with SIMEX in speed of action? What would explain the similarities or differences?

6. The Treasury Committee of the House of Commons published a report in December 1996 criticizing the BoE for poor supervision when evaluating banks' internal controls, communicating among its own staff, and applying its own rules. It suggested a conflict of interest, since BOE both supervises and promotes London as a financial center. The Committee recommended removing the Department of Trade and Industry from supervision (due to securities operations) so that the Treasury Department alone would be responsible for financial regulation. J. Blitz, *MPs Hit at Bank of England's Role over Barings*, Financial Times, Dec. 17, 1996. In July 1998, all financial sector supervisory activities were consolidated within the new Financial Supervisory Agency, with the banking supervisors transferred from the Bank of England. In June 2000, the U.K. passed the Financial Services and Markets Act, formally replacing the very decentralized supervision, that characterized U.K. regulation during the Barings crisis, with a super-regulator. *FSM Bill Finally Clears Parliament, Full Implementation Seen Next Year,* Bureau of National Affairs, Inc. June 2000 at 3.

6. THE AFTERMATH: WINDING DOWN AND TRANSFERRING OWNERSHIP

The exchanges wound down Barings' loss-making positions and BoE arranged for its sale in the manner described below.

SINGAPORE. SIMEX took Barings' loss-making positions on Monday, February 27, 1995 and announced it would wind them down by March 10. SIMEX refused to reveal the size of Barings' open positions and the price at which it acquired them. SIMEX said the information would have made it harder to get a good liquidation price. Foreign dealers doing business with SIMEX said they wanted to know the amounts in order to know whether SIMEX itself was sound. Several refused to pay margins until Singapore's central bank stated on Monday February 27 that SIMEX would not use those fees to meet its other obligations.

By Wednesday March 1, SIMEX had wound down most of Barings' positions. By March 16, it had either liquidated or transferred all the positions. SIMEX left untouched a US$ 300 million letter of credit it had arranged from local financial institutions, a small compensation fund, and the $200 million collective liability of its members for losses. After SIMEX returned S$47m ($33.6m) to BFS, which had held this cash before the collapse, ING Barings claimed the money because it had acquired BFS and paid the claims of its trade creditors. The UK High Court ruled instead that ING Barings did not have priority over other creditors, notably bond holders.

One reason Barings' margins with SIMEX were adequate may have been that the stock index price recovered somewhat on February 28 (only to fall on March 1). One question was whether the Singapore government helped in any way. The Monetary Authority of Singapore had foreign exchange reserves of $60 billion. The government had a fiscal surplus of S$10 billion.

JAPAN. OSE revealed the size of Barings' long futures positions with it: 16,937 contracts on February 24. Losses were estimated at the equivalent of $175 million on February 28. The OSE's average acquisition price per contract was ¥18,180. Its average sale price was ¥16,800. OSE froze the positions of Barings' clients on February 27.

Daiwa Securities was appointed to liquidate the OSE positions. Daiwa sold 49.9% on March 1 and 50.1% on March 2. The market price dropped on March 1, but rose March 2. One broker was reported as saying that there was "no point in going bearish .... Everyone would have lost."

OSE's reserves, built by member firms, were ¥6.1 billion against futures losses and ¥2.3 billion against stock losses. But OSE did not have to call on them. Margins supplied by BSJ, the only member of the Barings Group to operate on the OSE, were sufficient.

UNITED KINGDOM. The Bank of England took over Baring Brothers on February 27. Having decided that Barings posed no systemic risk, the Bank of England was prepared to let it fail but preferred to find a buyer. Several foreign banks were interested. The Bank of England accepted ING Bank's offer.

The acquisition arrangement identified how ING Bank would deal with Barings' creditors, which included the following groups:

-   securities firms that were creditors of Barings in the course of business.

-   banks, mainly in Japan, that had loaned to fund Barings' margin calls.

-   depositors in Barings' merchant bank, who were owed £2.5 billion. About 40% were other banks and 60% were 3,000 non-bank clients, including municipalities and pension funds. Bank of England immediately froze the money; in the worst case, 75% of deposits to £15,000 had deposit insurance.

- banks like Deutsche Bank that as part of a transaction like a currency exchange had transferred funds to Barings' merchant bank but not yet received the funds the merchant bank owed it when the Bank of England closed Barings (Herstatt risk).

- owners of funds managed by Barings' units; 5% of the funds' £27.8 billion ($43 billion) in assets was in cash and Barings merchant bank held about £600 million, commingling it with the bank's own funds and using it to meet the margin calls in February 1995.

- investors in about $550 million of bonds issued by financing subsidiaries of Barings PLC and guaranteed by it.

- investors in a bond of £100 million issued by Barings PLC.

Two other groups were potential claimants when Bank of England started its negotiations. The extent of their claims would not be known until later. As it happened, neither had claims, but this would not have been known until late in the acquisition talks.

- SIMEX and OSE, whose margin calls had not been met after February 23 at the latest.

- securities customers whose margins were mingled with those of Barings in a single account at SIMEX and which would take several days at least to unscramble.

ING Bank acquired Barings' securities, asset management, and merchant banking operations (which particular subsidiaries were included is not clear). For this, it paid £1 and promised the Bank of England to invest £660 million more to pay the debts of those operations. ING Bank agreed to repay a $150 million loan from Barings BV to BSL, which ING had acquired (it is not clear if this amount was part of the £660 million). After writing off Leeson's losses and the cost incurred when the exchanges prematurely closed their derivative contracts with Barings upon its liquidation, only £62 million was left to meet unexpected costs of the acquired units.

ING Bank did not acquire Barings PLC, the group's holding company, and some of its other subsidiaries. It refused to accept liability for $300 million in notes issued by an offshore financing vehicle. Euroclear declared half of this, an FRN, in default March 10. ING Bank offered to pay 7.5% of the face value of £100 million in subordinated perpetual bonds Barings PLC had issued in 1994. Large UK insurers were major investors and considered law suits against Barings' directors and Ernst & Young, the administrator, for ignoring the bondholders in the acquisition.

It was not initially clear that ING Bank would have to, or want to, acquire Barings' operations in Japan because of their large debt. The extent of Barings' Japanese subsidiaries' losses was not clear. Since ING Bank eventually agreed to invest ¥10 billion in the subsidiaries, losses were probably in that magnitude. The losses would have included borrowing to finance its margin calls, overdrafts, and guarantees (most without collateral). The major creditors were 15 Japanese banks; 15-20 US and UK securities firms were less exposed.

Eventually ING Bank decided to acquire the Japanese operations, with MOF's approval on March 9. The timing suggests that this acquisition was not integral to ING's agreement with the Bank of England.

The acquisition solved many problems that might otherwise have led to litigation. Deutsche Bank, for example, prepared to sue but then decided not to when ING Bank acquired Barings. BB&Co would now be able to pay Deutsche Bank. But opportunity costs accompanied the efforts to resolve Barings' crisis. For example, 20 Barings unit trusts had independent trustees, but the Bank of England nevertheless froze about £650 million in assets until March 2.

The ripple beyond Barings was minor. During the first week of the crisis, the Bank of England had to lend funds short term to a small UK bank that could not tap the money markets because of depositor nervousness.

After cleaning up, Britain and Singapore set about to find out what happened, eventually producing the BoE Report and the Singapore Report. The two inspections teams did not cooperate. Indeed, each was kept at arms'-length from the other. The BoE Report described how its investigators were required to apply to a Singapore court for access to information held by the judicial managers responsible for liquidating BFS's positions there. The court declined to give access because it could not find sufficient benefit to BFS of doing so. The Singapore finance minister refused to allow the BoE investigators access to materials held by the authors of the Singapore Report. As a result, the BoE investigators were unable to evaluate the role of regulators abroad and the records of BFS's Singapore operations. The authors of the Singapore Report also encountered barriers in London.

Law suits were launched by various parties to the fiasco. For example, Barings' auditor, Coopers & Lybrand, was sued for negligence by the bank's administrators for up to £1bn ($1.6bn). The case reached the courtroom in October 2001, after KPMG replaced Ernst & Young as administrator, and some predicted it could last, with appeals, to 2010. Coopers, in turn, had decided to sue nine ex-directors and managers for this amount. See J. Kelly and J. Gapper, *Ex-Barings Chiefs to be Sued by Bank's Auditors*, Financial Times, Nov. 30-31, 1996; M. Peel, *Barings Creditors Demand Cut in Fees*, Financial Times, Aug. 13, 2001; and J. Eaglesham, *Auditors' Failure to Detect Leeson Fraud Blamed for Bank's Downfall*, Financial Times, Oct. 3, 2001.

At steep discounts, vulture funds had bought many of the £150 million of FRNs issued by Barings and acquired a majority stake. In late 1998, these funds voted to reject an arbitrator's proposal that ING, Coopers &

Lybrand, and Deloitte & Touche pay bondholders 60% of the FRNs' face value. The funds believed they could negotiate a better settlement. Other bondholders had wanted to settle. The vulture funds similarly prevented a settlement with Coopers in July 2001.

Notes and Questions

1.   Review the Windsor Declaration and the declaration implementing it (below). Do they provide for enough cooperation among supervisors to protect against more problems like Barings? If not, what further cooperation would you recommend?

2.   Consider the time it took both exchanges to wind down Barings' positions. Was it fast? Slow? What might account for this?

3.   What does the Bank of England's resolution of the Barings crisis suggest about the allocation of risk in futures and options? Which creditors does the Bank of England appear to favor? How would its resolution of the crisis look to Japanese creditors? Do you see any parallels with the handling of BCCI? Should investors in bonds issued or guaranteed by the holding company add the Bank of England to their list of culpable parties along with Barings' directors and the administrator?

4.   What does the failure of the U.K. and Singapore investigators to cooperate say about the ability of regulators to cooperate in the future? What would explain their failure to cooperate in the investigations?

5.   Other Barings-type losses surfaced after Mr. Leeson's activities left the front page. National Westminster Bank (NatWest), a leading UK bank caught the attention of options traders for over a year by appearing to underprice options it traded. In late February 1997, NatWest announced losses of more than £50 million on OTC interest rate options and fired five traders. The traders had been reviewed consistently by controllers, but apparently the model all used was too simple for the complex trades. Since the options were not exchange-traded, market prices were not readily available and the bank relied on the traders' estimates of the options' value. The model permitted the traders to set off options with different risk profiles against one another. See G. Gapper, *When the Smile is Wiped Off*, Financial Times, Mar. 8-9, 1997, and D. Shirreff, *Lessons from NatWest*, Euromoney, May 1997. In 1999, Scudder Kember Investments, Inc. discovered that a derivatives trader in Boston had miscoded, forged, or failed to submit order tickets from 1997 to late 1998, incurring losses of $16 million by the time he was discovered. *Scudder Kemper Investments Has Barings-Type Scare*, 1 Derivatives Report 2 (Jan. 2000).

6.   In November 2000, ING decided to sell the U.S. operations of Barings and end the separate existence, and name, for the rest of the operations. C. Pretzlik, *Interest in ING Sell-Off in US*, Financial Times, Nov. 22, 2000.

7. INTERNATIONAL EFFORTS TO AVOID ANOTHER BARINGS CRISIS

When the Barings crisis broke, the regulators of many futures and options markets in East and Southeast Asia, Europe, and North America quickly became involved. Mary Shapiro, the chairman of the CFTC, played a leading role coordinating a regulatory response.

From the crisis came a belief among regulators and players in the industry that cooperative efforts were essential to avoid a recurrence of the Barings crisis. To that end, they formulated the principles described in the following documents. As you read them, consider these two questions:

1. If these understandings had existed from 1993, could they have averted the Barings crisis?

2. Do the agreed principles solve the major problems revealed by the Barings crisis?

a. THE WINDSOR DECLARATION

Meeting May 16-17, 1995 in Windsor, U.K., representatives of financial futures and options regulators from 16 countries agreed to certain steps they hoped would strengthen international supervision. They embodied these in the Windsor Declaration, which is presented below. The "Authorities" represented included regulators from Australia, Brazil, Canada, France, Germany, Hong Kong, Italy, Japan, Netherlands, Singapore, South Africa, Spain, Sweden, Switzerland, the U.S., and the U.K.

The authorities addressed issues related to:

+ Co-operation between market authorities
+ Protection of customer positions, funds and assets
+ Default procedures
+ Regulatory co-operation in emergencies

Their points of consensus related to all "markets": futures and options exchanges, and clearing houses. They agreed:

a) to "support, subject to appropriate confidentiality protections, mechanisms to improve prompt communication of information relevant to material exposures and other regulatory concerns" among market regulators and authorities.

b) to "review the adequacy of existing arrangements to minimize the risk of loss through insolvency or misappropriation and enhance such arrangements as appropriate" in order to protect customers and reduce systemic risk.

c) to promote, in the context of national insolvency regimes, "national provisions and market procedures that facilitate the prompt liquidation and/or transfer of positions, funds and assets, from failing members of futures exchanges." The authorities recognized the importance of "effective margining systems [to] mitigate the risk of losses arising from the inability of solvent participants to close out or manage their exposures to a failing market member."

d) to "support measures to enhance emergency procedures at financial intermediaries, market members and markets and to improve existing mechanisms for international co-operation and communication among market authorities and regulators."

These four goals led the authorities to agree to promote the following activities. See Article II:

✦ Active surveillance within each jurisdiction of large exposures by market authorities and/or regulators as appropriate.

✦ Development of mechanisms to ensure that customer positions, funds and assets can be separately identified and held safe to the maximum extent possible and in accordance with national law.

✦ Enhanced disclosure by the markets of the different types and levels of protection of customer funds and assets which may prevail, particularly when they arc transferred to different jurisdictions, including through omnibus accounts.

✦ Record-keeping systems at exchanges and clearing houses and/or market members which ensure that positions, funds and assets to be treated as belonging to customers can be satisfactorily distinguished from other positions, funds and assets.

✦ Enhanced disclosure by markets to participants of the rules and procedures governing what constitutes a default and the treatment of positions, funds and assets of member firms and their clients in the event of such a default.

✦ The immediate designation by each regulator of a contact point for receiving information or providing other assistance to other regulators and/or market authorities and the means to assure twenty-four hour availability of contact personnel in the event of disruption occurring at a financial intermediary, market member or market.

✦ Review of existing lists and assuring maintenance by IOSCO of an international regulatory contacts list.

✦ The development by financial intermediaries, market members or markets and regulatory authorities of contingency arrangements, or a review of the adequacy of existing arrangements, and enhancement as appropriate.

To implement these activities, the authorities recommended that "the appropriate international bodies" carry out certain studies. IOSCO would take the lead.

Notes and Questions

1.   In June 1995, the Futures Industry Association published a follow up report.   Members of the FIA included major futures and options exchanges and major firms operating in the markets.   After recommending action for exchanges and clearing houses concerning member and customer protection, margin requirements, information, transfers of customer property, and risk assessment and management for exchanges, the FIA proposed action on legal issues. These follow:

FUTURES INDUSTRY ASSOCIATION,
FINANCIAL INTEGRITY RECOMMENDATIONS FOR FUTURES AND OPTIONS MARKETS AND MARKET PARTICIPANTS
(1995).

Bankruptcy Issues

21.   The bankruptcy or other relevant laws of each jurisdiction should provide for (or at least not prevent) the prompt close out of positions and/or transfer of customer positions and property from a defaulted broker/intermediary to another broker/intermediary. Where necessary, exemptions from any automatic "stay" or similar provisions should be implemented in order to permit such transfers or close outs to be made.

22.   The bankruptcy or other relevant laws of each jurisdiction should clearly specify the rights of customers and brokers/intermediaries upon the default of a clearinghouse, broker/intermediary or depository with respect to the customer and proprietary assets held by such clearinghouse, broker/intermediary or depository, including any priority rights granted to customers with respect to such assets.

23.   Margin or settlement payments made to or from a broker/intermediary or exchange/clearinghouse should be protected from reversal in a bankruptcy proceeding.

24.   Legislators and regulatory authorities should attempt to harmonize conflicting bankruptcy regimes in different jurisdictions in order to provide, to the maximum extent possible, for consistent treatment of customer positions and property upon the bankruptcy of a clearinghouse, a depository or a broker/intermediary. In addition, the bankruptcy or other relevant laws should ensure that brokers/intermediaries and clearinghouses are permitted to exercise rights of netting and set-off in the event of a default by a customer, broker/intermediary or clearinghouse.

Coordination and Oversight by Regulatory Authorities

25.   Regulatory authorities in different jurisdictions should, to the extent practicable, harmonize conflicting regulatory requirements with respect to market participants operating or trading in multiple

jurisdictions. As part of this effort, regulatory authorities in each jurisdiction should clarify the scope of their authority with respect to domestic persons trading or engaging in other activities outside the jurisdiction and with respect to the trading or other activities of non-domestic persons within the jurisdiction.

26.   Appropriate systems of regulatory oversight (which may include delegations of oversight responsibilities to exchanges, clearinghouses or other self-regulatory organizations) should be established and enforced in each jurisdiction. Such systems should include oversight and periodic reviews of the operations and activities of exchanges, clearinghouses, brokers/intermediaries and, where appropriate, other market participants.

b. MARCH 1996 DECLARATION FOR INFORMATION SHARING

Almost a year after the Windsor Declaration, futures and options regulators pushed further in their effort to open lines of communication and information sharing. Many supervisory authorities signed the Declaration on Cooperation and Supervision of International Futures Markets and Clearing Organizations in March 1996. The idea was that the authorities, both regulators and some self-regulatory organizations, would share specific types of information in carefully defined circumstances. Key to this was the agreement to assure confidentiality.

The authorities defined events that would permit one to request information from another. "An Authority may make a Request if, within the ordinary course of its existing supervisory responsibilities, it becomes aware that any of the following events has occurred with respect to a Member of a Party:

(A) A large decrease in Owner's Equity in any six month period.

(B) A Member's cumulative net Variation Payments over ten consecutive business days for proprietary and non-customer positions which are unusually large in relation to the Member's Owner's Equity.

(C) A Member's cumulative net Variation Payments over six consecutive months for proprietary and non-customer positions are unusually large in relation to Member's Owner's Equity.

(D) A Member's net Variation Payments for customer positions for one business day which are of unusually large size in relation to the Member's Owner's Equity.

(E) Total positions in a contract registered in a Member's name which represent at least 50% of the total long or short positions in that contract, the Open Interest of which is greater than 25,000 but less than 100,000.

(F) Total positions in a contract registered in a Member's name which represent at least 25% of the total long or short positions in that contract, the Open Interest of which exceeds 100,000.

(G) A Member, Affiliate or a firm with a substantial commercial relationship to the Member experiences an event that is not listed but in the opinion of an Authority is of a similar magnitude, and the Authority determines that it has reasonable grounds to seek information in accordance with Article 3 of this Declaration.

The declaration left the definition of "large" and "unusually large" to the discretion of the Requesting Authority.

The request could "only be for information . . . relevant to the event that actually gave rise to the Request, and may relate only to information which the Requested Authority either maintains or has access to under relevant Laws, Rules and Regulations." It could go to any authority "that regulates a Party to which: (A) the affected Member; (B) an Affiliate of the Member; or (C) a firm with a substantial commercial relationship with the Member belongs." Oral requests had to be confirmed in writing and the confirmation had to contain specified information about the event, required data, purpose, and use.

An authority that receives a request agreed to "use reasonable efforts to obtain information from: (A) its records; (B) any other Authority in the jurisdiction of the Requested Authority which has access to relevant records; or (C) any other source in the jurisdiction of the Requested Authority from which such information might appropriately be sought." If cost became an issue, the requesting and requested authorities would consult. If local law interfered with the response, the requested authority would "use its best efforts to facilitate the delivery of information to the requesting Party or to its Authority."

The authority receiving information agreed to use it only to carry out its supervisory responsibilities and never "contrary to conditions relating to the use of that information imposed by the Requested Authority to give effect to Laws, Rules or Regulations in force in the Requested Authority's jurisdiction." No information could "be used for competitive advantage."

Confidentiality was to be preserved. The two authorities would "advise each other of the applicability of the Laws, Rules or Regulations which govern the provision, use and confidentiality of information which may be exchanged under this Declaration."

Notes and Questions

1. Some exchanges began to respond to the concerns being expressed about the risk of trading futures and options in such an environment. The London Clearing House announced that its members would provide up to £150m "if a party trading through the exchange defaults on its obligations." See P. John, *LCH Provides Crisis Cover for Derivatives*, Financial Times, Aug. 6, 1996. In the U.S., clearing members of the CME, CBOT, and Board of Trade Clearing Corporation would be subject to risk-based capital rules effective January 1, 1998. The new

rules would require members to hold "adjusted net capital in excess of the greatest of:

1.   Minimum dollar balances [set by the]... clearing organizations; or

2.   10% of ... customer and 4% of noncustomer (excluding proprietary) risk maintenance margin/performance bond requirements [based on the portfolio's price and volatility] for all ...futures and options on futures; or

3.   ...Minimum capital requirements [of the SEC or CFTC].

Previously, the higher SEC early warning level had been used. Non-customers are mainly other exchange members. The rules extend to the accounts of foreign customers trading in foreign markets, which had not been subject to capital rules before. See Chicago Mercantile Exchange/Chicago Board of Trade, and Board of Trade Clearing Corporation, *Risk Based Capital Requirement*, undated memorandum.

2.   The CFTC refined its Large-Trader Reporting System. Exchanges were to report, for each clearing member, by proprietary long and short positions of the member and each customer, as well as buy and sell orders, above specified amounts (e.g. 25 to 1000 open contracts). The CFTC surveillance staff aggregates related accounts across members and exchanges. The staff may contact traders for more information. The CFTC acknowledged as a major problem that many customers trade through intermediaries. See CFTC *Backgrounder*, No. 1-01, October 2001.

3.   Financial Accounting Standard 133 requires reporting companies to disclose the fair market value of their derivatives on their balance sheets, marking them to market. In a survey, some companies reported that they reduced their use of derivatives because the requirements were onerous. *Accounting Rule Change Hits Use of Derivatives*, Financial Times, June 13, 2001 (no author).

4.   Debate rages between those worried about the systemic dangers posed by the derivatives markets and those who deride the worriers. Many people, including U.S. Congressmen, believe the problem is big, though they often are speaking of the OTC markets. The enormous notional growth implies that operations outstrip systems. The complexity eludes the senior managers who are supposed to evaluate the systems and the risks, but must instead rely on the traders themselves, exposing the firm to possible fraud. The many imponderables cripple efforts to calculate exposures. Intra-day swings may be large. The industry responds that the risk is vastly overstated. Nothing has happened yet, say supporters. From the perspective of a U.S. bank regulator looking at the futures and options markets, how serious would you find these concerns?

5.   Several U.S. governmental initiatives were directed at the futures and options markets during 1994-5. The U.S. executive proposed taxing futures and options to raise $59 million a year. The Clinton Administration had proposed this once before and the Bush

Administration had proposed it three times. The U.S. exchanges observed that trading would move abroad "in a nanosecond" See L. Morse, *Traders Condemn Plan to Tax Futures*, Financial Times, Feb. 8, 1995. Five bills to regulate derivatives were introduced in Congress in 1994 and early 1995. One proposed a Federal Derivatives Commission that would merge the SEC and CFTC. Most were concerned with off-exchange activity.

6. Singapore integrated its legal regime for securities and derivatives. The draft Securities and Futures Act streamlined licensing, increased disclosure, tightened insider trading rules, and enhanced the MAS's enforcement powers, granting extra-territorial reach of "conduct within Singapore in relation to securities or futures contracts listed and traded overseas; and conduct outside Singapore in relation to securities and futures contracts listed or traded in Singapore." *Omnibus Securities, Futures Bill, Financial Advisers Bill Introduced*, Bureau of National Affairs, Oct. 2001, at 18.

7. Alerted by the Barings crisis to the potential dangers in clearing futures and options, regulators in the BIS systematically examined the problems in Clearing Arrangements for Exchange-Traded Derivatives, Mar. 1997. The report concluded that "clearing houses simply cannot be made fail-safe." It suggested stress testing to identify points of vulnerability. It welcomed the trend toward real time gross settlement (RTGS) payment systems and electronic trading as devices to monitor intraday risk to the exchanges and manage it by collecting cash margins intraday. The BIS looked forward to systems permitting final intraday transfers of securities that served as collateral for members. The BIS identified four major cross-border issues. First, contracts and collateral denominated in foreign currencies created special problems. For example, exchanges holding margin collateral in currencies other than that of the contract took on foreign exchange risk. Second, foreign members of a clearing house could, if they had no local presence, generate risk for the clearing house if their resources were based in another country. Third, collateral held in a foreign jurisdiction raised similar problem. Could the clearing house reach it readily? Finally, links between clearing houses in foreign countries created risk for the participants. One type was the clearing link, in which a "home" exchange for a contract is the primary counterparty even though an "away" exchange may temporarily act as a counterparty when it trades the same contract, but only until the home exchange opens. A second type is the mutual offset, in which members of several exchanges trading the same contract chose the exchange at which to hold the contract. When a position is transferred from the exchange on which the trade was executed to another exchange, the executing exchange takes a position at the second exchange and the second becomes a counterparty to a position at the executing exchange. The two exchanges must post initial margins with each other and make variation payments. In this process, they incur institutional risks that must be managed.

Links To Other Chapters

In earlier Chapters we saw many of the instruments that make up the assets underlying futures and options: the bonds traded on domestic and offshore markets (Chapters 2, 5, 8 and 12), the eurocurrency deposits (Chapter 9), and the foreign exchange instruments traded around the world (Chapter 6).

Futures and options are part of the wave of innovation that swept international finance beginning in the 1980s. Securitization (Chapter 13) and swaps (Chapter 17) are other examples. Motivating much of the innovation is the investors' desire to reduce risk. The same motive propels many institutional investors to diversify their portfolios internationally (Chapter 20).

The futures and options markets further integrate domestic financial markets. This tendency is also at work in the global offerings of bonds (Chapter 12) and equities (20) and in the competition and cooperation among exchanges, whether for futures and options or for stocks and bonds (Chapter 14).

The major tool to protect the futures and options markets, margining, supplements the capital adequacy rules seen earlier for banks and securities firms in these markets (Chapter 4). Many basic rules governing these markets appear in the readings about major countries (Chapters 2, 3, 5, and 8). The payments system, a possible tool of national control over the development of futures and options markets outside the country, is examined in detail in Chapter 10.

Finally, the still very limited use of futures and options on organized exchanges in developing countries contrasts with the dynamism of securities markets in emerging markets (Chapter 20).

CHAPTER SEVENTEEN

SWAPS

In this Chapter, we look at the most important OTC derivative, swaps. Unlike futures and options, this market is not based on an exchange. Instead, like the foreign exchange market, it consists of specific contracts negotiated and settled by individual parties (counterparties).

We begin the Chapter with a description of the two most widely used swaps, interest rate and currency swaps, an examination of why parties use them, and some characteristics of the overall market. Next we examine the risk of swaps, with particular attention to new forms of swaps like credit derivatives. A key question is whether swap risks are different and greater than risks involved in traditional banking activity, deposit-taking and lending. Our examination of risk concentrates on credit risk and market risk. This sets the scene for a discussion of important regulatory issues, disclosure standards, capital requirements, dealer liability and netting.

A. SWAP TRANSACTIONS AND MARKETS

We start with a description of some standard swap transactions.

1. SWAP TRANSACTIONS

S. HENDERSON, SWAP CREDIT RISK: A MULTI-PERSPECTIVE ANALYSIS

International Banking and Corporate Financial Operations 41-47
(K. Lian, H. Kee, C. Cheong, and B. Ong. eds., 1989)
(Henderson).

I. Description of Swaps

Regardless of form, the underlying principle of a swap is the agreement of each of two parties to provide the other with a series of cash flows, based on fixed or floating interest rates and in the same or different currencies. At the outset, the parties view the respective values of the two streams as equal. In other words, when the agreement is formed, the present values of the respective cash flows at the current prevailing interest rates and, if applicable, exchange rates are equal. Virtually all common interest rate indices are regularly used in swaps: US dollar fixed, prime, London interbank offered rate

(LIBOR), bankers' acceptance, treasury bill, certificate of deposit, commercial paper and zero coupon rate, and a further variety of rate indices for other currencies. All major convertible currencies are swapped.

A typical interest rate swap agreement obligates the first party to pay an amount equal to the interest which would accrue on an agreed amount during a given period at one type of interest rate and obligates the second party to pay an amount equal to the interest which would accrue on that agreed amount during the period at another type of interest rate. To the extent that payment dates are simultaneous, the parties typically would net the payments, with the party owing the larger amount paying the difference to the other party. The economic relationship of the parties under a simple interest swap agreement is illustrated in the following diagram of a swap between Party X, in this instance a company which is about to incur a LIBOR-based debt but which would prefer a long-term fixed rate financing at a favourable rate, and Party A, a bank which is about to incur a fixed rate debt but which would prefer financing on a LIBOR basis:

Figure 1 *

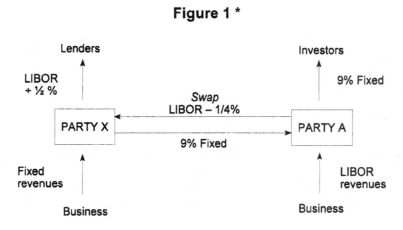

* For illustration purposes all numbers and percentages herein are based on hypothetical figures and are not meant to imply that the rates are current market rates.

A typical currency swap involves an agreement under which the first party agrees to pay an amount in one currency, usually at periodic intervals, and the second party agrees to pay an amount in a different currency at the same or different intervals. These amounts may be expressed as either stated amounts due at stated times (in which case the interest rate and principal components are implicit in the specified amounts) or in terms of interest accruing on principal amounts in different currencies plus payment of those principal amounts at maturity. It is not uncommon to have the notional interest rates in a currency swap calculated on different bases so that effectively the interest rate swap and the currency swap are combined. Payments, even if due on the same date, are usually not netted but are paid gross. The economic relationship of the parties in a combined currency and interest rate swap agreement is illustrated in the following diagram of a swap between Party C, a company with LIBOR dollar liabilities and Swiss franc revenues, and Party X, in this instance a company with fixed rate Swiss franc liabilities and dollar revenues.

Figure 2

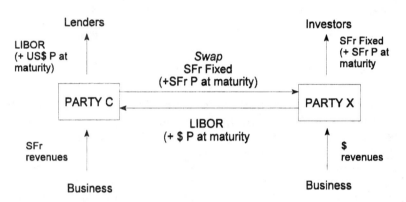

Parties entering into swaps for the above reasons are termed 'end-users,' i.e. parties using the swap for direct financing, asset and liability management or investment purpose. In fact, parties desiring a swap on similar terms, but from reverse perspectives, may not have a commercial relationship with each other, may not be in the business of making credit decisions or may not be able to find counterparties directly. Each would prefer to deal with a strong credit financial institution acting as an intermediary. The intermediary financial institution would, in effect, stand in the middle by entering into matching reverse agreements with each party, thereby bearing the credit risk of each and retaining a spread in the transaction. Each agreement would normally be independent of, and not even refer to, the other. Indeed, the end-users would normally not know of the existence of the other counterparty. Thus, the typical swap is not one illustrated in Figure 1 or 2, but a swap in which one or more financial institutions act as intermediary between end-users.

Figure 4

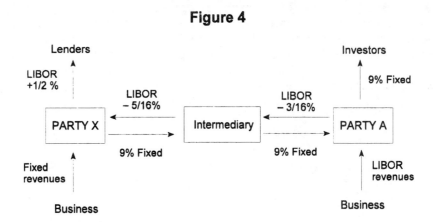

As intermediaries refined their swap funding capabilities, the critical mass of swaps developed to the point that these swaps themselves became an instrument which, while not tradeable, developed many indicia of tradeability. An early swap innovation was the termination of swaps for a fee.   Intermediaries noted that termination was often more profitable than the intermediated swap spread itself had been. As it was logical to view a termination as if it were a sale and a realization on the value intrinsic in the swap, swap specialists began to think in terms of trading, particularly as competition drove down swap margins. Also as a result of increased competition for swap-related financings, intermediaries began to commit to swaps prior to obtaining hedging swaps. Delay while a hedging swap was sought would mean loss of the desired swap and related financial services, such as an underwriting position. The risk posed by the absence of a hedging swap focused attention on the means of temporarily hedging swap risk, or 'warehousing' a swap, until the match could be found. Once these temporary hedging techniques were developed, swap institutions were able and began to quote swap prices on a regular basis.

Trading indicia were simulated through the entering into, terminating and assigning of swaps and the quoting of swap prices, coupled with the use of sophisticated portfolio hedging activities.[2] Many swap institutions began to view themselves as 'dealers' in swaps, rather than as extenders of corporate financial services or credit. The swap market began to take coherent form with the creation of the International Swap Dealers Association Inc (ISDA), now composed of more than 90 major financial institutions.

The vast majority of swaps written therefore represent, at least from one of the party's point of view, a financial service or a dealing function of a financial institution which enters into swaps in the ordinary course of its business in order to earn either spreads between matching swaps, a profit on their swaps portfolio on an aggregate basis or a combination thereof. Some (but by no means all) commercial banks view their swap activity primarily as part of their business in providing financial services to their customers. Even if these banks often do not enter into exactly matching swaps (at least for interest rate swaps), and hedge their risk on a portfolio basis, they may still view their primary function as one of providing a financial accommodation. Most investment banks (and many commercial banks), on the other hand, view their swap activity primarily as part of their dealing activities. Their profit is perceived as deriving from the entry, transfer and termination of swaps on a portfolio basis.

.   .   .

The interest rate swap in Figure 1 only involves an exchange of interest payments, not of principal (the notional amount). The only relevance of the notional amount is for the calculation of the interest payments. The maturity of the swap (the time period over which interest payments will be exchanged) is typically 3-10 years, much longer than forward interest rate contracts.

2. WHY PARTIES DO SWAPS

The following excerpt looks at why parties enter into swap transactions.

---

[2] If Party X wishes to terminate a swap with a dealer, a typical dealer would agree to do so on payment of a fee to or by Party X, depending on rates at the time. An "assignment' by a dealer of its swap with Party X to another dealer is accomplished through:

(1) termination of the dealer's swap with Party X,
(2) Party X entering into a swap on similar terms with the 'assignee' and
(3) the "assignee' paying a fee to, or receiving a fee from, the 'assignor'.

This requires the consent of all parties, including Party X, and the two-step documentation, and is thus obviously not as smooth a process as selling a negotiable instrument which does not have mutual payment obligations. In a termination or assignment, the fee payable is roughly the Agreement Value of the swap, described below.

GROUP OF THIRTY, DERIVATIVES:
PRACTICES AND PRINCIPLES
July 1993, at 34-43 (G-30 Derivatives Study).

II. Who Uses Derivatives and Why?

The participants in derivatives activity can be divided into two groups—end-users and dealers. End-users consist of corporations, governmental entities, institutional investors, and financial institutions. Dealers consist mainly of banks and securities firms, with a few insurance companies and highly rated corporations (mainly energy firms) having recently joined the ranks. An institution may participate in derivatives activity both as an end-user and a dealer. For example, a money-center bank acts as an end-user when it uses derivatives to take positions as part of its proprietary trading or for hedging as part of its asset and liability management. It acts as a dealer when it quotes bids and offers and commits capital to satisfying customers' demands for derivatives.

Derivatives permit end-users and dealers to identify, isolate, and manage separately the fundamental risks and other characteristics that are bound together in traditional financial instruments. Desired combinations of cash flow, interest rate, currency, liquidity, and market source characteristics can be achieved largely by separable choices, each independent of the underlying cash market instrument. As a result, management is able to think and act in terms of fundamental risks.

The next section describes specific uses of derivatives by different groups of end-users.

End-Users

Derivatives are used by end-users to lower funding costs, enhance yields, diversify sources of funding, hedge, and express market views through position taking.

Corporations According to the Survey of Industry Practice, over 80% of the private sector corporations consider derivatives either very important (44%) or imperative (37%) for controlling risk. Roughly 87% of the reporting private sector corporations use interest rate swaps, while 64% use currency swaps and 78% use forward foreign exchange contracts. For option-based derivatives, 40% use interest rate options and 31% use currency options.

Different uses of derivatives by corporations are discussed in more detail below.

Lowering Funding Costs through Arbitrage Opportunities or Issuance of Customized Instruments Derivatives allow corporations to lower funding costs by taking advantage of differences that exist between capital markets. They allow the principle of comparative advantage to be applied to financing. Where financial markets are segmented nationally or internationally, whether due to market or regulatory barriers or to different perceptions of credit qualities in various markets, the use of derivatives has delivered unambiguous cost savings for borrowers and higher yields for investors.

For example, a borrower may issue debt where it has a comparative advantage, and use a currency swap to achieve funding in its desired currency at a lower funding cost than a direct financing. A borrower generating savings in this way is, in effect, using a swap to exploit an arbitrage between the financial markets involved. Similarly, borrowers are able to achieve savings by issuing structured securities tailored to meet specific investor requirements. Then, the borrowers use swaps to achieve the borrowing currency and structure they need.[9]

The Connection Between Swaps and Financing: *In light of the significant reductions in funding costs that swap arbitrage can achieve, evaluating swap opportunities has become a crucial consideration in issuing bonds. That is, the choice of market and timing of issuance is driven by relative swap opportunities. It has been estimated that from 1985 to 1989, the volume of international new issues that were swap driven increased steadily, reaching 70% of international U.S. dollar new issue volume and 53% of total international new issue volume. Today all major borrowers monitor their funding opportunities regularly by evaluating the relative pricings for new issues and swaps across markets worldwide. See* Global Swap Markets *(IFR Publishing, 1991), Table 3.*

Diversifying Funding Sources By obtaining financing from one market and then swapping all or part of the cash flows into the desired currency denominations and rate indices, issuers can diversify their funding activities across global markets. Placing debt with new investors may increase liquidity and reduce funding costs for the issuer.

Funding Operations in Multiple Countries at Lowest Cost For international corporations, borrowing needs in a particular country or countries may be too small to be funded cost effectively through the local capital markets. It may be cost effective, however, to borrow more than they need in those capital markets and swap excess debt into the other needed currencies.

Hedging the Cost of Anticipated Issuance of Fixed-Rate Debt Volatile interest rates create uncertainty about the future cost of issuing fixed-rate debt. Delayed start swaps, or forward swaps, can be used to "lock in" the general level of interest rates that exists at the time the funding decision is made. Such hedging

---

[9] In the early days of the swap market, funding could be obtained at savings of as much as 50 basis points (0.50%) given the significant arbitrage opportunities that then were possible. Today arbitrage savings are more likely to be in the range of 10 to 25 basis points (0.10% to 0.25%).

eliminates general market risk. It does not eliminate, however, specific risk-the risk that an issuer's funding cost may move out of line with the funding cost of other borrowers, due to factors related principally to the issuer.

. . .

Managing Existing Debt or Asset Portfolios As its assessment of economic prospects changes, a company may want to change the characteristics of its existing debt portfolio-either the mix of fixed- and floating-rate debt or the mix of currency denominations. Interest rate swaps can be used to adjust the ratio of fixed- to floating-rate debt, while currency swaps can be used to transform an obligation in one currency into an obligation in another currency, changing the currency mix of the debt portfolio.

Making Small Business Loans and Adding Lending Capacity Using Interest Rate Swaps: *Two of the primary lenders to McDonald's U.S. franchisees use swaps to better accommodate franchisees' needs for financing. One of these lenders had accumulated a large portfolio of fixed-rate loans to the franchisees. It sold participations in these loans in the secondary market to investors who were willing to buy a portion of the portfolio if they could receive a floating-rate return. Interest rate swaps were used to convert the fixed-interest payment stream on the participations to the floating rate that investors desired. This freed lending capacity so the bank could make additional loans to franchisees. Another lender manages a special purpose corporation which issues commercial paper to fund franchisee loans. It uses interest rate swaps to offer McDonald's franchisees either floating- or fixed-rate funding.*

Volatile interest rates may affect the value of a firm's assets as well as its liabilities. To protect the firm's net worth from interest rate risk, corporate treasurers increasingly take account of the interest rate sensitivity of both assets and liabilities in designing hedges. Interest rate swaps can be used to adjust the average maturity or interest rate sensitivity of a company's debt portfolio so that it more closely matches the interest rate sensitivity of the asset side of the balance sheet, reducing the exposure of the company's net worth or market value to interest rate risk.

Roughly 78% of the private sector corporations responding to the Survey indicate that they use derivatives to manage or modify the characteristics of their existing liabilities and assets.

Managing Foreign Exchange Exposures Both importers and exporters are exposed to exchange rate risk. As a result of this transactional exposure, an importer's profit margin can, and often does, evaporate if its domestic currency weakens sharply before purchases have been paid for. International firms with overseas operations also face translation exposure as the values of their overseas assets and liabilities are translated into domestic currency for accounting purposes. The competitive position of many domestic producers also is subject to change with major movements in foreign exchange rates. Currency swaps and foreign exchange forwards and options can be used to create hedges of those future cash flows and reduce the risk from currency fluctuations.

. . .

Managing Sovereign Debt with Currency Swaps: *Finland is a highly rated sovereign and an active borrower in the international capital markets. The government of Finland, through the Ministry of Finance, has actively used swaps to lower its effective cost of debt and manage the currency composition of its foreign liabilities to hedge foreign exchange risks. During the period 1987-1990, Finland entered into approximately 50 swaps with notional principal equivalent to U.S. $50-200 million at a time. Roughly 30% of the government's total outstanding foreign debt was swapped, with most swaps being related to newly issued debt. Swaps were used in 1990 to achieve funding costs of 30-50 basis points below LIBOR. They were also used to configure the currency composition of Finland's foreign liabilities in the direction of its official currency basket. The Finnish mark was pegged to the value of the currency basket. The Ministry used currency swaps to access the lowest-cost offshore debt markets, while translating the currency composition of the debt portfolio to the desired mix. Substantial changes in the debt composition were achieved through swaps. For example, although the actual share of the Japanese yen in the external debt was 23- in 1989, currency swaps were used to reduce the effective share to 12- in 1989 and 5- in 1990. See "Government Use of Cross Currency Swaps" in* Cross Currency Swaps *(Business One Irwin, 1992) edited by Carl Beidleman.*

. . .

Institutional Investors

Enhancing Yields Through Arbitrage Opportunities The earliest use of swaps by institutional investors involved asset swaps, in which the cash flows from a particular asset are swapped for other cash flows, possibly denominated in another currency or based on a different interest rate. Institutional investors use derivatives to create investments with a higher yield than corresponding traditional investments. They might do this when securities trade poorly because of some unattractive feature. In such a case, an investor may purchase the securities, neutralize the undesirable feature with a suitable derivatives transaction, and create, for example, a synthetic fixed-rate investment with a higher yield than comparable fixed-rate instruments of the same credit quality.

Managing Exposures to Alternative Assets Institutional investors have recently begun to use derivatives, especially interest rate and equity swaps, to manage their exposure to debt and equity markets, both domestic and international. The immediate appeal is the ability to quickly and effectively adjust exposures-between debt and equity or among different equity classes-without incurring substantial transaction and custodial costs. There is also potential to enhance yields. The availability of equity swaps on the major international equity indices allows investors to diversify globally and adjust their portfolios in a cost-effective manner.

Eliminating Currency Risk Some institutional investors wish to benefit from investment in or exposure to foreign debt or equity markets without necessarily incurring foreign exchange risk. For instance, a Japanese investor might want to earn a return based on the S & P 500 Index but payable in yen at a predetermined exchange rate. A family of swaps called "quanto" swaps have been designed to meet the growing demands of investors for investment diversification without currency risk.

Global derivatives are now used widely by financial institutions to manage the interest rate and foreign exchange risk arising from a variety of activities. Eighty-four percent of the financial institutions responding to the Survey indicate that they use derivatives for hedging market risks arising from new financings, 77% use them to manage their existing assets and liabilities, 39% use them to offset option positions embedded in the institution's assets and liabilities, 39% use them to hedge transaction exposures, and 46% use them to hedge translation exposures.

Dealers

The Function of Dealers Early in the evolution of OTC derivatives, financial institutions-including investment banks, commercial banks, merchant banks, and independent broker-dealers-acted for the most part as brokers finding counterparties with offsetting requirements with regard to notional amount, currencies, type of interest to be paid, frequency of payments, and maturity. They then negotiated on behalf of the two parties. Acting as agent or broker for a fee, the institutions took no principal position in the transactions and, hence, were not exposed to credit or market risk.

Most financial institutions found their role soon evolved beyond brokering to acting as dealers, offering themselves as counterparties or principals to intermediate customers' requirements. Transactions, however, were immediately matched or hedged by entering into an opposing transaction such as a "matched swap." Each pair of transactions was dealt with separately and discretely. As a result, the dealer's book of business was relatively simple to monitor and manage. This new role, however, required a commitment of capital since dealers now faced credit risk and some limited market risk.

The next step in the evolution of dealer activities was the "warehousing" of derivatives transactions. Dealers would temporarily hedge a swap-typically with a cash security or futures position-until a matched transaction could be found to replace the temporary hedge. This advance in risk management practice increased the ability of dealers to accommodate customer needs.

Today, major dealers have moved from the "warehouse" approach to a "portfolio" approach, wherein the dealer simply takes the customer's transaction into its portfolio or book of derivatives and manages the net or residual risk of its overall position. Each new transaction is decomposed into its component cash flows and risk factors and aggregated with all previous transactions. The focus of risk management changes from individual transactions to portfolio exposures. This has led to a marked improvement in the ability of dealers to accommodate a broad spectrum of customer transactions, and has improved their ability to monitor and manage the various components of market risk, regardless of the transactions from which the risks derive.

By quoting bid and offer prices, dealers provide liquidity and continuous availability of derivatives transactions. To supply the immediacy demanded by end-users, dealers use their own inventory, or establish new positions, and manage the resulting risk. They are compensated by earning a return from a bid-ask spread. In addition, dealers can take market risk positions to express market views in the expectation of profiting from favorable movements in prices or rates.

Dealers also provide an arbitrage function, identifying and exploiting anomalies between derivatives and underlying cash market instruments, thereby enhancing market liquidity and pricing efficiency. Finally, dealers earn a return for the amount of financial engineering that goes into developing customized and structured transactions that meet specific customer needs.

Types of Dealers Dealing in derivatives has tended to concentrate among principals possessing not only the requisite technology and know-how but also ample capital and credit appraisal experience. Banks have become the dominant derivatives players, but they hold no monopoly.[11] Securities firms, insurance companies, and high-rated corporates (especially in the energy area) are deploying capital and credit experience to run swap books to profit from both dealing and position-taking activity.

The credit standing of the dealer is very important. Several dealers have created special purpose derivatives product companies which

---

[11]Based on a ranking in *The World's Major Swap Dealers* (Swaps Monitor Publications, Inc., November 1992) for year-end 1991, 19 of the top 25 dealers in interest rate and currency swaps were banks; four were security firms; and two were insurance companies. Out of the 25 dealers from around the world, 14 were U.S. based. Of the top 25 dealers in foreign exchange forwards, 24 were banks, while one was a securities firm.

benefit from the support of a strong parent or shareholder. Some dealers have established separately capitalized, triple-A rated, derivatives vehicles.

Use of derivatives is particularly important to banks. It appears that banks that use derivatives have faster growth in their loan portfolios, hold lower levels of capital (substituting risk management for capital), tend to be larger (reflecting fixed costs of start-up), and have less exposure to interest rate risk. E. Brewer III, W. Jackson, and J, Moser, *The value of using interest rate derivatives to manage risk at U.S. banking organizations,* Federal Reserve Bank of Chicago, Economic Perspectives 49 (3Q 2001). It also appears that use of derivatives by non-financial institutions is modest. If the median non-financial firm were to simultaneously experience a three standard deviation change in interest rates, exchange rates and commodity prices, it would collect only $15 million from its entire derivatives portfolio, a quite modest amount compared to firm size and cash flows. W. Guay and S. Kothari, *How Much do Firms Hedge with Derivatives,* Working Paper (Draft, March 2001).

Studies have also highlighted the significant use of derivatives by sovereigns, G. Piga, *Do Governments Use Financial Derivatives Appropriately? Evidence from Sovereign Borrowers in Developed Economies,* 4 International Finance 189 (2001). While use of derivatives may just be another tool for reducing the cost of borrowing, it can also be used to window dress public accounts, thereby decreasing apparent deficits. This may be done to achieve better credit ratings (if use is not transparent) or to meet deficit limits, as under the EU Stability Pact.

3. OVERALL MARKETS

The estimates of swaps outstanding vary widely. According to Swaps Monitor, *Data on the Global Derivatives Market*, there were $62.4 trillion in notional amounts of swaps outstanding, 58.5 trillion in interest rates, and 3.9 in currency, as of June 2000. The total of $62.4 trillion compares with $8.7 trillion in 1992. According to BIS, as of June 2000, contracts in dollars accounted for 27.5% of notional amounts outstanding on single-currency interest rate contracts, while the euro accounted for 35.7%, and the dollar figured on one side of 90% of all foreign exchange swaps. BIS Quarterly Review (March 2001). Swaps activity is highly concentrated. As of 1991, the top eight dealers accounted for 58 percent of the worldwide notional interest rate and currency swaps. G-30 Study at 61. See also GAO, Financial Derivatives 36 (1994) (GAO Report). As of June 30, 2000, the two largest dealers, JP Morgan Chase and Deutsche Bank, controlled 23% and 11% respectively of the notional value of interest rate swap contracts outstanding, Swaps Monitor, *Data on the Global Derivatives Market* (2000).

Notes and Questions

1. Consider the following two $100 million 5 year interest rate matched swaps entered into between Bank A (AAA credit rating) and Company B (BBB credit rating) with Swap Bank, when the yield on the 5 year treasury bond was 9%:

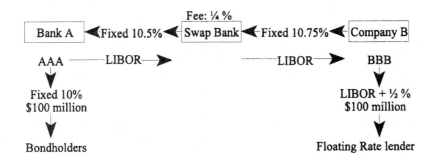

Assume Bank A's cost of floating rate funding would be LIBOR and Company B's cost of fixed rate funding would be 11¾. Is Bank A at risk if Company B fails to pay Swap Bank?

Why would Company B enter into this transaction? Has Company B hedged or reduced its interest rate risk? Would Company B be better off, post-swap, if interest rates increased or decreased. How about Bank A?

2. Did Company B reduce its pre-swap floating rate funding cost by entering into the transaction described in note 1?   This would be determined by the following calculation:

Analysis of Company B's Savings

1. Direct Cost (to floating lender):   (LIBOR + ½%)
2. Swap cost (to Swap Bank):   (10¾%)
3. Swap Revenue (from Swap Bank):   LIBOR
4. Net Cost (3 - (1 + 2))   11¼%
5. Cost Savings: ½% (11¾ - 11¼)

In this transaction Company B saved ½% by entering into this transaction. Did Bank A reduce its funding cost by entering into this transaction? What was the total funding cost savings of entering into this transaction? What are the essential conditions for having funding cost savings in this transaction? Does it follow from the fact that there are funding cost savings for Bank A that Bank A has reduced its risk by entering into this transaction? If Bank A is willing to engage in this transaction, why would it not simply loan money to Company B at a rate below its bond borrowing rate?

Most versions of the comparative funding cost advantage theory of swaps are based on the idea that the higher credit rated party has a bigger advantage in borrowing at fixed rates. Thus, in our example, we see that the difference in borrowing costs between Bank A and Company B is greater for fixed rates (175 basis points) than floating rates (50 basis points). Empirical studies have confirmed this. Floating rate payers have a higher mean S&P bond rating than fixed rate payers. L. Wall and J. Pringle, *Alternative Explanations of Interest Rate Swaps: A Theoretical and Empirical Analysis*, 18 Financial Management 59 (1989). See also D. Duffie and J. Liu, *Floating-Fixed Credit Spreads,* Financial Analysts Journal 76 (May/June 2001), which finds that if a debt issuer default risk is independent of a change in interest rates, the sign of floating-fixed spreads is determined by the term structure of the risk-free forward interest rate. If there is an upward sloping curve, the floating-fixed rate spread increases.

One might expect arbitrage to eliminate the profitable opportunities of entering into a swap, that the difference in fixed rates charged by the swap counterparty and bond investors would be eliminated. Nonetheless, swap-driven bond issuance still accounts for the bulk of issuance in the Euromarket. In 1994, about 60% of all bond issues had swaps attached to them. *Is Arbitrage Dead*, Euromoney, Oct. 1995, at 80.

While the credit ratings of swap users like Company B may be lower than their bank counterparties, they are considerably higher than firms in general. A Federal Reserve Board study found that the credit rating of firms reporting OTC derivatives that have a senior debt rating is significantly better than all firms with senior debt ratings. Indeed, the ratio of expected default rates for the typical derivative user to the typical firm representing all the firms in the sample was almost exactly one-half. Note that the maximum credit risk-weighting for derivative contracts under the Basel Accord is 50% as compared with 100% for other credit obligations of private obligors. V. Bhasin, On the Credit Risk of OTC Derivative Users (Federal Reserve Board Finance and Economics Discussion Series No. 95-50, 1995).

3. Let's assume Bank A wants to hedge or speculate on interest rates. Why not use interest rate futures/options rather than swaps? How would these alternatives compare with respect to liquidity, maturities, credit risk and nature of participants.

4. The Swap Bank earns a bid-asked spread of 25 basis points in the transaction described in note 1. The bank has bid 10.5% fixed to buy LIBOR, but offers to sell LIBOR for 10.75% fixed. Swap dealers regularly quote bid and ask prices on fixed-floating swaps. Does the Swap Bank

have any risk in this transaction? How would the Swap Bank determine its bid-ask prices?

5. In 1995, the swaps community contemplated the possibility of negative interest rates on the floating side of Yen swaps. As of October, Tibor (the Tokyo interbank offering rate) was .5% or 50 basis points. Given that the floating rate side of a swap is often quoted at some discount from Tibor, e.g. Tibor minus 75 basis points, the floating rate could have gone negative. In this example it would be -25 basis points. What should this mean for the obligations of the parties? Would the fixed rate payer have to pay the promised fixed rate *plus* 25 basis points, or just the fixed rate—the latter alternative would assume there was a floor of zero percent on the floating rate? Obviously, this matter could be handled by contract for new swaps, and ISDA suggested language in the standard documentation for swaps that would permit parties to select one of the alternatives. ISDA, Negative Interest Rates (1995).

6. Consider (and diagram) the two following 5 year currency swaps. Issuer A swaps $40 million for ¥5 billion with Swap Dealer, and pays Swap Dealer 5.50% fixed on ¥5 billion in return for 9.40% fixed on $40 million. Issuer B swaps ¥5 billion with Swap Dealer for $40 million and pays Swap Dealer 9.90% fixed on $40 million in exchange for 5.10% fixed on ¥5 billion. Issuer A has raised the $40 million by issuing bonds paying 9.40% fixed, and Issuer B has raised the ¥5 billion by issuing bonds paying 5.50% fixed. The current spot foreign exchange rate between the dollar and yen is assumed to be US $1.00 = ¥125 ($40 million = ¥5 billion).

How are the fixed interest rate payments on these currencies determined. Do you think they are the current interest rates on the dollar and the yen? Why would these two issuers enter into these swaps? Suppose issuer A, a Japanese company, issued a dollar equity warrant (bond cum warrant) instead of a straight bond, with an interest rate of 2%. The lower rate is due to the warrant feature. What is the impact on the issuer?

7. Consider the FX risk on the currency swap described in note 6. Assume that the dollar-yen rate changes to $1 = ¥100 during the life of the swap. What is the FX risk for A and B?

8. What role do you think regulatory and tax factors play in parties entering into swap transactions? Consider the following: "A case of tax and regulatory arbitrage through swaps occurred in 1984, when Japan still treated interest 'income' on zero-coupon bonds as nontaxable capital gain, whereas accruing interest 'payments' on zeros were tax deductible by U.S. borrowers. Financing packages utilizing swaps were devised in the market to exploit the discrepancy, enabling a number of U.S. borrowers to procure cheap dollar funding, effectively at the expense of the Japanese taxpayer." JP Morgan, *Swaps: Versatility at Controlled Risk*, World Financial Markets, Apr. 1991, at 17. U.S. borrowers could

issue zero-coupon yen denominated bonds to Japanese investors and swap the proceeds for dollars.

9. Does the Japanese zero coupon case indicate that swaps are an important tool for regulatory and tax arbitrage? Were the Japanese powerless to stop this? If swaps are an important tool, then they may play an important role in liberalizing domestic capital markets.

10. An interesting study has shown that changes in bank portfolios of commercial and industrial loans are positively related to banks' participation in interest rate swaps. This suggests that swaps allow banks to better manage the interest rate exposure of their loan portfolios, and that regulatory restraints on swaps could result in lower lending growth. E. Brewer III, B. Milton and J. Moser, *The Effect of Bank-Held Derivatives on Credit Accessibility*, Federal Reserve Bank of Chicago, Working Paper Series, Issues in Financial Regulation, Apr. 1994.

11. Swaps may also be used to minimize other taxes. Consider equity swaps, for example. In a simple "total return" equity swap a foreign party (F) would enter into a swap with a U.S. party (D) under which F pays D annually X% (the interest on a Treasury bill) and an amount equal to any depreciation in the value of 100 shares of USCo, a U.S. issuer. D pays F an amount equal to the dividends paid on USCo and any appreciation in its value. F gets the X% to pay D by investing in a U.S. Treasury bond (paying D the interest on the bond compensates him for his carrying cost on buying the stock), while D hedges its risk by acquiring USCo stock. F has, in effect, invested in U.S. Co. and a Treasury bond but pays no U.S. withholding taxes. If F had invested directly in stock and the Treasury bond, he would have been subject to withholding payments on dividends (as we have seen in Chapter 12, interest payments on the bond are exempt). R. Avi-Yonah and L. Schwartz, *Virtual Taxation—Source-Based Taxation in the Age of Derivatives*, Derivatives 247 (May/June 1997).

12. Historically swaps have been entered onto off exchanges, compared to on exchange instruments like futures and options. Indeed, the bank dominated swap market is a major competitor to the exchanges. The on-off exchange distinction is now breaking down. In 2002, the Chicago Board of Trade began trading a 10 year interest rate swap and will soon trade a five year contract. So far, the volume is modest; through April 2002, yearly volume was about 123,000 contracts. Chicago Board of Trade, *Monthly Statistics* (April 2002). This compares with 17.3 million futures contracts on U.S. Treasury bonds. The trading unit for the CBOT swaps is the notional price of the fixed-rate side of a plain vanilla swap. In this context plain vanilla denotes a swap that has a principal equal to $100,000 and that exchanges semiannual interest payments at a fixed 6% per annum for floating interest rate payment based on 3-month LIBOR. Chicago Board of Trade, *Interest Rate Swap Complex, 5-Year and 10-year* (2002). In a related development, Liffe launched a Swapnote in March

2001, a future on euro interest-rate swaps. N. Tait, *CBOT to launch swaps futures,* Financial Times, July 19, 2001. How would you compare the costs and benefits of exchange-traded and off-exchange swaps?

B. CREDIT AND MARKET RISKS IN SWAPS

While we have already touched upon risks in swaps, we now turn to a more focused examination of credit and market risks.

1. THE NATURE OF CREDIT RISK

Henderson at 49-65.

. . .

A. DEFINITION OF CREDIT RISK

The risk incurred by a counterparty entering into a swap with Party X can be analysed as consisting of two parts: the rate risk and the credit risk of Party X. The rate risk (including currency risk if applicable as well as interest rate risk) is that, based on movement of rates in the future, the counterparty will be the net payor under the swap. Worded another way, after all payments have been made, the payments made by the counterparty will turn out to have been more valuable than those received by it. This is the risk that the swap becomes unfavourable to it. This risk can be and is hedged, as illustrated in all the examples above.[5]

It should be noted that the swap is almost always independent of the position which it is hedging or which is hedging it. Whether the swap is viewed as hedged by other positions or as itself hedging those positions, the result is the same: if the swap terminates, the counterparty is then exposed because of the continued existence of those positions. As swaps are hedged either explicitly or implicitly, the counterparty has no rate risk as long as Party X performs.

Thus, exposure arises if rates have moved in such a way that the swap is favourable to the counterparty (which means that the corresponding hedge is unfavourable) and Party X does not perform. Swap credit risk is this risk of the failure of Party X to perform under those circumstances.

---

[5] A party which hedges itself through general asset and liability management techniques may have no direct hedge in place and, in fact, may have an open position. The party may be taking a view on rates. Indeed, every party that incurs a loan takes a view on rates when it determines whether or not it wishes to borrow at fixed or floating rates. This position represents as real a hedge as does a specific, matching hedge. For the balance of this Chapter, it will be assumed that a swap is hedged even if only through the taking of a managed open position for which it has bargained in the swap.

B. QUANTIFICATION OF CREDIT RISK

The sensible means of quantifying that risk is through measuring the cost of replacing the cash flows under the swap if Party X defaults and the swap terminates. Since swaps involve reciprocal obligations and the possibility of bilateral cash flows, depending on rate movements there will almost certainly be a gain or loss to the counterparty if the swap terminates: a gain if, in recreating the future cash flows, the value of the termination of the counterparty's liability to pay under the swap exceeds its cost of replacing its income under the swap; and a loss, if termination of its liability is worth less than its cost of replacing its income under the swap.

This quantification cannot be precisely calculated in advance, that is to say prior to an actual default, since the counterparty does not know how rates will move and what their level will be at an indefinite time in the future. At best, when entering into the swap a rough estimate can be made of the range of exposures depending on theoretical rate movements. At the time of Party X's default, however, the measurement of the counterparty's gain or loss on replacement can be calculated precisely through the cost of one or a combination of several alternative transactions: a replacement swap on similar terms but commencing on the date the original swap is terminated and running through the original term; a combination of borrowing and investing in order to recreate the remaining cash flows under the swap agreement; or the use of forward rate agreements, futures, options, caps, floors and other instruments to recreate the hedge which the swap was serving.

Replacement of the cash flows of an interest rate swap through a combination of borrowing and investment can be illustrated as follows:

Figure 5

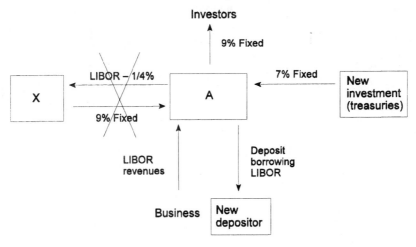

(A's loss = Present value of 2 1/4% pa over the remaining term.)

The basic financial gain or loss at a given time is equal to the then present value of the difference for each future payment date between the fixed rate on the investment or borrowing (depending on whether the gain or loss is viewed from the perspective of the fixed rate recipient or payor) and the rate on the swap.

Replacement of the cash flows through a new swap can be illustrated as follows:

Figure 6

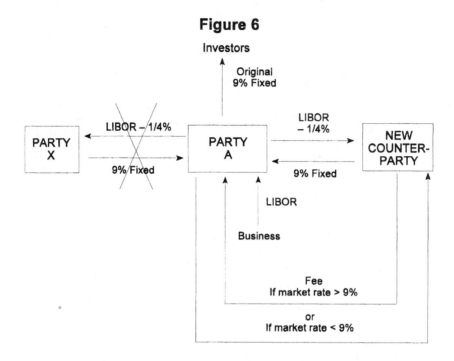

The basic financial gain or loss of a party at a given time is equal to the front-end fee which the party could receive or would have to pay to a third party in consideration of the third party entering into the replacement swap given rates current in the swap market at the time of replacement.

The right to terminate, calculate gain or loss in each swap, and claim for losses is set forth in the lengthy but standardized swap agreements on the forms published by the ISDA. These agreements are described below, but it may be useful at this point to describe several elements which will be necessary for the balance of this Chapter.

C. DETERMINATION OF GAINS AND LOSSES: AGGREGATION

Each ISDA agreement is a master agreement which provides that all swaps done between Party X and the counterparty under the master shall be regarded as integral parts of a single agreement. This being the case, if Party X defaults generally or on one swap, the agreement provides that the counterparty may terminate all (but not less than all) swaps with Party X. The measure of damages, the counterparty's gain or loss, is calculated through reference to the average cost of a replacement swap with respect to each swap (the mark-to-market value, the Agreement Value, at the time of each terminated swap). The gains and losses of all swaps are then netted, with one resulting figure being used as the counterparty's gain or loss on termination. This termination of all swaps and netting of gains and losses on termination is generally termed 'aggregation'.

. . .

D. DOCUMENTATION

Once the initial credit analysis is satisfactorily completed and allocation is made against credit lines, the counterparty will control its swap credit risk with Party X on an ongoing basis through contractual provisions in the swap agreement. A party's ongoing commercial concerns about the creditworthiness of its counterparty will be most directly reflected in its attitude towards the substantive credit controls in the document: the requirement for closing documents, representations and warranties, covenants and events of default. Warranties and closing documents lend assurance to each party at the commencement of the transaction as to the other party's requisite legal, tax and commercial status and the absence of certain credit-sensitive events. Covenants and events of default set forth the commercial and credit standards with which each party must comply on an ongoing basis failing which the other party will no longer wish to maintain its credit exposure to that party. The key enforcement provisions of a swap agreement, those which provide the remedy for breach of the substantive credit controls, are found in the clauses which entitle the non-defaulting party to terminate the swap agreement and recover its losses resulting from termination or to exercise any other remedies produced by law, as discussed above.

Documentation controls can be analysed in the context of the form of documentation and of the ongoing policing of compliance with its provisions.

1. Form of documentation

. . .

The ISDA was initially formed to expedite documentation through the development of standard terms. The first step was publication of the ISDA's 1985 and 1986 Editions of the Code of Standard Wording, Assumptions and Provisions for Swaps (Swaps Code). The 1985 edition was primarily concerned with financial provisions and provisions relating to compensation on early termination. The 1986 edition of the Swaps Code reiterated the existing provisions of the 1985 edition and added more extensive credit related provisions. Each edition together with minor amendments is a compendium of standard terms from which the parties to a swap may freely choose in a separately drafted, negotiated and executed agreement.

Finally, in 1987 the ISDA published two master agreements, presented on printed forms. The first master, prepared by an ISDA working group in New York (the Rate Swap Master), is for US dollar interest rate swaps only, incorporates terms from the 1986 edition of the Swaps Code and is governed by New York law. The second, prepared by an ISDA working group in London (the Rate and Currency Swap Master), is for rate swaps in any currency as well as currency swaps, does not incorporate Swaps Code terms (since the Swaps Code contemplates only dollar rate swaps), and has been drafted to be governed by either New York or English law. However, the provisions in the two agreements are nearly identical in substance, except to the extent necessary for the London agreement to accommodate currency transactions and non-dollar rate swaps. In addition, a pamphlet, ISDA's 1987 Interest Rate and Currency Exchange Definitions, has been prepared for optional use as a companion to the Rate and Currency Swap Master in the same way that the 1986 Swaps Code is a companion (albeit required) for the Rate Swap Master. Indeed, these 1987 Definitions are patterned after the financial provisions of the Swaps Code, setting forth definitions of rates and related terms for swaps involving 15 currencies.

Each of the agreements consists of two parts, the first of which sets forth the basic terms of the master and the second of which is a Schedule on which some of those terms may be completed, supplemented or varied. Specially tailored cross-default provisions, additional covenants to be complied with by certain kinds of counterparties, and special clauses relating to credit support, such as guarantees and collateral, must be added to the Schedule under 'Other Provisions'. Another provision, to be completed in the Schedule, facilitates the designation of the third parties that will be providing credit support (e.g. a guarantee or a letter of credit) or that will be relevant for purposes of the cross-default clause, if appropriate. The ISDA has published a User's Guide to assist in the process of 'customization'.

Existence of the ISDA agreements has had a strong effect on bringing documentation into a 'market acceptable' form and has greatly facilitated the growth of the swap market on the basis of prudent documentation and reduced backlogs. However, standardization discourages provisions which may be desired by a particular institution either for credit purposes or because of the unique character of the counterparty (such as UK local councils) or its jurisdiction. Dealers are increasingly reluctant to require provisions which, while perhaps desirable in principle, meet market resistance, require the sort of negotiation which the Swaps Code and master agreements were intended to avoid and which could result in the deal being lost. This reluctance even exists where the forms provide for insertion of various types of clauses or for modifications which are readily visible. For instance, the agreements provide space for insertion of a description of financial information required on execution, but this is often not utilized (particularly outside of the USA) and, indeed, often meets market resistance when a party attempts to utilize it. Credit terms which would be regarded as mandatory in more traditional credits are thus often not required in swaps.

. . .

E. CONTROL THROUGH SECURITY, GUARANTEES AND SUBORDINATION

The counterparty may wish further to control its credit exposure to Party X through guarantees, collateral or the existence of a protective cushion of subordinated debt, as in other financial transactions.

. . .

As the Henderson piece explains, a counterparty is only exposed to credit risk when the swap is in the money, i.e. has a positive value. The value of a swap, referred to as its mark-to-market value, can be calculated as the present value of the net payments the holder expects to receive over the life of the contract. An alternative expression of the same value is replacement cost, the cost of obtaining a replacement swap on the same terms and for the time remaining on the initial swap should the counterparty default.

As an example, consider the interest rate swap in note 1 above. Assume that at the end of the third year of the swap, the market rate for the five year swap is 12.75% fixed for LIBOR. This means the swap is in the money (a good deal) for Company B, since it would now cost Company B 12.75% rather than 10.75% to get LIBOR. The replacement cost is the present discounted value of this two percent differential (multiplied by the notional amount of the swap) over the remaining 2 year life of the swap. Company B would have to pay $2,000,000 ($100,000,000 × .02) more in each interest period to obtain LIBOR. Using the current 2 year swap rate (12.75) as the discount rate, the replacement cost would be $2,000,000/1.1275 + 2,000,000/(1.1275)^2 = \$3,347,081$. This cost would only be incurred if Company B's counterparty, Swap Bank, defaulted.

Consider the position of Company A under the same scenario of a 2% rise in interest rates. It is out of the money; it has made a bad deal. In the market, it could get 12.75% for LIBOR, while under its contract it is only getting 10.50%. The loss in the value of its contract is the present discounted value of the 2.25 percent differential in fixed rates (12.75 - 10.50) over the remaining 2 year life of the swap. Company A will be receiving $2,250,000 ($100,000,000 × .0225) less than the market would pay in each interest period. Using the current two year swap rate of 12.75 as the discount rate, the loss would be $2,250,000/1.1275 + 2,250,000/(1.1275)^2 = \$3,765,468$. This is a market loss for Company A, assuming A's fixed rate exposure is not hedged.

Finally, consider the position of Swap Bank. It is in the money on its contract with Company A (it would have to pay more now to get LIBOR) and out of the money on its contract with Company B (it could now get more for LIBOR in the market). Swap Bank does have a credit risk on its contract with Company B, but absent default, its market loss on its contract with B is offset by its market gain on its contract with A.

This analysis of risk looks at gains or losses on the contract at a fixed point in time, two years into the contract. Suppose we want to predict the risk of the contract over the life of the swap. Let's go back to credit risk and Company B's position. We know that Company B stands to lose about $3.3 million if Swap Bank were to default at the end of two years. This is referred to as current exposure. But B might stand to lose even more money if interest rates further increased and Swap Bank then defaulted. This is referred to as future or potential exposure.

A principal methodology used to estimate potential exposure over the remaining life of a swap is the Monte Carlo simulation. The remaining life of the swap is analyzed on the basis of simulations which model movements in swap rates based on different assumptions of interest rate volatility.

A study by K. Simons, *Interest Rate Structure and the Credit Risk of Swaps*, New England Economic Review, July-Aug. 1993, at 23, performed a Monte Carlo simulation for interest rate swaps of various maturities. The study used matched pairs of swaps to control for market risk, i.e. gain on one swap would be exactly offset by loss on the other. This approach allows for isolation of credit risk. Interest rate predictions were based on two scenarios. The first assumed that interest rates follow a random walk in accordance with historical volatility and further assumes that changes are lognormally distributed around a mean corresponding to historical volatility. The second used the forward interest rates implied by the shape of the swap yield curve (maturity on horizontal axis, percentage yields on vertical axis) as a forecast of expected future swap interest rates. The results were as follows:

Table 2: Exposure on a Matched Pair of Swaps as a
Percentage of Notional Principal

Swap Maturity	10-Year Flat Rate	10-Year Rising Rate	7-Year Flat Rate	7-Year Rising Rate	5-Year Flat Rate	5-Year Rising Rate	3-Year Flat Rate	3-Year Rising Rate	1-Year Flat Rate	1-Year Rising Rate
Confidence Interval										
99%	11.22	13.07	7.78	9.49	5.12	6.44	2.25	2.79	.34	.36
95%	8.28	9.24	5.67	6.79	3.59	4.64	1.63	2.02	.24	.25
90%	6.93	7.57	4.71	5.54	3.06	3.75	1.37	1.66	.20	.21
75%	5.12	5.33	3.37	3.75	2.22	2.54	.98	1.13	.14	.14
Mean Expected Lifetime Exposure	4.03	4.27	2.68	2.97	1.74	2.00	.77	.87	.10	.10

The values in the Table indicate the expected replacement costs over the lifetime of the swap. The "flat rate" is based on the random walk methodology, while the "rising rate" is based on the shape of the swap yield curve. The results are interpreted as follows. For a swap with a remaining life of 10 years, the flat rate exposure will be no more than 8.28 and the rising rate exposure will be no more than 9.24 percent of the notional amount in 95% of the cases, while the mean expected lifetime exposure is 4.03 and 4.27 percent under the two respective methodologies. The mean expected lifetime exposure is calculated by averaging the expected exposure for each period. The lower mean expected lifetime exposures take into account the fact that the risk reduces as the swap approaches maturity since fewer periods remain in which the difference between the initial and the current rate can accumulate.

Notes and Questions

1. The G-30 Derivatives Study gave the following estimates for the gross replacement costs of the derivatives portfolio of the 50 largest U.S. bank holding companies.

Table 7

Derivatives Exposure by Lead Banks of 50 Largest U.S. Bank Holding Companies

(Year-End 1990-1992)

Gross Replacement Costs

	Interest Rate Contracts		Currency Contracts		Combined Exposure
Year	$ Billion	Percent of Notional Principal	$ Billion	Percent of Notional Principal	$ Billion
1990	26.2	1.15	76.3	2.82	102.5
1991	47.8	1.61	99.4	3.70	147.2
1992	49.7	1.61	94.3	2.98	144.0

The gross replacement cost is the mark-to-market value for OTC derivatives contracts with positive replacement cost, including swaps, forwards, purchased options, when-issued securities, and forward deposits accepted. Exchange-traded contracts and foreign exchange contracts with less than 14 days maturity are excluded.

Source: Consolidated Reports of Condition and Income.

Can these results for interest rate contracts (which include futures/options and swaps) be squared with the Simons study? Why would exposure on currency contracts be higher than on interest rate contracts. The G-30 Study stated that the "total replacement cost of $144.0 billion represents less than 11% of the market value of the assets of these banks and 120% of their total capital." *Id.* This was at year-end 1992. On the other hand, a 1994 study by the International Monetary Fund (IMF), International Capital Markets Part 2: Systemic Issues in International Finance at 27, reports that replacement cost was $170 billion for the 10 largest U.S. banks, or 17.3% of their assets, as of September 1992 (U.S. banks must report replacement cost to the Federal Reserve Board). What do you think replacement cost was in the spring of 1994, after the U.S. experienced a sudden surge in interest rates?

2. How would you compare the credit and market risks to a bank on an interest rate swap with those from lending. Banks that lend typically have exposure to interest rate risk, for example if they have a mismatch between long-term fixed rate assets and short-term floating rate liabilities. Is this just like entering a swap in which a bank pays a fixed rate and receives a floating rate?

The actual credit risks on swaps, like loans, not only depend on the credit rating of the counterparty, but also on security provisions. Some swap arrangements require the out-of-the money participant to provide collateral or "mark-to-market" payments to the in-the-money participant.

In 1992, Citicorp had $135 billion in loans compared to $217 billion in interest rate swaps. Does this mean it has more total risk from swaps than loans?

3. How can a Swap Dealer deal with market risk? One possibility, as in our paradigm interest rate swap, is to enter into a matched swap with another counterparty. In practice, however, it is very difficult to run a swaps portfolio that is entirely matched. One way to deal with this is to use non-swap interest rate contracts, futures, forwards or options, to hedge swap exposure. However, these hedges are "dynamic" since they need to be adjusted over time due to the fact that non-swap interest rate contracts have a shorter maturity than swaps. Indeed, a major problem in estimating the market risk to a particular institution from swaps is deciding to what extent swap risks are offset or hedged by positions in other instruments. It should be noted that dealers mark-to-market their derivatives portfolio daily in order to assess their value.

4. The ISDA Master Agreement was revised in 1992 and is currently in the process of being revised in 2002.

2. REDUCING COUNTERPARTY RISK

Dealing in swaps is a very competitive business, reflected in the narrowing of dealer spreads over time. Does the competitiveness of a dealer depend on having a low credit risk?

M. PELTZ, WALL STREET'S TRIPLE-A FOR EFFORT
Institutional Investor, May 1993, at 93-98.

Investors in the derivatives markets have discovered a fundamental law of risk that's similar to the first law of thermodynamics governing conservation of energy. Risk never disappears, it just changes form. "Over-the-counter derivatives allow investors to lay off market risk very accurately," Securities and Exchange Commissioner J. Carter Beese Jr. noted last March. But hedging, he continued, "certainly has its own price tag. [Customers] are, in effect, trading market risk for credit risk."

Not if they can help it, however. When several financial institutions were down-graded during the recession to humble single-A status, many users of interest rate and currency swaps shifted business to the highest-rated banks and firms or demanded that counterparties put up collateral. Now, says attorney Kenneth Raisler, co-head of Sullivan & Cromwell's commodities, futures and derivatives group, "if you don't have the credit rating, people won't deal with you."

Single-A doesn't cut it. Most swappers insist on double-A or better. So to counter the advantage of triple-A banks like swaps powerhouse J.P. Morgan & Co., investment banks have cobbled together "credit-enhanced" derivatives subsidiaries. (The Comptroller of the Currency has informally dissuaded commercial banks from forming such units.) The first triple-A sub, Merrill Lynch Derivative Products, was separately capitalized upon its debut in November 1991 so that it would survive even if parent Merrill Lynch were to go bankrupt. To guarantee a top rating (see box, page 92), MLDP was endowed with a cool $350 million, or about $117 million per "A."

———————

As the above article recounts, U.S. bank regulators did not allow banks (Citibank and Continental Illinois were denied permission in 1992) to set up AAA subsidiaries. This changed for the first time in May 1996 when the Office of the Comptroller of the Currency permitted NationsBank to do so, stating "This allows domestic banks to remain competitive with U.S. investment banks and foreign banks in the area of derivative dealing." O. de Sennerpont Domis, *NationsBank Gets OCC Nod on Derivatives*, American Banker, May 20, 1996. Why would they be against this? Should banks be concerned about the competitive impact? In 1996, Dai-Ichi Kangyo (DKB), a large Japanese bank, reached an agreement that would allow it to funnel its derivatives business through Merrill Lynch Capital Services' triple-A rated derivatives conduit. Due to concern over the creditworthiness of the bank, DKB thought it desirable to use a triple-A entity, and found it cheaper to use Merrill Lynch's existing entity, which had excess capital, than to spend $300 million to capitalize its own. An excellent summary of the characteristics of the 15 triple-A rated conduit vehicles outstanding as of August 1998 is set forth in Swaps Monitor (August 24, 1998), at p. 4.

Indeed, a May 1996 study of the Federal Reserve Bank of New York generally questions the efficacy of the use of AAA companies, given their substantial capital investment. These entities have garnered a relatively small percentage of the swaps market. In fact, the biggest of these companies, Merrill Lynch Derivatives Products and Salomon Swapco had derivatives books at the end of 1994 with notional values of only $91 billion and $67 billion, respectively, with each book representing less than 7 percent of their parents' derivative books. E. Remolona, W. Bassett, and In Sun Geoum, *Risk Management by Structured Derivative Product Companies*, 2 Economic Policy Review (Federal Reserve Bank of New York) 17, 22 (1996). Another problem with these companies is that their risk may not be entirely segregated from that of their parents since AAAs typically hedge customer transactions with mirror transactions with parents. If parents were to default on the mirror transactions, or have an increased risk of defaulting, the AAA would itself be at increased risk and its AAA rating might be jeopardized.

The preceding article suggests that pricing in the swaps market does not materially take counterparty creditworthiness into account. Why would that be? R. Litzenberger, *Swaps: Plain and Fanciful*, 47 Journal of Finance 831, 836-838 (1992), gives three reasons: First, assuming that bankruptcy probabilities are independent of interest rate levels, gains from the default of a counterparty are just as likely as losses. If you are a fixed-rate payer, you gain from your counterparty's bankruptcy if rates go down, but lose if rates go up. If, however, low interest rates are associated in general with more bankruptcies, and fixed rate payers are generally more risky than floating rate payers, floating rate payers are more likely to lose if rates go down, i.e. when fixed rate payers default. Second, under the one-way payment rules, the solvent party may not have to pay the defaulting party (more on this later). Third, there is protection against credit risk. Deterioration in credit ratings may terminate swaps, or there may be collateral.

While many dealers report that they do not quote different rates for counterparties of different credit quality, dealers do require their counterparties to establish credit lines, and lower quality credits get smaller credit lines than those with higher credit. One study has stated: "Suppose that traders of one firm do not offer different prices to different credit risk counterparties but ration them depending on their credit quality. A low rating company will reach the maximum of its credit line faster than a high rating company. It will have to obtain a quote from a globally less favorable dealer [a dealer uniformly charging higher rates, eds.]. At equilibrium, in the market, participants may obtain different rates from different dealers even though no dealers give different quotes to different companies." D. Cossin and H. Pirotte, *Swap Credit Risk: An Empirical Investigation on Transaction Data,* J. of Banking & Finance 1351 (1997). The study, in fact found, that credit ratings affected swap prices in the aggregate by 3.8 basis points with the biggest impact for non-rated companies.

Notes and Questions

1. Do you think AAA swap dealers reduce risk?

2. Do you agree with Litzenberger's analysis?

3. In March 1999, the CFTC approved an application of the London Clearing House (LCH), which clears and settles trades on London financial exchanges, for an exemption from regulation that would permit it to clear and settle OTC derivatives, beginning with plain vanilla interest rate swaps and forward exchange rate agreements. The name of the service is SwapClear. Under the plan, two parties in a swap deal would convert their bilateral agreement into separate agreements with the LCH. The plan envisions that contracts with the LCH as counterparty would require less capital than would otherwise be the case. This may result from the advantages of netting with one rather than several counterparties. N. Tait and E. Luce, *Clearing services proposal for OTC derivatives*, Financial Times, June 17, 1998. SwapClear will impose both initial and variation margin requirements based on daily marking-to-

market of the value of the swap. The service was launched in September 1999. What do you think of this plan?

3.   MORE EXOTIC SWAPS

The material has focused on plain vanilla swaps. While these constitute a very substantial percentage of all swaps outstanding, there are more customized or exotic swaps. We look at two: diff swaps and credit derivatives.

a.   DIFF SWAPS

A Diff is an exchange of interest payments calculated with respect to different currencies but payable in one currency. Let's take a specific example. Assume we have a 5 year Diff for DM 100 million in which Company A agrees to receive DM LIBOR (currently 8%) from Company B in exchange for paying B $ LIBOR + 50 basis points ($ LIBOR currently being 3%).

A's current cash flow on the swap is positive, A pays B DM 3.5 million (100 million X .035) and receives DM 8 million (100 million X .08). This looks like a great deal for A, but is it? What would you expect the yield curves for German and U.S. interest rates to look like?

The first reported diff was done by Sallie Mae arranged by Credit Suisse. Sallie Mae issued a $105 million 3 yr floating note in July 1991 with a coupon of DM Libor -160 BP, with all payments in dollars. The initial coupon was 7.90% which was equivalent to U.S. Libor plus 128 bp. Sallie Mae then did a Swap with CS in which Sallie Mae paid CS U.S. Libor-for DM Libor -160 BP. What was Sallie Mae trying to accomplish?

Is a Diff more or less risky than the plain vanilla swaps? Consider the problems that a dealer in diffs might have in hedging its exposure on these instruments.

M. PALSEY, THE LAST PIECE OF THE JIGSAW
Euromoney, Nov. 1993, at 29-31.

. . .

Diffs are easy to describe and almost impossible to hedge. The swap writer undertakes to receive Libor in one currency, usually dollars, and to pay Libor in another currency with that payment stream denominated in dollars. This creates two correlation problems.

First, the dealer is exposed to the correlation between the two Libors. This can be avoided relatively easily using a pair of interest rate swaps, by buying bonds or using futures or FRAS.

Second, there is the correlation between interest rates and FX rates. Suppose the swap writer is paying Deutschemark Libor in dollars and receiving dollar Libor. He is funding the Deutschemark Libor payout through the Deutschemark swap market, so even if interest rates remain the same he is exposed to the risk that the dollar will strengthen leaving him short of Deutschemarks to pay off the dollar liability. Hedging this risk means taking a view on the correlation between interest rates and FX rates.

Does the bank believe that a rise in Deutschemark interest rates will affect the $/Dm rate? If so, exactly how strong is the correlation effect-to what extent does the bank believe that any rise in Deutschemark rates (and so in the amount of money it must pay out to the counterparty) will be compensated for by a strengthening of the Deutschemark against the dollar?

"Customers are basically getting the bank to remove the uncertainty between the relationship of interest rates and currency values, that is to guarantee that movements in European interest rates will have no impact on the value of the currency. The problem we have is that if we take a position to hedge against the most likely scenario, that is that when European rates fall European currencies will weaken, and it doesn't happen, then we lose money," says Ronald Tanemura, a director at Salomon Brothers.

The correlation problem in the case of diffs is particularly acute. A corporate hedger's rationale for using one shows why. Before the ERM meltdown, a corporation with Libor-based sterling liabilities found itself paying interest rates that bore no relationship to the economic environment in which it operated. Treasurers saw that US rates were more obviously tied to the real economy and decided to take advantage of this by opting to swap dollar Libor for sterling Libor in dollars. If the US recession were prolonged, dollar Libor would remain low, while levels of political support for high European interest rates looked strong. The political and economic factors that drive FX and interest rate correlations make those correlations difficult to predict and subject to sudden, extreme movements.

Need to Quantify

So how do dealers hedge the risk? The simple answer is that they don't. "Correlation risk is essentially unhedgeable," says one trader. "Providers of these products are taking correlation views, over- or under-hedging and basically being optimistic that what is unhedgeable today will be hedgeable in a couple of years." They can overhedge with expensive foreign exchange options, desirable because diff pricing is related to FX volatility and is therefore option-like, or in the interest rate futures markets.

· · ·

Further consider the problems of Proctor & Gamble which lost $102 million on a diff swap.

CORPORATE HEDGING, HARD SOAP
The Economist, Apr. 16, 1994 at 82.

When things go wrong, the first instinct of Americans is often to phone their lawyer. The same holds for American corporations. On April 12th Proctor & Gamble, a consumer-goods maker, grimly announced that it had lost $102m, after tax, on two interest-rate swaps. Edwin Artzt, P & G's chairman, said he was considering suing Bankers Trust (BT), the bank that had sold it the loss-making swaps, on the ground that these instruments were inappropriate for managing his firm's interest-rate risk.

They were: the swaps bought by P & G about a year ago ("diff" swaps in traders' jargon) are complex even by the standards of that most arcane of markets. They were based on the hope that German and American three-year interest rates would converge more slowly than the market thought they would. If so, P & G would cash in, having leveraged its bet by as much as ten times. But the bet started to go badly wrong towards the end of 1993. German and American interest rates converged. Every hundredth of a percentage point of that convergence cost P & G about $400,000. Since three-year rates have converged by 2.5%, it is easy to see how P & G lost about $100m.

b.   CREDIT DERIVATIVES

A fast growing area of swaps is credit derivatives. The total global credit derivatives market in 2001 was over $1 trillion from a base of $180 billion in 1997. Insurance companies have about a 25 percent market share. Financial Services Authority, *Cross-sector risk transfers* (May 2002) (FSA Study), p. 3.

One variation of this product, a credit default swap, allows a counterparty (usually a financial institution) to buy protection against default of an asset, a loan or bond or receivable, by paying a derivatives dealer, the seller of protection, a periodic fee, expressed as a percentage of face value in basis points. The seller of protection is required to acquire credit-impaired assets at a given price (physical settlement) or to pay the difference between that price and the current value of the assets (cash settlement) in the case of a "credit event." An example of cash settlement would be as follows: "Thirty days after a company defaults (e.g. it fails to make a bond coupon payment) its bonds are valued at 30 cents on the dollar. If the notional of a cash-settled credit default swap referencing that entity's bonds is $10 million, the protection 'seller' would be required to make a payment of $7 million to the protection 'buyer.'" Moody's Investor Service, *Structured Finance, Special Report, Understanding The risks in Credit Default Swaps* (March 16, 2001) (Moody's).

The contingent payment amount made by the seller of protection is often determined by the percentage decline in a reference security whose value would be correlated with the asset that deteriorated. For example, where the protected asset was a bank loan to Company X, the reference security might be Company X's publicly issued bonds. The payoff depends on the value of the relative credits, the loans and bonds. In such arrangements, the definition of a "credit event," the event triggering a payment, is crucial. This definition, and others of importance to credit derivatives, is now covered in an ISDA master agreement issued in January 1998 with definitions revised in 1999. The standard credit events for a corporate swap issuer include bankruptcy, payment default, merger, "cross acceleration," "cross default," credit downgrade, repudiation and restructuring. The problem of defining credit events for sovereign issuers, who do not go bankrupt in a conventional sense, is more difficult. M. Hughes, *Areas of Legal Risk in Sovereign-Linked Credit Derivatives,* Butterworths Journal of International Banking and Financial Law (April 1999).

A credit default swap could be linked to an interest rate swap. For example, if Bank A had a 10-year interest rate swap exposure to Company and it wanted to hedge the risk of the company, it could enter into a swap with a third party (TP) under which it would make periodic payments to TP, and TP would pay Bank A in the event Company defaulted on the interest rate swap. The amount of the default payment would be linked to Company A bonds with similar maturities to the swap.

Another type of credit derivative is the total return swap in which the buyer of protection pays to the seller of protection the total return on an asset, such as a loan or bond, in return for a given payment. For example, Bank B which owns XYZ bond, would agree to pay all positive returns on the bond to dealer (all bond cash flows plus positive mark to market movements) in exchange for a fee, e.g. LIBOR plus specified basis points, and loss protection on the bond (negative mark to market movements). See Bank of England, Supervision and Surveillance, Discussion Paper, *Developing A Supervisory Approach to Credit Derivatives,* November 1996. For another example, an equity investor who thinks the German DAX index (a stock market index) will fall over the next six months might enter into a swap on which he pays the DAX return every month in exchange for receiving 1-month DM LIBOR plus a spread. See H. Kat, *Financial Engineering, Credit Derivatives: A New Addition to the Derivatives Toolbox,* Derivatives (November/December 1997).

Credit derivatives work in an opposite direction from securitization. Banks have used securitization techniques to get risky loans off their balance sheets. Credit derivatives allow the banks to keep loans on their balance sheets but transfer the default risk to counterparties. This has the potential of reversing the long-term trend of the growth of the capital markets at the expense of the banking markets.

Still another innovation is a tax rate swap which allows a specific hedge against a change in tax rates. A company (A) had entered into a large leasing transaction providing tax benefits and, therefore, increased profits which would be lost if corporate tax rates fell. Many companies (B), of course, have lower profits if tax rates increase. The swap involved approximately $30 million, the profits sought to be protected. Morgan Grenfell arranged a swap by which A made payments to B if tax rates increased and B made payments to A if tax rates decreased. The pricing of the swap presumably involved estimates of the probabilities of tax rate changes. T. Corrigan, *Tax Rate Swap Deal Opens a Fresh Vista*, Financial Times, Aug. 18, 1994. See generally A. Bomfin (Federal Reserve Board), *Understanding Credit Derivatives and their Potential to Synthesize Riskless Assets*, Working Paper (July 11, 2001) for a good overview of credit derivatives.

Notes and Questions

1. While exotic swaps are a small percentage of total swaps issued, they do raise different risks than plain vanilla swaps, and may require specialized rules. One problem with the risks is that they cannot easily be hedged or eliminated the way plain vanilla swaps can by engaging in a second swap that offsets the original. This is due to the customized nature and limited quantity of such swaps—the exotic swap market is not liquid.

2. S. Henderson, *Credit Derivatives at a Crossroads?*, Journal of International Banking and Financial Law (May 2001) has written about an important issue relating to credit derivatives, the definition of the credit event "Restructuring" as defined in the 1999 ISDA Credit Derivatives Definitions. The definitions list specific events which are typical of debt restructurings and introduces a condition whereby the Credit Event only occurs if the restructuring results from a deterioration in the creditworthiness of the reference entity. The problem arose when Conseco, Inc., a U.S. consumer finance company restructured its maturing bank loans in response to an impending liquidity crisis. The problem was whether this was a restructuring under the definition; the consensus was that it was since it resulted from a deteriorating financial condition but as a legal matter the situation was not entirely clear. Given that a restructuring occurred the buyer of the protection was entitled to receive a payment from the seller of protection in return for the physical delivery of assets. Certain buyers delivered bonds, a type of Conseco debt that had deteriorated more than the loans which were the subject of the restructuring.

This possibility arose due to the fact that the underlying ISDA documentation allows the parties to adopt a broad range of Deliverable Obligations. In a particular swap, the Deliverable Obligation can be so broad as to include both bonds or loans, although the parties are free to define the Deliverable Obligation much more narrowly, e.g. to particular kinds of loans. See 1999 ISDA Credit Derivative Definitions, Sections 2.14-2.19 and the long form confirmation. Some have suggested that when restructurings of the type in Conseco occur, that only short-dated bond should be deliverable, maturing reasonably close to the maturity date of the swap (these bonds would lose less value than those with longer maturities). Indeed, ISDA has provided in its May 11, 2001 Restructuring Supplement to the 1999 Credit Derivative Definitions that a credit protection buyer can only deliver a Deliverable Obligation that has a final maturity date no later than the Restructuring Maturity Limitation Date, which is a date that is the earlier of thirty months after the date that the restructuring of an obligation is legally effective or the latest final maturity date of any restructured Bond or Loan. Is this more desirable than allowing the parties to make their own choices in particular transactions?

The ISDA documentation for credit derivatives is extremely complex and generally offers the parties choices of terms with respect to 30 variables, e.g. credit event or deliverable obligation. This has led credit derivatives teams at JP Morgan and Morgan Stanley, two of the major players in the business, to simplify the documentation by fixing 22 of the variables, including what is a credit event. This will cut down negotiation time and transaction costs. R. Bream, *Move to align credit default contracts,* Financial Times, November 23, 2001.

3. Credit derivative swaps can also be securitized. A SPV, as a seller of protection, would enter into a credit default swap with a financial institution. The SPV would receive a fee for the protection from the financial institution and if a credit default occurred on the referenced credits, e.g. bonds or loans held by the financial institution, the SPV would make payments to the financial institution. The SPV would then transfer its risk to the capital market. Through synthetic collateralized debt obligations (CDOs) or credit-linked notes (CLNs) investors would become sellers of protection to the SPV. The investors would receive a return on their notes and receive back their investment at term absent a credit event. In the event, a credit event occurred, the SPV would make payments to the financial institution and investors would experience losses of principal. Typically in a synthetic CDO, the financial institution retains the first loss piece, while the mezzanine tranches are securitized and sold to investors. Moody's, supra, at 3; FSA Study, supra, at 12.

4. Should bank regulators be concerned with the legal issues relating to the definition of restructuring? Was the Conseco case a problem for the buyer or the seller of protection? Which of these parties is more likely to be a bank? See generally, *The swaps emperor's new clothes,* The Economist, February 10, 2001.

5. Clearly, credit derivatives are closely related to insurance. An easy way to conceptualize the transaction is that the buyer of protection

is buying insurance against credit risk from the seller of protection. The documentation and writing about these transactions seeks to avoid talking about the transactions in these terms largely because of regulatory concerns. If the contracts were regarded as insurance they might be subject to regulation by insurance regulators (posing the threat of control over terms) or become ultra vires for institutions that could not provide insurance, e.g. banks in some countries. See D. Nirenberg and R. Hoffman, *Are Credit Default Swaps Insurance?*, Derivatives Report 7 (December 2001).

6. Credit derivatives are written on sovereign debt. Indeed, when Argentina failed to timely meet its debt payments, hedge funds submitted substantial claims to dealers. The issue arose, however, as to whether there had actually been a default within the meaning of the derivatives contract. J. Chaffin, *Bondholders making their way to court,* Financial times, December 22/23, 2001. Indeed, the interest of bondholders and derivatives counterparties could diverge, with bondholders ready to agree to a restructuring that was not a "default" and with buyers of protection preferring a default.

7. Enron has generated some significant litigation over surety bonds issued to back credit extended to Enron. Insurers issued surety bonds to JP Morgan that guaranteed that Enron would make good on $965 million in oil and gas forward contracts. The surety bonds were substitutes for credit derivatives but apparently, unlike credit derivatives, permit the insurer (seller of protection) fraud and misrepresentation defenses. G. Silverman and A. Hill, *JP Morgan and insurers go to court over Enron*, Financial Times, January 15, 2002. The insurers claimed that they thought they were insuring a trade which, in reality, was a disguised loan.

4. SYSTEMIC RISK AND PRUDENTIAL REGULATION

a. THE EXTENT OF SYSTEMIC RISK

The G-30 Derivatives Study, at 60-64, concluded that there should not be a lot of concern over the systemic risk that might arise from derivatives activity (including swaps). In particular, it noted that the notional amounts of derivatives overstate the size of the market (only replacement value should be relevant), that the participants understand the complexities, that the markets are not highly concentrated, and that credit risks are less in derivatives than traditional lending (because swap counterparties are generally more creditworthy). Nonetheless, there has been an outcry for more regulation by congressional committees and some regulators. Should we be worried about the risks of swaps? A 1992 ISDA Default Survey, which surveyed swap dealers accounting for over 70% of the market, found that the cumulative losses over the history of the involvement of these firms with swaps was $358.36 million, or about

.011% of the notional amount of swaps outstanding as of December 31, 1991.

A 1995 central bank survey of the over-the-counter derivatives markets concludes that these markets have successfully withstood several interest rate cycles and episodes of large changes in exchange rates, and that the price shocks will have less impact than price changes in the debt securities markets. It generally sees derivatives as decreasing rather than increasing systemic risk due to their widespread use in hedging. J. Kambhu, F. Keane, and C. Benadon, *Price Risk Intermediation in the Over-the-Counter Derivatives Markets: Interpretation of a Global Survey,* 2 Economic Policy Review (Federal Reserve Bank of New York) 1 (1996).

Nonetheless, there were some losses in 1997 that called into question the accuracy of computer models used by dealers to control risks. Bank of Tokyo-Mitsubishi Bank Ltd. incurred a $50 million loss and costs of $33 million in unwinding a portfolio composed of swaps and options linked to movements in U.S. interest rates. It attributed these losses to its computer model which overvalued its position. This report came only weeks after National Westminster Bank PLC announced that mispricing of interest rate options at its banking unit, NatWest Markets, cost the bank about $138.8 million. S. McGee, *Bank of Tokyo Blames Loss on Bad Model,* Wall Street Journal, March 28, 1997. If dealer VAR (value-at-risk) models are flawed, current estimates of potential losses may be too low. Many believe that whatever risks swaps present, they reduce the overall risk to swap dealers because swaps are used by these institutions to match or hedge other interest rate or currency positions. However, a 1996 study of U.S. bank holding companies indicated that overall use of swaps increased rather than decreased the interest rate risk of these institutions. B. Hirtle, *Derivatives, Portfolio Composition and Bank Holding Company Interest Rate Exposure,* Wharton School Financial Institutions Center Working Paper 96-43, Draft, November 8, 1996.

The studies cited above do not focus on losses to non-bank counterparties, such as the $102 million loss in the case of Proctor & Gamble. Other substantial user losses have also been reported. A large investment fund of Wisconsin public money reported a $95 million loss due to leveraged swaps based on Mexican and European interest rates. G. Knecht, *Wisconsin Fund Records a Loss on Derivatives*, Wall Street Journal, March 24, 1995. The most noteworthy loss on OTC derivatives was in the case of the Orange County Fund where losses were estimated at $2.5 billion. But these losses were not due to swaps, but mostly to inverse floating rate derivatives which generated less interest, and thus losses, when interest rates increased in 1994. L. Jereski, *Orange County Fund Losses Put at 2.5 Billion*, Wall Street Journal, December 12, 1994. Merrill Lynch, the major defendant in the Orange County case, settled its suit in 1998, L. Wayne and A. Pollack, *Merrill Makes Strategic Move in Ending Suit,* New York Times, June 4, 1998.

b.   PRUDENTIAL STANDARDS

A key development in 1994 was the formulation by various regulators of prudential guidelines for the derivative operations of banks, largely motivated by concern with systemic risk.   The formulation of these standards reflected continue unease about the adequacy of banks' risk management systems.   This concern was reflected in the results obtained from a survey of some major swap dealers by the BIS Committee on Banking Supervision.   Bankers were asked to compute their exposure on a swap portfolio under certain specified parameters such as a 10 day holding period and a 99% confidence level.   Exposure calculations varied at the extreme ends by a factor of eight.   This could mean (actual numbers are not available) from $30 to $240 million.   *Danger—Kids at Play*, Euromoney, March 1995, at 43.   On the other hand, the Group of Thirty has reported, on the basis of a survey of 300 dealers and 600 end-users, that derivative risks are now well managed by banks, although end-users (including non-dealer banks) lag substantially behind.   Derivatives: Practices and Principles: Follow-up Surveys of Industry Practice, Dec. 1994.

The BIS Committee on Banking Supervision has set forth three basic principles of risk management: (1) appropriate oversight by boards of directors and senior management; (2) adequate risk management process that integrates prudent risk limits, sound measurement procedures and information systems, continuous risk monitoring and frequent management reporting; and (3) comprehensive internal controls and audit procedures.   Risk Management Guidelines for Derivatives, July 1994. Similar standards have been formulated by IOSCO, Operational and Financial Risk Management Control Mechanisms for Over-the Counter Derivative Activities of Regulated Securities Firms, July 1994.   Both reports discuss the question of how specific regulators should be about management calculation of risk exposure.   In May 1995, BIS and IOSCO issued a joint report, Framework for Supervisory Information About the Derivatives Activities of Banks and Securities Firms.   This is a very detailed statement and represented a breakthrough for collaboration between bank and security regulators at the international level.

In 1998, the BIS Committee on Payment and Settlement Systems and the Euro-currency Standing Committee, issued a report on the ways in which firms seek to control their risks in swap transactions, OTC Derivatives: Settlement Procedures and Counterparty Risk Management, September 1998.

As a formal matter, the derivatives activities of banks in the United States are highly regulated by bank supervisors.   This regulation involves detailed examination of their activities as well as the capital requirements discussed below.   The Office of the Comptroller of the Currency in the United States has been very active in this area.   See OCC Banking Circular (BC) 277, Oct. 27, 1993; and OCC, Bulletin No. 94-32, Questions and Answers About BC 277, May 10, 1994. However, there is no regulatory framework for supervision of the derivatives activities of securities firms by the SEC or CFTC. Securities firms are not generally regulated for safety and soundness except through capital requirements, and unregistered affiliates of such firms dealing in swaps are not even subject to capital requirements.

Perhaps in an attempt to head off more formal regulation, in March 1995 six major securities firms*, in cooperation with the SEC and CFTC, agreed to adopt a *Framework for Voluntary Oversight* (Voluntary Framework) under which the firms would undertake to have certain management controls, submit quantitative reports covering credit risk exposures, evaluate risk relative to capital and adopt guidelines for dealing with non-professional counterparties to derivatives contracts.

Should securities firms generally be submitted to the same regulatory framework for their derivatives activities as are banks? This was the basic proposal put forward by Jim Leach, the Chairman of the House Banking Committee, in H.R. 20, introduced on January 4, 1995. It would have created a Federal Derivatives Commission to among other things set principles and standards for federal supervision of all financial institutions. The SEC would have enforced the standards with respect to securities firms. Nothing came of this proposal, however.

One way to reduce the risk on swaps is to require collateral. Increasingly swaps require the losing side to post collateral. This is, of course, similar to variation margins on futures contracts. The Chicago Mercantile Exchange has abandoned its three year effort to offer a swaps collateral depository which would have been charged with receiving and accepting collateral on swaps transactions between major swaps dealers. 10 Swaps Monitor, No. 24 (September 29, 1997).

Some have advocated moving swaps trading to exchanges with margin requirements and guaranteed settlement typical of futures exchanges. See D. Folkerts-Landau and A. Steinherr, *The Wild Beast of Derivatives: To be Chained Up, Fenced in or Tamed?, in* Finance and the International Economy: The Amex Bank Review (1994). As we saw, this is now beginning to happen.

The underlying concern with losses in the swap market is that it could lead to systemic risk, a widespread breakdown of financial markets. Many assume such risk would manifest itself through interlinked failures, i.e. A's failure imposes losses on its counterparty B which fails, and so on. No analysis has been done to ascertain whether such an event is likely. If VAR estimates are reasonably accurate and dealers have relatively dispersed risks with a variety of counterparties, rather than highly

*Credit Suisse First Boston, Goldman Sachs, Morgan Stanley, Merrill Lynch, Salomon Brothers, and Lehman Brothers.

concentrated exposures, such a scenario seem quite unlikely. A 1996 study by L. Wall, E. Tallman and P. Abken, *The Impact of a Dealer's Failure on OTC Derivatives Market Liquidity During Volatile Periods,* Federal Reserve Bank of Atlanta, Working Paper 96-6, June 1996, poses a different systemic risk scenario. The authors describe their paper as follows (footnotes omitted):

> Our paper exploits the idea long-standing in the banking literature that a bank failure results in a temporary loss of credit quality information on that bank's clients. We apply Wall's intuition that information losses may be a key component of the costs of intermediary failure to the derivatives market. In particular, the dealer failure forces good, solvent firms of the failed dealer to seek hedges with other dealers. However, by forcing good firms to look for a new derivatives dealer, the dealer failure provides camouflage for insolvent firms looking to speculate with a dealer that does not know their credit status. That is, insolvent firms can mimic good firms because other dealers cannot quickly verify credit quality information to distinguish good from bad firms. If the firms could give the remaining dealers some time to analyze their credit quality then the dealers could separate the good firms from the insolvent ones. However, during periods of market turbulence a delay of a day (or even a few hours) in reestablishing the hedge could result in substantial losses to the good firm. The resulting pooling equilibrium will impose at best additional costs (pooling losses) on the good firms but may also cause good firms to leave the market completely. Thus, there are costs imposed on derivatives users caused by the loss of credit information from the failure of their derivatives dealer, and these costs may be high enough to cause a collapse of the market.

This paper shows that such an event would be unlikely but not impossible. Is this a serious concern?

c.   THE ROLE OF THE CFTC AND "LEGAL CERTAINTY"[*]

During the 1990's there was considerable doubt as to whether the CFTC had jurisdiction over swap transactions. This issue was not merely theoretical since if the CFTC had jurisdiction, absent an exemption from the Commodity Exchange Act granted by the CFTC, swap contracts would be possibly invalid and unenforceable.

The history of the issue of legal certainty is well detailed in The Report of The President's Working Group, *Over-the-Counter Derivatives Markets and the Commodity Exchange Act* (November 1999). The Congress previously addressed the legal status and enforceability of OTC derivative contracts in the Futures Trading Practices Act of 1992 (FTPA)

---

[*]This section is based largely on the testimony Professor Scott gave before the U.S. House Committee on Banking and Financial Services on July 19, 2000, on an earlier version of the new legislation.

which amended the CEA to provide the CFTC with the authority to grant exemptions from the CEA for transactions for which an exemption was in the public interest, where the parties were "appropriate persons," large institutions, and where the exemption would not have a material adverse effect on the ability of the CFTC to fulfill its duties under the CEA.

Pursuant to this authority, and the intent of the Congress, in 1993 the CFTC adopted the Swap Exemption which exempted certain swaps entered into by "eligible swap participants" from the provisions of the Act. Eligible swap participants included all "appropriate persons" as defined by FTPA, plus the Commission added any natural person with assets exceeding $10 million. However, in order to qualify for the exemption, swap agreements had to meet certain conditions. Swaps could not be "part of a fungible class of agreements that are standardized as to their material economic terms." The creditworthiness of the parties to the swap agreement had to be a material consideration in entering into the swap. In this regard, the Commission's commentary stated that the exemption did not extend to transactions that are subject to a clearing system where the credit risk of individual members of the system is replaced by a system of mutualized risk, which would be the case where a clearinghouse became the counterparty to transactions. Finally, the swap could not be entered into or traded through a "multilateral transaction execution facility" (MTEF). The Commission's commentary explained (no definition was provided in the text of the exemption) that an MTEF was a "physical or electronic facility in which all market makers and other participants that are members simultaneously have the ability to execute transactions and bind both parties by accepting offers which are made by one member and open to all members of the facility."

What were the "legal certainty" problems under the Swap Exemption? First, there was the continuing possibility that the CFTC might change the Swap Exemption. This concern was heightened by its issuance of its concept release, Over-the-Counter Derivatives, 63 Fed. Reg. 26,114 (1998), requesting comment on how, if at all, the swaps market could be regulated, and the general perception of OTC market participants that the CFTC wanted to even the playing field of competition between OTC derivatives and exchange-traded derivatives regulated by the CFTC.

A second concern with the Swap Exemption had to do with the lack of clarity of the conditions establishing the Exemption. For example, what exactly was a fungible class of standardized agreements? Were "plain vanilla" interest rate and foreign currency swaps entered into under standard documentation of the International Swaps and Derivatives Association (ISDA) such a fungible class of standardized agreements? What exactly was a MTEF?

And just as important was the third concern, the rationale for the conditions. Why shouldn't standardized swaps, or swaps where the credit of the counterparty was not a concern, or swaps traded through a MTEF be excluded from CFTC jurisdiction? The clear reason for the conditions was the desire of the CFTC to take jurisdiction over swaps the more they looked like futures and options traded on regulated exchanges. Exchange-traded derivatives have standardized terms, mutualized credit, and arguably some form of multilateral trading. No attempt was made, however, to articulate why the public interest required regulation of OTC derivatives with these characteristics. The issue here was not really legal certainty. It was rather what the substantive conditions should be for excluding transactions from CFTC regulation.

On December 21, 2000, the Congress passed the Commodity Futures Modernization Act (CFMA) that attempted to resolve these issues. Section 103 of the Act, entitled "Legal Certainty for Excluded Derivative Transactions" defines the conditions under which swaps and other OTC derivatives will be excluded from CEA jurisdiction. It sets forth two routes for exclusion.

Route 1 Exclusion

Under the first route, the transaction must be between "eligible contract participants (ECPs)" and the transaction must not be executed on a "trading facility". The definition of "eligible contract participants," set forth in §3(12) is the counterpart to the definition of "appropriate persons" in the Swap Exemption.

An ECP includes a list of qualifying persons <u>acting for their own account</u>: (1) regulated financial institutions (including banks, insurance companies, investment companies, broker-dealers, futures commission merchants) or arrangements (commodity pools); (2) corporations or other entities with total assets of at least $10 million, obligations backed by a letter of credit, or a net worth of $1,000,000 and enters into the transaction "in connection with the conduct of the entity's business or to manage the risk associated with an asset or liability owned or incurred or reasonably likely to be owned or incurred by the entity in the conduct of the entity's business"; (4) certain employee benefit plans; (5) various national and international governmental entities; and (6) a natural person with assets exceeding $10 million or $5 million where the person enters into the transaction "in order to manage the risk associated with an asset owned or liability incurred, or reasonably likely to be owned or incurred by the individual," e.g. for hedging. In addition, the same ECPs (except for investment companies or a natural person) can act as <u>brokers or agents</u> for other ECPs. The CFTC may add to the list of ECPs acting either for their own account or as agents, fiduciaries or investment managers.

The first route to exclusion prohibits use of a "trading facility" which is defined in §3 (33) of CFMA as a physical or electronic trading facility in which "multiple participants have the ability to execute or trade agreements...by accepting bids and offers made by other participants that are open to multiple participants" in the facility. However, the same definition provides that the term "trading facility" does not include an electronic system "to negotiate the terms of and enter into bilateral transactions as a result of communications exchanged by the parties and not from interaction of multiple orders within a predetermined, nondiscretionary automated trade matching algorithm."

Route 2 Exclusion: Electronic Trading Facility (ETF)

Subsection (2) of Section 103 establishes three conditions for exclusion: (1) the transactions must be entered into on a "principal-to-principal basis" by parties trading for their own account or as agents to the extent permitted under the ECP definition; (2) the parties must be "eligible contract participants"; and (3) the transaction must be executed on an electronic trading facility. The Subsection (2) route does not allow (without specific Commission approval) any agency transactions.

Covered Swap Agreements of Banks

In addition to these exclusions, Section 407 of CFMA provides that "covered swap agreements" of banks are exempt from the CEA. A covered swap agreement is essentially any swap that would be excluded from the CEA under either of the two routes described above. While some thought the legislation might exclude any swap offered by banks, regardless of whether it was excluded under either of the two routes, this did not come to pass.

Finally, Section 120 of CFMA provides that no transactions between ECPs shall be unenforceable "based solely on the failure of the agreement, contract, or transaction to comply with the terms and conditions of an exemption or exclusion from any provision of this Act or regulations of the Commission."

There are a number of problems with this approach. In our view any new legislation in this area should fulfill at the minimum three objectives: (1) ensure by legislation (as opposed to CFTC regulation) that OTC derivatives are not subject to the CEA; (2) formulate clear and certain rules that accomplish the exclusion; and (3) make sure these rules are justified by public policy concerns. Section 5 fails on all three criteria.

Continuing Exemption through Regulation

Section 103 continues to give the CFTC substantial discretionary authority over whether certain swap transactions are excluded from CEA coverage. Under both routes to exclusion, generally one must be an ECP to participate in swap transactions excluded from the CEA. While the proposed legislation does determine that certain parties are ECPs, e.g. banks, it leaves to the CFTC the option of adding to the list. Qualification as an ECP is particularly important given that Section 22 only insures contract enforceability for ECPs.

Of equal importance, the CFMA creates many new terms. The major problem with these terms is that they will create legal uncertainty, as detailed below. The CFTC will acquire substantial power over the conditions of the exclusion of OTC derivatives through its power to issue interpretations or regulations clarifying these terms.

Creation of New Legal Uncertainty

Section 103 together with the relevant definitions in Section 101, are replete with new terms and concepts that will create significant uncertainty as to whether a given OTC transaction is excluded from the CEA. Indeed, more uncertainty will be created than existed under the old Swap Exemption where most of these new terms and concepts were not used. Some examples follow:

1. Under the ECP definition, corporations with a net worth of at least $1 million can engage in excluded transactions if the transactions are "in connection with the conduct of the entity's business or to manage the risk associated with an asset or liability owned or incurred or reasonably likely to be incurred by the entity in the conduct of the entity's business." This type of subjective purpose test is inherently uncertain since the purpose of a particular transaction will not be clear on its face.

2. Under the Subsection (2) route to exclusion, trading on an electronic facility can be done on a "principal-to-principal" basis but not on an agency basis. Whether or not a particular party is acting as agent or principal may be difficult to determine in particular cases—it will call into play the general law of agency. Furthermore, a party will not easily be able to determine whether his counterparty is acting in such a capacity.

3. The Subsection (1) route to exclusion prohibits use of a "trading facility". Such a facility includes a system where the acceptance of bids and offers are open to multiple participants and where there is an "interaction of multiple orders within a predetermined, nondiscretionary automated trade matching and execution algorithm," but does not include a system "to negotiate the terms of and enter into bilateral transactions as a result of communications exchanged by the parties." Suppose a system is open to multiple participants, who post bids and offers, and results in bilateral transactions. Whether or not it will be excluded or covered by the CEA results from a determination as to whether there was an interaction of the orders in a "nondiscretionary automated trade matching and execution algorithm." Whether or not a system has such an algorithm and whether or not it is nondiscretionary will create uncertainty.

4. OTC derivatives that are electronically traded under Subsection (2) are restricted to "principal-to-principal" transactions whereas non-traded OTC transactions under Subsection (1) can be engaged in on an

agency basis. It will be difficult to determine whether a particular system for entering into transactions does or does not involve trading.

Unjustified Underlying Policies

Many of the new legal uncertainty problems have been created out of a desire to limit which parties can participate in OTC derivative transactions. For example, individuals with a net worth of under $10 million, or corporations with a net worth of less than $1 million, cannot participate in these transactions directly as principals, nor can they participate through financial firms acting as their agents. These same parties are free, however, to trade in risky exchange-traded derivatives, penny stock markets, and other types of risky investments. There is no documented abuse of such investors in OTC derivative markets—the Working Group was unable to point to any; indeed the participation of retail investors in such markets is currently minuscule. Yet we risk creating huge uncertainty in the broader wholesale market out of a theoretical concern with retail investors being defrauded. This makes no sense. A cynic might view the proposed approach in CFMA as designed to fence off exchange-traded derivatives markets from competition with OTC derivatives markets for retail investors, a market segmentation that is completely unjustifiable on public policy grounds. Retail investors can be protected through state and federal fraud laws. If serious abuses come to light, which would justify regulation, Congress can intervene at that time.

CFMA only allows for the trading of OTC derivatives on an electronic trading facility, and then only on a principal-to-principal basis. It is entirely arbitrary to permit OTC derivatives to be traded on an electronic facility rather than in person. The only possible reason for this distinction is to advantage the physical trading of exchange-traded derivatives, which is not good public policy.

Finally, it is unclear why CFMA would only permit electronic trading where the acceptance of bids and offers are open to multiple participants" and where there is an "interaction of multiple orders within a predetermined, nondiscretionary automated trade matching and execution algorithm" whatever the meaning of such qualifications. This seems to be a continuation of the MTEF exclusion under the Swap Exemption. Working Group Report, at 19. The only purpose of such an exclusion seems to be to advantage the use of such systems for exchange-traded derivatives. Nowhere in the Working Group Report is a justification for this exclusion set forth.

A Preferable Approach

A preferable approach would be that derivatives based on non-agricultural products, including all financial derivatives, would be outside the CEA, unless a trading facility for such transactions has specifically requested to be covered and regulated under CEA. Under this approach, transactors would have the choice of trading any financial derivative, whether a future, option or swap, either over-the-counter or an exchange. This would remove the CFTC from any regulatory role, unless the parties to transactions consent to its jurisdiction. Further, it provides complete legal certainty. If the parties have not consented to CFTC jurisdiction, a transaction would not be subject to CEA. This alternative recognizes that OTC derivatives contracts have become more functionally equivalent over time to exchange-traded derivatives, and that it is arbitrary to force some to be regulated by the CEA while excluding others. The exchanges would be free to set up trading facilities unregulated by the CEA just the way any other transactors could. Indeed, the CFMA moves in this direction by subjecting certain wholesale exchange traded derivatives to less regulation.

The result would not necessarily mean that all financial derivatives would be traded outside the CEA and the jurisdiction of the CFTC. If transactors and investors believed that these rules were necessary, because they provided needed regulation, they would choose to become subject to the CEA. This would be similar to the choice investors make internationally in trading on a more highly regulated exchange where stocks have dual listings, or the choice securities markets make in issuing stock under the laws of jurisdictions requiring significant disclosure.

This approach would abandon the rearguard action of CFMA in trying to protect the organized exchanges from competition from the OTC market by forcing retail investors or certain type of trading arrangements under the jurisdiction of the CFTC. The organized exchanges currently have less than a 14% market share in financial derivatives and their share is falling. If the CFTC wants to reverse this trend, it will adopt regulations that investors and transactors find attractive and necessary. It is undesirable to force retail investors to participate in less efficient markets, and it is undesirable to hamper the development of efficient trading systems outside the CEA.

Notes and Questions

1. Do you agree with our prescription for what to do about CFTC regulation of swaps?

2. A number of new electronic trading facilities are being established to trade swaps, which will automate much of the individual negotiations now conducted. For example, SwapsWire, backed by 23 leading participants in the swaps market, is designed to automate derivatives dealing, allowing dealers to display prices and book deals electronically. J. Sandman, *SwapsWire Set to Expand Testing with Member Firms*, Security Industry News, April 23, 2001. Would such an arrangement be excluded from CEA coverage by CFMA?

3. In the spring of 2002, the Congress began reconsidering whether it had made the right decision in removing swaps from CFTC regulation. This was prompted, in large part, by the use of commodity OTC derivatives by Enron which some believe may have affected energy prices in California.

C. DISCLOSURE REQUIREMENTS

There are several different types of disclosure requirements for swaps: accounting rules, public disclosure of information for purposes of financial reporting, and disclosure of information to market participants or regulators.

1. ACCOUNTING

Until June 1998, generally accepted accounting principles did not directly address income and balance sheet accounting for swaps. Industry practice is to record the net difference in interest payments on interest rate swaps. Neither the notional amount nor the market value of swaps entered into for hedging purposes is recorded on the balance sheet. Dealers in swaps must mark their positions to market on the balance sheet, and record changes in value on the income statement. GAO Report at 96.

There are two accounting problems caused by hedges. When an entity has two perfectly offsetting positions that are measured using different valuation techniques—one at cost (typically the hedged item) and one at market—the picture presented will not reflect the true financial situation. Another problem arises when an entity has two perfectly offsetting positions but one is not recognized and the other is. If hedging items were marked-to-market there would be an artificial timing mismatch in the realization of gains and losses on the two items. Hedge accounting basically allows deferral of gains and losses on the hedging item until they are realized on the hedged item. This is done by incorporating the gain or loss on the hedging item into the carrying amount of the hedged item.

This approach depends on knowing when one position is hedging another one and when it is not. *Accounting for Futures Contracts*, Statement of Financial Accounting Standard 80, ¶ 4, defines a hedge as follows:

> The contract [the hedge] reduces that exposure [on the hedged item] and is designated as a hedge. At the inception of the hedge and throughout the hedge period, high correlation of changes in (1) the market value of the futures [hedge] contract(s) and (2) the fair value of, or interest income or expense associated with the hedged item(s) shall be probably so that the results of the futures contract(s) will

substantially offset the effects of price or interest rate changes on the exposed item(s)....

The difficulties of identifying a hedge—for example, what is a "high correlation"—led the Financial Accounting Standards Board (FASB), a private professional organization that sets accounting standards, to attempt to formulate a new approach.

In November 1994, FASB proposed eliminating deferral accounting for hedges altogether. All derivatives, including swaps, would be marked-to-market on the balance sheet. However, gains and losses would only be reflected in income for derivatives entered into for trading purposes. For non-trading derivatives, gains and losses resulting from market changes would only be reflected in an equity account; they would only be reflected in earnings when realized. Adoption of this approach would avoid the hedge accounting model of the past that required a one-to-one accounting linkage between the hedging and hedged items. J. Adams, *Simplifying Accounting for Derivative Instruments, Including Those Used for Hedging, in* Highlights of Financial Reporting Issues (Financial Accounting Standards Board ed., 1995).

This approach was opposed by industry groups because it would deprive them of the value of hedging; there would be timing differences between recognition of income on swaps which were marked-to-market and other assets like loans that could not be marked-to-market. It also would not have permitted hedge accounting for "anticipated transactions," where a position is taken on a derivative in anticipation of taking a position on another asset, e.g. X enters into an interest rate swap under which X pays floating for fixed in anticipation of acquiring a floating rate liability. See G. Benston and S. Mian, *Financial Reporting of Derivatives: An Analysis of the Issues, Evaluation of Proposals, and a Suggested Solution*, 4 Journal of Financial Engineering 217, 230-231 (1996).

The accounting issue has been one of the most contentious ever faced by FASB. Indeed, some industry groups sought to set up an organization to "oversee" FASB, but the SEC came strongly to FASB's defense indicating it would oppose any initiative by any group that sought to undermine FASB's independence.

FASB's subsequent proposal, in the form of an Exposure Draft, *Accounting for Derivative and Similar Financial Instruments and for Hedging Activities* (June 20, 1996), continued to require that all derivatives be marked-to-market but also permitted using gains or losses in the value of underlying assets to offset the value of derivatives used in certain hedging transactions. Unlike the hedge deferral model in which gains/losses on derivatives are deferred until the time gains/losses are recognized on the hedged items, this proposal accelerated the gains/losses on the hedged items. This would only be possible, however, where the hedged item had a market value, e.g. traded debt or equity. Unlike its earlier proposal, the full change in value of the hedged item would not be realized—only the amount of the change of the derivative. This means a bank with a derivative that gained $10 would only have to report a $10 swing in the price of the hedged item, even if that hedged item actually lost $15. See D. Schiela, *FASB Closes in on Standard on Accounting for Derivatives and Hedging*, Derivatives 33, September/October 1996. Under a deferral approach, no gain/loss would be realized on the derivative until gain/loss was recognized on the hedged item.

The Exposure Draft does not solve the basic problem of hedge accounting—deciding what is and is not a hedge, and it is this issue which has been a main focus of criticism. For example, in order to use hedge accounting, the Exposure Draft requires that changes in the fair value of the derivative must offset substantially all of the changes in the fair value of the hedged item. This would preclude a risk management strategy matching a swap to a fixed rate debt when the swap has a shorter term. See J. Johnson, *Derivatives Draft Dissed, Where to Now, FASB?*, Derivatives 201, March/April 1997.

On August 29, 1997, FASB issued a new draft statement, subsequently revised on September 12, 1997. *Statement of Financial Accounting Standards No. 13X, Accounting for Derivative Instruments and For Hedging Activities*. This continued the basic approach in the 1996 draft with two major changes. First, only the portion of the gain or loss on a hedged asset or liability attributable to the risk being hedged is eligible for accelerated earnings recognition. The 1996 Exposure Draft proposed that the entire gain or loss on a hedged item (incorporating all risk components) be eligible for accelerated earnings recognition. Suppose that a bank was hedging a fixed rate bond asset with an interest rate swap paying fixed and receiving floating. Any change in the value of the bond due to changes of interest rates would be recognized on an accelerated basis; however, changes in the value of the bond due to changes in the credit rating of the issuer would not. Measurement of which gain or loss to count will be difficult.

Second, all gain and loss on the hedged item can be recognized in current earnings even if it is not fully offset by the gain and loss on the hedging item (this assumes that the gain or loss is attributable to the nature of the risk being hedged). This reversed the position taken in the 1996 Draft. The reversal was based on the adoption of the first modification discussed above.

The financial industry continued to attack the FASB proposals and brought the matter to the U.S. Congress. S. 1560, introduced by Senator Faircloth in November 1997 would have prevented banks from having to implement the FASB proposals unless the standards were approved by bank regulators (who currently oppose them), and H.R. 3165 introduced by Rep. Baker in February 1998 would effectively shift standards setting in accounting from FASB to the SEC (although the SEC favors the FASB proposals), and give companies the right to mount a legal challenge to accounting standards. Chairman Greenspan of the Federal Reserve Board urged FASB to eliminate its proposals and require only large companies to disclose the fair market value of their derivatives in supplements to their financial statements. E. McDonald and S. Frank, *FASB Rejects Fed Chairman's Request to Soften Proposed Rule on Derivatives*, Wall St. Journal, August 12, 1997. Despite the political attacks and criticism from the industry, FASB issued its *Accounting for Derivative Instruments and Hedging Activities,* Statement of Financial Accounting Standards No. 133 on June 1, 1998, which was originally to be effective for fiscal years beginning after June 15, 1999. For calendar year companies this would be January 1, 2000. In May 1999, FASB delayed the effective date for a year due to difficulties companies were experiencing in implementing the change.

One of the strongest complaints of the financial industry results from the necessity to report changes in the value of hedging items in current income without being able to offset with changes in the value of the hedged items where the hedged items have no fair market value. This is a huge problem in cases where interest rate swaps hedge long-term deposits since such deposits are valued at face value. Banks have said they might be less likely to hedge their interest rate risk under the new FASB proposals. B. McConnell, *Debate Rages On Derivatives Plan by FASB,* American Banker, January 8, 1998.

On June 15, 2000, FASB issued Statement 138, amending Statement 133 in certain technical respects. This was part of the work of the FAS 133 Derivatives Implementation Group (DIG) to help resolve particular implementation issues

2. FINANCIAL REPORTING

Requirements for financial reporting have until recently come almost exclusively from accounting standards. However, the SEC has formulated disclosure requirements for public companies, and the Basel Committee and IOSCO have issued guidelines for financial institutions.

a. ACCOUNTING STANDARDS

Accounting standards provide a baseline for financial disclosure. SFAS 119 *Disclosure about Derivative Financial Instruments and Fair Value of Financial Instruments*, Oct. 1994[*] requires the disclosure of the following

---

[*] Some of the requirements of SFAS 119 already applied to swaps under two prior statements, FASB Statement No. 105, *Disclosure of Information about Financial Instruments with Off-Balance Sheet Risk and Financial Instruments with Concentrations of Credit Risk*, Mar. 1990, and FASB Statement No. 107, *Disclosures about Fair Value of Financial Instruments*, Dec. 1991.

information either in the body of the financial statements or in the accompanying footnotes:

- the amounts, nature, and terms of each class of derivatives, including differentiation between instruments held or issued for purposes of trading and purposes other than trading;

- the average, maximum, and minimum aggregate fair values during the reporting period of each class of derivatives held or issued for trading purposes, with differentiation between assets and liabilities;

- the net gains or losses arising from derivatives trading activities during the reporting period and where those net gains or losses are reported in the income statement;

- a description of the entity's objective for each class of derivatives held or issued for purposes other than trading and how these instruments are reported in financial statements; and

- a description of anticipated transactions for which the risks are hedged with derivatives, including the expected time frame for the transactions, the amount of related hedging gains and losses that are explicitly deferred, and the transactions or other events that result in recognition of the deferred gains and losses.

The SFAS encourages but does not require disclosure of quantitative information about interest rate risk or other market risks of derivatives that is consistent with the way the entity manages those risks. It also encourages such disclosures about other assets and liabilities.

b. THE SEC RULES

In February 1997, the SEC adopted its long awaited disclosure rule. Securities and Exchange Commission, Disclosure of Accounting Policies for Derivative Financial Instruments and Derivative Commodity Instruments and Disclosure of Qualitative and Quantitative Information About Market Risk Inherent in Derivative Financial Instruments, Other Financial Instruments, and Derivative Commodity Instruments, 62 Federal Register 6044 (1997). With respect to disclosure of accounting policies, the Commission observed that accounting treatment of derivatives was complicated by the absence of comprehensive policies—this is, of course, what FASB is working on. It also noted that while SFAS 119 emphasized the disclosure of accounting policies, it did not give specific instructions of how to do so.

The Commission rule, 17 C.F.R. §210.4-08, requires disclosure of: (1) each method used to account for derivatives, (2) types of derivatives accounted for under each method, (3) the criteria required to be met for each accounting method used (e.g. the manner in which the risk reduction, correlation, designation and/or effectiveness tests are applied for hedge accounting), (4) the accounting method used if the specified criteria are not met, (5) the accounting for the termination of derivatives designated as hedges or used to affect directly or indirectly the terms, fair values, or cash flows of a designated item, (6) the accounting for derivatives if the designated item matures, or is sold, extinguished, terminated, or, if related to an anticipated transaction, is no longer likely to occur, and (7) where and when derivatives and their related gains or losses are reported in the statements of financial position, cash flows, and results of operations.

As for disclosures of quantitative and qualitative information, the SEC rule, 17 C.F.R. §229.305, is limited to required disclosures of market risk; other risks, like credit risks, are not covered. With respect to quantitative information, the Commission allows registrants to choose among three alternatives: tabular presentation, sensitivity analysis, or value at risk.

Tabular presentation includes information about fair values of instruments, expected principal or transaction cash flows, weighted average effective rates or prices, and other relevant market risk information. The tabular information would be presented for different risk exposure categories, e.g. interest rate risk, and within the foreign currency exchange rate risk category by functional currency (the currency of the primary economic environment of the registrant).

The Commission rule further provides that at a minimum instruments should be distinguished by the following characteristics: "(i) [f]ixed rate or variable rate assets or liabilities, (ii) long or short forwards or futures, (iii) written or purchased put or call options, (iv) receive fixed or receive variable interest rate swaps, (v) the currency in which the instruments' cash flows are denominated." Instructions to Paragraph 305(a).

Sensitivity Analysis permits registrants "to express the potential loss in future earnings, fair values, or cash flows of market risk sensitive instruments resulting from one or more selected hypothetical changes in interest rates, foreign currency exchange rates..." and other similar market price changes. 62 Federal Register 6049.

Value at Risk analysis expresses the potential loss in fair values, earnings, or cash flows of market risk sensitive instruments over a selected period of time with a selected likelihood of occurrence from changes in interest rates, foreign currency exchange rates, and other relevant market rates or prices. Registrants are required to report either: "(i) the average, high and low amounts, or the distribution of value at risk amounts for the reporting period, (ii) the average, high and low amounts, or the distribution of actual changes in fair values, earnings, or cash flows from market risk sensitive instruments occurring during the reporting period, or (iii) the percentage or number of times the actual changes in fair values, earnings or cash flows from market risk sensitive instruments that exceeded the reported value at risk amounts during the reporting period." *Id*.

The rules also require disclosure of the model assumptions and parameters underlying the registrant's value at risk model. At a minimum, this would include how loss was defined by the model, a general description of the modeling technique, e.g. historical or Monte Carlo simulation, how options are dealt with, the types of instruments covered and relevant model parameters, such as holding period and confidence interval.

With respect to qualitative information, the SEC rule is less specific. It acknowledges that SFAS 119 already requires that certain qualitative disclosures be made.

Securities industry representatives have questioned whether the rules requiring particular types of disclosure will inhibit the development of new ways to manage and measure risk; the SEC has dismissed these objections given the flexibility provided as to what type of method of disclosure to use and how to apply the particular method selected. A more genuine issue is the value obtained by such disclosures given the difficulties of comparing information as between different financial statements.

Finally, the Commission has provided that registrants supplying forward looking information pursuant to its rule, outside of the financial statement, would be protected from liability by a safe harbor made available by the Private Securities Litigation Reform Act of 1995, Pub. L. No. 104-67, 109 Stat. 737 (1995).

A study in 2001 concluded that the SEC's required risk disclosures may have drawbacks. It found that derivative users may have more complex evaluations of risk than perhaps the SEC anticipated, that the flexibility permitted in presenting risk may lead investors to form inconsistent risk perceptions for the same underlying economic situation and that since certain quantitative disclosure is not required, inappropriate risk assessments can occur. L. Hodder, L. Koonce and M. McNally, *SEC Market Risk Disclosures: Implications for Judgment and Decision Making,* 15 Accounting Horizons 49 (2001).

c. THE BASEL COMMITTEE-IOSCO GUIDELINES

In February 1999, the Basel Committee and IOSCO issued a joint report on Disclosure. Recommendations for Public Disclosure of Trading and Derivative Activities, Consultative paper issued jointly by the Basel Committee on Banking Supervision and the Technical Committee of the International Organization of Securities Commissions. This was followed up on by a subsequent paper, Recommendations for Public Disclosure of Trading and Derivatives Activities of Banks and Securities Firms (October 1999). The recommendations generally cover similar ground as the SEC rules, but in much less detail. There are two major differences, however. The Recommendations are not binding, and are addressed to a wider set of risks, credit and liquidity risk as well as market risk.

3. MARKET REPORTING

The BIS, through the Working Group of the Euro-currency Standing Committee of the Central Banks of the Group of Ten countries, put forward a discussion paper on Public Disclosure of Market and Credit Risks by Financial Intermediaries (Sept. 1994). The paper is known as the Fisher Report, after the Chairman of the group, Peter R. Fisher, then Executive Vice President of the Federal Reserve Bank of New York. The Report seems concerned with the need for disclosure to market participants in order that participants may correctly assess their risks of dealing with each other.

The Report recommends that all financial intermediaries should move in the direction of publicly disclosing periodic quantitative information which expresses, in summary form, the estimates relied upon by the firm's management of:

- the market risks in the relevant portfolio or portfolios, as well as the firm's actual performance in managing the market risks in these portfolios;

- the counterparty credit risks arising from its trading and risk management activities, including current and potential future credit exposure as well as counterparty credit worthiness, in a form which permits evaluation of the firm's performance in managing credit risk.

The Report envisions disclosure of value at risk analysis of derivatives portfolios for market risks. The Report suggests that what might be disclosed, as an example, would be the high, low, and average value-at-risk for holding periods of one-day, and two-weeks, that occurred during the reporting period. The Report, however, does not suggest mandating any particular method of calculating market risk.

The Report provides various graphic examples of the types of disclosure possible. What would you conclude from the following?

Example D: Summary comparison of portfolio performance with value-at-risk
—— The frequency at which daily changes in portfolio value exceeds
   daily value-at-risk

Possible alternatives:
(1) The histogram of the ratio of daily variation in
    portfolio value to daily value-at-risk

(2) The five or ten largest one-day changes in
    portfolio values and relevant value-at-risk

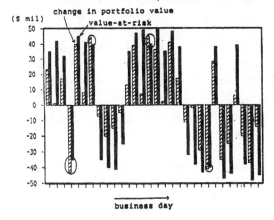

($ mil)

change in portfolio value
value-at-risk

The frequency at which
daily changes in
portfolio value exceeded
daily value-at-risk = 4 days

business day

As for credit risks, basic information would consist of current credit
exposure (net replacement values when close-out netting arrangements
are in place, otherwise gross replacement values), broken down by credit
quality class, and/or counterparty type. It might also include further
breakdowns by maturity, estimates of future credit exposure, and
measures of losses over the reporting period. Again, no particular form
of disclosure is envisioned.

Questions

1. Should there be a difference among disclosures required for
purposes of accounting, financial reporting and to market participants?

2. Which accounting approach would you favor: mark-to-market of all
instruments, deferred hedging, or accelerated hedging as adopted by
FASB?

3. Should the SEC have promulgated disclosure standards for
derivatives? Why doesn't the SEC deal with credit risk? Should it have
dealt with the issue of accounting disclosure before FASB had completed
its efforts? As between the three alternatives for quantitative disclosure,
tabular presentation, sensitivity and value at risk, which is preferable?

D.   CAPITAL REQUIREMENTS FOR SWAPS

A principal way of dealing with the risks of swaps to financial institutions is through capital requirements.

1. THE BASEL ACCORD: CREDIT RISK

Under the Basel Accord capital rules for credit risk, which we covered in Chapter 4, swaps are dealt with as a special type of off-balance sheet asset. Swaps must first be converted into asset equivalents and are then risk weighted under the normal Basel risk-weight categories, subject to a maximum risk weight of 50%. Thus, a swap with an OECD sovereign would have a 0 percent risk weight, whereas a swap with a private obligor would have a 50 percent risk weight.

The following excerpt describes how the Accord handles the conversion of swaps into asset equivalents.

H. SCOTT AND S. IWAHARA, IN SEARCH OF A LEVEL PLAYING FIELD: THE IMPLEMENTATION OF THE BASEL ACCORD IN JAPAN AND THE UNITED STATES
49-54 (Group of Thirty Occasional Paper No. 46, 1994).

The Basel Accord permits countries to use one of two methods in calculating the asset equivalents of these contracts, the original exposure or current exposure method. At the Basel conference Japan strongly pushed to permit countries to use either method. The United States has required banks to use the current exposure method.

. . .

Suppose Company A and Company C seek to enter into a fixed-floating rate swap through Intermediary Bank B on the following terms:

Notional principal	$10 million
Maturity	3 years
Floating index	6 months LIBOR (currently 8.5%)
Floating reset period	Every 6 months
Fixed rate	T bill rate + 70 basis points (current T bill rate = 8%)
B's profit (spread)	10 basis points

This transaction can be diagramed as follows:

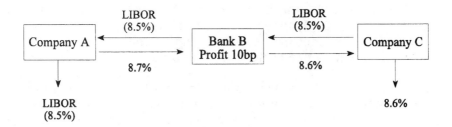

   Note that Intermediary Bank B has entered into two independent contracts. Under its contract with Company A, it pays A a floating rate of 8.5 percent and receives a fixed rate of 8.7 percent. Under its contract with Company C, it pays C a fixed rate of 8.6 percent (8.7 - profit of 0.1) and receives a floating rate of 8.5 percent.

. . .

   Under the current exposure method, the conversion process has two steps. First, a bank marks to market the replacement cost of contracts with a positive value (in the money). This reflects the cost the bank would incur if it entered into a new swap on the same terms. Second, the bank calculates the potential future credit exposure on the contract based on its residual maturity. This calculation reflects the potential risk of loss from counterparty default. Contracts with a residual maturity of less than one year are deemed to have no future exposure; contracts with one year and over are deemed to have 0.5 percent risk.* The asset equivalent amount is the sum of these two calculations: replacement cost plus future exposure.

   On the date on which these contracts are entered into, there is no replacement cost-they are entered into at market prices. Since both contracts are for one year and over, the asset equivalent amount of the two contracts is $10,000,000 x .005 x 2, or $100,000. The two contracts would generate risk-weighted assets of $50,000 ($100,000 x .50), and a capital requirement of $4,000 ($50,000 x .08).

   Suppose that at the end of one year, interest rates have increased so that Bank B would now have to pay Company D a fixed rate of 8.95 percent to get a six-month LIBOR floating rate, if Company C defaulted.

* Under the 1995 Netting Amendment, the following factors apply to swaps:

Maturity	Interest Rate	Exchange Rate
One year or less	0.0%	1.0%
Over one year to five years	0.5%	5.0%
Over five years	1.5%	7.5%

. . .

In this situation, Bank B would have a loss of 0.25 percent of $10,000,000, or $25,000 for each of the two remaining years on the two contracts, the difference between receiving a fixed rate from A of 8.70 percent and paying a fixed rate to D of 8.95 percent. This loss would be discounted to present value using an appropriate discount rate derived from interest rate yield curves for each of the two one-year periods remaining on the contract. If one assumed a flat yield curve at 9 percent for each period, the replacement cost would be $43,978. The potential future exposure, $100,000, would be unchanged since the two contracts have two years to run. The credit equivalent amount would be the sum of replacement cost and future exposure, $143,978, and the cost of capital would be $5,759 ($143,978 x .50 x .08).

. . .

Looking at our 5 year interest rate swap paradigm, the capital requirements for Bank A under the current exposure method (assuming the notional amount was 1000), at inception, would be (1000 x .005) x .50 = 2.5, or .25% of the notional amount. Of course, if the swap went into the money the capital charge would increase by the amount of the positive value times the 50% risk weight. The 50% risk weight seems justified by the fact that the default rates for swap users are about one half the default rate for all firms. V. Bhasin, *On the Credit Risk of OTC Derivative Users,* Finance and Economics Discussion Series 95-90, Division of Research and Statistics and Division of Monetary Affairs, Federal Reserve Board, November 1995, at p. 26. We discuss at the end of this Chapter how netting would affect capital requirements.

2. BASEL ACCORD: MARKET RISK AMENDMENTS

In 1996, BIS adopted capital requirements for market risk which we have already generally reviewed in Chapter 4. These requirements covered swaps, as well as debt and equity securities, and permit the models-based approach as an alternative to prescribed BIS methodology. We examine here the prescribed methodology. You should look back to Chapter 4 to refresh your memory about the models-based approach.

a. DEBT SECURITIES AND INTEREST RATE SWAPS

Interest rate swaps are dealt with in connection with market risk for debt securities (in Chapter 4 we only looked at market risk for equities). The requirements only apply to debt securities (including interest rate swaps) on a bank's trading book. These are a bank's proprietary positions "which are intentionally held for short-term resale and/or which are taken on by the bank with the intention of benefitting in the short-term from actual and/or expected differences between their buying and selling prices, or from other price or interest-rate variations, and positions in financial instruments arising from matched principal brokering and market making, or positions taken in order to hedge other elements of the trading book." Bank for International Settlements, Amendment to The Capital Accord to Incorporate Market Risks, Jan. 1996, §I.2, at 1 (Amendment). The Amendment does, nonetheless, allow banks to exclude from their trading books derivative products such as swaps which are taken on explicitly to hedge positions on the banking book. *Id*. §I.3, at 2. The market risk capital requirements for swaps are in addition to those for credit risk. This contrasts with debt or equity securities which are only subject to the market risk requirements. *Id*. §I.13, at 4.[*] Swaps on the banking book will continue to be governed by the current credit risk requirements and will not be subject to an additional charge for market risk.

The capital requirements for debt securities are, like those for equities, based on a building block approach, in which the specific risk of the instrument (related to the issuer) and the general risk of the market (for example, movement of interest rates) are separately taken into account. However, swaps are treated like government securities, as having no specific market risk. A detailed examination of these requirements is set forth in Part I of the Appendix to this Chapter.

b. FOREIGN EXCHANGE POSITIONS AND CURRENCY SWAPS

The approach to capital for foreign exchange positions is less complicated. The bank first calculates its net open currency position in each currency. On a currency swap, the bank would be short on the currency it must deliver and long on the currency it will receive at the end of the swap. Thus, a U.S. bank that had swapped $40 million for ¥5 billion would be long the dollars and short the yen.

The amount of the bank's net position in each currency is then converted at current spot rates into the bank's reporting currency, i.e. dollars for a U.S. bank. The capital charge would be 8% of the higher of its long or short positions.

c. MODELS-BASED APPROACH

The models-based approach specifies certain parameters, relevant to swaps, that must be used in models. Models must use a minimum of six interest rates (for different maturities)—the BIS methodology, as we have seen, uses thirteen. The models must also use exchange rates between

[*] Debt and equity securities, on the other hand, would not be subject to market risk requirements on the trading book.

the bank's domestic currency and each foreign currency in which the bank has a significant position.

3. THE SEC BROKER-LITE RULE

As we learned in Chapter 4, the capital requirements for securities firms are generally set by the SEC through their Net Capital Rule. The SEC has, however, adopted special capital rules for broker-dealer affiliates engaged in OTC derivative transactions which have been dubbed the Broker-Dealer Lite (BDL) rules. SEC Release No. 34-40594 (October 23, 1998). Many OTC derivative transactions, such as swaps, are generally not considered securities under the securities laws (as discussed below), and thus a corporation solely engaging in such transactions would not be a regulated broker-dealer and, therefore, would not be subject to SEC capital requirements. However, many firms engaged in swap transactions also engage in other OTC derivative transactions that are considered securities, such as OTC options on equity securities or on U.S. government securities, and are thus are subject to SEC capital requirements. The combination of the products permits firms to net positions against counterparties with whom the firms have engaged in transactions both types of transactions, those considered securities and those not so considered. The SEC has asserted that U.S. firms subject to such requirements have located their business abroad to escape from U.S. capital requirements (an other broker-dealer regulations like margin requirements).

As a response, the SEC has modified its net capital requirements, and other regulations, for such firms (OTC firms). OTC firms have to hold $100 million in tentative net capital and at least $20 million in net capital. OTC firms, unlike fully regulated securities firms, are not required to subtract most unsecured receivables (like accrued net interest payments on swaps) nor are they be required to subtract unrealized gains (the amount by which swaps are in the money).

Alternatively, OTC firms can use value-at-risk models to compute capital under which market losses predicted by the model would be subtracted from capital. Modeling is subject to certain parameters like those of Basel, e.g. 99 percent confidence level with an assumed 10 day holding period, including the requirement that the amount of capital determined by the model be multiplied by a factor of 3 to 4 depending on backtesting results, the degree to which the model successfully predicts losses.

Firms using models have to make a two part deduction from capital for credit risk. First, for each counterparty, an OTC firm must take a charge equal to the net replacement value in the account of the counterparty multiplied by 8% and further multiplied by a counterparty factor, ranging from 20% to 100%, based on the counterparty's credit rating. Its approach to counterparty risk is more nuanced than Basel's. Second, an OTC firm must take an additional charge when it has concentrated risk with one counterparty. When replacement value for one counterparty exceeds 25% of the OTC firm's net capital, the deduction ranges from 5% of the net replacement value in excess of 25% of the OTC dealer's tentative net capital for a highly rated counterparty to 50% of net replacement value over 25% of tentative net capital for lower rated counterparties.

Notes and Questions

1. How does a bank know whether a swap is subject to credit risk or market risk? Does it make sense to talk about swaps being part of a bank's trading book?

2. How would you evaluate the credit rules for capital?

(a) The rules for future exposure use a coefficient of 0.5 for all interest rate swaps without regard to the currency of the notional amount (the same is true for volatilities for debt securities under the market risk proposal). Does this make sense?

(b) In the example used from the Scott and Iwahara article, Swap Bank is considered to have two separate swap positions, each generating a capital charge. Does that make sense?

(c) As the Simons study shows, the timing of the peak exposure for different swaps varies with their maturities. Do the credit rules take this into account?

(d) Should the credit rules for diff swaps be the same as for other interest rate swaps?

(e) Under the Voluntary Framework for the six securities firms, current credit risk is net replacement cost by counterparty multiplied by the applicable historic default ratios published by rating agencies. The ratings would take into account an estimate of average maturity. In no case would a default ratio be below 0.001. How does this compare with the Basel approach? Which is preferable?

Potential credit risk, is calculated by multiplying market risk for each counterparty (using a 99 percent confidence level and a 10 business day holding period), ignoring collateral arrangements, by the counterparty's applicable default ratio. Aggregate potential credit risk would equal the sum, for all counterparties, of these calculations of individual counterparty potential credit risk. How does this compare with the Basel approach? Which is preferable? In particular, what do you think of using a 10 business day holding period for credit risk purposes?

3. How would you evaluate the market rules for capital?

(a) The market rules for debt securities appear to generate higher capital requirements than do the credit rules. Does this make sense?

(b) Will it be difficult to tell whether a swap on the trading book is hedging a position on the banking book? How would one go about figuring this out?

4. Should market risk capital requirements focus on the risk of specific instruments, like debt securities or swaps, or instead look at the portfolio risk of all of a bank's assets? How would these two approaches be different? For an excellent treatment of the general issue of capital for swaps, see B. Darringer, *Swaps, Banks and Capital: An Analysis of Swap Risks and A Critical Assessment of the Basel Accord's Treatment of Swaps*, 16 University of Pennsylvania Journal of International Business Law 259 (1995).

5. Under the standardized approach of the new Basel capital proposals, for qualifying credit derivatives, assets covered by the derivatives are assigned a risk weight that is the weighted average of the obligor's risk weight and the protection provider's risk weight, Basel Committee on Banking Supervision, *Consultative Document, The New Basel Capital Accord* (January 2001), para. 130. Under the foundation IRB approach, qualifying credit derivatives may be assigned the lower of the risk-weight of the obligor or seller of protection, para. 418. This would be a change from current Basel rules where the risk-weight is determined by the risk-weight of the seller of protection. FSA Study, Annex D, at 1.

The Federal Reserve Board has provided specific rules for credit derivatives used by banks. In August 1996, the Board issued guidance for the treatment of credit derivatives on the banking book, Board of Governors of the Federal Reserve System, *Supervisory Guidance for Credit Derivatives*, SR 96-17 (August 12, 1996). This guidance provides that total rate of returns and credit default swaps should be treated as creating synthetic asset positions of the banks creating the credit protection; thus they are treated like loans. For the bank receiving the credit protection, the bank may have an exposure to either the counterparty on the swap, or on the underlying asset, depending on the degree to which the receiving bank has transferred ownership of the underlying asset to the credit protecting bank. The guidance allows a bank to use credit derivatives to reduce its exposure from an obligor by entering into an offsetting credit derivative transaction, thus capital required for a loan can be replaced by the capital required by a credit derivative. Thus, banks have the potential to substitute a 20% risk-weighting of an OECD bank providing credit protection for the 100% risk-weighting on a loan to a private obligor. In June 1997, the Board issued guidance on risk-based capital treatment of credit derivatives held in the trading book, Board of Governors of the Federal Reserve System, *Application of Market Risk Capital Requirements to Credit Derivatives*, SR 97-18 (June 13, 1997). The fundamental idea is that credit derivatives on the trading book are exposed to three different kinds of risk: counterparty credit risk, general market risk and specific risk, and rules are provided for calculating each type of risk. This description relies heavily on L. Darby, III, *Recent Regulatory Developments Affecting Credit Derivatives,* Derivatives 235 (May/June 1998).

Note that if the risk-weight of the seller of protection is lower than the risk-weight of the obligor, a financial institution may have an incentive to transfer the risk to reduce capital requirements. See FSA Study, at 19 noting that management of regulatory capital was the most important application of credit derivatives in 1999, and the fifth most important reason in 2002 (the reason for the change is unclear). Further note that under the current accord, where the risk-weight of an OECD bank is 20%, compared with the risk-weight of other corporates, including insurance companies, of 100%, insurance companies would be somewhat disadvantaged. However, this disadvantage is counterbalanced by the fact that insurance companies are not covered by Basel at all, and are generally subject to lower capital requirements than banks. Thus, insurance companies may be able to use their lower capital requirements to compensate the buyers of protection for the higher risk weights they will receive. Insurance companies will be at a greater advantage under Basel II because the risk-weights of banks and insurance companies will both be determined by ratings.

This risk-weight charge under Basel II is subject to an additional legal risk charge of 15%, where the seller of protection is neither a sovereign, central bank or bank. Basel Committee on Banking Supervision, *Consultative Document, The Standardized Approach to Credit Risk* (January 2001), paras. 204, 216. This adjustment is based in part on doubts about the coverage and enforceability of documentation. Do you think a 15% charge is justified? Note that this gives banks a new advantage over insurance companies. Is this justified?

E.   ENFORCEABILITY ISSUES

This section deals with two important "legal" issues about swaps, their enforceability by dealers against users, and the validity of netting arrangements in bankruptcy.

1.   LIABILITY OF DERIVATIVES DEALERS

We begin with an overview of the theories of dealer liability, and then turn to the Bankers Trust litigation in the U.S. with Proctor & Gamble, and its litigation in the U.K. with Dharmala, an Indonesian conglomerate.

a. OVERVIEW

H. SCOTT, LIABILITY OF DERIVATIVE DEALERS
The Future for the Global Securities Market 271 (F. Oditah ed. 1996).

[Derivatives] activity has produced, by some accounts, at least 30 multimillion dollar derivative suits in the United States...by customers against major securities firms that advised them about derivatives or entered into derivatives transactions with them in the 1990s. *Gibson Greetings v. Bankers Trust Co.*, CV No. C-1-94-620 (S.D. Ohio, filed September 12, 1994) involved a claim for $32 million in compensatory damages and *Proctor & Gamble v. Bankers Trust Co.*, CV No. C-1-94 735 (S.D. Ohio, filed October 27, 1994) involved a claim for $195 million. *Gibson* was settled for approximately $14 million [some report $6 million] in 1994.   The real blockbuster was *Orange County Investment Pool v. Merrill Lynch & Co.*, Ch. 9 Case No. SA 94-22272-JR, Adv. No. SA 94-1045-JR (C.D.B.R. Cal., filed January 12, 1995) in which Orange County sued for $3 billion in damages.

Although there is great variety in the derivative transactions behind the different litigations, many of the transactions were swaps reflecting bets that interest rates would stay constant during 1993 and 1994. The *P&G* and *Gibson* derivatives were complex interest rate swaps where either a rise in short term or long term rates would very quickly put the parties in the red. Orange County involved structured notes called inverse floaters which represented a direct bet that interest rates would stay constant or decline.

The complaints in these various litigations are based on a combination of common law and statutory claims that can be broken down into four main categories: ultra vires, fraud, suitability and contract. This article examines each theory, as well as the exposure of dealers to regulatory sanctions.

1. **Ultra Vires.** The basic ultra vires claim is that the customer corporation was prohibited by law from engaging in a particular transaction. For example, Orange County claims that the transactions it entered into with Merrill Lynch were prohibited by the California Constitution because they required Orange County to become indebted in excess of Orange County's income and revenue for the year. Similarly, in *Lehman Bros. Commercial Corp. v. China International United Petroleum and Chemicals Co., Ltd. ("UNIPEC")*, No. 94-CIV-8304 (S.D.N.Y., filed November 15, 1994), UNIPEC claims that its foreign exchange swaps were in violation of Chinese laws prohibiting all persons, except those approved by the State Administration of Exchange Control, from engaging in foreign exchange transactions.

The possibility of ultra vires swap contracts was a risk well known since the English case of *Hazell v. Hammersmith* [1992] 2 AC 1 where the House of Lords decided that thousands of interest rate swaps entered into by local authorities with banks were ultra vires and therefore void. The resulting mark-to-market losses to the banks have been estimated to be in excess of £500 million.

In U.S. corporate law, the ultra vires defense to contract liability has limited application. Corporate charters are now written in very broad terms and, where they are more limited, courts will allow apparent or inherent authority to trump the lack of actual authority. Courts are particularly reluctant to apply the doctrine when it is only invoked to avoid the losing side of a contractual bet and would not have been invoked if the bet had been profitable. As a matter of economic analysis, these limitations on the doctrine make sense. Generally, it would be cheaper for corporate owners to monitor their agents' compliance with a corporate charter than it would be for third parties contracting with the corporation.

If the Orange County contracts were subjected to this analysis, it might be quite difficult to hold the swap contracts ultra vires. The Treasurer of Orange County quite likely had apparent authority to enter into the contracts even if he did not have actual authority. And clearly the County is seeking to avoid unprofitable contracts which it might well have profited on. Economically, it would seem a lot cheaper for the state or the county to monitor contractual compliance with the state constitution than it would be for the derivative dealer, particularly where the capacity issue involves novel or difficult issues of interpretation of the enabling statutes or constitution. The problem is not simply solved by obtaining a covenant of capacity from a counterparty. Such covenant would not likely be binding absent capacity.

Of course, Orange County is not a private corporation. One could well argue that the validity of the ultra vires defense should be different in the public contracts area because it is seeking to protect the public fisc for the benefit of taxpayers. On the other hand, why should one private firm rather than the public as a whole bear the loss for imprudent actions of public agents?

2. **Fraud**. The fraud claims arise either out of common law or statutory law related to securities and commodities, the Securities Act of 1933, the Securities Exchange Act of 1934 (together the "Securities Laws") or the Commodity Exchange Act. As the common law generally imposes no duty to reveal all material information, plaintiffs have a strong incentive to fit the derivative transaction in question into coverage of the Securities Laws or the Commodity Exchange Act. Coverage under these laws hinges on whether certain derivatives are deemed securities or commodities, a matter as yet undecided by the courts.

However, as a result of the *Gibson Greetings* case, the CFTC and the SEC both initiated investigations of Bankers Trust that resulted in consent orders whereby Bankers Trust agreed to pay a $10 million fine. See *In re BT Securities Corp.*, Rel Nos. 33-7124, 34-35136, 3-8579, Fed. Sec. L. Rep. (CCH) [1994-1995 Decisions] ¶85,477 (December

22, 1994). Both the SEC and CFTC concluded that Bankers Trust had committed fraud in the sale of certain derivatives. In fact, the SEC concluded that two of the twelve types of derivative transactions involving swaps were securities, and the CFTC concluded that all twelve derivatives were some type of commodity option or future contract. Subsequent to the SEC order, P&G amended its complaint to include causes of action based on violations of the Securities Laws. It is still unclear which derivatives are deemed to be securities. The SEC order appears to take the position that swaps which can be characterized as options on securities, or indexes of securities, are securities. Thus, the two derivatives that the SEC deemed to be securities were interest rate swaps whose value was determined in reference to certain T-bill rates. However, the definition of "security" in the '34 Act is extremely broad and might cover all derivatives. As the Supreme Court stated in *Reves v. Ernst & Young*, 494 U.S. 56, 61 (1990), Congress enacted a definition of "security" that was "sufficiently broad to encompass virtually any instrument that might be sold as an investment."

Assuming that a derivative is considered a security, the dealer in such a security would have an obligation to disclose material information about the security to a buyer. A major difficulty is encountered in determining what is material information with respect to a particular derivative. This issue has been addressed in a number of forums.

. . .

[There is a discussion of various disclosure standards already covered above.] One effort has touched on disclosure from the dealer - investor perspective. Representatives from various dealer groups, including the International Swaps and Derivatives Association, on August 17, 1995 issued "Principles and Practices for Wholesale Financial Market Transactions." The preparation of the Principles was coordinated by the Federal Reserve Bank of New York. The Principles do not mandate any disclosure. Section 4.2.2 entitled "Reliance on Investment Advice" provides that a "Participant *may* communicate to its counterparty economic or market information relating to Transactions and trade or hedging ideas or suggestions. All such communications (whether written or oral) should be accurate and not intentionally misleading." (emphasis added). Section 4.2.3 entitled "Transaction Information" puts the onus on the investor in obtaining information. It provides that:

A Participant should either ask questions and request additional information or seek independent professional advice when it does not have a full understanding of either the risks involved in a Transaction or the fit between a Transaction and its desired risk profile. A counterparty should answer such questions and respond to such requests for additional information in good faith, and the information provided should be accurate and not intentionally misleading. A participant should expect that, if it does not expressly ask questions or request additional information with respect to a transaction, its counterparty will assume that the Participant understands the transaction and has all the information it needs for its decision-making process.

The Principles seem to adopt a common law fraud approach under which disclosure is voluntary and only actionable when inaccurate or intentionally misleading, as contrasted with the Securities law approach in which disclosure is mandatory, and the failure to disclose material information is actionable. Also, there is some difficulty in making an investor responsible for not asking the right question. How does one know what he doesn't know?

. . .

OTC derivatives are different from most other securities (including exchange-traded derivatives like futures and options) in one important respect--they are generally offered to and often designed for a particular customer, not the general investing public. This has at least one important consequences. Disclosure needs can be judged in the context of particular investors. Disclosure needed by the Treasurer of P&G could well be different than that needed by less sophisticated investors. Where securities are generally offered to a wide range of investors it is not feasible to tailor disclosure requirements to particular investors, whereas it is feasible for OTC derivatives. In effect, the disclosure issue tends to merge with the suitability issue discussed below.

3. **Suitability**. Suitability claims appear in two forms: the pure suitability claim and the disclosure suitability claim. In the pure suitability claim the plaintiff claims that the defendant violated his duty to recommend and sell only suitable investments. In order to recover, the plaintiff must prove that the investments were unsuitable, the defendant had a duty not to recommend or sell unsuitable investments, the defendant acted with some level of intent, and that the plaintiff reasonably relied on the defendant's recommendation in purchasing the security. Plaintiffs have pointed to four different sources of rules that can create the duty to recommend or sell only suitable investments: the common law of fiduciary duty, Rule 10b-5 of the '34 Act, the New York Stock Exchange's (NYSE) Know Your Customer Rule, and the National Association of Securities Dealers' (NASD) Suitability Rule.

In *P&G* and *Gibson Greetings* plaintiffs have tried to show that the derivative dealers assumed the role of advisor to the plaintiff and thus assumed fiduciary duties. Other plaintiffs have supplemented this argument with appeal to the NYSE's Know Your Customer Rule and the

NASD Suitability Rule. It is currently unclear whether a private right of action exists under these two rules, but it appears that violations of the rules can at least be a factor in determining whether dealers have committed fraud under Rule 10b-5 by selling unsuitable investments. Dealers may have a defense that the plaintiff either knew, or by reasonable investigation could have known, that the investments were unsuitable.

The central issue in this area is whether a large sophisticated investor should have a suitability claim. While this may seem dubious, the City of San Jose effectively utilized a 10b-5 suitability claim to win a jury verdict against multiple brokerage firms.

A plaintiff's sophistication alone is generally not dispositive of whether a given investment is suitable. An investment bet with a 100-1 payoff would not appear suitable for a sophisticated retiree with limited resources. Courts rather determine suitability based on the investment objectives of the plaintiff. If a defendant recommends a speculative investment to an investor that he knows is pursuing conservative investment goals, one might conclude it was done with fraudulent intent. However, one might argue that sophistication is quite relevant in this context. If the sophisticated retiree accepts the risky bet, perhaps he has changed his investment objectives.

Sophistication is clearly relevant to the issue of reasonable reliance. If the plaintiff knew or could have known that the investment was unsuitable to his investment objectives, there is a strong argument that he should not be allowed to recover.

The disclosure suitability claim is a mixture of a pure suitability claim and a fraud claim. The complaint is that the dealer committed fraud not by recommending or selling an unsuitable security, but by doing so without disclosing that the investment was unsuitable. The sophisticated investor is likely to argue that he reasonably relied on the recommendation given what he was told, but would not have done so if he knew all the facts. The disclosure suitability claim could properly be applied to a sophisticated investor since even a sophisticated investor would be unable to judge the suitability of an investment to his risk preferences without knowing the material risks of the investment.

The Principles also deal with the suitability issue. Section 4.2.2. provides:

> Absent a written agreement or an applicable law, rule or regulation that expressly imposes affirmative obligations to the contrary, a counterparty receiving ... communications should assume that the Participant is acting at arm's length for its own account and that such communications are not recommendations or investment advise on which the counterparty may rely.

Only if an investor informs a dealer that it wishes to rely on its advice, the dealer agrees to do business on that basis and the investor gives the dealer information about his financial situation, will the dealer incur any responsibility for recommending suitable investments.

The drafters explicitly rejected an "alternative approach" that would require a dealer to determine the suitability of an investment recommendation. Their commentary states, "the alternative approach would undermine the finality of agreed Transactions, and create tremendous uncertainty regarding the economic risk position of participants." *Principles*, at 7.

In March 1995 six major securities firms, in cooperation with the SEC and CFTC, agreed to adopt a *Framework for Voluntary Oversight* ("Voluntary Framework") under which the firms would undertake to have certain management controls, submit quantitative reports covering credit risk exposures, evaluate risk relative to capital and adopt guidelines for dealing with non-professional counterparties to derivatives contracts.   While the Voluntary Framework, like the Principles, generally takes an arm's length approach, it goes significantly further in placing affirmative obligations on dealers. In "Counterparty Relationships," II.C (Nature of Relations), it states:

> In cases where existing transaction documentation does not expressly address the nature of the relationship between the professional intermediary and its nonprofessional counterparty and the professional intermediary becomes aware that the nonprofessional counterparty believes incorrectly that the professional intermediary has assumed advisory or similar responsibilities towards the nonprofessional counterparty with respect to a prospective OTC derivative transaction, the professional intermediary should take steps to clarify the nature of the relationship.

It goes on to provide in II.E:

> *Specific Transaction Proposals.* In circumstances where a professional intermediary, at the express request of a nonprofessional counterparty, formulates a specific OTC derivative transaction proposal that is tailored to particular transactional objectives specified by the counterparty, the professional intermediary should formulate the transaction proposal in good faith based on the information and objectives specified by the counterparty and subject to the terms of the parties' contractual arrangement.

And II. F further provides:

> *Special Situations.* In circumstances where a nonprofessional counterparty has expressly requested assistance in evaluating an OTC derivative transaction in which the payment formula is particularly complex or

which includes a significant leverage component, the professional intermediary should offer to provide additional information, such as scenario, sensitivity or other analyses, to the nonprofessional counterparty or should recommend that the counterparty obtain professional advice.

The Voluntary Framework clearly imposes more obligations on dealers than does the Principles. This partially reflects the different orientation of the regulators involved. The first concern of the SEC in the Voluntary Framework would be to protect investors whereas the first concern of the Federal Reserve Bank of New York in the Principles would be to protect the safety and soundness of banks by limiting their liability. One significant difficulty in this area arises from the proliferation of suitability rules. While none of the private rules are binding, they could well be invoked or cited by courts.

4. **Contract.** There are two main types of contract claims. The first is that an investor is not bound by his investment agreement. For example, UNIPEC argues that it was not bound by its agreement because it was made by an agent with no authority to bind the corporation, and Gibson argued that a swap with Bankers Trust was not binding because it was made under economic duress in a situation of financial emergency. UNIPEC's argument is a first cousin to the ultra vires argument examined earlier. While UNIPEC does not claim the corporation had no power to enter into the contract, it does claim that the particular agent who entered into the contract had no corporate authority. While it remains to be seen whether the agent had apparent authority even if he lacked actual authority, obviously the claim that an agent acted beyond his authority is a standard one and should not be surprising in the derivatives context.

The second type of claim is that the contract should embody certain prior oral understandings reached between the parties or, if it does not, that there was no meeting of the minds and thus no contract at all. P&G claims that it never agreed to the secret and proprietary Bankers Trust early lock-in pricing model as a term of its derivative transactions. UNIPEC claims that it had an oral agreement with Lehman Brothers to close out all transactions if they reached a net debt position of $5 million (later raised to 8 million). Again, this is just a standard contract claim. Obviously if derivatives dealers breach their contracts they may be held liable. The implications of this claim is that the key characteristics of the instruments may have to be documented and agreed in writing.

5. **Regulatory Actions.** The SEC and CFTC actions show that derivatives dealers are exposed to federal agency actions, based on the concerns of these agencies with investor protection. Bank dealers are also exposed to actions by bank regulators. A written Agreement between the Federal Reserve Bank of New York and Bankers Trust of December 5, 1994, Fed. Banking L. Rep. (CCH) [Current] ¶90,332,

focuses on Bankers Trust's leveraged derivatives (LDT) business. The Fed's concern is that bank holding companies under its supervision will be damaged by allegations and recoveries based on claims of fraud. Therefore, the remedial measures required by the Agreement require greater disclosure of risks to customers, greater transparency of pricing and better control over the actions of people involved in marketing and selling derivatives.

For example, the Fed's order requires that BT shall conduct its LDT Business in a manner which seeks to reasonably ensure that each LDT customer has the capability to understand the nature and material terms, conditions, and risks of any LDT entered into with the customer. It further provides that BT shall distribute to each customer written term sheets and sensitivity analyses designed to illustrate a broad range of outcomes and distribution of risks at maturity. BT must constantly update its customers as to risks. The Agreement also provides that BT will update its customer as to the value of positions entered into. It is unclear to what extent the practices set forth in the Agreement will be applied to the derivatives business of other banks.

6. **Conclusion**. Derivatives dealers face serious threats of liability to sophisticated investors under the various theories of liability examined herein. From the normal perspective of the securities laws, this might appear routine; dealers are just being held accountable for how they sell new investment products, and securities laws have always been applied to sophisticated investors (albeit somewhat differently than to unsophisticated investors). And there is nothing much new about the doctrine of ultra vires or holding parties to contractual obligations. But since many securities dealers are banks, and since significant legal exposures could affect their safety and soundness, there may be a concern about applying normal rules in this situation. The solution to this problem, in my opinion, is not to change the standards, but to make them clearer. Currently, there is much confusion as to what needs to be disclosed with respect to particular derivatives, and what the proper suitability standards should be. Hopefully, these issues will soon be addressed by the SEC.

There is a significant need to improve the documentation of derivatives transactions; they cannot be documented like standard securities trades. The documents cover such matters as:

- The relationship of the parties, e.g. is the dealer acting as an advisor or merely a seller.
- The investment objectives of the customer and the suitability of the derivative given such objectives.
- The material properties of the derivative (this could be tailored for individual products against a standard baseline for "plain vanilla" products).
- Any ongoing reporting duties of the dealer with regard to the value or properties of the product.

b.   P&G LITIGATION

The *P&G v. Bankers Trust* case was settled in May 1996. It involved two swaps. In November 1993, the parties entered into a $200 million interest rate swap (the 5/30 swap) with a term of five years in which P&G received fixed rate interest at the then current five year rate and P&G paid a floating rate at the prevailing commercial paper (CP) rate minus 75 basis points plus an Additional Amount commencing in November 1994. The Additional Amount was to be determined in May 1994 on the basis of treasury rates. The higher those rates, the higher the Additional Amount. Thus, if the Additional Amount was 35 basis points, P&G would pay the CP rate minus 40, rather than the initial rate of CP minus 75. When interest rates dramatically increased in 1994, the Additional Amounts became very significant; under the formula, P&G was required to pay the CP rate *plus* well over 1000 basis points.

The second swap entered into in 1994 was a 162.8 million DM swap with a term of almost five years matching an existing DM swap. The DM swap was structured so that P&G would, if certain DM rates remained stable, save 100 basis points on its existing swap. DM rates did not remain stable with the result that P&G was required to pay over 1600 additional basis points. S. Henderson, *Derivatives Litigation in the United States, in* Swaps and Off-Exchange Derivatives Trading: Law and Regulation (1996). The two swaps are also described in *Proctor & Gamble Company v. Bankers Trust Company et. al*, 1996 U.S. Dist. Lexis 6435 (U.S.D.C. S.D. Ohio, May 8, 1996) (*P&G*).

Various documents produced in discovery in this case became available to the press. They contained various potentially damaging statements by Bankers Trust. In one example, a Bankers Trust salesman responded to an another employee's question as to how the salesman had obtained a derivative customer's confidence: "Funny business, you know? Lure people into that calm and then just totally f__ `em." G. Knecht, *P&G Can Add Racketeering to its Claims*, Wall Street Journal, Oct. 4, 1995.

In *P&G supra*, the federal district court dismissed most of P&G's claims against Bankers Trust. In particular, it found that swaps were not securities under federal or state securities laws. It noted that the transactions in question were different than those that were the subject of the SEC's enforcement action, where the SEC had found the swaps were securities since they could be characterized as options. Moreover, it noted that the SEC's finding had no binding effect on the court. The court also found that Bankers Trust owed no fiduciary duty to P&G. Nonetheless, the court did find that under New York law Bankers Trust had a duty to disclose "material information to plaintiff both before the parties entered into the swap transactions and in their performance, and also a duty to deal fairly and in good faith during the performance of swap transactions." But P&G had to prove by clear and convincing evidence, and not mere preponderance, that Bankers Trust had failed to meet its disclosure obligations. *P&G* at 16. This would seemingly impose greater disclosure obligations than those contemplated by the Principles.

In *Société Nationale d'Exploitation Industrielle des Tabacs et Allumettes v. Salomon Brothers,* Index No. 113154/96 (Supreme Court, February 11, 1998) (on file with authors), the court dismissed plaintiff's claim against Salomon for breach of fiduciary duty, citing *P&G.* Since the court failed to find that Salomon had agreed to act in a fiduciary capacity, it imposed no fiduciary obligations on Salomon, and that the fact that Salmon may have possessed superior knowledge of the transactions did not mean it was a fiduciary. The opinion did not deal with the duties of disclosure of a non-fiduciary.

The May 1996 settlement, following this decision, reportedly required Bankers Trust to absorb as much as $150 million, or 83% of P&G's loss, on the two swaps. L. Hays, *Bankers Trust Settles Dispute with P&G,* Wall Street Journal, May 10, 1996.

c. THE DHARMALA LITIGATION

A 1995 English decision, *Bankers Trust v. Dharmala*, Q.B. Div.'l Comm. Ct. 1994 Folio Nos. 2168 and 1396 (1995), is the most extensive court decision to date involving dealer liability on swaps. Dharmala is an Indonesian conglomerate engaged in commercial and financial activities. Two swaps were involved. Swap 1, a two year interest rate swap on $50 million, was entered into on January 19, 1994. It has two parts. Under part one, Dharmala was to pay BT at the rate of 6 month U.S. dollar Libor and was to receive the same plus a 125 basis point margin. In effect, BT paid Dharmala 125 basis points per annum over 6 month U.S. dollar Libor. Under part two, Dharmala paid BT a 5% fixed rate annual rate and received interest at 5% multiplied by the fraction N/183. N was defined as the "actual number of days in a six month period during which Libor was less than 4.125%." If the LIBOR rate was never less than 4.125%, BT would pay nothing on this part of the swap, and Dharmala would lose 3.75%; it would receive 1.25% on part one, and pay out 5.00% on part two. This would mean a maximum two year loss of $3.75 million ($50 million x .0375 x 2). At the time Swap 1 was entered into, 6 month Libor was 3.625% (the Federal Reserve Board's Fed Funds rate was then 3%). On February 4, the Fed Funds rate was raised by 25 basis points pushing Libor up to over 3.85%.

On February 16, 1994, the parties canceled Swap 1 and entered into Swap 2, what BT termed a "Barrier Swap". Swap 2 was also for two years at $50 million but was more complex and riskier. It was a "leveraged" swap since under the formula, a small movement in interest rates against Dharmala imposed on Dharmala a disproportionate increase in liability. As originally agreed, Swap 2 had the two following parts. Under part one, Dharmala received annual interest at the 6 month U.S. dollar Libor rate plus 125 basis points. On part two, Dharmala would pay interest at the 6 month U.S. dollar Libor rate less 225 basis points per annum, plus a "Spread". In effect, leaving the Spread aside, Dharmala received 350 basis points (3.5%), or $1.75 million, per year.

"Spread" was to be zero if the 6 month Libor did not go above a 5.25% barrier during a "look" period, the first 12 months of the swap (February 16, 1994 - February 16, 1995). If at any time during that 12 months the rate did pass through the barrier, then "Spread" was to be determined on February 16, 1995, for each of the two years of the swap, by taking (6 month Libor on February 16, 1995 ÷ 4.50%) - 1. If 6 month Libor were 6% on February 16, the spread would be .33 or $16.5 million per year ($50 million x .33) and Dharmala would have a net obligation to BT of $14.75 million (16.5 - 1.75). This formula was further complicated by two changes. The nominal amount of $50 million was divided into two tranches of $25 million. On one tranche, the barrier was raised to 5.3125%. Also, it was agreed that Dharmala would receive its $1.75 million in advance, discounted to $1.7 million.

Interest rates continued to rise in 1994, so that by May 1994 Swap 2 had a negative value to Dharmala for the remaining terms of $45 million (a BT estimate based on the forward Libor rate), and if rates continued to move up, the situation would get worse, and a lawsuit resulted. BT contended that by December 1994 it was owed approximately $65 million. Dharmala sought to rescind the swaps principally on the grounds of BT's misrepresentation and failure to meet its duty of care by explaining the swaps, and the contention that the swaps were unsuitable and also sued for damages.

Some facts about the parties. The chief player for BT was Mr. Hyun, a U.S. citizen born and brought up in New York. He majored in East Asian studies at Yale, graduating in 1985 and joining BT in 1987. During the transactions at issue he was the managing director of BT's Singapore office and had been extremely important in building up a substantial derivatives business. He was described by the court as a "master in the field of derivatives." The chief player for Dharmala was the Indonesian Finance Director, Mr. Thio, aged 38, who attended high school in Singapore and received an MBA from California State University. He was assisted by a Malaysian Mr. Kong, aged 39, the financial controller, who had an accounting degree from Kent University in England. It appears that Dharmala had limited experience in dealing with swaps before its transactions with BT, although it had entered into a complex yen-based swap with CS First Boston and had rejected previous BT swap proposals as too risky.

Some facts about the dealings of the parties before they entered into the two swaps. As to Swap 1, Hyun made a presentation but it is unclear whether he presented the formula on which the swap was based and worked out its operation under different scenarios, although it was clear that he indicated the maximum downside was 3.75%. The swap was presented in a written proposal as an "attractive interest cost reduction structure that will reduce [Dharmala's] interest exposure on its U.S. Dollar liabilities by 1.25 percent per annum for the next three years" and contained a written economic forecast of interest rates that were low compared with a majority of other economists. BT did not disclose that Swap 1 had a negative market value to Dharmala of $2 million at the time it was entered into.

As for Swap 2, BT represented that it had "a superior risk/return profile" to Swap 1, and contended that it was "unlikely" for interest rates to rise beyond the 5.25% barrier. BT's letter proposal was accompanied by a graphed sensitivity analysis showing outcomes at various assumed interest rates but did not extend far enough to show that Dharmala's liability was virtually unlimited if interest rates rose above the barrier. The court found the presentation unbalanced. BT did not disclose that Swap 2 had a negative value to Dharmala of $8 million at the time it was entered into. It is not clear how the court determined this negative value since research has shown that the pricing of these "barrier options" is not precise. D. Leisen, *Valuation of Barrier Options in a Black-Scholes Setup with Jump Risk,* 3 European Finance Review 319 (1999).

With respect to the misrepresentation issue, the court found that BT had not represented, as claimed by Dharmala, that the swaps were safe and suitable and could be replaced at no cost. The court further found that the economic forecasts, while more optimistic than those made by others, were based on proper research and reasonable. While the court found that BT's presentation on Swap 2 was unbalanced, it concluded that Dharmala was capable of doing its own analysis and did not fully rely on BT's representations. The court further found that it was not up to BT to judge whether the swaps were suitable for Dharmala; Dharmala could make its own judgment on that question. The court also rejected the duty of care claim finding that BT had no duty to disclose the market value of the swaps at their inception. The court gave BT judgment on its claims on Swap 2.

Notes and Questions

1.   The CFMA of 2000 contains new provisions of the '33 and '34 Acts bearing on the issue of whether swaps are securities. Section 301, which amends the GLB Act, provides that any "swap agreement" (defined to include interest rate, currency, derivative and other similar agreements) subject to individual negotiation between eligible participants is not a security if no material term of the agreement is based "on the price, yield, value, or volatility of any security or any group or index of securities, or any interest therein." Neither non-security based or security-based swap

agreements are required to be registered, Section 302. However, security-based swap agreements are subject to the liability provisions of Section 17(a) of the '33 Act, Section 302(b), and Section 10(b) of the '34 Act (and thus Rule 10b-5), Section 303(d).

2. How should *Dharmala* come out under U.S. law? Do you think BT made adequate disclosures to Dharmala? If not, how should that affect the outcome of the case? In 1999, the Federal Reserve Board charged Guillaume Fonkenell, a trader at Bankers Trust in New York, with a breach of fiduciary duty, violations of safe and sound banking practices, and a scheme to defraud in connection with the Dharmala transaction. Allegedly, Fonkenell was involved in the development of the barrier swap which was marketed to various clients abroad, including Dharmala. The heart of the charge was that Fonkenell had constructed a formula designed to hide the leverage in the second transaction. The spread formula of (6 month Libor on February 16, 1995 ÷ 4.50%) -1. The Fed contended that "[d]ividing the formula by 4.50% is mathematically equivalent to multiplying the formula by 22.2," and that nowhere in the proposal was this amount of leverage pointed out. In the Matter of Guillaume Fonkenell, Notices of Charges and of Hearing, Docket No. 98-032-B-1, 98-032-CMP-1 (May 7, 1999). The Fed charges were held not to be supported by the facts by an Administrative Law Judge in June 2000, and the Fed dismissed the charges on March 14, 2001.

The Fed's charge order indicates that Bankers Trust settled its case with Dharmala for a payment of $12.5 million, even though it contended that Dharmala owed it $65 million.

3. Did BT's conduct in *Dharmala* conform to the requirements of the "Principles" and the "Voluntary Framework"?

For excellent commentary on *Dharmala*, see J. Quitmeyer, *An English Case, Dharmala, Looks at the Relationship Between the Dealer and Counterparty*, 1 Derivatives 160 (1996); D. Petkovic, *Derivatives and the Banker's Duties of Care*, 14 International Banking and Financial Law 93 (1996).

4. In November 1995, Bankers Trust settled a suit brought by Air Products, a chemical company, for $67 million. In October 1995, the U.S. District Court in Lehman Brothers Commercial Corp. v. Minmetals International Non-Ferrous Metals Trading Co., 94 Civ. 8301 (S.D.N.Y. 1995) permitted a Chinese metal trading company to counterclaim for fraud and lack of suitability in Lehman's breach of contract case involving foreign exchange and swap transactions. 65 BNA's Banking Report 724 (1995).

5. The Orange County debacle led to a lengthy investigation by the SEC of Merrill Lynch. In August 1998, the SEC charged the firm with negligent conduct for allegedly failing to warn investors of the risks they were taking in buying the county's notes. Simultaneous with the charge,

Merrill settled the suit for $2 million. Merrill had previously settled a civil suit with the county for $437 million and had paid $30 million to resolve a criminal investigation by the Orange County district attorney. Wall St. Journal, August 25, 1998. Would CFMA change the result of this case?

6.   Customers may also face liability on derivatives deals. Gibson Greetings, Inc., which settled its dispute with Bankers Trust, was charged by the SEC with violations of securities laws' requirements of financial reporting of its losses and potential risks, as well as failures to maintain accurate internal record-keeping and internal controls. These charges were settled in 1996 by the entry of cease and desist orders committing Gibson to avoid such violations in the future. 65 BNA Banking Report 619 (1995).

7.   Derivatives played a role in the Asian financial crisis of 1998. One of Indonesia's banks lost several hundred million dollars on derivative bets on the rupiah. And J.P. Morgan & Co. was forced to make huge provisions in its 1997 earnings because of its failure to be paid $500 million on derivatives contracts with South Korean financial institutions. R. Borsuk and D. McDermott, *Indonesian Bank Faces Currency Losses,* Wall St. Journal, March 9, 1998. The Morgan case is in litigation. *Morgan's Korean Problems Involve a Complex Swap Structure,* 11 Swaps Monitor, No. 9 (February 23, 1998).

8.   There have been several English cases dealing with the calculation of the amount of settlement when one party defaults on its swap obligations. See S. Henderson, *English Cases Dealing with Settlement Provisions of the ISDA Master Agreement,* Butterworths Journal of International Banking and Financial Law (June 2000). In one of the cases there reviewed, *Peregrine Fixed Income Ltd (in liquidation) v. Robinson Department Store plc,* Commercial Court Claim No. 2000-Folio 277 (May 18, 2000), Peregrine, a Hong Kong financial institution and Robinson, a Thai retailer, had entered into a swap transaction under which Peregrine had no future payments and Robinson had to make 25 annual payments with a present value of $87 million. Peregrine became insolvent and under the ISDA agreement it was necessary to determine the value of the contract to Peregrine.

This was done under the Market Quotation method (which the parties had specified), in which three quotes are obtained to determine what dealers would pay to become Robinson's counterparty. The quotes were $750,000, $9.5 million and 25.5 million. These quotes were obtained two years after the Peregrine insolvency (it is unstated why Robinson waited so long to get them). They reflected the fact that Robinson had itself become insolvent by that time, so that dealers deeply discounted any obligation that Robinson might have to them. The parties had not specified the alternative Loss Method of calculating the Settlement Amount, under which one includes "any loss of bargain, cost of funding, or, at the election of such party [here Robinson, the party entitled to make the calculation], loss or cost incurred" as a result of termination. The Loss Method also applies if application of the Market Quotation Method "would not (in the reasonable belief of the party making the determination) produce a commercially reasonable result." Although Robinson argued that application of the Market Quotation Method did produce a commercially reasonable method, the Court concluded otherwise and sustained Peregrine's claim for $87 million. Do you agree with the result? See A. Gauvin, *Is ISDA Documentation Reliable in case of Early Termination of the Master Agreement?*, 118 The Banking Law Journal766 (2001).

9. Are bank regulators justified in regulating the derivatives business of banks on the grounds of concern with potential bank legal liability? Aren't regulators' incentives to protect banks from liability? The "Principles" which were "coordinated" by the Federal Reserve Bank of New York were widely criticized by user groups who have accused the dealers and Fed of excluding them from the process in which the Principles were formulated. 66 BNA Banking Report 636 (Apr. 15, 1996).

10. Can U.S. banks and securities firms avoid U.S. legal requirements by conducting their swaps business off-shore?

2. NETTING AND BANKRUPTCY

a. CHERRY PICKING

The following Memorandum describes how the U.S. has handled the bankruptcy issue.

CRAVATH, SWAINE & MOORE, MEMORANDUM FOR THE INTERNATIONAL SWAPS AND DERIVATIVES ASSOCIATION, INC., OVER-THE-COUNTER DERIVATIVES TRANSACTIONS: NETTING UNDER THE U.S. BANKRUPTCY CODE, FIRREA AND FDICIA
(December 20, 1993).

This memorandum examines the treatment under the United States Bankruptcy Code (the "Bankruptcy Code"),[1] the Financial Institutions Reform, Recovery, and Enforcement Act of 1989 ("FIRREA")[2] and the Federal Deposit Insurance Corporation Improvement Act of 1991 ("FDICIA")[3] of over-the-counter derivatives transactions

[1] 11 U.S.C. § 101 *et seq.*

[2] Pub.L. No. 101-73, 103 Stat. 183 (1989).

[3] Pub.L. No. 102-242, 105 Stat. 2236 (1991).

("Transactions") that are documented under an ISDA Master Agreement.

. . .

B. Background

In structuring a contractual relationship, parties will often negotiate an ISDA Master Agreement that is structured as a complete contract containing payment provisions, representations, agreements, events of default, termination events, provisions for early termination, methods for calculating termination payments and other provisions. An ISDA Master Agreement may cover multiple Transactions, the economic terms of which are documented in separate confirmations exchanged between the parties and which each constitutes a supplement or amendment to the relevant ISDA Master Agreement. Accordingly, participants in the derivatives markets might include within one ISDA Master Agreement, for example, interest rate swaps, currency swaps, equity index swaps, as well as Physically Settled Transactions.

. . .

The ISDA Master Agreements provide that on each payment date all amounts otherwise owing in the same currency under the same Transaction are netted so that only a single amount is owed in that currency. The ISDA Master Agreements also provide, if the parties so elect, for such netting of amounts in the same currency among all Transactions identified as being subject to such election that have common payment dates and booking offices. *See* Section 2 of the ISDA Master Agreements. The obligation of each party to make scheduled payments or deliveries with respect to the Transactions is subject to the conditions that (i) no event of default in respect of the other party (including, without limitation, a payment or delivery default) has occurred and continues and (ii) no early termination date has occurred or been designated. *See* Section 2(a) of the ISDA Master Agreements. The failure by a party to make a payment or delivery with respect to any Transaction or the insolvency of that party constitutes an event of default under the ISDA Master Agreements as it relates to all Transactions. *See* Sections 5(a)(i) and (vii) of the ISDA Master Agreements. Finally, the default-based termination of any other specified derivatives transactions between the parties constitutes an event of default under the ISDA Master Agreements. *See* Section 5(a)(v) of the ISDA Master Agreements.

. . .

In the event of a default-based termination, the ISDA Master Agreements provide for a lump-sum amount (reflecting the positive or negative values of all Transactions) to be calculated on the early termination date (commonly referred to as "close-out netting").

. . .

The ISDA Master Agreements also require the parties to elect between the "First Method" of calculating termination payments and the "Second Method". Under the First Method, in the case of an event of default, if the lump-sum termination amount is positive, it is paid by the defaulting party to the nondefaulting party, but, if it is negative, no payment is due; the nondefaulting party is not required to make a termination payment to the defaulting party after an event of default. Under the Second Method, if the lump-sum termination amount is a positive number, the defaulting party will pay it to the nondefaulting party; if that amount is a negative number, the nondefaulting party will pay the absolute value of that number to the defaulting party.

. . .

On November 9, 1992, in the case of Drexel Burnham Lambert Products Corp. v. Midland Bank, PLC, [7] Judge Pollack of the U.S. District Court for the Southern District of New York held that "[t]he so-called 'Limited Two-Way Payments Clause' ... is enforceable". This memorandum, however, does not address the enforceability of the First Method (formerly called limited two way payments) or the Second Method (formerly called full two way payments), because resolution of this issue would have no impact upon the conclusions reached herein.

. . .

V. "SWAP AGREEMENT" UNDER THE BANKRUPTCY CODE AND FIRREA

A. Bankruptcy Code

1. *Background: Definitions.* On June 25, 1990, legislation amending the Bankruptcy Code to deal expressly with a "swap agreement" was signed into law. The Bankruptcy Code now provides:

(i) an express exemption from the automatic stay contained in Section 362 to allow non-bankrupt parties to set off any mutual obligations arising under or in connection with any "swap agreement" following a bankruptcy filing and to use any collateral held to satisfy amounts due from the bankrupt party;

(ii) express recognition that parties will be entitled to exercise contractual rights to terminate a "swap agreement" and net or offset

---

[7] No. 92 Civ. 3098 (S.D.N.Y. Nov. 9, 1992).

termination values and payment amounts under such "swap agreement"; and

(iii)   express protection for transfers in good faith under a "swap agreement" against a trustee's power to avoid payments and other transfers made within 90 days (or in some cases one year) prior to a bankruptcy filing.

. . .

3.   *Right to Terminate and Exercise Netting Provisions.* Section 560 of the Bankruptcy Code, 11 U.S.C. § 560, preserves a swap participant's contractual right to terminate a "swap agreement" and offset or net out any termination or payment amounts owed under it in the event that the other party to the agreement files a bankruptcy petition or becomes insolvent, or in the event that a trustee or custodian is appointed for the party. A contractual right is defined to include a right arising under common law, under law merchant, or by reason of normal business practice, whether or not the right is evidenced in writing.

One principal effect of this provision is to override Section 365(e) of the Bankruptcy Code, 11 U.S.C. § 365(c), which otherwise generally would prevent a nonbankrupt party from using the bankruptcy filing as a basis for exercising a typical bankruptcy default provision in order to terminate a "swap agreement". Equally important, by permitting a party to "net out any termination values," Section 560 of the Bankruptcy Code, 11 U.S.C. § 560, makes clear that the provisions contained in an ISDA Master Agreement for close-out netting will be enforceable upon termination of a "swap agreement."

. . .

B. FIRREA[*]

On August 9, 1989, FIRREA was signed into law. Among other things, FIRREA significantly revised the powers of the FDIC as the receiver or conservator for an insolvent financial institution and extended its powers to cover almost all banks and savings institutions in the United States.

1.   *Background: Definitions.* FIRREA provides that, in the case of *receivership,* subject to certain limitations, a party to a qualified financial contract will be entitled to:

(i) exercise any contractual right to terminate or liquidate a qualified financial contract as a result of the appointment of the receiver;

---

[*] Note that the Bankruptcy Code, and therefore the discussion above, does not apply to financial institutions; thus, the necessity for the FIRREA netting provisions, eds.

(ii) exercise any rights under any security arrangement relating to any qualified financial contract; and

(iii)   exercise any right to "offset or net out any termination value, payment amount or other transfer obligation arising under or in connection with [one] or more [qualified financial contracts]".

. . .

3. *Netting.* A key provision of FIRREA expressly addresses the concerns of swap participants over whether netting provisions will be enforced. It protects the rights of parties to swap agreements and other qualified financial contracts to "offset or net out any termination value, payment amount, or other transfer obligation arising under or in connection with [one] or more [qualified financial contracts]." This provision, together with the anti-cherry-picking provisions described below, should ensure that credit exposures to an insolvent institution can be calculated fairly on a net basis as long as the "swap agreement" so provides-an ISDA Master Agreement does so provide.

4. *Selective Repudiation.* FIRREA provides that, in any *transfer* of assets of an insolvent institution, the receiver or conservator may not "cherry-pick" among qualified financial contracts between the insolvent institution and any particular counterparty. Instead, if any qualified financial contract with a given counterparty is transferred, all qualified financial contracts with that counterparty must be transferred to the same party (together with all claims relating thereto).

In some circumstances with several separate agreements for qualified financial contracts, there is a risk that a receiver or conservator could (without effecting any transfer of assets) "cherry-pick" by selectively repudiating only disadvantageous qualified financial contracts. If, however, all the Transactions documented under an ISDA Master Agreement fall within the definition of "swap agreement", then selective repudiation will not pose a problem because there is only *one* agreement to repudiate or honor. Under FIRREA, the treatment of a master agreement as one "swap agreement" is specifically addressed as follows:

"(vii) TREATMENT OF MASTER AGREEMENT AS 1 SWAP AGREEMENT.-Any master agreement for any agreements described in clause (vi)(I) together with all supplements to such master agreement shall be treated as 1 swap agreement."

V. FDICIA

. . .

In the event a court did not treat an ISDA Master Agreement as one agreement or did not (or could not) apply the analysis concerning the Bankruptcy Code and FIRREA set forth in Section IV above, a counterparty still may be able to rely on FDICIA to enforce the close-out netting provisions in an ISDA Master Agreement with certain U.S. entities. Congress recently enacted FDICIA, which recognizes the enforceability of the netting of payment obligations between two "financial institution[s]" under a "netting contract", "notwithstanding any other provision of law" and notwithstanding any "stay, injunction, avoidance, moratorium or similar proceeding or order, whether issued or granted by a court, administrative agency, or otherwise."

France passed a similar law in December of 1993, but one major issue remained:

THE HOLES IN NETTING
Euromoney, Apr. 1994, at 54.

It took the French parliament more than five years to adopt the Group of 12's 1988 recommendation that netting be recognized in bankruptcy.

When it finally did, on December 31 last year, French bankers were delighted because the move reduced their obligation to cover risk. "The new provisions for netting will enable French banks to balance their total exposure," says Patrick Stevenson, a managing director at Banque Paribas.

Unfortunately, that may not be true if the banks work with foreigners.

When netting is in place, bankruptcy administrators, which normally have broad freedom to decide what debts are paid when a company goes bankrupt, must take account of offsetting payment obligations. This is particularly important when companies trade derivatives such as swaps, where each counterparty owes the other a sum of money.

The new law permits netting for French banks and similar institutions that operate in the credit markets, including insurance companies-but foreign institutions are eligible only if they have "similar status."

Financial lawyers complain that the law does not explain this term. "The definition of the foreign institutions which may benefit from the new rules relating to netting is unclear," says Pierre Chabert, a lawyer with Cleary, Gottlieb, Steen & Hamilton in Paris. "An unregulated affiliate of a US bank, a broker-dealer, a fund manager or a foreign investment advisor would probably not qualify under these new rules."

Notably unprotected are the foreign derivative product companies that banks have set up to handle their trading. "It is not clear that special-purpose derivative units organized outside France would have the benefits of the legislation available to them," complains Ed

Nalbantian, of Watson, Filey, Williams. Also unprotected, he says, are foreign insurance companies.

In theory, the Bank of France or the treasury could approve netting for these institutions. But since the law does not provide for such approvals, lawyers point out, the courts might not recognize them.

This seems to be one area where neither the Bank of France nor the ministry of the economy has the power to intervene. Either parliamentary action will be required to make the law clearer, or a lot of cases will have to go through the courts.

——————

The problems with the scope of the French law were corrected with the enactment of Law No. 96-597, Loi de modernisation des activités financières, in July 1996. As now revised, the netting rules apply to any contract where one of the parties is a provider of investment services (prestataire de services d'investissement). This term is defined as an investment company or bank with authorization to provide investment services. The term "investment company," is defined as any entity (other than a bank) which as its regular and principal business provides investment services. S. Mouy & E. Nalbantian, *France Modernizes Collateralization and Netting*, International Financial Law Review 26, September 1996. A European Union Netting Directive now makes netting effective across the Community. A. Hudson, *The European Netting Directive*, European Financial Services Law 309, November 1996.

Japanese law was quite unclear on the validity of netting. Legislation to uphold netting was introduced in the Diet on March 10, 1998 and took effect in December 1998. In Italy, another country where the validity of netting was unclear, a new law took effect in July 1998. 11 Swaps Monitor, No. 11 (April 6, 1998).

b. ONE-WAY PAYMENTS

Schuyler K. Henderson explores the relative merits of the two approaches to the termination of swap transactions, one way or two way payments, where one party to the agreement is in default.

S. HENDERSON, SHOULD SWAP TERMINATION PAYMENTS BE ONE-WAY OR TWO-WAY
International Financial Law Review, Oct. 1990, at 27-32.

The 1987 ISDA Interest Rate and Currency Exchange Agreement and the 1987 ISDA Interest Rate Swap Agreement (collectively referred to as the ISDA Agreements, using the same defined terms) provide that a defaulting party will never receive payment of its net value, if any, in terminated swap transactions. An alternative approach, which is beginning to be used by some major swap dealers, is for the non-defaulting party to pay over its gain resulting from termination. The gain would approximate, but be somewhat less than, a defaulting party's loss of its net value on termination.

Termination

A swap transaction can be terminated on a date (the early termination date) before its scheduled termination date by one party acting alone on either of two bases: a termination event with respect to itself or, in some cases, the other party (generally a 'no fault' event beyond the control of the parties, such as supervening illegality or change in tax law but also including certain merger events); or an event of default with respect to the other party.

Because of the movement of rates since inception of the swap, and also at times because of the mismatch of payments made prior to the early termination date, a termination of the swap transactions and their future cash flows without a cash settlement will generally favour one party at the expense of the other. If a swap transaction has become 'out-of-the money' or unfavourable for a party, it has a negative value, and termination results in a gain to it. If the swap transaction is 'in-the-money' or favourable for a party, it has a positive value for the party, and termination results in a loss to it.

On termination, the amount of gain or loss under the ISDA Agreements is determined by first calculating two components: unpaid amounts and settlement amounts.

A party's unpaid amounts are payments (plus interest) which were scheduled to be, but were not, made before the early termination date. These payments may not have been made because either the payer defaulted or the payment was deferred because the payee was in default.

. . .

Settlement provisions

Counterparties invariably provide in their agreements that, where early termination is based on a termination event, two-way payments applies. Under this method, the non-affected party's settlement amount (positive or negative) is aggregated with any unpaid amounts (always positive) owing to the non-affected party and, from this sum (which may be positive or negative), any unpaid amounts owing to the affected party are subtracted. The resulting amount, if positive, is paid over by the affected party. If the amount is negative, the non-affected party would pay the absolute value of that amount to the affected party.

Where early termination is based on an event of default, most dealers generally provide in their agreement that one way payments applies. The non-defaulting party would calculate the aggregate of its settlement amount and unpaid amounts owing it and subtract unpaid amounts owing to the defaulting party, as above. If the resulting amount is positive, the defaulting party is obliged to pay that amount to the non-defaulting party. If the resulting amount is negative, there is no obligation imposed on the non-defaulting party to make any payment to the defaulting party. This method is referred to as 'one-way payments.'

There is concern that there may be a penalty aspect with respect to forfeiture of unpaid amounts otherwise owing to a defaulting party. If the settlement amount was zero and there were unpaid amounts owing to the defaulting party (for instance, as the result of deferral by reason of a potential event of default with respect to the defaulting party at the time payment was due to it), no payment of those unpaid amounts would be made. Some dealers modify one-way payments so that the settlement amount, if it is a negative number, will be treated as equalling zero and the two unpaid amounts will be compared. If the unpaid amounts owing to the defaulting party exceed those owing to the non-defaulting party, the non-defaulting party would in this situation, and this situation alone, pay the excess to the defaulting party. This method of settlement is referred to as 'modified one-way payments.' A variation is 'two pool damages.' Here, if a party has fully performed some transactions (eg, purchased caps), the market quotations for these transactions are not included in the settlement amount, but are included as an unpaid amount owing to the party, and modified one-way payments is applied.

However, in modified one-way payments a negative settlement amount cannot be used to reduce unpaid amounts owing to the non-defaulting party. For instance, if the settlement amount was negative, unpaid amounts owing to the non-defaulting party were positive and unpaid amounts owing to the defaulting party were zero, under one-way payments the defaulting party would effectively be able to reduce unpaid amounts owing to the non-defaulting party by the amount of the negative settlement amount. Under modified one-way payments, the settlement amount would be deemed to be zero and the defaulting party would not be able to reduce its payment. Although it eliminates the forfeiture issue as to unpaid amounts, modified one-way payments may create a greater risk of being regarded as an unenforceable penalty, since it may impose a payment obligation on the defaulting party in excess of the non-defaulting party's loss.

. . .

To summarise, in either one-way payments or modified one-way payments the defaulting party does not receive any net value which it had in the terminated swap transactions except to the extent, in one-way payments, it reduces any net unpaid amounts otherwise payable to the non-defaulting party. In conditional two-way payments, the defaulting party would receive the non-defaulting party's gain on termination after assurance that all other liabilities and costs have been satisfied.

Calculating termination payments

($000's) Non-defaulting party's loss or gain from termination			($000's) Non-defaulting party's loss or gain from termination	
Settlement amount	= -1,000		Settlement amount	= 1,000
+ Unpaid amounts owing non-defaulting party	= 100		+ Unpaid amounts owing non-defaulting party	= 100
- Unpaid amounts owing defaulting party	= 50		- Unpaid amounts owing defaulting party	= 50
Net loss (gain) of non-defaulting party	= (950)		Net loss (gain) of Non-defaulting party	= 1,050

Calculation of termination payments

	Limited two-way payments	Modified limited two-way payments	Two-way payments		Limited two-way payments	Modified limited two-way payments	Two-way payments
	-1,000	0	-1,000		+1,000	+1,000	+1,000
	+100	+100	+100		+ 100	+ 100	+ 100
	-50	-50	-50		- 50	- 50	- 50
	-950	50	-950		1,050	1,050	1,050
Amount owing by:				Amount owing by:			
Defaulting party =	0	50	0	Defaulting party =	1,050	1,050	1,050
Non-defaulting party =	0	0	950	Non-defaulting party =	0	0	0

One-way payments: the arguments for

Avoiding rewarding a defaulting party: in principle, a party should not be able to benefit from its wrongful act or event of default. Many institutions oppose, on an emotional level, making payments to a defaulting party.

Inducement not to breach: one-way payments creates a powerful incentive for a counterparty to honour its obligations and not default. Two-way payments creates an incentive to breach.

Bargaining leverage: one-way payments strengthens the non-defaulting party's bargaining position in negotiating with an in-the-money defaulting party which is resisting termination. At the time of desired termination, if it appears prudent to do so, the non-defaulting party could waive the right not to make payment and agree to pay, perhaps a reduced amount, on conditions similar to those set out in conditional two-way payments. In several default situations, defaulting parties have been able to negotiate either orderly payouts on, effectively, a two-way payment basis or agreed novations of their swap portfolios.

Windfall: with one-way payments, a non-defaulting party might obtain a gain, a 'windfall', through the cancellation without cost of a disadvantageous contract (and, if hedged, continue to benefit from a corresponding advantageous contract or contracts). The active market participant should anticipate that at some times it will be the losing, in-the-money counterparty and unable to recover its loss. At other times it will be an out-of-the-money counterparty and be entitled to retain its gain. The windfalls would balance the losses.

Enforceable: in the most active swap jurisdiction (the United States), the risk of inability to terminate has been greatly diminished and the risk of 'cherry-picking' has apparently been eliminated. This results from the Financial Institutions Reform, Recovery and Enforcement Act, 1989 (FIRREA) with respect to banks and savings and loan institutions and as a result of recent legislation with respect to corporations subject to the US Bankruptcy Code (Bankruptcy Swap Amendment). Enforcement risks presented by one-way payments in the context of a US bankruptcy, referred to below, have therefore been substantially reduced.

. . .

Arguments against one-way payments

Status as a dealer: a dealer holds itself out as a market-maker and generally is expected to and does offer quotes for terminating a swap transaction. Exercise of one-way payments by a dealer is inconsistent with this role and expectation. This has a number of ramifications discussed below.

No "reward" to defaulting party in two-way payments: there is no net benefit or reward to a defaulting party receiving a payment on termination. The value the defaulting party had in the agreement, which is now lost, will exceed any payment it receives on default. In addition, payments are often made to defaulting parties in bilateral financial arrangements such as repos, exchange-traded futures and FX netting agreements. The purpose of two-way payments in these situations is to provide greater certainty of enforcement and to preserve the soundness of the dealing market (including orderly distribution of assets to creditors), not to be generous to defaulters. It is consistent with the orderly settlement of the defaulting parties' swap portfolios referred to in Bargaining leverage above (but would not present the risks to orderly settlement posed by actions which were taken by a few non-defaulting parties in each of those situations which refused to co-operate and attempted to retain their windfall).

One-way payments will not reduce defaults: the event of default may be involuntary and unintentional (such as a bankruptcy or an event of default relating to an affiliate). Onerous contractual provisions, such as one-way payments, will not affect the defaulting party's actions relating to those defaults. ...

Cherry Picking

Bankruptcy-questionable enforceability of one-way payments:
despite the improved situation in the United States following the
Bankruptcy Swap Amendment, insolvency laws in some other
jurisdictions provide that the non-defaulting party will not be able to
terminate after formal insolvency proceedings have commenced,
regardless of whether one-way payments or two-way payments are
used. In addition, one-way payments could in these jurisdictions draw
the attention of the bankruptcy representative to related legal issues.
For instance, the representative might challenge the "single
agreement" concept and attempt to 'cherry-pick' among the swap
transactions, ie assuming (or assuming and assigning) those swaps
where the insolvent party is in-the-money and rejecting those where it
is out-of-the-money (leaving the solvent party obligated on the former
with only a claim for damages on the latter).

. . .

Just to be clearer with respect to Henderson's Chart, focus on the left
hand side example. For ease of reference let's refer to Party A as the
non-defaulting party and Party B as the defaulting party. As shown on
the top of the Chart, Party A owes B 1000. This means the swap is in
the money for B, not A (based on replacement value quotes). Party A also
owes 50 to B in "unpaid amounts." These are payments which were
scheduled to be made but which have not been made. Also, B owes 100
in "unpaid amounts" to A. Thus, B has a gain of 950.

Column 1 shows the result under the earlier swap documentation
rules if Party B defaulted. All payments are netted. Since A owes B a
settlement amount of 1000, but is on net owed 50 in unpaid amounts (is
owed 100, but owes only 50), the net of all payments is -950. The
standard swap rule was that the non-defaulting party makes no net
payments to the defaulting party; thus A makes no payments to B.

How did that compare with the normal termination rule, e.g. where
the contract was at an end, or the parties mutually agreed to terminate?
Column 3 shows this. Here the rule is two-way payments, the party out
of the money, A, pays the party in the money, B, 950, the net of all
payments.

How would a modified limited two-way payment rule change this?
This is shown in Column 2. The issue of the payment of the settlement
amount is separated from that of the payment of unpaid amounts. A does
not pay B the settlement amount since B has defaulted. But since, on
net, B owes A 50 in unpaid amounts, B pays A 50.

The right hand example deals with the situation where the non-defaulting party has a gain. Here the result is always the same. B must always pay A the net amount, 1000 + 50 (net of unpaid amounts).

Notes and Questions

1. Assume Party A and Party X have three swap contracts between them, and that marking each contract to market, and calculating replacement value, there are some contracts favorable to Party A, but others that are favorable to Party X.

	X	A	
1.	+200,000	-200,000	(A owes X)
2.	+500,000	-500,000	(A owes X)
3.	-800,000	+800,000	(X owes A)

So, in this example, on net, X owes A 100,000. Before the U.S. passed the new law what was X's risk if A were to go bankrupt?

2. Does the new U.S. law protect A against the cherry-picking risk? Would it depend on whether X was a U.S. company or a foreign company? The ISDA 1992 Master Swap Agreement provides that the governing law is either English or New York. Assuming netting is valid in England, does this choice of law provision protect swap parties against cherry-picking risk?

3. The European Union, in implementing the BIS Netting Amendment, has adopted a Directive permitting national supervisors to take bilateral netting into account in setting capital requirements but the validity of netting is still left to national law. Council Directive 96/10, 1996 O.J. (L 85/17).

4. What would you advise a client to do with respect to one-way or two-way payments in a swap contract?

3. NETTING AND CAPITAL REQUIREMENTS

We turn again to capital requirements. The issue here is how the capital requirements deal with the netting issue. The credit rules of the original Basel Accord did not permit swaps to be netted among the same counterparties. Thus, in the example in Note 1, the values of the contracts could not be netted for capital purposes.

The Basel capital requirements now do permit bilateral netting of swaps (those between the same counter-parties) with respect to replacement values and future exposure values. Basel Capital Accord: Treatment of the Credit Risk Associated with Certain Off-Balance-Sheet Items (Basel Committee 1994) (replacement values) and Basel Capital Accord: Treatment of Potential Exposure for Off-Balance-Sheet Items (Apr. 1995) (1995 Netting Amendment) (future exposure values). U.S.

bank regulators have allowed bilateral netting of replacement values on the same terms as proposed by the Basel Supervisors Committee, Board of Governors of the Federal Reserve System, Capital Adequacy Guidelines, Final Rule, 59 Federal Register 62987 (1994); Board of Governors of the Federal Reserve System, Final Rule, 60 Federal Register 46170 (1995).

With respect to replacement value, suppose Banks A and B have entered into two swap contracts which have the following values to Bank A:

	Replacement Value	Future Exposure
#1	1000	3000
#2	-500	700

A is in the money on #1 and out of the money on #2. Thus, if the swap were to terminate today due to B's default A would have a claim in B's bankruptcy of 500 after the swaps were netted. The asset equivalent amounts for Bank A of these two swaps, with respect to replacement values, is 500 with netting rather than 1000.

The permissibility of bilateral netting is subject to certain requirements. Supervisors must be assured that a bank has:

(1) a netting contract or agreement with the counterparty which creates a single legal obligation, covering all included transactions, such as that the bank would have either a claim to receive or obligation to pay only the net sum of the positive and negative mark-to-market values of included individual transactions in the event a counterparty fails to perform due to any of the following: default, bankruptcy, liquidation or similar circumstances;

(2) written and reasoned legal opinions that, in the event of a legal challenge, the relevant courts and administrative authorities would find the bank's exposure to be such a net amount under:

— the law of the jurisdiction in which the counterparty is chartered and, if the foreign branch of a counterparty is involved, then also under the law of the jurisdiction in which the branch is located;

— the law that governs the individual transactions; and

— the law that governs any contract or agreement necessary to effect the netting.

(3) The national supervisor, after consultation when necessary with other relevant supervisors, must be satisfied that the netting is enforceable under the laws of each of the relevant jurisdictions; procedures in place to ensure that the legal characteristics of netting arrangements are kept under review in the light of possible changes in relevant law.

Contracts containing walkaway clauses (one-way payments) will not be eligible for netting for the purpose of calculating capital requirements pursuant to this Accord. A walkaway clause is a provision which permits a non-defaulting counterparty to make only limited payments, or no payment at all, to the estate of a defaulter, even if the defaulter is a net creditor.

Notes and Questions

1. Should we permit netting of future exposures as well as replacement values?

2. Does the Netting Amendment set forth tough enough standards for determining the enforceability of netting? Why is BIS worried about swap enforceability in three possible jurisdictions?

3. Should the SEC and Fed have a joint approach to capital requirements for derivatives dealers?

Links to Other Chapters

Swaps, as well as futures and options (Chapter 16) and securitized instruments (Chapter 13) raise crucial problems of dealing with financial innovation. From a regulatory point of view, the focus has been on capital (generally reviewed in Chapter 4) and netting. Netting issues are crucial not only for swaps, but with respect to the payment system (Chapter 10) and clearance and settlement (Chapter 15). The development of swaps, like other euromarket products, has in part responded to the inefficiencies or regulatory restrictions in national markets, which we have reviewed for the U.S. (Chapters 2 and 3) and Japan (Chapter 8).

APPENDIX

I. CAPITAL REQUIREMENTS FOR DEBT SECURITIES

The capital requirements for debt securities depend on the maturities of the obligation and the coupon rate. Swaps are treated as two notional debt securities with the relevant maturities. Fixed-rate instruments are allocated according to the residual term to maturity and floating-rate instruments according to the next repricing date. *Id.* §III.19, at 15. Go back to our interest rate swap paradigm (the transaction in note 1, at p. 995 of this Chapter) and assume that the LIBOR swap rate reset every 3 months. At the outset, Bank A would be considered to have a short position (the position it had to pay) in a three month security and a 5 year long position in the fixed rate swap (the position it is paid). Over the 5 years, the fixed rate leg of the swap would decrease in maturity, and the floating rate swap would decrease in maturity every three months, e.g. after the elapse of one month of time, it would be a two-month security, and at the end of three months would again revert to a three-month security.

Swap Bank would not have any position because of its exactly matched book (Swap bank is completely hedged). Close matches might also not require capital, e.g. if the coupons on offsetting fixed rate swaps were within 15 basis points of each other, and the maturities of the swaps were close.

We set out below a hypothetical debt securities portfolio taken from a 1993 BIS report first proposing market risk requirements. Bank for International Settlements, The Prudential Supervision of Netting, Market Risks and Interest Rate Risk (1993) (Market Risk Proposals), Annex 4.

Debt securities
Sample market risk calculation

Time-band	Issuer	Position	Specific risk Weight (%)	Specific risk Charge	General market risk Weight (%)	General market risk Charge
0- 1 mo.	Treasury	5,000	0.00	0.00	0.00	0.00
1- 3 mos	Treasury	5,000	0.00	0.00	0.20	10.00
3- 6 mos	Qual Corp	4,000	0.25	10.00	0.40	16.00
6- 12 mos	Qual Corp	(7,500)	1.00	75.00	0.70	(52.50)
1- 2 yrs	Treasury	(2,500)	0.00	0.00	1.25	(31.25)
2- 3 yrs	Treasury	2,500	0.00	0.00	1.75	43.75
3- 4 yrs	Treasury	2,500	0.00	0.00	2.25	56.25
3- 4 yrs	Qual Corp	(2,000)	1.60	32.00	2.25	(45.00)
4- 5 yrs	Treasury	1,500	0.00	0.00	2.75	41.25
5- 7 yrs	Qual Corp	(1,000)	1.60	16.00	3.25	(32.50)
7- 10 yrs	Treasury	(1,500)	0.00	0.00	3.75	(56.25)
10- 15 yrs	Treasury	(1,500)	0.00	0.00	4.50	(67.50)
10- 15 yrs	Non Qual	1,000	8.00	80.00	4.50	45.00
15- 20 yrs	Treasury	1,500	0.00	0.00	5.25	78.75
> 20 yrs	Qual Corp	1,000	1.60	16.00	6.00	60.00

Specific risk	229.00	
Residual general market risk		66.00

How would our paradigm swap be dealt with (assuming it was on the trading book)? The 100 million fixed rate 5 year leg would at the outset be like a 4-5 year Treasury security with a market risk weight of 2.75. This risk weight is generated from the risk weight table of the Amendment, *id*. §II.12, at 12:

Table 1
Maturity Method: time-bands and weights

Coupon 3% or more	Coupon less than 3%	Risk Weight
up to 1 month	up to 1 month	0.00%
1 to 3 months	1 to 3 months	0.20%
3 to 6 months	3 to 6 months	0.40%
6 to 12 months	6 to 12 months	0.70%
1 to 2 years	1.0 to 1.9 years	1.25%
2 to 3 years	1.9 to 2.8 years	1.75%
3 to 4 years	2.8 to 3.6 years	2.25%
4 to 5 years	3.6 to 4.3 years	2.75%
5 to 7 years	4.3 to 5.7 years	3.25%
7 to 10 years	5.7 to 7.3 years	3.75%
10 to 15 years	7.3 to 9.3 years	4.50%
15 to 20 years	9.3 to 10.6 years	5.25%
over 20 years	10.6 to 12 years	6.00%
	12 to 20 years	8.00%

Risk-Weights

The Amendment describes the derivation of these weights as follows: "The first step in the calculation is to weight the positions in each time-band by a factor designed to reflect the price sensitivity of those positions to assumed changes in interest rates." *Id.* at §II.11, at 11. Notice that one set of volatility weights is used for interest rates on instruments denominated in different currencies, even though separate charge calculations (reporting ladders) must be made for instruments in different currencies.

In our paradigm example, let's look at Bank A's position, assuming that the swap was for 1000 rather than for $100 million. In the calculation of residual market risk, the fixed rate swap leg (the long) would generate a charge of 27.50, 2.75% of the notional amount, and the floating rate swap leg (the short) would generate a charge of (2.00), .20% of the notional amount. The overall net charge (before offsets) for the swap position would be 25.50 (netting the long position against the short one), or 2.55% of the notional amount. This would increase the general market risk of the hypothetical portfolio from 66.00 to 91.50.

The next step of the analysis involves vertical and horizontal offsets. The Table below sets forth calculations which will be explained in the following text:

Calculation of capital charge						Charge
1. Specific Risk						229.00

2. Vertical offsets WITHIN SAME TIME-BANDS

Time-band	Longs	Shorts	Residual*	Offset	Disallowance	Charge
3-4 yrs	56.25	(45.00)	11.25	45.00	10.00%	4.50
10-15 yrs	45.00	(67.50)	(22.50)	45.00	10.00%	4.50

3. Horizontal offsets WITHIN SAME TIME-ZONES

	Longs	Shorts	Residual*	Offset	Disallowance	Charge
Zone 1						
0-1 mo.	0.00					
1-3 mos	10.00					
3-6 mos	16.00					
6-12 mos		(52.50)				
Total						
Zone 1	26.00	(52.50)	(26.50)	26.00	40.00%	10.40
Zone 2						
1-2 yrs		(31.25)				
2-3 yrs	43.75					
3-4 yrs	11.25					
Total						
Zone 2	55.00	(31.25)	23.75	31.25	30.00%	9.38
Zone 3						
4-5 yrs	41.25					
5-7 yrs		(32.50)				
7-10 yrs		(56.25)				
10-15 yrs		(22.50)				
15-20 yrs	78.75					
> 20 yrs	60.00					
Total						
Zone 3	180.00	(111.25)	68.75	111.25	30.00%	33.38

4. Horizontal offsets BETWEEN TIME-ZONES

	Longs	Shorts	Residual*	Offset	Disallowance	Charge
Zone 1 & Zone 2	23.75	(26.50)	(2.75)	23.75	40.00%	9.50
Zone 1 & Zone 3	68.75	(2.75)	66.00	2.75	100.00%	2.75

5. Total capital charge

Specific risk	229.00
Vertical disallowances	9.00
Horizontal disallowances	53.16
(offsets within same time-zones)	12.25
(offsets between time-zones)	66.00
Residual general market risk	369.41
Total	

* Residual amount carried forward for additional offsetting as appropriate.

Vertical Offsets

The idea behind vertical offsets is to deal with the problem that the calculation of residual market risk assumed that the interest rate sensitivity of every instrument within one of the 13 time bands was the same, even though different instruments within the same time band will not react uniformly to changes in interest rates. For this reason, the Committee did not want to fully allow longs to offset shorts, and therefore applies a "vertical disallowance factor" of 10% to the smaller of the long or short position.

In the hypothetical portfolio, this disallowance is applied to both the 3-4 and 10-15 year time bands where there are both long and short positions. Thus, for the 3-4 year time band, where the charge for the short position of (45.00) is smaller than the charge for the long position, 56.25, it becomes the offset, and generates an additional charge of 4.50, 10% of 45. Our swap has just increased the charge for the long positions in the 4-5 time band and therefore requires no vertical offset. However, in the 1-3 months time band, our swap now generates a short position charge of (2.00) generated by the swap to go along with the existing 10 charge on the long. Since (2.00) is the smaller, there would be an additional vertical offset of .20, 10% of 2.

Horizontal Offsets

The idea behind horizontal offsets is to limit the netting between maturity bands in the calculation of market risk (the first calculation). In getting the 66 general market risk charge, shorts in one time band were netted off against longs in another time band. Based on observed correlations, BIS believes that the likelihood of divergent movements is lower for nearer segments of the yield curve and higher for more distant segments. 1993 Market Risk Proposal at 19. Thus, the Amendment provides for two rounds of partial "horizontal" offsetting, first between the net positions in each of the three zones (zero to one year, one year to four years and over four years), and subsequently between the net positions in the different zones. These disallowance result in a greater recognition of hedging for offsets taking place within the same zone than for offsets between different zones. The horizontal disallowances are set forth below:

Table 2
Horizontal Disallowances

Time-band		within the zone	between adjacent zones	between zones 1 and 3
Zone 1	0- 1 mo.	40%	40%	100%
	1- 3 mos			
	3- 6 mos			
	6- 12 mos			
Zone 2	1- 2 yrs	30%		
	2- 3 yrs			
	3- 4 yrs			
Zone 3	4- 5 yrs		40%	
	5- 7 yrs			
	7- 10 yrs			
	10- 15 yrs	30%		
	15- 20 yrs			
	over 20 yrs			

The zones for coupons less than 3% would be 0 to 12 months, 1 to 3.6 years, and over 3.6 years

Within the Zone

How does our swap affect the calculation of horizontal offsets within the same time zone? Our swap has increased the shorts in Zone 1 by (2.00) to (54.50) but does not lead to any additional charge, because the longs are less than the shorts. Our swap has increased the longs in Zone 3 by 27.50 to 207.50, but again there is no impact because the disallowance is applied to the smaller short position. Notice that the disallowance factor is higher in Zone 1 (40%) than in Zones 2 or 3. This seems to be because rates are believed to be more volatile, or rates on different instruments within the Zone are believed to be less correlated, in the shorter Zone 1 maturities.

Between Zones

Let's now take the second offset, horizontal offsets between time zones. Before taking the swap into account, Zone 1 has an overall short position of (26.50) (also the Zone 1 residual) and Zone 2 has an overall long position of 23.75 (also the Zone 2 residual). This produces an offset of 23.75, the smaller long position, and a charge of 9.50 (40% of 23.75). The same type of calculation is performed for Zones 1 and 3. Zone 3 has an overall 68.75 long. Zone 2's position is now considered net of the offset against Zone 1, or short (2.75). This is the residual produced by the first offset between Zones 1 and 2. The offset is 2.75, the smaller position, and the charge is 2.75 (100% of 2.75). Larger disallowances are set where positions between more distant time zones have been offset, 1 and 3 (100%) compared to 1 and 2 (40%).

Now let's look at the effect of our swap. The short leg of our swap with a charge of (2.00) will increase the Zone 1 residual to (28.50) and the long leg of our swap with a charge of 27.50 will increase the Zone 3 residual to 96.25 (68.75 + 27.50). This will not result in any increased charge in the Zone 1-2 calculation since the long position is still the smallest, but it does increase the Zone 1-2 residual to short (4.75)---(23.75 - (28.50)).

There will, however, be an increase in the Zone 1-3 calculation. The Zone 3 residual or longs (it's the same) is increased to 96.25 as against the Zone 1 residual (as now carried forward) of (4.75). The disallowance of 100% is applied against the smaller (4.75) to produce a charge of 4.75, as compared with the original charge of 2.75. The swaps thus increase the offset charge by 2.00.

The total capital charge for the swaps alone, and for all debt securities, including the swaps, is set forth below:

	Swaps	All Debt Securities
Specific Risk	0.00	229.00
Vertical disallowances	.20	9.20
Horizontal disallowances		
(within same zone)	0.00	53.16
(between zones)	2.00	14.25
Residual General Market Risk	25.50	91.50
Total Charge	27.50	397.11

The 27.50 swap charge represents about 2.8% of the 1000 notional amount of the swap. Recall that under the existing credit risk approach the charge for the swap would have been .25%. This comparison only holds true at the inception of the swap. The .25% credit risk charge can increase if the swap has positive value, and the market risk charge will decrease over the life of the fixed rate swap leg. Nonetheless, it would appear that the market risk requirements are significantly more onerous than the credit risk ones.[*]

---

[*] The Amendment offers an alternative methodology, the so-called "duration method" in which the price sensitivity of each position is calculated separately. The method can only be used with the supervisor's consent.

II. FUTURE EXPOSURE UNDER THE 1995 NETTING AMENDMENT

The Netting Amendment provides that the potential future credit exposure be multiplied by the specified add-on factors. The formula set out below then reduces the add-ons for transactions subject to legally enforceable netting agreements. The add-on for netted transactions (A_{Net}) would equal the average of the add-on as presently calculated (A_{Gross}),[**] reduced by the ratio of net current replacement cost to gross current replacement cost (NGR), and the A_{Gross}.

$$A_{NET} = 0.5 * A_{GROSS} - 0.5 * NGR * A_{GROSS}$$

where

NGR = level of net replacement cost/level of gross replacement cost for transactions subject to legally enforceable netting agreements

A_{GROSS} = equals the sum of notional principal amounts of all transactions subject to legally enforceable netting agreements times the appropriate add-on factors

Using this formula, banks will always hold capital against potential exposure as the net add-on can never be zero. In this context, the NGR can be seen as somewhat of a proxy for the impact of netting on potential future exposure but not as a precise indicator of future changes in net exposure relative to gross exposure, reflecting the fact that the NGR and potential exposure can be influenced by many idiosyncratic properties of individual portfolios. With the weight at 0.5, the reduction in add-on, assuming an NGR of 0.5, would be 25%. A simple example of calculating NGR is set out below.

Simple example of calculating the net to gross ratio

Transaction	Counterparty 1		Counterparty 2		Counterparty 3	
	Notional amount	Mark-to-market value	Notional amount	Mark-to-market value	Notional amount	Mark-to-market value
Transaction 1	100	10	50	8	30	-3
Transaction 2	100	-5	50	2	30	1
Gross Replacement Cost(GR)		10		10		1
Net Replacement Cost (NR)		5		10		0
NGR (per counterparty)	0.5		1		0	
NGR (aggregate)	$\Sigma NR/\Sigma GR = 15/21 = 0.71$					

U.S. bank regulators altered the BIS formula in implementing the capital requirements for potential future exposures by giving more weight to the risk reducing potential of netting. The BIS formula only weights the NGR, which reflects the netting, at 50%. The U.S. regulators have given it a 60% weight, thereby adopting the following formula:

$$A_{NET} = 0.4 * A_{GROSS} - 0.6 * NGR * A_{GROSS}$$

60 Federal Register 46170, 46173 (1995). Under the 2000 proposed revisions of the Basel Accord, the 50% ceiling on counterparty risk weightings would be removed, para. 42.

The current rules have been modified somewhat for credit derivatives which combine credit and market risk. Board of Governors of the Federal Reserve Board, Division of Banking Supervision and Regulation, SR 97-18, June 13, 1997.

CHAPTER EIGHTEEN

OFFSHORE
MUTUAL FUNDS

Mutual funds are investment vehicles which allow investors to purchase interests representing pro rata shares of the net assets of a pool of securities and other assets. Such funds can be public or private. An open-end fund engages in a continuous offering of its shares and will permit investors to redeem shares at current net values. A closed-end fund engages in one offering and does not generally permit share redemptions. Investors exit from their investments by selling their shares to other investors in a secondary market. Mutual funds have emerged as the preferred investment vehicle for most individual investors, since they allow inexpensive diversification of risk under the management of a qualified expert adviser. As of 1999, 41% of U.S. households invested in mutual funds; and total mutual fund assets in the U.S. had skyrocketed from about $716 billion at the end of 1986 to over $6 trillion. Investment company assets outside the U.S. increased from under $1 trillion in 1988 to $3.5 trillion in 1999. Investment Company Institute, *Fact Book 2000*; Investment Company Institute and Securities Industry Association, *Equity Ownership in America* (1999). There is great potential for growth for foreign investment in mutual funds, as in France and the U.K. As of 1996, only one in ten households in these countries invests in mutual funds, and the ratios are even lower in the rest of the world. As of 1996, it was estimated that foreign investment advisers managed $141 billion of investment company assets in the United States, or 4.8% of total industry assets, while U.S. firms managed $56.6 billion in mutual funds outside the United States, or 3.7% of the non-U.S. mutual fund market. See Response of the Investment Company Institute to IOSCO Cross-Border Marketing Survey, November 14, 1996.

Generally speaking, an offshore mutual fund is a fund organized in a foreign nation, as opposed to onshore funds which are organized in the United States. Offshore funds are most often sponsored by well-known financial institutions. Sponsors may receive annual management fees, commissions, placement fees, and/or an agreed initial fee that may represent a small percentage of the money invested in the fund. The sponsors of the offshore funds appoint professional managers to advise the fund on daily operations. Investment advisers of offshore funds are often located in foreign financial centers and are thereby able to identify investment opportunities and make qualified investment decisions regarding the foreign securities of which a foreign fund is often comprised.

Offshore mutual funds enable investors to take advantage of the globalization of the economy and further diversify their risk while minimizing the possible disadvantages stemming from unfamiliarity with foreign securities. Meanwhile, the offshore mutual funds provide a stream of capital to foreign corporations. Investors worldwide can also invest in foreign securities through U.S. mutual funds that invest in foreign securities. As we shall see, however, for tax and regulatory reasons U.S. investors tend to invest only in U.S. funds and foreign investors in offshore funds. This is a remarkable pattern given the level of cross-border activity in the primary securities markets.

Offshore funds generally take either of two organizational forms: a contract or unit trust form, most often used by German, Japanese or British funds, or a corporate form, used by Mexican and French funds.[*] The common organizational structure taken by U.S. funds is the corporate form. In the contract form, the fund is a creation of its sponsor or manager and is monitored by an independent trustee or government regulator. In the corporate form, the fund is created as a separate entity. The corporate fund is owned and theoretically managed by its shareholders through a board of directors.

A. UNITED STATES REGULATORY BARRIERS TO OFFSHORE MUTUAL FUNDS

The U.S. mutual funds market is often regarded as the most difficult mutual fund market for an offshore fund to penetrate. Some funds choose not to register in the U.S. because of highly stringent U.S. disclosure requirements, and corporate form requirements, combined with the expense of U.S. registration. However, the Securities & Exchange Commission allows foreigners to freely invest in American mutual funds, and permits foreign mutual funds to freely purchase American securities without having to register.

Since 1954, only 13 foreign investment companies have registered with the SEC. Of the 13 foreign investment company registrants, no more than four are still operating in the United States. Even more striking is the fact that since 1973, no foreign investment company has been approved by the SEC to register in the United States.

---

[*] See D. Silver, *Meeting the Demand for Pooled Investments in a World Market* 9, Investment Company Institute (Sept. 24, 1991).

1. THE INVESTMENT COMPANY ACT OF 1940

The Investment Company Act of 1940 (the 1940 or '40 Act)* was enacted to address potential abuses in pooled securities funds such as the pyramiding of funds and uncontrolled conflicts of interest. Administered by the SEC, the 1940 Act applies by its terms to all investment companies, including both U.S. and offshore mutual funds. In its inclusive interpretation by the SEC, the 1940 Act defines "investment companies" to include any entity, incorporated or not, which:

- is or holds itself out as being engaged primarily, or proposes to engage primarily, in the business of investing, reinvesting or trading in securities (a subjective test)

- is engaged or proposes to engage in the business of investing, reinvesting, owning, holding or trading in securities and owns or proposes to acquire investment securities having a value exceeding 40 per cent of the issuer's total assets (an objective test)

The definition of 'security' includes stocks, bonds, notes, certificates of interest or participation in any profit-sharing agreement, certain options, evidences of indebtedness, investment contracts (that is, an arrangement where the person invests money in a common enterprise expecting profits principally from the efforts of a third party), and undivided interests in oil or gas or mineral rights.

---

* 15 U.S.C. 80a (1988). The 1940 Act provides:

No investment company organized or otherwise created under the laws of the United States or of a State and having a board of directors, unless registered under section 80a-8 of this title, shall directly or indirectly -

(1) offer for sale, sell, or deliver after sale, by the use of the mails or any means or instrumentality of interstate commerce, any security or any interest in a security, whether the issuer of such security is such investment company or another person; or offer for sale, sell, or deliver after sale any such security or interest, having reason to believe that such security or interest will be made the subject of a public offering by use of the mails or any means or instrumentality of interstate commerce;

(2) purchase, redeem, retire, or otherwise acquire or attempt to acquire, by use of the mails or any means or instrumentality of interstate commerce, any security or any interest in a security, whether the issuer of such security is such investment company or another person;

(3) control any investment company which does any of the acts enumerated in paragraphs (1) and (2) of this subsection;

(4) engage in any business in interstate commerce; or

(5) control any company which is engaged in any business in interstate commerce. The provisions of this subsection shall not apply to transactions of an investment company which are merely incidental to its dissolution.

Section 7(d) of the 1940 Act[*] prohibits a foreign investment company from using jurisdictional means such as the U.S. mails or any other method of interstate commerce to offer or sell its securities (or shares of its funds, for our purposes) in connection with a public U.S. offering, unless the SEC issues an order permitting the foreign investment company to register under the '40 Act. Section 7(d) only applies to foreign funds which have more than 100 U.S. resident "beneficial owners" of fund shares. The 100 beneficial owner limit applies to the foreign fund, even if the shares are primarily offered abroad.

When Section 7(d) applies, the foreign fund will be barred from selling shares in the U.S. unless the SEC issues an order permitting the fund to register (with the SEC), and the fund then indeed registers. Section 7(d) authorizes the SEC to issue an order 'permitting' registration only if the SEC finds that it is both legally and practically feasible to enforce the provisions of the 1940 Act against the foreign investment company, and that the issuance of such an order is consistent with public interest and SEC notions of investor protection.

In order to register under the 1940 Act, a foreign investment company will often have to restructure its fund substantially. While the '40 Act does not explicitly require that mutual funds be organized under a corporate structure, it does impose restrictions that assume such a structure, including the requirements of a board of directors to oversee the fund's operations and contractual obligations, and shareholder voting to elect board members and approve fundamental changes in the nature of the fund and its management. The biggest obstacle for many European and Japanese funds is that they are structured under a more contractual or trust-like model in which the investors' money does not form part of the investment company's own assets, but rather is treated as a collection of separate funds bought by the investment company in the form of securities for the unit holders.

---

[*] 15 U.S.C. 80a-7(d) provides:
No investment company, unless organized or otherwise created under the laws of the United States or of a State, and no depositor or trustee of or underwriter for such a company not so organized or created, shall make use of the mails or any means or instrumentality of interstate commerce, directly or indirectly, to offer for sale, sell, or deliver after sale, in connection with a public offering, any security of which such company is the issuer. Notwithstanding the provisions of this subsection and of section 80a-8(a) of this title, the Commission is authorized, upon application by an investment company organized or otherwise created under the laws of a foreign country, to issue a conditional or unconditional order permitting such company to register under this subchapter, and to make a public offering of its securities by use of the mails and means or instrumentalities of interstate commerce, if the Commissioner finds that, by reason of special circumstances or arrangements, it is both legally and practically feasible effectively to enforce the provisions of this subchapter against such company and that the issuance of such order is otherwise consistent with the public interest and the protection of investors.

In 1954, to clarify the criteria that a foreign fund would need to satisfy before the SEC would issue a 7(d) order, the SEC adopted Rule 7d-1, 12 C.F.R. §270.7d-1. The following are among the Rule 7d-1 requirements: (1) the foreign applicant's charter and by-laws must contain the substantive provisions of the 1940 Act; (2) all parties involved with the management and investment of the funds must file an agreement stating that each will comply with the 1940 Act; (3) at least a majority of the directors and officers of the applicant foreign fund must be U.S. citizens, and of these, a majority must reside in the United States; (4) all of the foreign fund's assets must be maintained in a U.S. bank; and (5) the applicant's principal underwriter and auditor must be U.S. entities.

Following up its adoption of Rule 7d-1, the SEC issued a release in 1975 called Guidelines for Filing of Application for Order Permitting Registration of Foreign Investment Companies (the Guidelines or 7d-1 guidelines), 40 Federal Register 45,424 (1975) to set forth standard conditions for foreign funds seeking 7(d) orders. The Guidelines state that "compliance with the conditions and arrangements in Rule 7d-1 need not necessarily be the only means of satisfying the statutory standards." The SEC emphasized its willingness to consider exemptive applications under Section 6(c) of the '40 Act for any offshore fund that could not meet all of the standards of Rule 7d-1, but that proposed alternative methods for protecting investors and for assuring that the provisions of the Act could be adequately enforced against it.

Consider the following application for an exemption from general SEC registration requirements which was subsequently withdrawn after the SEC announced it would hold a hearing on the application. 48 Federal Register 23342 (1983).

UNION-INVESTMENT GESELLSCHAFT m.b.h.
SECURITIES AND EXCHANGE COMMISSION
INVESTMENT COMPANY ACT OF 1940
Release No. 12863, Dec. 1, 1982

NOTICE IS HEREBY GIVEN that Union-Investment-Gesellschaft m.b.h. ("Union-Investment" or "Applicant"), a West German management company, filed an application on behalf of Unifonds, a West German mutual fund, on August 5, 1980, and an amendment thereto on October 8, 1982, for an order of the Commission pursuant to Section 7(d) of the Investment Company Act of 1940 ("Act") permitting registration of the Applicant under the Act so that it may sell Unifonds shares in the United States, and pursuant to Section 6(c) of the Act granting exemptions from [various provisions of the Act]

. . .

According to the application, Unifonds is one of the three largest mutual funds in West Germany, having over $900 million in assets comprised of cash and a diversified portfolio made up solely of securities of West German issuers that are listed or traded on West German stock exchanges. Under West German law, Unifonds is a "separate estate"; it has no legal personality or existence. It is an unincorporated collection of assets. It has no employees, cannot transact business, and can neither sue nor be sued. Union-Investment is one of West Germany's oldest management companies. It advises and administers five separate funds, one of which is Unifonds. Consequently, Union-Investment is the entity that issues shares in Unifonds, and has filed the application on its behalf.

According to the application, Union-Investment is owned by 40 shareholder banks whose liability as owners is limited to the amount of their respective contributions. Applicant states that these banks, not the shareholders of Unifonds, vote on matters concerning Union-Investment, including the election of its Aufsichtsrat ("Board of Supervisors").

. . .

A. Registration of Applicant Under the Act to Allow Sale of Unifonds Shares in the United States.

Section 7(d) of the Act prohibits foreign investment companies from making a public offering in the United States unless they first receive an order of the Commission based upon a finding that "by reason of special circumstances or arrangements, it is both legally and practically feasible effectively to enforce the provisions of [the Act] against such company and that the issuance of such order is otherwise consistent with the public interest and the protection of investors." Rule 7d-1 sets forth for Canadian management investment companies certain conditions and arrangements for compliance with the standard of enforceability stated in Section 7(d). Those conditions and arrangements have also, in the past, been used as guidelines for non-Canadian investment companies wishing to sell their shares in the United States although strict conformity with Rule 7d-1 is not a requirement. Rule 7d-1 provides that "conditions and arrangements proposed by investment companies organized under the laws of other countries will be considered by the Commission in light of the special circumstances and local laws involved in each case."

. . .

Applicant states that, because of the reasons outlined below, it has difficulties complying with many of the provisions of Rule 7d-1 because of the West German regulatory system and West German business practices, but that the operation of West German law and the conditions and arrangements to which it has consented in its application, together with the application of those provisions of the Act from which it does not request exemption, provide the means for it to meet the enforceability standard of Section 7(d).

. . .

Applicant declares that its corporate executives and Unifonds' distributor, custodian and accountant under West German law are not permitted to be United States citizens or residents. Furthermore, Union-Investment states that under West German business practice those persons have no personal liability toward fund shareholders. Therefore, such persons and entities will not enter into any agreements to comply with the Act, nor will they consent to the jurisdiction of United States courts and appoint agents for service of process here. However, Union-Investment, which is liable to the shareholders of Unifonds under West German law, has undertaken to comply with those provisions of the Act from which it is not exempted, and will consent to jurisdiction of United States courts and will appoint an agent for service of process. Also, Union-Investment has agreed that the Commission may revoke any order issued on this application in the event of a violation of such order. In addition, according to Applicant, all of Unifonds' assets must be held in West Germany in Unifonds' custodian bank or, for some of its cash deposits, in Union-Investment's shareholder banks. Under West German law, all sales transactions must take place at Unifonds' custodian bank in Frankfurt. Thus, in many cases, the United States courts will not have jurisdiction over the persons associated with Union-Investment, Unifonds' assets or the transactions in Unifonds shares.

Moreover, it may be difficult for the Commission or a shareholder to enforce an injunction or bring a criminal action against the European executives of Union-Investment or to attach, liquidate or distribute any of the assets of Union-Investment or Unifonds, all of which will be kept in West Germany. The assets can be liquidated and distributed according to West German law only, and jurisdiction over any distribution lies solely in the courts in Frankfurt. Union-Investment has, however, attempted to compensate for the unavailability of assets in the United States with which to satisfy a judgment by undertaking to arrange for and maintain, in a form satisfactory to the staff of the Commission, an irrevocable letter of credit in an initial amount of $1 million, and thereafter in an amount equal to five percent of the value of Unifonds shares then outstanding in the United States, with the amount of the letter of credit to be adjusted monthly in order to maintain such five percent relationship. This letter of credit will be drafted and issued so as to be payable, effectively, to any person (or persons) who has obtained a judgment of a United States court against Union-Investment for violation of the securities laws of the United States, provided that Union-Investment has refused to satisfy such judgment after demand for satisfaction. Finally, according to

Applicant, it will not be possible to inspect or audit the books and records of either Union-Investment or Unifonds, as the originals of such items will be kept in West Germany and Union-Investment asserts that it would be too expensive to ship duplicates to this country.

Applicant asserts that, despite its inability to comply with many of the provisions of Rule 7d-1, the special circumstances of this case warrant permitting Union-Investment to register here. It asserts that West Germany has an extensive system of regulation with oversight of the activities of management companies by each fund's respective custodian bank and by the Bundesaufsichtsamt fuer das Kreditwesen ("BAK") – the agency in West Germany that regulates investment companies operating there. In addition, Applicant states that West German law imposes a fiduciary duty upon managers of an investment company to operate the fund on behalf of the fund's shareholders. Applicant submits that the conditions and arrangements discussed herein, which have been agreed to as prerequisites for obtaining a Commission order under Section 7(d), together with the protections afforded by the West German regulatory system, meet the standard of enforceability enunciated in Section 7(d). Applicant further submits that the policies of facilitating the international flow of capital and practicing reciprocity with friendly nations argue for granting permission to Union-Investment to register here.

In order to facilitate granting its requested order under Section 7(d) of the Act, Union-Investment has made certain undertakings and agreed to certain conditions being imposed in such order. Specifically, Union-Investment has undertaken that, with respect to the financial statements of Unifonds, those statements will meet the requirements of Regulation S-X (except for such differences that have been agreed upon by representatives of the Commission's staff and Applicant), despite the fact that such statements filed with the Commission and sent to United States investors will be prepared in accordance with West German generally accepted accounting principles. Such financial statements will reconcile the differences between West German accounting principles and generally accepted accounting principles in the United States. Union-Investment has also agreed that such financial statements will be audited on a basis that substantially complies with United States generally accepted auditing standards, and that it will engage United States independent public accountants for the purpose of consulting with its independent West German accountants as to such standards. Such financial statements will contain an audit report that is substantially equivalent to an audit report that would be issued by an independent public accountant in the United States under similar circumstances, and will not be prepared on a basis that would result in a qualification in the accountant's report other than qualifications which are beyond the control of Union-Investment to cure.

Applicant has also undertaken that it will register Unifonds as an investment company under the Act, that it will register Unifonds shares sold to United States investors under the Securities Act of 1933 ("1933 Act") and will file all appropriate disclosure documents prepared in the prescribed manner, with the exception that Union-Investment will report the aggregate amount of remuneration paid to its management and the aggregate amount of brokerage fees paid to its shareholder banks, and provided that Union-Investment will be permitted to discuss with the staff the possible modification or inapplicability of certain items in the disclosure forms.

. . .

b. Request for Exemptions from the Provisions of Certain Sections of the Act.

Pursuant to Section 6(c) of the Act, Applicant has requested exemptive relief from many provisions of the Act in order to accommodate Unifonds' status as a registered investment company under the Act with West German law and business practices. Such exemptive requests are summarized below.

Section 6(c) provides that the Commission may exempt any person from the provisions of the Act if and to the extent that such exemption is necessary or appropriate in the public interest and consistent with the protection of investors and the purposes fairly intended by the policy and provisions of the Act.

Applicant has requested exemption from Sections 30(a) and 30(d) in order to be able to prepare and file its required periodic Commission and shareholder reports with such modifications as discussed above.

. . .

Applicant represents that it needs an exemption from the bonding requirements of Section 17(g) of the Act and Rule 17g-1 thereunder because BAK policy would prohibit it from obtaining a bond to protect United States investors unless it provided bonding protection for all Unifonds' shareholders, which, it further represents, would put Applicant at a competitive disadvantage with other West German investment companies. As a condition to granting this exemption, Union-Investment consents to disclose to its United States investors that, although those investors are protected under West German Law against acts of theft or embezzlement of Unifonds' assets, Union-Investment's employees are not bonded, and there is no assurance that Union-Investment's assets will be adequate to cover a loss.

. . .

Applicant states that owing to the structure of the West German investment company industry and the provisions of West German law, which do not embody the concept of independent directors, it needs an exemption from those provisions of the Act dealing with disinterested directors: Sections 10(a), (b) and (g); 15(c) and 32(a). . . . Applicant argues that West German law provides substitute safeguards for these provisions. With respect to Section 10(a), Applicant represents that West German law imposes a duty on management to act in the interest of Unifonds' shareholders, and it provides for independent review of management by Unifonds' custodian bank and by the BAK, both of which may bring suit against Union-Investment for management's failure to so act. The BAK may also dismiss a manager who is unfit professionally or who violates laws regulating West German investment companies. Applicant argues that the functions of Sections 10(b) and (g), to prevent conflicts of interest, are fulfilled by provisions of West German law that prohibit members of the Advisory Board and the Board of Supervisors from participating in the daily decisions concerning allocation of brokerage and the investment of assets for Unifonds.

. . .

The application also requests exemptive relief so that Applicant may engage in certain affiliated transactions which are typical of West German business practices. Applicant requests exemptions from Sections 10(f) and 17(a), (b) and (e)(2) to be able to continue to use its shareholder banks as depositary banks and as principal underwriters and brokers, and to buy securities from and sell securities to such banks and members of its Advisory Board. Applicant represents that, instead of prohibiting affiliated transactions, West German law prohibits any borrowing of fund assets by anyone except to the extent that cash is deposited in shareholder banks. It also prohibits members of a Board of Supervisors and Board of Managers from buying property from or selling property to a fund. Applicant states that conflicts of interest are also prevented by a prohibition against participation in daily investment decisions by members of the Board of Supervisors and the Advisory Board, and by limitations on the terms of all transactions, rather than the proscription of affiliated transactions. For example, Applicant states that, although the purchase of securities from and sale of securities to affiliates, including shareholder banks, is permitted by West German law, restrictions are placed on the price and type of security that may be bought or sold. Applicant represents that transactions which meet such restrictions would meet the standard of Section 17(b).

Applicant states that, to the extent its shareholder banks serve as depositories for Unifonds' cash, there may be non-compliance with Section 17(a)(3). It represents, however, that West German law prohibits the participation of the members of the Board of Supervisors in any decision concerning the allocation of cash deposits and requires Unifonds' fund manager to make such allocations for the benefit of Unifonds' shareholders.

. . .

Finally, Applicant requests an exemption from Section 17(f) of the Act. Applicant represents that, under West German law, Union-Investment must keep its assets in West Germany in a West German custodian bank, which plays a substantial regulatory role. Applicant further represents that, while Unifonds' custodian bank is not regulated by U.S. laws, it is regulated pursuant to the German Banking Act, and West German law provides protections equivalent to those provided by Section 17(f) and the rules thereunder by requiring that (1) the custodian bank keep Unifonds' assets in a restricted account where they cannot be pledged, assigned, encumbered or transferred except for the account of Unifonds; (2) the BAK approve the selection of the custodian bank and remove it if it is unqualified to perform its regulatory functions; (3) the custodian bank keep vouchers reflecting the value, date, object of and parties to each transaction in Unifonds' account; (4) the BAK or Bundesbank (the West German banking regulatory agency) appoint an auditor to perform a regular audit of the Unifonds account including an examination of its portfolio transactions; (5) Union-Investment be liable to Unifonds for assets stolen or embezzled by any employee, including the four members of its Board of Managers or by Unifonds' fund manager, who are the only five persons with access to Unifonds' assets; and (6) Unifonds' cash deposits be protected against a bank failure by the Deposit Protection Fund.

Therefore, Applicant submits that granting it the exemptive relief it has requested under Section 6(c) of the Act is appropriate in the public interest and consistent with the protection of investors.

. . .

Notes and Questions

1. Should the SEC have allowed Union-Investment to register under 7(d)? Would denial have been justified on national treatment grounds? In the 1960-1973 period, the SEC permitted a number of foreign funds from Canada, Australia, Bermuda, the United Kingdom and South Africa to register, although there have been no further registrations (or applications) since that time. Why were these countries' funds permitted to register? Why do you think there were no applications apart from the one of Union-Investment after the 1970s?

2. Assuming application of U.S. rules effectively precludes foreign funds from registering in the U.S., is that a concern to the United States or to U.S. investors?

3. Note that Regulation S rules for debt securities apply to mutual fund offerings. See 17 C.F.R. §230.903. How does this affect offshore funds? See Chapter 2. Suppose the foreign fund would attract substantial U.S. investor interest, would it have to wait 40 days after its initial offering to permit a U.S. investor to invest? Is this a problem?

4. While this Chapter generally looks at offshore funds, there are also important issues relating to the custody of foreign securities of U.S. funds. Section 17(f) of the Investment Company Act generally permits a U.S. fund to maintain its assets only in custody of a U.S. bank and its foreign branches, a member of a U.S. securities exchange, the fund itself, or a U.S. securities depository, e.g. DTC. In 1984, the SEC adopted rule 17f-5 which expanded the foreign custody arrangements available to funds by permitting them to maintain their assets with an "eligible foreign custodian," which included a foreign bank with more than $200 million in equity and a foreign securities depository that operates either the central system for the handling of securities in that country or a transnational system, e.g. Euroclear. The rule, however, imposed detailed obligations on a fund's board of directors with respect to placing assets in a foreign country and the selection of the foreign custodian.

These rules were changed in 1997, effective June 1998. Securities and Exchange Commission, Custody of Investment Company Assets Outside the United States, Final Rule, 62 Federal Register 26293, May 16, 1997. The amendments expanded the class of foreign banks and securities depositories that may serve as custodians of fund assets by eliminating capital requirements that would otherwise block the selection of a suitable custodian without seeking relief from the Commission. The amended rule required instead that the selection of a foreign custodian be based on whether the fund's assets will be subject to reasonable care by the custodian, after considering all relevant factors, including the custodian's financial strength, its practices and procedures, and internal controls. The "reasonable care" standard raises a host of questions, probably the most important of which is whether reasonableness should be based on local or U.S. practices. Thus, would it be reasonable for Indian custodians to post stock certificates endorsed and ready for transfer to the local registrar by mail, as was the case before a large fraud occurred? D. Platt, *Investing Abroad: New Lessons from Rule 17f-5,* Security Industry News, September 8, 1997.

The amendments also eliminated the requirement that the board consider "prevailing country risks" in choosing a custodian on the grounds that these risks were appropriately considered when investing not in making custody decisions. Once the decision is made to invest in a country, given that some securities can only be held in custody in the country of the investment, such country risk was unavoidable.

Finally, the amendments permitted fund directors to play an oversight role with respect to the custody of fund assets overseas by permitting the board to delegate its duties to select and monitor foreign custodians to others, e.g. a global bank custodian.

In some countries, there is a compulsory depository for local shares. Mutual funds have argued that custodians must make a reasonable care determination for such compulsory depositories as part of their responsibility to assess reasonable care of all depositories. Custodians, on the other hand, have argued that they often do not have sufficient information to do so because the depositories may be government or quasi-government agencies that do not disclose the needed information, and because such a determination is irrelevant since such depositories are compulsory. The custodians argue that the use of compulsory depositories is entailed in the decision of a fund to invest in a particular country. The SEC came down on the side of the funds, but the issue was still controversial. C. Kentouris, *Funds Can Require Custodians to Select Foreign Custodians,* Securities Industry News, March 9, 1998. The effective date of the rule was extended to February 1, 1999.

In April 1999, the Commission proposed to further amend rule 17f-5 and to enact a new rule 17f-7, as a result of learning that its 1997 rules continued to present problems for the use of foreign securities depositories. Release No. IC-23815, April 29, 1999. Bank custodians refused to accept delegated responsibility to make findings regarding funds' use of most foreign securities depositories. As a result, in May 1998 the Commission suspended the compliance date for many of the 1997 rule changes. Proposed rule 17f-7 was adopted on April 27, 2000, Release No. IC-24424. The Rule eliminates the requirements that certain findings be made by the fund board, its investment adviser or global custodian, and that certain specified terms appear in depository rules for participants. Instead, the Rule establishes certain standards for foreign securities depositories eligible to be used by funds, and requires the global custodian to furnish a fund with a risk analysis of the foreign depository, through exercising reasonable care. Decisions to maintain assets with a depository are to be made by the fund and its adviser and not by the custodian.

a.   MIRROR FUNDS

The SEC recognizes that it may be too burdensome for a foreign mutual fund company to offer the same level of investor protection as a U.S. mutual fund and that it may be impossible for a foreign investment company to restructure its fund so that it complies with U.S. laws and regulations while complying with the laws and regulations in its home country. As an alternative, the SEC has recommended that foreign fund advisers organize mirror funds in the U.S. and then register these mirror funds to offer shares to U.S. investors.* A mirror fund is a separate U.S.-organized company that invests in the same foreign securities in which the foreign fund invests.

The establishment of mirror funds has been employed widely by foreign investment companies. As of March 1992, 269 foreign investment advisers representing 36 countries had registered in the United States under the Investment Advisers Act of 1940. *Protecting Investors: A Half-Century of Investment Company Regulation*, SEC Staff Report (Extra Edition) Fed. Sec. L. Rep. (CCH) No. 1504 (May 29, 1992) at 197 n.38, many of which are believed to be mirror funds. However, it appears that many foreign funds are reluctant to undertake the establishment of mirror funds due to the high additional costs and losses in economies of scale that would result from operating separately from the foreign investment company.

In addition, a mirror fund is generally unable to make representations about the previous history of success that the overseas foreign investment company may have had prior to the mirror fund's organization. However, the SEC has ruled that during the first year of a U.S. mirror fund's organization, the mirror's prospectus may include information about the recent performance of its non-U.S. mirror. Growth Stock Outlook Trust, Inc., SEC No-Action Letter (Apr. 15, 1986).

The SEC has approved the use of "cloning" technology in connection with mirror funds, as described below.

BANQUE INDOSUEZ LUXEMBOURG.
SECURITIES AND EXCHANGE COMMISSION
Response of the Office of Chief Counsel, Division of Investment
Management, Dec. 10, 1996

BISL is a Luxembourg bank that has developed software designed to facilitate the management and operation of legally distinct "mirror" portfolios by a single investment adviser ("cloning"). In the cloning process, separate funds having identical or substantially similar investment policies are linked in a group of cloned portfolios with a common investment adviser and common custodian/administrator ("cloned funds"). Cloning is conducted through software operating on the premises of a fund's custodian.

.   .   .

You state that the cloning process consists of two core functions -- one that facilitates "bunched" trades among the cloned funds and one

---

* See Applications of Foreign Investment Companies Filed Pursuant to Section 7(d) of the Investment Company Act of 1940, 49 Federal Register 55, 55-56 (1984) (to be codified at 17 C.F.R. pt. 271) (proposed Jan. 3, 1984).

that rebalances cloned funds that have experienced different cash flows. The cloning software facilitates aggregated buy and sell orders when a group of cloned funds has net inflows or outflows of capital on an aggregate basis or in response to the adviser's investment decisions. You state that the software's "bunching" function can be modified to refrain from aggregating orders to the extent legally necessary or otherwise deemed advisable by the investment adviser.

You state that the rebalancing function keeps cloned funds in parallel, notwithstanding the fact that the individual funds will inevitably experience different inflows or outflows of capital on any given trading day. This is accomplished by causing a fund with net sales at the end of the day to use the cash received from its net sales to purchase a "strip" of the portfolio of a fund that had net redemptions on the same day. The fund with net redemptions would then use this cash to satisfy its redemptions. You state that BISL as the funds' custodian will conduct the rebalancing process through book-entry transactions between the cloned funds' positions. To the extent that securities are held by subcustodians, you indicate that BISL employs an omnibus arrangement pursuant to which securities are maintained in a single account at each sub-custodian in the name of BISL on behalf of its customers.

Analysis

The use by U.S. registered investment companies of BISL's cloning process raises a number of issues under the Investment Company Act, which are addressed below. First, the cloning program could itself be deemed an "investment company" under Section 3(a) of the Investment Company Act. Second, the aggregation of orders by BISL on behalf of U.S. registered funds and other clients participating in the cloning program may raise joint transaction issues under Section 17(d). Finally, BISL's role as custodian of a cloned fund group may raise an issue under Section 17(f) of the Act.

Section 3(a)

Certain investment advisory programs that are designed to provide substantially identical investment advice to individual clients may be subject to regulation as investment companies. Section 3(a)(1) of the Investment Company Act defines "investment company" generally to include any "issuer" which is engaged primarily in the business of investing, reinvesting, or trading in securities. The definition of "issuer" includes any organized group of persons, whether or not incorporated, that issues or proposes to issue any security. An investment advisory program could be considered to be an issuer because the client accounts in the program, taken together, could be considered to be an organized group of persons. Investors in the program could be viewed as purchasing securities in the form of investment contracts. If an investment advisory program is deemed to be an "issuer," it also would be deemed to be an investment company because it is engaged in the business of investing, reinvesting, or trading in securities.

In determining whether an investment advisory program should be regulated as an investment company, the staff generally would consider whether the treatment received by clients in the program is sufficiently individualized to distinguish it from the fungible investment that arises from participation in an investment company. You note that participants in the cloning program, including registered investment companies, will maintain individualized characteristics, such as individualized investment policies. You represent in this regard that the cloning software can be modified to provide for individualized treatment of participating funds, by permitting any cloned fund to "opt out" of a transaction that would cause the fund to violate an investment restriction. You further represent that the assets of registered investment companies and other participants in the cloning program will not be pooled, but will be recorded separately on BISL's books, and that each participant will retain individualized ownership of securities and funds. For these reasons, you maintain that a group of cloned funds involving registered investment companies and other institutional investors would not constitute an "investment company" within the meaning of Section 3(a) of the Investment Company Act.

Section 17(d)

Section 17(d) of the Investment Company Act provides that the Commission may adopt rules restricting participation by a registered investment company in joint transactions with affiliated persons, or with affiliated persons of affiliated persons, for the purpose of preventing or limiting participation by such company on a basis different from or less advantageous than that of any other participant. Rule 17d-1 generally prohibits an affiliated person of a fund (which includes its adviser), or an affiliated person of such person, from participating in, or effecting any transaction in connection with, any "joint enterprise or other joint arrangement or profit-sharing plan" in which such fund is a participant unless the Commission grants an exemptive order. The rule defines "joint enterprise or other joint arrangement or profit-sharing plan" broadly to include any type of plan or arrangement whereby a fund and an affiliated person have a joint and several participation in, or share in the profits of, such enterprise. In determining whether to grant an exemptive order, the rule requires the Commission to consider whether the participation by the fund is on a basis different from, or less advantageous than, that of other participants.

Your letter raises issues under Section 17(d) because BISL proposes to aggregate orders on behalf of U.S. registered funds and other clients participating in the cloning program that may be affiliated persons of the registered funds. The staff has taken the position that the mere aggregation of orders for advisory clients, including a registered fund, does not violate Section 17(d) when registered funds participate on terms no less advantageous than those of any other participant. If a portfolio manager allocates trades in such a way as to disadvantage a registered investment company, however, a joint enterprise or arrangement raising Section 17(d) concerns may result.

You assert that cloning is consistent with Section 17(d) and Rule 17d-1 because of the equality of the terms on which all members of a cloned group participate in any transaction initiated by the cloning software. You represent that the aggregation function of the cloning program is substantially identical to the system of aggregating orders described in the SMC Capital letter and that, therefore, all members of the cloned fund group would participate in portfolio transactions on equal terms.

. . .

Conclusion

We would not recommend that the Commission take enforcement action[.]

. . .

b.   MASTER/FEEDER FUNDS

Another possible technique for offering the same or similar funds to both U.S. and foreign investors is the master/feeder fund structure. This is a multi-tiered structure, where feeder funds with substantially identical investment objectives pool their assets by investing in a single portfolio (master fund), as illustrated in the diagram A below.

Diagram A

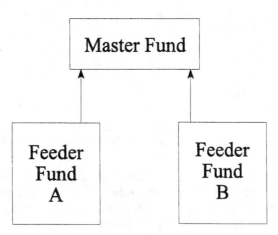

Feeder funds invest only in the master fund and all investment activity for the portfolio within the master/feeder fund structure takes place at the master fund level. The master fund management fees are allocated to the feeder funds. The master fund must adopt the most restrictive portfolio investment limitations imposed by regulation applicable to the feeder funds. Thus, if one of the feeder funds is a U.S. mutual fund, the master must adhere to '40 Act compliance. See D. Smith, *Master/Feeder Funds*, The Global Navigator, State Street Bank & Trust Company, July 1996.

The use of master/feeder funds can encounter problems in complying with the regulation of multiple jurisdictions, as set forth below.

G. KENYON, GLOBALIZATION OF THE MUTUAL FUNDS INDUSTRY—THE U.S. PERSPECTIVE

29 S&P's Review of Securities & Commodities Regulation 61 (1996)

. . .

Although international master/feeder structures are now possible under U.S. law, the theoretical possibilities presently exceed the practical applications. To date, international master/feeder structures that include registered mutual funds qualified for sale in the United States generally have restricted their offshore sales to private placements. In practice, it has proven difficult to reconcile the SEC's requirements, described above, with those imposed by other regulatory bodies as a pre-condition to making public offerings in their respective jurisdictions. Probably the most significant example is the interplay between the U.S. requirements described above and the requirements applicable to funds that qualify under the UCITS Directive, the legislation that facilitates pan-European public offerings within the member states of the European Union. The UCITS Directive currently precludes the use of master/feeder structures. Although legislation has been under consideration that would permit a UCITS to adopt a master/feeder structure, this legislation would require the use of a master fund that was itself a UCITS. Because a UCITS must necessarily be organized in a member state of the European Union, this requirement would be in direct opposition to the U.S. requirement that the master fund be organized under U.S. law.

. . .

The laws of the United States and other major jurisdictions place certain constraints on a master fund's investment program as well as its legal structure. Because a master/feeder feed complex employs a common investment portfolio that must conform with all applicable regulatory requirements, the investment program offered to all investors must comply with the strictest requirement to which any investor is subject. This consequence is sometimes referred to as the "highest common denominator" effect.

For example, a U.S. registered mutual fund is subject to restrictions on its ability to borrow or otherwise leverage its portfolio, and these restrictions have been interpreted by the SEC in a manner that has important implications for the ability of a fund to pursue certain investment strategies. Because of the common investment portfolio, the investment program of all non-U.S. investors would also be subject to this requirement.

Even where the regulatory regimes of several jurisdictions follow consistent themes, the "highest common denominator effect" can be significant. For example, a hypothetical master fund able to qualify under the laws of both the United States and the European Union would be restricted from having more than 10 percent of its assets invested in securities that were not traded on a 'regulated market,' as required by the UCITS Directive, and restricted from having more than 15 percent of its assets in illiquid securities (i.e. securities that are not readily marketable), as required by the SEC. While there is substantial overlap between the two restrictions, many securities would be covered by one restriction and not by the other.

Another issue of considerable importance to fund sponsors is the ability of feeder funds to advertise the track record of their master fund, or of their master fund's predecessor, or to assume such performance as their own for ongoing reporting purposes. The SEC staff has stated that a newly created feeder fund can assume the performance history of its master fund. The staff has also stated that where an existing fund becomes a feeder fund by exchanging its assets for shares of an operating master fund and, after such a reorganization, the new feeder fund resembles its master fund more closely than it resembles its predecessor fund, the new feeder fund should assume the adjusted performance data of the master fund for periods prior to the reorganization. However, the no-action letters described above each involved the ability of a U.S. registered investment company to assume the track record of another U.S. registered investment company. It is not clear that the SEC staff would take the same position in the context of an international master/feeder complex (e.g. one in which a fund that has compiled a favorable track record in Europe seeks to contribute its assets to a U.S. master fund). The staff has traditionally been quite restrictive in permitting mutual funds to advertise the performance of other accounts managed by the same investment adviser. Moreover, the National Association of Securities Dealers, which has substantive review authority over mutual fund advertisements used by any U.S. broker-dealer, generally takes the position that the use of past performance information from related accounts in marketing and sales literature is impermissible.

. . .

Notes and Questions

1.   How would you compare the costs and benefits of using a mirror fund, with cloning technology, to using a master/feeder structure? Which is preferable?

2.   Do the availability of mirror fund and master/feeder funds make it relatively unimportant whether there are regulatory obstacles to foreign funds selling shares to investors in the United States?

3.   Restrictions on entry by offshore mutual funds is not a policy unique to the United States. Traditionally, the Japanese investment trust markets remained virtually closed to U.S. investment advisers, making it impossible to use the mirror fund approach. In early 1995, however, the United States and Japan reached an agreement to open up the Japanese market. Measures by the Government of the U.S. and the Government of Japan Regarding Financial Services, 34 International Legal Materials 617 (1995).

4.   A key part of setting up an offshore fund is the selection of the domicile. Low taxes and the economic and political environment are important factors, as they are for offshore banking centers. The domiciles of choice close to the United States have been the Bahamas, Bermuda, the Cayman Islands, and Curacao. See generally, J. Press, *Critical Accounting, Tax and System Issues,* in Hedge Funds, eds. J. Lederman and R. Klein 199 (1995). In Europe, Luxembourg and Dublin have been the leaders. In mid-1995, funds domiciled in Luxembourg exceeded $341.6 billion. *Funds Continue to Grow,* Investors Chronicle, May 26, 1995.

5.   Offshore funds must make sure they are truly offshore to escape regulation. The SEC has generally granted no-action relief to offshore funds that provide administrative support from the U.S. as long as the funds' principal administrative offices are outside the U.S.   U.S. connections are also an important tax consideration, discussed below.

c.   THE PRIVATE FUND EXEMPTION: SECTION 3(c)(1) AND THE TOUCHE REMNANT DOCTRINE

Another possibility to consider for foreign funds is use of the private fund exemption under Section 3(c)(1) of the 1940 Act.   Originally emerging as part of an SEC No-Action Letter to Touche, Remnant & Co.,*

---

*   Touche, Remnant & Co., SEC No-Action Letter, [1984-1985 Transfer Binder] Fed. Sec. L. Rep. (CCH) 77,810, at 79,141 (July 27, 1984). The 1940 Act excludes from its coverage a company that has no more than 100 security holders and is neither making nor plans to make a public offering of its securities, 15 U.S.C. 80a-3(c)(1), because the 1940 Act is limited to companies in which there is "a significant public interest." H.R. Rep. No. 2337.

Section 3(c)(1), permits an exemption from Section 7(d) and the 1940 Act to any issuer of securities, as long as the entity does not offer the shares to the public and the shares are beneficially owned by no more than 100 U.S. residents.

For a foreign investment company to comply with the 100 person beneficial ownership provision of §3(c)(1), before it commences a U.S. offer, it must account for all shareholders of the specific fund, including pre-existing U.S. resident shareholders. To prevent large groups of investors from investing as one entity for the purpose of circumventing the 100 beneficial owner exemption, the 1940 Act stipulates that for purposes of determination of a fund's number of investors, all investors in an entity formed for the sole purpose of investing in a fund will be counted individually, rather than as a single entity.

Due to the restrictive nature of the 100 beneficial owner limit of Section 3(c)(1), many foreign investment companies will either refuse to offer their shares in the U.S. under §3(c)(1) or will make it very difficult for U.S. investors to buy shares in their funds. Such actions are taken by foreign investment companies in fear that one additional U.S. beneficial owner would set them over the limit and cause them to be no longer exempt from the Act. How do changes in fund ownership subsequent to the initial private offering affect compliance with the exemption? Consider the following SEC no-action letter.

INVESTMENT FUNDS INSTITUTE OF CANADA
SECURITIES AND EXCHANGE COMMISSION
Response of the Office of Chief Counsel, Division of Investment
Management, Mar. 4, 1996

The Investment Funds Institute of Canada ("IFIC") is the national association of the Canadian investment fund industry. You state that the overwhelming majority of IFIC members do not offer or sell their shares in the United States, although some funds offer and sell their securities in private placements to not more than 100 U.S. investors. You state that IFIC has requested no-action relief on behalf of its members organized under the laws of Canada because some of those members are concerned that they may inadvertently become subject to the Investment Company Act through the relocation of Canadian securityholders to the United States. Specifically, IFIC seeks assurance that the staff would not recommend enforcement action to the Commission under Section 7(d) if a Canadian fund that is not registered under the Investment Company Act has more than 100 U.S. residents as securityholders, as long as the 100 investor limit is exceeded because securityholders who purchased their securities while residing outside the United States subsequently relocate to the United States.

· · ·

In applying the Touche Remnant position, the Division staff has indicated that once a foreign investment company uses U.S. jurisdictional means in connection with a private offering of its securities in the United States, the issuer must count all U.S. residents that beneficially own its securities for purposes of determining compliance with the 100 U.S. securityholder limit. Thus, the position contemplates that issuers count toward this limit both beneficial owners of securities privately placed in the United States, as well as U.S. residents who beneficially own securities issued and acquired outside the United States. A foreign investment company whose securities are beneficially owned by more than 100 U.S. residents is effectively prevented from privately placing securities in the United States, even though some or all of the U.S. holders may have acquired their securities outside the United States. In addition, a foreign investment company that has offered its securities privately to 100 or fewer U.S. investors in reliance on the Touche Remnant position would become subject to regulation under the Investment Company Act if it subsequently exceeded the 100 investor limit as a result of the relocation of foreign securityholders to the United States or purchases of the fund's securities by U.S. residents in secondary market transactions outside the United States. This application of the Touche Remnant position has been criticized as unfairly subjecting a foreign investment company to U.S. regulation solely as a result of the actions of investors who are outside the control of the investment company.

Discussion

You maintain that under the Touche Remnant position as applied by the staff, the relocation of Canadian securityholders from Canada to the United States places Canadian funds that have conducted private placements of their securities in the United States, or that intend to conduct such private placements, in a difficult position. To avoid the application of Section 7(d), as interpreted by the Touche Remnant position, the funds may be required to cause investors who have become U.S. residents to terminate their investment in the funds through mandatory redemptions, transfers or otherwise. You represent, however, that many Canadian funds have not anticipated the regulatory concern created by the presence of U.S. resident securityholders. Consequently, under the governing documents of many Canadian funds, mandatory redemptions or transfers are not permitted. Moreover, even if such redemptions or transfers are permitted, a fund may be unaware of the change in residence of its shareholders for some time, and would be subject to regulation under the Investment Company Act. You contend that funds should not be required to amend their governing documents and make mandatory redemptions simply because of the independent actions of their shareholders.

You note that the funds could seek an order from the Commission under Section 7(d) allowing them to register under the Investment

Company Act. You maintain, however, that Section 7(d) effectively requires a foreign investment company to structure itself and operate in a manner identical to that of a U.S. investment company. You point out that the staff has recognized that many foreign investment companies do not consider registration to be a viable option, because foreign investment companies are structured to comply with regulatory systems that differ greatly from the Investment Company Act.

You propose that the Division modify the scope of the Touche Remnant position with respect to the definition of who must be counted toward the 100 U.S. investor limit. Specifically, you propose that for purposes of counting U.S. resident securityholders under the Touche Remnant position, foreign funds be permitted to distinguish between U.S. resident beneficial owners of securities purchased in private offerings in the United States (and any subsequent U.S. resident transferees of such securities) ("Private Offering Holders"), and U.S. resident beneficial owners who were not U.S. residents when they purchased their securities (and subsequent U.S. resident transferees of such securities) ("Non-U.S. Holders"). You propose that a foreign fund should have to count only the private Offering Holders towards the 100 beneficial owner limit. Under your proposal, a Canadian fund could not effect a private placement of securities to U.S. investors unless, at the conclusion of the private placement, the total number of private Offering Holders of the fund's securities does not exceed 100. The fund would also have to monitor the number of Private Offering Holders on a ongoing basis to ensure that the number does not exceed 100.

You represent that, with respect to Non-U.S. Holders, the funds' activities would be limited to continuing to provide the following services: (1) the mailing of securityholder reports, account statements, proxy statements and other materials that are required to be provided by Canadian provincial law and the funds' governing documents; (2) processing of redemptions and payment of dividends and distributions; (3) processing of transfers of ownership; and (4) the issuance of securities pursuant to a dividend reinvestment plan. You further represent that Non-U.S. Holders who purchase additional securities from a Canadian fund would have to be counted as Private Offering Holders of the fund. Non-U.S. Holders would not be permitted to exchange securities among funds within the same Canadian fund complex.

You assert that your proposal is consistent with the policy considerations underlying the Touche Remnant position, because foreign funds relying on this position, by the limited nature of their activity in the United States, would have sought no competitive advantage over domestic funds. You also maintain that these funds should not create significant regulatory concerns because investors who purchase securities of foreign funds outside the United States do so in reliance on the investor protections afforded under foreign law and not the Investment Company Act. Moreover, you argue that foreign investors who become United States residents after purchasing fund securities abroad do not have a reasonable expectation that changing their residence would subject a foreign fund to regulation under the Investment Company Act.

The legislative history of the Investment Company Act indicates that, despite Section 7(d), Congress anticipated that there would be some "leakage" of foreign fund securities into the United States. This legislative history appears to support the view that a valid U.S. regulatory interest in a foreign fund would not arise simply because foreign purchasers of securities of a foreign fund subsequently relocate to the United States. Regulatory concern under the Investment Company Act is, in our view, more appropriately triggered by activities undertaken by or on behalf of a foreign investment company, rather than by activities of the company's securityholders that occur outside the influence of the company or its affiliates.

We would not recommend enforcement action to the Commission under the Investment Company Act if a fund organized outside the United States that is not registered under the Investment Company Act permits more than 100 U.S. residents to remain beneficial owners of the fund's securities, if

(1) the fund has not publicly offered or sold its securities in the United States;

(2) the fund and its agents or affiliates have not engaged in activities that could reasonably be expected, or are intended, to condition the U.S. market with respect to the fund's securities, such as placing an advertisement in a U.S. publication;

(3) the fund and its agents or affiliates have not engaged in activities that could reasonably be expected, or are intended, to facilitate secondary market trading in the United States with respect to the fund's securities;

(4) the fund and its agents or affiliates have not knowingly engaged in a deliberate marketing strategy, adopted directly by the fund's manager or other entity responsible for the business and affairs of the fund, that is calculated to result in the sale of securities to foreign investors who are relocating to the United States;

(5) the 100 U.S. investor limit is exceeded solely because Non-U.S. Holders (i.e., beneficial owners who purchased their securities while residing outside the United States) have relocated to the United States; and

(6) the fund's activities with respect to Non-U.S. Holders are limited to providing the following services: (a) the mailing of securityholder reports, account statements, proxy statements and other materials that are required to be provided by foreign law and the fund's governing documents; (b) the processing of redemption requests and payment of dividends and distributions; (c) the mechanical

processing of transfers of ownership; and (d) the issuance of securities pursuant to a dividend reinvestment plan.

. . .

Note

As an alternative to using §3(c)(1), under §3(c)(7) of the Investment Company Act, added by the National Securities Markets Improvement Act of 1996, funds can offer shares to an unlimited number of "qualified" purchasers, generally those with more than $5 million in investments. Under this alternative while fund sales are not restricted to 100 U.S. persons, but all sales must be made to qualified investors, and the fund must comply with detailed rules to assure that only such investors buy the fund. M. Parry and T. Harman, *The New Qualified Purchaser Fund Rules*, 30 Securities & Commodities Regulation 195 (September 24, 1997).

d. HEDGE FUNDS AND THE LONG-TERM CAPITAL MANAGEMENT DEBACLE

The term hedge fund originated in the 1960s to refer to speculative investment vehicles using sophisticated hedging and arbitrage techniques in the corporate equities market. Legally, it is a private fund exempt from the securities laws. This is a fast growing segment of the mutual funds industry, with assets under management close to $600 billion, about 10% of total mutual funds assets of $6 trillion. "Hedge Funds, The Latest Bubble, " Economist, September 2001. The founder of the hedge fund is reported to be Alfred Winslow Jones, a sociologist and business writer. He used short selling and leverage to increase returns with limited downside risk. T. Caldwell, *Introduction: The Model for Superior Performance,* in Hedge Funds, J. Lederman and R. Klein, eds. 1 (1995). Today, these funds engage in a wide variety of speculative activity including derivative and foreign exchange transactions. Their sponsors are financial stars like George Soros who some believe can move markets. While there is a significant amount of money in about 2,500 to 3,000 of such funds, an estimated $300 billion in capital supporting assets of $800 billion to $1 trillion, there is far more equity in public mutual funds, approximately $5 trillion. Report of The President's Working Group on Financial Markets, *Hedge Funds, Leverage, and the Lessons of Long-Term Capital Management* (April 1999) ("Hedge Fund Report"), p. 1.

Hedge funds are generally organized as investment partnerships and interests in them constitute securities. However, hedge funds are offered privately and only to wealthy investors. This enables the funds to avoid regulation under the 1933 and 1934 Securities Acts. In addition, hedge funds have avoided regulation under the 1940 Act by restricting sales to 100 persons. With the 1996 amendments, the funds are now being offered to "qualified investors." See L. Jereski, *A New Breed of Hedge Fund is on the Prowl*, Wall Street Journal, April 29, 1997. In 2000, it was estimated that total U.S. hedge funds had $350 billion in assets compared to $28 billion in European funds. A. Skorecki, *Europe's hedge funds are growing apace*, Financial Times, October 27, 2000. But European funds are growing. In April 2001, Deutsche Bank announced plans to increase its own hedge funds portfolio by $500 million, bringing its total to $4 billion. Financial Times, April 12, 2001.

Long-Term Capital Management, L.P. (LTCM) was an extremely successful hedge fund created in 1994 which by August 1998 had levered around $4.8 billion in capital into more than $125 billion in assets and several times more off-balance sheet. LTCM was a Delaware limited partnership but the fund that it operated, Long-Term Capital Portfolio, L.P. (the Fund), was a Caymans Island partnership that employed a "hub-and-spoke structure to provide a number of different funds.

LTCM's balance sheet leverage ratio of 25 to 1 compared with the average leverage ratio of 2 to 1 for all hedge funds. The fund's returns were over 40% in both 1995 and 1996, far in excess of the average return of about 17% of all hedge funds in these years. LTCM engaged in a huge number of trades on its books, 60,000 as of August 1998. It held positions of over $50 billion in long and short securities, and had futures contracts of over $500 billion, swaps contracts of more than $750 billion, and options and other OTC derivatives of over $150 billion. Hedge Fund Report, pp. 11-12. The fund was run by John Meriwether, a legendary bond trader at Salomon, who had resigned from Salomon after the firm disclosed a series of improper bids at U.S. Treasury note auctions. Meriwether worked closely with a cast of finance stars, including David Mullins Jr., a former Harvard Business Professor and Vice Chairman of the Federal Reserve Board, and two Nobel Prize winners, Robert Merton of the Harvard Business School and Myron Scholes of Black-Scholes model fame. In October 1998, it came to light that LTCM had lost more than 90% of its capital and had been bailed out, with an infusion of $3.6 billion in exchange for 90% of the equity, by a consortium of 14 Wall Street banks who were both lenders to and counterparties of LTCM, and had huge exposures. For example, Chase acknowledged a $3.2 billion exposure, which comes to 13% of its tangible equity, mostly collateralized. See Hedge Fund Report, pp. 10-14. *How the Salesmanship and Brainpower Failed at Long-Term Capital*, Wall St. Journal, November 16, 1998; *Collateral Damage*, Euromoney, November 1998.

LTCM engaged primarily in convergence and relative value trades. "For example, recently issued (so-called on-the-run) U.S. Treasury bonds typically traded at slightly lower yields (higher prices) than comparable maturity but older (so-called off-the-run) Treasury bonds. If the spread were sufficiently wide, LTCM might purchase the off-the-run bond, and sell short the lower-yielding on-the-run bond. With attractive financing rates, this position would make money if held to maturity. The position also stood to make significant profits if the yield spread, and hence the value differential narrowed." Harvard Business School, *Long-Term Capital Management, L.P. (A),* Case N9-200-007 (October 27, 1999) (This case contains an excellent analysis of LTCM's various trades). LTCM would stand to lose, however, if spreads widened.

Consider the following.

WILLIAM J. MCDONOUGH, PRESIDENT, FEDERAL RESERVE BANK OF NEW YORK, STATEMENT BEFORE THE COMMITTEE ON BANKING AND FINANCIAL SERVICES, U.S. HOUSE OF REPRESENTATIVES
October 1, 1998

.   .   .

Background

Long-Term Capital is an investment partnership that was started in 1994. It has many of the characteristics of a "hedge fund" in that it borrows money to leverage its capital and is only available to wealthy investors. The strategy of Long-Term Capital was to use complex mathematical formulas to identify temporary price discrepancies between different interest rates. For example, the firm might notice that the yield on corporate bonds relative to Treasury yields was higher than the range observed in recent years. If Long-Term Capital believed the former relationship would reassert itself, it would buy corporate bonds and sell short Treasury bonds. If the spread narrowed as expected, the firm would profit. If, however, the spread continued to widen, the firm would incur losses. This basic strategy and many complex variations was followed across many interest rate products in the U.S. and many overseas markets as well. The firm was active both in traditional securities markets, and perhaps more importantly, in derivative product markets such as futures, swaps, and options. Anticipating that some positions would move in their favor and some would move against them, the firm relied on diversification across a large number of product and geographic markets. Long-Term Capital proved quite successful at this strategy, generating returns in excess of 40 percent in 1995 and 1996, though somewhat less in 1997.

Perhaps their success went to their heads. Long-Term Capital took on larger and larger positions. They also leveraged their investments at higher levels, returning capital to their investors but not, apparently, reducing risks. We now also know that they took on significant positions in equity markets, through both swap and options contracts. The reputations of the Long-Term Capital partners, as traders and economists, and their initial success, appear to have contributed to so many counterparties' willingness to deal with them.

While hubris may have set them up for a fall, it was the extraordinary events of August in global markets that appears to have tripped them.

On August 17, the Russian government announced an effective devaluation of the ruble and declared a debt moratorium, shocking investor confidence all over the world. Over subsequent days and weeks, equity and debt markets the world over became increasingly volatile, with U.S. equity markets falling and the spreads between U.S. Treasury securities and higher-yielding debt instruments widening sharply. The correction of stock prices was not of exceptional size or concern and, indeed, had been anticipated by a number of astute market observers. However, the abrupt and simultaneous widening of credit spreads globally, for both corporate and emerging-market sovereign debt, was an extraordinary event beyond the expectations of investors and financial intermediaries.

The unusual widening of credit spreads also caused significant losses at Long-Term Capital. As markets around the world moved in the same direction at the same time, the diversification on which Long-Term had previously relied failed them utterly. Instead of offsetting positions, their losses were compounded. At the same time, the volatility in equity markets caused further losses. On September 2, the partners of Long-Term Capital sent their investors a letter acknowledging 52 percent losses on the year through August 31 and that they were seeking an injection of capital to sustain the firm. The existence of this letter became widely known and reported within a few days.

.   .   .

By Friday, September 18, with the efforts to raise new capital still unsuccessful -- and with an increasing number of people now aware of Long-Term's plight because of the efforts to bring in new investors -- events seemed to come to a head. With market conditions particularly unsettled that day, I made a series of calls to senior Wall Street officials to discuss overall market conditions. Let me take a moment to put those calls in context. One important objective of the Federal Reserve is to assure financial stability. Particularly in times of stress, it is essential that the Federal Reserve continue to take the pulse of the market. One way to do that is through candid and open communication with key market participants. Everyone I spoke to that day volunteered concern about the serious effect the deteriorating situation of Long-Term could have on world markets.

Also on the 18th, one of the firms that had been working with Long-Term to raise new capital asked the Long-Term Capital partners if the firm could share the information it had with us. The partners at Long-Term Capital responded that they would prefer to present the information themselves and called me to arrange such a presentation.

After conferring with Chairman Greenspan and Secretary Rubin, we agreed that a visit to Long-Term Capital's offices was needed. A team from the New York Fed, led by Peter Fisher, the head of our Markets Group, and joined by Treasury Assistant Secretary Gary Gensler, met with the Long-Term Capital partners at their offices on Sunday, September 20. During this meeting, we learned the broad outlines of Long-Term Capital's major positions in credit and equity markets, the difficulties they were having in trying to reduce these positions in thin market conditions, their deteriorating funding positions and an estimate of their largest counterparty exposures. The team also came to understand the impact which Long-Term Capital's positions were already having on markets around the world and that the size of these positions was much greater than market participants imagined.

The New York Fed's Judgments

There are several ways that the problems of Long-Term Capital could have been transmitted to cause more widespread financial troubles. Had Long-Term Capital been suddenly put into default, its counterparties would have immediately "closed-out" their positions. If counterparties would have been able to close-out their positions at existing market prices, losses, if any, would have been minimal. However, if many firms had rushed to close-out hundreds of billions of dollars in transactions simultaneously, they would have been unable to liquidate collateral or establish offsetting positions at the previously-existing prices. Markets would have moved sharply and losses would have been exaggerated. Several billion dollars of losses might have been experienced by some of Long-Term Capital's more than 75 counterparties.

These direct effects on Long-Term Capital's counterparties were not our principal concern. While these losses would have been considerable, and would certainly have adversely affected the firms experiencing them, this was not, in itself, a sufficient reason for us to become involved.

Two factors influenced our involvement. First, in the rush of Long-Term Capital's counterparties to close-out their positions, other market participants -- investors who had no dealings with Long-Term Capital -- would have been affected as well. Second, as losses spread to other market participants and Long-Term Capital's counterparties, this would lead to tremendous uncertainty about how far prices would move. Under these circumstances, there was a likelihood that a number of credit and interest rate markets would experience extreme price moves and possibly cease to function for a period of one or more days and maybe longer. This would have caused a vicious cycle: a loss of investor confidence, leading to a rush out of private credits, leading to a further widening of credit spreads, leading to further liquidations of positions, and so on. Most importantly, this would have led to further increases in the cost of capital to American businesses.

Let me be clear: had we not just experienced in August precisely this type of shock to our credit markets, had we not just seen a sudden, worldwide straining of investor confidence, had there not already been underway a flight of capital away from private credit and into Treasury securities, were much of the world not experiencing financial strain, then our judgments about the risks to the American economy of an abrupt and disorderly close-out of Long-Term Capital may well have been different. But, in the circumstances that did in fact exist, it was my judgment that the American people, whom we are pledged to serve, could have been seriously hurt if credit dried up in a general effort by banks and other intermediaries to avoid greater risk.

In light of these risks, the responsible public policy objective was to get together those with a direct financial interest in an orderly rescue of Long-Term Capital, to discuss its problems openly and objectively, to provide a sounding board for solutions, and if necessary, a calming influence. In my view, we achieved this objective.

What did the New York Fed do?

Because events were moving swiftly, and with my approval and support, my colleague Mr. Fisher invited representatives of the three firms, which we felt had the greatest knowledge of the situation at Long-Term Capital and a strong interest in seeking a solution, to an early morning meeting on September 22nd. The three firms were Goldman Sachs, Merrill Lynch, and J.P. Morgan.

Continuing discussions which commenced the day before, Mr. Fisher explained our interest in being aware of developments and in reducing the risk of an abrupt and chaotic close-out of Long-Term Capital. The firms present stated that they were not aware of any other initiatives then being actively pursued, to resolve Long-Term Capital's problems. They voiced their own concerns about the risks to the markets of a close-out scenario. They discussed various approaches to stabilizing Long-Term Capital including the concept of a "collective industry" or consortium approach. However, they all agreed that work on a collective option should not preclude parallel efforts by anyone; indeed, that if any firm or group of firms wished to step forward and take Long-Term Capital itself or Long-Term Capital's positions onto their balance sheets that this would be the most desirable outcome. In the absence of any other solutions, the firms dispatched two working groups to Long-Term Capital's offices in Connecticut to consider the feasibility of "lifting" the fixed-income and the equity positions out of Long-Term Capital. A third working group met at one of the firm's offices downtown to develop the idea of a consortium approach. By mutual agreement another firm, UBS, a Swiss bank, was added to this core group and to each of the three working groups. However, no one from the New York Fed participated in any of the working groups.

At no point in this early morning meeting, nor at any stage last week, was there discussion of the use of public monies--Federal

Reserve or otherwise. No Federal Reserve or government guarantees, actual or implied, were offered, discussed or solicited.

Later that afternoon, we participated in a conference call to review the progress of the working groups. Two of the working groups concluded that a "lifting" of the fixed income and equity positions was not feasible. The third group developed a consortium approach, which was deemed feasible. Every one agreed that the consortium approach should be "last ditch", and that parallel solutions should still be encouraged.

The four firms met at the Federal Reserve at 7:00 p.m. A draft term sheet was reviewed which provided detail with respect to the consortium approach. The terms and conditions were debated, altered in some places, and ultimately refined so that the four firms could present it to a wider group. Although Federal Reserve officials were present at the meeting, we did not participate in the discussion about terms and conditions.

At about 8:30 p.m., a meeting of a wider group involving 13 firms began. Meanwhile, some representatives of the Core Group called Long-Term Capital to discuss the terms and conditions of the consortium approach. Federal Reserve officials did not participate in any conversations with Long-Term Capital regarding the terms and conditions. In the meeting with the wider group, Peter Fisher explained the importance of avoiding a disorderly close-out of Long-Term Capital's positions. He also underscored the desirability of parallel efforts to resolve the problem. It was agreed that the group would reconvene at 10:00 a.m. the following morning. It was clear to everyone that time was of the essence.

I returned to New York from London around midnight. During the early morning hours, I called various foreign central bank officials to inform them of the situation. At about 9:30 a.m. my colleagues and I met with the Core Group to review the status of the situation. A few minutes before the start of the scheduled 10:00 a.m. meeting, one of the Core Group firms told me that an investor group [Goldman Sachs - Warren Buffett] would make an offer to acquire the Long-Term portfolio. I called one of the representatives of the investor group to confirm this development. The offer was subsequently conveyed to Long-Term Capital by that investor group and a response was requested by 12:30 p.m.

After a brief consultation with the Core Group, I decided that the effort to proceed with the consortium approach needed to be suspended for a short time until the alternative offer could be considered. As noted earlier, the consortium approach was seen as a "last resort". Consequently, the meeting about the consortium approach was adjourned at about 10:50 a.m., to reconvene at 1:00 p.m.

At 12:30 p.m., I learned that the alternative offer had not been accepted and would not be extended. Shortly after 1:00 p.m., the meeting about the consortium approach resumed. This was now the only solution being pursued. During the next five hours, the private sector participants discussed every aspect of the terms and conditions. At the end of that discussion, 14 banks and securities firms agreed to participate in the recapitalization, with three firms contributing smaller amounts than the other eleven. Two firms declined to participate.

I want to emphasize a few points. First, this was a private sector solution to a private-sector problem, involving an investment of new equity by Long-Term Capital's creditors and counterparties. Second, although some have characterized this as a "bailout", control of the Long-Term Portfolio passed over to this 14 firm creditor group and the original equity holders have taken a severe hit. Finally, no Federal Reserve official pressured anyone, and no promises were made. Not one penny of public money was spent or committed.

Issues that should concern us

It is far too early to state categorically the lessons to be learned from Long-Term Capital. What I can say is that we are focused on three specific issues, all relating to leverage and how we are able to observe it through the eyes of our bank examiners. Let me emphasize, yet again, that the Federal Reserve has no regulatory authority over hedge funds and no regulatory authority over Long-Term Capital.

The first issue relates to credit analysis. Our supervisory guidance generally, and with respect to hedge funds specifically, stresses the importance of knowing the borrower and the business purpose of the borrower's transactions. In 1994, the Federal Reserve issued a supervisory letter emphasizing the importance of financial analysis of counterparties, including hedge funds, which can quickly adjust their risk profile. There is a question whether adequate credit analysis was performed by creditors of Long-Term Capital, which needs to be examined carefully during the next few weeks. If credit analysis was deficient, we need to learn how and why before we can make pronouncements that will avoid repetition of our Long-Term Capital experience.

The second issue relates to derivatives activities and a concept called future potential exposure, which is a measure of the likely price movements based on recent years experience. With respect to derivatives, the current market value is captured by financial statements prepared in accordance with generally accepted accounting principles, but not the potential future exposure. To fully understand the degree and effect of leverage in Long-Term Capital's derivatives-related strategies, it would have been necessary to measure the potential future exposure in a rigorous and conservative manner. Whether sufficient information was made available to

Long-Term Capital's counterparties, including its banks, and adequately analyzed by those counterparties, remains to be seen.

A third question concerns stress testing in the credit analysis of hedge funds and the structuring of margin agreements. Stress testing simulates the effects on a portfolio if many asset relationships simultaneously move adversely far beyond historical observation. We recognize that stress testing is a developing discipline, but it is clear that adequate testing was not done with respect to the financial conditions that precipitated Long-Term Capital's problems. In a recent supervisory letter on credit underwriting generally, we emphasized the importance of stress testing. Effective risk management in a financial institution requires not only modeling, but models that can test the full range of financial transactions across all kinds of adverse market developments. Whether such models existed and, if so, whether they were effective, are issues that we need to address.

In the aftermath of Long-Term Capital, we need to pursue these leverage-related issues, and others, in conjunction with our colleagues at the Federal Financial Institutions Examinations Council. The insights that we gain should be of value to bank supervisors, and for the study of the Long-Term Capital matter that is to be done by the President's Working Group on Financial Markets, announced by Secretary Rubin last Friday.

.   .   .

Some more facts to round out the picture. As McDonough alluded to, LTCM experienced substantial losses from its equity positions. Some of these positions were arbitrage investments betting on takeover outcomes. LTCM had wandered a long way from interest rate convergence bets based on sophisticated computer models. Much of the collateral securing the lenders and counterparties was in the form of repos. In a repo transaction, LTCM borrowed money by offering liquid securities as collateral, agreeing to repurchase the securities at a fixed time. It appears that many lenders lent at close to the full value of these securities, many of which had dropped in value by September 1998, and that this drop had not been fully covered by additional collateral. R. Clow and R. Atlas, *Wall Street and the Hedge Funds, What Went Wrong*, Institutional Investor (1998). Moreover, margin on collateral tends to be called from one to two days after the position has been marked to market. It is also important to note that LTCM made very few disclosures to investors about their portfolio, stressing that if investors needed such information they should go elsewhere. Lack of disclosure was justified by proprietary concerns over LTCM's trading strategy. It appears that LTCM's take it or leave it attitude, when combined with their past success, enhanced the allure of investing in the fund. LTCM was the only notable hedge fund that required a creditor bailout.

Hedge funds generally rebounded in the fourth quarter of 1998, producing average net returns of nearly 10%. Indeed, it is estimated that American hedge funds made average returns in 11.7% in 1998 as a whole. *Hedge funds, Trimmed, not axed*, The Economist, February 27, 1999. LTCM itself was reportedly up 12% through April 1999. However, in 2000 many of the largest hedge funds, like those of George Soros, announced their withdrawal from "large-scale and aggressive" hedge fund investing, due to significant losses, 21% for the $8.24 billion Quantum Fund and 32% for the $1.2 billion Quota Fund, as of April 2000. W. Lewis and J. Chaffin, *Soros to curtail hedge fund activity after fall in returns,* Financial Times, April 29/30, 2000. The Basel Committee on Banking Supervision and IOSCO, *Review of Issues relating to HLIs*, March 2001, found that leverage of hedge funds had been significantly reduced by 2001.

Notes and Questions

1.   While most of this Chapter has focused on open-end mutual funds, consider whether sale of closed-end fund shares to U.S. investors in the secondary market could cause a closed-fund to lose its private offering exemption. Could Rule 144A be used to avoid this problem?

2.   Should the U.S. generally permit U.S. investors to buy unregistered closed-end mutual fund shares in the secondary market? Currently, hedge funds are prevented by U.S. laws from advertising, on the theory that only institutional or wealthy investors can invest in the funds. The Managed Funds Association, which represents U.S. hedge funds, has proposed that hedge funds be able to place "tombstone" ads, which would give the basic facts about the fund including that only accredited investors can invest. The Investment Company Institute which represents public mutual funds objects, saying advertising bans are necessary to protect the average investor. A. Beard, *Hedge funds call on SEC to lift long-time advertising ban*, Financial Times, April 11, 2001. What do you think?

3.   As part of its new policies for the offer of securities over the Internet, SEC Release No. 33-7516, 34-39779, March 23, 1998, see Chapter 2, the SEC also adopted rules for the offer of mutual funds over the Internet which closely parallel the rules for securities. General precautionary measures are required for foreign funds making offers targeted exclusively offshore, while offshore offers by U.S. funds will be required to use more specific precautions like passwords. A foreign fund which is simultaneously making an Internet offshore public offer and a U.S. private offer must include in its general precautionary measures a disclaimer that reflects the existence of two separate offers and indicates that the Internet offer is not being made in the United States.

4.   With respect to LTCM, what was the role of the New York Federal Reserve Bank? Was it merely a fact-finder and meeting convener? What

justified their involvement? Reserve Bank President McDonough talks about the fear of a collapse in financial markets; interestingly this issue was downplayed in the Hedge Fund Report, p. 17, which talked about potentially sizeable losses for LTCM counterparties—major financial firms—amounting to $300 million to $500 million. There is no assertion that markets would have seized up or that any of these losses would have bankrupted counterparties.

F. Edwards, *Hedge Funds and the Collapse of Long-Term Capital Management,* 13 Journal of Economic Perspectives 189 (1999) offers the following possible justifications for Fed intervention. First, the financial markets were fragile following the Russian debt default in August. Investors were demanding huge premia for all emerging market securities. A bankruptcy of LTCM could lead to a liquidation of its derivatives portfolio, with potential large losses for its counterparties who were in the money. Since under U.S. bankruptcy law, as well as the laws of other major countries, such liquidations would not be prevented by the automatic stay—such positions are exempt—there would be a rush of creditors to liquidate "[a]s they all ran for the door, very few could get through before prices collapsed—especially since LTCM's positions constituted a sizeable portion of the total outstandings in some assets." Id., at 202. Edwards calls this a "funnel effect." Second, there could be a "knock-on" effect as other financial institutions with positions similar to LTCM suffered losses. Third, there could be a "chain reaction" since losses could result in bankruptcies which could cause further losses and bankruptcies to counterparties, including major banks and securities firms. If the chain reaction effect was a serious concern, why not avoid rescuing LTCM and provide liquidity to banks and securities firms experiencing difficulties?

C. Furfine, *The Costs and Benefits of Moral Suasion,* Working Paper, September 25, 2001, has found that the federal funds markets did not restrict credit to the nine major creditors of LTCM in the period preceding its rescue. The evidence, he argues, suggests that the market never believed that these institutions had a significant probability of default, thus raising further doubt as to whether there was really a systemic risk problem. Furfine further found that large banking organizations started paying lower interest rates after the resolution of the LTCM crisis. This could be because the market viewed these institutions as safer because they avoided the LTCM problem or because the Fed's action was perceived as an extension of the too-big-to-fail policy.

5. McDonough makes reference to a third-party offer that was rejected. Edwards gives the following account of the offer: "John Meriwether, LTCM's managing partner had turned down a $4 billion cash offer by Warren Buffett, Goldman Sachs and AIG, Inc. to take over LTCM that would have reduced the remaining stake of LTCM's partners to just 5 percent and would have fired Meriwether. Meriwether claimed that he

was unable to accept the Buffett offer because it did not allow sufficient time (he was reportedly given 45 minutes) for him to obtain the needed approvals...In particular, LTCM's numerous counterparties would have had to agree to an assignment of their derivative contracts to the Buffett group, and LTCM would have had to cash out its investors at what could have been viewed as an artificial net asset value." Edwards goes on to report that the failure to accept the offer made Meriwether and the partners substantially better off. Id., at note 6, p. 200. Did the NY Fed play a role in the rejection of the Buffett offer? As a result of the meeting between the Fed and creditors on September 22, the next day the consortium agreed to put in additional capital of $3.625 billion in exchange for 90% of the remaining equity.

6. Should regulation be enacted forcing hedge funds to make material disclosures to investors? How about to bank investors? Should regulation limit hedge fund leverage ratios, and if so how? The Basel Committee on Banking Supervision has suggested strengthening bank management of risks to highly leveraged institutions (HLIs), in a report entitled *Banks' Interactions with Highly Leveraged Institutions* (January 1999). This was followed by a second report, *Banks' Interactions with Highly Leveraged Institutions: Implementation of the Basel Committee's Sound Practices Paper* (January 2000). Would adequate risk management by banks fully address the issues raised by LTCM?

7. The Hedge Fund Report stressed that potential losses to counterparties were limited as a result of closeout (right to terminate), netting and collateral provisions. The Report raised the issue as to what would have happened if LTCM had gone bankrupt under Cayman law. Had that been the case, a foreign receiver could have sought to enjoin actions of U.S. creditors to liquidate collateral under Section 304 of the Bankruptcy Code with potential detrimental consequences to such creditors. The Report recommended an amendment to the Bankruptcy Code to prevent such a possibility in the future. Hedge Fund Report, pp. 27-28. A bill pending in Congress, as of March 2000, would have required the largest hedge funds to disclose publicly certain financial and risk management data. The bill did not pass. Is this a good idea? Is it necessary to protect investors? Would it enable regulators to assess the impact of the systemic impact of a hedge fund failure? See generally, B. Eichengreen, *The Regulator's Dilemma: Hedge Funds in the International Financial Architecture,* 2/3 International Finance 411, 431-434 (1999). Should capital risk-weights be increased for banks loaning to hedge funds?

8. Some like Mahathir Mohamad, the prime minister of Malaysia, have blamed hedge funds, and in particular George Soros, for destabilizing exchange rates and playing a major role in causing the Asian financial crisis. However, this seems highly unlikely given that the major source of capital outflow was attributed to the failure of foreign banks to renew short-term loans to Asian banks, and that hedge funds are small

compared to other portfolio investors. Whereas pension funds, mutual funds and insurance companies hold about $25 trillion in assets worldwide, hedge funds control at most about $1 trillion. M. Baily, D. Farrell, and S. Lund, *The Color of Hot Money,* 79 Foreign Affairs 99 (2000). As a related matter, mutual funds in general and particularly hedge funds have been accused of worsening financial crises by pulling money out of countries at the first sign of distress. A study by E. Borensztein and R. Geloo, *A Panic Prone Pack? The Behavior of Emerging Market Mutual Funds*, IMF Working Paper 00/198, December 2000, found that funds do make substantial withdrawals, and tend to do so one month before a crisis. Contrary to some pundits, these funds do not shun all emerging markets when some go bad; the funds withdrawing from Russia in 1998 invested in Latin America even though Latin America was seen as suffering from contagion, p. 11.

2. THE INVESTMENT ADVISERS ACT OF 1940

An offshore mutual fund contemplating selling its shares in the US must also consider the restrictions imposed by the Investment Adviser's Act of 1940 (Investment Advisers Act). Under the Investment Advisers Act, regardless of the fund involved, any person, whether a foreign or U.S. citizen, who advises 15 or more U.S. clients, or solicits the advisory business of U.S. citizens, or advises any SEC-registered fund, must register with the SEC. The Investment Advisers Act poses only a limited obstacle to offshore funds as the investment adviser registration process is relatively simple and inexpensive, albeit somewhat time-consuming. To register as an investment adviser with the SEC, an individual must file the registration form (FORM ADV) which requires the listing of owners, prior securities convictions and injunctions, and the distribution of a brochure on business operations for the examination of prospective clients. The Investment Advisers Act also mandates the annual filing of a balance sheet and detailed record-keeping, both personal and fund-related. While the Investment Advisers Act imposes no qualification or examination requirements of its own, very often prospective U.S. advisers must register in each state in which they do business and comply with each of these respective states' own qualification or examination requirements.

Aside from its registration requirements, the Investment Advisers Act imposes limitations on the methods of investment service provision. Among these restrictions are: limitations on performance fees, advertising and affiliate-related transaction limitations, client asset segregation, and the imposition of general fiduciary obligations to clients. Due to these requirements, many foreign advisers try to exempt themselves from the Investment Advisers Act. One partial solution is the establishment and registration of a separate U.S. advisory subsidiary. A foreign adviser seeking this option must comply with guidelines which ensure that the subsidiary is truly separate from its parent adviser. In effect the foreign investment adviser might be "cloned" by a U.S.-affiliated adviser.

B. TAX CONSIDERATIONS

Tax considerations play a critical role in the structure of the global mutual funds market. Generally, they result in a segregation of the market so that U.S. investors do not invest in foreign funds, and foreign investors do not invest in U.S. funds. The following pieces lay out the general tax situation.

TAX CONSIDERATIONS AFFECTING CROSS-BORDER SALES OF U.S. FUNDS

Appendix A to Response of Investment Company Institute to IOSCO Cross-Border Marketing Survey, Nov. 14, 1996

A. Applicable Tax Provisions

The different tax laws of multiple jurisdictions may make a US fund less attractive to non-US investors than a domestic or "home-country" fund with a comparable investment objective and management style. The tax laws that may be relevant in determining whether a foreign fund will be a good investment from a tax perspective include the laws of: (1) the country where the fund is domiciled, (2) the investor's country of residence and (3) countries where the fund invests, other than its country of domicile. Tax treaties between these countries also can be significant.

B. Tax Considerations for Investors

In ascertaining the tax consequences of investing in a home-country or an offshore fund, a number of issues may be relevant. First, an investor must consider "timing issues", i.e., whether and when a fund distributes ordinary income and/or capital gain. In general, an investor will prefer a fund that retains rather than distributes its income because current distributions of income accelerate the payment of tax.

Second, the "character" of the income received by the fund's shareholders must be considered. For example, an investor in a fund that makes no distributions would receive any earnings of the fund only in the form of capital gains arising upon redemption of the fund's shares. By contrast, an investor in a foreign fund required to make distributions of its income and realized gain generally will be required to treat the entire amount of these distributions as ordinary income, because the tax laws of the investor's home country will not recognize the capital gain character of a dividend distribution from a fund. Most fund investors would prefer to receive capital gains instead of ordinary income, because many countries offer favorable tax treatment to capital gains.

Third, withholding taxes -- which may be imposed on the fund's receipt of income from sources outside the fund's country of domicile as well as on the fund's distributions of its income to shareholders -- can impact the investor's return. In some cases a shareholder can receive credits against home country tax for withholding taxes incurred by the fund with respect to its earnings or by the shareholder with respect to his distributions.

C. Consequences of Various Tax Rules

1. Tax Rules Applicable to Fund Distributions

Whether a fund distributes to shareholders or retains its ordinary income and realized capital gains can have significant tax consequences. One consequence of investing in a fund that distributes its income is current taxation of the fund distribution in the investor's country of residence. US funds, for example, are required to distribute essentially all of their income and capital gains on a calendar year basis. By contrast, investment in a fund that retains or rolls-up its income usually results in deferral of current taxation.

A second consequence of investing in a "distributing" fund is that the investor has no control over the timing of the income and, consequently, may have less flexibility in planning transactions to minimize overall tax liability. An investor in a fund that rolls up its income can control the timing of receipt of income by determining when redemptions will be made.

Income deferral from investing in a "roll-up" fund also can result in a conversion of ordinary income to capital gain realized when the fund shares are redeemed. This "character" conversion is particularly beneficial where the investor's country of residence provides favorable tax treatment for capital gains. Character conversion also could be important if the fund's country of residence imposes withholding tax on dividend distributions but not on capital gains.

Additional character of income issues may arise for a distributing fund. First, where a fund distributes income that retains its character in the fund's country of residence (e.g., long-term capital gains of the fund which retain their character as long term capital gains in the US when distributed to US shareholders), the issue presented is whether the investor's country of residence will respect the character of the distribution (which may result in favorable tax treatment) or will treat it as an "ordinary" dividend. A second "character" issue arises where a fund distributes income that does not retain its character in the fund's country of residence, e.g., short-term capital gains of the fund which are treated as ordinary income when distributed to shareholders in the US. Here, the question presented is whether the investor's country of residence nevertheless will treat the income as retaining its capital gains character.

2. Anti-Deferral Regimes

Some countries have tax rules, similar to the passive foreign investment company ("PFIC") rules of US law, designed to reduce or eliminate benefits that otherwise might arise from investing in non-distributing "roll-up" funds and certain other foreign entities. These tax regimes take many forms, including (1) the imposition of a mark to market regime and "penalties" designed to eliminate the tax deferral benefit of investing in roll-up funds and (2) the use of a formula to determine the fund's deemed taxable income. Depending on the particular nature of the rules, a disincentive for investing in an offshore fund may be created.

3. Withholding Tax Rules

Two types of withholding tax considerations can affect the attractiveness of investing in offshore funds. The first consideration relates to withholding by the offshore fund's country of residence on distributions made by the fund and/or redemptions of the fund's shares. The second relates to withholding by the countries in which the fund invests. The impact of these withholding taxes may depend on whether an investor can claim credits against home-country tax for the withheld foreign taxes.

a. Withholding by the Fund's Country of Residence

Withholding tax by the fund's country of residence can impact the decision to invest in an offshore fund in several ways. First, withholding tax reduces the dividend distribution received by foreign investors.[2] Where the investor's country of residence provides a credit against tax for foreign taxes paid (a "foreign tax credit"), the withholding of tax in the fund's country of residence may create only a "cash flow" consideration,[3] since the tax is withheld at the time of the cash distribution and the credited tax is typically applied against future taxes owed.[4] Second, where the withholding tax is not creditable, the

---

[2] In certain circumstances, withholding is imposed upon fund distributions of income that would not be subject to withholding if received directly by the foreign investor. For example, distributions by a US fund of its interest income and capital gains on assets held for one year or less (short-term capital gains) are treated under US law as dividends -- which are subject to 30 percent US withholding tax (often reduced by treaty to 15 percent) -- when paid to foreign shareholders. The same interest income and short-term capital gains are exempt from US withholding tax when received by foreign investors from direct investments in the U.S.

[3] If the procedures required for claiming the foreign tax credit either are time consuming or are deemed by the taxpayer to be too burdensome relative to the benefits of claiming the credit, withholding creates administrative burden as well.

[4] For example, assume a $100 fund dividend attributable to interest income from the fund's bond portfolio. Assuming a foreign investor in a US fund that can claim foreign tax credits, the investor ultimately would receive the full benefit of a $100 dividend from a US fund ($85 in cash and the remaining $15 as a foreign tax credit), but the "cash flow" would be less (since only $85, rather than $100, would be received directly from the fund.)

amount of any tax withheld represents a permanent reduction in the investment return on the fund shares. Moreover, if withholding tax is imposed on an investor exempt from tax in its country of residence (e.g., a pension plan), a permanent reduction in investment return occurs unless the taxes withheld are refunded.

b. Withholding by the Countries in which the Fund Invests

Additional tax considerations relate to withholding tax imposed by the countries in which an offshore fund invests. First, the source-country withholding tax imposed upon investment income (e.g., dividends and interest) paid to the offshore fund generally can not be recouped by the investor resident in a third country. In general, an investor's residence country will not provide credits both for withholding tax imposed on dividends paid to the investor *and* for the tax withheld on payments made to the offshore fund. This loss is exacerbated if the offshore fund is not eligible for tax treaty benefits. Absent treaty benefits, source-country withholding on income paid to an offshore fund typically is imposed at a withholding rate (e.g., 30 percent) that is significantly higher than the treaty rate (e.g., 15 percent). As a result, the treaty network of the country in which the fund is domiciled can affect the relative attractiveness of investing in that fund. For example, if the investor's country of residence has a treaty with a source country, but the offshore fund's country of residence does not, a domestic fund would have an advantage over an offshore fund investing in the same source country.

· · ·

TAX ASPECTS OF THE INTERNATIONALIZATION OF THE INVESTMENT FUND INDUSTRY
Memorandum of Sullivan & Cromwell, July 1990

III. U.S. TAXATION OF RICs, PFICs AND THEIR SHAREHOLDERS

For the purposes of the analysis below, it is assumed that where investors of a foreign country (an "FC") invest in a U.S. mutual fund, the fund will qualify as a RIC for U.S. tax purposes. Conversely, where a U.S. investor purchases an interest in a fund organized in an FC, it is assumed that -- quite apart from the FC tax consequences -- the FC fund will constitute a PFIC for U.S. tax purposes.

· · ·

A. RICs

Description. A RIC is a U.S. domestic corporation or business trust, registered with the Securities and Exchange Commission as an investment company under the provisions of the Investment Company Act of 1940, which elects to be a RIC for a taxable year and satisfies certain requirements relating to:

- the source of its income (broadly, at least 90% must be derived from securities or securities transactions); and

- the diversification of its assets (broadly, at least 50% must be represented by securities, subject to certain limitations, cash or cash items, and not more than 25% may be invested in the securities of any one issuer other than those of governments or other RICs).

Taxation of income. If a RIC distributes all of its income (including long-term capital gains) annually, it may deduct the amount of dividends paid when computing its taxable income, with the result that its distributed net income can be passed through to shareholders free of tax at the RIC level. If a RIC fails to distribute at least 90% of its income (other than long-term capital gains) by March 15 of the succeeding taxable year, it will lose its exemption, and it may incur a 4% excise tax if less than 98% of its income (other than long-term capital gains) is not distributed before the end of the calendar year.

Taxation of capital gains. Retained long-term capital gains are taxed at the RIC level at the rate of 34%. However, the RIC may elect to include the undistributed gains in its shareholders' income as a deemed dividend. If the election is made, shareholders receive a credit for the tax paid by the RIC (and in appropriate cases may even obtain a refund) and are entitled to increase the basis in their shares by 66% of the amount of the deemed dividend (*i.e.*, that amount is effectively treated as reinvested by the shareholders), which is relevant primarily to shareholders who are residents and citizens of the U.S. In practice, it is believed that RICs ordinarily distribute all their long-term capital gains, as well as ordinary income.

Distributed long-term capital gains keep their character in the hands of shareholders (though, at the present time, this is relevant primarily to non-U.S. resident shareholders as described below, but pending legislation would make it relevant to U.S. shareholders as well.

Withholding tax on dividends. In the case of shareholders who are not residents or citizens of the U.S., dividends are subject to a withholding tax of 30%, unless a reduced rate is available under an applicable double tax treaty between the U.S. and the relevant shareholder's country of residence. However, no U.S. tax is withheld from long-term capital gain dividends or deemed dividends thereof (because such gains are not considered to be fixed or determinable annual or periodic gains).

The U.S. withholding tax, whether reduced by treaty or not, applies to all distributions by a RIC even though the RIC derives some or all of its income (a) from outside the U.S., whether or not the "pass-through" election (described below) is in effect, or (b) from U.S. source interest which would be exempt from withholding if the interest were paid directly to the nonresident shareholders. A non-U.S. resident shareholder will thus always receive dividends from a RIC subject to deduction of U.S. withholding tax, but will not be able to claim a credit or deduction against such U.S. tax for any foreign taxes paid by the RIC on foreign source income out of which the dividend is paid, or to claim an exemption for the portion of the dividend that is paid out of U.S. source interest income which would be exempt from withholding if received directly by the shareholder.

Foreign tax credits. If more than 50% in value of a RIC's assets consists of stock or securities in foreign corporations, the RIC may elect to "pass-through" any foreign taxes it pays to shareholders who are U.S. residents or citizens.[9] If the RIC so elects:

- any foreign taxes paid by the RIC will be treated as having been distributed to the U.S. shareholders, who may claim a credit or deduction for such taxes; and

- the U.S. shareholders will treat as foreign source income, for foreign income inclusion and tax credit limitation purposes, the amount of foreign taxes included as a result of the election, in addition to the amount of actual dividends from the RIC which represents income from foreign countries.

In the case of shareholders who are not U.S. residents or citizens, the effect of the election is to increase the amount treated as having been distributed as a dividend (and on which the withholding tax is imposed) and thus to reduce the net cash received by the shareholders.

. . .

Whether the "pass-through" provisions of the U.S. tax law will be effective for shareholders who are not U.S. residents is to be decided under the laws of the countries where the shareholders are resident. No treaties deal with the matter and no country is known to have given effect to the pass-through in the absence of a treaty.

. . .

B. PFICs

Description. A non-U.S. fund will constitute a PFIC if 75% or more of its gross income is "passive income" (which includes dividends and interest, and net gains from property which produces such income) or 50% or more of its assets produce, or are held for the production of,

---

[9]   *See* Section 853 of the Code. This feature is relied on by the so-called "country funds", *i.e.*, funds that invest solely in the securities of the government and corporations in one particular country, and by "global" and "world" funds, *i.e.*, funds that invest in the securities of issuers in a number of countries outside the U.S.

passive income. The relevant rules apply irrespective of the size of an investor's shareholding or the extent of holdings by U.S. taxpayers in the aggregate, provided the fund is not 50% or more owned by U.S. persons (in which case other rules apply which are outside the scope of this memorandum).

. . .

Qualified electing fund. If a U.S. taxpayer who is an investor in a PFIC elects to treat the PFIC as a "qualified electing fund" (a "QEF") and the PFIC complies with prescribed requirements concerning the provision of information,[13] the U.S. taxpayer is taxable currently on its share of the PFIC's undistributed earnings, and subsequent distributions of those earnings are not taxable.

Not a QEF. If a U.S. taxpayer does not elect to treat a PFIC as a QEF (or if the PFIC does not comply with the information requirements), the U.S. taxpayer will be taxable when it receives an "excess distribution" or sells its share in the PFIC. The gain in the case of a sale is not treated as a capital gain (where that makes a difference) and, in the case of both a sale and an excess distribution, an interest charge is imposed (in addition to the regular tax) to reflect the value of deferring the tax. An "excess distribution" is generally the amount of the distribution received during a taxable year in excess of 125% of the average of the distributions during the three preceding years. In this way, the previous benefits of investing in a "roll-up" fund (*i.e.*, one that accumulates its income, with investors realizing their gains in the form of capital gain on the disposal of their interests in the fund), assuming there is a capital gains tax rate differential, are greatly reduced.

Foreign tax credits. A U.S. resident investor in a PFIC will not normally be entitled to a credit for any foreign taxes paid by the PFIC (other than those withheld from distributions made by the PFIC), unless the investor is a corporation owning 10% or more of the PFIC's voting stock and is thus entitled to the deemed paid credit.

. . .

---

[13] The fund must ordinarily provide an annual information statement which contains information concerning the fund's fiscal year, the shareholder's share of the fund's ordinary earnings and net capital gains, distributions to the shareholder and a statement that the fund will permit the shareholder to inspect the fund's relevant books and records. *See* Notice 88-125, 1988-2 C.B. 535. It may therefore be the case that, save where a significant proportion of its investors are U.S. residents, an offshore fund may not wish to provide the required statement, thus preventing a U.S. taxpayer's election from taking effect.

V. TAXATION OF INVESTMENTS BY FUNDS
IN COUNTRIES OUTSIDE THE CO

Where an investment fund invests in the securities of issuers organized in other countries, dividends and interest received from those issuers may be subject to deduction of foreign withholding tax, as discussed in Part IV, but a crucial further question is whether the withholding tax is the only foreign tax that will be imposed.

In this respect, a distinction needs to be drawn between a fund investing and trading in securities, and between income received in the form of dividends and interest, and gain arising from the sale or disposal of the securities.

A. Investing vs. Trading

In many countries, a non-resident will only be subject to withholding tax, and not income tax at ordinary rates, if it invests in securities (*i.e.*, acquires securities for the purpose of obtaining a flow of income in the form of dividends or interest), as opposed to trades or deals in securities or carries on a securities business (*i.e.*, acquires the securities with a view to resale at a profit).

It will in some cases also be important to ascertain whether a fund will be treated as trading or carrying on business within (as opposed to without) an FC and whether the fund's operations will result in its being treated as having a permanent establishment in that FC. There may be concerns, in particular, if a fund uses local brokers or other agents.

The U.S. Internal Revenue Code provides that trading in stocks, securities or commodities (regardless of the frequency, size or extent of the transactions) will not ordinarily constitute the conduct of a U.S. trade or business by a non-U.S. fund, if the fund does not have an office or other fixed place of business in the U.S. through which such transactions are effected.[21] In addition, in order to deal with the concern of foreign investors that the grant of discretionary authority to a U.S. agent might result in the forfeiture of the statutory exemption, the relevant rules were modified by the Foreign Investors Tax Act of 1966 to make it clear that such trading through a resident broker, commission agent, custodian or other independent agent - even if that person has discretionary authority - will not constitute a U.S. trade or

---

[21] *See* Section 864(b)(2)(C) of the Code and Treas. Regs. Sections 1.864-2(c) and (d).

business provided that the non-U.S. fund does not have its principal office located in the U.S.[23]

. . .

B. Capital Gains

A number of countries do not impose capital gains tax with respect to gain realized on the sale of property situated within the country, where the vendor is a non-resident. However, some countries do make non-residents liable, even where the non-resident has held the property as an investment (and has not traded or dealt in the property).

Australia, for example, taxes gain realized by non-residents on the sale of shares in private corporations and on the sale of shares in public corporations where the non-resident owns 10% or more of that corporation's stock. France and Canada have similar rules. And it has recently been proposed in the U.S. Foreign Tax Equity Bill of 1990 that the U.S. should tax gain in respect of holdings by non-U.S. residents of 10% or more of the shares in the U.S. corporation.

The possible imposition of tax on any gain realized will thus be a further factor to be considered by a fund which proposes investing in the securities of foreign issuers. From a U.S. viewpoint, it should be noted that U.S. investors in a fund that has made a "pass-through" election may not get a credit for any non-U.S. capital gains tax paid by

---

[23] Treas. Reg. Section 1.864(c)(2)(iii) formerly stated that a corporation could only have one principal office and provided (by way of the so-called "Ten Commandments") that "a foreign corporation which carries on most or all of its investment activities in the U.S. but which maintains a general business office or offices outside the U.S. in which its management is located will not be considered as having its principal office in the U.S. if all or a substantial portion of the following functions is carried on at or from an office or offices located outside the U.S.:

(1) communicating with its shareholders (including the furnishing of financial reports);

(2) communicating with the general public;

(3) soliciting sales of its own stock;

(4) accepting the subscriptions of new stockholders;

(5) maintaining its principal corporate records and books of account;

(6) auditing its books of account;

(7) disbursing payments of dividends, legal fees, accounting fees, and officers' and directors' salaries;

(8) publishing or furnishing the offering and redemption price of the shares of stock issued by it;

(9) conducting meetings of its shareholders and board of directors; and

(10) making redemptions of its own stock."

[This regulation was repealed by the enactment of the 1997 Taxpayer Relief Act. Although these activities can now be performed in the United States for tax purposes, securities law concerns may still dictate that some or all of these activities are performed outside of the United States, eds.]

a RIC because the gain likely will be treated as U.S. (rather than foreign) source income, regardless of where the sale occurs.

VI. CONCLUSIONS

. . .

A. U.S. Residents

Due to the PFIC rules, there will be no tax advantages for a U.S. resident purchasing an interest in a "tax haven" fund that invests in FCs, as opposed to purchasing shares in either an RIC that invests in FCs (and "passes through" foreign tax credits) or in a "transparent" fund organized in a non-tax haven FC. Moreover, U.S. residents will not generally be entitled to any credit for taxes withheld on dividends and interest paid to non-U.S. funds, while they will be entitled to such credits where an investment is made in a RIC which satisfies the requirements for "passing through" such credits.

B. Non-U.S. Residents

Solely from a tax viewpoint, it appears that residents in a number of countries outside the U.S. may not be significantly disadvantaged by purchasing shares in a RIC, as opposed to purchasing an interest in a fund organized in their home country or elsewhere.

That general statement is subject to a number of qualifications, however. One is that residents of countries which tax capital gains favorably may be able to purchase interests in an "accumulation" fund and realize their investments by selling the interests (and realizing a deferred and lower or untaxed capital gain), rather than by receiving income distributions (which would be taxed as and when received). Thus the U.S. tax law requirement that RICs must distribute substantially all their income in order to be exempt from corporate level taxation *may* disadvantage RICs with respect to those residents, in comparison with funds that can accumulate income without paying a corporate level tax because the CO either (a) imposes no taxes or (b) grants an exemption to funds from general corporation taxes.

It has been suggested that, in order to eliminate that disadvantage, a RIC should be permitted to make distributions to non-U.S. resident shareholders in shares of the RIC equal in value to their aliquot shares of the cash which is retained and reinvested. The share distribution would be treated as satisfying the distribution requirement but not as constituting a distribution which was subject to U.S. withholding tax. In order for the proposal to be effective, however, the relevant FCs would have to treat the share distribution as not constituting current income but as the equivalent of an accumulation of undistributed income.

A further disadvantage of investing via a RIC is that income and short-term gain distributions will be subject to U.S. withholding tax, whether made from U.S. or non-U.S. source income. Although a non-U.S. shareholder may be able to claim a credit in its home country for the U.S. tax, the shareholder will typically not obtain a credit for non-U.S. withholding taxes paid by a RIC in respect of the non-U.S. source income received by the RIC, whether or not the RIC qualifies for and makes the "pass-through" election for U.S. tax purposes. In principle, it is difficult to justify the imposition of U.S. withholding tax on income and short-term gains derived from non-U.S. sources in the case of a fund, and it has been proposed that the U.S. tax law should be changed in this respect in order to make U.S. funds more tax efficient for non-U.S. resident investors.

The question of providing non-U.S. shareholders with a credit for non-U.S. withholding taxes paid by a RIC in respect of non-U.S. source income received by the RIC can only be resolved by the countries where the shareholders reside. Other countries may not be willing to provide relief, however, so long as the U.S. does not provide such relief to U.S. taxpayers with respect to PFICs.

In the case of bond and money market funds, RICs are disadvantaged by the imposition of U.S. withholding taxes on distributions to non-resident investors, on the theory that the distributions are dividends without regard to the extent to which the income of the fund consists of U.S. source interest income which, if paid directly to the investors or to an FC fund, would be exempt from U.S. withholding tax under the Code or applicable double tax treaties. As in the case of non-U.S. source income of RICs, proposals have been made that distributions should be exempt from the withholding tax to the extent that the income of the RIC consists of interest and interest equivalents which would be exempt from withholding tax if paid directly to non-residents.

. . .

Notes and Questions

1. What U.S. tax consequences prevent U.S. investors from investing in offshore mutual funds? What changes, if any, would you make in U.S. tax law to promote such investment? Note that negative tax consequences for offshore investors would not be a consideration for tax-exempt investors like pension funds. However, the U.S. Employee Retirement Income Security Act (ERISA) may impose limitations on use of offshore funds. For example, if employee benefit plan investors hold 25 percent or more of the shares of a fund, the fund's assets, in addition to shares of the fund, will be regarded as plan assets for purposes of applying various ERISA reporting, fiduciary and custody requirements.

2. In 1997, Congress created an alternative to the imposition of interest on distributions of non-QEF PFICs effective 1998. Under I.R.C. 1296, a U.S. person holding an investment in a PFIC may elect to mark

the fund shares to market and to pay a tax on any gain of the shares (as measured by net asset value) over the taxpayer's adjusted basis in such shares. Does this solve the problem of having an investment in a non-QEF?

3. What U.S. tax consequences prevent foreign investors from investing in U.S. mutual funds? What changes, if any, would you make in U.S. tax law to promote such investment?

4. How would you compare globalization in the market for primary securities, with globalization in the mutual funds market? Is there a euromarket for mutual funds?

Links to Other Chapters

The last questions above invite one to consult Chapter 2 on International Aspects of U.S. Securities Markets, as well as treatment of international securities in Europe, in Chapter 6, and Japan, in Chapter 8, Section II. Also see Chapter 12 on Eurobonds and Global Bonds.

PART III

EMERGING MARKETS

Developing countries and the former socialist countries now in transition raise special issues for international finance. Despite huge differences among them, these countries when contrasted to the more developed markets offer very different risks and rewards. This is because their basic institutions, such as law, accounting, corporate governance, and even government, are often not well developed. In addition, their economic performance varies much more dramatically over time than that of the developed countries. While this raises the risk for financial firms, savers, and even users of funds, the high potential upside is a tantalizing lure. Since major industrial countries have economic and political stakes in developing and transition countries, the governments of industrial countries intervene in financial markets involving developing countries. This too changes the balance of risk and reward.

This part deals with three types of international finance involving emerging markets. Project finance has been a burgeoning area of activity and legal practice. Chapter 19 examines it in the context of a large power project in the Philippines. Cross-border investment in emerging markets by foreign institutional investors like pension funds has been one of the most dynamic activities in international finance. Much of this investment is in newly privatized companies. Chapter 20 deals with that subject by focusing on the Mexican Telmex offer and the impact of the peso crisis that followed it. Emerging market debt, raised internationally, has funded development but also contributed to the collapse of many economies. Chapter 21 deals with the debt problem that began in the 1960s, the crises this generated in subsequent years, and the efforts to deal with these crises.

CHAPTER NINETEEN

PROJECT FINANCE

A. INTRODUCTION

In April 1993, work began on an electric power plant project in Pagbilao, the Philippines. Consisting of two large coal-fired generators, the plant would be developed for the government's National Power Company (Napocor) by the Hopewell Group of Hong Kong, with Mitsubishi Corporation of Japan as the main builder, for a total cost of $933 million. After construction, scheduled to end no later than April 30, 1996 for the first generator and July 31, 1996 for the second, Hopewell would own and operate the plant for 25 years and then transfer ownership to Napocor at no cost. This was a BOOT project: build, own, operate, transfer.

The project was significant for several reasons. For the Philippines, it would become the largest coal-fired plant in the country, serving a region including the capital, Manila, that was starved for power. Hopewell was managed by Gordon Wu, a Hong Kong resident and Princeton educated engineer, who takes credit for originating BOT/BOOT projects in China in the late 1970s. And its financing was particularly important: Pagbilao launched the government's new strategy of relying on the private sector to fund major infrastructure projects, such as power. Supplementing the private funds was support from the government-owned export-import banks of Japan and the United States, as well as three multilateral agencies, the Asian Development Bank, the International Finance Corporation (part of the World Bank), and the Commonwealth Development Corporation.

Project finance, such as this, started to play an increasingly important role in cross-border financial flows in the mid-1980s in many regions of the world. In Asia by the early 1990s, direct investment, of which project finance was a major part, dominated even the booming portfolio investment as a source of cross-border finance. The Philippines was particularly successful in attracting foreign investment to infrastructure projects. Its legal regime for BOT projects was among the best in Asia.

This Chapter describes the situation in the Philippines when the project and its financing were being negotiated in the early 1990s, explains the country's need for power, gives background on project finance, and presents the arrangements for the Pagbilao project, emphasizing its financing. As you read, identify the risks for parties to a BOT/BOOT project and evaluate the way the parties to the Pagbilao project allocated the risks.

B.   THE PHILIPPINES

The Philippines was a tropical country of about 65 million people in 1993. Culturally and linguistically diverse, it boasted 988 different languages, though most people spoke at least one of four major languages, including Tagalog and English. Filipinos were spread across 7,000 islands of an archipelago, with two-thirds concentrated on the two big islands of Luzon (in the north) and Mindanao. Over 85% were Catholic; other large groups were Protestant and Muslim. Most of the material for this part comes from Europa Publications Ltd., III The Europa World Year Book 1995, 2454 (1995) and World Bank, World Development Report 188 (1996).

A short political history. A colony of Spain for over 300 years when the United States took possession in 1898, the Philippines was occupied by Japan during World War II and became independent in 1946. After a series of peaceful transfers of power from one elected president to another, Ferdinand Marcos became president in 1965. In 1972, nearing the end of his second term and facing a constitutional limit of two terms, he declared martial law (which only ended in 1981). Guerilla activity in the country, sometimes quite serious, had increased. During this period, the Philippines was of great strategic importance to the U.S., which used its military bases on the islands as a key logistical center for activities in the Pacific, particularly near East and Southeast Asia and notably Vietnam. Marcos ruled by decree until a new constitution was approved by referendum, after which he was re-elected twice. Political fraud was seen as rampant during the campaigns.

Public criticism of Marcos' rule centered on "croney capitalism," the close link between the political elite and business elite, a highly concentrated group of families whose wealth derived from land-owning and, more recently, control over financial-industrial conglomerates. Criticism grew more intense after 1977, when Benigno Aquino, Jr., an opposition leader, was sentenced to death for murder and subversion, though the sentence was stayed. When his party won local elections in 1980, Aquino was released and went to the United States for medical treatment. On his return in 1983, he was assassinated at the airport. This set the stage for political change, uniting the opposition. In February 1986, after a presidential campaign both Marcos and his opponent Corazon Aquino, the widow of Benigno Aquino, claimed they had won. Marcos' acting Chief of Staff, Lieutenant-General Fidel Ramos, responded to a call from the defense minister to help Aquino and rallied troops protected by unarmed crowds to support Aquino. Offered sanctuary in Hawaii by the U.S. government, Marcos left the country after a stand-off and Aquino took office. Marcos' supporters, including many senior military officers, wanted to restore him to power and attempted several coups, some posing serious threats to the Aquino government. Guerilla activity persisted. The Aquino government responded and was accused by Amnesty International of allowing the military to abuse human rights; some 550 "extra-judicial" killings were said to have occurred from 1988 to 1992. Marcos died in exile in 1989. His wife Imelda, who had been politically active during the Marcos regime, later returned to the Philippines, where she fought many civil suits charging corruption and won a seat in the House of Representatives.

The Aquino presidency was followed in 1992 by that of Fidel Ramos. He opened ties to the business community. He was a Protestant opposed during the election by the leaders of the country's Catholic Church. The coalition supporting Aquino formally split and Ramos formed a new party with Corazon Aquino's support. Voters gave Ramos a plurality of 24% among the eight official candidates. He increased his support in 1995 elections for both legislative chambers. Ramos had completed the negotiations started by Aquino with the U.S. government to close its military bases by the end of 1992. Crime and political warfare became major issues for him. Among other concerns, abduction of the rich was frequent. Many senior judges were accused of accepting bribes. Military disaffection persisted. Almost 600 private armies, supported by politicians and landowners, could not be disbanded. Armed political groups, including Communists and Muslim separatists, continued to fight. Ramos initiated peace talks punctuated by periodic fighting. The Constitution limits a president to one non-renewable term of six years.

The economy. A thriving country in the 1960s, the Philippines saw its economy wither afterwards, particularly during the Marcos era. Gradually during the period 1956-73, the government displaced market forces as the key allocator of resources. The financial system came under the direction of the central bank, which guided lending to sectors that received the government's imprimatur for economic or political reasons. From 1974-81, government control intensified through regulation, price controls, and credit allocation, though the formal role of the central bank was reduced. After 1981 a slow, bumpy process of liberalization began. In the late 1980s, the Aquino government hastened the process with fiscal austerity, privatization, and liberalization, including foreign investment laws. In 1992, the government ended exchange control. The financial system remained weak as a method of resource allocation. The banks were burdened by bad loans, the money and capital markets still suffering from years of direct and very harmful government involvement. Natural disasters, such as the eruption of Mt. Pinatubo in 1991, cost the country dearly in human and financial resources.

Key Indicators for the Philippines					
	Philippines			All lower-middle countries†	East Asia and Pacific countries†
Indicator	1980	1994	1980-1994		
Real GNP per cap. growth p.a.			1.7%*	-1.2*	6.9
Real growth of industry p.a.			-0.9,0.9**	na	9.7, 13.4**
Industry/GNP	39	33		na, 36	39, 42
Gross domestic investment/GNP	29	24		na, 26	29,36
Gross domestic savings/GNP	24	18		na, 25	28, 37
Gov't deficit/GNP	4.1	1.9		n.a.	n.a.
Population growth p.a.			2.4,2.2**	1.7, 1.4**	1.6, 1.4**
Urban/total population	38	53		47, 56	22, 32
Workforce: % in industry	15.	15.***		26,27	14, 16
Adult literacy (%)		95		na	91
Energy use per capita	277	364		na, 1,540	405, 670
Official dev't aid/GNP	0.9	1.7		1.3, 1.1	0.7, 0.8
Current account deficit/GNP	-6.2	-4.5		n.a.	n.a.
International reserves (months of imports covered)	4.6	3.1		n.a.	n.a.
Source: World Bank, World Development Report 1996 at 188 on. p.a. = per annum † Periods correspond to periods for Philippines data * 1985-94 **1980-90,1990-94 ***1990					

In 1994, the Philippines was ranked by the World Bank as a lower-middle income country, number 56 out of 133 (where 1 is lowest) in GNP per capita for all countries. In 1994, GNP grew 5% and inflation was down from a high of 19% in 1991 to about 10% a year. Income distribution remained concentrated: the top 20% of the population received almost 50%, while the lowest 20% got under 10%. Almost 50% of the workforce was in agriculture, mostly peasant, and barely 10% paid taxes. Health problems were severe: infant mortality and malnutrition were more serious than in most lower-middle income countries. The standard of living was so far behind that of the Asian Tigers that some estimated if the Philippines could grow at 8% p.a. it would take 20 years to reach the 1995 living standard of Thailand or 50 years to reach Korea's. But the Philippines had high literacy, its people were proficient in English, and a high proportion was college graduates. See E. Luce, *Asian Tiger in Hard Training*, Financial Times, Oct. 2, 1995, at I of Special Survey. See the adjacent table for other key indicators of the Philippines economy.

Foreign trade was important to the Philippines. Exports of manufactured goods increased from 37% of all exports of goods in 1980 to 76% in 1994. The fastest growing component was electrical machinery. Just over 50% of exports went to the U.S. and Japan. Fuel fell as a share of all imports from 28% in 1980 to 12% in 1994; about 45% of all imports came from Japan and the U.S. Imports consistently exceeded exports, and the deficit in the country's current account balance (goods, services, and transfers, including most importantly for the Philippines, workers' remittances) rose from $2.1 billion in 1980 (against exports of $8 billion) to $3.3 billion in 1994 (against exports of $24 billion).

Foreign resources were fueling development more than before: from 1980 to 1994, net private capital inflows almost quintupled to $4 billion. External debt, which had snowballed during the Marcos regime, grew from $17 billion (54% of GNP and 234% of exports) in 1980 to $39 billion (60% of GNP and 190% of exports) in 1994. Most of the debt was owed to private lenders. Equity investment mainly took the form of direct investment, giving control. Over the period 1991-3, net direct investment was about $1.5 billion, while net portfolio was $14 million, according to the IMF. Direct investments approved by the Board of Investment (not the same as annual flows) rose from $1.7 bn in 1991 to $4.6 bn in 1995. Asian investors dominated, accounting for 37% in 1994. Many American companies had started their Asian operations in the Philippines, which had effectively been a U.S. colony for 50 years.

Notes and Questions

1. Evaluate the Philippines from the point of view of an American company considering FDI in the country in 1993. What are the major risks? How could they be managed?

2. What would be the major reasons the Philippines would be interested in FDI? What would be the main concerns of the Philippine government about FDI in the country?

C.   THE PHILIPPINES' NEED FOR POWER

As early as 1987, the Government recognized that the country faced a serious shortfall in power. Until then, the Department of Energy regulated electric utilities through concessions. Only Napocor, its wholly-owned company, could generate and transmit power through seven grids for the country. The few private, municipal, and rural utilities were not significant. The country drew over half of its power from thermal plants using imported oil, and most of the rest from coal and hydroelectric sources. Rates were the second highest in Asia because so much of the power was oil-based. See J. Galang, *Gaining on the Neighbours*, Financial Times Survey, Sep. 12, 1994, at I.

In July 1987, the government authorized the private sector to construct and run power plants. Many projects began to be negotiated, but the process was very slow and the lead time to actual production was many years. Despite the policy, the crisis grew as demand grew. By 1991-2, the Philippines suffered severe power shortages lasting 5 to 12 hours a day. The Government tried to end unnecessary consumption. Businesses, institutions, and homes bought electric generators that caused serious health hazards; for example, respiratory diseases in Metro Manila increased 20%.

Projections into the near future painted an even more dire picture. If GDP grew at only 4% a year peak demand would be 5,002 megawatts (MW) by the year 2000 and Napocor would need to add 250-300 MW capacity each year. But many existing plants were over 25 years old and scheduled to be phased out soon.

The Philippines faced such an acute crisis due to power shortages that in April 1993 the Congress gave President Ramos emergency powers to deal with it. Without the powers, the law would require bids for each plant, which would be very time consuming. Had the government built itself, individual bids would be needed for each major component of a plant, even more time-consuming. Ramos encouraged private groups to take on new power projects because the red tape surrounding government-run projects would have delayed the initiatives. In 1994, 11 new power plants began to operate, promising up to 1,074 MW. The crisis became less acute, but brownouts and blackouts continued around the Manila area.

Notes and Questions

1. Evaluate the advantages and disadvantages to the Philippines of relying on the private development of energy.

2. The World Bank study confirmed the wisdom of using the private sector for infrastructure projects. A major reason for the government to carry out a project is that, because its credit rating is better than private sector borrowers, it will pay less for debt to finance the project. On the other hand, the government is less efficient and likely to generate longer delays to completion. Using a power plant as an example, the Bank noted that if construction costs equal 70% of all costs and with interest rates at

10%, a 20% construction cost overrun or a 2 year delay in completion would raise the unit price of power 15%. (It said that government power projects commonly cost 35% above budget.) Suppose a private developer would have had to pay 13% for debt. The government's borrowing advantage would permit a unit cost 20% lower than what the private developer could offer. To offset the effect of cost overruns, the government would have to have a 6% advantage in debt markets. See World Bank, World Development Report 1994 (1994) at 91.

3. Is there anything about the long-term supply and demand conditions for power in the Philippines that could concern private developers of these power projects? What could they do to protect themselves?

D.   PROJECT FINANCE IN GENERAL

1.   FOREIGN DIRECT INVESTMENT

Foreign direct investment (FDI), of which project finance was a sub-type, gave the foreign investor equity control of a company in the host country. FDI dominated cross-border private investment into developing and many other countries after World War II until the mid-1970s. U.S. investors led, partly because their's was one of the only capital surplus countries after the war and partly because the dollar became overvalued against many other currencies while it served as reserve currency. The OECD calculated the types of financial resources that all developing countries had received from 1960-72. Most resources were from official sources (industrial governments, IMF and World Bank, primarily). The stock of FDI equaled about one-third of the official resources, but was almost three times the lending by banks, mainly short-term debt. See Organization for Economic Co-Operation and Development, Total External Liabilities of Developing Countries (1974) at 7.

In the mid-1970s, bank loans surpassed FDI in developing countries. The OECD reported the following changes, which as flows are not comparable to the preceding table. Bonds were a very small portion for all developing countries, but played a larger role for Asian borrowers. Note that the method of calculation changes at 1982.

During the 1980s, FDI once again became important, while bank and bond funding fell in the wake of the international debt crisis that began in 1982 (see table).

Components in the Increase of Resource Transfers to Developing Countries, 1970-90				
Source of Resource Transfer	1970	1982	1982*	1990
Total increase (=100%)	$ 51 bn	$ 98 bn	$116 bn	$144 bn
	% of total			
Official assistance	41%	36%	32%	48%
Multilateral	4	7	6	7
Official export credit	8	12	12	4
FDI	20	14	11	22
Banks, Bonds	16	23	37	13
Private flows	na	na	**	4
Private grants	4	8	2	3

* Method of calculation changed   ** < .05%
Source: See OECD, Development Co-operation 1983 Review (1983) at 53 and 1991 Review (1991) at 113.

Portfolio investment, primarily in equity, started in the late 1980s (see private flows in the table) and picked up substantially after 1990. Issuers from the Philippines, for example, raised $536 billion in 1991-3 and another $947 billion in 1994. See IMF, Private Market Financing for Developing Countries, Nov. 1995, at 25. But in Asia, portfolio investment never displaced FDI. The IMF reported that from 1991-5, for Asia, net FDI flows were $156 billion, against net portfolio investment of only $71 billion. This differed from developing and transition countries as a whole, for which the flows were about equal over the same period. See IMF, International Capital Markets, Sep. 1996, at 86.

Notes and Questions

1. How would relative exchange rates among the industrial countries affect the investors' relative roles in FDI?

2. What about FDI would concern developing countries? What could they do about it? How would these host governments affect the investors?

3. Why might direct investment be more important, relative to portfolio investment, in Asia than in other regions?

4. What might explain the changes in the relative importance of official assistance to countries?

2. CONTROL OF FDI IN THE PHILIPPINES

The Philippine government wanted to encourage foreign investment. The following summary of the country's investment policies was prepared by one of the leading accounting firms in the Philippines.

SGV & CO., DIRECT INVESTMENT
Euromoney, The 1996 Guide to the Philippines, July 1996, at 12-13.

The Philippines encourages private investments, both domestic and foreign, in industry, agriculture, mining and other sectors of the economy. Generally, anyone, regardless of nationality, is welcome to invest in the Philippines. For certain economic activities, restrictions on foreign investors are primarily on the extent of ownership of a domestic enterprise rather than on nationality. The Philippine Constitution safeguards foreign investments by guaranteeing:

- Protection from expropriation without just compensation;
- Remittance of profits, capital gains, and dividends;
- Repatriation of investments;
- Ability to obtain foreign exchange to repay foreign obligations.

The recently revised FIA (Foreign Investment Act) of 1991 permits 100% foreign ownership in activities not covered by the Foreign Investment Negative List (FINL), which lists specific areas where foreign ownership is limited up to a maximum of 40%. Foreigners, however, may own up to 100% of domestic market enterprises and up to 100% of export market enterprises that sell at least 60% of their production abroad, if the paid-in capital is at least $200,000. However, if such enterprises involve advanced technology as determined by the Department of Science and Technology, or employ at least 50 direct employees, then only a $100,000 minimum paid-in capital is required.

The FIA simplified foreign investments by eliminating the multiple registrations that used to make investments a difficult process. Foreigners investing in domestic enterprises under the FIA need to register only with the SEC in cases of partnerships and corporations, and with the Bureau of Trade Regulation and Consumer Protection (BTRCP) in cases of sole proprietorships. However, foreigners investing in export enterprises also need to register with the BOI for the purpose of reporting on compliance with export requirements.

When it was passed into law in 1991, the FIA represented a landmark piece of legislation that marked a departure from the decade-old policy of protectionism. Since then, the Philippine Congress has continually made new moves to further liberalize the FIA. The government recently approved the reduction in the minimum paid-in capital requirement for domestic market-oriented enterprises. Another measure has been passed further liberalizing the entry of foreign investments in areas such as import and wholesale trading, insurance, travel agencies, convention and conference organizing, etc. These laws are consistent with the Government's overall objective of further opening the Philippines to business.

Meanwhile, foreign investors wishing to avail of incentives from the Government can refer to the Omnibus Investments Code of 1987 which offers a comprehensive scheme of benefits for investments covered by the priority areas, as well as the Special Economic Zone Act of 1995 which grants special incentives to projects locating in Ecozones.

Fiscal incentives and other benefits as outlined in the Omnibus Investments Code are accorded to qualified projects registered with the BOI. Among the major benefits available under the Code are income tax holidays of six years for pioneer projects and four years for non-pioneer projects, additional deductions for training expenses, permanent resident status for foreign investors and immediate family, and employment of foreign nationals. These incentives are generally perceived by investors as necessary and useful to improve the viability of their projects.

Furthermore, among the major incentives available to Ecozone enterprises, developers and bankers are tax- and duty-free importation of capital equipment and a 5% final tax on gross income earned in lieu of all national and local taxes. Gross income earned is defined as gross revenues less allowable deductions which typically refer to direct costs such as costs for raw materials, direct labour, depreciation of capital equipment, financing charges for the acquisition of capital equipment, etc.

Since the Constitution forbade foreign ownership of land, the Government increased the maximum lease period from 50 to 75 years. Utilities exploiting a natural resource had to be in the hands of citizens. But it continued to require all foreign investment, portfolio or direct, equity or debt, to register with the central bank in order for the investment to be serviced. All foreign exchange transactions for these projects had to go through authorized foreign exchange banks.

Notes and Questions

1. Why, besides the worry about bureaucracy, might the government want private development of infrastructure projects? Why would it be interested in foreign developers?

2. How would potential foreign investors be likely to view the Philippines' policy toward FDI? To what extent would government policy explain the relatively unimportant role of portfolio investors?

3. PROJECTS AND PROJECT FINANCE

Project finance funded projects that depend on their own cash flow to repay the investors according to obligations defined by contract. This was called limited recourse finance. In normal conditions the creditors would be paid from the cash flows of the project. Back up support existed, but if a problem occurred the investors could not look for more general support from, for example, the government of the country in which the project is located. The earliest projects were to extract minerals, which earned foreign exchange. Many later projects earned their income in domestic funds. They often built infrastructure, which included public utilities (like power, water, or telecommunications), public works (roads, dams, canals), and other forms of transport (urban railways, ports, and airports, for example). Infrastructure grew fast over the last decades. For example, in middle income countries, power production per capita grew 55% each decade from 1960 to 1990.

Much infrastructure development in the early years took place under the direct control of government agencies. One study found that from 1980-89 the governments of 8 middle income countries devoted almost 60% of public investment to infrastructure. See World Bank, World Development Report 1994, the main source for this and the following paragraphs. The wave of privatization swept through these sectors in the mid-1980s and many countries began looking for ways to develop infrastructure using private firms. The World Bank found that during 1988-92, of the $62 billion in total privatizations in developing countries, almost $20 billion was for infrastructure and $4 billion of this was for power generation. Another $1 billion was for power distribution.

In late 1993, a total of 148 major infrastructure projects were identified world wide as being underway and another 358 in the pipeline. Of those underway, 77 were in middle-income countries and 16% of these were in the power sector (69% were in transport). Middle income countries had another 179 infrastructure projects, with value of $77 billion, in the pipeline. Although the study did not report how many of these pipeline projects involved power projects, one can assume the number was significant. Despite the rapid growth of power infrastructure, the need persisted for much more development. For middle-income countries, although power generating capacity (measured by '000 kilowatts/million population) grew from 175 in 1975 to 373 in 1990, it still fell far short of the 2,100 capacity found on average in high income economies.

The power sector differs from some other types of infrastructure in important ways. Providers of power can compete with one another, for example, while other types of infrastructure, such as urban and rural roads, are not amenable to competition. Projects in the power sector raise special issues of the government's role in what is supposed to be a private activity. According to the World Bank (see World Development Report 1994, at 100) power

> project sponsors focus on the credibility and solvency of their buyer, typically a government utility that transmits and distributes power. The instrument that protects the power supplier is the "take-or-pay" contract, or power purchase agreement. Under such a contract, the buyer agrees to pay a specified amount regardless of whether the service is used. The government thus provides a contract compliance guarantee....

The question is under what circumstances this sort of government guarantee is good policy since project finance is supposed to depend on the project's cash flow. This goes to the overall structure of the project.

An overview of the structure of a major international project and the risks involved is given in the following material:

P. WOOD, PROJECT FINANCE, SUBORDINATED DEBT AND STATE LOANS
(1996) at 3-9.

Basic structure

To give an initial bird's eye view, the typical basic structure (of project finance) is as set out below.

1. A single-purpose project company is formed to build and operate the project. The shares in the project company are owned by the project sponsors who enter into a shareholders' joint venture agreement between themselves governing their rights and duties as shareholders.

2. A syndicate of banks enter into a credit agreement to finance the construction of the project. The banks are paid out of the proceeds of the project product after completion. There may be several classes of lending banks, e.g. international banks lending foreign currency; local banks lending domestic currency for local costs; export credit agencies lending or guaranteeing credits to finance suppliers to the project of their national equipment; and international agencies lending guaranteeing development credits (World Bank, Asian Development Bank, African Development Bank, European Bank for Reconstruction and Development). ... The agency may lend on a conduit basis so that the banks are sub-participants with the result that, although the banks take risk, the lender of record is the agency. ...

The project company grants the financiers the maximum security available locally over the assets. There may be an intercreditor agreement between the creditors.

3. The balance of the finance needed is provided by the project sponsors, either by way of equity subscriptions or subordinated debt or both.

4. The project sponsors may guarantee the loans under full or limited guarantees during the high-risk pre-completion period.

5. The main commercial contracts are as follows:

- A construction contract whereby a contractor agrees to construct the project. The contractor's obligations may be bonded by surety companies or banks. The project sponsors or others may give a completion guarantee to the project company guaranteeing that completion will take place by a long-stop date.

- There may be equipment supply contracts whereby manufacturers agree to supply the equipment for the project. These contracts may also be bonded.

- Suppliers agree to supply to the project once it is operational, e.g. fuel for a power project, unrefined oil for refining, or raw materials for processing.

- Purchasers (or off-takers) - who are often also project sponsors - agree to buy the project product when the project is completed. The proceeds of sale are used to pay operating expenses, the loans and profits to sponsor shareholders. But in many projects there are no initial long-term purchase contracts for the project product and pay-out depends on market prices, e.g. oil prices or traffic through a tunnel or over a bridge.

- An operator (often also a project sponsor) enters into an operating and maintenance agreement with the project company to operate the project in return for a fee.

6. Often the government grants a concession to the project company to build and operate the concession, e.g. an oil or gas production licence, a mining concession, or a permit to build and operate a power plant or pipeline. These concessions vary from one-off mining concessions to routine permits, e.g. planning and environmental permissions from local authorities. The concession may be of the build-operate-transfer type whereby the government transfers the land to the project company on terms that it is to be re-transferred after a period sufficiently long to repay the finance and to give the project sponsors a reasonable profit margin.

7. Other typical ancillary contracts are:

-   Interest hedge agreements whereby a bank agrees with the project company to pay amounts equal to interest on the loans over a specific rate so as to protect the project from increases in the interest rate during the life of the project. Less commonly, there may also be a currency hedge agreement to protect the project from depreciation of the local currency receipts from the project product (e.g. power supplies) against the foreign currency loan.

-   Insurance policies (damage, third party liability, and sometimes environmental, delay in start-up, business interruption and, unusually, political risk).

-   Direct agreements whereby the project contractors agree with the lenders not to cancel their project contracts on a default by the project company if the lenders perform the contracts.

-   Appointments of independent experts to advise the lenders, e.g. engineers and insurance brokers.

-   Special contracts applicable to the project, e.g. in power projects, electricity grid connection agreements, and steam supply agreements in cogeneration projects producing both electricity and steam. In mobile telephone or cable projects, there will be interconnect agreements with the main telecommunications operator.

8. Feasibility studies and information memorandum. In order to be bankable, projects require an initial feasibility study prepared by experts, e.g. engineering, construction, and technical consultants instructed by the sponsors.

The sponsors also prepare an information memorandum with the help of the banks in order to solicit banks interested in participating in the credit. This contains a description of the project, the terms of the financing, and cash-flow forecasts showing the financial feasibility of the project on the basis of certain assumptions, e.g. as to completion date, construction costs, productivity, market price, interest rates and exchange rates. These assumptions are adjusted to show the impact of the worst case, e.g. high interest rates plus low market prices - usually known as a sensitivity analysis.

. . . Inevitably because of the project risks, this information memorandum is a key document and its accuracy is warranted by the borrower in the credit agreement.

Project Risks Outlined

By way of an overview, it is helpful to outline the main project risks and to give examples of how they are met in the documentation. The essence of project finance is identifying the risks and determining who should bear them.

-    Completion risk. This is the risk that the project will not be completed on time or at all, e.g. because of technology failures, costs overruns, force majeure or necessary variations. If the project is late, interest will run up and perhaps not be covered by the projected cash flows. Project lenders are often not prepared to take non-recourse completion risk and require either a completion guarantee or a guarantee of the loans until completion provided by the project sponsors.

-    Permitting risk. This is the risk that official licences and consents for the project will not be forthcoming or be subject to costly conditions, e.g. construction, environmental or extractive consents from the host government. Lenders are reluctant to lend so long as the project may be blocked or delayed by the absence of a necessary permit. Hence, the important permits cannot be left to later, but must be settled - or completely assured - before non-recourse money is lent. Some minor consents might be dealt with by drawdown milestones, but usually the absence of a critical consent is fatal to early drawdown, i.e. the obtaining of all necessary consents is a condition precedent to borrowings under the credit agreement.

-    Price risk. This is, for example, the risk of volatile markets or government price controls. The risk covers both supplies to the project and sales by the project. The risk is sought to be dealt with by the matching of contracts and the pass-through of risks to the purchasers of the project product or the services. Matching might include a detailed pass-through to the purchasers of fuel/raw material costs, operating costs, tax costs, debt service costs and any dividend cost. The ideal is that a creditworthy purchaser should agree to pay a price for the project product which covers the project costs and the loans, whether or not the project produces.

-    Resource risk. This is, for example, the risk of the adequacy of reserves of gas, minerals, people who want to transport themselves through the tunnel, and the like. This is assessed by initial expert evaluations and an engineer's report. The lenders may keep a cushion retention account financed out of proceeds, and monitor continued viability by cover rations ...

-    Operating risks. This covers, for example, manpower costs, maintenance costs, technology, operating supply costs and the like. These risks are sometimes met by pass-through of extra costs to the purchaser of the product, sometimes by proceeds retention accounts, and are monitored by cover ratios.

-    Casualty risk. This is the risk of damage to the project and is usually met as far as possible by insurance in which the deductibles and exclusions are important. There may also be delay in start-up and business interruption insurance. The latter is often expensive and available for short periods only.

-     Technology risk. Does the project involve sophisticated unproven technology? Is there a risk of latent defects? This is assessed by expert evaluations, and sometimes by retention accounts to cover the projected cost of maintaining the project.

-     Political risk. This used to be a very considerable risk in the lesser developed countries but may be less so now in view of the decreasing popularity of the corporatist state and the ending of the wave of redistributive newly-independent regimes. But history tends to repeat itself, albeit in different guises.

Political risk relates to such matters as increased taxes and royalties, employment controls (work permits, local management), compulsory monopoly sales, sales in local currency only, revocations or changes to the concession, export prohibitions, exchange controls on proceeds, excessive environmental clean-ups, forced governmental or local participation in shares, planning or construction controls and the refusal of import licences for essential foreign equipment. The expropriation may be creeping or constructive as opposed to an outright nationalisation. Government price controls within a utility sector fall within this area.

The protections are various and may include:

-     externalisation of the project company by forming it abroad (often not practicable or particularly helpful);

-     external law and jurisdiction for the main documents so as to insulate the contracts from local changes of law - ... - but the licence or concession is invariably governed by local law or sometimes public international law;

-     external accounts for proceeds (there are limits to this because if the local tap is turned off, then all that is left in the foreign bucket is what is in it plus the dregs in the pipeline);

-     political risk insurance (expensive);

-     export credit guarantees from foreign government export credit agencies;

-     contractual sharing of political risk between the lenders and external project sponsors (e.g. by providing that the sponsors will guarantee the loan to the extent that a loss is caused by a specified political risk, such as expropriation without compensation, although more commonly the banks take political risk and the sponsors commercial risk);

-     government or regulatory agency undertakings to cover (a) policies on taxes, royalties, prices, monopolies, etc., (b) non-termination of the concession if the banks agree to take over, and (c) the grant of a new concession to a bank vehicle if necessary pursuant to rights of the banks to step-in and take over a project;

- the involvement of a supra-national agency with diplomatic clout; and

- ideally, external guarantees or quasi-guarantees such as take-or-pay contracts, investments undertakings or completion guarantees from foreign credit-worthy parties.

- Environmental risk. This contemplates such matters as pollution and clean-up costs on abandonment. These are difficult to meet completely but may be mitigated to some extent by an initial environmental audit and by insurance. But one cannot cover potential future legal changes in advance.

- Exchange rate risk. This is the risk that, for example, the currency of the price paid for the project product depreciates in relation to the currency of the loan, so that the loan is uncovered by sale proceeds. This may be met by currency swaps or options, but it would be unusual for currency swaps or options to be available for the whole period of the loan (e.g. anything from seven to twelve years or more), even if there is a market for the currency in question.

- Interest rate risk. This is the risk of higher interest rates than expected. It may be met by interest cap or interest swap agreements. ...... Again, it may be difficult to purchase interest contracts in the market for whole life of the project for all of the revenue streams. The credit risk of the counterparty is an additional factor.

- Insolvency risk. This is the risk of the insolvency of contractors, project sponsors, suppliers, purchasers, even insurers or a syndicate bank. This is inherent in project risk and is a bank credit risk which they are used to evaluating. This is their metier. Ultimately the credit strength of the sponsors, whether or not there is recourse to sponsors, is crucial. Banks often take the credit risk of the purchasers of the product or users of the project: construction contractor risk usually has to be bonded.

Notes and Questions

1. In July 1987, the Philippine Government issued Executive Order No. 215, which provided for the private sector to build, own, and operate power stations. Soon the policy was embodied in a statute, Republic Act No. 6957, which granted the private sector the right to engage in infrastructure projects through several means: build, own, and transfer (BOT), build, own, operate, and transfer (BOOT), or build and transfer (BT).

2. What are the special attributes of project finance? Which types of risk are likely to be the most serious to a foreign investor in a project's

equity? Debt? How does the basic structure Wood outlines allocate these risks?

3.   As you read the description of the Pagbilao power project below, ask how closely its structure conforms to that outlined by Wood. How did the parties allocate the risks identified by Wood? Specifically, how did the senior lenders protect themselves against completion risk, operating risk, price risk, risks related to financial markets (such as interest and foreign exchange rate change), and country risk?

4.   Model codes have appeared that countries may use to guide their own legislation for projects. These include the United Nations Commission on International Trade Law guidelines for law governing privately financed infrastructure projects, The OECD model concession law (in draft), the European Bank for Reconstruction and Development Secured Transactions Model Law, and the OECD Convention on Combating Bribery of Foreign Public Officials in International Business Transactions. Rules governing dispute resolution are offered by the International Chamber of Commerce, the World Bank's Convention on the Settlement of Investment Disputes between States and Nationals of Other States, the London Court of International Arbitration, and the New York Convention on the Recognition and Enforcement of Arbitral Awards of 1958, as well as bilateral investment treaties. E. Hayes and A. Cumings, *Taming the Risks of Project Finance*, International Financial Law Review, May 2001, at 27.

E.   THE PAGBILAO POWER PROJECT

When the Philippines Government announced in 1987 that it wanted the private sector to develop power plants, the Hopewell Holding Ltd (HHL) group, based in Hong Kong, quickly opened discussions. Hopewell had led major BOT power projects in China and the Philippines. It could offer experience with offtake contracts, turnkey construction, limited recourse financing, fuel supply arrangements, and many of the other elements of the Pagbilao project. Internationally respected, it had a reputation for good work and timely completion. It ranked among the top 20 companies on the Hong Kong Stock Exchange. As the Pagbilao project was being closed, Hopewell reorganized its power project companies, allowing the group to go public. These changes in corporate structure did not affect the underlying relationships and are not described here.

In 1993, Hopewell Energy International, Ltd (HEIL) and Napocor concluded an Energy Conversion Agreement (ECA). HEIL had two years to arrange the Pagbilao Power Project. The ECA described the parameters of the project, including implementation, fuel supply, basic costs (ultimately fixed at $933 million), payments, energy tariffs, and financing.

HEIL would build, own, operate, and then transfer the plant as is and at no cost to Napocor after 25 years.

The ECA set target dates:

Commence work:	April 30, 1993
Complete Unit 1	April 30, 1996
Complete Unit 2	July 31, 1996
Complete Power Station	July 31, 1996

The arrangements led in late April 1993 to a bundle of contracts (the Agreements).

The Agreements described a complex structure, pictured in the following chart. Hopewell Power (Philippines) Corporation (HPPC), a roughly 87% subsidiary of HEIL, would be the project company. HEIL promised Napocor it would be jointly and severably liable for all of HPPC's obligations. The contractors building the plant were Mitsubishi Corp. of Japan, the leader, and Slipform Engineering Ltd, a member of the Hopewell Group. Napocor would make key contributions during construction. Once the plant was operating, Hopewell Tileman Ltd would

Major Participants in the Pagbilao Project

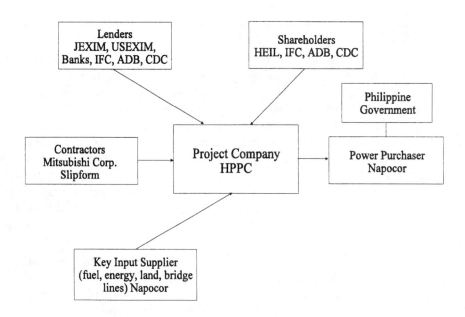

manage it, assisted by a specialist firm that would provide technical support. Throughout construction and the first 25 years of operations, HPPC would own the plant and be primarily responsible for it. Napacor agreed to supply the fuel (coal) needed to run the plant and to buy all power it produced according to the agreed tariff.

Many contracts documented the arrangement. Loan agreements included the Common Agreement (described later in this Chapter), separate agreements between HPPC and CDC, IFC, JEXIM, the Citibank syndicate, and U.S. EXIM. Security documents included a trust (described below), a mortgage trust, an assignment and security, and a pledge, all involving the company, the trustee, and usually the sponsor and one or more lenders. Several completion support agreements were designed to ensure the turnkey project was finished on time. In addition, the Project Documents included the ECA, the turnkey contract, and related agreements.

Pagbilao would receive several incentives because it qualified as a "pioneer" for the Omnibus Investments Code of 1987. These included a 6 year income tax holiday from the start of operations, tax free imports of capital equipment for several years, a tax credit for domestic capital equipment, and the right to employ foreigners. HPPC faced several problems ultimately resolved in its favor. Several lawsuits tried to block construction. Issues of the Project's environmental impact had to be settled by the government.

Notes and Questions

1. Why would the Philippines Government and Hopewell prefer to work through a locally incorporated subsidiary of Hopewell (HPPC) rather than formal joint venture?

2. How significant is it that the government and others contract with various units in the Hopewell group, most incorporated abroad, rather than the parent company itself? What would account for this arrangement? What is the function of the Hopewell parent?

3. What does each of the main parties to this project bring to it? What are its major concerns? As you read the following, please consider how the senior lenders protect themselves.

1. CONSTRUCTION

The Agreements described the plant, its technology, components, fuel supply, and site. The plant would be built according to international standards as described. Mitsubishi, selected by bid to be the lead member of the construction consortium, would have overall responsibility. The other member, Slipform Engineering Ltd, an HHL subsidiary based in Hong Kong, had done similar work on a project in China. It would be responsible for civil construction work. HPPC, as owner, would supervise, aided by Hopewell Tileman Ltd, another Hopewell Holding subsidiary, as representative. The supervisors would review all engineering designs, monitor procurement and quality, ensure construction met contract requirements, monitor progress, testing, and transfer, and assure compliance with governmental approvals and law.

Of the total project costs of $933 million, direct costs were $535 million for mechanical and electrical work, $167 million for civil construction, $166 million for interest and finance charges, and $65 million for other indirect costs (eg., lawyers' fees).

The construction consortium agreed to accept a lump sum price. If the units did not meet guaranteed standards, the consortium would pay liquidated damages, providing a performance bond in support. The consortium would buy insurance for the plant, equipment, and vehicles. HPPC would retain 5% of all payments (other than civil and architectural works) until 30 days after it certified the second generator reliable. The consortium warranted against defective equipment and workmanship for two years. Failure to complete the project on time would result in liquidated damages up to an agreed portion of the contract price. Testing of the first generator was to occur six months before it was due to start operating and testing of the second, four months before operations.

HPPC would buy insurance to cover construction risks, including:

- Marine Cargo Insurance (including war and strike risks) covering imports of plant, equipment, machinery and materials to the Project site;

- Contract Works Insurance covering loss or damage to the Project works during the construction and testing/commissioning periods. Extended maintenance cover will be included and specifications will include requirement for riot and strike, design defects, etc.

- Business Interruption Insurance covering loss, specified standing charges, interest and fees due to delay in start up of the project as a result of damage during transit to site and during construction, testing and commissioning;

- Third Party Liability Insurance covering legal liabilities to third parties for injury or damage arising from construction, testing/commissioning and maintenance; and

- Other local insurances such as workmen's compensation and motor insurance for the Company's personnel and vehicles.

The sponsors, HEIL and HPPC, would be rewarded for early completion and penalized if they were late. The reward was that HEIL would receive directly 50% of the capacity fees and energy fees (described in the following section), after deducting expenses, earned during the period before the target completion dates. The reward was called a Bonus

Dividend. As a shareholder, it would also receive its pro rata share of the remaining 50%. For delays over 30 days, Napocor could claim for each day and generator, $10,000 the first 60 days and $24,7000 beyond that, to a ceiling of $16 million. HEIL had to post a $16 million bond when it signed the ECA, which was reduced 50% after the first generator was built. Hopewell was not able to complete the project early, despite having started before financing was completely arranged. Hopewell accused Napocor of failing to do what it had promised.

Napocor agreed to provide at no cost several essential inputs for construction, including the electricity needed for construction, a bridge and power line to the Pagbilao Grande Island, and the land for the site. Napocor retained ownership and paid all real estate taxes and assessments. It agreed to pay all other taxes except for net income tax and construction fees. It would pay for testing and start-up.

The finance ministry stated that the obligations of Napocor had the full faith and credit of the Republic, which would make sure that Napocor would be able to discharge them. Any dispute would be resolved using the Australian Commercial Disputes Center in Sydney, Australia under the rules of UNCITRAL. The government waived sovereign immunity.

Government agencies agreed to give the approvals identified in the Agreements as necessary. For example, the Central Bank needed to approve procedures for foreign exchange transactions. Many other government agencies were involved: the Board of Investment (e.g., to permit 100% foreign ownership of HPPC), Securities and Exchange Commission (e.g., that HEIL did not need a license to do business in the country), Department of Finance, Department of Environment and Natural Resources, Napocor, National Economic and Development Authority (as to the project's significance), National Electrification Administration, Energy Regulatory Board, Department of Justice, Regional Development Council for the region, local governments, Insurance Commission, Immigration Commission, local deed registry, and local registry for chattel mortgages.

The parties distinguished between two types of *force majeure*. These were:

Type A Events

Other than as referred to in paragraph B below, any war, declared or not or hostilities, or of belligerence, blockade, revolution, insurrection, riot, public disorder, expropriation, requisition, confiscation or nationalization, export or import restrictions by any governmental authorities, closing of harbors, docks, canals, or other assistances to or adjuncts of the shipping or navigation of or within any place, rationing or allocation, whether imposed by law, decree or regulation by, or by compliance of industry at the insistence of any governmental authority, or fire, unusual flood, earthquake, volcanic activity, storm, typhoons, lightning, tide (other than normal tides), tsunamis, perils of the sea, accidents of navigation or breakdown or injury of vessels, accidents to harbors, docks, canals, or other assistances to or adjuncts of the shipping or navigation, epidemic, quarantine, strikes or combination of workmen, lockouts or other labour disturbances, or any other event, matter or thing, wherever occurring, which shall not be within the reasonable control of the party affected thereby; or

Type B Events

War, declared or not or hostilities occurring in or involving the Republic of the Philippines, or of belligerence, blockade, revolution, insurrection, riot, public disorder, expropriation, requisition, confiscation or nationalization by or occurring in or involving the Republic of the Philippines, export or import restrictions by any governmental, regional or municipal authorities of or within the Republic of the Philippines, closing of harbors, docks, canals, or other assistances to or adjuncts of the shipping or navigation of or within the Republic of the Philippines, rationing or allocation, whether imposed by law, decree or regulation by, or by compliance of industry at the insistence of, any governmental authority of or within the Republic of the Philippines, or any other event, matter or thing, wherever occurring, which shall be within the reasonable control of Napocor or the government of the Republic of the Philippines or any agency or regional or municipal authority thereof.

Napocor promised to buy the project if certain events occurred during construction or operation. These events included agreed changes in circumstances (notably law, regulation, the status of the site, government approvals) that adversely affected Hopewell's rate of return, Type B *force majeure* events, a decision by Napocor to close the plant (permissible only 20 years or more after completion), or Napocor's failure to ensure timely payment. If the buy out occurred before completion, Napocor would pay all Hopewell's actual and incurred costs plus 10%. If after completion, it would pay the present value of all remaining Capacity Fees (except fixed operating fees).

Notes and Questions

1. How do the parties deal with construction risks identified in the article by Wood? How do the incentives and penalties work? How useful is the distinction between Type A and B events in the *force majeure* clause likely to be? Do the parties address other risks? Are there important risks that they ignore? Why?

2. Is this a non-recourse project? What is the function of the government, Napocor, and Hopewell during construction?

3. How much risk did Hopewell take by starting before financing was complete? Why would it do this?

2. OPERATIONS

Once the plants were operational, the parties' obligations and remuneration changed. HPPC remained in charge overall, but it would be assisted by Hopewell Tileman Power Systems Corp, a sister company with operational experience. Also providing technical support would be an international operations and management contractor that specialized in running coal-fired thermal power plants. Though 15 expatriates would be employed in key roles in the work force of 467 people, Hopewell planned to place overall management authority in local hands by the year 2000. It had done so in its earlier projects in the Philippines and in China.

An agreement governed operations and maintenance. Hopewell, as operator, agreed to comply with all relevant laws, control the budget, comply with the ECA and fuel supply arrangements, guarantee performance, and train staff.

Payment would take the form of capacity fees and energy fees. Capacity fees, accounting for over 90% of income, were fixed in the contract as flat fees per KW/month. Rates were fixed for four types of capacity: capital costs (accounting for over 80% of all capacity fees), fixed operating costs, infrastructure costs, and service (return on investment). Energy fees had two parts. One part paid a flat rate per KW hour calculated in U.S. dollars and pesos. For the output above the first 75% of the generator's capacity, the dollar rate was 5% lower than for the output at or below 75%, but the peso rate did not change. The second part of the energy fee added a bonus for efficient fuel use and deducted a penalty for inefficient use. All energy fees and the fixed operating fee were indexed to adjust for inflation in fixed and variable costs. The dollar portion was indexed to Japanese and U.S. export prices and the peso portion to the official Metro Manila consumer price index. Dollar payments, the bulk, were to be made to Hopewell's account in New York. Peso payments were made to its Manila account.

The parties based these fees on scenarios that assumed the plant would operate at 80% capacity even though the plant could readily produce 5% more. The scenarios estimated costs for the first year of operation and increased costs 6% each following year. The parties concluded that the return on equity investment would only fall slightly with construction cost overruns of 10% or if no energy fees were paid.

Other bonuses and penalties were provided. HPPC agreed to a maximum "net heat rate" which, if exceeded, would generate penalty payments from HPPC and if met would bring bonus payments to it. Other penalties applied if station downtime exceeded that allowed by the Agreements.

HPPC will buy insurance against operating risks, including:

- Material Damage Insurance covering loss or damage to the completed Project on an "all risks" basis;

- Machinery Breakdown Insurance covering loss or damage to mechanical and electrical equipment resulting from breakdown or derangement;

- Business Interruption Insurance covering specified standing charges, interest and fees as a result of interruption in the operation of the completed Project following material damage or breakdown;

- Third Party Liability Insurance covering legal liabilities to third parties for injury or damage resulting from the operation of the Project; and

- Other local insurances such as workmen's compensation and motor insurance.

Napocor promised to buy all the energy the plant produced. It would pay capacity fees based on the capacity HPPC offered up to a maximum of 85% and energy fees based on Napocor's actual requests for energy.

Notes and Questions

1. What is the function of the capacity and energy fees?

2. Evaluate the assumptions underlying the calculation of the fees. How well do they protect the parties?

3. The impact of the 1997 financial crisis in Asia led to proposals to change the allocation – or at least the presentation – of exchange risk. A writer in the Philippines proposed two ways to allocate exchange risk. Instead of automatically passing on to consumers the sometimes very large impact of local currency devaluation, it would be wiser to have the government give a sovereign guaranty of exchange rates in the form of a "shadow" adjustment of the price of energy (or whatever commodity the project produced). The benefits of the project to the country would justify the government bearing this risk and its cost. Second, multilateral agencies (see the next section of this chapter) would offer insurance for any differential between the rate changes anticipated by the project (and priced in it) and actual changes. R. Gavieta, *Currency Exchange Risk and Financing Structure: A Southeast Asia Developing Country Perspective*, The Journal of Project Finance 49, Winter 2001.

4. Why specify such a detailed list of types of insurance? Why not simply specify insurance as needed or standard practice in the industry?

5. During the late 1990s and early 2000s, major insurance companies offered a growing array of policies for non-traditional risks in project finance and other single asset endeavors. Traditional insurance includes insurance for finite risk, excess loss, and political risk, as well as financial

and performance guarantees. On the non-traditional side is insurance for "currency, commodity, operating and credit risks–risks that previously were borne by a company's shareholders or creditors. Rating agencies are increasingly willing to consider non-traditional insurance as mitigating risk in projects they rate, even reducing the spread against investment-grade debt when the project is not investment grade. It seems that only the risk of revenue shortfalls that are in the control of management are necessarily beyond the appropriate scope of insurance, to avoid moral hazard. But the insurance companies are still reluctant to take on risks with a high-dollar loss per claim, such as the risks of new technologies or a country at war. P. Alderdiece, H. Horwich, and R. Feldman, *Risk Finance for Project Finance: The Expanding Horizon of Credit Enhancement*, The Journal of Project Finance 30, Winter 2001.

6. Does Napocor's role effectively leave the project in private hands?

F. FINANCING PAGBILAO

Financing for Pagbilao took the form of equity ($235 million) and debt ($698). HEIL held 86.95% of HPPC's shares and three multilateral institutions -- the International Finance Corporation (IFC), the Asian Development Bank (ADB), and the Commonwealth Development Corporation (CDC) -- held the rest in equal proportions. The shareholders paid HPPC the peso equivalent of their dollar obligations. HEIL paid for part of its equity stake by capitalizing its preparatory expenditures.

Senior debt of $698 million was provided by the Japanese Export-Import Bank (JEXIM) ($220 million), a consortium of banks acting with it ($147 million), a construction loan from a Citicorp-led syndicate of banks ($185 million) replaced by a loan from the U.S. Export-Import Bank (U.S. EXIM) when operations began, and loans from the multilaterals ($152 million). All loans matured in ten years (except that from the Citicorp syndicate, the CDC, and a small loan). In addition, the contractors and sponsor (HEIL) agreed to provide $200 million in subordinated loans to HPPC to fund pre-completion cost overruns and funding shortfalls. The amount would be reduced to $100 million after the first generator was done. These sources are described below.

The major lenders were the two export-import banks, owned by their governments, and two consortia or syndicates of commercial banks. The Japanese lending group included five Japanese and two German banks' Japanese units. The group gave such a large portion of the loan because Mitsubishi Corp was the lead contractor. JEXIM's dollar loan was made without recourse at a fixed interest rate of 8%. JEXIM acted as agent for the bank syndicate, whose dollar loan carried a floating rate of LIBOR (then about 4.5%) plus 2.15%. The banks' loan had limited insurance from the Japanese Ministry of International Trade and Industry. Both

matured in 10 years.   The U. S. export credit differed somewhat in
amount and structure.   The next section describes this sort of export
finance and the U.S. Export-Import Bank in more detail.

Financing for the Pagbilao Project ($ millions)

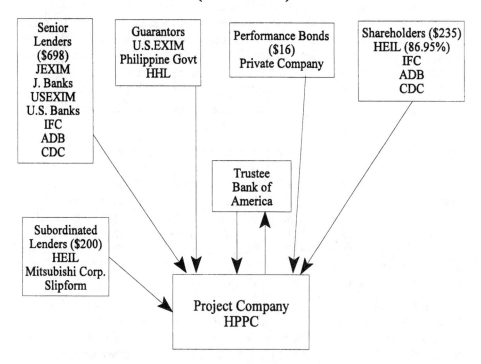

Note: Members of each group, and the groups, are also related by various contracts.   For
example, the senior lenders have an agreement among themselves, as do the shareholders.
Both the senior lenders and the owners have appointed specialist firms to monitor the
project and advise them.

1. OFFICIAL EXPORT CREDIT: U.S. EXPORT-IMPORT BANK

Projects that needed equipment or other inputs from another country
often found they could draw on official export credit.   Most industrial
countries and many others had quasi-independent government agencies
dedicated to financing their countries' exporters, in the belief that
importers were swayed not only by the quality of goods or equipment, but
also by cost.   To the extent that exporters competing from different
countries could not distinguish their goods according to quality, price was
critical and, people reasoned, the cost of credit could be an important
factor in cost.   Indeed, where the buyer needed to borrow to make the

purchase, cheap credit could make a high-cost product competitive by reducing the total amount the borrower paid over the life of the loan.

The U.S. Export-Import Bank, founded in 1934, was a statutory corporation directed by a president and board appointed by the U.S. President. The view in the mid-1930s was that exports could help the U.S. economy climb out of its depression. Congress had to renew the charter every 4 years. U.S. EXIM was financed by Congressional appropriations. It was to supplement private capital rather than compete with it.

U.S. EXIM's portfolio of services broadened over the last few decades. It initially made loans to a buyer/borrower equal to 95% of the value of the U.S. exports being purchased. In the 1970s, its practices changed in response to competitive pressure from other countries. Many exporting countries used their export-import banks as competitive tools, offering loans at below-market interest rates and subsidizing them to do so. Often they gave mixed credits, combining export credits and foreign aid to lower the price of credit even further. Borrowers in developing countries knew a good thing when they saw it and began to play the export-import banks off against one another, bargaining the rates down even further. U.S. EXIM responded at two levels. It diversified its services, offering a variety of loans for different purposes and adding guarantees and insurance to its portfolio. Guarantees required only 25% of the capital U.S. EXIM had to allocate to loans, allowing U.S. EXIM to leverage its resources more.

Working through the Organization for Economic Cooperation and Development (OECD), U.S. EXIM sought a consensus to limit export credit pricing to market rates and eliminate financing that mixed export credits and aid. Gradually the OECD won support. Eventually, its members agreed to an Arrangement setting minimal standards. The IMF summarized the *Arrangement on Guidelines for Officially Supported Export Credits*, prepared by the Export Credit Group of the OECD. See M. Kuhn, B. Horvath, and C. Jarvis, Officially Supported Export Credits, Mar. 1995, at 6 ("Official Credits"). The most important elements were:

- a cash payment at least 15% of the export contract's value;
- repayment at regular intervals, with a 5 year limit for richer importing countries and a 10 year limit for poorer ones;
- "minimum interest rates linked to market rates;"
- "minimum levels of concessionality for 'tied-aid' financing."

Not all countries practiced what was preached, but most tried to appear to be in compliance with the agreed standards. U.S. EXIM allowed up to 15% foreign content in the U.S. export package, stayed within the OECD's maximum repayment terms, and would finance local costs in the importing country up to a ceiling of 15% of the U.S. contract value.

By the mid-1990s, U.S. EXIM offered medium- and long-term loans and guarantees, facilities to support bank credit, and programs for aircraft finance, projects, insurance, and working capital guarantees primarily for small and medium-sized businesses' exports. Its fiscal year 1996 program budget was $894 million, which it estimated supported exports of almost $15 billion. This was only 2% of total U.S. exports, in contrast to support from the Japanese Export-Import Bank amounting to 32% of Japanese exports and from the French agency of 18%. Nevertheless, U.S. EXIM boasted that since 1991 it supported $76 billion of U.S. exports, which generated 1 million jobs. Since 1980, it financed $126 billion of exports, sustaining losses of only $2.4 billion for an enviably low loan loss ratio of 1.9%.

In the early 1990s, export credits were an important source of external debt for all developing and transitional countries. The credits were particularly important for the 20 largest recipients, of which the Philippines was one. Its debt to official export credit agencies doubled from $4 billion in 1987 to $8.1 billion in 1992. See the following table which, with much of the following paragraphs, is from Official Credits.

Developing Countries and Transitional Economies: Composition of External Debt, 1992		
	Total Debt and Share by Type	
Type of Debt	**All Developing and Transitional Countries**	**Top 20 Recipients of Export Credits**
Total ($ billions) (=100%)	$1,731	$ 960
Share of: Export credits	21%	26%
Official development aid	8	8
Other bilateral	11	5
Multilateral	16	15
Official debt subtotal	56	55
Banks and other	44	45
Source: Official Credits at 7.		

The Philippines was low in the Top 20. At the top was Russia and the former USSR, which accounted for 13% of the Top 20's debt, or $47.5 billion, in 1992 Export-Credit Borrower' Club. The top 5 accounted for

42% of the debt of all developing and transitional countries to export-credit agencies: China ($32 billion), plus Brazil, Mexico, and Indonesia (about $22 billion each). Export credit varied in relative weight in the portfolios of the debtor countries. It was relatively low in the Philippines, at 20% in 1992. It was of much greater importance for Nigeria at 63% (Nigeria, owing $18 billion, ranked as the 8th largest debtor), Iran at 56% (owing $17 billion and ranking 10th), and Algeria at 49% (owing $21 billion and ranking 7th). A major problem for export credit banks was that many borrowing countries lagged when it came to repaying. Arrears and unrecovered claims were high in Brazil ($12 billion, about 55% of its total), Nigeria ($14 billion, 78% of total), Russia and the former USSR ($14 billion, 29%) and Iran ($4 billion, 24%). Even the Philippines appeared on this list in 1992, owing arrears of $2 billion, or 25% of the total. It corrected this problem when it rescheduled its official external debt in December 1995 through a formal inter-governmental mechanism known as the Paris Club.

Arrears, a serious global problem for creditors of developing countries since the 1980s debt crisis, raised the difficult question for export credit agencies of when they should not lend or give guarantees to support exports. Some loans faced much higher country risk than others. Repayment mattered to the export-credit agencies. They measured their performance in net cash flow, consisting of income from premiums plus recoveries minus claims paid out. By this measure, their performance in the early 1990s was nothing to emulate. In each of those four year, they recorded negative cash flows from $500-700 million. See Official Credits at 11. The result was that many export credit agencies became more sensitive to risk and priced accordingly or even cut off their services for some countries.

Notes and Questions

1. How risky would the Philippines appear to a commercial lender? An export credit agency? How significant is the Philippines inclusion in the Top 20? How significant is its arrears and the resolution of the problem? What do you make of the fact that the Philippines was in arrears when the Pagbilao project was financed? Should U.S. EXIM and JEXIM have participated in the financing?

2. What is the function of export-credit banks? Some export credit agencies saw their role as an insurer, while others saw it as export promotion. How would these different perceptions have affected their activities? How would they explain the need for and components of the OECD Arrangement? How would importing countries view the Arrangement? Why would the U.S. government want to promote such an arrangement when governments of other major industrial countries did not?

a. DIRECT LOANS

U.S. EXIM made direct loans to buyers, but the amount of the loan varied with the degree of foreign content in the U.S. exports. With 10-15% foreign content, the U.S. EXIM loan would be for up to 85% of the contract price. The buyer had to pay 15% in cash. If the goods had 15-50% foreign content, U.S. EXIM financed only the portion with the U.S. content and it would not finance exports with more than 50% foreign content. The bank disbursed funds directly to the U.S. exporter. U.S. EXIM charges fees based on its assessment of the credit-worthiness of the borrower or guarantor, the country risk, and the maturity of the loan. But U.S. EXIM's policy was not to lend for a project during the construction period when there was a risk that construction might not be completed. Instead, it offered only a political risk guarantee to banks lending to support the exports during construction. After construction, U.S. EXIM would provide credit.

This was what happened with Pagbilao. The Citibank syndicate loaned HPPC funds to finance its purchase of the U.S. equipment for the project, but their loan only lasted through the construction phase. U.S. EXIM guaranteed the political risk of their loan. U.S. EXIM ensured that its criteria (such as US content) were met. The Citibank syndicate had two groups of about 18 banks each, one of banks incorporated in the Philippines that would lend in pesos to meet local costs and the other of banks based abroad that would lend in dollars to pay for the U.S. goods. When Pagbilao became operational, U.S. EXIM's own direct loan to HPPC replaced the Citibank syndicate: HPPC used the proceeds from the U.S. EXIM loan to repay the Citibank group. U.S. EXIM charged fees for all its services, in line with its published rates. New York law governed the various contracts.

Project finance had become increasingly important to U.S. EXIM. In June 1994, it established a Project Finance Division. During its first year, the division approved eight projects generating over $2 billion in US exports. Its general policies included requirements that projects have long-term contracts extending beyond the maturity of the U.S. EXIM funding, that project costs and pricing should be market-based, and that revenues should be largely in hard currency to reduce currency risk.

b. THE POLITICAL RISK GUARANTEE FROM U.S. EXIM

U.S. EXIM provided its political risk guarantee to the eight banks in the Citibank syndicate that had loaned $185 million to HPPC. The guarantee covered payments of principal and interest as they became due, regardless of whether they were accelerated, but did not cover penalties. U.S. EXIM received a commitment fee and a fee of about 2% of the disbursed loans. U.S. EXIM would succeed to the rights and interests that the lenders it compensated had in all unpaid amounts. Political risk included Transfer Risk, Expropriation, and Political Violence.

Transfer risk was non-payment that occurred solely because the borrower could not lawfully obtain dollars in a market in the Philippines or transfer the dollars to the lenders. The borrower had to make an irrevocable deposit in local currency within 90 days after the dollar payment was due. The barriers could include any law, order, decree, or regulation by an authority within the de facto control of the Philippine government. The borrower could not have any lawful market through which it could make the payment. The barrier could not have been caused by the action of the borrower, the lenders, or Citibank as agent. It could not be the result of a rule in a country other than the Philippines. The lenders could not have known at the time of the loan that the borrower would face this barrier. U.S. EXIM would pay compensation in dollars if all these conditions were met.

Expropriation occurred by the act of a government agency that had de facto control over the part of the Philippines where HPPC operated. That agency must have caused the default, violating international law by:

- preventing the Borrower from paying when payment is due;

- depriving the Borrower of control or disposal of its property or its ability to operate the project;

- canceling previously issued authorizations to import the item being exported after shipment; or

- substantially causing the default or depriving the Agent, Lenders, or Trustee of fundamental creditors' rights, such as rights to levy against security or commercial guarantees.

This also included U.S. Government restrictions on export of the goods (but no other acts of the U.S. Government). The default must have persisted for 90 days. Expropriation did not include acts resulting from (according to the agreement):

(a) any law, decree, regulation or administrative action of the Government of the Philippines which:

(i) is not by its express terms for the purpose of nationalization, confiscation or expropriation (including by not limited to intervention, condemnation or other taking),

(ii) is reasonably related to constitutionally sanctioned governmental objectives,

(iii) is not arbitrary,

(iv) is based upon a reasonable classification of entities to which it applies, and

(v) does not violate generally accepted principles of international law; or

(b) an action in accordance with any agreement voluntarily made by the Borrower, Agent, Guaranteed Lenders or Trustee [defined later in this Chapter]; or

(c) a provocation or instigation by the Agent, Guaranteed Lenders or Trustee, including corrupt practice which is unlawful at the time under the laws of the United States or the Philippines, provided that (i) actions taken in compliance with a specific request of the Government of the United States or (ii) any reasonable measure taken in good faith by the Agent, Guaranteed Lenders or Trustee, by way of a judicial, administrative or arbitral proceeding respecting any action in which the Government of the Philippines is involved shall be deemed not to be provocations or instigations under this Section 6.02 (c); or

(d) the insolvency of, or creditor's proceedings against, the Borrower under applicable law; or

(e) bona fide exchange control actions by the Government of the Philippines (or its instrumentalities or state enterprises); or

(f) any action which (i) is lawful under the laws of the Philippines of the type described in [this agreement], and (ii) is taken by the Government of the Philippines in any capacity or through the exercise of any powers as shareholder, director or manager of the Project; provided, however, the shares in question have not been acquired through an act or series of acts that, under the criteria set forth in Article VI, constitute Expropriation; or

(g) Any abrogation, impairment, repudiation or breach by the Government of the Philippines (or its instrumentalities or state enterprises) of any undertaking, agreement or contract relating to the Project or Items, provided that the foregoing exclusion shall not preclude a claim otherwise eligible under this Article VI; or

(h) Any action or actions by the Government of the Philippines (or its instrumentalities or state enterprises) that terminate or restrict the use of or maintenance of the Retention Account [defined later in this Chapter] or any offshore accounts of the Borrower, provided that the foregoing exclusion shall not preclude a claim otherwise eligible under this Article VI or Article V related to the Retention Account or any account of the Borrower (or the Proceeds thereof), which, in either case, has been transferred to the Philippines from offshore; ....

Political violence that directly caused default in a payment due on the loan obligated U.S. EXIM to pay compensation. Political violence referred to any violent act intended to achieve a political end. Examples included war, hostile acts of armed forces, civil war, revolution, insurrection, civil strife, terrorism, or sabotage. It specifically did not include acts done primarily to accomplish goals of labor or students.

Notes and Questions

1. Wood says above that political risk insurance is expensive. Why would the parties to Pagbilao be willing to bear this risk?

2. Does the protection provided by U.S. EXIM meet the political risks this project would encounter in the Philippines? What political risks are not covered? Why? How serious are they?

3. Why would U.S. EXIM not be prepared to lend during the Pagbilao construction but be willing to provide political risk insurance?

2. MULTILATERAL FUNDING

Three of the investors, the IFC, ADB, and CDC, took both equity and debt interests in HPPC. They were called multilateral institutions because each was established and controlled by the governments of many countries: the IFC as part of the World Bank group had government members from all regions of the world; the ADB's government members were primarily from Asia, the region served by the development bank, but also from industrial countries elsewhere; and the Commonwealth Development Corporation was owned and managed by members of the Commonwealth, the successor to the former British empire.

The involvement of these three institutions went beyond simply providing money to fund the project. The following sections present background information about two, the IFC and ADB.

a. INTERNATIONAL FINANCE CORPORATION

The IFC is a part of the World Bank group, which is described in Chapter 1. In its own operations, the World Bank actively promoted infrastructure projects with its own battalions of technical specialists in fields ranging from agricultural technology to water resources. The IBRD loaned to member governments at market rates, applying market tests to projects proposed by member recipients. It built a strong reputation in international capital markets as one of the best credits, given its excellent track record managing both assets (borrowers did not default, at least until the early 1990s) and liabilities (it always met its obligations) and the callable capital subscriptions of the industrial governments that were its major shareholders. (This reputation was weakening in the late 1990s as some debtors failed to service their loans on schedule.) By the early 1990s, the World Bank had assets of about $150 billion, outstripping any other multilateral or bilateral development aid agency. The group had become the elephant that nobody could ignore in the development pond.

The World Bank group evolved as the IBRD saw the need for other forms of development finance. The IFC was established in 1956 to promote private sector development. The International Development Association (IDA) was created in 1960 as a sister agency to provide very low cost concessional long-term funds for projects in the poorest countries.

IDA was funded by subscriptions and grants from member governments and some of the World Bank's profit. The other member was the Multilateral Investment Guarantee Agency (MIGA), established in 1988.

The IFC paralleled the World Bank in important ways. It had 170 countries as shareholders by the mid-1990s. The top five held 45.4%: U.S. (22.5%), Japan (6.7%), Germany (5.6%), France (5.3%), and the U.K. (5.3%). The World Bank's president was the president of IFC and also IDA.

Unlike the World Bank, the IFC could invest in private entities. It gradually carved a niche analyzing investment opportunities in developing countries and helping them solve investment problems, whether of information or structure. It did so with its own debt and equity investments in firms, by mobilizing other investors, and by helping the process with advice and technical assistance. Thus the IFC helped governments privatize. Its trust fund helped secure funding for projects in 50 countries. The IFC became a major source of data and expertise about emerging markets, advising 50 countries about stock market development by the mid-1990s. It offered risk management tools, such as swaps or securitization, to firms in developing countries. And it managed a portfolio of investments designed to prime the pump for private investors, domestic or foreign, in developing countries. Over 40 years, it invested more than $30 billion in 1,700 businesses and 120 member countries.

By the mid-1990s, the IFC had a staff of over 1,300, organized by key industries (agribusiness, capital markets, chemicals, oil and gas, power) and by regions. Its portfolio had grown fast: its own loans and equity investment approvals rose from $1.8 billion in 1992 to $2.5 billion in 1994 and $3.2 billion in 1996. Worldwide, it had outstanding investments of almost $20 billion in over 260 projects, mostly in the form of long-term loans. It also helped a growing number of firms in developing countries raise funds from foreign banks and equity investors; these approvals rose from $1.4 billion in 1992 to $4.5 billion in 1994 and $4.9 billion in 1996. All told, it reported portfolio investments in 985 companies (including regional and global financial institutions), valued at $9.8 billion committed funds and $7.8 billion actually disbursed.

From this, IFC generated substantial "net income," similar to what most private firms would call profit. IFC was a development agency, so it ploughed this money back into its operations. It borrowed $3 billion in 1996.

Leverage was key to the IFC's activities. It never invested alone and it relied on others to manage the project; it was a passive investor that might hold the shares long-term and then sell on the domestic market. The prospect of a strong supply of private international bank credit for a project, for example, would prompt the IFC to reduce its anticipated direct stake, as long as the scale was commercially viable. IFC calculated that in 1996, for every $1 of its own funds, other investors contributed $5.13.

Infrastructure projects in Asia were important to IFC. Infrastructure accounted for 28% of all IFC's own and supplemental funding, more than any other sector in 1996. It dedicated to infrastructure about 20% of its 53 projects in 12 Asian countries that year (including 3 regional projects), drawing almost $1 billion of IFC's own funds.

In the lead up to the Pagbilao project, the IFC had a coordinating role. For example, it prepared and updated the information memorandum that was circulated to prospective parties.

b.   ASIAN DEVELOPMENT BANK

Regional development banks emulated the World Bank within their region. The Inter-American Development Bank (IDB) led, followed by the Asian Development Bank, the African Development Bank (AfDB), the European Investment Bank (EIB), European Bank for Reconstruction and Development (EBRD) and other funds for smaller regions. Their share of total lending by multilateral institutions appears in the adjacent table. For contrast, the table includes lending by the World Bank and IMF, as well as developing and transition countries' total external debt.

All multilateral institutions faced the serious continuing problem of heavily indebted borrowing countries that could not service their loans on schedule. Between 1980 and 1995, 65 countries rescheduled their debt at least once. Of these, 35 were low-income, 14 lower-middle, and 16 other middle. By 1995, 23 had graduated from reschedulings (including 9 lower-middle countries, of which the Philippines was one), 24 had rescheduling agreements in effect (including 3 lower-middle income countries), and 18 needed further reschedulings (including 2 lower middle). The poorest countries suffered most from bad debt. Only 4 of had graduated. Their external debt grew from 2.7 times their exports in 1983 to 5.6 times in 1993. As a share of real GDP, however their debt fell from a peak of 4% in 1985 to 1% in 1993. The problem was that the countries needed foreign exchange to service their debt. Lenders and aid donors devoted much time to trying to resolve, or at least ameliorate, this problem. At the end of 1995, the Philippines again rescheduled, so "graduation" was a relative and slippery term. See Official Financing.

The ADB opened in 1966 as a multilateral development bank for the region of Asia. At the time of the Pagbilao project, governments of 40 Asian countries (holding 60% of the shares) and 16 other countries (holding 40%) owned it (and the number rose to 57 by 2000). The top shareholders were: Japan and the U.S. (16.054% each), China (6.628%), India (6.512%), Australia (5.952%), Indonesia (5.602%), Canada (5.381%), Germany (5.381%), and Korea (5.182%).

These governments subscribed almost $46 billion in capital, actually paying-in only $3.5 billion. Debt ($13.7 billion) and reserves ($6.6 billion) raised these resources for ordinary operations. In addition, the ADB had special funds, financed by donations, to support special activities. One, of $18.7 billion, was the Asian Development Fund and another, of $630 million, was the Technical Assistance Special Fund.

Based in Manila, the ADB was more under the influence of Japan than the U.S. Its president was traditionally nominated by the Japanese government, for example.

External Debt of Developing Countries to Multilateral Institutions, 1980-94							
Multilateral Institution	**Annual Average**						
	1980-4	**1985-9**	**1990**	**1991**	**1992**	**1993**	**1994**
Total External Debt* of Developing Countries ($ bns)			$1,104			$1,246	$1,331
Total Debt to Multi- laterals ($ bns)	$93	$193	$244	$265	$272	$291	S309
	as % of total multilateral debt						
World Bank	51%	56%	58%	57%	56%	56%	57%
IBRD	33	39	39	38	36	35	35
IDA	17	17	19	19	20	20	21
Regional Development Banks	12	15	19	19	21	21	22
AfDB	1	2	3	4	4	5	5
AsDB	4	4	6	7	7	8	9
IDB	8	9	9	9	9	9	8
European institutions	3	4	5	5	5	5	5
Others	7	6	5	5	5	5	3
IMF	27	20	14	14	14	13	14

Source: A. Boone, Official Financing for Developing Countries, Dec. 1996, at 46 ("Official Financing").   Sums may not total due to rounding.   * Excludes short-term debt (*ibid* at 7).

Like the World Bank, the ADB made loans and equity investments to help its developing members grow, provided technical assistance to prepare and execute development projects and programs, promoted public and private investment, and helped members coordinate development plans and policies. In 1996, 22% of its $5.5 billion in loans were for energy and 77% of its disbursed loans ($3.8 billion) were for projects. Its private sector lending was about 5% of total loans and had started only in the mid-1980s. Of its $138 million in technical assistance grants, 10% were for energy. Between 1991 and 1996, its annual net income fluctuated between $513 million and $660 million. In 1994, the proportion of concessional to nonconcessional funds was 62% for IBRD/IDA and 59% for ADB. See Official Financing at 48.

The ADB reported 13 projects in the Philippines, most in agriculture, agro-industry, social infrastructure, education, and health, in 1996.

Notes and Questions

1. What is the economic function of multilaterals? Some said their primary role was to help developing countries. Yet the interest rates they charged on their loans were substantially higher than the interest rate for the loans from the US and Japan banks. Why?

2. How well did the IFC's Pagbilao role conform to its general policy and practice?

3. Why would HHL not just have hired a leading consulting firm to perform the advisory functions of the IFC?

4. Does the presence of multilateral lenders in the Pagbilao project suggest it was not commercially viable? What was their function for the project?

3. COMMON ARRANGEMENTS

In a variety of combinations, the parties agreed to common approaches to issues. The senior lenders agreed about how to share collateral, procedures for consultation, and other matters. The shareholders entered a common agreement. The following subsections describe two such arrangements, one to standardize conditions, the other to facilitate payment to the senior lenders.

a. THE COMMON AGREEMENT

HPPC and each of the Senior Lenders entered an agreement, governed by New York law, setting out common representations, warranties, covenants, and other terms that would apply to all the agreements. The Common Agreement defined terms, set forth principles of construction, gave the financing plan, and then detailed the conditions precedent to initial and all disbursements, the representations and warranties, affirmative and negative covenants, and events of default.

Some elements may be summarized: the debt/equity ratio may not exceed 75/25. The independent engineer will not have disapproved any payments to the contractors. HPPC will consult with any lender about any adverse report of the engineer. All necessary government approvals remain in full force. HPPC has no subsidiaries or equity interests in any other person. HPPC must maintain records and make regular reports as stipulated.

The following material from the agreement illustrates some of the important or special arrangements:

Representations and Warranties

Submission to Law and Jurisdiction. As of the Initial Borrowing Date, the choice of governing law for each of the respective Project Documents will be recognized in the courts of the Republic, and those courts will recognize and give effect to any judgment in respect of any Project Document obtained against the Company or HEIL in the courts the jurisdictions of which the Company has submitted. ...

Single-Purpose Company. The company has not traded or incurred any liabilities other than in connection with its participation in the transactions contemplated by the Project Documents.

Status of the Senior Loans. The Obligations constitute direct, unconditional, and general obligations of the Company and rank not less than pari passu as to priority of payment with all other Indebtedness of the company .... or where such Indebtedness is secured by a Permitted Lien. Except as permitted by ..... the Agreement, the Company has not secured or agreed to secure any such Indebtedness by any Lien upon any of its present or future revenues or assets or capital stock.

Negative Covenants

6. 03 *Dividends: Restricted Payments.* (a) The Company will not declare or pay any dividends, or return any capital, to its stockholders or authorize or make any other distribution, payment or delivery of property or cash to its stockholders as such, or redeem, retire, purchase or otherwise acquire, directly or indirectly, for consideration, any shares of any class of its capital stock now or hereafter outstanding (or any options or warrants issued by the Company with respect to its capital stock), or set aside any funds for any of the foregoing purposes, unless:

(i) such dividend or other action is permitted by applicable law;

(ii) no Default or Event of Default is then in existence (or would be in existence after giving effect to such dividend or other action);

(iii) such dividend or other action is permitted under the Trust and Retention Agreement; and

(iv) either such dividend is a Bonus Dividend or in the case of a cash dividend or distribution, such dividend or distribution is made only after the Project Completion Date and if, after giving effect to such dividend or distribution, (a) the Long-term Debt to Equity Ratio would not exceed 65:35 and

(b) the Senior Debt Annual Cover Ratio would be no less than 1.4:1

(b) *Payments of principal and interest on the Sponsor Subordinated Loans* permitted by the Trust and Retention Agreement shall not be deemed restricted by Section ... (a) above.

6.09 *Other Transactions.* The Company will not enter into any partnership, profit-sharing, or royalty agreement or other similar arrangement whereby the Company's income or profits are, or might be, shared with any other Person, or enter into any management contract or similar arrangement whereby its business or operations are managed by any other Person, other than the Project Management Agreement and the Operation and Maintenance Agreement.

6.11 *No Other Business.* The Company will not carry on any business other than in connection with the completion and operation of the Project and will take no action whether by acquisition or otherwise which would constitute or result in any material alteration to the nature of that business.

Events of Default

7.06 *Project Events.* (a) (i) Any of the Operating and Maintenance Agreement, the Project Management Agreement and the Technical Support Agreements shall be assigned or otherwise transferred, materially amended or prematurely terminated (other than by reason of any default on the part of the Lenders or the Trustee) by any other party thereto other than with the written consent of the Required Lenders and no alternative arrangement satisfactory to the Required Lenders has been effected within 30 days thereof or (ii) any of the Project Documents (other than the Operating and Maintenance Agreement, the Project Management Agreement and the Technical Support Agreements) shall be assigned or otherwise transferred, materially amended or prematurely terminated by any party thereto other than with the written consent of the Required Lenders; or

(b) the Company shall cease to have the right to possess and use the Site; or

(c) any event shall have occurred which entitles the Company or NAPOCOR to give a notice under ... the Energy Conversion Agreement; or

(d) the Company shall abandon the Project or otherwise cease to pursue the operation of the Project in accordance with standard industry practice, or shall (except as permitted by [this agreement]) sell or otherwise dispose of any of its interest in the Project; or

(e) the Company shall fail to maintain any of the insurance policies described in ...[this agreement]; or

(f) the Project Completion Date shall not have occurred by February 6, 1997; ...

7.07 *Material Adverse Change.* One or more events, conditions or circumstances (including without limitation Force Majeure as defined in Articles 14.1 (a) and 14.1 (b) of the Energy Conversion Agreement) shall exist or shall have occurred which, in the reasonable judgment of the Required Lenders, would adversely affect the ability of the Company or HHL or either of the Turnkey Contractors) in a material respect to meet as required their respective obligations hereunder or under any of the Loan Documents, the Energy Conversion Agreement or the Shareholders Agreement; ...

7.09 *Ownership of the Borrower.* (a) HHL shall cease to maintain Control (as defined below) of the Company or shall sell, transfer, assign or otherwise dispose of (each a "Transfer"), or create or permit to exist any Lien on or in respect of any shares of capital stock of HEIL if, after giving effect to such Transferor Lien, HHL owns directly or indirectly, or possesses voting power in respect of, capital stock of HEIL representing less than fifty-one (51%) of total voting power of HEIL (for purposes of this Section 7.09, "Control" means the possession, directly or indirectly, of the power to direct or cause the direction of the management and policies of a Person, whether through ownership of voting securities, by contract, or otherwise); or

(b) HEIL shall cease to maintain Control of the Company [HPPC] or shall Transfer or create or permit to exist any Lien on or in respect of any shares of capital stock of the Company if, after giving effect to such Transfer or Lien, HEIL owns of record or beneficially, or possesses voting power in respect of, capital stock of the Company representing less than sixty-seven (67%) of total voting power of the Company; or

(c) the Company or HEIL shall, without the prior consent of the Required Lenders, issue or have outstanding any securities convertible into or exchangeable for its capital stock or issue or grant or have outstanding any rights to subscribe for or to purchase, or any options or warrants for the purchase of, or any agreements, arrangements or understandings providing for the issuance (contingent or otherwise) of, or any calls, commitments or claims of any character relating to, its capital stock, other than as provided in the Financial Plan, the Shareholders Agreement, and the Board of Investments Approval; ...

Other events of default include:

- failure to pay any senior loan principal on time or interest within 7 days after the date it was due;
- default, beyond the grace period, on debt exceeding $1 million by HEIL, Hopewell Tileman Power, Slipform, or Hopewell Tileman Ltd, or exceeding $10 million by HHL;
- a bankruptcy decree against HPPC, HEIL, Hopewell Tileman Power, Hopewell Tileman Ltd., Slipform, or Mitsubishi;
- judgments not fully insured against HPPC or HEIL of more than $10 million) or, before the project completion date, against HHL ($10 million), Slipform ($5 million), or Mitsubishi ($20 million).

When an event of default occurs, each lender may notify HPPC to declare its loan, or the entire loan if by Citibank or the JEXIM banks, immediately due and payable. The loan documents specify the parties' rights toward the trust and security (see next section). If a bankruptcy decree is entered or if Napocor buys the plant, all loans immediately become due and payable without notice and any obligation to lend more ends. The definition of "Required Lenders" is given in the next section.

Notes and Questions

1. Overall, evaluate the protection given by the Common Agreement to the various parties. Who are the major beneficiaries? What are their principal forms of protection?

2. What accounts for the limitations in HPPC's activities?

3. Who stands to lose most if the events of default occur? Are the events under their control?

4. How effectively has HHL separated itself from the risks of the project?

b. THE TRUST ARRANGEMENT

HPPC, HEIL, HHL, the contractors in their capacity as subordinated lenders, Mitsubishi Hong Kong as a subordinated lender that made the loan due from Mitsubishi Corporation as contractor, the senior lenders, and Bank of America as trustee, made a trust and retention agreement subject to New York law. The same parties, other than the lenders and trustee, made an Assignment and Security Agreement creating for the Trustee and the benefit of the lenders and Mitsubishi Hong Kong security for the obligations. The agreement set priorities among claimants to income streams and security, and procedures for acting if a default might have occurred.

HPPC and HEIL instructed other parties that would owe the project money, such as Napocor for purchases of energy, or insurers if claims were made, to pay those funds to the Trustee. The Trustee set up a "Retention Account" in its New York office to hold the funds. Most forms of income for the project would be paid into the trust. Most would be dollar accounts, but the Trustee would keep Peso receipts as pesos unless otherwise instructed. Subaccounts would hold different types of proceeds: funds from HPPC's sale of energy to Napocor, insurance payments, liquidated damages paid by the sponsor or contractors for late delivery, funds from the subordinated loans (completion support), and funds from reserves and a security letter of credit. The funds were held for the benefit of the senior lenders then, subordinated to them, Mitsubishi Hong Kong and finally HPPC as residual beneficiary. Only the Trustee controlled the Retention Account.

A Diagram to the Parties to the Trust Agreement

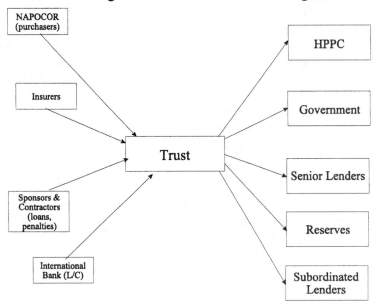

The Trust Agreement set priorities for accounts from which withdrawals from the Retention Account would be made if no event of default had occurred. These were, in order, the accounts holding:

- sales proceeds,
- reserves to service senior debt,
- completion support (for the first four purposes, below), and
- liquidated damages (for the same purposes).

The Trust Agreement also set priorities for recipients of those withdrawals. These were, in order:

1. operating and maintenance costs up to total construction costs until completion and then an amount equal to the estimated quarterly cost of operations (on-going);

2. taxes (as due);

3. senior debt service (as due);

4. payment of senior debt principal (as due);

5. reserves to service all senior debt over the next six months (ongoing);

6. payments due to contractors on certain subordinated debt (when due);

7. interest and arrears due on the remaining subordinated debt (when due);

8. reserves to service all senior debt over the next twelve months (ongoing);

9. principal due on the remaining subordinated debt; and

10. as HPPC directs.

The Trustee would rely, to determine the amounts due, on quarterly reports submitted by HPPC and the lenders. When an "extraordinary casualty" occurred, the Trustee could release up to $7.5 million to HPPC in any one fiscal year. The Trustee would also pay any bonus due to HPPC, on the instructions of the Required Lenders (a majority of the senior lenders as explained below). By written notice in advance, the Required Lenders could prevent the Trustee from paying HPPC, HHL, HEIL, or Slipform if they asserted a breach of contract.

HPPC was obliged to have a leading international bank issue a "security letter of credit" immediately after the first scheduled repayment of the senior loans. The one-year LC would be payable to the Trustee. The amount of the LC would be 33% of the amount left after subtracting $46 million from the funds remaining in the Retention Account after all uses (1-10) had been satisfied. The Required Lenders could instruct the Trustee to draw on the Security LC according to circumstances specified in the Common Agreement. If a new LC was not received within 30 days of the expiration of the old one, the proceeds from the old one could be deposited in the Security Subaccount. The Trustee could pay senior debt service and principal from this subaccount if the proceeds, reserve, and completion support sub-account lacked funds. Any remaining amounts would meet operating and maintenance costs if funds were not available.

The Trust Agreement also gave the Trustee authority over liquidated damage payments owed by the sponsors or contractors to Napocor.

When a lender alleged default, the rules changed. Any lender could do so in writing. The Trustee's powers depended on whether a large majority of lenders agreed with the allegations. The "Required Lenders" are those senior lenders which hold 75% or more of the loans committed (before drawdown) or outstanding (if drawn) and are 75% of the number of lenders. For this calculation, JEXIM spoke for the Japanese banks and Citibank spoke for the syndicate members. If the Required Lenders did not act after the allegation, the Trustee would not take any enforcement action for six months. The Required Lenders (including the alleging lenders) could determine that the event was cured, in which case the Trustee would take no action. They may waive defaults on covenants, but not on payments of the senior loans or the Mitsubishi loan. If the Required Lenders instructed the Trustee not to enforce the security, no action may be taken for a two year period from the first notice. After that, the Trustee must enforce for the benefit of all lenders, by declaring all obligations due and taking any necessary court action. The Trustee will pay first all senior lenders, then Mitsubishi, then HPPC.

The Trust Agreement says clearly that no one lender has any right to disturb or prejudice the rights of other lenders or seek priority over others. The only way to enforce security arrangements is as provided in the agreement.

Notes and Questions

1.   In many Asian countries, the civil law tradition was not clear about whether BOT and other types of projects were subject to private law, treating the state as another private party, or to laws governing the state. In the latter case, the bureaucracy could play an important role. This is one more reason to apply the law of a major financial center rather than the host.

2.   Given the role of Napocor and the Philippines government, is this project really non-recourse?

3.   How does the Trust Agreement protect senior lenders? Where do they stand in the order of priorities? Why? How flexible are the provisions?

4.   How well do the various agreements protect senior lenders from political risk? Consider also the role of Eximbank and the multilateral lenders.

5.   Overall, how well does the structure of the Pagbilao project resolve the problems with foreign direct investment encountered by investors and host countries in the past?

6.   Beginning in 1996, insurance companies offered political risk insurance (PRI) for investors in bonds issued for project finance. Five years later, five insurers offered capital market PRI, as it was called. Like the Pagbilao financing, the issuer built a debt serve reserve account

offshore that funded the insured Trustee paying the investors in the notes. D. Galvao, *Political Risk Insurance: Project Finance Perspectives and New Developments,* Journal of Project Finance, Summer 2001, at 35.

7.   The currency crisis in Asia, discussed in Chapter 21, slowed the growth of projects and project finance in that region.   It raised questions about the viability of many projects underway in the affected countries, including the Philippines.   The crisis led governments in the countries to cancel many planned projects and slow the development of others.   Even without governmental delays, the collapse of the host country's currency often made a project economically unviable.   Organizing firms suffered. In 1996, Asia accounted for 30% of deals in project finance and 33% of the funds raised, so the Asian crisis was quite damaging.   Hopewell was hit by the crisis.   In October 1997, it announced that it was setting aside $647 million to provide against losses on a Thai mass transit project that had collapsed.   Hopewell was hardly unique among construction firms. Banks and law firms that provided supporting services were also hit.

Even more serious for financial markets, however, was the prospect that projects still being financed might default.   Moody's announced in April 1998 that four power projects in Indonesia could default on $855 million bonds they issued.   One project was postponing its start, and many believed it would never start.   For three projects already operating, the state-owned power company appeared unlikely to be able to pay the project for the power in the near future at the agreed price.   Devaluations of 50% of the rupiah's value against the dollar meant that the power companies would have to impose huge rate increases to raise the rupiah needed to pay the dollar values of the loans.   Since huge rate increases were politically difficult and economically short sighted for the project, the investors faced possible renegotiation of their agreements.   In a project-related bond market of $32 billion in principal, no bond had been renegotiated, at least in recent memory.   Renegotiating publicly traded bonds was much more complicated than renegotiating syndicated loans, which were a much larger source of funds for projects.   A survey of more than 800 banks revealed that their project financings fell from $76 billion in 1997 to $34.5 billion in 1997.   See S. Davies, *Indonesia Projects 'At Risk Of Default',* Financial Times, April 16, 1998 and L. Lucas, Erie Silence Sweeps Construction Sites, Financial Times, April 5, 1998. Ultimately, the Philippines government did not seek to renegotiate the BOT power projects.

8.   In April 2000, the Philippines government presented a Power Reform bill to the legislature.   If enacted, the bill would privatize Napocor.   The IMF, World Bank, and ADB had made its privatization key to their release of further loans to the Philippines.   Subsidies for Napocor were a major cause of the government's large fiscal deficit.   Napocor needed the subsidies because its sale of power earned less than had been projected.   Actual demand for power had turned out to be lower than

demand projected when Napocor undertook the Pagbilao project, and others. The privatization ran into stiff political opposition. Then at the end of 2000, impeachment proceedings for the country's president dominated the political agenda. A special body reviewed Napocor's contracts to find ways that would reduce its obligations to pay minimum off-takes of 75% even when the plants only actually used 40% of capacity. W. Arnold, *Philippines Set to Privatize Power Company*, New York Times, Apr. 11, 2000; Manila Times Internet Edition, *Palace Urged to Review Napocor IPP Deals*, Apr. 22, 2001.

The Philippine Electric Power Reform Act was passed in June 2001. The government was to restructure the industry, privatize Napocor's assets and liabilities, open generation and distribution to competition, and transfer transmission to a National Transmission Corporation. The government would assume up to Pesos 200 billion ($4 billion) of Napocor's debts and Napocor would assess consumers for the remainder. During the transition, a new Power Sector Assets and Liabilities Management Corp. (PSALM) would own generation assets, all liabilities, contracts with independent power producers (IPPs) and other assets" to be sold to private investors. Cross subsidies, from industrial to retail users, for example, would end. The ADB and Japanese Import-Export Bank released about $1 billion in loans they had been holding until the bill passed. US Asean Business Council, Inc. Press Release, June 5, 2001.

The plan was to sell Napocor's power plants, after removing its debt, to foreign buyers. In early 2002, however, the government had a difficult time finding buyers. While private distributors would keep their monopolies over residential buyers, they would compete for industrial ones, reducing power cost which were higher in the Philippines than any other country in Asia. Although distributors would keep their monopoly over power lines, the law required them to allow competitors access at rates set by government. R. Landingin, *Meralco Prepares to Exploit New Era in Philippine Power*, Financial Times, June 26, 2001.

By March 2002, Napocor's debt had reached Pesos 310 billion ($6.1 billion), of which 57% was owed to multilateral and bilateral creditors, 15% to bond holders, and the remaining 28% to banks. PSALM announced that rather than prepay all loans, some of which extended to 2028, they would refinance. Since PSALM's life ended in 2026, one question was what would happen to the remaining two years of debt. The government said it hoped to complete Napocor's privatization by June 2002. H. Madrilejos-Reyes, *Napocor Debts Up By 6.16%*, Manila Times, Mar. 8, 2002; R. Domingo, *Government Shelves Roadshow for Napocor's Transco*, Inquirer News Service, Mar. 12, 2002.

What effect would Napocor's privatization have on the lenders to the Pagbilao project? Are they protected against this eventuality?

Links to Other Chapters

Although project finance raises many issues not covered elsewhere in this textbook, its analysis of risk reflects that in the material about capital adequacy (Chapter 4) and foreign exchange (Chapter 6). Some of the key lenders are banks from the U.S (Chapter 3) and Japan (Chapter 8). One of the major types of credit is the syndicated eurocurrency loan (Chapter 9). And many of the factors prompting the government of the Philippines to delegate the building and operation of the power plant to a private group arise in our discussion of privatization (Chapter 20).

CHAPTER TWENTY

EMERGING MARKETS: PRIVATIZATION AND INSTITUTIONAL INVESTORS

A. INTRODUCTION

The growth of stock markets in many developing countries outstripped that in industrial countries since the mid–1980s. Fueling this growth was an almost insatiable appetite for emerging market securities on the part of investors worldwide. Apparently radical change in the countries' economic policies attracted the investors. A key change was privatization, as governments sold state owned enterprises to the private sector.

In 1989, the new president of Mexico, Carlos Salinas de Gortari, announced that the government would divest itself of its controlling interest in Telefonos de Mexico, S.A. de C.V. (Telmex). A Harvard trained economist, he took office in a close and bitter election in which he had promised to reform the country's economy. In his first year, he started with banks nationalized in late 1982. Then he looked beyond the financial sector. Telmex was the third largest company in Mexico, ranked by assets.

This Chapter describes the steps taken by the government to sell its shares in Telmex. It starts with background about privatization worldwide. It describes circumstances in Mexico that prompted the government's action and Telmex during the period before 1989/90. Two options were to divest only on the Mexican stock exchange and to sell the Government's full share in a block to foreign investors; both routes are explored.

The actual privatization had two stages. The first, in 1990, transferred voting control (but not all of the government's portion of the capital) to a private consortium of Mexicans and foreign investors. The second stage, in 1991, sold much of the government's remaining stake in Telmex on equity markets in Mexico, the U.S., Japan, and Europe. Institutional investors, such as pension funds, were major buyers. The Chapter gives information about them and factors that propelled them on emerging markets.

As you read the Chapter, consider why the government would privatize Telmex as it did. Were there reasonable alternatives? What were the risks for the parties? Why did the investors show such interest in the company's 1991 offering?

B.   PRIVATIZATION IN THE 1980S AND 1990S

Government control of business seemed to be a permanent feature of the landscape in almost every country well into the 1970s. When Margaret Thatcher became U.K. prime minister in 1979, she set out to reverse this trend in her country and soon officials were devising ways the government could divest itself of productive firms. Momentum picked up as other industrial and developing countries saw benefits for themselves in the early and mid–1980s. Then communist countries across Eastern Europe and Asia shifted toward market economics and the prospect of the largest asset transfer in the history of the world raised dazzling prospects.

In 1994, the U.S. Congress, as overseer of foreign aid programs funding private investment in Eastern Europe and elsewhere, requested an explanation of the privatization process. The executive director of Price Waterhouse's international privatization group gave the following description.

J. WADDELL, TESTIMONY BEFORE THE SMALL BUSINESS COMMITTEE OF THE U.S. HOUSE OF CONGRESS
(Apr. 14, 1994).

What is Privatization?

Privatization is the process of transferring productive operations and assets from the public sector to the private sector. Broadly defined in this fashion, privatization is much more than selling an enterprise to the highest bidder, as it includes contracting out, leasing, private sector financing of infrastructure projects, liquidation, mass privatization, etc. My testimony will argue that there is no single "best" approach to privatization; the appropriate privatization path depends on the goals that the government is seeking to attain, the individual circumstances facing the enterprise and the economic and political context of the country.

It should be noted that privatization is fundamentally a political process as well as a commercial and economic process. Privatization changes the distribution of power within a society, as it diminishes control of the economy by the state and government-appointed managers. Workers often feel threatened by the potential changes inherent in privatization, although employees frequently benefit from the process. As a result, public support is a major consideration in any privatization program and many of the choices made in designing and implementing transactions reflect the need for such support. Two consequences flow from this factor: 1) choices of approaches are sometimes altered due to "political" considerations, meaning that equity must be promoted in the privatization strategy, and 2) program implementation must be objective and fair to avoid adverse publicity.

What are the Goals of Privatization?

Many, varied goals are often pursued through privatization programs. These goals often fall along two principal dimensions: 1) broad social or macroeconomic goals, and 2) enterprise specific or macroeconomic goals.

Macroeconomic goals are numerous. Fundamentally, privatization is advocated as a means to reduce the government's role in the economy, partly as a philosophical matter (as in the UK) but principally because governments have performed badly in that role. Many countries can attribute substantial portions of their external debt to liabilities of state-owned enterprises and significant portions of government budgets are devoted to paying subsidies or otherwise assisting loss-making state-owned enterprises. Government's objectives in these situations is often simply to extricate themselves from these financial commitments, and focus scarce resources instead on education, infrastructure, and social welfare.

A second macroeconomic goal of privatization is to promote the development of the private sector by "levelling the playing field" and ending subsidized competition from state-owned enterprises. There is a danger in some countries that emerging private businesses face unfair competition from state enterprises that have access to credit and other inputs at below market rates and better access to government distribution channels. In order to give the private sector a fair opportunity to compete and thrive, state-owned enterprises are privatized.

A third goal of privatization, is to obtain the sales proceeds and use them to finance shortfalls in the government's budget or retire some of the public sector debt. While it is widely recognized that focusing on sales proceeds may be short-sighted and ignore other important outcomes of privatization, it is a fact that many governments are strongly influenced by the availability of funds from privatization.

A fourth goal is to broaden share ownership so that the public has mechanisms for saving money and participating in the economies of their countries.

The macroeconomic goals of privatization focus mostly on the potential improvements that private sector operators will bring to an enterprise to improve this performance and increase chances of survival. These goals recognize the need to improve enterprise efficiency by introducing new technology and financing sources, improving the quality of the product, enhancing marketing-especially in the international market, providing information systems, and generally improving the management of the enterprise. Obviously successful changes of this nature, when applied to a number of individual enterprises, will have significant macroeconomic implications as well.

A final comment on the goals of privatization is to note that in most countries privatization is but one part of a broad program of structural reform. This is most evident in former Communist countries, where privatization is an element of the process of developing a market economy and its associated financial institutions. In such cases, the privatization program designed should take into account the broader economic goals that are being pursued, as well as the goals specific to the enterprise.

What Types of Privatization Techniques Can Be Used?

There are a variety of techniques that can be selected to use in privatizing state-owned enterprises of activities. These techniques include the following:

Small business auctions—A normal procedure for privatizing small businesses is to auction them to the highest bidder. Especially when dealing with truly small businesses, such as sole proprietorships and small partnerships, it is advantageous to sell to a single bidder. Given the size of the enterprises, elaborate bid evaluations and valuations are not appropriate and will only serve to delay the process. Auctions also create a dramatic setting to promote the visibility of privatization and allow for broad participation, and they are truly transparent, in the sense that all participants can see for themselves how the process was conducted and identify the high bidder.

Auctions are generally not appropriate for larger enterprises because the bids will not be as readily comparable: the quality of the new ownership group becomes important—what technology will it bring, is it well-financed, what investments will it commit to making, where will it market the product, will it close the business to limit competition, etc.?

Strategic investors—Larger enterprises are often sold on a case-by-case basis, by soliciting technically and financially capable investors to acquire the enterprise. In soliciting the investors, the seller normally conducts a thorough review of the business and prepares material describing the business and its equipment, workforce, financial condition, markets, and prospects. This information is circulated to a group of candidate investors that express initial interest in the business. These investors then submit bids outlining the terms under which they would purchase shares of the enterprise. The offers will discuss the percentage of shares to be purchased, what debts will be assumed, future investment plans and the financing associated with the expansion, any anticipated changes to the underlying business or the workforce, actions required by the government (sometimes requesting measures such as tariff protection), and other significant factors. Because bids received in this fashion are not readily comparable, the seller must prepare a valuation of the enterprise and the bids received, analyze the strengths and weaknesses of the bidding groups, and then engage in a significant amount of negotiation with the highest ranked bidder. This process is often lengthy, as there are significant but difficult issues at stake.

Trade sales have significant disadvantages in that they can take a long period of time and substantial expense to conduct. Because of the substantial amount of negotiation often involved, they also have the aura of "back room deals" being conducted and are susceptible to complaints from bidders that the decision process was unfair—particularly when the bids are structured very differently.

Initial Public Offerings (IPOs)—Initial Public Offerings are the sale of shares directly to the public. Most of the privatizations conducted in the United Kingdom during the 1980's were done through IPOs. Because the potential buying public includes a large number of unsophisticated investors, relatively more information and higher quality information needs to be prepared to conduct an IPO. A valuation of the enterprise is prepared and a pricing strategy is developed that reflects the valuation, but seeks to ensure that the offer is sufficiently attractive that the shares available can be sold. IPOs have the virtue of stimulating interest among the general public in financial markets and increasing share ownership in society. They are also less subject to negotiated agreements than trade sales, although the negotiations between the selling government and its agent, the underwriter, may be elaborate.

The disadvantages of IPOs are that they do not bring new capital to the enterprise and do not bring in new managerial talent or resources. As a result, IPOs should only be used if the performance of existing management is satisfactory. In addition, IPOs are very time consuming and expensive to conduct, and they generally require the existence of a formal stock exchange and broker network or other distribution mechanism to be implemented effectively.

Joint Ventures—A common form of privatization in some parts of the world—especially China—is the joint venture. Under a typical joint venture, an investor approaches the government and offers to contribute something of value to an enterprise, such as capital, management, or technology, and in return receives a share of the ownership of the newly constituted business. Joint ventures are often attractive to governments that are not fully supportive of privatization because the government does not relinquish all control of the enterprise. Over time, and with new investments, it may be possible to minimize government control by diluting its ownership interest.

There are several significant disadvantages to joint ventures as a form of privatization. Because of the government's continued involvement, many of the goals of privatization set forth at the outset of my testimony are not met: the government remains involved in management and its liability for poor performance is retained. In addition, joint ventures are subject to the same complaints about lack of transparency and participation as trade sales—sometimes even more so due to the fact that joint ventures are often proposed by the investor on an exclusive basis and are less subject to standardization than trade sales.

Mass Privatization Programs—One of the significant innovations in privatization techniques during the last few years is the development of mass privatization programs. In concept, mass privatization programs avoid the time and expense of case-by-case transactions and involve the general public by distributing shares for free or in exchange for specially created privatization vouchers. The mechanics of mass privatization programs are similar to IPOs, except that vouchers are used to purchase shares, rather than cash. As a result, significantly less analytical time is required and disclosure requirements are greatly reduced. The virtues of a speedy process, which I discuss in the next section, cannot he overestimated, particularly in the transitional economies of the former Communist world.

The disadvantages of the mass privatization programs lie principally in the diffusion of ownership across broad groups and in the critical role that management is able to play in the privatization process. It is argued that subsequent restructuring of enterprises will be more difficult due to these factors. Offsetting this argument to some degree is the fact that potential investors in these enterprises can negotiate with the new owners—rather than the government—and can make investments into the enterprise in return for shares, rather than have their funds go into the state treasury. Both of these factors are valued by investors.

Build–Own–Operate/Build–Own–Transfer Programs. Governments facing severe needs for infrastructure investments increasingly turn to the private sector to finance, build, and operate the needed facilities. In return, the government gives certain assurances to the investor and pays fees for the services provided. This technique has proved useful in attracting additional capital into infrastructure investments and alleviating critical shortages of power and transportation, especially in Asia.

The disadvantages of these programs are that they are often very difficult and time consuming to negotiate and structure. Because these programs are relatively new and involve financing of new projects—not assets that are already existing—many difficult issues emerge that have not previously been confronted.

Liquidation—State-owned enterprises with very limited prospects for survival are sometimes liquidated and their assets auctioned to the private sector. Sometimes these "liquidated" enterprises continue as going concerns; in other cases their assets are sold separately, liquidation ends the government's commitment to support an enterprise and lays the groundwork for private sector investment—if the product has a market and it can be manufactured efficiently.

Liquidation is normally a last resort, used when the government has no realistic alternatives. In this sense, it is applicable only in a limited set of circumstances.

Notes and Questions

1. The author describes several options available to governments wishing to privatize. Consider which of these options would be most appropriate to each of two countries with large state owned enterprises, one fitting profile (a) and the other profile (b):

   a. A leading industrial country with a deep and broad stock market, large banks, sophisticated accounting systems and investors, moderate domestic savings, no exchange controls, good pools of managers, and a legal system that resolves commercial disputes quickly and predictably.

   b. A former Communist country with no working financial system, a small inactive stock market, banks with minimal capital and bad debts equalling at least 30% of all loans, government officials and a population with limited understanding of how a market economy works, a legal system unequipped to resolve private commercial disputes, minimal domestic savings eroded by serious inflation, and a private sector consisting of only small family owned firms.

2. Analysis of the performance of privatized firms raised questions about the wisdom of investing in them. A study by analysts at Morgan Stanley reported that in Western Europe issues by firms privatized from 1988-94 performed less well, as of June 1996, than the rest of their domestic market, using total compound annual return as the measure. The exception was the U.K., which accounted for about half of all privatized firms. There privatized and other issues performed equally well. See R. Lapper, *The Fruits of Privatisation*, Financial Times, June 11, 1996, at 22.

3. During the 1990s, the amounts raised from privatization rose dramatically, from $29.9 billion in 1990 to $153.8 billion in 1997, then retreated to only $114.5 billion in 1998 as the Asian crisis took its toll. About 75% of these funds was raised in OECD countries. Although less was raised in both OECD and non-OECD countries in 1998, the non-OECD countries registered the biggest drop that year, about 50%. Only in the telecommunications sector did privatization proceeds actually rise

in non-OECD countries. OECD, *Privatization Trends*, Financial Market Trends, Feb. 1999, at 129.

C.   MEXICO'S EVOLVING ECONOMY

In the 1970s and early 1980s, the growth of the Mexican economy depended on production and export of its massive petroleum reserves, among the largest in the world. The quadrupling of the oil price in 1973–4 and doubling in 1979 made Mexico appear to be one of the strongest developing economies. The country also exported agricultural products mainly to the United States, where its goods encountered protective barriers. These farm goods came from northern Mexico, which boasted a modern agricultural technology. Most of the population, however, were peasant farmers on small subsistence plots. The manufacturing sector, itself protected by high tariffs and quotas, was weak. Its workforce was almost entirely in Mexico City. The government fixed the cost of many domestic goods. The peso was fixed to the dollar although inflation rates were much higher in Mexico than in the U.S. Mexican state owned enterprises had borrowed more than any other developing country from foreign banks. U.S. banks dominated, but banks from Japan and Europe actively competed. In late 1979, the government encouraged private sector firms and individuals to borrow on the eurocurrency market as well. By 1981, many in Mexico realized that as the price of oil weakened, the country's economic strategy would founder. Along with sophisticated foreign investors and financial institutions, they began to shift their assets out of pesos and mainly into dollars, in the form of real estate investments and bank deposits in the United States. Flight capital reached billions of dollars.

In August 1982, the government of Mexico shocked the international financial world by declaring a moratorium on servicing the country's foreign debt, imposing exchange controls, and massively devaluing the peso. Inflows of foreign private capital stopped abruptly.

S. BAVARIA, MEXICO COMES BACK TO MARKET: THE MIRACLE RECOVERY
Investment Dealer's Digest Inc., Dec. 10, 1990, at 16 (Bavaria).

. . .

The nation's foreign debt then was over $100 billion and virtually unserviceable. In just a few years newly oil-rich Mexico had borrowed its way into bankruptcy, with the eager assistance of the world's leading commercial banks. Falling oil prices brought a heady—but bogus—prosperity to a brutal halt. A country that for years had enjoyed solid growth and low inflation faced punishing recession, with triple-digit inflation threatening to soar completely out of control.

The business community was reeling from major shocks: massive currency devaluation, the freezing of dollar bank accounts, the nationalization of the mighty private banks. As much as $20 billion in flight capital had left a gaping hole in the balance of payments. Exchange controls, long the ultimate taboo, were imposed in a desperate attempt to conserve foreign exchange.

Outgoing President Jose Lopez Portillo was openly reviled, while blatant corruption among government officials became the stuff of outrage. Things were bad and destined to get still worse.

Mexico's creditors, led by then Federal Reserve governor Paul Volcker, rallied. Rather than declaring default, they restructured the outstanding loans several times. Foreign governments, also led by the U.S., increased aid to Mexico. The peso was linked to the dollar and devalued in small steps to adjust for inflation differentials. Over the years, the trade balance improved, the country returned to servicing its debt, and the banks' relative exposure in Mexico fell.

Much of the credit for this recovery went to President Salinas' predecessor, President Miguel de la Madrid. For sixty years, a party known as the PRI dominated Mexican politics. Every six years the outgoing president would nominate his successor after Byzantine negotiations in secret within the PRI. Some noted a tendency to alternate between spokesmen for the more liberal and more conservative wings of the PRI. The party's grip on the electoral process had assured an overwhelming majority at the polls. President Salinas' predecessor adopted the austerity programs urged on him by foreign governments and the International Monetary Fund. When Salinas took office in 1989, public discontent with the economic crisis translated into a very close call at the polls; many PRI opponents accused it of fraud as Salinas barely slipped by. It looked as though the PRI was about to lose control of the government. Salinas pledged to reform not only the economy but the political system. Neither promised to be easy.

In 1990, the country had a population of 81 million. The government budget deficit was Pesos 23 trillion (or $7.7 billion at Pesos 3000 to $1). Balance of payments reserves had grown $3.4 billion. Gross domestic product, or total annual output, was Pesos 669 trillion ($223 billion). By 1990, according to Bavaria,

With the strong support of the US, his government has decreased external debt from $100 billion to $80 billion. Economic growth has finally regained its momentum, with GDP growing at 3% in 1989 and a projected 4% in 1990.

Salinas has encouraged unprecedented liberalization of Mexico's xenophobic foreign investment regulations. And he is now pushing the heretofore unthinkable; a free trade agreement with the gringos. With Presidents Bush and Salinas engaged in what has been described as a "love fest" as they lay plans for a North American free trade agreement, Mexico enjoys the best relations it has ever had with its northern neighbor.

THE NEW MODEL DEBTOR
The Economist, Oct. 6, 1990, at 85.

· · ·

- The government kept its promise to cut public spending. In 1986 and 1987 the budget deficit was 16% of GDP; in 1988 it fell to 12.3%, in 1989 to 5.8%. This year the deficit will be about 3% of GDP, according to CIEMEX–Wharton, Mexico's leading private forecaster. As Mr. Pedro Aspe, Mexico's finance minister, proudly points out, the cut in the deficit is equivalent to that envisaged by America's Gramm–Rudman act several times over—except that it happened.

- After an initial devaluation of 20%, the government fixed the peso's exchange rate against the dollar in February 1988. Later it began to devalue daily, but at a rate equivalent to only 14% a year—well below the country's inflation rate of 60%. Since May the rate of devaluation has been even slower. This strong-peso policy has its risks (principally of declining competitiveness); but it has helped to anchor domestic prices and reduce inflationary expectations.

- Latin America's other governments froze prices and wages more or less indiscriminately and all at once. Mexico's plan, unlike the others, was supported by business and the unions. It let prices adjust before the plan took effect, and called on a few big firms to keep prices down, but only for one or two months at a time. Prices and wages could adjust somewhat between periods, preventing relative costs from moving too far out of line.

- Mexico opened its economy to imports. First, tariffs replaced import quotas. Then the tariffs were steadily reduced. The free flow of imports, together with the frequent adjustment of relative prices, ensured that shortages (with some exceptions, such as meat) were rare, and never threatened to destroy the programme. Since 1987 the "shortage ratio" (the proportion of shops that were out of stock of a product they normally sold) has wavered around 10%. Shortages in Argentina during the Austral plan and Brazil during its Cruzado plan have been much worse—60% and 25% respectively.

- The government negotiated a deal on foreign debt in March 1990.

The cut in debt-service payments was no more than $4 billion a year—smaller than originally hoped for. But the deal has boosted private-sector and foreign confidence in the economy, and interest rates have now fallen to their lowest levels since 1981.

Inflation remains the country's biggest macroeconomic worry. Mr. Aspe says he will reduce the inflation rate by buying up the government's domestic debt with money earned from privatisation sales. But few if any countries have cut inflation from three digits to one without suffering a fearsome recession. Mexico will not be the exception.

Underlying inflation may be lower than the official 30%, because the government has raised public-sector prices much more than other prices in order to cut subsidies to state-owned industries. In December 1989 subway fares rose 30%, which by itself added four percentage points to the inflation rate. Since then the government has raised electricity prices by 300%, telephone charges by 400%, and so on. Mr. Salinas therefore argues that the current inflation rate does not reflect "macroeconomic imbalances". Unfortunately, these once-and-for-all rises will fuel inflation by pushing up wage demands and encouraging businesses, when they can, to raise their own prices. There is evidence that this is already happening.

Most Mexicans, mind you, must be disappointed with the results so far. Real wages have fallen for eight consecutive years; they are barely half what they were in 1982. Some 30% of Mexicans live in poverty, roughly the same proportion as in 1980. This year the economy will grow by 2–3%, half what it achieved in the 1960s and 1970s. Inflation will be close to 30% this year, ten percentage points higher than last year. The trade balance has suffered from the country's open-door policies. In 1985 Mexico ran a trade surplus of $8 billion; this year, despite the influence of Mr. Saddam Hussein on oil prices, the country may run a deficit.

Before you call that a failure, look at Latin America's other big debtors. It is more than likely that, if Mexico had failed to reform its economy, its people would already have suffered even more. The real test, however, will come in the next few years. Wages and economic growth seem likely to pick up; inflation, though high, should remain manageable. Crucially, the government is now in a position to tackle Mexico's appalling social problems, and to improve the country's deteriorating infrastructure. In the mid–1980s such ambitions would have been dismissed out of hand.

Notes and Questions

1. General purpose syndicated eurocredits, studied in Chapter 9, were the form of many of the bank loans to Mexico in the 1970s and early 1980s. What seems to have prompted Mexico to rely on this source of funds? If banks had made substantial loans to Mexico and then begun to realize that the economy was weakening in the early 1980s, how easily could they stop lending and reduce their exposure? To determine the weakness of these loans to Mexico before August 1982, how readily could their real value be fixed? As you read this Chapter, compare syndicated loans as a source of foreign capital for Mexico with the foreign funding for Telmex.

2. Consider the management of Mexico's 1982 debt crisis. For the next 6 years, Mexico got prompter treatment and more funds from the U.S. and other governments than other large debtor countries. Part of the reason was that the Mexican government's economic policy seemed to address the country's macroeconomic problems. What other factors do you think might have prompted the U.S. to play an active role resolving the crisis? As you read this Chapter, ask if these other reasons would affect investors in Telmex equity instruments.

3. From the sketch of Mexico, would you say it more closely resembles country (a) or country (b) in the question at the end of the previous section?

D.   TELMEX UNDER GOVERNMENT CONTROL

Telmex did not start as a government-owned firm. In 1947, foreign investors set it up to buy a Swedish firm's telephone business in Mexico. Three years later, Telmex acquired its only national competitor from International Telephone and Telegraph Company. Independent local companies ceased to exist in 1981. From then, Telmex became "the only licensed supplier of fixed link public telecommunications services in Mexico." By 1990, Telmex owned "all public exchanges, the nationwide network of local telephone lines and the principal public long-distance telephone transmission facilities." The prospectus continues:

TELEPHONOS DE MEXICO, S.A. DE C.V., PROSPECTUS
(May 13, 1991) (Prospectus).

A group of Mexican investors acquired the Company in 1953, but from the 1950s onward the Government was closely involved in the Company's strategic and financial planning. In 1972 the Government acquired the majority of the Company's capital stock, and in 1976 a new concession was granted to serve as a general framework for the Company's activities. In 1989 Telmex decentralized its internal organization, creating five operational divisions and four administrative divisions.

At December 31, 1990, the Mexican telephone system comprised 5.4 million lines in service, or 6.6 lines in service per 100 inhabitants, and 10.3 million telephone sets. It was the eighteenth-largest national telephone system in the world based on the number of lines in service at year-end 1988.

The business of the Company and the rates it charges for telephone services are subject to comprehensive regulation by the Communications Ministry under the Communications Law, the Telecommunications Regulations and the Concession. The regulatory regime applicable to the Company changed substantially in 1990.

Telmex provides basic telephone services, consisting of international long-distance, domestic long-distance and local telephone service. Of the consolidated revenues of the Company in 1990, approximately 29.1% was attributable to international long-distance service, approximately 35.5% to domestic long-distance service and approximately 31.6% to local service.

———

Rates, through 1989, were below cost for local service and far above cost for international service, 90% of which was with the United States and Canada. New customers had to buy Telmex shares or bonds at a premium over their market value to have new lines installed. Problems were rife, according to Bruce Wasserstein, whose firm advised a foreign investor during privatization.

B. WASSERSTEIN, REALITIES
OF CROSS–BORDER FINANCE

Talk Given at Harvard Law School (Oct. 25, 1993) (Wasserstein).

In 1990, Mexico, the 13th largest world economy, ranked 83rd in phone line per capita. The average waiting period for a new line was three years. Mexico's access to capital markets had been restricted throughout the 1980's, and *Telmex* was constrained in its ability to make necessary investments in equipment and technology. This resulted in a telephone system in which completed calls were the exceptions rather than the norm. Lines were so often crossed that dialers commonly opened a conversation by asking "*A donde hablo?* "*Where* am I speaking?

The Company had been managed with little emphasis on operating efficiency. An audit after the sale found $300 million of equipment scattered in 105 *Telmex* warehouses throughout the country. The Consortium found the opposite problem with maintenance centers: They were too centralized. All of the repair crews in Mexico City, which has 20 million residents, were crammed into 11 buildings. In one center there were 300 repair trucks—and one exit. It took an hour and a half each morning simply to roll all of the trucks onto the street.

Telmex has nearly twice as many employees per line as the average Bell company. Accordingly, productivity was always substandard. Repair crews traditionally sold their services to the highest bidder. For example, *Telmex* linemen for years refused to use rain-proof cable, complaining it was too slippery to handle. Similarly, operators for years labored at 1940s vintage switchboards.

———

In 1990, Telmex had assets of $9.6 billion, total long-term debt of $2.7 billion, and total stockholders' equity of $5.3 billion. Its operating income was $1.05 billion. Its workforce of 65,200 was one of the largest in Mexico aside from the government.

The Telmex capital structure was relatively straight-forward at this point. There were two classes of stock, AA and A shares. They had identical rights except for voting. AA shares could only be owned by Mexican citizens because Mexican law, described shortly below, required that Telmex be controlled by Mexicans. The A shares could be owned by anyone. The distribution of voting rights and the capital stock was as follows:

	Distribution of voting rights	Distribution of capital stock
Class AA:	51%	51%
Class A:	49	49

The Government owned 55.9% of Telmex capital stock, the AA shares and a small portion of the A shares. The public owned 44.1% of Telmex stock, the majority of the A shares. The A shares were traded on the Mexican Stock Exchange. Mexico's government-owned banks took positions in A Shares and Nacional Financiera (Nafin), a government owned bank, accounted for on average 10% of all A share trades on the Mexican exchange and on some occasions even 35%.

About 60% of the A shares were held as A Share American Depositary Shares (ADSs) quoted on NASDAQ. Prices of the A shares moved in tandem on the Mexican stock exchange and NASDAQ, although they were not exactly equal. On the Mexican stock exchange trading in A shares was in pesos; the U.S. dollar value of A shares moved steadily up from $0.34 in early 1989 to $3.35 on May 9, 1991. Trading was in dollars on NASDAQ. Before 1990, shares of two other Mexican companies also had ADRs. During 1990, five more Mexican companies joined them.

Notes and Questions

1. From 1970–76, Mexico's president enforced a nationalistic policy that relied on direct government intervention in the economy. This general strategy would encourage the government to take control of Telmex in 1972. What else might explain why the government acquired control of Telmex then?

2. The reading in Section B above lists several goals of privatization. Which of these goals would be likely to motivate President Salinas' decision to sell most of the government's stake in Telmex? How would these goals affect the privatization option he might choose?

3. How might the fact that the public already owned 44.1% of Telmex shares and that 60% of this was already traded on NASDAQ affect the options open to President Salinas?

E.   TRADITIONAL OPTIONS THE GOVERNMENT COULD USE TO SELL ITS TELMEX STAKE

Among the ways to privatize described in Section B are what might be called two traditional options: a sale on the national stock exchange and a sale to a small group of foreigners who would take full control of the company. This section describes the Mexican stock exchange and the laws governing foreign investment in Mexico. As you read it, consider the extent to which these two traditional options were available to President Salinas for the sale of the government's Telmex stock.

1.   THE MEXICAN STOCK EXCHANGE

a.   BACKGROUND INFORMATION

The following paragraph from the prospectus describes the exchange:

The Mexican Stock Exchange, located in Mexico City, is the only stock exchange in Mexico. Founded in 1907, it is organized as a corporation whose shares are held by 26 brokerage firms, which are exclusively authorized to trade on the floor of the Exchange. Trading on the Mexican Stock Exchange takes place principally on the floor of the Exchange, which is open between the hours of 10:30 a.m. and 1:30 p.m., Mexico City time, each business day. The Mexican Stock Exchange operates a system of automatic suspension of trading in shares of a particular issuer as a means of controlling excessive price volatility. Each day a price band is established, with the upper and lower limits being a specified percentage above and below a reference price, which is initially the day's opening price. For Telmex the specified percentage is 15%. If during the day a bid or offer is accepted at a price outside this band, trading in the shares is automatically suspended for one hour. When trading resumes, the high point of the previous band becomes the new reference price in the event of a rise in the price of a security and the low point of the previous band becomes the new reference price in the event of a fall in the price of a security. If it becomes necessary to suspend trading on a subsequent occasion on the same day, the suspension period lasts one and a half hours. Suspension periods in effect at the close of trading are not carried over to the next trading day.

In 1990, the ten most actively traded equity issues represented 66.6% of the total volume of equity issues traded on the Exchange. A Shares of the Company were the most actively traded equity issue in 1990, accounting for 17.6% of total shares traded on the Exchange.

b.   GOVERNMENT POLICY TOWARD THE STOCK MARKET

The government had started developing its capital markets in the mid–1970s. Mexico adopted a Securities Market Law in 1975. Institutional development followed the law. The country opened a central depository institution for shares in 1978, a Stock Market Law Academy in 1979, a Mexican Brokerage Houses Association, a Mexican Capital Markets' Institute, and a Contingency Fund in 1980. The debt crisis plunged the stock market index to below its level in 1975, but it more than recovered by 1985.

The National Securities Commission (the CNV), which reports to the Ministry of Finance and Public Credit, regulates the stock market. According to Guillermo Barnes Garcia, a finance ministry official who spoke at a Seminar on Financial Sector Liberalization and Regulation at Harvard Law School in June 1990;

> The Securities Market Law issued in 1975 substantially improved the structure and efficiency of securities markets. This law has been updated several times, the most recent in December 1989. As previously mentioned, the law passed in 1975 introduced two important changes for the financial system: the operation of brokerage houses instead of individual brokers and a far more active role of the National Securities Commission in supervision and promotion.

> In 1978 the law was reformed to include the centralized depository institution for shares (INDEVAL). In 1980, the law was complemented in order to take into account the requirements to public offers of shares, bonds or other obligations to be previously approved by the National Securities Commission. In 1983 the concept "insider information" was defined and incorporated in the law, with sanctions to be applied to those who profited from it. In 1985, the Contingency Fund was created with the full participation of the stock exchange and the brokerage houses. Several additions in the law were included, to require the formal approval of the National Securities Commission of the corporation's balance sheets previous to dividend payments. In 1986 branches of INDEVAL where approved within the country.

> In December 1989, Congress passed a new legislation which is having a significant impact on the structure of the financial system. The main objectives of the reform were (1) enlarge competition and efficiency within the financial system, (2) allow an expansion in the amount of private investment, both domestic and foreign, (3) increase the operation autonomy of the banks, allowing an addition in the amount of private investment (restricted by law to 34% until May

1990), and giving private sector investors a greater role managing the banks.

The Securities Market Law was also reformed to correct abuses in the securities industry and to encourage increased competition. The main amendments include:

— authorization of shelf registration for companies that meet listing and quarterly reporting requirements;

— authorization of Mexican brokerages to open branches abroad;

— authorization of arbitrage operations in Mexican stocks traded in New York;

— authorization for firms to invest in money market accounts at banks and brokerage firms (previously limited to individuals);

— authorization of foreign investment in Mexican stock without voting rights through the national financial global trust mechanism;

— the introduction of stronger penalties for investors found to have used insider information;

— promotion of a securities rating agency, on the model of Moody's and Standard & Poor's.

c.   COMPARISONS WITH OTHER STOCK MARKETS

Mexico's exchange was among the largest in emerging markets and it equaled the combined volume of the four other leading Latin American exchanges. The following tables show the size and growth of the Mexican stock market and compare the number of its listed companies to those on other exchanges. For reference, 1990 market capitalization in some other countries was (in billions): U.S.—$3,090, Japan—$2,918, France—$342, and Canada—$242.

Number of Listed Companies, End 1991

Country	Number	Country	Number
Brazil	570	Mexico	209
Chile	221	Taiwan	221
France	839	Thailand	276
Greece	126	UK	1,915
India	6,500*	USA	6,742
Japan	2,107	Venezuela	66
Korea	686		

* Estimated

INTERNATIONAL FINANCE CORPORATION, EMERGING STOCK MARKETS

Factbook (1992).

Mexico, 1982-1991
(Currency amounts in millions)

	1982	1983	1984	1985	1986	1987	1988	1989	1990	1991
A. Number of listed companies										
Bolsa Mexicana de Valores	206	163	160	157	155	190	203	203	199	209
B. Market capitalization										
1) In pesos	165,826	432.435	423.009	1,418,168	5,496.862	18,415.504	31,977.806	60,514.035	96,472.097	303.271.345
2) In U.S. dollars	1,719	3,004	2.197	3.815	5,952	8,371	13,784	22,550	32,725	98,178
C. Trading value										
1) In pesos	44,071	133.505	362.491	606,106	2,349.694	21,436.504	13,026.825	15,421.436	34,574.647	95,724.515
2) In U.S. dollars	781	1.112	2.160	2,360	3,841	15,554	5,732	6,232	12,212	31,723
3) Turnover ratio	20.5	44.6	84.8	65.8	68.0	179.3	51.7	33.3	44.0	47.9
D. Local Index										
1) BMV General Index (Nov 1978=0.7816)*	0.7	2.5	4.0	11.2	47.1	105.7	211.5	418.9	628.8	1,431.5
2) Change in index (%)	-28.5	261.8	64.7	177.3	320.6	124.3	100.2	98.0	50.1	127.6
E. IFC Emerging Markets Data Base										
1) Number of stocks	21	21	22	26	26	26	52	52	54	56
2) Share of market cap. (%)	35.4	38.4	62.6	36.6	56.3	36.9	64.1	65.5	62.5	51.6
3) P/E ratio	.	.	.	.	10.5	6.2	5.0	10.7	13.2	14.6
4) P/BV ratio	.	.	.	.	1.0	0.8	0.7	1.0	1.3	2.6
5) Dividend yield (%)	219	7.6	4.3	6.5	2.6	3.9	3.0	2.1	3.4	0.8
6) Total return index (Dec 84=100)	438	88.4	100.0	118.5	236.4	215.8	448.3	770.9	1,002.8	2,048.7
7) Change in index (%)	-750	101.6	13.1	18.5	99.6	-8.7	107.7	71.9	30.1	104.3
F. Economic data										
1) Gross domestic product (US$)	166.965	142.736	171.300	177,476	129.858	140.375	174.201	199,662	237,748	-
2) Change in consumer price index (%)	58.9	101.8	65.5	57.7	86.2	131.8	114.2	20.0	26.7	18.8
3) Exchange rates (end of period)	96.4800	143.9299	192.5599	371.6997	923.5000	2,200.0000	2,320.0000	2,683.5000	2,948.0000	3,089.0000
4) Exchange rates (average of period)	56.4017	120.0935	167.8275	256.8713	611.7698	1,378.1800	2,272.5660	2,474.4609	2,831.1166	3,017.5194

a The BMV General Index was divided by 1,000 in May 1991. This series reflects that division.
- Not available.

Notes and Questions

1.   All told, the Telmex privatization in 1990–1 raised over $3 billion. Could the Mexican government have done this through an offer on the Mexican stock exchange?

2. FOREIGN INVESTMENT IN MEXICO AND POLICY TOWARD IT

For over 50 years, Mexico had rules containing or prohibiting the ability of foreigners to control Mexican business. About the time of World War II, foreign control of the country's oil industry was ended by fiat. Soon after, foreigners were prohibited from owning banks in Mexico. Mexicans wanted to assure the country's independence from economic as well as political domination.

Mexico's foreign investment law was designed to protect the country from foreign control. The prospectus explained the policy and its effect:

> Ownership by non-Mexicans of shares of Mexican enterprises in certain economic sectors, including telephone services, is regulated by the 1973 Law to Promote Mexican Investment and Regulate Foreign

Investment (the "Foreign Investment Law") and the 1989 Regulations thereunder (the "Foreign Investment Regulations"). The National Commission on Foreign Investment (the "Foreign Investment Commission") is responsible for administration of the Foreign Investment Law and Regulations. In order to comply with restrictions on the percentage of their capital stock that may be owned by non-Mexican investors, Mexican companies typically limit particular classes of their stock to Mexican ownership. Under the administrative practice of the Foreign Investment Commission, a trust for the benefit of one or more non-Mexican investors may qualify as Mexican if the trust meets certain conditions that will generally ensure that the non-Mexican investors do not determine how the shares are voted.

Non–Mexicans may not own more than 49% of the capital stock of a Mexican corporation in the telephone business. No foreign state may own shares directly or indirectly in it.

A Mexican company with foreign owners of its shares must register those owners, including a depositary for ADSs, with the National Registry of Foreign Investment. No unregistered foreign owner may vote its shares or receive dividends for those shares.

Questions

1. Many countries have had rules to limit foreign investment. Many of these countries have been removing or reducing those limits through formal changes in the laws. Mexico has been reluctant to do so. What might account for Mexico's concern about foreign domination of its economy?

2. How does this law affect the ability of the Mexican government to sell its shares in Telmex? Is it a serious obstacle?

F. THE TRANSFER OF CONTROL OVER TELMEX TO THE CONSORTIUM

1. THE WINNING BIDDERS

The government decided to sell its control to a private group. Three groups bid initially.

- Southwestern Bell, with France Telecom and Grupo Carso as partners. Salomon Brothers advised Southwestern Bell. Wasserstein, Perella advised France Telecom.

- GTE Corp., Telefonica de Espana, and Acciones y Valores (a Mexican securities firm).

- NYNEX, BCE, and Casa de Bolsa Inverlat Associates.

The winner, the Southwestern Bell consortium, paid $1.8 billion for the shares. Of this, the Mexican partner, Grupo Carso, provided 51%. Bell effectively beat the GTE group. The NYNEX group had withdrawn shortly before the bids were submitted. Wasserstein described the members of the winning group:

GRUPO CARSO—led by Mexican industrialist Carlos Slim is an entrepreneurial organization with a splendid track record in running diverse enterprises. Mr. Slim's partners have included such impressive multi-nationals as Philip Morris and Michelin. Grupo Carso has had experience in basic industry, finance, retailing and real estate, all of which had application in making *Telmex* a world class provider of telecom services. Carlos Slim's personal knowledge, credibility and project management expertise made him the leading contender in the fight for *Telmex*.

SOUTHWESTERN BELL—was and continues to be one of the most highly regarded U.S. telecommunications companies with a reputation for particular excellence in cellular communications, telephone directories, general marketing and customer service skills. Furthermore, 2000 miles of common border made for significant interest in *Telmex*.

FRANCE TELECOM—has substantial experience in rapid modernization, having built up the French network from 4 million access lines in 1971 to approximately 28 million lines today, a compound annual growth rate of almost 11% sustained over two decades. This achievement is particularly relevant given the government's requirement that access lines growth in Mexico be no less that 12% a year for five years, more than double *Telmex's* historical growth level. A fully integrated telephone company, France Telecom enjoys expertise in long distance telephony, satellite and network administration, and most other aspects of telecommunications.

2. THE NEW CAPITAL STRUCTURE

The government transferred to the winning consortium all of the AA stock in Telmex and with it 51% of the votes. But at the same time Telmex's capital stock was increased 1.5 times by the addition of a new type of share, the L share. The L share effectively had no voting power. This remained with the AA and A shares, which now accounted for 40% of Telmex's total capital stock and 100% of its voting stock. As a result, the consortium received only 20.4% of the company's entire capital stock because the new non-voting share was added.

All AA and A shareholders were entitled to 1.5 L shares for each AA or A share they held. The government had held all AA shares and some A shares, amounting for 55.9% of Telmex capital, as described above.

When it transferred the AA shares to the winning consortium, it was still entitled to receive the L shares for the AA shares it transferred. It also held Telmex shares subject to an option by the consortium to buy them later. And some shares were set aside for Telmex employees. Each A share in the hands of the public or the government also entitled its holder to 1.5 L shares, so the public's share of the total capital remained unchanged. The table shows the shift in ownership.

Owner groups	Before sale to winning consortium	After sale to winning consortium
Government	55.9%	26.0%
Government subject to option of controlling shareholders		5.1
Consortium		20.4
Employees of Telmex		4.4
Public	44.1	44.1

The impact of these changes on voting rights was different. The AA shares could still be owned only by Mexicans, while anyone could own A shares. Only the AA and A shares had voting power. The following table compares changes in the distribution of shares by voting rights and by class. The L shareholders could only elect 2 of the board's 19 directors, so they were treated as having no vote.

	Distribution by class of stock				
	of voting rights		of capital stock		
	AA	A	AA	A	L
Before the L share dividend	51%	49%	51%	49%	
At the L share dividend (12/20/91)	51	49	20.4	19.6	60.0

The consortium received the AA shares in trust, which gave it 20.4% of all shares and 51% of voting rights. Among members of the consortium, beneficial ownership in the trust was distributed to Grupo Carso (28% itself and 23% through 50 other Mexican investors), and 25% to each of the two foreign members. Grupo Carso had 51% of the vote to control the trust.

Mexican laws were interpreted in a way that allowed this arrangement. The prospectus explained:

> Pursuant to a decision dated August 10, 1990 of the Foreign Investment Commission, the L Shares, because of their limited voting rights, are not taken into account in determining compliance with this

restriction. Accordingly, the L Shares are not restricted to Mexican ownership. The A Shares, which represent approximately 49% of the combined AA Shares and A Shares, are also unrestricted. The AA Shares, however, which must always represent at least 51% of the combined AA Shares and A Shares, may be owned only by holders that qualify as Mexican investors as defined in the Company's by-laws. The criteria for an investor to qualify as Mexican under the by-laws are stricter than those generally applicable under the Foreign Investment Law and Regulations. A holder that acquires AA Shares in violation of the restrictions on non-Mexican ownership will have none of the rights of a shareholder with respect to those AA Shares.

As a consequence of these limitations, non-Mexican investors cannot under Mexican law own a majority of the Company's voting stock except through trusts that effectively neutralize the votes of non-Mexican investors. The Controlling Shareholders, which include non-Mexican corporations as beneficial owners of 49% of the AA Shares, own the AA Shares through a trust that has been approved by the Foreign Investment Commission for this purpose.

In addition to the limitations on share ownership, the Foreign Investment Law and Regulations and the Concession require that Mexican shareholders retain the power to determine the administrative control and the management of the Company. Violation of this prohibition may render the Concession void.

Foreign states are prohibited under the by-laws and the Communications Law from directly or indirectly owning shares of the Company. The Telecommunications Regulations and the Concession provide, however, that foreign state-owned enterprises organized as separate entities with their own assets may own minority interests in the Company or any number of shares with limited voting rights. In the opinion of Santamarina y Steta, the Company's Mexican counsel, ownership of A Shares or L Shares by such foreign state-owned companies, or by pension or retirement funds organized for the benefit of employees of state, municipal or other governmental agencies, will not be considered direct or indirect ownership by foreign states for the purposes of the by-laws or the Communications Law.

3. THE MODIFIED CONCESSION

Mexican laws were modified to embody the government's new policies. Some new rules set standards that Telmex would have to meet. Others provided incentives to the new owners to meet these standards. The prospectus explained. As you read it, identify incentives and performance standards.

PROSPECTUS

General

The Communications Law, adopted in 1940, and the Telecommunications Regulations, adopted in October 1990, provide the general legal framework for the regulation of telecommunications services in Mexico. Under the Communications Law and the Telecommunications Regulations, a provider of public telecommunications services, such as Telmex, must operate under a concession granted by the Communications Ministry. Such a concession may only be granted to a Mexican citizen or corporation and may not be transferred or assigned without the approval of the Communications Ministry. Telmex's current Concession was granted in 1976 and amended in August 1990.

Substantial changes in the regulatory regime applicable to the Company occurred in 1990, including the amendment of the Concession, the adoption of the Telecommunications Regulations and the elimination of excise taxes on telephone services.

Supervision

The Communications Ministry is the government agency principally responsible for regulating telecommunications services. The Ministry's approval is required for any change in the by-laws of the Company and for any issuance of debt or equity securities to finance construction of the telecommunications network. It also has broad powers to monitor the Company's compliance with the Concession, and it can require the Company to supply it with such technical, administrative and financial information as it may request. The Company must submit its service expansion plans to the Ministry for publication, and the Ministry is authorized to require the Company to modify certain technical plans in response to objections from other interested parties. The Company must also advise the Ministry quarterly of the progress of its expansion program. Finally, under the Company's by-laws the Communications Ministry may appoint one member and one alternate member of the Company's Board of Directors, and the Concession requires such a provision through August 1993.

Until 1990, the annual budget of the Company required approval by the Ministry of Budget and Planning; and until December 1990, when the Government ceased to own a majority of the full voting stock of the Company, the Company's rates were subject to the approval of the Ministry of Finance and Public Credit.

The Communications Law gives certain rights to the Government in its relations with concessionaires. For example, it provides that the Government may require a 50% discount on services provided by the Company to the Government. The federal judiciary currently receives such a discount. The legislative branch and the executive branch of the Government do not currently receive such a discount, although they have exercised their right to do so in the past. If they were to receive such a discount, the Company does not expect that its revenues would be materially affected. The Government also has the right to take over the management of the Company in cases of imminent danger to internal security or the national economy. The Government has used this power, most recently in 1986, to ensure continued service during labor disputes. The Communications Law also provides that the Company may not sell or transfer any of its assets unless it gives the Government a right of first refusal. If the Government declines to exercise its right, the Company's unions also have a right of first refusal.

Rates

The Communications Law and the Telecommunications Regulations provide that the basis for setting rates of a telecommunications concessionaire is set forth in its concession.

Through 1990, the Company's rates were established separately for each category of service by the Communications Ministry, upon application by the Company. Under the 1990 amendment to the Concession, beginning in 1991 the Company's rates for basic telephone services, including installation, monthly rent, measured local service and long-distance service, are subject to a ceiling on the price of a "basket" of such services weighted to reflect actual volume of each service during the preceding period. Within this aggregate "price cap", the Company is free to determine the structure of its own rates. Approval of the Communications Ministry is not required for rates to take effect, although the Company must publish its rates and register them with the Ministry. The Communications Ministry also has the power, subject to the basis set forth in the Concession for determining rates, to modify rates when required in the public interest.

The price cap varies directly with the NCPI, permitting the Company to raise nominal rates to keep pace with inflation. The Concession also provides that, beginning on January 1, 1997, the price cap will be adjusted downward periodically to pass on the benefits of increased productivity to the Company's customers. The adjustment will be 3% per year for 1997 and 1998. Beginning on January 1, 1999 and every four years thereafter, the Communications Ministry will set the amount of the periodic adjustment of the price cap, following administrative proceedings, to permit the Company to maintain an internal rate of return equal to the Company's weighted average cost of capital.

A principal goal of the Government in establishing the price cap system was to permit the Company to increase local service rates to meet its costs and to reduce long-distance rates in anticipation of possible competition beginning in August 1996. The Company is required under the Concession and the Telecommunications Regulations to eliminate cross subsidies between different categories of services, subject to specified exemptions such as rural telephone services. In order to further this and other public policy objectives, several provisions of the Concession modify the application of the price cap in the initial years of its application. These include mandatory reductions in installation charges for new telephone lines, a mandatory increase in domestic long-distance rates that took effect on January 1, 1991, and permitted increases in basic monthly rent in 1991 that are partially excluded from the calculation of the price cap.

The Company is currently free to set its prices free of rate regulation for "value-added" services extending beyond basic telephone services. These services include the Integrated Digital Network, private circuits, directory services and new services based on digital technology such as call waiting, speed calling and automatic re-dialing. The Company is required to register the rates it charges for value-added services, and the Communications Ministry has power under the Telecommunications Regulations to begin regulating rates for such services if it determines that there is no effective competition and that the Company is abusing monopoly power in pricing such services. Rates for cellular mobile telephone services are regulated under separate concessions.

Taxation of Telephone Services

Through 1989 the Government imposed a high level of taxation of telephone use. In 1989, for example, telephone charges were subject to an excise tax that ranged from 22% on international long-distance calls to 72% on local commercial service charges, and to a value added tax of 15% calculated on the aggregate of the charges plus the excise tax. Beginning on January 1, 1990, excise taxes no longer apply to telephone charges. Also beginning on January 1, 1990, the Company is subject to a tax on revenues from telephone services.

Expansion and Modernization Requirements

As amended in 1990, the Concession requires the Company to expand, improve and modernize its telephone network. In particular, the Company must (i) during the period between August 10, 1990 and December 31, 1994, expand the number of lines in service by an average minimum annual rate of 12%; (ii) expand its services to rural areas, and in particular provide each town in Mexico with more than 500 inhabitants (as determined by the 1990 Census) with at least one public telephone booth or agency for providing long-distance services by December 31, 1994; (iii) expand the number of public telephone booths from a current density of 0.8 booths per 1,000 inhabitants to 2 booths per 1,000 inhabitants by the end of 1994 and 5 booths per 1,000 inhabitants by the end of 1998; and (iv) reduce the maximum waiting time for installation of telephone service (in cities with automatic exchanges) to six months by 1995 and to one month by the year 2000.

The amended Concession also sets forth extensive goals for the quality of the Company's services, including reductions in line failures, reductions in repair time, reductions in the time required to obtain a dial tone, improvements in the percentage of calls completed on the first attempt, and reductions in installation time.

Competition

The Telecommunications Regulations and the 1990 amendment to the Concession contain various provisions designed to introduce competition in the provision of communications services. In general, the Communications Ministry is authorized to grant concessions to other parties for the provision of any of the services provided by the Company under the Concession, except that, as long as the Company is in compliance with the Concession, no competing provider of domestic or international long-distance services may operate before August 1996. After August 1996 the Communications Ministry may grant concessions to other long-distance carriers. The Company is required to permit any other concessionaire to connect to its network and, after December 31, 1996, it must permit other long-distance telephone networks to be connected in a manner that enables customers to choose the network by which their calls are carried. The Company is also required to permit users of its telephone network to resell excess capacity, except that until August 1996 it is not required to permit the resale of any excess capacity for use in providing long-distance services. Concessions are not required to operate certain private local telecommunications networks or to provide value-added services, although other authorizations may be required.

Termination of the Concession

The Concession provides that it will remain in force until 2026, and that it may be renewed by the Company for an additional fifteen years subject to additional requirements the Communications Ministry may impose.

The Concession provides that upon its expiration the Government is entitled to purchase the telecommunications assets of the Company at a price determined on the basis of an appraisal by a public official, and the Telecommunications Regulations provide that upon expiration of the Concession the Government has a right of first refusal to acquire the telecommunications assets of the Company. The Communications Law, however, provides that upon expiration of the Concession the telecommunications assets of Telmex will revert to the Government free of charge. There is substantial doubt as to whether the provisions of the Concession and the Telecommunications Regulations would prevail, and accordingly there can be no assurance that upon expiration of the Concession the telecommunications assets of the Company would not revert to the Government free of charge.

The Communications Law and the Concession include various provisions under which the Concession may be terminated before its scheduled expiration date. Under the Communications Law, the

Communications Ministry may cause early termination of the Concession in certain cases, including (i) failure to expand telephone services at the rate specified in the Concession; (ii) interruption of all or a material part of the services provided by Telmex; (iii) transfer or assignment without Ministry approval of the Concession or any asset used to provide telephone service; (iv) violation of the prohibition against ownership of Telmex shares by foreign states; (v) any material modification of the nature of the Company's services without prior Ministry approval; and (vi) breach of certain other obligations under the Communications Law. In addition, the Concession provides for early termination by the Communications Ministry following administrative proceedings in the event of (i) a material and continuing violation of any of the conditions set forth in the Concession; (ii) material failure to meet any of the service expansion requirements under the Concession; (iii) material failure to meet any of the requirements under the Concession for improvement in the quality of service; (iv) engagement in any telecommunications business not covered by the Concession and requiring prior approval of the Communications Ministry; (v) following notice and a cure period, failure without just cause to allow other concessionaires to interconnect their telephone networks to the Company's telephone network; or (vi) bankruptcy of the Company.

The Communications Law provides that in the event of early termination of the Concession for specified causes, including violation of the prohibition on ownership of the Company's shares by foreign states, the Company would forfeit all of its telecommunications assets to the Government. In the event of early termination of the Concession for any other cause, the Communications Law provides that a portion of the Company's telecommunications assets would revert to the Government free of charge, and that the Company may be required to dismantle the remaining portion. There is substantial doubt as to whether the provisions of the Concession and the Telecommunications Regulations regarding the consequences of expiration of the Concession would apply to mitigate the provisions of the Communications Law in the event of early termination.

Notes and Questions

1.   Be sure you understand this transfer of ownership and the reasons for it. Compare it to the privatization options in Section B above. Which does it resemble? Why? What would the consortium members bring in addition to money?

2.   Compare the old and new capital structures. What accounts for the added complexity? Does the new capital structure reflect the spirit of the foreign investment laws?

3.   How does the modified concession protect Mexico now that the government no longer controls Telmex? Compare the performance requirements with the incentives given to the restructured company. How complete is this privatization?

4.   Why would the consortium want to enter this transaction? What incentives are given to them?

5.   Suppose the consortium manages Telmex successfully and the company is very profitable. Should the consortium be concerned about anything? Evaluate the rules governing the termination of the Concession from the perspective of members of the winning group.

G. THE OFFER OF TELMEX SHARES IN WORLD MARKETS

In May 1991, the government sold another 14% of its Telmex shares in a $2.17 billion global public offering. The funds went to the government. The offering consisted of 100 million L shares offered in Mexico and 70 million American Depositary Shares (ADSs), each representing 20 L shares. At the time, about 2.2 billion AA shares, 2.1 billion A shares, and 6.4 billion L shares were outstanding.

1. THE EVOLUTION OF THE TELMEX CAPITAL STRUCTURE

Although the L shares had been issued in 1991 as a stock dividend to all Telmex shareholders, they were not to be distributed until the closing of the May 1991 combined share offer. The government, which had held the AA shares, had been able to separate and hold its rights to the L shares when it delivered the AA shares to the trust for the consortium. The trust, therefore, held no L shares. In effect, at the time of the offering, only A shares had associated L shares, each A carrying the right to 1.5 L shares. The A shareholders, however, were not allowed to deliver the L shares separately from the A shares until after the May closing. When the A shares (or the ADSs for them on NASDAQ) were traded before the May closing, their L shares were traded with them.

After the May closing, L shares would be listed on the Mexican Stock Exchange. The A shares remained listed on the exchange and the A ADSs remained on NASDAQ.

Also after the May closing, any AA or A share could be exchanged for one L share, subject to limits to protect the integrity of the overall allocation of voting power among AA, A, and L shares. The AA or A shareholder make the exchange as long as all AA shares would not represent less than 20% of the Company's outstanding stock or 51% of the combined AA and A shares.

From January 1, 2001, each L share could be exchanged for an AA share, provided the AA and A shares together never exceeded 51% of Telmex outstanding stock and AA shares continued to be subject to limits on non-Mexican ownership.

After the privatization, ownership of Telmex had been distributed among several groups, including the government. The government's ownership of all shares had fallen from almost 56% before the sale to the consortium to just under 10% after the public offering.

Owner groups	Before sale to winning consortium	After sale to winning consortium	After May 1991 offering
Government	55.9%	26.0%	9.5%
Government subject to option of controlling shareholders		5.1	5.1
		20.4	20.4
Consortium		4.4	5.8
Employees of Telmex	44.1	44.1	59.2
Public			

The offering would shift voting rights and the distribution of the stock among the three categories of shares in the following ways:

	Distribution by class of stock				
	of voting rights		of capital stock		
	AA	A	AA	A	L
Before the L share dividend	51%	49%	51%	49%	60.0
At the L share dividend (12/20/91)	51	49	20.4	19.6	
After the combined public offering and A to L exchanges	64	36	20.4	11.5	68.1

2. THE AMERICAN DEPOSITARY RECEIPTS

The ADSs on the L shares would be listed on the New York Stock Exchange. Morgan Guaranty Trust Company was to serve as the depositary for the L Shares. The depositary would issue American Depositary Receipts evidencing American Depositary Shares. Each ADS would represent 20 L Shares. The Banco Nacional de Mexico, as custodian, would hold the L shares. Any L shareholder could place the shares with the custodian and receive ADSs from the depositary. Any ADS holder could surrender the ADSs to the depositary and receive L shares. Cash payments of dividends on L shares would be converted promptly by the depositary into U.S. dollars and distributed to ADS holders. Mexico would impose no taxes on any distribution or on capital gains.

The following table gives an overview of the evolution of Telmex's share structure.

EVOLUTION OF TELMEX CAPITAL STRUCTURE
(ownership of total capital (%))

SHAREHOLDERS	1989/90. OWNERSHIP BEFORE THE L ISSUE			STEP 1. L SHARE. OWNERSHIP AFTER THE L ISSUE		
	AA	A	TOTAL	AA	A	L
GOVERNMENT	51.0	4.9	55.9	20.4	2.0	33.5
PUBLIC	---	44.1	44.1	---	17.6	26.5
TOTAL	51.0	49.0	100.0	20.4	19.6	60.0
VOTES	51.0	49.0	100.0	51.0	49.0	---

SHAREHOLDERS	STEP 2. SELL CONTROL. OWNERSHIP AFTER THE SALE TO THE CONSORTIUM				STEP 3. GLOBAL OFFER. AFTER ADS OFFERING BEFORE A TO L CONVERSIONS			
	TOTAL	AA	A	L	TOTAL	AA	A	L
GOVERNMENT	26.0	---	2.0	24.0	9.5	---	2.0	7.5
GOV'T FOR CONSORTIUM'S OPTION	5.1	---	---	5.1	5.1	---	---	5.1
CONSORTIUM	20.4	20.4	---	---	20.4	20.4	---	---
TELMEX EMPLOYEES	4.4	---	---	4.4	5.8	---	---	5.8
PUBLIC	44.1	---	17.6	26.5	59.2	---	17.6	41.6
TOTAL	100.0	20.4	19.6	60.0	100.0	20.4	19.6	60.0
VOTES	100.0	51.0	49.0	---	100.0	51.0	49.0	---

SHARES	EXCHANGE	SHARES	EXCHANGE
A	MEXICAN	L	MEXICAN
A ADS	NASDAQ	L ADS	NYSE

Notes and Questions

1.   Why would an A shareholder, after the May 1991 closing, want to exchange its shares for L shares? In the first two months after the May closing, about 70% of all A ADR holders converted into L shares in ADR form, one-for-one. Only 1.2% of A shareholders in Mexico opted to convert into L shares. Moreover, in the U.S. market, the L ADSs never traded at a discount to the A ADSs. Why would investors trading ADSs in Telmex A shares on NASDAQ want to switch to L shares? What do they gain and what do they lose? Why would investors trading Telmex A shares in Mexico not want to switch to L shares?

2.   Which privatization option, described in Section B above, does this offer resemble? What would have motivated the government to take this route? How does this offer benefit privatization in Mexico? How would it benefit Telmex?

3. What accounts for the complex nature of this offer? Is the offer and its structure consistent with the spirit of the Mexican foreign investment law?

4. What is likely to be the relation between the L shares traded on the Mexican Stock Exchange and the L ADSs traded on the New York Stock Exchange? Would you expect pricing in one market to lead the other? If so, what are the implications for the country whose exchange follows the other? A study of three factors that might affect the price of ADRs concluded that the price of the underlying shares was most important, but the relevant exchange rates and the US market index also affect ADR prices. M. Kim, A. Szakmary, and I. Mathur, *Price Transmission Dynamics Between ADRs and Their Underlying Foreign Securities*, 24 Journal of Banking & Finance, 1359 (2000). Foreign ownership of a company does not affect share volatility, according to another study, unless the shares are cross-listed, because trading volume rises and information increases. M. Coppejans and I. Domowitz, *The Impact of Foreign Equity Ownership on Emerging Market Share Price Volatility*, 3 International Finance 95 (2000). What would happen if most trading took place on a deep foreign exchange, as it does for the Telmex shares and ADRs?

H. DEMAND FOR THE TELMEX OFFER

The market for the Telmex offer was institutional investors in the U.S., Europe, and Japan. Less than a decade earlier, pension funds, insurance companies, and mutual funds showed little interest in foreign equities, particularly in developing countries. Regulations that limited their freedom to invest were sometimes said to be the reason: a U.S. insurance company might be allowed to invest no more than 5% of its assets in foreign securities. A German pension fund would be required to invest a large part of its assets in government debt, ostensibly because these carried no or low risk, and also limited to investing only 30% of its funds in equity. But these rules were not so binding, since few funds pushed against the regulatory ceilings. German pension funds, for example, invested barely 3% of their funds in equity.

This section describes pension funds, an increasingly major force in international markets, and their role in emerging markets. It then sketches the way the Telmex offer was marketed around the world and reports the buyers by region. As you read it, consider why pension funds would be attracted to the Telmex offer.

1. PENSION FUNDS AS INSTITUTIONAL INVESTORS

Pension funds are among the largest sets of investors in the world. At the end of 1993, U.S. pension fund assets were $3.65 trillion, just over half the total worldwide of $6.9 trillion. Their assets exceeded the total output of any country in the world except the U.S. Among major industrial countries, pension funds' assets as a percentage of GDP ranged in 1993 from a high of 84% in Holland and Switzerland, 76% in the U.K., 60% in the U.S., and 45% in Canada, down to 28% in Japan and a mere 7% in Germany. So in many countries pension funds were extraordinarily powerful investors. U.S. funds held over one-third of all equity of U.S. listed companies, a share that grew steadily from 19% in 1980. See Research and Information Center, State Street Bank and Trust Company (State Street), The Impact of Pension Investments on the World's Financial Market Structure (Aug. 3, 1994). In a comparison that brings pension funds' investments more up to date, the OECD reported that the total financial assets of all OECD pension funds grew from $3.8 trillion in 1990 to $6.8 trillion in 1996. OECD, *Recent Statistics on OECD Institutional Investors*, Financial Market Trends, Feb. 1999, at 147.

OECD pension assets grew 3.5 times faster than personal income in those countries over the last 25 years, so fund managers faced growing pressure to deploy their assets productively. State Street explains the funds' investment style:

Pension Investment Styles

Pension funds have a voracious appetite for investments that satisfy a unique set of investment styles and characteristics. Their investments are distinguished from corporate or individual investments by a particular set of rules and preferences. While maximizing returns and reducing risk are the predominant considerations in all financial investments, a more systematic approach is taken by pension investors:

— Pension investment must be "prudent," barring highly risky and irrational investment decisions.

— Pension fund sponsors are particularly concerned with the need to match assets with liabilities, the future payouts of the plans.

— Pension investments are professionally managed, guided by modern portfolio management theories regarding asset allocation and risk control. A diversified, balanced portfolio is a trademark of pension funds.

— Pension investment is more strongly inclined to quantitative methods, including indexing and passive investments, and portfolio performance is analyzed and benchmarked carefully.

— Pension investments are long-term, designed to provide funding for long-term liabilities. Long investment horizons and aggressive yield assumptions attract many pension funds to high-yield investments and newly developed investment instruments. One of the keys to managing a pension fund is viewing asset allocation and targets in terms of decades rather than quarters.

— Meeting aggressive yield targets requires careful analysis and quantification of risk. Risk, whether it pertains to emerging market investment or derivative instruments, has become a commodity that can be bought and sold.

This systematic approach contrasts with that of individual investors, many of whom are either excessively risk-averse or dangerously speculative. Sometimes, individual investors combine the two ends of the spectrum to develop a "balanced" portfolio, half of which is CD and half is highly speculative instruments. Pension funds tend to have a different idea of diversification.

The structures, assumptions and theories intrinsic to pension investment are transforming the financial services industry drastically and permanently.

2. PENSION FUNDS IN INTERNATIONAL FINANCIAL MARKETS

The funds moved into international financial markets rather recently. State Street described the situation in 1994.

Let's look at some statistics. The InterSec Research Corporation estimates that total cross-border investment by pension funds reached $725 billion in 1993. The U.K., Germany, Netherlands, Japan and the U.S. are among the most aggressive international investors.

Exhibit 3 shows the top seven countries in terms of pension asset accumulation for 1993. Note that U.S. pension funds invest a substantially lower percentage of their assets overseas than do other major international investors. Since total U.S. pension assets dwarf those of other countries, however, U.S. pension funds rank among the leaders in global investment.

Although total U.S. cross-border investment is substantial and U.S. pensions are the most globally active of all U.S. investor groups, cross-border assets as a percentage of total assets is a relatively small 7%. That is far below the conservative recommendation of 15%, the progressive recommendation of 20% and the U.K. pension industry practice of 28%. This leaves room for substantial growth in the dollar value of U.S. pension funds' international holdings. ... Since 1987, U.S. pension investment overseas has grown at an annual rate of 25%, dramatically higher than the 6% growth for U.S. pension assets as a whole.

The flow of cross-border investing has greatly accelerated in 1993. Many pension funds have made their first international forays this year; others, particularly the largest ones, have aggressively increased their foreign exposure. The California Public Employees' Retirement System, which manages $78 billion of assets, began to invest overseas only about five years ago and now has about 15.5% of its assets—some $12 billion—invested in foreign markets. Overseas investments of U.S. pension funds are expected to grow at a slightly reduced pace of 23% per year over the next five years, reaching 10% of total assets by 1997.

The scale of investment flows indicates a structural shift in pension investment strategy. The quests for diversification and higher returns are the two driving forces behind globalization. When U.S. pension funds began to invest in foreign equities a dozen years ago, a key reason was diversification—other markets would not move in sync with the U.S. domestic market. Although the globalization of financial markets is increasing the correlation among world markets, advantages can still be gained from diversification.

The globalization of pension investments is breaking down financial barriers. According to a recent study by the International Monetary Fund, home-country bias (an unjustified preference for the domestic securities market) caused U.S. institutional investors to earn 2% less in annual return than global investment would have produced. In Germany, the cost of home-country bias is 9%. Globalized pension investments, for both traditional pensions and 401(k)-type plans, are clearly in the best interest of both pension sponsors and beneficiaries.

Exhibit 3

Non-Domestic Investment as a Percentage of Total Pension Assets (1993)

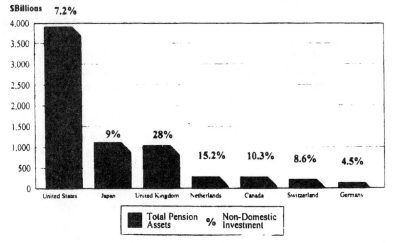

Source: InterSec Research Corp

STATE STREET BANK AND TRUST COMPANY

In October, the European Community voted to limit cross-border investments by pensions to 20% of total assets in the unified Europe. Some member countries want to use the restriction to limit capital outflows. The proposed 20% limit is already high compared with the current U.S. level of 7% of international investment and with European practices in general, except the U.K., Ireland and the Netherlands.

These three countries, however, account for 83% of current European assets and appear to be completely uninterested in the 20% cap. It remains to be seen how this issue will be resolved.

3. PENSION FUNDS IN EMERGING MARKETS

Pension funds still invest only a very small portion of their assets in emerging markets. In the following articles, State Street gives some broad brush comparisons, while Faber portrays the thinking of individual fund managers. State Street:

> Emerging markets have become one of the fastest growing areas of international investment. In the U.K., one survey estimates that $1 of every $3 of new investment is channeled into emerging markets.

> Much of the increased demand for emerging market securities comes from pension investors. Among the most aggressive are U.K. funds, which have allocated 5.5% of their total assets to emerging markets, an allocation almost equal to their U.S. investment. By comparison, U.S. pension investments are still heavily biased toward Europe and Japan, although a process of asset allocation restructuring is well underway. In the past three years, U.S. pension sponsors have dramatically increased their exposure to these markets. At the end of 1992, they had invested approximately US $8.5 billion in emerging markets. Although this still represents little more than 0.2% of total assets, it reflects an average growth rate of 50% during 1991 and 1992. Emerging market investments jumped an additional 35% in the first six months of 1993.

> The potential for further emerging market investment is tremendous, considering that these markets represent 20% of global GDP and 12% of the capitalization of the world's equity markets .... Their economies are estimated to grow at about 2.5 times the rate of those of industrialized countries. Some financial consultants recommend a 3% to 6% asset allocation to emerging markets.

D. FABER, U.S. PENSIONS EXPLORE EMERGING MARKETS
Institutional Investor, Apr. 1993, at 52.

. . .

U.S. pension funds—even a few public plans—have become the newest, and still somewhat tentative, explorers of third-world markets. The main attraction is the prospect of spectacular riches, but growing liquidity and the proliferation of vehicles for, and guides to, investing in emerging markets have helped to overcome lingering reservations. ...

Pension funds of multinational companies and the bolder foundations and endowments formed the early expeditionary party, investing modest sums in third-world markets in their modern-day infancy in the mid–1980s. Since then these institutions have by and large become more aggressive in allocating funds to the developing world. ...

Public funds, many of which didn't get into international investing of any sort until three to five years ago, are also beginning to set aside a small portion of their assets for emerging markets. No one, however, seems precisely sure how much U.S. pension money has flowed into emerging markets, in part because it has happened so quickly. But a sophisticated guess is one half of one percent of total pension assets, or around $18 billion. The potential for further investments is thus considerable: Emerging markets represent 13 percent of global GNP and 6 percent of the capitalization of all equity markets. ...

The U.S. institutions with the most experience in third-world investments tend to be the pension funds of top 50 companies and the largest endowments. Antoine van Agtmael, president of Emerging Markets Management, one of the largest of the emerging-markets specialist firms, ... says he's seeing interest both from smaller corporate pension funds and from the larger ones that just hadn't gotten around to investing before. ...

The largest, and by far the most important, prospective emerging-markets investors, however, are public funds. ...

The larger the fund, whether public, private or endowment, the more likely it is to invest in emerging markets. Twenty-eight percent of foundations and endowments with more than $1 billion in assets use an emerging-markets specialist. For equivalent corporate and public funds, the comparable proportions are 15 percent and 10 percent, respectively. Moreover, 5 percent of the large public funds and 13 percent of the corporate ones expect to hire a specialist this year. ...

The Dictator Drawback
Those that do commit tend to be timid about it. Douglas Lemon Jr., chief investment officer for the $10 billion Arizona State Retirement System, has adopted a deliberate approach typical of plan sponsors.

Arizona has allocated $50 million to emerging markets. ... "A lot of toe dipping will go on until people become a lot more comfortable," says Lemon. Many funds, he notes, took a bath investing directly in South America during the 1960s: "Every time you thought you had something good, a new dictator took over and nationalized the industries."

Arizona's 0.5 percent emerging-markets allocation is smaller than most, even for a public fund. Nevertheless, few plan sponsors are expected to reach the 3 percent to 6 percent allocation recommended by consultants for another two years. Their initial allocations will be on the order of 1 percent, say plan sponsors, and after they gain some experience, they may move up to the recommended zones.

Even for plans that have been in emerging markets for a number of years, though, allocations typically comprise no more than 3 percent of assets and 10 to 15 percent of international exposure. Frank Russell's Castelin notes that a 3 percent allocation is close to the true investable market capitalization of emerging markets as a proportion of all the world's stock markets. ...

Lawrence Speidell is international portfolio manager at Batterymarch Financial Management, which runs $500 million in emerging-market equities through various regional funds. He confides that he's often asked, "Why should we invest in countries that oppress their people, ravage their environment and take jobs away from American workers?" His answer: Economics is more important than politics; a rising standard of living is the best protection for the people and the resources of nations; investment in support of free trade is important for world growth; and economic reforms need the early support of foreign investors.

.   .   .

Patience Needed

Experts advise wide geographical diversification for an initial exposure to emerging markets, which have low relative correlations. PGGM's Keijzer suggests a two-tiered approach: go with a global mandate first, then move to a smaller allocation for regional managers. Unless a country fund is the only way to play a market, stay away from it, most plan sponsors counsel. Devoting too much cash to one market undermines the benefits to be gained by diversifying. "We considered going with country funds, but quickly dropped that idea in favor of letting a manager decide where we should be," says Scott Malpass, the University of Notre Dame's investment officer.

To truly benefit from emerging markets, investors must reconcile themselves to being in for the long haul. "This is the growth area for the next ten to twenty years," states Wilshire's Nesbitt. A long-term mindset can also help console plan sponsors when emerging markets suffer a setback, as they inevitably will from time to time. A disruption in a country with putative political stability, like Mexico, would undoubtedly slow the stream of funds into emerging markets. But Fisher and many other managers and consultants now feel certain that the markets are sufficiently well established to surmount their own vulnerability to volatility.

As for the danger that emerging markets will prove so popular that too much money will end up chasing too few stocks, the massive privatization of government-owned assets, such as telephone companies, should assure an adequate supply of shares indefinitely. Add to that the possibility that China, Brazil or India will blossom in the same way Mexico has, and liquidity should be no problem, experts say.

The beauty of emerging markets is precisely that—that new ones are *always* emerging. As a Mexico or a Thailand develops beyond the parameters that define "emerging," another country is certain to take its place. This process has been going on for a long time, notes Genesis' Paulson–Ellis: "In the nineteenth century I think [the emerging market] was called America."

A simple explanation for the relative lack of pension fund investment in emerging markets is their small relative size. The following table compares the market capitalization of the Group of 7 countries with some leading emerging stock markets over a decade. Their growth suggests where emerging markets got their name. The following table is from J. Mullin, *Emerging Equity Markets in the Global Economy*, Federal Reserve Bank of New York Quarterly Review, Summer 1993, at 71.

Table 7

Total Market Capitalization: 1981–91

	1981		1986		1991	
	Billions of U.S. Dollars	Percent of GDP	Billions of U.S. Dollars	Percent of GDP	Billions of U.S. Dollars	Percent of GDP
Canada	106	36	166	46	267	45
France	38	7	150	20	374	31
Germany	63	9	258	29	394	25
Italy	24	6	140	23	154	13
Japan	431	37	1,842	93	3,131	93
United Kingdom	181	35	440	78	1,003	99
United States	1,333	44	2,637	62	4,180	74
Group of Seven markets	2,176	33	5,632	60	9,503	65
All developed markets	2,502	--	6,367	--	10,760	--
Argentina	2	2	2	2	19	17
Brazil†	13	5	42	16	43	9
Chile	7	22	4	24	28	93
Mexico	10	4	6	5	98	40
India	7	4	14	6	48	16
Korea	4	6	14	13	96	37
Thailand	1	3	3	7	36	41
Malaysia	15	61	15	54	59	127
Taiwan	5	11	15	19	125	74
Nine emerging markets	64	6	115	12	551	32
All emerging markets tracked by International Finance Corporation	83	--	145	--	643	--

Sources: International Finance Corporation, *Emerging Stock Markets Factbook*, various issues; and International Monetary Fund, International Financial Statistics.
Note: Capitalization data refer to the market value of shares listed on domestic exchanges, including shares associated with international placements and those used to back American depository receipts.
† Sao Paulo only.

Note

1. As U.S. and European pension funds continued to increase the portion of their funds invested in foreign securities, the advantages of diversification came under scrutiny. The IFC found great variation in emerging markets' correlation with U.S. markets over a five year period.

IFC Total Return Correlation Index
December 1988 - December 1993
(1.00 is complete correlation)

Correlation with US S&P 500

Latin America		Asia	
index	0.20	index	0.45
Peru	0.48	Malaysia	0.41
Mexico	0.38	Philippines	0.37
Chile	0.19	Thailand	0.33
Brazil	0.18	Pakistan	0.22
Argentina	0.07	Taiwan	0.04
		India	-0.14
		Korea	-0.16

Source: International Finance Corporation, Emerging Markets Factbook 104 (1994)

But perhaps 5 year periods hid important relationships. As volatility increased on exchanges around the world, so did the correlation in their price movements, found another study. This would be unfortunate for investors seeking to diversify by investing abroad. They would most want the benefits of diversification when large downward price movements occurred during volatile times, such as the market crash of 1987. Study by Bruno Solnik, Hautes Etudes Commerciales, reported in *Global Diversification Has Its Downside And May Not Be the Strongest Safety Net*, Wall Street Journal, June 14, 1994. Perhaps, also, the recent wave of ADRs and other forms of investment had increased market correlation. During the first six months of 1994 Latin American stock prices correlated twice as much (0.44) with the US S&P 500 as they had during 1993, according to a third study. N. Ramachandran, Rogers, Casey & Associates, reported in *The Trouble with Togetherness*, Institutional Investor, Oct. 1994, at 115.

4. THE TELMEX OFFER: MARKETING TO INSTITUTIONAL INVESTORS

Goldman Sachs lead managed the global offering. In the following material, Goldman summarizes the marketing and its results. The first chart lists the places Goldman's roadshow team went to sell the offer to investors. The second shows the results of the offering: how much was sold in four different areas, the fee distribution, and the lead managers. The third chart gives more information about the international part of the offering. The final chart shows allocation relative to demand, by region. The offer was oversubscribed in every region, but more in some than others. As you read these, consider why demand might have been so relatively strong in some regions and not in others.

Marketing

Summary of Roadshow Attendance

City	Total No. Attendees	No. Institutions Represented
Tokyo	145	106
Paris	92	78
Copenhagen	27	17
Frankfurt	51	38
Edinburgh	14	13
Zurich	14	13
Geneva	68	61
London	68	61
Houston	44	21
Denver	24	12
Baltimore	19	13
Philadelphia	21	17
San Francisco	47	36
Los Angeles	45	20
Montreal	50	13
Toronto	160	52
Minneapolis	16	11
Chicago	62	32
New York — Breakfast	24	18
— Lunch	224	157
Boston	70	48
Total	1,285	837

The Telmex International Roadshow had an unprecedented attendance of almost 1,300 investors representing over 800 institutions worldwide

Syndication

Structure of the Global Offering

	Combined Offering	Mexico	United States	International[a]	Japan
Type of Security Sold[b]	Ordinary Shares/ADRs	Ordinary Shares	ADRs	ADRs	ADRs
Size of Tranche					
—Shares of ADRs	79,750,000	115,000,000[c]	44,000,000[d]	25,000,000	5,000,000
—Dollars (millions)	$2,173.2	$156.7	$1,199.0	$681.3	$136.3
Percent of Offering	100.0%	7.2%	55.2%	31.3%	6.3%
Percent of Govt. Ownership	57.9	4.2	32.0	18.2	3.6
Percent of Total Equity	15.0	1.1	8.3	4.7	0.9
Offer Price	$27.25/ADR	4,090 pesos/share	$27.25/ADR	$27.25/ADR	$27.25/ADR
Gross Spread per ADR	$1.22(4.5%)				
—Underwriting	27¢				
—Management	25¢				
—Selling	70¢				
Lead Manager(s)		Acciones y Valores Invetsora Bursal	Goldman Sachs (Co-lead Managers: Bear Stearns, Merrill Lynch)	CSFB Deutsche Bank Goldman Sachs Paribas S.G. Warburg Wood Grundy	Nomura
Goldman Sachs' Role	Global Coordinator		Lead Manager	Co-Lead Manager (Lead Manager of ROW)	Co-Lead Manager

Banco Internacional ● ISEFI   Global Agent of the Mexican Government

(a) Includes offerings in Canada, France, Germany, Switzerland, the U.K. and the rest of the world.
(b) Banamex is the custodian for all the ordinary shares and Morgan Guaranty is the ADR Depositary Bank.
(c) Equal to 5,750,000 ADRs; includes overallotment option exercised in Mexico for 15,000,000 L shares on May 13, 1991.
(d) Includes overallotment option exercised in the US market for 4,000,000 L ADRs on June 5, 1991.

The Telmex offering constitutes the first simultaneous offering of shares in the Mexican, US and international markets

Syndication

Breakdown of the International Offering

	Total International Offering	Canada	France Belgium and Luxembourg	Germany and Austria	Switzerland and Liechtenstein	United Kingdom	Rest of World
Size of Tranche							
—ADRs	25,000,000	2,760,000	3,000,000	2,040,000	3,000,000	11,000,000	3,200,000
—Dollars (Millions)	$681.3	$75.2	$81.8	$55.6	$81.8	$299.8	$87.2
Percent of Offering	31.3%	3.5%	3.8%	2.6%	3.8%	13.8%	4.0%
Percent of Govt. Ownership	18.2	2.0	2.2	1.5	2.2	8.0	2.3
Percent of Total Equity	4.7	0.5	0.6	0.4	0.6	2.1	0.6
Syndicate Managers							
—Lead Manager		Wood Grundy	Paribas	Deutsche	CSFB	S.G. Warburg	Goldman Sachs
—Co-lead Managers		Goldman Sachs	Banque Indosuez	Dresdner	Goldman Sachs	Baring Brothers	S.G. Warburg
		Scotia McLeod	Goldman Sachs	Goldman Sachs	Swiss Bank Corp.	Goldman Sachs	

Regional syndicates were essential to ensure focussed marketing and depth of distribution

Allocation

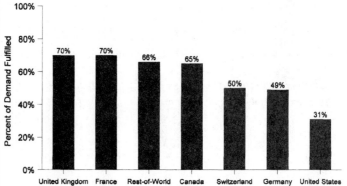

Regional Allocations Relative to Demand (a)

Telmex shares were oversubscribed in all the regional markets and unsatisfied demand helped strengthen the after-market.

Percent of Demand Fulfilled

United Kingdom 70% · France 70% · Rest-of-World 66% · Canada 65% · Switzerland 50% · Germany 49% · United States 31%

(a) These figures are based on regional demand estimates. Estimates were not available for Mexico and Japan syndicates

Notes and Questions

1. What would account for the relative distribution of the tranches among the four regions: Mexico, U.S., International, and Japan? What explains Japan's share?

2. What might account for the regional allocations relative to demand? Specifically, what might explain the U.S. share?

3. How important is control over Telmex likely to be to institutional investors like the pension funds? Why? What other factors are likely to be more important to them?

4. The following items are said to affect institutional investors' interest in emerging markets. How did Mexico deal with these potential problems, in the Telmex offer and in its development of its stock market? Would the investors in the Telmex ADSs care much about these items?

  a. restrictions on capital inflows;

  b. restrictions on repatriation of dividends and capital;

  c. limited market transparency;

  d. illiquid and shallow stock markets;

  e. unreliable broker networks; and

  f. limited financial instruments.

5. According to Goldman Sachs, in the first two months after the offer, the New York Stock Exchange was the home market for Telmex. Trading on peak days is "as much as 85% of all trading activity in Telmex." The L shares trading on the Mexican stock exchange represented up to 40% of all Telmex trading on peak days.

I. THE DECEMBER 1994 PESO CRISIS

On December 20, 1994, the Mexican government devalued the peso 15% against the dollar to 25 cents/peso and two days later let the peso float. It fell almost 50% in four weeks. Foreign investors in Telmex ADSs and other Mexican securities reeled. Mutual funds specializing in Mexican paper saw their price fall 5% on December 21 alone and plummet after that. Chapter 21 describes the crisis and its aftermath for emerging market debt.

1. THE IMPACT OF THE CRISIS ON EMERGING STOCK MARKETS

Mexico's stock market index fell from 2600 at the start of December 1994 to below 1500 in early March before it began to recover. By mid-April, it passed 1900. The market proved sensitive to the apparent success or failure of efforts to resolve the crisis in Mexico and abroad. As the government raised interest rates to 50% and higher in order to strengthen the peso, equity investors saw the damage of high rates to Mexican firms. As the government drew on the US credit line, investors concluded the country was indeed in very bad shape. A Mexican development bank, Nacional Financiera, began to buy shares to create demand. When the government was able to roll over a maturing debt issue, the market rallied a bit. When it became clear on January 30 that the US Government's January support package would fail, the market fell almost 3%. It rose over 10% the day after Clinton announced the second package. Later in February, as the belt-tightening policies Mexico would need to follow became clear, the market fell again.

Mexico's crisis was contagious. Other Latin American markets quickly took a turn for the worse. The prices of leading traded Latin American companies collapsed; their index fell from 490 in early January to 400 in mid-January then, after quickly recovering to 470 in late January, fell to 270 in early March. It recovered to 370 a month later. The major markets—in Argentina, Brazil, Chile, and Peru—fell quickly in late December. Argentina, Brazil, and Peru continued to fall through mid-March to 60% of their end-1994 values. Some investors believed these countries' currencies were overvalued. By early March, Argentina had sought substantial help from the IMF, as depositors withdrew substantial dollar deposits from the country's banks. Also in early March, Brazil devalued the real and actively tried to distinguish its economy from Mexico's in the eyes of investors. See P. Coggan and A. Sharpe, *Bargain Hunters*, Financial Times, Apr. 13, 1995.

Investors differentiated among Latin American countries to some extent.   The market in Chile stayed close to its end-1994 values. Investors saw Chile as having a consistently better managed economy. Demand for many closed end mutual funds invested in Latin America remained strong enough for the funds' shares to be traded at a premium over their portfolio value. One reason given was that fund investors had not withdrawn from the funds to the same extent that local markets had fallen, suggesting that they expected the markets to turn around. See E. Browning, *Heard on the Street*, Wall Street Journal, Mar. 15, 1995.

Asian exchanges were also hit. During January 1995, the biggest declines (11-13%) were in Pakistan, Philippines, China, India, South Korea, and Taiwan. Smaller declines hit Hong Kong, Thailand, Malaysia, Indonesia, and Singapore. Countries with the largest falls had domestic problems pre-dating the tequila effect. Pakistan's exchange, for example, had fallen 10% during the last quarter of 1994. By mid-February, most Asian emerging markets had started to grow. Hong Kong, Malaysia, and Thailand made up any fall. Investors were said to have decided Clinton's second aid package was a good sign that major governments would help emerging markets.

Many investors in the US, at least, planned to maintain or increase their investment in emerging markets in 1995 despite the Mexican crisis.

In a survey of investments during January and February 1995, 46% of the 50 companies questioned had reduced their exposure to emerging markets and 34% actually increased it. Indeed, only 26% planned to reduce their exposure in Latin America (other than Mexico). See *It Doesn't Have to be American*, Euromoney, Apr. 1995, at 45.

Stock markets recovered by early 1996. Mexico's stock index finished higher at the end of March 1996 than its peak in late 1994. By May 1999, Mexico's stock market index reached 6,000. A. Mandel-Campbell, *Foreign Funds Drive Mexico*, Financial Times, May 19, 1999. Foreign funds began to return to other Latin American exchanges. Despite the crisis, total returns on Latin American stock markets exceeded those on Asian markets by over 100% for the period 1989 to mid-1995, according to the IMF.

ADR markets continued to grow, fueled more by European issuers than those from developing countries. Nevertheless, by 1995, Mexico boasted 50 ADRs, ranking it the fifth largest home country (behind the UK, Australia, South Africa, and Hong Kong). The impact of ADRs on the Mexican exchange was mixed, according to one study. The Mexican market suffered from greater volatility because of the ADRs, but competition among brokers in Mexico increased, benefitting investors. See I. Domowitz, J. Glen, and A. Madhavan, International Cross-Listing, Ownership Rights and Order Flow Migration: Evidence from Mexico (1995).

Portfolio investment in developing countries was not expected to reach its 1993 levels even by 1997. The following table reports the sources of net external financing for major emerging markets from 1993-8.

Major Emerging Market Economies' External Finance ($ billions)						
Sources (net)	**1993**	**1994**	**1995**	**1996**	**1997e**	**1998e**
External financing	211.7	198.5	254.6	298.0	229.3	171.5
Portfolio Equity	40.4	27.3	24.4	33.2	19.4	22.5
Direct Equity	48.5	64.1	75.7	93.3	114.4	106.5
Commercial banks	30.2	40.8	90.8	103.5	-3.7	2.4
Nonbank private creditors	70.4	40.2	16.7	65.2	70.0	40.1
Official flows	22.3	26.1	46.9	2.8	29.7	30.8
Resident lending/other	-71.6	-79.9	-81.9	-116.2	-101.8	-69.0
Reserves excl. gold (- = increase)	-61.4	-46.6	-94.1	-85.1	-49.9	-60.7

Source: Institute for International Finance, Capital Flow to Emerging Economies, Sep. 19, 1996.
e = estimate

2. TELMEX AND THE CRISIS

Several years into its transition, Telmex could boast $3 billion in 1993 profits on $8 billion in sales, foreign investors who had put $18 billion in it, a 26% weight on the Mexican IPC index, 18% of the stock market's capitalization, and 23% of its trading volume. Telmex benefitted from the wealth and power of its principal Mexican owner, Carlos Slim, who was the richest man in the country. On the other hand, Telmex had a bad reputation for service and only 8.8 phones existed for each 100 people. See C. Torres, *Future Is on the Line for Mexico's Telephone Company*, Wall Street Journal, June 29, 1994.

The crisis hit Telmex on and off the exchanges. Its L ADS's high on the NYSE in 1994 was $76, but by early March 1995 it traded at $25. The following chart shows the L ADS prices from late November 1994 to mid-April 1995. The price of the L shares on the Mexican exchange moved just the same in dollar terms. Telmex announced a loss during the first quarter of 1995 of P. 390 million ($67 million) because of foreign exchange losses of P. 4.3 billion. Telmex had sharply cut its capital expenditures to reduce costs. This worried investors, who expected that Telmex would be hurt by new legislation to increase competition in both local and long-distance markets in 1997. See D. Dombey, *Telmex Blames Heavy Forex Loss for Fall into Red*, Financial Times, Apr. 29, 1995.

The Mexican government seemed to be proceeding with its plan to open the country's phone market to competition. In July 1994, it issued rules permitting unlimited competition and forcing Telmex to give competitors access to its exchanges. Only the fees due from new entrants remained to be set. Foreign firms were positioning themselves. AT&T entered a joint venture in November 1994 with a major industrial conglomerate, Grupo Alfa, in which Carlos Slim held a 15% share. Other companies, like MCI and Motorola, entered similar ventures with Mexican firms. Telmex's original partners were seen as inexperienced with the complex billing software that Telmex needed to keep a high market share, so Telmex allied with Sprint. France Telecom SA was negotiating a substantial stake in Sprint at the time.

Telmex ADS Price, November 1994 to mid-April 1995

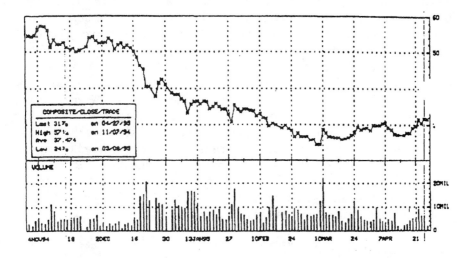

Source: Bloomberg

The Mexican Government sought ways to offset the likely damage of this expected competition to Telmex, which depended on long-distance revenues to show a profit. A revised fee schedule in 1995 gave Telmex a subsidy to offset the losses on its domestic services since the profits from long distance service would not subsidize domestic services as much as in the past. Another source of help was an agreement between Mexico and the US Government that as long as Telmex had at least 75% of the northbound phone traffic it would be entitled to handle 75% of the southbound traffic regardless of which foreign carrier originated the call. T. Bardacke, *Tough Times for Telmex as Mexico Prepares to Open Market*, Financial Times, Nov. 17, 1994.

In April 1995, the Mexican government decided not to charge fees to new entrants into the phone market, despite its need for foreign currency. Instead, the government set modernization of the phone system as its primary goal. Telmex's ADSs fell 1.2% on the news. The government promised that Telmex could increase rates on its local services.

The recession in 1995 hurt Telmex, so that its net sales fell 6% below the 1994 level. Nevertheless, the company was able to securitize $280 million of telephone receivables in international markets in early 1996. The Mexican government set up a regulatory commission for telecommunications, anticipating the end of Telmex's monopoly. And Carlos Slim spun his company's interest in Telmex off into a separate firm, apparently to protect his company from loss if Telmex should suffer. But by 1996, his company was buying Telmex stock.

The prospect of a competitive telecommunications industry in 1997 was bracing. Telmex began to connect its exchanges to competitors' long-distance lines in January 1997, having already lowered its long-distance prices in anticipation. Two rivals launched an advertizing blitz to announce the new regime. They were linked, respectively, to MCI and ATT and expected to invest $1 billion each by 2000. A 20% p.a. growth was forecast in the long-distance market and Telmex's rivals hoped to win a 40% market share by 2000. But in June 1997, 70% of Mexican customers in 26 cities opted, by choice or inertia, to stay with Telmex as their long distance carrier, leaving its rivals a small share of the market. The rivals, however, argued that government policy continued to support Telmex to their disadvantage. Anticipating this challenge, Telmex had invested $11 billion since it was privatized. It cut costs and diversified. Mexico City's phone system was much improved. A Telmex subsidiary dominated the limited cellular phone market.

3. TELMEX AND THE WTO

Telmex's business in, and competition with firms from, the U.S. led to several conflicts potentially within the ambit of the WTO. In late 1997, Telmex won FCC preliminary approval to enter the U.S. market with Sprint, targeting Hispanic communities in the Southwest. But ATT and MCI froze payments due to Telmex and challenged Telmex's entry into the U.S. market. As a result, Telmex threatened to seek redress from the World Trade Organization.   In the meantime, Telmex reported a substantial drop in net revenue in 1997. Local rates were still not up to market prices and Telmex was expected to continue to subsidize them for at least two more years from the connection fees paid by its competitors. See D. Dombey, *Winds of Change Snuff Old Problems*, Financial Times, Oct. 28, 1996; L. Crawford, *Telmex Chief Plans US Move This Year*, Financial Times, Jan. 13, 1997; J. Preston, *A Telecom Revolucion in Mexico*, New York Times, Nov. 14, 1996, H. Tricks, *AT&T Threatens to Halt Telmex Payments*, Financial Times, February 9, 1998; H. Tricks, *Telmex Threatens to Complain to the WTO*, Financial Times, February 25, 1998; and *Telmex Net Falls 22% As More Competition Erodes Market Share*, Wall Street Journal, October 22, 1997.

Telmex retained 99% of the domestic market in mid-2000. It leveraged this power to impose onerous conditions on long-distance competitors, because they had to use Telmex to reach almost all of their Mexican customers. In an action urged by the U.S. competitors, the FTC fined Telmex's U.S. subsidiary $100,000 for unfair practices and high interconnection costs. Then in July 2000, the U.S. trade representative, Charlene Barshevsky, started a process to bring Mexico before the WTO. She was responding to complaints from U.S. companies like AT&T and WorldCom that Telmex was keeping them out of phone markets in Mexico, with the help of the country's regulators. The U.S. said that "Telmex overcharges to connect local calls to the long-distance networks, applies unfair fees for incoming international long-distance phone calls, and denies competitors the high-traffic lines they need for Internet service." A. DePalma, *U.S. Seeks W.T.O. Talks On Mexican Phone Market*, New York Times, July 29, 2000. Telmex agreed in September to divest its wireless holdings and the value of its ADRs rose 20% in one week. Then Mexican regulators, trying to avoid the WTO, ordered Telmex to cut its interconnection rates 63% and the U.S. put its action on hold. In April 2001, the U.S. gave Mexico until June 1 to remove the barriers still in place, or the WTO arbitration would proceed. A. Mandel-Campbell, *Please Hold, Mexican Callers*, Financial Times, May 16, 2000; A. Mandel-Campbell, *Telmex To Shed Wireless Arms*, Financial Times, Sep. 11, 2000; G. Gori, *Trade Dispute More Likely as Telmex Sues on Connection Fees*, New York Times, Nov. 1, 2000; A. Mandel-Campbell and E. Alden, *US Warns Mexico on Telecoms*, Financial Times, Apr. 3, 2001.

Questions

1. Why would the sharp peso devaluation hurt the price of the Telmex L ADS, which was traded in dollars on the NYSE?

2. What lessons should an institutional investor draw from the Mexican rescue package? How, if at all, should the package affect investments in Mexico? In other Latin American countries? In Asia? To what extent can governments of major industrial countries be expected to support an emerging market? How does this package compare with those for the 1982 debt crisis in Mexico? What would account for differences? Who was being helped by the two rescue packages?

3. What lessons should an institutional investor draw from the tequila effect? Where was the contagion serious? Why? How capable are investors to distinguish among countries? Why would they move as a herd, when they do? To the extent that they do, is the behavior similar to that of the banks that made syndicated loans in the 1970s and early 1980s?

4. In April 1996, does the Telmex L ADS look attractive? How would recent government policies affect the value of the ADS? To what extent have investors in the L ADS diversified away from US risks?

5.   Compare the discipline the securities market imposed on Mexico, before and after the December 1994 crisis, with the discipline imposed by the banks that made syndicated loans to Mexico 12 to 20 years earlier.

Links To Other Chapters

The Telmex offering raises issues that appear throughout the book. This is a global offering, like those discussed in Chapter 12. Some of the syndication techniques used to market the security worldwide remind one of those described in Chapter 9. Capital adequacy rules affect the capabilities of the underwriters to do their job (Chapter 4).

Access to the major national markets was very important. The choice of ADRs as a vehicle to reach the American investors and the factors that influence decisions to make a public or private offer, or both, appear as topics in Chapter 2. The problems faced by Japanese equity investors are described in Chapter 8.

The relationship of the ADS and its underlying stock are vitally affected by exchange rates (Chapter 6) and clearing and settlement (Chapter 15). The exchanges in Mexico and the U.S. cooperate as well as compete (Chapter 14).

The offering suggests important trends in the relative importance of the debt and equity markets (Chapter 1). The ADR is a type of derivative (Chapters 15 and 16) that is found increasingly in international markets.

Chapter 21 describes the currency crisis in Asia, as does Chapter 1 for Korea.

CHAPTER TWENTY-ONE

EMERGING MARKET DEBT

A. INTRODUCTION

On international markets, borrowers from developing countries have a spotty record of debt service extending back over 150 years or longer. In response their creditors, and the home governments of those creditors, devised various ways to discourage default and recover the debt.

In the 19th century, Europeans bought bonds issued by "railroads and mines in Spain, Austria, Turkey, and Russia, banks in Egypt, Mexico, Haiti, and the Balkans, nickel in Caledonia, guano in Peru, the canal at Panama." H. Feis, Europe, The World's Banker (1936) at 64. Bonds financed the construction of U.S. railroads. Waves of default swept the world during economic depression and war: 1873, 1893, 1914-18, 1929, and 1939-45 were bad years for creditors.

Borrowers from many countries defaulted. One borrower was the khedive, or ruler, of Egypt from 1863 to 1879, Pasha Ismail. Egyptian cotton rode an export boom during the U.S. Civil War, when prices soared worldwide. The Khedive issued bonds in the U.K. and France to finance "grandiose schemes, including irrigation project, schools, palaces, the construction of the Suez Canal and the extensions of Egyptian rule in the Sudan. Much of the money was wasted." *Columbia Encyclopedia*, 3rd Ed. (1963) at 1052. Then came the depression of 1873, and the Pasha could not repay the debt on schedule.

The 19th century solution to default was straight forward. The British government, supported by France, led the effort to help the Pasha service his debt. In 1876, they set up a bondholders commission to help the Pasha manage his finance. After an armed uprising in 1879, Britain sent troops. Its consul general took de facto control of Egypt's government. Ismail's son replaced the father as pasha. The parties agreed to reschedule the debt over a 30 year period and Britain agreed to retain control of Egypt's government pending full payment. British capital and skills integrated Egypt into the British empire as a valuable agricultural producer and a market for British goods. This was an outcome Pasha Ismail had probably not looked for when he started to borrow. See R. Mabro and S. Radwan, The Industrialization of Egypt, 1839-1973 (1976) at 19. It was echoed so widely then that former U.S. president U.S. Grant warned the emperor of Japan, during a visit there, not to let his country borrow in international markets if it wanted to retain its independence.

A century later, creditor governments seemed no less interested in protecting their lenders but were more circumspect when enforcing the claims.

Since the 1960s, many different types of credit flowed to borrowers in emerging markets, which include developing, or less developed, countries ("LDCs") and those in transition from communism. The debt includes loans from other governments (called official bilateral debt) and multilateral agencies such as the World Bank, and banks, as well as international bonds, notes, and short-term credit instruments. For this chapter, the debt does not include cross-border portfolio investment in domestic bonds issued by private entities in the countries.

The crises are more frequent now than before 1914 and the techniques to resolve them have become more complex. Generally, the external debt crisis combines with a foreign exchange crisis to cripple the borrowing country. A systematic comparison appears in M. Bordo and A. Schwartz, *Measuring Real Economic Effects of Bailouts: Historical Perspectives on How Countries in Financial Distress Have Fared With and Without Bailouts*, NBER Working Paper 7701, May 2000. The authors cast doubt on the effectiveness of the central institution now used to deal with the crises, the International Monetary Fund. Compared to countries that did not turn to the IMF, those that did may have performed worse according to various macro aggregates, such as the decline and growth of real GDP overall and per capita, and the ratio of consumption to GDP during and after the crisis. As you read this chapter, please consider the role of the IMF in managing the crises.

This chapter describes the major types of debt raised on international markets: syndicated borrowing during the 1970s and early 1980s, the coerced lending that grew out of the 1982 debt crisis, and the later voluntary credit as some of the developing countries reestablished their credibility in international markets for bank loans and bonds. Major debt crises accompanied this lending—the 1982 collapse, the Mexican crisis of 1994-1995, the Asian financial crisis of 1997, default on emerging market bonds in Russia and Ecuador, and Argentina's collapse. The chapter also presents the solutions to these crises, such as they were.

The adjacent table records the outstanding external debt of 157 low and middle income developing countries periodically from 1970. The countries include Korea and Mexico, as well as many poorer economies. The table separately reports debt owed or guaranteed by the government, which includes companies, such as a national airline, in which the government holds over 50% of the shares. Long-term debt has an original maturity of over one year. Other private creditors include manufacturers, exporters, bank loans guaranteed by export credit agencies, and other suppliers. Lines A and B are the only identifiable debt of the public sector. It is not possible to distinguish between public and private non-guaranteed short-term debt.

External Debt Outstanding of All Developing Countries: ($ billions, end of year)						
Creditors	**1970**	**1980**	**1985**	**1990**	**1995**	**1999**
A. Public and publicly guaranteed long term debt	**47**	**365**	**742**	**1,115**	**1,433**	**1,542**
of which: Commercial banks	4	124	278	257	174	219
Bonds	2	13	32	107	257	365
Other private creditors	8	52	103	145	138	81
Bilateral official creditors	26	127	222	397	573	533
Multilateral creditors	7	49	108	208	290	345
B. Use of IMF credit	**1**	**12**	**na**	**35**	**na**	**79**
C. Subtotal (A + B)	56	377		1,149		1,621
D. Short-term debt (all types of creditors and borrowers)	**9**	**139**	**164**	**245**	**428**	**407**
E. Private non-guaranteed long-term debt	**15**	**71**	**na**	**66**	**na**	**536**
F. Total (A + B + D + E)	73	587		1,460		2,564
Note: Commercial banks, bonds, and other private creditors as % of line C	*25%*	*50%*		*44%*		*41%*

Source: World Bank *Global Development Finance* (2001) supplemented by data from the World Bank. na = not available. Multilateral creditors include the World Bank, regional development banks, but not the IMF, which is separately listed.

The table reveals an almost 30 fold increase over 40 years in the external long-term debt owed or guaranteed by the public sector in developing countries (line A). We call this sovereign debt. It rose from $56 billion in 1970 to $1.6 trillion in 1999. As a comparison, long-term debt owed by private sector borrowers (and not guaranteed by the government) was only a third of the sovereign debt in 1999.

This period saw a shift in the relative importance of private lenders–banks, bond markets, and others–compared to public lenders–bilateral and multilateral agencies. From a low share of 25% in 1970, private lenders increased their portion to just over 50% in 1980, only to see it fall to 41% in 1999. Public creditors again took the lead. Among private lenders, a sea change was in the shift from bank to bond debt. In 1970, bank debt was twice that of bond debt, $4 billion compared to $2 billion. As late as 1990 bank debt still dominated, over twice as high as bonds, or $257 billion compared to $107 billion. In 1999, the tables had turned. Bond debt was over 1½ times as high as bank debt, $365 billion compared to $219 billion.

Among official creditors, the growth of lending by the IMF was the largest. It rose 100 times from 1970 to 1999 (from $800 million to $79 billion). Its funds largely address financial crises in developing countries. Other official creditors lend to finance economic projects as well as to resolve crises.

Finally, the maturity of the credit shifted to short-term debt from long-term. We lack numbers for sovereign short-term compared to sovereign long-term overall for the period, but one can compare short-term debt of sovereigns and the private sector to long-term sovereign debt. Short-term was about 1/6th of all loans in 1970, about 1/5th in 1990, and about 1/4th by 1999.

In summary, sovereign debt grew substantially, the private creditor share of this debt rose but is decreasing again, debt extended by private creditors shifted from banks to investors in bonds, IMF crisis lending grew enormously, and an increasing portion of sovereign debt seems to be short-term.

B. SYNDICATED BANK LOANS TO DEVELOPING COUNTRIES, THE 1982 DEBT CRISIS, AND ITS RESOLUTION

1. LENDING BY BANKS TO BORROWERS FROM DEVELOPING COUNTRIES TO 1982

Until the early 1970s, the major cross-border flow of funds to emerging markets was from official sources (government or multilateral), supplemented by foreign direct investment and credit to support exports to the borrowers. In 1970, for example, of $14.7 billion in total net financial flows to developing countries, $7.9 billion came from official bilateral and multilateral sources, and another $3.5 billion was direct investment. Banks made export credits of $2.1 billion and other loans of $0.7 billion, which was 19% of total net flows. A mere seven years later, the share of bank loans doubled to 39% of total flows, which was $48 billion. Organization for Economic Cooperation and Development, *Development Cooperation Review 1970* and *1977* (1971 and 1978).

Much of the new bank lending allowed borrowing countries to finance huge deficits in the balance of trade caused by the first oil shock, the sudden quadrupling in the oil price in 1973. All oil importing countries were hurt and needed to finance their deficits. To fund these deficits, they borrowed hard currency largely from banks and then they borrowed to service their bank debt. Since the oil exporting countries deposited much of their huge trade surpluses in international banks, people said the banks were recycling the oil money. The U.S. Treasury estimated that in 1974 the oil producers placed $22.5 billion of their $71 billion current account surplus in eurocurrency markets. Office of International Banking and Portfolio Investment, U.S. Treasury Department, *Estimates of the Disposition of OPEC Investable Surplus*, 1974-1979 (June 13, 1980); P. Wellons, *World Money and Credit: The Crisis and Its Causes* (1983) at 43 (Wellons 1983).

The banks loaned the money in various ways, but their major instrument was the medium-term floating-rate syndicated eurocurrency loan or eurocredit. Chapter 9 describes this financial market, the institutions in it, and the major provisions of a eurocredit contract. Most international banks had a relatively low level of exposure to non-oil producing developing countries (NODCs), although they had started to offer eurocredits to NODCs around 1970. Demand from industrial countries was low because most were in recession. Particularly after 1973, NODC borrowers, who were mainly governments, government agencies, or government-owned enterprises, paid much higher spreads than borrowers in industrial countries. For example, in 1976, the mean spread was 1.87% for borrowers in NODCs and 1.29% for those in large OECD countries. Wellons 1983, at 55.

The bond market was not a significant source of funds for NODCs. In 1976, for example, NODCs received $21 billion in net new bank loans and only $2 billion in net new bonds, which was twice the average annual flow since 1971. IMF, International Capital Markets: Recent Developments (Sep. 1980), Table 13.

The second oil shock, when OPEC doubled the price in 1979, made this reliance on banks untenable. The major NODC borrowers were in Latin America. Their current account deficits almost tripled from $4.5 billion in 1973 to $11.3 in 1978. Their borrowing grew, resulting in a capital account deficit of $20.5 billion in 1978. Now the banks had substantial exposure to the borrowers and the borrowers were much in debt. In these circumstances, the banks were much less willing to lend to them but if they stopped completely the borrowers would not be able to service the outstanding debt. So they continued to lend, but increasingly short term and at a slower rate.

Banks eagerly increased their lending to oil-producing countries, such as Mexico. Given the ability of OPEC to impose its price on the world, this exposure seemed safe. From December 1978 to December 1981, banks increased their loans to Mexico by 138% from $23.3 billion. By comparison, they increased their lending to other Latin American countries by only 84% from $55.9 billion. By 1982, 1,400 banks had loaned foreign currency to Mexican borrowers, mainly the government or banks and enterprises that it owned, but also to some private borrowers. P. Wellons, *Passing the Buck* (1987) at 239

(Wellons 1987).

2. THE COLLAPSE IN 1982

Mexico failed to service its debt in August 1982, sought help from its stunned creditors, and set off a crisis lasting 10 years for some countries and still underway for others. Almost immediately, other developing countries with large debts to banks also failed to pay. According to W. Cline, *International Debt: Systemic Risk and Policy Response* (1984) at 5 (Cline 1984), four major factors from 1974 to 1982 led to the crisis. First, the increase in the real cost of oil (the nominal cost increase in excess of U.S. inflation) was $260 billion. Second, the U.S. central bank dramatically increased U.S. interest rates to counter a persistent inflation. Dollar LIBOR, on which so much eurocredit was based, rose from a low of 5% in 1976 to almost 17% in 1981, adding $41 billion to the borrowers' debt service costs. Third, the NODCs' exports earned less than in the past, creating a loss of $79 billion. The combined effect of the second and third factors was that the ratio of their real debt servicing costs to their exports, a common measure of the relative burden of a country's debt, rose from 6% in 1975 to over 20% in 1982. The fourth factor was the world recession in 1981-82 that reduced the NODCs' exports by $21 billion. In total, these four factors explain $401 billion of the $482 billion increase in the NODCs' debt from 1973 to 1982.

Between August 1982 and October 1983, 28 countries including Mexico rescheduled their debt. Sixteen were Latin American. They owed banks $239 billion, but the debt was concentrated in four countries—Mexico, Brazil, Venezuela, and Argentina—that owed $176 billion or 79% of the total. These four countries owed the nine largest U.S. banks $39 billion, which was 130% of their capital. All NODCs owed these nine banks 221% of their capital. Wellons 1987 at 225, Cline 1984 at 22.

These countries failed to service their debt as it became due, which most people would describe as default, but they were not technically in default according to the terms of the loan agreements. That was because most syndicated loans provided that a majority of the participating banks had to decide that the loan was in default and instruct their agent bank to take action against the borrower. Almost all participating banks decided not to declare their borrowers in default. Had default been declared, many banks, including the biggest ones in the U.S., would have had to recognize the loss. U.S. accounting rules required a bank to record a loss when the loan was in default but permitted it not to recognize a loss when the loan was rescheduled, or even when payments were missed. This was true even when the real value of the loan was much lower than its face value or the prospect of total repayment at market rates was impossible. But the banks with the most exposure lacked the reserves to absorb such a huge loss, nor was their capital adequate. Their strategy had to be to buy time, building their provisions and capital until they could afford to write off the losses. Their vulnerability and importance in their home financial systems raised the specter of economic crisis if they collapsed.

This prompted their home governments to look for ways to buy time.

3. RESOLVING THE CRISIS

In the months leading up to August 1982, Mexico's finance minister traveled incognito to Washington, D.C. regularly to confer with Paul Volcker, Chairman of the Federal Reserve Board, about the imminent collapse. When Mexico finally announced that it was imposing a moratorium on servicing its debt, the U.S. was prepared. Within days, a rescue package was announced, before banks had committed to any new funds. To provide liquidity, the U.S. Commodity Credit Corporation loaned $1 billion to Mexico, the Bank for International Settlements provided a $1 billion swap, and a U.S. oil reserve fund advanced $1 billion against future purchases of oil from Mexico. Shortly after that, the Fed itself loaned almost $1 billion short term, pending funds from the IMF. Because of the moratorium, which lasted for a year, none of these funds serviced the banks' loans. Working closely with the U.S. government, in November the IMF provided a $3.7 billion loan, to be drawn over three years, on the condition that in 1983 the banks make new loans to Mexico of $5 billion, which they did. Prodded by the U.S. and other governments, and the IMF, the 1,400 banks rescheduled $19.5 in largely short term loans originally due by December 1984, at higher spreads and for a rescheduling fee of ½%. Volcker tried, but failed, to raise much new money from other G-5 governments. Cline 1984 at 31 and Wellons 1987 at 236.

The exercise to inject new funds and reschedule both official and bank loans took place under the guidance of Paul Volcker and the Fed, the U.S. Treasury, and the IMF. They rallied other countries' regulators and made sure the banks followed the plan. They herded the banks with formal and informal tools. Banks that did not want to lend more learned that the IMF's new funds were contingent on the banks' new money. The bank that threatened to sue a debtor in the hope of being repaid immediately found its Federal Reserve Bank warning it to reconsider or risk unstated, but possibly dire, sanctions. The links between the official and private efforts were tight.

This Mexican rescue moved much faster than the rescues of other major debtors. Brazil, for example, took several months to receive short-term loans of $400 million from the Fed, $1.53 billion from the U.S. Treasury, and $1.2 billion from the BIS. These were replaced by a loan of $5.9 billion from the IMF to be drawn over three years, $4.4 billion in new loans from the banks, and $4.9 billion in rescheduled long term loans due in 1983, with a higher spread than before the crisis (2%) and a 1 ½% fee. Cline 1984 at 31-32.

This phase of managing the debt crisis saw coordinated lending by the IMF, World Bank, governments, and banks. Mexico set a new standard in September 1984, when it reduced its spread to 1% over LIBOR, and reduced fees. Soon each major country had signed a multi-year rescheduling agreement (MYRA) for loans coming due over the next five or so years and received from the banks longer term funds for balance of payments shortfalls. The banks did not lend voluntarily. They were coerced by the IMF with the support of the major central banks and particularly Paul Volcker, and their governments. The IMF insisted that the banks reschedule and provide new credit if any official help was to be given, including Paris Club arrangements (see below). The countries, however, did not recover and kept rescheduling.

The negotiations to reschedule the banks' loans took place along side other negotiations about rescheduling official credit. The Paris Club, whose core members are industrial countries, managed the rescheduling of most official debt. The Paris Club was established in 1956 to help reschedule Argentine debt. Since 1979, the French treasury has housed the Paris Club and provided a modest staff. The Paris Club acts as a partial mediator between creditor and debtor governments, advised by the IMF and the World Bank. In the Paris Club discussions, the lenders and borrower agree to general terms for rescheduling, then each creditor government negotiates its own new agreement bilaterally with the debtor government.

Over time, conventions evolved to guide the Paris Club. Comparability of terms requires creditors not in the Paris Club to accept a rescheduling of their loans to the borrower that is no less onerous than that adopted by the Paris Club. Certain debt must be fully paid on time and is not rescheduled: loans from multilateral agencies like the World Bank; interbank deposits (after they were included in some of the early reschedulings, the Bank of England won an exemption to protect the interbank market); and trade credits such as letters of credit (although they were included in restructurings of the debt of Brazil, Philippines, and Morocco). See M. Rahnama-Moghadam, D. Dilts, H. Samavati, *The Clubs of London & Paris: International Dispute Resolution in Financial Markets*, 53 Dispute Resolution Journal 71 (Nov. 1998) at 72 (Rahnama-Moghadam *et al*); K. Clark, *Sovereign Debt Restructurings: Parity of Treatment Between Equivalent Creditors in Relation to Comparable Debts* (1986) (Clark 1986), and IMF, Official Financing for Developing Countries (April 1994 and Feb. 1998) (IMF 1994 and IMF 1998, respectively).

The London Club is a forum housed in London—the center of the eurocurrency market—to help private banks reschedule their loans to developing country governments. The London Club has no secretariat. It does not follow rigorous formal procedures, but it has a common practice. For each debtor government, the creditor banks appoint a Bank Advisory Committee of the 12 to 15 banks with the largest stakes, led by the bank that has the most exposure. The committee negotiates an agreement in principle with the debtor government. All lending banks approve and then sign it. Rahnama-Moghadam *et al*.

As noted by a specialist in this field, Lee Bucheit, in *Sovereign Debtors and Their Bondholder*, (2000) (Bucheit 2000) at 11:

> Although these committees were careful to describe themselves as merely 'communications links' with the sovereign debtor, in fact they operated as fully-fledged negotiating committees. Both the financial and the legal terms

of the serial debt rescheduling packages for dozens of countries during the 1980s were hammered out between the sovereign borrowers and their bank advisory committees. . . .

Bank advisory committees had two major weaknesses. First, they operated on the principle that each bank on the committee must concur with every aspect of a transaction before it could be presented to the banking community at large. In practice, this unanimity rule gave each committee bank a veto power that, if used, could stall negotiations for months on end. Second, even after a deal was struck with the committee, the only tools for securing acceptance by non-committee banks were fraternal persuasion by fellow bankers and, when necessary, a nudge from bank regulators. These features of the bank advisory committee process meant that complicated transactions such as Brady bond exchanges could take years to negotiate and many months to close.

In the reschedulings, the banks organized by home country. On the advisory committee, the bank with the most exposure usually took the lead for other banks from the same country. Among the German banks, for example, Dresdner bank accounted for 25% of loans to Mexico, so it took the lead for the other German banks. The steering committee member had to make sure that the other banks it represented would agree to the terms it negotiated with the debtor country.

Remarkably few banks tried to sue to recover the payments due to them. One reason was that their central bankers pushed them very hard to take part in the debt restructurings, even if they had only a very small exposure to the country. Another may be the limited likelihood that they would actually recover the money owed to them. Bucheit, in *To Sue is Human, To Levy is Sublime*, International Financial Law Review (May 1992) at 12, explains the problem. Sovereign debtors have only limited assets outside their country. Certain assets, such as the embassy (and perhaps the reserves of the central bank), cannot be seized. State-owned enterprises may have assets abroad. The national airline has airplanes. A national oil company may have income abroad. The problem is that these enterprises are legally separate from the government, even if it owns them. So the question is when the court will pierce the corporate veil. Bucheit summarizes U.S. case law:

> Mere ownership by the sovereign of the agency or instrumentality will not be sufficient to defeat the presumption of separate status. Among other things, US courts will look at factors such as whether the instrumentality is established as a separate juridical entity, whether it has the power to sue and be sued, the power to hold and sell property, the ability to run its own financial affairs and the authority to manage its own personnel matters. Only if it can be shown that the entity is so extensively controlled by its sovereign owner that a relationship of principal and agent is created, or if the corporate form of the instrumentality is abused in a manner that works a fraud or injustice, will the presumption against recognising the separate juridical personality of such an enterprise be overcome.

(For relevant U.S. legislation, see the Foreign Sovereign Immunities Act, 28 U.S.C. §§ 1330, 1391, 1441(d), 1602-1611.) European countries follow the same rule. Bucheit points out that the government has so many ways to affect the activities of a state owned enterprise that such a rule may be too limited. For example, exchange controls can affect the ability of the airline to service its own debt. Distinctions between solvent and weak state owned enterprises are often illusory for a creditor.

On balance, official sources allowed the banks to reduce their exposure to the NODCs. A comparison of the NODCs' balance of payments reveals that banks changed from being net suppliers of funds before 1982 to net takers of funds after that. From 1975 to 1981, NODCs received and used $724 billion (receipts and uses are equal). Banks provided 33.7% of the net sources of funds for NODCs and only took 14.4% of funds used. So during this period, banks were net suppliers of funds (supplying 33.7% and using only 14.4%). From 1982 to 1985, the role of the banks reversed even though they provided new funds to many troubled countries. The NODCs received and used $361 billion. Banks supplied only 19.7% of this but took 27.8%, becoming net users of NODCs' funds during the period. Who supplied the funds that they took during the second period? Official sources of funds did. During 1975 to 1981, official sources accounted for 31.4% of all funds. During 1982 to 1985, official sources accounted for 48.9%. Since the banks' share fell from 33.7% to 19.7% and other sources remained steady at just over 30%, the net effect is that official funds allowed the banks to reduce or slow the growth of their net exposure to NODCs between 1982 and 1985. Wellons 1987 at 248.

Notes and Questions

1. Why not just let the private debtors work out solutions themselves? Many banks, particularly those with smaller stakes, argued that they were coerced into lending new money and rescheduling the loans. After all, the IMF and the Fed linked new official lending to the banks' rescheduling. What would the banks have done if official funds were not involved? Who coerced whom? Why?

2. The strategy was to reschedule existing loans and supply new money. This suggests that the problem is one of liquidity and so one needs only to stretch out repayment and provide temporary liquidity. Later events proved this wrong.

3. How new were the "new" funds supplied by banks? Why not reduce the debt rather than reschedule it? Why not let the banks write off the bad debts as they came due? Why delay this?

4. When a government intervenes in financial markets to rescue one or more banks faced with loss, the danger of moral hazard exists. Banks may anticipate the intervention and lend without adequately pricing for risk because they can count on the government's intervention. How would this response to the crisis affect moral hazard for banks' international lending in the future?

5.   What is the argument for favoring some creditors over others? Why exclude certain types of credit and creditors from rescheduling? Why separate official and private creditors (Paris and London clubs)? Why exempt short-term debt (particularly short-term trade credits, but sometimes also bank credits) and only reschedule medium- and long-term debt?

6.   Before the crisis, many different government agencies raised money in international markets. These included the central government (sometimes through the treasury), separate government authorities, and some parastatal companies (like a government-owned development bank). In the restructuring negotiations, these debts were consolidated and one government entity (e.g., the finance ministry or the central bank) became the sole obligor. From the point of view of the lenders, was this appropriate? Would a bank that originally loaned money to the state oil company, that earned some foreign exchange by selling oil abroad, find the substitution of the finance ministry (on behalf of the government) acceptable? Or should the original debtor agencies have stayed as parties to the rescheduling?

7.   The sharing clause in a eurocredit gives each participating bank the right to its pro rata share in any repayment made to any participant in that loan. Two versions exist, according to M. Walker and L. Bucheit, *Legal Issues in the Restructuring of Commercial Bank Loans to Sovereign Borrowers*, in M. Gruson and R. Reisner, eds., *Sovereign Lending: Managing Legal Risk* (1984) at 459. The version preferred by U.S. banks requires any bank receiving more than its share to buy participations from the other banks with cash to equalize all positions. The other version simply requires the bank to distribute cash ratably among the other participants. In a restructuring of many sovereign debts, should a universal sharing provision link all borrowers? Should Creditor A who receives a payment from Debtor D, due according to Loan A, be required to share than payment with Creditor B who made Loan B, an unrelated contract?

8.   Should the events of default in a restructuring agreement include failure to comply with performance criteria set in an IMF loan agreement or stabilization program? Later parts of this chapter describe some of the IMF requirements. Should an event be the failure to obtain official credit of an anticipated amount?

9.   Should the debtor be required to release to the banks participating in a restructuring agreement the information that it gives the IMF confidentially? Suppose that some information is politically sensitive. Should that matter?

10. Is it good policy to treat low income countries differently?

C. THE TRANSITION FROM COERCED TO VOLUNTARY CREDIT: THE BOND MARKETS IN THE LDC DEBT CRISIS

For almost 10 years after 1982, bank lenders rescheduled their loans and gave new credit involuntarily. Those with large exposures saw no alternative.

A bank with a small exposure was pressed by its home central bank to stay in the game. The first effort to move beyond simple rescheduling of debt, the Baker Plan, was replaced by the Brady plan and Brady bonds, but lenders participated in both involuntarily to some extent. As the Brady plan began to work, countries were able to return to markets in which creditors would lend voluntarily.

1. THE BAKER PLAN

The Baker Plan, named for the U.S. Treasury Secretary, James Baker, was announced in 1986. It set targets for new loans to help 17 countries with the greatest debt, most in Latin America, restructure their economies. Over three years, banks would lend $20 billion in new money, long term and at rates similar to those of the multi-year rescheduling agreements (MYRAs). This would in effect finance 33% of the interest due on the $250 billion in bank loans outstanding. Multilateral development banks would lend $10 billion long term each year, replacing the shorter term IMF credits as they became due for repayment. The debtor governments were to adopt better economic policies, which included opening to foreign investment. See Cline 1995 at 208.

The point of the plan was to require new funds as a supplement to the reschedulings that were already underway in the MYRAs. Even though the MYRAs stretched the repayment periods of the defaulted loans into the long term, few lenders voluntarily provided new credit to the debtor countries. The countries continued to negotiate MYRAs, with terms like those for Mexico, during the years of the Baker Plan. The Baker Plan reinforced "concerted" lending. New bank lending was linked to new loans from the multilaterals, giving commercial banks an incentive to lend.

The failure of the Baker Plan was acknowledged by 1988. Both the official creditors and the banks supplied much less new money than the plan required. Banks actually loaned $12.8 billion to the 10 countries that adopted acceptable economic policies. Long negotiations often collapsed over the macroeconomic policies of the government. Brazil and Argentina, for example, failed to comply with standards in their IMF programs. A collapse in the oil price in1986 undermined the recovery of Mexico and other heavily indebted producers. The countries' debt was not being reduced. During the 1980s, the same country would go through several MYRAs. Brazil, for example, entered four MYRAs in less than a decade. The need to reschedule rescheduled loans signaled the failure of this approach to the debt crisis.

During the Baker Plan period, banks took different routes to reduce their problem debts, setting the stage for the Brady Plan, discussed below. European banks were willing to capitalize interest due from the borrowers, but U.S. banks were not because they feared it would require recognizing losses. Banks began to build provisions for the bad debt so that they could write it off. In 1987, Citicorp, for example, set aside $3 billion, while the Bank of Boston raised its provisions for bad loans over 50%. By 1987, the large U.S. banks had increased their capital and slowed the growth of lending to developing countries, reducing their vulnerability. Cline 1995 at 214-15.

2. TRADING LDC DEBT DURING THE REFINANCINGS OF THE MID-1980S

Most eurocredit agreements gave each participating bank notes showing the principal and the procedure to calculate interest owed on each payment date. The agreement specified whether the bank could negotiate the note.

A secondary market in negotiable notes on sovereign loans existed in rudimentary form since the 1970s and grew after 1982. One estimate puts trading at $600 million face value in 1983 and $15 billion by 1987. Trading was in small amounts, perhaps $1 or $2 million and, because the market was not transparent, rates for the same loan could vary a lot. The main suppliers of paper were U.S. regional banks and European banks, but perhaps 250 banks and 50 non-financial corporations participated in the trading. These companies, such as IBM and Volkswagen, swapped the debt they acquired for equity in local companies, a way to invest at a discount in the countries. R. Buckley, *Emerging Markets Debt: An Analysis of the Secondary Market* (1999) at 70, 130 (Buckley 1999). Discounts on the face value varied. In early 1986, Chilean debt traded at 65-69% and Argentine debt at 62-66%. This market was informal, thin, volatile, and not transparent. See Buckley 1999 at 71. In addition, swaps began of bank debt for equity, natural resources (such as land), or some other asset or public good.

Debtor governments could buy back their own debt in this market. In 1985, for example, Chile allowed its companies and individuals to buy Chile's foreign debt on the secondary market and convert the asset into local currency. Chile's government bought the debt at a discount as well and retired it. Banks opposed buy backs. In their view, the buy backs allowed the debtors to avoid servicing their debt. If borrowers could buy back, they would have an incentive to default on the loans to reduce the cost of servicing them.

Documentation of trades evolved during the 1980s from individually negotiated agreements to standard formats followed by the major traders. Thus by the late 1980s, "the assignment agreements of the eight largest traders contained clauses on virtually identical matters cast in substantially similar wording." Buckley 1999 at 240. According to Buckley 1999 at 41:

> The usual layout was three to four pages of standard text followed by schedules into which were inserted the details of the credit being assigned, the consideration for the assignment [cash or other loans], and details of payment offices and addresses for notices. The schedules would also contain any non-standard clauses required for this particular transaction. Typical standard terms addressed the following matters: assignment and assumption; allocation of payments under the credit; representation and warranties; and a host of miscellaneous 'boilerplate' type provisions.

In the mid-1980s, the large U.S. banks wanted to reduce their bad debt, but the regional banks sought to withdraw from the LDC debt market. In 1987,

Argentina offered to let the regional banks convert their outstanding loans at a discount to par into "exit bonds" offered by the Argentine government, with interest rates below market. Exit bond holders would not have to supply new money. But the discount was so big that no bank bought Argentine exit bonds at that time. The innovation, however, set the stage for the Brady plan.

3. DEBT AND DEBT SERVICE REDUCTION: BRADY BONDS

The Bush Administration, having just taken office in 1989, launched a new approach to the LDC debt problem. The idea was to bring permanent relief using market-based debt and debt-service reduction and forgiveness to countries adopting strong economic reform programs. J. Clark, *Debt Reduction and Market Reentry Under the Brady Plan*, Federal Reserve Bank of New York Quarterly Review (Winter 1993-94), at 38.

The initiative led to a market for "Brady Bonds." The object was to reduce total debt, in contrast to the rescheduling approach tried earlier. The government of the debtor country issued the bonds in exchange for outstanding debt in arrears to banks, at a negotiated discount related to the market price of the notes traded in the secondary market. The bonds took many forms, but were distinguished by the collateral that secured most, but not all, of them.

- Securing the principal were U.S. Treasury zero coupon bonds issued for that purpose by the U.S. government and held in escrow. The issuer of Brady Bonds purchased the U.S. bonds, mostly financed by borrowing from a $34 billion fund established by the IMF, World Bank, and Japanese Exim Bank. Remaining funds were supplied by the countries and, to a smaller extent, some new money from the banks.

- Securing interest payments were other securities held in escrow. These securities amounted to 7% to 13% of the expected present value of interest streams that were secured. Clark at 42. Commonly, the security would be callable after a default on interest due at any point in the life of the bond and for defaults continuing for an agreed period of time, such as 12 or 18 months, or up to a ceiling.

The first Brady Bond, issued by Mexico, is described in the following excerpt.

Debt reduction and interest relief were crucial (see Buckley 1999 at 102). Since the LDC debt traded at large discounts in the secondary market, Mexico could argue that the markets—and the banks that sold the notes they held into the market—recognized the debt would be written down. Mexico argued that it should be able to share in that discount.

Buckley 1999 at 102-107.

The Brady Plan

Secretary Brady proposed a series of individual market-based transactions in which (i) creditors would be invited to participate voluntarily, (ii) debt relief would be tied into the conversion of loans into collateralised bonds, (iii) debtor nations would be permitted to repurchase their own discounted debt on the secondary market and (iv) debt-equity schemes would be promoted. The proposal was seen as an expression of increased urgency from the U.S. government about the resolution of the debt crisis, a strong call for the development of capital-market-based solutions, and an official acceptance that some debt forgiveness was essential. At long last, it seemed, the calls for debt relief were to be heeded.

The Brady proposal dealt only with debt to commercial banks. [It offered no official debt forgiveness. Only in the late 1990s did official creditors forgive debt, and only to low income countries.]

The first Brady-style restructuring was of Mexico's debt as its strategic importance to the U.S. was seen as likely to result in the most favourable precedent for other debtor nations and at the time Mexico was in relatively good economic health. Negotiations began in earnest between Mexico and its commercial bank creditors in May 1989. An agreement in principle was announced in July, the terms sheet distributed to banks in September, the debt reduction package signed in February 1990, and the bonds issued late March 1990. It was a slow process dragging hundreds of resistant banks to the table. Mexico's Brady scheme represented a significant departure from Secretary Brady's proposals as it was a one-off scheme in which creditor participation was effectively compulsory. The U.S. Treasury swiftly accepted the virtues of necessity and embraced the bonds as a product of the Brady proposals. Many banks were reportedly 'disgusted' with the deal but in the end had to go along with it. The die had been cast for future Brady-style restructurings.

The banks were offered a choice from the following three options for their Mexican loans.

1. The banks could have their loans converted into newly issued 30-year bonds paying Libor plus 13/16 per cent with principal discounted 35 per cent from the loans. Repayment of principal would be guaranteed by zero coupon bonds issued for the purpose by the U.S. Treasury acquired by Mexico and held in escrow. In addition there would be a rolling guarantee of 18 months interest.

2. The banks could have their loans converted into "par bonds" - bonds with the same face value as the loans which paid interest at the discounted fixed rate of 6.25 per cent. The term and collateral for these bonds were as for the discounted principal bonds considered above.

3. The banks could elect to participate in new loans to Mexico in the coming four years to the extent of 25 per cent of their medium and long-term exposure to Mexico.

The new money option contained a paradox. It was crucial that sufficient banks opt for new money as it would be required to assist with the payment of interest on the Brady bonds and for Mexico's continued economic growth and might be required to assist with the acquisition of the collateral for these bonds. However, the extension of new money eroded the debt-reduction effect of the proposal and if too many banks opted for new money there may have been a net increase in Mexico's indebtedness.

This approach of offering the banks a range of restructuring options was known as the "menu" approach. It allowed banks to choose the option which most suited their view on interest rates and debtor prospects and their individual tax, regulatory and accounting situation.

The prospects of the Brady proposal were greatly enhanced by a letter of 14 July 1989 from the SEC to David Mulford, Under Secretary of the Treasury which 'clarified' the application to the Mexican Brady restructuring of Financial Accounting Standards No. 15, 'Accounting by Debtors and Creditors for Troubled Debt Restructurings' (FAS 15). The relevant part of FAS 15 provides that if, in full settlement of a debt, a creditor receives assets of which the fair value is less than the recorded value of the debt, then the creditor must record the shortfall as a loss. If an active market exists, fair value is market value. In the absence of such a market, fair value is to be estimated based on expected cash flows discounted for risk.

David Mulford is commonly regarded as the Washington architect of the Brady Plan and he had requested, and doubtless shaped, the letter of 14 July 1989 from the SEC. In the name of applying FAS 15 to Mexico's restructuring, the SEC wrote that a loss need not be recognised if 'the total future undiscounted cash receipts specified by the new terms of the loan, including receipts designated as both principal and interest, equal or exceed the book value of the loan.' This letter is a remarkable document. Upon this criterion the banks could accept Mexico's Brady Bonds in exchange for their loans without having to recognise a loss notwithstanding that shortly after issue the par bonds were trading at 42 per cent of face value and the discount bonds at 63 per cent. The analysis in this SEC letter represents the apotheosis of the popular debt crisis game of images and mirrors by treating interest as principal and making the value of money in 30 years equal to its value today. By ensuring that Brady bonds could be accepted by banks without provisions or write-downs, the SEC made the Mexican restructuring far more palatable for U. S. banks; at the cost of turning reality on its head. The turning of water into wine should perhaps be reserved for higher authorities than the SEC.

This restructuring was of all of Mexico's medium and long-term debt to the commercial banks: some $54 billion. A great deal of arm-twisting by regulators was required to secure the participation of all banks. Many were very reluctant to participate but bankers find overt pressure from their home regulators difficult to resist. Banks elected to convert 41 per cent of total indebtedness into discounted principal bonds, 49 per cent into discounted interest ('par') bonds, and to advance new money for the remaining 10 per cent. Of the three options, new money was to prove by far the most lucrative and Citibank's foresight in taking that option exclusively was richly rewarded. Yet in 1990 substantial pressure was needed to make banks holding the required 10 per cent of exposure agree to advance new money.

Bank Choices in the Mexican Restructuring			
Country	*Par Bond*	*Discount Bond*	*New Money*
France	79%	9%	12%
United States	58%	24%	19%
Japan	18%	81%	0%
Canada	48%	52%	0%
Germany	80%	20%	0%
United Kingdom	48%	45%	6%

The terms of the bonds differed from the loans in a number of respects. The bonds were negotiable instruments designed to be traded and the sharing clause and mandatory prepayments clause typical of syndicated bank loans were absent.

The acquisition of the collateral for these bonds was funded by $1.3 billion from Mexico, $2 billion from Japan, and $3.7 billion from the IMF and the World Bank. In committing World Bank and IMF funds to this purpose, the United States was for the first time, putting taxpayers funds into the resolution of the debt crisis - a politically courageous act within the U.S. Nevertheless, the Plan has been severely criticised for affording inadequate debt relief, criticisms with which this author agrees. . . .

The Brady restructuring failed to help Mexico at all on one important measure. Mexico's net annual transfer to the banks before the restructuring was $3.24 billion. After the restructuring it was $3.59 billion. This is because before Brady most of the interest payments were funded by new money. Once again, however, figures do not tell the full story. The Brady process served an important function in breaking the upward spiral of total indebtedness and in reducing the demands on the scarce time of government ministers and civil servants which arose from the periodic restructurings of the 1980s. In Clark's words, 'The Brady restructurings did not achieve significantly more near-term cash flow relief for debtors than the previous approach. But they did provide a more stable long-run financial framework that, in combination with structural reforms by debtors and a favorable environment of lower global interest rates, helped to restore market access.' Shortly after the Mexican restructuring, the commercial banks negotiated agreements with the Philippines, Costa Rica, Venezuela and Morocco in that order.

Many people assumed that the use of bonds would reduce the frequency of restructurings. One reason was that, unlike syndicated loans, bonds had no clause for sharing. Sharing clauses limit direct action against the issuer by forcing a lender who sues and collects from a debtor to share the proceeds with the others participating in the loan. Bond holders could sue and expect to recover amounts owed to them. They would not be forced to cooperate with other lenders in restructuring agreements. Practical reasons keep sharing clauses out of bond agreements, according to A. Yianni, *Resolution of Sovereign Financial Crises—Evolution of the Private Sector Restructuring Process*, Bank of England Financial Stability Review (June 1999) at 78 (Yianni 1999). Bond instruments and their holders are diverse. Their sheer number would make it very difficult to identify and reach those entitled to share the proceeds.

Later Brady Bonds differed from Mexico's and each other, leading to multiple forms of the instrument. Venezuela, for example, followed Mexico by a year, offering five options: collateralized par bonds or discount bonds; new money bonds, equal to 20% of the bank's loans; 17 year temporary interest reduction bonds in exchange for loans; or the bank could sell its Venezuela loans to the country's government at about the going rate in the secondary market, 45% of face value.

Twenty-one countries adopted a Brady package. Two-thirds took place in 1990. They included (see IMF, *Private Market Financing for Developing Countries* (Nov. 1995) at 7 (IMF 1995)):

Africa and Mid-East	Asia	Latin America
Jordan	Philippines	(continued)
Mozambique		Chile
Niger	Europe	Costa Rica
Nigeria	Bulgaria	Dominican
Sao Tome and	Poland	Republic
Principe		Ecuador
Uganda	Latin America	Guyana
Zambia	Argentina	Mexico
	Bolivia	Uruguay
	Brazil	Venezuela

Countries allowed banks to select different options from the Brady menu. The value of the options they chose, the amount of debt they restructured, and the cost of that restructuring appear in the following table. The IMF concluded that the "cost per unit of debt reduction (the buyback equivalent price)" was "in line with the secondary market price of the bank claims at the time of the agreement in principle." It was also important that the price of the bonds reflect the discounted price of the debt being traded in the secondary market. That discounted price was the market's valuation of the debt. Bonds issued in exchange for that debt would be traded. If the value of the bonds on the secondary market were to fall substantially below the price at issue, the drop would undermine the credibility of the Brady Bonds as market-based instruments (IMF 1995 at 6- 7):

Commercial Bank Debt- and
Debt-Service-Reduction Operations
(21 Countries from 1988 to 1995)

	$ billions
a. Debt restructured by these operations (face value)	$170.2
b. Total debt- and debt-service reduction (DDSR) (present value)	76.0
i. Debt reduction	
Buyback	14.0
Discount exchange	21.8
ii. Debt-service reduction	
Principal collateralized par bond	19.9
Other par bond	1.5
iii. Prepayments through collateralization	18.8
c. Cost of reduction (principal and interest guarantees and buyback costs at closing)	25.2
d. Total DDSR/Debt restructured [b/a]	Ratio
i. Average (# countries)	44.6 (21)
ii. Low end of range (# of countries)	30.7 (1)
iii. High end of range (# of countries)	100.0 (9)

The timing of the negotiations created problems for the issuer if prices moved a certain way. According to Clark at 45, the interest rates and guarantees were

fixed at the time of agreement in principle, not indexed to movements in market rates before completion of the deal. As a result, movements in rates could shift the overall pricing and also favor some options over others. This problem did not arise with the early bank packages, but emerged as an important issue for Argentina and Brazil, which saw a fall in long-term interest rates following agreement in principle with banks on a restructuring menu. These declines, to the extent they were unhedged, increased the cost of the Treasury zero coupon bonds used to secure the Brady bonds' principal . . . . [Had the issuer not been bound by the interest rate prevailing at the time of agreement in principle, it could have received the lower rate when the deal was completed. This raised] collateral costs for both the par and discount bonds. The cost increase was more pronounced for the par bonds because they had a larger principal amount to be secured. In addition, when the gap narrowed between market rates and the agreed fixed rates for the par bonds, banks strongly preferred the par option, which became more costly for the debtors. In both cases the countries sought a 'rebalancing' or reallocation of choices away from the unexpectedly less concessional par exchange.

According to Bucheit 2000 at 12:

> By the time the Brady process ended in the mid-1990s (with transactions for Ecuador, Panama, Peru and the Ivory Coast), more than half of the affected debt stock had already traded into the hands of non-bank investors. Despite this tectonic shift in the composition of the creditor group, even the later Brady deals were negotiated by sovereign borrowers with their respective commercial bank advisory or steering committees, just like the old rescheduling packages. Non-bank holders of the debt were not invited to participate in these negotiations.

> A number of non-bank creditors questioned the logic of negotiating these later Brady transactions with committees composed exclusively of commercial banks when the deals would ultimately be presented -- on a take it or leave it basis -- to a creditor class in which commercial banks were a minority. This grievance was aggravated by the fact that most of the Brady instruments designed by bank advisory committees were collateralized in ways that accommodated the special regulatory needs of commercial bank lenders. Non-bank investors generally viewed these collateral features as unnecessary and cumbersome.

The Brady Program achieved some of its goals. By 1994, the banks' built their loan loss provisions and wrote off substantial bad loans. Most notably, many of the countries saw their economies recover and gradually became eligible to return to financial markets. Bank claims on the Brady 17[1] traded on the secondary market. The market value of these claims rose from 34% of the face value in 1990 to 70% in late 1994 (before the Mexico crisis discussed in the next section). Private capital began to flow into these countries again. After net outflows from 1983 to 1988, net inflows to Latin American countries rose from about $3 billion in 1990 to over $50 billion in 1993. The problems of the low income countries, however, remained and seemed intractable. See IMF 1995 at 10, 15.

In the secondary market, traders were at first uncertain how to value some of the contingencies. One example is the guarantee of interest for 18 months after one default at any time. Banks wanted the guarantee to lengthen the time before they would have to give a loan non-accrual status, which is 90 days after it is in arrears. The guarantee would extend the period from 3 months to 21 months, and reduce the borrower's bargaining power during the first 3 months

---

[1] The original 15 major participating countries were Argentina, Bolivia, Brazil, Chile, Colombia, Ecuador, Ivory Coast, Mexico, Morocco, Nigeria, Peru, the Philippines, Uruguay, Venezuela, and the former Yugoslavia. Two more countries were added soon after that.

of arrears. But in the early years those trading the instruments could not assign useful probabilities of default to these new instruments. So they treated the guarantee as existing for only the first 18 months, which they saw as undervaluing the instruments. See Buckley 1999 at 124-25.

The secondary market for Brady Bonds grew through 1997, then trading slowed. The range of investors in emerging market debt broadened with the advent of Brady Bonds. High yield investors moved from U.S. junk bonds to this emerging market debt. Then institutional investors entered: pension funds and insurance companies from the U.S. and non-banks from Europe. Even retail buyers entered. Also in the early 1990s, the main sellers were regional U.S. banks. Larger U.S. banks unloaded some of their holdings. Japanese banks started to sell. Buckley 1999 at 130. The following table shows the growth of trading in Brady Bonds and other emerging market debt, from 1993, when reliable data began to be collected.

Emerging Market Instruments: Trading Volume (U.S.$ billions)						
Instruments	1993	1994	1995	1996	1997	1998
Total	1,979	2,766	2,739	5,297	5,916	4,174
Brady Bonds	1,021	1,684	1,580	2,690	2,403	1,541
Non-Brady Eurobonds	177	159	211	568	1,335	1,021
Loans	274	244	175	249	305	213
Local Markets Instruments	NA	524	593	1,274	1,506	1,176
Derivatives (Options, etc.)	57	142	179	471	367	223

Source: Emerging Market Traders Association 1998 Annual Report, pp. 12-13

Market practices became increasingly standard as traders adopted similar norms. They founded the Emerging Market Traders Association in 1990. It designed standard comprehensive terms for loan assignments. It introduced an automated trade confirmation and matching system in 1995. Not only did it largely eliminate error between execution and trade, but it made pricing transparent. EMTA began to distribute volume and price data almost in real time. Buckley 1999 at 240.

Beside Brady Bonds, borrowing countries used many other ways to reduce their debt. As mentioned, they could enter the secondary markets and buy back their debt, usually at large discounts. Some countries allowed investors to swap debt they held for equity in local companies. Some allowed swaps that would use the proceeds of the debt to protect the environment in the country (debt for nature swaps) or to fund teaching projects in the country (debt for education swaps).

Brady Bonds, generally subject to either English or New York law, adopted the New York rule for modifying the bonds. New York law requires the consent of each bond holder to any proposal to modify the terms for paying the bond. English law allows a super-majority holding 67% or 75% of the value of the bonds to modify payment terms and impose the change on the minority. Of course, the terms of a bond subject to New York law may specify that a super-majority may amend it. Yianni 1999 at 80.

The major development, however, was the growth of voluntary credit to many of these governments through the bond market.

4. BRADY BOND HOLDOUTS: ELLIOTT ASSOCIATES

Vulture funds threatened Brady Bond restructurings. They bought defaulted loans from banks at a discount, then held out for payment at full value. Four months after the government of Peru announced its Brady Bond package in 1995, Elliott Associates, LP paid two banks $11.4 million for loans guaranteed by the government of Peru in 1983 with a face value of $20.7 million. Elliott rejected the Brady offers, then sued Peru and a borrower in New York courts for full payment and won a judgment of $55.7 million in 2000. But Peru had little property there. "Elliot's lawyers came up with a creative solution. They intercepted and attached the payments that were to be made to the other creditors, i.e., the ones who had agreed to the Brady Plan debt restructuring." M. Gulati and K. Klee, *Sovereign Piracy*, 56 Business Lawyer, February 2001 at 635 (Gulati and Klee, the source of much of this section). Elliott won a judgment from a New York court that funds Chase Bank, the agent for the Brady Bonds, would use to service the bonds were Peru's property. The court restrained Chase from paying them.

Peru learned of the judgment and, rather than transfer funds to Chase in New York, Peru tried to service the debt through Euroclear in Belgium. At the first instance Belgian court, Elliott lost its *ex parte* request for an order restraining Euroclear from "either accepting money from Peru or paying it to the other creditors." On appeal, the Court of Appeals reversed, restraining JPMorgan as operator of Euroclear. Peru settled after Elliott won an *ex parte* decision from the Belgian Court of Appeals just before Peru would have been in default on the Brady Bonds. Gulati and Klee, 636. See Court of Appeals of Belgium, LP Elliott Associates, Petitioner, General Docket No. 2000/QR/92, Sep. 26, 2000.

Elliott argued that the *pari passu* clause in the 1983 loan agreement required the debtor to pay all creditors, including Elliot, *pro rata*. The clause stated that the government's obligations "rank at least pari passu in priority of payment with all other External Indebtedness" of the government "and interest thereon." An expert opinion from Professor Andreas Lowenfeld, of New York University Law School, argued that the pari pasu clause "entitles each Lender to share equally and ratably with any other holder of External Indebtedness as defined" (this included investors in Brady Bonds). Any funds available should be divided among all debt holders, including Elliott, *pro rata*.

Critics of the Belgian decision argued that it misinterpreted the clause and would have terrible consequences for sovereign debt. Gulati and Klee argued that the clause ensures the borrower cannot create "a class of creditors whose claims will rank senior in priority to the lending claims of the current creditors. In the corporate debt context, this means that no other lender will enjoy a priority in a liquidation distribution of the borrower's assets." Since sovereigns cannot be liquidated, the "clause works as a covenant by the borrower that it will not bestow a legally senior priority status on certain lenders." In their view, the clause for sovereigns is "about the alteration of payment priorities by law." Gulati and Klee, 640.

Their reasoning has several strands. First, no sovereign would agree to treat all external debt the same. Sovereigns expect to service unsecured multilateral creditors (IMF, World Bank) differently from bilateral and private creditors. Pro rata payments would force the sovereign to default on all loans. Second, the Belgian court's interpretation would empower holdouts to do much greater damage to sovereign debt restructuring than the alternative interpretation. Speculators would buy as much sovereign debt as they could and then demand to be paid the entire amount. Third, although no cases decide the meaning of the clause, leading experts like Bucheit and Wood opine that paying one creditor before another does not violate the clause. Fourth, other clauses in loan agreements provide for pro rata interests or against preferential treatment. The "'mandatory prepayment clause' that restricts non-ratable prepayments to others . . . [or] the 'sharing clause' that says that whatever one lender receives has to be shared ratably with others" are examples. If the *pari passu* clause means *pro rata*, these other clauses would be unnecessary. In their view, the market answer to a broad interpretation of the clause will be for restructurings to use exit consents (discussed at the end of this chapter) "that gut the ability of the holdouts to use the pari passu clause." Gulati and Klee, 646, 650.

5. GROWTH OF THE VOLUNTARY MARKET FOR EMERGING MARKET BONDS

Countries that were caught in the 1982 crisis were able to start issuing bonds on international markets, without help, in the early 1990s. The countries that were part of the crisis but were recovering by 1989 issued less than $1 billion that year. By 1993, ten recovering countries issued $23.2 billion. This signaled substantial improvement in their economies. Mexico particularly was growing again and attracting large capital inflows.

Bond issuers emerging from the 1980s debt crisis, such as Brazil, paid junk-bond premiums (500 basis points). Cline, who sought to isolate the price effect of debt forgiveness from other factors (such as high inflation) concluded that "A country that asked for debt forgiveness now pays about 75 basis points above what it would otherwise pay in the international bond market." Bad economic conditions when the bonds were issued explained much of the rest of the premium paid by the issuers. Cline 1995 at 451-55.

Notes and Questions

1. Who benefitted from the various solutions from August 1982 through the Baker Plan, and who bore the costs? Did all banks benefit? How well did U.S. exporters like these solutions? The U.S. public?

2. Was the Brady plan an improvement over the 1980s reschedulings?

3. Was the debt reduction significant enough? Was debt reduction preferable to default?

4. Was the Brady Program correct in allowing the banks to choose among the options? What if all had opted for debt reduction options? What if all opted for new money? How attractive would par and discount exchanges be to the countries?

5. Many investors in the secondary markets appear to have been residents of the issuing countries. They bought the bonds with hard currency that they may have held abroad against the laws of the country and used debt/equity swaps to invest back into the country. Is this a serious abuse of Brady bonds?

6. Which interpretation of the *pari passu* clause do you agree with, that of Elliott or Gulati and Klee? Has Elliott discovered an effective way to attach substantial assets of defaulting sovereign debtors?

7. The borrrowers entered the voluntary bond market relatively soon, once the Brady packages took effect. Yet as they did so, syndicated lending to these borrowers remained low. What accounts for this? Was Mexico wise to have accepted debt forgiveness, given the 75 bp premium?

D. MEXICO'S DECEMBER 1994 PESO CRISIS: THE IMPACT ON THE MEXICAN GOVERNMENT'S DOLLAR AND PESO DEBT SECURITIES

The next major debt crisis hit on December 20, 1994, when the Mexican government devalued the peso 15% against the dollar to 1 peso for 25 cents and two days later let the peso float. It fell almost 50% in four weeks. Over the past year, the Mexican economy had become increasingly unbalanced, with imports growing much faster than exports but no adjustment in the value of the peso.

1. THE CRISIS: PLAYERS AND INSTRUMENTS

Each week since 1991, the Mexican government auctioned Tesobonos, short term peso denominated securities indexed to the dollar, usually maturing in 91 days. To mid-1993, these were less than 2% of the government's debt. By

August 1994, they had risen to 54%. Their initial attraction to the government was that, being short-term, their interest was low compared to longer term instruments. Non-residents owned almost 80% of all outstanding Tesobonos by December 1994. IMF November 1995 at 48, Buckley 1999 at 164. Tesobonos worth the equivalent of $28 billion were due through 1995. Of this, over $4 billion was due in January and early February. Also outstanding was an equally large volume of Cetes, short-term government notes (usually for 91 days) denominated in pesos. They were auctioned weekly. Because the government paid interest on Cetes that was two to four times the U.S. T-bill rate during 1994, over half of them were owned by non-residents by mid-1994. Mexico refinanced by rolling both securities over, but as financial conditions in Mexico worsened, many investors withdrew. The government tried to attract investors by raising interest rates. Those on Cetes reached as high as 90% (annualized) but even these prices failed to stop the outflow or attract new funds.

The crisis hit barely three weeks into the administration of Mexico's new president, Ernesto Zedillo, a newcomer to elected office. His finance minister visited New York just before Christmas to defend the government's actions in person to representatives of about 100 institutional investors. They accused the government of breaking its promise to maintain the peso's value against the dollar. Since 1991, the peso had devalued only 9% against the dollar even though Mexican consumer prices rose almost 30% in the same period. During 1994, rather than devalue, the government had spent close to $20 billion to defend the peso as the country's reserves dwindled to $6 billion. The country ran a $30 billion trade deficit.

The link between the foreign exchange and debt crises was the Tesebonos and Cetes, and the country's debt created an urgent need to act. During the time before devaluation, Mexico kept the value of the peso steady against the dollar by intervening in the market, using its reserves. The net outflow during 1994 drained Mexico's reserves. Mexico devalued because it no longer had the reserves to support the peso at the old rate. Devaluation meant that the foreign holders of Cetes would receive much less, in dollars, than before. Those who had not rolled over their loan had been paid in pesos and converted the payment into dollars or other foreign currency. Now the pesos they receive would buy many fewer dollars.

The Mexican government then raised the interest rates on Cetes to get investors to roll over their securities or to attract new investors. This raised the peso amount the government would have to pay and the holders would want to convert, putting even more pressure on the peso exchange rate. The Tesebonos were indexed to the dollar, so their peso value rose as the peso fell against the dollar. This put still more downward pressure on the peso exchange rate. Investors in Tesebonos and Cetes saw a substantial rise in their risk, and withdrew rather than roll over the securities. No investors offset the outflow of dollars. No rollovers increased the demand for dollars. Both reduced the funds available to the government. Investors saw large volumes of the two instruments coming due between January and March, well in excess of Mexico's reserves. They concluded the situation was untenable. The crises in the debt and exchange markets fed on each other. As demand for the peso evaporated and the government lost the ability to intervene to support the peso, the currency fell precipitously against the dollar. Even more people and companies tried to convert from the peso and the currency's downward spiral on foreign exchange markets continued. The government faced stark choices: would it have to declare a moratorium on servicing the debt or even end peso convertibility into other currencies?

The crisis seems to have surprised most investors. In the run-up to the

Dollar/peso Jan 94- Dec 95 monthly average

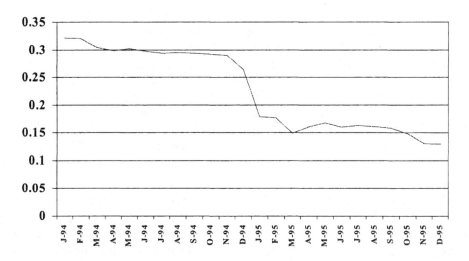

crisis, secondary markets ambiguously reflected the worsening financial situation in Mexico. The discount on traded bank claims on Mexico rose from a low of 6% at the start of 1994 to just above 20% mid-year. In the secondary market, Brady Bonds fell 17% in the same period. IMF November 1995 at 12, 14. Yields on Tesobonos rose from about 5% in the first quarter of 1994 to about 9% through November, when they rose steeply to 25% before the market for them closed. Yields on Cetes were about 10% from January to April 1994, when they rose to 20%. They stayed there until December, when they rose steeply to over 40%, then to almost 90% in February 1995. IMF *International Capital Markets* Aug. 1995 at 56. The mid-year rate increases could have been due solely to growing political violence in Mexico at that time.

2. THE RESCUE PACKAGE

The Clinton administration rallied to Mexico's aid in January 1995. The U.S. government concluded that the peso's free fall would hurt Mexico, the U.S., and other developing countries (see the next section). Led by the new Treasury Secretary and former investment banker Robert Rubin, the U.S. Government quickly arranged a $9 billion credit line at the Federal Reserve on which the Mexicans could draw to maintain peso convertibility and stop its fall. The Bank for International Settlements (BIS) assembled a $5 billion loan from several central banks that would serve as a bridge until the IMF could advance funds. By late January, the IMF offered a $7.8 billion loan. Canada stood ready to lend just over $1 billion. Several private banks offered to arrange a $3 billion syndicated loan. And the Clinton administration asked Congress to enable it to guarantee up to $40 billion in bonds the Mexican government would issue at the U.S. treasury bond rate. Mexico would put future oil revenues in escrow as a guarantee. Mexico drew some of the Fed credit line, but nothing else during January.

Despite bipartisan support among leaders in the House and Senate, the new Republican majority in the U.S. Congress was unwilling to approve the guarantee facility quickly. Many members balked at what they saw as bailing out not Mexico but foreign investors who should have known better. They complained that U.S. securities firms had enriched themselves, having earned $133 million a year underwriting Mexican securities from 1992 to 1994 and $305 million underwriting Latin American securities. These firms should not be helped by bailing out the customers who had invested in Tesebonos and Cetes. U.S. banks had outstanding loans of $16 billion to Mexico and $41 billion to all of Latin America which, as a share of capital, was much less than in 1982. R. Smith, R. McGough, and T. Vogel, Jr, *U.S. Securities Firms and Mutual Funds Have Big Bucks Riding on Mexico Rescue*, Wall Street Journal, Feb. 1, 1995.

On January 31, President Clinton announced a second package by executive order to avoid Congress, dropping the first package. The U.S. Exchange Stabilization Fund, which was set up to stabilize the dollar and held $25 billion in yen and DM, would exchange into dollars up to $20 billion, then swap the dollars for pesos with Mexico for 3 to 5 years. Mexico would pay a fee for the swap and set aside oil revenues as security. (In fact, the U.S. only advanced $12.5 billion, $10.5 billion as medium-term swaps and $2 billion as short-term swaps.) The IMF would lend $17.8 billion, three times more than it had ever loaned before. Of this, $7.8 billion was funded by the IMF. The remainder was to be funded by non-BIS central banks. IMF International Capital Markets, Aug. 1995 at 63. According to the IMF, this was the largest package it had ever given, both in amount and as a multiple of a country's quota (it was 688% of Mexico's quota). IMF, *IMF Approves US$17.8 Billion Stand-By Credit for Mexico*, Feb. 1, 1995. Canada and the private banks would advance the roughly $4 billion committed earlier (though the banks ultimately failed to assemble the syndicate). Some BIS member governments were to lend $10 billion, but ended up not having to do so. Mexico would make and implement major economic reforms. Reaction was mixed in Congress and abroad. Several European governments expressed doubt that the Mexican crisis posed any systemic risk.

By mid-April 1995, Mexico was announcing a turn-around but recovery was slow and painful. A crisis in the financial sector forced the Government to reclaim control of many banks. They had been nationalized after the 1982 crisis, and later privatized. The government said that it had to take ownership again to keep them afloat. Between July and November, the peso fell 33% against the dollar and the government intervened in foreign exchange markets to prevent a free fall. Nevertheless, the government regularly serviced its obligations to the U.S. It repaid $700 million of the short-term swap ahead of schedule in October 1995 and another $1.2 billion in February 1996. It repaid $7 billion of the medium term swap in July 1996 and the remainder three years ahead of schedule in 1997. It financed the 1996 payment by issuing $6 billion of floating rate notes. Later that year it issued a $750 million global bond. In 1996, GDP grew 3.5%. Mexico had not rescheduled or defaulted on its debt. The currency did not stabilize against the U.S. dollar until mid-1999, when it reached about 10 pesos to U.S. $1.08, and hovered there into 2001.

Critics of President Clinton's emergency package disputed its legality. In an article titled *Adventures in the Zone of Twilight: Separation of Powers and National Economic Security in the Mexican Bailout*, 105 Yale Law Journal 1311 (1996), R. Covey argued that Clinton's use of the Emergency Stabilization Fund was improper. The President lacked statutory or constitutional authority without a formal appropriation by Congress. Neither the ESF statute, its legislative history, or past usage permitted the funds to be used to help Mexico. Nor did the President have independent constitutional authority to use the money.

In May 2000, Mexico's deposit insurance authority IPAB prepaid a $2.5 billion debt it owed Citibank as part of the bank's 1998 acquisition of a troubled Mexican bank. The government agency had agreed to buy $2.5 billion of the bank's bad debt, paying over 8 years. Citibank, calculating it would lose $300 million in interest over the remaining 6 years of the debt, sued in Mexican courts to prevent the prepayment. D. Fineren, *Mexico's Debt Situation Takes a New Twist*, New York Times, June 27, 2000; P. Fritsch, *How Citibank's Deal To Buy Mexican Bank Turned Into a Standoff*, Wall Street Journal, Sep. 20, 2000.

3. IMPACT OF THE CRISIS ON OTHER EMERGING MARKETS: THE TEQUILA EFFECT

Mexico's crisis affected the exchange and capital markets. The peso crisis weakened the dollar because investors believed that the U.S. would have to support Mexico and that Mexico's crisis would damage U.S. exports. Mexican firms were hurt by the high interest rates. The Mexican stock exchange fell substantially.

Mexico's crisis was selectively contagious. Financial flows into other Latin American countries quickly fell and outflows rose as capital fled. Argentina, Brazil, and other countries asked the IMF for emergency help. But investors differentiated among Latin American countries to some extent. The stock market in Chile stayed close to its end-1994 values. Investors saw Chile as having a consistently better managed economy. Years earlier, during the 1970s, the country had begun to open trade. It cut government costs, privatized many companies, fixed the exchange rate to the dollar, and substantially reduced inflation. It reformed the structure of the economy, relying on exports to grow, and strengthened its capital markets, increasing domestic savings. It used capital controls to limit the inflow of private capital and moderate its dependence on foreign debt. Cline 1995 at 287. Asian countries were also hit, particularly in their stock markets. But most recovered within several months.

Major Emerging Market Economies' External Finance ($ billions)					
Sources (net)	1993	1994	1995	1996	1997e
External financing	211.7	198.5	254.6	298.0	229.3
Commercial banks	30.2	40.8	90.8	103.5	-3.7
Direct Equity	48.5	64.1	75.7	93.3	114.4
Nonbank private creditors	70.4	40.2	16.7	65.2	70.0
Portfolio Equity	40.4	27.3	24.4	33.2	19.4
Official flows	22.3	26.1	46.9	2.8	29.7
Resident lending/other	-71.6	-79.9	-81.9	-116.2	-101.8
Reserves excl. gold (- = increase)	-61.4	-46.6	-94.1	-85.1	-49.9
Source: Institute for International Finance, Capital Flow to Emerging Economies, Sep. 19, 1996. e = estimate					

The Mexican crisis led to an important change in external financial flows to developing countries, as shown in the adjacent table. In 1993, non-bank private lenders (such as companies buying a government's dollar notes, or financing trade) and portfolio investors accounted for 52% of external finance. By 1995, their share was down to 16%. Increased lending by banks, governments and multilaterals, and foreign direct investment replaced them. Private portfolio flows to developing countries continued but at a lower rate. But as large countries like Russia or Argentina had crises, emerging market funds that were diversified across countries encountered problems because of the weight of the countries in their portfolios. Argentina, for example, accounted for 23%-24% of many indices. After Argentina's problems surfaced in late 2000, investors sold their Argentine assets, the prices of Argentine debt declined, the overall value of the fund fell. As the funds pull back from their investments in emerging markets generally, demand falls for the securities of other emerging markets. This is one vehicle for contagion. See J. Wiggins and V. Boland, *Argentine Contagion Reaches Other Markets*, Financial Times, Apr. 25, 2001.

Questions

1. Why should the U.S. rescue Mexico? Was the rescue package appropriate?

2. To what extent can governments of major industrial countries be expected to support local and foreign currency securities issued by the government in an emerging market and bought by foreigners?

3. How did the resolution of the 1994/95 Mexican crisis differ from the resolution of the 1982 Mexican crisis? Were the crises different?

4. Why was a Brady Bond approach not used in the 1994/95 Mexican crisis?

E. THE ASIAN FINANCIAL CRISIS OF 1997: FOREIGN BANKS' FOREIGN CURRENCY LOANS TO LOCAL BANKS AND COMPANIES

Just as the tequila effect wound down, the exchange rates for many countries in East and Southeast Asia collapsed, pulling them into a calamitous financial crisis. Starting in mid-1997 with Thailand, the attacks spread to the Malaysia, Philippines, Indonesia, and Korea within six months. Each of the countries managed its foreign exchange rate, generally tying its currency to the dollar or a basket dominated by the dollar. Foreign exchange markets bet that the country could not maintain the current rate. Each country tried unsuccessfully to prove the bet was wrong.

1. THE CRISIS: PLAYERS AND INSTRUMENTS

At the center of the storm was the unexpected withdrawal of short-term foreign currency lending by foreign banks to banks and companies in these Asian countries. By mid-1999, several of the countries seemed to be recovering. Korea reported positive economic growth for the twelve months ending March 31, 1999, for example.

The debate about the causes of the crisis is fierce. One view emphasizes the dominant role of poor domestic economic policy and the weakness of the domestic financial institutions as contributing factors to the collapse. This view is not shared by all observers. Another view explains the collapse as a panic of external investors and bad policy by the IMF and other institutions that stepped in to help the countries respond. S. Radelet and J. Sachs, in *The Onset of the*

East Asian Financial Crisis, Harvard Institute for International Development, Mar. 30, 1998, acknowledge significant domestic weaknesses but argue that these problems were known for many years. For Sachs and Radelet, the rapid reversal of private capital flows from in-coming to out-going defined the crisis for the five countries. Net external inflows of funds grew from $47.4 billion in 1994 to $92.8 billion in 1996. The suppliers were about 60% private commercial banks, with equity investors and non-banks providing almost 40%. Official funding was negligible and the countries' reserves grew. Private flows reversed in 1997. Net, $12.1 billion flowed out of the countries. The swing from $93 billion inflows in 1996 to $12 billion outflows in 1997 represented a total loss of $105 billion to the five countries in a year, amounting to 9% of GDP. Of this, 75% represented the collapse of lending by commercial banks. The banks with the biggest exposure in the five countries were from Japan (see following Table).

Table: International Claims Held By Foreign Banks-- Distribution by country of origin (Billions of dollars)

	Total Outstanding	Japan	U.S.A.	Germany	All others
Mid-1997					
Indonesia	58.7	23.2	4.6	5.6	25.3
Malaysia	28.8	10.5	2.4	5.7	10.2
Philippines	14.1	2.1	2.8	2.0	7.2
Thailand	69.4	37.7	4.0	7.6	20.1
Korea	103.4	23.7	10.0	10.8	58.9
Sub-total	274.4	97.2	23.8	31.7	121.7
Total, all reporting countries*		404.4	166.3	301.2	

"Claims held by banks from:" spans Japan, U.S.A., Germany, All others.

* Reporting countries include G-10 plus Austria, Denmark, Finland, Ireland, Luxembourg, Norway, Spain, plus 15 financial centers

Source: Radelet and Sachs (Bank for International Settlements)

Foreign banks loaned mainly to banks in Korea, mainly to non-bank commercial borrowers in Indonesia, and more to non-banks than banks elsewhere, according to Radelet and Sachs. They argue that, except for Korea, the foreign banks are unlikely to have loaned in reliance on an implicit guarantee from the host government.

The imbalance leading to the crisis, say Radelet and Sachs, was that so much of their external debt was short-term that it exceeded most countries' reserves. In these circumstances, reserves were inadequate to service all short-term debt as it became due. A rational response by a lender concerned about possible delinquency would be simply to lend only short term and refuse to roll over its loan when due, forcing repayment and allowing this lender to escape before reserves ran out. The problem was most severe in Korea. In mid-1997,

67% of Korea's debt to foreign banks was short term. This $67.5 billion was over twice the size of Korea's reserves. The ratio of short-term debt to reserves was 1.7 for Indonesia and 1.5 for Thailand. It was 0.8 for Philippines and only 0.6 for Malaysia.

2. THE RESCUE PACKAGE FOR KOREA

Korea negotiated a three year $57 billion assistance package on December 4, 1997. The IMF provided a stand-by arrangement of $21 billion, the World Bank and ADB provided $14 billion, and G-7 countries contributed $22, but only if the multilaterals' funds proved inadequate. Korea could only draw $8 billion in the first instalment and the remaining installments were to be advanced over two or more years as Korea complied with the structural reforms the IMF required for its economy. See the Introductory Chapter to this book.

The December package assumed that it would allow Korea to service its external debt as payment came due, in part because foreign lenders would now be willing to roll over their short-term credit. But foreign banks decided that the package would not solve Korea's problems and withdrew rather than roll over their loans. This threatened to sabotage Korea's recovery.

In late December, the U.S. government intervened. The IMF and G-7 governments agreed to advance very soon the funds due otherwise in later installments, provided the banks restructured $28 billion in longer-term loans. The banks acquiesced in late January and the restructuring agreement was completed at the end of March 1998. The restructuring permitted the banks to exchange existing loans for 1-3 year loans backed by Korean government guarantees. Interest rates were at 2.25 - 2.75% over Libor. Korea could repay at six-month intervals without prepayment penalties. Korea paid most of its external short-term debt and then increased its reserves, the two main uses of the $55 billion aid package. At home, Korea allowed one-third of its merchant banks, funded by domestic creditors including banks, to close. The assistance package was not used mainly to recapitalize Korean banks, clean up the domestic financial system, or stimulate the economy.

For this help, the IMF required from Korea a contractionary fiscal policy, tight domestic credit, the closure of the many unviable banks and financial institutions to limit losses, enforcement of capital adequacy standards and recognition of huge loan and FX losses, full repayment of foreign debt backed by funds mobilized by the IMF, and restructuring of domestic industry to increase competition. Equity investors in Korea suffered substantial losses and bonds were trading at 400 basis points off U.S. treasuries as compared with 60 off before the crisis. The country went through very painful change and the impact of the crisis was felt for years. In 2000, for example, large conglomerates threatened or declared bankruptcy. Domestic banks continued to require substantial government funding. C. Lee and Reuters, *Creditors Agree Funds for Daewoo*, Financial Times, Nov. 30, 2000; S. Len, *South Korea to Spend $44 Billion More to Support Banks*, New York Times, Sep. 23, 2000.

As Korea recovered with strong growth and international reserves of $100 billion by 2001, the danger to many was that it would revert to the former directly interventionist polices before the structural changes adhered. Indeed, the government repaid the last tranche of the IMF loan in August 2001. That year, when the Korean stock market fell to 1998 levels, the government announced that the National Pension Fund would invest $4.4 billion to revive the market.   It guaranteed corporate bonds being issued by troubled companies, such as Hynix Semiconductor. The government's management of the crisis resulted in the its owning "several big commercial banks, two of the three biggest investment trusts and a life insurer. Indirectly the government owns some truly big companies, such as Daewoo, Ssangyong and, soon, Hyundai. . . ." *Micro-meddler,* The Economist, May 5, 2001. In mid-2001, the finance ministry proposed to place its staff in key positions of the Financial Supervisory Service, to run it.   The FSS was set up in 1998 to separate supervision from policy, which the finance ministry retained. A. Harney, *Seoul Repays Final Part of Loan from IMF,* Financial Ties, July 24, 2001; D. Kirk, *Korea to Use Pension Money to Bolster its Stock Market,* New York Times, Apr. 5, 2001; D. Kirk, *South Korea Is Guaranteeing Debt of Distressed Companies,* New York Times, May 17, 2001.

While fear that a default could trigger failures of foreign banks was a real concern in the Latin America debt crisis of the 1980s, it was not in Asia. At the end of 1997, foreign banks had about $100 billion in foreign currency loans to Koreans, most short-term. The U.S. banks had loaned $10 billion, barely 6% of the capital of the top 10 U.S. banks. Japanese bank loans of $24 billion represented about 9% of the capital of Japanese banks. This was small even assuming an extremely improbable default on all debt. If the problem was seen as regional, the numbers were also manageable. Foreign bank loans to Indonesia, Malaysia, the Philippines and Thailand only totaled $171 billion. In the worst case, the few foreign banks at serious risk could receive targeted support from their own central banks. Many saw it as foolish to funnel funds through debtor countries so all foreign banks got aid.

Notes and Questions

1.   Should Korea have defaulted? After all, most borrowers were in the private sector, not governmental. Korea's major borrowers were private banks controlled de facto by the government. In other countries, such as Indonesia, the borrowers were private companies. The main problem with a bailout is that it creates moral hazard. Since lending banks do not lose money making bad loans, they make more of them. This runs counter to the idea that the foreign banks' job is to discipline each borrower by assessing its risk and gearing the cost and amounts of credit to that risk. Prospective loss keeps the banks careful.

   a.   Treasury Secretary Rubin argued that Korean default on foreign bank debt might trigger capital flight and reduce access to new private capital. Is this argument convincing in the case of Korea? Does the solution discriminate against capital markets?

b. If a Korean default risked contagion, causing lenders to pull out of other countries, should the default be averted?

c. If Korea defaulted, would that create moral hazard by signaling other debtors that they could take on more unsupportable debt in the future? Some people argue that defaults would dry up future funding. How compelling is this? How compelling is the counter argument that the very possibility of the bailout makes the debtor country more reckless in borrowing?

d. If Korea were about to default, would significant national security concerns of the lending countries, such as the country's relations with North Korea, justify preventing the default?

2. Prime Minister Mahathir Mohamad, of Malaysia, explained the crisis in his country as largely due to foreign speculators, such as George Soros and the hedge funds that had played an important role in the 1992-93 currency crises in Europe. But for them, he said, the Asian crisis would not have occurred. Bailey, Farrell, and Lund came to the opposite conclusion. Their analysis of the financial flows in and out of the five crisis countries showed that bank lending shifted from large net inflows (75% of all foreign investment) before the crisis to large net outflows after. Portfolio investors (including hedge funds) shifted from much smaller net inflows before the crisis to continued net inflows of half the volume after. Bailey et al. at 103 attribute the banks' behavior to the nature of their contracts:

> Bank loans are mostly illiquid, fixed-price assets—they cannot be quickly converted into cash, and once priced, their interest rate does not go up and down to reflect new information about a borrower (except in the case of a breach of contract or a default). Because the "price" of a loan—the interest rate—does not automatically adjust to changing market conditions, banks adjust the quantity of lending instead. A bank can avoid a default by simply declining to roll over its loan if it sees a borrower in trouble.

The authors note that hedge funds are small players, accounting for only 4% of the assets of the big institutional investors worldwide. They acknowledge that hedge funds did bet against currencies like the Thai baht just before the crisis, but quote one trader in Thailand who asked "Who wasn't betting against the baht?" M. Baily, D. Farrell, and S. Lund, *The Color of Hot Money*, 79 Foreign Affairs, Mar./Apr. 2000 at 99. Do you agree with the explanation of the banks' behavior given by Bailey et al?

3. Yet another view is that the Asian crisis was the result of asset bubbles in each country. In this view, the crises in Korea and Southeast Asia were caused by the same factors that led to the financial and economic crisis in Japan (described in Chapter 8). Do the crises seem comparable?

4. What role did law and the legal systems of the countries play in the crises? In a recent study for the Asian Development Bank, both Korea and

Malaysia (and four other countries) were found to be in transition from a legal system that supported the government's interventionist economic policies to one that supported more market oriented economic policies. In the earlier periods, legal procedures relied on substantial bureaucratic discretion and substantive laws that supported allocation of resources by the state. As economic policies liberalized in these countries, procedures became less discretionary and substantive laws supported resource allocation by private parties much more. A major problem was that the transition was underway, not complete. In particular, the procedural aspects of the law had not adjusted to the newer paradigm. Courts were politically weak and lacked adequate resources, for example. Institutions took a long time to change. See K. Pistor and P. Wellons, *The Role of Law and Legal Institutions in Asian Economic Development*, 1960-1995 (1999). As part of the IMF-sponsored adjustment, the Asian crisis countries began to amend their laws. For example, new or amended bankruptcy laws were passed in February 1998 by Korea and March 1998 by Thailand.

5.   For an excellent overall view of the Asian financial crisis and its possible solutions, see M. Goldstein, *The Asian Financial Crisis, Causes, Cures, and Systemic Implications* (June 1998). Goldstein argues that the criticism of the bailout is overstated. He contends that "the rescue packages go primarily for purposes other than to prevent rescheduling of debt to private creditors; namely they go to cushion the (inevitable) recession in the crisis countries, to help to rebuild international reserves, and to help recapitalize the banking system." At p. 38. Goldstein supplies no data to substantiate this point, and the IMF has not released data to show what it anticipated its funds would be spent on. The point about building reserves has a robbing Peter to pay Paul quality if existing reserves are used to pay foreign creditors and IMF money is used to replace them. Part of the problem may lie in the assumptions the IMF makes as to what will happen after giving aid. If the IMF assumed that its contribution would have the effect of stopping foreign capital outflows (banks would roll over their credits) and strengthening the won, less of the IMF money would have to be used to actually pay the foreign creditors, and more could be used for other purposes. However, if this were not the case—and it was not in Korea (or in Latin America in the 1980s)—more or all of the funds would have to be used to pay off the creditors. Suffice it to say the funds can be used for this purpose, and most often are. Goldstein himself acknowledges that the decision *not* to rely more heavily on rescheduling of short-term bank debt in Korea was a mistake. Id. at 39.

F. SOVEREIGN DEFAULT ON RESCHEDULED SECURITIES AND VOLUNTARY BONDS: RUSSIA

In 1999, Russia defaulted on instruments it had issued as part of an earlier debt rescheduling, as well as bonds it had issued voluntarily. The defaults contravened market expectations: debtor governments were supposed to refrain from defaulting on instruments that had been rescheduled.

The financial turmoil that hit Russia in 1998 affected many forms of outstanding government debt, some in roubles held by foreigners and some in foreign currency. Russia chose to treat different types of debt differently.

1. THE CRISIS: PLAYERS AND INSTRUMENTS

During the 1990s, Russia's government relied increasingly on short-term debt to fund its deficits. In 1993, it began issuing short-term rouble bonds called GKOs. In 1995, it started issuing medium-term rouble bonds called OFZs. Their values grew from the equivalent of $4 billion in 1994 to $45 billion at the beginning of 1997 and $64 billion at the beginning of 1998. The government's total external debt was $150 billion in August 1998, when the crisis hit. This was 33% of GDP. Two-thirds of the external debt was incurred during the Soviet era. The government had recently rescheduled the Soviet debt, including MinFins (dollar bonds issued by the Soviet government amounting to $11 billion). It had issued four eurobonds and incurred other debt to private creditors. See B. Horrigan, *Debt Recovery by Foreign Investors in Post-Crisis Russia*, European Business Journal 88 (1999) (Horrigan).

Investors in rouble debt, notably GKOs, included Russian banks and non-residents. Prudential rules in Russia mandated bank investment in liquid securities of low risk, and the GKOs seemed to qualify. Banks had invested 35% of their assets in GKOs by late 1997. Foreigners were gradually allowed to invest and trade rouble notes, notably GKOs, in the domestic market. They held 30% of all GKOs by late 1997.

After the Asian crisis hit, investors began to withdraw from Russia, draining perhaps $5 billion in just one month, November 1997, for example. Political uncertainty, limits on foreign investment, and weak financial indicators prompted further outflow. Yields on government debt rose to offset the outflows and government debt service costs rose. The rising domestic rates hurt the rouble; rather than attract new capital inflows, they signaled the weakness of the economy. Reserves fell from $24 billion in mid-1997 to $18 billion in January 1998 and $15 billion in June 1998.

On August 17, 1998, the government and central bank ended support for the rouble and suspended trading in GKOs and OFZs. They decreed that GKOs maturing between August 17, 1998 and December 31, 1999 would become new securities with characteristics not then defined. They placed a 90-day moratorium on repaying hard currency loans from non-residents, paying margin calls, and paying forward currency contracts. The government prohibited foreign investment in rouble assets due in one year or less.

The economy spiraled down over the next weeks. The rouble collapsed against the dollar. The stock market collapsed. Banks stopped lending, as the value of their holdings of GKOs evaporated. Close to illiquid, they froze accounts and stopped making transfers and inter-bank payments.

Later the initial panic passed, but the situation was dire. Russia had about $150 billion in foreign debt outstanding (other than the GKOs), of which $17.5 billion was due in 1999. Only in late 1999 did people begin to speak as though the crisis was over.

2. THE RESPONSE

Russia's strategy was to service debt selectively and restructure the rest. It continued to honor its eurobonds. It restructured the GKOs. It negotiated with the London Club to restructure the commercial debt, and write off some. It asked the Paris Club to restructure and write-off the debt to official creditors. Bucheit 2000 at 13-14 described the process. Russia used a "full negotiation with a 1980s style advisory committee."

> . . . Russia reconstituted in 1999 the former commercial bank advisory committee that handled the first rescheduling of this debt. . . . Some members of the old committee who no longer held significant positions in the debt were dropped from the committee, and two new members active in secondary market trading of the paper were added. Russia commenced negotiations with this committee, styled the London Club Advisory Committee, in mid-1999. Russian Eurobonds, issued after the demise of the former Soviet Union, were not included in these negotiations and were serviced normally.

These latter negotiations lasted into 2000. In part, all parties were buying time. Russia earned foreign exchange by exporting oil. The price of oil was rising substantially in 1999 and into 2000. Russia reported a $30 billion trade surplus for 1999 and the best economic growth in the 1990s. This reassured creditors that Russia could service rescheduled debt and strengthened Russia's hand.

Restructuring GKOs. In August, when Russia defaulted on the GKOs, their value was $40 billion and foreigners held about 30%. But as the rouble fell against the dollar, so did the value of the GKOs. Six months later, they were worth only $11.5 billion at prevailing exchange rates and foreigners held less than 20%, according to Buckley 1999 at 202. Soon after the crisis started, the major Western foreign holders of GKOs formed a Creditors' Group in London led by Deutsche Bank and representing only foreign banks, and negotiations began.

The government converted the frozen GKOs in March 1999 and reorganized the market in June. It extended the notes' maturity from below 12 months to an average of about 30 months and reduced the face value of those outstanding by 33% in nominal terms and 67% allowing for inflation. The market, however, was illiquid and secondary market yields were 60% in late 1999. IMF, *World Economic Outlook*, Oct. 1999 at 63. The IMF, in *The GKO OFZ Novation*, Russian Federation: Recent Economic Developments, 108, Sep. 1999, described the novation that arose from several months of acrimonious negotiations. All but 20% of the payments received had to be deposited in restricted ruble accounts. Non-residents who owned the accounts could repatriate the funds only after depositing them in a non-interest bearing account for a year. Alternatively, they could bid in four sales of foreign currency (up to about $50 million each) at rates at most 20% below market By some calculations, foreign investors would receive only 5 cents on the dollar. Russian institutional investors would receive a bit more. Non-residents who did not agree to the novation would not be able to repatriate them for five years.

London Club debt. In 1993, Russia assumed the debt incurred by the Soviet Union and this accounted for about 67% of the country's debt at the time of the crisis. In October 1997, the London Club restructured $26 billion Russia owed commercial creditors, which consisted of about 10,000 different loan agreements. The principal of this debt was evidenced by a rescheduling agreement and its notes were called PRINS. Past due interest accrued through 1997 was exchanged for Luxembourg-listed interest notes called IANS that were functionally bonds. Bucheit 2000. Some of the banks quickly sold their notes in the secondary market. In 1997, trading of Russian debt accounted for 11% of all trading in emerging market securities. See Buckley 1999 at 205.

In 1998 and 1999, Russia defaulted on payments due on PRINS. It asked the London Club to restructure and perhaps write off amounts coming due. According to Horrigan, "Restructuring of London Club debt is . . . problematic, since the lANs and PRINS are held by thousands of banks, investment funds and individuals, complicating the process of garnering the creditor consents necessary to permit a restructuring to occur." Some of these investors were hedge funds that expected a high return. Others were Russian banks that, perhaps anticipating a settlement, bought PRINS in late 1999 at big discounts.

Russia and the London Club reached agreement and in August 2000 Russia offered its commercial creditors a restructuring. The creditors would write off 33% of $32 billion in debt from the Soviet era and swap the 67% for long term low interest eurobonds. *All Friends Now*, The Economist, Feb. 19, 2000; *Russian Debt Holders To Be Offered New Deal*, Financial Times, Aug. 18, 2000.

Paris Club debt. The $40 billion due to other governments had been restructured in 1996 by the Paris Club. The debt is unsecured principal and interest, according to Horrigan. About half was owed to the German government. In late 1998, Russia defaulted on $685 million it owed the German and French governments. Asked in 1999 to write off some of this debt, the Paris Club declined. It deferred to the IMF, which in December 1999 wanted Russia to meet the conditions for IMF credit before receiving more official funds. Only in April 2001, when Russia and Germany (which held the largest share of Paris Club debt) seemed about to reach an accommodation, did restructuring of the Paris Club debt seem possible. Russia was able to take a tough stance because income from its oil exports gave it economic muscle. A. Ostrovsky and H. Simonian, *Russia and Germany Head for Debt Accord*, Financial Times, Apr. 24, 2001.

Debt to Multilateral Institutions. Of the $26 billion that Russia owed multilateral agencies, $19 billion was owed to the IMF and $4.7 billion of that came due in 1999. IMF debt cannot be rescheduled, according to the terms of the loans. Russia also was due to pay the World Bank $800 million in 1999. Russia met these payments on schedule. From late 1999, however, the IMF was unwilling to disburse additional funds to Russia. The country had promised to make many structural changes, such as enacting a new bankruptcy law. But it had failed to accomplish many of these conditions on schedule. The IMF delayed disbursing funds until Russia met these conditions. Not everyone accepted this as the reason for the delay. Some saw it as pressure to end the war in Chechnya. B. Aris, *Living With a Lie*, Euromoney, Jan. 2000 at 75.

Other debt. Russia made the payments due in 1999 on the $16 billion in outstanding eurobonds. According to Horrigan, "Default on such obligations would trigger cross-defaults accelerating the entire indebtedness, and would also effectively exclude Russia from world capital markets for the foreseeable future." Of the $32 billion in outstanding trade credit, $2.5 billion was due in 1999. Russia serviced this debt.

Creditors of banks renegotiated individually with the bank. Their leverage was limited because they could not force the bank into bankruptcy because no law existed for bank insolvency. A major concern to foreign creditors was the banks' forward currency contracts. Recent court cases in Russia held that the agreements were illegal as gambling and could not be enforced. By the end of 1999, most had been renegotiated and the lower amount paid.

Notes and Questions

1. Should Russia be permitted to treat some debt differently from other debt?

2. Suppose foreign investors in GKOs and OFZs looked to the courts to enforce their contractual rights. How effective would this remedy be likely to be?

3. Would the fact that Russia possesses a very large supply of nuclear warheads be likely to have affected its creditors' treatment of its debt? How?

4. Like the Tequila effect, the Russian crisis spilled over into other transition countries, particularly those with close economic ties to Russia, such as former members of the Soviet Union. Their currencies fell 30% to 80% against the dollar as their exports to Russia dropped. Output declined. The financial sectors of these countries weakened significantly and confidence in them ebbed further. Capital flowed out. IMF, World Economic Outlook, Oct. 1999 at 66-70.

G. SOVEREIGN DEFAULT ON BRADY BONDS AND EUROBONDS: ECUADOR

Like Russia's, Ecuador's default contravened market expectations. Many investors believed that a country would continue to service Brady Bonds and eurobonds even though its debt to banks was in default. Ecuador scotched this belief in 1999.

1. THE CRISIS: PLAYERS AND INSTRUMENTS

Hit by El Nino, falling prices for key export commodities, and increasing financial costs, as well as unable to make essential domestic banking and other structural reforms, the government of Ecuador defaulted on its Brady bonds in August 1999.

Ecuador's external debt, at the end of 1998, consisted of $5.8 billion in Brady bonds, $3.6 billion in bank loans, $2.8 billion to multilateral agencies, $1.1 billion of official bilateral loans, a eurobond of $0.7 billion, and trade credits of $0.6 billion. Three of the four Brady bond issues took place in February 1995, according to P. Graf, *Ecuador's External Debt Problem*, BIS *International Banking and Financial Market Developments*, Nov. 1999 at 6, and all were listed in Luxembourg:

- A $1.9 billion par bond repayable in a single amount after 30 years. The coupon, payable May and November, steps up gradually from 3.25 to 5% after 10 years. Principal is guaranteed by a zero coupon U.S. treasury bond. Interest carries a 5% rolling guarantee.

- A $1.4 billion discount bond also repayable in a single amount after 30 years. Interest is LIBOR plus 13/16ths, payable February and August. Principal is guaranteed by a zero coupon U.S. bond. Interest carries a 7% rolling 12 month guarantee. The bonds are registered only.

- A $2.4 billion past due interest (PDI) bond payable in 21 increasing semiannual installments from February 2005 and paying interest semiannually at LIBOR + 13/16ths. It had no guarantees. The bonds may be bearer or registered.

- A $190 million interest equalization bond (IEB) payable in increasing semiannual installments from June 1995, with semiannual interest of LIBOR + 13/16ths. By starting with interest rates below market and ending with rates above market the IEB "equalized" rates across the life of the loan. It had no guarantees and was issued in December 1994.

The government did not pay the interest coupons due on the discount and PDI bonds at the end of August 1999. It requested 30 days to restructure them, but found no takers. According to the IMF November 1999:

At the end of September the government decided to pay the coupon on the PDI and asked investors to use the interest guarantee attached to the

Discount bond to meet the coupon payment on this issue. However, it was then reported that a group of investors had decided to seek an 'acceleration' of this bond (i.e., to seek full payment immediately).

In order to maintain access to the international capital markets, the government intended to continue servicing the rest of its liabilities. However, this would have implied an unequal treatment of creditors. In the event, in late October it decided to defer interest payments on its Par Brady bonds as well as its outstanding eurobonds, and to seek a renegotiation of this Paris Club and domestic debt.

2. THE RESCUE PACKAGE: EXCHANGE FOR GLOBAL BONDS

The IMF's response was measured. Initially, it was not willing to provide Ecuador with emergency funds that would allow the country to service the debt. Lenders saw this as a response by the IMF to its critics during the Asian financial crisis, and a signal that the IMF would not bail out foreign lenders. They believed that the IMF was trying to "bail in" creditors that had been exempted from restructurings of the past. By March 2001, however, the IMF was about to complete a stand-by program with Ecuador. It was expected to disburse $120 million by the end of April. This would be part of $2 billion in support to be provided by the IMF, World Bank, and Inter-American Development Bank.

A Connecticut hedge fund that had invested $10 million in the discount Brady bonds spearheaded the decision by 35% of the bondholders to vote on September 27, 1998 to accelerate the bonds (25% was needed). Acceleration had several potential effects that did not materialize. The holders of the discount bond could sue to enforce their rights, but did not choose to do so. The hedge fund did receive, however, a seat on the consultative group later assembled by Ecuador. Acceleration allowed holders of other bonds and debt to accelerate as well because it was an event of default in all the Brady bonds and many of the credits. But no other creditors chose to accelerate.

On July 27, 2000, the government of Ecuador offered to exchange US dollar Global Bonds due 2012 and 2030 for the Brady Bonds and the eurobonds. Ecuador declined to negotiate and set up a formal consultative group representing the creditors. According to Bucheit 2000 at 13-14:

> Ecuador, . . . rather than attempt to reconstitute the commercial bank advisory committee with which the Ecuador Brady deal had been negotiated in 1993-94, . . . invited eight of the larger institutional holders of its bonds to sit on a Consultative Group. The announced function of this Group was not to negotiate the terms of an exchange offer for Ecuador's bonds, but rather to provide a formal medium through which Ecuador could communicate with the bondholder community and receive the views of bondholders on issues relevant to an eventual exchange offer..

Bondholders who chose the 2030 Bonds would receive an amount equal to the par value of the shorter bonds being retired (the old bonds), or discounted from 42% to 60% from the par value of the longer old bonds. The 2030 Bonds would pay interest of 4% in the first year, stepping up to 10% from 2006 on. Their holders would also receive cash payments for interest that was overdue on the old bonds. Bondholders who chose the 2012 Bonds had to accept a discount 35% greater than on the 2030 Bonds. They would receive 12% interest. Ecuador would only issue 2012 Bonds with a total face value of $1.25 billion, and would give priority to holders of shorter old bonds. Almost 97% of the bondholders accepted the offer and Ecuador reduced the aggregate value of its bond obligations by almost 40%. L. Buchheit, *How Ecuador Escaped the Brady Bond Trap*, International Financial Law Review, 17, Dec. 2000; Republic of Ecuador, *Offer to Exchange*, Offering Circular, Jul. 27, 2000.

Ecuador accepted several important limits. Principal reinstatement was one. If the government defaulted on servicing the 2030 Bonds in the first 10 years, it would automatically issue more of the Bonds. The additional Bonds would reinstate the principal on the old bonds that the bondholders had relinquished. Mandatory debt management guidelines required Ecuador to retire an agreed portion of the outstanding 2030 Bonds starting 11 years after issue and 2012 Bonds starting 6 years after issue. The purpose was to avoid relying on Ecuador's ability to make a bullet payment at the end, while recognizing that the parties could not set a repayment schedule with any confidence in 2001. Since Ecuador could be buying the Bonds in the secondary market, it would provide a liquidity that investors want. If Ecuador failed to manage its debt as required, it would have to retire the excess bonds at par.

The impact on the Brady bond market was expected by some to be dire. Moody's Investors Service, for example, expected the Ukraine, Pakistan, Moldova, and Romania to consider defaulting on their Brady bonds. Ivory Coast defaulted in late April 2000. This, it was predicted, would increase the risk premium on Brady bonds and hurt the issuers. *See* Luce and Moss 1999. The BIS's Graf noted after a few months, however, that the market distinguished between the paper of Ecuador and other countries, and that the average price of Brady bonds fell in the last part of 1999.

Notes and Questions

1. Why would Ecuador decide to treat all creditors equally? Should it have done so?

2. At the September 1999 meeting, Ecuador had proposed that the bondholders activate the guarantee of interest on the discount bond and the par bond. But Ecuador failed to muster the 25% of the bondholders needed to do this. Should the holders of the discount Brady bond have voted to exercise the interest guarantee rather than accelerate the bond? What might have accounted for the decision that they took? Would your analysis be affected by the fact that 50% of the bondholders would be needed to repeal the acceleration?

3. Why would most of the holders of the accelerated bond choose to accept Ecuador's offer rather than pursue the recovery of their bond through the New York courts, if necessary?

4. Under what circumstances is it appropriate or essential for public sector creditors–such as the U.S. government or the IMF–to take the lead in the rescheduling of a country's debt? When should private sector creditors resolve the debt problems on their own?

5. Compare the process followed by Ecuador with that used by Russia, described above, and Pakistan. Pakistan first discussed issues with creditors informally and then made a unilateral offer to bondholders. Bucheit 2000 at 13-14:

> Pakistan had large Eurobond payments coming due in December 1999. Pakistan did not convene a negotiating committee of creditors or even establish a formal consultative body along the lines of Ecuador. Instead, the Pakistan authorities privately contacted some of the country's larger Eurobond holders to explain the country's financial difficulties and to seek their views on a possible restructuring. On the basis of these consultations, Pakistan made a unilateral exchange offer for the bonds in November 1999. More than 90% of the bondholders eventually accepted the offer.

6. The following table compares four debt crises and their solutions. In what important ways, if any, do the natures of the crises differ?

Key dimensions	Mexico '82	Korea '97	Russia '98	Ecuador '99
Instruments				
Bank loans	Yes	Yes	Yes	Yes
Bonds	-	-	Yes	Yes
Official loans	Yes	-	Yes	Yes
Maturity profile	ST < MT	ST > MT	ST, MT	MT, LT
Borrowers	Gov't	Banks, Co's	Gov't,bank	Gov't
Big banks' loans	> capital	< capital	< capital	small

ST is Short Term loans and MT is Medium Term loans

7. Do the differences in the natures of the crises affect the solutions? Is moral hazard a greater concern in some cases than others? See the following table.

Solutions	Mexico '82	Korea '97	Russia '98	Ecuador '99
Any default?	Yes	No	Yes	Yes
IMF/World Bank funds used?	Yes	Yes	No	Not yet
New private money given?	Yes	No	No	Not yet
Debt rescheduled?	Yes	Later	Yes	Yes
Debt reduced?	Yes	No	Yes	Yes
Use Brady bonds?	Yes	No	No	No

3. WHEN PUBLIC SECTOR ISSUERS DEFAULT ON VOLUNTARY BONDS: EXIT CLAUSES

As the Brady bonds, which banks were to some extent forced to buy, gave way in the early 1990s to bonds issued to investors who bought them voluntarily, many investors were said to assume that the risk of default on bonds was much less than for syndicated bank loans. By 2000, that view may seem hard to justify, but earlier investors noted that after the 1982 crisis bonds were not rescheduled. They mentioned the impracticality of getting the very large number of diverse bondholders to be able to reach a consensus on any proposal by an issuer in default. And some believed that bondholders were much more likely to turn to courts for help than the bank lenders ever were.

Now that governments have defaulted on both Brady and other bonds, investors face the process of restructuring the bonds. Most sovereign bonds are governed by New York State or English law, as described above. Those subject to New York law generally require the agreement of all bondholders to changes in payment (amounts and due dates). This is difficult. English law usually allows a supermajority (66 2/3% - 75%) of bondholders to approve even payment amendments and bind all holders.

The issuer's alternative is to offer bondholders an exchange of "existing bonds for new debt instruments. . . . It was the presence of a unanimity rule in the amendments clauses of commercial bank loan agreements that forced the Brady process to be implemented through loan-for-bond exchanges, rather than amendments to the existing loan contracts. Those who do not accept the exchange keep the old bonds, with the "full legal rights and remedies under those instruments." Their threat of on-going litigation is serious. Bucheit, *Sovereign Debtors and Their Bondholders*, Unitar 2000 at 3 (Bucheit 2000).

Ecuador used exit amendments that would reduce the protection offered by the old bonds and so encourage holders of those bonds to tender them for the Global Bonds. New York law permitted the bondholders to make any amendments by majority vote except those matters concerning payment, which required 100% approval. Holders who accepted the offer to switch also agreed to the exit amendments of the old bonds that concerned matters other than payment. For example, exit amendments removed the cross-default, cross-acceleration, and negative pledge clauses in the old bonds. The amendments also removed covenants to make annual reports, include the old bonds in later conversions, keep the bonds listed, and prevent the government from buying old bonds while they were in default. A simple majority of the holders of the old bonds could impose these changes. Since anyone who kept the old bonds would be much less protected than before, the exit amendments would induce the others to accept the Global Bonds. An issue was how to bind the remaining holders of the bonds to the new amendments.

Notes and Questions

1. Is the repurchase of bonds by the issuer an appropriate way for a government to deal with debt crisis?

2. Are exit amendments an appropriate way to encourage bond holders to participate in a bond novation? Suppose many more governments than Ecuador used them to prod reluctant investors to exchange their bonds. How would that affect the evolution of the international bond market? Should government that issue many bonds try to discourage countries like Ecuador from using exit amendments?

3. Under what circumstances do the crises examined here suggest that creditors should turn to the courts to enforce their contractual rights? When is this approach not useful?

H. SOVEREIGN DEFAULT ON DOMESTIC BONDS: TURKEY

While the crises dealt with above involved IMF help in servicing foreign currency debt, the focus of the Turkish crisis was government debt due in domestic currency.

The crisis began in November 2000 when Demir Bank, a medium-sized bank, failed. It had invested substantially in 1 to 1½ year government securities which it funded by borrowing in the overnight market. The mismatch exposed the bank to interest rate risk and short-term interest rates began to rise in July 2000. When other banks stopped lending to Demir Bank in November, the bank sold its government securities. The big increase in the supply of government paper in the secondary markets pushed interest rates on government debt up to 100% and primary dealers stopped giving quotes on government paper. At this point, foreign investors still held a large share of government Lira securities. They sold and converted their Lira receipts to foreign currency. As confidence in the country's foreign exchange position evaporated, capital flowed out of Turkey. In a few days, Turkey's reserves fell 20%. People anticipated the rapid depletion of reserves if the crisis was not resolved quickly.

To help stem the outflow, the IMF supplemented the outstanding standby credit of $3.7 billion it had granted in December 1999 by $7.3 billion in December 2000, adding many conditions to restructure the economy.

Before the economic restructuring could take effect, however, a political battle over corruption between Turkey's president and prime minister battered public confidence even more. Large capital outflows resumed in January 2001. As pressure mounted on the Lira, Turkey was forced to abandon its crawling peg against the dollar, a regime previously encouraged by Stanley Fisher, the second highest ranking IMF official. (See Chapter 6 for the criticisms of crawling peg regimes.) Turkey was unable to comply with the conditions of the IMF stabilization program.

The immediate problem facing Turkey was the large government short-term debt in Lira. Much of this debt–the equivalent of about $20 billion–was due within the next six months. The government had planned, as in the past, simply to roll it over at current rates. But if the outflow continued, it would reduce the supply of funds in domestic markets, which would in turn push interest rates up even more and raise the servicing costs to unacceptably high levels for the government. The government lacked funds in its budget to meet existing debt service, let alone an increase. It could not simply print more Lira to service the domestic debt. That would hurt the economy. Inflation was already over 100%. Even higher inflation would worsen the exchange rate.

On the horizon was a threat to Turkey's financial system like that in the crisis in Korea, a danger of which the IMF was keenly aware. Private Turkish banks were the main investors in the government's short term Lira paper. They had financed their purchases of government debt by borrowing funds denominated in foreign currency, mainly Deutschmark, from foreign banks. Suppose that the government were to default on its short term Lira debt. That would make it impossible for Turkish banks to service their foreign currency debt. This could force the government to step in, renegotiating the external credit to the banks and taking responsibility for servicing the new debt, perhaps even guaranteeing it as Korea's government did.

The rescue options were limited, in the IMF view. The market needed to be confident that the government could service its short-term Lira debt without damaging the economy. Renewed confidence would reverse the outflow of funds from the country. Investors would return to government Lira securities.

The IMF designed another assistance program. The government would receive a larger standby credit. This would be doubly beneficial. To the extent the government drew on the funds, it could use them to service its short term Lira debt. Even if it did not draw on them, the public would see that it could do so if needed. IMF lines of credit would show investors that Turkey could draw on adequate funds, without inflating the economy, to service its debt. Investors would then keep their own funds in the country. In these two ways, the IMF hoped to restore confidence in Turkey's economy and domestic financial markets. If capital flight could be reversed, or at least stopped, the government could weather the crisis.

So in mid-May 2001, the IMF expanded its standby credit to $19 billion. The IMF would immediately provide $3.8 billion, and disburse another $9 billion by the end of the year if Turkey complied with the conditions of the help, which included the following. The government was to put a lid on the growth of money, make structural changes in its banking sector, and implement other changes in the economy. It would improve the court system, to help enforce the law.   The government would form a committee of specifically identified officials to design a plan, by September 2001, that would combat corruption and improve governance, and rewrite the code of conduct for government officials. *Letter of Intent to IMF from the Prime Minister of Turkey*, May 3, 2001, at 9. Foreign banks with loans to Turkish banks had already been pressed by their home governments to roll over the loans. The foreign banks' supervisors, working with the IMF, put in place a system to monitor performance. In addition, the World Bank added another $1.8 billion for specified projects to the $5 billion in loans that it was already providing. *IMF Executive Board Approves $8 billion Augmentation fo Stand-By Credit for Turkey*, IMF Survey, May 21, 2001; S. Fidler, *Turkish Crisis Set to Test US Aversion to Bail-Outs*, Financial Times, Mar. 2, 2001; L. Boulton and S. Fidler, *Turkey Wins Backing for $19bn Loans*, Financial Times, May 16, 2001; D. Frantz, *Turkish Bailout is Joined to a Political Overhaul*, New York Times, May 18, 2001.

Events did not unfold as hoped, however. The IMF only disbursed the $3.8 billion in August, after insisting on agreed changes that Turkey delayed. By November, Turkey and the IMF realized that the economy was not performing as expected and the country would need $10 billion more in external financing than it could earn or raise. They identified September 11 as a major cause. It accounted for large declines in tourism, exports, funding from international financial markets, and foreign direct investment.   So economic growth collapsed. Turkey did not implement the agreed structural changes on schedule.   The IMF agreed that it had largely done so by February 2002, restructuring the banking sector, for example.

The IMF agreed in February to increase its potential funding from $19 billion to $31 billion. Of the $12 billion in new money, half would be used to repay $6 billion coming due to the IMF in 2002, in effect lengthening the maturity by 4 years. Turkey could draw down $5 billion in2002, $2 billion of the $4 billion in money still undrawn from the May 2001 arrangement and another $3 billion in new money.   It would receive the funds in four tranches as it met other conditions, such as reducing public sector employment, setting formal inflation targets, and privatizing state banks. The IMF released one tranche in mid-April 2002 as inflation slowed to 70%.   To win the next tranche, Turkey would have to reduce public employment a lot. IMF Press

Release No. 02/7, *IMF Managing Director Sees Impressive Commitment by Turkey to Economic Reforms*, Feb. 4, 2002; M. Munir, *Banks Face Up to Survival Tests*, Euromoney, Feb. 2002, at 120; L. Boulton, *IMF To Approve Loan To Turkey*, Financial Times, Apr. 16, 2002.

This new money was seen as "further evidence of the willingness of the fund's largest member states to act generously with countries that are seen as strategically important to the war against terrorism and are also pursuing aggressive economic reform programmes." The US had "strongly supported" the new money "to prevent destabilisation in a key regional ally." E. Aiden, *Turkish Reforms Bring $16bn IMF Loan*, Financial Times, Feb. 5, 2002.

Notes and Questions

1. Before taking office, senior officials in the Bush Treasury Department actively spoke out against bailouts and the role of the IMF. Is their support for the IMF-led help to Turkey consistent with their earlier positions?

2. Some say that Turkey's strategic position explains the help it receives. What criteria make a borrowing government strategic? How many of the other countries examined above are strategic? Is assistance like that given to Turkey consistent with the country's stability and strategic position in the long-run?

3. Should IMF assistance be restricted to dealing with foreign currency debt only?

I. SOVEREIGN DEFAULT ON ALL DEBT: ARGENTINA

Argentina captured the title for the largest sovereign default when it defaulted on its $141 billion external debt in late December 2001. Many accused the IMF of contributing to the default. Often the criticism is that the IMF is too rigid in demanding policies that the government cannot accomplish. In the case of Argentina, one set of critics found the IMF too lenient with the Argentine government before the crisis.

1. OVERVIEW OF EVENTS LEADING TO THE COLLAPSE

Although the crisis spun out of control during 2001, its genesis traces back a decade. In 1991, the government adopted a Currency Board, fixing the peso equal to one US dollar under the guidance of then Economy Minister Domingo Cavallo. With tight money, the initial effect was to end very high inflation. The government's large fiscal deficits promoted economic growth of 4% p.a. from 1994 to 1998, but external debt doubled in the same period and imports flowed into the country.

In April 2001, the third year of recession, the government recalled Cavallo as Economy Minister. He instituted an austerity program that promised a zero fiscal deficit and he suggested weakening the peso/dollar link (see

Chapter 6). Gradually these policies, coupled with low commodity prices and the devalued currency of competing countries, produced bankruptcies, unemployment, financial and economic crisis, runs on banks, riots, and capital flight conservatively estimated at $13 billion.

By November 2001, Cavallo proposed to reduce the interest payable on the government's domestic and foreign debt to balance the budget. The Argentine stock index fell to 200. from 650 in January 2000. Argentine ADRs had fallen by 50%.

The crisis came to a head the next month. The government became increasingly desperate to avoid default and devaluation. Depositors fled the banks, credit evaporated, and interest rates soared. The government limited bank depositors to $250 cash withdrawals a week and controlled transfers of funds out of Argentina. It reduced the interest payments on $45 billion of government bonds held by local investors. It made local banks roll over $360 million of Treasury bills and seized assets of pension funds in order to avoid a formal default on public debt.

In late December the government defaulted on its debt and the next month it ended the 1:1 peso:dollar rate and the Currency Board.

The role of the IMF and Argentina's treatment of foreign creditors follow.

2. THE PRE-COLLAPSE ROLE OF THE IMF

During the two years leading up to the crisis, the IMF loaned Argentina funds repeatedly. U.S. government officials were involved in each IMF decision. The IMF allowed Argentina a three year standby loan of $7 billion in March 2000, four months after a new government took office. The IMF raised the standby to $14 billion in January 2001. Six months later, a spokesman for the IMF and the U.S. National Security Advisor, Condoleezza Rice, fearing a premature stock and bond market rally in Argentina based on hopes of aid, both said on the same day that there were no plans to give the country special help. The rally stopped. But the IMF raised its standby again to $22 billion on September 7, 2001. The September arrangement let Argentina draw about $6 billion immediately, another $6 billion in 2002, and $1.3 billion in 2003, but allowed Argentina to draw immediately $3 billion of the later funds if it improved the structure of government debt. In January 2002, the IMF extended by one year repayment of a $933 million loan due that month. J. Fuerbringer, with R. Stevenson, *No Bailout Is Planned For Argentina*, New York Times, July 14, 2001.

Each agreement included specific targets for economic reform. For example, in March 2001, the government agreed to reduce the deficit of the central and provincial governments substantially, describing how this would be done. The government agreed to reform labor law and the social security system, and to introduce competition in the energy and telecommunications sectors. It would improve social assistance by making delivery more efficient. But in January 2001, the IMF agreed to accept only a small reduction in the government deficit in the short run and repeated the need to restructure energy and telecommunications. Then in September 2001 the IMF required Argentina to eliminate the federal deficit immediately. Argentina had passed a zero deficit law that required increasing taxes and cutting spending, including wages and pensions. The IMF expected these policies "to result in a lasting decline in the risk premium on Argentine debt and of domestic interest rates, thus creating conditions for a modest recovery of real GDP growth in the final quarter of 2001." IMF, *IMF Augments Argentina Stand-By Credit to $21.57 Billion,*" Press Release No. 01/37, Sep. 7, 2001.

The government failed to achieve the zero deficit quickly. Many provincial governors refused to take part. So in December, the IMF delayed releasing $1.26 billion to Argentina from the September 2001 package. The World Bank and Inter-American Development Bank froze another $1.1 billion. Soon after, Argentina defaulted.

After the default and currency collapse, the IMF reviewed its role during the past year. It had not imposed rigid policies on the government. Rather, ownership of the plan was in Argentina, as Economics Minister Cavallo had said in October 2001. Rather than accepting blame for the collapse because it had withheld funds in December, the IMF said the zero deficit policy "flowed logically and necessarily from the currency board, which was the Argentines' own decision." That is, Argentina could not have both a currency board fixing the peso to the dollar and a fiscal policy that allowed domestic inflation to exceed inflation in the U.S. The combination led to an overvalued peso that strangled exports, sent the economy into recession and, as tax receipts fell, enlarged the fiscal deficit.

The IMF suggested that, far from being a dictator, it may have capitulated repeatedly to a large member country that was on the edge, for fear of being seen to push it over. The IMF knew that the government could not sustain its growing debt yet, rather than withhold new funds until Argentina met the debt-reduction conditions, the IMF increased the standby twice. The IMF's former deputy managing director, Stanley Fischer, said some countries spread rumors that the IMF loan being negotiated was for a large amount (more than the IMF wanted to advance), then told the IMF that a figure below the rumored amount would send a bad signal to the market. Argentina seems to have negotiated adroitly. A. Beattie, *IMF Seeks to Draw Lessons from Turmoil in Argentina*, Financial Times, Jan. 2, 2002.

Critics of the IMF said that it should have led a bailout like that for Mexico, infusing $50 billion that would jump start the economy. The Bush administration, far from allowing this, had prevented the IMF in December 2001 from advancing the standby funds.

3. TREATMENT OF FOREIGN CREDITORS BEFORE DEFAULT

Argentina's external bond holders first welcomed the Carvallo regime, then doubted it. In June 2001, the government swapped about $30 billion in short-term external bonds for new bonds with longer maturities. The interest on the new bonds was a higher-than-market long-term rate as a sweetener but the government still saved $16 billion in interest over the next four years. Two of the 12 investment banks had to withdraw as managers, however, when they learned that research by one of them published before the offer may have violated U.S. securities law. C. Krauss, *Bond Sale Seems to Signal Easing of Argentine Crisis*, New York Times, June 13, 2001; T. Catan, *Banks Pull Out of Argentine Debt Swap*, Financial Times, June 2/3, 2001.

In late October and November, the government asked investors to swap up to $95 billion of bonds due in the next decade for ones paying much lower interest and postponing full payment for three years. The swap would let the government pay $4 billion less in interest each year. This could help the government because the $10 billion interest it was about 20% of its budget. Investors holding one-third of the bonds were Argentine institutions, such as banks and pension funds, and assumed to be the main target. But President de la Rúa also visited Wall Street, arguing that the offer would be better than an outright default. Foreign rating agencies said that the swap was a form of default and rated bonds eligible for the swap as being in default. In the event, some local investors–including banks–accepted the offer. For foreign investors, Argentina hoped to make a global offer for all bonds sometime between January and March 2002, but events outdistanced it.

In December, the government tried again to court foreign creditors, meeting the Emerging Markets Creditors Association (established in late 2000) in New York in a search for common ground to restructure the $132 billion, which was mostly in bonds. President Bush announced that he supported these efforts but did not offer Argentina any funds.

4. ARGENTINA AFTER DEFAULT

In the months after the crisis, the new Duhalde government, the fifth since mid-December, instituted capital controls. In late March, it limited daily buying by individuals to $1,000 and companies, $10,000. It halved the daily operating time of exchanges to 3.5 hours. It limited the amount of dollars banks and business could hold. It limited the ability of investors and brokers to buy stock in the U.S., where they traded in dollars at a premium over the peso market. It tried to shield the banking sector, which were severely hurt by controls, devaluation, and loss of confidence. Even so, banks were expecting to fire 10% to 20% of their staff. In the interim, the government made discounted loans to provincial and national government agencies, paying with new pesos. M. Mulligan, *Argentine Rescue Plan 'Back to Square One,'* Financial Times, May 14, 2002;   L. Rohter, *Peso Down Steeply, Argentines Strengthen Currency Curbs*, New York Times, Mar. 26, 2002.

Most banks in Argentina were insolvent although the restrictions on payments slowed the drain of their reserves. The government had forced the banks to convert their dollar assets at Peso 1 equals $1 while converting their dollar liabilities at Peso 1 equals $1.4 as a sop to depositors. The banks lost about $9bn as a result. But long-term solutions eluded the government. By late May 2002, the legislature had twice defeated the central bank's proposal to force holders of the frozen time deposits to accept a swap of 10 year floating rate government bonds. M. Mulligan, *Argentine Rescue Plan 'Back to Square One,'* Financial Times, May 14, 2002; M. Mulligan, *Argentina Intervenes over Credit Agricole Offshoots*, Financial Times, May 21, 2002.

Major foreign banks, which dominated much of Argentina's banking system, wrote down huge amounts or withdrew. Provisions were set up for problem loans by Citibank ($2.1 bn), HSBC ($1.5 bn), and FleetBoston ($1.4 bn). Two Spanish banks wrote off their entire investments in Argentina ($2.9 bn total). The Bank of Nova Scotia of Canada and Credit Agricole ($278m) did the same and refused to inject further funds. R. Lapper, *Banks Count Cost of Stake in Argentina*, Financial Times, May 13, 2002. M. Mulligan, *Argentina Intervenes over Credit Agricole Offshoots*, Financial Times, May 21, 2002.

Argentina's government and big companies lost access to foreign credit. The government's creditors waited for signs of a recovery plan that might work, including an IMF arrangement. A few hedge funds holding a form of credit derivative called default swaps were reported to be preparing to sue their counterparties. Others formed the Argentine Bondholders Committee. A concern for the prospective debt rescheduling was how the government would propose to treat the investors who swapped into bonds with lower interest and longer maturities in November 2001. Among corporate debtors, Telecom Argentina stopped servicing its $3.4 billion external debt in March. It was not alone. J. Chaffin, *Bondholders Making Their Way to Court*, Financial Times, Dec. 22-23, 2001; C. Denny, *Argentina Chokes on 'Tough Love,'* Guardian, Apr. 3, 2002; B. Boccara, *Analysis: Argentina*, Standard & Poor's, Jan. 11, 2002; T. Catan and S. Silver, Telecom *Argentina Defaults on $3.3bn of Debt Repayments*, Financial Times, Apr. 3, 2002.

The central bank continued to service its debt to the World Bank, paying $680m in May 2002, and is paying other multilateral agencies in the hope of receiving further funding from them. M. Mulligan, *Argentine Rescue Plan 'Back to Square One,'* Financial Times, May 14, 2002.

The IMF insisted that it would not provide more funds until Argentina made essential changes. First, Argentina was to eliminate barriers to exit from its bankruptcy law, such as prohibiting the cram down. The government submitted reforms to Congress in April. Second, the Provinces would have to accept limits on their spending and could not issue scrip as an alternative to local or foreign currency, as they had done. The Provinces promised to do so in April. Finally, the budget deficit had to be reduced a lot. The Federal and provincial governments worked toward a package of reforms that would satisfy the IMF, but in late May 2002 the Governor of Buenos Aires refused to sign an austerity pact with IMF-mandated limits on the federal government's deficit because it would push the province much deeper into deficit. Pressure from politically powerful provinces led the central bank to take control in late May 2002 of three banks, with assets of $1.2bn, owned by Credit Agricole of France. Their credit to grain growing regions of the country made them important. BBC, *Argentina: Government Agrees to Amend Laws in Order to Comply with IMF Demands*, BBC Monitoring Service, Apr. 12, 2002; M. Mulligan, *Argentina Intervenes over Credit Agricole Offshoots*, Financial Times, May 21, 2002.

The future looked bleak. GNP was projected to fall 15% in 2002, adding a fourth year to the recession. The foreign exchange rate collapsed 72% from January to May, so that one dollar equaled 3.5 pesos. Prices rose an estimated 30% since January. The fear is a return of hyper-inflation. M. Mulligan, *Argentine Rescue Plan 'Back to Square One,'* Financial Times, May 14, 2002; M. Mulligan, *Argentina Intervenes over Credit Agricole Offshoots*, Financial Times, May 21, 2000; M. Mulligan, *Argentine Rescue Plan 'Back to Square One,'* Financial Times, May 14, 2002; M. Wolf, *Argentina on the Road to Ruin*, Financial Times, May 1, 2002.

Links To Other Chapters

Emerging market debt first appears as a topic in Chapter 1, which presents the 1997-98 financial crisis in Korea. Rules governing the issuance of foreign debt securities in the U.S. and the activities of U.S. investors in international securities are discussed in Chapter 2. Prudential rules governing banks are important to the growth of emerging market debt, and capital adequacy rules are at the center of these rules (Chapter 4).

The markets include those for syndicated loans (Chapter 9), eurobonds and global securities (Chapter 12), and to some extent derivatives (Chapters 16 and 17). Foreign creditors play an important role in project finance, which often includes structured securities (Chapter 19). Institutional investors in emerging market securities are discussed in Chapter 20.

The crises that engulf debtor countries draw on foreign exchange markets (Chapter 6). They raise issues that resemble those faced by Japan (Chapter 8).

The underlying issues that concern international financial architecture are raised in Chapter 22.

PART IV

INTERNATIONAL FINANCIAL ARCHITECTURE

This concluding Part of the book focuses on two subjects. Chapter 22 deals with reforms of the international financial system to deal with the continuous problems of emerging market debt and financial instability examined in Chapter 21. These efforts have greatly accelerated the pace of globalized regulation that have been generated by the problems of interaction between developed economies. Chapter 23 deals with the consequences of September 11 to the international financial system, and details how the United States and the world have built on anti-money laundering efforts to fight terrorism through controls in the financial system.

CHAPTER TWENTY-TWO

REFORM OF THE INTER-NATIONAL FINANCIAL SYSTEM

The Asian financial crisis triggered an outpouring of proposals for reforming the international financial system aimed primarily at preventing international financial crises and dealing better with them when they do occur. These proposals are referred to as the new International Financial Architecture (IFA). An excellent review of these proposals is found in B. Eichengreen, *Toward a New International Financial Architecture* (1999). This Chapter focuses on some key areas of IFA: the role of the IMF in dealing with debt crises, the possible need for an international bankruptcy system and collective action clauses in bond contracts, promulgation and enforcement of international banking standards, and the advisability of capital controls. We do not deal here with the issue of exchange rate systems. Suffice it to say that many economists have criticized pegged rates and have advocated moving more towards floating rates or currency boards, see e.g. Council of Foreign Relations, *Independent Task Force Report on Safeguarding Prosperity in a Global Financial System: The Future International Financial Architecture* (2000) (CFR Report), pp. 13-15. In the big picture, we seem to be moving, however haltingly, toward more global regulation to match our more global economy, and this trend may pose some significant dangers to the continued health of that economy.

A. THE ROLE OF THE IMF

Chapter 21, which dealt with emerging market debt, raised many of the background issues concerning the role of the IMF in dealing with debt crises. One central concern has been the moral hazard created by the use of IMF funds to pay off foreign creditors. How to deal with this issue has spawned an active debate.

In November 1998, the U.S. Congress established the International Financial Institutions Advisory Commission, dubbed the Meltzer Commission for its Chairman, Allan Meltzer. The Commission's mission was to consider the future roles of international financial institutions including most prominently the IMF. The Meltzer Commission recommended that the IMF be restructured as a smaller institution with three responsibilities: collect financial and economic data, provide advice without conditions relating to economic policy and "to act as a quasi-lender of last resort to solvent emerging economies by providing short-term liquidity assistance to countries in need under a mechanism designed to avoid the abuse of liquidity assistance to sponsor bail outs and under a system that would not retard the development of those institutions within the recipient country that would attract capital from commercial sources...."

The Meltzer Commission would end IMF long-term lending tied to policy conditions. This would preclude the type of lending now pending for Russia. The Commission further proposed that liquidity lending only be to countries meeting minimum prudential standards, that it not be tied to policy reforms, that it should be limited to illiquid not insolvent borrowers, and that it should not be used to salvage insolvent domestic financial institutions or to protect foreign lenders from losses. The Commission further proposed that the short-term loans be for a maximum of 120 days with one permissible rollover, should carry a penalty interest rate, and should require that the IMF be given priority in payment over all other lenders. At the same time, the Commission recommended that the IMF, the World Bank and the regional development banks write-off in their entirety all claims against heavily indebted poor countries.

The Meltzer Commission's recommendations were criticized by U.S. Treasury Secretary Lawrence Summers for putting a straitjacket on the IMF's response to crisis. While he agreed with the emphasis of moving from long-term to short-term lending, he disagreed with the pre-qualification conditions imposed on short-term lending. 74 BNA Banking Report 592 (March 27, 2000). Stanley Fisher, the Deputy Managing Director of the IMF, disagreed with the short-term lending approach and has emphasized the role of the IMF in promoting economic reform. Others, including Joseph Stiglitz former chief economist and vice president of the World Bank, have rejoined that IMF macroeconomic policy of budget cutting and tighter monetary policies was often mistaken. *What I Learned at the World Economic Crisis,* The New Republic, April 17 & 24, 2000. To this point Stiglitz said that the IMF staff frequently "consists of third-rank students from first-rate universities," id., at 7.

The CFR Report seems to take a more moderate approach to IMF reform, pp. 12-13, 15-16. It proposed that international bonds be required to contain collective action clauses because this would facilitate rescheduling of bonds and reduce moral hazard. We discuss this proposal later in the Chapter. The CFR Report was critical of the size of IMF rescue packages. It observed that in the overwhelming majority of the cases, the Fund's normal lending limits (100 percent of a country's quota or IMF subscription annually and 300 percent of quota cumulatively) ought to be sufficient, but that IMF loans to Mexico (1995), to Thailand and Indonesia (1997) and to Brazil (1999) were in the neighborhood of 500-700 percent of Fund quotas, while the loan to South Korea (1997) was 1,900 percent of its quota.

The CFR also proposed to address moral hazard by having the IMF make known that it will provide emergency financial assistance only when there is a good prospect of the recipient's country achieving "balance of payments viability" in the medium term. Further, in "extreme cases" in which the "existing debt profile is clearly unsustainable," the IMF would expect, as a condition for its support, that debtors engage in good faith discussion with their private creditors to achieve a more sustainable debt and debt-servicing profile, and that no category of debt would be presumed exempt from such discussions. In such cases, the IMF would recognize a temporary payments standstill, say for 30-60 days, during which time "the IMF would encourage debtors to seek an agreement that is nondiscriminatory between foreign and domestic holders of debt and to provide creditor banks with timely and reliable information on interbank exposures to the country. Likewise, the Fund would encourage creditor banks to maintain interbank lines and to refrain from legal challenges during the period of the standstill." Id, at 64.

On the other hand the CFR was willing to entertain larger rescue packages in the "rare situations" of widespread cross-border contagion of financial crises where failure to intervene would threaten the world's economy. This would be done by creating a new "contagion facility" that would replace the existing Supplemental Reserve Facility (SRF) and the Contingency Credit Line (CCL).

The SRF was introduced in 1997 to supplement the normal Fund borrowing arrangements to provide financial assistance for exceptional balance of payments difficulties "owing to a large short-term financing need resulting from a sudden and disruptive loss of market confidence such as occurred in the Mexican and Asian financial crises of 1995 and 1997." International Monetary Fund, *How We Lend* (March 27, 2000). Repayments are to be made within 2½ years.

In April 1999, the IMF's Executive Board agreed to provide Contingent Credit Lines (CCL) only to member countries with strong economic policies as a precautionary line of defense against future balance of payments problems that might arise from international financial contagion. Countries apply in advance for pre-qualification The CCL provides short-term financing to overcome balance of payments difficulties "that can arise from a sudden and disruptive loss of market confidence due to contagion, that is, circumstances that are largely beyond the member's control and stem primarily from adverse developments in international capital markets consequent upon developments in other countries." International Monetary Fund, *IMF Tightens Defenses Against Financial Contagion by Establishing Contingent Credit Lines,* April 25, 1999. In September 2000, the IMF adopted changes to its CCL program after noting that no country has used its program. The IMF lowered the intensity of monitoring arrangements used to assure the strong economic policies requirement, made the availability of resources in a crisis more automatic, and reduced the rate of charge. The initial surcharge was reduced from 300 to 150 basis points, and then rise over time to 350 basis points. International Monetary fund, *IMF Board Agrees on Changes to Fund Financial Facilities,* September 18, 2000. But as of late 2001, still no country had applied for pre-qualification. Doing so might be regarded as a signal that a country expects its currency to be attacked. M. Feldstein, *Economic and Financial Crises in Emerging Market Economies: Overview of Prevention and Management,* NBER Working Paper 8837 (March 2002).

Treasury Secretary Summers in a *Statement to the International Monetary and Financial Committee,* April 16, 2000, set forth the U.S. agenda for Fund reform. He proposed that all Fund lending in the future should be based on the principle that charges should escalate the longer countries have Fund money outstanding. In addition, he proposed that the CCL be clearly reserved for financing before a crisis and that its price be decreased, and that the commitment fee be dropped because "there is a tension between charging a commitment fee for an instrument that is most successful if it is not activated, and reimbursing the fee if the instrument is activated." Also, he thought it should be clear that countries that have committed to a specific policy program with regular performance reviews, and have fulfilled those commitments, be able to draw on the CCL.

Reiterating his preference for shorter term lending, Summers advocated reserving use of the EFF, the Extended Financing Facility for longer term lending, for countries requiring bold structural reforms like lower-income transition countries.

Summers went on to suggest the following operational guidelines for debt rescheduling:

> [I]ts programs should put strong emphasis on medium-term financial sustainability, and aim to strike an appropriate balance between the contributions of official external creditors, including the IFIs, and private external creditors. The IMF should encourage the country to aim for balance in treatment of different classes of private creditors, and to involve all classes of material creditors. The Fund should not micromanage the details of any debt restructuring or debt reduction negotiations. Rather, the IMF should underline the possible consequences to the country of

any failure to secure the necessary contribution from private creditors on appropriate terms. These could include the need for a program revision to provide for additional adjustment by the country concerned or the option of reduced official financing. And finally, the IMF should be prepared to lend into arrears if a country has suspended payments but is seeking to work cooperatively and in good faith with its private sector creditors and is meeting other program requirements.

On the other hand, the Geneva based International Centre for Monetary and Banking Studies proposed in September 1999 that the Executive Board that runs the Fund should be made independent with directors given long terms of office and forbidden from taking instructions from the governments that appointed them. They specifically criticized U.S. government pressure that led to the 1998 loan to Russia despite the fact that the country could not comply with IMF conditions.

Notes and Questions

1. What justifications are there for the IMF lending money to countries before there is a reduction in or at least a rescheduling of debt on concessionary terms? Is moral hazard a serious concern given that in most cases creditors or investors have lost money?

2. The CFR study envisions preventing IMF lending until there is a plan for reducing or rescheduling existing debt and this would be accomplished by having a 30-60 days payments standstill, a measure that would play a key role in the discussion of an international bankruptcy system which follows. Will this work?

3. Can the lending activities of the IMF be rationalized as part of the need for an international lender of last resort? C. Goodhart and H. Huang, *A Simple Model of an International Lender of Last Resort,* IMF Working Paper/00/75 (April 2000), argue that it is the fragility of the world's banking system and the limited ability of a domestic central bank to provide international liquidity that causes currency crisis, which further triggers a banking crisis. While the international banking market can supply liquidity this comes at the cost of international financial contagion. The international lender of last resort (ILLR) could supply the liquidity without the risk of contagion. But the IMF does not have the unlimited resources, the hallmark of domestic central banks. Could the IMF role in lending to Korea during the Asian crisis or to Mexico in the 1994 Peso Crisis, or to Russia in 1998, be justified as fulfilling its role as lender of last resort? Are all crises liquidity crises?

Anna Schwartz has proposed abolishing the IMF entirely, *Time to Terminate the ESF and the IMF* (August 26, 1998). Schwartz observes that it is no longer serving its original purpose, to defend fixed-exchange rates, and has tried to become an ILLR. In her view, it cannot serve this function because it cannot create high-powered money, bank reserves, and that its official resources are limited. In her view, the power to make loans to foreign governments should belong to Congress and not to an international organization. Further, she argues that the IMF is not lending to solvent borrowers, as is required for an ILLR., as evidenced in the Korean crisis where it bailed out insolvent Korean banks.

4. What would be the impact of limiting IMF long-term lending and reducing the size of such lending? Would this help remedy the moral hazard problem? Would it improve debtor country economic policies? Would it reduce the likelihood of financial crises?

5. What will be accomplished by having the charge for IMF lending go up as the maturity of the loan increases? Will this reduce borrowing from the IMF?

6. Do you agree with the Summers criticism of the Meltzer Commission? Would it put a straightjacket on responses to financial crises, or would it just put the straightjacket on the IMF?

7. In the Latin debt crisis in the '80s, debtor countries led the charge for debt moratoria and forgiveness. The only Asian country to raise such suggestions in the Asian crisis was Indonesia. Why didn't South Korea and Thailand do so?

8. Before the Asian crisis, the IMF had a formal policy of not lending into arrears—it would not lend money to a country that had defaulted and was thus in arrears. Of course, what was actually a "default" was open to interpretation. This made IMF assistance conditional on the absence of default. That policy has now been changed, the Board of the Fund having decided that it would lend into arrears on a case-by-case basis. International Monetary Fund, *A Guide to Progress in Strengthening the Architecture of the International Financial System,* April 28, 1999. Is this a good change?

B. THE MODIFICATION OF BOND CLAUSES

One important issue in the IFA discussion is whether bond clauses should be modified to facilitate rescheduling. An increasing part of cross-border debt is held in the form of bonds rather than loans. Dealing with bondholders in the case of a financial crises is much more difficult than dealing with a much smaller group of lenders with a long history of experience and collaboration in dealing with debt crises. Moreover, lenders are much more subject to moral suasion with regard to debt restructuring.

The difficulties of restructuring bond debt are likely to be greater with American-style international bonds, the most prevalent style of bonds issued by emerging market countries. Such instruments, unlike British-style bonds, do not include provisions for qualified majorities, e.g.

75%, to modify the terms of the bond, to impose such modifications on bondholders, and to limit the initiation of litigation, e.g. to grab debtor assets. British-style bonds do permit a qualified majority of bondholders to modify bond terms, and they require that all litigation be brought by the trustee, acting upon a direction from bondholders, typically holders of 25 percent of principal. Litigation through a trustee results in sharing. This limitation on initiating suits prevents creditors with small exposures from suing on their own. An excellent discussion on bond issues is contained in International Monetary Fund, Policy Development and Review Department, *Involving the Private Sector in Forestalling and Resolving Financial Crises* 47-64 (1999).

The IMF is encouraging sovereigns to move toward British-style bonds but the market has as yet shown no interest. The G-7 is considering issuing their own British-style bonds as a demonstration effect. Some argue that the presence of such clauses would make it easier for countries to wiggle out of their contracts and thus would increase borrowing costs. Others point to the adverse signaling effect of inclusion of British clauses. See B. Eichengreen, *Toward a New Financial Architecture* 65-70 (1999). In any event, such clauses could only be inserted in newly issued bonds, and would thus have little impact for years to come since most bonds would contain the old American–style covenants.

Absent an agreement of bondholders to reschedule, whether under a unanimity or qualified majority rule, all is not lost for the debtor country. A restructuring of the bonds can be achieved through an exchange offer under which the debtor may try to make new bonds more attractive than old ones through higher interest rates or by declaring that new bonds would have priority for payment. Such exchange offers were made in the case of Pakistan in 1999 and the Ukraine in 2000. Thus, in the Pakistan exchange, the government announced that it "does not propose to make any offers to holders of the Existing Notes other than this Exchange Offer. Accordingly, the Republic does not propose to settle amounts due under Existing Notes with holders who do not participate in the Exchange Offer on terms which are more favourable than those contained in the Exchange Offer." The Islamic Republic of Pakistan, Offer to Exchange U.S. Dollar 10 per cent Notes due 2002/2005, Offering Memorandum dated November 15, 1999, at A-5, as cited in L. Buchheit and G. Gulati, *Exit Consents in Sovereign Bond Exchanges*, 48 UCLA Law Review 59 (2000). As Buchheit and Gulati point out, however, this may cause old bondholders to accelerate unmatured principal, which usually only requires a vote of 25% of the bondholders, and cause litigation.

Once bonds are amended, non-tendering bondholders, sometimes referred to as rogue creditors, can sue to collect the bonds. In the worst case this could cause the old bondholders to attach the stream of payments due on the new bonds and divert those funds to the accelerated payout of the old bonds. They propose a solution to this problem by amending the old bonds to make them unattractive to those who remain behind, i.e. by precluding acceleration or waivers of sovereign immunity. The bondholders who agree to the exchange would consent to the amendment, a so-called exit consent, just before tendering their old bonds for new ones. Their incentive to do so would be to protect their claims on new bonds against claims of old bondholders. They argue that such exit consents have withstood legal challenge in New York. Exit amendments cannot change provisions in bonds requiring unanimous consent of all bondholders. Typically this includes the amount and date of payments, and currency of such payments. Id., at n.79, p. 80. Other clauses, such as waiver of sovereign immunity or consent to jurisdiction could be changed. It would not appear that an exit amendment could preclude "rogue" creditors suing to collect on old bonds because this would be inconsistent with the unanimous consent required to alter payment terms.

Another issue in bond contracts is whether they should contain sharing clauses like syndicated loans which would require any person receiving payment to share the proceeds pro-rata with all other bondholders. The prospect of suing an issuer only to turn over any monetary recovery to other bondholders might deter such litigation in the first place, making it easier for the issuer to restructure the bonds. This would also deter "vultures" from buying distressed bonds with the idea of bringing such litigation. Despite their popularity in the loan market such sharing clauses are not customary for bonds.

Creditors fear such sharing clauses, like majority action clauses, may make it easier for debtors to default, and debtors fear requiring such clauses might increase interest rates on their borrowings. B. Eichengreen and A. Mody, *Would Collective Action Clauses Raise Borrowing Costs?*, National Bureau of Economic Research, Working Paper No. 7458 (January 2000), found that clauses facilitating collective action in fact reduced borrowing costs for the most creditworthy issuers, who benefit from being able to have an orderly restructuring. This may be because an orderly restructuring minimizes acrimonious disputes, unproductive negotiations and extended periods when no debt service is paid and growth is depressed by debt overhang. Id., at 2. They also found, however, that for less creditworthy issuers, the opposite seemed true. The authors conjecture this was because the advantages of orderly restructuring were offset "by the moral hazard and default risk associated with the presence of renegotiation-friendly loan provisions." Id., at 3. However, T. Becker, A. Richards and Y. Thaicharoen, *Bond Restructuring and Moral Hazard: Are Collective Action Clauses Costly,* Working Paper, August 2001, have found that collective action clauses do not increase yields for either higher or lower-rated issuers. A major difference in methodology between the two studies is whether to consider the choice of clauses by sovereigns to be endogenous, meaning that borrowers that anticipate having to restructure choose the English law majority action clauses and those that do not chose the U.S. unanimous consent clauses. Eichengreen and Mody believe this happens and design their methodology accordingly. Becker et. al do not.

Notes and Questions

1. Would you favor making clauses facilitating collective action mandatory in sovereign debt issues?

2. Are exit amendments a better solution than collective action clauses?

C. An International Bankruptcy System

The following study was written after the Mexican crisis of 1995.

B. EICHENGREEN AND R. PORTES, CRISIS? WHAT CRISIS? ORDERLY WORKOUTS FOR SOVEREIGN DEBTORS
Centre for Economic Policy Research, pp. 28-54 (1995).

4.2.1   Defining property rights and their enforcement

In contrast to the position of a private company where all its assets will usually be available to creditors, for several reasons only a very small proportion of a state's assets will be available for execution. Most of the country's assets will be located in its own territory and may therefore be beyond the reach of any court or tribunal. Exports can be transferred to private (third-country) owners before they leave the debtor state's borders. Foreign courts will only allow the creditor's rights to be enforced against the debtor if property rights are clearly defined in the debtor's jurisdiction. While the debtor state may have some assets within the jurisdiction of the courts in another country, it is frequently very difficult to levy execution against such assets, because of the law of sovereign immunity. Although most states no longer accord sovereign immunity from suit in an action in respect of a loan transaction or other debt instrument, states still enjoy a wide immunity from execution against their property. Unless the state has waived that immunity or the property is clearly in use for commercial purposes, execution or prejudgment attachment will not be available in most jurisdictions.

The United States Foreign Sovereign Immunities Act, Section 1610(a)(2), goes further and precludes execution even against commercial property unless it has a connection with the subject matter of the action against the foreign state (a requirement which also features in a draft convention produced by the International Law Commission). Embassy bank accounts in most states and the treatment of central bank accounts varies (though in the United Kingdom such accounts enjoy absolute immunity). Even if immunity has been waived in respect of state property, property in the hands of separate legal entities will not be liable to execution in respect of obligations entered into by the state unless the forum state can be persuaded to lift the corporate veil.

. . .

4.6   An international bankruptcy court or tribunal

. . .

Supervising the negotiation of a reorganization plan would not be within the power of the International Court of Justice, for example, which has jurisdiction only over cases between states, not between a state and private parties (such as private foreign creditors). This has led to proposals (for example Sachs, 1995; Greenwood and Mercer, 1995) for the creation of an international arbitral tribunal with jurisdiction over debt disputes between states or between states and private creditors, possibly as an agency of the International Monetary Fund.

Creation of the tribunal, funding for its operations and binding status for its determination could be provided by an international treaty or by an amendment to the IMF Articles of Agreement. Alternatively, the tribunal could be a self-standing entity independent of the Fund, possibly relying on staff support from it or another multilateral institution. There are two issues here. One is whether implementation is feasible: whether such a tribunal could override national laws, whether it could act in binding arbitration, or whether it would be limited to coordination, conciliation and advice.

. . .

The tribunal would then help creditors and the debtor to negotiate a debt restructuring. Were the IMF given this role, it would proceed under authority vested in it by Article V(2)(b), which empowers the IMF to perform financial and technical services if authorized to do so by its members. The process would involve examining the economic and financial situation of the country, the stance of policy and the state of the international financial markets. The relevant officials would consult with representatives of the creditors, perhaps encouraging the establishment of a creditors' representative committee. The plan would entail reorganization of the debt and policy adjustments by the debtor government. It would come into operation if approved by the debtor government and a majority (perhaps qualified) of creditors. The facility or tribunal could have the power to cram down generally agreed settlement terms. The plan might entail agreement by the creditors to provide new money, although this would be difficult to enforce where the governments's liabilities take the form of bonded debt.   This provides a rationale for empowering the facility to grant seniority to new funds and/or inject new money of its own.

There are several distinctions that might delineate the scope of such a tribunal: type of debt instrument (bond or bank loan); residence of lender; 'proper law' of the debt contract; currency of denomination of the debt (domestic or foreign). A key question is whether limits on recourse and the decisions of the tribunal should apply to domestic as well as foreign creditors. Many of the inefficiencies that these institutions are designed to avert can arise equally from the actions of domestic and foreign residents. Both can and do hold the foreign-currency liabilities of governments, and the actions of both classes of creditor have the capacity to provoke a run on official reserves. In the recent Mexican crisis, for example, much of the flight from government debt appears to have been on the part of Mexican residents. Any attempt to expand differential treatment to domestic and foreign creditors would open the door to all manner of circumvention, with one group employing the other as its surrogate.

To produce an effective standstill and impose an effective reorganization plan, the jurisdiction of the tribunal might therefore have to apply equally to domestic and foreign investors. Which government liabilities would fall under the jurisdiction of the tribunal would be for the government and its creditors to decide when specifying the terms of the loan agreement; a government could always exclude such clauses from the contracts underlying its domestic currency liabilities. If the right of recourse of dissident creditors to the tribunal were specified in the original bond covenant, as described above, this would not pose obvious problems.

How would the activities of such a tribunal differ from existing IMF procedures for dealing with countries in financial distress? First, allowing the tribunal to invoke the standstill would deal with the 'verification problem' and thereby mitigate the damage to the country's reputation of the suspension of debt service payments. Reputation will be preserved only if the markets believe that financial distress was not the debtor's 'fault'; but then the contingency responsible for the crisis must be independently verifiable. The theory of 'escape clauses' suggests that measures of this sort can be invoked without damage to a government's reputation only when the contingency in response to which they are utilized is independently verifiable. The difficulty of verification explains why governments have been reluctant to employ unilateral suspensions in practice.

To the extent that the problem was judged to be the debtor's fault, of course, a standstill might still be justifiable, but then the debtor's reputation *should* suffer. Independent endorsement of a standstill could also limit contagion to other countries and other assets, in so far as the tribunal could point out the specific circumstances that warranted suspension of service on a class of obligations of a given debtor. The moral hazard - the 'strategic' use of a standstill to pressure creditors - would be limited by the possibility that it would not be approved.

Under the tribunal proposal, this body would assume the role of 'referee' more directly than the IMF does currently. Binding status for its determinations would eliminate the problem of 'holdout' by a minority of creditors. An ability to assign seniority to new funds would diminish problems of illiquidity. Alternatively, a tribunal which worked in concert with the IMF could ameliorate the problem of injecting new money directly.

To limit moral hazard and improve *ex-ante* efficiency might require strengthening the powers of the IMF, by allowing it to impose stronger policy conditionality on governments in return for allowing them to make use of the binding arbitration powers of the tribunal. It might be provided that only countries which had met IMF conditionality *ex ante* could have recourse to this binding arbitration *ex post*. This assumes that the IMF would be able to avoid the obvious time inconsistency problem. Though it would be in its interest to announce that binding arbitration would be extended only to countries that had met its conditionality, after the fact it might have every incentive to make an exception, which would weaken the incentive for countries to satisfy its conditions in the first place.

The tribunal would not possess the powers of a national court to enforce seizure of collateral, given sovereign immunity. Granting seniority to new money would require a treaty agreed between debtor and creditor nations which would then have to be implemented in national law. (Alternatively, this could be provided for by agreement in advance as part of the loan agreement or bond covenant, as described in section 4.2 above.) Creating an arbitral tribunal with the power to require dissident creditors to accept a majority-approved restructuring would require an international treaty.

.   .   .

Securing the support of creditor-country governments would not be straightforward either. The industrial countries might be reluctant to participate if doing so raised the possibility that they might be forced to surrender significant independence. In principle, there is no reason why such procedures should be limited to developing countries. Given the amounts of money involved, it can be argued that it is potentially more important for the international community to consider ways of providing 'orderly workouts' in the developed world. But it is not clear that the governments of high-income countries would see a need to subject themselves to the authority of the tribunal. Allowing some countries to announce that they were prepared to participate only as creditors, however, would threaten to label the others as second-class citizens in the eyes of the capital markets.

There has been much debate about the idea of adopting some form of an international bankruptcy system. A main feature of such a system is the automatic stay, which prevents creditors from bringing actions to collect their debts, including foreclosures on assets. Those favoring bailouts have justified them on the basis of the difficulty in preventing creditors from engaging in a race to grab the debtor country's assets. Stanley Fisher, *Mechanism Must be Found to Avoid Moral Hazard in Crises, IMF Deputy Says,* 69 Banking Report 623, October 20, 1997. This might include official reserves held outside the country or new borrowed funds flowing into the country. See M. Miller and L. Zhang, *Sovereign Liquidity Crises: The Strategic Case for a Payments Standstill,* Discussion Paper No. 1820 (Centre for Economic Policy Research 1998), p. 4. Such seizures would presumably arise because no court or international tribunal could prevent them. This has led those opposing bailouts to favor the bankruptcy process on the theory the protection of debtor assets will make bailouts less necessary. However, it is far from clear that seizure of assets is a significant problem at all, given the small percentage of sovereign assets outside the debtor country. While the sovereign may be the shareholder of companies with significant assets outside the country, e.g. state owned airlines, these assets would not ordinarily be available to satisfy sovereign debts through the normal operation of limited liability principles.

Most advocates of an international bankruptcy process believe that it would help reduce bailouts and therefore moral hazard. For example, Jeffrey Sachs has argued that a system facilitating debtor defaults through an orderly bankruptcy process would be an alternative to the current IMF lending process, that is if debtors could have orderly defaults IMF lending would not be necessary. *Do We Need an International Lender of Last Resort,* Frank D. Graham Lecture, Princeton University, April 20, 1995. An interesting variant of this view is put forward by E. Fernandez-Arias and R. Hausmann, *The Redesign of the International Financial Architecture from a Latin American Perspective: Who Pays the Bill,* Inter-American Development Bank, Research Department, Working Paper 440 (December 2000) (Arias and Hausmann).

These authors generally oppose a system in which private sector involvement (PSI), e.g. debt reduction or rescheduling, is imposed before public assistance is given. They argue that this requires the private sector to participate in a non-existing program, delays help, while the country situation deteriorates, until an accommodation with the private sector can be reached, and that public support may be necessary for private debt reduction, as with the Brady Plan. Moreover, they argue that under forced PSI, governments would be less likely to call in the IMF because this would cause the private sector to withdraw funds before debt reduction or rescheduling was imposed.

The authors, however, state "we favor the alternative in which official support is ample and PSI is demanded only when necessary, and then in a way in which the burden is shared according to clear rules not subject to abuse. This mechanism would define a standard of 'excusable default' that would ensure flexibility when needed. An international bankruptcy court, for example, would fit this characterization. In that case, under insolvency conditions PSI would kick in according to international law, coordinated and supplemented by official support. . . . This court would authorize domestic borrowers not to repay when the country is deemed unable, rather than simply unwilling, to pay. . . .By transferring the power to authorize nonpayment to an independent court that does not have a willingness-to-pay problem, this arrangement provides more flexibility while keeping sovereign risk under control."

The debate over the need for sovereign bankruptcy procedures greatly accelerated in late November 2001 after a speech by Anne Krueger, the new First Deputy Managing Director of the International Monetary Fund (the number two position), *International Financial Architecture for 2002: A New Approach to Sovereign Debt Restructuring,* November 26, 2001. This was later refined some four months later, *New Approaches to Sovereign Debt Restructuring: An Update on our Thinking*, April 1, 2002. The major change in the interim was to lessen the role of the IMF in the process and to increase the control of creditors.

Krueger's proposal has the following elements. First, the sovereign debtor would be protected against legal actions after a suspension of payments by a stay of fixed duration but potentially renewable. Initially, the IMF would determine whether to trigger the stay, but later it would be left to a majority vote of creditors. It is unclear what criteria the IMF would use to grant the stay. Krueger rejects the alternative of giving the debtor the unilateral right to declare a stay on the ground that "this would clearly be open to abuse."

Second, the process would only continue if the debtor was negotiating in good faith and protecting creditor interests, and if it was adopting appropriate economic policies. The creditors would judge the first for themselves. The issue of appropriate economic policies would apparently be left to the judgment of the IMF.

Third, new private financing would be encouraged. A super-majority of creditors would be given the power to subordinate the claims of all private creditors to claims arising after the stay took effect.

Fourth, approval of the final restructuring agreement would be left to a super-majority of creditors but the decision "would clearly be influenced by the Fund's assessment of whether the terms of the agreement adequately reduce the debt burden to a sustainable level." If they did not, the Fund would withhold further financing.

Fifth, all creditors would be bound by the final restructuring agreement, thus ending the threat from rogue creditors.

Krueger envisioned the need to create an independent judicial organ, insulated from the IMF staff and management "to adjudicate disputes and oversee voting." What this means exactly is unclear.

When the proposal was first put forward in November 2001, it appeared it might receive immediate support from the Bush Treasury; but that did not happen. In the same week in April 2002 that Krueger put forward her modified proposals, John Taylor, the Undersecretary of the Treasury for International Affairs, rejected this proposal in favor of the adoption of contractual approach, the use of majority-action bond clauses. J. Taylor, *Sovereign Debt Restructuring: A U.S. Perspective,* Remarks at a conference on "Sovereign Debt Workouts: Hopes and Hazards," Institute for International Economics, April 2, 2002. However, later that month Secretary of the Treasury O'Neill indicated that the Bush Administration supported bond clause modifications in the short-run, but wanted to pursue exploration of the IMF proposal for the longer term. Statement of Treasury Secretary Paul H. O'Neill at the International Monetary and Financial Committee Meeting (IMF policy committee), April 20, 2002. See also Paul Martin, Canadian Finance Minister, *There's a better way,* May 8, 2002, indicating that the G7 finance ministers support the IMF initiative: "[e]stablishing a structure analogous to an international bankruptcy court is the ultimate answer, and we must work toward it."

Creditors still oppose the idea. The Institute of International Finance (IIF), which is a major international creditors group, has alternatively proposed: (1) establishing a consultative mechanism for restructurings; (2) using collective action clauses in bonds; and (3) designing a targeted legal action to address vulture funds (e.g. the *Elliott* problem). Letter from Charles H. Dallara, Managing Director of IIF, to The Honorable Gordon Brown (English Chancellor of the Exchequer), Chairman of the International Monetary and Financial Committee, April 9, 2002. Brown has taken IIF up on their vulture fund proposal by asking officials in England to draw up measures to restrain them. R. Bennett, *Crackdown on 'vulture funds' proposed by finance minister,* Financial Times, May 6, 2002.

Consider the following.

H. SCOTT, WHAT PROBLEMS IS A NEW INTERNATIONAL BANKRUPTCY REGIME DESIGNED TO SOLVE?

Discussion Paper for "A Bankruptcy Court for Sovereign Debt," Brookings Panel on Economic Activity, April 4-5, 2002

A key issue in the debate over reform of the international financial system is whether to adopt a new international bankruptcy regime for sovereign debt, and an important aspect of that debate is the lack of consensus about the problems that such a regime would be designed to solve and whether it would solve them. My remarks are focused on a new bankruptcy regime rather than a new court, because the former does not necessarily entail the latter. The authors of the three papers in this symposium all have quite different conceptions of the problems, as do other important protagonists.

Bulow's paper, like his past articles on this subject, is focused on the need to reduce bailouts of developing-country debt by International Financial Institutions (IFIs) and governments in the industrial countries, so as to achieve more optimal flows of private capital to emerging markets. Sachs' paper sees two different roles for the bankruptcy process: avoiding a creditor grab race for the sovereign debtor's assets, and giving the sovereign debtor a new start by substantially reducing its debt. White's paper mainly addresses two objectives that differ from both Bulow's and Sachs', preventing rogue creditors from upsetting private debt reorderings and making sure defaulting countries have adequate sources of funds, through granting seniority to creditors who lend in the wake of a default. The U.S. Treasury, in the form of John Taylor's statement during the same week as this conference, has yet a different objective. He wants to reduce the uncertainty of the current process by providing a more orderly structure for resolving crises when they occur. Finally, the purpose of the IMF proposal offered by Anne Krueger is more encompassing. In her proposal last November she said her "aim is to create a catalyst that will encourage debtors and creditors to come together to restructure unsustainable debts in a timely and efficient manner."

Krueger's latest proposal for a sovereign debt restructuring mechanism (SDRM) contains the following elements: a stay for some fixed duration on creditors' seizure of a troubled debtor's assets, reform of the debtor's economic policies as part of the bankruptcy plan, seniority for creditors who lend after the petition for a stay, and a mechanism enabling a supermajority of creditors to bind other creditors to a plan. How does this proposal relate to the objectives identified by Krueger herself, Taylor, and the others?

The relationship between Krueger's SDRM and reducing bailouts is not clear. One could argue that this objective could be achieved more directly than through adoption of an SDRM, by placing restraints on crisis lending by the IFIs. This could be done in a variety of ways. Under the proposal by Adam Lerrick and Allan Meltzer, IMF support would be limited to a commitment to buy the debt of defaulting sovereigns at some discount from the price being offered by the sovereign. Under a proposal offered jointly by the Bank of Canada and the Bank of England, there would be procedures like those adopted in the United States in 1991 under the Federal Deposit Insurance Corporation Improvement Act for official lending to failed banks. Lending would only be permitted when there is a threat to the stability of the international monetary system and only after approval by a supermajority of the IMF's executive board.

Krueger's proposal for an SDRM addresses the bailout problem more indirectly. The idea is that pressure for IMF lending would be lessened if the SDRM offered a mechanism by which a troubled sovereign debtor and its creditors could reach an agreement to reduce the sovereign's debt. One reason that IMF lending has been so prevalent is that there is no workable mechanism for reducing debt. Indeed, the argument would be that the IMF could not risk the chaos, economic and political, that might ensue in the absence of its lending unless an alternative debt reduction process were in place. Of course, in the short term, this is proving wrong in Argentina. One can just say no, without an SDRM. One wonders how long such a policy would be sustainable, however.

Even if an SDRM existed, nothing would ensure its use, at least under the current versions of the proposal. A country would *choose* to use the procedure, and then would be permitted to do so only if it met some threshold test of insolvency, in the sense that it was unable to service its debt. A country could well choose not to use the procedure even though to do so offered the prospect of cutting its debt burden. It might fear being cut off from market access in the future and prefer to solve the problem through a bailout. And, as the Argentine case currently illustrates, as do the examples of Ecuador and Russia in the 1990s as well as the Latin American crises in the early 1980s, a country does not need an SDRM to default and restructure its debt. Thus the proposed SDRM will lead to increased debt reduction and fewer bailouts only if sovereigns prefer that outcome. Most heavily indebted poor countries will, but what about countries like Brazil, Korea, or Turkey?

Is a bankruptcy procedure necessary to avoid the rush to seize a sovereign's assets when the sovereign defaults, as Sachs has contended? This depends at the outset on how exposed the sovereign's assets are to such seizure. There is little empirical evidence that this is a serious problem. Sovereign default should not put at risk the assets of state enterprises, such as state-owned airlines, because these are separate entities from the sovereign. It is unlikely that these assets would be collapsible into those of the sovereign as a matter of course. Certain assets, like those of the central bank, enjoy absolute immunity, that is, immunity that cannot be waived. Nonetheless, the creditor grab race remains a concern. A stay, if binding on all countries, would prevent the seizure of sovereign assets once a default occurred.

Is a bankruptcy procedure necessary to bind rogue creditors? White does not think so. She, like Taylor, thinks this could be done through the use of U.K. style collective action clauses in which a supermajority of creditors could bind all others. The problem is that such clauses have not been adopted, probably because of the increased cost of issuing bonds that have them. As Taylor has suggested, this problem could be overcome by requiring such clauses as a condition for IMF programs or by subsidizing such clauses through lower IMF charges for borrowing. But this would not solve the problem of outstanding bonds without such clauses.

Some have argued that majority action clauses are really not necessary given the alternative possibility of using exit consents. Under this technique, as used in conjunction with an exchange offer as in Ecuador, those tendering the old bonds vote to poison them by changing all of their nonpayment terms (payment terms themselves on bonds issued under New York law cannot be changed without unanimous consent). For example, the tendering creditors could vote to retract any waivers of sovereign immunity or to prohibit the bonds from being listed, thus making them much less attractive to hold. But although this might increase the tender rate, the vulture creditor looking to realize the face value of the old bond would still hold the bond and sue. And the prospect of finding sovereign assets to attach to satisfy such judgments is significant. This is the lesson of the case involving Elliott Associates and Peru, where vulture creditors refused to tender old bonds for new Brady bonds, and then, in an action in a Brussels court, attached interest payments that were to be made on the Brady bonds through Euroclear system. Peru's decision to settle this claim makes future actions of this kind more likely.

Bulow thinks the problem could be addressed by the United States repealing the Foreign Sovereign Immunities Act of 1976 (FSIA), and that other countries should similarly repeal their foreign sovereign immunity acts. The idea is that the FSIA is bad because it permits creditors to seize sovereign assets in the United States in satisfaction of their claims. This is far from clear. The FSIA does permit creditors to seize nonexempt assets in connection with commercial activity of the sovereign, and the Supreme Court has held, in *Republic of Argentina* v. *Weltover*, that issuance of a bond constitutes a commercial activity. But it does not follow that creditors would have no remedies in the absence of the FSIA. In its absence, the jurisdiction of U.S. courts would be determined by international law, which generally itself provides a commercial activity exception to sovereign immunity. This exception could only be eliminated by international agreement. So neither exit consents nor repeals of sovereign immunity provisions are likely to solve the problem of rogue creditors.

We are therefore back to majority action clauses, but the problem remains that today's outstanding bonds do not have these clauses. Furthermore, as Krueger points out, even if these clauses existed in all *bonds*, "a country with an unsustainable debt burden will require a comprehensive restructuring across a broad range of indebtedness, potentially including different bonds issued under different jurisdictions, bank loans, trade credits, and some official claims." This is a fundamental point. The very existence of corporate bankruptcy laws responds to the collective action problem in trying to provide such a process through private contract. Although Alan Schwartz has argued that the state should permit parties to contract for the corporate bankruptcy system they prefer, such contracting would take place against a default system of law, in the shadow of the law. Such a default is missing in Taylor's exclusive reliance on private contract.

Is a bankruptcy procedure necessary to ensure the continued flow of funds to defaulting debtors, as White contends? Not if the lender providing new financing enjoys seniority, as the IMF clearly does, and as do all official creditors to a degree. But if we are seeking to minimize assistance from governmental institutions, it is necessary to ensure seniority for private postdefault creditors. This would be impossible to achieve through subordination agreements, because preexisting creditors are unlikely to agree to subordination without substantial compensation, and the transactions costs of subordination negotiations would be high. Thus seniority for new money could only be ensured through some international agreement, which could be part of a new SDRM.

To conclude, I believe it is relatively clear that private contracting alone will not be able to achieve the various objectives I have examined, although it can play an important role, particularly in the shadow of a default rule. I think we should focus in the future on issues of implementation of an SDRM, such as who will administer this procedure, what types of debt should be covered, whether any creditors should enjoy seniority, and how the "plan" of reorganization with respect to the sovereign's future economic policies should be handled. Whatever procedure is adopted must, however, be flexible and responsive to the political and foreign policy concerns of creditor governments. In the pinch, and perhaps more often, one must be able to override the SDRM. This counsels against entrusting authority to any independent court, as Krueger's latest proposal suggests, at least if the jurisdiction of the court cannot be restrained where necessary.

The black hole in the SDRM proposal is: What happens to the debt if, even with majority voting rules, the sovereign and its creditors cannot agree on a plan? Liquidation is not a practical alternative. Corporate cramdown, as White points out, is judged against a liquidation benchmark—all classes of creditors must get what they would have received in liquidation. Like liquidation itself, this benchmark is unavailable for sovereign bankruptcies.

One solution might be to require that bankruptcy creditors get no less in bankruptcy than the their debt would be worth absent bankruptcy. The market would be able to value newly issued debt. However, one could probably not rely on the actual market value of the old debt to make a determination of what creditors would receive absent bankruptcy (assuming there was a market in the instrument) because that value might be heavily influenced by expectations of what would happen in bankruptcy. One might look, however, to valuation models to determine what the debt was worth.

Finally, it is unlikely that politics would permit private creditors to impose an economic plan on the debtor, as in corporate bankruptcy. This suggests that the debtor's interlocutor about future economic plans be the IMF, with input, as at present, from the private creditors.

Notes and Questions

1. Article VIII Section 2(b) of the IMF Articles of Agreement provides: "Exchange contracts which involve the currency of any member and which are contrary to the exchange control regulations of that member maintained or imposed consistently with this Agreement shall be unenforceable in the territories of any member. In addition, members may, by mutual accord, cooperate in measures for the purpose of making the exchange control regulations of either member more effective, provided that such measures and regulations are consistent with this Agreement." Later in this Chapter we will look at a package of reforms, backed by the G-7 countries, to strengthen the "architecture" of the international financial system. One proposal would amend this article to provide for the imposition of stays on creditor litigation to facilitate an orderly sovereign debt renegotiation. Presumably such an amendment would create a binding international rule, but who would have the power to impose the stay, a debtor country, a court of a debtor country, or the IMF? Could one create a new international bankruptcy court through an amendment to Article VIII Section 2(b)?

2. Some argue that a stay against creditors would be a bad idea because it would make it easier for debtor countries to default. Institute of International Finance, *Involving the Private Sector in Resolution of Financial Crises in Emerging Markets* (April 1999). But absent an IMF bailout, a debtor may have no choice but to default when foreign reserves dry up. Application of the stay insures fairness among creditors and facilitates debtor reorganization once default becomes inevitable. For a general approach to using bankruptcy laws for sovereign debt, see S. Schwarcz, *Sovereign Debt Restructuring: A Bankruptcy Reorganization Approach,* 85 Cornell L. Rev. 956 (2000).

3. The causes of the Korea and Thailand crises in 1997 were not sovereign debt crises, but banking crises. Local banks were unable to repay foreign bank creditors on short-term loans because the countries ran our of foreign exchange reserves. Should such banking crises be subject to similar bankruptcy procedures as sovereign debt crises, or could these problems be handled by local bankruptcy laws? Note that most countries, like the United States, do not subject local banks to the bankruptcy laws that apply to other companies.

4. Arias and Hausmann, for example, seem to suggest that only insolvent country debtors be permitted to use a bankruptcy process, probably because they believe that if such a procedure were more generally available countries would abuse it. But in what sense can a country ever become insolvent? Most countries, certainly those involved in the Asian crisis, were not insolvent. They could have obtained the necessary resources to service debt through increased taxation and reduced spending. Given this fact, should they be allowed to default, or go into any form of bankruptcy procedure? Arias and Hausmann fear

abuse but couldn't the market discipline such abuse by withdrawing funds, or charging hefty premiums, in the future?

Note that in the U.S. a company can declare bankruptcy without demonstrating it is insolvent. Of course, the result may be a liquidation, a remedy one can hardly envision applying to a country. Note also that in Chapter 11 reorganizations, creditors obtain substantial leverage because the failure to approve a plan can push the debtor back into a Chapter 7 liquidation. Again, this is not possible with sovereigns. Does this mean the Chapter 11 analogy does not work for sovereigns? Also, given the reluctance of sovereigns to default, would any country make use of Chapter 11?

5. A key feature of the U.S. bankruptcy system is that new post-petition loans gets priority over old debt. As applied to sovereigns, would this priority give sufficient incentives to new lenders so as to avoid IMF or other governmental lending?

6. The decision of the Court of Appeals of Brussels in *LP Elliott Associates,* General Docket No. 2000/QR/92, September 26, 2000, was rendered ex parte. It was based in large part on the interpretation of a *pari passu* clause in a guaranty by Peru of the existing bonds, as offered in a supporting affidavit by Professor Andreas Lowenfeld of New York University School of Law. The guaranty provided that "the obligations of the Guarantor hereunder do rank and will rank at least *pari passu* in priority of payment with all other External Indebtedness of the Guarantor, and interest thereon. Lowenfeld claimed, and the court accepted, that the clause meant that payments on the new bonds could not have priority over payments on the old bonds. This meant that the payments on the old bonds had to be made if any payments were to be made on the new Brady bonds. This interpretation has been hotly contested. M. Gulati and K. Klee, *Sovereign Piracy,* 56 Business Lawyer 636 (2001). These authors claim that the *pari passu* clause only prevents a debtor from creating a class of more senior ranking debt in the context of bankruptcy and does not require pro rata debt payments.

7. What should be the role of the IMF in an international bankruptcy process? Should it come up with the "reorganization" plan, basically the macro plan for the debtor, or should this be left to the private creditors. In this connection, recall Stiglitz's criticisms of IMF macro policy.

8. Do you think it would be a good idea to establish an international bankruptcy court to deal with sovereign debt defaults? What would be the role of such a court?

9. In 1997, Japan suggested that a $100 billion fund, created and financed by Asian countries, be created to help countries deal with the crisis. The fund would have been entirely independent from the IMF. This idea was criticized on the ground that it would undercut the IMF and create moral hazard—the existence of such a fund would make

countries more likely to borrow. *An Asian IMF?,* The Economist, September 27, 1997. It was also clear the U.S. did not want Japanese regional initiatives which it would not control. This proposal never materialized but what do you think of it? Does this create any greater moral hazard than does the IMF bailout system? In May 2000, the Japanese tabled another idea. It proposed establishing a coordinated network of currency swap facilities with other Asian countries. Countries with excess reserves would swap their own currencies with countries whose currencies were under attack. The Japanese stressed that its facilities would not bypass IMF conditionality on lending. P. Montagnon and C. Mai, *Japan Offers plan to avert financial crises in Asia,* Financial Times, May 6/7, 2000. In May 2001, 13 Asian countries agreed to implement the currency swap arrangement, the so-called Chiang Mai initiative. J. Thornhill and E. Luce, *East Asia Seeks its own voice,* Financial Times, May 14, 2001.

10. The IMF and the World Bank have put forward a special initiative for heavily indebted poor countries (HIPC). These are countries that have an unsustainable debt burden. Countries who have adopted a Poverty Reduction Strategy Paper and have made progress in implementing the strategy can qualify. These are economic policies that the IMF approves. Qualifying countries will receive sufficient funds to reduce their debt to sustainable levels once satisfactory assurances have been received by other creditors. Bilateral and commercial creditors are generally expected to reschedule obligations coming due, with a 90 percent reduction in net present value. The total cost of the initiative for multilaterals and other official creditors, for providing assistance to 34 countries, is estimated at about $36 billion. International Monetary Fund, *Debt Relief under the Heavily Indebted Poor Countries Initiative, A Factsheet,* March 2002. By early 2002, 22 poor countries had made substantial progress in negotiating debt relief under the HIPC initiative.

It is far from clear whether countries that obtain HIPC debt relief will avoid reincurring unsustainable levels of debt in the future without concessionary grants and loans going forward. This is due to their inability to make necessary fiscal adjustments without severe social welfare costs. S. Edwards, *Debt Relief and Fiscal Sustainability,* NBER Working Paper No. 8939 (May 2002).

D. INTERNATIONAL BANKING STANDARDS

Even before the Asian crisis struck, bank regulators were urging that regulation of banks be strengthened in emerging markets so as to promote domestic economic growth and to avoid systemic spillover of bank bankruptcies to the rest of the world. This has created a demand for international bank regulation standards.

1. AN INTERNATIONAL BANKING STANDARD

The G-7 countries (Canada, France, Germany, Italy, Japan, the United Kingdom, and the United States) at the Lyons summit in 1996, largely in response to the Mexican crisis of 1994, directed finance ministries and central banks to come up with proposals for emerging market banking supervision in time for the June 1997 Denver summit. This led to or stimulated various efforts to develop some form of international banking standards.

Morris Goldstein in *The Case for an International Banking Standard* (Institute for International Economics 1997) has championed the approach of developing and enforcing an international banking standard (IBS). He bases the need for such a standard on the fact that since 1980, domestic banking crises have been a common feature of the world's financial system. At least 14 countries had banking crises so serious that total losses or costs ranged from 10% to 55% of GDP. These countries were:

Latin America	Industrial	Africa	Other
Argentina	Spain	Benin	Israel
Chile	Japan	Ivory Coast	Bulgaria
Venezuela		Mauritania	Hungary
Mexico		Senegal	
		Tanzania	

Other countries had very serious banking crises that did not quite result in quite such large costs: Finland, Norway, and Sweden. The cost of resolving banking crises in developing and transition countries since 1980 has been estimated to be about $250 billion, which equaled an average of four years of development assistance from all sources during the same period. The major concern is that such crises may have spillover effects on other countries; indeed this concern with international transmission of systemic risk underlies much of U.S. regulation of foreign banks.

It is questionable whether there is the same global concern about banking crises in developing countries. This is largely because banks from some developing countries have very few linkages with developed countries, i.e. they do not operate in other countries and do not do much cross-border business. It is also questionable whether country banking crises are the major problem. After all, BCCI, which triggered many of the U.S. regulatory reforms, had nothing to do with a country crisis—it was a failure of a poorly regulated multinational bank.

Goldstein uses the existence of these crises to argue that the world needs an International Banking Standard ("IBS") to prevent these crises. His IBS would include the following four policies, among others:

a. Public disclosure. Banks would be required to furnish timely and accurate information on their financial condition to investors. A balance sheet, income statement, large off-balance sheet exposures, and major concentrations of credit and market risk should be consolidated globally in accordance with international accounting standards and certified by an independent external auditor. Serious penalties would apply for false or misleading data. Banks would disclose their ratings, or lack of them, from international credit rating agencies.

b. Bank capital. The IBS would require adherence to the Basel risk-weighted capital standards which are examined at length in Chapter 4. To qualify as strong, banks in a relatively volatile operating environment would apply a 'safety factor' if their recent history of loan defaults, restructured loans, and/or government assistance to troubled banks was significantly higher than the OECD average over, say, the past five years. The safety factor could require a 1.5 capital multiple, so that a 12% risk-weight would apply instead of the ordinary 8%.

c. Safety net. The safety net for banks would consist of the following features, mimicking features of U.S. banking regulation:

(1) government deposit insurance is retained for small depositors; (2) deposit insurance premiums paid by banks are risk weighted. . .; (3) banks become subject to progressively harsher regulatory sanctions (e.g., eliminating dividends, restricting asset growth, and changing management) as their capital falls below multiple capital-zone trip wires: (4) . . . well capitalized banks receive 'carrots' in the form of wider bank powers and lighter regulatory oversight; (5) regulators' discretion is sharply curtailed (with respect to initiating 'prompt corrective actions' and resolving a critically undercapitalized bank at least cost to the insurance fund. . .; (6) . . . the insurance fund is generally prohibited from protecting uninsured depositors or creditors at a failed bank if this would increase the loss to the deposit insurance fund; and (7) provision is made for a discretionary, systemic-risk override to protect all depositors in exceptional circumstances. . . but [its] activation requires explicit, unanimous approval by the most senior economic officials and subjects any bailout to increased accountability. . .Id. at 46-47.

d. Consolidated supervision and cooperation among host- and home-country supervisors. The IBS would require participants to implement the 1992 Basel rules:

(1) all international banks be supervised on a globally consolidated basis by a capable home-country supervisor; (2) home-country supervisors be able to gather information from their cross-border banking establishments; (3) before a cross-border banking establishment is created, it receive prior consent from both the host- and home-country authorities; and (4) host countries have recourse to

certain defensive actions (e.g., prohibit the establishment of banking offices) if they determine that conditions (1)-(3) are not being satisfied. . ..Id. at 50.

Goldstein's proposal raises the question of whether one standard set of rules could be applied to all banks in all countries. As we have already seen in our examination of the Basel Accord, the future of regulation may be more "models"- based, where regulators pass on models used by banks to control risks, rather than mandating specific rules. The same could be said for countries. There may be several valid ways for countries to supervise banks, not just one incorporated in an IBS. This suggests that, at most, international regulators should pass on country approaches rather than mandate one approach.

Goldstein would have the IMF and World Bank enforce his standards. We have great difficulty with this idea. Neither of these organizations is particularly expert in banking regulation, and would be called upon to enforce rules that others who were expert, like BIS, had formulated. Could BIS enforce these rules? It seems unlikely.

In October 1996, the Basel Committee on Banking Supervision and the Offshore Group of Banking Supervisors issued a report entitled *The Supervision of Cross-Border Banking* which addressed various proposals for overcoming problems in supervising the cross-border operations of international banks. These problems were of two kinds. First, home country supervisors had difficulty in obtaining necessary information about foreign operations as a result of secrecy laws and impediments to on-site inspections by home country supervisors. Second, host and home country supervisors had no common standard to assess the adequacy of each other's supervision, and supervisory gaps continued to exist as a result of "booking offices in the form of so-called 'shell branches', parallel-owned banks, i.e. 'sister' institutions in under-regulated financial centres. . ." Id., at 2. The Report encouraged the Offshore Group (a forum for supervisory cooperation of supervisors in certain offshore financial centres) and other regional groups to adopt common standards, and offered its own checklist of principles in that regard. However, the Basel Committee stated that it did "not wish its Secretariat to become directly involved in an exercise of this nature [monitoring compliance with standards] because of the moral hazard involved in appearing to give a 'seal of approval.'" Id., at 18.

The moral hazard may be that monitoring by the Basel Committee, by issuing the seal of approval, would take local regulators off the hook of doing their own day-to-day jobs. We doubt this would happen. It would be well understood that Basel approval was a necessary but not sufficient condition for adequate regulation. The real problem is political; a small group of elite OECD central bankers do not think they will be able to pass judgment on developing countries'—or for that matter each other's—banking systems.

If there is no current body to enforce the standards, the temptation would be to create a new one, but that would be extremely difficult to do. An alternative would be to assign responsibility to particular countries involved with transactions, i.e. the home or host country. This was the approach of the Basel Concordats, and is also the direction largely taken in S. Key and H. Scott, *International Trade in Banking Services: A Conceptual Framework* (Group of Thirty 1991).

2. THE INTERNATIONAL FINANCIAL ARCHITECTURE APPROACH

The G-7 countries have formulated their own approach to financial institution reform, mainly focusing on banks, as part of the International Financial Architecture. The general idea is to establish workable guidelines for supervision and regulation of banks that should be observed by all countries.

In April 1997, the BIS Committee on Banking Supervision issued a Consultative Paper on *Core Principles for Effective Banking Supervision*. It formulated 25 "Core Principles" for Effective Banking Supervision under the headings of Licensing and Structure, Prudential Regulations and Requirements, Methods of Ongoing Bank Supervision, Information Requirements, Formal Powers of Supervisors and Cross-Border Banking. These principles were later issued in final form in September 1997. They are quite general. The first Principle, a precondition for effective supervision in all areas, conveys the generality of the approach. It provides:

> An effective system of banking supervision will have clear responsibilities and objectives for each agency involved in the supervision of banks. Each such agency should possess operational independence and adequate resources. A suitable legal framework for banking supervision is also necessary, including provisions relating to the authorisation of banking establishments and their ongoing supervision; powers to address compliance with laws as well as safety and soundness concerns; and legal protection for supervisors. Arrangements for sharing information between supervisors and protecting the confidentiality of such information should be in place.

The G-10 deputies (deputy finance ministers and senior central bank officials), together with representatives of emerging market economies, known as the Working Party on Financial Stability in Emerging Market Economies, issued another report, also in April 1997, *Financial Stability in Emerging Market Economies*. This goes beyond the topics dealt with in the BIS *Core Principles*, and deals with such issues as accounting standards, payment systems, and competition. Its strategy for achieving stability has four major components: (1) development of an international consensus on the key elements of a sound financial and regulatory system by representatives of the G-10 and emerging economies (this would be the

Core Principles); (2) formulation of sound principles and practices by international groupings of national authorities with relevant expertise and experience such as the Basel Committee, the IAIS (the accounting standards organization) and IOSCO; (3) use of market discipline and market access channels to provide incentives for the adoption of sound supervisory systems, better corporate governance and other key elements of a robust financial system; and (4) promotion by multilateral institutions such as the IMF, the World Bank and the regional development banks of the adoption and implementation of sound principles and practice. One might call these "soft" principles since they would not be binding on particular countries nor enforced by any international body. These objectives were further elaborated in the Working Group Report on Strengthening Financial Systems of the G-22 countries of October 1998 (Working Group Report of 1998). One important addition to the prior statements on banking supervision was the stress on developing improvements in the techniques of asset valuation and loan loss provisioning as related to accounting standards.

In 1999, the Basel Committee issued a key paper further elaborating standards for banking regulation. *Core Principles Methodology* (October 1999) sets forth a methodology for testing whether countries are in compliance with the Core Principles. The Committee recognized that effective banking supervision required a set of preconditions to be in place: (1) sound and sustainable macroeconomic policies; (2) a well-developed public infrastructure, i.e. effective courts, accountants and auditors; (3) effective market discipline, e.g. financial transparency and effective corporate governance; (4) procedures for the efficient resolution of problems in banks; and (5) mechanisms for providing an appropriate level of systemic protection (or public safety net).

While the Basel Committee has taken the lead in promulgating standards, the IMF and World Bank, through their pilot Financial Sector Assessment Program (FSAP) introduced in May 1999, have undertaken to assess whether the Basel standards are being complied with. These are called Core Principles Assessments (CPA). As of November 2000, 22 CPAs had been made. Most of the countries surveyed at that time were developing countries, but Canada was also included (probably on the what's good for the goose is good for the gander principle). The average time spent in a country making the assessment was about 3 weeks. The surveys found a wide range of compliance with particular Core Principles (CPs). Six countries had weak compliance with 14-99 CPs, while five countries had weak compliance with 0-5 CPs. This assessment has also led to some feedback to the Basel Committee on the standards themselves. It is up to countries as to whether to publish the assessments. Performance on standards is taken into account by the Fund in making lending and other decisions regarding country assistance. See International Monetary Fund, *Experience with Basel Core Principle*

Assessments, April 12, 2000; International Monetary Fund, *Financial Sector Assessment Program (FSAP) A Review: Lessons from the Pilot and Issues Going Forward,* November 27, 2000. By December 2001, CPs had been surveyed in 36 countries, 22 of which have been published. International Monetary Fund, *Quarterly Report on the Assessment of Standards and Codes—December 2001,* February 6, 2002.

The scope of the FSAP is wider than just the Basel banking standards, and covers the IMF's Code of Good Practices on Transparency in Monetary and Financial Policies, the Basel Committee on Payment and Settlement Systems' Core Principles for Systematically Important Payment Systems, IOSCO's Objectives and Principles of Securities Regulation, and the International Association of Insurance Supervisors' Insurance Core Principles, and FSAPs in some countries have covered these other areas.

The Financial Stability Forum (FSF) was created in 1999, in part to coordinate efforts of various international regulatory bodies. It brings together three representatives, finance ministers, central bankers and financial regulators, from each G-7 country. In addition, the IMF and World Bank have two members each, as does the Basel Committee on Banking Supervision, IOSCO and the International Association of Insurance Supervisors. Finally, the Bank for International Settlements itself, OECD, the Basel Committee on Payment and Settlement and the Basel Committee on Global Financial Systems each have one seat, for a grand total of 35. The Chair is Andrew Crockett, the general manager of BIS. The FSF has a small secretariat and no formal enforcement power. Nor does it have any direct representation from emerging market countries. The objective of the forum is to coordinate the policy actions of its members. A summary of its ever widening range of activities is set forth in FSF, *Ongoing and Recent Work Relevant to Sound Financial Systems,* March 14, 2002.

Given its small secretariat, at least for now, it is unlikely that the FSF could take any operational role. It appears that the IMF is assuming this responsibility. The FSF, in its *Report of the Follow-Up Group on Incentives to Foster Implementation Standards,* August 31, 2000, the FSF has identified what it considers 12 key international standards. In addition to those subject to FSAPs, as discussed above, they include: IMF standards on fiscal policy transparency and data dissemination, the World Bank's Principles and Guidelines on Effective Insolvency Systems, the OECD's Principles of Corporate Governance, IASC's International Accounting Standards, the International Federation of Auditors Committee's (IFAC) International Standards on Auditing, and the Financial Action Task Force's Recommendations on Money Laundering. FSF issued its *Final Report of the Follow-Up Group* on September 6/7 2001. While it found increasing worldwide awareness and understanding of the standards, implementation of the standards lagged behind.

In the FSF's discussion of incentives, two interesting ideas appear. First, the FSF states that FSF members should encourage the voluntary disclosure in prospectuses for international sovereign bond issues on observance of relevant standards, and also encourage the use of such information by banks in assessing lending risks. Also, FSF suggests that its members should give greater weight to a foreign jurisdiction's observance of relevant standards in making market access decisions and in the supervision and regulation of subsidiaries or branches of institutions from that jurisdiction or of domestic institutions dealing with counterparties in that jurisdiction.

The IFA does generally contemplate more transparency about IMF programs in order to facilitate countries being subject to market discipline although the IMF has stated that the benefits of transparency must be balanced against the IMF's role as confidential policy advisor and the need to have candor in communications to the IMF from the countries.

Another important contribution to regulatory coordination is represented by the Joint Forum, composed of the Basel Committee on Banking Supervision, IOSCO and the International Association of Insurance Supervisors, housed at BIS. It has initiated important work comparing principles of regulation across the banking, securities and insurance industries. Joint Forum, *Core Principles,* November 2001. This work is also highly relevant to the regulation of financial conglomerates, firms which engage in all of these activities. See Joint Forum on Financial Conglomerates, *Supervision of Financial Conglomerates,* February 1999.

Notes and Questions

1. Why, if at all, should the banking crises described by Goldstein be of international concern, that is to countries other than those in which a particular crisis occurred?

2. In what areas of international financial regulation have we already developed international financial standards? You will have to briefly review the prior chapters to answer that question. Have these standards been mainly developed in banking or securities regulation? Have they been successful?

3. Do you agree with Goldstein about the need for an International Banking Standard to deal with banking crises? How would you compare the G-7 approach of Strengthening Financial Architecture to that favored by Goldstein? Should we have binding international standards that are enforced? If so, how and by whom could such standards be enforced? Could the new Financial Stability Forum (see Section F) be the enforcer? Do the IMF and World Bank have the expertise to assess whether countries are complying with principles formulated by the Basel Committee?

4. Is it likely that countries will be able to comply with the Core Principles? It can be argued that the Core Principles mimic supervisory standards in developed countries (particularly the United states), assume a well trained body of supervisors and sophisticated bankers, and thus are inappropriate for many countries. Further, there is little proof that use of such standards will make financial crises less likely. Indeed, such strict standards, which give government officials tremendous power, seem to be more likely to increase corruption in many countries. It may be far better to design mechanisms which give more sway to private sector control of excesses, e.g. disclosure, mandatory issuance of subordinated debt. These were the findings of a survey of regulatory and supervisory policies in 107 countries. J. Barth, G. Caprio, Jr., and R. Levine, *Bank Regulation and Supervision: What Works Best,* Second Draft, April 2, 2001.

5. The Group of Thirty has suggested that financial institutions create voluntary standards for global risk management. *Global Institutions, National Supervision and Systemic Risk,* A Study Group Report (1997). It has argued that regulators alone will be unable to deal with preventing the kinds of risks that can bring down banks or banking systems and that over regulation may stifle the financial system and ultimately the real economy. Is this approach more likely to work in emerging or developed countries, or neither?

6. M. Goldstein, *IMF Structural Program*, Working Paper, December 2000, examines the IMF's conditionality policies, finding that the number of conditions in assistance packages had vastly expanded with the result that compliance could not be adequately assessed. The IMF has indicated that it wants to streamline its conditionality approach, but it remains to be seen what this means in practice. IMF, Communiqué of the International Monetary and Financial Committee of the Board of Governors of the International Monetary Fund, para. 11, April 29, 2001. Would streamlining conflict with the idea that the Fund should include FSAP results in deciding whether to assist countries? There is also sharp disagreement whether IMF conditionality in any form, streamlined or broad, actually improves country performance. The Meltzer Commission, supra at p. 35, concluded that numerous studies show its failure. Not surprisingly the IMF has a different view, M. Khan and S. Sharma, *IMF Conditionality and Country Ownership of Programs,* IMF Working Paper, September 2001.

E. CAPITAL CONTROLS

Capital controls come in many forms. They can restrict inward or outward capital flows or both. They can be administrative, controlling capital flows by outright prohibitions, explicit quantitative limits or an approval procedure. Capital controls can also be indirect or market-based, taking the form of dual or multiple-exchange rate systems, explicit taxation, indirect taxation in the form of non-interest bearing compulsory reserve/deposit requirements or other price or quantity restrictions.

In dual exchange rate systems, different exchange rates apply to different kinds of transactions. They have typically been used where authorities did not want to maintain exchange rates by generally imposing higher interest rates. Foreign exchange rates for trade and inward investment are generally exempted, thus allowing local currencies to depreciate against dollar for such transactions and imposing higher costs for those exchanging local currency in connection with such transactions, e.g. importers. IMF, *Country Experiences with the Use and Liberalization of Capital Controls* (September 1999) (IMF Study).

Many arguments have been used to justify capital controls. For example, second-best arguments identify situations in which capital controls may compensate for market imperfections such as information asymmetry. In addition, policy implementation arguments are invoked, primarily to permit monetary policy autonomy, usually aimed at lower interest rates while preventing the currency from depreciating. Also, capital controls may be justified as protecting monetary and financial stability, as where short-term interbank inflows reflect inadequate risk assessment by local or foreign banks. And capital controls can also be imposed to support policies of financial repression to provide cheap government financing. Id, at 3.

S. Radelet and J. Sachs, *The East Asian Financial Crisis: Diagnosis, Remedies, Prospects,* Brookings Papers on Economic Activity 1:1998, have proposed to impose inward capital controls to limit countries' short-term borrowings. Joseph Stiglitz, the former chief economist at the World Bank, also favors such an approach. Much of the steam behind new calls for inward capital controls comes from the exposure of Korea and Thailand to sharp outflows of short-term capital in the Asian crisis, where there were no significant inward controls, and the ability of Chile to use inward controls to limit the inflow of short-term capital.

Chile imposed capital controls in June 1991 when a surge of capital inflows threatened a significant appreciation of the currency with the result that the central bank faced a problem in managing money supply. Originally, all portfolio inflows were subject to a 20 percent reserve deposit that earned no interest. For maturities of less than a year, the deposit applied for the duration of the credit, while for longer maturities, the reserve requirement was only for one year. Certain transactions were exempted, like trade flow, foreign currency deposits in commercial banks, and foreign direct investment. The controls were initially readily avoided by misdescribing the purpose of the inflow so as to qualify for an exemption. The Chilean authorities responded in July 1992 by raising the reserve requirement to 30 percent and extending coverage to trade credit and loans related to direct foreign investment. In 1995, the controls were further extended to investments by Chilean residents in Chilean stocks traded on the New York Stock Exchange and to international bond issues. IMF Report, Part II (country studies), p. 5; S. Edwards, *How Effective are Capital Controls?*, National Bureau of Economic Research, Working Paper No. 7413 (November 1999).

The purpose of the Chilean controls was not to reduce short-term inflows in order to reduce the possibility of sudden outflows, the objective of Radelet and Sachs. The purpose was more traditional, to reduce upward pressure on the Chilean peso, which would interfere with the Chilean export promotion policy, and preserve monetary policy autonomy. Since the mid 1980s, the Chilean Central Bank had pursued a disinflation policy by targeting real interest rates. However, high rates attracted capital inflow, putting pressure on money creation. Reserve requirements were apparently higher on short-term capital because this capital was thought to be more speculative and controllable. Were the Chilean controls successful in achieving their objectives? It appears that the controls clearly affected the maturities of inflows but the aggregate inflows were not affected. The controls also appeared to generate a small and temporary increase in interest rates giving the Central Bank some aid in controlling inflation. And the controls resulted in a small, 2.5 percent, depreciation in the peso. On the other hand, there was an increase in the cost of domestic capital, particularly for small firms that could not evade the controls. J. De Gregorio, S. Edwards, R. Valdes, *Controls on Capital Inflows: Do They Work,* National Bureau of Economic Research, Working Paper No. 7645 (April 2000). The IMF Report concludes that there "is no discernible evidence that the [reserve requirements] had an effect on the exchange rate path or total capital inflows." IMF Report, Part II, at 6. These studies fail to comment on another cost of controls—possible corruption associated with avoiding controls.

E. Kaplan and D. Rodrik examine the September 1998 Malaysian capital controls in *Did the Malaysian Capital Controls Work?* NBER Working Paper 8142 (February 2001). In 1997, in order to stem the decline of the ringgit (MR) in the wake of the Asian financial crisis in Thailand and Korea, Malaysian authorities followed orthodox policies, raising interest rates and cutting spending, without effect. Consumption and investment demand decreased as a result of capital flows. Malaysia was intent on reflating the economy through lowering interest rates, but any attempt to do so was undercut by growing speculation against the ringgit in offshore markets, mainly Singapore. Institutions borrowed ringitt at double or triple the prevailing interest rates in Malaysia to purchase dollars and bet in favor of the ringgit's collapse. It is against this background that capital controls were imposed in September 1998 along with a new fixed rate of exchange of MR against the dollar of 3.80, about 10% higher than the rate at which the MR was trading against the dollar immediately preceding the adoption of controls.

Kaplan and Rodrik find that the capital controls worked. Malaysia was able to lower interest rates and make the fixed-exchange rate regime work without creating a black market. The authors leave open the issue of whether the controls intensified cronyism and had negative implications for political governance. One important point the authors make is that the imposition of capital controls avoided the necessity of going to the IMF for assistance. In this respect, capital controls may perform a similar function to the adoption of an international system for automatic stays or payment standstills, discussed above.

Capital controls have long been opposed by the IMF which has consistently tried to prohibit countries from imposing capital controls on the ground that they distort international capital flows and are ultimately unenforceable. See Stanley Fisher, *Capital-Account Liberalization and the Role of the IMF* in *Should the IMF Pursue Capital- Account Convertibility,* No. 207 Princeton Essays in International Finance (1998) has begun to reconsider this issue. It has recently begun to hedge this view, stating that while "there remain differences of view on the merits of capital controls, it is generally agreed that controls cannot substitute for sound macroeconomic policies, although they may provide a breathing space for corrective action." Report of the Acting Management Director to the International Monetary and Financial Committee on Progress in Reforming the IMF and Strengthening the Architecture of the International Financial System (April 12, 2000), p. 14.

The Monetary and Financial Committee (formerly called the Interim Committee) of the IMF has favored another approach—raising the cost of short-term cross-border capital flow to the borrowers. The specific proposals are to "[m]ake capital requirements [for banks] a function of the type of funding; have the monetary authority charge banks for the existence of sovereign guarantees; and on the lending side, assign higher risk weighting to interbank lines under the Basel Capital Accord." *International Monetary Fund, A Guide to Progress in Strengthening the Architecture of the International Financial System*, April 28, 1999, p. 9. Federal Reserve Board Chairman Greenspan has suggested that banks might be required to post reserve requirements for loans from foreign banks. What do you think of these various proposals?

In the past, arguments on unenforceability of capital controls have focused on the inability to prevent firms or individuals from taking funds out of the country, capital flight, as opposed to controls to prevent funds from coming into a country. Do the two cases present the same or different enforcement problems?

F. THE DANGERS OF GLOBAL REGULATION

The Asian financial crisis has triggered a new demand for international solutions to the problems of globalization in an increasingly interdependent world. These solutions, broadly conceived, result in increased power for international institutions, whether they be the IMF, the Basel Committees or newly created institutions like the Financial Stability Forum. These institutions are increasingly being relied upon to formulate and enforce international standards. Their growing importance parallels that of the WTO in trade.

It is not yet clear how the work of the various fora, e.g. BIS, IOSCO, IMF, World Bank, will be coordinated. One possibility is the Financial Stability Forum (FSF), created in 1999. The objective of the forum is to coordinate the policy actions of its members. Given its small secretariat, at least for now, it is unlikely that the FSF could take any operational role. It appears that the IMF is assuming this responsibility.

There could be substantial costs if this development towards international regulation proceeds unchecked. It could result in the transfer of significant power to undemocratically controlled institutions. The American voters and their elected officials may be unable to control these institutions in the way they have done in the past since we are quickly moving to a bipolar (with EMU) and probably a tripolar world (with the economic recovery of Japan) in which the U.S. will increasingly have to share economic power. One key point in favor of FSF is that it is more directly within the control of the major economic powers than is IMF; however it lacks in resources. Perhaps the point is that any international institution with the necessary resources to deal with emerging market problems, like the IMF, will have a bureaucracy with its own agenda.

A single set of mandated international rules will be more inflexible and less adaptable rules than multiple rules of sovereigns which compete with each other to attract financial institution activity. It is highly unlikely that the same rules fit all. Further, the advisability of mandated rules, in general, is contradicted by our recent experience with financial innovation (derivatives)—that regulators often do not know what to do. Indeed, this is behind the development of models-based regulation and the self-regulation approach of the Group of Thirty. See D. Llewellyn, *The Institutional Structure of Regulatory Agencies,* in How Countries Supervise Their Banks, Insurers and Securities Markets, ed. N. Courtis (1999) for an excellent checklist of the pros and cons of centralized international regulation.

One general alternative to international rules is the home-country approach. This envisions international cooperation on the issue of which country should regulate what, but leaves the content of the regulation to the regulating country. See H. Scott and S. Key, *International Trade in*

Banking Services: A Conceptual Framework, Group of Thirty, Occasional Paper 35 (1991); E. Kapstein, *Governing the Global Economy, International Finance and the State* (1994). It is probably desirable for a few core principles, such as non-discrimination and national treatment, to be adopted at the international level. Such rules are currently embodied in the GATS Treaty and various statements of OECD. But this is a far cry from having such organizations concretely apply such rules to financial matters. In our view, much of the impetus for international rules is premised on the spillover effect of financial crises, but this has proven to be quite limited—the Asian crisis did not spillover into the West. More importantly, it is premised on IMF bailouts: developed countries are trying to limit the cost of bailouts by improving the financial systems of emerging market countries. We would generally prefer to let the market work by allowing defaults and the consequent restructuring. From this point of view, the most urgent reforms are those facilitating orderly sovereign defaults.

The call for international rules sometimes ignores the tendency for firms to locate their activities in jurisdictions with the optimal amount of regulation—although, as we have seen, this may not be the jurisdiction with the least amount of regulation. As long as there are jurisdictional holes in the international order, regulation havens that do not subscribe to international rules, there may be significant limits on enforcing international rules, and this problem may be intensified by the Internet and the development of electronic money.

However, as we have discussed in various places in this book, for example Chapter 9 on the eurodollar market, institutions are only able to locate operations abroad to escape regulation because host countries are not willing to reach out unilaterally or in concert to stop these offshore activities. They have adequate tools to do so, through cutting off market access to firms located offshore, e.g. the U.S. could say Bahamian corporations cannot do business in the United States, cutting off use of their payment systems, e.g. the U.S. could say Bahamian corporations could not have accounts at U.S. banks, or use such accounts to transfer funds, or penalizing citizens doing business with such companies, e.g. the U.S. could say any U.S. underwriter of securities of a Bahamian corporation, whether they were sold in the U.S. or abroad, would pay a fine. But some of these tools are very costly to U.S. financial institutions, such as monitoring obligations placed on U.S. banks in connection with money laundering, or may be ineffective unless done on a multilateral level

In recent years, there seems to be a new willingness of developed countries to act in unison to prevent offshore centers from being used to evade regulation and taxes. Part of the recent effort has been led by the Financial Stability Forum which has recommended that the IMF bring offshore centers into their FSAPs and that "international standards" formulated by the G-7 with respect to cross-border information sharing be implemented. For example, "[e]ach supervisor should have general statutory authority to share its own supervisory information with foreign supervisors, in response to requests, or when the supervisor believes it would be beneficial to do so." These standards have come out of the U.S.'s development of effective consolidated supervision requirements for foreign banks following BCCI, discussed in Chapter 3. Financial Stability Forum, *Report of the Working Group on Offshore Centres,* April 5, 2000. In addition the Financial Action Task Force has developed the FATF Recommendations on combating money laundering, see e.g. FATF, *FATF on Money Laundering, The Forty Recommendations* (no date). And the OECD has formulated proposals for possible counter-measures against tax havens, see M. Peel, *Crackdown taxes patience of offshore finance centres,* Financial Times, October 17, 2000.

In March 2001, there were signs that these efforts were having some impact, J. Kingston, *Grenada shuts down 17 banks in clean-up of financial sector,* Financial Times, March 13, 2001. If these efforts continue, it will be harder to evade the effectiveness of global regulation. The issue will remain as to whether such global regulation is desirable.

Links to Other Chapters

Much of this Chapter builds on Chapter 21 where we deal with emerging markets. Basic issues of systemic risk, which this Chapter raises, appear generally in Chapter 2 and more specifically in terms of the payments system (Chapter 10) and clearance and settlement (Chapter 15).

The immediate causes of international financial crises include bank cross-border lending, which played a central role in the 1982 LDC debt crisis (see Chapter 9), plus portfolio investment and positioning in foreign exchange markets, which were key to the 1992-93 crises in the European Monetary System (Chapter 6). More generally, weak regulation by banks' home governments may play a role (Chapter 3).

Other chapters also examine international rules, most notably the Basel Capital Accord (Chapter 4) and international accounting standards (Chapter 2). Moreover, the EU's financial services directives offer a model for the home country approach (Chapter 5). And the experience with offshore markets, e.g. swaps in Chapter 17, raises the general question of whether "international" rules can work given offshore centers that may not subscribe. Indeed, the question of advisability of international regulation is raised throughout this book.

CHAPTER TWENTY-THREE

RESPONDING TO TERRORISM THROUGH THE INTERNATIONAL FINANCIAL SYSTEM

The events of September 11, 2001 shook the world. One of the important parts of the U.S. and worldwide response was to try to cut off funding to terrorists and to track terrorists through their use of the financial system. This has resulted in the freezing of certain terrorist accounts on a coordinated worldwide basis. The operation of such freezes was explored in Chapter 11. This Chapter focuses on how the U.S. and other countries have built on past efforts to stop money laundering to fight terrorism. In addition, it looks at whether countries, in particular the United States, should back up the private sector in providing insurance against terrorism.

A. MONEY LAUNDERING AND ANTI-TERRORISM [*]

1. NATURE OF THE PROBLEM

Before September 11, 2001, the U.S. had in place, along with many other countries, rules designed to stop money laundering. This is the process in which criminal activities like drug trafficking generate large cash receipts which are deposited in the banking system of major countries, where the drugs are sold, and then moved to offshore banking centers or into legitimate businesses. The point of anti-money laundering laws was twofold. First, to make it harder to deposit such cash without

---

[*] We have been greatly aided in preparing this Chapter by James Gillespie, *Follow the Money: Tracing Terrorist Assets*, Paper written for the Harvard Law School Seminar on International Finance (2002) (on file with authors.)

attracting attention from authorities and second, to record information about such deposits or wire transfers which could later be used to investigate criminal activities.

The financing of terrorism differs from money laundering in some important respects. First, the source of funding is different. Although some funding may come from illegal activities in the form of cash, much of the funding does not. It can come from rich individuals like Bin Laden or from terrorist states such as Iraq. These parties will already hold funded bank accounts, albeit under cloaked identities; their funding will often not start with cash deposits.

Second, the amount of individual funds transfers and the total amount of funds to support terrorism appear to be less than is generated by criminal activities such as drug trafficking. The wire transfers involved in 9-11 were quite small. Although we have no estimates of the amount of funds used for terrorism, it is likely to be considerable less than the estimates of total funds laundered, $600 billion to $2 trillion per year.

Third, the origin of terrorist funding will often be external to the major economic powers, given who the terrorists are, and funds will then be moved to operatives inside the major economic powers. Criminal proceeds, however, are usually generated in the major markets and then moved offshore.

Dennis M. Lormel, Chief, Financial Crimes Section, Federal Bureau of Investigation, Statement for the Record, House Committee on Financial Services, Subcommittee on Oversight and Investigations, Washington, D.C., February 12, 2002, testified that the 19 hijackers involved in 9-11 opened 24 domestic bank accounts at four different banks. The following financial profile was developed from the hijackers' domestic accounts.

Account profile

- Accounts were opened with cash/cash equivalents in the average amount of $3,000 to $5,000.
- Identification used to open the accounts were visas issued through Saudi Arabia or the U.A.E.
- Accounts were opened within 30 days after entry into the U.S.
- All accounts were normal checking accounts with debit cards.
- None of the hijackers had a social security number.
- They tended to open their accounts in groups of three or four individuals.
- Some of the accounts were joint accounts with others.
- Addresses used usually were not permanent (i.e. mail boxes, etc.) and changed frequently.
- Hijackers would often use the same address/telephone numbers on the accounts.

- No savings accounts or safe deposit boxes were opened.
- Hijackers would open their accounts at branches of large well known banks.
- The majority of hijackers (12) opened accounts at the same bank.

Transaction profile

- Some accounts would directly receive/send wire transfers of small amounts to foreign countries UAE, Saudi Arabia, Germany.
- Hijackers would make numerous attempts of cash withdrawals which often would exceed the limit of the debit card.
- High percentage of withdrawals were from debit cards vs. low percentage of checks written.
- Numerous balance inquiries were made.
- Hijackers would often travel domestically.
- There was a tendency to use Western Union to wire money.
- One deposit would be made and then the money would trickle out a little at a time.
- Account transactions did not reflect normal living expenses for rent, utilities, auto payments, insurance, etc.
- There was no normal consistency with timing of deposits/disbursements.
- Funding for normal day to day expenditures was not evident from transactions.
- Overall transactions are below reporting requirements.
- Funding of the accounts dominated by cash and overseas wire transfers.
- ATM transactions occur where more than one hijacker present (uninterrupted series of transactions involving several hijackers at the same ATM).
- Use of debit cards by hijackers who did not own affected accounts.

International Activity

- Three of the hijackers supplemented their financing by opening foreign checking accounts and credit card accounts at banks located in the UAE.
- While in the U.S., two of the hijackers had deposits made on their behalf by unknown individuals.
- Hijackers on all four flights purchased traveler's checks overseas and brought them to the U.S. These traveler's checks were partially deposited into their U.S. checking accounts.
- Three of the hijackers (pilots/leaders) continued to maintain bank accounts in Germany after moving to the U.S.
- Two of the hijackers (pilots/leaders) had credit cards issued by German banks and maintained those after moving to the U.S.

- It is suspected that other unknown foreign accounts exist that were opened by the hijackers to further supplement the financing of the September 11, 2001, attacks.
- One of the hijackers (pilot/leader) received substantial funding through wire transfers into his German bank in 1998 and 1999 from one individual.
- In 1999, this same hijacker opened an account in the UAE, giving power of attorney over the account to this same individual who had been wiring money to his German account.
- More than $100,000 was wired from the UAE account of the hijacker to the German account of the hijacker in a 15-month period.

It is unclear what one does with the profiles. Are they really useful in identifying terrorists? If banks were to run the account profile against their existing accounts it is highly doubtful whether terrorists, as opposed to Arab students, would be identified, and the cost of making such checks would be extremely high. This raises a general problem about cost-benefit calculations with regard to anti-terrorist policies. Suppose there was a very low probability that a terrorist would be identified, say less than .5%, but that a terrorist act in the future might involve a nuclear bomb. Should governments require the banks to make the assessment? Certainly, one would want to use the cheapest way of making the identification, e.g. it might be cheaper to check the visas of all Arab students. There is an additional issue as to who should pay for these measures. Should the costs be imposed on the banks, and therefore the banks' customers, or should they be deferred by taxpayers more generally?

A further problem with terrorism financing is that it is often done outside the formal financial system. One of the methods used is Hawala which is prevalent in Arab countries as well as in southern Africa and southern Asia. Hawala operates through a network of agents who maintain running balances with each other that are periodically settled. It very much resembles the system used for cross-border payments in Europe before the invention of the modern banking system. Lets take an example. Suppose Somali A is in Minneapolis (where there are 50,000 Somalis) and wants to send money to Somali B in Somalia. She takes cash to a local Hawala agent who issues her a receipt. The local agent telephones or faxes another agent in Somalia who give out cash to the beneficiary, Somali B. Over time, there will be movement in both directions. As a result each agent will have a net position, one positive and the other negative. The two agents will settle in person by cash, commodities or through conventional payment systems. The system was set up to provide a cheap payment system to poor people who do not have bank accounts and is now being used to make payments to terrorists.

For an excellent overview of how money laundering and terrorist funding works, and some of the differences, see Financial Action Task Force on Money Laundering, *Report on Money Laundering Typologies 2001-2002* (February 1, 2002).

2. THE UNITED STATES RESPONSE

The United States has responded to the terrorist threat by modifying its money laundering rules. On October 26, 2001 President Bush signed into law the Uniting and Strengthening America by Providing Appropriate Tools to Intercept and Obstruct Terrorism Act of 2001 ("USA PATRIOT Act"). Title III of this Act is the International Money Laundering Abatement and Anti-Terrorist Financing Act of 2001 which both amends existing anti-money laundering law and imposes new requirements.

a. U.S. ANTI-MONEY LAUNDERING LAW: THE BASICS

This Section describes the key features of the basic anti-money laundering law together with PATRIOT Act amendments. The description of the basic law relies heavily on Wilmer, Cutler and Pickering, *Anti-Money Laundering Guidance for Financial Institutions,* January 30, 2001 and the information on the PATRIOT Act relies heavily on Sullivan & Cromwell, Financial Institutions Group, *Anti-Terrorism Law Changes, Expands Responsibilities of Financial Institutions,* 77 BNA Banking Report 835 (November 19, 2001).

The core of U.S. anti-money laundering law is the Bank Secrecy Act of 1970 (BSA), which has been frequently amended. The BSA authorizes the Secretary of the Treasury to regulate record keeping and reporting requirements for banks and other financial institutions, and to require financial institutions and some other private businesses and citizens to report certain kinds of financial transactions. In addition, banks are required by their regulators to "know your customer." (KYC). FinCEN is the agency created by Treasury to deal with money laundering issues.

i. Suspicious Activity Reporting

Every bank operating in the United States must where warranted file a suspicious activity report (SAR). After December 31, 2001, money services businesses have also been required to do so.

Regardless of the amount involved, a bank must file a SAR when the bank believes it was an actual or potential victim of a criminal violation or has a substantial basis for believing that its own people were so involved. Banks must also file SARs, depending on the size of aggregate transactions, where a suspect of a crime can be detected ($5000 or more), where a crime is suspected but no suspect has been identified ($25,000 or more), or when the bank suspects that a transaction involves funds derived from illegal activities, is designed to evade regulations, or has no apparent purpose ($5000 or more).

Pursuant to the PATRIOT Act amendments, Section 356, Treasury has issued a proposed rule-making which would require all broker-dealers to also file SARs, 66 Federal Register 67670 (December 31, 2001).

ii. Currency Transaction Reporting

Every financial institution, including banks and securities firms, must file a report for each non-exempted "deposit, withdrawal, exchange of currency or other payment or transfer, by, through, or to the financial institution which involves a transaction in currency of more than $10,000" in one business day. 31 C.F.R. §103.22(b). Multiple transactions of less than $10,000 by the same person must be aggregated. Transactions with certain persons who generate large currency transactions in the normal course of business, such as other banks, large corporations listed on an exchange, and government agencies, are exempt from reporting. Pursuant to the PATRIOT Act amendments, the U.S. Treasury has adopted an Interim Rule, extending this requirement to nonfinancial businesses, 66 Federal Register 67680 (December 31, 2001).

iii. Wire (Funds) Transfer Requirements

Under the so-called Travel rule, for any transmittal of funds of $3000 or more, involving more than one financial institution, each financial institution must forward certain information to the next financial institution. This facilitates the tracing of laundering transactions between U.S. and foreign financial institutions. Certain transmittals are exempt, for example, where both the transmitter and the recipient are a U.S. bank. All transmittal orders must include: the transmitter's name, address and account number; the identity of the transmitter's financial institution, the amount, the execution date and the recipient's financial institution. Certain recipient information must also be included if the bank receives it, i.e. name, address, account number and any specific identifier. In addition, financial institutions must keep records of wire transfers of $3000 and over.

iv. Know Your Customer

In December 1998, the Federal Reserve Board and other U.S. banking regulators promulgated proposed KYC regulations, 63 Federal Register 67,516 (December 7, 1998.) The basic idea was that banks must know their customers and their businesses to decide whether they are engaged in suspicious or illegal activities. The KYC regulation would have required, among other things, that banks determine the sources of funds and the normal and expected transactions of their customers. The proposal was withdrawn due to thousands of comments complaining of invasion of privacy. Banks were also opposed due to the significant new costs that would be imposed. The regulatory agencies have, however, adopted examination guidelines, referred to as "enhanced due diligence" requiring many of the KYC practices.

In addition to the procedures described above, additional regulatory guidance exists for so-called high-risk banking products, private banking and correspondent banking. "High-risk" in this context refers to banking transactions that have a high-risk of involving money laundering.

v. Private Banking

Private banking involves the provision of banking services to high net worth individuals, including money management and financial advice. Such services often involve setting up offshore facilities and banking arrangements. Banking regulators give guidance on how to handle these activities so as to minimize the possibility of money laundering. See e.g. Fed Guidance on Private Banking Activities, SR-97-19, June 30, 1997. For example, private banking often involves the creation of Personal Investment Companies (PICs), offshore legal entities to hold client assets and to keep confidential the name of the beneficial owner. Banks are advised to use extra caution in dealing with the beneficial owners, and following heightened KYC type policies. On October 30, 2000, a group of large international financial institutions released a set of anti-money laundering guidelines for private banking known as the Wolfsberg Principles. They include the principle that numbered or alternate name accounts will only be accepted if the bank has established the identity of the client and the beneficial owner.

b. KEY ADDITIONS OF THE PATRIOT ACT: "SPECIAL MEASURES" AND CORRESPONDENT OR SHELL BANKING

i. Special Measures

Section 311 of the PATRIOT Act authorizes the Treasury to designate certain jurisdictions, institutions or types of transactions as posing particular threats for anti-money laundering or anti-terrorism investigations, and to require financial institutions to take additional steps to monitor those transactions, including heightened reporting or record keeping, all of which can be done through Executive Order. Factors to be taken into account with respect to jurisdictions include:

- evidence of terrorist activity in that jurisdiction.
- bank secrecy provisions, and similar benefits for non-residents.
- quality of bank supervision.
- imbalances between the volume of financial transactions and real economy.
- designations of the jurisdiction as an 'offshore haven' by international experts.

- prevalence of corruption in that country.

For foreign institutions and types of transactions, the criteria are similar, and similarly broad:

- whether the institution or transaction is commonly used to facilitate money laundering.
- whether that type of transaction has any legitimate purpose.
- whether the proposed regulatory action will "continue...to guard against international money laundering."
   31 U.S.C. §5318A(c)(2)(B)

The Secretary may require a domestic financial institution or domestic financial agency to maintain records and file reports concerning the aggregate amount of transactions or with regard to particular transactions. The following information can be required: (1) the identity and address of the transaction participants (including the originator of a funds transfer); (2) the legal capacity in which a participant is acting; (3) the beneficial owner of the funds; and (4) a description of the transaction. The Secretary may also require domestic financial institutions or agencies to ascertain the beneficial ownership of an account that is opened or maintained by a foreign person in the United States.

ii. Correspondent Accounts

Terrorists and money launderers can make use of the correspondent banking system to cover their tracks. While a U.S. bank is in the position to take measures to assure that its foreign respondent banks (foreign banks holding accounts with it) have taken similar measures with respect to its customers as are required by U.S. law of the U.S. bank with respect to its customers, it has no way of knowing whether sub-respondents of the foreign bank (foreign banks which bank with the foreign bank) have done so. Lets take an example. Assume Terrorist A has an account in the Bank of Somalia. Bank of Somalia in turn holds an account with BNP-Paribas, a large French bank, and BNP holds an account with Citibank, N.Y. Terrorist B sends funds to Terrorist A who holds an account at Citibank. Citibank can try to assure that its bank respondents like BNP take precautions against terrorists opening accounts and keeps records to permit tracking of transactions after-the-fact. But Citibank cannot know whether Bank of Somalia does so, and may not even know that Bank of Somalia is a respondent of BNP.

The PATRIOT Act tries to address the problem of correspondent accounts in a variety of ways. First, Section 312 adds a new section 5318(i) to the BSA which imposes a general due diligence obligation on U.S. banks that have correspondent accounts. Institutions must establish procedures and controls that are reasonably designed to detect and report instances of money laundering through those accounts. Second, a higher level of due diligence may be imposed on banks maintaining correspondent accounts for three categories of foreign banks: (1) foreign banks operating outside the United States under an "offshore banking license," which is a license to conduct banking activities which prohibits the licensed entity from conducting banking activities with local citizens or in local currencies; (2) banks operating under a license in a foreign country that has been designated as noncooperative with international anti-money laundering principles by an intergovernmental group of which the U.S. is a member (like the Financial Action Task Force, FATF, discussed below); and (3) foreign banks operating under a license issued by a foreign country that has been designated by the Secretary as warranting special measures.

Additional due diligence requires U.S. banks to ascertain the ownership of the foreign bank, conduct enhanced scrutiny of the correspondent account to guard against money laundering and report any suspicious transactions and determine whether the foreign bank provides correspondent accounts to other foreign banks and if so, which ones. Also, they are required to determine what these second-tier foreign banks do to prevent money laundering or terrorist financing. It is far from clear how U.S. banks will obtain such information from their respondent or sub-respondent. It is also unclear how far up the correspondent chain such procedure is to be used. Suppose in our earlier example, the Bank of Somalia banks with a Lichtenstein bank which in turn banks with BNP. Citibank would have to ask BNP who its respondents were. Assuming BNP would or could disclose such information, Citibank would have to get due diligence information from the Lichtenstein bank, but it is unclear it would have to do so from the Bank of Somalia.

In addition, new section 5318(k) of the BSA requires any covered financial institution that provides a correspondent account to a foreign bank to maintain records of the foreign bank's owners and agent in the United States designated to accept service of legal process for its records regarding the correspondent account and permits the Secretary and the Attorney General to subpoena those records. If a foreign bank fails to comply, a financial institution must terminate the account upon notice from the Secretary or Attorney General.

Even stronger requirements apply to "shell banks." Section 313 of the PATRIOT Act prohibits covered financial institutions from establishing or maintaining a correspondent account for a shell bank and to take reasonable steps to assure that correspondent accounts of foreign banks are not being used indirectly by shell banks, e.g. where a shell bank banks with BNP which banks with Citibank. A shell bank is a foreign bank that does not have a "physical presence" in any country. A foreign bank does have a physical presence if it maintains a place of business at a fixed physical address in the foreign bank's licensing jurisdiction at which the bank has one or more full-time employees, maintains operating records, and is subject to inspection by the foreign bank's licensing banking authority. Shell banks affiliated with U.S. banks are generally exempt. Treasury has issued Interim Rules, 66 Federal Register 59342 (November 27, 2001) and proposed rules, 66 Federal Register 67460 (December 28, 2001), implementing the subpoena power and shell bank requirements. Both rules provide safe harbors if U.S. banks obtain specified model certifications from their foreign bank customers. Senate Banking Chairman Paul Sarbanes has criticized the certification approach to the extent it substitutes certification for due diligence. 78 BNA Banking Report 192 (February 4, 2002).

3. INTERNATIONAL INITIATIVES

a. FINANCIAL ACTION TASK FORCE (FATF)

Work on identifying jurisdictions that pose money laundering threats has been carried on by the FATF, an organization of 29 countries including the United States. FATF, *Review to Identify Non-Cooperative Countries or Territories: Increasing The Worldwide Effectiveness of Anti-Money Laundering Measures,* June 22, 2000. The FATF was founded by the Group of Seven nations in 1989 to foster money laundering controls worldwide.

In 1990, FATF issued *Forty Recommendations on Money Laundering* which have been repeatedly endorsed by major countries. The Recommendations call for the criminalization of money laundering, international cooperation in money laundering cases, and a wide range of money laundering control duties for financial institutions, including customer identification, mandatory suspicious activity reporting and due diligence. In May 2002, FATF issued a Consultation Paper, *Review of the FATF Forty Recommendations*, seeking comment on proposed changes in the Forty Recommendations. The measures would generally put more obligations on financial institutions to adopt KYC polices and enhance suspicious transaction reporting. It also discusses the application of the standards to a broad range of financial institutions and would impose obligations on some non-financial businesses and professions (including lawyers). In line with the PATRIOT Act, it would impose heightened obligations with respect to correspondent banking. It would also impose special requirements on dealings with political leaders and electronic and other non face-to-face transactions. In addition, the paper discusses problems of identifying the beneficial owners of "corporate vehicles" and trusts, and the use of bearer shares.

In March 2001, the Basel Committee on Bank Supervision weighed in on money laundering. The Committee stated its focus was on the integrity and safety and soundness of banks rather the crime prevention agenda of FATF. Nevertheless, their recommendations cover some of the same territory, e.g. KYC programs. Basel Committee on Banking Supervision, *Consultative Document, Customer due diligence for banks*, January 2001.

FATF has also formulated certain principles to determine when a *jurisdiction* was not taking adequate measures to combat money laundering: (1) loopholes in financial regulation; (2) lack of regulatory mechanisms to identify beneficial owners of accounts; (3) obstacles to international cooperation, such as laws prohibiting information exchange; and (4) inadequate resources devoted to prevent and detect money laundering. These requirements were further elaborated in February 2000 by setting forth twenty five criteria which would be used to make these determinations. FATF, *Report on Non-Cooperative Countries and Territories* (2000). As of September 7, 2001, nineteen jurisdictions were identified as non-cooperating countries and territories (NCCTs), including Egypt, Israel, Nauru, the Philippines and Russia.

The FATF's direct involvement in anti-terrorism stems from October 2001 when it issued *8 Special Recommendations on Terrorist Financing*. The recommendations provide that countries should:

- ratify and implement all applicable UN instruments.
- criminalize the financing of terrorism and associated money laundering.
- freeze and confiscate terrorist assets.
- report suspicious transactions related to terrorism.
- cooperate with other states' investigations relating to the financing of terrorism.
- eliminate or regulate alternative remittance systems.
- require more complete record-keeping regarding wire transfers.
- review laws relating to non-profits that may be exploited for terrorist purposes.

FATF has set a June 2002 date for compliance with these recommendations, FATF, *Self-Assessment Questionnaire: FATF Special Recommendations on Terrorist Financing* ¶2, January 31, 2002. Thus, as yet, FATF has not assessed publicly the extent to which countries comply with these recommendations, i.e. there is no NCCT list for terrorism. As indicated above, such a determination would trigger additional due diligence requirements under the PATRIOT Act.   It appears many countries will not meet the June deadline, *Follow the money,* The Economist, June 1, 2002.

b. THE INTERNATIONAL MONETARY FUND

The previous chapter on International Regulation has described the efforts of the IMF in monitoring and assessing the implementation of international standards through the Financial Sector Assessment Program. The IMF Directors have generally agreed in November 2001 that the FATF 40 recommendations on money laundering should become part of that process, following the development of an appropriate methodology and assessment procedure.   IMF, *Intensified Fund Involvement in Anti-Money Laundering Work and Combating the Funding of Terrorism,* November 5, 2001. This report contemplates that the Fund would have a similar role with respect to FATF's anti-terrorist funding recommendations.

c. THE UNITED NATIONS

On September 28, 2001, the Security Council of the United Nations adopted Resolution 1373 under Chapter VII of the UN Charter, which authorizes the Security Council "to maintain or restore international peace and security," through measures binding on all members. This resolution requires countries to criminalize terrorist funding, freeze terrorist assets, prohibit terrorists from obtaining financial services and cooperate with criminal investigations of other countries.   This was followed up four months later with Resolution 1390 which essentially establishes an international embargo on financial, military, political or any other form of aid to Osama bin Laden, Al Quaeda or the Taliban. The UN resolutions require action by the Security Council which, given the current Mideast problems, is likely to disagree on the meaning of terrorism which is left undefined by the resolutions.

Prior to September 11, the United Nations General Assembly approved the International Convention for the Suppression of Financing of Terrorism, signed by 132 states, but only ratified by 24 (not including the United States). The Convention largely overlaps the UN resolutions.

d. THE EUROPEAN UNION DIRECTIVE

On December 4, 2001, the European Union adopted a Directive on prevention of the use of the financial system for the purpose of money laundering.   Directive 2001/97/EEC, O.J. L344/6, December 28, 2001. This amended a prior Directive on money laundering, Directive 91/308/EEC, O.J. L166/77, June 28, 1991.

The most interesting part of the new Directive is that its anti-money laundering prohibitions are imposed not only on financial institutions but on a wide array of other persons, including auditors, external accountants, tax advisers, notaries, real estate agents, dealers in high value goods, and attorneys. The Directive exempts independent members of professions like attorneys from reporting requirements where the information is obtained in connection with representation of a client unless the attorney is herself involved in the money laundering. Moreover, it permits attorneys to make their reports to the bar rather than to governmental agencies.

4. ADDITIONAL MEASURES

What additional measures might be considered beyond those set forth above. First, FATF could promulgate a NCCT country list with respect to anti-terrorist funding measures and then establish international sanctions for violations. It is relatively clear that the U.S. cannot rely exclusively on unilateral measures, particularly where terrorist financing circumvents the U.S. banking system entirely. While such circumvention would be difficult for terrorist activities that occur in the United States, it could easily be done where American interests were attacked abroad. And even when the U.S. banking system is involved, the tiering nature of correspondent accounts necessitates cooperation of other countries in enforcing their own anti-terrorist measures. FATF would seem preferable to the United Nations as the agency to formulate international standards, given its composition and expertise. The IMF could monitor and assess country compliance.

However, there is the additional issue of sanctions. As of yet, the international financial system has not established sanctions for the violation of banking standards generally; they are still precatory and resemble guidelines more than binding rules. This is unacceptable when it comes to terrorism. However, given the disagreement on what actually constitutes terrorism, it may be difficult to get international agreement on sanctions. Such disagreement has already manifested itself in the freezing of terrorist assets. For example, Germany and France, the latter with a significant local Arab population and strong international Arab ties, have ordered their banks to block accounts of just 140 of the 192 people and entities on the U.S. list, leaving untouched organizations like Hamas, the Palestinian group that has taken responsibility for many suicide bombings in Israel. M. Phillips and I. Johnson, *U.S.-European Divisions Hinder Drive to Block Terrorists' Assets,* Wall Street Journal, April 11, 2002. It is conceivable, however, that there will be less disagreement over matters pertaining to regulation of the financial system than there is over the freezing of particular accounts.

A second possibility might be the establishment of national registries of bank accounts which are accessible to other countries, or perhaps even to other countries' financial institutions under certain conditions. Germany is planning to implement such a system. The German register will list the name, date and place of birth of all account holders, as well as the date when the account was opened, the name of the bank and the account number. This plan has been criticized by some as impinging on bank secrecy. H. Simonian, *Germany plans central bank account register*, Financial Times, October 6/7, 2001.*

Linked national registries could greatly aid in the detection or tracking of terrorism. For example, suppose a foreigner in the United States, who was a Pakistani student from Germany, deposited substantial funds in a U.S. bank, and further suppose the bank filed an SAR. The FBI could check with German authorities as to whether the individual had funds in a German bank account. If not, further enforcement measures could be taken. Further, suppose that this same student committed an act of terrorism in the U.S. Law enforcement agencies would be able to determine in which countries the individual had accounts. Of course, this assumes that terrorists would only be able to open accounts under their real identities, perhaps a heroic assumption. Difficult issues would be encountered in establishing which law enforcement agencies, and perhaps in limited circumstances which financial institutions, would be granted access to these data bases, and under what conditions such access would be granted.

A third possibility would be to try to eliminate informal payment mechanisms like Hawala which bypass the official banking system. Such elimination would obviously be quite difficult. However, one could try to increase the costs of such system by steering legitimate transactions into the formal system through reducing the costs of holding accounts and through educational initiatives. With fewer legitimate transactions, the costs of maintaining such networks for illegitimate transactions would increase.

A fourth and fifth possibility are much more radical, contemplating fundamental changes in the current international banking system. The U.S. could prohibit second tier correspondent banking in the United States. Thus no foreign bank could access the U.S. payment system without holding an account directly in the United States. U.S. banks would be required to obtain assurances from all foreign banks whose

---

* The proposal for an international deposit registry was developed in Philippe Scharf, *Money Laundering, terrorist financing and the global financial system: structure, evolution and proposals to ameliorate and protect the system*, LLM Paper, Harvard Law School, May 2002 (on file with authors).

accounts it held that that bank was not accessing its U.S. account on behalf of any other foreign bank. Thus, if a Bank in Somalia wanted to access the U.S. payment system it would have to hold an account with a U.S. bank. If the Treasury believed that such a bank, or Somalia itself, was not adequately complying with anti-terrorist funding policies, such an account could be prohibited. The Secretary has this power today under the PATRIOT Act, but it is unlikely that the Bank of Somalia would ever hold a direct correspondent account in the U.S. It is free under the existing regime to access the U.S. indirectly.

This proposal founders largely on the cost it would impose on international banking. It is more efficient for many small foreign banks to hold accounts with foreign correspondents rather than to establish direct access to the U.S. banking system. The same pattern obtains within the U.S. where a small country bank in Pennsylvania that receives wire transfers for its customers from a California bank will do so through an account at a Philadelphia bank rather than opening an account with the California bank. Further, foreign banks currently serving as correspondent banks for smaller foreign banks would vigorously oppose such a measure because of the loss of business. Of course, such added costs should properly be weighed against the terrorist savings.

Finally, one could envision another radical change. Cash could be banned entirely in favor of electronic banking systems that permitted the tracking of transactions. A step along this road would be to ban cash transactions (not just require reporting) of over relatively small amounts. Without cash, terrorists could arguably be more easily tracked. In our view these kind of more radical solutions will only be seriously considered if the cost of terrorism increases dramatically.

B. REINSURANCE CRISIS

It has been estimated by the IMF that the U.S. costs of the 9-11 attack was $21 billion, D. Milverton, *IMF Estimates Cost of Terror Attacks at $21 Billion, Predicts Recovery in 2002,* Wall Street Journal, December 19, 2001. Other estimates put the losses at between $50 billion and $70 billion. N. Evans, *Insurance's catastrophic year impels it onto banks' terrain,* Euromoney, January 2002 (*Catastrophic Year*). It is further estimated that $35 billion in these losses were covered by reinsurance, obligations of reinsurance companies to pay off on underlying insurance contracts. Actually, in the case of the World Trade Center's destruction, many reinsurance companies were primary insurers. Many of these reinsurers declared substantial losses in 2001 (over and above reserves). For example, Swiss Re declared a $118 million loss, its first in 135 years. Premium rates on renewals went up substantially for policies on which there was a terrorist risk. By mid-December, according to the Institute of Actuaries, rates for aviation insurance went up on average by 600-800%, while property and casualty rates generally rose by 50% and ins some cases by 100%. In a bid to replenish losses and to take advantage of the new rates, the insurance industry has raised a substantial amount of capital, apparently over $20 billion, and many in the reinsurance industry are predicting a strong recovery. See H. Lux, *Reinsurance,* Institutional Investor, April 2002; *Catastrophic Year*, supra.

It is unclear to what extent projects are not proceeding due to the added risk of terrorism, either because of the added expense or the unavailability of insurance or reinsurance. The lack of affordable terrorist insurance seems to have impacted the New York property market, P. Taylor, *Insurance question clouds NY property market,* Financial Times, November 20, 2001. Outside New York, there does not appear to be any systematic evidence of a serious problem, M. Miller, *No Terror Insurance, But Lenders Still Lending,* American Banker, January 7, 2002.

In November 2001, the U.S. House passed a bill under which the U.S. government would assume part of the risk of terrorism. If industry losses from an event exceeded $1 billion, the government would pay 90% of additional losses up to $100 billion. The government would be reimbursed by assessments on insurers for payments up to $20 billion, and could assess commercial policy holders for any additional losses. In addition, limitations would be put on tort actions. Most importantly there would be no punitive damages and a 20% cap on attorneys fees. This engendered substantial opposition from the Trial Lawyers Association and their congressional allies. The Senate has yet to pass the legislation. Its plan would have required the industry to take the first $10 billion in losses and participate in losses up to $100 billion.

The Shadow Financial Regulatory Committee issued the following Statement No. 172 on this matter on December 3, 2001.

Statement of the Shadow Financial Regulatory Committee
on Terrorism Insurance

Estimates of insured property and business losses in excess of $50 billion from the destruction of the World Trade Center and uncertainty concerning the future course of terrorism have caused reinsurers around the world to threaten withdrawal of terrorism coverage. Primary property and casualty insurance companies have indicated that, unless the government steps in to provide last resort reinsurance coverage, they therefore will seek to exclude terrorism risk from new and renewal insurance contracts beginning in 2002. Banks that finance buildings and other facilities are less likely to lend when there is a risk that the collateral will be destroyed with no insurance behind it. Increases in loan rates, denials of financing for new construction, or the defaulting of loans to weak borrowers would involve significant, economy-wide costs.

Some evidence indicates that insurance markets are beginning to digest the September 11th attacks and subsequent events. Significant amounts of capital are being raised to support the sale of insurance and reinsurance. Although it is not clear how much new capital would be devoted to supplying terrorist coverage without government intervention, it is plausible that at least some reinsurers, who are in the business of taking and spreading risks in exchange for premiums, would be willing to take on the newly evident risks.

Nevertheless, the insurance industry consensus is that there will be relatively little terrorism coverage after January 2002, in large part because of the potential for enormous loss and the inability to price the risk of loss accurately. The Administration, the insurance industry, and members of Congress have considered a number of plans for the federal government to assume substantial portions of terrorism insurance risk—and thus encourage the inclusion of terrorism coverage in insurance contracts coming into force in 2002 and future years. The House passed a terrorism insurance bill on November 29. Several bills have been introduced in the Senate, most notably a bill co-sponsored by Senator Gramm, which incorporates some features of an earlier Administration proposal.

Given the possibility of significant, short-term disruptions in insurance markets with material detrimental spillovers on economic activity, the enactment of some form of federal backstop for terrorist coverage is probably prudent. A key issue is whether the current problems in insuring against terror are long term or short term. Barring any large and unexpected increase in the threat of attacks, the Committee believes that over time – and a relatively short time – private insurance markets will be able to price and devote the resources necessary to provide terrorism coverage efficiently.

An appropriate federal backstop for terrorism insurance coverage should reflect the following principles:

1. Any program should be temporary, structured so that the insurance industry will take on full responsibility for terrorism losses relatively quickly, and include built-in phase-outs over two or at most three years with strong sunset provisions.

2. There should be a substantial layer of private risk-bearing before government assistance kicks in and risk-sharing by private insurers and reinsurers once any threshold for assistance is reached. That approach would mimic private insurance/reinsurance for catastrophes. Consistent with insurers' ability to adapt and the rapid phase-out of assistance, the threshold for government assistance should increase each year.

3. Intervention should avoid any direct government charge for assistance or government approval of premium rates. Efforts to set rates or impose rate regulation as a "price" for the government absorbing some terrorism risk

should be firmly resisted. Although there is some public interest in holding down rate increases, that interest is best served by getting the private sector back in the business of insuring against terrorism risk as quickly as possible—a task that rate regulation can only delay.

4. A backstop program should avoid mandating that an insurer offer coverage to all policyholders as a condition for participating in the government program. Such mandates might lead to government intervention in pricing decisions.

A program that reflects these principles would target the short-run problems, encourage private sector risk spreading, and reduce the potentially adverse effects of federal subsidies on private sector risk assessment, risk management, and claims adjustment.   On a longer-term basis, allowing insurers and reinsurers to accumulate some amount of capital (reserves) on a tax-deferred basis would make insuring potentially large losses from terrorism (or natural disasters) cheaper and more abundant. It would make future problems less likely.

The terrorism insurance bill approved by the House on November 29 would pay 90% of losses after $1 billion in aggregate industry losses or at lower levels of loss for individual insurers, to be paid back over time by assessments on insurers and, for large levels of loss, by surcharges on policyholders. The Committee believes that the thresholds for assistance in the House bill are too low and that the bill is excessively complex. The combination of low thresholds and potentially large assessments to be repaid over time might produce a long-term program.

The bill introduced by Senator Gramm would have the government pay 90% of losses above $10 billion each year for two years without a repayment feature. The Treasury could extend the program for a third year to cover losses above a $20 billion threshold. The Committee believes that the $10 billion threshold is more appropriate than the much lower amounts in the House bill and that a higher threshold would make sense for the second year.   The Committee urges the Congress to develop an appropriate compromise that would incorporate the best features of both bills and otherwise reflect the principles set forth above.

Notes and Questions

1.   How effective do you think current U.S. policies on anti-terrorist funding will be in significantly reducing such funding?

2.   Should we favor the development of internationally linked central registries of bank accounts? Would it be more effective than current policies? What costs would it impose on the system? Would you favor any of the other more radical changes discussed in the materials?

3.   Do you think the difference between money laundering and terrorist funding requires different policies in combating them?

4.   Should the U.S. government provide reinsurance for terrorism? If so, how?

Links to Other Chapters

This Chapter requires a basic understanding of the payment system as dealt with in Chapter 10. The related issue of asset freezes is taken up in Chapter 11.

GLOSSARY*

ABS. See Asset-based securities.

ACE. A European trade confirmation and matching service.

ADR. See American Depositary Receipts.

Allotments. A method of distributing previously unissued shares in a limited company in exchange for a contribution of capital. The company accepts the application by dispatching a letter of allotment to the applicant stating how many shares have been allotted.

American Depositary Receipts (ADR). Receipt for the shares of a foreign-based corporation held by a U.S. bank entitling the shareholder to all dividends and capital gains. Instead of buying shares of foreign-based companies in overseas markets, Americans can buy shares in the U.S. in the form of an ADR.

American Shares. Also called **American Depository Shares.** See American Depositary Receipts.

Amortization. The process of treating as an expense the annual amount deemed to waste away from a fixed asset. This accounting procedure gradually reduces the cost value of a limited life or intangible asset through periodic charges to income.

Arbitrage. Profiting from differences in price when the same security, currency, or commodity is traded on two or more markets. For example, an arbitrageur simultaneously buys one contract of gold in the New York market and sells one contract of gold in the Chicago market, locking in a profit because at that moment the price on the two markets is different. Index arbitrage exploits price differences between stock index futures and underlying stocks.

Article 65. A section of Japan's Securities and Exchange Law, often referred to as the Japanese Glass-Steagall because of its resemblance to the U.S. Glass-Steagall Act.

Asset-backed securities (ABS). Bonds or notes backed by loan paper or accounts receivable originated by banks, credit card companies, or other providers of credit.

Asset freeze. Government action that prevents the owner of assets from using or selling them.

---

*Sources:
H. Bonham, *The Complete Investment and Finance Dictionary* (2001); P. Moles and N. Terry, *The Handbook of International Financial Terms* (1997); G. Bannock and W. Manser, *The Penguin International Dictionary of Finance* (2nd ed. 1995); *The New Palgrave Dictionary of Money and Finance* (P. Newman, M. Milgate and J. Eatwell eds., 1994); *A Dictionary of Finance* (Oxford Paperback Reference 1993); *Barron's Dictionary of Finance and Investment Terms* (3rd ed. 1991).

Bank Law of 1981. Law regulating Japanese banks and branches of foreign banks located in Japan.

Bankers acceptance. Corporate note which bank agrees to pay.

Base. The rate of interest used as a basis by banks for the rates they charge their customers. In practice most customers will pay a premium over base rate to take account of the bank's risk involved in lending, competitive market pressures, and to regulate the supply of credit.

Basis point. A standard unit of measure for bond yields which equals 1/100 of 1 percent; 1 percent equals 100 basis points.

Basel Committee on Banking Supervision. An international banking regulatory group established in 1974 and consisting of representatives from the G-10 countries, Switzerland and Luxembourg.

Basel Concordat. This agreement, made in Switzerland in 1975 and revised in 1983, regulates international banking. Parent countries (those in which a bank is incorporated or has its main business activities) are primarily responsible for overseeing solvency; parent and host countries (those in which a bank's foreign branches are located) share responsibility for monitoring liquidity.

Benchmark. Point in an index or rate that is important, and that can be used to compare with other figures.

Beneficial owner. Person who enjoys the benefits of ownership even though title is in another name. When shares of a mutual fund are held by a custodian bank or when securities are held by a broker in street name, the real owner is the beneficial owner, even though, for safety or convenience, the bank or broker holds title.

Benelux countries. An association of countries in western Europe, consisting of Belgium, the Netherlands, and Luxembourg.

BHC (Bank Holding Company). Company that owns or controls one or more banks or other bank holding companies, as defined in the U.S. Bank Holding Company Act of 1956. Such companies must register with the Board of Governors of the Federal Reserve System and hence are called registered bank holding companies.

BHCA (Bank Holding Company Act). See BHC.

BIF (Bank Insurance Fund). Federal Deposit Insurance Corporation (FDIC) unit providing deposit insurance for banks other than thrifts.

"Big bang". Major change in operation of the London Stock Exchange (LSE) on 26 October 1986. Changes included the abolition of LSE rules mandating a single-capacity (restricting firms to acting only as broker, dealer or jobber etc.), the abolition of fixed commission rates charged by stockbrokers to their clients, the closure of the trading floor of the stock exchange in favor of off-the-floor telephone dealing, and a major expansion in dealing with international securities. Also refers generally to radical financial reform, as in Japan in 1997.

Bill discount market. The part of the U.K. money market consisting of banks, discount houses, and bill brokers. By borrowing money at short notice from commercial banks or discount houses, bill brokers are able to discount bills of exchange, especially Treasury bills, and make a profit.

BIS (Bank for International Settlements). An international bank originally established in 1930 as a financial institution to coordinate the payment of war reparations between European central banks. It was hoped that the BIS, with headquarters in Basel, would develop into a European central bank but many of its functions were taken over by the International Monetary Fund (IMF) after World War II. Since then the BIS has fulfilled several roles including acting as a trustee and agent for various international groups, such as the OECD, European Monetary Agreement, etc. The frequent meetings of the BIS directors have been a useful means of cooperation between central banks, especially in combating short-term speculative monetary movements. Since 1986 the BIS has acted as a clearing house for interbank transactions in the form of European Currency Units (ECU). The BIS also promulgates international capital adequacy standards.

Blue sky laws. State laws in the USA regulating securities.

BoE. Bank of England.

Bonds. Any interest-bearing or discounted government or corporate security that obligates the issuer to pay the bondholder a specified sum of money, usually at specific intervals, and to repay the principal amount of the loan at maturity. Bondholders have an IOU from the issuer, but no corporate ownership privileges, as stockholders do.

> **convertible.** These bonds give their owners the privilege of exchanging them for other specified assets, usually other securities of the issuing company, at some future date and under prescribed conditions.
>
> **corporate.** Bonds whose issuer is a corporation.
>
> **domestic.** Bonds issued within a country by local issuers.
>
> **floating rate.** Bonds with a variable interest rate usually linked to a specified benchmark such as the LIBOR.
>
> **foreign.** Bonds issued in a country other than that of the issuer.
>
> **global.** Bonds launched simultaneously in the major markets with a single worldwide price.
>
> **government.** Bonds whose issuer is a government.
>
> **high grade.** Bond rated triple-A or double-A by Moody's or Standard & Poor's rating service.
>
> **high yield.** Bond with a high yield.
>
> **international.** See Eurobonds.
>
> **Samurai.** Bonds offered by a non-resident issuer in Japan and denominated in Japanese yen.
>
> **Shogun.** Bonds offered by a non-resident issuer in Japan and denominated in U.S. dollars.
>
> **straight.** Fixed-rate bonds--the usual kind.

Book entry securities. Securities that are not represented by a certificate but by book entries on the books of a custodian bank.

Bookrunner. Lead underwriter of securities or loans.

Bourse. The French term for stock exchange

Brady bond exchanges. An initiative by the first Bush Administration using market-based debt and debt-service reduction and forgiveness to bring permanent relief to countries adopting strong economic reform programs.

Breaking the syndicate. Terminating the investment banking group formed to underwrite a securities issue. More specifically, terminating the agreement among underwriters, thus leaving the members free to sell remaining holdings without price restrictions. The agreement among underwriters usually terminates the syndicate 30 days after the selling group, but the syndicate can be broken earlier by agreement of the participants.

Bretton Woods. A conference (official title: the United Nations Monetary and Financial Conference) held at Bretton Woods, New Hampshire, USA, in July 1944, called to consider the postwar organization of international monetary relations and resulting in the establishment of the International Bank for Reconstruction and Development (World Bank) and the International Monetary Fund (IMF).

Bubbles. An inflated price of a security or asset that far exceeds the true value of that security or asset. When the bubble "bursts" the price of that security or asset falls precipitously until it reaches a more realistic level. For example, in the early 1600's Dutch tulip prices rose until they tulips were worth more than gold. Eventually the bubble burst, bringing prices down to more realistic levels.

Build, operate, transfer (BOT) and **build, own, operate, transfer (BOOT)** refer to forms of project finance in which host government gives the project company a concession to construct the project, mange its operations and, after an agreed period, transfer the project to the government or one of its agencies. BOOT refers to circumstances in which the project company owns the project's assets until transfer occurs.

Bulge. Quick, temporary price rise that applies to an entire commodities or stock market, or to an individual commodity or stock.

Bulge-bracket firms. Large securities firms.

CAD (Capital Adequacy Directive). A set of capital adequacy rules issued in 1993, affecting banks located in the EU.

Call account. Short-term bank account paying interest and on which funds can be withdrawn on call.

Call option. Right to buy a specified number of shares at a specified price by a fixed date. See option.

Cap. See collar.

Capitalization. The total value at market prices of a company's or market's securities.

CBOT (Chicago Board of Trade). A Chicago-based commodity and futures exchange.

CDS. Certificates of deposit.

CEDEL (Centrale de Livraison de Valeurs Mobilières). One of the two settlement systems for trading in Eurobonds and other international securities, established in Luxembourg in 1970. See also Euroclear.

Central bank swaps. In international monetary relations, the opening by one central bank of a line of credit in its own currency against the opening of an equivalent line of credit in another currency by the relevant central bank.

Certificate of deposit. Debt instrument issued by a bank that usually pays interest. Institutional CDS are issued in denominations of $100,000 or more, and individual CDS start as low as $100. Maturities range from a few weeks to several years. Interest rates are set by competitive forces in the marketplace.

CFTC (Commodities Futures Trading Commission). Established by Congress in 1974 to regulate futures securities.

Cherry picking. Selectively repudiating only disadvantageous financial contracts.

CHIPS (Clearing House Interbank Payment System). Electronic clearing house for funds transfer.

Chokoku funds. Japanese bond trusts similar to U.S. money market mutual funds.

Clearing. The offsetting of liabilities or purchases and sales between two parties. See clearinghouse.

Clearinghouse. Any institution that settles mutual indebtedness between a number of participants, such as CHIPS.

Closed-End Mutual Fund. A mutual fund which engages in one offering and does not generally permit share redemptions. Investors exit from their investments by selling their shares to other investors in a secondary market.

CME (Chicago Mercantile Exchange). A Chicago-based securities and commodities exchange.

CNS (Continuous Net Settlement). Method of securities clearing and settlement that uses a clearinghouse, such as the National Securities Clearing Corporation, and a depository, such as Depository Trust Company, to match transactions to securities available in the firm's position, resulting in one net receive or deliver position at the end of the day.

Collar. Two interest-rate options combined to protect an investor against wide fluctuations in interest rates. One, the cap, covers the investor if the interest rate rises against him or her; the other, the floor, covers the investor if the rate of interest falls too far.

Collateralized mortgage obligations (CMOs). Mortgage-backed bonds.

Commercial paper (CP). Short-term corporate debt usually maturing in 90 days or less.

Concessional finance. Funding, generally in the form of a loan supplied by official lenders, advanced at terms below the market rate for the borrower. Usually the interest rate is low and the maturity extended beyond what private lenders would provide.

Conservator. See receiver.

Convertible securities. Shares or bonds that are exchangeable for a set number in another form at a prestated price.

Counterparty. A person who is a party to a contract.

CRA. U.S. Community Reinvestment Act of 1977 requiring banks to serve their communities.

Cross-acceleration. A loan provision that allows creditors to accelerate the servicing and repayment of the loan when another loan meets the requirements of acceleration.

Cross-border trading. Trading by investors located in foreign countries who use a domestic exchange to perform their trades.

Cross-default. A loan provision that allows creditors to declare the loan in default when another loan meets the requirements of default.

Cross-exchange trading. Trading stocks on stock exchanges located in a market other than the issuer's home market.

Deliverable. A security deliverable on a certain date.

Depositary receipts. See American Depositary Receipts.

> **International, Continental, and European depositary receipts.** The equivalent to ADRs, held in foreign countries.

Derivatives. Financial instruments whose value is based on that of another security or its underlying asset. Derivatives include futures, options, swaps, and warrants.

Devaluation. A decrease in the value of a currency relative to the currencies of other countries or to a fixed standard such as gold.

DKV. German securities clearing system.

Dollar LIBOR. The rate of interest on LIBOR deposits or loans denominated in dollars. See LIBOR.

Dragon bond market. The emerging bond markets in the Pacific basin, including Indonesia, Malaysia, the Philippines, and Thailand.

DTB (Deutsche Terminborse). German stock exchange.

DTC (Depository Trust Company). Central securities depository in U.S. where stock and bond certificates are exchanged.

DVP (Delivery versus Payment). Securities industry procedure, common with institutional accounts, whereby delivery of securities sold is made to the buying customer's bank in exchange for simultaneous payment.

EC (European Community). Now known as EU or European Union.

ECB (European Central Bank). Though this bank currently exists only on paper, its creation is planned in the treaty for EMU.

ECP (Euro-commercial paper). Commercial paper issued in a eurocurrency, the market for which is centered in London.

ECU (European Currency Unit). A currency medium and unit of account created in 1979 to act as the reserve asset and accounting unit of the European Monetary System. The value of the ECU is calculated as a weighted average of a basket of specified amounts of European Union currencies.

EMI (European Monetary Institute). Institute to help coordinate monetary policy among the European central banks and prepare the arrangements for the ESCB.

EMS (European Monetary System). A European system of exchange-rate stabilization involving the countries of the European Union.

EMTN. Euro-commercial paper with a maturity term of several years.

EMU (Economic and Monetary Union). The planned merger of the currencies of the member states of the European Union.

EOC (Euroclear Operations Center).

ERM (Exchange Rate Mechanism). Exchange-rate system of the European Union.

ESCB (European System of Central Banks). A proposed European central banking system intended to take effect as part of EMU.

EU. European Union.

EUCLID. The telecommunications system of Euroclear.

Eurobond. Bonds that are a) underwritten by an international syndicate, b) offered simultaneously to investors in a number of countries, c) outside the jurisdiction of any single country, and d) in unregistered form.

 Eurodollar. Eurobonds offered in U.S. currency.

 Euroyen. Eurobonds offered in Japanese currency.

Eurocheque. A standardized cheque accepted in 39 countries. It can be made out in any desired amount, often in local currency, and must be used with an EC Card, a combination debit/ATM card used in the EU.

Euroclear. One of the two clearing and settlement systems for Eurobonds and other international securities, operated by the Brussels branch of the Morgan Guaranty Trust Co. of New York. The other is CEDEL.

Eurocurrency market. Market for supplying and borrowing eurocurrencies.

Euroloan. A loan made in a eurocurrency.

Euromarket. A market centered in London that emerged in the 1950s for financing international trade. Its main business is in eurobonds, euro-commercial paper, euronotes, and eurocurrencies.

Euronote. A form of euro-commercial paper consisting of short-term negotiable bearer notes. They may be in any currency but are usually in dollars or ECUs. The euronote facility is a form of note issuance facility set up by a syndicate of banks, which underwrites the notes.

Exchange-traded. Traded in a stock exchange rather than over the counter.

Exchange offers. Offers to exchange one set of securities for another.

Exchange rate volatility. The fluctuations in the rate of exchange between currencies.

Export credit agency. An institution to provide financing for a county's exports, usually established, controlled, and funded by the government of the country.

FASB. Financial Accounting Standards Board, accounting standards setting organization in the U.S.

FBSA. U.S. Foreign Bank Supervision Act of 1991.

FBSEA. U.S. Foreign Bank Supervision Enhancement Act of 1991.

FDI (foreign direct investments). Investment in the capital of foreign businesses.

FDIC (Federal Deposit Insurance Corporation). U.S. federal agency established in 1933 that guarantees (within limits) funds on deposit in member banks and thrift institutions and performs other bank regulatory functions. In 1989, Congress passed savings and loan association bailout legislation that reorganized FDIC into two insurance units: the Bank Insurance Fund (BIF) continues the traditional FDIC functions with respect to banking institutions; the Savings Association Insurance Fund (SAIF) insures thrift institution deposits, replacing the Federal Savings and Loan Insurance Corporation (FSLIC), which ceased to exist.

Federal Reserve Bank (FRB). One of the 12 U.S. banks that, with their branches, make up the Federal Reserve System. These banks are located in Boston, New York, Philadelphia, Cleveland, Richmond, Atlanta, Chicago, St. Louis, Minneapolis, Kansas City, Dallas, and San Francisco. The role of each Federal Reserve Bank is to monitor the commercial and savings banks in its region to ensure that they follow Federal Reserve Board regulations and to provide those banks with access to emergency funds from the discount window. The reserve banks act as depositories for member banks in their regions, providing money transfer and other services.

Federal Reserve Board. Governing board of the U.S. Federal Reserve System. Its seven members are appointed by the President of the United States, subject to Senate confirmation, and serve 14-year terms.

Fedwire. A high-speed electronic link in the USA between the 12 Federal Reserve Banks and the Treasury, used to move large sums of money for themselves and their customers.

FIBV. Federation Internationale des Bourses de Valeurs (International Federation of Stock Exchanges). A private foundation that exchanges information on international stock markets.

Financial intermediaries. A bank, building society, finance house, insurance company, investment trust, etc., that holds funds borrowed from lenders in order to make loans to borrowers.

Financial leverage. Debt in relation to equity in a firm's capital structure.

Financial Reform Act of 1992. Amends Japan's Securities and Exchange Law, its Banking Law, and other statutes.

Firewall restrictions. Restrictions on dealings between a bank and its affiliates to protect bank solvency.

FIRICA. U.S. Financial Institutions Regulatory and Interest Control Act of 1978.

FIRREA. U.S. Financial Institutions Reform, Recovery, and Enforcement Act of 1989. Legislation to resolve the crisis affecting savings and loan associations.

Fixed-price offering. Method of pricing underwritten securities by which the price remains fixed as long as the syndicate remains in effect. In contrast, Eurobonds, which are also sold through underwriting syndicates, are often offered on a basis that permits discrimination among customers; i.e., the underwriting spread may be adjusted to suit the particular buyer.

Floating exchange rate. Movement of a currency's exchange rate in response to changes in the market forces of supply and demand; also known as flexible exchange rate. The opposite of the floating exchange rate is the fixed exchange rate system. See also par value of currency.

Floor. See collar.

Foreign Exchange and Foreign Trade Control Law (FECL). Japanese law governing foreign-exchange and other international matters.

Forward markets. Markets where there is a contract to buy or sell a currency at a fixed price in the future, without a corresponding offsetting transaction.

Fourth market. Direct trading of large blocks of securities between institutional investors to save brokerage commissions. The fourth market is aided by computers, notably by a computerized subscriber service called Instinet, an acronym for Institutional Networks Corporation.

FRB. See Federal Reserve Bank, Federal Reserve Board.

Friction costs. Costs associated with transactions, such as fees, risks.

FRN (floating rate note). Debt instrument with a variable interest rate. Interest adjustments are made periodically, often every six months, and are tied to a money-market index such as Treasury bill rates. Also known as a floater.

Futures. An agreement to buy or sell a fixed quantity of a particular commodity, currency, or security for delivery at a fixed date in the future at a fixed price. Unlike an option, a futures contract involves a definite purchase or sale and not an option to buy or sell; it therefore may entail a potentially unlimited loss.

G-7 (Group of Seven). Group formed by the seven leading industrial nations (USA, Japan, Germany, France, UK, Italy, and Canada) in order to foster economic and political coordination.

G-10 (Group of Ten). The ten industrial nations that agreed in 1962 to lend money to the International Monetary Fund (IMF). They are Belgium, Canada, France, Italy, Japan, Netherlands, Sweden, Germany, US, and USA.

GAAP. Generally accepted accounting principles.

GATT (General Agreement on Tariffs and Trade). A trade treaty that has been in operation since 1948.

GDP (gross domestic product). The monetary value of all the goods and services produced by an economy over a specified period.

GDR (global depositary receipt). Also called **GDS (global depositary shares).** See ADR.

Gensaki. The Japanese money market for the resale and repurchase of medium- and long-term government securities.

Glass-Steagall. U.S. legislation of 1933 separating banking and securities businesses.

Globex. International after-hours screen trading system developed in 1992 dealing in currency futures and options.

Gold standard. A former monetary system in which a country's currency unit was fixed in terms of a specific quantity of gold bullion.

Grey market. A market in shares that have not been issued but are due to be issued in a short time.

Group of Thirty. A 'think tank' composed of 30 high-level individuals drawn from central banks, commercial bank management, the economics profession and finance ministries in both developed and developing countries.

Haircuts. Securities industry term referring to the formulas used in the valuation of securities below current market prices for the purpose of calculating a broker-dealer's net capital. The haircut varies according to the class of a security, its market risk, and the time to maturity.

Hedge fund. Form of private mutual fund which engages in a range of speculative activities ("hedge" is quite a misnomer).

Hedging. Strategy used to offset investment risk. A perfect hedge is one eliminating the possibility of future gain or loss.

Herstatt risk. The risk of loss in a foreign exchange transaction, where one side of the bargain is completed, but the other is not. Named after the Herstatt Bank of Germany which failed in 1974.

IBA. U.S. International Banking Act of 1978.

IBBEA. U.S. Interstate Banking and Branching Efficiency Act of 1994.

ICA. U.S. Investment Company Act of 1940 regulating mutual funds.

IDTCA. U.S. Interest and Dividend Tax Compliance Act of 1983.

IFS (international finance subsidiary). Subsidiary created and used to escape tax provisions in the international bond market; revisions in the tax code have made its use largely unnecessary.

ILLR. International lender-of-last-resort. See lender-of-last-resort.

IMF (International Monetary Fund). A specialized agency of the United Nations established in 1945 to promote international monetary cooperation and expand international trade, stabilize exchange rates, and help countries experiencing short-term balance of payments difficulties to maintain their exchange rates.

Impact day. The day on which the terms of a new issue of shares are made public.

Index. Statistical composite that measures changes in the economy or in financial markets, often expressed in percentage changes from a base year or from the previous month.

Indexes also measure the ups and downs of stock, bond, and commodities markets, reflecting market prices and the number of shares outstanding for the companies in the index. Some well-known indexes are the New York Stock Exchange Index, the American Stock Exchange Index, Standard & Poor's Index, and the Value Line Index. Subindexes for industry groups such as beverages, railroads, or computers are also tracked. Stock market indexes form the basis for trading in index options.

Index fund. Mutual fund whose portfolio matches that of a broad-based index such as Standard & Poor's Index and whose performance therefore mirrors the market as a whole.

Interbank lending. The money market in which banks borrow or lend money among themselves.

Interest rate parity. Relationship between changes of exchange-rates and interest rates between countries.

Intermediated credit. Credit arranged by a broker, bank, or agent.

International Primary Marketing Association (IPMA). A London-based membership group for euro-issuers.

Investment Adviser's Act of 1940. U.S. legislation that requires all investment advisers to register with the Securities and Exchange Commission. The Act is designed to protect the public from fraud or misrepresentation by investment advisers.

Investment grade securities. Those with a rating ranging from AAA to BBB.

IOSCO (International Organization of Securities Commissioners). International regulatory body for securities.

IPO (initial public offering). Corporation's first offering of stock to the public.

ISDA. International Swaps and Derivatives Association.

Issue price. The price at which a new issue of shares is sold to the public. Once the issue has been made the securities will have a market price, which may be above (at a premium on) or below (at a discount on) the issue price.

Issuer. Legal entity that has the power to issue and distribute a security.

JSDA. Japanese Securities Dealers Association.

Junior security. Security with lower priority claim on assets and income than a senior security.

Keiretsu. A Japanese company group formed by interlocking shareholdings. Keiretsu normally contain a bank. They differ from Zaibatsu in that the bank is not the group holding company, post-war legislation having reduced a bank's permitted shareholding in a company to 5%.

LBO (leveraged buy-out). Takeover of a company, using borrowed funds. Most often, the target company's assets serve as security for the loans taken out by the acquiring firm, which repays the loans out of cash flow of the acquired company. Management may use this technique to retain control by converting a company from public to private.

LDC. Less developed country.

LDC (London Dollar Clearing Scheme). A net settlement system for clearing dollar transactions outside the U.S.

Legal tender. Money that must be accepted in discharge of a debt.

Lender-of-last resort. An institution, normally a central bank, that stands ready to lend to the commercial banking system when the later is in overall shortage of funds. This power is often used by central banks to avert bank failures.

Letter of credit. A non-negotiable order from a bank to a bank abroad, authorizing payment to a named person of a particular sum of money or up to a limit of a certain sum.

LIBOR (London Interbank Offered Rate). The rate of interest offered on loans to first-class banks in the London interbank market for a specified period (usually three or six months). The rate may apply to sterling or Eurodollars. The corresponding rate for deposits is the interbank market bid rate (IBMBR), the interbank bid rate (IBBR) or the London interbank bid rate (LIBID). Some other financial centers have interbank bid and offer rates, e.g., the Paris interbank offered rate (PIBOR) and the Tokyo interbank offered rate (TIBOR).

LIFFE (London International Financial Futures Exchange). A London financial futures market to provide facilities within the European time zone for dealing in options and futures contracts, including those in government bonds, stock-and-share indexes, foreign currencies, and interest rates.

Limit orders. Order to buy or sell a security at a specific price or better. The broker will execute the trade only within the price restriction.

Liquidity. Ability of assets to be converted into cash without significant loss.

Locked-in. Unable to take advantage of preferential tax treatment on the sale of an asset because the required holding period has not elapsed.

Long position. A position held by a dealer in securities, commodities, currencies, etc., in which holdings exceed sales, because the dealer expects prices to rise enabling a profit to be made by selling at the higher levels. Compare short position.

Managed account. Investment account consisting of money that one or more clients entrust to a manager, who decides when and where to invest it.

Mandate. A written authority given by one person (the mandator) to another (the mandatory) giving the mandatory the power to act on behalf of the mandator. Issuers of securities give mandates to their underwriters.

Margin account. Brokerage account allowing customers to buy securities with money borrowed from the broker.

    initial margin. Collateral deposited with a broker, when opening a trading account, to cover possible losses.

    maintenance margin. Collateral kept with a broker to cover possible trading losses.

Mark-to-market. The daily valuation of securities at market prices.

Market makers. A dealer who maintains firm bid and offer prices in a given security by standing ready to buy or sell the security at publicly quoted prices.

Market order. Order to buy or sell a security at the best available price.

Master feeder fund. A multi-tiered structure for mutual funds, whereby separate feeder funds with substantially identical investment objectives pool their assets by investing in a single portfolio (master fund).

MATIF (Marché à Terme Internationale de France). French futures exchange.

MBS. See mortgage-backed security.

Medium-term note. An unsecured note issued in a eurocurrency with a maturity of about three to six years.

Mezzanine debt. A term signifying an intermediate stage in a financing operation.

Mirror fund. A mutual fund that invests in the same securities as another mutual fund, e.g. a U.S.-organized fund that invests in the same securities in which the foreign fund invests.

MJDS (Multi-jurisdictional Disclosure System). SEC disclosure system streamlining offerings made jointly in the U.S. and Canada.

MOF. Japan's Ministry of Finance.

Mortgage backed security (MBS). Security backed by mortgages.

Multilateral agency or **multilateral organization.** An institution established by treaty. Governments are members and supply the capital. A secretariat carries out its mandate. Examples include the Asian Development Bank or the International Finance Corporation.

Multiple (price-earnings ratio). Price of a stock divided by its earnings per share.

Mutual fund. A system of group investment which allow investors to purchase interests representing pro rata shares of the net assets of a pool of securities and other assets.

Mutual recognition. EU approach to regulation; it requires each country to recognize the validity of other member countries' laws, regulations, and administrative practices and is intended to preclude the use of national rules to restrict access to financial markets.

NASD (National Association of Securities Dealers). A self-regulatory organization of securities dealers that set up and now regulates NASDAQ and the OTC market.

NASDAQ (NASD Automated Quotation System). Owned and operated by NASD, a computerized system that provides price quotations for securities.

NASDAQ National Market System (NMS). A system providing information on the quoted price of stocks, the latest price paid, the high and low for the day and the current volume. NMS brokers are required to report this information through the system within 90 seconds of the trade.

National Securities Clearing Corporation. Securities clearing organization formed in 1977. It clears securities traded on the NYSE and NASDAQ.

NCD (negotiable certificates of deposit). Large-dollar amount, short-term certificates of deposit that can be negotiated to third parties. Such certificates are issued by large banks and bought mainly by corporations and institutional investors.

Negative pledge. Negative covenant or promise that states the borrower will not pledge any of its assets.

Netting. The process of setting off matching sales and purchases against each other.

Net debit cap. Limits on the maximum net debit position of clearinghouse participants; intended to reduce the risk of settlement defaults.

NIF (note issuance facility). A means of enabling short-term borrowers in the eurocurrency markets to issue euronotes with maturities of less than one year when the need arises, rather than having to arrange a separate issue of euronotes each time they need to borrow.

Non-recourse finance. An investment whose servicing and repayment depends only on the profitability of the underlying project and not on any other source.

Notional principal. The notional amount of an obligation used as a basis of calculation, as with interest rate swaps.

Novation. The replacement of one legal agreement by a new obligation, with the agreement of all the parties.

NYSE (New York Stock Exchange). The leading U.S. stock exchange and largest in the world in terms of market capitalization.

OCC (Office of the Comptroller of the Currency). Office of the U.S. Department of Treasury responsible for regulating national banks.

OCC (Options Clearing Corporation). A New-York based clearinghouse that clears option contracts.

OECD (Organization for Economic Cooperation and Development). Organization formed in 1961 and based in Paris to promote cooperation among industrialized member countries on economic and social policies.

Off- balance sheet exposures. Potential exposures to loss not reflected on a balance sheet, e.g. bank issued letters of credit.

Offering circulars. See Prospectus.

Offering period. Period during which a public offering is made.

Open-end Mutual Fund. An mutual fund which engages in a continuous offering of its shares and permits investors to redeem shares at current net values.

Open-outcry system. Quoting prices, making offers, bids, and acceptances, and concluding transactions by word of mouth in a commodity market or financial futures exchange, usually in a trading pit.

Operational risk. Risk that loss will result from the breakdown of a systems operational component such as hardware, software, or communications.

Options. A contract giving its beneficiary the right to buy or sell a financial instrument or a commodity at a specified price within a specified period.

    naked. Option for which the buyer or seller has no underlying security position.

Order-driven. Denoting a market in which prices are determined by the publication of orders to buy or sell shares, with the objective of attracting a counterparty.

OSE. Osaka Stock Exchange.

OTC (over the counter). Market in which securities transactions are conducted through a telephone and computer network connecting dealers in stocks and bonds, rather than through an exchange.

Overdraft. A loan made to a customer by allowing an account to go into debit, usually up to a specified limit (the overdraft limit). Interest is charged on the daily debit balance.

Parastatal. An organization founded and owned by a government but a legally separate person.

Pass through. Security, representing pooled debt obligations repackaged as shares, that passes income from debtors through the intermediary to investors. The most common type of pass-through is a mortgage-backed certificate, usually government-guaranteed.

Pathfinder prospectus. An outline prospectus concerning the flotation of a new company in the UK; it includes enough details to test the market reaction to the new company but not its main financial details or the price of its shares. Pathfinder prospectuses are known in the USA as red herrings.

Peg. To fix something to another standard; for example, to fix an exchange rate to the price of another country's currency or to the price of gold.

Perpetual. Bond that has no maturity date, is not redeemable, and pays a steady stream of interest indefinitely; also called annuity bond. The only notable perpetual bonds in existence are the consols first issued by the British Treasury to pay off smaller issues used to finance the Napoleonic Wars (1814).

> **perpetual FRN.** A floating rate note having no maturity, i.e., not to be repaid; used chiefly as an investment instrument.

Phillips Curve. The proposition that, other things equal, the rate at which the nominal wage level changes is a decreasing function of the level of the unemployment rate.

Pink Sheets. U.S. National Quotation Bureau publications listing the bid and offer prices of the securities available in the over-the-counter markets.

POP Directive (publication of prospectus). An EU direction requiring information disclosure in the form of a prospectus, before a securities offering.

PORTAL. U.S. system operated by the NASD for qualified investors to trade in unregistered securities.

Praecipium. Fee given to the lead manager of an underwriting.

Preferred stock. Stock that pays dividends at a specified rate and that has preference over common stock in the payment of dividends and the liquidation of assets. Most preferred stock is cumulative; if dividends are passed (not paid for any reason), they accumulate and must be paid before common dividends. A passed dividend on noncumulative preferred stock is generally gone forever.

Premium. An amount in excess of the issue price of a share or other security. When dealings open for a new issue of shares, for instance, it may be said that the market price will be at a premium over the issue price.

Price dumping. Discounting on an issue price in order to sell the issue, usually one initially priced too high. Fixed-price reofferings are intended to eliminate this practice.

Primary offering. Any sale of a new issue of a stock or bonds. Not the same as an initial public offering (IPO), which refers only to a company's first public sale of stock.

Prime. Interest rate banks charge to their most creditworthy customers.

Private placements. Sale of unregistered stocks, bonds, or other investments directly to an institutional investor like an insurance company.

Privatization. The process of selling a publicly owned company to the private sector.

Professionals' exemption. General practice under many foreign regulatory regimes of allowing the sale of securities to large institutions and market professionals with few regulations.

Proprietary trading systems. Screen-based automated trading systems typically owned by broker-dealers.

Prospectus. Formal written offer to sell securities that sets forth the plan for a proposed business enterprise or the facts concerning an existing one that an investor needs to make an informed decision.

Public float. The proportion of a corporation's stocks held by the public rather than by insiders.

Public offering. Offering to the investment public, after registration requirements have been complied with, of new securities, usually by an investment banker or a syndicate made up of several investment bankers, at a public offering price agreed upon between the issuer and the investment bankers.

Public style covenants. Fewer and less restrictive than the covenants found in many private placements, these covenants are used in loan agreements to specify the criteria with which the bond issuer in a public offering has to comply.

Purchasing power parity. Parity between two currencies at a rate of exchange that will give each currency exactly the same purchasing power in its own economy.

Put option. Gives the option holder the right to sell an asset -- at a set time, for a set price.

QIB. Under SEC Rule 144A, a qualified institutional buyer.

Quote-driven. Denoting an electronic stock-exchange system in which prices are determined by the quotations made by market makers or dealers. The London Stock Exchange and NASDAQ System use quote-driven arrangements. Compare order driven.

RAP. Regulatory accounting principles, which may differ from generally acceptable accounting principles (GAAP) or tax accounting principles.

Rating system. Evaluation of securities investment and credit risk, performed by private services such as Fitch's, Moody's, and Standard & Poor's. Ratings range from AAA (best) to D.

Receiver. Also called a conservator. Court-appointed person who takes possession of, but not title to, the assets and affairs of a business or estate that is in bankruptcy.

Redemption. The repayment at maturity of a bond or other document certifying a loan, by the borrower to the lender.

Regulation D. Refers to both SEC rule exempting certain securities offerings from registration and Federal Reserve Board (FRB) Regulation specifying reserve requirements for banks.

Regulation K. FRB regulation of international banking.

Regulation O. FRB regulation on loans to bank insiders.

Regulation S. SEC regulation governing applicability of U.S. securities laws to foreign offers of securities.

Regulation Q. FRB regulation that used to set ceilings on rates of interest paid by banks on their deposits.

REIT (Real Estate Investment Trust). A company that manages a portfolio of real estate investments.

Repatriate. The return of capital from a foreign investment to investment in the country from which it originally came.

Replacement cost risk. Risk of loss resulting from a credit default.

Repurchase agreement (repo). A transaction whereby funds are borrowed through the sale of short-term securities, usually governments, on the condition that the instruments are repurchased at a given date.

Risk-weighted assets. The assets, shown on the balance sheet of a bank, that have had a risk weighting applied to them.

Rollovers. The extension or reissuing of an instrument of debt upon its date of maturity.

RTGS (real-time gross settlement system). Payment system like Fedwire in which each transaction is finally settled as it occurs, without netting.

RUF (revolving underwriting facility). See NIF.

Saitori. Members of the Tokyo Stock Exchange who act as intermediaries between brokers. They cannot deal on their own account or for non-members of the exchange; they may only be allowed to deal in a limited number of stocks.

SEAQ (Stock Exchange Automated Quotation System). System of quoting stocks on London Stock Exchange.

Second Banking Directive. An EU directive governing the provision of banking in the EU.

SEC (Securities and Exchange Commission). U.S. agency for the regulation of the markets in securities set up in 1934.

Secondary market. Exchanges and over-the-counter markets where securities are bought and sold subsequent to original issuance in the primary market.

Secretariat. Within an international organization, the administrative office that supports the governing body.

Selling concession. Discount at which securities in a new issue offering (or a secondary distribution) are allocated to the members of a selling group by the underwriters. Since the selling group cannot sell to the public at a price higher than the public offering price, its compensation comes out of the difference between the price paid to the issuer by the underwriters and the public offering price, called the spread. The selling group's portion, called the concession, is normally one half or more of the gross spread, expressed as a discount off the public offering price.

SESC. Securities and Exchange Surveillance Commission, Japan.

Shelf registration. SEC Rule 415 adopted in the 1980s, which allows a corporation to comply with registration requirements up to two years prior to a public offering of securities. With the registration "on the shelf," the corporation, by simply updating regularly filed annual, quarterly, and related reports to the SEC, can go to the market as conditions become favorable with a minimum of administrative preparation.

Short position. For commodities, contract in which a trader has agreed to sell a commodity at a future date for a specific price; for stocks, shares that an individual has sold short (by delivery of borrowed certificates) and has not covered as of a particular date.

SIMEX (Singapore International Mercantile Exchange).

Sovereign lending. A loan made by a bank to a foreign government.

Spot markets. Markets in which goods or currencies are sold for cash and delivered immediately.

Spread. The difference between the buying and selling price made by a dealer.

SPV (Special Purpose Vehicle). An entity used to issue securities in the securitization process.

Stabilization. Intervention in new issues market by an underwriter to keep the market price from falling below a given price during the offering period.

Stagflation. Term coined by economists in the 1970s to describe the previously unprecedented combination of slow economic growth and high unemployment (stagnation) with rising prices (inflation).

Stick position. The amount of an allotment unsold at the close of an offering period.

Straddle. A strategy used by dealers in traded options or futures. In the traded option market it involves simultaneously purchasing a put and call option; it is most profitable when the price of the underlying security is very volatile.

Strike price. Also called exercise price, this is the price at which the stock or commodity underlying a call or put option can be purchased (call) or sold (put) over the specified period.

Subordinated debt. A debt that can only be claimed by an unsecured creditor, in the event of a liquidation, after the claims of secured creditors have been met.

Subscription. Agreement of intent to buy newly issued securities.

Swap. Exchange of obligations as with interest rates and currency swaps.

> **basis swap.** Interest rate swap in which the same type of interest rate obligations are swapped (floating for floating or fixed for fixed) but the basis of the two rates are different, e.g. floating LIBOR for floating PIBOR.
>
> **commodity swap.** Exchange of two commodities to be reexchanged at future date.
>
> **currency swap.** An interest rate swap consisting of the exchange of two streams of interest in different currencies, as well as the principal amounts.
>
> **interest rate swap.** A transaction under which two streams of interest rate payments are exchanged, usually floating for fixed.
>
> **matched swap.** Swap which is hedged by another swap.

Swaption. An offer to enter into a swap contract.

SWIFT (Society for Worldwide International Financial Telecommunications). A credit-transfer system between banks.

Syndicated loan. A very large loan made to one borrower by a group of banks.

Tanshi. A market maker in the Japanese money market.

Tax haven. A country or independent area that has a low rate of tax and therefore offers advantages to individuals or companies that can arrange their affairs so that their tax liability falls at least partly in the low-tax haven.

TEFRA. U.S. Tax Equity and Fiscal Responsibility Act of 1982.

Third market trading. Nonexchange-member broker/dealers and institutional investors trading over-the-counter in exchange-listed securities.

TIFFE. Tokyo International Financial Futures Exchange.

Tokyo Dollar Clearing. Japanese system for clearing dollar payments among banks.

Tombstone. Advertisement placed in newspapers by investment bankers in a public offering of securities.

Trade comparison. The process of confirming and matching the terms of a securities transaction.

Tranche. A predetermined part of a financial transaction (from the French, meaning 'slice').

Transfers. In banking, the movement of money from one bank account to another.

    correspondent. A transfer involving two or more banks.

    in-house. A transfer between accounts at the same bank.

Transparency rules. Rules designed to the extent that to which transaction prices and volumes in a securities market are visible to all market operators.

Treasury bills. Short-term securities with maturities of one year or less, issued at or at a discount from face value.

Trust Indenture Act of 1939. U.S. law requiring all corporate bonds and other debt securities to be issued under an indenture agreement approved by the SEC and providing for the appointment of a qualified trustee free of conflict of interest with the issuer.

Unit Trust Fund. United Kingdom mutual fund which is regulated by a trust deed, the trustees being separate from management.

Universal banking system. System in which banks can engage in businesses other than banking, e.g. securities.

VAR (Value-At-Risk). The potential profit and losses on one's investments over a defined period of time.

Warrants. Type of security, often issued together with a bond or preferred stock, that entitles the holder to buy a proportionate amount of common stock at a specified price, usually higher than the market price at the time of issuance, for a period of years or to perpetuity.

Wind down. Set in order the affairs of a failed institution.

Withholding taxes. Tax deducted at source from dividends or other income paid to non-residents of a country.

Yankee securities. Dollar-denominated securities issued in the U.S. by foreign issuers.

Yield. The income from a security as a proportion of its current market price.

Zaibatsu. A large interlocking grouping of Japanese companies, similar to a US trust or a German Konzern; dominated by a bank, holding controlling interests in the other members of the group. The zaibatsu have been largely outmoded by legislation since the Second World War, their place being taken by the keiretsu.

Zero coupon rate. Refers to the effective rate of interest from bonds that do not provide interest payments, but rather are sold at a discount from their par value.

INDEX

References are to Pages.

†

ISBN 1–58778–433–5